COBOL

From Micro to Mainframe

SECOND EDITION

ROBERT T. GRAUER

University of Miami

CAROL VAZQUEZ VILLAR

University of Miami

PRENTICE HALL

Englewood Cliffs, New Jersey 07632

Library of Congress Cataloging-in-Publication Data
Grauer, Robert T., 1945–
COBOL : from micro to mainframe / Robert T. Grauer, Carol Vazquez Villar
p. cm.
Includes index.
ISBN 0-13-138686-7
1. COBOL (Computer program language) I. Vazquez Villar, Carol
II. Title
QA76.73.C25G734 1994 93-21235
005.13'3—dc20 CIP

To Marion, Benjy, and Jessica
To Mario, Mom & Dad, and Fefa

TRADEMARK INFORMATION

CA-Realia® is a registered trademark of Computer Associates International, Inc.

ANSI Acknowledgment: COBOL is an industry language and is not the property of any company or group of companies, or of any organization or group of organizations. No warranty, expressed or implied, is made by any contributor or by the CODASYL COBOL Committee as to the accuracy and functioning of the programming system and language. Moreover, no responsibility is assumed by any contributor, or by the committee, in connection therewith. The authors and copyright holders of the copyrighted materials used herein

> FLOW-MATIC (trademark of Sperry Rand Corporation), Programming for the UNIVAC® I and II, Data Automation Systems copyrighted 1958, 1959, by Sperry Rand Corporation; IBM Commercial Translator Form No. F 28-8013, copyrighted 1959 by IBM; FACT, DSI 27A5260-2760, copyrighted 1960 by Minneapolis-Honeywell

have specifically authorized the use of this material in whole or in part, in the COBOL specifications. Such authorization extends to the reproduction and use of COBOL specifications in programming manuals or similar publications.

U.S. Government Restricted Rights: The SOFTWARE and documentation is provided with RESTRICTED RIGHTS. Use, duplication, or disclosure by the Government is subject to restrictions as set forth in subdivision (b)(3)(ii) of The Rights in Technical Data and Computer Software clause at 252.227-7013. Contractor/manufacturer is Computer Associates International, Inc., One Computer Associates Plaza, Islandia, NY 11788-7000.

Should you have any questions concerning the Maintenance and License Agreement, or these RESTRICTED RIGHTS, or should you want to contact Computer Associates for any other reason, please call (516) 342-5224.

The author and publisher of this book have used their best efforts in preparing this book. These efforts include the development, research, and testing of the theories and programs to determine their effectiveness. The author and publisher make no warranty of any kind, expressed or implied, with regard to these programs or the documentation contained in this book. The author and publisher shall not be liable in any event for incidental or consequential damages in connection with, or arising out of, the furnishing, performance, or use of these programs.

A Paramount Communication Company
Englewood Cliffs, New Jersey 07632

Printed in the United States of America
10 9 8 7 6 5 4 3 2 1

ISBN 0-13-138686-7

Prentice-Hall International (UK) Limited, *London*
Prentice-Hall of Australia Pty. Limited, *Sydney*
Prentice-Hall Canada Inc., *Toronto*
Prentice-Hall Hispanoamericana, S.A., *Mexico*
Prentice-Hall of India Private Limited, *New Delhi*
Prentice-Hall of Japan, Inc., *Tokyo*
Simon & Schuster Asia Pte. Ltd., *Singapore*
Editora Prentice-Hall do Brasil, Ltda., *Rio de Janeiro*

Acquisitions Editor: *Bill Zobrist*
Editor-in-chief: *Marcia Horton*
Production Editor: *Greg Hubit*
Text Designer: *Gary Palmatier*
Cover Designer: *Bruce Kenselaar*
Production Coordinator: *Linda Behrens*
Supplements Editor: *Alice Dworkin*

Contents

Chapter 4: The Identification, Environment, and Data Divisions 73

Chapter 5: The Procedure Division 97

Chapter 6: Debugging 139

Chapter 7: Editing and Coding Standards 169

Chapter 8: Data Validation 195

Chapter 9 : More About the Procedure Division 229

Chapter 10: Screen I-O 265

Chapter 11: Introduction to Tables 301

Chapter 12: Table Lookups 331

Chapter 13: Multilevel Tables 363

Chapter 14: Sorting 403

Chapter 15: Control Breaks 435

Chapter 16: Subprograms 475

Chapter 17: Sequential File Maintenance 515

Chapter 18: Indexed Files 549

Preface

COBOL: From Micro to Mainframe is a truly comprehensive work, providing in a single source all subjects normally covered in the one-year COBOL sequence. The scope is extensive, ranging from an introduction to COBOL, to maintaining sequential and nonsequential files. The text and accompanying software comprise a total package designed to satisfy all of your COBOL needs, regardless of whether you are using a mainframe or a PC.

All listings are machine independent and thus are applicable to classes running on either a mainframe or a PC; indeed, it is not only possible to address both audiences, but easy and necessary as COBOL is COBOL regardless of the platform on which it is executed. The text provides instruction in ANS standard COBOL rather than the nonexistent PC COBOL or mainframe COBOL.

The Software

- A COBOL compiler: CA-Realia® Classroom COBOL is a fully functional compiler that enables students to run all projects on a PC. It is limited only by the size of the program it can accept (500 lines), but subprograms can be nested to any level, and each subprogram can contain 500 lines.
- Utility programs: A debugger, editor, linker, and indexed file utility provide everything necessary for serious COBOL programming. The debugger can monitor a program as it executes, establish break points, display intermediate results in watch windows, and so on. The full-featured editor is tied to the COBOL listing and facilitates the correction of compilation errors. The linker produces an executable load module, and the indexed file utility creates and/or prints (multiple key) indexed files.
- Data disk: The data disk contains every COBOL program in the text as well as data files for the nearly one hundred student projects. The availability of the sample listings enables students to reproduce and/or modify any of the programs without the tedium of data entry and further enhances the learning experience. The data disk can be used in a mainframe environment to upload files to the mainframe to provide students with data files for programming assignments.

Improvements in the Second Edition

The second edition incorporates suggestions from many students and instructors who have used the first edition. Many new features have been added with the following items of special interest:

- A change in orientation to emphasize COBOL-85 as opposed to COBOL-74 (in the first edition). All chapters focus on the newer compiler, and the programs are written to take advantage of its enhancements. Every chapter ends with a discussion of the limitations of COBOL-74 to prepare students for the conversions they will encounter in industry.
- Improvements in software: All software has been upgraded and the compiler fully supports screen I/O. Four utilities (a debugger, editor, linker, and indexed-file utility) have been added or enhanced.
- New chapters on screen I/O, subprograms, and data validation with supporting COBOL programs on these crucial topics.
- Extended table coverage with three chapters devoted entirely to table processing. There is an introductory chapter, a separate chapter for table lookups, and a third chapter on multilevel tables.
- A conscious attempt to develop continuity from chapter to chapter by extending programs across chapters; for example, the data validation program in Chapter 8 creates a valid transaction file, which is input to the program in Chapter 9. Many of the programming assignments are developed in similar fashion; that is, the output of one project is input to another.
- An increased number of programming projects (nearly 100), which appear in an appendix at the end of the text. The assignments are presented in the same format as the illustrative programs.
- A thorough reworking of the Classroom COBOL documentation and associated hands-on exercises with all material placed in two appendices. Information is provided about previously undocumented features, such as compiler switches to compile under EBCDIC or ASCII. Detailed hands-on exercises take the reader through the editor and debugger.

Benefits and Features

All of the features that have made the first edition successful have been retained and carried over into the second edition. These include:

- Immediate entry into COBOL programming, beginning in Chapter 1. Programming is learned by doing, and the book has students writing a complete program from the very beginning. Chapter 2 continues the discussion by having them execute the program of Chapter 1 in a thorough introduction to the programming process.
- 30 illustrative COBOL programs reinforce the discussion in the text and serve as both pedagogical aids and subsequent reference material. Every program is presented in a uniform and detailed format, including program narrative, record layouts, report layouts, test data, and processing specifications.

- A thorough discussion of structured methodology, hierarchy charts, pseudocode, and top-down testing is presented in Chapter 3 and followed throughout. Students learn the proper way to develop programs early on and follow the procedure throughout the text.
- An abundance of short-answer (true-false and fill-in) questions, COBOL problems, and programming projects for every chapter, with answers to the odd-numbered questions provided in an appendix.
- Programming tips, dispersed throughout the text, that go beyond the syntactical rules of COBOL, and suggest stylistic considerations to make programs easier to read and maintain.
- Extensive use of graphic aids, featuring a two-color presentation, with abundant use of figures to further clarify the presentation.
- System concept presentations at the beginning of most chapters as COBOL instruction has come to require additional material beyond the language itself. There are detailed discussions of control breaks, data validation, techniques for table lookups and initialization, sorting, the balance line algorithm for file maintenance, and the organization of indexed files.

Acknowledgments

We are especially grateful to our editors at Prentice Hall, Marcia Horton and Bill Zobrist, without whom this project would not have been possible. We are indebted to Mark Sokol of Computer Associates for making Classroom COBOL available. Farrell Collins and Jeff Friedman, also of Computer Associates, provided invaluable support along the way.

We also want to thank the many other individuals who helped bring this project to its successful conclusion. Greg Hubit is the consummate professional who supervised the production from beginning to end, and who was always available, no matter what the day or hour. Jennifer has an eagle eye and was a superb proofreader. Gary Palmatier and Robaire Ream of Ideas to Images put manuscript and art together to produce the finished typeset product. Tom McElwee, our marketing manager at Prentice Hall, developed the innovative campaign that made the book a success. Alice Dworkin, also of Prentice Hall, coordinated the Instructor's Manual and Test Bank.

We also want to acknowledge our reviewers, who through their comments and constructive criticism, made this a far better book:

Robert V. Binder, Robert Binder Systems Consulting, Inc.
Dinon Boyer, University of Akron
Rick Byars, University of Texas at Austin
Jan De Lassen, Brigham Young University
Ida M. Flynn, University of Pittsburgh
Frank T. Gergelyi, NJIT
Ken Goldsmith, University of Miami
Carol C. Grimm, Palm Beach Community College
Ann W. Houck, Pima Community College
David Lee
James W. Payne, Kellogg Community College

Wendell L. Pope, Utah State University
Daniel H. Rindfleisch, Computer Specialist with Federal Government
Nick Ross, University of Illinois at Chicago
Daniel R. Rota, Robert Morris College
Richard H. Saracusa, Northeastern University
Ron Teemley, DeVry Institute of Technology
Donat Valcourt, Northeastern University
Ron Williams, McLennon Community College
Jackie Zucker, University of Miami

A final word of thanks to the unnamed students at the University of Miami who make it all worthwhile. And, most of all, thanks to you, our readers, for choosing this book. Please feel free to contact us with any comments and suggestions. We can be reached most easily on the Internet.

Robert Grauer
RGRAUER@UMIAMI.MIAMI.EDU

Carol Vazquez Villar
CVILLAR@UMIAMI.MIAMI.EDU

Introduction

CHAPTER OUTLINE

OBJECTIVES

After reading this chapter you will be able to:

- Define the terms: field, record, and file.
- Name two techniques used to express program logic.
- Identify the four divisions of a COBOL program.
- State the six COBOL language elements.
- State the rules for creating a programmer-supplied name; distinguish between examples of valid and invalid names.
- State the difference between numeric and nonnumeric literals; recognize valid and invalid examples of each.
- Follow the logic of a simple program as expressed in a flowchart or pseudocode.

OVERVIEW

This book is about computer programming. In particular, it is about COBOL, a widely used commercial programming language. Programming involves the translation of an algorithm (a precise means of solving a problem) into a form the computer can understand. Programming is necessary because, despite reports to the contrary, computers cannot think for themselves. Instead, they do exactly what they have been instructed to do, and these instructions take the form of a computer program. The advantage of the computer stems from its speed and accuracy. It does not do anything that a human being could not do, given sufficient time and memory capacity.

We begin our study of computer programming by describing a simple problem and then developing the logic and COBOL program to solve it. This rapid entrance into COBOL is somewhat different from the approach followed by most textbooks, but we believe in learning by doing. There is nothing very mysterious about COBOL programming, so let's get started.

The First Problem

Our first problem is set in the context of a university, and involves a set of student records, one record per student. Each record contains the student's name, number of completed credits, and major. Implicit in this statement are the definitions of three fundamental terms: field, record, and file. A ***field*** is a basic fact, such as the name, address, major, grade point average, or number of completed credits. A ***record*** is a set of fields, and a ***file*** is a set of records. Thus, if there were 1,000 students, there would be 1,000 records (one for each student), each consisting of five fields, and comprising a single student file.

To clarify this relationship, we create four hypothetical students for our problem: John Adams, Amelia Earhart, Orville Wright, and Georgia O'Keeffe. There are many facts about each of our students, but our problem utilizes only three:

Figure 1.1 Fields, Records, and Files

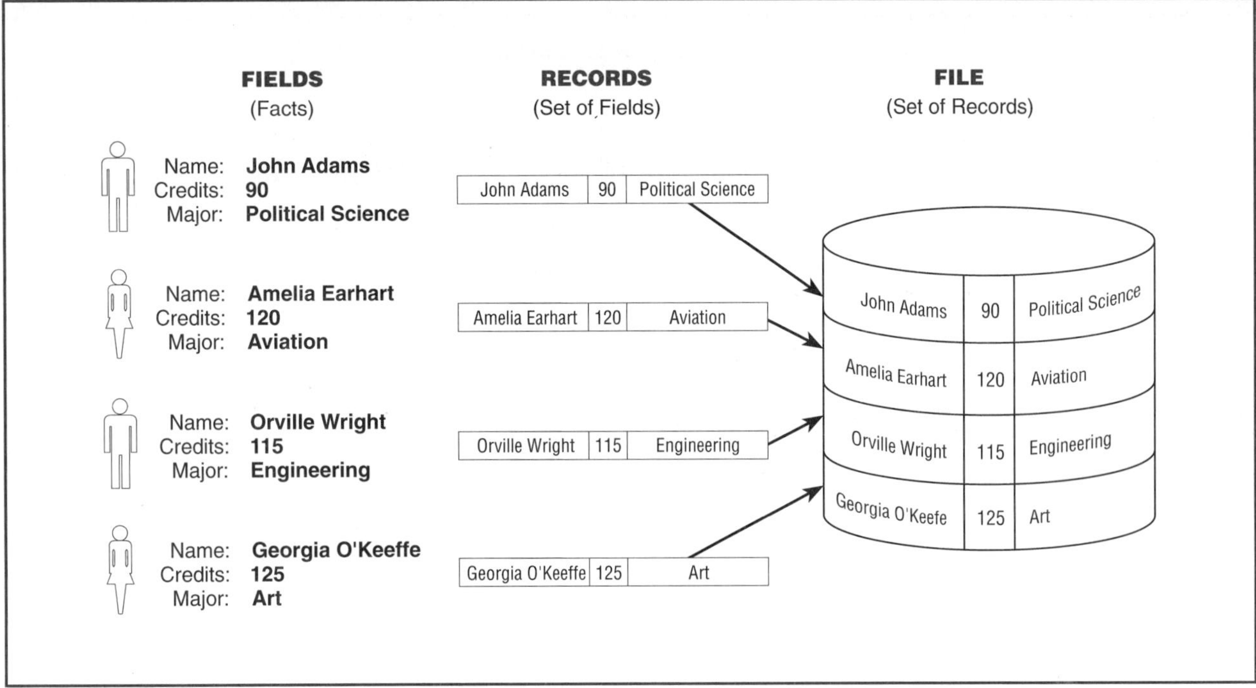

name, major, and credits completed. Figure 1.1 represents these concepts in pictorial fashion. Each fact about each student comprises a single field. The three fields collectively make up that student's record. The four records (one for each of our students) compose the student file.

The problem is to process the file of student records and produce a list of engineering students who have completed more than 110 credits. It is a typical problem, in that its solution will address the three elements common to all computer applications: input, processing, and output. As shown in Figure 1.2, the student file, just defined, is the ***input***; this file is ***processed*** by determining which students are engineering majors with more than 110 credits; and consequently, a report is created as ***output***, reflecting these students.

The input to a computer program; that is, the precise arrangement of the various fields in each incoming record, has to be specified exactly. Figure 1.3a is a common way to communicate this information, and shows that the student's name is contained in positions 1–25, the number of credits in positions 26–28, and the student's major in positions 29–43. Note too, that every record in a given file must have the identical record layout.

In similar fashion, the report produced as output is also precisely designed. Figure 1.3c shows a print layout chart, in which descriptive information appears on line one, with the names of selected students in columns 9–33 of subsequent lines. Observe also that the location of the name field is different in the input and output records (positions 1–25 and 9–33, respectively), and that each input record contains three fields, but that each line of output has been designed to contain only one field.

Programming Specifications

It is important that programming specification—that is, the input, processing, and output requirements—be presented in a clear and unambiguous fashion.

Figure 1.2 Input, Processing, and Output

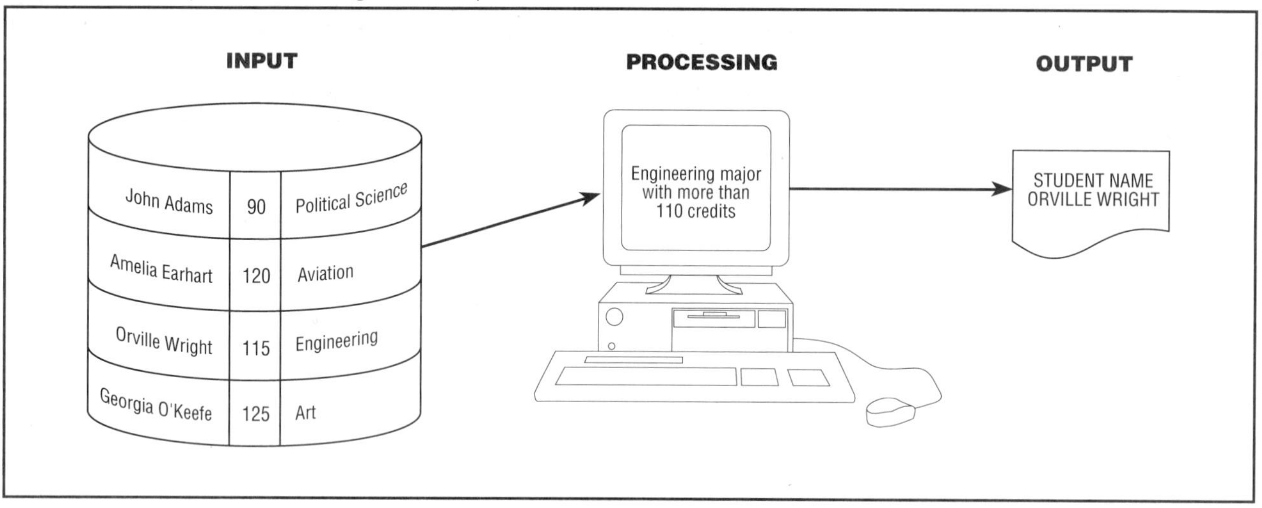

Figure 1.3 Engineering Senior (Input and Output)

STUDENT NAME	CREDITS	STUDENT MAJOR
1 2 3 4 5 6 7 8 9 10 11 12 13 14 15 16 17 18 19 20 21 22 23 24 25	26 27 28	29 30 31 32 33 34 35 36 37 38 39 40 41 42 43

(a) Student Record Layout

```
JOHN ADAMS               090POLITICAL SCI
AMELIA EARHART           120AVIATION
ORVILLE WRIGHT           115ENGINEERING
GEORGIA O'KEEFE          125ART
```

(b) Test Data

```
1            STUDENT NAME
2          XXXXXXXXXXXXXXXXXXXXXXXXX
3          XXXXXXXXXXXXXXXXXXXXXXXXX
```

(c) Print Layout

Accordingly, the authors have adopted the format shown below, and use it throughout the text for both illustrative programs and student assignments. The programming specifications begin with the program name and a brief narrative, followed by a detailed description of the various requirements. Note, too, that the specification document is entirely self-contained, and that if the person preparing the specifications has done a complete job, there will be little need for the programmer to seek additional information.

PROGRAMMING SPECIFICATIONS

Program Name: Engineering Senior Program

Narrative: This program processes a file of student records and prints the name of every student who is an engineering major with more than 110 credits.

Input File(s): STUDENT-FILE

Input Record Layout: See Figure 1.3a

Test Data: See Figure 1.3b

Report Layout: See Figure 1.3c

Processing Requirements:

1. Print a heading line.
2. Read a file of student records.
3. For every record, determine whether that student has a major of engineering and has completed more than 110 credits.
4. Print the name of every student who satisfies the requirements in item 3 above. Single-space the output.

Required Logic

Let us imagine momentarily that the student records are physically in the form of manila folders, stored in a filing cabinet, and further that a clerk is available to do our work. Our problem is to instruct the clerk on how to go through the folders. We would say something to the following effect:

Repeat steps 1 through 4 until there are no more folders:

1. Select a folder.
2. Examine the folder to see if that student is an engineering major *and* has more than 110 credits.
3. If the student meets both qualifications, write the student's name on a running list.
4. Return the folder to the file cabinet.

Stop

In essence, we have prepared a series of instructions for the clerk to follow. If our instructions are correct and if they are followed exactly, then the clerk will produce the desired results.

A ***computer program*** is a set of instructions, written according to a precise set of rules, which the computer interprets and subsequently executes. Unlike the clerk, however, the computer always follows our instructions exactly. In other words, *the computer does what we tell it to do, which is not necessarily what we want it to do.* A human clerk, on the other hand, has a mind of his or her own and can question or alter erroneous instructions. Since the computer does precisely what it is told, it is imperative that you strive to write logically correct programs. Accordingly, you must expend significant effort *prior to actual coding* to develop a program's logic correctly. Two common techniques for expressing that logic are ***flowcharts*** and ***pseudocode.***

Flowcharts

A flowchart is a pictorial representation of the logic inherent in a program. It is the translation of a problem statement into a logical blueprint that is subsequently incorporated into the COBOL program. A flowchart to list the engineering students with more than 110 credits is shown in Figure 1.4.

A flowchart uses blocks with specific shapes to indicate the nature of an operation. Using Figure 1.4 as a guide, we see that a diamond-shaped block indicates a decision, a parallelogram depicts input or output, an ellipse shows the beginning or end, and a rectangle implies straightforward processing. A rectangle with vertical lines implies that the processing within the rectangle will be expanded into a flowchart of its own.

To understand the flowchart in Figure 1.4, consider the nature of a READ statement. The function of a READ instruction is to obtain a record, but there will always be a point when a READ is attempted and no record is found, that is, when all the records in the file have already been read. Since one does not know in advance how many records a file contains, the READ instruction must also test for the ***end-of-file*** condition. Thus, if a file contains two records, it is actually read three times (once for each record, and once to sense the end-of-file condition).

The flowchart in Figure 1.4 begins with a start block (block 1), and continues with various housekeeping blocks. Housekeeping consists of statements that are done once at the start of processing, for example, opening files (block 2), reading the first record (block 3), and writing a heading at the start of a report (block 4). Control then passes through a connector block (block 5) to a decision statement (block 6).

If the end-of-file has not been reached, control goes to the PROCESS-RECORDS block, which is expanded in the right side of the figure. Each incoming record is checked in block 9 to determine if it meets both qualifications. If so, that student's name is written to the output report in block 10; if not, control goes directly to the connector in block 11. (Note that both the true and false branches for the condition in block 9 meet at a single connector in block 11.) The next record is read in block 12, and the PROCESS-RECORDS block is finished. Control then moves to the left side of the figure, to the connector in block 5 to the end-of-file test in block 6. Eventually, when the end-of-file has been reached, control will pass to close files (block 7), then to the stop statement in block 8.

To better understand how the flowchart works, we can use the test data of Figure 1.1 and play computer, by running the data through the flowchart. Execution begins by opening the files, reading the first record (John Adams), and writing the heading line. The end-of-file has not been reached, so block 6 directs flow to block 9, the test for engineering majors with more than 110 credits. John Adams fails the test, so control passes to the connector in block 11, to the READ in block 12, whereupon the data for Amelia Earhart are read into memory. Control flows through

Figure 1.4 Flowchart to Select Engineering Seniors

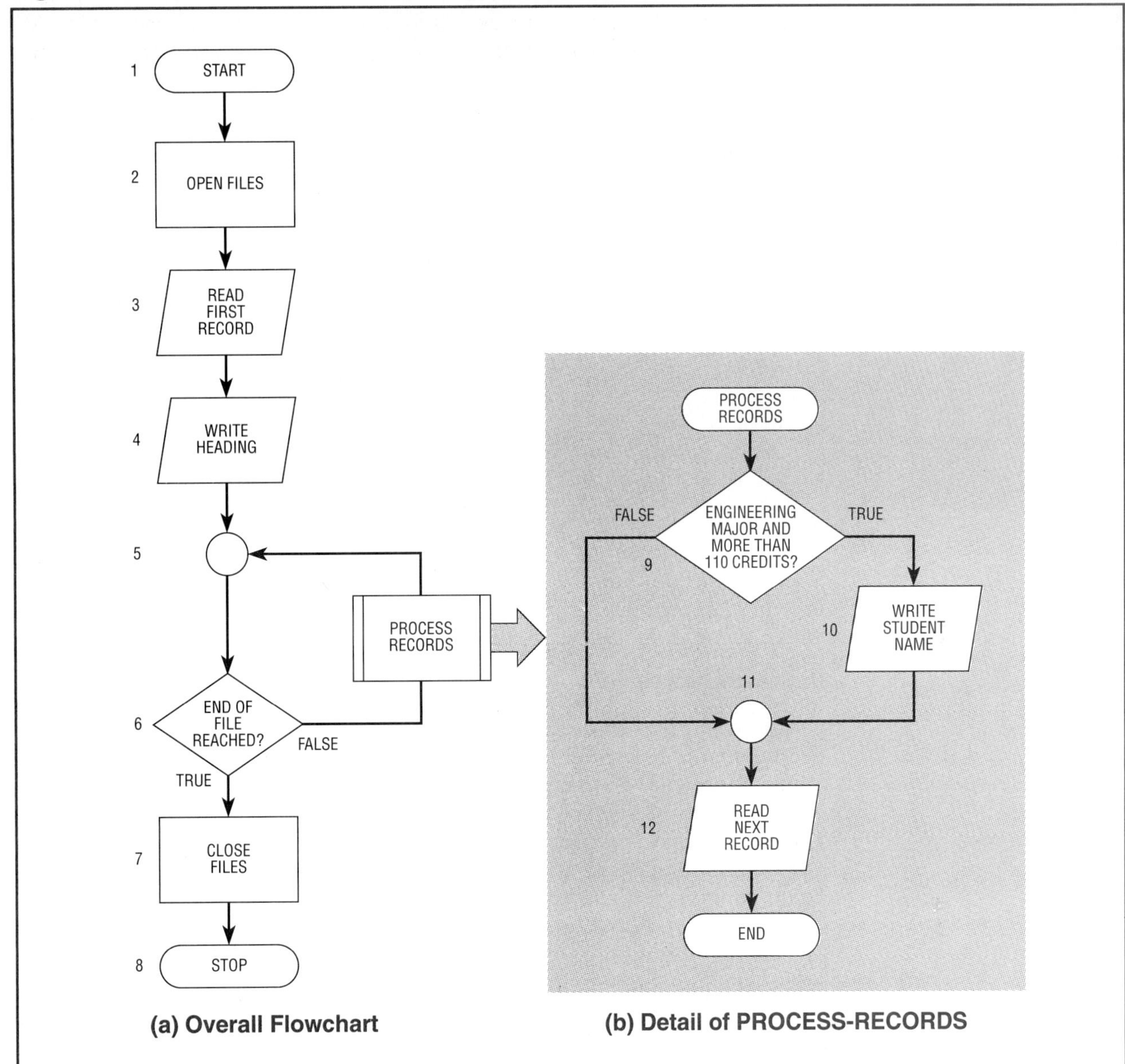

the connector of block 5, to the end-of-file test in block 6, and then to the qualification test in block 9. Amelia Earhart fails the test, again passing control to the connector in block 11, to the READ in block 12, at which point Orville Wright is read into memory. However, Wright is an engineering major with more than 110 credits, so he passes the test and his name is written in block 10.

The data for Georgia O'Keeffe are read in block 12, and control flows once more to the connector in block 5, to the end-of-file test in block 6. Realize, however, that even though O'Keeffe is the last record, the end-of-file condition has *not* yet been detected. O'Keeffe fails the qualification test, whereupon control flows to the READ in block 12. This time the end-of-file is detected so that, when control again reaches the end-of-file test in block 6, processing will be directed to the CLOSE FILES and STOP statements in blocks 7 and 8.

TABLE 1.1 The Flow chart and Test Data

BLOCK & DESCRIPTION		TIMES EXECUTED	EXPLANATION
1	Start	1	At beginning of program
2	Open files	1	At beginning of program
3	Initial read	1	Reads the first record (Adams)
4	Write heading	1	At beginning of program
5	Connector	5	Entered five times
6	End-of-file test	5	Once for each of four records; once to sense end-of-file condition
7	Close files	1	Once, before execution stops
8	Stop	1	Executed once, at program's end
9	Qualifying test	4	Once for each student
10	Write	1	Executed for Wright only
11	Connector	4	Entered four times
12	Read	4	Reads every record but the first, and detects the end-of-file condition

It is useful to summarize this discussion by tabulating the number of times each block in Figure 1.4 is executed. This is shown in Table 1.1.

Pseudocode

Pseudocode expresses a program's logic more concisely than a flowchart. One definition of pseudocode is *neat notes to oneself,* and since programmers do this naturally, pseudocode has replaced the traditional flowchart in many installations. Consider Figure 1.5, which contains identical logic to the flowchart in Figure 1.4, albeit in a more concise fashion.

As shown in Figure 1.5, the logic of most programs can be divided into three major portions: ***initialization***, ***processing***, and ***termination***. Initialization is done once at the start of processing—for example, opening files, reading the first record in a file, and writing a heading. This is followed by a series of instructions that are executed repeatedly, once for each incoming record; e.g., each record is evaluated for an engineering major with the requisite number of credits. If both conditions are met, the name will be written on the registrar's list; if the conditions are not met,

Figure 1.5 Pseudocode

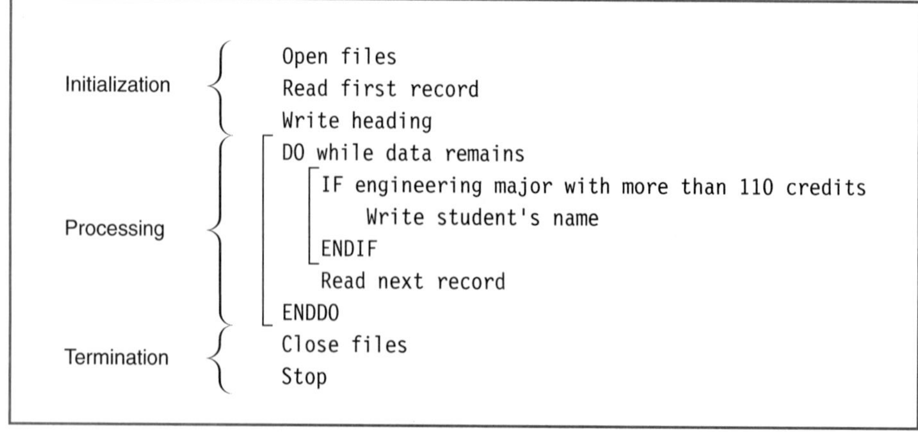

nothing further is done with the particular record. When *all* of the records in the file have been read, the loop is finished, and a termination routine is entered to print a total or simply stop processing.

Figure 1.5 also contains vertical lines connecting the words IF and ENDIF, and DO and ENDDO. This notation indicates two of the basic building blocks (***selection*** and ***iteration***) of a discipline known as ***structured programming*** which is fully explained in Chapter 3.

Pseudocode uses instructions similar to those of a computer language to describe program logic, but is *not* bound by precise syntactical rules found in formal programming languages. For example, the vertical lines referred to previously are the authors' convention and do not necessarily appear in the pseudocode of others. Nor is pseudocode bound by any rules for indentation, which is done strictly at the discretion of the person using it. The purpose of pseudocode is simply to convey program logic in a straightforward and easily followed manner.

A First Look at COBOL

We proceed to the COBOL program in Figure 1.6, which corresponds to the flowchart in Figure 1.4 and the pseudocode in Figure 1.5. The syntactical rules for COBOL are extremely precise, and you are certainly *not* expected to remember them after a brief exposure to Figure 1.6. The authors believe, however, *that immediate exposure to a real program is extremely beneficial in stripping the mystical aura that too often*

Figure 1.6 The First COBOL Program

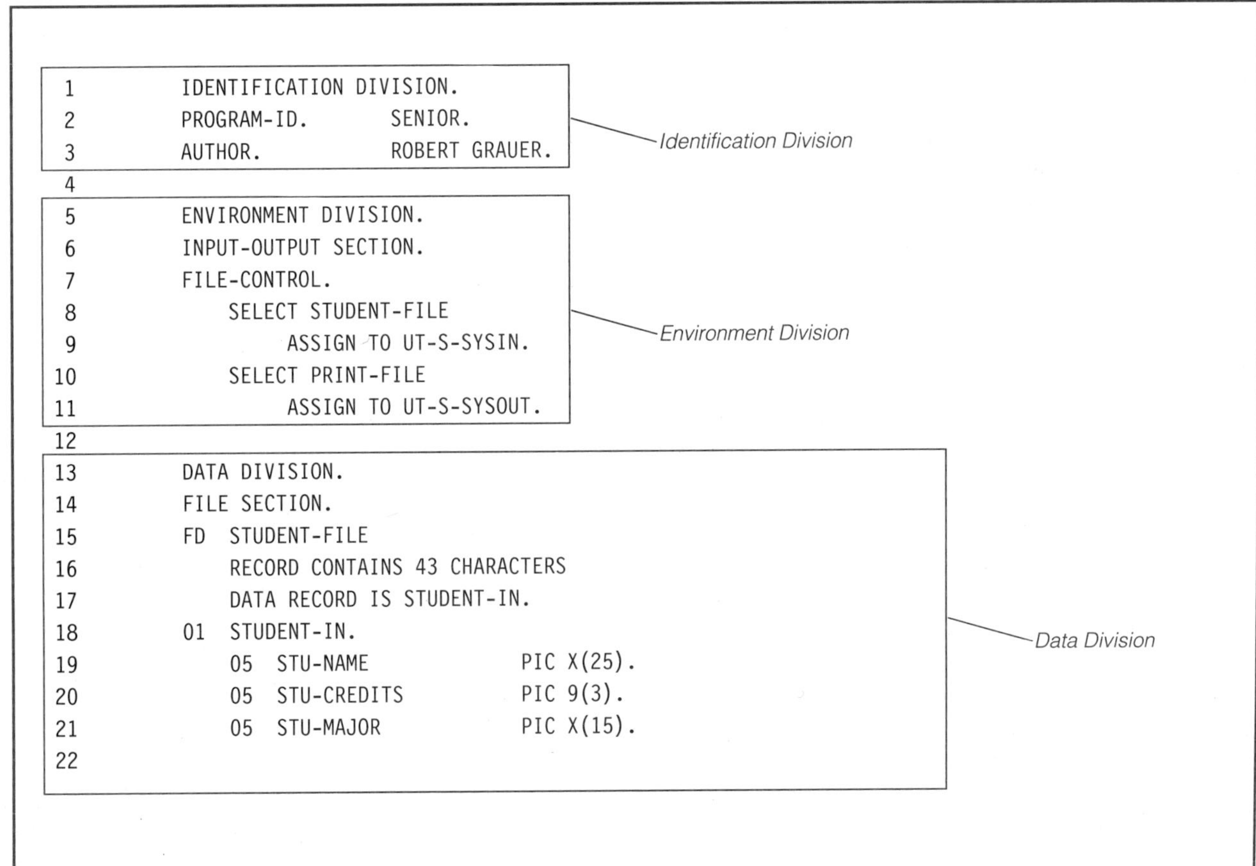

```
IDENTIFICATION DIVISION.
PROGRAM-ID.        SENIOR.
AUTHOR.            ROBERT GRAUER.

ENVIRONMENT DIVISION.
INPUT-OUTPUT SECTION.
FILE-CONTROL.
    SELECT STUDENT-FILE
         ASSIGN TO UT-S-SYSIN.
    SELECT PRINT-FILE
         ASSIGN TO UT-S-SYSOUT.

DATA DIVISION.
FILE SECTION.
FD  STUDENT-FILE
    RECORD CONTAINS 43 CHARACTERS
    DATA RECORD IS STUDENT-IN.
01  STUDENT-IN.
    05  STU-NAME             PIC X(25).
    05  STU-CREDITS          PIC 9(3).
    05  STU-MAJOR            PIC X(15).

```

Figure 1.6 *(continued)*

```
       FD  PRINT-FILE
           RECORD CONTAINS 132 CHARACTERS
           DATA RECORD IS PRINT-LINE.
       01  PRINT-LINE                PIC X(132).

       WORKING-STORAGE SECTION.
       01  DATA-REMAINS-SWITCH       PIC X(2)      VALUE SPACES.

       01  HEADING-LINE.
           05  FILLER                PIC X(10)     VALUE SPACES.
           05  FILLER                PIC X(12)     VALUE 'STUDENT NAME'.
           05  FILLER                PIC X(110)    VALUE SPACES.

       01  DETAIL-LINE.
           05  FILLER                PIC X(8)      VALUE SPACES.
           05  PRINT-NAME            PIC X(25).
           05  FILLER                PIC X(99)     VALUE SPACES.
```

Data Division

```
       PROCEDURE DIVISION.
       PREPARE-SENIOR-REPORT.
           OPEN INPUT  STUDENT-FILE
                OUTPUT PRINT-FILE.
           READ STUDENT-FILE
               AT END MOVE 'NO' TO DATA-REMAINS-SWITCH
           END-READ.
           PERFORM WRITE-HEADING-LINE.
           PERFORM PROCESS-RECORDS
               UNTIL DATA-REMAINS-SWITCH = 'NO'.
           CLOSE STUDENT-FILE
                 PRINT-FILE.
           STOP RUN.

       WRITE-HEADING-LINE.
           MOVE HEADING-LINE TO PRINT-LINE.
           WRITE PRINT-LINE.

       PROCESS-RECORDS.
           IF STU-CREDITS > 110 AND STU-MAJOR = 'ENGINEERING'
               MOVE STU-NAME TO PRINT-NAME
               MOVE DETAIL-LINE TO PRINT-LINE
               WRITE PRINT-LINE
           END-IF.
           READ STUDENT-FILE
               AT END MOVE 'NO' TO DATA-REMAINS-SWITCH
           END-READ.
```

Procedure Division

surrounds programming. Further, Figure 1.6 will become easier to understand after some brief explanation.

Every COBOL program consists of four divisions, which must appear in the following order:

`IDENTIFICATION DIVISION`	The Identification Division contains the program name and author's name.
`ENVIRONMENT DIVISION`	The Environment Division associates the file names referenced in a program to the input and output (I/O) devices recognized by the operating system.
`DATA DIVISION`	The Data Division describes the record layout of the incoming record(s) and the location of data in the generated report.
`PROCEDURE DIVISION`	The Procedure Division contains the program logic, that is, the instructions the computer is to execute in solving the problem.

Since COBOL is intended to resemble English, you may be able to get an overall sense of what is happening, merely by reading the program. We provide an intuitive explanation and reiterate that, at this time, you should in no way be concerned with the precise syntax of the language; that is, our present intent is to teach COBOL by example, with the short-term objective of achieving a conceptual understanding of a COBOL program.

The Identification Division

The **IDENTIFICATION DIVISION** (Lines 1–3) appears at the beginning of every program. It serves to identify the program (SENIOR) and the author (Robert Grauer). There is nothing complicated about this division, and it has no effect on the results of the program.

The Environment Division

The **ENVIRONMENT DIVISION** (lines 5–11) contains the INPUT-OUTPUT SECTION, which describes the files used by the program. The engineering senior program uses two files, an input file containing the student records and an output file for the report. Both of these files are defined in SELECT statements.

The names chosen by the programmer for these files (that is, STUDENT-FILE and PRINT-FILE) are assigned to logical devices known to the operating system, by the SELECT statement and associated ASSIGN clause. Line 8, for example, ties the incoming STUDENT-FILE to the logical device, UT-S-SYSIN; this tells the operating system to read the file containing the incoming student records from the device UT-S-SYSIN. (The name of the device, such as UT-S-SYSIN, is installation dependent and varies from computer to computer.)

The Data Division

The **DATA DIVISION** (lines 13–39) describes all data elements used by the program. It is divided into two sections, the FILE SECTION (lines 14–26) and the WORKING-STORAGE SECTION (lines 28–39).

The **FILE SECTION** contains file description (FD) entries for files previously defined in SELECT statements. The FD for STUDENT-FILE extends from line 15 to line 17 and contains clauses that describe the physical characteristics of the file. The FD is followed by a ***record description,*** which defines the various fields within the record (lines 18–21).

The statements within the record description are preceded by ***level numbers,*** in this example, 01 and 05. The level number 01 is special and indicates the beginning of a ***record description*** entry. The fields within a record are defined through a series of PICTURE clauses (PIC is an acceptable abbreviation), which indicate the ***type*** and ***size*** of the field. A picture of 9's indicates a numeric field, whereas a picture of X's signifies an alphanumeric field. The number in parentheses indicates the size of the field; for example, PIC 9(3) indicates a three-position numeric field, and PIC X(25) is a 25-position alphanumeric field. The PICTURE clauses in lines 19–21 of Figure 1.6 are consistent with the record description in the original problem statement.

The **WORKING-STORAGE SECTION** (lines 28–39) is used to define any data names that do not appear in an input or output file. The programming specifications called for two distinct print lines (a heading line and a detail line), each of which contains a different format as per the print layout of Figure 1.3. Accordingly, two different 01 entries are defined, HEADING-LINE and DETAIL-LINE, each with a different layout. The function of DATA-REMAINS-SWITCH will be made clearer after an examination of the Procedure Division.

The Procedure Division

The **PROCEDURE DIVISION** (lines 41–67) contains the logic required to solve the problem. The Procedure Division is divided into ***paragraphs,*** with each paragraph consisting of one or more sentences.

The first paragraph, PREPARE-SENIOR-REPORT, extends from line 42 to line 53. It begins by opening the files, then reading the first student record. The PERFORM statement in line 48 transfers control to the paragraph WRITE-HEADING-LINE (lines 55–57), which prints the heading, then returns control back to line 49 in the PREPARE-SENIOR-REPORT paragraph. This too is a PERFORM statement, which transfers control to the paragraph PROCESS-RECORDS (lines 59–67), which processes incoming student records until the data file is exhausted.

The IF statement in line 60 determines whether an incoming record meets both qualifications, that is, whether the student is an engineering major and has more than 110 credits. If both conditions are met, that student's name is written to the output report. The IF statement extends to the END-IF ***scope terminator*** in line 64; that is, if the condition in line 60 is met, *every* statement between the condition and the END-IF in line 64 will be executed. Note, too, that three COBOL statements are required to produce a detail line; the incoming name is moved to the output name in line 61, the detail line is moved to the print line in line 62, and the line is written in line 63.

The action of the PERFORM statement is explained with the aid of Figure 1.7. The PERFORM statement in line 49 transfers control to the paragraph PROCESS-RECORDS, until DATA-REMAINS-SWITCH = 'NO', that is, until the data file is empty. Accordingly, the last statement of the performed routine is a READ statement to read the next record. When the end-of-file is reached, the AT END clause of the READ statement will move 'NO' to DATA-REMAINS-SWITCH to terminate the PERFORM; the READ statement itself is ended by the END-READ scope terminator. Control then returns to the statement under the PERFORM statement (to line 51), which closes the files, and finally to the STOP RUN statement, which terminates the program.

Figure 1.7 Procedure Division Logic

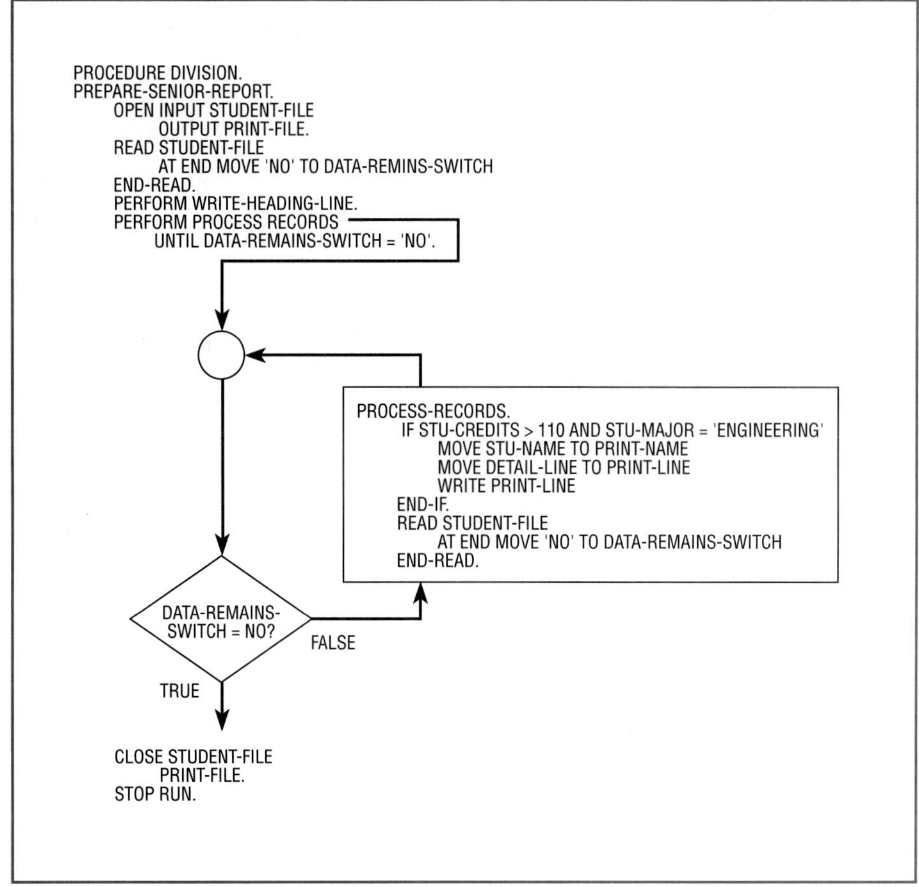

Test Data

Figure 1.8 contains test data and the associated output produced by the program in Figure 1.6. (Five more records have been added to provide additional examples.) You should be able to state the reasons why individual records were not selected for the output report; for example, Amelia Earhart and Alex Bell were rejected for the wrong major and an insufficient number of credits, respectively. (Can you identify all nine of our famous students?)

Elements of COBOL

Although you are not yet expected to write a COBOL program, you should be able to follow simple programs like the one in Figure 1.6 intuitively. This section begins a formal discussion of COBOL so that you will eventually be able to write an entire program.

COBOL consists of six language elements: reserved words, programmer-supplied names, literals, symbols, level numbers, and pictures.

Reserved Words

Reserved words have special significance to COBOL and are used in a rigidly prescribed manner. They must be spelled correctly, or the compiler will not be able

Figure 1.8 Test Data and Associated Output

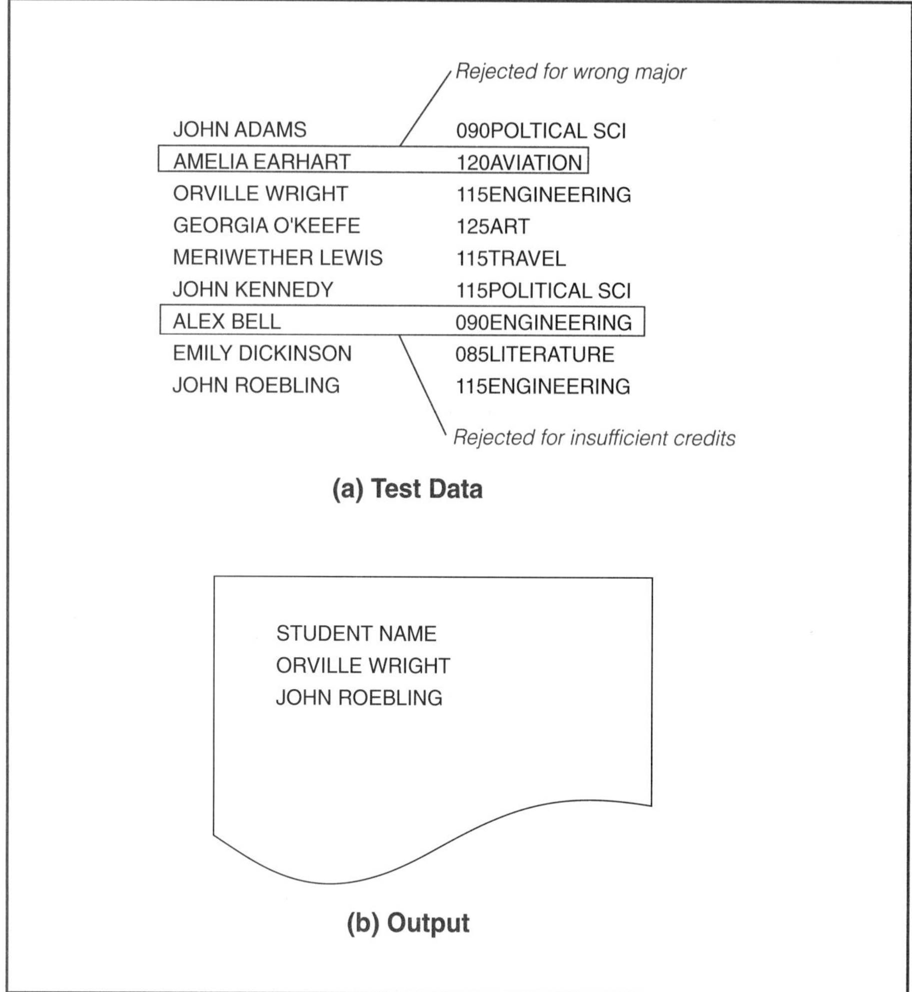

to recognize them. The list of reserved words varies from compiler to compiler. A comprehensive list of reserved words is given in Appendix C. The beginner is urged to refer frequently to this appendix for two reasons: (1) to ensure the proper spelling of reserved words used in his or her program; and (2) to avoid the inadvertent use of reserved words as programmer-supplied names.

Programmer-Supplied Names

You, the programmer, supply names for paragraphs, data elements, and files. A ***paragraph name*** is a tag to which the program refers, for example, PROCESS-RECORDS or PREPARE-SENIOR-REPORT in Figure 1.6. ***Data names*** are the elements on which instructions operate, for example, STU-NAME, STU-CREDITS, and STU-MAJOR in Figure 1.6. ***File names*** are specified in several places throughout a COBOL program, but their initial appearance is in the Environment Division, for example, STUDENT-FILE and PRINT-FILE in Figure 1.6. All programmer-supplied names are chosen according to the following rules:

1. A programmer-supplied name may contain the letters A to Z, the digits 0 to 9, and the hyphen; no other characters are permitted, not even blanks.

2. A programmer-supplied name may *not* begin or end with a hyphen.
3. A programmer-supplied name must be 30 characters or fewer in length.
4. A reserved word may *not* be used as a programmer-supplied name.
5. Data names must contain at least one letter.
6. Paragraph names may be all numeric.

Table 1.2 illustrates examples of the rules associated with programmer-supplied names.

TABLE 1.2 Programmer-Supplied Names

PROGRAMMER-SUPPLIED NAME	EXPLANATION
SUM	**Invalid**—reserved word
SUM-OF-X	**Valid**
SUM OF X	**Invalid**—contains blanks
SUM-OF-X-	**Invalid**—ends with a hyphen
SUM-OF-ALL-THE-XS	**Valid**
SUM-OF-ALL-THE-XS-IN-ENTIRE-PROGRAM	**Invalid**—more than 30 characters
GROSS-PAY-IN-$	**Invalid**—contains a $
12345	**Valid** as a paragraph name but *invalid* as a data name

Literals

A ***literal*** is an exact value or constant. Literals are of two types, ***numeric*** (a number) or ***nonnumeric*** (a character string). Literals of both types appear throughout a program and are used to compare the value of a data name to a specified constant. Consider line 60 of Figure 1.6:

```
IF STU-CREDITS  > 110 AND STU-MAJOR  = 'ENGINEERING'
```

In the first portion of the statement, STU-CREDITS is compared to 110, a numeric literal. Numeric literals adhere to the following rules:

1. A numeric literal can be up to 18 digits long.
2. A numeric literal may begin with a leading (leftmost) plus or minus sign.
3. A numeric literal may contain a decimal point, but it may *not* end with a decimal point.

The second part of the IF statement contains a nonnumeric literal, 'ENGINEERING'. Nonnumeric literals adhere to the following rules:

1. A nonnumeric literal is enclosed in apostrophes (or quotation marks) as specified by the compiler.
2. A nonnumeric literal may be up to 160 characters in length.
3. A nonnumeric literal may contain anything, including blanks, numbers, and reserved words, but not another apostrophe (or quotation mark).

Examples of both numeric and nonnumeric literals are shown Table 1.3.

TABLE 1.3 Numeric and Nonnumeric Literals

LITERAL	EXPLANATION
123.4	Valid numeric literal
'123.4'	Valid nonnumeric literal
+123	Valid numeric literal
'IDENTIFICATION DIVISION'	Valid nonnumeric literal
123.	Invalid numeric literal—may not end with a decimal point
123-	Invalid numeric literal—the minus sign must be in the leftmost position

Symbols

Symbols are of three types—punctuation, arithmetic, and relational, as listed in Table 1.4.

TABLE 1.4 Symbols

CATEGORY	SYMBOL	MEANING
Punctuation	.	Denotes end of COBOL entry
	,	Delineates clauses
	' or "	Sets off nonnumeric literals
	( )	Encloses subscripts or expressions
Arithmetic	+	Addition
	-	Subtraction
	*	Multiplication
	/	Division
	**	Exponentiation
Relational	=	Equal to
	>	Greater than
	<	Less than
	>=	Greater than or equal to
	<=	Less than or equal to

The use of relational and arithmetic symbols is described in detail later in the text, beginning in Chapter 4. A period terminates an entry, and its omission (in the absence of a scope terminator) can cause difficulty. A comma, on the other hand, is entirely optional, and its omission (or inclusion) has no effect whatsoever on the program. The use of commas is discouraged, however, as a comma can be mistaken for a period on older printers, which tend to blur the output.

Level Numbers

Level numbers describe the relationship of items in a record. For example, under STUDENT-FILE in Figure 1.6, there was a single 01-level entry and several 05-level entries. In general, the higher (numerically) the level number, the less significant the entry; thus 05 is less important than 01. Entries with higher numeric values are said to belong to the levels above them. Thus, in Figure 1.6 the several 05-level entries belong to their respective 01-level entries.

PICTURE Clauses

Pictures describe the nature of incoming or outgoing data. A picture of 9's means the entry is numeric; a picture of X's means the entry is alphanumeric, that is, it can contain letters, numbers, and special characters. (Alphabetic pictures, with a picture of A, are seldom used; even names can contain apostrophes or hyphens, which are alphanumeric rather than alphabetic in nature.) Level numbers and pictures are discussed more fully in Chapter 4.

A Second Look at COBOL

Figure 1.9 contains a relabeled version of the Engineering Senior Program and represents a second look at COBOL. This time our intention is to emphasize the various COBOL elements as they appear in a complete program.

Figure 1.9 The Engineering Senior Program (A Second Look)

```
1     IDENTIFICATION DIVISION.
2     PROGRAM-ID.        SENIOR.
3     AUTHOR.            ROBERT GRAUER.
4
5     ENVIRONMENT DIVISION.
6     INPUT-OUTPUT SECTION.
7     FILE-CONTROL.
8         SELECT STUDENT-FILE
9              ASSIGN TO UT-S-SYSIN.
10        SELECT PRINT-FILE
11             ASSIGN TO UT-S-SYSOUT.
12
13    DATA DIVISION.
14    FILE SECTION.
15    FD  STUDENT-FILE
16        RECORD CONTAINS 43 CHARACTERS
17        DATA RECORD IS STUDENT-IN.
18    01  STUDENT-IN.
19        05  STU-NAME          PIC X(25).
20        05  STU-CREDITS       PIC 9(3).
21        05  STU-MAJOR         PIC X(15).
22
23    FD  PRINT-FILE
24        RECORD CONTAINS 132 CHARACTERS
25        DATA RECORD IS PRINT-LINE.
26    01  PRINT-LINE            PIC X(132).
27
28    WORKING-STORAGE SECTION.
29    01  DATA-REMAINS-SWITCH   PIC X(2)      VALUE SPACES.
30
```

Programmer-supplied file name appears in several places (see lines 43, 45, 51, and 65)
PICTURE clauses describe incoming record and are consistent with the data in Figure 1.3
Reserved words

Figure 1.9 *(continued)*

```
31      01  HEADING-LINE.
32          05  FILLER              PIC X(10)     VALUE SPACES.
33          05  FILLER              PIC X(12)     VALUE 'STUDENT NAME'.
34          05  FILLER              PIC X(110)    VALUE SPACES.
35
36      01  DETAIL-LINE.
37          05  FILLER              PIC X(8)      VALUE SPACES.
38          05  PRINT-NAME          PIC X(25).
39          05  FILLER              PIC X(99)     VALUE SPACES.
40
41      PROCEDURE DIVISION.
42      PREPARE-SENIOR-REPORT.
43          OPEN INPUT  STUDENT-FILE
44               OUTPUT PRINT-FILE.
45          READ STUDENT-FILE
46              AT END MOVE 'NO' TO DATA-REMAINS-SWITCH
47          END-READ.
48          PERFORM WRITE-HEADING-LINE.
49          PERFORM PROCESS-RECORDS
50              UNTIL DATA-REMAINS-SWITCH = 'NO'.
51          CLOSE STUDENT-FILE
52                PRINT-FILE.
53          STOP RUN.
54
55      WRITE-HEADING-LINE.
56          MOVE HEADING-LINE TO PRINT-LINE.
57          WRITE PRINT-LINE.
58
59      PROCESS-RECORDS.
60          IF STU-CREDITS > 110 AND STU-MAJOR = 'ENGINEERING'
61              MOVE STU-NAME TO PRINT-NAME
62              MOVE DETAIL-LINE TO PRINT-LINE
63              WRITE PRINT-LINE
64          END-IF.
65          READ STUDENT-FILE
66              AT END MOVE 'NO' TO DATA-REMAINS-SWITCH
67          END-READ.
```

Reserved words (PROCEDURE DIVISION., line 41)

Programmer-supplied paragraph name (PERFORM PROCESS-RECORDS, line 49; PROCESS-RECORDS., line 59)

Numeric literal (110, line 60)

Nonnumeric literal ('ENGINEERING', line 60)

Observe, for example, the definition of a ***file name***, STUDENT-FILE, in the SELECT statement of line 8, and its subsequent appearance in the FD of line 15, and the OPEN, READ, and CLOSE statements of lines 43, 45, 51, and 65. Notice the definition of the various ***data names*** in lines 19–21 (accomplished through level numbers and PICTURE clauses) and the subsequent appearances in the Procedure Division. Note the consistency of the paragraph name in the PERFORM statement of line 49 and the paragraph header in line 59. Observe that literals appear in the IF statement of line 60 and in the AT END clause of the READ statement (lines 46 and 66). Finally, note the abundant use of COBOL reserved words (PROCEDURE, DIVISION, WORKING-STORAGE, SECTION, and so on) throughout.

SUMMARY

Points to Remember

- A field is a basic fact, such as the name, address, major, grade point average, or number of completed credits. A record is a set of fields, and a file is a set of records.
- Every computer application consists of input, processing, and output.
- The computer cannot think for itself but must be told precisely what to do. This is done through a series of instructions known as a program.
- The computer does not do anything that a human being could not do if given sufficient time. The advantages of a computer stem from its speed and accuracy.
- A flowchart and/or pseudocode represent the logic embodied in a computer program.
- Every COBOL program contains four divisions, which appear in the sequence: Identification, Environment, Data, and Procedure.
- COBOL contains six language elements; reserved words, programmer-supplied names, literals, symbols, level numbers, and pictures.

Key Words and Concepts

Alphabetic data
Alphanumeric data
Arithmetic symbol
End-of-file
Field
File
Flowchart
Initialization
Level number
Nonnumeric literal
Numeric data
Numeric literal
Paragraph
Processing
Programmer-supplied name
Programming specifications
Pseudocode
Punctuation symbol
Record
Record description
Relational symbol
Reserved words
Scope terminator
Symbol
Termination
Test Data

COBOL Elements

```
DATA DIVISION
ENVIRONMENT DIVISION
FILE SECTION
IDENTIFICATION DIVISION
INPUT-OUTPUT SECTION
PICTURE
PROCEDURE DIVISION
WORKING-STORAGE SECTION
```

FILL-IN

1. All computer applications consist of ____________, ____________, and ____________.
2. The divisions of a COBOL program appear in the order: ____________, ____________, ____________, and ____________.
3. A ____________ is a pictorial representation of the logic in a program.
4. ____________ may be described as neat notes to oneself.
5. A diamond-shaped block in a flowchart indicates a ____________.
6. ____________ ____________ have special significance to COBOL and must be used in a rigidly prescribed manner and be spelled correctly.
7. A ____________-____________ ____________ may contain the letters A to Z, the digits 0 to 9, and the hyphen.
8. ** is the COBOL symbol for ____________.
9. =, > , and < are examples of ____________ symbols in COBOL.
10. A ____________ is a set of records.
11. A record consists of one or more ____________.
12. A ____________ is a set of instructions to a computer.

TRUE/FALSE

1. Nonnumeric literals may not contain numbers.
2. Numeric literals may not contain letters.
3. A data name may not contain any characters other than letters or numbers.
4. The rules for forming paragraph names and data names are exactly the same.
5. A data name may not consist of more than 30 characters.
6. A nonnumeric literal may not contain more than 30 characters.
7. A numeric literal may contain up to 18 digits.
8. There are four divisions in a COBOL program.
9. The divisions of a COBOL program may appear in any order.
10. Data description appears in the Identification Division.
11. A record contains one or more fields.
12. A file is a set of records.
13. Computers can think for themselves.
14. No statement in a computer program may be executed more than once.
15. A rectangle is the standard flowchart symbol for a decision block.
16. Reserved words may appear in a nonnumeric literal.
17. Reserved words may be used as data names.

18. Pseudocode serves the same function as a flowchart.
19. Pseudocode must be written according to precise syntactical rules.
20. The COBOL compiler needs to be installed every time a program is executed.

PROBLEMS

1. Indicate whether the entries below are valid as data names. If any entry is invalid, state the reason.
   a. NUMBER-OF-TIMES
   b. CODE
   c. 12345
   d. ONE TWO THREE
   e. IDENTIFICATION-DIVISION
   f. IDENTIFICATION
   g. HOURS
   h. GROSS-PAY
   i. GROSS-PAY-IN-$
2. Classify the entries below as being valid or invalid literals. For each valid entry, indicate whether it is numeric or nonnumeric; for each invalid entry, state why it is invalid.
   a. 567
   b. 567.
   c. -567
   d. +567
   e. +567.
   f. '567.'
   g. 'FIVE SIX SEVEN'
   h. '-567'
   i. 567-
   j. 567+
   k. '567+'
3. a. Which division(s) contain paragraph names?
   b. Which division(s) contain the SELECT statement(s)?
   c. Which division(s) contain level numbers?
   d. Which division(s) contain data names?
   e. Which division(s) contain reserved words?
   f. Which division(s) contain PICTURE clauses?
   g. Which division(s) do not contain file names?
4. Given the COBOL program in Figure 1.6, indicate what changes would have to be made if
   a. We wanted music students rather than engineering students.
   b. We wanted students with 60 or fewer credits.
   c. The student major was contained in columns 60–74 of the incoming record.
   d. We wanted engineering students *or* students with 110 credits or more.

   Note: Treat parts (a), (b), (c), and (d) independently.

5. Which division in a COBOL program contains
   a. The File Section?
   b. Statements to open and close files?
   c. The description of incoming data?
   d. The description of outgoing data?
   e. The author's name?
   f. The program's name?
   g. Statements to read information?
   h. Statements to write information?

6. Your programming supervisor has drawn a flowchart for you to code. He left the flowchart on his dining room table at home, and unfortunately his three-year-old son, Benjy, cut it up into pieces with a pair of scissors. Your supervisor has collected the pieces (shown in Figure 1.10) and has asked you to rearrange them properly into a correct flowchart; do so. The flowchart is to read a file with each record containing three unequal numbers, A, B, and C. Write out the greater of the two sums (A + B) and (B + C) for each record only if A is less than 50. Develop the equivalent pseudocode.

7. World Wide Sales, Inc., wishes to promote one of its employees to head the South American Division. The selected employee must speak Spanish, be 40 or younger, and hold a college degree. The programming manager has prepared the necessary flowchart (see Figure 1.11), but unfortunately Benjy and his scissors got to it first (see Problem 6). Your job is to put the flowchart together. Note that there may be more than one employee who qualifies for the position. Accordingly, the flowchart includes the necessary logic to count and print the number of qualified employees and to print the name of every such employee. Develop the equivalent pseudocode.

8. Figure 1.12 contains a COBOL program to process a file of employee records and print the names of programmers under 30. Using Figure 1.6 as a guide, restore the missing information so that the program will run as intended.

Figure 1.10 Flowchart Blocks for Problem 6

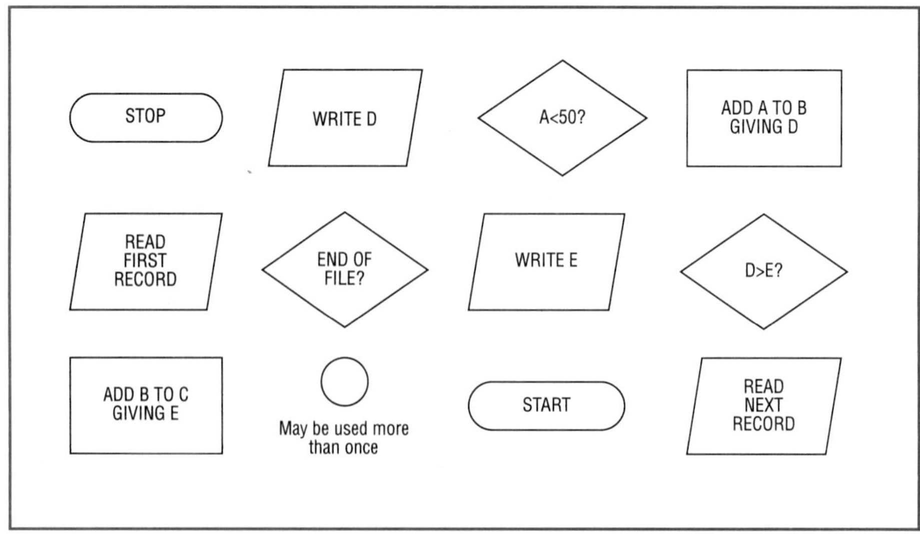

Figure 1.11 Flowchart Blocks for Problem 7

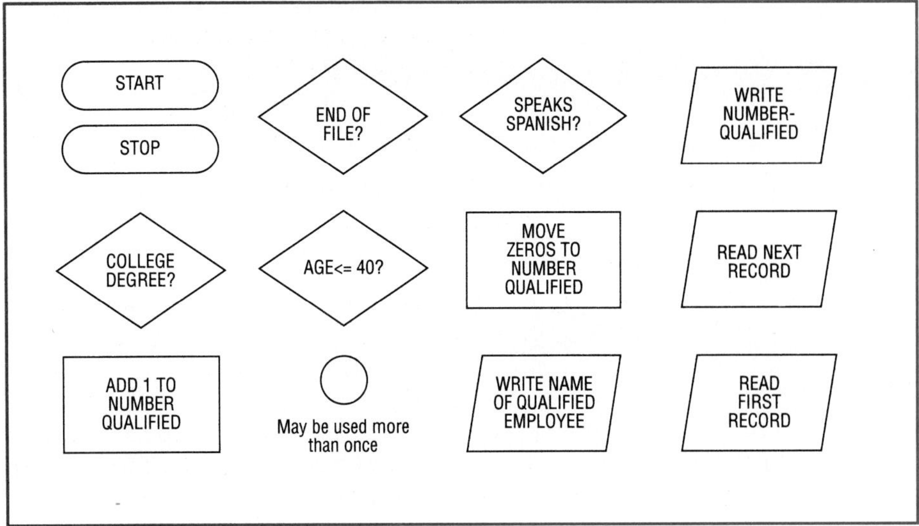

Figure 1.12 COBOL Listing for Problem 8

```
IDENTIFICATION DIVISION.
PROGRAM-ID.  FIRSTTRY.
1 __________ GRAUER.

ENVIRONMENT DIVISION.
INPUT-OUTPUT SECTION.
FILE-CONTROL.
    SELECT EMPLOYEE-FILE
        ASSIGN TO UT-S-SYSIN.
  2 ______ PRINT-FILE
        ASSIGN TO UT-S-SYSOUT.

3 ____________
FILE SECTION.
FD  EMPLOYEE-FILE
    RECORD CONTAINS 44 CHARACTERS
    DATA RECORD IS EMPLOYEE-RECORD.
01  EMPLOYEE-RECORD.
    05  EMP-NAME                PIC X(25).
    05  EMP-TITLE               PIC X(10).
    05  EMP-AGE                 PIC 99.
    05  FILLER                  PIC XX.
    05  EMP-SALARY              PIC 9(5).
```

Figure 1.12 COBOL Listing for Problem 8 *(continued)*

```
       FD   ________ 4
           RECORD CONTAINS 132 CHARACTERS
           DATA RECORD IS PRINT-LINE.
       01  PRINT-LINE.
           05  FILLER                  PIC X.
           05  PRINT-NAME              ________ 5
           05  FILLER                  PIC X(2).
           05  PRINT-AGE               PIC 99.
           05  FILLER                  PIC X(3).
           05  PRINT-SALARY            PIC 9(5).
           05  FILLER                  PIC X(94).

     6 ____________________
       01  END-OF-DATA-FLAG            PIC X(3)       ________ 7
       PROCEDURE DIVISION.
       MAINLINE.
         8 ____  INPUT EMPLOYEE-FILE
               OUTPUT PRINT-FILE.
           MOVE SPACES TO PRINT-LINE.
           MOVE 'SALARY REPORT FOR PROGRAMMERS UNDER 30' TO PRINT-LINE.
           WRITE PRINT-LINE
              AFTER ADVANCING 2 LINES.
           READ EMPLOYEE-FILE
               AT END MOVE 'YES' TO END-OF-DATA-FLAG
           END-READ.
         9 _______ PROCESS-EMPLOYEE-RECORDS
               UNTIL END-OF-DATA-FLAG = 'YES'.
           CLOSE EMPLOYEE-FILE
                PRINT-FILE.
           STOP RUN.

       PROCESS-EMPLOYEE-RECORDS.
           IF EMP-TITLE = 'PROGRAMMER' AND EMP-AGE < 30
               MOVE SPACES TO PRINT-LINE
               MOVE EMP-NAME TO PRINT-NAME
               MOVE ________ TO PRINT-AGE          10
               MOVE EMP-SALARY TO PRINT-SALARY
               WRITE PRINT-LINE
           END-IF.
           READ EMPLOYEE-FILE
               AT END MOVE ______ TO END-OF-DATA-FLAG     11
           END-READ.
```

2

From Coding Form to Computer

CHAPTER OUTLINE

OBJECTIVES

After reading this chapter you will be able to:

- State the rules associated with the COBOL coding sheet, and enter a program appropriately.
- Distinguish between compilation and execution; describe the function of a link program.
- Describe the environmental differences between a PC and a mainframe as they relate to execution of COBOL programs.
- Compile, link, and execute a COBOL program.
- Find and correct simple errors in compilation or execution.

OVERVIEW

This chapter continues with the engineering senior program of Chapter 1, describing how to actually run a COBOL program. We discuss the COBOL coding form and its associated rules, the use of an editor (or word processor) to create COBOL programs and/or data files, and the procedure for submission to the computer. We describe the compile, link, and execute sequence. We also prepare you for the errors you will inevitably make, discuss fundamentals of debugging, and alert you to the subtle differences between the two standards in use today, COBOL-74 and COBOL-85.

At the conclusion of the chapter we ask you to run the engineering senior program of Chapter 1. *Seeing is believing* may be a cliché, but it is only after you have seen output from your own program that the material truly begins to make sense. Suffice it to say then, that the sooner you are on the computer, the sooner you will appreciate the subtleties inherent in programming.

From Coding Form to Computer

Chapter 1 ended with presentation of a completed COBOL program, and a discussion of the elements that make up the COBOL language. The program, however, is not yet in a form suitable for execution on the computer, and much has to be done in order for this to be accomplished. That is the overriding objective of this chapter.

The flowchart in Figure 2.1 depicts the various steps in solving a problem through use of a computer. The first step is to obtain a clear statement of the problem, containing a complete description of the input and desired output. The problem statement should also contain detailed processing specifications. It is not enough, for example, to say calculate a student's grade point average; instead the method for calculating the average must be provided as well.

Once the input, output, and processing specifications have been enumerated, a hierarchy chart (see Chapter 3) is created, then a flowchart or pseudocode is developed. Careful attention to these steps will simplify the subsequent program and increase the likelihood it will be correct.

Coding is the translation of the hierarchy chart, flowchart, and/or pseudocode into COBOL. Coding must be done within the well-defined rules of COBOL regarding

Figure 2.1 The Programming Process

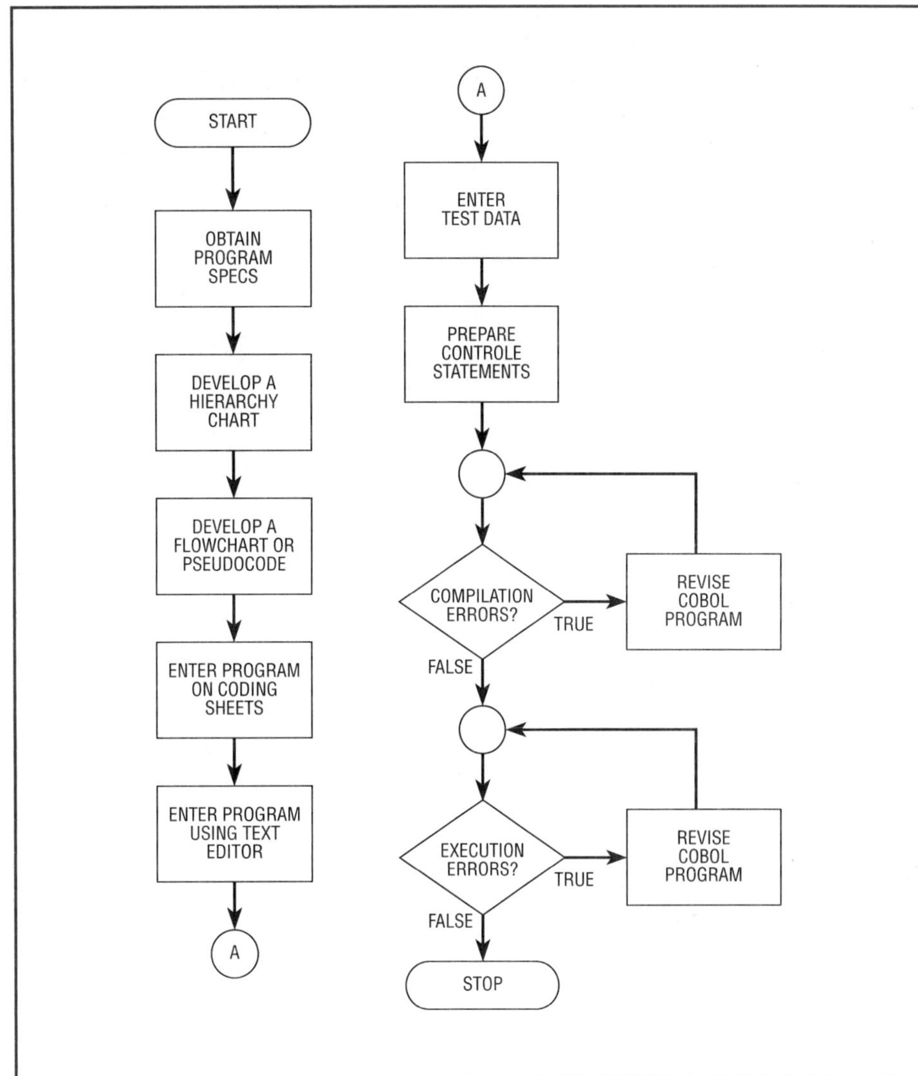

the placement of various statements in specific areas of the coding form. After coding, the program is entered into a file suitable for input to a computer through use of an editor.

The program is then submitted to the computer in conjunction with a set of control statements. The latter provide information to the operating system as to the location of the COBOL program and/or its associated data. The control statements vary greatly from installation to installation.

Next comes compilation in which the COBOL program is translated into machine language. Initial attempts at compilation are apt to identify several errors, due to misspellings, missing periods, misplaced parentheses, etc. Corrections are made, and the program is recompiled. Only after the compilation has been successfully completed can we proceed to execution.

During execution the computer does exactly what it was instructed to do, which may be different from what you want it to do. For example, if OR were substituted for AND in line 60 of the engineering senior program, the program would select *either* engineering majors *or* seniors. Either way, it would function differently from the original, logically correct version, although the program would still compile cleanly. Corrections are made, the program is recompiled, and testing continues.

The presence of the two decision blocks in Figure 2.1 indicates the iterative nature of the entire process. Few, if any, programs compile correctly on the first try—hence the need to recode specific statements. Similarly, programs may not execute properly on the first attempt, and thus the need to revise the program, recompile, reexecute, and so on.

The COBOL Coding Form

The COBOL compiler is very particular about the information it receives, and requires a program to be written within its well-defined syntax. For example, division and section headers are required to begin between columns 8 and 11, whereas most other statements begin in or past column 12. There are additional rules for continuation (what happens if a statement does not fit on one line), comments, optional sequencing of source statements in columns 1–6, and program identification in columns 73–80.

The rules of the coding sheet are summarized in Table 2.1, and illustrated in Figure 2.2. The latter shows completed forms for the engineering senior problem of Chapter 1. Several features in Figure 2.2 bear mention. Note in particular the wavy line under various PIC entries to indicate that identical information is to be entered on subsequent lines. Of greatest import, however, is the conformity between the entries in Figure 2.2 and the COBOL requirements of Table 2.1.

Coding sheets are not mandatory and you can use ordinary paper instead. You will find, however, that programming is much easier, if you are well organized. A good start is to have the program neatly entered in appropriate columns before sitting down at the computer.

Use of an Editor

Once a program has been written on coding sheets, it is entered through an editor (or word processor) into a file for subsequent input to the computer. In all likelihood you are already familiar with a word processor, and can use that to create and edit COBOL programs as well. Accordingly, be sure you can do all of the following:

1. Save the program as an unformatted (ASCII text) file, with a file name of your own choosing, consistent with the computer on which you will execute the program.
2. Retrieve the file, then resave it after making additional modifications.
3. Toggle between the insertion and replacement modes to change characters within a statement, and/or to insert and/or delete statements within a program.
4. Print a listing of the file.

You will also find it useful to learn the commands to:

1. Set tabs to move to designated columns; for example, columns 8 and 12 for the A and B margins, respectively.
2. Search and/or replace character strings.
3. Move to specified places within the program; for example, the beginning or end, a particular line, the start of the Procedure Division, and so on.

The availability of an on-line editor facilitates programming to an extent that was unimaginable to tens of thousands of COBOL programmers of the 1960s and

TABLE 2.1 Rules for the COBOL Coding Form

COLUMN	EXPLANATION AND USE
1–6	***Optional sequence numbers***; If this field is coded, the compiler performs a sequence check on incoming COBOL statements by flagging any statements out of order. Although some commercial installations encourage this option, we advise against it, especially since you are entering your own programs, and the more you type, the more chance for error.
7	An asterisk in column 7 indicates a ***comment***, while a hyphen is used for the ***continuation of nonnumeric literals*** (described further on page 180). Comments may appear anywhere in a program; they are shown on the source listing but are otherwise ignored.
8–11	Known as the ***A margin***; Division headers, section headers, paragraph names, FD's, and 01's all begin in the A margin.
12–72	Known as the ***B margin***; All remaining entries begin in or past column 12. COBOL permits considerable flexibility here, but individual installations have their own requirements. We, for example, begin PICTURE clauses in the same column, for example, column 37, for better readability. (We shall discuss this further in Chapter 7.)
73–80	***Program identification***; a second optional field, which is ignored by the compiler. Different installations have different standards regarding use of this field.

Figure 2.2 The COBOL Coding Form

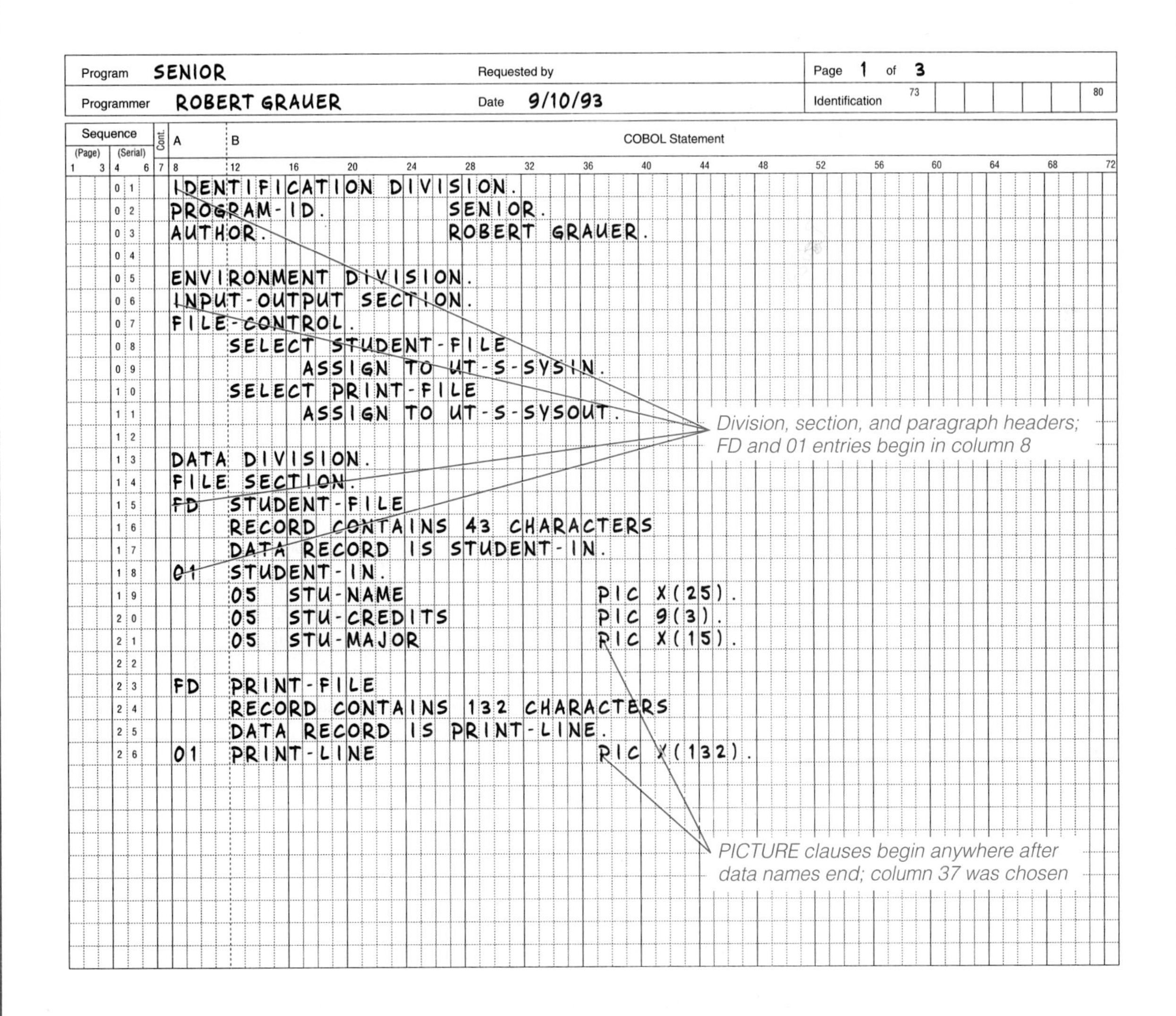

Program SENIOR Requested by Page 1 of 3
Programmer ROBERT GRAUER Date 9/10/93 Identification

```
IDENTIFICATION DIVISION.
PROGRAM-ID.                 SENIOR.
AUTHOR.                     ROBERT GRAUER.

ENVIRONMENT DIVISION.
INPUT-OUTPUT SECTION.
FILE-CONTROL.
    SELECT STUDENT-FILE
           ASSIGN TO UT-S-SYSIN.
    SELECT PRINT-FILE
           ASSIGN TO UT-S-SYSOUT.

DATA DIVISION.
FILE SECTION.
FD  STUDENT-FILE
    RECORD CONTAINS 43 CHARACTERS
    DATA RECORD IS STUDENT-IN.
01  STUDENT-IN.
    05  STU-NAME                PIC X(25).
    05  STU-CREDITS             PIC 9(3).
    05  STU-MAJOR               PIC X(15).

FD  PRINT-FILE
    RECORD CONTAINS 132 CHARACTERS
    DATA RECORD IS PRINT-LINE.
01  PRINT-LINE                  PIC X(132).
```

Figure 2.2 *(continued)*

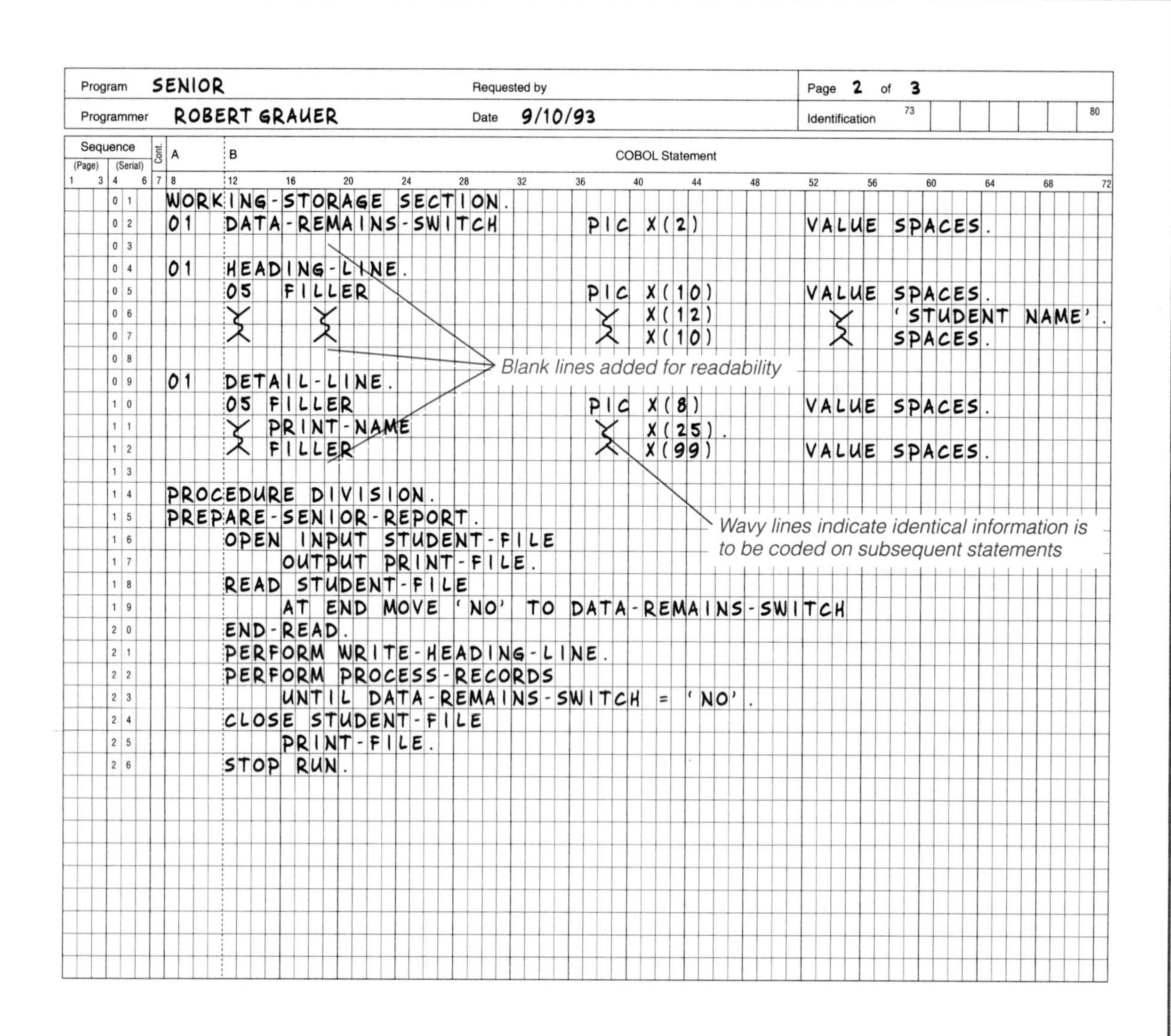

Program SENIOR	Requested by	Page 2 of 3
Programmer ROBERT GRAUER	Date 9/10/93	Identification

```
       WORKING-STORAGE SECTION.
       01  DATA-REMAINS-SWITCH          PIC X(2)     VALUE SPACES.

       01  HEADING-LINE.
           05  FILLER                   PIC X(10)    VALUE SPACES.
                                            X(12)          'STUDENT NAME'.
                                            X(10)          SPACES.

       01  DETAIL-LINE.
           05  FILLER                   PIC X(8)     VALUE SPACES.
               PRINT-NAME                   X(25).
               FILLER                       X(99)    VALUE SPACES.

       PROCEDURE DIVISION.
       PREPARE-SENIOR-REPORT.
           OPEN INPUT STUDENT-FILE
                OUTPUT PRINT-FILE.
           READ STUDENT-FILE
                AT END MOVE 'NO' TO DATA-REMAINS-SWITCH
           END-READ.
           PERFORM WRITE-HEADING-LINE.
           PERFORM PROCESS-RECORDS
                UNTIL DATA-REMAINS-SWITCH = 'NO'.
           CLOSE STUDENT-FILE
                 PRINT-FILE.
           STOP RUN.
```


early 1970s. COBOL itself is over 30 years old, and for much of its existence the punched card and batch processing (often with turnaround times of several hours or more) was the way in which programs were submitted. Students today are far more fortunate in the available technology, taking for granted the ability to execute a program many times in a single session, instead of having to wait hours (or days) to retrieve a single run, wait hours more for the next run, etc.

The Compile, Link, and Execute Sequence

The material on the coding sheet and use of an editor is straightforward, and should pose little difficulty. The execution of a COBOL program, however, is more complex, and is explained in conjunction with Figure 2.3. The figure shows the execution of three distinct programs, a ***compiler***, ***linker*** (or linkage-editor on IBM mainframes), and ***load module***, each of which is necessary to produce the list of engineering seniors. Realize, too, that the process described in Figure 2.3 is required for any COBOL program, even one as simple as the engineering senior example.

Figure 2.2 *(continued)*

Program SENIOR — Requested by — Page 3 of 3
Programmer ROBERT GRAUER — Date 9/10/93 — Identification

```
       WRITE-HEADING-LINE.
           MOVE HEADING-LINE TO PRINT-LINE.
           WRITE PRINT-LINE.

       PROCESS RECORDS.
           IF STU-CREDITS > 110 AND STU-MAJOR = 'ENGINEERING'
                MOVE STU-NAME TO PRINT-NAME
                MOVE DETAIL-LINE TO PRINT-LINE
                WRITE PRINT-LINE
           END-IF.
           READ STUDENT-FILE
                AT END MOVE 'NO' TO DATA-REMAINS-SWITCH
           END-READ.
```

Procedure Division statements begin in or past column 12

Optional indentation to indicate these statements "belong" to the IF

The procedure begins with the COBOL ***compiler***, a program that accepts a COBOL (source) program as input, and produces a machine-language (object) program as output. The result of the compilation, the object program, is input into a second program called the ***linker***, that combines the object program with subroutines and other object modules to produce a load module. Execution of the compiled COBOL program takes place in the third step as the ***load module*** accepts input data and produces an output report.

The execution of the various programs in Figure 2.3 does not happen through wishful thinking, but through specification of commands to the ***operating system*** to describe these programs and their associated data files. Every operating system has its own specific commands, but the underlying concept is the same, namely that three different programs (a compiler, linker, and load module) are required. It will be necessary, therefore, to learn the commands for your particular configuration in order to compile, link, and execute a COBOL program.[1]

---

1. Appendices A and B describe the CA-Realia® Classroom COBOL compiler that accompanies this text and the associated DOS commands for use on a PC.

Figure 2.3 Compile, Link, and Execute Sequence

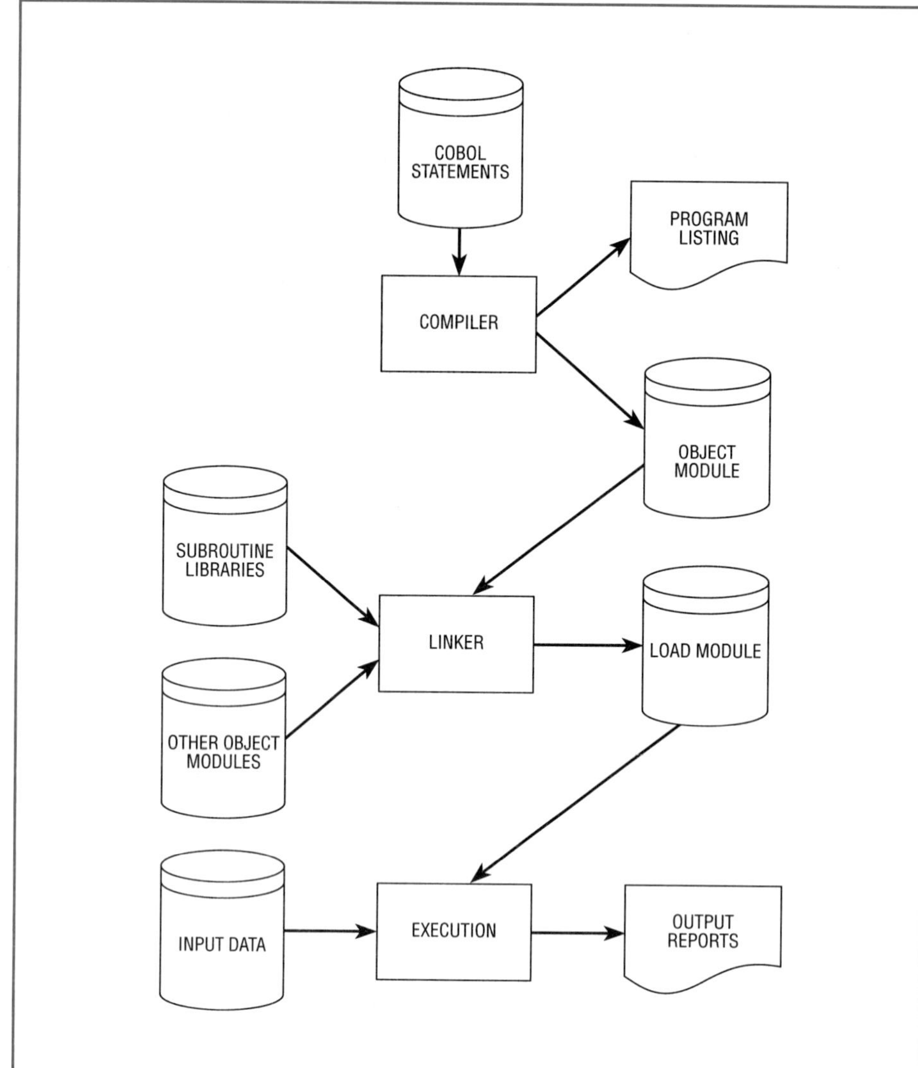

Learning by Doing

One learns by doing. This time-worn axiom is especially true for programming. We have covered a lot of material since you first began reading Chapter 1. Now it is time to put everything together and actually run your first program. Enter the program on the coding sheets in Figure 2.2, using the appropriate editor. Prepare the necessary control statements for the operating system. Create your own test data, or use Figure 1.8a. Submit the job and retrieve your output.

We believe—in fact we are very sure—that after you receive your first computer printout, many things will fall into place. Nevertheless, the first program is in many ways the most difficult you will attempt, and you should be prepared for problems along the way. The difficulty is not in the program's complexity (the engineering senior program is logically trivial). Nor is it in the COBOL syntax, in that the program uses only a fraction of the COBOL features you will eventually employ. The problems arise in interacting with the computer, using the editor, entering the proper commands to the operating system, and so on. Murphy's Law is perhaps the most eloquent statement of what to expect, and thus you should be prepared for any or all of the ensuing errors.

Errors in Entering the Program

The errors that occur as you enter the program are potentially the most damaging, especially if you spend hours entering the program and then forget to save it, save it incorrectly, or delete it unintentionally. A suggested course of action for your first attempt is to enter only the first two lines of the program, save these, log off the system, then log on and retrieve the file. In this way you are sure you know how to use the editor. Other frequent errors are to enter information in the wrong columns, to misuse a tab key, and so on.

Errors in Operating System Commands

The syntax of operating system commands has to be followed exactly, in order for the system to do your bidding. Simple mistakes result in baffling errors; for example, *Bad command or file name,* when you misspell an MS-DOS command, and/or fail to indicate the proper subdirectory where the command is located. In similar fashion the control statements submitted on a mainframe must be syntactically correct, or everything else will fail. Invalid job streams result in the system being unable to execute the job, leaving you with the most frustrating of all messages, *Job not run due to JCL error.*

Errors in Compilation

A ***compilation error*** occurs whenever you violate a rule of COBOL, for example, misspelling a reserved word or misplacing a period. The result of the error is that the compiler is unable to translate a portion of the COBOL program to machine language, and any subsequent attempt at execution will (most likely) be incorrect.

Consider, for example, Figure 2.4a, which contains a slightly modified version of the Engineering Senior Program of Figure 1.6, in which lines 59–64 have been

Figure 2.4 Engineering Senior Program with Compilation Errors

```
 1        IDENTIFICATION DIVISION.
 2        PROGRAM-ID.         SENIORCE.
 3        AUTHOR.             ROBERT GRAUER.
 4
 5        ENVIRONMENT DIVISION.
 6        INPUT-OUTPUT SECTION.
 7        FILE-CONTROL.
 8            SELECT STUDENT-FILE
 9                 ASSIGN TO UT-S-SYSIN.
10            SELECT PRINT-FILE
11                 ASSIGN TO UT-S-SYSOUT.
12
13        DATA DIVISION.
14        FILE SECTION.
15        FD  STUDENT-FILE
16            RECORD CONTAINS 43 CHARACTERS
17            DATA RECORD IS STUDENT-IN.
18        01  STUDENT-IN.
19            05  STU-NAME            PIC X(25).
```

Figure 2.4 *(continued)*

```
         05  STU-CREDITS         PIC 9(3).
         05  STU-MAJOR           PIC X(15).

     FD  PRINT-FILE
         RECORD CONTAINS 132 CHARACTERS
         DATA RECORD IS PRINT-LINE.
     01  PRINT-LINE              PIC X(132).

     WORKING-STORAGE SECTION.
     01  DATA-REMAINS-SWITCH     PIC X(2)      VALUE SPACES.

     01  HEADING-LINE.
         05  FILLER              PIC X(10)     VALUE SPACES.
         05  FILLER              PIC X(12)     VALUE 'STUDENT NAME'.
         05  FILLER              PIC X(110)    VALUE SPACES.

     01  DETAIL-LINE.
         05  FILLER              PIC X(8)      VALUE SPACES.
         05  PRINT-NAME          PIC X(25).
         05  FILLER              PIC X(99)     VALUE SPACES.

     PROCEDURE DIVISION.
     PREPARE-SENIOR-REPORT.
         OPEN INPUT  STUDENT-FILE
              OUTPUT PRINT-FILE.
         READ STUDENT-FILE
             AT END MOVE 'NO' TO DATA-REMAINS-SWITCH
         END-READ.
         PERFORM WRITE-HEADING-LINE.
         PERFORM PROCESS-RECORDS
             UNTIL DATA-REMAINS-SWITCH = 'NO'.
         CLOSE STUDENT-FILE
               PRINT-FILE.
         STOP RUN.

     WRITE-HEADING-LINE.
         MOVE HEADING-LINE TO PRINT-LINE.
         WRITE PRINT-LINE.

     PROCESS-RECORDS
         IF STU-CREDITS > 110 AND STU-MAJOR = 'ENGINEERING'
             MOVE STU-NAME TO PRINT-NAME
             MOVE DETAIL-LINE TO PRINT-LINE
             WRTE PRINT-LINE.
         END-IF.
         READ STUDENT-FILE
             AT END MOVE 'NO' TO DATA-REMAINS-SWITCH
         END-READ.
```

Period missing after paragraph header

WRITE is misspelled
Period does not belong before END-IF terminator

(a) COBOL Listing

Figure 2.4 *(continued)*

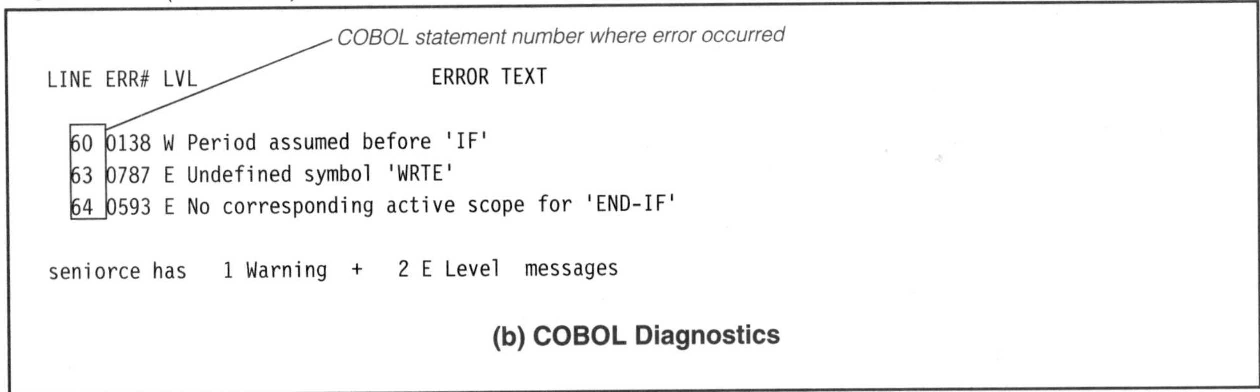


```
LINE ERR# LVL                    ERROR TEXT

 60 0138 W Period assumed before 'IF'
 63 0787 E Undefined symbol 'WRTE'
 64 0593 E No corresponding active scope for 'END-IF'

seniorce has   1 Warning  +   2 E Level  messages
```

(b) COBOL Diagnostics

changed to produce compilation errors. Figure 2.4b shows the resulting compiler diagnostics. The error message associated with line 60 is caused by the missing period (after the paragraph header) in line 59. The diagnostic in line 63 resulted from misspelling a reserved word, and the diagnostic in line 64 is produced by the superfluous period in line 63.

Compiler diagnostics are discussed fully in Chapter 6. Corrections are made, and the program is recompiled. Only after the compilation has been successfully completed should we proceed to execution.

Errors in Execution

Execution errors occur after compilation and are generally due to errors in logic. Figure 2.5a contains yet another version of the engineering senior program in which the credits test was *deliberately* omitted in line 60. The program is syntactically correct and will compile without error; it is, however, logically incorrect and hence the associated output in Figure 2.5b is wrong. (Review the original program specifications and test data; Alex Bell should not be selected because of an insufficient number of credits.)

Figure 2.5 Engineering Senior Program with Execution Errors

```
 1          IDENTIFICATION DIVISION.
 2          PROGRAM-ID.       SENIOREE.
 3          AUTHOR.           ROBERT GRAUER.
 4
 5          ENVIRONMENT DIVISION.
 6          INPUT-OUTPUT SECTION.
 7          FILE-CONTROL.
 8              SELECT STUDENT-FILE
 9                   ASSIGN TO UT-S-SYSIN.
10              SELECT PRINT-FILE
11                   ASSIGN TO UT-S-SYSOUT.
12
13          DATA DIVISION.
```

Figure 2.5 *(continued)*

```
FILE SECTION.
FD  STUDENT-FILE
    RECORD CONTAINS 43 CHARACTERS
    DATA RECORD IS STUDENT-IN.
01  STUDENT-IN.
    05  STU-NAME            PIC X(25).
    05  STU-CREDITS         PIC 9(3).
    05  STU-MAJOR           PIC X(15).

FD  PRINT-FILE
    RECORD CONTAINS 132 CHARACTERS
    DATA RECORD IS PRINT-LINE.
01  PRINT-LINE              PIC X(132).

WORKING-STORAGE SECTION.
01  DATA-REMAINS-SWITCH     PIC X(2)      VALUE SPACES.

01  HEADING-LINE.
    05  FILLER              PIC X(10)     VALUE SPACES.
    05  FILLER              PIC X(12)     VALUE 'STUDENT NAME'.
    05  FILLER              PIC X(110)    VALUE SPACES.

01  DETAIL-LINE.
    05  FILLER              PIC X(8)      VALUE SPACES.
    05  PRINT-NAME          PIC X(25).
    05  FILLER              PIC X(99)     VALUE SPACES.

PROCEDURE DIVISION.
PREPARE-SENIOR-REPORT.
    OPEN INPUT  STUDENT-FILE
         OUTPUT PRINT-FILE.
    READ STUDENT-FILE
        AT END MOVE 'NO' TO DATA-REMAINS-SWITCH
    END-READ.
    PERFORM WRITE-HEADING-LINE.
    PERFORM PROCESS-RECORDS
        UNTIL DATA-REMAINS-SWITCH = 'NO'.
    CLOSE STUDENT-FILE
          PRINT-FILE.
    STOP RUN.

WRITE-HEADING-LINE.
    MOVE HEADING-LINE TO PRINT-LINE.
    WRITE PRINT-LINE.

PROCESS-RECORDS.
    IF STU-MAJOR = 'ENGINEERING'
        MOVE STU-NAME TO PRINT-NAME
        MOVE DETAIL-LINE TO PRINT-LINE
        WRITE PRINT-LINE
```

Credits test missing (callout to the line IF STU-MAJOR = 'ENGINEERING')

Figure 2.5 *(continued)*

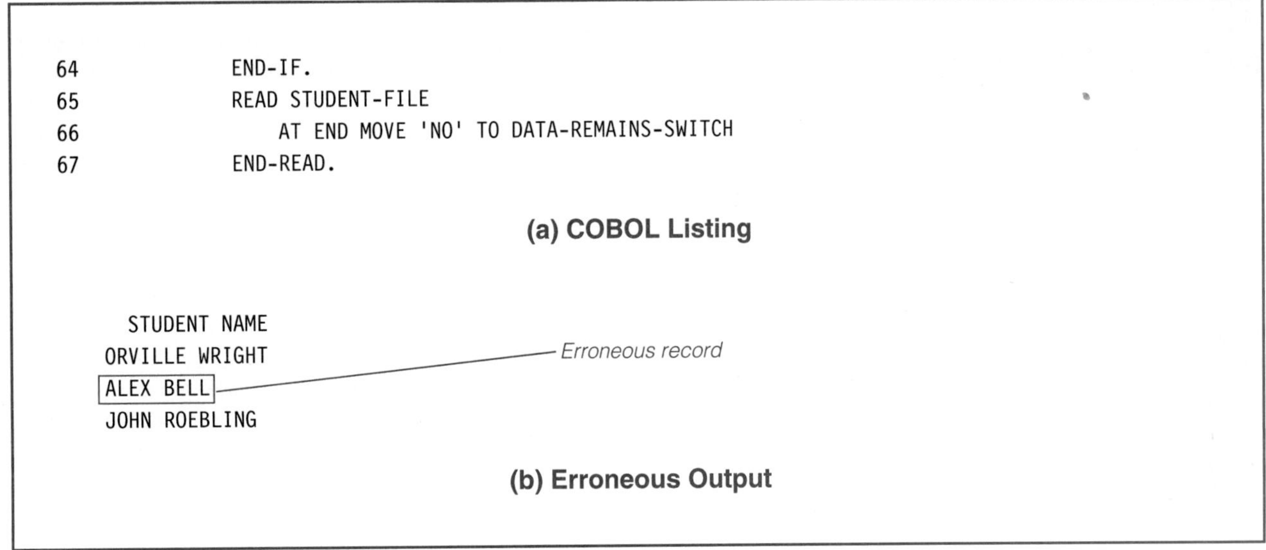

```
64             END-IF.
65             READ STUDENT-FILE
66                 AT END MOVE 'NO' TO DATA-REMAINS-SWITCH
67             END-READ.
```

(a) COBOL Listing

```
  STUDENT NAME
ORVILLE WRIGHT
ALEX BELL          ---- Erroneous record
JOHN ROEBLING
```

(b) Erroneous Output

It is important to remember, therefore, that *a computer does exactly what it is instructed to do, which may be different from what you want it to do.* In other words if you (incorrectly) tell the computer to ignore the credits test, then that is precisely what the program will do.

Errors In Data Input

A program may also produce erroneous output, even if it is logically correct, when the data on which the program operates are invalid. If, for example, the *erroneous* data in Figure 2.6 are submitted to the *valid* program in Figure 2.2, neither Orville Wright nor John Roebling will be selected! Wright's major appears in the data as ENGINEER, whereas line 60 in the program is looking for ENGINEER*ING*. Roebling's credits are entered in the wrong column. In other words, a computer operates on data exactly as it is submitted, with no regard for its correctness. Stated another way, the output produced by a program is only as good as its input, or put even more simply, ***garbage in, garbage out,*** giving rise to the well known acronym, ***GIGO.***

Figure 2.6 Erroneous Input Data

```
JOHN ADAMS           090POLITICAL SCI
AMELIA EARHART       120AVIATION
ORVILLE WRIGHT       115ENGINEER        ---- "Engineering" is spelled incorrectly
GEORGIA O'KEEFFE     125ART
MERIWETHER LEWIS     115TRAVEL
JOHN KENNEDY         115POLITICAL SCI
ALEX BELL            090ENGINEERING
EMILY DICKINSON      085LITERATURE
JOHN ROEBLING         115ENGINEERING    ---- Data entered in wrong columns
```

Evolution of COBOL

COBOL was introduced in 1959 through the efforts of Captain Grace Murray Hopper of the United States Navy. It was designed to be an open ended language, capable of accepting change and amendment. It was also intended to be a highly portable language; i.e., a COBOL program written for an IBM mainframe computer should run equally well on any other computer with a COBOL compiler. Over the years the needs of an evolving language, and the desire for compatibility among vendors have given rise to several COBOL standards, two of which are in common use today, ***COBOL-74*** and ***COBOL-85***.

All of the listings in this text are written to take advantage of features in the newest standard, COBOL-85. We think it important to emphasize COBOL-85 (de-emphasize COBOL-74) because COBOL-85 has been the current standard for several years. Industry, however, is slow to change, and even as this book is written in 1993, many (perhaps most) of industry's currently running COBOL programs adhere to COBOL-74. The reason for the slow conversion is the subtle ***incompatibilities*** that exist between the two compilers. In theory, a program written under the earlier compiler is supposed to run without modification under the later compiler. In practice, however, this is not always the case.

Consider, for example, the incompatibility brought about by the introduction of new features and associated new reserved words, words such as CONTENT, EVALUATE, FALSE, OTHER, TEST, and so on. A programmer writing under COBOL-74 could logically have used any or all of these words as data names, which posed no problem under the older compiler, but which produces numerous compilation errors under COBOL-85. Thus, a blanket conversion by an installation of its hundreds (thousands, or tens of thousands) of COBOL programs, would prove disastrous, unless each program was manually checked for compatibility with the new standard.

Many installations support both compilers, using COBOL-74 to maintain existing programs and COBOL-85 for new development. It is important, therefore, that you become aware of the differences between the two standards. Accordingly, we end most chapters with a section describing differences between the standards as they relate to the program discussed in that chapter.

Figure 2.7 represents our final look at the engineering senior program as it would be implemented in COBOL-74. Note the following differences between this program and the COBOL-85 implementation of Figure 1.6:

Figure 2.7 Engineering Senior Program (COBOL-74 Implementation)

```
IDENTIFICATION DIVISION.
PROGRAM-ID.       SENIOR74.
AUTHOR.           ROBERT GRAUER.

ENVIRONMENT DIVISION.
CONFIGURATION SECTION.
SOURCE-COMPUTER.  IBM-PC.
OBJECT-COMPUTER.  IBM-PC.
INPUT-OUTPUT SECTION.
FILE-CONTROL.
    SELECT STUDENT-FILE
        ASSIGN TO UT-S-SYSIN.
    SELECT PRINT-FILE
        ASSIGN TO UT-S-SYSOUT.

DATA DIVISION.
```

CONFIGURATION SECTION is required

Figure 2.7 *(continued)*

```
FILE SECTION.
FD  STUDENT-FILE
    LABEL RECORDS ARE STANDARD
    RECORD CONTAINS 43 CHARACTERS
    DATA RECORD IS STUDENT-IN.
01  STUDENT-IN.
    05  STU-NAME              PIC X(25).
    05  STU-CREDITS           PIC 9(3).
    05  STU-MAJOR             PIC X(15).

FD  PRINT-FILE
    LABEL RECORDS ARE STANDARD
    RECORD CONTAINS 132 CHARACTERS
    DATA RECORD IS PRINT-LINE.
01  PRINT-LINE                PIC X(132).

WORKING-STORAGE SECTION.
01  DATA-REMAINS-SWITCH       PIC X(2)      VALUE SPACES.

01  HEADING-LINE.
    05  FILLER                PIC X(10)     VALUE SPACES.
    05  FILLER                PIC X(12)     VALUE 'STUDENT NAME'.
    05  FILLER                PIC X(110)    VALUE SPACES.

01  DETAIL-LINE.
    05  FILLER                PIC X(8)      VALUE SPACES.
    05  PRINT-NAME            PIC X(25).
    05  FILLER                PIC X(99)     VALUE SPACES.

PROCEDURE DIVISION.
PREPARE-SENIOR-REPORT.
    OPEN INPUT  STUDENT-FILE
         OUTPUT PRINT-FILE.
    READ STUDENT-FILE
        AT END MOVE 'NO' TO DATA-REMAINS-SWITCH.
    PERFORM WRITE-HEADING-LINE.
    PERFORM PROCESS-RECORDS
        UNTIL DATA-REMAINS-SWITCH = 'NO'.
    CLOSE STUDENT-FILE
          PRINT-FILE.
    STOP RUN.

WRITE-HEADING-LINE.
    MOVE HEADING-LINE TO PRINT-LINE.
    WRITE PRINT-LINE.

PROCESS-RECORDS.
    IF STU-CREDITS > 110 AND STU-MAJOR = 'ENGINEERING'
        MOVE STU-NAME TO PRINT-NAME
        MOVE DETAIL-LINE TO PRINT-LINE
        WRITE PRINT-LINE.
    READ STUDENT-FILE
        AT END MOVE 'NO' TO DATA-REMAINS-SWITCH.
```

LABEL RECORDS clause is required

END-IF scope terminator is not recognized in COBOL-74

1. COBOL-74 requires a CONFIGURATION SECTION with both a SOURCE-COMPUTER and an OBJECT-COMPUTER paragraph, to indicate the computer on which the program will compile and execute. The CONFIGURATION SECTION is optional in COBOL-85, and since these entries are treated as comments by the compiler, they are omitted in the COBOL-85 listing.
2. COBOL-74 requires the LABEL RECORDS clause in a file description to indicate whether standard, nonstandard, or no labels are in effect. (A label contains information about a file such as the date it was created and the intended expiration date.) The clause is optional in COBOL-85 where its omission defaults to LABEL RECORDS ARE STANDARD.
3. Scope terminators (END-IF and END-READ) are not permitted in COBOL-74 and hence do not appear in Figure 2.7. Scope terminators are optional in COBOL-85, but are used throughout the text because of advantages that will be clearly explained in Chapter 7.

Despite these differences the COBOL-74 implementation of the engineering senior program is upward compatible with COBOL-85; that is, the program in Figure 2.7 will run *without* modification under the new compiler. The converse is not true; the COBOL-85 listing in Figure 1.6 will not run under the earlier standard.

There's Always a Reason

We expect that you completed the chapter with little difficulty and that you were able to successfully run the engineering senior program. There will be times, however, when not everything will go as smoothly and so we relate a favorite anecdote ("Mystery of the Month," PC World Magazine, April 1983) that is as relevant today as when it was written. As you read our tale, remember that a computer does exactly what you tell it to do, which is not necessarily what you want it to do. It is a source of wonderful satisfaction when everything works, but also the cause of nearly unbelievable frustration when results are not what you expect.

Our story concerns a manager who purchased a PC and began to use it enthusiastically. Unfortunately, the feeling did not rub off on his assistant, who was apprehensive of computers in general, but who finally agreed to try the new technology.

As is frequently the case, the assistant's experience with the computer was as frustrating as the manager's was rewarding. Every time the assistant tried using the computer an error message appeared, yet when the manager tried the same procedure it worked fine. Finally, manager and assistant went through a systematic comparison of everything they did: turning the machine on and off, handling disks, using the keyboard, etc. They could find no difference in their procedures and could not account for the repeated disk errors which plagued the assistant but left the manager alone.

Just as they were about to give up the manager noticed that his assistant was wearing a charm bracelet. He looked closely, and sure enough one of the charms was a tiny magnet containing just enough force to interfere with reading the disk. The assistant stored the bracelet in a drawer and the machine has been fine ever since.

The point of our story is that there is always a logical reason for everything a computer does or does not do, although discovering that reason may be less than obvious. You are about to embark on a wonderful journey toward the productive use of a computer, with a virtually unlimited number of potential applications. Be patient, be inquisitive, and enjoy.

SUMMARY

Points to Remember

- The A margin consists of columns 8–11 whereas the B margin is defined as columns 12–72. Division and section headers, paragraph names, FD's, and 01-level entries must begin in the A margin; all other entries begin in the B margin (that is, in or past column 12).
- The execution of a COBOL program is a three part process, involving three distinct programs—a compiler, a linker, and the resultant load module. The means of communicating information about these programs (and their associated files) is dependent on the operating system.
- A compiler is a computer program that translates a higher-level (problem-oriented) language such as COBOL into machine language; the input to a compiler is referred to as a source program, whereas the output is an object program.
- The linker combines the output produced by the compiler, with additional object modules (such as subroutines and/or Input/Output modules) to produce a load module.
- Execution of the COBOL program occurs when the load module processes the input file(s) to produce the required reports.
- COBOL-74 is intended to be upward compatible with COBOL-85 although subtle incompatibilities do exist between the two standards. The converse is not true, as COBOL-85 programs will not run under the earlier standard.

Key Words and Concepts

A margin
ASCII file
B margin
COBOL-74
COBOL-85
Coding form
Comments
Compilation error
Compiler
Continuation
Debugging
Editor
Execution error
GIGO
Incompatibility
Load module
Object program
Operating system
Source program
Test data

FILL-IN

1. A ______________ translates a ______________ language into an ______________ language.
2. ______________ is the most recently approved COBOL standard, but ______________ is still widely used in industry.

3. The ______________ is in columns 8 to 11 of the coding sheet.
4. A comment is indicated by an ______________ in column ______________.
5. Entries that are not required to begin in the A margin may begin anywhere in columns ______________ to ______________.
6. Division headers and paragraph names must begin in the ______________.
7. An ______________ is used to enter programs into the computer.
8. The compile, link, and execute process requires the execution of ______________ distinct programs.
9. ______________ is the process of finding and correcting errors in a program.
10. Picture clauses may begin anywhere within the ______________ margin.
11. The output of compilation is input to a second program called the ______________.
12. A clean compile (does/does not) guarantee that the resulting program execution will be correct.
13. Different mainframe computers will most likely use (different/identical) COBOL compilers.
14. Misspelling a reserved word will result in a ______________ error.
15. Entering test data in the wrong columns will result in an ______________ error.

TRUE/FALSE

1. A compiler translates a machine-oriented language into a problem-oriented language.
2. A well-written program will always produce correct results, even with bad data.
3. A compiler is a computer program.
4. The COBOL compiler for an IBM mainframe is identical to the compiler for a PC.
5. A COBOL program can run on a variety of computers.
6. Division headers must begin in the A margin.
7. Division headers must begin in column 8.
8. Section headers must begin in column 12.
9. Paragraph names must begin in column 8.
10. PICTURE clauses may appear in column 12 or after.
11. If a program compiles correctly, then it must execute correctly.
12. Columns 1–6 are never used on the coding sheet.
13. The use of columns 73–80 is optional.
14. Column 8 is used as a continuation column.
15. All editors have identical commands.
16. All computers use the same operating system.
17. Successful execution of the COBOL compiler produces a load module.

PROBLEMS

1. Figure 2.8a contains data for the COBOL program in Figure 2.8b, which will process a file of employee records and print the names of all programmers under 30.

Figure 2.8 COBOL Program and Associated Data for Problems 1 & 2

```
WALT BECHTEL             PROGRAMMER34  39700
NELSON KERBEL            PROGRAMMER23  30000
MARGOT HUMMER            PROGRAMMER30  45000
CATHY BENWAY             DATA BASE 23  50000
JUD MCDONALD             DATA BASE 29  55000
JACKIE CLARK             PROGRAMMER22  47500
LOUIS NORIEGA            PROGRAMER 24  42500
JEFF SHEESLEY            ANALYST   28  46400
```

(a) Data

```
IDENTIFICATION DIVISION.
PROGRAM-ID.  FIRSTTRY.
AUTHOR.      GRAUER.

ENVIRONMENT DIVISION.
INPUT-OUTPUT SECTION.
FILE-CONTROL.
    SELECT EMPLOYEE-FILE
        ASSIGN TO UT-S-SYSIN.
    SELECT PRINT-FILE
        ASSIGN TO UT-S-SYSOUT.

DATA DIVISION.
FILE SECTION.
FD  EMPLOYEE-FILE
    RECORD CONTAINS 44 CHARACTERS
    DATA RECORD IS EMPLOYEE-RECORD.
01  EMPLOYEE-RECORD.
    05  EMP-NAME               PIC X(25).
    05  EMP-TITLE              PIC X(10).
    05  EMP-AGE                PIC 99.
    05  FILLER                 PIC XX.
    05  EMP-SALARY             PIC 9(5).

FD  PRINT-FILE
    RECORD CONTAINS 132 CHARACTERS
    DATA RECORD IS PRINT-LINE.
01  PRINT-LINE.
```

Figure 2.8 *(continued)*

```
           05  FILLER                  PIC X.
           05  PRINT-NAME              PIC X(25).
           05  FILLER                  PIC X(2).
           05  PRINT-AGE               PIC 99.
           05  FILLER                  PIC X(3).
           05  PRINT-SALARY            PIC 9(5).
           05  FILLER                  PIC X(94).

       WORKING-STORAGE SECTION.
       01  END-OF-DATA-FLAG            PIC X(3)      VALUE SPACES.
       PROCEDURE DIVISION.
       PREPARE-PROGRAMMER-REPORT.
           OPEN INPUT EMPLOYEE-FILE
               OUTPUT PRINT-FILE.
           MOVE SPACES TO PRINT-LINE.
           MOVE 'SALARY REPORT FOR PROGRAMMERS UNDER 30' TO PRINT-LINE.
           WRITE PRINT-LINE
              AFTER ADVANCING 2 LINES.
           READ EMPLOYEE-FILE
               AT END MOVE 'YES' TO END-OF-DATA-FLAG
           END-READ.
           PERFORM PROCESS-EMPLOYEE-RECORDS
               UNTIL END-OF-DATA-FLAG = 'YES'.
           CLOSE EMPLOYEE-FILE
                PRINT-FILE.
           STOP RUN.

       PROCESS-EMPLOYEE-RECORDS.
           IF EMP-TITLE = 'PROGRAMMER' AND EMP-AGE < 30
               MOVE SPACES TO PRINT-LINE
               MOVE EMP-NAME TO PRINT-NAME
               MOVE EMP-AGE TO PRINT-AGE
               MOVE EMP-SALARY TO PRINT-SALARY
               WRITE PRINT-LINE
           END-IF.
           READ EMPLOYEE-FILE
               AT END MOVE 'YES' TO END-OF-DATA-FLAG
           END-READ.
```

(b) COBOL Program

a. Compile, link, and execute the COBOL program, using the appropriate commands for your system. (The program is on the data disk that accompanies this book.)

b. Are any potential problems introduced by checking age rather than date of birth?

c. Would processing be simplified if the employee records contained an abbreviated title code (for example, 010) rather than an expanded title (for example, programmer)? Are there any other advantages to storing codes rather than expanded values?

2. Modify the program in Figure 2.8b to accommodate all of the following.
   a. Employee age is stored in positions 38 and 39 of the incoming record.
   b. The report should list all employees under age 30 who earn at least $30,000, regardless of title.
   c. The report should include the title of all selected employees in positions 41–52.

3. Match each item with its proper description.

___	1. A Margin	a.	An asterisk in column 7
___	2. B Margin	b.	First line of any COBOL program
___	3. Comment	c.	Often appears in data names
___	4. IDENTIFICATION DIVISION	d.	Columns 12 through 72
___	5. PROCEDURE DIVISION	e.	Contains the logic of a program
___	6. Hyphen	f.	Limited to 160 characters, and enclosed in quotes or apostrophes
___	7. Nonnumeric literal	g.	Where division, section, and paragraph headers begin
___	8. Reserved word	h.	Translates COBOL to machine language
___	9. Compiler	i.	Preassigned meaning
___	10. Literal	j.	A constant; may be numeric or nonnumeric

4. Indicate the starting column (or columns) for each of the following.
   a. Division headers
   b. Comments
   c. Paragraph names
   d. Statements in the Procedure Division (except paragraph names)
   e. WORKING-STORAGE SECTION
   f. FD
   g. 01 entries
   h. 05 entries
   i. PICTURE clauses
   j. OPEN statement
   k. WRITE statement
   l. SELECT statement

5. Explain how it is possible for a program to compile perfectly, be logically correct, and still produce invalid results; provide specific examples in conjunction with the engineering senior program.

A Methodology for Program Development

CHAPTER OUTLINE

OBJECTIVES

After reading this chapter you will be able to:

- Describe how a hierarchy chart is developed; discuss three criteria for evaluating a completed hierarchy chart.
- Define structured programming; describe its three fundamental building blocks and an optional extension.
- Explain the one entry point/one exit point philosophy of structured programming.
- Differentiate between structured programming and structured design; distinguish between a functionally oriented technique and one that is procedurally oriented.
- Describe what is meant by top down design and implementation.

OVERVIEW

We stated at the outset that programming is best learned by doing, and so our objective in the first two chapters was to put you on the computer as quickly as possible. Thus, we jumped immediately into COBOL, without giving much thought to the underlying logic of the program you developed. While that approach works well initially, it is also important for you to learn how to properly design programs, so that they will work correctly, and further so that they can be easily read and maintained by someone other than yourself.

Accordingly, this chapter presents a methodology for program development, embracing the techniques of structured design, structured programming, and top down testing. We stress that structured design is functionally oriented and describes what is to be accomplished; structured programming, on the other hand, is procedurally oriented and focuses on how the objectives of the program will be realized. The discussion includes hierarchy charts, pseudocode, flowcharts, and Warnier-Orr diagrams.

The presentation is of a practical nature, and stresses application rather than theory. Accordingly, we introduce a new program at the beginning of the chapter, and develop the methodology in the context of that program. We begin with presentation of the program specifications.

The Tuition Billing Program

This section contains the specifications for a new problem, known simply as the tuition billing program. The requirements are straightforward and parallel those of many other COBOL programs, namely to print a heading line(s) at the start of processing, one or more detail lines for every record processed, and a total line(s) at the end of processing. As simple as these specifications may be, it is critical that you avoid the temptation to rush immediately into COBOL, and concentrate instead on designing the program you will eventually write.

The approach we follow begins with a determination of the most general function the program is to accomplish, then divides that task into smaller and smaller pieces, until the requirements of each piece are clearly recognized. Initially the design process may seem superfluous in that you are confident of your ability to begin coding immediately. Rest assured, however, that design is productive work, and does in fact pay dividends in the long run. A well-designed program is far more likely to be correct than one written off-the-cuff. Moreover, and this may be the argument that most appeals to you, a well-designed program will ultimately be completed in less time than one that is poorly designed or one that has no design at all.

PROGRAMMING SPECIFICATIONS

Program Name: Tuition Billing Program

Narrative: This program processes a file of student records, computes and prints the tuition bill for each student, and prints the total amounts for all students.

Input File(s): STUDENT-FILE

Input Record Layout: See Figure 3.1a

Test Data:

```
SMITH          JB15Y0000230
JAMES          HR15 0500245
BAKER          SR09 0500350
PART-TIMER     JR03Y0000300
JONES          PL15Y0000280
HEAVYWORKER    HM18 0000200
LEE            BL18 0000335
CLARK          JC06 0000310
GROSSMAN       SE07 0000215
FRANKEL        LF10 0000350
BENWAY         CT03 0250395
KERBEL         NB04 0000100
```

Report Layout: See Figure 3.1b

Processing Requirements:

1. Print a suitable heading at the beginning of the report.
2. Read a file of student records.
3. Process each record read by:
   a. Computing an individual bill, equal to the sum of tuition, union fee, and activity fee, minus a scholarship (if any), by:
      i. Calculating the tuition due, at a rate of $200 per credit.
      ii. Billing the student $25 for the union fee, if there is a "Y" in the Union Member position.
      iii. Computing the activity fee based on the number of credits taken:

ACTIVITY FEE	CREDITS
$25	6 or fewer
$50	7 - 12
$75	more than 12

Figure 3.1 Record Layouts for Tuition Billing Program

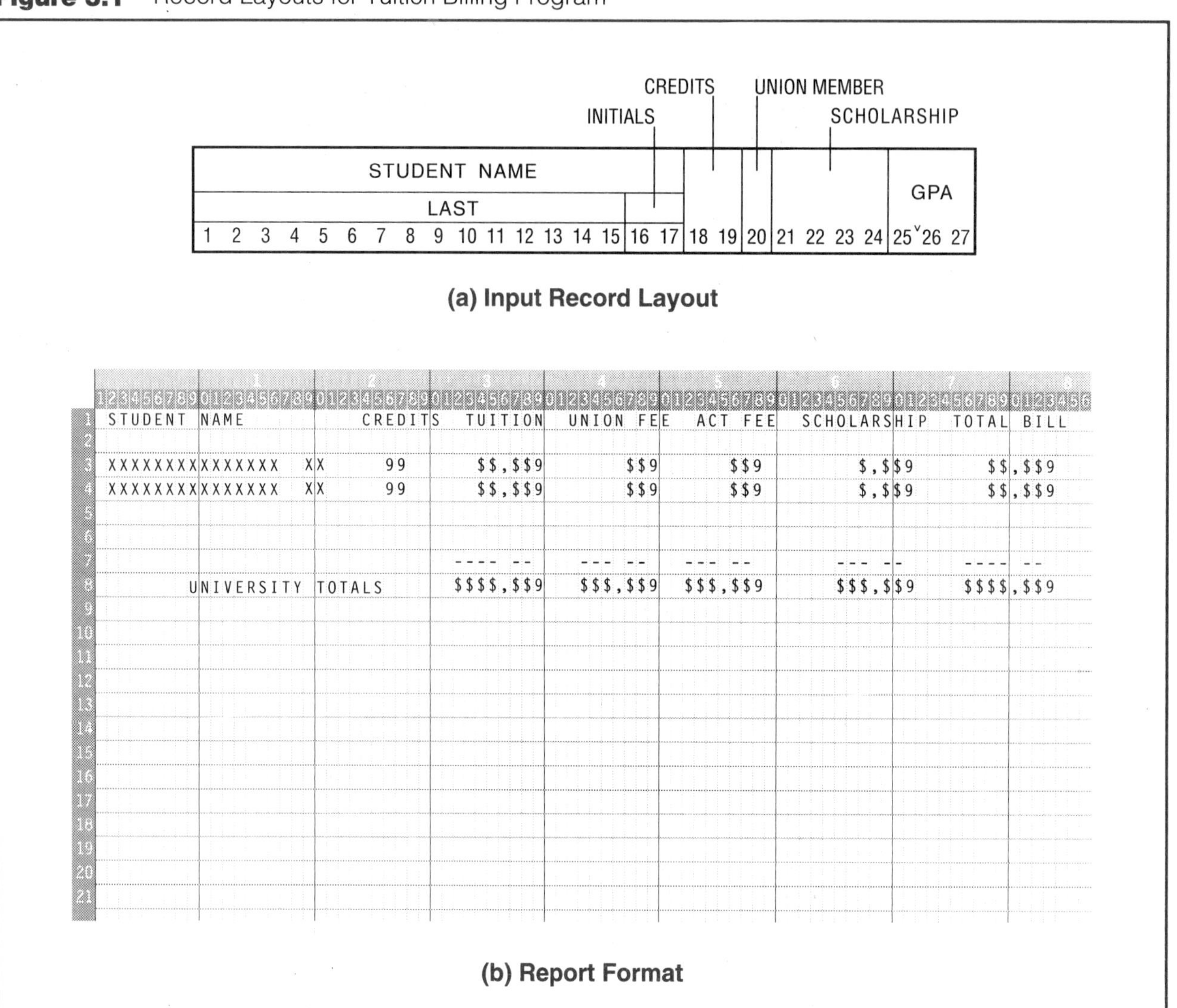

iv. Awarding a scholarship equal to the amount in the incoming record if, and only if, the GPA is greater than 2.5. (Observe that in the test data on the previous page James does *not* qualify for the $500 scholarship he would otherwise have been awarded.)

v. Incrementing the university totals for tuition, union fee, activity fee, scholarship, and overall total.

b. Printing a detail line for each record read.

4. Print a total line at the end of the report.

Structured Design

Structured design identifies the tasks a program is to accomplish, then relates those tasks to one another in a ***hierarchy chart.*** Figure 3.2 contains a very basic example, applicable to any COBOL program. The hierarchy chart divides the program into its functional components, for example, initialization, processing, and termination, and indicates the manager/subordinate relationships between these components. In this example all three modules are subordinate to the module labeled any COBOL program.

To better appreciate the significance of a hierarchy chart and its role in program development, consider Figure 3.3, depicting the hierarchy chart for the tuition billing program. The development takes place in stages, beginning at the top and working down to the bottom. At every level, the major function(s) are subdivided into other functions that are placed on the next lower level in the hierarchy chart. Those functions are in turn further subdivided into still other functions, until finally the lowest-level functions cannot be further subdivided.

The specifications for the tuition billing problem suggest a suitable name for the highest-level module, PREPARE-TUITION-REPORT. This in turn is divided into its basic functions of initialization (consisting of WRITE-HEADING-LINE and READ-STUDENT-FILE), processing (PROCESS-STUDENT-RECORD), and termination (WRITE-UNIVERSITY-TOTALS). Levels 1 and 2 of the hierarchy chart are shown in Figure 3.3a.

Of these four modules, only one, PROCESS-STUDENT-RECORD, needs to be subdivided. In other words ask yourself which additional lower-level functions should be included under PROCESS-STUDENT-RECORD in order to process individual student records. The program specifications contain the requirement to compute the individual's bill, increment the university totals to include the amount just computed, and write a detail line for the particular student. Each of these tasks requires its own module as indicated in Figure 3.3b. In addition, PROCESS-STUDENT-RECORD must also read the next record so that the program can continue. (The module READ-STUDENT-FILE appears twice in the hierarchy chart; on level two to read the first record, and on level three to read all subsequent records. The necessity for the dual appearance stems from a limitation in COBOL-74 rather than a requirement of structured design).

The development of a hierarchy chart continues until its lowest-level modules cannot be further subdivided, that is, until the designer believes they can be easily translated into programming statements. The decision is *subjective* in that there is no single correct answer; you could, for example, stop at three levels or continue to a fourth level as in Figure 3.3c. We chose to divide COMPUTE-INDIVIDUAL-BILL into four additional modules: COMPUTE-TUITION, COMPUTE-UNION-FEE, COMPUTE-ACTIVITY-FEE, and COMPUTE-SCHOLARSHIP.

The hierarchy chart is now complete and consists of four levels, each of which will correspond to a PERFORM statement in the eventual COBOL program;

Figure 3.2 Overall COBOL Hierarchy Chart

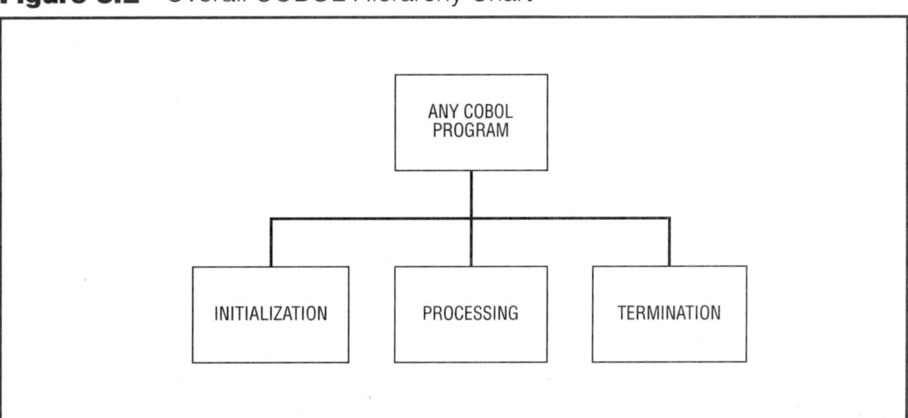

Figure 3.3 Hierarchy Chart for Tuition Billing Program

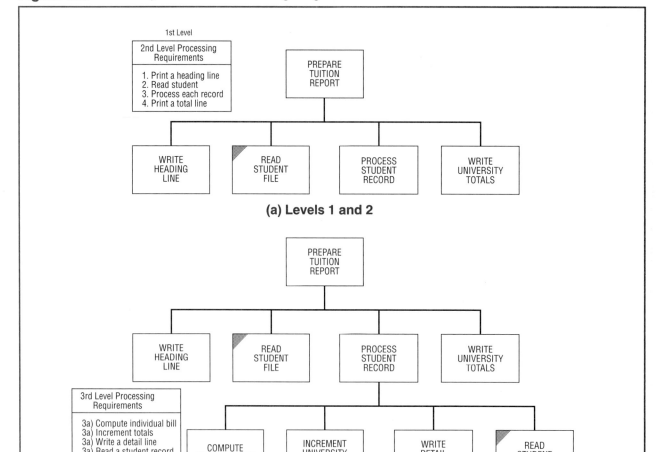

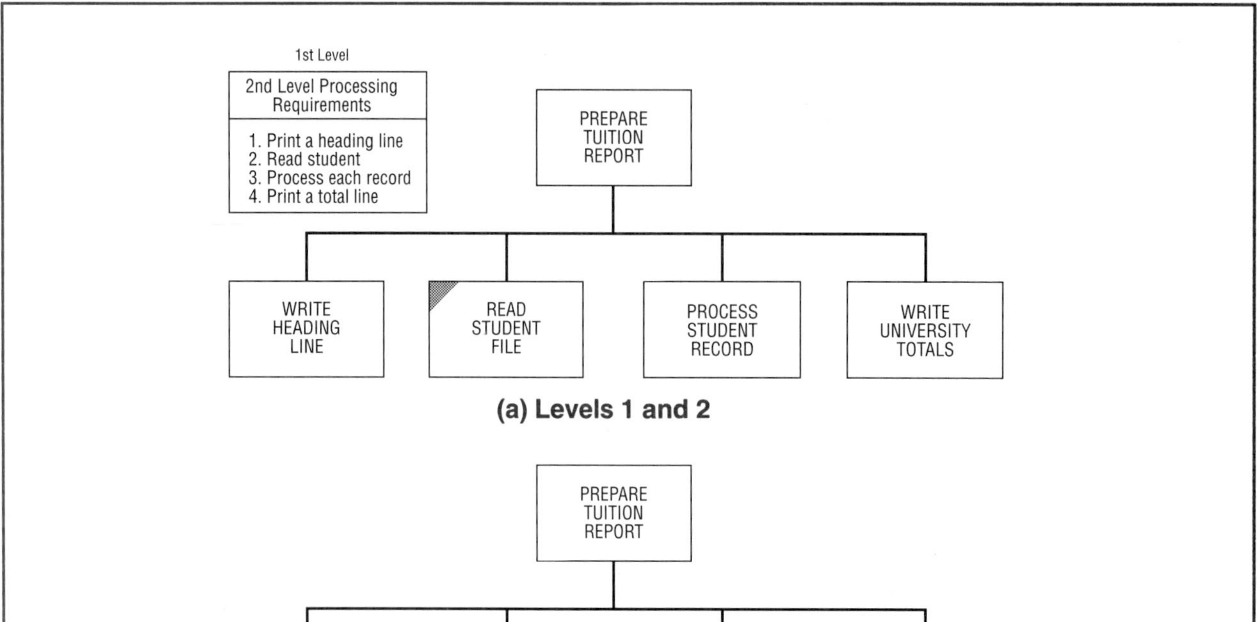

that is, the module (paragraph) on level one will perform the modules (paragraphs) on level two, those on level two will perform the modules on level three, and so on. The hierarchy chart does not specify how often these paragraphs will be called, nor does it indicate the conditions for calling one subordinate in lieu of another. In other words, the hierarchy chart indicates only what functions are necessary, but not when they are executed. It contains no decision-making logic, nor does it imply anything about the order or frequency in which various paragraphs within a program are executed. That, in turn, is specified within the logic of the program, developed according to the discipline of structured programming as discussed later in the chapter.

Evaluating the Hierarchy Chart

As we have already indicated, the decision of how many modules to include in a hierarchy chart and how they should be related to one another is necessarily subjective. Nevertheless, there are certain evaluation criteria that result in selecting one design over another. Among these are the following:

Figure 3.3 *(continued)*

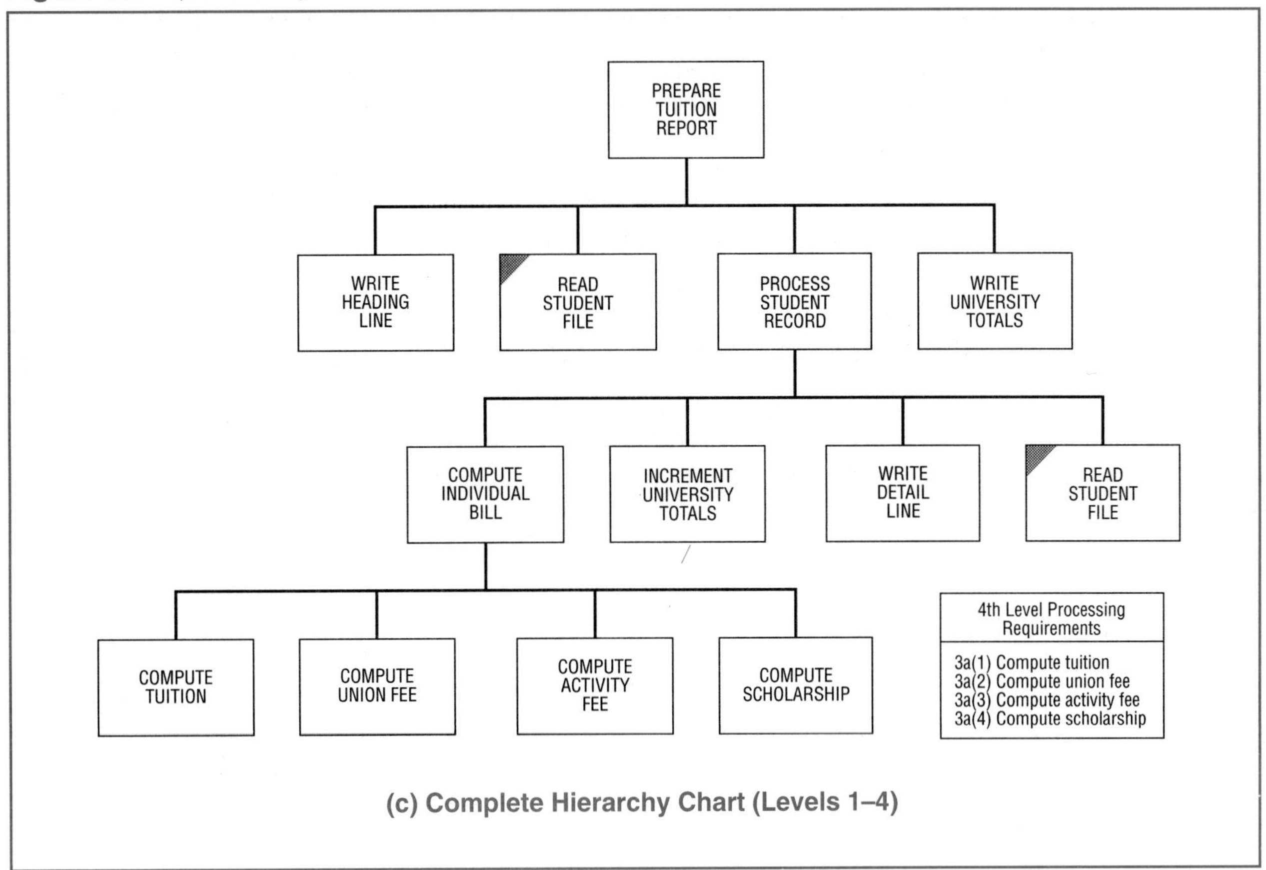

(c) Complete Hierarchy Chart (Levels 1–4)

1. Is the hierarchy chart complete?
2. Are the modules functional?
3. Is there effective span of control?

Completeness

A hierarchy chart must be complete; that is, it has to provide for every function required by the program as specified in the programming specifications. You test for completeness level by level, starting at the top of the hierarchy chart, and working your way down, one level at a time, by asking the question, "Do the subordinate modules at the next level completely develop their corresponding modules at this level?" If the answer is yes, move to the next module on the present level, or to the first module on the next level, and repeat the question. If the answer is no, add functions as necessary and continue to the next module.

For example, begin with the completed hierarchy chart of Figure 3.3c and ask yourself whether the modules on level two are adequate to expand the single module of level one; that is, do the four modules on level two completely expand the PREPARE-TUITION-REPORT module to which they are subordinate? The answer is yes, so you move to level three and see whether the modules on this level adequately expand the PROCESS-STUDENT-RECORD module from level two. Once again the answer is yes, and so you progress to level four. The process continues until you have checked every module on every level and are satisfied that all necessary functions are included.

Functionality

Every module in a hierarchy chart should be dedicated to a *single* function, the nature of which should be clear from examining the module's name. Each of the module names in Figure 3.3 consists of a verb, adjective (or two), and an object—for example, COMPUTE-INDIVIDUAL-BILL or WRITE-DETAIL-LINE. Indeed, if a module cannot be named in this way, its function is probably not well defined and thought should be given to revising the hierarchy chart.

Stated another way, you should reject (or redesign) any module that does not appear to be functional; that is, modules whose names contain:

1. More than one verb—for example, READ-AND-WRITE.
2. More than one object—for example, EDIT-NAME-AND-ACCOUNT-DATA.
3. Nondescriptive or time-related terms—for example, HOUSEKEEPING, TERMINATION-ROUTINE, INITIALIZATION, or MAINLINE.

Another way of expressing the need for functional modules is to strive for module independence; that is, the internal workings of one module should not affect those of another. Perhaps you have already been associated with a working program in which changes were implemented, only to have some other, apparently unrelated, portion of the program no longer work properly. The problem may be due to paragraphs in the program being unnecessarily dependent on one another.

What we are saying is that in an ideal situation, changes made to one paragraph should not affect the results of any other. In a more practical sense, the paragraphs have to be somewhat related, otherwise they would not be parts of the same program; however, the amount of interdependence between paragraphs should be minimized to the greatest extent possible. With respect to Figure 3.3, for example, a change in the procedure for computing the union fee should not affect how the activity fee is determined. That is because the modules COMPUTE-UNION-FEE and COMPUTE-ACTIVITY-FEE are functional in their own right, and consequently are independent of one another.

Span of Control

The ***span of control*** of a module is the number of subordinates it contains. In Figure 3.3, for example, the span of control of both PREPARE-TUITION-REPORT and COMPUTE-INDIVIDUAL-BILL is four. An effective span of control (for hierarchy charts associated with COBOL programs) is generally from two or three to seven, although that may vary depending on the situation. You should, however, avoid extremes in either direction. Programs with ineffective spans of control (too many subordinates or too few) are poorly designed and difficult to follow and/or maintain.

Structured Programming

Let us pause for a moment to see what has been accomplished. We have taken the original problem and divided it into a series of manageable pieces, each of which describes a particular job that needs to be accomplished. In other words, we have said what needs to be done to solve the problem, but have not as yet said how we will solve it. That in essence is the difference between structured design and structured programming.

A structured program is one consisting entirely of three types of logic structures: sequence, selection (a decision), and iteration (a loop). The fact that these structures (or basic building blocks) are sufficient to express any desired logic was first postulated in a now-classic paper by Bohm and Jacopini.[1]

The elementary building blocks of structured programming are shown in flowchart form in Figure 3.4. Flowcharts use special symbols to communicate information. A rectangle indicates a processing statement, a diamond indicates a decision, and a small circle connects portions of the flowchart. All of the flowcharts have one key feature in common, namely, a *single entry point* and a *single exit point*; that is, there is only one way to enter each structure and only one way to leave.

The ***sequence*** structure in Figure 3.4a specifies that the program statements are executed sequentially, in the order in which they appear. The two blocks, A and B, may denote anything from single statements to complete programs, and it is clear that there is a single entry point and a single exit point to the structure.

The ***selection*** (or IF . . . THEN . . . ELSE) structure in Figure 3.4b specifies a choice between two actions. A condition is tested with one of two outcomes; if

1 Bohm and Jacopini, "Flow Diagrams, Turing Machines and Languages with Only Two Formation Rules," *Communications of the ACM* (May 1966).

Figure 3.4 The Building Blocks of Structured Programming

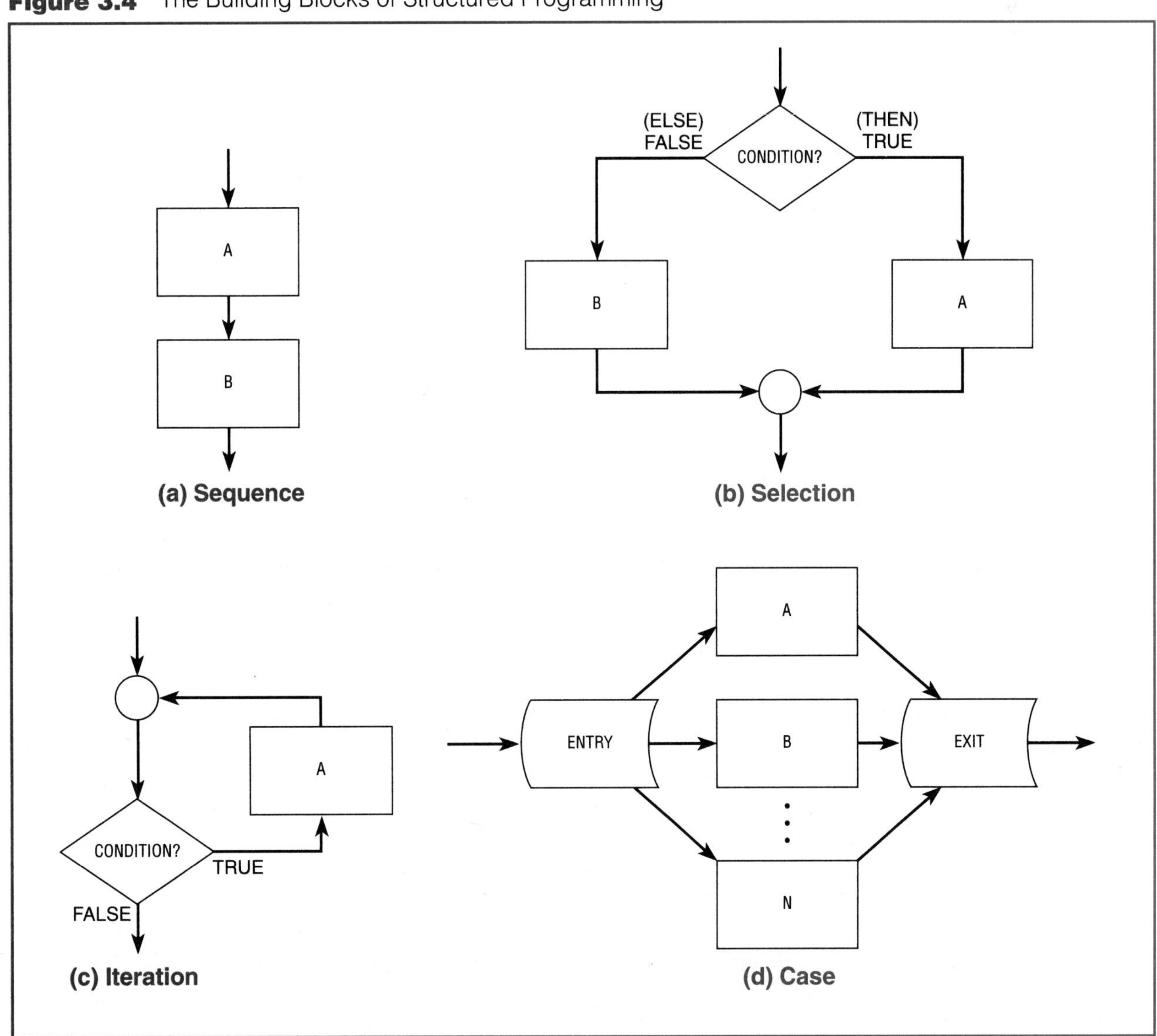

the condition is true, block A is executed, while if it is false, block B is executed. The condition itself is the single entry point, and both paths meet to form a single exit point.

The ***iteration*** (or DO . . . WHILE) structure in Figure 3.4c specifies repeated execution of one or more statements while a condition is true. A condition is tested and, if it is true, block A is executed after which the condition is retested. If, however, the condition is false, control passes to the next sequential statement after the iteration structure. Again, there is a single entry point and a single exit point from the structure.

The ***case structure*** in Figure 3.4d expresses a multibranch situation. Although case is actually a special instance of selection, it is convenient to extend the definition of structured programming to include this fourth type of building block. The case structure evaluates a condition and branches to one of several paths, depending on the value of the condition. As with the other building blocks, there is one entry point and one exit point.

Sufficiency of the Basic Structures

The theory of structured programming says simply that an appropriate combination of the basic building blocks may be derived to solve any problem. This is possible because an entire structure (sequence, selection, iteration, or case) may be *substituted* anywhere block A or B appears. Figure 3.5 shows a combination of the basic structures to illustrate this concept.

Figure 3.5 is essentially a selection structure. However, instead of specifying a single statement for the true or false branches, as was done in Figure 3.4, a complete building block is used instead. Thus, if condition-1 is true, an iteration structure is entered, whereas, if it is false, a sequence structure is executed. Both the iteration and sequence structures meet at a single exit point which becomes the exit point for the initial selection structure.

Figure 3.5 Sufficiency of the Basic Structures

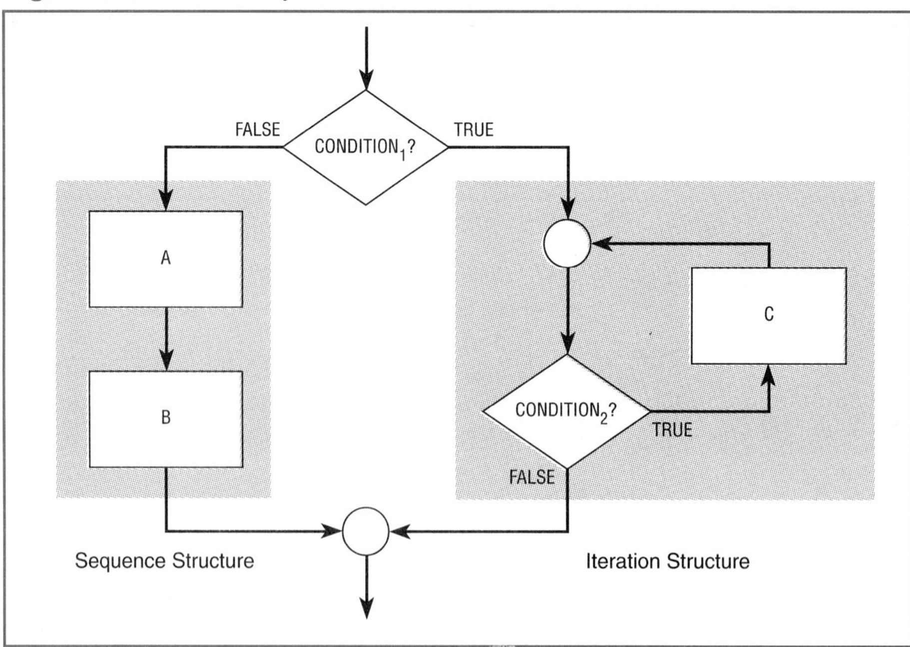

Expressing Logic

We now turn our attention to ways in which programmers express logic, to themselves and to others. We begin with the traditional flowchart, then move to newer techniques more closely associated with structured programming: pseudocode and Warnier-Orr diagrams.

The Traditional Flowchart

Every programmer is familiar with the traditional ***flowchart*** as described in Chapter 1. Although flowcharts have declined in popularity, they remain in widespread use, primarily for documentation. Our personal preference is to use pseudocode, but we include Figure 3.6 for completeness. The decision as to which technique to use is between you and your instructor.

Pseudocode

The fact that most programmers write simple notes to themselves prior to coding a program gave rise to ***pseudocode***, a technique associated with structured programming. As we indicated in Chapter 1, pseudocode is defined simply as neat notes to yourself, and uses statements similar to computer instructions to describe logic. Figure 3.7 represents the building blocks of structured programming as they would be written in pseudocode and corresponds to the flowcharts shown in Figure 3.4.

Pseudocode comes into play after the design phase of a program has been completed, and prior to actual coding. Recall that a hierarchy chart is *functional* in nature and indicates *what* has to be done, but not necessarily *when* or *how*. Pseudocode, on the other hand, is *procedural* and contains sequence and decision-making logic. In other words, pseudocode connects the modules in a hierarchy chart through loops and decision making.

To better appreciate how pseudocode expresses programming logic, consider Figure 3.8, which contains pseudocode for the tuition billing program. Two versions of the pseudocode are presented—an initial attempt in Figure 3.8a, and an expanded (more detailed) version in Figure 3.8b. Both versions are equally appropriate, with the choice between them depending entirely on the individual, and the level of detail he or she desires.

The logic is straightforward and begins with the steps for initialization; to open files, write a heading line(s), and read the first record. Then, a loop (or iteration structure) is entered in which the program computes the student's bill (tuition plus union and activity fees minus scholarship), increments the university totals to include this amount, writes a detail line, and finally reads the next student record. The statements in the loop are executed continually until all the records have been read, at which point university totals are written, and the program terminates.

Pseudocode has a distinct block structure that is conducive to structured programming. It is not, however, bound by formal syntactical rules (although some organizations have implemented standards), nor does it have specific rules of indentation, which is done strictly at the programmer's discretion. Its only limitation is a restriction to the building blocks of structured programming (sequence, selection, iteration, and case).

With practice, pseudocode can be developed quickly and easily. Good pseudocode should be sufficiently precise to be a real aid in writing a program, while informal enough to be understood by nonprogrammers. The informality of

Figure 3.6 Flowchart for Tuition Billing Program

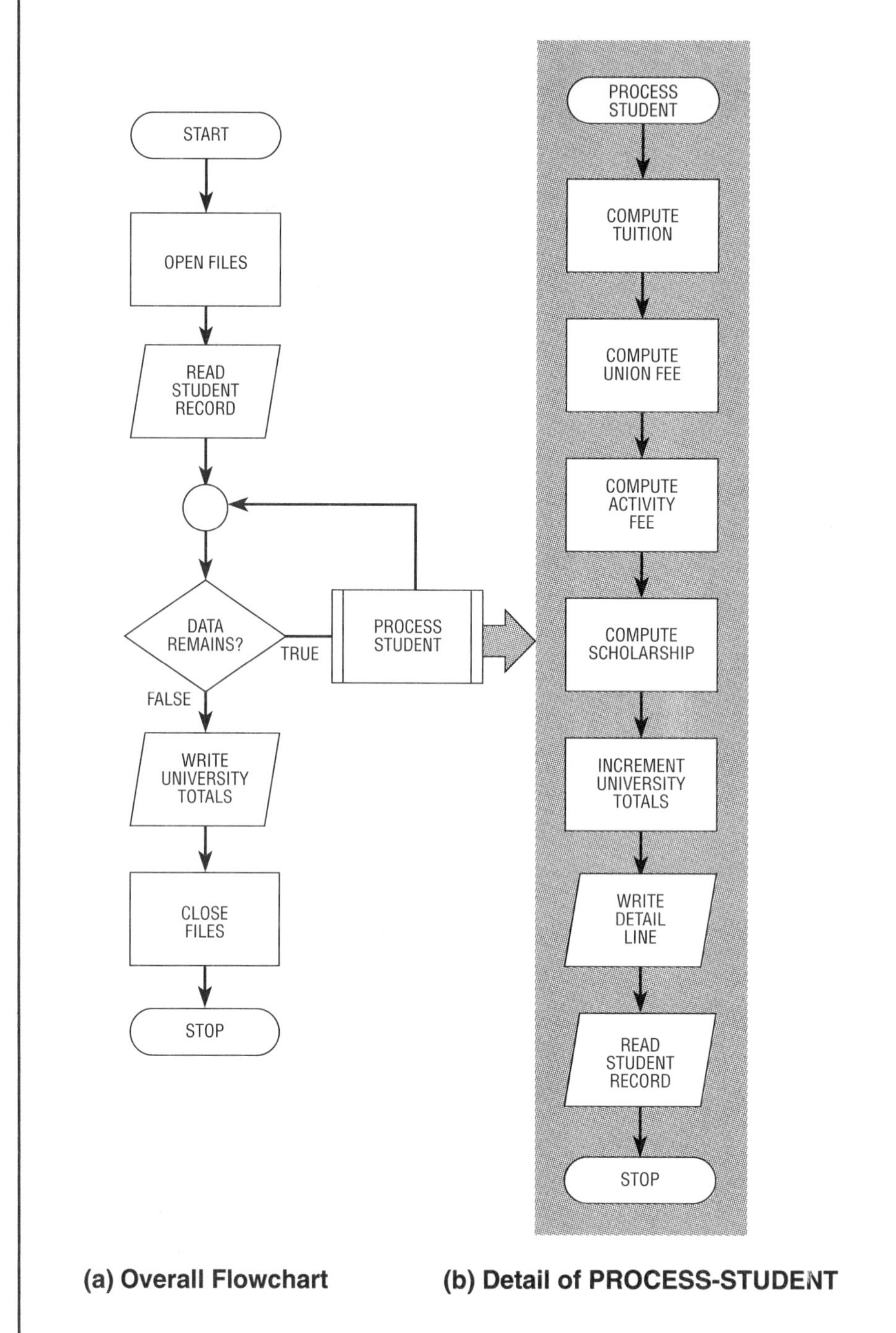

the technique precludes exact rules, but we urge the use of consistent conventions to make it easier to read. Our suggestions:

1. Indent for readability.
2. Use ENDIF, ENDDO, and ENDCASE to indicate the end of a logic structure; use vertical lines to indicate the extent of a block.

Figure 3.7 Pseudocode for Building Blocks

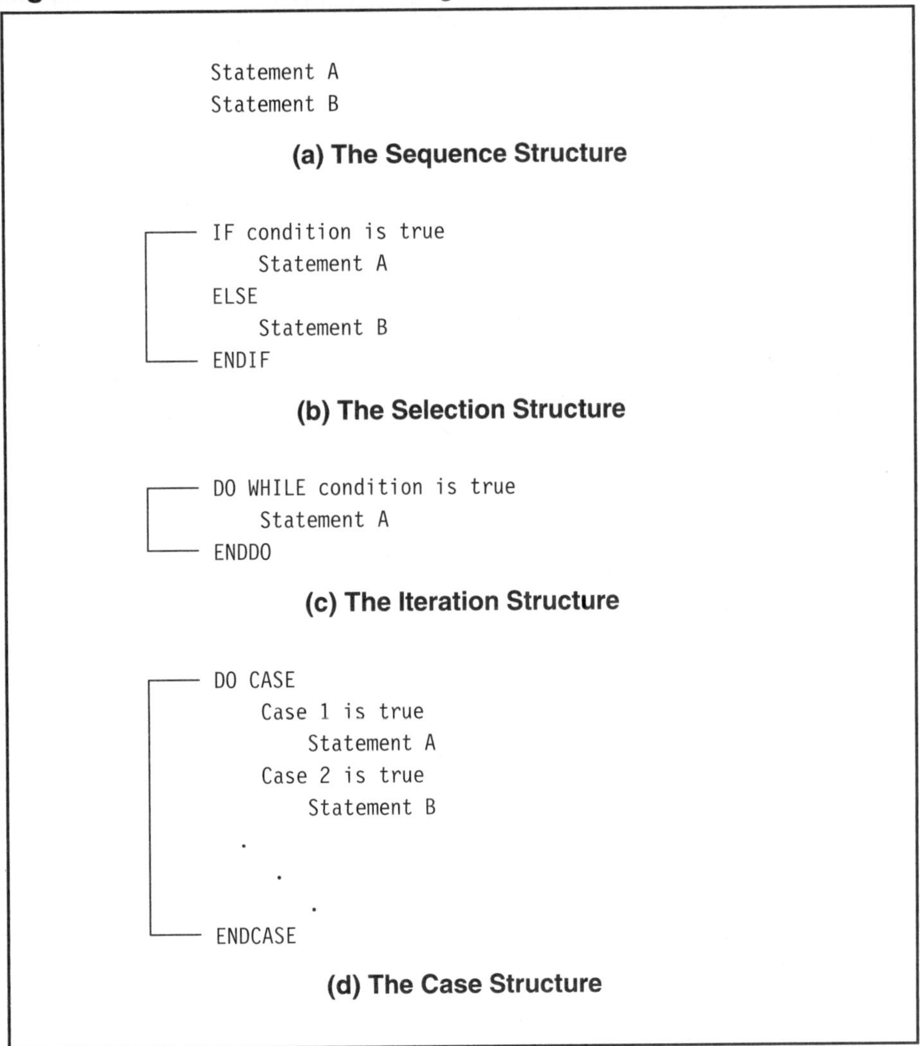

Statement A
Statement B
(a) The Sequence Structure
IF condition is true
Statement A
ELSE
Statement B
ENDIF
(b) The Selection Structure
DO WHILE condition is true
Statement A
ENDDO
(c) The Iteration Structure
DO CASE
Case 1 is true
Statement A
Case 2 is true
Statement B
.
.
.
ENDCASE
(d) The Case Structure

3. Use parenthetical expressions to clarify statements associated with the ELSE portion of an IF statement.
4. Minimize or avoid the use of adjectives and adverbs.

Warnier-Orr Diagrams

Warnier-Orr diagrams (named for their co-developers, Jean-Dominique Warnier and Kenneth Orr) combine elements of structured design and structured programming. The diagrams use specific symbols to represent the basic building blocks of structured programming, then combine these elements in hierarchical fashion.

Figure 3.9 shows how the basic building blocks of structured programming would be represented in a Warnier-Orr diagram. Sequential statements (Figure 3.9a) are listed vertically, one under the other, and are grouped in braces. A plus sign enclosed in a circle indicates selection, and is placed between the true and false conditions of the selection structure (a bar denotes the false condition). Parentheses indicate iteration (Figure 3.9c), with the number inside the parentheses indicating

Figure 3.8 Pseudocode for Tuition Billing Program

```
Open files
Write heading line(s)
Read STUDENT-FILE at end indicate no more data
DO WHILE data remains
    Compute tuition
    Compute union fee
    Compute activity fee
    Compute scholarship
    Compute bill
    Increment university totals
    Write detail line
    Read STUDENT-FILE at end indicate no more data
ENDDO
Write university totals
Close files
Stop run
```

(a) Initial attempt

```
Open files
Write heading line(s)
Read STUDENT-FILE at end indicate no more data
DO WHILE data remains
    Compute tuition = 200 * credits
    IF union member
        Union fee = $25
    ELSE
        Union fee = 0
    ENDIF
    DO CASE
        CASE credits <= 6
            Activity fee = 25
        CASE credits > 6 and <= 12
            Activity fee = 50
        CASE credits > 12
            Activity fee = 75
    END CASE
    IF gpa > 2.5
        Scholarship = Scholarship amount
    ELSE (no scholarship)
        Scholarship = 0
    ENDIF
    Compute Bill = Tuition + Union fee + Activity fee - Scholarship
    Increment university totals
    Write detail line
    Read STUDENT-FILE at end indicate no more data
ENDDO
Write university totals
Close files
Stop run
```

(b) Detailed pseudocode

Figure 3.9 Warnier-Orr Diagrams for Building Blocks

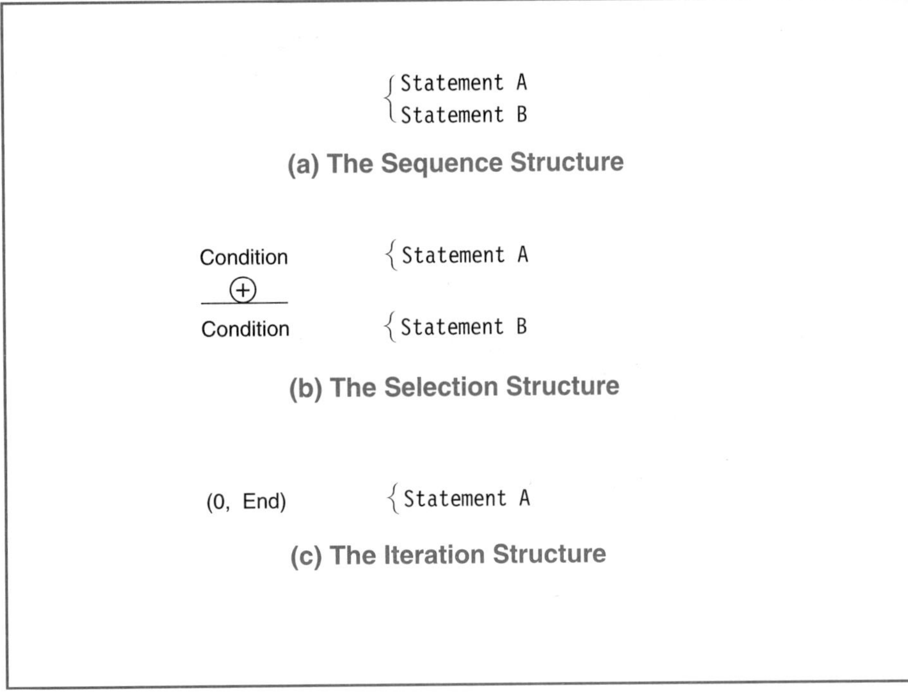

how often the loop is to be performed. A variable number of iterations is implied by enclosing two numbers, for example (0, End) to indicate execution until an end-of-file condition is reached. There is no specific notation for the case construct.

Figure 3.10 contains a Warnier-Orr diagram for the tuition billing program. The diagram depicts the same manager/subordinate relationships as the hierarchy chart of Figure 3.3c, but unlike the hierarchy chart, is read from left to right rather than from top to bottom. The diagram also contains additional information not found in the hierarchy chart, namely the logic to indicate how often, and in what sequence, subordinate modules are executed.

Top-Down Testing

All programs require extensive testing to ensure that they conform to the original specifications. However, the question of when coding ends and testing begins is not as straightforward as it may appear, and gives rise to the philosophy of ***top-down testing.***

Top-down testing suggests that coding and testing are parallel activities, and espouses the philosophy that testing begins even before a program is completely finished. This is accomplished by initially coding the intermediate- and/or lower-level paragraphs as ***stubs,*** that is, partially coded paragraphs whose purpose is to indicate only that the paragraph has been executed. The stub paragraphs do no useful work per se, and are used only to test the overall flow of the program. The rationale is that the highest (and most difficult) modules should be tested earlier and more often than the lower-level routines; the latter contain detailed but often trivial logic, and are least important with respect to the overall program flow.

Figure 3.11 is an example of such a program. It is *complete* in the sense that it contains a paragraph for every module in the hierarchy chart of Figure 3.3, yet *incomplete* in that most of its paragraphs consist of a single DISPLAY statement.

Figure 3.10 Warnier-Orr Diagram for Tuition Billing Program

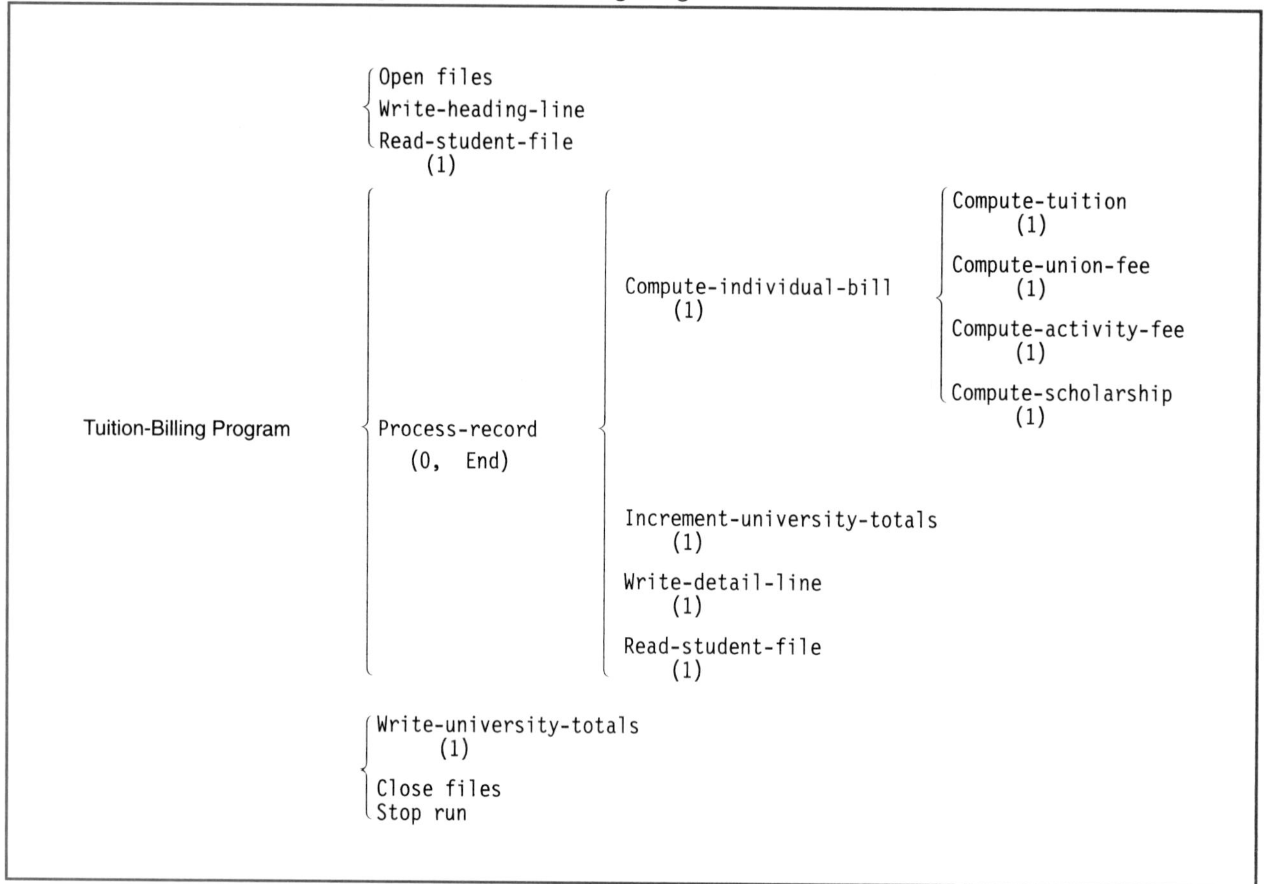

(DISPLAY is one of the most useful statements in COBOL as it allows the programmer to print a message on the screen—for example, DISPLAY "COMPUTE-INDIVIDUAL-BILL paragraph has been entered"—or to print the contents of a data name—for example, DISPLAY STUDENT-RECORD—without having to open a file. The DISPLAY statement is covered in Chapter 6.)

The program in Figure 3.11 was tested with the data of Figure 3.12a, and produced the output of Figure 3.12b. You may not think that much has been accomplished, but closer examination shows that all of the paragraphs in the program were executed, and further that they were executed in the correct sequence. The testing has demonstrated that the overall program flow is correct.

Execution began with the paragraph PREPARE-TUITION-REPORT followed by the the paragraph WRITE-HEADING-LINE. The record for the first student (JB Smith) was read, and the paragraph PROCESS-STUDENT-RECORD was entered. The paragraph COMPUTE-INDIVIDUAL-BILL was executed next, and called its four subordinates to compute the tuition, union fee, activity fee, and scholarship. The paragraphs to increment university totals and to write a detail line were also called. The data for the second student (HR James) was read, and PROCESS-STUDENT-RECORD (and all its subordinates) were re-executed. Eventually the end of file was reached, the paragraph WRITE-UNIVERSITY-TOTALS was executed, and the program ended.

Yes, the program requires additional development, but the hardest part is over. Any errors that may have existed in the highest-level modules have already

Figure 3.11 Tuition Billing Program with Stubs

```
IDENTIFICATION DIVISION.
PROGRAM-ID.    TUITION3.
AUTHOR.        CAROL VAZQUEZ VILLAR.

ENVIRONMENT DIVISION.
INPUT-OUTPUT SECTION.
FILE-CONTROL.
     SELECT STUDENT-FILE
         ASSIGN TO UT-S-SYSIN.

DATA DIVISION.
FILE SECTION.
FD  STUDENT-FILE
    RECORD CONTAINS 27 CHARACTERS.
01  STUDENT-RECORD          PIC X(27).

WORKING-STORAGE SECTION.
01  DATA-REMAINS-SWITCH     PIC X(2)    VALUE SPACES.

PROCEDURE DIVISION.
PREPARE-TUITION-REPORT.
    DISPLAY 'PREPARE-TUITION-REPORT paragraph entered'.
    OPEN INPUT  STUDENT-FILE.
    PERFORM WRITE-HEADING-LINE.
    PERFORM READ-STUDENT-FILE.
    PERFORM PROCESS-STUDENT-RECORD
        UNTIL DATA-REMAINS-SWITCH = 'NO'.
    PERFORM WRITE-UNIVERSITY-TOTALS.
    CLOSE STUDENT-FILE.
    STOP RUN.

WRITE-HEADING-LINE.
    DISPLAY 'WRITE-HEADING-LINE paragraph entered'.

READ-STUDENT-FILE.
    READ STUDENT-FILE
        AT END MOVE 'NO' TO DATA-REMAINS-SWITCH
    END-READ.

PROCESS-STUDENT-RECORD.
    DISPLAY ' '.
    DISPLAY 'PROCESS-STUDENT-RECORD paragraph entered'.
    DISPLAY 'Student record being processed: ' STUDENT-RECORD.
    PERFORM COMPUTE-INDIVIDUAL-BILL.
    PERFORM INCREMENT-UNIVERSITY-TOTALS
    PERFORM WRITE-DETAIL-LINE.
    PERFORM READ-STUDENT-FILE.
```

Display statement shows current record

Figure 3.11 *(continued)*

```
COMPUTE-INDIVIDUAL-BILL.
    DISPLAY '   COMPUTE-INDIVIDUAL-BILL paragraph entered'.
    PERFORM COMPUTE-TUITION.
    PERFORM COMPUTE-UNION-FEE.
    PERFORM COMPUTE-ACTIVITY-FEE.
    PERFORM COMPUTE-SCHOLARSHIP.

COMPUTE-TUITION.
    DISPLAY '   COMPUTE-TUITION paragraph entered'.

COMPUTE-UNION-FEE.
    DISPLAY '   COMPUTE-UNION-FEE paragraph entered'.

COMPUTE-ACTIVITY-FEE.
    DISPLAY '   COMPUTE-ACTIVITY-FEE paragraph entered'.

COMPUTE-SCHOLARSHIP.
    DISPLAY '   COMPUTE-SCHOLARSHIP paragraph entered'.

INCREMENT-UNIVERSITY-TOTALS.
    DISPLAY '   INCREMENT-UNIVERSITY-TOTALS paragraph entered'.

WRITE-DETAIL-LINE.
    DISPLAY '   WRITE-DETAIL-LINE paragraph entered'.

WRITE-UNIVERSITY-TOTALS.
    DISPLAY ' '.
    DISPLAY 'WRITE-UNIVERSITY-TOTALS paragraph entered'.
```

Program stub

been found, and were easier to correct than had testing been deferred. Of course, later versions of the program can still contain bugs, but these errors will occur in lower level modules where correction is generally easier. The more difficult problems will already have been resolved in the initial tests, and that is precisely the goal of top-down testing.

We urge you to implement the top-down approach to program testing, and offer Figure 3.13 as our last word on the subject. In the traditional mode of Figure 3.13a, no testing is done until the weekend before the program goes live (or your assignment is due). Inevitably last-minute panic sets in, giving rise to overtime and chaos, an environment unlikely to produce logically correct programs. By contrast, the top down approach of Figure 3.13b provides a more uniform testing pattern, beginning almost immediately with the project's inception and continuing throughout its duration. The results are vastly superior.

Figure 3.12 Testing the Tuition Billing Program

```
SMITH          JB15Y0000230
JAMES          HR15 0500245
BAKER          SR09 0500350
PART-TIMER     JR03Y0000300
JONES          PL15Y0000280
HEAVYWORKER    HM18 0000200
LEE            BL18 0000335
CLARK          JC06 0000310
GROSSMAN       SE07 0000215
FRANKEL        LF10 0000350
BENWAY         CT03 0250395
KERBEL         NB04 0000100
```

(a) Test Data

```
PREPARE-TUITION-REPORT paragraph entered
WRITE-HEADING-LINE paragraph entered

PROCESS-STUDENT-RECORD paragraph entered
Student record being processed: SMITH          JB15Y0000230
  COMPUTE-INDIVIDUAL-BILL paragraph entered
  COMPUTE-TUITION paragraph entered
  COMPUTE-UNION-FEE paragraph entered
  COMPUTE-ACTIVITY-FEE paragraph entered
  COMPUTE-SCHOLARSHIP paragraph entered
  INCREMENT-UNIVERSITY-TOTALS paragraph entered
  WRITE-DETAIL-LINE paragraph entered

PROCESS-STUDENT-RECORD paragraph entered
Student record being processed: JAMES          HR15 0500245
  COMPUTE-INDIVIDUAL-BILL paragraph entered
  COMPUTE-TUITION paragraph entered
  COMPUTE-UNION-FEE paragraph entered
  COMPUTE-ACTIVITY-FEE paragraph entered
  COMPUTE-SCHOLARSHIP paragraph entered
  INCREMENT-UNIVERSITY-TOTALS paragraph entered
  WRITE-DETAIL-LINE paragraph entered
   .
      .
         .
PROCESS-STUDENT-RECORD paragraph entered
Student record being processed: KERBEL         NB04 0000100
  COMPUTE-INDIVIDUAL-BILL paragraph entered
  COMPUTE-TUITION paragraph entered
  COMPUTE-UNION-FEE paragraph entered
  COMPUTE-ACTIVITY-FEE paragraph entered
  COMPUTE-SCHOLARSHIP paragraph entered
  INCREMENT-UNIVERSITY-TOTALS paragraph entered
  WRITE-DETAIL-LINE paragraph entered

WRITE-UNIVERSITY-TOTALS paragraph entered
```

(b) Output of Stubs Program

Figure 3.13 Advantages of Top-Down Testing

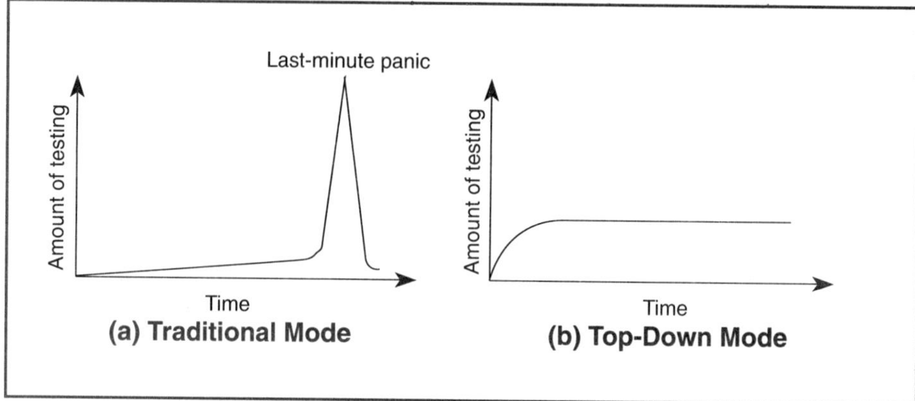

SUMMARY

Points to Remember

- Structured design is a functionally oriented technique that identifies the tasks a program is to accomplish, then relates those tasks to one another in a hierarchy chart.
- The modules in a hierarchy chart correspond one to one with paragraphs in a COBOL program. A module (paragraph) can be entered only from the module immediately above it, and must return control to that module when execution is complete.
- A hierarchy chart is evaluated for completeness, functionality, and span of control.
- Structured programming is procedural in nature and contains decision-making logic depicting the sequence in which the program tasks will be executed.
- A structured program consists entirely of the basic building blocks of sequence, selection, and iteration; a fourth construct, case, is commonly included in the definition of structured programming.
- Each of the elementary building blocks in structured programming has one entry point and one exit point.
- Flowcharts and/or pseudocode (defined as neat notes to yourself) describe the logic in a program. Warnier-Orr diagrams combine elements of structured design and structured programming.
- Top down testing begins early in the development process, even before a program is completely coded; it is accomplished through the use of program stubs.

Key Words and Concepts

Bohm and Jacopini
Case structure
Flowchart
Functional technique
Hierarchy chart
Iteration structure
One entry point/one exit point
Procedural technique
Program stub
Pseudocode
Selection structure
Sequence structure
Span of control
Structured design
Structured programming
Top-down development
Warnier-Orr diagram

FILL-IN

1. The fundamental building blocks of structured programming are: ______________, ______________, and ______________.
2. The ______________ construct is a fourth structure, which is convenient for expressing multibranch situations.
3. All of the basic building blocks of structured programming have ______________ entry point and ______________ exit point.
4. In the iteration, or DO WHILE construct, the condition is tested (before/after) the procedure is executed.
5. The primary tool of structured design is the ______________ ______________.
6. ______________ diagrams combine elements of a hierarchy chart and pseudocode.
7. A hierarchy chart is evaluated according to the criteria of ______________, ______________, and ______________.
8. Structured design is a ______________ oriented technique, whereas structured programming is ______________ in nature.
9. ______________, rather than flowcharting, is the most common technique for expressing program logic.
10. Each module in a ______________ ______________ represents a ______________ in a COBOL program.
11. ______________ — ______________ is the management term for the number of subordinate modules.
12. A well-chosen paragraph name should indicate the function of that paragraph, and consist of a ______________, ______________, and ______________.
13. ______________ and ______________ are the individuals credited with first postulating the structured theorem.
14. Structured (programming/design) is intended to produce a ______________ solution with the same components and relationships as the problem it is intended to solve.
15. A program should be tested from the (top down/bottom up).

TRUE/FALSE

1. A structured program is guaranteed not to contain logical errors.
2. Structured programming can be implemented in a variety of programming languages.
3. INITIALIZATION and TERMINATION are good module names.
4. The logic of any program can be expressed as a combination of only three types of logic structures.
5. The one entry/one exit philosophy is essential to structured programming.
6. Decision making should generally occur in higher-level, rather than lower-level, modules.
7. The case construct is one of the three basic logic structures.
8. A flowchart is the only way to communicate program logic.
9. Pseudocode has precise syntactical rules.
10. A program's hierarchy chart is developed from the bottom up.
11. A program must be completely coded before testing can begin.
12. A Warnier-Orr diagram combines elements of structured design and structured programming.
13. READ-WRITE-AND-COMPUTE is a good module name.
14. A single COBOL paragraph should accomplish many functions for optimal efficiency.
15. Program testing should be concentrated in the last 25% of the development phase.
16. A span of control from 15 to 25 COBOL paragraphs is desirable for the highest-level modules.
17. The optimal number of modules in a system is equal to the number of programmers available for coding.
18. A module in a hierarchy chart can be called from another module on its own level.

PROBLEMS

1. Given the flowchart in Figure 3.14, respond "true" or "false" to the following on the basis of the flowchart.
   a. If $X > Y$ and $W > Z$, then *always* add 1 to B.
   b. If $X < Y$, then *always* add 1 to D.
   c. If $Q > T$, then *always* add 1 to B.
   d. If $X < Y$ and $W < Z$, then *always* add 1 to D.
   e. There are no conditions under which 1 will be added to both A and B simultaneously.
   f. If $W > Z$ and $Q < T$, then *always* add 1 to C.
2. Assume that a robot is sitting on a chair, facing a wall a short distance away. Restricting yourself to the basic building blocks of structured programming, develop the necessary logic to have the robot walk to the wall and return to its initial position. Express your solution in pseudocode. The robot understands the following commands:

Figure 3.14 Flowchart for Problem 1

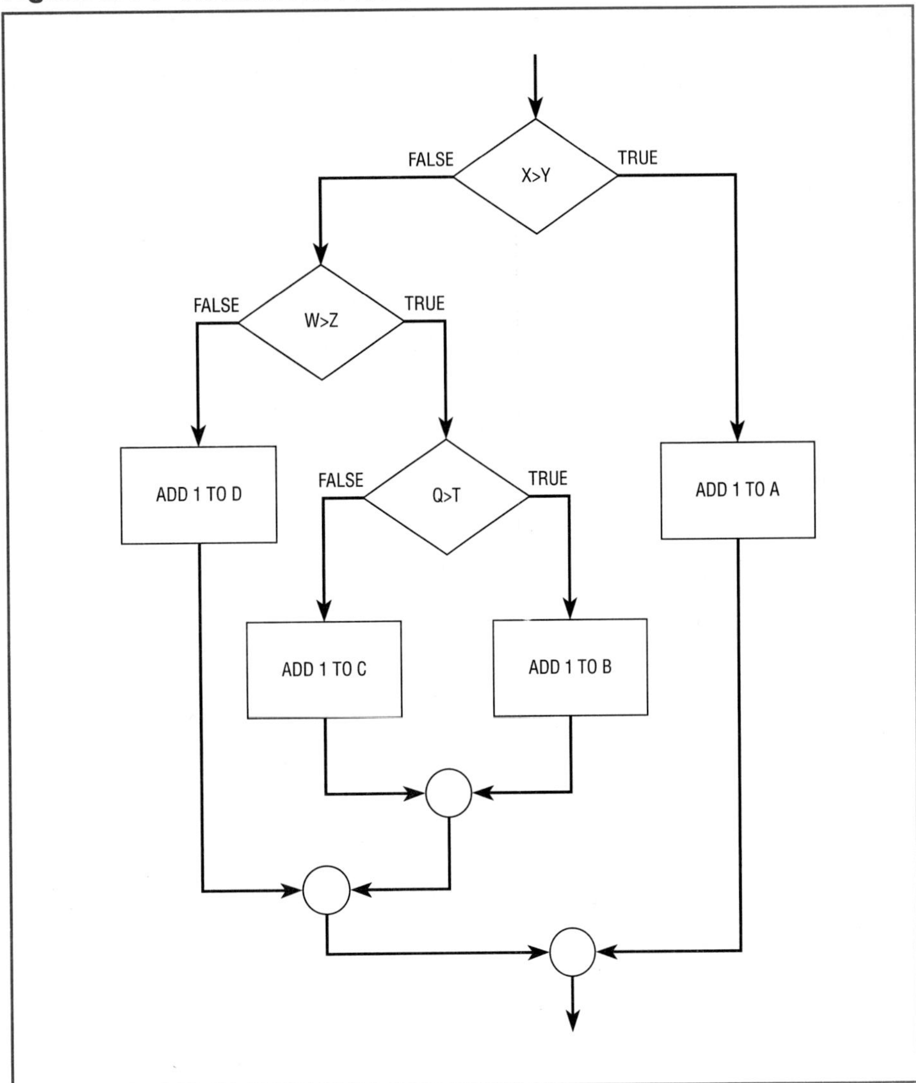


```
STAND
SIT
TURN (turns right 90 degrees)
STEP
```

In addition, the robot can raise its arms and sense the wall with its fingertips. (However, it cannot sense the chair on its return trip, since the chair is below arm level.) Accordingly the robot must count the number of steps to the wall or chair by using the following commands:

```
ADD (increments counter by 1)
SUBTRACT (decrements counter by 1)
ZERO COUNTER (sets counter to zero)
ARMS UP
ARMS DOWN
```

The wall is assumed to be an integer number of steps away. Select a volunteer to act as the robot, and see whether the submitted solutions actually accomplish the objective.

Figure 3.15 Flowchart for Problem 3

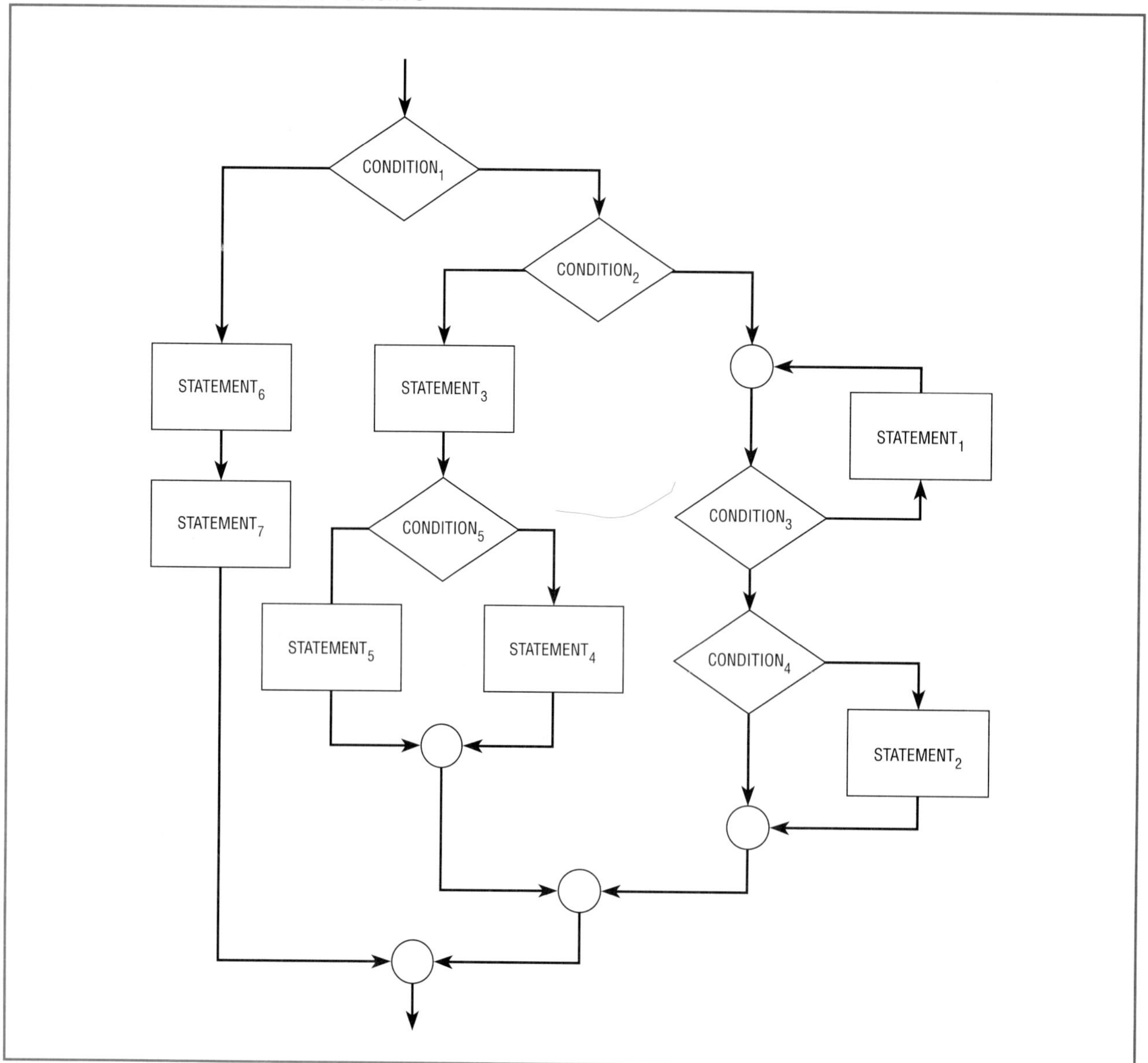

3. Identify the elementary building blocks in Figure 3.15. Be sure you get all of them (the authors can find eight).
4. Indicate the output that will be produced by each of the following DISPLAY statements.
   a. DISPLAY 'STUDENT RECORD'.
   b. DISPLAY STUDENT-RECORD.
   c. DISPLAY 'STUDENT RECORD IS ' STUDENT-RECORD.
   d. DISPLAY.
   e. DISPLAY STUDENT-NAME, SOC-SEC-NUM.
5. This non-data-processing problem specifically avoids a business context, and was chosen because you are unlikely to have a preexisting bias toward a solution.

Develop a hierarchy chart to allow a user to play a series of tic-tac-toe games interactively against a computer. The following modules were used in the author's solution: PLAY-SERIES, PLAY-GAME, CLEAR-BOARD, GET-USER-MOVE, VALIDATE-USER-MOVE, CHECK-FOR-WINNER, UPDATE-BOARD, GET-COMPUTER-MOVE, DISPLAY-BOARD, DISPLAY-MESSAGE. (The last module, DISPLAY-MESSAGE, may be called from several places.) The module names should in themselves be indicative of the module functions.

6. Again we have chosen a nonbusiness problem to give you further practice with structured design. This time you are asked to develop a hierarchy chart for the game of blackjack (also known as "21"). The game is played with a deck of 52 cards (or more commonly with multiple decks). The player places a bet, and the player and dealer are each dealt two cards. Both of the player's cards are face up (showing), but one of the dealer's cards is hidden. The player is asked whether he or she wishes to draw additional card(s), after which the dealer has the same option (provided the player has not gone over 21). The player closest to 21 (without going over) wins. The rules of the game require the dealer to draw with 16 or less, and stand (not draw) with 17 or more. Your hierarchy chart should contain the necessary modules to keep a running total of the player's winnings (or losses) as well as the following special situations:
   a. Doubling down—if the player's first two cards total 11, he or she may double the bet and receive one additional card.
   b. Purchasing insurance—if the dealer's "up" card is an ace, the player may place an additional side bet. If the dealer has "blackjack," the player receives a payout of 2 to 1 on the side bet, but loses the initial bet. If the dealer does not have blackjack, the side bet is lost and play continues.
   c. Splitting pairs—if the player has a pair, he or she may double the bet and play two hands.

The Identification, Environment, and Data Divisions

CHAPTER OUTLINE

OBJECTIVES

After reading this chapter you will be able to:

- Describe the COBOL notation and determine the appropriate syntax for any statement.
- Complete the Identification Division of a COBOL program.
- Complete the Environment Division of a COBOL program.
- Code a record description to show hierarchical relationships among fields containing numeric and alphanumeric entries.
- Code a Working-Storage Section to define various print lines.
- Explain the use of an assumed decimal point.

OVERVIEW

The overall approach of this book is to provide a rapid introduction to computer programming; thus we presented a complete COBOL program in Chapter 1. Our objective at that time was to put you on the computer immediately, without too much concern for the syntactical rules, which you must eventually master.

We move now to a formal study of COBOL, beginning with a notation that fully explains the variations permitted within any COBOL statement. The chapter focuses on the Identification, Environment, and Data Divisions, and concludes with a COBOL listing expanding on this material.

COBOL Notation

COBOL is an English-like language with inherent flexibility in the way a particular entry may be expressed. In other words, there are a number of different, but equally acceptable, ways to say the same thing. It is necessary, therefore, to develop a standard notation to provide a clear and unambiguous means of indicating precisely what is, and is not, permitted within any given statement. The notation is illustrated in Figure 4.1 and adheres to the following conventions:

1. Lowercase letters signify programmer-supplied information—for example, identifier-1 or literal-1.
2. Uppercase letters indicate reserved words—for example, IF, GREATER, or THAN.
3. Uppercase letters that are underlined are required; uppercase letters that are not underlined are optional reserved words.
4. Brackets [ ] symbolize an optional entry—for example, [NOT].
5. Braces { } imply that one of the enclosed items must be chosen—for example, a choice is required between identifier-1, literal-1, and arithmetic expression-1.
6. Three dots . . . mean that the last syntactical unit can be repeated an arbitrary number of times.

Figure 4.1 COBOL Notation

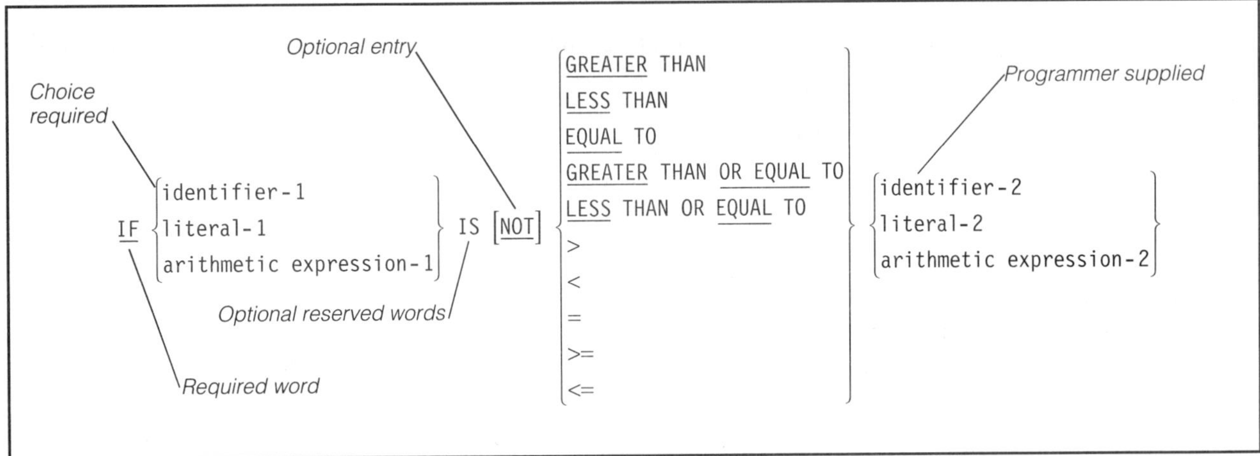

The example in Figure 4.1 is associated with the condition portion in the IF statement. IF is underlined and appears in capital letters, indicating it is a required reserved word. It is followed by a set of braces containing three options, one of which must be chosen. The reserved word IS appears in uppercase letters but is not underlined, meaning its use is optional. The brackets surrounding NOT imply that the clause is optional, but if the clause is chosen, NOT is required because it is underlined.

The next set of braces indicates a second mandatory choice among five relationships: GREATER THAN, GREATER THAN OR EQUAL TO, LESS THAN, LESS THAN OR EQUAL TO, or EQUAL TO. The reserved words THAN and TO are not underlined and are, therefore, optional. Alternatively, you can choose the appropriate symbol: >, >= <, <=, or = instead of spelling out the relationship. The third set of braces indicates yet another choice, this time from the entries identifier-2, literal-2, and arithmetic expression-2.

Returning to the engineering senior problem of Chapter 1, in which STU-MAJOR is compared to engineering, we see that all of the following are acceptable as the condition portion of the IF statement:

```
IF STU-MAJOR IS EQUAL TO 'ENGINEERING'
IF STU-MAJOR EQUAL 'ENGINEERING'
IF 'ENGINEERING' IS EQUAL TO STU-MAJOR
IF STU-MAJOR = 'ENGINEERING'
```

Identification Division

The **IDENTIFICATION DIVISION** is the first of the four divisions in a COBOL program. Its function is to provide identifying information about the program, such as author, date written, and security. The division consists of a division header and up to six paragraphs:

```
IDENTIFICATION DIVISION.
PROGRAM-ID.         program-name.
[AUTHOR.            [comment-entry] ... ]
[INSTALLATION.      [comment-entry] ... ]
[DATE-WRITTEN.      [comment-entry] ... ]
[DATE-COMPILED.     [comment-entry] ... ]
[SECURITY.          [comment-entry] ... ]
```

The division header and PROGRAM-ID paragraph are the only required entries. The five remaining paragraphs are optional (as indicated by the COBOL notation), and only the DATE-COMPILED paragraph merits special mention. If the paragraph is specified, the compiler will insert the current date during program compilation. (The paragraph is redundant, however, since most compilers automatically print the date of compilation on the top of each page.) A completed Identification Division is shown:

```
IDENTIFICATION DIVISION.
PROGRAM-ID.            FIRSTTRY.
AUTHOR.                ROBERT  T.  GRAUER.
INSTALLATION.          UNIVERSITY OF MIAMI.
DATE-WRITTEN.          MARCH 16, 1993.
DATE-COMPILED.         The compiler supplies compilation date.
SECURITY.              TOP SECRET-INSTRUCTORS  ONLY.
```

Coding for the Identification Division follows the general rules described in Chapter 2. The division header and paragraph names begin in the A margin, with all corresponding entries beginning in or past column 12 (B margin).

Environment Division

The ENVIRONMENT DIVISION contains two sections:

1. The CONFIGURATION SECTION identifies the computers for compiling and executing the program, usually one and the same.
2. The INPUT-OUTPUT SECTION associates the files in the COBOL program with the files known to the operating system.

The nature of these functions makes the Environment Division dependent on the computer on which you are working; that is, the Environment Division for a program on a VAX is different from that for a program on an IBM mainframe.

Configuration Section

The **CONFIGURATION SECTION** is enclosed in brackets within the COBOL notation and is therefore optional. An abbreviated format is shown below:

```
[CONFIGURATION SECTION.
[SOURCE-COMPUTER.  computer-name.]
[OBJECT-COMPUTER.  computer-name.]]
```

The section header and paragraph names begin in the A margin whereas the computer-name entries begin in or past column 12. The CONFIGURATION SECTION does little to enhance (the documentation of) a COBOL program and is typically omitted.

Input-Output Section

The **INPUT-OUTPUT SECTION** associates the files in a COBOL program with files known to the operating system. It contains a FILE-CONTROL paragraph, which in turn contains a **SELECT** statement for every file in the program. Syntactically it has the format:

```
[INPUT-OUTPUT SECTION.
 FILE-CONTROL.
     SELECT file-name-1 ASSIGN TO implementor-name.]
```

A program may be written without any files and hence the INPUT-OUTPUT section is optional. (See Chapter 10 on screen I/O for an example of a program written without any files.)

The section header (INPUT-OUTPUT SECTION) and paragraph name (FILE-CONTROL) begin in the A margin (columns 8 through 11). The SELECT statements for the individual files begin in the B margin (column 12 and beyond).

The precise format of the ***implementor-name*** in the SELECT statement varies from compiler to compiler, with the example below taken from lines 8 through 11 in the engineering senior problem. The example is for an IBM mainframe.

```
INPUT-OUTPUT SECTION.
FILE-CONTROL.
    SELECT STUDENT-FILE
        ASSIGN TO UT-S-SYSIN.
    SELECT PRINT-FILE
        ASSIGN TO UT-S-SYSOUT.
```

The dependence of the Environment Division on the individual computer installation bears repeating. You should consult either your instructor or your computer center for the proper statements to use in your program.

Data Division

The Data Division describes the data items that appear in a program. It contains several sections, two of which, the FILE SECTION and the WORKING-STORAGE SECTION, will be discussed in this chapter. Two other sections, the SCREEN SECTION and the LINKAGE SECTION, are presented in later chapters.

File Section

The **FILE SECTION** is the first section in the Data Division and contains a file description (FD) for every file previously defined in a SELECT statement in the Environment Division. (If, however, a program is written without any files, then the FILE SECTION will not appear.) The file description is followed by the associated record description which is accomplished through PICTURE clauses and level numbers. Each of these elements is discussed in turn.

File Description (FD) The ***file description*** (FD) provides information about the physical characteristics of a file. It contains four clauses, all of which are optional, and which may appear in any order. The final entry, however, must be terminated by a period. An abbreviated format for the file description is as follows:

```
FD  file-name
    [BLOCK CONTAINS integer-1 RECORDS ]
    [RECORD CONTAINS integer-1 CHARACTERS]
    [LABEL {RECORDS ARE} {OMITTED }]
    [      {RECORD IS  } {STANDARD}]
    [DATA RECORD IS data-name-1].
```

The **BLOCK CONTAINS** clause is used to speed up input/output operations for files on tape or disk, by reducing the number of physical records (blocks) in a file, and thus reducing the number of times the input/output device is accessed. In other words, it is more efficient to access a disk once and read a block containing 10 records, than it is to access the disk 10 times and read each record individually. The ***blocking factor*** is defined as the number of ***logical records*** in a ***physical record***. The concept is illustrated in Figure 4.2 where the records of Figure 4.2a are unblocked, whereas those in Figures 4.2b and 4.2c have blocking factors of 2 and 3, respectively.

The higher the blocking factor, the fewer the number of physical records, and the more efficient the processing. Thus, the blocking factor should always be as high as possible, within the limitations of the physical device. The actual determination of the blocking factor need not concern us now; what is important is the implementation of blocking in a COBOL program.

Assume, for example, a blocking factor of 5, with the associated entry, BLOCK CONTAINS 5 RECORDS. The initial execution of the READ statement places a block of 5 logical records in memory, with only the first record available to the program. The second (third, fourth, and fifth) execution of the READ statement makes a new logical record available, without a corresponding physical operation taking place. In similar fashion the sixth execution of the READ statement will bring a new physical record into the I/O area, with new logical records made available on the seventh through tenth executions of the READ statement. All of this is automatically done for the programmer as long as the BLOCK CONTAINS statement is specified in the COBOL FD.

Figure 4.2 Blocked versus Unblocked Records

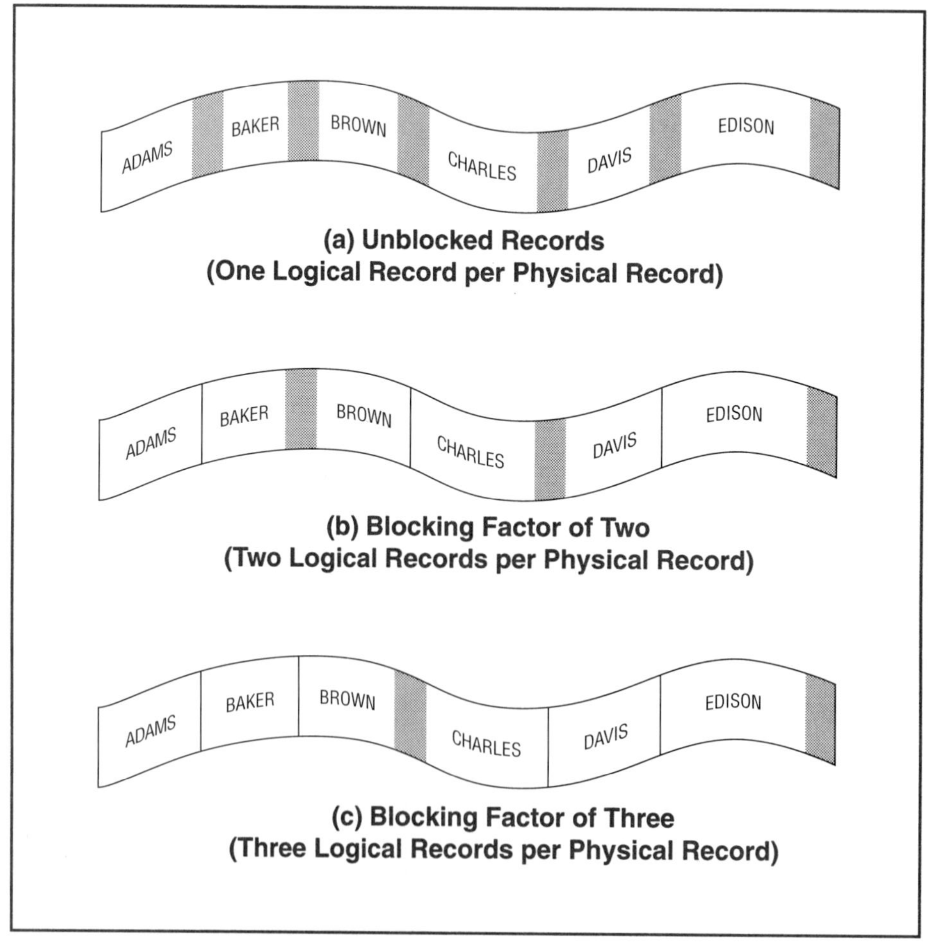

COBOL programs that are written to run on an IBM mainframe typically contain the entry, BLOCK CONTAINS 0 RECORDS. This entry does not mean what it says literally, but rather that the block size will be entered at execution time.

The **RECORD CONTAINS** clause indicates the number of characters in a record and is useful for documentation. The clause also causes the compiler to verify that the sizes of the individual data items sum to the stated value.

The **LABEL RECORDS** clause determines whether or not label processing is to take place. Label records appear at the beginning and end of files stored on tape or disk, and contain information about the file, such as the date created, the logical record size and the block size. Label records are created automatically whenever a file is opened as output and are checked automatically whenever a file is opened as input. Label processing is necessary to ensure that the proper file is being processed. The LABEL RECORDS clause is optional and its omission defaults to standard labels.

The DATA RECORD clause specifies the name of the 01 entry (or entries) associated with the particular file. It has limited value in documentation and has no other function. An example of a completed FD is shown below:

```
FD  STUDENT-FILE
    BLOCK CONTAINS 10 RECORDS
    RECORD CONTAINS 43 CHARACTERS
    LABEL RECORDS ARE STANDARD
    DATA RECORD IS STUDENT-IN.
```

Record Description A file description is followed by an associated ***record description*** that conveys the following information:

1. The size and type of each field within a record
2. The order in which the fields appear
3. The relationship of the fields to one another

through a combination of PICTURE clauses and level numbers.

PICTURE Clause A **PICTURE** clause describes the size and type of a field. The ***size*** of a field is equivalent to the number of characters (positions) in the field. The ***type*** of field is either numeric or alphanumeric, and is denoted by a 9 or an X, respectively, in the associated PICTURE clause. A ***numeric item*** can contain the numbers 0 – 9, whereas an ***alphanumeric item*** may contain A – Z (alphabetic), 0 – 9 (numeric), and/or special characters.

The size of a field is indicated by the number of times the 9 or X is repeated. A data item with a picture of XXXX or X(4) is a four-position alphanumeric field. In similar fashion 999 or 9(3) denotes a three-position numeric field. (Alphabetic data items, denoted by an A in the associated PICTURE clause, are seldom used because even a field as simple as a person's name can contain apostrophes or hyphens, which are alphanumeric rather than alphabetic in nature.)

Level Numbers ***Level numbers*** describe the relationships that exist between fields within a record. Each field is classified as either a group item or an elementary item. A ***group item*** is a field that can be further divided—an ***elementary item*** can not.

Consider, for example, Figure 4.3, which depicts a student examination record. The field STUDENT-NAME is a group item because it is divided into three fields: LAST-NAME, FIRST-NAME, and INIT. LAST-NAME, FIRST-NAME, and INIT, however, are elementary items, since they are not further divided. In similar fashion, SS-NUM is an elementary item. EXAM-SCORES is a group item, as are MATH and ENGLISH. ALG, GEO, READ, etc., are elementary items.

Figure 4.3 Student Exam Record

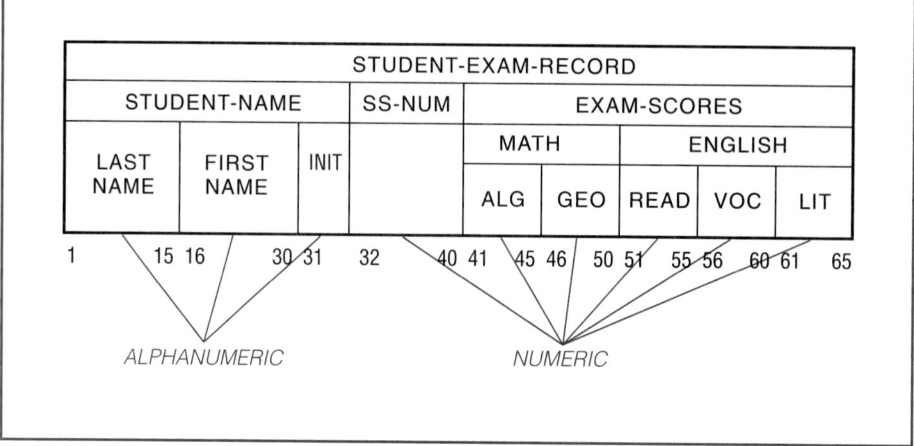

Level numbers and PICTURE clauses are used in Figure 4.4 to define a record corresponding to the STUDENT-EXAM-RECORD in Figure 4.3. Two equivalent sets of COBOL statements (Figures 4.4a and 4.4b) are presented and follow the rules below:

1. The level numbers within a record description can assume any value from 01 to 49 inclusive.
2. The level number 01 denotes the record as a whole.
3. Any level number from 02 to 49 can be used for field(s) within the record, so long as elementary items have a numerically higher number than the group item to which they belong.
4. An elementary item *must* have a PICTURE clause—a group item *cannot* have a PICTURE clause.

In Figure 4.4 STUDENT-EXAM-RECORD has a level number of 01 to indicate the record as a whole. STUDENT-NAME is a subfield of STUDENT-EXAM-RECORD; hence it has a higher level number (05). LAST-NAME, FIRST-NAME, and MID-INITIAL are subordinate to STUDENT-NAME and thus have a higher level number (10). SOC-SEC-NUM and EXAM-SCORES are also subfields of STUDENT-EXAM-RECORD and have the same level number as STUDENT-NAME. EXAM-SCORES is subdivided into two group items, MATH and ENGLISH, which in turn are further subdivided into elementary items.

Every elementary item must have a PICTURE clause, whereas a group item cannot have a PICTURE clause. Thus, LAST-NAME has the entry PICTURE IS X(15) to denote a 15-position alphanumeric field; STUDENT-NAME, however, is a group item and does not have a PICTURE clause. The parentheses in a PICTURE clause imply repetition; that is, the entry 9(5) for ALGEBRA depicts a 5-position numeric field.

There is considerable latitude within COBOL as to the specification of level numbers and PICTURE clauses. You can, for example, choose any level numbers from 02 to 49 to describe subordinate fields; for example, 04, 08, and 12 are used in Figure 4.4b as opposed to the levels 05, 10, and 15 in Figure 4.4a. The 01 level is used in both figures for the record as a whole.

Figure 4.4 Level Numbers and PICTURE Clauses

```
01  STUDENT-EXAM-RECORD.
    05  STUDENT-NAME.
        10  LAST-NAME            PICTURE IS X(15).
        10  FIRST-NAME           PICTURE IS X(15).
        10  MID-INITIAL          PICTURE IS X.
    05  SOC-SEC-NUM              PICTURE IS 9(9).
    05  EXAM-SCORES.
        10  MATH.
            15  ALGEBRA          PICTURE IS 9(5).
            15  GEOMETRY         PICTURE IS 9(5).
        10  ENGLISH.
            15  READING          PICTURE IS 9(5).
            15  VOCABULARY       PICTURE IS 9(5).
            15  LITERATURE       PICTURE IS 9(5).
```

(a) Initial Coding

```
01  STUDENT-EXAM-RECORD.
    04  STUDENT-NAME.
        08  LAST-NAME            PIC X(15).
        08  FIRST-NAME           PIC X(15).
        08  MID-INITIAL          PIC X.
    04  SOC-SEC-NUM              PIC 9(9).
    04  EXAM-SCORES.
        08  MATH.
            12  ALGEBRA          PIC 99999.
            12  GEOMETRY         PIC 99999.
        08  ENGLISH.
            12  READING          PIC 99999.
            12  VOCABULARY       PIC 99999.
            12  LITERATURE       PIC 99999.
```

(b) Alternative Specification

The PICTURE clause itself can assume any one of four forms: PICTURE IS, PICTURE, PIC IS, or PIC. Parentheses may be used to signal repetition of a picture type; that is, X(3) is equivalent to XXX. Figure 4.4b is the exact equivalent of Figure 4.4a with emphasis on the aforementioned flexibility.

Assumed Decimal Point Incoming numeric data may not contain *actual* decimal points. On first reading, that statement may be somewhat hard to accept. How, for example, does one read a field containing dollars and cents? The answer is an assumed (implied) decimal point as illustrated in the COBOL entry:

```
05  HOURLY-RATE    PICTURE IS 99V99.
```

Everything is familiar except the V embedded in the PICTURE clause. The V means an ***implied decimal point***; that is, HOURLY-RATE is a four-digit (there are

Figure 4.5 Assumed Decimal Point

INCOMING RECORD:	DATA DIVISION RECORD DESCRIPTION:	VALUES:
	01 INCOMING-DATA-RECORD.	
9ˇ87|65ˇ4|3|ˇ210	05 FIELD-A PIC 9V99. →	9.87
	05 FIELD-B PIC 9V99. →	65.4
	05 FIELD-C PIC 9. →	3
	05 FIELD-D PIC V999. →	.210

four 9's) numeric field, with two of the digits coming after the decimal point. Simply stated, the V indicates the position of the decimal point.

To check your understanding, assume that 9876543210 is found in positions 1–10 of an incoming record and that the following Data Division entries apply:

```
01  INCOMING-DATA-RECORD.
    05  FIELD-A          PIC 9V99.
    05  FIELD-B          PIC 99V9.
    05  FIELD-C          PIC 9.
    05  FIELD-D          PIC V999.
```

The values of FIELD-A, FIELD-B, FIELD-C, and FIELD-D are 9.87, 65.4, 3, and .210, respectively, as shown in Figure 4.5. FIELD-A is contained in the first three positions with two of the digits to the right of the decimal point. FIELD-B is contained in the next three positions (i.e., 6, 5, and 4) with one digit to the right of the decimal point. FIELD-C is contained in position 7 with no decimal places. Finally, FIELD-D is contained in positions 8, 9, and 10, with all three to the right of the decimal.

Working-Storage Section

The **WORKING-STORAGE SECTION** defines any data name that was not previously referenced in the FILE SECTION, that is, any data name that does not appear in a file. The WORKING-STORAGE SECTION contains data names to store the results of calculations, switches to control the execution of performed paragraphs, and/or data names to hold constants needed by the program. The WORKING-STORAGE SECTION will also define various print lines (a heading, detail, and/or total line) required by a program.

Figure 4.6 contains a WORKING-STORAGE SECTION for an expanded version of the engineering senior program to count the number of qualified students. There are separate record descriptions for the counters and constants needed by the program, as well as a separate record description (01 entry) for each type of print line.

A **FILLER** entry defines a field that is not referenced elsewhere in the COBOL program. The layout of DETAIL-LINE, for example, begins with eight spaces, followed by the value of PRINT-NAME, an additional 10 spaces, the value of PRINT-MAJOR, and a final set of 74 spaces to complete the print line. The three fields containing spaces are not referenced anywhere else in the program yet need to be accounted for—hence the FILLER entry.

The word FILLER is optional, however, and could be omitted as shown in the definition of TOTAL-LINE. The entries under TOTAL-LINE look strange initially, but make perfect sense when your realize that the "missing" FILLER entries are not

Figure 4.6 The Working-Storage Section

```
WORKING-STORAGE SECTION.

01  COUNTERS-AND-SWITCHES.
    05  TOTAL-STUDENTS           PIC 9(3)      VALUE ZEROS.
    05  DATA-REMAINS-SWITCH      PIC X(2)      VALUE SPACES.

01  PROGRAM-CONSTANTS.
    05  REQUIRED-CREDITS         PIC 999       VALUE 110.
    05  REQUIRED-MAJOR           PIC X(10)     VALUE 'ENGINEERING'.
    05  REQUIRED-GPA             PIC 9V99      VALUE 3.00.

01  HEADING-LINE.
    05  FILLER                   PIC X(10)     VALUE SPACES.
    05  FILLER                   PIC X(12)     VALUE 'STUDENT NAME'.
    05  FILLER                   PIC X(110)    VALUE SPACES.

01  DETAIL-LINE.
    05  FILLER                   PIC X(8)      VALUE SPACES.
    05  PRINT-NAME               PIC X(25).
    05  FILLER                   PIC X(10)     VALUE SPACES.
    05  PRINT-MAJOR              PIC X(15).
    05  FILLER                   PIC X(74)     VALUE SPACES.      FILLER IS OPTIONAL IN COBOL-85

01  TOTAL-LINE.
    05                           PIC X(4)     VALUE SPACES
    05                           PIC X(14)    VALUE 'TOTAL STUDENTS'.
    05                           PIC X(2)     VALUE SPACES.
    05  TOT-STUDENTS             PIC 9(3)     VALUE ZEROS.
    05                           PIC X(110)   VALUE SPACES.

01  DASHED-LINE
    05  FILLER                   PIC X(132)   VALUE ALL '-'.
```

referenced in the Procedure Division, and hence their omission has no effect on the remainder of the program.

VALUE Clause The **VALUE** clause initializes the contents of a data name within the WORKING-STORAGE SECTION and has the general form:

```
VALUE IS literal
```

Literals are of three types—numeric, nonnumeric, and figurative constants. Numeric literals—for example, 110 or 3.00—contain a number and are used in calculations. Nonnumeric literals, such as 'ENGINEERING', contain a character string and are enclosed in apostrophes or quotations marks. (Additional rules for numeric and nonnumeric literals were presented in Chapter 1.)

A ***figurative constant*** (ZERO or SPACE) is a COBOL reserved word with a pre-assigned value. The singular and plural forms of a figurative constant are interchangeable; that is, one can use SPACE or SPACES, or ZERO, ZEROS, or ZEROES.

Figurative constants are *not* enclosed in quotation marks. COBOL also permits the use of the **ALL** literal to repeat a character string.

The VALUE clause associated with a particular data name must be consistent with the corresponding PICTURE clause; that is, it is *incorrect* to use a nonnumeric literal with a numeric picture clause or a numeric literal with a nonnumeric picture. Consider:

```
REQUIRED-CREDITS    PIC 999    VALUE 110.              (valid)
REQUIRED-MAJOR      PIC X(10)  VALUE 'ENGINEERING'.    (valid)
REQUIRED-CREDITS    PIC 999    VALUE '110'.            (invalid)
REQUIRED-MAJOR      PIC X(10)  VALUE ENGINEERING.      (invalid)
```

REQUIRED-CREDITS is defined as a numeric item and must have a numeric value. In similar fashion, REQUIRED-MAJOR is defined as alphanumeric and requires an alphanumeric VALUE clause.

The Tuition Billing Program

The tuition billing program was introduced in Chapter 3 in conjunction with structured programming and design. The stubs program did not, however, show the detailed output as presented in the programming specifications, because the objective at that time was only to test the overall flow of the program. It is necessary, therefore, to return to the original specifications to develop the Identification, Environment, and Data Divisions. We will, however, amplify the development of the Data Division by presenting three figures that relate various portions of the programming specifications to their associated COBOL entries.

Programming Specifications

Figure 4.7a displays the input record layout from the programming specifications; Figure 4.7b shows the corresponding FD and record description. STUDENT-RECORD corresponds to the record as a whole and thus is assigned the level number 01. STUDENT-RECORD in turn is divided into the subordinate fields STU-NAME (which is further divided into STU-LAST-NAME and STU-INITIALS), STU-CREDITS, STU-UNION-MEMBER, and STU-SCHOLARSHIP. STUDENT-RECORD and STU-NAME are group items and do not have a PICTURE clause; all of the other data names are elementary items and have a PICTURE clause. An implied decimal point appears within the PICTURE clause for STU-GPA.

Figure 4.8a excerpts the processing specifications for the computation of a student's bill; Figure 4.8b shows the associated record description as it appears in WORKING-STORAGE. The entries in Figure 4.8b are not required by COBOL per se, and are included to facilitate documentation and maintenance. It would be possible, for example, to use the constants 200 and 25 in the Procedure Division rather than the corresponding data names PRICE-PER-CREDIT and UNION-FEE. The data names, however, facilitate program maintenance; that is, a change in the value of a constant is easier to implement in the Data Division than (in multiple statements) in the Procedure Division.

Figure 4.9a contains the programming specifications for the heading and detail lines; Figure 4.9b shows the associated COBOL entries. Note carefully the exact correspondence between the COBOL entries and report layout. The print layout calls for 10 spaces between the literals STUDENT NAME and CREDITS; thus there is a 10 position FILLER entry between these literals within the COBOL entries.

Figure 4.7 Development of a COBOL Program (File Section)

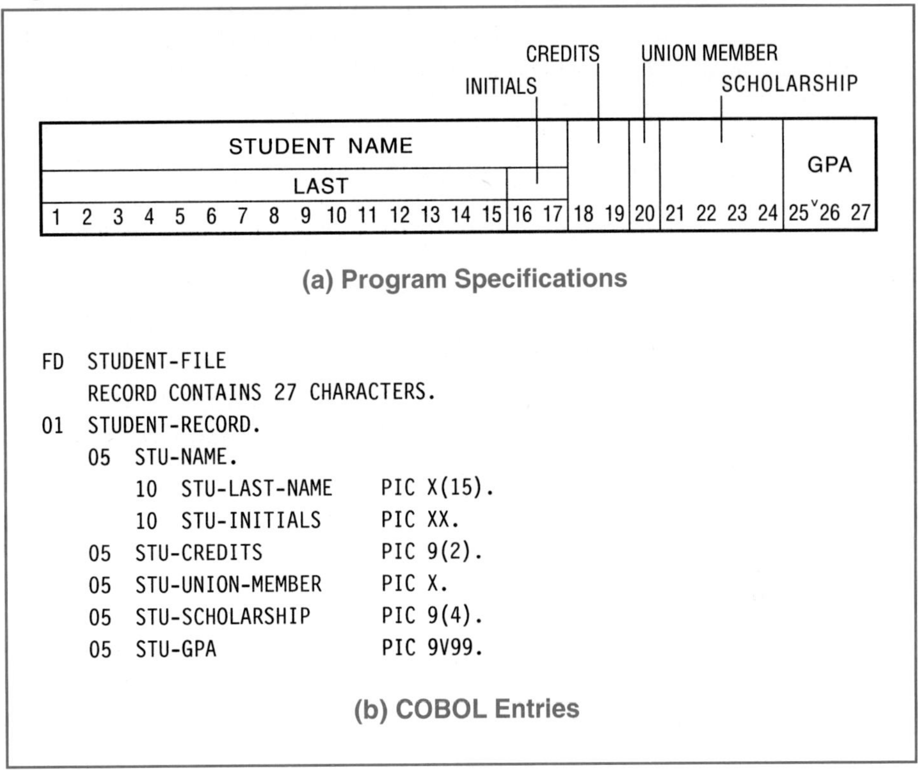

(a) Program Specifications

```
FD  STUDENT-FILE
    RECORD CONTAINS 27 CHARACTERS.
01  STUDENT-RECORD.
    05  STU-NAME.
        10  STU-LAST-NAME      PIC X(15).
        10  STU-INITIALS       PIC XX.
    05  STU-CREDITS            PIC 9(2).
    05  STU-UNION-MEMBER       PIC X.
    05  STU-SCHOLARSHIP        PIC 9(4).
    05  STU-GPA                PIC 9V99.
```

(b) COBOL Entries

Figure 4.8 Development of a COBOL Program (Constants and Rates)

1. Calculate tuition due at the rate of $200 per credit.
2. The union fee is $25.
3. Compute the activity fee based on the number of credits taken; $25 for 6 credits or less, $50 for 7 to 12 credits, and $75 for more than 12 credits.
4. Award a scholarship equal to the amount in the incoming record if, and only if, the GPA is greater than 2.5.

(a) Excerpt from the Program Specifications

```
WORKING-STORAGE SECTION.
01  CONSTANTS-AND-RATES.
    05  PRICE-PER-CREDIT        PIC 9(3)   VALUE 200.
    05  UNION-FEE               PIC 9(2)   VALUE 25.
    05  ACTIVITY-FEES.
        10  1ST-ACTIVITY-FEE    PIC 99     VALUE 25.
        10  1ST-CREDIT-LIMIT    PIC 99     VALUE 6.
        10  2ND-ACTIVITY-FEE    PIC 99     VALUE 50.
        10  2ND-CREDIT-LIMIT    PIC 99     VALUE 12.
        10  3RD-ACTIVITY-FEE    PIC 99     VALUE 75.
    05  MINIMUM-SCHOLAR-GPA     PIC 9V9    VALUE 2.5.
```

(b) COBOL Entries

Figure 4.9 Development of a COBOL Program (Print Lines)

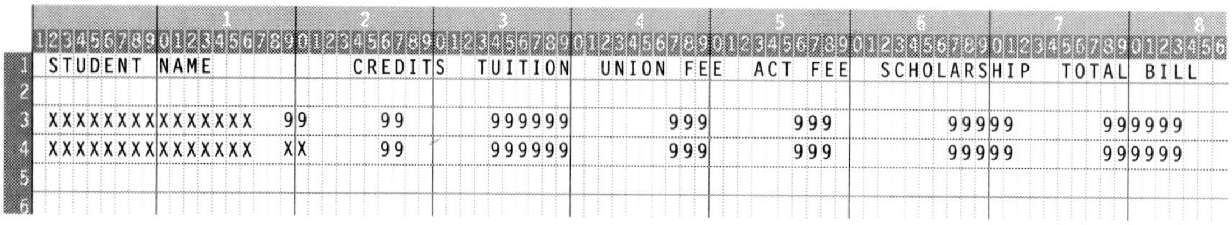

```
 STUDENT NAME          CREDITS  TUITION  UNION FEE  ACT FEE  SCHOLARSHIP  TOTAL BILL

 XXXXXXXXXXXXXXX  99     99      999999       999      999        99999      999999
 XXXXXXXXXXXXXXX  XX     99      999999       999      999        99999      999999
```

(a) Report Layout

```
01  HEADING-LINE.
    05  FILLER               PIC X        VALUE SPACES.
    05  FILLER               PIC X(12)    VALUE 'STUDENT NAME'.
    05  FILLER               PIC X(10)    VALUE SPACES.
    05  FILLER               PIC X(7)     VALUE 'CREDITS'.
    05  FILLER               PIC X(2)     VALUE SPACES.
    05  FILLER               PIC X(7)     VALUE 'TUITION'.
    05  FILLER               PIC X(2)     VALUE SPACES.
    05  FILLER               PIC X(9)     VALUE 'UNION FEE'.
    05  FILLER               PIC X(2)     VALUE SPACES.
    05  FILLER               PIC X(7)     VALUE 'ACT FEE'.
    05  FILLER               PIC X(2)     VALUE SPACES.
    05  FILLER               PIC X(11)    VALUE 'SCHOLARSHIP'.
    05  FILLER               PIC X(2)     VALUE SPACES.
    05  FILLER               PIC X(10)    VALUE 'TOTAL BILL'.
    05  FILLER               PIC X(48)    VALUE SPACES.

01  DETAIL-LINE.
    05  FILLER               PIC X        VALUE SPACES.
    05  DET-LAST-NAME        PIC X(15).
    05  FILLER               PIC X(2)     VALUE SPACES.
    05  DET-INITIALS         PIC X(2).
    05  FILLER               PIC X(5)     VALUE SPACES.
    05  DET-CREDITS          PIC 9(2).
    05  FILLER               PIC X(6)     VALUE SPACES.
    05  DET-TUITION          PIC 9(6).
    05  FILLER               PIC X(7)     VALUE SPACES.
    05  DET-UNION-FEE        PIC 9(3).
    05  FILLER               PIC X(6)     VALUE SPACES.
    05  DET-ACTIVITY-FEE     PIC 9(3).
    05  FILLER               PIC X(8)     VALUE SPACES.
    05  DET-SCHOLARSHIP      PIC 9(5).
    05  FILLER               PIC X(6)     VALUE SPACES.
    05  DET-IND-BILL         PIC 9(6).
    05  FILLER               PIC X(49)    VALUE SPACES.
```

(b) COBOL Entries

COBOL Entries

Figure 4.10 contains the completed entries for the first three divisions. (The completed Procedure Division appears at the end of Chapter 5.) The Identification Division is unchanged from the stubs program in Chapter 3 and contains only the required PROGRAM-ID paragraph and an optional AUTHOR paragraph. The Environment Division has expanded slightly to include an additional SELECT statement for the print file (lines 10 and 11).

The Data Division, however, has grown significantly. The FILE SECTION contains the FD for the incoming student record (lines 15 and 16) followed by the associated record description in lines 17 through 24. A file description has also been added for PRINT-FILE. Note, too, the correspondence between the SELECT statements in the Environment Division and the associated FD entries in the Data Division.

The programming specifications call for multiple calculations for each student (tuition, union fee, activity fee, scholarship) as well as university totals for each item. Each of these calculations requires a separate data name in WORKING-STORAGE to store the result. Observe, therefore, the definition of the elementary items IND-TUITION, IND-ACTIVITY-FEE, and so on, which appear together (for convenience) under the group item INDIVIDUAL-CALCULATIONS (line 33). In similar fashion, the elementary items UNI-TUITION, UNI-ACTIVITY-FEE, and so on, appear under the group item UNIVERSITY-TOTALS (line 40). There is also a separate 01 entry to hold the constants and rates required by the program (lines 47–56).

The program requires several different types of print lines—a heading line, a detail line, and a total line, each with a different format. Thus, there are separate 01 entries for HEADING-LINE (lines 58–73), DETAIL-LINE (lines 75–92), and TOTAL-LINE in lines 107–121. Note, too, the separate entry for DASH-LINE (lines 94–105), which makes use of the ALL literal to establish a row of dashes. Look carefully at the use of the FILLER and associated VALUE clauses in each of these print lines, to create the necessary literal information, and the correspondence between these entries and the COBOL specifications.

Figure 4.10 Identification, Environment, and Data Divisions for Tuition Billing Program

```
1       IDENTIFICATION DIVISION.
2       PROGRAM-ID.    TUITION5.
3       AUTHOR.        CAROL VAZQUEZ VILLAR.
4
5       ENVIRONMENT DIVISION.
6       INPUT-OUTPUT SECTION.
7       FILE-CONTROL.
8           SELECT STUDENT-FILE
9               ASSIGN TO UT-S-SYSIN.
10          SELECT PRINT-FILE
11              ASSIGN TO UT-S-SYSOUT.
12
```

Figure 4.10 Identification, Environment, and Data Divisions for Tuition Billing Program *(continued)*

```
DATA DIVISION.
FILE SECTION.
FD  STUDENT-FILE
    RECORD CONTAINS 27 CHARACTERS.
01  STUDENT-RECORD.
    05  STU-NAME.
        10  STU-LAST-NAME     PIC X(15).
        10  STU-INITIALS      PIC XX.
    05  STU-CREDITS           PIC 9(2).
    05  STU-UNION-MEMBER      PIC X.
    05  STU-SCHOLARSHIP       PIC 9(4).
    05  STU-GPA               PIC 9V99.

FD  PRINT-FILE
    RECORD CONTAINS 132 CHARACTERS.
01  PRINT-LINE                PIC X(132).

WORKING-STORAGE SECTION.
01  DATA-REMAINS-SWITCH       PIC X(2)  VALUE SPACES.

01  INDIVIDUAL-CALCULATIONS.
    05  IND-TUITION           PIC 9(4)  VALUE ZEROS.
    05  IND-ACTIVITY-FEE      PIC 9(2)  VALUE ZEROS.
    05  IND-UNION-FEE         PIC 9(2)  VALUE ZEROS.
    05  IND-SCHOLARSHIP       PIC 9(4)  VALUE ZEROS.
    05  IND-BILL              PIC 9(6)  VALUE ZEROS.

01  UNIVERSITY-TOTALS.
    05  UNI-TUITION           PIC 9(6)  VALUE ZEROS.
    05  UNI-UNION-FEE         PIC 9(4)  VALUE ZEROS.
    05  UNI-ACTIVITY-FEE      PIC 9(4)  VALUE ZEROS.
    05  UNI-SCHOLARSHIP       PIC 9(6)  VALUE ZEROS.
    05  UNI-IND-BILL          PIC 9(6)  VALUE ZEROS.

01  CONSTANTS-AND-RATES.
    05  PRICE-PER-CREDIT      PIC 9(3)  VALUE 200.
    05  UNION-FEE             PIC 9(2)  VALUE 25.
    05  ACTIVITY-FEES.
        10  1ST-ACTIVITY-FEE PIC 99    VALUE 25.
        10  1ST-CREDIT-LIMIT PIC 99    VALUE 6.
        10  2ND-ACTIVITY-FEE PIC 99    VALUE 50.
        10  2ND-CREDIT-LIMIT PIC 99    VALUE 12.
        10  3RD-ACTIVITY-FEE PIC 99    VALUE 75.
    05  MINIMUM-SCHOLAR-GPA  PIC 9V9   VALUE 2.5.

01  HEADING-LINE.
    05  FILLER                PIC X     VALUE SPACES.
    05  FILLER                PIC X(12) VALUE 'STUDENT NAME'.
    05  FILLER                PIC X(10) VALUE SPACES.
    05  FILLER                PIC X(7)  VALUE 'CREDITS'.
```

STU-NAME is a group item with two elementary items

Implied decimal point

VALUE clauses initialize data names

Separate areas for heading and detail lines

Figure 4.10 *(continued)*

```
           05  FILLER               PIC X(2)  VALUE SPACES.
           05  FILLER               PIC X(7)  VALUE 'TUITION'.
           05  FILLER               PIC X(2)  VALUE SPACES.
           05  FILLER               PIC X(9)  VALUE 'UNION FEE'.
           05  FILLER               PIC X(2)  VALUE SPACES.
           05  FILLER               PIC X(7)  VALUE 'ACT FEE'.
           05  FILLER               PIC X(2)  VALUE SPACES.
           05  FILLER               PIC X(11) VALUE 'SCHOLARSHIP'.
           05  FILLER               PIC X(2)  VALUE SPACES.
           05  FILLER               PIC X(10) VALUE 'TOTAL BILL'.
           05  FILLER               PIC X(48) VALUE SPACES.
```

Separate areas for heading and detail lines

```
       01  DETAIL-LINE.
           05  FILLER               PIC X     VALUE SPACES.
           05  DET-LAST-NAME        PIC X(15).
           05  FILLER               PIC X(2)  VALUE SPACES.
           05  DET-INITIALS         PIC X(2).
           05  FILLER               PIC X(5)  VALUE SPACES.
           05  DET-CREDITS          PIC 9(2).
           05  FILLER               PIC X(6)  VALUE SPACES.
           05  DET-TUITION          PIC 9(6).
           05  FILLER               PIC X(7)  VALUE SPACES.
           05  DET-UNION-FEE        PIC 9(3).
           05  FILLER               PIC X(6)  VALUE SPACES.
           05  DET-ACTIVITY-FEE     PIC 9(3).
           05  FILLER               PIC X(8)  VALUE SPACES.
           05  DET-SCHOLARSHIP      PIC 9(5).
           05  FILLER               PIC X(6)  VALUE SPACES.
           05  DET-IND-BILL         PIC 9(6).
           05  FILLER               PIC X(49) VALUE SPACES.
```

Separate areas for dash and total lines

```
       01  DASH-LINE.
           05  FILLER               PIC X(31) VALUE SPACES.
           05  FILLER               PIC X(8)  VALUE ALL '-'.
           05  FILLER               PIC X(2)  VALUE SPACES.
           05  FILLER               PIC X(8)  VALUE ALL '-'.
           05  FILLER               PIC X(2)  VALUE SPACES.
           05  FILLER               PIC X(7)  VALUE ALL '-'.
           05  FILLER               PIC X(6)  VALUE SPACES.
           05  FILLER               PIC X(7)  VALUE ALL '-'.
           05  FILLER               PIC X(5)  VALUE SPACES.
           05  FILLER               PIC X(7)  VALUE ALL '-'.
           05  FILLER               PIC X(49) VALUE SPACES.

       01  TOTAL-LINE.
           05  FILLER               PIC X(8)  VALUE SPACES.
           05  FILLER               PIC X(17)
                   VALUE 'UNIVERSITY TOTALS'.
           05  FILLER               PIC X(8)  VALUE SPACES.
           05  TOT-TUITION          PIC 9(6).
```

Figure 4.10 *(continued)*

```
           05  FILLER             PIC X(6)  VALUE SPACES.
           05  TOT-UNION-FEE      PIC 9(4).
           05  FILLER             PIC X(5)  VALUE SPACES.
           05  TOT-ACTIVITY-FEE   PIC 9(4).
           05  FILLER             PIC X(7)  VALUE SPACES.
           05  TOT-SCHOLARSHIP    PIC 9(6).
           05  FILLER             PIC X(6)  VALUE SPACES.
           05  TOT-IND-BILL       PIC 9(6).
           05  FILLER             PIC X(49) VALUE SPACES.
```

LIMITATIONS OF COBOL-74

The CONFIGURATION SECTION, SOURCE-COMPUTER, and OBJECT-COMPUTER entries are optional in COBOL-85 but are required in COBOL-74. The LABEL RECORDS clause is optional in COBOL-85 but is required in COBOL-74.

The BLOCK CONTAINS clause is optional in both compilers, but its omission has different effects. Omitting the clause in COBOL-85 causes the system to take the blocking factor from the operating environment (and is equivalent to the IBM entry BLOCK CONTAINS 0 RECORDS). Omission of the clause in COBOL-74 defaults to the implementor-designated number, regardless of what was specified in the control statements to the operating system.

COBOL-85 allows two new relationships, GREATER THAN OR EQUAL TO and LESS THAN OR EQUAL TO, in the condition portion of an IF statement. These were not allowed in COBOL-74, which used NOT LESS THAN as the equivalent of GREATER THAN OR EQUAL TO.

The word FILLER is optional in COBOL-85, whereas it is required in COBOL-74.

SUMMARY

Points to Remember

- COBOL notation is the standardized form used to express permissible COBOL formats. Uppercase letters indicate COBOL reserved words, whereas lowercase letters denote programmer-supplied information. Brackets [ ] imply an optional entry, whereas braces { } indicate a choice between required entries. Any underlined item is required.
- The PROGRAM-ID paragraph is the only required entry in the Identification Division; the AUTHOR paragraph is strongly recommended. The

Environment Division contains the FILE-CONTROL paragraph that defines the files used in a program through SELECT statements.

- The FILE SECTION contains a file description for every file previously defined in a SELECT statement in the Environment Division. The file description is followed by a record description to describe the fields within a file.
- The PICTURE clause indicates the size and type of a data name. An elementary item always has a PICTURE clause, whereas a group item does not. Level numbers assume values from 01 to 49 inclusive, with 01 assigned to the record as a whole. Level numbers need not be assigned consecutive values.
- The WORKING-STORAGE SECTION contains additional record descriptions for data names not found in the FILE SECTION. VALUE clauses assign an initial value to a data name of a numeric literal, a nonnumeric literal, or a figurative constant.

Key Words and Concepts

Alphanumeric item
Assumed (implied) decimal point
Blocking factor
Braces
Brackets
COBOL notation
Detail line
Elementary item
Figurative constant
File description
Group item
Heading line
Level numbers
Logical record
Numeric item
Physical record
Record description
Size
Total line
Type

COBOL Elements

```
ALL
ASSIGN
AUTHOR
BLOCK CONTAINS
DATA RECORD IS
DATE-COMPILED
DATE-WRITTEN
FD
FILE SECTION
FILE-CONTROL
FILLER
INPUT-OUTPUT SECTION
INSTALLATION
LABEL RECORDS
PICTURE
PROGRAM-ID
RECORD CONTAINS
SECURITY
SELECT
SPACES
VALUE
WORKING-STORAGE SECTION
ZEROS
```

FILL-IN

1. The ______________ Division is the first division in a COBOL program.
2. The ______________ paragraph is the only required entry in the Identification Division.
3. In the COBOL notation, ______________ indicate that one of the enclosed elements must be included.
4. Required reserved words are written in ______________ letters and are ______________.
5. Lowercase letters indicate ______________ ______________ information.
6. The Environment Division contains ______________ sections.
7. The ______________ statement ties a programmer-chosen file name to a system name.
8. A ______________ item is divided into one or more elementary items.
9. An elementary item always has a ______________ clause.
10. Level numbers appearing under a 01 record may range from ______________ to ______________.
11. The Data Division contains the ______________ and ______________ sections.
12. The presence of a V in a numeric picture indicates an ______________ decimal point.
13. Incoming numeric fields (may/may not) contain an actual decimal point.
14. ______________ denotes a field that is not referenced by name.
15. The ______________ ______________ specifies the number of ______________ records in one ______________ record.

TRUE/FALSE

1. The Identification Division may contain up to six paragraphs.
2. The PROGRAM-ID paragraph is the only required paragraph in the Identification Division.
3. Square brackets indicate a required entry.
4. Braces imply that one of the enclosed entries must be chosen.
5. A COBOL program that runs successfully on a PC would also run successfully on a mainframe with no modification whatever.
6. A level number may assume any value from 01 to 49.
7. A 01-level entry cannot have a PICTURE clause.
8. All elementary items have a PICTURE clause.
9. A group item may have a PICTURE clause.
10. 01-level entries may appear in both the File and Working-Storage Sections of the Data Division.

11. A data name at the 10 level will always be an elementary item.
12. A data name at the 05 level may or may not have a PICTURE clause.
13. PICTURE, PICTURE IS, PIC, and PIC IS are all acceptable forms of the PICTURE clause.
14. PICTURE IS 9(3) and PICTURE IS 999 are equivalent entries.
15. The File Section is required in every COBOL program.
16. An incoming numeric field may contain an actual decimal point.
17. The RECORD CONTAINS clause is required in an FD.

PROBLEMS

1. Consider the accompanying time card. Show an appropriate record description for this information in COBOL; use any PICTURE clauses you think appropriate.

Time-Record							
Name			Number	Date			Hours
First	Middle	Last		MO	DA	YR	

2. In which division(s) do you find the
   a. PROGRAM-ID paragraph?
   b. FILE-CONTROL paragraph?
   c. CONFIGURATION SECTION?
   d. WORKING-STORAGE SECTION?
   e. FILE SECTION?
   f. FD's?
   g. AUTHOR paragraph?
   h. DATE-COMPILED paragraph?
   i. INPUT-OUTPUT SECTION?
   j. File names?
   k. Level numbers?
   l. SELECT statements?
   m. VALUE clauses?
   n. PICTURE clauses?

3. Given the following record layout:

```
01  EMPLOYEE-RECORD.
    05  SOC-SEC-NUMBER          PIC 9(9).
    05  EMPLOYEE-NAME.
        10  LAST-NAME           PIC X(12).
        10  FIRST-NAME          PIC X(10).
        10  MIDDLE-INIT         PIC X.
    05  FILLER                  PIC X.
    05  BIRTH-DATE.
        10  BIRTH-MONTH         PIC 99.
        10  BIRTH-DAY           PIC 99.
        10  BIRTH-YEAR          PIC 99.
    05  FILLER                  PIC X(3).
```

```
05  EMPLOYEE-ADDRESS.
    10  NUMBER-AND-STREET.
        15  HOUSE-NUMBER     PIC X(6).
        15  STREET-NAME      PIC X(10).
    10  CITY-STATE-ZIP.
        15  CITY             PIC X(10).
        15  STATE            PIC X(4).
        15  ZIP              PIC 9(5).
05  FILLER                   PIC X(3).
```

a. List all group items.

b. List all elementary items.

c. State the record positions in which the following fields are found:
   - SOC-SEC-NUMBER
   - EMPLOYEE-NAME
   - LAST-NAME
   - FIRST-NAME
   - MIDDLE-INIT
   - BIRTH-DATE
   - BIRTH-MONTH
   - BIRTH-DAY
   - BIRTH-YEAR
   - EMPLOYEE-ADDRESS
   - NUMBER-AND-STREET
   - HOUSE-NUMBER
   - STREET-NAME
   - CITY-STATE-ZIP
   - CITY
   - STATE
   - ZIP

4. Given the following record layout (assume that FIELD-I is the last entry under FIELD-A),

```
01  FIELD-A
    05  FIELD-B
        10  FIELD-C
        10  FIELD-D
    05  FIELD-E
    05  FIELD-F
        10  FIELD-G
        10  FIELD-H
        10  FIELD-I
```

answer true or false.

a. FIELD-C is an elementary item.

b. FIELD-E is an elementary item.

c. FIELD-E should have a picture.

d. FIELD-F should have a picture.

e. FIELD-B must be larger than FIELD-C.

f. FIELD-C must be larger than FIELD-D.

g. FIELD-C must be larger than FIELD-H.

h. FIELD-B and FIELD-D end in the same column.

i. FIELD-A and FIELD-I end in the same column.

j. FIELD-E could be larger than FIELD-F.

k. FIELD-D could be larger than FIELD-E.

l. FIELD-F and FIELD-G start in the same column.

5. Use the COBOL notation introduced at the beginning of the chapter and the general format of the FD entry to determine whether the following are valid FD entries.

a. `FD EMPLOYEE-FILE.`

b.
```
FD EMPLOYEE-FILE
     BLOCK CONTAINS 10 RECORDS
     RECORD CONTAINS 100 CHARACTERS
     LABEL RECORDS ARE STANDARD
     DATA RECORD IS EMPLOYEE-RECORD.
```

c.
```
FD EMPLOYEE-FILE
     BLOCK 10 RECORDS
     RECORD 100 CHARACTERS
     LABEL RECORDS STANDARD
     DATA RECORD EMPLOYEE-RECORD.
```

6. Indicate whether each of the following entries is spelled correctly and whether it is syntactically valid.

a. ENVIRONMENT DIVISION

b. WORKING-STORAGE-SECTION

c. IDENTIFICATION-DIVISION

d. WRITTEN-BY

e. DATA-DIVISION

f. FILE SECTION

g. PROGRAM ID

h. DATE-WRITTEN

i. DATE-EXECUTED

j. INPUT-OUTPUT SECTION

k. FILE-CONTROL SECTION

l. DATE DIVISION

m. COMMENTS

The Procedure Division

CHAPTER OUTLINE

OBJECTIVES

After reading this chapter you will be able to:

- Write the OPEN, CLOSE, READ, and WRITE statements necessary for sequential file processing.
- Describe the purpose of the priming (initial) READ statement, and place it correctly in the Procedure Division.
- Discuss the rules of the MOVE statement as they apply to numeric and alphanumeric fields.
- Describe the PERFORM statement; show how this statement is used to process a file until all of its records have been read.
- Describe the IF statement and how it is used with and without an ELSE clause; explain the significance of the END-IF scope terminator.
- Use the EVALUATE statement to implement a case (multibranch) construct.
- State the hierarchy of operations for a COMPUTE statement; describe the individual arithmetic statements, ADD, SUBTRACT, MULTIPLY, and DIVIDE.
- Describe the ROUNDED and SIZE ERROR options as they apply to any of the arithmetic statements.
- Explain the relationship between a Procedure Division and its associated hierarchy chart.

OVERVIEW

This is a long chapter—the longest in the text. It focuses on the Procedure Division, which is the portion of a COBOL program that contains the logic. The chapter is long because it presents the many statements needed to write a basic program such as the tuition billing program introduced in Chapter 3.

We begin with the COBOL statements used for I/O (input/output) operations; OPEN, CLOSE, READ, and WRITE, and continue with the STOP RUN statement to terminate program execution. We learn about the PERFORM statement to implement a loop, the IF statement to implement the selection structure, and the EVALUATE statement to implement a case structure. We study the MOVE statement to copy data from one location to another and end with the arithmetic statements: COMPUTE, ADD, SUBTRACT, MULTIPLY, and DIVIDE.

The chapter concludes with the completed COBOL listing for the tuition billing program of Chapter 3.

OPEN

The **OPEN** statement initiates processing for a file. It indicates the nature of the file (input or output) and ensures that a specific device is available for the I/O operations. The OPEN statement also performs validation functions in conjunction with the LABEL

RECORDS clause of the FD; for example, if label records are specified for an input file, the OPEN statement checks the header label of that file to ensure that the proper file is available for processing. An abbreviated format of the OPEN statement is:

```
OPEN { {INPUT } file-name-1 . . . } . . .
       {OUTPUT}
```

The syntax of the OPEN statement indicates a mandatory selection for the type of file—INPUT is used for a file that is read, whereas OUTPUT is used for a file that is written to. The brackets and ellipsis associated with file-name-2 imply that multiple files can be opened in the same statement as was done in lines 43 and 44 of the engineering senior program in Figure 1.6:

```
OPEN INPUT STUDENT-FILE
     OUTPUT PRINT-FILE.
```

Each file referenced in an OPEN statement must have been previously defined in a SELECT statement in the Environment Division, and in a corresponding FD in the Data Division. All files must be opened before they can be accessed; the operating system will terminate execution of a COBOL program that attempts to read (or write) an unopened file.

CLOSE

The **CLOSE** statement is executed when access to a file is no longer necessary, such as when all records have been read from an input file or when all records have been written to an output file. The CLOSE statement releases the I/O devices associated with the file; it also writes trailer labels at the end of files on disk or tape in conjunction with the LABEL RECORDS clause of the FD. All open files should be closed before processing terminates. The format of the CLOSE is simply:

```
CLOSE file-name-1 [, file-name-2 ...]
```

The brackets and ellipsis associated with file-name-2 indicate that multiple files can be closed in the same statement. The type of file, INPUT or OUTPUT, is not specified when the file is closed because the distinction between input and output is no longer important. Lines 51 and 52 in the engineering senior program provide an example:

```
CLOSE STUDENT-FILE
      PRINT-FILE.
```

A CLOSE statement can appear anywhere within a program but typically appears immediately before the program terminates, that is, immediately before the STOP RUN statement.

READ

The **READ** statement transfers data from an open file into memory, provided a record is available. If, however, no record is present—that is, the ***end-of-file*** condition has been reached—control passes to the statement(s) following the AT END clause. An abbreviated format of the READ statement is shown below:

```
READ file-name
     AT END statement
[END-READ]
```

The END-READ scope terminator is optional but strongly recommended. The READ statement is illustrated in lines 45–47 of the engineering senior program.

```
READ STUDENT-FILE
    AT END MOVE 'NO' TO DATA-REMAINS-SWITCH
END-READ.
```

Placement of the READ Statement

The engineering senior program in Figure 1.6 contained two distinct READ statements. There was an initial, or priming, READ in lines 45–47 and a second READ statement as the *last* instruction of the performed paragraph (lines 65–67). The necessity for *both* statements is explained by considering Figure 5.1, which shows correct and incorrect ways to process a file of transactions.

Figure 5.1a, the *incorrect* implementation, causes the last record of INPUT-FILE to be processed twice. To see how this happens, consider a file with only two records, A and B, realizing that such a file is read three times—once for each record and once to sense the end of file. Realize, too, that the PERFORM statement evaluates the UNTIL condition *before* branching (a detailed description of the PERFORM statement is found in an upcoming section).

In Figure 5.1a, record A is read the first time PROCESS-RECORDS is performed, with execution continuing through the remainder of the PROCESS-RECORDS paragraph, at which point DATA-REMAINS-SWITCH is still set to 'YES'. Hence, PROCESS-RECORDS is executed a second time, during which time it reads and processes record B. Since DATA-REMAINS-SWITCH is still set to 'YES', PROCESS-RECORDS is executed a third time, during which the end-of-file condition is sensed immediately. Execution continues, however, to the end of the paragraph, causing the last record (record B) to be processed twice.

In the *correct* implementation of Figure 5.1b, an initial (priming) READ is executed *before* performing the paragraph PROCESS-RECORDS, which also contains a READ statement. The first time PROCESS-RECORDS is performed, it processes record A, and its *last* statement reads record B. Since DATA-REMAINS-SWITCH is still set to 'YES', PROCESS-RECORDS is executed a second time to process record B, with the ending READ statement sensing the end-of-file condition. DATA-REMAINS-SWITCH is set to 'NO', which in turn terminates the PERFORM statement.

WRITE

The **WRITE** statement transfers data from memory to the printer (or other open output device). Consider:

```
WRITE record-name

    [ {AFTER }            {integer [LINE ] } ]
    [ {BEFORE} ADVANCING  {        [LINES] } ]
    [                     {PAGE            } ]
```

The ADVANCING option controls the line spacing on a printer; for example, specification of AFTER ADVANCING 3 LINES produces triple spacing (the printer skips two lines and writes on the third). Conversely, specification of the BEFORE option first writes the line, then skips the designated amount. Specification of

Figure 5.1 Placement of the READ Statement

```
PREPARE-TUITION-REPORT.
    .
     .
      .
    MOVE 'YES' TO DATA-REMAINS-SWITCH.
    PERFORM PROCESS-RECORDS
        UNTIL DATA-REMAINS-SWITCH = 'NO'.
    .
     .
      .
PROCESS-RECORDS.
    READ INPUT-FILE
        AT END MOVE 'NO' TO DATA-REMAINS-SWITCH
    END-READ.
    .
     .
      .
```

First statement of performed paragraph is the READ

(a) Incorrect Implementation

```
PREPARE-TUITION-REPORT.
    .
     .
      .
    MOVE 'YES' TO DATA-REMAINS-SWITCH.
    READ INPUT-FILE
        AT END MOVE 'NO' TO DATA-REMAINS-SWITCH
    END-READ.
    PERFORM PROCESS-RECORDS
        UNTIL DATA-REMAINS-SWITCH = 'NO'.
    .
     .
      .
PROCESS-RECORDS.
    .
     .
      .
    READ INPUT-FILE
        AT END MOVE 'NO' TO DATA-REMAINS-SWITCH
    END-READ.
```

Initial READ is executed once and only once

Last statement of performed paragraph is another READ

(b) Correct Implementation

PAGE, in lieu of LINES, will cause output to begin on top of a new page. Omission of the ADVANCING option defaults to single spacing. The examples below

```
WRITE PRINT-LINE.
WRITE PRINT-LINE
    AFTER ADVANCING 2 LINES.
WRITE PRINT-LINE
    AFTER ADVANCING PAGE.
```

will single space, double space, and advance to the top of a new page, respectively.

The WRITE statement contains a *record* name, whereas the READ statement contains a *file* name. The record name in the WRITE statement will appear as a 01 entry in the File Section of the Data Division. The file in which it is contained will appear in SELECT, FD, OPEN, and CLOSE statements.

STOP RUN

The format of the **STOP RUN** statement is simply:

```
STOP RUN
```

The STOP RUN statement terminates execution of a COBOL program and returns control to the operating system. [STOP RUN need not be (and typically is not) the last physical statement in the program.] All files should be closed prior to executing the STOP RUN statement.

MOVE

The **MOVE** statement copies data from one location to another; for example, the statement MOVE A TO B copies the value in location A to location B. The value of A is in two places after the move has taken place, while the initial value of B is gone (having been replaced by the value of A). The syntax of the MOVE statement is:

```
MOVE {identifier-1} TO identifier-2 [identifier-3] . . .
     {literal-1   }
```

Consider the following examples:

1. MOVE 200 TO PRICE-PER-CREDIT.
2. MOVE 'ABC UNIVERSITY' TO SCHOOL-NAME.
3. MOVE STU-NAME TO PRINT-NAME.
4. MOVE ZEROS TO TOTAL-NUMBER.
5. MOVE SPACES TO PRINT-LINE.

Example one moves a numeric literal, 200, to the data name PRICE-PER-CREDIT. Example two moves a nonnumeric literal, 'ABC UNIVERSITY', to SCHOOL-NAME. Example three copies data from an input area to an output area for subsequent printing. Examples four and five use the figurative constants, ZEROS and SPACES, to initialize a counter and print line, respectively.

The brackets and ellipsis associated with identifier-3 in the COBOL syntax indicate the same item can be moved to multiple data names. Thus the single statement:

```
MOVE 10 TO FIELD-A FIELD-B FIELD-C.
```

is equivalent to the three individual statements:

```
MOVE 10 TO FIELD-A.
MOVE 10 TO FIELD-B.
MOVE 10 TO FIELD-C.
```

Restrictions on the MOVE Statement

The results of a MOVE statement depend on the type of data in the sending and/or receiving field. We concentrate initially on MOVE statements involving only elementary items, since these statements are by far the most common. Recall (from Chapter 4) that elementary data items may be of four types:

Numeric	Numeric data items, numeric literals, and the figurative constants, ZERO, ZEROS, or ZEROES.
Alphabetic	Alphabetic data items and the figurative constants, SPACE and SPACES
Alphanumeric	Alphanumeric data items, nonnumeric literals and the figurative constants, SPACE and SPACES
Numeric Edited	Numeric edited data items (to be discussed in Chapter 7)

In theory a MOVE statement could involve any combination of these four types; in actuality, however, certain types of moves are not permitted as indicated by Table 5.1. (You do not have to commit the table to memory; simply be aware that certain restrictions exist, and know where to turn should questions arise later.)

TABLE 5.1 Rules of the MOVE Statement (Elementary Data Items)

SENDING FIELD	RECEIVING FIELD			
	ALPHABETIC	**ALPHANUMERIC**	**NUMERIC**	**NUMERIC EDITED**
Alphabetic	Valid	Valid	Invalid	Invalid
Alphanumeric	Invalid	Valid	Invalid	Invalid
Numeric	Invalid	Integers only	Valid	Valid
Numeric Edited	Invalid	Valid	Valid	Invalid

At first glance Table 5.1 seems overwhelming, but a second look shows it to make intuitive sense. You cannot, for example, move an alphanumeric field to an alphabetic field (because the alphanumeric field may contain numbers, which are invalid in an alphabetic field). You can, however, do the move in the opposite direction; that is, you can move an alphabetic field to an alphanumeric field.

Even Table 5.1 does not tell us everything we need to know about the MOVE statement. What happens, for example, when moves with like fields (an alphanumeric sending field to an alphanumeric receiving field) involve PICTURE clauses of different lengths? Additional explanation is required as explained in the next two sections.

Alphanumeric Field to Alphanumeric Field

Data moved from an alphanumeric field to an alphanumeric field are moved one character at a time from left to right. If the receiving field is larger than the sending field, it is padded on the right with blanks; if the receiving field is smaller than the sending field, the rightmost characters are truncated.

Alphanumeric moves are illustrated in Table 5.2. Example (a) is trivial, in that the sending and receiving fields have the same picture clause. In example (b) the sending field is one character longer than the receiving field; hence the rightmost character is truncated. Data are moved from left to right one character at a time; thus A, B, C, and D are moved in that order, and E is dropped. In example (c), however, the receiving field is one character longer than the sending field. A, B, C, D, and E are moved in that order, and a blank is added at the right.

TABLE 5.2 Illustration of the MOVE Statement: Alphanumeric Sending Field to Alphanumeric Receiving Field

	SENDING FIELD		RECEIVING FIELD	
	PICTURE	**CONTENTS**	**PICTURE**	**CONTENTS**
(a)	X(5)	A B C D E	X(5)	A B C D E
(b)	X(5)	A B C D E	X(4)	A B C D
(c)	X(5)	A B C D E	X(6)	A B C D E ␣

Numeric Field to Numeric Field

All moves involving numeric fields maintain decimal alignment. If the integer portion of the receiving field is larger than that of the sending field, high-order (insignificant) zeros are added to the receiving field. If, however, the integer portion of the receiving field is smaller than that of the sending field, the high-order (significant) digits of the sending field are truncated.

In similar fashion if the decimal portion of the receiving field is larger than that of the sending field, low-order zeros are added. And finally, if the decimal portion of the receiving field is smaller than that of the sending field, the extra positions are truncated. These points are clarified in Table 5.3.

TABLE 5.3 Illustration of the MOVE Statement: Numeric Sending Field to Numeric Receiving Field

	SENDING FIELD		RECEIVING FIELD	
	PICTURE	**CONTENTS**	**PICTURE**	**CONTENTS**
(a)	9(5)	1 2 3 4 5	9(5)	1 2 3 4 5
(b)	9(5)	1 2 3 4 5	9(4)	2 3 4 5
(c)	9(5)	1 2 3 4 5	9(6)	0 1 2 3 4 5
(d)	9(3)V99	1 2 3 ‸ 4 5	9(3)	1 2 3
(e)	9(3)V99	1 2 3 ‸ 4 5	9V99	3 ‸ 4 5
(f)	9(3)	1 2 3	9(3)V99	1 2 3 ‸ 0 0

Example (a) is trivial. Example (b) attempts to move a five-position field to a four-position field. Since decimal alignment is always maintained, the leftmost digit (i.e., the *most significant* digit) is truncated. Example (c) moves a five-position sending field to a six-position receiving field, causing the addition of a leading (nonsignificant) zero. The sending field in example (d) has two digits after the decimal point, but the receiving field has none. Hence the 4 and 5 do not appear in the receiving field. Example (e) truncates the most significant digits. Example (f) adds two nonsignificant zeros to the receiving field.

Group Moves

The preceding discussion concerned MOVE statements in which the receiving field was an elementary item. The results are very different if a group item is involved, because *if the receiving field is a group item, the move takes place as though the receiving field were an alphanumeric item, with padding or truncation on the right as necessary.* MOVE statements involving group items often produce unexpected results and should be avoided.

PERFORM

The **PERFORM** statement transfers control to a procedure (paragraph) elsewhere in the program, allowing the program to be divided into functional modules. An abbreviated format of the PERFORM statement is:

```
PERFORM procedure-name
    [UNTIL condition]
```

Consider first the statement *without* an UNTIL clause as illustrated below:

```
    COMPUTE TUITION = CREDITS * CHARGE-PER-CREDIT.
    PERFORM WRITE DETAIL-LINE.
    ADD 1 TO NUMBER-OF-STUDENTS.
    .
     .
      .
WRITE-DETAIL-LINE.
    MOVE STUDENT-NAME TO PRINT-NAME.
    MOVE TUITION TO PRINT-TUITION.
    WRITE PRINT-LINE AFTER ADVANCING 2 LINES.
WRITE-TOTAL-LINE.
```

Transfer to

Return to

The statement PERFORM WRITE-DETAIL-LINE transfers control to the first statement in the paragraph WRITE-DETAIL-LINE. When every statement in WRITE-DETAIL-LINE has been executed (i.e., when the next paragraph name is encountered), control returns to the statement immediately after the original PERFORM, in this case, to the ADD statement.

A loop (iteration) is implemented through inclusion of an UNTIL clause. The condition in the UNTIL clause is tested *before* the paragraph is executed, and if the condition is not met, control is transferred to the designated paragraph. When the paragraph has completed execution, the condition is retested, and if it (the condition) is still not met, the paragraph is executed a second time. The process continues until the condition is finally satisfied. Consider:

```
    PERFORM PROCESS-RECORDS
        UNTIL DATA-REMAINS-SWITCH = 'NO'.
    .
     .
      .
PROCESS-RECORDS.
    .
     .
      .
    READ STUDENT-FILE
        AT END MOVE 'NO' TO DATA-REMAINS-SWITCH
    END-READ.
```

The paragraph PROCESS-RECORDS is executed repeatedly until DATA-REMAINS-SWITCH equals 'NO', that is, until there are no more incoming records. The last statement of the performed paragraph is a READ statement, so that when the end of file is reached, DATA-REMAINS-SWITCH will be set to 'NO'. This causes the next test of the UNTIL condition to be successful and prevents further execution of the PROCESS-RECORDS paragraph.

IF

The **IF** statement is one of the most powerful statements in COBOL. Our present concern, however, is with only a few of the available options, with additional consideration deferred to Chapter 8. An abbreviated format of the IF statement is

```
IF condition THEN
     statement-1
[ELSE
     statement-2 ]
[END-IF]
```

The IF statement is terminated by the optional (but highly recommended) END-IF scope terminator and/or a period. Consider:

```
IF STU-CREDITS > 110 AND STU-MAJOR = 'ENGINEERING'
    MOVE STU-NAME TO PRINT-NAME
    MOVE STU-CREDITS TO PRINT-CREDITS
    MOVE STU-GPA TO PRINT-GPA
    WRITE PRINT-LINE
END-IF.
```

If the condition is true, then *every* statement between the IF (condition) and the END-IF (and/or period) will be executed. Hence, when an engineering senior is processed, three MOVE statements and one WRITE statement are executed. If, however, the condition is false, then all four statements—three MOVEs and a WRITE—are bypassed.

As indicated, the IF statement is terminated by the END-IF scope terminator and/or a period, and the inclusion of both appears redundant. (Many programmers do, however, use both entries.) END-IF, despite the fact that it is an optional entry, has distinct advantages (as will be explained in Chapter 7) and should be used in every instance.

The ELSE Clause

The **ELSE** clause is optional as implied by the square brackets in its syntax. Figure 5.2a contains an ELSE clause, whereas it is omitted in Figure 5.2b. If the condition in Figure 5.2a is true, statement-1 is executed; whereas if it is false, statement-2 is executed—in either case execution continues with statement-3. Figure 5.2b, however, omits the ELSE clause so that if the condition is false, the IF statement is terminated immediately.

Indentation

Indentation in an IF statement is extremely important to emphasize a programmer's understanding of a statement's intended effect. Consider Figure 5.3, which contains a flowchart and corresponding COBOL code.

Figure 5.2 The IF Statement

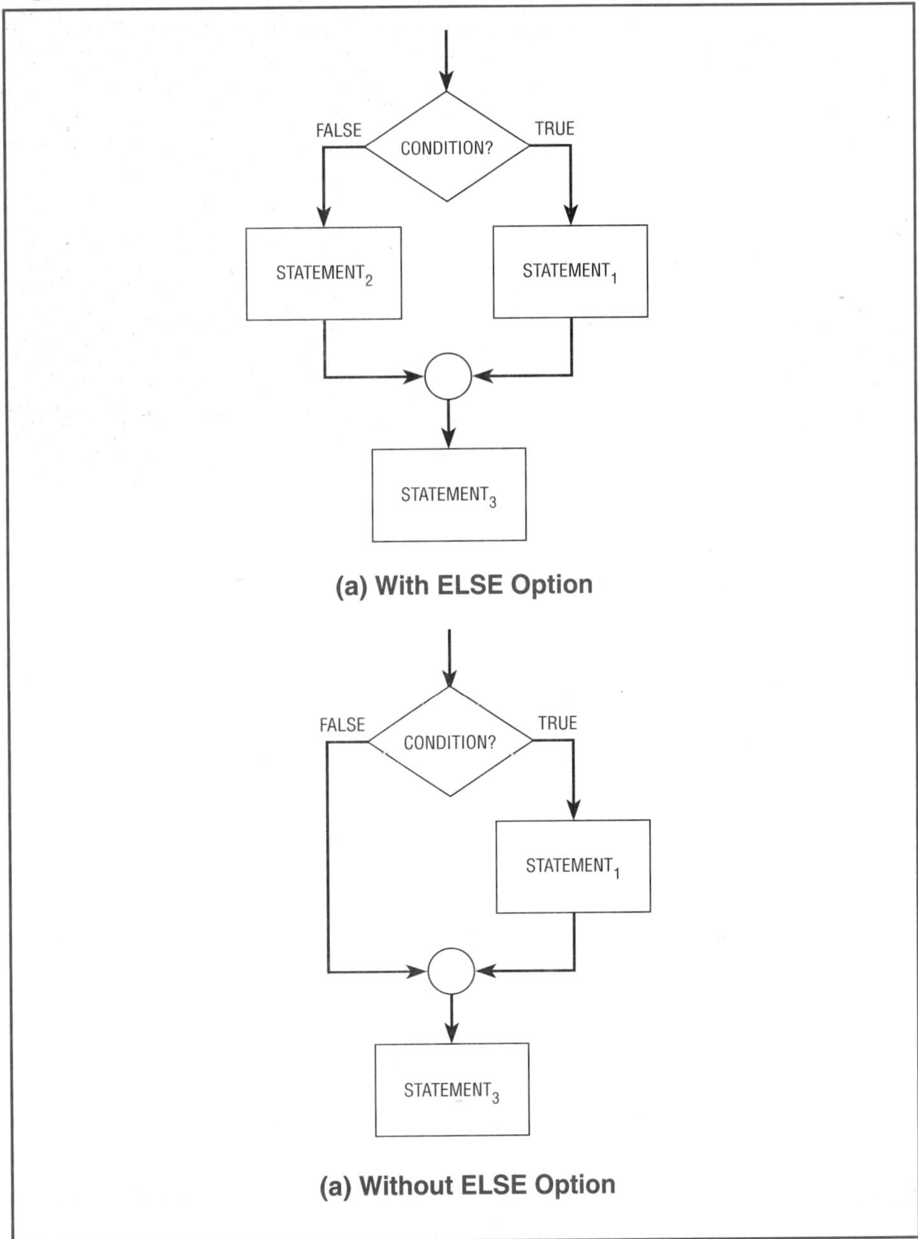

(a) With ELSE Option

(a) Without ELSE Option

The flowchart in Figure 5.3a indicates that if the condition A = B is true, the statements MOVE 1 TO C and MOVE 1 TO D are to be executed. If, however, the condition is false, then the statements MOVE ZERO TO C and MOVE ZERO TO D are to be executed instead. In either case—that is, whether the condition is true or false—we are to write a detail line. The latter is indicated by the IF and ELSE branches meeting in a common exit point, which leads to the final WRITE statement.

The COBOL code in Figure 5.3b is carefully aligned to reflect this interpretation. Recall that the rules of COBOL require only that an IF statement appear in the B margin, that is, in columns 12–72. Hence the indentation in Figure 5.3b is done solely for the purpose of making a program easier to read, rather than to satisfy a

Figure 5.3 The ELSE Clause/II

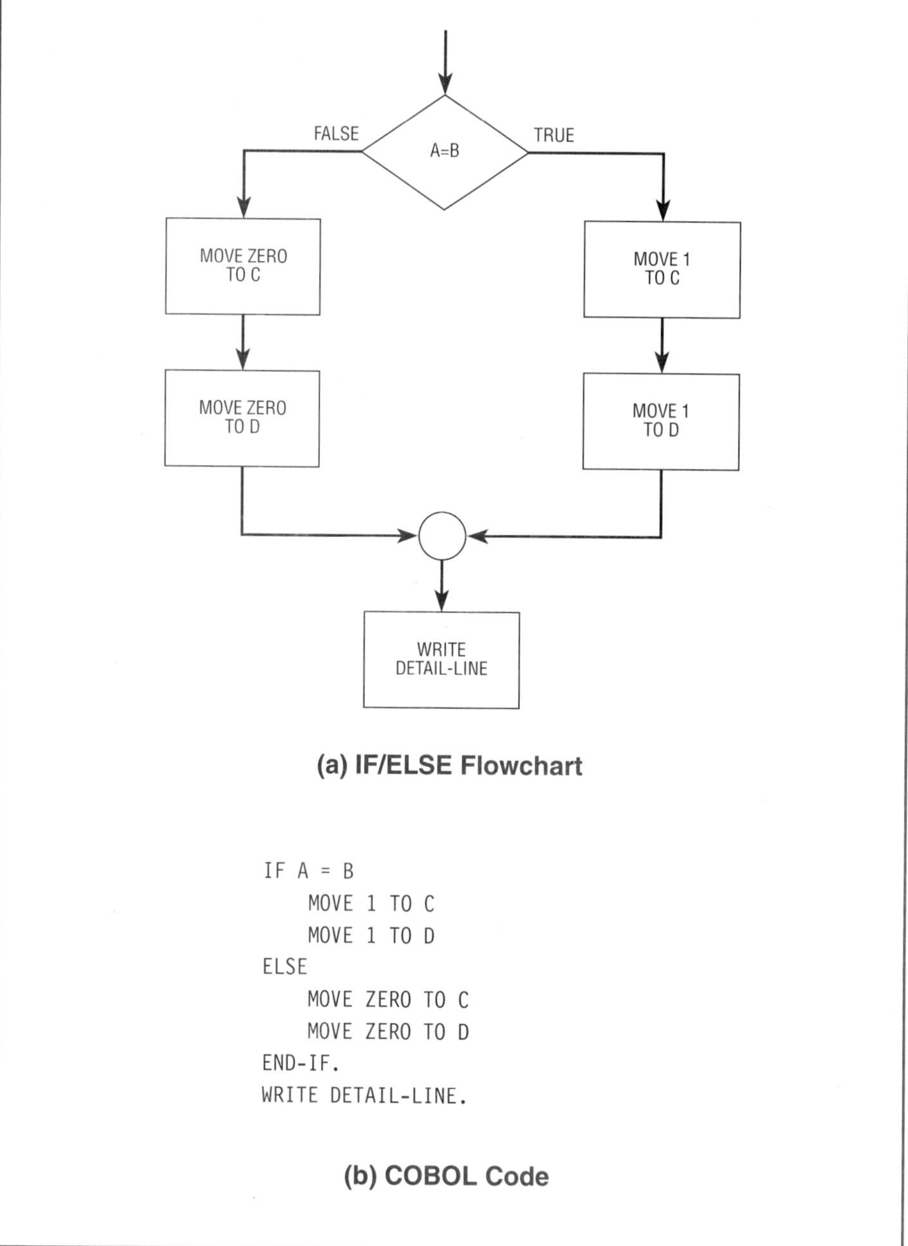


```
IF A = B
    MOVE 1 TO C
    MOVE 1 TO D
ELSE
    MOVE ZERO TO C
    MOVE ZERO TO D
END-IF.
WRITE DETAIL-LINE.
```

(b) COBOL Code

rule of COBOL. Nevertheless, proper indentation is essential and goes a long way to improve the quality of your work. Accordingly, we suggest the following guidelines:

1. Begin the IF statement in column 12.
2. Put the word ELSE on a line by itself and directly under the IF.
3. Indent detail lines associated with either the IF or ELSE four columns.
4. Put END-IF on a line by itself directly under the IF statement.

EVALUATE

The **EVALUATE** statement implements the case (multibranch) construct of structured programming. It has what first appears to be a rather complicated syntax, but in actuality is quite easy to use. Consider:

```
         ┌identifier-1┐
         │expression-1│
EVALUATE ┤TRUE        ├
         │FALSE       │
         └            ┘

  ┌      ┌condition-1┐                            ┐
  │WHEN  ┤TRUE       ├ imperative-statement-1 . . .├
  │      │FALSE      │                            │
  └      └           ┘                            ┘

  [WHEN OTHER imperative-statement-2]

[END-EVALUATE]
```

An example of the EVALUATE statement is shown below in conjunction with the tuition billing program presented in Chapter 3. The specifications for the program indicate that activity fee is dependent on the number of credits ($25 for 6 credits or fewer, $50 for 7 to 12 credits, and $75 for 13 credits or more). Consider:

```
EVALUATE TRUE
    WHEN STU-CREDITS <= 6
       MOVE 25 TO IND-ACTIVITY-FEE
    WHEN STU-CREDITS > 6 AND STU-CREDITS <= 12
        MOVE 50 TO IND-ACTIVITY-FEE
    WHEN STU-CREDITS > 12
        MOVE 75 TO IND-ACTIVITY-FEE
END-EVALUATE.
```

The different conditions (i.e., the ranges for the number of student credits) are presented in the various WHEN clauses. The END-EVALUATE scope terminator is a required entry.

Arithmetic Statements

COBOL does arithmetic in one of two ways. It has individual statements for the basic arithmetic operations (addition, subtraction, multiplication, and division), and a COMPUTE statement that combines multiple operations into one statement. As you shall see, the COMPUTE statement is generally easier to use, and so we begin with it. Note, too, that all of these statements have optional ROUNDED and SIZE ERROR clauses, which are discussed prior to the individual statements.

The ROUNDED Clause

The **ROUNDED** clause (in any arithmetic statement) causes COBOL to carry a calculation to one more decimal place than is specified in the result field. If the value of the extra decimal place is 5 or larger, the answer is rounded up; if it is 4 or less, the answer is unchanged. If the ROUNDED clause is omitted, COBOL truncates any extra decimal positions regardless of their value. Table 5.4 shows the effect of the ROUNDED option in which the values of A and B are added to produce a value for C.

TABLE 5.4 The ROUNDED Clause

DATA NAME	A	B	C
PICTURE	**9V99**	**9V99**	**9V9**
Value before execution	123	456	(immaterial)
Value after execution of			
ADD A B GIVING C	123	456	57
ADD A B GIVING C ROUNDED	123	456	58

Both of the examples in Table 5.4 add the same numbers (1.23 and 4.56) to produce a sum of 5.79. Both examples also specify the same PICTURE clause for the sum, which contains only a single decimal place. The first statement, however, does not contain the ROUNDED clause, and hence the .09 is truncated, leaving 5.7 as the final answer. The second example contains the ROUNDED clause, producing a more accurate 5.8.

The SIZE ERROR Clause

The **SIZE ERROR** clause is available for all arithmetic statements and produces a warning when the result of calculation is too large for the designated field. Consider:

```
05  HOURLY-RATE          PIC 99.
05  HOURS-WORKED         PIC 99.
05  GROSS-PAY            PIC 999.
.
  .
    .
    COMPUTE GROSS-PAY = HOURLY-RATE * HOURS-WORKED.
```

Let us assume that HOURLY-RATE and HOURS-WORKED are 25 and 40, respectively. The result of the multiplication should be 1,000. GROSS-PAY, however, is defined as a three-position numeric field and is too small to hold the result. Hence its value is *truncated* and only the three rightmost digits are retained; in other words, GROSS-PAY becomes 000.

The situation is prevented by the inclusion of the SIZE ERROR clause:

```
COMPUTE GROSS-PAY = HOURLY-RATE * HOURS-WORKED
    ON SIZE ERROR PERFORM ERROR-ROUTINE
END-COMPUTE.
```

This time, if the results of the computation are too large and exceed the size allotted in the PICTURE clause, control passes to the statement(s) following the SIZE ERROR clause. The latter contains an error routine to display an error message or take other corrective action.

COMPUTE

The **COMPUTE** statement combines multiple arithmetic operations into a single statement of the form:

```
COMPUTE {identifier-1 [ROUNDED]}...= expression-1

    [ON SIZE ERROR imperative-statement-1]

[END-COMPUTE]
```

The COMPUTE statement first calculates the value of the expression on the right side of the equal sign, then stores that value in the data name on the left. The expression within the COMPUTE statement consists of data names, numeric literals, arithmetic symbols, and parentheses. Spaces should precede and follow arithmetic symbols. A space is also required before a left parenthesis and after a right parenthesis.

Parentheses are used to clarify, and in some cases, alter the sequence of, operations within an expression, but anything contained within parentheses must also be a valid expression. Expressions are evaluated according to the following rules:

1. Anything contained in parentheses is evaluated first as a separate expression.
2. The symbols +, –, *, /, and ** denote addition, subtraction, multiplication, division, and exponentiation, respectively. Exponentiation is done first, then multiplication or division, then addition or subtraction.
3. If rule 2 results in a tie (e.g., if both multiplication and division are present), then evaluation proceeds from left to right.

Table 5.5 contains examples to illustrate the formation and evaluation of expressions in a COMPUTE statement.

TABLE 5.5 The COMPUTE Instruction

DATA NAME	A	B	C	COMMENTS
Value *before* execution	2	3	10	Initial Values
Value *after* execution of				
COMPUTE C = A + B.	2	3	5	Simple addition
COMPUTE C = A + B * 2.	2	3	8	Multiplication before addition
COMPUTE C = (A + B) * 2.	2	3	10	Parenthesis evaluated first
COMPUTE C = A ** B.	2	3	8	Algebraically, $c = a^b$
COMPUTE C = B ** A.	2	3	9	Algebraically, $c = b^a$

Table 5.6 should further clarify the use of this all-important statement. This table contains several algebraic expressions and the corresponding COMPUTE statements to accomplish the intended logic.

TABLE 5.6 The COMPUTE Instruction *(continued)*

ALGEBRAIC EXPRESSION	COBOL COMPUTE
$x = a + b$	`COMPUTE X = A + B.`
$x = \frac{a+b}{2}$	`COMPUTE X = (A + B) / 2.`
$x = \frac{(a+b)c}{2}$	`COMPUTE X = (A + B) * C / 2.`
$x = \frac{a+b}{2c}$	`COMPUTE X = (A + B) / (2 * C).`
$x = \sqrt{a}$	`COMPUTE X = A ** .5.`
$x = \frac{a^2 + b^2}{c^2}$	`COMPUTE X = (A ** 2 + B ** 2) / C ** 2.`

ADD

The **ADD** statement has two basic formats:

```
ADD {identifier-1} . . . TO {identifier-2 [ROUNDED]} . . .
    {literal-1   }

    [ON SIZE ERROR imperative-statement-1]

[END-ADD]
```

```
ADD {identifier-1} . . . TO {identifier-2}
    {literal-1   }          {literal-2   }

    GIVING {identifier-3 [ROUNDED]} . . .

    [ON SIZE ERROR imperative-statement-1]

[END-ADD]
```

In the first format the value of identifier-2 is *replaced* by the result of the addition; in the second format the value of identifier-2 is *unchanged*, because the result is stored in identifier-3 (and beyond). The word TO is *required* in the first format, but *optional* in the second. The three dots in either format indicate that identifier-1 or literal-1 can be repeated as many times as necessary (so that multiple items can be added together.)

Examples 5.1 and 5.2 illustrate the ADD statement. The first instruction adds the values of A and B (5 and 10) to the value of C (20), and puts the sum of 35 back into C. Example 5.2, however, does not include the initial value of C in the calculation; it adds the values of A and B (5 and 10), and places the sum of 15 in C.

Example 5.1 `ADD A B TO C`

	A	B	C
Before execution:	5	10	20
After execution:	5	10	35

Example 5.2 `ADD A TO B GIVING C`

	A	B	C
Before execution:	5	10	20
After execution:	5	10	15

Table 5.7 contains additional examples of the ADD statement, with all examples operating on the *initial* values of A, B, and C (5, 10, and 30, respectively). The last example changes the values of both B and C.

TABLE 5.7 The ADD Instruction

DATA NAME	A	B	C
Value before execution	5	10	30
Value after execution of			
ADD A TO C.	5	10	35
ADD A B TO C.	5	10	45
ADD A TO B GIVING C.	5	10	15
ADD A 18 B GIVING C.	5	10	33
ADD A 18 B TO C.	5	10	63
ADD 1 TO B C.	5	11	31

SUBTRACT

The **SUBTRACT** statement has two formats:

```
SUBTRACT {identifier-1} . . . FROM {identifier-2 [ROUNDED]} . . .
         {literal-1   }

         [ON SIZE ERROR imperative-statement-1]

[END-SUBTRACT]
```

```
SUBTRACT {identifier-1} . . . FROM {identifier-2}
         {literal-1   }            {literal-2   }

         GIVING {identifier-3 [ROUNDED]} . . .

         [ON SIZE ERROR imperative-statement-1]

[END-SUBTRACT]
```

In the first format the initial value of identifier-2 is replaced by the result of the subtraction. In the second format the initial value of either identifier-2 or literal-2 is unchanged, as the result is stored in identifier-3 (and beyond).

Examples 5.3 and 5.4 illustrate the SUBTRACT statement. In Example 5.3 the SUBTRACT statement causes the value of A (5) to be subtracted from the initial value of B (15) and the result (10) to be stored in B. Only the value of B was changed.

In the FROM . . . GIVING format of Example 5.4 the value of A (5) is subtracted from the value of B (15), and the result (10) is placed in C. The values of A and B are unchanged, and the initial value of C (100) is replaced by 10. Table 5.8 contains additional examples.

Example 5.3 `SUBTRACT A FROM B`

	A	B
Before execution:	5	15
After execution:	5	10

Example 5.4 SUBTRACT A FROM B GIVING C

	A	B	C
Before execution:	5	15	100
After execution:	5	15	10

TABLE 5.8 The SUBTRACT Instruction

DATA NAME	A	B	C	D
Value before execution	5	10	30	100
Value after execution of				
SUBTRACT A FROM C.	5	10	25	100
SUBTRACT A B FROM C.	5	10	15	100
SUBTRACT A B FROM C GIVING D.	5	10	30	15
SUBTRACT 10 FROM C D.	5	10	20	90

MULTIPLY

The **MULTIPLY** statement has two formats:

```
MULTIPLY {identifier-1} BY {identifier-2 [ROUNDED]} . . .
         {literal-1   }

      [ON SIZE ERROR imperative-statement-1]

[END-MULTIPLY]
```

```
MULTIPLY {identifier-1} BY {identifier-2}
         {literal-1   }    {literal-2   }

      GIVING {identifier-3 [ROUNDED]} . . .

      [ON SIZE ERROR imperative-statement-1]

[END-MULTIPLY]
```

If GIVING is used, then the result of the multiplication is stored in identifier-3 (and beyond). If GIVING is omitted, then the result is stored in identifier-2 (and beyond).

Example 5.5 MULTIPLY A BY B

	A	B
Before execution:	10	20
After execution:	10	200

Example 5.6 `MULTIPLY A BY B GIVING C`

	A	B	C
Before execution:	10	20	345
After execution:	10	20	200

Table 5.9 contains additional examples of the MULTIPLY statement. As in the previous examples, the instructions operate on the initial values of A, B, and C.

TABLE 5.9 The MULTIPLY Instruction

DATA NAME	A	B	C
Value before execution	5	10	30
Value after execution of			
MULTIPLY B BY A GIVING C.	5	10	50
MULTIPLY A BY B GIVING C.	5	10	50
MULTIPLY A BY B.	5	50	30
MULTIPLY B BY A.	50	10	30
MULTIPLY A BY 3 GIVING B C.	5	15	15

DIVIDE

The **DIVIDE** statement has two formats. In the second format, the primary distinction is between the words BY and INTO, which determine whether identifier-2 is the divisor or the dividend. As with the other arithmetic statements, the GIVING option implies that the result is stored in identifier-3 so that the initial value of identifier-2 or literal-2 is unchanged. Only the second format makes explicit provision for storing the remainder.

```
DIVIDE {identifier-1} INTO {identifier-2 [ROUNDED]} . . .
       {literal-1   }

       [ON SIZE ERROR imperative-statement-1]

[END-DIVIDE]
```

```
DIVIDE {identifier-1} {INTO} {identifier-2} GIVING {identifier-3 [ROUNDED]} . . .
       {literal-1   } {BY  } {literal-2   }

       [REMAINDER identifier-4]

       [ON SIZE ERROR imperative-statement-1]

[END-DIVIDE]
```

In Example 5.7 the value of B (50) is divided by the value of A (10), and the quotient (5) replaces the initial value of B. In Example 5.8, which uses the GIVING option, the quotient goes into C, the remainder into D, and the values of A and B are

PROGRAMMING TIP

Use the COMPUTE Statement for Multiple Arithmetic Operations

The COMPUTE statement should always be used when multiple arithmetic operators are involved. Consider two sets of equivalent code:

Poor Code:

```
MULTIPLY B BY B GIVING B-SQUARED.
MULTIPLY 4 BY A GIVING FOUR-A.
MULTIPLY FOUR-A BY C GIVING FOUR-A-C.
SUBTRACT FOUR-A-C FROM B-SQUARED GIVING RESULT-1.
COMPUTE RESULT-2 = RESULT-1 ** .5.
SUBTRACT B FROM RESULT-2 GIVING NUMERATOR.
MULTIPLY 2 BY A GIVING DENOMINATOR.
DIVIDE NUMERATOR BY DENOMINATOR GIVING X.
```

Improved Code:

```
COMPUTE X = (-B + (B ** 2 - (4 * A * C)) ** .5) / (2 * A).
```

Both sets of code apply to the quadratic formula,

$$X = \frac{-B + \sqrt{B^2 - 4AC}}{2A}$$

It is fairly easy to determine what is happening from the single COMPUTE statement, but next to impossible to realize the cumulative effect of the eight arithmetic statements. Interpretation of the unacceptable code is further clouded by the mandatory definition of data names for intermediate results, RESULT-1, RESULT-2, etc.

Parentheses are often required in COMPUTE statements to alter the normal hierarchy of operations; for example, parentheses are required around 2 * A in the denominator. If they had been omitted, the numerator would have been divided by 2 and then the quotient would have been multiplied by A. Sometimes the parentheses are optional to the compiler but should be used to clarify things for the programmer. The parentheses around 4 * A * C do not alter the normal order of operations and hence are optional.

Individual arithmetic statements are preferable to the COMPUTE statement when only a *single* operation is required. Hence, ADD 1 TO COUNTER is easier to read than COMPUTE COUNTER = COUNTER + 1.

unaffected. Example 5.9 parallels 5.8 except that BY replaces INTO, resulting in a quotient of zero and a remainder of 10. Table 5.10 contains additional examples of the DIVIDE statement.

Example 5.7 `DIVIDE A INTO B.`

	A	B
Before execution:	10	50
After execution:	10	5

Example 5.8 `DIVIDE A INTO B GIVING C REMAINDER D.`

	A	B	C	D
Before execution:	10	51	13	17
After execution:	10	51	5	1

Example 5.9 `DIVIDE A BY B GIVING C REMAINDER D.`

	A	B	C	D
Before execution:	10	51	13	17
After execution:	10	51	0	10

TABLE 5.10 The DIVIDE Instruction

DATA NAME	A	B	C
Value before execution	5	10	30
Value after execution of			
DIVIDE 2 INTO B.	5	5	30
DIVIDE 2 INTO B GIVING C.	5	10	5
DIVIDE B BY 5 GIVING A.	2	10	30
DIVIDE A INTO B C.	5	2	6
DIVIDE A INTO B GIVING C.	5	10	2
DIVIDE 3 INTO A GIVING B REMAINDER C.	5	1	2

Assumed Decimal Point

Arithmetic is performed on decimal as well as integer fields. You must be aware of the decimal point, and in particular, *be sure to define the field holding the result with a sufficient number of decimal places.* Consider Example 5.10, in which A and B have pictures of 99 and 99V9, respectively.

Example 5.10 `ADD A TO B.`

	A	B
Before execution:	1 2	3 4^5
After execution:	1 2	4 6^5

In the example, field B is stored with an implied decimal point. The compiler generates instructions to add an integer number (12) to a number with one decimal place (34V5). It maintains decimal alignment, obtains 46V5 as an answer, and stores the result in field B.

Now consider what happens if the operation is reversed, that is, ADD B TO A. The result of the addition is still 46V5; however, the field that stores the sum, A, is defined without a decimal point; hence, the .5 will be truncated. *It is critical, therefore, to define the receiving field with a sufficient number of decimal places.* Table 5.11 contains additional examples. In each instance the instruction is assumed to operate on the initial values of A, B, and C.

TABLE 5.11 Arithmetic on Fields with Assumed Decimal Points

DATA NAME	A	B	C
PICTURE	**99**	**99V9**	**99V99**
Value before execution	12	345	4712
Value after execution of			
ADD B TO A.	46	345	4712
ADD A TO B.	12	465	4712
ADD B TO C.	12	345	8162
ADD C TO B.	12	816	4712
ADD C TO A.	59	345	4712
ADD A TO C.	12	345	5912

The Tuition Billing Program

The tuition billing program was first presented in Chapter 3, where we produced the hierarchy chart, pseudocode, and stubs program. We continued the development of the program in Chapter 4, with specifics of the Identification, Environment, and Data divisions. Now we are able to write the Procedure Division and complete the program.

We emphasize, however, that the Procedure Division is not written from scratch, but is developed from work already done in Chapters 3 and 4. Consider, therefore, Figure 5.4, which contains the hierarchy chart and detailed pseudocode, and most importantly the *already working* stubs program. The stubs program is complete in the sense that it contains all of the paragraphs needed for the eventual program; it is incomplete because many of its paragraphs exist as one sentence DISPLAY statements that need to be expanded to perform the indicated task. The most difficult work has already been done, however, because the testing in Chapter 3 demonstrated that the overall program flow is correct.

Thus, it is relatively simple to expand the various stub paragraphs in favor of more detailed Procedure Division statements presented in this chapter. The paragraphs can be implemented one (or several) at a time; for example, begin with the paragraph to write a heading line, expand it, then test it to be sure it executes correctly. Develop the paragraph to write a detailed line, then expand the paragraphs to compute the individual amounts (tuition, union fee, activity fee, and scholarship), testing each paragraph to be sure it works properly. Finally, add the paragraphs to increment the university totals and write the summary line at the end of the report.

The completed program is shown in Figure 5.5. The Identification, Environment, and Data divisions were developed at the end of Chapter 4 and are

Figure 5.4 Developing the Procedure Division

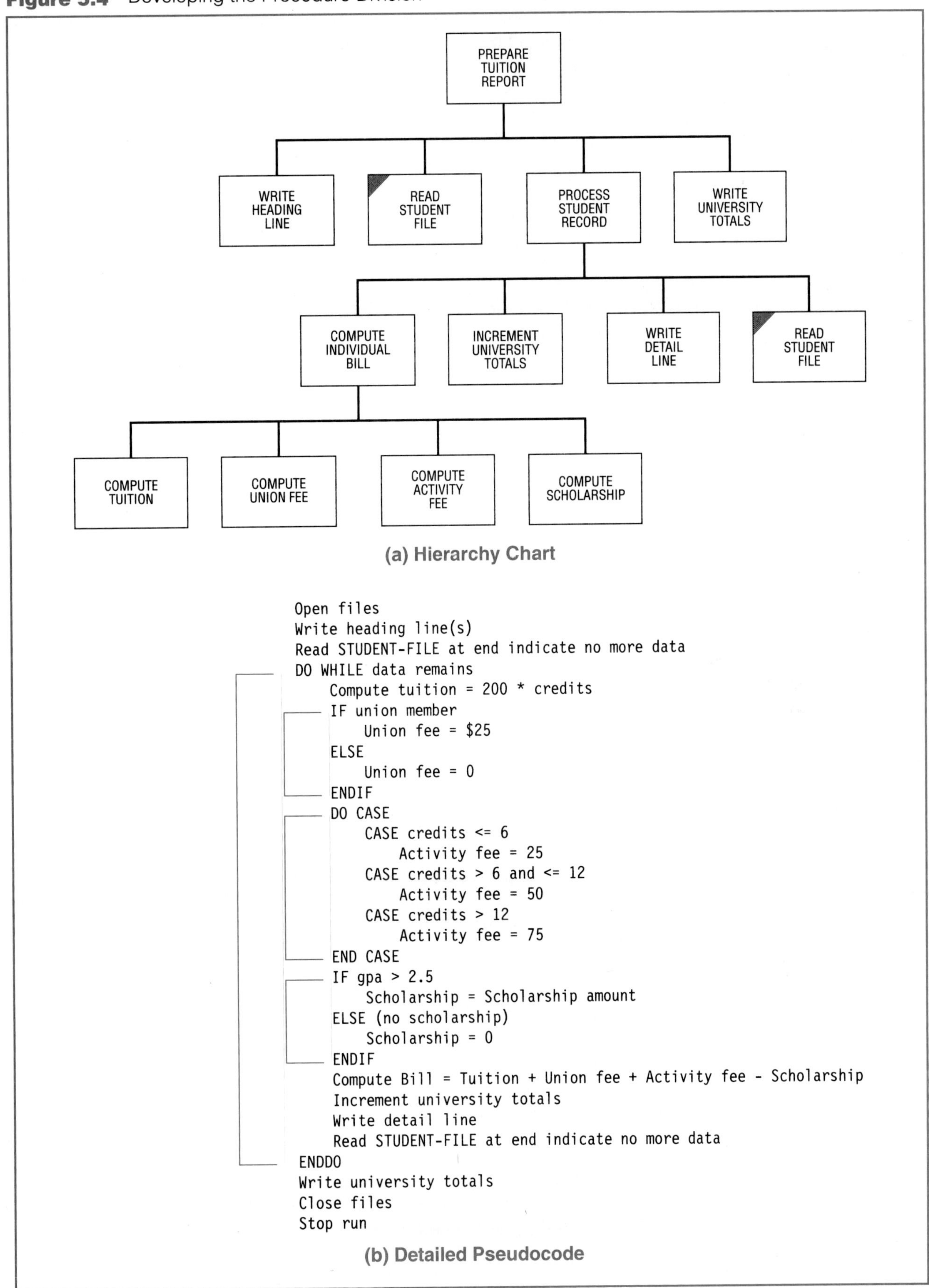

(a) Hierarchy Chart

```
Open files
Write heading line(s)
Read STUDENT-FILE at end indicate no more data
DO WHILE data remains
    Compute tuition = 200 * credits
    IF union member
        Union fee = $25
    ELSE
        Union fee = 0
    ENDIF
    DO CASE
        CASE credits <= 6
            Activity fee = 25
        CASE credits > 6 and <= 12
            Activity fee = 50
        CASE credits > 12
            Activity fee = 75
    END CASE
    IF gpa > 2.5
        Scholarship = Scholarship amount
    ELSE (no scholarship)
        Scholarship = 0
    ENDIF
    Compute Bill = Tuition + Union fee + Activity fee - Scholarship
    Increment university totals
    Write detail line
    Read STUDENT-FILE at end indicate no more data
ENDDO
Write university totals
Close files
Stop run
```

(b) Detailed Pseudocode

Figure 5.4 *(continued)*

```
PROCEDURE DIVISION.
PREPARE-TUITION-REPORT.
    DISPLAY 'PREPARE-TUITION-REPORT paragraph entered'.
    OPEN INPUT  STUDENT-FILE.
    PERFORM WRITE-HEADING-LINE.
    PERFORM READ-STUDENT-FILE.
    PERFORM PROCESS-STUDENT-RECORD
        UNTIL DATA-REMAINS-SWITCH = 'NO'.
    PERFORM WRITE-UNIVERSITY-TOTALS.
    CLOSE STUDENT-FILE.
    STOP RUN.
WRITE-HEADING-LINE.
    DISPLAY 'WRITE-HEADING-LINE paragraph entered'.

READ-STUDENT-FILE.
    READ STUDENT-FILE
        AT END MOVE 'NO' TO DATA-REMAINS-SWITCH
    END-READ.

PROCESS-STUDENT-RECORD.
    DISPLAY ' '.
    DISPLAY 'PROCESS-STUDENT-RECORD paragraph entered'.
    DISPLAY 'Student record being processed: ' STUDENT-RECORD.
    PERFORM COMPUTE-INDIVIDUAL-BILL.
    PERFORM INCREMENT-UNIVERSITY-TOTALS
    PERFORM WRITE-DETAIL-LINE.
    PERFORM READ-STUDENT-FILE.

COMPUTE-INDIVIDUAL-BILL.
    DISPLAY '  COMPUTE-INDIVIDUAL-BILL paragraph entered'.
    PERFORM COMPUTE-TUITION.
    PERFORM COMPUTE-UNION-FEE.
    PERFORM COMPUTE-ACTIVITY-FEE.
    PERFORM COMPUTE-SCHOLARSHIP.

COMPUTE-TUITION.
    DISPLAY '  COMPUTE-TUITION paragraph entered'.

COMPUTE-UNION-FEE.
    DISPLAY '  COMPUTE-UNION-FEE paragraph entered'.

COMPUTE-ACTIVITY-FEE.
    DISPLAY '  COMPUTE-ACTIVITY-FEE paragraph entered'.

COMPUTE-SCHOLARSHIP.
    DISPLAY '  COMPUTE-SCHOLARSHIP paragraph entered'.

INCREMENT-UNIVERSITY-TOTALS.
    DISPLAY '  INCREMENT-UNIVERSITY-TOTALS paragraph entered'.

WRITE-DETAIL-LINE.
    DISPLAY '  WRITE-DETAIL-LINE paragraph entered'.

WRITE-UNIVERSITY-TOTALS.
    DISPLAY ' '.
    DISPLAY 'WRITE-UNIVERSITY-TOTALS paragraph entered'.
```

(c) Stubs Program

Figure 5.5 The Tuition Billing Program

```
IDENTIFICATION DIVISION.
PROGRAM-ID.    TUITION5.
AUTHOR.        CAROL VAZQUEZ VILLAR.

ENVIRONMENT DIVISION.
INPUT-OUTPUT SECTION.
FILE-CONTROL.
    SELECT STUDENT-FILE
        ASSIGN TO UT-S-SYSIN.
    SELECT PRINT-FILE
        ASSIGN TO UT-S-SYSOUT.

DATA DIVISION.
FILE SECTION.
FD  STUDENT-FILE
    RECORD CONTAINS 27 CHARACTERS.
01  STUDENT-RECORD.
    05  STU-NAME.
        10  STU-LAST-NAME     PIC X(15).
        10  STU-INITIALS      PIC XX.
    05  STU-CREDITS           PIC 9(2).
    05  STU-UNION-MEMBER      PIC X.
    05  STU-SCHOLARSHIP       PIC 9(4).
    05  STU-GPA               PIC 9V99.

FD  PRINT-FILE
    RECORD CONTAINS 132 CHARACTERS.
01  PRINT-LINE                PIC X(132).

WORKING-STORAGE SECTION.
01  DATA-REMAINS-SWITCH       PIC X(2)  VALUE SPACES.

01  INDIVIDUAL-CALCULATIONS.
    05  IND-TUITION           PIC 9(4)  VALUE ZEROS.
    05  IND-ACTIVITY-FEE      PIC 9(2)  VALUE ZEROS.
    05  IND-UNION-FEE         PIC 9(2)  VALUE ZEROS.
    05  IND-SCHOLARSHIP       PIC 9(4)  VALUE ZEROS.
    05  IND-BILL              PIC 9(6)  VALUE ZEROS.

01  UNIVERSITY-TOTALS.
    05  UNI-TUITION           PIC 9(6)  VALUE ZEROS.
    05  UNI-UNION-FEE         PIC 9(4)  VALUE ZEROS.
    05  UNI-ACTIVITY-FEE      PIC 9(4)  VALUE ZEROS.
    05  UNI-SCHOLARSHIP       PIC 9(6)  VALUE ZEROS.
    05  UNI-IND-BILL          PIC 9(6)  VALUE ZEROS.

01  CONSTANTS-AND-RATES.
    05  PRICE-PER-CREDIT      PIC 9(3)  VALUE 200.
    05  UNION-FEE             PIC 9(2)  VALUE 25.
    05  ACTIVITY-FEES.
```

Figure 5.5 *(continued)*

```
            10  1ST-ACTIVITY-FEE PIC 99    VALUE 25.
            10  1ST-CREDIT-LIMIT PIC 99    VALUE 6.
            10  2ND-ACTIVITY-FEE PIC 99    VALUE 50.
            10  2ND-CREDIT-LIMIT PIC 99    VALUE 12.
            10  3RD-ACTIVITY-FEE PIC 99    VALUE 75.
        05  MINIMUM-SCHOLAR-GPA  PIC 9V9   VALUE 2.5.

    01  HEADING-LINE.
        05  FILLER               PIC X     VALUE SPACES.
        05  FILLER               PIC X(12) VALUE 'STUDENT NAME'.
        05  FILLER               PIC X(10) VALUE SPACES.
        05  FILLER               PIC X(7)  VALUE 'CREDITS'.
        05  FILLER               PIC X(2)  VALUE SPACES.
        05  FILLER               PIC X(7)  VALUE 'TUITION'.
        05  FILLER               PIC X(2)  VALUE SPACES.
        05  FILLER               PIC X(9)  VALUE 'UNION FEE'.
        05  FILLER               PIC X(2)  VALUE SPACES.
        05  FILLER               PIC X(7)  VALUE 'ACT FEE'.
        05  FILLER               PIC X(2)  VALUE SPACES.
        05  FILLER               PIC X(11) VALUE 'SCHOLARSHIP'.
        05  FILLER               PIC X(2)  VALUE SPACES.
        05  FILLER               PIC X(10) VALUE 'TOTAL BILL'.
        05  FILLER               PIC X(48) VALUE SPACES.

    01  DETAIL-LINE.
        05  FILLER               PIC X     VALUE SPACES.
        05  DET-LAST-NAME        PIC X(15).
        05  FILLER               PIC X(2)  VALUE SPACES.
        05  DET-INITIALS         PIC X(2).
        05  FILLER               PIC X(5)  VALUE SPACES.
        05  DET-CREDITS          PIC 9(2).
        05  FILLER               PIC X(6)  VALUE SPACES.
        05  DET-TUITION          PIC 9(6).
        05  FILLER               PIC X(7)  VALUE SPACES.
        05  DET-UNION-FEE        PIC 9(3).
        05  FILLER               PIC X(6)  VALUE SPACES.
        05  DET-ACTIVITY-FEE     PIC 9(3).
        05  FILLER               PIC X(8)  VALUE SPACES.
        05  DET-SCHOLARSHIP      PIC 9(5).
        05  FILLER               PIC X(6)  VALUE SPACES.
        05  DET-IND-BILL         PIC 9(6).
        05  FILLER               PIC X(49) VALUE SPACES.

     01  DASH-LINE.
         05  FILLER               PIC X(31) VALUE SPACES.
         05  FILLER               PIC X(8)  VALUE ALL '-'.
         05  FILLER               PIC X(2)  VALUE SPACES.
         05  FILLER               PIC X(8)  VALUE ALL '-'.
         05  FILLER               PIC X(2)  VALUE SPACES.
         05  FILLER               PIC X(7)  VALUE ALL '-'.
```

Figure 5.5 *(continued)*

```
           05  FILLER              PIC X(6)  VALUE SPACES.
           05  FILLER              PIC X(7)  VALUE ALL '-'.
           05  FILLER              PIC X(5)  VALUE SPACES.
           05  FILLER              PIC X(7)  VALUE ALL '-'.
           05  FILLER              PIC X(49) VALUE SPACES.
       01  TOTAL-LINE.
           05  FILLER              PIC X(8)  VALUE SPACES.
           05  FILLER              PIC X(17)
                   VALUE 'UNIVERSITY TOTALS'.
           05  FILLER              PIC X(8)  VALUE SPACES.
           05  TOT-TUITION         PIC 9(6).
           05  FILLER              PIC X(6)  VALUE SPACES.
           05  TOT-UNION-FEE       PIC 9(4).
           05  FILLER              PIC X(5)  VALUE SPACES.
           05  TOT-ACTIVITY-FEE    PIC 9(4).
           05  FILLER              PIC X(7)  VALUE SPACES.
           05  TOT-SCHOLARSHIP     PIC 9(6).
           05  FILLER              PIC X(6)  VALUE SPACES.
           05  TOT-IND-BILL        PIC 9(6).
           05  FILLER              PIC X(49) VALUE SPACES.
       PROCEDURE DIVISION.
       PREPARE-TUITION-REPORT.
           OPEN INPUT STUDENT-FILE
                OUTPUT PRINT-FILE.
           PERFORM WRITE-HEADING-LINE.
           PERFORM READ-STUDENT-FILE.
           PERFORM PROCESS-STUDENT-RECORD
                UNTIL DATA-REMAINS-SWITCH = 'NO'.
           PERFORM WRITE-UNIVERSITY-TOTALS.
           CLOSE STUDENT-FILE
                 PRINT-FILE.
           STOP RUN.
       WRITE-HEADING-LINE.
           MOVE HEADING-LINE TO PRINT-LINE.
           WRITE PRINT-LINE
               AFTER ADVANCING PAGE.
           MOVE SPACES TO PRINT-LINE.
           WRITE PRINT-LINE.
       READ-STUDENT-FILE.
           READ STUDENT-FILE
               AT END MOVE 'NO' TO DATA-REMAINS-SWITCH
           END-READ.
       PROCESS-STUDENT-RECORD.
           PERFORM COMPUTE-INDIVIDUAL-BILL.
           PERFORM INCREMENT-UNIVERSITY-TOTALS
           PERFORM WRITE-DETAIL-LINE.
```

Initial (priming) READ statement

Figure 5.5 *(continued)*

```
           PERFORM READ-STUDENT-FILE.

       COMPUTE-INDIVIDUAL-BILL.
           PERFORM COMPUTE-TUITION.
           PERFORM COMPUTE-UNION-FEE.
           PERFORM COMPUTE-ACTIVITY-FEE.
           PERFORM COMPUTE-SCHOLARSHIP.
           COMPUTE IND-BILL = IND-TUITION + IND-UNION-FEE +
              IND-ACTIVITY-FEE - IND-SCHOLARSHIP.

       COMPUTE-TUITION.
           COMPUTE IND-TUITION = PRICE-PER-CREDIT * STU-CREDITS.

       COMPUTE-UNION-FEE.
           IF STU-UNION-MEMBER = 'Y'
              MOVE UNION-FEE TO IND-UNION-FEE
           ELSE
              MOVE ZERO TO IND-UNION-FEE
           END-IF.

       COMPUTE-ACTIVITY-FEE.
           EVALUATE TRUE
               WHEN STU-CREDITS <= 1ST-CREDIT-LIMIT
                   MOVE 1ST-ACTIVITY-FEE TO IND-ACTIVITY-FEE
               WHEN STU-CREDITS > 1ST-CREDIT-LIMIT
                   AND STU-CREDITS <= 2ND-CREDIT-LIMIT
                       MOVE 2ND-ACTIVITY-FEE TO IND-ACTIVITY-FEE
               WHEN STU-CREDITS > 2ND-CREDIT-LIMIT
                   MOVE 3RD-ACTIVITY-FEE TO IND-ACTIVITY-FEE
               WHEN OTHER
                   DISPLAY 'INVALID CREDITS FOR: ' STU-NAME
           END-EVALUATE.

       COMPUTE-SCHOLARSHIP.
           IF STU-GPA > MINIMUM-SCHOLAR-GPA
              MOVE STU-SCHOLARSHIP TO IND-SCHOLARSHIP
           ELSE
              MOVE ZERO TO IND-SCHOLARSHIP
           END-IF.

       INCREMENT-UNIVERSITY-TOTALS.
           ADD IND-TUITION      TO UNI-TUITION.
           ADD IND-UNION-FEE    TO UNI-UNION-FEE.
           ADD IND-ACTIVITY-FEE TO UNI-ACTIVITY-FEE.
           ADD IND-SCHOLARSHIP  TO UNI-SCHOLARSHIP.
           ADD IND-BILL         TO UNI-IND-BILL.

       WRITE-DETAIL-LINE.
           MOVE STU-LAST-NAME TO DET-LAST-NAME.
           MOVE STU-INITIALS TO DET-INITIALS.
           MOVE STU-CREDITS TO DET-CREDITS.
```

Last statement of performed paragraph is a second READ

IF statement ends with END-IF scope terminator and implements selection structure

EVALUATE statement implements case structure

Comparison done on numeric fields with implied decimal places

Figure 5.5 *(continued)*

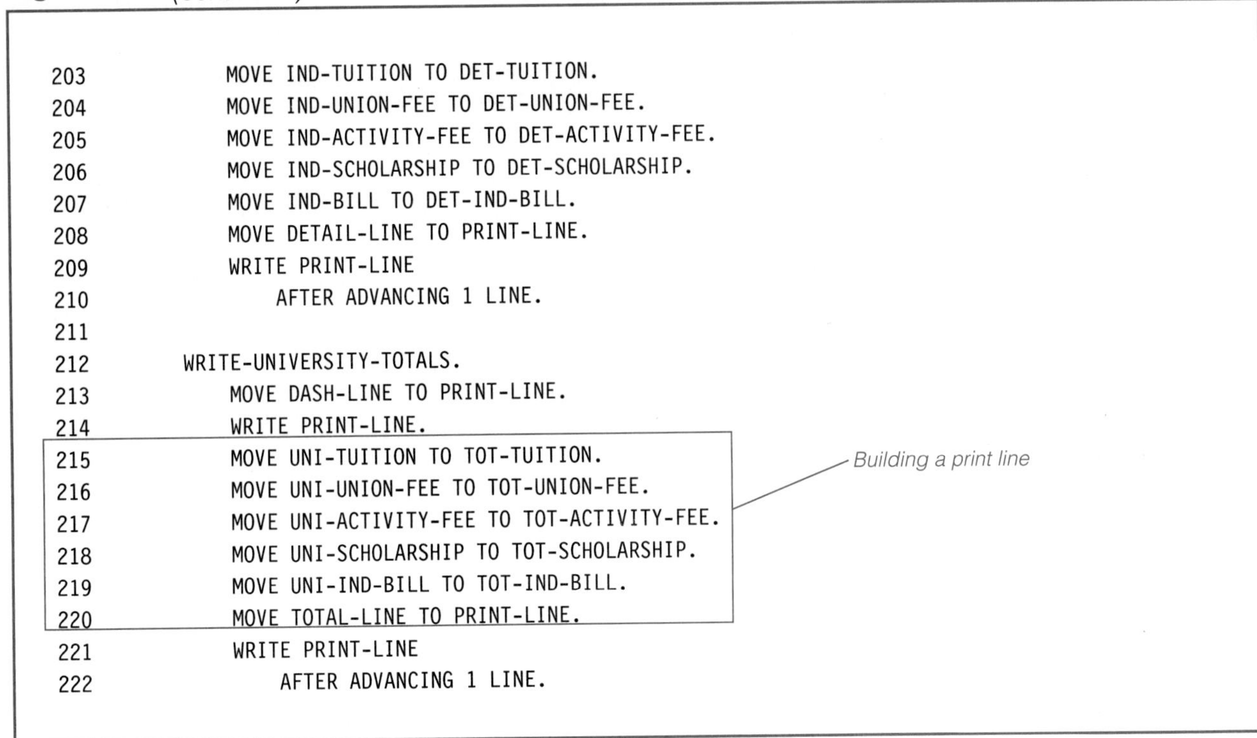

```
203          MOVE IND-TUITION TO DET-TUITION.
204          MOVE IND-UNION-FEE TO DET-UNION-FEE.
205          MOVE IND-ACTIVITY-FEE TO DET-ACTIVITY-FEE.
206          MOVE IND-SCHOLARSHIP TO DET-SCHOLARSHIP.
207          MOVE IND-BILL TO DET-IND-BILL.
208          MOVE DETAIL-LINE TO PRINT-LINE.
209          WRITE PRINT-LINE
210              AFTER ADVANCING 1 LINE.
211
212      WRITE-UNIVERSITY-TOTALS.
213          MOVE DASH-LINE TO PRINT-LINE.
214          WRITE PRINT-LINE.
215          MOVE UNI-TUITION TO TOT-TUITION.
216          MOVE UNI-UNION-FEE TO TOT-UNION-FEE.
217          MOVE UNI-ACTIVITY-FEE TO TOT-ACTIVITY-FEE.
218          MOVE UNI-SCHOLARSHIP TO TOT-SCHOLARSHIP.
219          MOVE UNI-IND-BILL TO TOT-IND-BILL.
220          MOVE TOTAL-LINE TO PRINT-LINE.
221          WRITE PRINT-LINE
222              AFTER ADVANCING 1 LINE.
```


copied directly from Figure 4.10. The completed program appears somewhat formidable the first time you see it, but it has been developed over the last three chapters, and you should have no difficulty in following. We suggest you take it in pieces and review sections of the text as you need them with respect to the following:

1. The Identification Division in lines 1–3 contains only the PROGRAM-ID and AUTHOR paragraphs.
2. The Environment Division in lines 5–11 contains the SELECT statements for the two required files.
3. The FD's in lines 15–16 and 26–28 correspond to the SELECT statements in the Environment Division.
4. The description for the incoming data in lines 17–24 matches the program specifications of Chapter 3.
5. Separate 01 entries are defined for individual and total calculations (lines 33–38 and 40–45); also data names for the constants and rates are established in lines 47–56.
6. Heading, detail, dashed, and total lines are described separately in WORKING-STORAGE (lines 58–73, 75–92, 94–105, and 107–121, respectively); note the use of VALUE clauses to initialize the various print lines.
7. The paragraphs in the Procedure Division correspond one to one with the blocks in the hierarchy chart of Figure 5.4a.
8. An initial READ statement in line 128 is followed by the PERFORM statement in lines 129 and 130 to execute PROCESS-STUDENT-RECORD (lines 148–152) until there are no more records. The last statement of the performed paragraph is a second READ statement. The combination of these statements implements the overall logic in the pseudocode of Figure 5.4b.

9. An EVALUATE statement in lines 173–183 computes the activity fee according to the number of credits taken.

10. Separate paragraphs in the Procedure Division compute an individual bill (lines 154–160), increment university totals (lines 192–197), and write a detail line (lines 199–210).

11. Multiple MOVE statements are required within the paragraph to write a detailed line (lines 199–210), with each statement moving a computed value (such as IND-TUITION) to the corresponding entry in the print line (DET-TUITION). The need for both data names will be more apparent after the material on editing in Chapter 7. The paragraph to write university totals requires similar treatment.

12. Multiple ADD statements are needed within the paragraph to increment university totals (lines 193–197). Each total is stored in a separate field and thus must be incremented separately.

Figure 5.6 Test Data and Output

```
SMITH          JB15Y0000230
JAMES          HR15 0500245
BAKER          SR09 0500350
PART-TIMER     JR03Y0000300
JONES          PL15Y0000280
HEAVYWORKER    HM18 0000200
LEE            BL18 0000335
CLARK          JC06 0000310
GROSSMAN       SE07 0000215
FRANKEL        LF10 0000350
BENWAY         CT03 0250395
KERBEL         NB04 0000100
```

(a) Test Data

```
STUDENT NAME            CREDITS  TUITION  UNION FEE  ACT FEE  SCHOLARSHIP  TOTAL BILL

SMITH            JB       15      003000     025       075       00000       003100
JAMES            HR       15      003000     000       075       00000       003075
BAKER            SR       09      001800     000       050       00500       001350
PART-TIMER       JR       03      000600     025       025       00000       000650
JONES            PL       15      003000     025       075       00000       003100
HEAVYWORKER      HM       18      003600     000       075       00000       003675
LEE              BL       18      003600     000       075       00000       003675
CLARK            JC       06      001200     000       025       00000       001225
GROSSMAN         SE       07      001400     000       050       00000       001450
FRANKEL          LF       10      002000     000       050       00000       002050
BENWAY           CT       03      000600     000       025       00250       000375
KERBEL           NB       04      000800     000       025       00000       000825
                                 --------  --------  -------    -------     -------
       UNIVERSITY TOTALS          024600     0075      0625      000750      024550
```

(b) Output

Test Data

The test data and associated output are shown in Figures 5.6a and 5.6b, respectively. The test data are identical to those used in the original stubs program; the output, however, is different and reflects the expanded Procedure Division of Figure 5.5. Note, too, the correspondence between individual records in the input data file and the associated lines in the printed report.

Observe, for example, that JB Smith, JR Part-Timer, and PL Jones each have a Y in column 20 of their input records, and that these are the only individuals who are charged a Union Fee. In similar fashion, James, Baker, and Benway are the only students with potential scholarships in the incoming data; James, however, does not have the requisite average and so he does not receive a scholarship. The student file has 12 records, and hence 12 students appear in the printed report.

In retrospect, the output produced isn't very pretty as it is unformatted and contains extraneous zeros throughout. (Editing is presented in Chapter 7 together with a final version of the program.)

Hierarchy Chart

The hierarchy chart was introduced initially as a design aid and developed before the program was written; it is also used as a documentation technique after coding is completed to better understand the overall program structure. The hierarchy chart depicts the functions inherent in a program, and is closely tied to the paragraphs in the Procedure Division. Observe therefore, the properties of the hierarchy chart in Figure 5.4a as they relate to the COBOL program in Figure 5.5.

1. Every box (module) in the hierarchy chart corresponds to a paragraph in the COBOL program. There are twelve different modules (the READ appears twice) in the hierarchy chart, and twelve paragraphs in the program.

2. Each paragraph in the COBOL program contains as many PERFORM statements as there are modules in the next lower level of the hierarchy chart. Thus the paragraph at the highest level, PREPARE-TUITION-REPORT, contains four PERFORM statements, one for each subordinate paragraph.

3. A paragraph can be entered only from the paragraph directly above it and must eventually return control to that paragraph. Hence, PROCESS-STUDENT-RECORDS is entered via a PERFORM statement in PREPARE-TUITION-REPORT. PROCESS-STUDENT-RECORDS in turn invokes four lower level paragraphs, each of which returns control to PROCESS-STUDENT-RECORDS, which eventually returns control to PREPARE-TUITION-REPORT.

4. Every module in a hierarchy chart (paragraph within a program) should be dedicated to a single function. The nature of that function should be apparent from the module's name and should consist of a verb, one or two adjectives, and an object.

Remember, too, that a hierarchy chart is very different from flowcharts or pseudocode. A hierarchy chart shows what has to be done, but not when; it contains no decision-making logic. Flowcharts and pseudocode, on the other hand, specify when and if a given block of code is executed. We say that hierarchy charts are *functional* in nature; they contain the tasks necessary to accomplish the specifications but do not indicate an order for execution. Pseudocode and flowcharts are *procedural* and specify logic.

COBOL Program Skeleton

Our objective is for you to write meaningful COBOL programs, not to memorize what must appear to be an endless list of rules. You must eventually remember certain things, but we have found the best approach is to pattern your first few COBOL programs after existing examples such as the tuition billing program. Everything you need to get started is contained in that program (Figure 5.5) if you will look at it carefully. As a further aid, Figure 5.7 contains a skeleton outline of a COBOL program and some helpful hints. Consider:

1. The four divisions must appear in the order: Identification, Environment, Data, and Procedure. Division headers begin in the A margin and always appear on a line by themselves.
2. The Environment and Data Divisions contain sections with fixed names. The Identification Division does not contain any sections. (The Procedure Division may contain programmer-defined sections; however, this is usually not done in beginning programs.)
3. The Data Division is the only division without paragraph names. In the Identification and Environment Divisions, the paragraph names are fixed. In the Procedure Division they are determined by the programmer. Paragraph names begin in the A margin.
4. Any entry not required to begin in the A margin begins in the B margin—that is, in or past column 12.
5. The program executes instructions sequentially, as they appear in the Procedure Division, unless a transfer-of-control statement such as PERFORM is encountered.
6. Every file must be opened and closed. A file name will appear in at least four statements: SELECT, FD, OPEN, and CLOSE. The READ statement also contains the file name of an input file, whereas the WRITE statement contains the record name of an output file.

LIMITATIONS OF COBOL-74

Scope terminators (e.g., END-IF, and END-READ) did not exist in COBOL 74; hence all scope terminators in Figure 5.5 must be removed for the program to compile under COBOL-74. The advantage of including scope terminators is explained further in Chapter 7.

The EVALUATE statement is also new to COBOL-85 and hence an alternative way to compute the activity fee (e.g., multiple IF statements) is required to develop the program under the older compiler.

The word TO is permitted as an optional reserved word in the GIVING form of the ADD statement in COBOL-85; it was not allowed in COBOL-74. THEN is an optional reserved word in the IF statement in COBOL-85 but was not allowed in COBOL-74.

Figure 5.7 Skeleton Outline of a COBOL Program

```
IDENTIFICATION DIVISION.
PROGRAM-ID.         PROGNAME.
AUTHOR.             JOHN DOE.

ENVIRONMENT DIVISION.
INPUT-OUTPUT SECTION.
FILE-CONTROL.
    SELECT INPUT-FILE
        ASSIGN TO UT-S-SYSIN.
    SELECT PRINT-FILE
        ASSIGN TO UT-S-SYSOUT.

DATA DIVISION.
FILE SECTION.
FD  INPUT-FILE
    RECORD CONTAINS 80 CHARACTERS.
01  INPUT-RECORD                 PIC X(80).

FD  PRINT-FILE
    RECORD CONTAINS 132 CHARACTERS.
01  PRINT-LINE                   PIC X(132).

WORKING-STORAGE SECTION
01  DATA-REMAINS-SWITCH          PIC X(2)    VALUE SPACES.
01  HEADING-LINE.
      .
        .
01  DETAIL-LINE.
      .
        .
01  TOTAL-LINE.
      .
        .

PROCEDURE DIVISION.
MAINLINE.
    OPEN INPUT INPUT-FILE
        OUTPUT PRINT-FILE.
    READ INPUT-FILE
        AT END MOVE 'NO' TO DATA-REMAINS-SWITCH
    END-READ.
    PERFORM PROCESS-RECORDS
        UNTIL DATA-REMAINS-SWITCH = 'NO'.
    CLOSE INPUT-FILE
          PRINT-FILE.
    STOP RUN.

PROCESS-RECORDS.
      .
        .
    READ INPUT-FILE
        AT END MOVE 'NO' TO DATA-REMAINS-SWITCH
    END-READ.
```

SELECT statements for input and output files

Controls performed paragraph

Housekeeping consists of opening files and the initial READ

Termination includes closing files and STOP RUN

Last line of performed paragraph is a second READ

SUMMARY

Points to Remember

- The READ statement typically appears twice in a COBOL program; as an initial (priming) read, and as the last statement of a performed paragraph to process a file until its records are exhausted.
- The PERFORM statement may be used with or without an UNTIL clause; the latter is used to implement a loop.
- The IF statement may be used with or without an ELSE clause; indentation is optional, but strongly suggested, in order to clarify intent.
- The EVALUATE statement implements the case structure and is used instead of multiple IF statements.
- The MOVE statement has several precisely defined rules, which govern the use of sending and receiving fields of different lengths and/or data types.
- Arithmetic is done in one of two ways: either through individual statements such as ADD, SUBTRACT, MULTIPLY, and DIVIDE, or through a COMPUTE statement which combines multiple operations.
- Parentheses may clarify and/or alter the normal sequence of operations; exponentiation, multiplication or division, addition or subtraction (and from left to right, if a tie).
- The hierarchy chart can be used as a design aid before a program is written, and as a documentation technique afterward.

Key Words and Concepts

Assumed (implied) decimal point	Hierarchy of operations
Decimal alignment	Indentation
Design aid	Priming (initial) read
Documentation	Pseudocode
Exponentiation	Receiving (destination) field
Group move	Scope terminator
Hierarchy chart	Source (sending) field

COBOL Elements

ADD	END-COMPUTE	EVALUATE	READ
ADVANCING	END-DIVIDE	GIVING	ROUNDED
CLOSE	END-EVALUATE	IF	SIZE ERROR
COMPUTE	END-IF	MOVE	STOP RUN
DIVIDE	END-MULTIPLY	MULTIPLY	SUBTRACT
ELSE	END-READ	OPEN	UNTIL
END-ADD	END-SUBTRACT	PERFORM	WRITE

FILL-IN

1. The ______________ statement permits multiple arithmetic operations in a single statement.
2. Most arithmetic statements have ______________ distinct formats.
3. Specification of the ______________ clause causes a calculation to be carried to one more place than is specified in the result field.
4. Exponentiation is indicated by ______________.
5. In the absence of parentheses exponentiation comes (before/after) multiplication.
6. If both multiplication and division are present, computation proceeds from ______________ to ______________.
7. The IF statement (does/does not) require an ELSE clause.
8. The effect of an IF statement is terminated by the presence of a ______________ or the presence of an ______________ clause.
9. ______________ is normally the last statement that is executed in any COBOL program.
10. A typical COBOL program usually has ______________ distinct READ statements.
11. A file containing N records is generally read ______________ times.
12. In COBOL, one reads a ______________ and writes a ______________.
13. Specification of ______________ ______________ ______________ in a WRITE statement causes the next line of output to begin on top of a new page.
14. The type of file—that is, INPUT or OUTPUT—appears in an ______________, but not in a ______________ statement.
15. When an alphanumeric field is moved to an alphanumeric field, data are moved ______________ character at a time, from ______________ to ______________.
16. If a five position alphanumeric field is moved to a four position alphanumeric field, the low order character is ______________.
17. A numeric move always maintains ______________ ______________.
18. A PERFORM UNTIL statement always tests the condition (before/after) performing the designated paragraph.
19. A numeric field (may/may not) be moved to an alphabetic field.
20. If a numeric field with PIC 999 is moved to a numeric field with PIC 99, the (most/least) significant digit will be truncated.
21. The ______________ ______________ option is available for all arithmetic statements, and indicates when the result of a computation is larger than its designated PICTURE clause.
22. The ______________ statement has been introduced to express a multibranch situation.

TRUE/FALSE

1. One ADD instruction can change the value of more than one data name.
2. Both GIVING and TO may be present in the same ADD instruction.
3. A valid ADD instruction may contain neither GIVING nor TO.
4. Both FROM and GIVING may appear in the same SUBTRACT instruction.
5. The use of GIVING is optional in the MULTIPLY statement.
6. The reserved word INTO must appear in a DIVIDE statement.
7. In the DIVIDE statement, the dividend is always identifier-1.
8. Multiplication and division can be performed in the same MULTIPLY statement.
9. Multiplication and addition can be performed in the same COMPUTE statement.
10. In a COMPUTE statement with no parentheses, multiplication is always done before subtraction.
11. In a COMPUTE statement with no parentheses, multiplication is always done before division.
12. Parentheses are sometimes required in a COMPUTE statement.
13. The COMPUTE statement changes the value of only one data name.
14. The IF statement must always contain the ELSE option.
15. The PERFORM statement transfers control to a paragraph elsewhere in the program.
16. A program may contain more than one STOP RUN statement.
17. STOP RUN must be the last statement in the Procedure Division.
18. The ADVANCING option is mandatory in the WRITE statement.
19. The READ statement contains a record name.
20. The WRITE statement contains a record name.
21. The OPEN and CLOSE statements are optional.
22. The END-IF scope terminator has little effect in an IF statement.
23. An IF statement can cause the execution of several other statements.
24. If the ELSE clause is satisfied in an IF statement, it can cause execution of several statements.
25. The ROUNDED clause is required in the COMPUTE statement.
26. The SIZE ERROR option is allowed only in the COMPUTE statement.
27. The SIZE ERROR option is required in the COMPUTE statement.
28. The EVALUATE statement facilitates implementation of the case construct.

PROBLEMS

1. Some of the following arithmetic statements are invalid. Identify those, and state why they are unacceptable.
   a. ADD A B C.
   b. SUBTRACT 10 FROM A B.
   c. SUBTRACT A FROM 10.
   d. ADD A TO B GIVING C.
   e. SUBTRACT A ROUNDED FROM B ROUNDED GIVING C.
   f. MULTIPLY A BY 10.
   g. MULTIPLY 10 BY A ROUNDED.
   h. MULTIPLY A BY 10 GIVING B C.
   i. DIVIDE A BY B.
   j. DIVIDE A INTO B.
   k. DIVIDE A INTO B GIVING C.
   l. DIVIDE B BY A GIVING C.
   m. COMPUTE X ROUNDED = A + B.
   n. COMPUTE X = 2(A + B).
   o. COMPUTE V = 20 / A - C.

2. Complete the table below. In each instance, refer to the *initial* values of A, B, C, and D.

DATA NAME	A	B	C	D
Value before execution	4	8	12	2
Value after execution of				
a. ADD 1 TO D B.				
b. ADD A B C GIVING D.				
c. ADD A B C TO D.				
d. SUBTRACT A B FROM C.				
e. SUBTRACT A B FROM C GIVING D.				
f. MULTIPLY A BY B C.				
g. MULTIPLY B BY A.				
h. DIVIDE A INTO C.				
i. DIVIDE C BY B GIVING D REMAINDER A.				
j. COMPUTE D = A + B / 2 * D.				
k. COMPUTE D = (A + B) / (2 * D).				
l. COMPUTE D = A + B / (2 * D).				
m. COMPUTE D = (A + B) / 2 * D.				
n. COMPUTE D = A + (B / 2) * D.				

3. Indicate the logical errors inherent in the following COBOL fragment:

```
FILE SECTION.
FD  EMPLOYEE-FILE
    .
      .
        .
FD  PRINT-FILE
    .
      .
        .
WORKING-STORAGE SECTION.
01  END-OF-FILE-SWITCH          PIC X(3)         VALUE 'YES'.
    .
      .
        .
PROCEDURE DIVISION.
PREPARE-EMPLOYEE-REPORT.
    MOVE HEADING-LINE TO PRINT-LINE.
    WRITE PRINT-LINE
        AFTER ADVANCING PAGE.
    OPEN INPUT EMPLOYEE-FILE
        OUTPUT PRINT-FILE.
    PERFORM PROCESS-RECORDS
        UNTIL END-OF-FILE-SWITCH = 'YES'.
    CLOSE EMPLOYEE-FILE.
    STOP RUN.
PROCESS-RECORDS.
    READ EMPLOYEE-FILE
        AT END MOVE 'YES' TO END-OF-FILE-SWITCH
    END-READ.
    .
      .
        .
```

4. Some of the following statements are invalid. Indicate those, and state why they are invalid. (Assume FILE-ONE and FILE-TWO are file names and RECORD-ONE is a record name.)
   a. OPEN INPUT RECORD-ONE.
   b. OPEN INPUT FILE-ONE OUTPUT FILE-TWO.
   c. OPEN INPUT FILE-ONE.
   d. CLOSE OUTPUT FILE-ONE.
   e. READ FILE-ONE.
   f. READ FILE-ONE AT END PERFORM END-OF-JOB-ROUTINE.
   g. READ RECORD-ONE AT END PERFORM END-OF-JOB.
   h. WRITE RECORD-ONE.
   i. WRITE RECORD-ONE AFTER ADVANCING TWO LINES.
   j. WRITE RECORD-ONE BEFORE ADVANCING TWO LINES.
   k. CLOSE FILE-ONE FILE-TWO.
   l. WRITE FILE-ONE.
   m. WRITE RECORD-ONE AFTER ADVANCING PAGE.

5. Write COBOL COMPUTE statements to accomplish the intended logic:

    a. $x = a + b + c$

    b. $x = \frac{a + bc}{2}$

    c. $x = a^2 + b^2 + c^2$

    d. $x = \frac{a + b}{2} - c$

    e. $x = a + b$

    f. $x = \sqrt{\frac{a^2 + b^2}{2c}}$

    g. $f = p(1 + i)^n$

    h. $f = \frac{((1 + i)^n - 1)}{i}$

    i. $x = \frac{(a + b)^c}{(d + e)^f}$

6. Given the following Procedure Division:

```
PROCEDURE DIVISION.
FIRST-PARAGRAPH.
    MOVE ZEROS TO FIELD-A FIELD-B.
    PERFORM SECOND-PARAGRAPH.
    PERFORM THIRD-PARAGRAPH.
    PERFORM SECOND-PARAGRAPH.
    STOP RUN.
SECOND-PARAGRAPH.
    ADD 10 TO FIELD-A.
    ADD 20 TO FIELD-B.
THIRD-PARAGRAPH.
    MULTIPLY FIELD-A BY FIELD-B GIVING FIELD-C.
    DIVIDE FIELD-A INTO FIELD-B GIVING FIELD-D.
```

    a. What are the final values for FIELD-A, FIELD-B, FIELD-C, and FIELD-D?
    b. How many times is each paragraph executed?

7. Complete the following table, showing the contents of the receiving field.

	SENDING FIELD		RECEIVING FIELD	
	PICTURE	CONTENTS	PICTURE	CONTENTS
a.	X(4)	H O P E	X(4)	
b.	X(4)	H O P E	9(4)	
c.	X(4)	H O P E	X(3)	
d.	X(4)	H O P E	X(5)	
e.	9(4)	6 7 8 9	X(4)	
f.	9(4)	6 7 8 9	9(3)	
g.	9(4)	6 7 8 9	9(5)	
h.	999V9	6 7 8 9	9(4)	
i.	999V9	6 7 8 9	9(4)V9	
j.	999V9	6 7 8 9	9(3)V99	
j.	999V9	6 7 8 9	99V99	

8. Supply Procedure Division statements as indicated:
   a. Code two equivalent statements, an ADD and a COMPUTE, to add 1 to the counter NUMBER-QUALIFIED-EMPLOYEES.
   b. Code a COBOL statement to add the contents of five fields, MONDAY-SALES, TUESDAY-SALES, WEDNESDAY-SALES, THURSDAY-SALES, and FRIDAY-SALES, storing the result in WEEKLY-SALES.
   c. Code a COBOL statement to subtract the fields FED-TAX, STATE-TAX, FICA, and VOLUNTARY-DEDUCTIONS, from GROSS-PAY, and put the result in NET-PAY.
   d. Code a single COBOL statement to calculate NET-AMOUNT-DUE, which is equal to the GROSS-SALE minus a 2% discount.
   e. Recode part (d), using two statements (a MULTIPLY and a SUBTRACT).
   f. Code a COBOL statement to compute GROSS-PAY, which is equal to HOURS-WORKED times HOURLY-RATE.
   g. Code a single COBOL statement to compute GROSS-PAY, which is equal to REG-HOURS-WORKED times HOURLY-RATE plus OVERTIME-HOURS times HOURLY-RATE times 1.5.
   h. Code a COBOL statement to determine AVERAGE-SALARY by dividing TOTAL-SALARY by NUMBER-OF-EMPLOYEES.
   i. Code a COBOL Compute statement equivalent to the algebraic formula.

$$x = \frac{(a+b)c}{de}$$

   j. Code a COBOL Compute statement equivalent to the algebraic formula.

$$x = \frac{-b+\sqrt{b^2-4ac}}{2a}$$

9. Write Procedure Division code for the flowchart in Figure 5.8.

Figure 5.8 Flowcharts for Problem 9

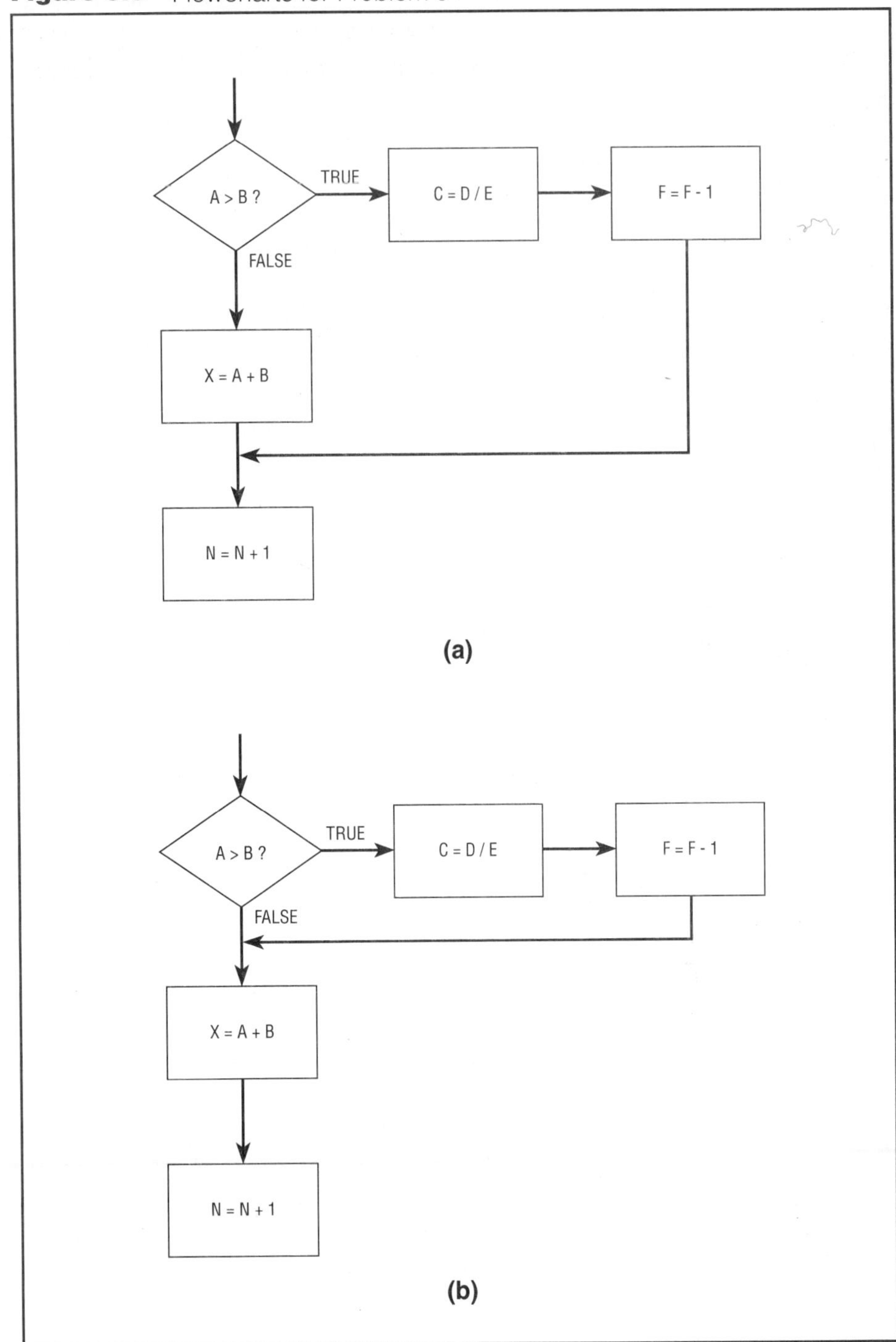

6 Debugging

CHAPTER OUTLINE

OBJECTIVES

After reading this chapter you will be able to:

- Distinguish between errors in compilation and execution; correct typical compilation errors.
- Generate a cross-reference listing; explain its utility in debugging.
- Use the DISPLAY statement as a debugging tool.
- Explain how an interactive debugger can be used to find and correct execution errors.
- Describe the use of file status codes in correcting data management errors.
- Explain what is meant by a structured walkthrough; be able to participate as reviewer, reviewee, moderator, or secretary.

OVERVIEW

Very few computer programs run successfully on the first attempt. Indeed, the programmer is realistically expected to make errors, and an important test of a good programmer is not whether he or she makes mistakes, but how quickly he or she is able to detect and correct the errors. Since this process is such an integral part of programming, an entire chapter is devoted to debugging. We consider errors in both compilation and execution.

Compilation errors occur during the translation of COBOL to machine language and are caused by a mistake in COBOL syntax, for example, a missing period or an entry in a wrong column. Execution errors result after the program has been translated to machine language and produce results that are different from what the programmer expected or intended.

Compilation errors are easy to find because the compiler produces an explicit error message. Execution errors are more difficult to detect and may require the use of additional debugging tools, such as the insertion of DISPLAY statements into a program and/or the use of an interactive debugger. The chapter also considers the structured walkthrough as a means of reducing errors before they occur.

Errors In Compilation

Compilation is the process of translating a source (COBOL) program into machine language. Any mistake in COBOL syntax causes the compiler to make an assumption in the interpretation of the statement in which the error occurs, or worse yet makes it impossible for the compiler to interpret the statement at all. Either way a ***compilation error*** results.

Some errors are less severe than others; for example, the compiler is generally able to guess the programmer's intent when periods are omitted in the Data Division, whereas it is unable to decipher a misspelled reserved word. Accordingly, most compilers provide different levels of ***compiler diagnostics*** (error messages) according to the severity of the error. CA-Realia® Classroom COBOL, for example, produces five types of error messages, which are listed in order of increasing severity. Other compilers have similar classifications. Consider:

I	Informational Diagnostics	Indicates a coding inefficiency or other condition (for example, an incompatibility with the ANS standard). The program will compile correctly.
W	Warning Diagnostics	The statement is syntactically correct, but the source of a potential problem. A program can compile and execute with several W-level diagnostics present; however, ignoring these messages could lead to errors in execution.
C	Conditional Diagnostics	The statement is incorrect as written, and requires the compiler to make an assumption in order to complete the compilation.
E	Error Diagnostics	A severe error in that the compiler cannot make corrections and therefore cannot generate object instructions. Any statement flagged as an E-level error is ignored and treated as if it were not present in the program.
S	Severe Diagnostics	An error of such severity that the compiler does not know what to do and cannot continue. S-level diagnostics are extremely rare, and you practically have to submit a dBASE program to the COBOL compiler to cause an S-level message.

The COBOL compiler tends to rub salt in a wound in the sense that an error in one statement can cause error messages in other statements that appear correct. For example, should you have an E-level error in a SELECT statement, the compiler will flag the error, ignore the SELECT statement, and then flag any other statements that reference that file even though those other statements are correct.

Often simple mistakes such as omitting a line or misspelling a reserved word can lead to a long and sometimes confusing set of error messages. The only consolation is that compiler errors can disappear as quickly as they occurred. Correction of the misspelled word or insertion of the missing statement will often eliminate several errors at once.

Proficiency in debugging comes from experience—the more programs you write, the better you become. You may correct the errors in the order they appear (our preference), or in the order of severity (from **S**evere, **E**rror, **C**onditional, **W**arning, to **I**nformational), or even haphazardly as you find them. Whichever way you choose, try to find the mistakes as quickly as possible and without wasting time. Moreover, don't spend too much time on any single error; instead, if you are stuck, skip the error temporarily and continue to the next, eliminating as many errors as you can before you recompile.

To give you a better feel of what to expect from your programs, we have taken the tuition billing program from Chapter 5 and deliberately changed several of the statements to cause compilation errors as shown in Figures 6.1 and 6.2. Each message in Figure 6.2 references a statement line number and error level and contains a brief explanation of the error. Some of the errors will be immediately obvious; others may require you to seek help. As you progress through this book and gain practical experience, you will become increasingly self-sufficient.

Figure 6.1 Tuition Billing Program with Compilation Errors

```
IDENTIFICATION DIVISION.
PROGRAM-ID.    TUIT6COM.
AUTHOR.        CAROL VAZQUEZ VILLAR.

ENVIRONMENT DIVISION.
INPUT-OUTPUT SECTION.
FILE-CONTROL.
    SELECT STUDENT-FILE
        ASSIGN TO UT-S-SYSIN.
    SELECT PRINT-FILE
        ASSIGN TO UT-S-SYSOUT.

DATA DIVISION.
FILE SECTION.
FD  STUDENT-FILE
    RECORD CONTAINS 27 CHARACTERS.
01  STUDENT-RECORD.
    05  STU-NAME.
        10  STU-LAST-NAME    PIC X(15).
        10  STU-INITIALS     PIC XX.
    05  STU-CREDITS          PIC 9(2).
    05  STU-UNION-MEMBER     PIC X.
    05  STU-SCHOLARSHIP      PIC 9(4).
    05  STU-GPA              PIC 9V99.

FD  PRINT-FILE
    RECORD CONTAINS 132 CHARACTERS.
01  PRINT-LINE               PIC X(132).

WORKING-STORAGE SECTION.
01  DATA-REMAINS-SWITCH      PIC X(2)  VALUE SPACES.

01  INDIVIDUAL-CALCULATIONS.
    05  IND-TUITION          PIC 9(4)  VALUE ZEROS.
    05  IND-ACTIVITY-FEE     PIC 9(2)  VALUE ZEROS.
    05  IND-UNION-FEE        PIC 9(2)  VALUE ZEROS.
    05  IND-SCHOLARSHIP      PIC 9(3)  VALUE ZEROS.
    05  IND-BILL             PIC 9(6)  VALUE ZEROS.

01  UNIVERSITY-TOTALS.
    05  UNI-TUITION          PIC 9(6)  VALUE ZEROS.
    05  UNI UNION FEE        PIC 9(4)  VALUE ZEROS.
```

Hyphens missing

Figure 6.1 *(continued)*

```
           05  UNI-ACTIVITY-FEE      PIC 9(4)  VALUE ZEROS.
           05  UNI-SCHOLARSHIP       PIC X(6)  VALUE ZEROS.
           05  UNI-IND-BILL          PIC 9(6)  VALUE ZEROS.

       01  CONSTANTS-AND-RATES.
           05  PRICE-PER-CREDIT      PIC 9(3)  VALUE 200.
           05  UNION-FEE             PIC 9(2)  VALUE 25.
           05  ACTIVITY-FEES.
               10  1ST-ACTIVITY-FEE PIC 99    VALUE 25.
               10  1ST-CREDIT-LIMIT PIC 99    VALUE 6.
               10  2ND-ACTIVITY-FEE PIC 99    VALUE 50.
               10  2ND-CREDIT-LIMIT PIC 99    VALUE 12.
               10  3RD-ACTIVITY-FEE PIC 99    VALUE 75.
           05  MINIMUM-SCHOLAR-GPA  PIC 9V9   VALUE 2.5.

       01  HEADING-LINE.
           05  FILLER               PIC X     VALUE SPACES.
           05  FILLER               PIC X(12) VALUE 'STUDENT NAME'.
           05  FILLER               PIC X(10) VALUE SPACES
           05  FILLER               PIC X(7)  VALUE 'CREDITS'.
           05  FILLER               PIC X(2)  VALUE SPACES.
           05  FILLER               PIC X(7)  VALUE 'TUITION'.
           05  FILLER               PIC X(2)  VALUE SPACES.
           05  FILLER               PIC X(9)  VALUE 'UNION FEE'.
           05  FILLER               PIC X(2)  VALUE SPACES.
           05  FILLER               PIC X(7)  VALUE 'ACT FEE'.
           05  FILLER               PIC X(2)  VALUE SPACES.
           05  FILLER               PIC X(11) VALUE 'SCHOLARSHIP'.
           05  FILLER               PIC X(2)  VALUE SPACES.
           05  FILLER               PIC X(10) VALUE 'TOTAL BILL'.
           05  FILLER               PIC X(48) VALUE SPACES.

       01  DETAIL-LINE.
           05  FILLER               PIC X     VALUE SPACES.
           05  DET-LAST-NAME        PIC X(15).
           05  FILLER               PIC X(2)  VALUE SPACES.
           05  DET-INITIALS         PIC X(2).
           05  FILLER               PIC X(5)  VALUE SPACES.
           05  STU-CREDITS          PIC 9(2).
           05  FILLER               PIC X(6)  VALUE SPACES.
           05  DET-TUITION          PIC 9(6).
           05  FILLER               PIC X(7)  VALUE SPACES.
           05  DET-UNION-FEE        PIC 9(3).
           05  FILLER               PIC X(6)  VALUE SPACES.
           05  DET-ACTIVITY-FEE     PIC 9(3).
           05  FILLER               PIC X(8)  VALUE SPACES.
           05  DET-SCHOLARSHIP      PIC 9(5).
           05  FILLER               PIC X(6)  VALUE SPACES.
           05  DET-IND-BILL         PIC 9(6).
           05  FILLER               PIC X(49) VALUE SPACES.
```

Alphanumeric picture is not permitted for numeric calculation

Period missing

Should be DET-CREDITS

Figure 6.1 *(continued)*

```

 01  DASH-LINE.
     05  FILLER                    PIC X(31) VALUE SPACES.
     05  FILLER                    PIC X(8)  VALUE ALL '-'.
     05  FILLER                    PIC X(2)  VALUE SPACES.
     05  FILLER                    PIC X(8)  VALUE ALL '-'.
     05  FILLER                    PIC X(2)  VALUE SPACES.
     05  FILLER                    PIC X(7)  VALUE ALL '-'.
     05  FILLER                    PIC X(6)  VALUE SPACES.
     05  FILLER                    PIC X(7)  VALUE ALL '-'.
     05  FILLER                    PIC X(5)  VALUE SPACES.
     05  FILLER                    PIC X(7)  VALUE ALL '-'.
     05  FILLER                    PIC X(49) VALUE SPACES.

 01  TOTAL-LINE.
     05  FILLER                    PIC X(8)  VALUE SPACES.
     05  FILLER                    PIC X(17)
             VALUE 'UNIVERSITY TOTALS'.
     05  FILLER                    PIC X(8)  VALUE SPACES.
     05  TOT-TUITION               PIC 9(6).
     05  FILLER                    PIC X(6)  VALUE SPACES.
     05  TOT-UNION-FEE             PIC 9(4).
     05  FILLER                    PIC X(5)  VALUE SPACES.
     05  TOT-ACTIVITY-FEE          PIC 9(4).
     05  FILLER                    PIC X(7)  VALUE SPACES.
     05  TOT-SCHOLARSHIP           PIC 9(6).
     05  FILLER                    PIC X(6)  VALUE SPACES.
     05  TOT-IND-BILL              PIC 9(6).
     05  FILLER                    PIC X(49) VALUE SPACES.

PROCEDURE DIVISION.
START.
    OPEN INPUT STUDENT-FILE
         OUTPUT PRINT-FILE.
    PERFORM WRITE-HEADING-LINE.
    PERFORM READ-STUDENT-FILE.
    PERFORM PROCESS-STUDENT-RECORD
         UNTIL DATA-REMAINS-SWITCH = 'NO'.
    PERFORM WRITE-UNIVERSITY-TOTALS.
    CLOSE STUDENT-FILE
          PRINT-FILE.
    STOP RUN.

WRITE-HEADING-LINE.
    MOVE HEADING-LINE TO PRINT-LINE.
    WRITE PRINT-LINE
        AFTER ADVANCING PAGE.
    MOVE SPACES TO PRINT-LINE.
    WRITE PRINT-LINE.

```

Reserved word used as paragraph name (annotation pointing to START.)

Figure 6.1 *(continued)*

```
143      READ-STUDENT-FILE.
144          READ STUDNET-FILE
145              AT END MOVE 'NO' TO DATA-REMAINS-SWITCH
146          END-READ.
147
148      PROCESS-STUDENT-RECORD.
149          PERFORM COMPUTE-INDIVIDUAL-BILL.
150          PERFORM INCREMENT-UNIVERSITY-TOTALS
151          PERFORM WRITE-DETAIL-LINE.
152          PERFORM READ-STUDENT-FILE.
153
154      COMPUTE-INDIVIDUAL-BILL.
155          PERFORM COMPUTE-TUITION.
156          PERFORM COMPUTE-UNION-FEE.
157          PERFORM COMPUTE-ACTIVITY-FEE.
158          PERFORM COMPUTE-SCHOLARSHIP.
159          COMPUTE IND-BILL = IND-TUITION + IND-UNION-FEE + IND-ACTIVITY
160                             - IND-SCHOLARSHIP.
161
162       COMPUTE-TUITION.
163           COMPUTE IND-TUITION =PRICE-PER-CREDIT * STU-CREDITS.
164
165       COMPUTE-UNION-FEE.
166           IF STU-UNION-MEMBER = 'Y'
167              MOVE UNION-FEE TO IND-UNION-FEE
168           ELSE
169              MOVE ZERO TO IND-UNION-FEE
170           END-IF.
171
172       COMPUTE-ACTIVITY-FEE.
173           EVALUATE TRUE
174               WHEN STU-CREDITS <= 1ST-CREDIT-LIMIT
175                   MOVE 1ST-ACTIVITY-FEE TO IND-ACTIVITY-FEE
176               WHEN STU-CREDITS > 1ST-CREDIT-LIMIT
177                   AND STU-CREDITS <= 2ND-CREDIT-LIMIT
178                       MOVE 2ND-ACTIVITY-FEE TO IND-ACTIVITY-FEE
179               WHEN STU-CREDITS > 2ND-CREDIT-LIMIT
180                   MOVE 3RD-ACTIVITY-FEE TO IND-ACTIVITY-FEE
181               WHEN OTHER
182                   DISPLAY 'INVALID CREDITS FOR: ' STU-NAME
183           END-EVALUATE.
184
185       COMPUTE-SCHOLARSHIP.
186           IF STU-GPA > MINIMUM-SCHOLAR-GPA
187              MOVE STU-SCHOLARSHIP TO IND-SCHOLARSHIP
188           ELSE
189              MOVE ZERO TO IND-SCHOLARSHIP
190           END-IF.
191
192       INCREMENT-UNIVERSITY-TOTALS.
```

Should be STUDENT-FILE

FEE extends past column 72

Missing space after =

Multiple definition in lines 21 and 81

Inconsistent PIC clauses in lines 23 and 37

Figure 6.1 *(continued)*

```
193          ADD IND-TUITION       TO UNI-TUITION.
194          ADD IND-UNION-FEE     TO UNI-UNION-FEE.
195          ADD IND-ACTIVITY-FEE  TO UNI-ACTIVITY-FEE.
196          ADD IND-SCHOLARSHIP   TO UNI-SCHOLARSHIP.
197          ADD IND-BILL          TO UNI-IND-BILL.
198
199      WRITE-DETAIL-LINE.
200          MOVE STU-LAST-NAME TO DET-LAST-NAME.
201          MOVE STU-INITIALS TO DET-INITIALS.
202          MOVE STU-CREDITS TO DET-CREDITS.
203          MOVE IND-TUITION TO DET-TUITION.
204          MOVE IND-UNION-FEE TO DET-UNION-FEE.
205          MOVE IND-ACTIVITY-FEE TO DET-ACTIVITY-FEE.
206          MOVE IND-SCHOLARSHIP TO DET-SCHOLARSHIP.
207          MOVE IND-BILL TO DET-IND-BILL.
208          MOVE DETAIL-LINE TO PRINT-LINE.
209          WRITE PRINT-FILE
210              AFTER ADVANCING 1 LINE.
211
212      WRITE-UNIVERSITY-TOTALS.
213          MOVE DASH-LINE TO PRINT-LINE.
214          WRITE PRINT-LINE.
215          MOVE UNI-TUITION TO TOT-TUITION.
216          MOVE UNI-UNION-FEE TO TOT-UNION-FEE.
217          MOVE UNI-ACTIVITY-FEE TO TOT-ACTIVITY-FEE.
218          MOVE UNI-SCHOLARSHIP TO TOT-SCHOLARSHIP.
219          MOVE UNI-IND-BILL TO TOT-IND-BILL.
220          MOVE TOTAL-LINE TO PRINT-LINE.
221          WRITE PRINT-LINE
222              AFTER ADVANCING 1 LINE.
```


Let us examine the errors:

```
42 E Unrecognizable word or literal 'UNION'
42 E Unrecognizable word or literal 'FEE'
```

Both errors result from omitted hyphens in the definition of UNI UNION FEE in line 42; that is, the compiler does not know how to handle what it thinks are three data names in a row (UNI, UNION, and FEE) and hence the error.

Correction: Insert hyphens to read UNI-UNION-FEE

```
62 W Period assumed before 'FILLER'
```

A level number must follow a completed statement, but the period ending line 61 has been removed. In this instance, the compiler assumes that the period is present, so no harm is done, but it is poor programming to permit such W-level diagnostics to remain. Moreover, there are situations in which a missing period can be very damaging.

Correction: Insert a period at the end of line 61.

Figure 6.2 Compilation Errors

```
LINE ERR# LVL                    ERROR TEXT

  42 0115 E Unrecognizable word or literal 'UNION'
  42 0115 E Unrecognizable word or literal 'FEE'
  62 0138 W Period assumed before 'FILLER'
 124 0348 W 'START' In invalid area; assumed valid
 124 0574 E Expected file-name; found 'START'
 144 0574 E Expected file-name; found 'READ'
 144 0786 E Undefined symbol 'STUDNET-FILE'
 146 0592 E No corresponding active scope for 'END-READ'
 159 0786 E Undefined symbol 'IND-ACTIVITY'
 163 0349 W Space assumed before 'PRICE-PER-CREDIT'
 163 0454 C Non-unique reference to 'STU-CREDITS' accepted
 174 0454 C Non-unique reference to 'STU-CREDITS' accepted
 176 0454 C Non-unique reference to 'STU-CREDITS' accepted
 177 0454 C Non-unique reference to 'STU-CREDITS' accepted
 179 0454 C Non-unique reference to 'STU-CREDITS' accepted
 187 0623 W Digits may be truncated during MOVE from 'STU-SCHOLARSHIP'
 194 0786 E Undefined symbol 'UNI-UNION-FEE'
 196 0752 E Data-name 'UNI-SCHOLARSHIP' invalid as numeric destination
 202 0454 C Non-unique reference to 'STU-CREDITS' accepted
 202 0786 E Undefined symbol 'DET-CREDITS'
 209 0678 E Record name not 01 level
 216 0786 E Undefined symbol 'UNI-UNION-FEE'
 218 0621 W Expected numeric data-name; found 'UNI-SCHOLARSHIP'; converted to numeric and accepted
```

```
124 W 'START' In invalid area; assumed valid
124 E Expected file-name; found 'START'
```

A subtle error and one that typically sends the beginner for help. START is intended as a paragraph name, and paragraph names must begin in the A-margin, so what's the problem? The difficulty is that START is a reserved word and cannot be used as a paragraph name.

Correction: Choose another name, for example, START-THE-PROGRAM

```
144 E Expected file-name; found 'READ'
144 E Undefined symbol 'STUDNET-FILE'
```

The compiler was expecting a valid file name but didn't find one because line 144 references STUD*NET*-FILE rather than STUDENT-FILE. You know they are the same, but the compiler does not and hence the error.

Correction: Change the file name to STUDENT-FILE in statement 144.

```
146 E No corresponding active scope for 'END-READ'
```

This error will disappear with the correction to the previous READ statement.

Correction: None required beyond the correction to line 144.

```
159 E Undefined symbol 'IND-ACTIVITY'
```

The error is subtle because the program file contains IND-ACTIVITY-FEE in line 35, yet the data name IND-ACTIVITY appears on the listing and is flagged as an error. The problem is that the COMPUTE statement extends beyond column 72, into columns 73–76, which are not interpreted by the compiler; that is, the compiler reads IND-ACTIVITY rather than IND-ACTIVITY-FEE.

Correction: Reformat the COMPUTE statement so that IND-ACTIVITY-FEE appears on the next line.

```
163 W Space assumed before 'PRICE-PER-CREDIT'
```

An easy error to find and correct. All relational symbols, as well as all arithmetic operators, must be preceded and followed by a blank.

Correction: Insert a space after the "=".

```
163 C Non-unique reference to 'STU-CREDITS' accepted
174 C Non-unique reference to 'STU-CREDITS' accepted
176 C Non-unique reference to 'STU-CREDITS' accepted
177 C Non-unique reference to 'STU-CREDITS' accepted
179 C Non-unique reference to 'STU-CREDITS' accepted
```

A nonunique error message implies that two or more data names are the same; in this instance STU-CREDITS is defined in line 21 and again in line 81 (the latter should be DET-CREDITS), and the compiler does not know which is which.

Correction: Restore uniqueness to the data name in line 81, by changing STU-CREDITS to DET-CREDITS.

```
187 W Digits may be truncated during MOVE from 'STU-SCHOLARSHIP'
```

The MOVE statement in line 187 moves the value of STU-SCHOLARSHIP (a four-position numeric field) to IND-SCHOLARSHIP (a three-position numeric field). The problem is that the sending field is larger than the receiving field, and thus the leftmost (most significant) digit may be truncated.

Correction: Increase the size of the PICTURE clause for IND-SCHOLARSHIP to PIC 9(4).

```
194 E Undefined symbol 'UNI-UNION-FEE'
```

The error message references UNI-UNION-FEE as an undefined symbol and is another example of how one error can cause several others. Hyphens were omitted in the definition of UNI-UNION-FEE in line 42, and thus (as far as the compiler is concerned) the data name UNI-UNION-FEE does not exist.

Correction: This diagnostic will disappear with the correction to line 42.

```
196 E Data-name 'UNI-SCHOLARSHIP' invalid as numeric destination
```

Arithmetic is permitted only on numeric data names. UNI-SCHOLARSHIP, however, was defined in line 44 as an alphanumeric rather than a numeric data name, and hence the error.

Correction: Change the PICTURE clause in line 44 from X(6) to 9(6).

```
202 C Non-unique reference to STU-CREDITS accepted
202 E Undefined symbol 'DET-CREDITS'
```

This error is identical to the earlier nonunique message from lines 163, 174, 176, 177, and 179.

Correction: This error will disappear after changing STU-CREDITS to DET-CREDITS in line 81.

```
209 E Record name not 01 level
```

A WRITE statement, such as the one in line 209, requires a record name rather than a file name.

Correction: Change line 209 to WRITE PRINT-LINE instead of WRITE PRINT-FILE.

```
216 E Undefined symbol 'UNI-UNION-FEE'
```

This error is identical to the one in line 194 and is due to the omitted hyphens in the definition of UNI-UNION-FEE.

Correction: None required beyond the previous correction to line 42.

```
218 W Expected numeric data-name; found 'UNI-SCHOLARSHIP'; converted to
numeric and accepted
```

This error is also due to the definition of UNI-SCHOLARSHIP (line 44) as alphanumeric (PIC X) rather than numeric and will disappear with the previous correction.

Correction: None required beyond the previous correction to line 44.

Common Compilation Errors

Compilation errors are a fact of life. Don't be discouraged if you have many compilation errors in your first few attempts, and don't be surprised if you have several pages of diagnostics. Remember that a single error in a COBOL program can result in many error messages, and that several errors often can be made to disappear with one correction. Before leaving the subject, it is worthwhile to review a list of common errors and suggested ways to avoid them:

Nonunique data names. This error occurs because the same data name is defined in two different records or twice within the same record. For example, CREDITS might be specified as an input field in STUDENT-FILE and again as output in a detail line. You can avoid the problem by prefixing every data name within a record by a unique prefix as shown below:

```
01  STUDENT-RECORD
    05  STU-NAME
        10  STU-LAST-NAME
        10  STU-INITIALS
    05  STU-CREDITS
    05  STU-UNION-MEMBER
    05  STU-SCHOLARSHIP
    05  STU-GPA
```

Omitted (or extra) periods. Every COBOL sentence should have a period. Omission in the first three divisions often results in the compiler's assumption of a period where one belongs, and such errors are generally harmless. The effect is far more serious in the Procedure Division, where missing and/or extra periods affect the generated logic.

Omitted space before or after an arithmetic operator. The arithmetic operators, **, *, /, +, and – all require a space before and after (a typical error for BASIC programmers, since the space is not required in that language).

Invalid picture clause for numeric entry. All data names used in arithmetic statements must have numeric picture clauses consisting of 9's, an implied decimal point, and an optional sign.

Conflicting picture and value clause. Numeric pictures must have numeric values (no quotes); nonnumeric pictures must have nonnumeric values (enclosed in quotes). Both entries below are *invalid.*

```
05  TOTAL    PIC 9(3)  VALUE '123'.
05  TITLE    PIC X(3)  VALUE 123.
```

Inadvertent use of COBOL reserved words. COBOL has a list of some 300 reserved words that can be used only in their designated sense; any other use results in one or several diagnostics. Some reserved words are obvious, for example, WORKING-STORAGE, IDENTIFICATION, ENVIRONMENT, DATA, and PROCEDURE. Others—such as CODE, DATE, START, and REPORT—are less obvious. Instead of memorizing the list or continually referring to it, we suggest this simple rule of thumb: *Always use a hyphen in every data name you create.* This will work more than 99% of the time.

Conflicting RECORD CONTAINS clause and FD record description. This is a common error, even for established programmers. It can stem from careless addition in that the sum of the pictures in the FD does not equal the number of characters in the RECORD CONTAINS clause. It can also result from other errors within the Data Division, for example, when an entry containing a PICTURE clause is flagged. (Remember that if an E-level diagnostic occurs, that entry will be ignored, and the count is thrown off.)

Receiving field too small to accommodate sending field. This is an extremely common error, often associated with edited pictures (editing is discussed in Chapter 7). Consider the entries:

```
05  PRINT-TOTAL-PAY     PIC $$,$$$.
05  WS-TOTAL-PAY        PIC 9(5).

MOVE WS-TOTAL-PAY TO PRINT-TOTAL-PAY.
```

The MOVE statement would generate the warning that the receiving field may be too small to accommodate the sending field. The greatest possible value for WS-TOTAL-PAY is 99,999; the largest possible value that could be printed by PRINT-TOTAL-PAY is $9,999. Even though the picture for the print field contains five $'s, one $ must always be printed along with the numeric characters, hence the warning.

Omitted (or extra) hyphens in a data name. This is a careless error, but one that occurs too often. If, for example, we define PRINT-TOTAL-PAY in the Data Division and then reference PRINT TOTAL-PAY in the Procedure Division, the compiler catches the inconsistency. It doesn't state that a hyphen was omitted, but indicates that PRINT and TOTAL-PAY are undefined.

A related error is the insertion of extra hyphens where they don't belong, for example, WORKING-STORAGE-SECTION or DATA-DIVISION.

Misspelled data names or reserved words. Too many COBOL students are poor spellers. Sound strange? How do you spell *environment*? One or many errors can result, depending on which word was spelled incorrectly.

Reading a record name or writing a file name. The COBOL rule is very simple—read a file and write a record—but many people get it confused. Consider:

```
FD  STUDENT-FILE
    DATA RECORD IS STUDENT-RECORD.

FD  PRINT-FILE
    DATA RECORD IS PRINT-RECORD.
```

Correct entries:

```
    READ STUDENT-FILE . . .
    WRITE PRINT-RECORD . . .
```

Incorrect entries:

```
    READ STUDENT-RECORD . . .
    WRITE PRINT-FILE . . .
```

Going past column 72. This error can cause any of the preceding errors as well as a host of others. A COBOL statement must end in column 72 or before; columns 73–80 are left blank or used for program identification. (The 72-column restriction does not apply to data.)

Errors in Execution

After a program has been successfully compiled, it can proceed to execution, and therein lie the strength and weakness of the computer. The primary attractiveness of the machine is its ability to perform its task quickly; its weakness stems from the fact that it does exactly what it has been instructed to do. The machine cannot think for itself; the programmer must think for the machine. If you were to inadvertently instruct the computer to compute tuition by charging $20 instead of $200 per credit, then that is what it would do.

To give you an idea of what can happen, we have deliberately altered the original tuition billing program of Chapter 5 and created a new program, shown in Figure 6.3. That, in turn, created the *invalid* output of Figure 6.4a, which at first glance resembles the valid output of Figure 6.4b (which is reproduced from Chapter 5). There are, however, several subtle errors in Figure 6.4a:

1. The university total for union fees is zero rather than a computed amount.

Figure 6.3 Tuition Billing Program with Execution Errors

```
IDENTIFICATION DIVISION.
PROGRAM-ID.    TUIT6EXE.
AUTHOR.        CAROL VAZQUEZ VILLAR.

ENVIRONMENT DIVISION.
INPUT-OUTPUT SECTION.
FILE-CONTROL.
    SELECT STUDENT-FILE
        ASSIGN TO UT-S-SYSIN.
    SELECT PRINT-FILE
```

Figure 6.3 *(continued)*

```
               ASSIGN TO UT-S-SYSOUT.

       DATA DIVISION.
       FILE SECTION.
       FD  STUDENT-FILE
           RECORD CONTAINS 27 CHARACTERS.
       01  STUDENT-RECORD.
           05  STU-NAME.
               10  STU-LAST-NAME    PIC X(15).
               10  STU-INITIALS     PIC XX.
           05  STU-CREDITS          PIC 9(2).
           05  STU-UNION-MEMBER     PIC X.
           05  STU-SCHOLARSHIP      PIC 9(4).
           05  STU-GPA              PIC 999.

       FD  PRINT-FILE
           RECORD CONTAINS 132 CHARACTERS.
       01  PRINT-LINE               PIC X(132).

       WORKING-STORAGE SECTION.
       01  DATA-REMAINS-SWITCH      PIC X(2)  VALUE SPACES.

       01  INDIVIDUAL-CALCULATIONS.
           05  IND-TUITION          PIC 9(4)  VALUE ZEROS.
           05  IND-ACTIVITY-FEE     PIC 9(2)  VALUE ZEROS.
           05  IND-UNION-FEE        PIC 9(2)  VALUE ZEROS.
           05  IND-SCHOLARSHIP      PIC 9(4)  VALUE ZEROS.
           05  IND-BILL             PIC 9(6)  VALUE ZEROS.

       01  UNIVERSITY-TOTALS.
           05  UNI-TUITION          PIC 9(6)  VALUE ZEROS.
           05  UNI-UNION-FEE        PIC 9(4)  VALUE ZEROS.
           05  UNI-ACTIVITY-FEE     PIC 9(4)  VALUE ZEROS.
           05  UNI-SCHOLARSHIP      PIC 9(6)  VALUE ZEROS.
           05  UNI-IND-BILL         PIC 9(6)  VALUE ZEROS.

       01  CONSTANTS-AND-RATES.
           05  PRICE-PER-CREDIT     PIC 9(3)  VALUE 200.
           05  UNION-FEE            PIC 9(2)  VALUE 25.
           05  ACTIVITY-FEES.
               10  1ST-ACTIVITY-FEE PIC 99    VALUE 25.
               10  1ST-CREDIT-LIMIT PIC 99    VALUE 6.
               10  2ND-ACTIVITY-FEE PIC 99    VALUE 50.
               10  2ND-CREDIT-LIMIT PIC 99    VALUE 12.
               10  3RD-ACTIVITY-FEE PIC 99    VALUE 75.
           05  MINIMUM-SCHOLAR-GPA  PIC 9V9   VALUE 2.5.

       01  HEADING-LINE.
           05  FILLER               PIC X     VALUE SPACES.
           05  FILLER               PIC X(12) VALUE 'STUDENT NAME'.
```

Implied decimal place missing (annotation pointing to `PIC 999.` of STU-GPA)

Figure 6.3 *(continued)*

```
       05  FILLER                 PIC X(10) VALUE SPACES.
       05  FILLER                 PIC X(7)  VALUE 'CREDITS'.
       05  FILLER                 PIC X(2)  VALUE SPACES.
       05  FILLER                 PIC X(7)  VALUE 'TUITION'.
       05  FILLER                 PIC X(2)  VALUE SPACES.
       05  FILLER                 PIC X(9)  VALUE 'UNION FEE'.
       05  FILLER                 PIC X(2)  VALUE SPACES.
       05  FILLER                 PIC X(7)  VALUE 'ACT FEE'.
       05  FILLER                 PIC X(2)  VALUE SPACES.
       05  FILLER                 PIC X(11) VALUE 'SCHOLARSHIP'.
       05  FILLER                 PIC X(2)  VALUE SPACES.
       05  FILLER                 PIC X(10) VALUE 'TOTAL BILL'.
       05  FILLER                 PIC X(48) VALUE SPACES.

   01  DETAIL-LINE.
       05  FILLER                 PIC X     VALUE SPACES.
       05  DET-LAST-NAME          PIC X(15).
       05  FILLER                 PIC X(2)  VALUE SPACES.
       05  DET-INITIALS           PIC X(2).
       05  FILLER                 PIC X(5)  VALUE SPACES.
       05  DET-CREDITS            PIC 9(2).
       05  FILLER                 PIC X(6)  VALUE SPACES.
       05  DET-TUITION            PIC 9(6).
       05  FILLER                 PIC X(7)  VALUE SPACES.
       05  DET-UNION-FEE          PIC 9(3).
       05  FILLER                 PIC X(6)  VALUE SPACES.
       05  DET-ACTIVITY-FEE       PIC 9(3).
       05  FILLER                 PIC X(8)  VALUE SPACES.
       05  DET-SCHOLARSHIP        PIC 9(5).
       05  FILLER                 PIC X(6)  VALUE SPACES.
       05  DET-IND-BILL           PIC 9(6).
       05  FILLER                 PIC X(49) VALUE SPACES.

   01  DASH-LINE.
       05  FILLER                 PIC X(31) VALUE SPACES.
       05  FILLER                 PIC X(8)  VALUE ALL '-'.
       05  FILLER                 PIC X(2)  VALUE SPACES.
       05  FILLER                 PIC X(8)  VALUE ALL '-'.
       05  FILLER                 PIC X(2)  VALUE SPACES.
       05  FILLER                 PIC X(7)  VALUE ALL '-'.
       05  FILLER                 PIC X(6)  VALUE SPACES.
       05  FILLER                 PIC X(7)  VALUE ALL '-'.
       05  FILLER                 PIC X(5)  VALUE SPACES.
       05  FILLER                 PIC X(7)  VALUE ALL '-'.
       05  FILLER                 PIC X(49) VALUE SPACES.

   01  TOTAL-LINE.
       05  FILLER                 PIC X(8)  VALUE SPACES.
       05  FILLER                 PIC X(17)
               VALUE 'UNIVERSITY TOTALS'.
```

Figure 6.3 *(continued)*

```
           05  FILLER                PIC X(8)  VALUE SPACES.
           05  TOT-TUITION           PIC 9(6).
           05  FILLER                PIC X(6)  VALUE SPACES.
           05  TOT-UNION-FEE         PIC 9(4).
           05  FILLER                PIC X(5)  VALUE SPACES.
           05  TOT-ACTIVITY-FEE      PIC 9(4).
           05  FILLER                PIC X(7)  VALUE SPACES.
           05  TOT-SCHOLARSHIP       PIC 9(6).
           05  FILLER                PIC X(6)  VALUE SPACES.
           05  TOT-IND-BILL          PIC 9(6).
           05  FILLER                PIC X(49) VALUE SPACES.

       PROCEDURE DIVISION.
       PREPARE-TUITION-REPORT.
           OPEN INPUT STUDENT-FILE
                OUTPUT PRINT-FILE.
           PERFORM WRITE-HEADING-LINE.
           PERFORM READ-STUDENT-FILE.
           PERFORM PROCESS-STUDENT-RECORD
                UNTIL DATA-REMAINS-SWITCH = 'NO'.
           PERFORM WRITE-UNIVERSITY-TOTALS.
           CLOSE STUDENT-FILE
                 PRINT-FILE.
           STOP RUN.

       WRITE-HEADING-LINE.
           MOVE HEADING-LINE TO PRINT-LINE.
           WRITE PRINT-LINE
               AFTER ADVANCING PAGE.
           MOVE SPACES TO PRINT-LINE.
           WRITE PRINT-LINE.

       READ-STUDENT-FILE.
           READ STUDENT-FILE
               AT END MOVE 'NO' TO DATA-REMAINS-SWITCH
           END-READ.

       PROCESS-STUDENT-RECORD.
           PERFORM READ-STUDENT-FILE.
           PERFORM COMPUTE-INDIVIDUAL-BILL.
           PERFORM INCREMENT-UNIVERSITY-TOTALS
           PERFORM WRITE-DETAIL-LINE.

       COMPUTE-INDIVIDUAL-BILL.
           PERFORM COMPUTE-TUITION.
           PERFORM COMPUTE-UNION-FEE.
           PERFORM COMPUTE-ACTIVITY-FEE.
           PERFORM COMPUTE-SCHOLARSHIP.
           COMPUTE IND-BILL = IND-TUITION + IND-UNION-FEE +
              IND-ACTIVITY-FEE - IND-SCHOLARSHIP.
```

READ statement incorrectly placed

Figure 6.3 *(continued)*

```
COMPUTE-TUITION.
    COMPUTE IND-TUITION = PRICE-PER-CREDIT * STU-CREDITS.

COMPUTE-UNION-FEE.
    IF STU-UNION-MEMBER = 'Y'
       MOVE ZERO TO IND-UNION-FEE
    ELSE
       MOVE UNION-FEE TO IND-UNION-FEE
    END-IF.

COMPUTE-ACTIVITY-FEE.
    EVALUATE TRUE
        WHEN STU-CREDITS <= 1ST-CREDIT-LIMIT
            MOVE 1ST-ACTIVITY-FEE TO IND-ACTIVITY-FEE
        WHEN STU-CREDITS > 1ST-CREDIT-LIMIT
            AND STU-CREDITS <= 2ND-CREDIT-LIMIT
                MOVE 2ND-ACTIVITY-FEE TO IND-ACTIVITY-FEE
        WHEN STU-CREDITS > 2ND-CREDIT-LIMIT
            MOVE 3RD-ACTIVITY-FEE TO IND-ACTIVITY-FEE
        WHEN OTHER
            DISPLAY 'INVALID CREDITS FOR: ' STU-NAME
    END-EVALUATE.

COMPUTE-SCHOLARSHIP.
    IF STU-GPA > MINIMUM-SCHOLAR-GPA
       MOVE STU-SCHOLARSHIP TO IND-SCHOLARSHIP
    ELSE
       MOVE ZERO TO IND-SCHOLARSHIP
    END-IF.

INCREMENT-UNIVERSITY-TOTALS.
    ADD IND-TUITION      TO UNI-TUITION.
    ADD IND-ACTIVITY-FEE TO UNI-ACTIVITY-FEE.
    ADD IND-SCHOLARSHIP  TO UNI-SCHOLARSHIP.
    ADD IND-BILL         TO UNI-IND-BILL.

WRITE-DETAIL-LINE.
    MOVE STU-LAST-NAME TO DET-LAST-NAME.
    MOVE STU-INITIALS TO DET-INITIALS.
    MOVE STU-CREDITS TO DET-CREDITS.
    MOVE IND-TUITION TO DET-TUITION.
    MOVE IND-UNION-FEE TO DET-UNION-FEE.
    MOVE IND-ACTIVITY-FEE TO DET-ACTIVITY-FEE.
    MOVE IND-SCHOLARSHIP TO DET-SCHOLARSHIP.
    MOVE IND-BILL TO DET-IND-BILL.
    MOVE DETAIL-LINE TO PRINT-LINE.
    WRITE PRINT-LINE
        AFTER ADVANCING 1 LINE.
```

Order of IF statement is reversed

ADD statement is missing for UNI-UNION-FEE

Figure 6.3 *(continued)*

```
211        WRITE-UNIVERSITY-TOTALS.
212            MOVE DASH-LINE TO PRINT-LINE.
213            WRITE PRINT-LINE.
214            MOVE UNI-TUITION TO TOT-TUITION.
215            MOVE UNI-UNION-FEE TO TOT-UNION-FEE.
216            MOVE UNI-ACTIVITY-FEE TO TOT-ACTIVITY-FEE.
217            MOVE UNI-SCHOLARSHIP TO TOT-SCHOLARSHIP.
218            MOVE IND-BILL TO TOT-IND-BILL.
219            MOVE TOTAL-LINE TO PRINT-LINE.
220            WRITE PRINT-LINE
221                AFTER ADVANCING 1 LINE.
```

Wrong field is moved to print line (callout for line 218)

2. The sum of the individual bills in the total line appears as 850 (the amount for the last record), rather than a running total of 24550.

3. The union fees are reversed for each student; for example, James and Baker are charged $25 when they should be charged nothing, and conversely, Part-Timer and Jones are charged nothing when their fee is $25.

4. The last record for NB Kerbel is processed twice; a related error is that the first record for Smith was omitted.

5. James was erroneously awarded a scholarship of $500; James, however, does not qualify because his average is below 2.5.

We emphasize that these execution errors are not contrived but are typical of students and beginning programmers. Even the accomplished practitioner can be guilty of similar errors when rushed or careless. Realize also that execution errors occur without fanfare. There are no compiler diagnostics to warn of impending trouble. The program has compiled cleanly, and there is nothing to indicate a problem.

The errors in Figure 6.3 are errors in execution, rather than compilation. The program compiled cleanly because it is *syntactically correct,* but it executed improperly because it is *logically incorrect.* Nevertheless, the program did precisely what it was instructed to do, which unfortunately, is not what the programmer wanted it to do. It is necessary, therefore, to find the source of each logic error as discussed below:

1. The totals for the university are computed in the paragraph INCREMENT-UNIVERSITY-TOTALS (lines 192–196) in which the individual amounts for the student being processed are added to the running university totals. Note, however, that the ADD statement for UNI-UNION-FEE is conspicuously absent and hence the value of UNI-UNION-FEE remains unchanged throughout the program.

2. UNI-IND-BILL is defined in line 45 and correctly incremented for each record in line 196; so far, so good. However, when the total line is built in line 218, IND-BILL rather than UNI-IND-BILL is moved to TOT-IND-BILL, causing the individual last bill (for Kerbel) to be printed as the total.

3. IND-UNION-FEE is calculated in a simple IF statement in lines 166–170, in which the IF and ELSE clauses are reversed; that is, the union fee is $25 for

Figure 6.4 Tuition Billing Report Comparisons—Invalid and Valid

4 Smith is missing
3 Union fees are reversed
5 Should not have a scholarship
2 Total is incorrect
1 Union fee was not summed
4 Last student appears twice

STUDENT NAME		CREDITS	TUITION	UNION FEE	ACT FEE	SCHOLARSHIP	TOTAL BILL
JAMES	HR	15	003000	025	075	00500	002600
BAKER	SR	09	001800	025	050	00500	001375
PART-TIMER	JR	03	000600	000	025	00000	000625
JONES	PL	15	003000	000	075	00000	003075
HEAVYWORKER	HM	18	003600	025	075	00000	003700
LEE	BL	18	003600	025	075	00000	003700
CLARK	JC	06	001200	025	025	00000	001250
GROSSMAN	SE	07	001400	025	050	00000	001475
FRANKEL	LF	10	002000	025	050	00000	002075
BENWAY	CT	03	000600	025	025	00250	000400
KERBEL	NB	04	000800	025	025	00000	000850
KERBEL	NB	04	000800	025	025	00000	000850
			--------	--------	-------	-------	-------
UNIVERSITY TOTALS			022400	0000	0575	001250	000850

(a) Invalid Output

STUDENT NAME		CREDITS	TUITION	UNION FEE	ACT FEE	SCHOLARSHIP	TOTAL BILL
SMITH	JB	15	003000	025	075	00000	003100
JAMES	HR	15	003000	000	075	00000	003075
BAKER	SR	09	001800	000	050	00500	001350
PART-TIMER	JR	03	000600	025	025	00000	000650
JONES	PL	15	003000	025	075	00000	003100
HEAVYWORKER	HM	18	003600	000	075	00000	003675
LEE	BL	18	003600	000	075	00000	003675
CLARK	JC	06	001200	000	025	00000	001225
GROSSMAN	SE	07	001400	000	050	00000	001450
FRANKEL	LF	10	002000	000	050	00000	002050
BENWAY	CT	03	000600	000	025	00250	000375
KERBEL	NB	04	000800	000	025	00000	000825
			--------	--------	-------	-------	-------
UNIVERSITY TOTALS			024600	0075	0625	000750	024550

(b) Valid Output (from Chapter 5)

students who belong to the union as indicated by a Y in the appropriate incoming field.

4. The *correct* implementation to process a file requires an initial (priming) READ in the paragraph PREPARE-TUITION-REPORT, as well as a second READ statement as the *last* statement in the paragraph PROCESS-STUDENT-RECORD. The errors for Kerbel and Smith occur because the latter READ statement was *incorrectly* moved to the beginning of the performed routine.

To understand the effect of the misplaced statement, consider a file with two records. The first record is read by the initial READ statement, after which the paragraph PROCESS-STUDENT-RECORD is entered. The second READ statement (incorrectly placed at the beginning of the paragraph) is executed immediately so that the first record is effectively lost.

Moreover, when the last statement in PROCESS-STUDENT-RECORD is executed, the end of file has not yet been reached. This in turn causes PROCESS-STUDENT-RECORD to be executed a *second* time, even though there are no more records. The end of file is sensed immediately in line 149, but the perform is not terminated until line 152, so that the intermediate statements are executed a second time for the previous record.

5. The definition of STU-GPA in line 24 incorrectly omits the implied decimal point in the PICTURE clause. Hence all incoming averages will be interpreted as ten times their true value (i.e., 2.5 will be stored as 25). Thus, all students will have an average greater than 2.5, and hence all students with potential scholarships will receive the award.

File Status Codes

Input/Output operations occur throughout the execution of a COBOL program and consequently are a source of frequent error. The statements in Figure 6.5 represent one of the most common types of student errors—attempting to read from a file that doesn't exist.

Figure 6.5 File Status Codes

```
SELECT STUDENT-FILE
    ASSIGN TO UT-S-SYSIN.
SELECT PRINT-FILE
    ASSIGN TO UT-S-SYSOUT.
```

(a) COBOL SELECT Statements

```
SET SYSIN=TUITION.DOT
SET SYSOUT=REPORT[N]
```

Filename spelled incorrectly

(b) DOS SET Commands

```
TUIT6COM COB     10140 06-10-92   6:28p
TUIT6EXE COB      9997 06-17-92   4:08p
TUIT6EXE LST     11112 06-17-92   4:08p
TUIT6EXE OBJ      3554 06-17-92   4:08p
TUIT6EXE SYM     12288 06-17-92   4:08p
TUIT6EXE EXE     33290 06-17-92   4:09p
TUIT6EXE MAP      1107 06-17-92   4:09p
TUITION  DAT       349 04-27-89  10:25p
```

The data file is TUITION.DAT

(c) Directory

```
File status 35 on C:TUITION.DOT
```

File status code indicates file is not present

(d) Attempted Execution

The COBOL SELECT statement ties a programmer-chosen file name to an implementor name. The operating system control statement—for example, a DOS SET statement on a PC—associates the implementor name with a specific file on disk. The combination of the two statements, SELECT and SET, associates a COBOL file, such as STUDENT-FILE in Figure 6.5a, with a file on disk, such as TUITION.DOT in Figure 6.5b.

The problem is that TUITION.DOT does not exist; look carefully at the directory in Figure 6.5c and see that it contains TUITION.DAT rather than TUITION.DOT. In other words the COBOL program is attempting to read from a file that isn't there, an impossible situation for the program, that leads to an execution error that terminates execution as shown in Figure 6.5d.

The cause of the error is easily determined, however, by examination of the associated ***file status*** code. (Table 18.1 on page 555 provides a listing of file status codes and their associated messages.) File status 35 indicates an I/O error in an OPEN statement that attempted to read from a file that wasn't present. All that is needed to correct the problem is to change the SET statement for SYSIN to reflect TUITION.DAT rather than TUITION.DOT.

Tips for Debugging

It was easy to find the execution errors just discussed because we created them in the first place, and hence we knew exactly where to look. In practice, however, it is not so easy and so we offer several suggestions to facilitate debugging.

The Cross-Reference Listing

A ***cross-reference listing*** is an alphabetical listing of all data names and paragraph names in a program, together with the statements in which they are referenced and/or modified. An abbreviated cross-reference listing for the program in Figure 6.3 is shown in Figure 6.6.

Figure 6.6 Abbreviated Cross-Reference Listing

NAME	LINE	LV	SEG	OFF	SIZE	TYPE	O/G	REFERENCE	
1ST-ACTIVITY-FEE	51	10	D00	275	2	DU		175R	
1ST-CREDIT-LIMIT	52	10	D00	277	2	DU		174R	176R
2ND-ACTIVITY-FEE	53	10	D00	279	2	DU		178R	
2ND-CREDIT-LIMIT	54	10	D00	281	2	DU		177R	179R
3RD-ACTIVITY-FEE	55	10	D00	283	2	DU		180R	
COMPUTE-ACTIVITY-FEE	172		C00		9	PAR		157E	
COMPUTE-INDIVIDUAL-BILL	154		C00		4	PAR		150E	
COMPUTE-SCHOLARSHIP	185		C00		10	PAR		158E	
COMPUTE-TUITION	162		C00		7	PAR		155E	
COMPUTE-UNION-FEE	165		C00		8	PAR		156E	
DASH-LINE	94	01	D00	552	132	GRP		212R	
DATA-REMAINS-SWITCH	31	01	D00	224	2	AN		130R	145M
DET-ACTIVITY-FEE	87	05	D00	475	3	DU		204M	
DET-CREDITS	81	05	D00	445	2	DU		201M	

DU signifies unsigned numeric

Paragraph

Referenced in line 130
Modified in line 145

Defined in line 31 and is a 01 level entry

2- byte alphanumeric field

Figure 6.6 Abbreviated Cross-Reference Listing

```
DET-IND-BILL                     91 05   D00   497     6  DU     206M
DET-INITIALS                     79 05   D00   438     2  AN     200M
DET-LAST-NAME                    77 05   D00   421    15  AN     199M
DET-SCHOLARSHIP                  89 05   D00   486     5  DU     205M
DET-TUITION                      83 05   D00   453     6  DU     202M
DET-UNION-FEE                    85 05   D00   466     3  DU     203M
DETAIL-LINE                      75 01   D00   420   132  GRP    207R
HEADING-LINE                     58 01   D00   288   132  GRP    137R
INCREMENT-UNIVERSITY-TOTALS     192      C00           5  PAR    151E
.
    .
        .
STUDENT-FILE                     15      D00   848    27  FD     1250    132C
                                                                 144R
TOT-ACTIVITY-FEE                116 05   D00   738     4  DU     216M
TOT-IND-BILL                    120 05   D00   761     6  DU     218M
TOT-SCHOLARSHIP                 118 05   D00   749     6  DU     217M
TOT-TUITION                     112 05   D00   717     6  DU     214M
TOT-UNION-FEE                   114 05   D00   729     4  DU     215M
TOTAL-LINE                      107 01   D00   684   132  GRP    219R
UNI-ACTIVITY-FEE                 43 05   D00   254     4  DU     194M    216R
UNI-IND-BILL                     45 05   D00   264     6  DU     196M
UNI-SCHOLARSHIP                  44 05   D00   258     6  DU     195M    217R
UNI-TUITION                      41 05   D00   244     6  DU     193M    214R
UNI-UNION-FEE                    42 05   D00   250     4  DU     215R
UNION-FEE                        49 05   D00   273     2  DU     169R
WRITE-DETAIL-LINE               198      C00           6  PAR    152E
WRITE-HEADING-LINE              136      C00              PAR    127E
WRITE-UNIVERSITY-TOTALS         211      C00           3  PAR    131E
```

FD for STUDENT-FILE

Group item

Referenced in line 215 but never modified

The cross-reference listing is somewhat overwhelming at first, but on closer examination, is seen to contain a wealth of information. Consider, for example, the entries for DATA-REMAINS-SWITCH. Reading from left to right (and omitting the SEG and OFF entries, which require a knowledge of assembler language), we see that DATA-REMAINS-SWITCH is defined in line 31, that it is a 01-level entry, that it is two bytes in length, and that it is an alphanumeric (AN) entry. The last two entries, 130R and 145M, reference statements in the Procedure Division; that is, DATA-REMAINS-SWITCH is *referenced* (by the UNTIL clause) in line 130 and *modified* (by the MOVE statement) in line 145.

Other data names in the cross-reference listing have different entries in the TYPE column depending on the type of data name. DU signifies an unsigned numeric field such as 1ST-ACTIVITY-FEE (signed numbers are discussed in Chapter 7). PAR, GRP, and FD denote a paragraph, group item, and file description, respectively.

The Procedure Division references in the cross-reference listing are invaluable in debugging. Consider, for example, the failure to increment the total union fee in the program of Figure 6.4, and how the nature of this error is immediately apparent from the cross-reference listing. The entry for UNI-UNION-FEE shows it to be referenced (by the MOVE statement in line 215) but never modified; that is, there is no statement to modify the value of UNI-UNION-FEE, indicating that the data name is never incremented and suggesting a missing ADD statement.

The cross-reference listing is available as a compiler option with most compilers.

DISPLAY Statement

It is often helpful to display intermediate results of a program as the program is being executed. One way to accomplish this is through the insertion of **DISPLAY** statements at strategic points in the program. The statement enables you to print the value of one or more data names and/or one or more literals without having to format a record description. Consider:

$$\underline{\texttt{DISPLAY}} \begin{Bmatrix} \texttt{identifier-1} \\ \texttt{literal-1} \end{Bmatrix} \left[\begin{Bmatrix} \texttt{identifier-2} \\ \texttt{literal-2} \end{Bmatrix} \right] \ldots$$

The DISPLAY statement produces the contents of each item listed in the order shown. For example,

1. DISPLAY STUDENT-RECORD.
2. DISPLAY 'Record being processed: ' STUDENT-RECORD.
3. DISPLAY 'COMPUTE-TUITION paragraph is entered'
4. DISPLAY 'Student data: ' STU-NAME ' ' STU-CREDITS.

Examples one and two both display the value of the data name STUDENT-RECORD; the second example, however, precedes the data name with a literal to facilitate interpretation of the output. Example three displays just a literal but could be used (in conjunction with similar DISPLAY statements in other paragraphs) to show the flow of program execution. Example four displays a literal and two data names.

Interactive Debugger

An ***interactive debugger*** monitors the execution of a COBOL program by pausing at designated points within the program, at which time you can display the value of a data name(s) or take other action. It is similar in concept to inserting a series of DISPLAY statements except it is far more flexible and easier to use.

Figure 6.7 shows the opening screen of the interactive debugger provided with the Realia compiler (see exercise 4 in Appendix B) as it would appear in conjunction with Figure 6.4. The highlighted statement (OPEN INPUT STUDENT FILE in the example) is the statement about to be executed pending instructions from the user, which are provided through a series of commands listed in the bottom portion of the screen.

You could, for example, tell the program to advance to the next statement, or you could continue execution to a designated break point, whereupon the debugger would again pause for further instruction. At any point you may examine and/or change the value of one or more data names. We have found the interactive debugger to be an invaluable tool and urge you to explore the capabilities of your compiler.

Figure 6.7 Interactive Debugging (REALDBUG)

```
Realia RealDBUG 1.02e | TUIT6EXE | Enter next command

     05  FILLER              PIC X(48) VALUE SPACES.

PROCEDURE DIVISION.
PREPARE-TUITION-REPORT.
    OPEN INPUT STUDENT-FILE
         OUTPUT PRINT-FILE.
    PERFORM WRITE-HEADING-LINE.
    PERFORM READ-STUDENT-FILE.
    PERFORM PROCESS-STUDENT-RECORD
         UNTIL DATA-REMAINS-SWITCH = 'NO'.
    PERFORM WRITE-UNIVERSITY-TOTALS.
    CLOSE STUDENT-FILE
          PRINT-FILE.
    STOP RUN.

WRITE-HEADING-LINE.

Advance     Breakpoint   Examine      Find defn    Goto range    Jump back
Look value  Next range   Program set  Quit Alt-F2  Range set     Step ranges
Trace       Unset range  View value   Where defn   eXecute set   0-9 Line num
CURSOR: ↑ ↓ →← Ctrl Tab →← Home CR  SCROLL: PgDn/Up F1 F2  HELP: Alt-F1,A-Z,0-9
```

Highlighted statement is about to be executed

The Structured Walkthrough

Although it is reasonable to expect errors, the programmer is also expected (reasonably) to find and correct them. Until recently, error detection and correction was a lonely activity. A programmer was encouraged to ***desk check***—that is, read and reread the code—in an attempt to discern logical errors before they occurred. Desk checking is still an important activity, but it is frequently supplemented by a newer technique, the ***structured walkthrough***.

The walkthrough brings the evaluation into the open. It requires a programmer to have his or her work reviewed formally and periodically by a peer group. The theory is simple—a programmer is too close to his or her work to see potential problems adequately and evaluate them objectively. The purpose of the walkthrough is to ensure that all specifications are met, and that the logic and its COBOL implementation are correct.

The earlier an error is found, the easier it is to correct and thus the single most important objective of a walkthrough is *early error detection*. Walkthroughs occur at several stages during a project, beginning in the analysis phase, where the purpose is to ensure that the systems analyst has understood the user's requirements. Walkthroughs occur again during the design phase, after the programmer has developed a hierarchy chart and/or associated pseudocode. Finally, walkthroughs occur during the implementation phase, during which the programmer presents actual code prior to testing.

Walkthroughs are scheduled by the person being reviewed, who also selects the reviewers. The programmer distributes copies of the work (for example, a hierarchy chart, pseudocode, or a COBOL program) prior to the session. Reviewers are supposed to study the material in advance so that they can discuss it intelligently. At the walkthrough itself, the programmer presents the material objectively, concisely, and dispassionately. He or she should encourage discussion and be genuinely glad when errors are discovered.

One of the reviewers should function as a ***moderator*** to keep the discussion on track. Another should act as a ***secretary*** and maintain an ***action list*** of problems uncovered during the session. At the end of the walkthrough the action list is given to the programmer, who in turn is expected to correct the errors and notify attendees accordingly. The objective of the walkthrough is to find errors, not to correct them. The latter is accomplished by the programmer upon receipt of the action list.

The preceding discussion may read well in theory, but programmers often dislike the walkthrough concept. The probable reason is that they dislike having their work reviewed and regard criticism of code as a personal affront, intended or otherwise. This attitude is natural and stems from years of working as individuals.

In addition, walkthroughs can and have become unpleasant and ego-deflating experiences. "Structured walkover" and "stomp through" are terms that have been applied to less-than-successful sessions. Only if the atmosphere is kept open and nondefensive, only if the discussion is restricted to major problems rather than trivial errors, and only if personality clashes are avoided can the walkthrough be an effective technique. To have any chance of success, programmers who function as both reviewer and reviewee must adhere to the following guidelines:

1. *The program, and not the programmer, is reviewed.* Structured walkthroughs are intended to find programming problems; they will not be used by management as an evaluation tool. No one should keep count of how many errors are found in an individual's work or how many errors one finds in someone else's. It is quite logical, therefore, to exclude the project manager—that is, the individual in charge of salaries and promotions—from review sessions.

2. *Emphasis is on error detection, not correction.* It is assumed that the individual being reviewed will take the necessary corrective action. Reviewers should not harp on errors by discussing how to correct them; indeed, no corrections whatever are made during a walkthrough.

3. *Everyone, from senior analyst to trainee, has his or her work reviewed.* This avoids singling out an individual and further removes any stigma from having one's work reviewed. It also promotes the give-and-take atmosphere that is so vital to making the concept work.

4. *A list of well-defined objectives for each session should be specified in advance.* Adherence to this guideline keeps the discussion on track and helps to guarantee productive discussions. Another guideline is to impose a predetermined time limit, from half an hour to two hours. Walkthroughs will eventually cease to be productive and degenerate into a discussion of last night's ball game, the new manager, the latest rumor, or some other "hot" topic. The situation should be anticipated and avoided, perhaps by scheduling walkthroughs an hour before lunch. If all of the walkthrough's objectives have not been met when the deadline is reached, schedule a second session.

5. *Participation must be encouraged and demanded from the reviewers.* A walkthrough will indeed become a waste of time if no one has anything to say. Let it be known in advance that each reviewer will be expected to make at least two comments, one positive and one negative. Alternatively, require each reviewer to come to the session with a list of at least three questions.

SUMMARY

Points to Remember

- Compilation errors occur in the translation of COBOL to machine language and result from a violation of COBOL syntax, for example, a misspelled data name or an entry in the wrong column.
- Execution errors develop after compilation has taken place, and are caused by improper logic and/or improper COBOL implementation of valid logic.
- A cross-reference listing is a valuable aid in debugging as it provides an alphabetical list of all data names and paragraph names in the program, together with the statements in which they are referenced and/or modified.
- A program may compile cleanly and be logically correct yet still fail to execute if there are problems with the associated data files. File status codes are provided by the operating system to help determine the cause of such data management errors.
- DISPLAY statements can be inserted at strategic points within a program to display intermediate results and facilitate debugging. An interactive debugger provides a similar capability but with less effort and more flexibility.
- A structured walkthrough is an open evaluation of an individual's work by a group of his or her peers, with the primary objective of detecting errors as soon as possible in the development cycle.

Key Words and Concepts

Action list
Compilation error
Compiler option
Cross-reference listing
Debugging
Desk checking
Early error detection
Execution error
File status codes
Interactive debugger
Moderator
Secretary
Structured walkthrough

COBOL Element

DISPLAY

FILL-IN

1. _______________ errors occur in the translation of COBOL to machine language.
2. _______________ errors occur after a program has been successfully translated to machine language.
3. Incorrect translation of valid pseudocode into COBOL will most likely produce _______________ errors.
4. Misspelling a reserved word will most likely produce a _______________ error.
5. If a program _______________ cleanly, it means only that the program has been successfully translated into machine language.
6. _______________ errors are accompanied by some type of error message, whereas _______________ errors are frequently undetected by the computer.
7. The process of peer review is known as a _______________ _______________.
8. The errors that are detected during a _______________ _______________ are entered on an _______________ _______________, which is maintained by the secretary.
9. The emphasis in a structured walkthrough is on error _______________, not error _______________.
10. One suggestion for conducting successful walkthroughs is to remember that the _______________, and not the _______________, is reviewed.
11. A _______________ _______________ _______________ is an alphabetical list of all data and paragraph names within a program.
12. _______________ _______________ _______________ are helpful in detecting errors in execution that pertain to data management.

TRUE/FALSE

1. If a program compiles with no diagnostics, it must execute correctly.
2. If a program compiles with warning diagnostics, execution will be suppressed.
3. If a program contains logical errors but not syntactical errors, the compiler will print appropriate warnings.
4. A COBOL program is considered data by the COBOL compiler.
5. An error in one COBOL statement can cause errors in several other, apparently unrelated, statements.
6. There are several different levels (of severity) of compilation errors.
7. Paragraph names begin in the A margin.
8. Spaces are required before and after arithmetic symbols.
9. Spaces are required before and after punctuation symbols.
10. A data name that appears in a COMPUTE statement can be defined with a picture of X's.
11. Data names may contain blanks.

12. The contents of columns 73–80 are ignored by the compiler.
13. In a COBOL program one reads a record name and writes a file name.
14. The emphasis in a structured walkthrough is on error detection rather than error correction.
15. Walkthroughs should be held for trainees only, as these are the individuals most likely to make mistakes.
16. Managers typically do not attend walkthroughs.
17. A walkthrough generally takes a minimum of two hours.
18. Walkthroughs should be restricted to the coding phase of a project.

PROBLEMS

1. Has your work ever been the subject of a structured walkthrough? Was the experience helpful or a waste of time, or worse? Are you looking forward to your next walkthrough?
2. Do you agree with banning managers from walkthroughs? Is it possible that the role of moderator in a walkthrough might best be filled by the project manager?
3. Do you agree with the authors' suggestions for successful walkthroughs? Are there any guidelines you wish to add to the list? To remove from the list?
4. Identify the syntactical errors in the COBOL fragment in Figure 6.8.
5. Identify the logical errors in the COBOL fragment in Figure 6.9. (Assume there are no other READ statements in the program.)
6. The COBOL fragment in Figure 6.10a is taken from a program that compiled cleanly but failed to execute. The DOS SET statements are shown in Figure 6.10b together with the associated error messages. (The File Status codes are found in Table 18.1, page 555.) Explain the problem.

Figure 6.8 COBOL Fragment for Problem 4

```
IDENTIFICATION DIVISION.
PROGRAM ID.  ERRORS.
ENVIRONMENT DIVISION.
INPUT-OUTPUT SECTION.
SELECT EMPLOYEE-FILE
    ASSIGN TO UT-S-EMPLOYEE.
DATA DIVISION.
FILE SECTION.
FD  EMPLOYEE-FILE
    RECORD CONTAINS 50 CHARACTERS
    DATA RECORD IS EMPLOYEE-RECORD.
    EMPLOYEE-RECORD.
    05  EMP-NAME                    PIC X(20).
    05  EMP-NUMBER                  PIC X(9).
    05  FILLER                      PIC X(20).
WORKING STORAGE SECTION.
10  END-OF-FILE-SWITCH              PIC X(3)     VALUE BLANKS.
```

Figure 6.9 COBOL Fragment for Problem 5

```
WORKING-STORAGE SECTION.
01  END-OF-FILE-SWITCH    PIC X(3)    VALUE 'YES'.
.
  .
PROCEDURE DIVISION.
MAINLINE.
.
  .
    PERFORM PROCESS-RECORDS
        UNTIL END-OF-FILE-SWITCH = 'YES'
.
  .
PROCESS-RECORDS.
    READ EMPLOYEE-FILE
        AT END MOVE 'YES' TO END-OF-FILE-SWITCH
    END-READ.
```

Figure 6.10 COBOL Fragment for Problem 6

```
    SELECT STUDENT-FILE
         ASSIGN TO UT-S-SYSIN.
    SELECT PRINT-FILE
         ASSIGN TO UT-S-SYSOUT.
.
  .
PROCEDURE DIVISION.
PREPARE-SENIOR-REPORT.
    READ STUDENT-FILE
        AT END MOVE 'NO' TO DATA-REMAINS-SWITCH
    END-READ.
    OPEN INPUT  STUDENT-FILE
         OUTPUT PRINT-FILE.
    PERFORM WRITE-HEADING-LINE.
    PERFORM PROCESS-RECORDS
        UNTIL DATA-REMAINS-SWITCH = 'NO'.
    CLOSE STUDENT-FILE
          PRINT-FILE.
    STOP RUN.
```

(a) COBOL Fragments

```
SET SYSIN=STUDENT.DAT
SET SYSOUT=STUDENT.RPT

File Status 47 on Unopened File
```

(b) DOS SET Statements and Error Message

7 Editing and Coding Standards

CHAPTER OUTLINE

OBJECTIVES

After reading this chapter you will be able to:

- List the complete set of COBOL editing characters.
- Differentiate between a numeric field and a numeric-edited field; predict the results when a numeric field is moved to a numeric-edited field.
- Understand the difference between an implied decimal point and an actual decimal point; state the role of each in editing.
- Describe the rules for signed numbers and the editing characters +, –, CR, and DB.
- Describe the rationale for coding standards that go beyond the syntactical requirements of COBOL.

OVERVIEW

The chapter introduces editing—the ability to dress up printed reports by inserting dollar signs, decimal points, and so on, into numeric fields prior to printing. The chapter also introduces the concept of signed numbers and the use of CR and DB, or a plus and minus sign, to indicate positive or negative results. All of this material is incorporated into the tuition billing program from Chapter 5.

The second half of the chapter develops the rationale for coding standards, or requirements imposed by an installation to increase the readability (and maintainability) of COBOL programs. We present a series of typical standards and show how they are incorporated into existing programs.

Editing

The importance of editing is best demonstrated by comparing outputs from two programs. Figure 7.1a contains the original (unedited) output produced by the tuition billing program of Chapter 5. Figure 7.1b contains edited output, produced by a modified version of the program, which is presented later in the chapter. The last line of Figure 7.1b displays a new student, Lucky One, whose scholarship grant exceeds the total amount of his bill, producing a credit of $150. (Lucky One is not shown in Figure 7.1a as the original program did not address signed numbers.) The superiority of the edited output speaks for itself.

The ***editing characters*** of Table 7.1 enable the kind of output shown in Figure 7.1b. Editing is achieved by incorporating these characters into the various PICTURE clauses within a COBOL program.

The editing characters are not associated with the numeric fields used in computations, as these fields may contain only digits, an implied decimal point, and an optional sign. Additional data names, known as ***numeric-edited fields***, are necessary within the program, and it is the picture clauses for the latter that contain editing characters from Table 7.1. In other words, arithmetic is performed on numeric fields, whose computed values are subsequently moved to numeric-edited fields, and the latter are printed.

Figure 7.1 Comparison of Outputs

STUDENT NAME		CREDITS	TUITION	UNION FEE	ACT FEE	SCHOLARSHIP	TOTAL BILL
SMITH	JB	15	003000	025	075	00000	003100
JAMES	HR	15	003000	000	075	00000	003075
BAKER	SR	09	001800	000	050	00500	001350
PART-TIMER	JR	03	000600	025	025	00000	000650
JONES	PL	15	003000	025	075	00000	003100
HEAVYWORKER	HM	18	003600	000	075	00000	003675
LEE	BL	18	003600	000	075	00000	003675
CLARK	JC	06	001200	000	025	00000	001225
GROSSMAN	SE	07	001400	000	050	00000	001450
FRANKEL	LF	10	002000	000	050	00000	002050
BENWAY	CT	03	000600	000	025	00250	000375
KERBEL	NB	04	000800	000	025	00000	000825
			--------	--------	-------	-------	-------
UNIVERSITY TOTALS			024600	0075	0625	000750	024550

(a) Without Editing

STUDENT NAME		CREDITS	TUITION	UNION FEE	ACT FEE	SCHOLARSHIP	TOTAL BILL
SMITH	JB	15	$3,000	$25	$75		$3,100
JAMES	HR	15	$3,000		$75		$3,075
BAKER	SR	9	$1,800		$50	$500	$1,350
PART-TIMER	JR	3	$600	$25	$25		$650
JONES	PL	15	$3,000	$25	$75		$3,100
HEAVYWORKER	HM	18	$3,600		$75		$3,675
LEE	BL	18	$3,600		$75		$3,675
CLARK	JC	6	$1,200		$25		$1,225
GROSSMAN	SE	7	$1,400		$50		$1,450
FRANKEL	LF	10	$2,000		$50		$2,050
BENWAY	CT	3	$600		$25	$250	$375
KERBEL	NB	4	$800		$25		$825
LUCKY ONE	FR	9	$1,800		$50	$2000	$150CR
			--------	--------	-------	-------	-------
UNIVERSITY TOTALS			$26,400	$75	$675	$2,750	$24,400

Student has been added to the original data

(a) With Editing

TABLE 7.1 Editing Characters

CHARACTER	MEANING	CHARACTER	MEANING
.	Actual decimal point	B	Blank
Z	Zero suppression	/	Slash
$	Dollar sign	CR	Credit character
,	Comma	DB	Debit character
*	Check protection	+	Plus sign
0	Zero	–	Minus sign

The relationship between numeric fields and numeric-edited fields is illustrated in Figure 7.2, which depicts the calculation of tuition as credits times the rate ($200 per credit). The incoming student record contains the field STU-CREDITS, with the calculated result defined in Working-Storage as IND-TUITION. The two fields are numeric, and do not contain any editing characters.

On the other hand, DETAIL-LINE contains two numeric-edited fields (DET-CREDITS and DET-TUITION), each of which holds one or more editing characters from Table 7.1. It is not necessary for you to know the precise function of the various editing characters at this time; you need only perceive the difference between numeric and numeric-edited fields.

The calculations within Figure 7.2 are done with the numeric fields (IND-TUITION and STU-CREDITS). Then, just prior to printing, the values in the numeric fields are moved to the corresponding numeric-edited fields, which are printed.

Let us consider the various editing characters from Table 7.1, in turn.

The Decimal Point

The ***actual decimal point*** is the most basic editing character. In reviewing this and other examples, it is essential that you remember that *any move of a numeric field to a numeric-edited field maintains decimal alignment.* Consider:

```
05  FIELD-A             PIC 9V99.
05  FIELD-A-EDITED      PIC 9.99.
```

FIELD-A is a numeric field, with two digits after an *implied* decimal point. FIELD-A-EDITED is a numeric-edited field containing an *actual* decimal point. All calculations are done using FIELD-A, which is moved to FIELD-A-EDITED prior to printing by means of the statement MOVE FIELD-A TO FIELD-A-EDITED. Thus:

	FIELD-A	FIELD-A-EDITED
Before move:	7^83	9.99
After execution:	7^83	7.83

The decimal point requires a position in FIELD-A-EDITED, but not in FIELD-A; that is, FIELD-A-EDITED is a *four*-position field, whereas FIELD-A requires only *three* positions.

Zero Suppression

One of the simplest editing requirements is to eliminate high-order (insignificant) zeros. For example, consider a numeric field defined with a PICTURE clause of 9(5), but whose value is 00120; in other words the two high-order positions contain insignificant zeros. It is likely that you would prefer the printed output to appear as 120, rather than 00120, which is accomplished by the statement MOVE FIELD-B TO FIELD-B-EDITED as shown:

```
05  FIELD-B             PIC 9(5).
05  FIELD-B-EDITED      PIC ZZZZ9
```

	FIELD-B	FIELD-B-EDITED
Before move:	00120	ZZZZ9
After execution:	00120	120

Figure 7.2 Numeric and Numeric-Edited Fields

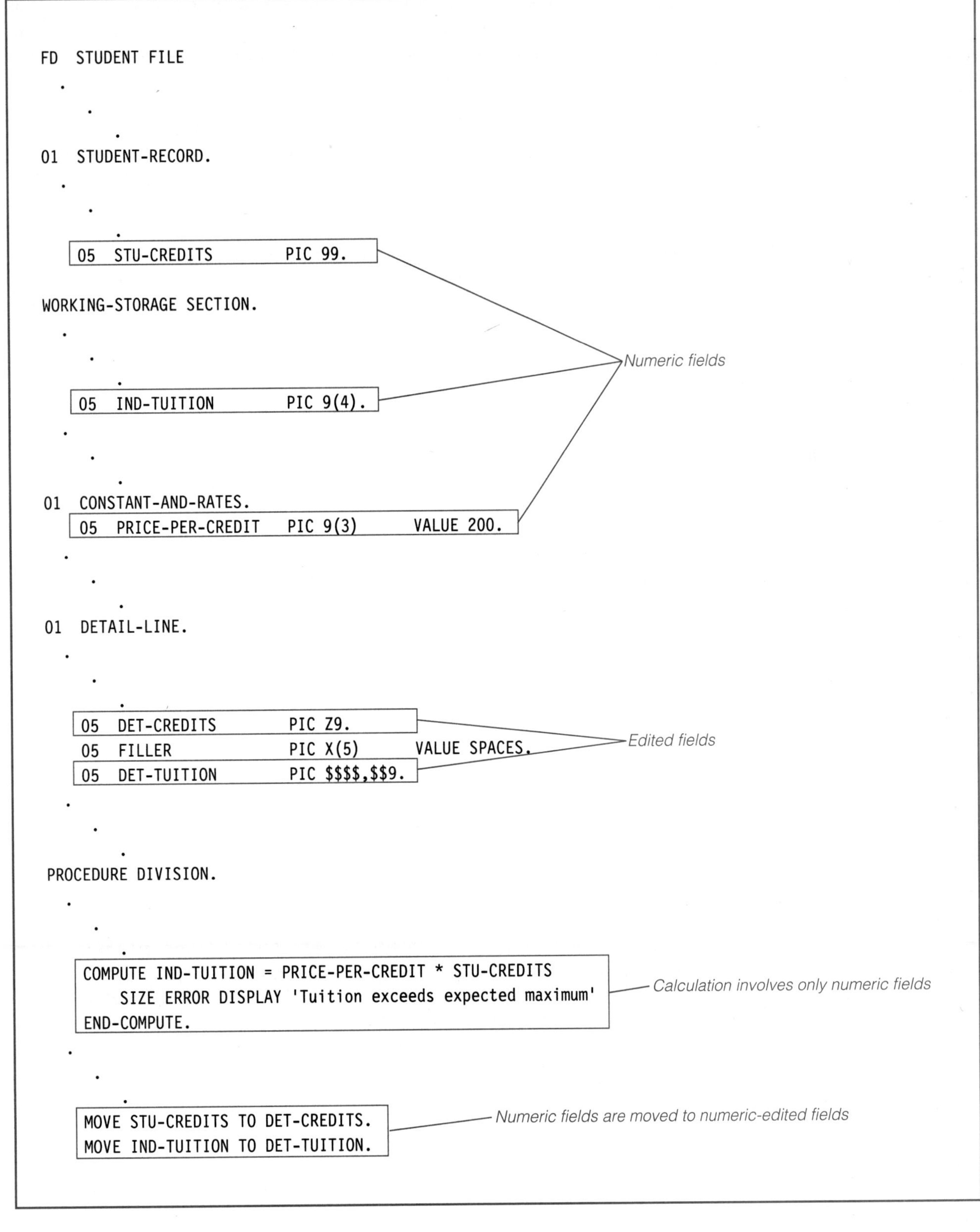
FD STUDENT FILE
01 STUDENT-RECORD.
05 STU-CREDITS PIC 99.
WORKING-STORAGE SECTION.
05 IND-TUITION PIC 9(4).
01 CONSTANT-AND-RATES.
05 PRICE-PER-CREDIT PIC 9(3) VALUE 200.
01 DETAIL-LINE.
05 DET-CREDITS PIC Z9.
05 FILLER PIC X(5) VALUE SPACES.
05 DET-TUITION PIC $$$$,$$9.
PROCEDURE DIVISION.
COMPUTE IND-TUITION = PRICE-PER-CREDIT * STU-CREDITS
SIZE ERROR DISPLAY 'Tuition exceeds expected maximum'
END-COMPUTE.
MOVE STU-CREDITS TO DET-CREDITS.
MOVE IND-TUITION TO DET-TUITION.
Numeric fields
Edited fields
Calculation involves only numeric fields
Numeric fields are moved to numeric-edited fields

The editing character Z indicates ***zero suppression***, and prevents the printing of leading zeros. However, as soon as the first significant digit is reached (the 1 in this example), all subsequent digits are printed. Note, too, that the picture for FIELD-B-EDITED has a 9 as the low-order character, to print a zero, rather than blank out the field entirely, in the event of a zero value.

Dollar Signs

The dollar sign is used as an editing character in one of two ways, either in a ***fixed*** or ***floating*** position. A single dollar sign in the numeric-edited picture will always print the dollar sign in the same (fixed) position. Consider the following data names with the statement MOVE FIELD-C TO FIELD-C-EDITED:

```
05  FIELD-C               PIC 9(4).
05  FIELD-C-EDITED        PIC $ZZZ9.
```

	FIELD-C	FIELD-C-EDITED
Before move:	0 0 4 3	$ Z Z Z 9
After execution:	0 0 4 3	$ 4 3

A floating dollar sign is obtained by using multiple dollar signs in the edited field. Consider the following data names in conjunction with the statement MOVE FIELD-D TO FIELD-D-EDITED:

```
05  FIELD-D               PIC 9(4).
05  FIELD-D-EDITED        PIC $$$$9.
```

	FIELD-D	FIELD-D-EDITED
Before move:	0 0 2 3	$ $ $ $ 9
After execution:	0 0 2 3	$ 2 3

A single (floating) dollar sign is printed before the first significant digit in the edited field, with the leading zero digits, if any, replaced by blanks. In other words, the floating dollar sign has the same effect as zero suppression. Note, too, that the receiving field must be at least one character longer than the sending field to accommodate the dollar sign; otherwise, a compiler warning results.

Comma

A ***comma*** used as an editing character causes a comma to be printed, provided a significant digit appears to the left of the comma. The comma will be suppressed, however, if it is preceded by leading zeros. Consider the following data names in conjunction with the statement MOVE FIELD-E TO FIELD-E-EDITED:

```
05  FIELD-E               PIC 9(4).
05  FIELD-E-EDITED        PIC $$,$$9.
```

	FIELD-E	FIELD-E-EDITED
Before move:	8 7 6 5	$ $, $ $ 9
After execution:	8 7 6 5	$ 8 , 7 6 5

The comma is printed in the indicated position. Suppose, however, that the contents of the sending field are less than 1,000, and that the statement MOVE FIELD-F TO FIELD-F-EDITED is executed in conjunction with the fields:

```
05  FIELD-F              PIC 9(4).
05  FIELD-F-EDITED       PIC $$,$$9.
```

	FIELD-F	FIELD-F-EDITED
Before move:	0 0 8 7	$ $, $ $ 9
After execution:	0 0 8 7	$ $ $ $ 8 7

The comma is suppressed because it was not preceded by a significant digit. Observe also how the comma is used in conjunction with a floating dollar sign.

Asterisks for Check Protection

The ***asterisk*** is used as a fill character to avoid blanks between a fixed dollar sign and the first significant digit as in $****87. Consider the following fields in conjunction with the statement MOVE FIELD-G TO FIELD-G-EDITED:

```
05  FIELD-G              PIC 9(5).
05  FIELD-G-EDITED       PIC $**,**9.
```

	FIELD-G	FIELD-G-EDITED
Before move:	0 0 0 8 7	$ * * , * * 9
After execution:	0 0 0 8 7	$ * * * * 8 7

The dollar sign will print in its fixed position, with asterisks replacing leading zeros. The use of the asterisk as a fill character is commonly referred to as ***check protection.***

Insertion Characters

The slash, blank, and zero (/, B, and 0, respectively) are ***insertion characters***, meaning that they are printed exactly where they appear in an edited field. Consider the following fields together with the statement MOVE FIELD-H TO FIELD-H-EDITED:

```
05  FIELD-H              PIC 9(6).
05  FIELD-H-EDITED       PIC 99/99/99.
```

	FIELD-H	FIELD-H-EDITED
Before move:	0 3 1 6 8 9	9 9 / 9 9 / 9 9
After execution:	0 3 1 6 8 9	0 3 / 1 6 / 8 9

FIELD-H-EDITED is an eight-position field and is typical of how a date field may be edited. Blanks and zeros may be inserted in similar fashion. Note, however, that the hyphen is ***not*** an insertion character and cannot, be used to place hyphens within a social security number.

Synopsis

Table 7.2 provides an effective review of the editing characters covered so far. Each entry in the table shows the result of a MOVE statement of a numeric source field to a numeric-edited receiving field. All of the examples maintain decimal alignment as required. (The ƀ which appears in several examples indicates a space.)

TABLE 7.2 Review of Editing Characters

SOURCE FIELD		RECEIVING FIELD	
PICTURE	**VALUE**	**PICTURE**	**EDITED RESULT**
a. 9(4)	0678	Z(4)	ƀ678
b. 9(4)	0678	$9(4)	$0678
c. 9(4)	0678	$Z(4)	$ƀ678
d. 9(4)V99	123456	9(4).99	1234.56
e. 9(4)V99	123456	$9(4).99	$1234.56
f. 9(4)V99	123456	$9,999.99	$1,234.56
g. 9(4)	0008	$$,$$9	ƀƀƀƀƀ$8
h. 9(4)V9	12345	9(4)	1234
i. 9(4)V9	12345	9(4).99	1234.50
j. 9(5)	00045	$****9	$***45
k. 9(9)	123456789	999B99B9999	123ƀ45ƀ6789
l. 9(4)	1234	$$,$$9.00	$1,234.00
m. 9(6)	080594	99/99/99	08/05/94
n. 9(6)	080594	Z9/99/99	ƀ8/05/94

Signed Numbers

Thus far we have considered only positive numbers, a rather unrealistic limitation. Numeric fields with negative values require an **S** in their PICTURE clause to indicate a ***signed field***, that is, a field that may contain either positive or negative values. If the sign (the S in the PICTURE clause) is omitted, the value of the data name will always be converted to a positive number, regardless of the result of the computation. Consider:

```
       05  FIELD-A          PIC S99    VALUE -20.
       05  FIELD-B          PIC 99     VALUE 15.
       05  FIELD-C          PIC S99    VALUE -20.
       05  FIELD-D          PIC 99     VALUE 15.
       .
         .
           .
   ADD FIELD-B TO FIELD-A.
       ADD FIELD-C TO FIELD-D.
```

Numerically, the sum of –20 and +15 is –5, and there is no problem when the result is stored in FIELD-A as in the first command. In the second command, however, the sum is stored in FIELD-D (an unsigned field), and thus it will assume a value of +5. Accordingly many programmers adopt the habit of always using signed fields to avoid any difficulty. Signed numbers require additional editing characters.

CR and DB

Financial statements use either the credit (**CR**) or debit (**DB**) character to indicate a negative number. In other words, the representation of a negative number can be either CR or DB, and depends entirely on the accounting system in use; some systems use CR, whereas others will use DB.

Table 7.3 contains four examples that should clarify the matter. In each instance, CR or DB appears only when the sending field is negative [examples (b) and (d)]. If the source field is positive or zero, CR and/or DB are replaced by blanks. The essential point is that COBOL treats CR and DB identically, and the determination of which negative indicator to use depends on the accounting system.

TABLE 7.3 CR and DB Editing Characters

	SOURCE FIELD		RECEIVING FIELD	
	PICTURE	**VALUE**	**PICTURE**	**EDITED RESULT**
a.	S9(5)	98765	$$$,999CR	$98,765
b.	S9(5)	-98765	$$$,999CR	$98,765CR
c.	S9(5)	98765	$$$,999DB	$98,765
d.	S9(5)	-98765	$$$,999DB	$98,765DB

Plus and Minus Signs

Table 7.4 illustrates the use of plus and minus signs. The repetition of a (plus or minus) sign within the edited PICTURE clause denotes a ***floating*** (plus or minus) ***sign***, which will appear in the printed field immediately to the left of the first significant digit. A single (plus or minus) sign, however, indicates a ***fixed*** (plus or minus) ***sign***, which prints in the indicated position.

Specification of a (fixed or floating) plus sign displays the sign of the edited field if the number is positive, negative, or zero [examples (a), (b), and (c)]. Specification of a minus sign, however, displays the sign only when the edited result is negative. The receiving field must be at least one character longer than the sending field to accommodate the sign; otherwise, a compiler warning results.

TABLE 7.4 Floating Plus and Minus Sign

	SOURCE FIELD		RECEIVING FIELD	
	PICTURE	**VALUE**	**PICTURE**	**EDITED RESULT**
a.	S9(4)	1234	++,+++	+1,234
b.	S9(4)	0123	++,+++	ƀƀ+123
c.	S9(4)	-1234	++,+++	-1,234
d.	S9(4)	1234	--,---	ƀ1,234
e.	S9(4)	0123	--,---	ƀƀƀ123
f.	S9(4)	-1234	--,---	-1,234
g.	S9(4)	1234	ZZ,ZZ9+	ƀ1,234+
h.	S9(4)	-1234	ZZ,ZZ9+	ƀ1,234-

BLANK WHEN ZERO Clause

The **BLANK WHEN ZERO** clause produces a blank field when the associated numeric value is zero. Although the same effect can be achieved with certain editing strings, such as ZZZZZ or $$$$$, there are times when the clause is essential. A field with dollars and cents—for example, $$$9.99, formatted to print a digit immediately to the left of the decimal point—will print $0.00. In similar fashion it might be desirable to blank out a date field with PIC Z9/Z9/Z9 if the values are unavailable. The inclusion of BLANK WHEN ZERO at the end of the PICTURE clause in all three instances will accomplish the desired result.

The Tuition Billing Program Revisited

We return once more to Figure 7.1, the example with which we began the chapter. The earlier version of the tuition billing program in Chapter 5 did not include editing characters, and so produced the output in Figure 7.1a. Now we incorporate the material just presented into a revised version of the program to produce the edited output of Figure 7.1b.

The necessary changes are highlighted in Figure 7.3, which compares edited and unedited PICTURE clauses. The changes affect only the detail (7.3a) and total

Figure 7.3 Edited versus Unedited PICTURE Clauses

```
                                  EDITED FIELDS                  UNEDITED FIELDS

01  DETAIL-LINE.
    05  FILLER                PIC X         VALUE SPACES.        PIC X      VALUE SPACES.
    05  DET-LAST-NAME         PIC X(15).                         PIC X(15).
    05  FILLER                PIC X(2)      VALUE SPACES.        PIC X(2)   VALUE SPACES.
    05  DET-INITIALS          PIC X(2).                          PIC X(2).
    05  FILLER                PIC X(5)      VALUE SPACES.        PIC X(5)   VALUE SPACES.
    05  DET-CREDITS           PIC Z9.                            PIC 9(2).
    05  FILLER                PIC X(4)      VALUE SPACES.        PIC X(6)   VALUE SPACES.
    05  DET-TUITION           PIC $$$$,$$9.                      PIC 9(6).
    05  FILLER                PIC X(6)      VALUE SPACES.        PIC X(7)   VALUE SPACES.
    05  DET-UNION-FEE         PIC $$$9      BLANK WHEN ZERO.     PIC 9(3).
    05  FILLER                PIC X(5)      VALUE SPACES.        PIC X(6)   VALUE SPACES.
    05  DET-ACTIVITY-FEE      PIC $$$9      BLANK WHEN ZERO.     PIC 9(3).
    05  FILLER                PIC X(6)      VALUE SPACES.        PIC X(8)   VALUE SPACES.
    05  DET-SCHOLARSHIP       PIC $$,$$$9 BLANK WHEN ZERO        PIC 9(5).
    05  FILLER                PIC X(4)      VALUE SPACES.        PIC X(6)   VALUE SPACES.
    05  DET-IND-BILL          PIC $$$$,$$9CR.                    PIC 9(6).
    05  FILLER                PIC X(47)     VALUE SPACES.        PIC X(49)  VALUE SPACES.
```

(a) Detail Line

```
01  TOTAL-LINE.
    05  FILLER                PIC X(8)      VALUE SPACES.        PIC X(8)   VALUE SPACES.
    05  FILLER                PIC X(17)                          PIC X(17)
            VALUE 'UNIVERSITY TOTALS'.                               VALUE 'UNIVERSITY TOTALS'.
    05  FILLER                PIC X(6)      VALUE SPACES.        PIC X(8)   VALUE SPACES.
    05  TOT-TUITION           PIC $$$$,$$9.                      PIC 9(6).
    05  FILLER                PIC X(2)      VALUE SPACES.        PIC X(6)   VALUE SPACES.
    05  TOT-UNION-FEE         PIC $$$$,$$9.                      PIC 9(4).
    05  FILLER                PIC X         VALUE SPACES.        PIC X(5)   VALUE SPACES.
    05  TOT-ACTIVITY-FEE      PIC $$$$,$$9.                      PIC 9(4).
    05  FILLER                PIC X(5)      VALUE SPACES.        PIC X(7)   VALUE SPACES.
    05  TOT-SCHOLARSHIP       PIC $$$$,$$9.                      PIC 9(6).
    05  FILLER                PIC X(4)      VALUE SPACES.        PIC X(6)   VALUE SPACES.
    05  TOT-IND-BILL          PIC $$$$,$$9CR.                    PIC 9(6).
    05  FILLER                PIC X(47)     VALUE SPACES.        PIC X(49)  VALUE SPACES.
```

(b) Total Line

(7.3b) lines. Computations are made within the program using the unedited PICTURE clauses found in INDIVIDUAL-CALCULATIONS and UNIVERSITY-TOTALS, then moved to edited PICTURE clauses found in DETAIL-LINE and TOTAL-LINE, respectively.

All of the calculations and editing are accomplished as illustrated earlier in Figure 7.2. The computed value of tuition, for example, is stored in the data name IND-TUITION with PIC 9(6), then moved to the edited field DET-TUITION with a PIC $$$$,$$9 prior to printing.

Observe the presence of a CR within the PICTURE clauses for both DET-IND-BILL and TOT-IND-BILL in Figures 7.3a and 7.3b, respectively. The CR is blanked out when students owe money to the university, but appears when the student is due a credit (Lucky One in Figure 7.1b). Note, too, the various BLANK WHEN ZERO clauses throughout Figure 7.3, which produce the more appealing edited output of Figure 7.1b contrasted to the zeros in Figure 7.1a.

Coding Standards

A good program is easily read and maintained by someone other than the author. Indeed, continuing success in a commercial installation depends on someone other than the author being able to maintain a program. Most installations impose a set of ***coding standards***, such as those described here, which go beyond the requirements of the COBOL compiler. These standards are optional for the student, but typical of what is required in the real world.

The next several pages suggest a series of coding standards for you to use. However, there are no absolute truths—no right or wrong—insofar as programming style is concerned. Different programmers develop slightly or even radically different styles that are consistent with the rules of COBOL and with the programmer's objective. The discussion that follows reflects the viewpoint of the authors and is necessarily subjective.

We begin with suggestions for the Data Division.

Data Division

Choose meaningful names. Avoid taking the easy way out with two- or three-character data names. It is impossible for the maintenance programmer, or even the original author, to determine the meaning of abbreviated data names. The usual student response is that this adds unnecessarily to the burden of writer's cramp. Initial coding, however, takes only 5–10% of the total time associated with a program (maintenance, testing, and debugging take the vast majority), and the modest increase in coding time is more than compensated by improvements in the latter activities.

Prefix all data names within the same FD or 01 with two or three characters unique to the FD; for example, OM-LAST-NAME, OM-BIRTH-DATE. The utility of this guideline becomes apparent in the Procedure Division if it is necessary to refer back to the definition of a data name.

Begin all PICTURE clauses in the same column. Usually in columns 36–48, but the choice is arbitrary. Do not be unduly disturbed if one or two entries stray from the designated column, because of long data names and/or indentation of level numbers.

Choose one form of the PICTURE clause. Choose PIC, PIC IS, PICTURE, or PICTURE IS and follow it consistently. PIC is the shortest and is as good as any.

PROGRAMMING TIP

Avoid Literals

The constant (literal) portion of a print line should be defined in Working-Storage, rather than moved to the print line in the Procedure Division. Consider the following:

Poor Code:

```
      MOVE 'STUDENT NAME          SOC SEC NUM  CREDITS  TUITION
   -  'SCHOLARSHIP FEES' TO PRINT-LINE.

      WRITE PRINT-LINE.
```

Hyphen required to continue nonnumeric literal

Improved Code:

```
01    HEADING-LINE.
      05                     PIC X(12)       VALUE 'STUDENT NAME'
      05                     PIC X(10)       VALUE SPACES.
      05                     PIC X(11)       VALUE 'SOC SEC NUM'.
      05                     PIC X(2)        VALUE SPACES.
      05                     PIC X(7)        VALUE 'CREDITS'.
      05                     PIC X(2)        VALUE SPACES.
      05                     PIC X(7)        VALUE 'TUITION'.
      05                     PIC X(3)        VALUE SPACES.
      05                     PIC X(11)       VALUE 'SCHOLARSHIP'.
      05                     PIC X(2)        VALUE SPACES.
      05                     PIC X(4)        VALUE 'FEES'.

      WRITE PRINT-LINE FROM HEADING-LINE.
```

The poor code illustrates continuation of a nonnumeric literal. The first line begins with an apostrophe before **STUDENT NAME** and ends *without* a closing apostrophe in column 72. The continued line contains a hyphen in column 7, and both a beginning and ending apostrophe.

The improved code may appear unnecessarily long in contrast to the poor code. However, it is an unwritten law that users will change column headings, and/or spacing at least twice before being satisfied. Such changes are easily accommodated in the improved code but often tedious in the original solution. Assume, for example, that four spaces are required between **CREDITS** and **TUITION**, rather than the two that are there now. Modification of the poor code requires that both lines in the **MOVE** statement be completely rewritten, whereas only a PICTURE clause changes in the improved version. Note, too, that the improved code can be rewritten to reduce the number of **FILLER** entries, and also to eliminate the word FILLER, as shown below.

```
01    HEADING-LINE.
      05                     PIC X(22)       VALUE 'STUDENT NAME'.
      05                     PIC X(13)       VALUE 'SOC SEC NUM'.
      05                     PIC X(9)        VALUE 'CREDITS'.
      05                     PIC X(10)       VALUE 'TUITION'.
      05                     PIC X(13)       VALUE 'SCHOLARSHIP'.
      05                     PIC X(4)        VALUE 'FEES'.
```

In this example each **VALUE** clause contains fewer characters than the associated **PICTURE** clause. Accordingly, alignment is from left to right, with the extra (low-order) positions padded with blanks.

Indent successive level numbers under a 01 consistently. For example, two or four columns. Leave gaps between adjacent levels (for example, 01, 05, 10, 15 or 01, 04, 08, 12) instead of using consecutive numbers; that is, avoid 01, 02, 03 (as discussed in Chapter 4). Use the same level numbers from FD to FD to maintain consistency within a program.

Avoid 77-level entries. 77-level entries have not been mentioned in the text, because current programming practice argues for their elimination. Nevertheless, they are apt to be found in existing programs and are discussed now for that reason.

A 77-level entry was originally defined as an independent data name with no relationship to any other data name in a program. (77-level entries are coded as elementary items in Working-Storage.) However, few if any data names are truly independent, and 77-level entries should be avoided for that reason. The authors, for example, have gotten along quite nicely by grouping related entries under a common 01 description. Consider the following:

Poor Code:

```
77  TUITION                 PIC 9(4)V99     VALUE ZEROS.
77  ACTIVITY-FEE            PIC 9(2)        VALUE ZEROS.
77  UNION-FEE               PIC 9(2)        VALUE ZEROS.
```

Improved Code:

```
01  INDIVIDUAL-CALCULATIONS.
    05  IND-TUITION         PIC 9(4)V99     VALUE ZEROS.
    05  IND-ACTIVITY-FEE    PIC 9(2)        VALUE ZEROS.
    05  IND-UNION-FEE       PIC 9(2)        VALUE ZEROS.
```

The improved code also uses a common prefix, which reflects the similarities among the related items. There is simply no reason to use the older approach of independent data items.

Procedure Division

Develop functional paragraphs. Every statement in a paragraph should be related to the overall function of that paragraph, which in turn should be reflected in the paragraph name. A well-chosen name will consist of a verb, one or two adjectives, and an object; for example, READ-STUDENT-FILE, WRITE-HEADING-LINE, and so on. If a paragraph cannot be named in this manner, it is probably not functional, and consideration should be given to redesigning the program and/or paragraph.

Sequence paragraph names. Programmers and managers alike accept the utility of this guideline to locate paragraphs in the Procedure Division quickly. However, there is considerable disagreement on just what sequencing scheme to use: all numbers, a single letter followed by numbers, and so on. We make no strong argument for one scheme over another, other than to insist that a consistent sequencing rule be followed. Some examples are A010-WRITE-NEW-MASTER-RECORD and 100-PRODUCE-ERROR-REPORT.

Avoid commas. The compiler treats a comma as noise; it has no effect on the generated object code. Many programmers have acquired the habit of inserting commas to increase readability. Though this works rather well with prose, it can have just the opposite effect in COBOL, because of blurred print chains, which make it difficult to distinguish a comma from a period. The best solution is to try to avoid commas altogether.

Use scope terminators. END-IF (see programming tip on page 182) is one of several scope terminators included in COBOL-85 that should be used whenever possible to

PROGRAMMING TIP

Use Scope Terminators

Scope terminators are one of the most powerful enhancements in COBOL-85, and in the opinion of the authors, justify in and of themselves, conversion to the new standard. In its simplest role a scope terminator is used in place of a period to end a conditional statement—for example, **END-IF** to terminate an **IF** statement. (A scope terminator and a period should not appear together unless the period also ends the sentence.)

One of the most important reasons for using scope terminators is that they eliminate the very subtle *column 73* problem which has always existed, and which is depicted below. The intended logic is straightforward, and is supposed to apply a discount of two percent on an order of $2,000 or more. The amount due **(NET)** is equal to the amount ordered less the discount (if any).

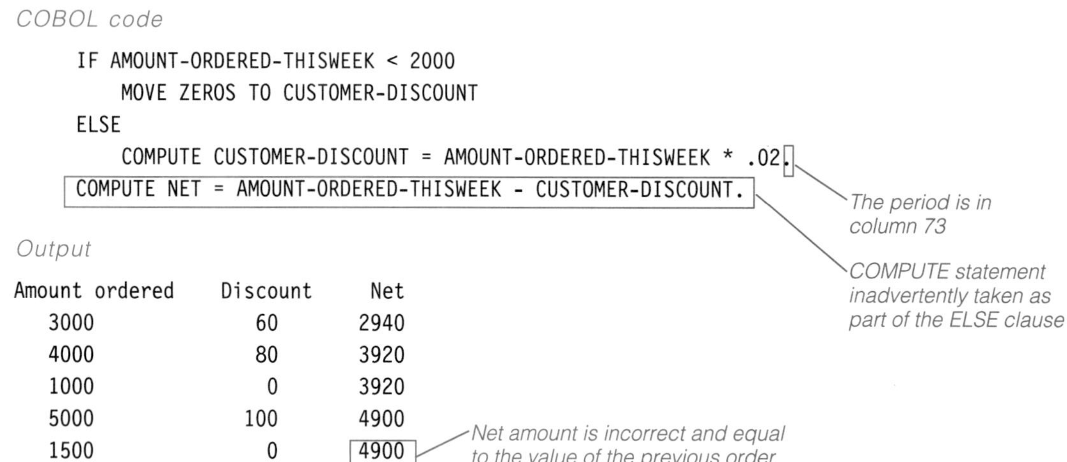
COBOL code
IF AMOUNT-ORDERED-THISWEEK < 2000
MOVE ZEROS TO CUSTOMER-DISCOUNT
ELSE
COMPUTE CUSTOMER-DISCOUNT = AMOUNT-ORDERED-THISWEEK * .02.
COMPUTE NET = AMOUNT-ORDERED-THISWEEK - CUSTOMER-DISCOUNT.
The period is in column 73
COMPUTE statement inadvertently taken as part of the ELSE clause
Output
Amount ordered Discount Net
3000 60 2940
4000 80 3920
1000 0 3920
5000 100 4900
1500 0 4900
Net amount is incorrect and equal to the value of the previous order

The COBOL statements appear correct, yet the output is wrong! In particular, *the net amounts are wrong for any order less than $2,000* (but valid for orders of $2,000 or more). The net amount for orders less than $2,000 equals the net for the previous order (that is, the net for an order of $1,000 is incorrectly printed as $3,920, which was the correct net for the preceding order of $4,000). The net amount for an order of $1,500 was printed as $4,900, and so on. Why?

The only possible explanation is that the **COMPUTE NET** statement is not executed for net amounts less than $2,000. The only way that can happen is if the **COMPUTE NET** statement is taken as part of the **ELSE** clause, and that can happen only if the **ELSE** is not terminated by a period. The period is present, however, so we are back at ground zero—or are we? *The period is present, but in column 73, which is ignored by the compiler.* Hence the visual code does not match the compiler interpretation, and the resulting output is incorrect. Replacing the period by the **END-IF** delimiter will eliminate this and similar errors in the future. (Remember, a period may appear *at the end of the sentence* after the **END-IF** terminator.)

terminate a conditional statement. The END-READ terminator should be used in similar fashion to end the conditional AT END clause in the READ statement.

Indent. Virtually all programmers indent successive level numbers in the Data Division, yet many of these same individuals do not apply a similar principle in the Procedure Division. The readability of a program is enhanced significantly by indenting subservient clauses under the main statements. Some examples:

```
READ STUDENT-FILE
    AT END MOVE 'NO' TO DATA-REMAINS-SWITCH
END-READ.

PERFORM 0020-PROCESS-A-RECORD
    UNTIL DATA-REMAINS-SWITCH   = 'NO'.

IF STU-UNION-MEMBER = 'Y'
    MOVE UNION-FEE TO IND-UNION-FEE
ELSE
    MOVE ZERO TO IND-UNION-FEE
END-IF.

COMPUTE IND-TUITION = PRICE-PER-CREDIT * STU-CREDITS
    SIZE ERROR DISPLAY 'Size error for individual tuition'
END-COMPUTE.
```

Both Divisions

Space attractively. The adoption of various spacing conventions can go a long way toward improving the appearance of a program. The authors believe very strongly in the insertion of blank lines throughout a program to highlight important statements. Specific suggestions include a blank line before all paragraphs, FDs, and 01 entries.

You can also force various portions of a listing to begin on a new page, by putting a slash in column 7 of a separate statement.

Avoid constants. A significant portion of maintenance programming (and headaches) could be avoided if a program is written with an eye toward change. Consider:

Poor Code:

```
    COMPUTE IND-TUITION = 200 * STU-CREDITS.
```

Improved Code:

```
WORKING-STORAGE SECTION.
01  CONSTANTS-AND-RATES.
    05  PRICE-PER-CREDIT        PIC 9(4)     VALUE 200.
.
   .
      .
PROCEDURE DIVISION.
.
   .
      .
    COMPUTE IND-TUITION = PRICE-PER-CREDIT * STU-CREDITS.
```

The improved code is easy to modify when (not if) the tuition rate changes as the only required modification is to the VALUE clause in Working Storage. The poor code requires changes to the appropriate Procedure Division statement(s), and if the constant 200 appears more than once in the Procedure Division, it is very easy to miss some of the statements in which the change is required. There is less possibility for error in the improved code.

Don't overcomment. Contrary to popular belief, the mere presence of comments does not ensure a well-documented program, and poor comments are sometimes worse than no comments at all. The most common fault is redundancy with the source code. Consider:

```
*    CALCULATE  NET PAY
     COMPUTE NET-PAY = GROSS-PAY - FED-TAX - VOL-DEDUCT.
```

The comment detracts from the readability of the statement because it breaks the logical flow as you read the Procedure Division. Worse than redundant, comments may be obsolete or inconsistent with the associated code, as is the case when program statements are changed during maintenance, and the comments are not correspondingly altered.

The authors certainly do not advocate the elimination of comments altogether, but argue simply that care, more than is commonly exercised, should be applied to developing them. One guideline is to provide a comment whenever the purpose of a program statement is not immediately obvious. Imagine, for example, that you are turning the program over to someone else for maintenance, and insert a comment whenever you would explain a statement to the other person. Comments should be used only to show *why* you are doing something, rather than *what* you are doing. Assume that the maintenance programmer is as competent in COBOL as you are; avoid using comments to explain how a particular COBOL statement works.

A Well-Written Program

Figure 7.4 is our final pass at the tuition billing program, with attention drawn to the application of the coding standards just developed. All data names within a 01 entry are given a common prefix: STU for entries in STUDENT-RECORD (lines 17–24), IND for data names under INDIVIDUAL-CALCULATIONS (lines 34–38), and so on. This guideline applies equally well to record descriptions in both the File and Working-Storage Sections.

Blank lines highlight 01 entries in the Data Division and paragraph headers in the Procedure Division. All PICTURE clauses are vertically aligned. Indentation is stressed in the Procedure Division with subservient clauses four columns under the associated statements.

Paragraph headers are sequenced and functional in nature. All statements within a paragraph pertain to the function of that paragraph, as indicated by its name. We have chosen a three-digit numerical sequencing scheme, in which the first digit reflects the hierarchy chart level and the remaining two digits reflect the order in which the paragraphs are performed.

Figure 7.4 A Well-Written COBOL Program

```
IDENTIFICATION DIVISION.
PROGRAM-ID.    TUITION7.
AUTHOR.        CAROL VAZQUEZ VILLAR.

ENVIRONMENT DIVISION.
INPUT-OUTPUT SECTION.
FILE-CONTROL.
    SELECT STUDENT-FILE
        ASSIGN TO UT-S-SYSIN.
    SELECT PRINT-FILE
        ASSIGN TO UT-S-SYSOUT.

DATA DIVISION.
FILE SECTION.
FD  STUDENT-FILE
    RECORD CONTAINS 27 CHARACTERS.
01  STUDENT-RECORD.
    05  STU-NAME.
        10  STU-LAST-NAME      PIC X(15).
        10  STU-INITIALS       PIC XX.
    05  STU-CREDITS            PIC 9(2).
    05  STU-UNION-MEMBER       PIC X.
    05  STU-SCHOLARSHIP        PIC 9(4).
    05  STU-GPA                PIC 9V99.

FD  PRINT-FILE
    RECORD CONTAINS 132 CHARACTERS.
01  PRINT-LINE                 PIC X(132).

WORKING-STORAGE SECTION.
01  DATA-REMAINS-SWITCH        PIC X(2)    VALUE SPACES.

01  INDIVIDUAL-CALCULATIONS.
    05  IND-TUITION            PIC 9(4)    VALUE ZEROS.
    05  IND-ACTIVITY-FEE       PIC 9(2)    VALUE ZEROS.
    05  IND-UNION-FEE          PIC 9(2)    VALUE ZEROS.
    05  IND-SCHOLARSHIP        PIC 9(4)    VALUE ZEROS.
    05  IND-BILL               PIC S9(6)   VALUE ZEROS.

01  UNIVERSITY-TOTALS.
    05  UNI-TUITION            PIC 9(6)    VALUE ZEROS.
    05  UNI-UNION-FEE          PIC 9(4)    VALUE ZEROS.
    05  UNI-ACTIVITY-FEE       PIC 9(4)    VALUE ZEROS.
    05  UNI-SCHOLARSHIP        PIC 9(6)    VALUE ZEROS.
    05  UNI-IND-BILL           PIC S9(6)   VALUE ZEROS.

01  CONSTANTS-AND-RATES.
    05  PRICE-PER-CREDIT       PIC 9(3)    VALUE 200.
    05  UNION-FEE              PIC 9(2)    VALUE 25.
    05  ACTIVITY-FEES.
```

Data names within 01 have common prefix

Blank lines appear before 01 entries

Figure 7.4 *(continued)*

```
                10  1ST-ACTIVITY-FEE PIC 99      VALUE 25.
                10  1ST-CREDIT-LIMIT PIC 99      VALUE 6.
                10  2ND-ACTIVITY-FEE PIC 99      VALUE 50.
                10  2ND-CREDIT-LIMIT PIC 99      VALUE 12.
                10  3RD-ACTIVITY-FEE PIC 99      VALUE 75.
            05  MINIMUM-SCHOLAR-GPA  PIC 9V9     VALUE 2.5.

        01  HEADING-LINE.
            05  FILLER               PIC X       VALUE SPACES.
            05  FILLER               PIC X(12)   VALUE 'STUDENT NAME'.
            05  FILLER               PIC X(10)   VALUE SPACES.
            05  FILLER               PIC X(7)    VALUE 'CREDITS'.
            05  FILLER               PIC X(2)    VALUE SPACES.
            05  FILLER               PIC X(7)    VALUE 'TUITION'.
            05  FILLER               PIC X(2)    VALUE SPACES.
            05  FILLER               PIC X(9)    VALUE 'UNION FEE'.
            05  FILLER               PIC X(2)    VALUE SPACES.
            05  FILLER               PIC X(7)    VALUE 'ACT FEE'.
            05  FILLER               PIC X(2)    VALUE SPACES.
            05  FILLER               PIC X(11)   VALUE 'SCHOLARSHIP'.
            05  FILLER               PIC X(2)    VALUE SPACES.
            05  FILLER               PIC X(10)   VALUE 'TOTAL BILL'.
            05  FILLER               PIC X(48)   VALUE SPACES.

        01  DETAIL-LINE.
            05  FILLER               PIC X       VALUE SPACES.
            05  DET-LAST-NAME        PIC X(15).
            05  FILLER               PIC X(2)    VALUE SPACES.
            05  DET-INITIALS         PIC X(2).
            05  FILLER               PIC X(5)    VALUE SPACES.
            05  DET-CREDITS          PIC Z9.
            05  FILLER               PIC X(4)    VALUE SPACES.
            05  DET-TUITION          PIC $$$$,$$9.
            05  FILLER               PIC X(6)    VALUE SPACES.
            05  DET-UNION-FEE        PIC $$$9    BLANK WHEN ZERO.
            05  FILLER               PIC X(5)    VALUE SPACES.
            05  DET-ACTIVITY-FEE     PIC $$$9    BLANK WHEN ZERO.
            05  FILLER               PIC X(6)    VALUE SPACES.
            05  DET-SCHOLARSHIP      PIC $$,$$$9 BLANK WHEN ZERO.
            05  FILLER               PIC X(4)    VALUE SPACES.
            05  DET-IND-BILL         PIC $$$$,$$9CR.
            05  FILLER               PIC X(47)   VALUE SPACES.

        01  DASH-LINE.
            05  FILLER               PIC X(31)   VALUE SPACES.
            05  FILLER               PIC X(8)    VALUE ALL '-'.
            05  FILLER               PIC X(2)    VALUE SPACES.
            05  FILLER               PIC X(8)    VALUE ALL '-'.
            05  FILLER               PIC X(2)    VALUE SPACES.
            05  FILLER               PIC X(7)    VALUE ALL '-'.
```

Figure 7.4 *(continued)*

```
       05  FILLER                 PIC X(6)     VALUE SPACES.
       05  FILLER                 PIC X(7)     VALUE ALL '-'.
       05  FILLER                 PIC X(5)     VALUE SPACES.
       05  FILLER                 PIC X(7)     VALUE ALL '-'.
       05  FILLER                 PIC X(49)    VALUE SPACES.

   01  TOTAL-LINE.
       05  FILLER                 PIC X(8)     VALUE SPACES.
       05  FILLER                 PIC X(17)
              VALUE 'UNIVERSITY TOTALS'.
       05  FILLER                 PIC X(6)     VALUE SPACES.
       05  TOT-TUITION            PIC $$$$,$$9.
       05  FILLER                 PIC X(2)     VALUE SPACES.
       05  TOT-UNION-FEE          PIC $$$$,$$9.
       05  FILLER                 PIC X        VALUE SPACES.
       05  TOT-ACTIVITY-FEE       PIC $$$$,$$9.
       05  FILLER                 PIC X(5)     VALUE SPACES.
       05  TOT-SCHOLARSHIP        PIC $$$$,$$9.
       05  FILLER                 PIC X(4)     VALUE SPACES.
       05  TOT-IND-BILL           PIC $$$$,$$9CR.
       05  FILLER                 PIC X(47)    VALUE SPACES.

   PROCEDURE DIVISION.
   100-PREPARE-TUITION-REPORT.
       OPEN INPUT STUDENT-FILE
            OUTPUT PRINT-FILE.
       PERFORM 210-WRITE-HEADING-LINE.
       PERFORM 230-READ-STUDENT-FILE.
       PERFORM 260-PROCESS-STUDENT-RECORD
            UNTIL DATA-REMAINS-SWITCH = 'NO'.
       PERFORM 290-WRITE-UNIVERSITY-TOTALS.
       CLOSE STUDENT-FILE
             PRINT-FILE.
       STOP RUN.

   210-WRITE-HEADING-LINE.
       MOVE HEADING-LINE TO PRINT-LINE.
       WRITE PRINT-LINE
           AFTER ADVANCING PAGE.
       MOVE SPACES TO PRINT-LINE.
       WRITE PRINT-LINE.

   230-READ-STUDENT-FILE.
       READ STUDENT-FILE
           AT END MOVE 'NO' TO DATA-REMAINS-SWITCH
       END-READ.

   260-PROCESS-STUDENT-RECORD.
       PERFORM 310-COMPUTE-INDIVIDUAL-BILL.
       PERFORM 330-INCREMENT-UNIVER-TOTALS
```

Data names within 01 have common prefix

Subservient Procedure Division clauses are indented

Figure 7.4 *(continued)*

```
           PERFORM 360-WRITE-DETAIL-LINE.
           PERFORM 230-READ-STUDENT-FILE.

       290-WRITE-UNIVERSITY-TOTALS.
           MOVE DASH-LINE TO PRINT-LINE.
           WRITE PRINT-LINE.
           MOVE UNI-TUITION TO TOT-TUITION.
           MOVE UNI-UNION-FEE TO TOT-UNION-FEE.
           MOVE UNI-ACTIVITY-FEE TO TOT-ACTIVITY-FEE.
           MOVE UNI-SCHOLARSHIP TO TOT-SCHOLARSHIP.
           MOVE UNI-IND-BILL TO TOT-IND-BILL.
           MOVE TOTAL-LINE TO PRINT-LINE.
           WRITE PRINT-LINE
               AFTER ADVANCING 1 LINE.

       310-COMPUTE-INDIVIDUAL-BILL.
           PERFORM 410-COMPUTE-TUITION.
           PERFORM 430-COMPUTE-UNION-FEE.
           PERFORM 460-COMPUTE-ACTIVITY-FEE.
           PERFORM 490-COMPUTE-SCHOLARSHIP.
           COMPUTE IND-BILL = IND-TUITION + IND-UNION-FEE +
              IND-ACTIVITY-FEE - IND-SCHOLARSHIP.

       330-INCREMENT-UNIVER-TOTALS.
           ADD IND-TUITION      TO UNI-TUITION.
           ADD IND-UNION-FEE    TO UNI-UNION-FEE.
           ADD IND-ACTIVITY-FEE TO UNI-ACTIVITY-FEE.
           ADD IND-SCHOLARSHIP  TO UNI-SCHOLARSHIP.
           ADD IND-BILL         TO UNI-IND-BILL.

       360-WRITE-DETAIL-LINE.
           MOVE STU-LAST-NAME TO DET-LAST-NAME.
           MOVE STU-INITIALS TO DET-INITIALS.
           MOVE STU-CREDITS TO DET-CREDITS.
           MOVE IND-TUITION TO DET-TUITION.
           MOVE IND-UNION-FEE TO DET-UNION-FEE.
           MOVE IND-ACTIVITY-FEE TO DET-ACTIVITY-FEE.
           MOVE IND-SCHOLARSHIP TO DET-SCHOLARSHIP.
           MOVE IND-BILL TO DET-IND-BILL.
           MOVE DETAIL-LINE TO PRINT-LINE.
           WRITE PRINT-LINE
               AFTER ADVANCING 1 LINE.

       410-COMPUTE-TUITION.
           COMPUTE IND-TUITION = PRICE-PER-CREDIT * STU-CREDITS.

       430-COMPUTE-UNION-FEE.
           IF STU-UNION-MEMBER = 'Y'
              MOVE UNION-FEE TO IND-UNION-FEE
           ELSE
```

Paragraph names are functional, i.e., verb, adjective, object

Continued line is indented

Paragraph names are functional, i.e., verb, adjective, object

IF/ELSE statement indented and ends with END-IF scope terminator

Figure 7.4 *(continued)*

```
            MOVE ZERO TO IND-UNION-FEE
        END-IF.

    460-COMPUTE-ACTIVITY-FEE.
        EVALUATE TRUE
            WHEN STU-CREDITS <= 1ST-CREDIT-LIMIT
                MOVE 1ST-ACTIVITY-FEE TO IND-ACTIVITY-FEE
            WHEN STU-CREDITS > 1ST-CREDIT-LIMIT
                AND STU-CREDITS <= 2ND-CREDIT-LIMIT
                    MOVE 2ND-ACTIVITY-FEE TO IND-ACTIVITY-FEE
            WHEN STU-CREDITS > 2ND-CREDIT-LIMIT
                MOVE 3RD-ACTIVITY-FEE TO IND-ACTIVITY-FEE
            WHEN OTHER
                DISPLAY 'INVALID CREDITS FOR: ' STU-NAME
        END-EVALUATE.

    490-COMPUTE-SCHOLARSHIP.
        IF STU-GPA > MINIMUM-SCHOLAR-GPA
           MOVE STU-SCHOLARSHIP TO IND-SCHOLARSHIP
        ELSE
           MOVE ZERO TO IND-SCHOLARSHIP
        END-IF.
```

IF/ELSE statement indented and ends with END-IF scope terminator

SUMMARY

Points to Remember

- A numeric field contains digits, an (optional) implied decimal point, and/or an optional sign. A numeric-edited field may contain any editing character. All calculations in a COBOL program are done on numeric fields, whose computed values are moved to numeric-edited fields prior to printing.
- Any move involving a numeric field and a numeric-edited field maintains decimal alignment.
- Only a signed numeric field can hold a negative value; that is, a numeric field cannot retain a negative value unless it has been defined with an S in its PICTURE clause.
- Coding standards are intended to improve the readability and maintainability of COBOL programs. They are imposed by individual installations and go beyond the requirements of COBOL.

Key Words and Concepts

Actual decimal point
Check protection
Coding standards
CR
DB
Decimal alignment
Editing
Editing characters
Fixed dollar sign
Floating dollar sign
Floating minus sign
Floating plus sign
Functional paragraph
Implied decimal point
Indentation
Insertion characters
Maintainability
Numeric field
Numeric-edited field
Prefixing data names
Readability
Receiving field
Sequencing paragraph names
Signed numbers
Source (sending) field
Zero suppression

COBOL Element

BLANK WHEN ZERO

FILL-IN

1. ______________ ______________ are a set of rules unique to each installation, which go beyond the rules of COBOL, to improve the readability of a COBOL program.
2. The editing characters, ______________ and ______________, will appear if and only if the sending field is ______________ and are suppressed otherwise.
3. The presence of multiple dollar signs in the PICTURE clause of an edited field indicates a ______________ dollar sign, whereas a single dollar sign indicates a ______________ dollar sign.
4. The ______________ is the character used for check protection.
5. The PICTURE clause of a numeric field may consist of 9's, a ______________ to indicate an implied decimal point, and the letter ______________ to indicate a signed field.
6. Continuation of a ______________ literal requires a ______________ in column ______________.
7. A well-chosen paragraph name consists of a ______________, ______________, and ______________ to indicate the function of that paragraph.
8. All data names within the same 01 record should begin with a common ______________.
9. ______________ of COBOL statements within the B margin does not affect compiler interpretation but goes a long way toward improving the readability of a program.
10. ______________ ______________ may be left before 01 records and paragraph names to enhance readability.

11. If a numeric field is defined without an S in its PICTURE clause, the field will never assume a ______________ value.
12. All calculations in a COBOL program are performed on (numeric/numeric-edited) fields.

TRUE/FALSE

1. Indentation within the B margin affects compiler interpretation.
2. Blank lines are not permitted within a COBOL program.
3. The COBOL coding standards for AT&T and IBM are apt to be identical.
4. COBOL requires that paragraph names be sequenced.
5. Data names should be as short as possible to cut down on the coding effort.
6. Indentation in COBOL is a waste of time.
7. A well-commented COBOL program should contain half as many comment lines as Procedure Division statements.
8. All continued statements require a hyphen in column 7.
9. COMPUTE-AND-WRITE is a good paragraph name.
10. Heading, detail, and total lines may be established as separate 01 entries in Working-Storage.
11. Every PICTURE clause requires a corresponding VALUE clause.
12. Arithmetic may be done on numeric-edited fields.
13. A positive field should always be defined with a CR in its PICTURE clause, whereas a negative field requires DB.
14. A single numeric-edited field may contain a dollar sign, comma, decimal point, asterisk, and the character string CR in its PICTURE clause.
15. The same numeric-edited field may contain both CR and DB in its PICTURE clause.
16. Hyphens may be used as insertion characters in a social security number.
17. Slashes may be used as insertion characters in a date.
18. The presence of CR or DB in a numeric-edited field implies that the sending field is signed.
19. Zero is a valid insertion character.

PROBLEMS

1. Supply PICTURE clauses for the receiving fields needed to accomplish the following:
   a. A floating dollar sign, omission of cents, printing (or suppression) of commas as appropriate, and a maximum value of $9,999,999.
   b. A fixed dollar sign, asterisk fill for insignificant leading zeros, printing (or suppression) of commas as appropriate, a maximum value of $9,999, and a trailing DB if the sending field is negative.

c. A fixed dollar sign, zero suppression of insignificant leading zeros, omission of commas in all instances, and a maximum value of $99,999.99.

d. A floating dollar sign, printing (or suppression) of commas as appropriate, a maximum value of $9,999.00, and a trailing CR if the sending field is negative.

2. Show the value of the edited result for each of the following entries:

	SOURCE FIELD		RECEIVING FIELD	
	PICTURE	VALUE	PICTURE	EDITED RESULT
a.	9(6)	123456	9(6)	________
b.	9(6)	123456	9(8)	________
c.	9(6)	123456	9(6).99	________
d.	9(4)V99	123456	9(6)	________
e.	9(4)V99	123456	9(4)	________
f.	9(4)V99	123456	$$$$$9.99	________
g.	9(4)V99	123456	$$$,$$9.99	________
h.	9(6)	123456	$$$$,$$9.99	________
i.	9(6)	123456	Z(8)	________
j.	9(4)V99	123456	$ZZZ,ZZZ.99	________

3. Show the edited results for each entry:

	SOURCE FIELD		RECEIVING FIELD	
	PICTURE	VALUE	PICTURE	EDITED RESULT
a.	S9(4)V99	45600	$$$$$.99CR	________
b.	S9(4)V99	45600	$$,$$$.99DB	________
c.	S9(4)	4567	$$,$$$.00	________
d.	S9(6)	122577	99B99B99	________
e.	S9(6)	123456	++++,+++	________
f.	S9(6)	-123456	++++,+++	________
g.	S9(6)	123456	----,---	________
h.	S9(6)	-123456	----,---	________
i.	9(4)V99	567890	$$$$,$$$.99	________
j.	9(4)V99	567890	$ZZZ,ZZZ.99	________
k.	9(4)V99	567890	$***,***.99	________

4. What, if anything, is wrong (either syntactically or logically) with the following PICTURE clauses?

a. $,$$$,$$9.99

b. 999999999

c. $$$$,$$$,$$$

d. $ZZZ.ZZ

e. $999V99

f. $999,999,999.99

g. $$$$$,$$9.99

5. Do you agree with all of the coding standards suggested by the authors? Can you suggest any others? Do you think the imposition of coding standards within an installation impinges on the creativity of individual programmers? Are coding standards worth the extra time and trouble they require?

6. Consider the following code:

```
01  AMOUNT-REMAINING            PIC 9(3)      VALUE 100.
01  WS-INPUT-AREA.
    05  QUANTITY-SHIPPED        PIC 99.
    05  REST-OF-A-RECORD        PIC X(50).
      .
          .
              .
    READ TRANSACTION-FILE INTO WS-INPUT-AREA
        AT END MOVE 'YES' TO EOF-SWITCH
    END-READ.
    PERFORM PROCESS-TRANSACTIONS
        UNTIL EOF-SWITCH = 'YES'.
      .
          .
              .
PROCESS-TRANSACTIONS.
    SUBTRACT QUANTITY-SHIPPED FROM AMOUNT-REMAINING.
    READ TRANSACTION-FILE INTO WS-INPUT-AREA
        AT END MOVE 'YES' TO EOF-SWITCH
    END-READ.
```

a. Why will AMOUNT-REMAINING never be less than zero?

b. What will be the final value of AMOUNT-REMAINING, given successive values of 30, 50, 25, and 15 for QUANTITY-SHIPPED?

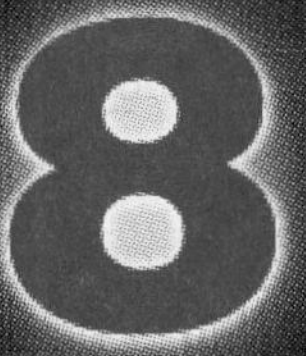

Data Validation

CHAPTER OUTLINE

OBJECTIVES

After reading this chapter you will be able to:

- Describe the importance of data validation and its implementation in a stand-alone edit program.
- Define the following validity tests: numeric test, alphabetic test, consistency check, sequence check, completeness check, date check, and subscript check.
- Describe the various types of conditions in an IF statement.
- Define a nested IF; indicate guidelines for proper indentation in coding such statements.
- Describe the advantages of the END-IF scope terminator; show how the scope terminator eliminates the need for the NEXT SENTENCE clause.
- Obtain the date (calendar and Julian) and time of execution; implement date checking in a program to ensure that the day and month are consistent.

OVERVIEW

This chapter introduces the concept of data validation, the process of ensuring that data entered into a system is as error-free as possible. It begins by describing various types of error checking, then focuses on the IF statement, the means by which data validation is implemented in COBOL. We cover the different types of conditions that exist within an IF statement (relation, class, sign, and condition name), the concept of a nested IF, and the importance of the END-IF scope terminator.

The second half of the chapter develops a stand-alone edit program to illustrate the implementation of data validation. The program is designed to process a file of incoming transactions, reject invalid transactions with appropriate error messages, and write valid transactions to an output file. The latter is then input to a reporting (or other) program.

Systems Concepts: Data Validation

A well-written program is not limited to merely computing answers, but must also validate the data on which those answers are based. Failure to do so results in programs that produce meaningless or inaccurate information, a situation described by the cliché GIGO (Garbage In, Garbage Out). It is the job of the programmer or analyst to ensure that a system remains as error-free as possible and that the "garbage" does not enter the system in the first place.

Incoming data may be validated within the program in which it is used or in a separate stand-alone edit program. The essential point is that incoming data *must* be checked; when and how this is done is of secondary importance. The following are typical types of data validation:

Numeric test. Ensures that a numeric field contains numeric data. Commas, dollar signs, decimal points, blanks, or other alphabetic characters are not numeric, and will cause problems in execution.

Alphabetic test. Analogous to a numeric test, except that alphabetic fields should contain only alphabetic data. Any errors detected here are typically less serious than for numeric fields.

Reasonableness (limit or range) check. Ensures that a number is within expected limits; that is, that a value does not exceed a designated upper or lower extreme.

Consistency check. Verifies that the values in two or more fields are consistent, for example, salary and job title. Other examples of consistency checks are an individual's credit rating and the amount of credit a bank is willing to extend, or (as used by the Internal Revenue Service) an individual's reported income and the zip code.

Existing code check. One of the most important tests, the omission of which produces countless errors. Consider:

```
IF SEX = 'M'
    ADD 1 TO NUMBER-OF-MEN
ELSE
    ADD 1 TO NUMBER-OF-WOMEN
END-IF.
```

It is decidedly poor practice to assume that an incoming record is female if it is not male. Both codes should be explicitly checked, and if neither occurs, a suitable error should be printed.

Sequence check. Ensures that incoming records are in proper order. It can also be used when one record is continued over several lines to ensure that the lines within a record are in proper sequence.

Completeness check. Verifies that data in all required fields are present; this check is normally used when new records are added to a file.

Date check. Ensures that an incoming date is acceptable—for example, that the day is from 1 to 31, the month from 1 to 12, and the year within a designated period, often just the current year. A further check is that the month and day are consistent with one another—for example, a date of April 31 is invalid.

Subscript check. Validates that a subscript or index is within a table's original definition. (Table processing is discussed fully in Chapter 11.)

Diligent application of data validation (sometimes referred to as defensive programming) minimizes the need for subsequent debugging. It assumes that errors will occur and takes steps to make them apparent to the programmer and/or user *before* a program terminates. Is it worth the extra time? Emphatically yes, especially if you have ever been called at two in the morning to hear that your program "bombed" because of invalid data.

The IF Statement

The importance of the *IF* statement is obvious, yet the large number of options make it one of the more difficult statements to master. Essential to any IF statement, however, is the condition, the portion of the statement that is evaluated as either true or false. Four types of conditions are possible: relational, class, sign, and condition-name, each of which is discussed in a separate section.

Relational Condition

The ***relational condition*** is the most common type of condition and has appeared throughout the book. As you already know there is considerable variation in the way the relational operator may be expressed. In all instances, however, the condition compares the quantities on either side of the relational operator to determine whether (or not) the condition is true.

The data type of the quantities being compared must be the same; for example, a numeric data item must be compared to a numeric literal and a nonnumeric data item to a nonnumeric literal. Failure to do so produces a syntax error during compilation. The relational condition is illustrated in Figure 8.1.

Figure 8.1 The Relational Condition

```
                       IS [NOT] GREATER THAN
                       IS [NOT] >
                       IS [NOT] LESS THAN
    identifier-1       IS [NOT] <                              identifier-2
IF  literal-1          IS [NOT] EQUAL TO                       literal-2
    expression-1       IS [NOT] =                              expression-2
                       IS [NOT] GREATER THAN OR EQUAL TO
                       IS [NOT] >=
                       IS [NOT] LESS THAN OR EQUAL TO
                       IS [NOT] <=
```

(a) Syntax

```
05  NUMERIC-FIELD              PIC 9(5).
05  ALPHANUMERIC-FIELD         PIC X(5).
.
   .
      .
IF NUMERIC-FIELD = 10 . . .           (valid entry)
IF NUMERIC-FIELD = '10' . . .         (invalid entry)
IF ALPHANUMERIC-FIELD = 10 . . .      (invalid entry)
IF ALPHANUMERIC-FIELD = '10' . . .    (valid entry)
```

(b) Examples

Class Test

The ***class test*** ensures that a field contains numeric or alphabetic data in accordance with its PICTURE clause. A valid numeric field will contain only the digits 0 to 9 (a sign is optional); blanks, decimal points, commas, and other editing characters are not valid as numeric characters. A valid alphabetic field will contain the letters A to Z (upper or lower case) and/or blanks. An alphanumeric field may contain any character; letters, numbers, and/or special characters.

The class test cannot be used indiscriminately; that is, a numeric test cannot be used for data names defined as alphabetic, nor can an alphabetic test be used for numeric data names. Either test, however, may be performed on alphanumeric items. The class test is illustrated in Figure 8.2

Figure 8.2 The Class Test

```
                                   { NUMERIC          }
IF identifier IS [NOT]             { ALPHABETIC       }
                                   { ALPHABETIC-UPPER }
                                   { ALPHABETIC-LOWER }
```

(a) Syntax

```
05  NUMERIC-FIELD                     PIC 9(5).
05  ALPHABETIC-FIELD                  PIC A(5).
.
    .
        .
IF NUMERIC-FIELD IS NUMERIC
    PERFORM DO-ARITHMETIC-CALCULATIONS
END-IF.

IF NUMERIC-FIELD IS NOT NUMERIC
    DISPLAY 'ERROR - NUMERIC FIELD CONTAINS INVALID DATA'
END-IF.

IF ALPHABETIC-FIELD IS ALPHABETIC
    DISPLAY 'ALPHABETIC FIELD CONTAINS UPPER AND/OR LOWER CASE LETTERS'
END-IF.

IF ALPHABETIC-FIELD IS NOT ALPHABETIC
    DISPLAY 'ALPHABETIC FIELD CONTAINS NON-ALPHABETIC DATA'
END-IF.
```

(b) Examples

Figure 8.3 The Sign Test

```
      {identifier           }         {POSITIVE}
   IF {                     } IS [NOT] {NEGATIVE}
      {arithmetic expression}         {ZERO    }
```

(a) Syntax

```
IF NET-PAY IS NOT POSITIVE
    PERFORM TOO-MUCH-TAXES
END-IF.

IF CHECK-BALANCE IS NEGATIVE
    PERFORM OVERDRAWN
END-IF.
```

(b) Examples

Sign Test

The ***sign test*** determines whether a numeric field is positive, negative, or zero. The test is of limited value and could in fact be replaced with the equivalent relational condition. Nevertheless, the sign test is illustrated in Figure 8.3.

Condition-Name Test

A ***condition name*** (88-level entry) is a special way of writing a relational condition that makes it (the condition) easier to read. Condition names are defined in the Data Division, then referenced in the Procedure Division as shown in Figure 8.4. Condition names are used for elementary items only.

The definition of a condition name in the Data Division simplifies subsequent coding in the Procedure Division; for example, IF FRESHMAN is equivalent to IF YEAR-CODE = 1. 88-level entries provide improved documentation in that IF FRESHMAN is inherently clearer than IF YEAR-CODE = 1.

The use of an 88-level entry also allows multiple codes to be grouped under a single data name; for example, VALID-CODES is defined as any value from 1 to 8. This in turn makes it possible to test for an invalid code with a simple IF statement as shown in Figure 8.4b. Note, too, that condition names permit a given value to appear under more than one classification; for example, records containing a 3 belong to JUNIOR, UPPER-CLASSMAN, and VALID-CODES.

Compound Test

Any two simple tests may be combined to form a ***compound test*** through the logical operators AND and OR. AND implies that both conditions must be satisfied for the IF to be considered true, whereas OR requires that only one of the conditions be satisfied. A flowchart is shown in Figure 8.5a depicting the AND condition. It requires that *both* A be greater than B *and* C be greater than D in order to proceed to TRUE. If either of these tests fails, the compound condition is judged false. The general format is:

```
                 {{AND}             }
IF condition-1   {{   } condition-2 } . . .
                 {{OR }             }
```

Figure 8.4 Condition Names (88-level entries)

```
88 data-name {VALUE IS  } {literal-1 [{THROUGH} literal-2]} . . .
             {VALUES ARE}            [{THRU   }          ]
```

(a) Syntax

```
 05  YEAR-CODE            PIC 9.
     88  FRESHMAN             VALUE 1.
     88  SOPHOMORE            VALUE 2.
     88  JUNIOR               VALUE 3.
     88  SENIOR               VALUE 4.
     88  GRAD-STUDENT         VALUES ARE 5 THRU 8.
     88  UNDER-CLASSMAN       VALUES ARE 1, 2.
     88  UPPER-CLASSMAN       VALUES ARE 3, 4.
     88  VALID-CODES          VALUES ARE 1 THRU 8.
.
   .
      .
IF FRESHMAN
    PERFORM WELCOME-NEW-STUDENTS
END-IF.

IF VALID-CODES
    PERFORM PROCESS-STUDENT-RECORD
ELSE
    DISPLAY 'INCOMING YEAR CODE IS IN ERROR'
END-IF.
```

(b) Examples

Figure 8.5b contains a flowchart for a compound OR in which only one of two conditions needs to be met for the condition to be considered true. Thus, if either A is greater than B or C is greater than D, processing is directed to TRUE.

Hierarchy of Operations

IF statements containing compound conditions can become difficult to interpret; for example, in the statement,

```
IF X > Y OR X = Z AND X < W ...
```

which takes precedence, AND or OR? To provide an unequivocal evaluation of compound conditions, the following hierarchy for evaluation is established:

1. Arithmetic expressions
2. Relational operators
3. NOT condition
4. AND (from left to right if more than one)
5. OR (from left to right if more than one)

Figure 8.5 Compound Conditions

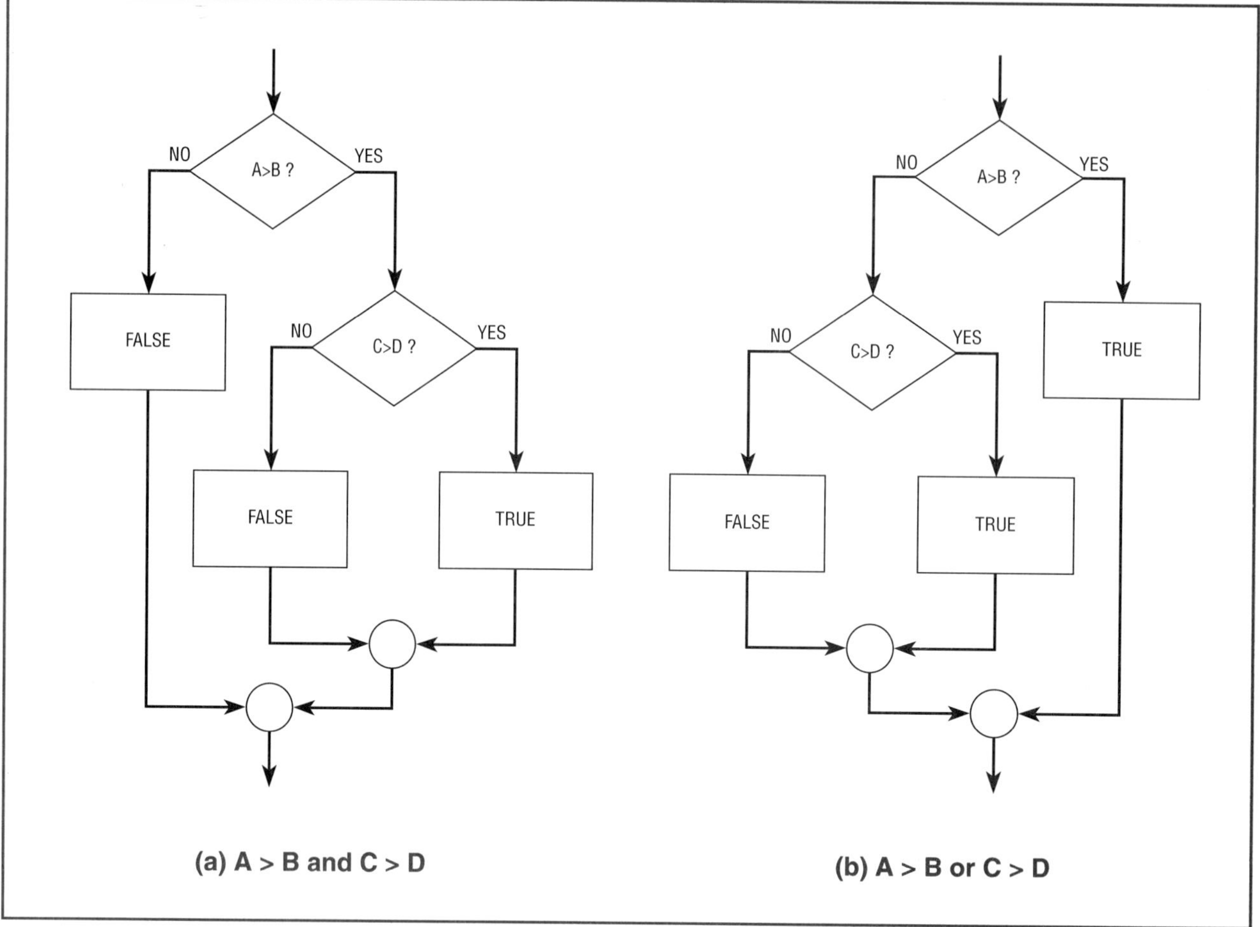

Thus, for the preceding statement to be true, either

```
X > Y
```

or

```
X = Z and X < W
```

Parentheses can (and should) be used to clarify the programmer's intent and the preceding statement is made clearer if it is rewritten as

```
IF X > Y OR (X = Z AND X < W) . . .
```

Parentheses can also *alter* the outcome in that the expression in parentheses is evaluated first. The following statement is *logically different* from the original statement:

```
IF (X > Y OR X = Z) AND X < W . . .
```

In this example the condition in parentheses (X > Y OR X = Z) is evaluated first, after which X is compared to W. Both conditions (the one in parentheses and X < W) must be true for the compound condition to be considered true.

Implied Conditions

The simple conditions within a compound condition often have the same subject as in the statement:

```
IF SALARY > 30000 AND SALARY < 40000
```

A more concise way of expressing this logic is with an ***implied condition***, which requires only the first occurrence of the subject; that is,

```
IF SALARY > 30000 AND < 40000
```

is equivalent to the earlier entry. If both the subject and relational operator are the same, then only the first occurrence of both needs to be written; that is,

```
IF DEPARTMENT = 10 OR 20
```

is equivalent to

```
IF DEPARTMENT = 10 OR DEPARTMENT = 20
```

Implied conditions are often confusing and the following are provided as additional examples:

```
IF X = Y OR Z        is equivalent to IF X = Y OR X = Z
IF A = B OR C OR D   is equivalent to IF A = B OR A = C OR A = D
IF A = B AND C       is equivalent to IF A = B AND A = C
```

Nested IFs

The general format of the IF statement is:

```
                                                 {ELSE   statement-2 . . . [END-IF]}
IF condition-1 THEN {statement-1 . . .  }        {ELSE   NEXT SENTENCE             }
                    {NEXT SENTENCE      }        {END-IF                           }
```

A ***nested IF*** results when either statement-1 or statement-2 is itself another IF statement, that is, when there are two or more IFs in one sentence. For example, consider

```
IF A > B
    IF C > D
        MOVE S TO W
        MOVE X TO Y
    ELSE
        ADD 1 TO Z
    END-IF
END-IF.
```

The ELSE clause is associated with the closest previous IF that is not already paired with another ELSE. Hence, in this example, Z is incremented by 1 if A is greater than B, but C is not greater than D. If, however, A is not greater than B, control passes to the statement immediately following the period with no further action being taken. (The END-IF scope terminator is optional in both instances, but is included as per our coding standard of Chapter 7 of always specifying the scope terminator.)

Figure 8.6 shows a flowchart and corresponding COBOL code to determine the largest of three quantities A, B, and C. (They are assumed to be unequal numbers.) Observe how the true and false branches of each decision block meet in a single exit point and how this corresponds to the COBOL code. Notice also how the indentation

Figure 8.6 Nested IF Statements

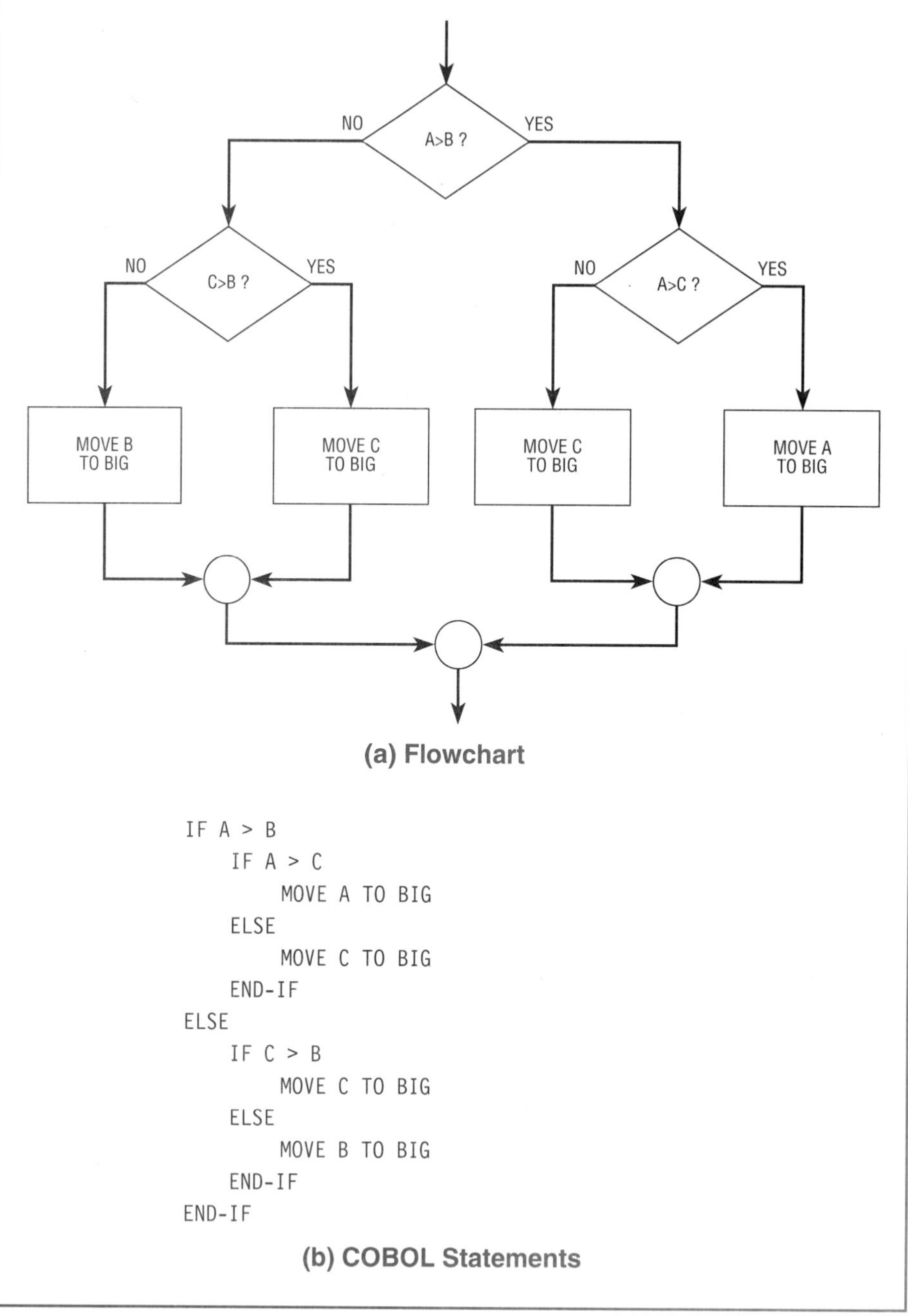

(a) Flowchart

```
IF A > B
    IF A > C
        MOVE A TO BIG
    ELSE
        MOVE C TO BIG
    END-IF
ELSE
    IF C > B
        MOVE C TO BIG
    ELSE
        MOVE B TO BIG
    END-IF
END-IF
```

(b) COBOL Statements

in the COBOL statement facilitates interpretation of the statement. (The compiler pays no attention to the indentation, which is done strictly for programmer convenience.)

We advocate careful attention to indentation and recommend the following guidelines:

1. Each nested IF should be indented four columns from the previous IF.
2. ELSE should appear on a line by itself directly under its associated IF.
3. Detail lines should be indented four columns under both IF and ELSE.

4. The END-IF scope terminator should always be used and appear on a line by itself directly under its associated IF.

These guidelines were used in Figure 8.6.

NEXT SENTENCE

The **NEXT SENTENCE** clause directs control to the statement following the period in an IF statement. It was an essential clause in COBOL-74 to implement certain types of nested IF statements, but is no longer needed due to the the END-IF scope terminator in COBOL-85. The use of NEXT SENTENCE is compared to the scope terminator in Figure 8.7.

Figure 8.7 Nested IF Statements/II

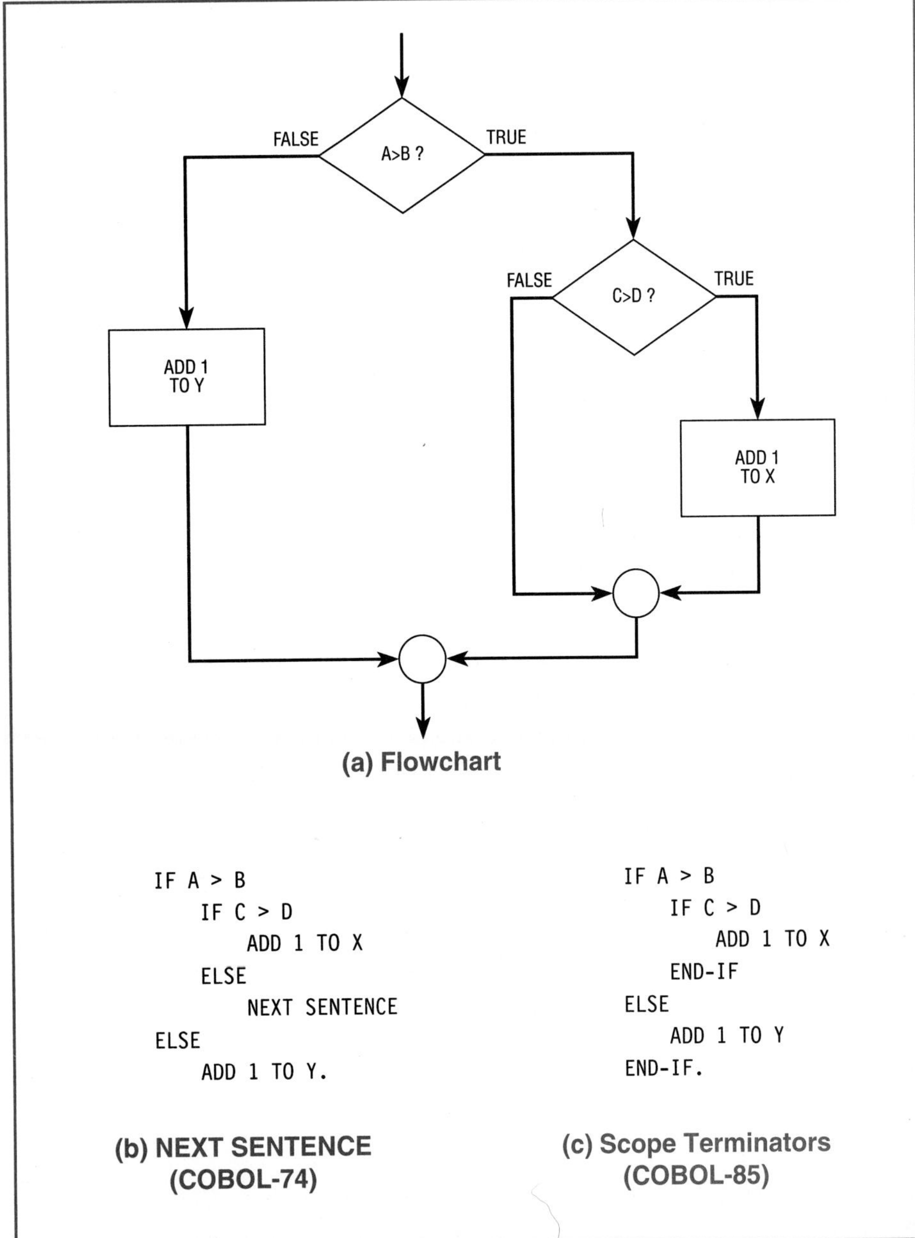

(a) Flowchart

```
IF A > B
    IF C > D
        ADD 1 TO X
    ELSE
        NEXT SENTENCE
ELSE
    ADD 1 TO Y.
```

(b) NEXT SENTENCE (COBOL-74)

```
IF A > B
    IF C > D
        ADD 1 TO X
    END-IF
ELSE
    ADD 1 TO Y
END-IF.
```

(c) Scope Terminators (COBOL-85)

The intended logic is to add 1 to X if A is greater than B and C is greater than D; if, however, A is greater than B, but C is not greater than D, no further action is to be taken. The NEXT SENTENCE clause in Figure 8.7b terminates the IF statement if the second condition (C > D) is not met. The identical effect is achieved by the END-IF scope terminator in Figure 8.7c.

ACCEPT Statement

The **ACCEPT** statement is used to obtain the day of the week, date, and/or time of program execution. Consider:

```
                                 ⎧DAY-OF-WEEK⎫
ACCEPT identifier-1 FROM ⎨DATE       ⎬
                                 ⎪DAY        ⎪
                                 ⎩TIME       ⎭
```

Identifier-1 is a programmer-defined work area that holds the information being accepted such as the DAY-OF-WEEK, DATE, DAY, or TIME. The DAY-OF-WEEK is returned as a single digit, from one to seven inclusive, corresponding to Monday through Sunday. (See Figure 9.8 in the next chapter.) DATE and DAY both reflect the current date, but in different formats. Specification of DATE places a six-digit numeric field into identifier-1 in the form *yymmdd;* the first two digits contain year; the next two, month; and the last two, the day of the month; for example, 930316, denotes March 16, 1993.

Specification of DAY, rather than DATE, returns a five-digit numeric field to the work area. The first two digits represent year and the last three the day of the year, numbered from 1 to 365 (366 in a leap year). March 16, 1993, would be represented as 93075, but March 16, 1992, as 92076, since 1992 is a leap year. (A date written in this format is known as a ***Julian date.***)

TIME returns an eight-digit numeric field, *hhmmsshh*, in a 24-hour system. It contains the number of elapsed hours, minutes, seconds, and hundredths of seconds after midnight, in that order, from left to right. 10:15 A.M. would return as 10150000, 10:15 P.M. as 22150000.

Calculations Involving Dates

Once the date of execution is obtained, it can be used for various types of date validation such as checking that an employee's hire date is within the current year. It can also be used in various calculations, for example, to compute an employee's age, or to determine which accounts haven't been paid in 30 days. Figure 8.8 illustrates how an employee's age may be calculated from the date of execution and the employee's birth date.

You should verify that the COMPUTE statement in Figure 8.8 works as intended, and further that it works for all combinations of data. This is best accomplished by "playing computer" and plugging in numbers. Accordingly, consider two examples:

Example 8.1

```
Date of birth: 3/73
Date of execution: 6/93
Expected age: 20 1/4
Calculation: 93 - 73 + (6 - 3)/12 = 20 + 3/12 = 20.25
```

Figure 8.8 The ACCEPT Statement

```
WORKING-STORAGE SECTION.

01  EMPLOYEE-RECORD.
    .
       .
    05  EMP-DATE-OF-BIRTH.
        10  EMP-BIRTH-MONTH             PIC 99.
        10  EMP-BIRTH-YEAR              PIC 99.

01  EMPLOYEE-AGE                        PIC 99V99.

01  DATE-WORK-AREA.
    05  TODAYS-YEAR                     PIC 99.
    05  TODAYS-MONTH                    PIC 99.
    05  TODAYS-DAY                      PIC 99.
    .
       .

PROCEDURE DIVISION.
    .
       .
    ACCEPT DATE-WORK-AREA FROM DATE.
    .
       .

    COMPUTE EMPLOYEE-AGE = TODAYS-YEAR - EMP-BIRTH-YEAR
        + (TODAYS-MONTH - EMP-BIRTH-MONTH) / 12.
```

Example 8.2

```
Date of birth: 9/73
Date of execution: 6/93
Expected age: 19 3/4
Calculation: 93 - 73 + (6 - 9)/12 = 20 + -3/12 = 19.75
```

The calculations are correct, and they work for both combinations of data; it doesn't matter whether the month of execution is before or after the birth month. (For simplicity only month and year were used in the calculation of age.)

The Stand-Alone Edit Program

The validation of incoming data is often done in a stand-alone edit program as opposed to the reporting program that processes the data. The sequence is shown in Figure 8.9. A transaction file is input to the edit program, which checks each incoming record for validity. Invalid transactions are rejected with an appropriate error message(s), whereas valid transactions are written to an output file. The valid transaction file (i.e., the output file from the edit program) is then input to a reporting program.

Figure 8.9 The Stand-Alone Edit Program

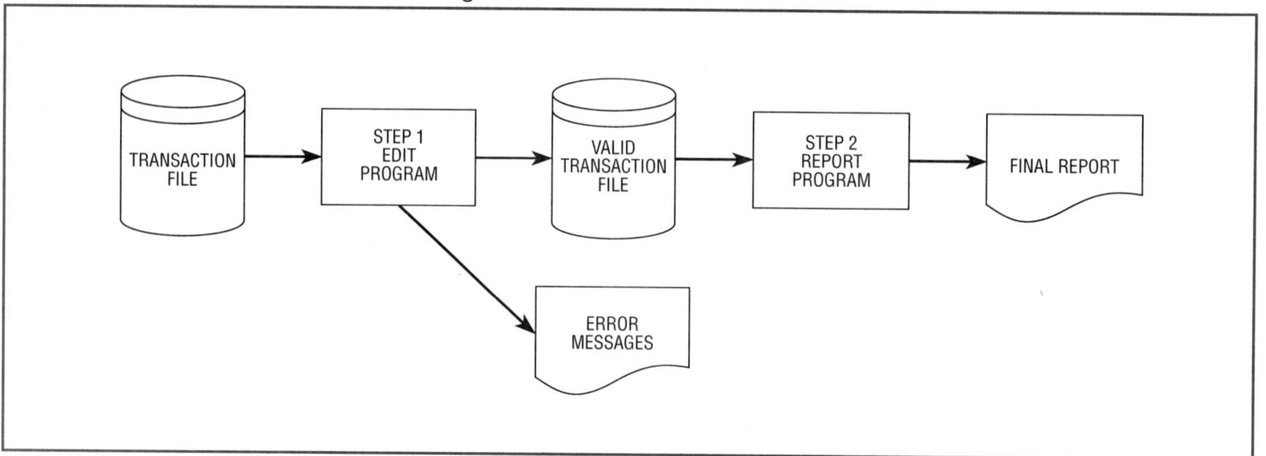

The flowchart in Figure 8.9 serves as an effective blueprint for the *combination* of programs that are developed in this chapter and the next. The programs are related to one another in that the output of the edit program in this chapter will be input to the reporting program in Chapter 9. Specifications for the edit program are given below, whereas the requirements of the reporting program are presented in Chapter 9.

PROGRAMMING SPECIFICATIONS

Program Name: Car Rental Validation

Narrative: The specifications describe a stand-alone edit program for car rental transactions, each of which is subject to multiple validity checks. Invalid transactions are to be rejected with appropriate error message(s), whereas valid transactions are to be written in their entirety to an output file; the latter will be input to a reporting program developed in the next chapter.

Input File(s): RENTAL-RECORD-FILE

Input Record Layout:

```
01  RENTAL-RECORD-IN.
    05  REN-CONTRACT-NO          PIC 9(6).
    05  REN-NAME.
        10  REN-LAST-NAME        PIC X(15).
        10  REN-FIRST-NAME       PIC X(10).
        10  REN-INITIAL          PIC X.
    05  REN-RETURNED-DATE.
        10  REN-RETURNED-YEAR    PIC 9(2).
        10  REN-RETURNED-MONTH   PIC 9(2).
        10  REN-RETURNED-DAY     PIC 9(2).
    05  REN-CAR-TYPE             PIC X.
    05  REN-DAYS-RENTED          PIC 99.
    05  REN-MILEAGE.
        10  REN-MILES-IN         PIC 9(6).
        10  REN-MILES-OUT        PIC 9(6).
        10  REN-MILEAGE-RATE     PIC 99.
    05  REN-INSURANCE            PIC X.
```

Test Data: See Figure 8.10a (Four errors are identified.)

Report Layout: See Figure 8.10b

Processing Requirements:

1. Read a file of car rental records.
2. Validate each input record for all of the following:
   a. A numeric contract number; print the message *Nonnumeric Contract Number* for any nonnumeric contract.
   b. The presence of both a first and last name; print the message *Missing last name* or *Missing first name* for a record missing either field. A middle initial is not required, but if present, the initial must be alphabetic; print the message *Nonalphabetic initial* as appropriate.
   c. A valid car type where the code is one of five values; E, C, M, F, or L. Print the message *Car type must be: E, C, M, F, or L* for any record with an invalid car type.
   d. Valid dates:
      (1) A valid month; that is, a month must be from 1 to 12; print the message *Month must be between 1 and 12* for any invalid month.
      (2) A valid day; that is, the day cannot exceed the maximum days in the corresponding month; print the message *Invalid Day* for any date that is inconsistent with the month—for example, April 31.
      (3) A valid date; that is, a date that is less than or equal to the system date; print the message *Date has not yet occurred* for any date in the future.
   e. A valid number of days rented where the number of days is numeric, is greater than zero, and less than or equal to 35. Print appropriate error messages for any condition that is not met; e.g., *Days rented must be numeric, Days rented must be > zero*, or *Refer to Long-Term Leasing.*

Figure 8.10 Transaction Files and Error Reports

```
123459BAKER          ROBERT   G930431F0500670000664025X      1 Invalid date
987651BROWN          PETER    G930112M1000353000352000N
999999JONES          TOM      J931309E35004500004600005Y     2 Inconsistent mileage
987655BROWNING       PAULA    J931024007002400002525 00Y
999777ELSINOR        TERRY    R921126F0500168000159005N
655443FITZPATRICK    DAN      T930532L0701000000987000C
987654SMITH          PAUL     G921213M0300510000500502Y
      PINNOCK                 1931012F1000342400331000N      3 Nonnumeric mileage
X93477BUTLER         JOHN     H930631C0000423000419075N
354679KERBEL         NORMAN   X930331E1000340000324300Y
264805CLARK          JANE     S921101F0700561500551200N
846440               SAM       921231XI500182300169802N      4 Invalid car type
233432BEINHORN       CATHY    B921122M0200123400113402Y
556564HUMMER         MARGO    R920815C0800234500123403Y
677844MCDONALD       JAMES     930123C0500423500402300N
886222VOGEL          JANICE   D930518F1200634500612302Y
008632TOWER          DARREN   R930429L0900700200689300N
```

(a) Transaction File

Figure 8.10 *(continued)*

ERROR REPORT AS OF 07/03/93

CONTRACT #	LAST NAME	ERROR MESSAGE & FIELD	CONTENTS
123459	BAKER	INVALID DAY	1 — 04/31
123459	BAKER	INSURANCE CODE MUST BE Y OR N	X
987651	BROWN	MILES DRIVEN UNREASONABLY LOW	DAYS: 10 MILES: 000010
999999	JONES	MONTH MUST BE BETWEEN 1 AND 12	13
999999	JONES	MILEAGE IN LESS THAN MILEAGE OUT	2 — IN: 004500 OUT: 004600
999999	JONES	NON-NUMERIC MILEAGE RATE	05
987655	BROWNING	CAR TYPE MUST BE: E, C, M, F, OR L	0
987655	BROWNING	DATE HAS NOT YET OCCURRED	10/24/93
987655	BROWNING	NON-NUMERIC MILES IN	002400
655443	FITZPATRICK	INVALID DAY	05/32
655443	FITZPATRICK	INSURANCE CODE MUST BE Y OR N	C
	PINNOCK	NON-NUMERIC CONTRACT NUMBER	
	PINNOCK	MISSING FIRST NAME	
	PINNOCK	NON ALPHABETIC INITIAL	1
	PINNOCK	DATE HAS NOT YET OCCURRED	10/12/93
	PINNOCK	NON-NUMERIC MILES OUT	3 — 003310
X93477	BUTLER	NON-NUMERIC CONTRACT NUMBER	X93477
X93477	BUTLER	INVALID DAY	06/31
X93477	BUTLER	DAYS RENTED MUST BE > ZERO	00
X93477	BUTLER	MILEAGE RATE OUT OF RANGE	75
846440		NON-NUMERIC CONTRACT NUMBER	846440
846440		MISSING LAST NAME	
846440		CAR TYPE MUST BE: E, C, M, F, OR L	4 — X
846440		DAYS RENTED MUST BE NUMERIC	I5
846440		MILES DRIVEN UNREASONABLY LOW	DAYS: I5 MILES: 000125

(b) Error Report

```
999777ELSINOR     TERRY    R921126F0500168000159005N
987654SMITH       PAUL     G921213M0300510000500502Y
354679KERBEL      NORMAN   X930331E1000340000324300Y
264805CLARK       JANE     S921101F0700561500551200N
233432BEINHORN    CATHY    B921122M0200123400113402Y
556564HUMMER      MARGO    R920815C0800234500123403Y
677844MCDONALD    JAMES     930123C0500423500402300N
886222VOGEL       JANICE   D930518F1200634500612302Y
008632TOWER       DARREN   R930429L0900700200689300N
```

(c) Valid Transaction File

f. Valid values for the mileage in and out:

(1) The values for both miles in and miles out must be numeric; print the message *Nonnumeric miles in* or *nonnumeric miles out*, respectively.

(2) The mileage reported when the car is turned in cannot be less than the mileage when the car was taken out; print the message *Mileage in less than mileage out* as appropriate.

(3) The number of miles driven must pass a reasonableness test of 10 miles or more per day; Display the message, *Miles driven unreasonably low* as appropriate.

g. The mileage rate must be numeric and less than or equal to 50 cents per day; print the message *Mileage rate out of range* for an invalid rate.

h. The value of the insurance field must be either Y or N; print the message *Insurance code must be Y or N* for an invalid value.

3. Any record that fails any validity test is to be rejected and omitted from the valid record file. It is quite possible that a given record may contain more than one error, and all errors are to be printed except where noted.

4. Valid records are to be written to a file.

Error Messages

The utility of a data validation program is determined by the number of potential errors that it can detect as well as the clarity of the resulting error messages. A truly useful program must check for a variety of errors and explain to the user the nature of any errors that are detected. These concepts are illustrated in Figure 8.10. The incoming transaction file is shown in Figure 8.10a, the associated error messages (in conjunction with the programming specifications) in Figure 8.10b, and the valid transaction file in Figure 8.10c.

The numbered callouts in Figure 8.10 highlight some of the erroneous transactions and the corresponding error message; for example, the date of April 31 is highlighted in the first transaction of Figure 8.10a as is the corresponding error message in Figure 8.10b. Three other erroneous transactions are similarly highlighted.

The individual error messages are fully descriptive and list both the contract number and last name of the associated transaction. In addition, the contents of the erroneous field(s) are shown to the right of the error message, making it even easier to correct the invalid transaction. Note, too, that the program can also detect *multiple* errors for the same transaction; for example, three errors are identified in the single transaction for Jones.

Pseudocode

The pseudocode in Figure 8.11 begins with statements to obtain the date of execution, write the heading for the error report, and read the first record. The main loop of the program is executed next and does the following:

1. The incoming transaction is assumed to be valid by moving 'YES' to a valid-record-switch.

2. The incoming transaction is subject to all of the individual validity checks, any one of which can set the valid-record-switch to 'NO'. Note, too, that since each transaction record is subject to *every* validity check, multiple errors can be detected for a single transaction.

3. The valid-record-switch is checked to see if the record is still valid, and if so, the transaction is written to the valid record file. If, on the other hand, the record is no longer valid, a blank line is written to the error report, which double spaces between the error messages for one transaction and the next.

Figure 8.11 Pseudocode

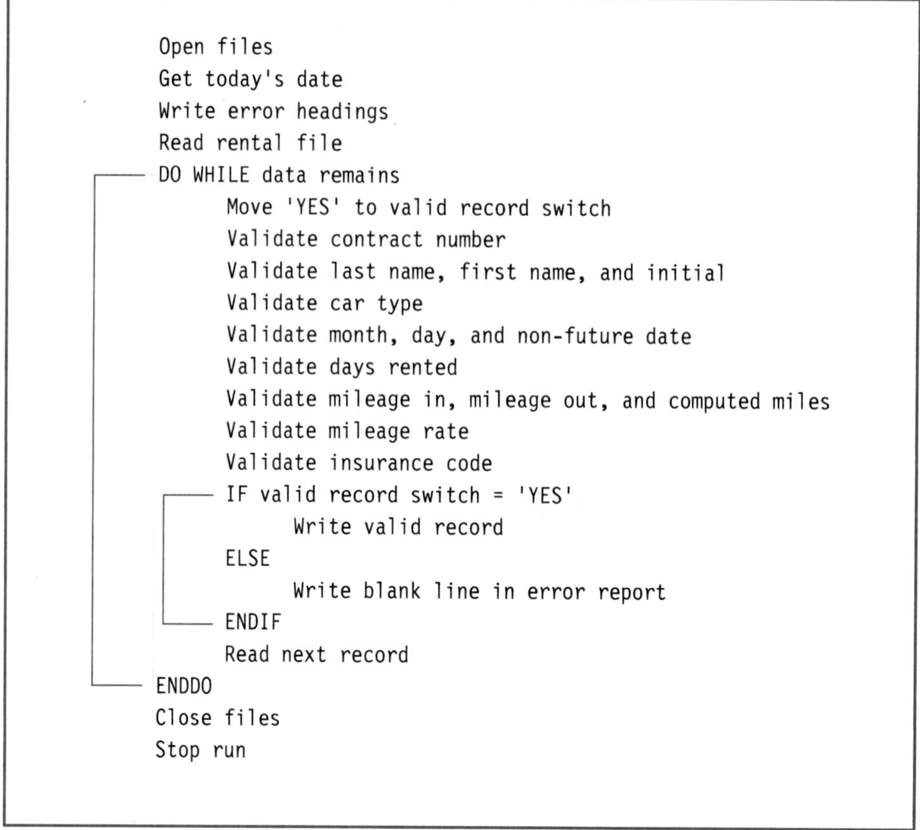

```
Open files
Get today's date
Write error headings
Read rental file
DO WHILE data remains
      Move 'YES' to valid record switch
      Validate contract number
      Validate last name, first name, and initial
      Validate car type
      Validate month, day, and non-future date
      Validate days rented
      Validate mileage in, mileage out, and computed miles
      Validate mileage rate
      Validate insurance code
      IF valid record switch = 'YES'
            Write valid record
      ELSE
            Write blank line in error report
      ENDIF
      Read next record
ENDDO
Close files
Stop run
```

4. The next record is read and the loop continues until the transaction file is exhausted.

The pseudocode is concise in that the specific nature of each error check is not shown; nevertheless it (the pseudocode) is an effective aid in writing the program.

Hierarchy Chart

The hierarchy chart for the data validation program is shown in Figure 8.12. The module CREATE-VALID-FILE sits at the top of the hierarchy chart and invokes four subordinates, one of which is PROCESS-RENTAL-RECORDS, which implements the main loop of the program.

PROCESS-RENTAL-RECORDS in turn has three subordinates, VALIDATE-RENTAL-RECORD to perform the individual error checks, WRITE-VALID-RECORD to write valid transactions to the output file, and READ-RENTAL-RECORD to read the next transaction. Each of the required validity checks is implemented in its own module, and all of these modules call a common routine to write an error message.

The Completed Program

The completed program is shown in Figure 8.13. It is considerably longer than the tuition billing program of the previous chapters, but nonetheless straightforward

Figure 8.12 Hierarchy Chart for Validation Program

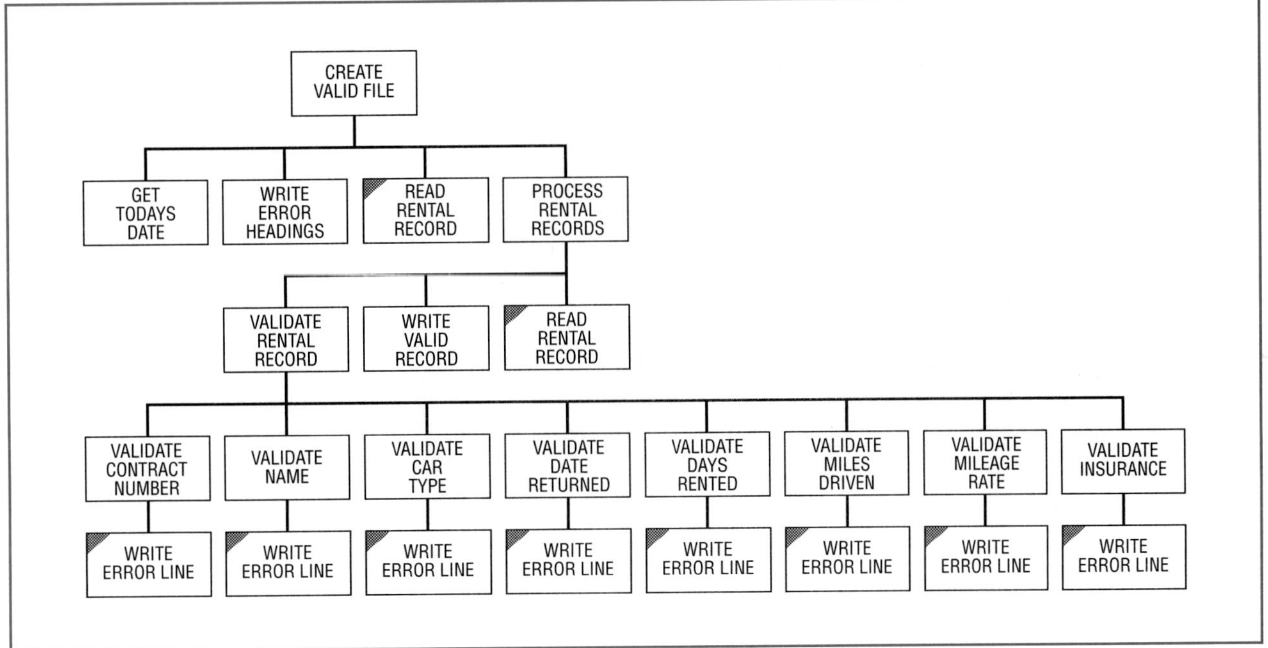

Figure 8.13 Data Validation Program

```
IDENTIFICATION DIVISION.
PROGRAM-ID.      VALCARS8.
AUTHOR.          CVV.

ENVIRONMENT DIVISION.
INPUT-OUTPUT SECTION.
FILE-CONTROL.
    SELECT RENTAL-FILE
        ASSIGN TO UT-S-SYSIN.
    SELECT VALID-RENTAL-FILE
        ASSIGN TO UT-S-SYSOUT.
    SELECT ERROR-FILE
        ASSIGN TO UT-S-ERRORS.

DATA DIVISION.
FILE SECTION.
FD  RENTAL-FILE
    RECORD CONTAINS 56 CHARACTERS.
01  RENTAL-RECORD.
    05  REN-CONTRACT-NO         PIC 9(6).
    05  REN-NAME.
        10  REN-LAST-NAME       PIC X(15).
        10  REN-FIRST-NAME      PIC X(10).
```

Figure 8.13 *(continued)*

```
            10  REN-INITIAL          PIC X.
        05  REN-RETURNED-DATE.
            10  REN-RETURNED-YEAR    PIC 9(2).
            10  REN-RETURNED-MONTH   PIC 9(2).
                88  VALID-MONTHS         VALUES 1 THRU 12.
                88  FEBRUARY             VALUE 2.
                88  30-DAY-MONTH         VALUES 4 6 9 11.
                88  31-DAY-MONTH         VALUES 1 3 5 7 8 10 12.
            10  REN-RETURNED-DAY     PIC 9(2).
        05  REN-CAR-TYPE             PIC X.
            88  VALID-CAR-TYPES          VALUES 'E' 'C' 'M' 'F' 'L'.
        05  REN-DAYS-RENTED          PIC 99.
            88  ZERO-DAYS-RENTED         VALUE  0.
            88  VALID-DAYS-RENTED        VALUES 1 THRU 35.
        05  REN-MILEAGE.
            10  REN-MILES-IN         PIC 9(6).
            10  REN-MILES-OUT        PIC 9(6).
            10  REN-MILEAGE-RATE     PIC 99.
                88  VALID-MILEAGE-RATES  VALUES 00 THRU 50.
        05  REN-INSURANCE            PIC X.
            88  VALID-INSURANCE          VALUES 'Y' 'N'.

    FD  VALID-RENTAL-FILE
        RECORD CONTAINS 56 CHARACTERS.
    01  VALID-RENTAL-RECORD          PIC X(56).

    FD  ERROR-FILE
        RECORD CONTAINS 132 CHARACTERS.
    01  ERROR-RECORD                 PIC X(132).

    WORKING-STORAGE SECTION.
    01  PROGRAM-SWITCHES.
        05  NO-DATA-REMAINS-SWITCH   PIC XXX VALUE SPACES.
            88 NO-DATA-REMAINS           VALUE 'NO'.
        05  VALID-RECORD-SWITCH      PIC X(3).
            88  VALID-RECORD             VALUE 'YES'.

    01  VALIDATION-CONSTANTS-AND-CALCS.
        05  MILES-PER-DAY-FACTOR     PIC 99  VALUE 10.
        05  EXPECTED-MILES           PIC 9(6).
        05  ACTUAL-MILES             PIC 9(6).

    01  ERROR-REASONS.
        05  NON-NUMERIC-CONTRACT-MSG PIC X(40)
              VALUE 'NON-NUMERIC CONTRACT NUMBER'.
        05  LAST-NAME-MSG            PIC X(40)
              VALUE 'MISSING LAST NAME'.
        05  FIRST-NAME-MSG           PIC X(40)
              VALUE 'MISSING FIRST NAME'.
        05  INITIAL-MSG              PIC X(40)
```

88-level entries define valid values

Table of error messages

Figure 8.13 *(continued)*

```
               VALUE 'NON ALPHABETIC INITIAL'.
           05  CAR-TYPE-MSG               PIC X(40)
               VALUE 'CAR TYPE MUST BE:  E, C, M, F, OR L'.
           05  MONTH-MSG                  PIC X(40)
               VALUE 'MONTH MUST BE BETWEEN 1 AND 12'.
           05  DAY-MSG                    PIC X(40)
               VALUE 'INVALID DAY'.
           05  FUTURE-DATE-MSG            PIC X(40)
               VALUE 'DATE HAS NOT YET OCCURRED'.
           05  NON-NUM-DAYS-RENTED-MSG    PIC X(40)
               VALUE 'DAYS RENTED MUST BE NUMERIC'.
           05  ZERO-DAYS-MSG              PIC X(40)
               VALUE 'DAYS RENTED MUST BE > ZERO'.
           05  LEASING-MSG                PIC X(40)
               VALUE 'REFER TO LONG-TERM LEASING'.
           05  NON-NUM-MILES-IN-MSG       PIC X(40)
               VALUE 'NON-NUMERIC MILES IN'.
           05  NON-NUM-MILES-OUT-MSG      PIC X(40)
               VALUE 'NON-NUMERIC MILES OUT'.
           05  LESS-THAN-MILES-MSG        PIC X(40)
               VALUE 'MILEAGE IN LESS THAN MILEAGE OUT' .
           05  INVALID-MILES-MSG          PIC X(40)
               VALUE 'MILES DRIVEN UNREASONABLY LOW'.
           05  NON-NUM-RATE-MSG           PIC X(40)
               VALUE 'NON-NUMERIC MILEAGE RATE'.
           05  MILEAGE-RATE-MSG           PIC X(40)
               VALUE 'MILEAGE RATE OUT OF RANGE'.
           05  INSURANCE-MSG              PIC X(40)
               VALUE 'INSURANCE CODE MUST BE Y OR N'.

       01  TODAYS-DATE.
           05  TODAYS-YEAR                PIC 99.
           05  TODAYS-MONTH               PIC 99.
           05  TODAYS-DAY                 PIC 99.

       01  HEADING-ERROR-LINE-ONE.
           05  FILLER                     PIC X(26) VALUE SPACES.
           05  FILLER                     PIC X(19)
                VALUE 'ERROR REPORT AS OF '.
           05  HDG-DATE.
               10  HDG-MONTH              PIC 99/.
               10  HDG-DAY                PIC 99/.
               10  HDG-YEAR               PIC 99.
           05  FILLER                     PIC X(79) VALUE SPACES.

       01  HEADING-ERROR-LINE-TWO.
           05  FILLER                     PIC X(10) VALUE 'CONTRACT #'.
           05  FILLER                     PIC XX    VALUE SPACES.
           05  FILLER                     PIC X(9)  VALUE 'LAST NAME'.
           05  FILLER                     PIC X(8)  VALUE SPACES.
```

Table of error messages

Figure 8.13 *(continued)*

```
           05  FILLER                    PIC X(21)
                  VALUE 'ERROR MESSAGE & FIELD'.
           05  FILLER                    PIC X(21) VALUE SPACES.
           05  FILLER                    PIC X(8)  VALUE 'CONTENTS'.
           05  FILLER                    PIC X(46) VALUE SPACES.

       01  ERROR-LINE.
           05  FILLER                    PIC XX    VALUE SPACES.
           05  ERR-CONTRACT-NO           PIC 9(6).
           05  FILLER                    PIC X(4)  VALUE SPACES.
           05  ERR-LAST-NAME             PIC X(15).
           05  FILLER                    PIC XX    VALUE SPACES.
           05  ERR-MESSAGE               PIC X(40).
           05  FILLER                    PIC XX    VALUE SPACES.
           05  ERR-CONTENTS              PIC X(23).
           05  FILLER                    PIC X(38)  VALUE SPACES.

       01  ERROR-DETAILS.
           05  ERR-MILES-IN-OUT.
               10  FILLER                PIC X(4) VALUE 'IN: '.
               10  ERR-MILES-IN          PIC 9(6).
               10  FILLER                PIC X(6) VALUE ' OUT: '.
               10  ERR-MILES-OUT         PIC 9(6).
           05  ERR-RETURNED-DATE.
               10  ERR-RETURNED-MONTH-DAY.
                   15  ERR-RETURNED-MONTH    PIC 99.
                   15  ERR-RETURNED-DAY      PIC /99.
               10  ERR-RETURNED-YEAR         PIC /99.
           05  ERR-EXPECTED-MILES.
               10  FILLER                PIC X(6) VALUE 'DAYS: '.
               10  ERR-DAYS-RENTED       PIC 99.
               10  FILLER                PIC X(9) VALUE '   MILES: '.
               10  ERR-MILES             PIC 9(6).

       PROCEDURE DIVISION.
       000-CREATE-VALID-RENTAL-FILE.
           OPEN INPUT  RENTAL-FILE
                OUTPUT VALID-RENTAL-FILE
                       ERROR-FILE.
           PERFORM 100-GET-TODAYS-DATE.
           PERFORM 200-WRITE-ERROR-HEADINGS.
           PERFORM 300-READ-RENTAL-RECORD.
           PERFORM 400-PROCESS-RENTAL-RECORDS
               UNTIL NO-DATA-REMAINS.
           CLOSE RENTAL-FILE
                 VALID-RENTAL-FILE
                 ERROR-FILE.
           STOP RUN.

       100-GET-TODAYS-DATE.
```

Separate output files for error messages and valid records

Figure 8.13 *(continued)*

```
           ACCEPT TODAYS-DATE FROM DATE.
           MOVE TODAYS-MONTH TO HDG-MONTH.
           MOVE TODAYS-DAY TO HDG-DAY.
           MOVE TODAYS-YEAR TO HDG-YEAR.

       200-WRITE-ERROR-HEADINGS.
           MOVE HEADING-ERROR-LINE-ONE TO ERROR-RECORD.
           WRITE ERROR-RECORD
               AFTER ADVANCING PAGE.
           MOVE HEADING-ERROR-LINE-TWO TO ERROR-RECORD
           WRITE ERROR-RECORD
               AFTER ADVANCING 2 LINES.
           MOVE SPACES TO ERROR-RECORD.
           WRITE ERROR-RECORD.

       300-READ-RENTAL-RECORD.
            READ RENTAL-FILE
               AT END MOVE 'NO' TO NO-DATA-REMAINS-SWITCH
            END-READ.

       400-PROCESS-RENTAL-RECORDS.
           MOVE 'YES' TO VALID-RECORD-SWITCH.
           PERFORM 500-VALIDATE-RENTAL-RECORD.
           PERFORM 600-WRITE-VALID-RECORD.
           PERFORM 300-READ-RENTAL-RECORD.

       500-VALIDATE-RENTAL-RECORD.
           PERFORM 510-VALIDATE-CONTRACT-NO.
           PERFORM 520-VALIDATE-NAME.
           PERFORM 530-VALIDATE-CAR-TYPE.
           PERFORM 540-VALIDATE-DATE-RETURNED.
           PERFORM 550-VALIDATE-DAYS-RENTED.
           PERFORM 560-VALIDATE-MILES-DRIVEN
           PERFORM 570-VALIDATE-MILEAGE-RATE.
           PERFORM 580-VALIDATE-INSURANCE.

       510-VALIDATE-CONTRACT-NO.
           IF REN-CONTRACT-NO NOT NUMERIC
              MOVE NON-NUMERIC-CONTRACT-MSG TO ERR-MESSAGE
              MOVE REN-CONTRACT-NO TO ERR-CONTENTS
              PERFORM 599-WRITE-ERROR-LINE
           END-IF.

       520-VALIDATE-NAME.
           IF REN-LAST-NAME = SPACES
               MOVE LAST-NAME-MSG TO ERR-MESSAGE
               MOVE SPACES TO ERR-CONTENTS
               PERFORM 599-WRITE-ERROR-LINE
           END-IF.
           IF REN-FIRST-NAME = SPACES
```

Obtain system date (ACCEPT TODAYS-DATE FROM DATE.)

Incoming records are assumed to be valid (MOVE 'YES' TO VALID-RECORD-SWITCH.)

Class test for numeric data (IF REN-CONTRACT-NO NOT NUMERIC)

Figure 8.13 *(continued)*

```
            MOVE FIRST-NAME-MSG TO ERR-MESSAGE
            MOVE SPACES TO ERR-CONTENTS
            PERFORM 599-WRITE-ERROR-LINE
        END-IF.
        IF REN-INITIAL NOT ALPHABETIC
            MOVE INITIAL-MSG TO ERR-MESSAGE
            MOVE REN-INITIAL TO ERR-CONTENTS
            PERFORM 599-WRITE-ERROR-LINE
        END-IF.

    530-VALIDATE-CAR-TYPE.
        IF NOT VALID-CAR-TYPES
            MOVE CAR-TYPE-MSG TO ERR-MESSAGE
            MOVE REN-CAR-TYPE TO ERR-CONTENTS
            PERFORM 599-WRITE-ERROR-LINE
        END-IF.

    540-VALIDATE-DATE-RETURNED.
        IF VALID-MONTHS
            IF 30-DAY-MONTH AND REN-RETURNED-DAY <= 30 OR
                 31-DAY-MONTH AND REN-RETURNED-DAY <= 31 OR
                 FEBRUARY AND REN-RETURNED-DAY <= 29
               IF REN-RETURNED-DATE > TODAYS-DATE
                   MOVE FUTURE-DATE-MSG TO ERR-MESSAGE
                   MOVE REN-RETURNED-MONTH TO ERR-RETURNED-MONTH
                   MOVE REN-RETURNED-DAY TO ERR-RETURNED-DAY
                   MOVE REN-RETURNED-YEAR TO ERR-RETURNED-YEAR
                   MOVE ERR-RETURNED-DATE TO ERR-CONTENTS
                   PERFORM 599-WRITE-ERROR-LINE
               END-IF
            ELSE
                MOVE DAY-MSG TO ERR-MESSAGE
                MOVE REN-RETURNED-MONTH TO ERR-RETURNED-MONTH
                MOVE REN-RETURNED-DAY TO ERR-RETURNED-DAY
                MOVE ERR-RETURNED-MONTH-DAY TO ERR-CONTENTS
                PERFORM 599-WRITE-ERROR-LINE
            END-IF
        ELSE
            MOVE MONTH-MSG TO ERR-MESSAGE
            MOVE REN-RETURNED-MONTH TO ERR-CONTENTS
            PERFORM 599-WRITE-ERROR-LINE
        END-IF.

    550-VALIDATE-DAYS-RENTED.
        IF REN-DAYS-RENTED NOT NUMERIC
            MOVE NON-NUM-DAYS-RENTED-MSG TO ERR-MESSAGE
            MOVE REN-DAYS-RENTED TO ERR-CONTENTS
            PERFORM 599-WRITE-ERROR-LINE
        ELSE
            IF ZERO-DAYS-RENTED
```

Class test for alphabetic data

Nested IF to implement date validation

Figure 8.13 *(continued)*

```
                MOVE ZERO-DAYS-MSG TO ERR-MESSAGE
                MOVE REN-DAYS-RENTED TO ERR-CONTENTS
                PERFORM 599-WRITE-ERROR-LINE
            ELSE
                IF NOT VALID-DAYS-RENTED
                    MOVE LEASING-MSG TO ERR-MESSAGE
                    MOVE REN-DAYS-RENTED TO ERR-CONTENTS
                    PERFORM 599-WRITE-ERROR-LINE
                END-IF
            END-IF
        END-IF.

    560-VALIDATE-MILES-DRIVEN.
        IF REN-MILES-IN NOT NUMERIC
            MOVE NON-NUM-MILES-IN-MSG TO ERR-MESSAGE
            MOVE REN-MILES-IN TO ERR-CONTENTS
            PERFORM 599-WRITE-ERROR-LINE
        ELSE
            IF REN-MILES-OUT NOT NUMERIC
                MOVE NON-NUM-MILES-OUT-MSG TO ERR-MESSAGE
                MOVE REN-MILES-OUT TO ERR-CONTENTS
                PERFORM 599-WRITE-ERROR-LINE
            ELSE
                IF REN-MILES-IN < REN-MILES-OUT
                    MOVE LESS-THAN-MILES-MSG TO ERR-MESSAGE
                    MOVE REN-MILES-IN TO ERR-MILES-IN
                    MOVE REN-MILES-OUT TO ERR-MILES-OUT
                    MOVE ERR-MILES-IN-OUT TO ERR-CONTENTS
                    PERFORM 599-WRITE-ERROR-LINE
                ELSE
                    COMPUTE EXPECTED-MILES =
                        MILES-PER-DAY-FACTOR * REN-DAYS-RENTED
                        SIZE ERROR DISPLAY 'SIZE ERROR EXPECT MILES'
                    END-COMPUTE
                    COMPUTE ACTUAL-MILES =
                        REN-MILES-IN - REN-MILES-OUT
                        SIZE ERROR DISPLAY 'SIZE ERROR ACTUAL MILES'
                    END-COMPUTE
                    IF ACTUAL-MILES < EXPECTED-MILES
                        MOVE INVALID-MILES-MSG TO ERR-MESSAGE
                        MOVE REN-DAYS-RENTED TO ERR-DAYS-RENTED
                        MOVE ACTUAL-MILES TO ERR-MILES
                        MOVE ERR-EXPECTED-MILES TO ERR-CONTENTS
                        PERFORM 599-WRITE-ERROR-LINE
                    END-IF
                END-IF
            END-IF
        END-IF.

    570-VALIDATE-MILEAGE-RATE.
```

SIZE ERROR clause in anticipation of unexpectedly large fields

Figure 8.13 *(continued)*

```
324            IF REN-MILEAGE-RATE NOT NUMERIC
325                MOVE NON-NUM-RATE-MSG TO ERR-MESSAGE
326                MOVE REN-MILEAGE-RATE TO ERR-CONTENTS
327                PERFORM 599-WRITE-ERROR-LINE
328            ELSE
329                IF NOT VALID-MILEAGE-RATES
330                    MOVE MILEAGE-RATE-MSG TO ERR-MESSAGE
331                    MOVE REN-MILEAGE-RATE TO ERR-CONTENTS
332                    PERFORM 599-WRITE-ERROR-LINE
333                END-IF
334            END-IF.
335
336        580-VALIDATE-INSURANCE.
337            IF NOT VALID-INSURANCE
338                MOVE INSURANCE-MSG TO ERR-MESSAGE
339                MOVE REN-INSURANCE TO ERR-CONTENTS
340                PERFORM 599-WRITE-ERROR-LINE
341            END-IF.
342
343        599-WRITE-ERROR-LINE.
344            MOVE 'NO ' TO VALID-RECORD-SWITCH.
345            MOVE REN-CONTRACT-NO TO ERR-CONTRACT-NO.
346            MOVE REN-LAST-NAME TO ERR-LAST-NAME.
347            MOVE ERROR-LINE TO ERROR-RECORD.
348            WRITE ERROR-RECORD.
349
350        600-WRITE-VALID-RECORD.
351            IF VALID-RECORD
352                MOVE RENTAL-RECORD TO VALID-RENTAL-RECORD
353                WRITE VALID-RENTAL-RECORD
354            ELSE
355                MOVE SPACES TO ERROR-RECORD
356                WRITE ERROR-RECORD
357            END-IF.
```

Common error routine sets switch to indicate invalid record and write error message

Valid transactions are written to a valid file, the ELSE clause writes a blank line before each group of invalid transactions

and easy to follow. The logic in the program parallels that of the pseudocode just developed, whereas the paragraphs in the Procedure Division correspond one to one with the modules in the hierarchy chart. The program complies completely with the processing requirements and also illustrates the various COBOL features presented earlier. Consider:

1. The use of condition names within the FD for RENTAL-RECORD (e.g., lines 28–31, 34, 36–37, etc.) to define valid values for the various input fields.
2. A table of error messages in lines 66–102; grouping the error messages in this way makes it easy to determine precisely which error checks are implemented. It also facilitates uniform formatting of the various error messages.

3. The ACCEPT statement in line 174 to obtain the system date; also the definition of TODAYS-DATE in WORKING-STORAGE to hold the date after it is read.
4. The MOVE statement to initialize VALID-RECORD-SWITCH to 'YES' for each incoming transaction record (line 195). A second MOVE statement in the WRITE-ERROR-LINE paragraph (line 344) to reset the switch to 'NO' if the current transaction fails any one of the validity tests.
5. Various class tests for numeric and alphabetic data as in lines 211 and 228.
6. A nested IF statement in lines 242–265 to implement the various types of date validation. A second nested IF statement in lines 287 through 321 performs the various checks on the incoming, outgoing, and computed mileage.
7. SIZE ERROR clauses within the COMPUTE statements, lines 306 and 310, in anticipation of unexpectedly large fields.
8. The IF statement in lines 351–357 that determines whether the transaction is written to the valid file. Note, too, the ELSE clause within this IF statement, which writes a blank line for every invalid record, which in turn puts a blank line before each group of invalid transactions in the error report.

LIMITATIONS OF COBOL-74

COBOL-85 introduced two additional relational conditions into the IF statement, GREATER THAN OR EQUAL TO and LESS THAN OR EQUAL TO; these conditions were not allowed in COBOL-74, which used NOT LESS THAN as the equivalent of GREATER THAN OR EQUAL TO and NOT GREATER THAN for LESS THAN OR EQUAL TO.

COBOL-85 enables the testing of upper- and/or lowercase letters through expansion of the alphabetic class test. In COBOL-85 the ALPHABETIC test is true for uppercase letters, lowercase letters, and the space character; the ALPHABETIC-UPPER test is true for uppercase letters and the space character; and the ALPHABETIC-LOWER test is true for lowercase letters and the space character. There were no UPPER/LOWER tests in COBOL-74 and the ALPHABETIC test was true only for uppercase letters and space characters.

The most significant change, however, is the introduction of the END-IF scope terminator, which did not exist in COBOL-74. We have already seen how the scope terminator eliminates the column-73 problem in conjunction with a "missing period" (page 182) and how it eliminates the need for the NEXT SENTENCE clause (Figure 8.7). The scope terminator also facilitates the nesting of conditional statements as shown in Figure 8.14.

Consider, for example, the flowchart of Figure 8.14a, and the contrasting implementations in COBOL-85 and COBOL-74 in Figures 8.14b and 8.14c, respectively. The END-IF terminator transforms a conditional statement to an imperative (complete) statement, making it possible to express the required logic as a single IF statement in COBOL-85. By contrast, the COBOL-74 implementation requires an additional PERFORM statement and is more difficult to follow.

Figure 8.14 Limitations of COBOL-74

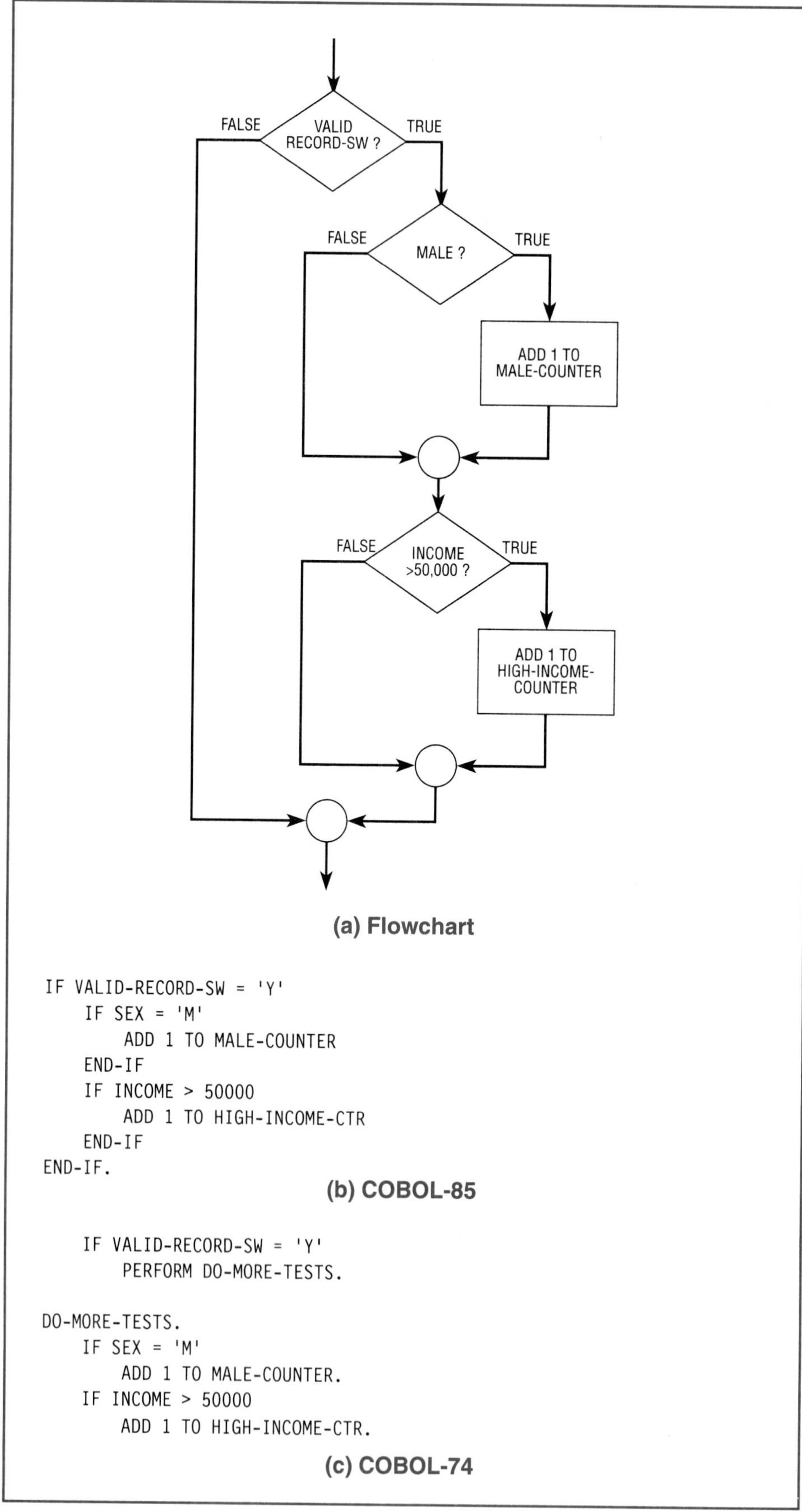

(a) Flowchart

```
IF VALID-RECORD-SW = 'Y'
    IF SEX = 'M'
        ADD 1 TO MALE-COUNTER
    END-IF
    IF INCOME > 50000
        ADD 1 TO HIGH-INCOME-CTR
    END-IF
END-IF.
```

(b) COBOL-85

```
    IF VALID-RECORD-SW = 'Y'
        PERFORM DO-MORE-TESTS.

DO-MORE-TESTS.
    IF SEX = 'M'
        ADD 1 TO MALE-COUNTER.
    IF INCOME > 50000
        ADD 1 TO HIGH-INCOME-CTR.
```

(c) COBOL-74

SUMMARY

Points to Remember

- Data validation is a critical portion of any system, as the output produced by any program is only as good as its input.
- Data validation is often done in a stand-alone edit program as opposed to the reporting program that processes the data; that is, the valid transaction file produced as output by the edit program becomes the input file to the reporting program.
- The ACCEPT statement is used to obtain the date of execution for use in implementing various types of date checks.
- There are four types of conditions in the IF statement: relation, class, sign, and condition name (88-level entries).
- Any two simple conditions may be combined to form a compound condition using the logical operators AND and OR. An IF statement may also use implied conditions, in which the subject and/or operation is understood.
- A nested IF statement contains two or more IF statements within a sentence. The scope of the condition in the IF statement is terminated by the ELSE clause, the END-IF scope terminator, and/or a period. The scope terminator is optional but strongly recommended in all instances.
- Indentation within an IF statement is not required by the compiler but recommended to facilitate the programmer's interpretation.
- The NEXT SENTENCE clause directs control to the statement immediately following the period and is required (in COBOL-74) to implement certain types of nested conditional statements. The END-IF scope terminator, introduced in COBOL-85, eliminates the need for the NEXT SENTENCE clause in all instances.

Key Words and Concepts

88-level entry
Alphabetic test
Class test
Completeness check
Compound test
Condition name
Consistency check
Data validation
Date check
Edit program
Existing code check
Implied condition
Limit check
Nested IF
Numeric test
Range check
Reasonableness check
Scope terminator
Sequence check
Sign test
Subscript check

COBOL Elements

```
ACCEPT          END-IF
AND             IF
DATE            NEXT SENTENCE
DAY             NOT
DAY-OF-WEEK     OR
ELSE            TIME
```

FILL-IN

1. Incoming data should be ______________ prior to being used in computations.
2. The valid transaction file produced as output by an edit program is ______________ to a reporting program.
3. A ______________ test ensures that numeric fields do in fact contain numeric data.
4. A ______________ check tests that a value does not exceed a designated upper or lower bound.
5. A ______________ check verifies that all required fields are present.
6. In evaluating a compound condition, AND comes (before/after) OR.
7. A condition name is also known as an ______________-level entry.
8. The ______________ ______________ clause directs control to the statement immediately following the period.
9. The ______________ scope terminator eliminates the need for the NEXT SENTENCE clause.
10. The statement, ACCEPT DATE-WORK-AREA FROM DATE requires specification of a user-defined work area in the form, ______________.

TRUE/FALSE

1. Output from a reporting program is typically input to an edit program.
2. The numeric class test can be applied to alphanumeric data.
3. The alphabetic class test can be applied to alphanumeric data.
4. The numeric class test can be applied to alphabetic data.
5. The alphabetic class test can be applied to numeric data.
6. A nested IF statement contains two or more IF statements within a single sentence.
7. The NEXT SENTENCE clause may be associated with either an IF or an ELSE.
8. The END-IF scope terminator eliminates the need for a NEXT SENTENCE clause.
9. The ACCEPT statement is used to obtain the date of execution.
10. DATE is a COBOL reserved word, containing the date of execution in the form yymmdd.
11. DAY and DATE produce the same results.
12. TIME returns a six-digit numeric field, indicating the time of program execution.

PROBLEMS

1. Recode the following statements to include scope terminators and proper indentation with the ELSE clause indented under the relevant IF.
   a. IF A > B, IF C > D, MOVE E TO F,
      ELSE MOVE G TO H.
   b. IF A > B, IF C > D, MOVE E TO F,
      ELSE MOVE G TO H, ELSE MOVE X TO Y.
   c. IF A > B, IF C > D, MOVE E TO F,
      ADD 1 TO E, ELSE MOVE G TO H,
      ADD 1 TO G.
   d. IF A > B, MOVE X TO Y, MOVE Z TO W,
      ELSE IF C > D MOVE 1 TO N,
      ELSE MOVE 2 TO Y, ADD 3 TO Z.

2. Given the nested IF statement:

```
IF SEX = 'M'
    PERFORM PROCESS-MALE-RECORD
ELSE
    IF SEX = 'F'
        PERFORM PROCESS-FEMALE-RECORD
    ELSE
        PERFORM WRITE-ERROR-MESSAGE
    END-IF
END-IF.
```

   and the logically equivalent code:

```
IF SEX = 'M'
    PERFORM PROCESS-MALE-RECORD
END-IF.
IF SEX = 'F'
    PERFORM PROCESS-FEMALE-RECORD
END-IF.
IF SEX NOT = 'M' AND SEX NOT = 'F'
    PERFORM WRITE-ERROR-MESSAGE
END-IF.
```

   a. Discuss the relative efficiency of the two alternatives.
   b. What would be the effect of changing AND to OR in the third IF of the second set of statements?
   c. What would be the effect of removing the word ELSE wherever it occurs in the first set of IF statements?

3. Are the two IF statements logically equivalent?

   Statement 1:

```
    IF A > B
        IF C > D
            ADD 1 TO X
        ELSE
            ADD 1 TO Y
        END-IF
    END-IF.
```

Statement 2:

```
IF A > B AND C > D
    ADD 1 TO X
ELSE
    ADD 1 TO Y
END-IF.
```

Try the following sets of values to aid in answering the question:

a. A = 5, B = 1, C = 10, D = 15.

b. A = 1, B = 5, C = 10, D = 15.

4. Company XYZ has four corporate functions: manufacturing, marketing, financial, and administrative. Each function in turn has several departments, as shown:

FUNCTION	DEPARTMENTS
MANUFACTURING	10, 12, 16-30, 41, 56
MARKETING	6-9, 15, 31-33
FINANCIAL	60-62, 75
ADMINISTRATIVE	1-4, 78

Establish condition-name entries so that, given a value of EMPLOYEE-DEPARTMENT, you can determine the function. Include an 88-level entry, VALID-CODES, to verify that the incoming department is indeed a valid department (any department number not shown is invalid).

5. Given the following COBOL definitions:

```
05  LOCATION-CODE          PIC 99.
    88  NEW-YORK               VALUE 10.
    88  BOSTON                 VALUE 20.
    88  CHICAGO                VALUE 30.
    88  DETROIT                VALUE 40.
    88  NORTH-EAST             VALUES 10 20.
```

Are the following entries valid as the condition portion of an IF statement?

a. IF LOCATION-CODE = '10'

b. IF LOCATION-CODE = 40

c. IF NEW-YORK

d. IF LOCATION-CODE = 10 OR 20 OR 30

e. IF NEW-YORK OR BOSTON OR CHICAGO

f. IF DETROIT = 40

Would the following be valid examples of MOVE statements?

g. MOVE 20 TO BOSTON.

h. MOVE 20 TO LOCATION-CODE.

i. MOVE '20' TO LOCATION-CODE.

6. Given the following pairs of IF statements, indicate whether the statements in each pair have the same effect:

a. IF A > B OR C > D AND E = F
   IF A > B OR (C > D AND E = F)

b. IF A > B OR C > D AND E = F
   IF (A > B OR C > D) AND E = F

c. IF A > B OR A > C OR A > D
   IF A> B OR C OR D

d. IF A > B
   IF A NOT < B OR A NOT = B

7. Consider the following code, intended to calculate an individual's age from a stored birth date and the date of execution.

```
01  EMPLOYEE-RECORD.
    05  EMP-BIRTH-DATE.
        10  BIRTH-MONTH     PIC 99.
        10  BIRTH-YEAR      PIC 99.
01  DATE-WORK-AREA.
    05  TODAYS-MONTH        PIC 99.
    05  TODAYS-DAY          PIC 99.
    05  TODAYS-YEAR         PIC 99.

PROCEDURE DIVISION.
    ACCEPT DATE-WORK-AREA FROM DATE.
    .
        .
            .
    COMPUTE EMPLOYEE-AGE = TODAYS-YEAR - BIRTH-YEAR
            + TODAYS-MONTH - BIRTH-MONTH.
```

There are two distinct reasons why the code will not work as intended. Find and correct the errors.

8. Implement the logic in Figure 8.15 with and without scope terminators, corresponding to the implementations in COBOL-74 and COBOL-85. Do you see any distinct advantages to the latter compiler?

Figure 8.15 Flowcharts for Problem 8

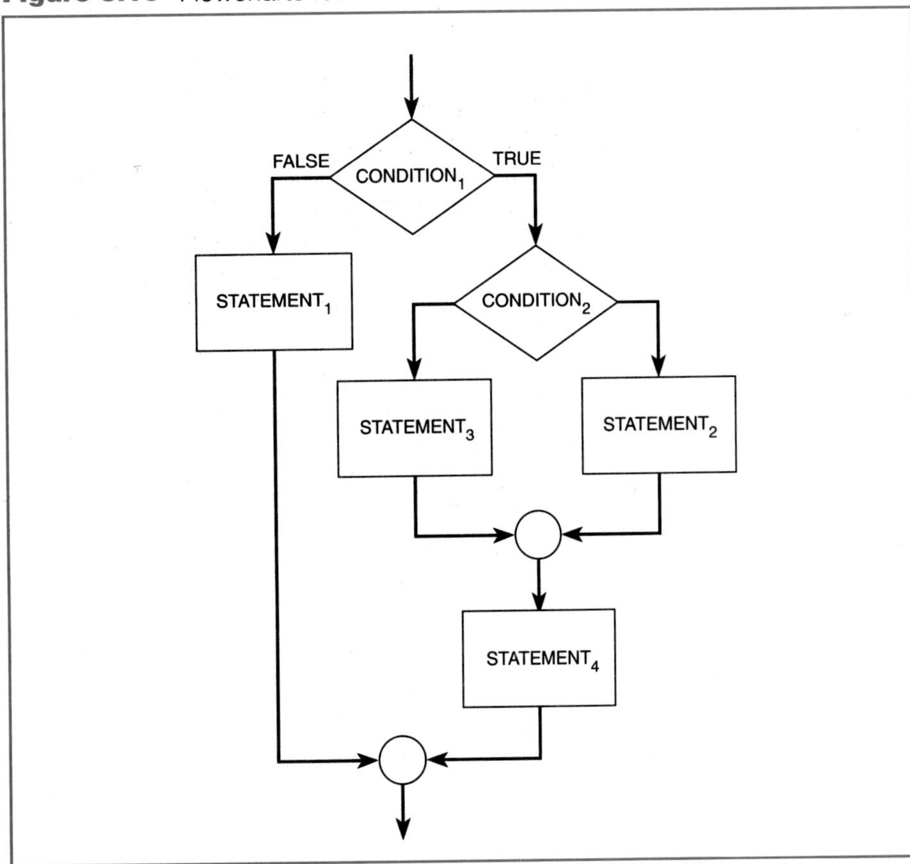

More About the Procedure Division

CHAPTER OUTLINE

OBJECTIVES

After reading this chapter you will be able to:

- Differentiate between the DO WHILE and DO UNTIL structures; describe how each is implemented in conjunction with a PERFORM statement.
- Define an in-line perform and a false-condition branch; explain how the combination of these features eliminates the need for a priming read statement.
- Differentiate between a paragraph and a section.
- Code the READ INTO and WRITE FROM statements in the Procedure Division.
- Use the INITIALIZE statement.
- Perform basic string processing operations through use of the INSPECT, STRING, and UNSTRING statements.
- Define a duplicate data name and use qualification to eliminate ambiguity; describe the use of the MOVE CORRESPONDING statement.

OVERVIEW

This chapter completes the two-program sequence begun in Chapter 8 by developing the reporting program for the valid transaction file. The program is also intended to illustrate a series of advanced Procedure Division statements that are presented in the chapter. Many of the statements are new to COBOL-85 and were not available in COBOL-74.

We begin with the PERFORM statement and include material on the TEST BEFORE and TEST AFTER clauses which correspond to the DO WHILE and DO UNTIL constructs of structured programming. The in-line perform is presented, as is the THROUGH clause, to perform multiple paragraphs; the use of sections in lieu of paragraphs is also covered. The READ INTO and WRITE FROM clauses are introduced to combine the effects of a MOVE statement with the indicated I/O operation. The ACCEPT statement is expanded to include the DAY-OF-WEEK clause, and the INITIALIZE statement establishes values for multiple data names in a single statement. The INSPECT, STRING, and UNSTRING statements are introduced to implement string processing operations. Duplicate data names, qualification, and the MOVE CORRESPONDING statement are introduced as well.

The program at the end of the chapter is designed very differently from the programs presented thus far as it uses an in-line perform and a false-condition branch to eliminate the priming read used in earlier programs. The program also makes extensive use of scope terminators throughout the Procedure Division.

PERFORM

A simple form of the PERFORM statement has been used throughout the text to implement the iteration construct of structured programming:

```
PERFORM procedure-name UNTIL condition
```

The condition in the UNTIL clause is tested *before* the procedure is executed, and if the condition is not met, control is transferred to the designated procedure. When the procedure has completed execution, the condition is retested, and if it (the condition) is still not met, the procedure is executed a second time. The process continues indefinitely until the condition is finally satisfied.

In actuality the PERFORM statement is considerably more complex with many additional options. Consider:

```
PERFORM [procedure-name-1 [{THROUGH} procedure-name-2]]
                           {THRU   }

        [WITH TEST {BEFORE} ] UNTIL condition-1
                   {AFTER }

        [imperative-statement-1 END-PERFORM]
```

TEST BEFORE/TEST AFTER

The optional TEST BEFORE/TEST AFTER clause is explained in conjunction with Figure 9.1. Figure 9.1a depicts the DO WHILE structure that has been used throughout the book, while Figure 9.1b illustrates the slightly different DO UNTIL structure. The difference between the two (aside from the semantics of switching the true and false branches) pertains to the sequence in which the condition and statement are executed.

The DO WHILE structure of Figure 9.1a tests the condition *before* executing Block A; the DO UNTIL structure in Figure 9.1b tests the condition *after* executing

Figure 9.1 The Iteration Structure

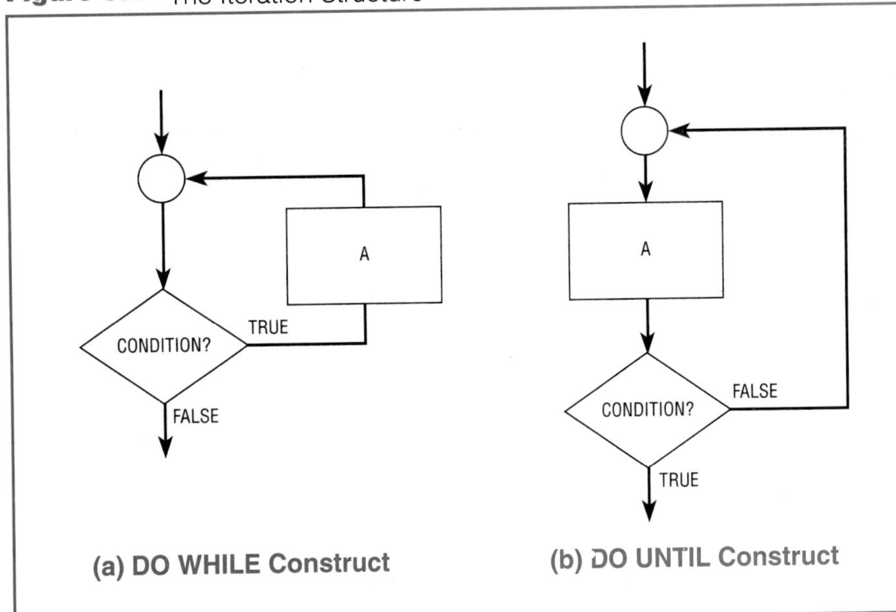

Block A. The DO WHILE structure does not execute Block A if the condition is initially false, whereas DO UNTIL guarantees that Block A is executed at least once.

The PERFORM statement includes the TEST BEFORE and TEST AFTER phrases, corresponding to a DO WHILE and DO UNTIL, respectively. Specification of TEST BEFORE tests the condition before performing the procedure, and corresponds to the DO WHILE. Specification of TEST AFTER performs the procedure and then tests the condition, and corresponds to a DO UNTIL. Omission of both TEST BEFORE and TEST AFTER (as has been done throughout the text) defaults to TEST BEFORE.

In-line PERFORM

The procedure-name is enclosed within brackets within the syntax of the PERFORM statement and thus is an *optional* entry. Omission of the procedure name produces an ***in-line perform,*** where the statements to be executed appear immediately below the PERFORM statement itself, as opposed to the out-of-line execution of a designated procedure elsewhere in the program. For example:

```
PERFORM
    Statement 1
    Statement 2
      .
      .  Other statements to be executed
      .
END-PERFORM
```

An in-line perform functions just as a regular PERFORM, except that the statements to be executed are contained entirely within the statement—that is, between PERFORM and END-PERFORM. Omission of the procedure name (that is, specification of an in-line perform) requires the END-PERFORM delimiter; conversely, the END-PERFORM may *not* be specified in conjunction with performing a paragraph.

Performing Sections

The procedure name in the PERFORM statement can be either a ***paragraph*** or a ***section.*** A paragraph consists of one or more sentences, whereas a section is made up of one or more paragraphs. Paragraph headers are required to begin in the A-margin (columns 8–11), whereas sentences begin in the B-margin (columns 12–72). The compiler recognizes the end of one paragraph when it senses the beginning of the next paragraph—that is, when it finds the next entry in the A-margin. Section headers also begin in the A-margin and are distinguished from paragraph headers by the reserved word SECTION.

When a paragraph is performed, control is transferred to the first sentence in that paragraph and remains in that paragraph until the next paragraph is reached. In similar fashion, if the procedure name in a PERFORM statement refers to a section (rather than a paragraph), control is transferred to the first paragraph in that section and remains in that section until the next section is reached.

The authors suggest that you avoid sections altogether (see tip on page 233); the material is included here because sections appear in many older COBOL programs.

PERFORM THRU

The THROUGH (THRU) clause executes all statements *between* the specified procedure names. The procedures may be paragraphs or sections, but procedure-name-1 must be physically before procedure-name-2 within the COBOL program.

PROGRAMMING TIP

Perform Paragraphs, Not Sections

The motivation behind this guideline is best demonstrated by example. Given the following Procedure Division, what will be the final value of X?

```
PROCEDURE DIVISION.

MAINLINE SECTION.
    MOVE ZERO TO X.
    PERFORM A.
    PERFORM B.
    PERFORM C.
    PERFORM D.
    STOP RUN.

A SECTION.
    ADD 1 TO X.
B.
    ADD 1 TO X.
C.
    ADD 1 TO X.
D.
    ADD 1 TO X.
```

The correct answer is 7, not 4. A common error made by many programmers is a misinterpretation of the statement **PERFORM A**. Since **A** is a *section* and not a *paragraph*, the statement **PERFORM A** invokes *every* paragraph in that section, namely, paragraphs B, C, and D, in addition to the unnamed paragraph immediately after the section header.

A **PERFORM** statement specifies a *procedure*, which is *either* a section *or* a paragraph, yet there is no way of telling the nature of the procedure from the **PERFORM** statement itself. Consequently, when a section is specified as a procedure, the unfortunate result is too often execution of unintended code. Can't happen? Did you correctly compute the value of **X?**

A common practice is to make procedure-name-2 a single-sentence paragraph consisting of the word EXIT. The EXIT statement causes no action to be taken; its function is to delineate the end of the PERFORM. Consider:

```
    PERFORM PROCESS-RECORDS THRU PROCESS-RECORDS-EXIT.
.
  .
    .
PROCESS-RECORDS.
.
  .
    .
PROCESS-RECORDS-EXIT.
    EXIT.
```

The only practical reason to use a PERFORM THRU statement with an EXIT paragraph is to enable *downward* branching to the EXIT statement depending on a condition within the paragraph. Although an argument could be made for this usage in limited instances, the need for such statements as GO TO PROCESS-RECORDS-EXIT should generally be avoided.

READ

The READ statement includes two important clauses—INTO and NOT AT END—that were not previously presented. Consider:

```
READ file-name RECORD [ INTO identifier ]
    [AT END imperative-statement-1]
    [NOT AT END imperative-statement-2]
[END-READ]
```

False-Condition Branch

The **NOT AT END** clause specifies an action for the false branch of a conditional statement; it is commonly used is in conjunction with a scope terminator and an in-line perform to eliminate the priming read, as shown in Figure 9.2.

Figure 9.2 Structure of a COBOL Program

```
    READ INPUT-FILE
        AT END MOVE 'NO' TO DATA-REMAINS-SWITCH.
    PERFORM PROCESS-RECORDS
        UNTIL DATA-REMAINS-SWITCH = 'NO'.


PROCESS-RECORDS.
    .
     .                 Procedure Division statements to process the current record
      .
    READ INPUT-FILE
        AT END MOVE 'NO' TO DATA-REMAINS-SWITCH.
```

(a) Priming Read

```
    PERFORM UNTIL DATA-REMAINS-SWITCH = 'NO'
        READ INPUT-FILE
            AT END
                MOVE 'NO' TO DATA-REMAINS-SWITCH
            NOT AT END
              .
               .       Procedure Division statements to process the current record
                .
        END-READ
    END-PERFORM.
```

(b) False Condition Branch with In-line Perform

The choice between the priming read in Figure 9.2a and the equivalent logic in Figure 9.2b is one of personal preference. The earlier listings (e.g., the tuition billing program in Chapter 5) used the priming read because it was required in COBOL-74 as the earlier compiler had neither the false-condition branch nor the in-line perform. Many programmers are, in fact, so accustomed to the priming read that they continue to use it even though it is no longer necessary. We prefer the in-line perform and false-condition branch, but both techniques are equally acceptable.

READ INTO

The **READ INTO** phrase causes the input record to be stored in two places: in the I/O area of the designated file *and* in the identifier name specified in the INTO phrase in Working-Storage. The statement is illustrated in Figure 9.3, where the input data are available in both EMPLOYEE-RECORD and WS-EMPLOYEE-RECORD. READ INTO is equivalent to the combination of a READ statement and a MOVE statement as shown:

```
READ EMPLOYEE-FILE
    AT END
        MOVE 'NO' TO DATA-REMAINS-SWITCH
    NOT AT END
        PERFORM PROCESS-THIS-RECORD
END-READ.
MOVE EMPLOYEE-RECORD TO WS-EMPLOYEE-RECORD.
```

Figure 9.3 The READ INTO Statement

```
FD  EMPLOYEE-FILE
    DATA RECORD IS EMPLOYEE-RECORD.
01  EMPLOYEE-RECORD            PIC X(60).
        .
           .
              .
WORKING-STORAGE SECTION.
01  FILLER                     PIC X(14)    VALUE 'WS BEGINS HERE'.
01  WS-EMPLOYEE-RECORD.
    05  EMP-NAME               PIC X(25).
           .
              .
                 .
PROCEDURE DIVISION.
           .
              .
                 .
     READ EMPLOYEE-FILE INTO WS-EMPLOYEE-RECORD
         AT END
             MOVE 'NO' TO DATA-REMAINS-SWITCH
         NOT AT END
             PERFORM PROCESS-THIS-RECORD
     END-READ.
```

The advantage of the READ INTO statement is in debugging. If a program ends prematurely, the first task is to identify the record being processed at the instant the problem occurred. The FD area is difficult to find, and identification of the specific logical record is further complicated by considerations of blocking. Working-Storage, however, is easy to find because of the literal WS BEGINS HERE. The technique is not sophisticated, but it does work. Once Working-Storage is found, you can identify the record in question as well as the values of all other data names defined in Working-Storage.

WRITE FROM

The **WRITE FROM** statement is analogous to READ INTO in that it combines the effects of a MOVE and a WRITE into a single statement. The general format of the WRITE statement is:

```
WRITE record-name [FROM identifier-1]

[                      {{identifier-2}  [LINE ]}]
[{BEFORE}              {{integer     }  [LINES]}]
[{AFTER } ADVANCING    {{mnemonic-name}        }]
[                      {{PAGE         }        }]
```

A single WRITE FROM statement, for example,

```
WRITE PRINT-LINE FROM HEADING-LINE
    AFTER ADVANCING PAGE.
```

is equivalent to the combination of a MOVE and a WRITE statement:

```
MOVE HEADING-LINE TO PRINT-LINE.
WRITE PRINT-LINE
    AFTER ADVANCING PAGE.
```

WRITE FROM can be used throughout a program to write heading, detail, and total lines.

INITIALIZE

The **INITIALIZE** statement sets multiple data names to initial values in a single statement. Consider:

```
INITIALIZE [identifier-1] . . .

[            {{ALPHABETIC          }                              }      ]
[            {{ALPHANUMERIC        }                              }      ]
[ REPLACING  {{NUMERIC             }  DATA BY  {identifier-2}     } . . .]
[            {{ALPHANUMERIC-EDITED }           {literal-1   }     }      ]
[            {{NUMERIC-EDITED      }                              }      ]
```

The brackets indicate that all parameters are optional; that is, INITIALIZE in and of itself is a valid statement that initializes all numeric items in a program to zeros, and all nonnumeric items to spaces. You can also restrict the INITIALIZE statement to one (data name or more,) initialize only specific categories of data names, and/or initialize to values other than zeros or spaces. Thus given the COBOL fragment:

```
01  GROUP-ITEM.
    05  NUMERIC-FIELD-1          PIC 9(4).
    05  NUMERIC-FIELD-2          PIC 9(4).
    05  ALPHANUMERIC-FIELD-1     PIC X(15).
    05  ALPHANUMERIC-FIELD-2     PIC X(20).
```

The statement INITIALIZE GROUP-ITEM is equivalent to:

```
MOVE ZEROS TO NUMERIC-FIELD-1.
MOVE ZEROS TO NUMERIC-FIELD-2.
MOVE SPACES TO ALPHANUMERIC-FIELD-1.
MOVE SPACES TO ALPHANUMERIC-FIELD-2.
```

In similar fashion, INITIALIZE GROUP-ITEM REPLACING NUMERIC BY ZERO is equivalent to:

```
MOVE ZEROS TO NUMERIC-FIELD-1.
MOVE ZEROS TO NUMERIC-FIELD-2.
```

And finally, INITIALIZE GROUP-ITEM REPLACING ALPHANUMERIC BY SPACES is equivalent to:

```
MOVE SPACES TO ALPHANUMERIC-FIELD-1.
MOVE SPACES TO ALPHANUMERIC-FIELD-2.
```

String Processing

It is often necessary to operate on individual characters within a field, when the field is alphanumeric. Operations of this type are called ***string processing*** operations, and are accomplished with the INSPECT, STRING, and UNSTRING statements in COBOL. Each of these statements is discussed in detail.

INSPECT

The INSPECT statement is a convenient way to replace one character (or character string) with another. Consider:

```
INSPECT identifier-1 REPLACING

{ CHARACTERS BY {identifier-2} [{BEFORE} INITIAL {identifier-3}] ...          }
                {literal-1   } [{AFTER }         {literal-2   }]               
{ {ALL    } {identifier-4} BY {identifier-5} [{BEFORE} INITIAL {identifier-6}] ... }
{ {LEADING} {literal-3   }    {literal-4   } [{AFTER }         {literal-5   }]     }
{ {FIRST  }                                                                   }
```

The INSPECT statement can be used with the editing characters of Chapter 7 as illustrated in Figure 9.4. Assume, for example, that social security number is stored as a nine-position field (with no hyphens) in the input record, but is to appear with hyphens in the printed report. The MOVE statement transfers the incoming social security number to an 11-position field containing two blanks (denoted by B in the PICTURE clause). The INSPECT statement replaces every occurrence of a blank in SOC-SEC-NUM-OUT by the desired hyphen.

Figure 9.4 The INSPECT Statement

```
01  RECORD-IN.
    05  SOC-SEC-NUM                 PIC 9(9).
    .
       .
          .
01  PRINT-LINE.
    05  SOC-SEC-NUM-OUT             PIC 999B99B9999.
    .
       .
          .
PROCEDURE DIVISION.
    .
       .
          .
    MOVE SOC-SEC-NUM TO SOC-SEC-NUM-OUT.
    INSPECT SOC-SEC-NUM-OUT REPLACING ALL ' ' BY '-'.
```

Another frequent use of the INSPECT statement is the elimination of leading blanks in numeric fields. (Numeric fields in COBOL should not contain anything other than the digits 0 to 9 and a sign over the rightmost (low-order) position.) Leading blanks can be replaced with zeros as follows:

```
INSPECT FIELD-WITH-BLANKS REPLACING LEADING ' ' BY '0'.
```

STRING

The STRING statement joins (concatenates) one or more fields and/or one or more literals into a single field. Thus a STRING statement has the same effect as a series of MOVE statements, except that the destination fields are one and the same. An abbreviated form of the COBOL notation for the STRING follows:

```
                                                        {identifier-3}
STRING {identifier-1} [identifier-2] . . . DELIMITED BY {literal-3   } . . .
       {literal-1   } [literal-2   ]                    {SIZE        }

       INTO identifier-4 [WITH POINTER identifier-5]

[END-STRING]
```

The above notation can be simplified, for our discussion, in the following manner:

```
STRING sending item INTO receiving field
```

A sending item may be either an identifier or a literal. Each sending item must be accompanied by a delimiting clause, which indicates when to stop moving characters from the sending field. The delimiter can take one of three forms:

1. An identifier name that contains the delimiting character(s),
2. A figurative literal or constant whose value is the delimiting character(s), or
3. SIZE, which transfers the entire contents of the sending item.

The delimiting character(s) itself is *not* transferred. Figure 9.5 contains an example of the STRING statement in which the components of an individual's name are stored separately, then put together to form a single character string. The application is not unusual in that a program often requires a person's name in two formats. It is easy, for example, to visualize the name (John H. Smith) as a single entity as it might appear on an address label. You would not, however, want to store the name as a single field as that would preclude the ability to obtain an alphabetical list on last name; that is you must have access to last name as a separate entity, in order to alphabetize a list. (See problem 3.)

Figure 9.5 The STRING Statement

```
05 NAME-IN-PIECES.
   10 LAST-NAME           PIC X(16)
   10 FIRST-NAME          PIC X(10)
   10 MIDDLE-INITIAL      PIC X.

05 ENTIRE-NAME            PIC X(29)
```

(a) Working-Storage Holding Areas

```
MOVE SPACES TO ENTIRE-NAME.
STRING FIRST-NAME DELIMITED BY SPACE
   ' ' DELIMITED BY SIZE
   MIDDLE-INITIAL DELIMITED BY SPACE
   ' ' DELIMITED BY SIZE
   LAST-NAME DELIMITED BY SPACE
   INTO ENTIRE-NAME
```

(b) STRING Statement

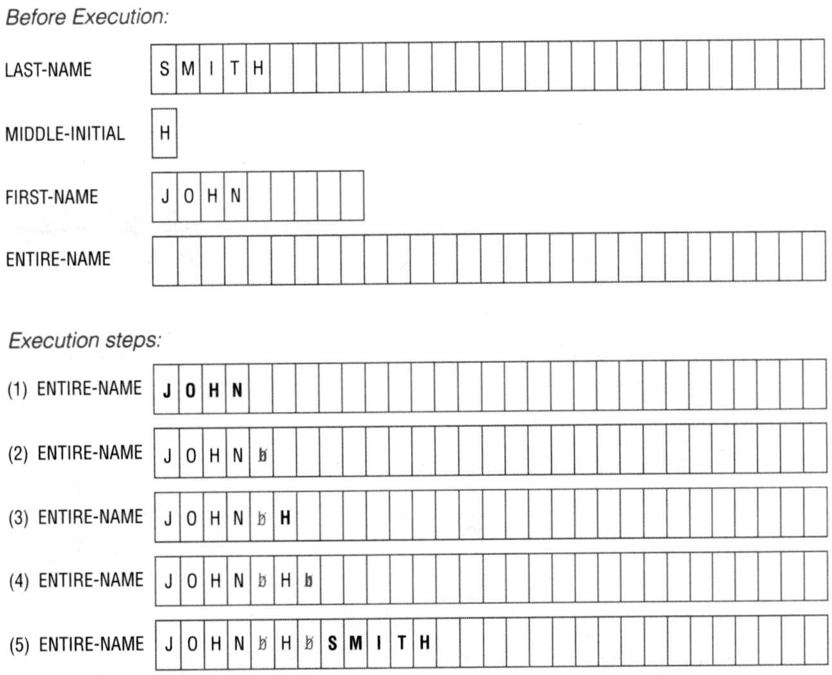

Before Execution:

LAST-NAME: S M I T H

MIDDLE-INITIAL: H

FIRST-NAME: J O H N

ENTIRE-NAME:

Execution steps:

(1) ENTIRE-NAME: **J O H N**

(2) ENTIRE-NAME: J O H N **b̸**

(3) ENTIRE-NAME: J O H N b̸ **H**

(4) ENTIRE-NAME: J O H N b̸ H **b̸**

(5) ENTIRE-NAME: J O H N b̸ H b̸ **S M I T H**

(c) Sequence of Transfer

The Data Division entries in Figure 9.5a define NAME-IN-PIECES to hold the individual fields, and ENTIRE-NAME to hold the concatenated result. Five distinct steps are required to string the individual fields together to form a single name:

1. Move FIRST-NAME to ENTIRE-NAME.
2. Move a space to ENTIRE-NAME after the first name.
3. Move MIDDLE-INITIAL to ENTIRE-NAME after the space.
4. Move a space to ENTIRE-NAME after the initial.
5. Move LAST-NAME to ENTIRE-NAME after the second space.

The STRING statement in Figure 9.5b accomplishes all five tasks and is illustrated in Figure 9.5c. The STRING statement executes as follows:

1. The characters in the FIRST-NAME field are moved (from left to right) to ENTIRE-NAME until a space is encountered (the delimiter), or the entire contents of FIRST-NAME are transferred.
2. The literal ' ' (delimiter is SIZE) is moved to the position following the last character of FIRST-NAME.
3. The MIDDLE-INITIAL is moved.
4. The literal ' ' (delimiter is SIZE) is moved to the position following the MIDDLE-INITIAL.
5. Finally, each character in LAST-NAME is moved until either a space is encountered (the delimiter), or the entire field is transferred.

UNSTRING

The UNSTRING statement breaks a concatenated field into its components and is the opposite of the STRING statement. An abbreviated form of the COBOL notation for the UNSTRING follows:

```
UNSTRING identifier-1 [DELIMITED BY {identifier-2} [OR {identifier-3}] . . . ]
                                    {literal-1   }      {literal-2   }

        INTO identifier-4

[END-UNSTRING]
```

We reverse the previous example and divide ENTIRE-NAME into its three components, FIRST-NAME, MIDDLE-INITIAL, and LAST-NAME, as shown in Figure 9.6. The UNSTRING statement operates from left to right on ENTIRE-NAME, moving characters into FIRST-NAME until a space is encountered, then into MIDDLE-INITIAL, and finally into LAST-NAME.

Reference Modification

Reference modification enables you to address a character string that was not explicitly defined—that is, a character string within an existing data name. This is done by specifying the leftmost (starting) position of the string within the data name and the length of the string, separating the parameters by a colon. The format for reference modification is shown below and is illustrated in Figure 9.7.

```
data-name (leftmost position: [length])
```

Figure 9.6 The UNSTRING Statement

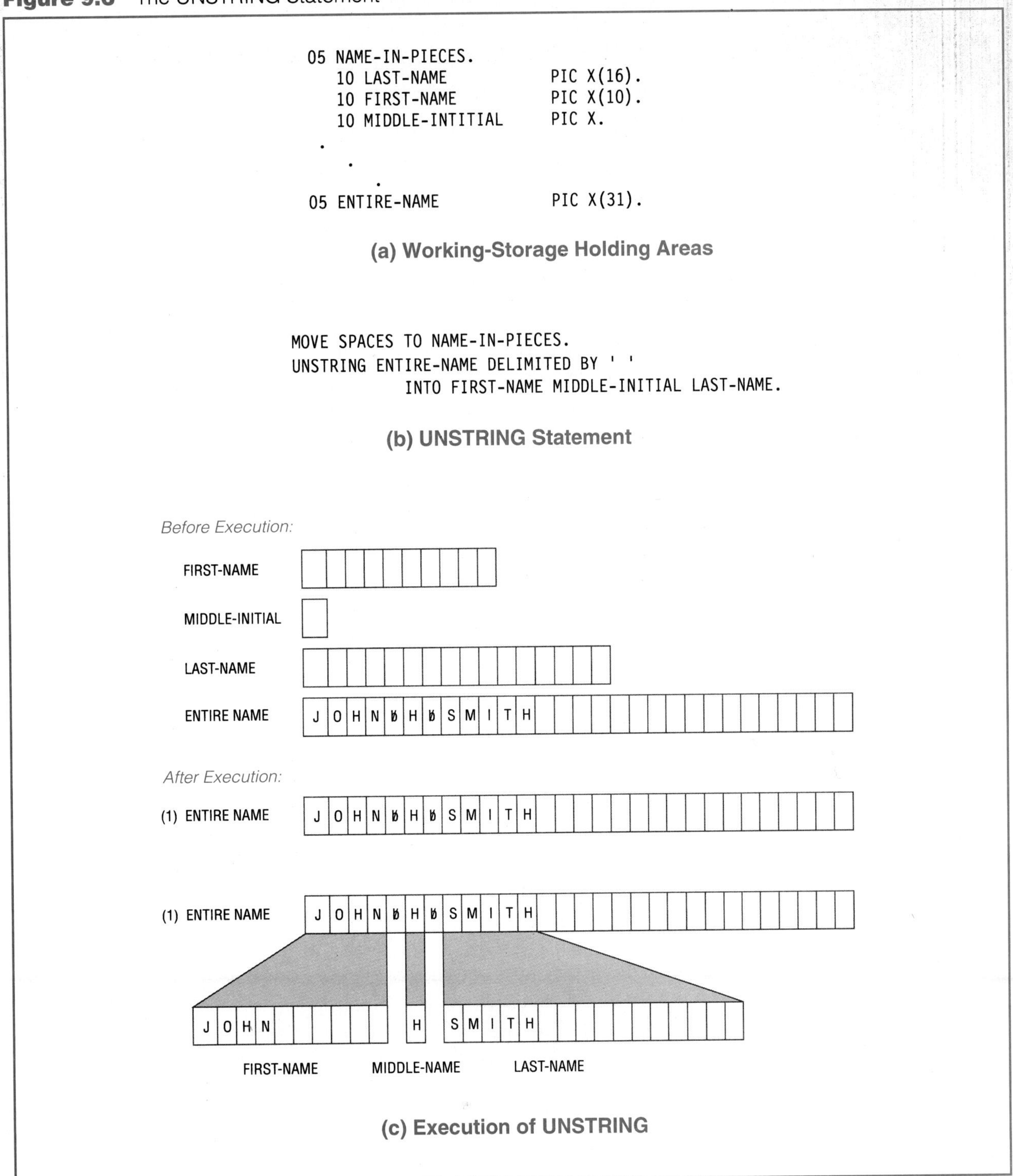

In Figure 9.7 TELEPHONE-NUMBER is defined as a 10 position field within an incoming record. Portions of this field are then moved to EDITED-PHONE-NUMBER through reference modification; for example, TELEPHONE-NUMBER (4:3) refers to positions 4, 5, and 6 within TELEPHONE-NUMBER. The specification of length is optional, and its omission defaults to the end of the data name; i.e., TELEPHONE-NUMBER (7:4) and TELEPHONE-NUMBER (7:) are equivalent.

Figure 9.7 Reference Modification

```
01  INCOMING-RECORD.
    .
      .
        .
    05  TELEPHONE-NUMBER          PIC X(10).
    .
      .
        .

01  EDITED-PHONE-NUMBER.
    05  FILLER                    PIC X     VALUE '('.
    05  AREA-CODE                 PIC X(3).
    05  FILLER                    PIC X     VALUE ')'.
    05  EXCHANGE                  PIC X(3).
    05  FILLER                    PIC X     VALUE '-'.
    05  DIGITS                    PIC X(4).
    .
      .
        .

    MOVE TELEPHONE-NUMBER (1:3) TO AREA-CODE.
    MOVE TELEPHONE-NUMBER (4:3) TO EXCHANGE.
    MOVE TELEPHONE-NUMBER (7:4) TO DIGITS.
```

ACCEPT

The **ACCEPT** statement was introduced in Chapter 8 to obtain the date of execution and implement various forms of date validation. The statement is expanded in this chapter to include the day of the week as well as the date. Consider:

```
                            { DATE        }
ACCEPT identifier-1 FROM    { DAY         }
                            { DAY-OF-WEEK }
```

The DAY-OF-WEEK clause returns an integer from 1 to 7 representing the day according to the following table:

INTEGER	DAY
1	Monday
2	Tuesday
3	Wednesday
4	Thursday
5	Friday
6	Saturday
7	Sunday

The ACCEPT statement is illustrated in Figure 9.8. The user defines a data name in Working-Storage—for example, DAY-CODE-VALUE in Figure 9.8a—then accepts

Figure 9.8 The ACCEPT Statement

```
01  DAY-CODE-VALUE              PIC 9.

01  TODAYS-DATE.
    05  TODAYS-YEAR             PIC 99.
    05  TODAYS-MONTH            PIC 99.
    05  TODAYS-DAY              PIC 99.

01  HDG-LINE.
    05  HDG-DAY-OF-WEEK         PIC X(9).
    05  FILLER                  PIC XX   VALUE ', '.
    05  HDG-DATE                PIC X(8).
```

(a) Working-Storage Entries

```
    ACCEPT DAY-CODE-VALUE FROM DAY-OF-WEEK.
    EVALUATE DAY-CODE-VALUE
        WHEN 1 MOVE '   Monday' TO HDG-DAY-OF-WEEK
        WHEN 2 MOVE '  Tuesday' TO HDG-DAY-OF-WEEK
        WHEN 3 MOVE 'Wednesday' TO HDG-DAY-OF-WEEK
        WHEN 4 MOVE ' Thursday' TO HDG-DAY-OF-WEEK
        WHEN 5 MOVE '   Friday' TO HDG-DAY-OF-WEEK
        WHEN 6 MOVE ' Saturday' TO HDG-DAY-OF-WEEK
        WHEN 7 MOVE '   Sunday' TO HDG-DAY-OF-WEEK
    END-EVALUATE.
```

(b) DAY-OF-WEEK Clause

```
    ACCEPT TODAYS-DATE FROM DATE.
    STRING TODAYS-MONTH '/' TODAYS-DAY '/' TODAYS-YEAR
        DELIMITED BY SIZE INTO HDG-DATE
    END-STRING.
```

(c) DATE Clause

the value from DAY-OF-WEEK into that data name. The subsequent EVALUATE statement expands the one-position code to a literal day.

The DATE and DAY clauses were described in Chapter 8 and represent the date (in the form yymmdd) and Julian date (in the form yyddd), respectively. The DATE clause is illustrated in Figure 9.8c for purposes of review.

Duplicate Data Names

Most programs require that the output contain some of the input, for example, name and social security number. COBOL permits the definition of ***duplicate data names*** in the Data Division, provided all Procedure Division references to duplicate names use the appropriate ***qualification***. We prefer *not* to use duplicate names because they violate the prefix coding standard discussed in Chapter 7, but they are used in older programs, and are covered here for completeness.

Qualification

The Data Division entries in Figure 9.9a contain several data names that appear in both STUDENT-RECORD and PRINT-LINE—for example, CREDITS—and any Procedure Division reference to CREDITS will produce a compiler error indicating a *nonunique data name.* This is because the compiler cannot determine which CREDITS (in STUDENT-RECORD or PRINT-LINE) is referenced. One solution is

Figure 9.9 Duplicate Data Names

```
01  STUDENT-RECORD.
    05  STUDENT-NAME                    PIC X(20).
    05  SOCIAL-SECURITY-NUM             PIC 9(9).
    05  STUDENT-ADDRESS.
        10  STREET                      PIC X(15).
        10  CITY-STATE                  PIC X(15).
    05  ZIP-CODE                        PIC X(5).
    05  CREDITS                         PIC 9(3).
    05  MAJOR                           PIC X(10).
    05  FILLER                          PIC X(3).
        .
          .
            .
01  PRINT-LINE.
    10  STUDENT-NAME                    PIC X(20).
    10  FILLER                          PIC XX.
    10  CREDITS                         PIC ZZ9.
    10  FILLER                          PIC XX.
    10  TUITION                         PIC $$,$$9.99.
    10  FILLER                          PIC XX.
    10  STUDENT-ADDRESS.
        15  STREET                      PIC X(15).
        15  CITY-STATE                  PIC X(15).
        15  ZIP-CODE                    PIC X(5).
    10  FILLER                          PIC XX.
    10  SOCIAL-SECURITY-NUM             PIC 999B99B9999.
    10  FILLER                          PIC X(47).
```

(a) Duplicate Data Names

```
MOVE CORRESPONDING STUDENT-RECORD TO PRINT-LINE.
```

(b) MOVE CORRESPONDING Statement

```
MOVE STUDENT-NAME OF STUDENT-RECORD
    TO STUDENT-NAME OF PRINT-LINE.
MOVE SOCIAL-SECURITY-NUM OF STUDENT-RECORD
    TO SOCIAL-SECURITY-NUM OF PRINT-LINE.
MOVE STREET OF STUDENT-RECORD
    TO STREET OF PRINT-LINE.
MOVE CITY-STATE OF STUDENT-RECORD
    TO CITY-STATE OF PRINT-LINE.
MOVE CREDITS OF STUDENT-RECORD
    TO CREDITS OF PRINT-LINE.
```

(c) Equivalent MOVE Statements

to *qualify* the data name, using **OF** or **IN**, and refer to CREDITS OF STUDENT-RECORD or CREDITS IN STUDENT-RECORD.

Qualification is sometimes necessary over several levels. For example, the use of STREET OF STUDENT-ADDRESS in the statement below is still ambiguous.

```
MOVE STREET OF STUDENT-ADDRESS TO OUTPUT-AREA.
```

The qualifier STUDENT-ADDRESS appears in both 01 records and thus the ambiguity was not resolved. Two levels of qualification are necessary to make the intent clear:

```
MOVE STREET OF STUDENT-ADDRESS OF STUDENT-RECORD TO OUTPUT-AREA.
```

Alternatively, you could skip the intermediate level and rewrite the statement as:

```
MOVE STREET IN STUDENT-RECORD TO OUTPUT-AREA.
```

OF and IN can be used interchangeably. Duplicate data names offer the advantage of not having to invent different names for the same item—for example, an employee name appearing in both an input record and output report. They also permit use of the MOVE CORRESPONDING statement which is *not* recommended by the authors, but which is covered for completeness.

MOVE CORRESPONDING

The syntax of the MOVE CORRESPONDING statement is:

```
MOVE {CORRESPONDING} identifier-1 TO identifier-2
     {CORR         }
```

The MOVE CORRESPONDING statement in Figure 9.9b is the equivalent of the individual MOVE statements in Figure 9.9c; that is, the single MOVE CORRESPONDING statement has the same effect as the five individual MOVE statements. The CORRESPONDING option searches every data name in STUDENT-RECORD for a matching (duplicate) data name in PRINT-LINE, then generates an individual MOVE statement whenever a match is found. It is very convenient because you have to code only the single MOVE CORRESPONDING statement.

The level numbers of the duplicate data names in Figure 9.9a do not have to match for a move to be generated—only the data names must be the same. The order of the data names in the 01 records is also immaterial; for example, SOCIAL-SECURITY-NUM is the second field in STUDENT-RECORD, and the next to last in PRINT-LINE. Two other conditions must be satisfied, however, in order for a move to be generated:

1. At least one item in each pair of CORRESPONDING items must be an elementary item; that is, STUDENT-ADDRESS of STUDENT-RECORD is not moved to STUDENT-ADDRESS of PRINT-LINE. (The elementary items STREET and CITY-STATE are moved instead.)

2. Corresponding elementary items are moved only if they have the same name and qualification, up to but not including identifier-1 and identifier-2. ZIP-CODE, for example, belongs directly to STUDENT-RECORD, but has an intermediate qualifier (STUDENT-ADDRESS) in PRINT-LINE, and thus ZIP-CODE is not moved.

The Car Billing Program

Our fundamental approach throughout the text is to learn by doing. To that end we have developed a complete COBOL program that incorporates the various statements presented in the chapter. Specifications follow in the usual format.

PROGRAMMING SPECIFICATIONS

Program Name: Car Billing Program

Narrative: This program processes the file of valid car rental records that was created in the validation program of Chapter 8 to produce a report reflecting the amounts owed by individual customers.

Input File(s):

```
RENTAL-FILE
01  RENTAL-RECORD-IN.
    05  REN-CONTRACT-NO          PIC 9(6).
    05  REN-NAME.
        10  REN-LAST-NAME        PIC X(15).
        10  REN-FIRST-NAME       PIC X(10).
        10  REN-INITIAL          PIC X.
    05  REN-RETURNED-DATE.
        10  REN-RETURNED-YEAR    PIC 9(2).
        10  REN-RETURNED-MONTH   PIC 9(2).
        10  REN-RETURNED-DAY     PIC 9(2).
    05  REN-CAR-TYPE             PIC X.
    05  REN-DAYS-RENTED          PIC 99.
    05  REN-MILEAGE.
        10  REN-MILES-IN         PIC 9(6).
        10  REN-MILES-OUT        PIC 9(6).
        10  REN-MILEAGE-RATE     PIC V99.
    05  REN-INSURANCE            PIC X.
```

Test Data: The input file used by this program was created by the data validation program of Chapter 8 and was shown earlier as Figure 8.10c. The data are repeated below for convenience:

```
999777ELSINOR        TERRY      R921126F0500168000159005N
987654SMITH          PAUL       G921213M0300510000500502Y
354679KERBEL         NORMAN     X930331E1000340000324300Y
264805CLARK          JANE       S921101F0700561500551200N
233432BEINHORN       CATHY      B921122M0200123400113402Y
556564HUMMER         MARGO      R920815C0800234500123403Y
677844MCDONALD       JAMES       930123C0500423500402300N
886222VOGEL          JANICE     D930518F1200634500612302Y
008632TOWER          DARREN     R930429L0900700200689300N
```

Report Layout: See Figure 9.10.

Processing Requirements:

1. Read the file of valid car rental records that was produced by the editing program of Chapter 8. No further validation is required in this program.

2. Calculate the amount due for each incoming record as a function of car type, days rented, miles driven, mileage rate, and insurance.
   a. The mileage rate is different for each customer and appears as a field in the incoming record; the mileage total is the mileage rate times the number of miles driven.
   b. The daily rate is a function of the type of car rented. Economy cars cost $15 a day, compact cars $20 a day, mid-size cars $24 a day, full-size cars $28 a day, and luxury cars $35 a day. The daily total is the daily rate times the number of days rented.
   c. Insurance is optional and is indicated by a 'Y' in the appropriate position in the incoming record. Insurance is $10.50 a day (for customers who choose it), regardless of the type of car rented.
   d. A customer's total bill consists of the mileage total, daily total, and insurance total as described in parts (a), (b), and (c).
3. A heading is required at the top of every page, as shown in Figure 9.10. Detail lines are to be double-spaced and limited to five per page.
4. A total line for all computed fields is required at the end of the report.

Figure 9.10 Car Rental Report

Mavis Car Rental Report   Saturday - 07/03/93   Page 2

Contract Number	Name	Date Returned	Car Type	Days Rented	Rental Total	Miles Driven	Mileage Rate	Mileage Total	Insurance Total	Amount Due
5-565-64	HUMMER, MARGO R.	08/15/92	C	8	160.00	1,111	.03	33.33	84.00	277.33
6-778-44	MCDONALD, JAMES	01/23/93	C	5	100.00	212	.00	0.00		100.00
8-862-22	VOGEL, JANICE D.	05/18/93	F	12	336.00	222	.02	4.44	126.00	466.44
										315.00

										$1,930.67

Mavis Car Rental Report   Saturday - 07/03/93   Page 1

Contract Number	Name	Date Returned	Car Type	Days Rented	Rental Total	Miles Driven	Mileage Rate	Mileage Total	Insurance Total	Amount Due
9-997-77	ELSINOR, TERRY R.	11/26/92	F	5	140.00	90	.05	4.50		144.50
9-876-54	SMITH, PAUL G.	12/13/92	M	3	72.00	95	.02	1.90	31.50	105.40
3-546-79	KERBEL, NORMAN X.	03/31/93	E	10	150.00	157	.00	0.00	105.00	255.00
2-648-05	CLARK, JANE S.	11/01/92	F	7	196.00	103	.00	0.00		196.00
2-334-32	BEINHORN, CATHY B.	11/22/92	M	2	48.00	100	.02	2.00	21.00	71.00

Program Design

The car billing program has two objectives: to complete the two-program sequence begun in Chapter 8 and to illustrate the Procedure Division statements presented in this chapter. Both objectives impact the design of the pseudocode and associated hierarchy chart.

The hierarchy chart in Figure 9.11 is written *without* the priming read of earlier programs. The highest-level module, PREPARE-RENTAL-REPORT, has three subordinates: GET-TODAYS-DATE, PROCESS-RENTAL-RECORDS, and WRITE-RENTAL-TOTALS. PROCESS-RENTAL-RECORDS in turn is the driving module of the program and performs four lower-level paragraphs: COMPUTE-INDIVIDUAL-BILL, WRITE-HEADING-LINES, WRITE-DETAIL-LINE, and INCREMENT-RENTAL-TOTALS. COMPUTE-INDIVIDUAL-BILL has three subordinate modules, COMPUTE-MILEAGE-TOTAL, COMPUTE-DAILY-TOTAL, and COMPUTE-INSURANCE-TOTAL to compute the components of a customer's bill.

The paragraph WRITE-HEADING-LINES is subordinate to PROCESS-RENTAL-RECORDS, which differs from an earlier hierarchy chart (page 119) that placed the heading routine on a higher level. The earlier structure, however, produced only a single heading at the start of processing, whereas the current requirement is to produce a heading at the top of every page; hence the heading routine will be executed several times and is subordinate to processing a record.

The pseudocode in Figure 9.12 takes advantage of the in-line perform and false-condition branch to eliminate the priming read used in earlier examples. The pseudocode also implements the required page heading routine by initializing the line counter to six and testing its value prior to writing each detail line. The heading

Figure 9.11 Hierarchy Chart

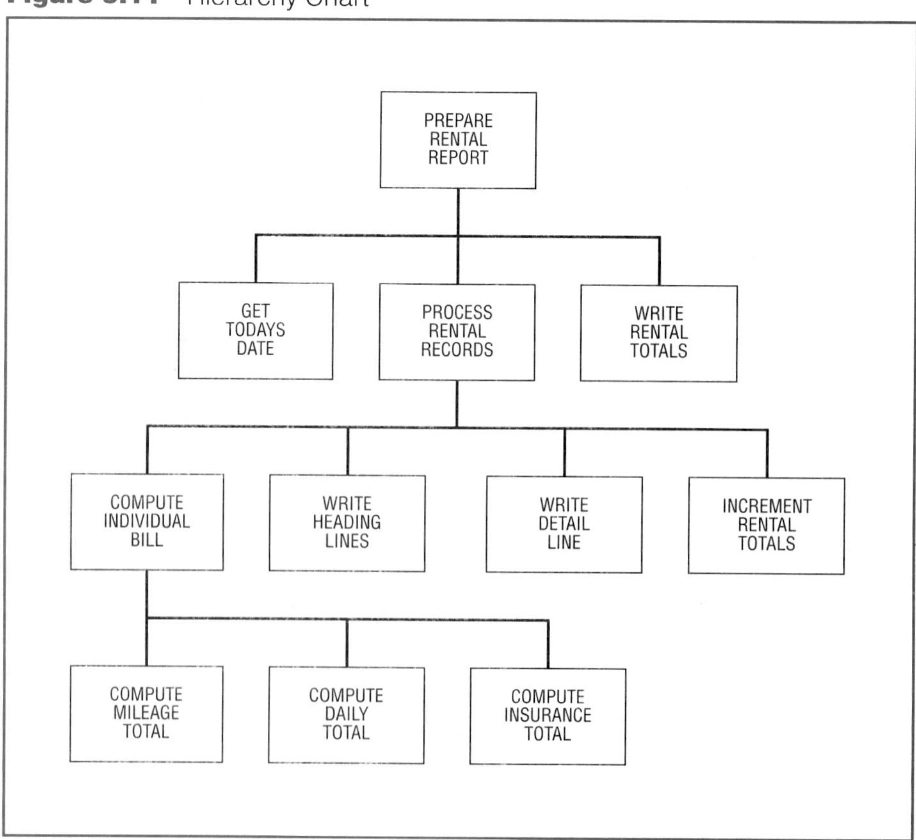

Figure 9.12 Pseudocode

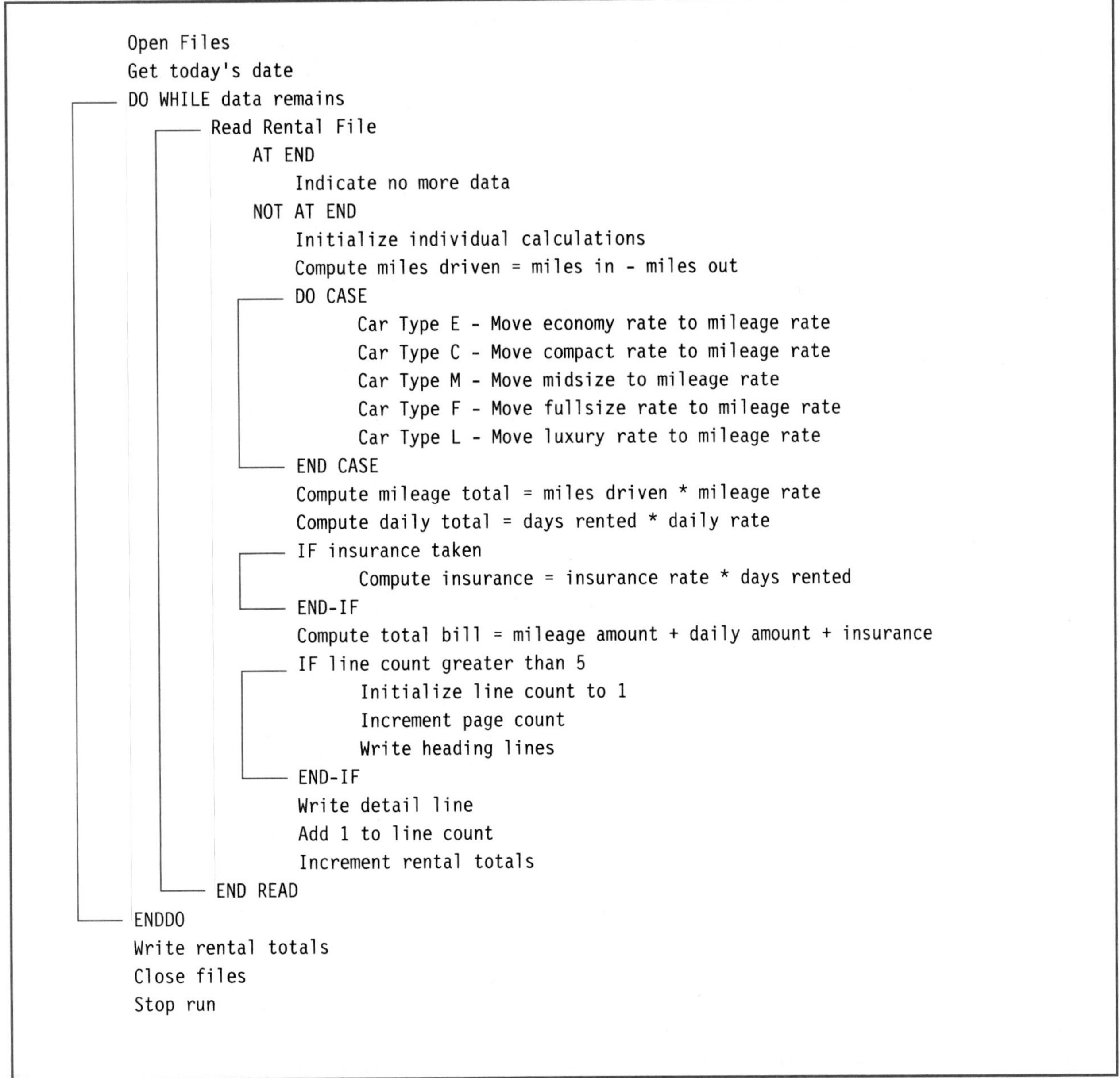

```
Open Files
Get today's date
DO WHILE data remains
    Read Rental File
        AT END
            Indicate no more data
        NOT AT END
            Initialize individual calculations
            Compute miles driven = miles in - miles out
            DO CASE
                Car Type E - Move economy rate to mileage rate
                Car Type C - Move compact rate to mileage rate
                Car Type M - Move midsize to mileage rate
                Car Type F - Move fullsize rate to mileage rate
                Car Type L - Move luxury rate to mileage rate
            END CASE
            Compute mileage total = miles driven * mileage rate
            Compute daily total = days rented * daily rate
            IF insurance taken
                Compute insurance = insurance rate * days rented
            END-IF
            Compute total bill = mileage amount + daily amount + insurance
            IF line count greater than 5
                Initialize line count to 1
                Increment page count
                Write heading lines
            END-IF
            Write detail line
            Add 1 to line count
            Increment rental totals
    END READ
ENDDO
Write rental totals
Close files
Stop run
```

will be written prior to the first detail record because it (the line counter) is greater than five (the desired number of lines per page). The line counter is then reset to one so that the heading will be produced for every fifth record.

The Completed Program

The completed program in Figure 9.13 illustrates many of the statements presented in the chapter. The logic of the program is straightforward and parallels the pseudocode just discussed. Several features of the program merit attention:

1. The combination of the in-line perform and false-condition branch (lines 209–216) to eliminate the priming read used in all previous programs.

Figure 9.13 The Completed Program

```
IDENTIFICATION DIVISION.
PROGRAM-ID.      CARSRPT.
AUTHOR.          CVV.

ENVIRONMENT DIVISION.
INPUT-OUTPUT SECTION.
FILE-CONTROL.
    SELECT RENTAL-FILE
        ASSIGN TO UT-S-SYSIN.
    SELECT PRINT-FILE
        ASSIGN TO UT-S-SYSOUT.

DATA DIVISION.
FILE SECTION.
FD  RENTAL-FILE
    RECORD CONTAINS 56 CHARACTERS.
01  RENTAL-RECORD                   PIC X(56).

FD  PRINT-FILE
    RECORD CONTAINS 132 CHARACTERS.
01  PRINT-LINE                      PIC X(132).

WORKING-STORAGE SECTION.
01  FILLER                          PIC X(14)
        VALUE 'WS BEGINS HERE'.

01  RENTAL-RECORD-IN.
    05  REN-CONTRACT-NO             PIC 9(6).
    05  REN-NAME.
        10  REN-LAST-NAME           PIC X(15).
        10  REN-FIRST-NAME          PIC X(10).
        10  REN-INITIAL             PIC X.
    05  REN-RETURNED-DATE.
        10  REN-RETURNED-YEAR       PIC 9(2).
        10  REN-RETURNED-MONTH      PIC 9(2).
        10  REN-RETURNED-DAY        PIC 9(2).
    05  REN-CAR-TYPE                PIC X.
    05  REN-DAYS-RENTED             PIC 99.
    05  REN-MILEAGE.
        10  REN-MILES-IN            PIC 9(6).
        10  REN-MILES-OUT           PIC 9(6).
        10  REN-MILEAGE-RATE        PIC V99.
    05  REN-INSURANCE               PIC X.

01  PROGRAM-SWITCHES.
    05  DATA-REMAINS-SWITCH         PIC XX  VALUE SPACES.
    05  NAME-POINTER                PIC 999 VALUE 1.

01  PAGE-AND-LINE-COUNTERS.
    05  LINE-COUNT                  PIC 9(2)     VALUE 6.
```

Definition of line counter in conjunction with heading routine

Figure 9.13 *(continued)*

```
           05  PAGE-COUNT                PIC 9(2)     VALUE ZEROS.
           05  LINES-PER-PAGE            PIC 9(2)     VALUE 5.

       01  DAILY-RATES.
           05  ECONOMY-RATE              PIC 9(3)V99  VALUE 15.
           05  COMPACT-RATE              PIC 9(3)V99  VALUE 20.
           05  MID-RATE                  PIC 9(3)V99  VALUE 24.
           05  FULL-RATE                 PIC 9(3)V99  VALUE 28.
           05  LUXURY-RATE               PIC 9(3)V99  VALUE 35.
           05  INSURANCE-RATE            PIC 99V99    VALUE 10.50.

       01  IND-BILL-INFORMATION.
           05  IND-MILES-DRIVEN          PIC 9(5).
           05  IND-DAILY-RATE            PIC 9(3)V99.
           05  IND-DAILY-TOTAL           PIC 9(4)V99.
           05  IND-MILEAGE-TOTAL         PIC 9(3)V99.
           05  IND-INSURANCE-TOTAL       PIC 9(3)V99.
           05  IND-AMOUNT-DUE            PIC 9(4)V99.

       01  TOTALS-FOR-REPORT.
           05  TOTAL-DAYS-RENTED         PIC 9(4)     VALUE ZEROES.
           05  TOTAL-DAILY-RENTAL        PIC 9(6)V99  VALUE ZEROES.
           05  TOTAL-MILES-DRIVEN        PIC 9(6)     VALUE ZEROES.
           05  TOTAL-MILEAGE             PIC 9(4)V99  VALUE ZEROES.
           05  TOTAL-INSURANCE           PIC 9(4)V99  VALUE ZEROES.
           05  TOTAL-AMOUNT-DUE          PIC 9(6)V99  VALUE ZEROES.

       01  TODAYS-DATE-AREA.
           05  TODAYS-YEAR               PIC 99.
           05  TODAYS-MONTH              PIC 99.
           05  TODAYS-DAY                PIC 99.

       01  DAY-CODE-VALUE                PIC 9.

       01  HEADING-LINE-ONE.
           05  FILLER                    PIC X(20)  VALUE SPACES.
           05  FILLER                    PIC X(25)
                   VALUE 'Mavis Car Rental Report'.
           05  FILLER                    PIC X(16)  VALUE SPACES.
           05  HDG-DAY                   PIC X(9).
           05  FILLER                    PIC X(3)   VALUE ' - '.
           05  HDG-DATE                  PIC X(8).
           05  FILLER                    PIC X(41)  VALUE SPACES.
           05  FILLER                    PIC X(5)   VALUE 'Page '.
           05  HDG-PAGE-NUMBER           PIC Z9.
           05  FILLER                    PIC X(3)   VALUE SPACES.

       01  HEADING-LINE-TWO.
           05  FILLER                    PIC X(8)  VALUE 'Contract'.
           05  FILLER                    PIC X(38) VALUE SPACES.
```

Definition of page counters in conjunction with heading routine

Figure 9.13 *(continued)*

```
101          05  FILLER                 PIC X(4)   VALUE 'Date'.
102          05  FILLER                 PIC X(5)   VALUE SPACES.
103          05  FILLER                 PIC X(3)   VALUE 'Car'.
104          05  FILLER                 PIC X(3)   VALUE SPACES.
105          05  FILLER                 PIC X(4)   VALUE 'Days'.
106          05  FILLER                 PIC X(6)   VALUE SPACES.
107          05  FILLER                 PIC X(6)   VALUE 'Rental'.
108          05  FILLER                 PIC X(4)   VALUE SPACES.
109          05  FILLER                 PIC X(5)   VALUE 'Miles'.
110          05  FILLER                 PIC X(2)   VALUE SPACES.
111          05  FILLER                 PIC X(7)   VALUE 'Mileage'.
112          05  FILLER                 PIC X(2)   VALUE SPACES.
113          05  FILLER                 PIC X(7)   VALUE 'Mileage'.
114          05  FILLER                 PIC X(2)   VALUE SPACES.
115          05  FILLER                 PIC X(9)   VALUE 'Insurance'.
116          05  FILLER                 PIC X(6)   VALUE SPACES.
117          05  FILLER                 PIC X(6)   VALUE 'Amount'.
118          05  FILLER                 PIC X(5)   VALUE SPACES.
119
120      01  HEADING-LINE-THREE.
121          05  FILLER                 PIC X      VALUE SPACES.
122          05  FILLER                 PIC X(6)   VALUE 'Number'.
123          05  FILLER                 PIC X(4)   VALUE SPACES.
124          05  FILLER                 PIC X(4)   VALUE 'Name'.
125          05  FILLER                 PIC X(29)  VALUE SPACES.
126          05  FILLER                 PIC X(8)   VALUE 'Returned'.
127          05  FILLER                 PIC X(2)   VALUE SPACES.
128          05  FILLER                 PIC X(4)   VALUE 'Type'.
129          05  FILLER                 PIC X(2)   VALUE SPACES.
130          05  FILLER                 PIC X(6)   VALUE 'Rented'.
131          05  FILLER                 PIC X(6)   VALUE SPACES.
132          05  FILLER                 PIC X(5)   VALUE 'Total'.
133          05  FILLER                 PIC X(3)   VALUE SPACES.
134          05  FILLER                 PIC X(6)   VALUE 'Driven'.
135          05  FILLER                 PIC X(4)   VALUE SPACES.
136          05  FILLER                 PIC X(4)   VALUE 'Rate'.
137          05  FILLER                 PIC X(4)   VALUE SPACES.
138          05  FILLER                 PIC X(5)   VALUE 'Total'.
139          05  FILLER                 PIC X(6)   VALUE SPACES.
140          05  FILLER                 PIC X(5)   VALUE 'Total'.
141          05  FILLER                 PIC X(9)   VALUE SPACES.
142          05  FILLER                 PIC X(3)   VALUE 'Due'.
143          05  FILLER                 PIC X(6)   VALUE SPACES.
144
145      01  DETAIL-LINE.
146          05  DET-CONTRACT-NO        PIC 9B999B99.
147          05  FILLER                 PIC X(3)   VALUE SPACES.
148          05  DET-NAME               PIC X(30).
149          05  FILLER                 PIC X(3)   VALUE SPACES.
150          05  DET-RETURN-DATE        PIC X(8).
```

Blanks are replaced in the INSPECT statement of line 302 (annotation to line 146)

Figure 9.13 *(continued)*

```
           05  FILLER                  PIC X(4)   VALUE SPACES.
           05  DET-CAR-TYPE            PIC X.
           05  FILLER                  PIC X(5)   VALUE SPACES.
           05  DET-DAYS-RENTED         PIC Z9.
           05  FILLER                  PIC X(5)   VALUE SPACES.
           05  DET-DAILY-TOTAL         PIC Z,ZZ9.99.
           05  FILLER                  PIC X(3)   VALUE SPACES.
           05  DET-MILES-DRIVEN        PIC ZZ,ZZ9.
           05  FILLER                  PIC X(5)   VALUE SPACES.
           05  DET-MILEAGE-RATE        PIC .99.
           05  FILLER                  PIC X(5)   VALUE SPACES.
           05  DET-MILEAGE-TOTAL       PIC ZZ9.99.
           05  FILLER                  PIC X(4)   VALUE SPACES.
           05  DET-INSURANCE-TOTAL     PIC ZZ9.99 BLANK WHEN ZERO.
           05  FILLER                  PIC X(4)   VALUE SPACES.
           05  DET-AMOUNT-DUE          PIC Z,ZZ9.99.
           05  FILLER                  PIC X(5)   VALUE SPACES.

       01  TOTAL-DASH-LINE.
           05  FILLER                  PIC X(59)  VALUE SPACES.
           05  FILLER                  PIC X(5)   VALUE ALL '-'.
           05  FILLER                  PIC X(3)   VALUE SPACES.
           05  FILLER                  PIC X(10)  VALUE ALL '-'.
           05  FILLER                  PIC XX     VALUE SPACES.
           05  FILLER                  PIC X(7)   VALUE ALL '-'.
           05  FILLER                  PIC X(11)  VALUE SPACES.
           05  FILLER                  PIC X(8)   VALUE ALL '-'.
           05  FILLER                  PIC XX     VALUE SPACES.
           05  FILLER                  PIC X(8)   VALUE ALL '-'.
           05  FILLER                  PIC XX     VALUE SPACES.
           05  FILLER                  PIC X(10)  VALUE ALL '-'.
           05  FILLER                  PIC X(5)   VALUE SPACES.

       01  TOTAL-LINE.
           05  FILLER                  PIC XX     VALUE SPACES.
           05  FILLER                  PIC X(6)   VALUE 'Totals'.
           05  FILLER                  PIC X(51)  VALUE SPACES.
           05  TOT-DAYS-RENTED         PIC Z,ZZ9.
           05  FILLER                  PIC X(2)   VALUE SPACES.
           05  TOT-DAILY-RENTAL        PIC $$$$,$$9.99.
           05  FILLER                  PIC XX     VALUE SPACES.
           05  TOT-MILES-DRIVEN        PIC ZZZ,ZZ9.
           05  FILLER                  PIC X(9)   VALUE SPACES.
           05  TOT-MILEAGE             PIC $$$,$$9.99.
           05  FILLER                  PIC X      VALUE SPACES.
           05  TOT-INSURANCE           PIC $$,$$9.99.
           05  FILLER                  PIC X      VALUE SPACES.
           05  TOT-AMOUNT-DUE          PIC $$$$,$$9.99.
           05  FILLER                  PIC X(5)   VALUE SPACES.
```

Figure 9.13 *(continued)*

```
       01  FILLER                           PIC X(12)
               VALUE 'WS ENDS HERE'.

       PROCEDURE DIVISION.
       000-PREPARE-RENTAL-REPORT.
           OPEN INPUT  RENTAL-FILE
                OUTPUT PRINT-FILE.
           PERFORM 100-GET-TODAYS-DATE.
           PERFORM UNTIL DATA-REMAINS-SWITCH = 'NO'
               READ RENTAL-FILE INTO RENTAL-RECORD-IN
                   AT END
                       MOVE 'NO' TO DATA-REMAINS-SWITCH
                   NOT AT END
                       PERFORM 200-PROCESS-RENTAL-RECORDS
               END-READ
           END-PERFORM.
           PERFORM 700-WRITE-RENTAL-TOTALS.
           CLOSE RENTAL-FILE
                 PRINT-FILE.
           STOP RUN.

       100-GET-TODAYS-DATE.
           ACCEPT TODAYS-DATE-AREA FROM DATE.
           STRING TODAYS-MONTH '/' TODAYS-DAY  '/' TODAYS-YEAR
               DELIMITED BY SIZE INTO HDG-DATE
           END-STRING.
           ACCEPT DAY-CODE-VALUE FROM DAY-OF-WEEK.
           EVALUATE DAY-CODE-VALUE
               WHEN 1 MOVE '   Monday' TO HDG-DAY
               WHEN 2 MOVE '  Tuesday' TO HDG-DAY
               WHEN 3 MOVE 'Wednesday' TO HDG-DAY
               WHEN 4 MOVE ' Thursday' TO HDG-DAY
               WHEN 5 MOVE '   Friday' TO HDG-DAY
               WHEN 6 MOVE ' Saturday' TO HDG-DAY
               WHEN 7 MOVE '   Sunday' TO HDG-DAY
           END-EVALUATE.

       200-PROCESS-RENTAL-RECORDS.
           PERFORM 300-COMPUTE-IND-BILL.
           IF LINE-COUNT > LINES-PER-PAGE
               PERFORM 400-WRITE-HEADING-LINES
           END-IF.
           PERFORM 500-WRITE-DETAIL-LINE.
           PERFORM 600-INCREMENT-TOTALS.

       300-COMPUTE-IND-BILL.
           INITIALIZE IND-BILL-INFORMATION.
           PERFORM 320-COMPUTE-MILEAGE-TOTAL.
           PERFORM 340-COMPUTE-DAILY-TOTAL.
           PERFORM 360-COMPUTE-INSURANCE-TOTAL.
```

In-line perform and false-condition branch drive program

ACCEPT statement obtains date of execution

Scope terminators are used throughout the Procedure Division

INITIALIZE statement resets initial values

Figure 9.13 *(continued)*

```
           COMPUTE IND-AMOUNT-DUE ROUNDED
               = IND-MILEAGE-TOTAL + IND-DAILY-TOTAL
                 + IND-INSURANCE-TOTAL
               SIZE ERROR DISPLAY 'SIZE ERROR ON AMOUNT DUE FOR '
                   REN-CONTRACT-NO
           END-COMPUTE.

       320-COMPUTE-MILEAGE-TOTAL.
           COMPUTE IND-MILES-DRIVEN
               = REN-MILES-IN - REN-MILES-OUT
           END-COMPUTE.
           COMPUTE IND-MILEAGE-TOTAL ROUNDED
               = IND-MILES-DRIVEN * REN-MILEAGE-RATE
               SIZE ERROR
                 DISPLAY 'COMPUTED BILL EXCESSIVELY LARGE'
           END-COMPUTE.

       340-COMPUTE-DAILY-TOTAL.
           EVALUATE REN-CAR-TYPE
               WHEN 'E' MOVE ECONOMY-RATE TO IND-DAILY-RATE
               WHEN 'C' MOVE COMPACT-RATE TO IND-DAILY-RATE
               WHEN 'M' MOVE MID-RATE TO IND-DAILY-RATE
               WHEN 'F' MOVE FULL-RATE TO IND-DAILY-RATE
               WHEN 'L' MOVE LUXURY-RATE TO IND-DAILY-RATE
               WHEN OTHER MOVE ZEROES TO IND-DAILY-RATE
           END-EVALUATE.
           MULTIPLY IND-DAILY-RATE BY REN-DAYS-RENTED
               GIVING IND-DAILY-TOTAL
               SIZE ERROR DISPLAY 'SIZE ERROR ON RENTAL TOTAL'
           END-MULTIPLY.

       360-COMPUTE-INSURANCE-TOTAL.
           IF REN-INSURANCE = 'Y'
               MULTIPLY INSURANCE-RATE BY REN-DAYS-RENTED
                   GIVING IND-INSURANCE-TOTAL
                   SIZE ERROR DISPLAY 'SIZE ERROR ON INSURANCE TOTAL'
               END-MULTIPLY
           END-IF.

       400-WRITE-HEADING-LINES.
           MOVE 1 TO LINE-COUNT.
           ADD 1 TO PAGE-COUNT.
           MOVE PAGE-COUNT TO HDG-PAGE-NUMBER.
           WRITE PRINT-LINE FROM HEADING-LINE-ONE
               AFTER ADVANCING PAGE.
           WRITE PRINT-LINE FROM HEADING-LINE-TWO
               AFTER ADVANCING 2 LINES.
           WRITE PRINT-LINE FROM HEADING-LINE-THREE.

       500-WRITE-DETAIL-LINE.
```

SIZE ERROR clause is used within COMPUTE statement

EVALUATE statement determines daily rate

Indentation increases readability

Figure 9.13 *(continued)*

```
           MOVE REN-CONTRACT-NO TO DET-CONTRACT-NO.
           INSPECT DET-CONTRACT-NO REPLACING ALL ' ' BY '-'.
           MOVE 1 TO NAME-POINTER.
           MOVE SPACES TO DET-NAME.
           STRING REN-LAST-NAME DELIMITED BY '  '
               ', ' DELIMITED BY SIZE
               REN-FIRST-NAME DELIMITED BY '  '
               INTO DET-NAME POINTER NAME-POINTER
           END-STRING.
           IF REN-INITIAL NOT = SPACES
               STRING ' ' REN-INITIAL '.' DELIMITED BY SIZE
                  INTO DET-NAME POINTER NAME-POINTER
               END-STRING
           END-IF.
           STRING REN-RETURNED-MONTH '/' REN-RETURNED-DAY '/'
               REN-RETURNED-YEAR DELIMITED BY SIZE
               INTO DET-RETURN-DATE
           END-STRING.
           MOVE REN-CAR-TYPE TO DET-CAR-TYPE.
           MOVE REN-DAYS-RENTED TO DET-DAYS-RENTED.
           MOVE IND-DAILY-TOTAL TO DET-DAILY-TOTAL.
           MOVE IND-MILES-DRIVEN TO DET-MILES-DRIVEN.
           MOVE REN-MILEAGE-RATE TO DET-MILEAGE-RATE.
           MOVE IND-MILEAGE-TOTAL TO DET-MILEAGE-TOTAL.
           MOVE IND-INSURANCE-TOTAL TO DET-INSURANCE-TOTAL.
           MOVE IND-MILEAGE-TOTAL TO DET-MILEAGE-TOTAL.
           MOVE IND-AMOUNT-DUE TO DET-AMOUNT-DUE.
           WRITE PRINT-LINE FROM DETAIL-LINE
               AFTER ADVANCING 2 LINES.
           ADD 1 TO LINE-COUNT.

       600-INCREMENT-TOTALS.
           ADD REN-DAYS-RENTED TO TOTAL-DAYS-RENTED
               SIZE ERROR DISPLAY 'SIZE ERROR ON TOTAL DAYS RENTED'
           END-ADD.
           ADD IND-DAILY-TOTAL TO TOTAL-DAILY-RENTAL
               SIZE ERROR DISPLAY 'SIZE ERROR ON TOTAL RENTAL'
           END-ADD.
           ADD IND-MILES-DRIVEN TO TOTAL-MILES-DRIVEN
               SIZE ERROR DISPLAY 'SIZE ERROR ON TOTAL MILES DRIVEN'
           END-ADD.
           ADD IND-MILEAGE-TOTAL TO TOTAL-MILEAGE
               SIZE ERROR DISPLAY 'SIZE ERROR ON TOTAL MILEAGE'
           END-ADD.
           ADD IND-INSURANCE-TOTAL TO TOTAL-INSURANCE
               SIZE ERROR DISPLAY 'SIZE ERROR ON TOTAL INSURANCE'
           END-ADD.
           ADD IND-AMOUNT-DUE TO TOTAL-AMOUNT-DUE
               SIZE ERROR DISPLAY 'SIZE ERROR ON TOTAL AMOUNT DUE'
           END-ADD.
```

STRING statement joins last name and first name

Line counter is incremented

Figure 9.13 *(continued)*

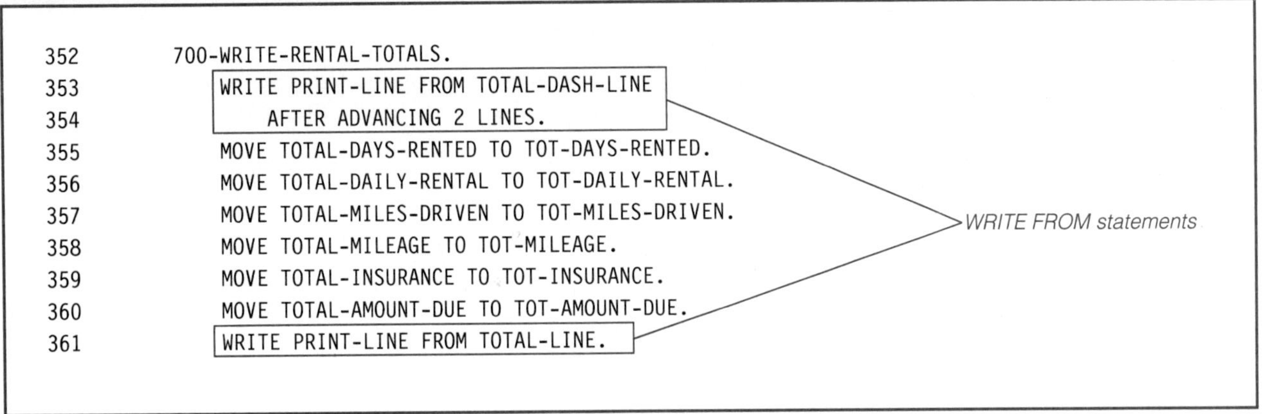

```
352        700-WRITE-RENTAL-TOTALS.
353            WRITE PRINT-LINE FROM TOTAL-DASH-LINE
354                AFTER ADVANCING 2 LINES.
355            MOVE TOTAL-DAYS-RENTED TO TOT-DAYS-RENTED.
356            MOVE TOTAL-DAILY-RENTAL TO TOT-DAILY-RENTAL.
357            MOVE TOTAL-MILES-DRIVEN TO TOT-MILES-DRIVEN.
358            MOVE TOTAL-MILEAGE TO TOT-MILEAGE.
359            MOVE TOTAL-INSURANCE TO TOT-INSURANCE.
360            MOVE TOTAL-AMOUNT-DUE TO TOT-AMOUNT-DUE.
361            WRITE PRINT-LINE FROM TOTAL-LINE.
```


(A period may not be present after the END-READ scope terminator because it is nested within the in-line perform statement. See problem 2 at the end of the chapter.)

2. The use of scope terminators throughout the Procedure Division—for example, END-READ in line 215, END-COMPUTE in lines 256 and 266, and END-IF in lines 242, 288, and 314.

3. The establishment of a heading routine (lines 290–298) and the associated definition of counters in Working-Storage, LINE-COUNT and PAGE-COUNT in lines 50 and 51. LINE-COUNT is tested prior to writing a detail line (lines 240–242). Since it was initialized to six (a value greater than the desired number of detail lines per page), a heading is written prior to the first detail record. The heading routine resets the line counter (line 291), which is subsequently incremented after every detail line is written (line 330). The page counter is also incremented in the heading routine (line 292), so that the page number can appear on the top of every page in the report.

4. The ACCEPT statement (line 223) to obtain the date of execution and again to accept the corresponding day of the week (line 227). The EVALUATE statement of lines 228–236 converts the numeric DAY-OF-WEEK code to its literal equivalent.

5. The INITIALIZE statement in line 247 to initialize the six data names defined under IND-BILL-INFORMATION.

6. The READ INTO statement in line 210 and the associated WS BEGINS HERE literal at the start of Working-Storage (lines 24–25) to facilitate debugging. The WRITE FROM statement is used throughout the Procedure Division with various print lines.

7. The indentation of subservient clauses throughout the Procedure Division to enhance the readability of the program. AT END and NOT AT END are indented under READ, AFTER ADVANCING is indented under WRITE, and so on. Blank lines are used throughout the program and appear before 01 entries in the Data Division and before paragraph headers in the Procedure Division.

8. The STRING statements in lines 305–309 and 311–313; the latter statements use the POINTER phrase to place the middle initial (if one is present) after the first name.

LIMITATIONS OF COBOL-74

The chapter focused on advanced statements in the Procedure Division, many of which were not available in COBOL-74. The most significant enhancements include scope terminators, the in-line perform, and false-condition branch, all of which are new to COBOL-85. The TEST BEFORE and TEST AFTER clauses are also new, as are the INITIALIZE statement and DAY-OF-WEEK clause.

The statements for string processing (INSPECT, STRING, and UNSTRING) were previously available in COBOL-74; reference modification, however, is new to COBOL-85. Duplicate data names, qualification, and the MOVE CORRESPONDING statement are unchanged from the earlier compiler.

SUMMARY

Points to Remember

- The PERFORM statement contains the optional TEST BEFORE and TEST AFTER clauses, corresponding to the DO WHILE and DO UNTIL iteration structures.
- The combination of an in-line PERFORM and false-condition branch within the READ statement eliminates the need for a priming read.
- The procedure-name in a PERFORM statement may be either a paragraph or a section. The THRU clause enables the execution of multiple procedures, which typically include an EXIT paragraph.
- READ INTO and WRITE FROM combine the effects of a MOVE statement with the indicated I/O operation. READ INTO is also used in conjunction with the literal WS BEGINS HERE to facilitate debugging.
- String processing is accomplished through the INSPECT, STRING, and UNSTRING statements, which provide flexibility in character manipulation.
- The ACCEPT statement includes the DAY and DAY-OF-WEEK clauses to obtain the date and corresponding day of the week on which a program executes.
- The INITIALIZE statement sets multiple data names to initial values in a single statement.
- Duplicate data names may be defined (but are *not* recommended) provided all Procedure Division references to the duplicate names use appropriate qualification. The MOVE CORRESPONDING statement is the equivalent of several individual MOVE statements.

Key Words and Concepts

DO UNTIL structure
DO WHILE structure
Duplicate (nonunique) datanames
False-condition branch
In-line perform
Procedure name
Qualification
Reference modification
Section
String processing

COBOL Elements

ACCEPT
DAY
DAY-OF-WEEK
EXIT
IN
INITIALIZE
INSPECT
MOVE CORRESPONDING
NOT AT END
OF
PERFORM THRU
PERFORM UNTIL
READ INTO
STRING
TEST AFTER
TEST BEFORE
UNSTRING
WRITE FROM

FILL-IN

1. The READ INTO statement causes each incoming record to be moved to ______________ areas.
2. The WRITE FROM statement is the equivalent of two statements, a ______________ and a ______________.
3. A ______________ consists of one or more paragraphs.
4. The ______________ statement causes no action to be taken and is often used to delineate the end of a PERFORM THRU statement.
5. Nonunique data names within a COBOL program may be ______________ using the reserved words ______________ or ______________.
6. The ______________ statement is a convenient way to replace leading blanks in a field with zeros.
7. String processing operations are accomplished through the ______________, ______________, and ______________ statements.
8. The READ statement includes an optional false-condition branch implemented by the ______________ ______________ ______________ clause.
9. The DO WHILE and DO UNTIL constructs of structured programming are implemented with the TEST ______________ and TEST ______________ clauses in the PERFORM statement.
10. ______________ ______________ makes it possible to address a string of characters contained within another string.

11. Omission of the procedure name in a PERFORM statement creates an ______________ perform.
12. The ______________ statement enables the initialization of multiple data types in a single statement.

TRUE/FALSE

1. The INSPECT statement facilitates the elimination of leading blanks.
2. A paragraph consists of one or more sections.
3. A PERFORM statement must include a procedure (paragraph or section) name.
4. Qualification over a single level will always remove ambiguity of duplicate data names.
5. The CORRESPONDING option is required if duplicate data names are used.
6. The STRING statement is used to combine several fields together.
7. For the CORRESPONDING option to work, both duplicate names must be at the same level.
8. The UNSTRING statement is used to separate a field into a maximum of three distinct fields.
9. The EXIT statement is required to delineate the end of a performed routine.
10. A PERFORM statement must specify either TEST BEFORE or TEST AFTER.
11. The READ statement may include both an AT END and a NOT AT END clause.
12. The READ statement must be terminated by an END-READ scope terminator.

PROBLEMS

1. Given the code:

```
PROCEDURE DIVISION.
MAINLINE SECTION.
FIRST-PARAGRAPH.
    PERFORM SEC-A.
    PERFORM PAR-C THRU PAR-E.
    MOVE 1 TO N.
    PERFORM PAR-G
        WITH TEST AFTER
        UNTIL N > 2.
    STOP RUN.
SEC-A SECTION.
    ADD 1 TO X.
    ADD 1 TO Y.
    ADD 1 TO Z.
PAR-B.
    ADD 2 TO X.
PAR-C.
    ADD 10 TO X.
```

```
PAR-D.
    ADD 10 TO Y
    ADD 20 TO Z.
PAR-E.
    EXIT.
PAR-F.
    MOVE 2 TO N.
PAR-G.
    ADD 1 TO N
    ADD 5 TO X.
```

a. How many times is each paragraph executed?

b. What are the final values of X, Y, and Z? (Assume they were all initialized to 0.)

c. What would happen if the statement ADD 1 TO N were removed from PAR-G?

2. Figure 9.14a contains a slightly modified version of the first paragraph in the car reporting program in which two periods have been added to produce the indicated compilation errors. Indicate the erroneous periods and explain why they produce the error messages.

Figure 9.14 COBOL Listing for Problem 2

```
204        PROCEDURE DIVISION.
205        000-PREPARE-RENTAL-REPORT.
206            OPEN INPUT  RENTAL-FILE
207                 OUTPUT PRINT-FILE.
208            PERFORM 100-GET-TODAYS-DATE.
209            PERFORM UNTIL DATA-REMAINS-SWITCH = 'NO'
210                READ RENTAL-FILE INTO RENTAL-RECORD-IN
211                    AT END
212                        MOVE 'NO' TO DATA-REMAINS-SWITCH.
213                    NOT AT END
214                        PERFORM 200-PROCESS-RENTAL-RECORDS.
215                END-READ.
216            END-PERFORM.
217            PERFORM 700-WRITE-RENTAL-TOTALS.
218            CLOSE RENTAL-FILE
219                  PRINT-FILE.
220            STOP RUN.
```

(a) Modified Procedure Division

```
209 W Explicit scope terminator END- 'PERFORM' assumed present
213 E AT END exception only valid for READ or SEARCH verbs
215 E No corresponding active scope for 'END-READ'
216 E No corresponding active scope for 'END-PERFORM'
```

(b) Error Messages

3. Is the following list of names in alphabetical order?

```
Joel Stutz
Maryann Barber
Shelly Parker
```

Your answer depends on the record layout, that is, whether Name is a single field or whether Last Name, First Name, and Middle Initial are defined as individual fields. Can you see the need to define separate fields for these items? Can you appreciate the utility of the STRING statement to concatenate the fields together when necessary?

4. Given the following Data Division entries:

```
01  EMPLOYEE-RECORD.
    05  EMP-NAME.
        10  EMP-LAST-NAME          PIC X(16).
        10  EMP-FIRST-NAME         PIC X(10).
        10  EMP-MIDDLE-INITIAL     PIC X.
    05  ADDRESS.
        10  EMP-STREET-ADDRESS     PIC X(20).
        10  EMP-CITY               PIC X(20).
        10  EMP-STATE              PIC XX.
        10  EMP-ZIP                PIC X(5).
```

Write the necessary STRING statements to create a mailing label with the format:

First-Name Middle-Initial Last-Name
Street-Address
City, State Zip

5. Given the following COBOL fragment:

```
01  DATE-WORK-AREA-1.
    05  YEAR-1                PIC 99.
    05  MONTH-1               PIC 99.
    05  DAY-1                 PIC 99.
01  DATE-WORK-AREA-2.
    05  YEAR-2                PIC 99.
    05  DAY-2                 PIC 999.
01  DATE-WORK-AREA-3.
    05  DAY-3                 PIC 9.

        .
          .
            .

    ACCEPT DATE-WORK-AREA-1 FROM DATE.
    ACCEPT DATE-WORK-AREA-2 FROM DAY.
    ACCEPT DATE-WORK-AREA-3 FROM DAY-OF-WEEK.
```

Indicate the stored values of each of the elementary items in the program. Assume a date of execution of March 16, 1993 (a Tuesday).

6. Given the following COBOL fragment:

```
01  DATE-WORK-AREA              PIC X(6).
01  EDITED-DATE.
    05  EDIT-MONTH              PIC XX.
    05  FILLER                  PIC X     VALUE '/'.
    05  EDIT-DAY                PIC XX.
    05  FILLER                  PIC X     VALUE '/'
    05  EDIT-YEAR               PIC XX.

         .
           .
             .

    ACCEPT DATE-WORK-AREA FROM DATE.
    MOVE DATE-WORK-AREA (3:2) TO EDIT-MONTH.
    MOVE DATE-WORK-AREA (5:2) TO EDIT-DAY.
    MOVE DATE-WORK-AREA (1:2) TO EDIT-YEAR.
```

Indicate the stored values of EDIT-MONTH, EDIT-DAY, and EDIT-YEAR. (Assume the same date as in the previous problem.)

7. Given the following COBOL definition:

```
01  GROUP-ITEM
    05  NUMERIC-FIELD-1             PIC 9(4).
    05  NUMERIC-FIELD-2             PIC 9(4).
    05  ALPHANUMERIC-FIELD-1        PIC X(15).
    05  ALPHANUMERIC-FIELD-2        PIC X(20).
```

What difference (if any) is there between the following statements?

a. `INITIALIZE.`
   and
   `INITIALIZE GROUP-ITEM.`

b. `INITIALIZE GROUP-ITEM.`
   and
```
   INITIALIZE GROUP-ITEM
      REPLACING NUMERIC DATA BY ZERO
               ALPHANUMERIC DATA BY SPACES.
```

c. `INITIALIZE GROUP-ITEM.`
   and
```
   MOVE ZEROS TO NUMERIC-FIELD-1 NUMERIC-FIELD-2.
   MOVE SPACES TO ALPHANUMERIC-FIELD-1 ALPHANUMERIC-FIELD-2.
```

10 Screen I-O

CHAPTER OUTLINE

OBJECTIVES

After reading this chapter you will be able to:

- Discuss the concept of screen I-O versus the file-oriented approach of earlier chapters.
- Describe the ACCEPT and DISPLAY statements; discuss at least three optional clauses for each statement.
- Describe the SCREEN SECTION and indicate why its use may be preferable to individual ACCEPT and DISPLAY statements.
- Differentiate between the background and foreground colors; implement a color scheme using ACCEPT and DISPLAY statements and/or the Screen Section.
- Describe how interactive data validation is implemented in a screen I-O program; contrast this technique to the batch-oriented procedure in Chapter 8.

OVERVIEW

The proliferation of the PC has increased the importance of screen I-O, whereby input to a program is received from the keyboard and output is displayed on the monitor. The specific options (color, highlighting, positioning, and so on) vary according to the particular keyboard or monitor (display terminal) and are *not* part of the COBOL-85 standard. Virtually all compilers, however, include these capabilities as an *extension* to the 85 standard, and hence we do our best to describe them in general fashion. The syntax is that of CA-Realia® Classroom COBOL that accompanies this text. (Classroom COBOL conforms to the X-Open standard, developed by of a consortium of software vendors including Microsoft, and has been proposed as an official extension to the 85 standard.)

The chapter begins with the ACCEPT and DISPLAY statements that are used for low-volume input and output and that reference specific line and column positions. Both statements contain an abundance of optional clauses that are illustrated in a final version of the tuition-billing program that first appeared in Chapter 5.

The second half of the chapter focuses on the Screen Section to define an entire screen as opposed to individual lines. We combine the data validation and reporting programs of Chapters 8 and 9 to produce an interactive program that validates data as it is entered, and produces an on-screen result.

ACCEPT

The **ACCEPT** statement enables data to be entered in specific positions according to a precise format. The statement contains a required identifier—that is, a data name to hold the input data, followed by optional clauses that can be entered in any order.

As indicated, the specific implementation for screen I-O is not defined in the COBOL-85 standard, but has been proposed as an extension to that standard. Our examples follow the syntax of Classroom COBOL that accompanies this text. Consider:

```
ACCEPT identifier [AT]

[LINE NUMBER {identifier }] [COLUMN NUMBER {identifier }]
             {integer-1  }                 {integer-2  }

[WITH [AUTO] [BACKGROUND-COLOR IS data-name] [{BELL}] [BLINK]
                                              {BEEP}

[FOREGROUND-COLOR IS data-name] [HIGHLIGHT] [SECURE] [REVERSE-VIDEO]

{LEFT-JUSTIFY } {SPACE-FILL} [TRAILING SIGN] [UNDERLINE] [UPDATE]]
{RIGHT-JUSTIFY} {ZERO-FILL }
```

The **LINE** and **COLUMN** clauses provide the location for the data. (The typical screen displays 25 lines of 80 columns.) Both clauses are optional with default actions as follows. Omission of the LINE clause defaults to line one if a previous screen element has not been defined, or to the existing line otherwise. Omission of the COLUMN clause defaults to column one if the LINE clause is also specified, and to the next column (after the last screen element) if the LINE clause is also omitted.

The **BACKGROUND-COLOR** and **FOREGROUND-COLOR** clauses specify the background and foreground colors, respectively, with the available colors listed in Table 10.1. Any of the sixteen listed colors may be specified for the foreground, but only the first eight (numbered from zero to seven) may be specified as the background. The default colors for the background and foreground are black and white, respectively, corresponding to white text on a black background.

TABLE 10.1 Foreground and Background Colors

INTEGER	COLOR
0	Black
1	Blue
2	Green
3	Cyan
4	Red
5	Magenta
6	Brown
7	White
8	Bright black (gray)
9	Bright blue
10	Bright green
11	Bright cyan
12	Bright red
13	Bright magenta
14	Bright brown (yellow)
15	Bright white

The **AUTO** clause terminates the ACCEPT statement when the last character in the data item has been entered; the user does not have to press the return key for processing to continue. If, however, multiple data names are entered into the same ACCEPT statement, the AUTO clause moves the cursor to the first character of the next item.

The **HIGHLIGHT**, **REVERSE-VIDEO**, **BLINK**, and **UNDERLINE** clauses are used for emphasis, and their intended effects are apparent: BLINK causes characters to blink on and off, UNDERLINE underlines each character as it is displayed on the screen, and HIGHLIGHT displays a field at its highest intensity. The REVERSE-VIDEO clause displays light characters on a dark background; that is, the characters are dark and the area surrounding the characters is light. The synonymous **BELL** and **BEEP** clauses sound the system's audio tone when the referenced data item is processed during execution of the ACCEPT statement.

The **ZERO-FILL** option displays a numeric item with high-order zeros, whereas the (default) **SPACE-FILL** clause displays data with zero suppression. The **RIGHT-JUSTIFY** clause makes operator-keyed characters align in the rightmost character position of the field and is for elementary items only. **LEFT-JUSTIFY** (the default) is for documentation only and has no effect. The SPACE-FILL, ZERO-FILL, LEFT-JUSTIFY, and RIGHT-JUSTIFY clauses are allowed only for elementary items.

The **UPDATE** option displays the initial value of the data item before the operator is prompted for new input, and if no new data are entered, the initial data are treated as though they were operator keyed. UPDATE is not allowed for a numeric-edited item.

The **SECURE** clause prevents the accepted data item from appearing on the screen and is useful in implementing ***password protection*** and/or other security considerations.

DISPLAY

The **DISPLAY** statement was introduced in Chapter 3 in conjunction with top-down testing and referenced again in Chapter 6 for use in debugging. In both instances the simplest form of the statement was used at strategic points in a program, to display messages and/or intermediate results to help monitor program execution. The DISPLAY statement also has many additional options to enhance its output. Consider:

```
DISPLAY {identifier-1}
        {literal-1   }

[AT LINE NUMBER {identifier-2}] [COLUMN NUMBER {identifier-3}]
                {integer-1   }                 {integer-2   }

[WITH [BACKGROUND-COLOR IS data-name] [{BELL}] [BLINK]
                                       {BEEP}

[FOREGROUND-COLOR IS data-name] [HIGHLIGHT] [REVERSE-VIDEO]

[UNDERLINE] [BLANK {SCREEN}]]
                   {LINE  }
```

Many of the clauses in the DISPLAY statement have been explained in conjunction with the ACCEPT statement; for example, you can use the LINE and COLUMN clauses to control the specific position where the displayed output is to appear. You can also emphasize the displayed message by blinking, beeping, underlining, or reverse video. You can (on a color monitor) implement a variety of color schemes for both the foreground (text) and background.

The DISPLAY statement also enables you to clear all or a portion of the screen prior to displaying a data element. The **BLANK SCREEN** clause clears the entire screen and leaves the cursor positioned in line 1, column 1. The **BLANK LINE** clause blanks the associated line beginning in column 1 unless a column is specified. Specification of either entry, BLANK SCREEN or BLANK LINE, also reactivates the default background and foreground colors.

The Tuition Billing Program Revisited

The tuition-billing program has appeared several times throughout the text. It was first presented in Chapter 3 in conjunction with structured methodology, used in Chapters 4 and 5 to introduce basic COBOL statements, and expanded in Chapter 7 to include editing characters. We continue now with one final version to illustrate screen I-O, whereby student data are accepted for one student at a time, after which the computed bill (for that student) is displayed on the monitor.

The programming specifications parallel the original problem statement on page 49 with minor modifications to reflect the interactive nature of screen I-O. Thus, unlike the original file-based program, which processed students until the input file was exhausted, the screen-based program accepts data for one student at a time, then asks the user whether data for another student are to be entered. The screen I-O program also imposes the requirement for a valid password prior to processing the first student, and it eliminates the calculation of university totals. The formal specifications follow in the usual format.

PROGRAMMING SPECIFICATIONS

Program Name: Tuition Billing Program (Screen Version)

Narrative: This program modifies the specifications for the original tuition billing program to accommodate screen I-O. Incoming records are to be entered one at a time via the keyboard with computed results for each student displayed as they are calculated.

Screen Layouts: The password is to be masked and entered as per the screen in Figure 10.1a, student data are to be entered according to the screen in Figure 10.1b, and the computed results displayed as in Figure 10.1c.

Processing Requirements:

1. Develop an ***interactive program*** to accept student data, then compute and display the student's bill. The program is to execute continually until it receives a response indicating that no more students are to be processed.
2. The program is to check for a valid password prior to accepting data for the first student. (The password is COBOL in either all upper- or all lowercase letters) The user is allowed a maximum of two tries to enter the password correctly, after which the program is to terminate with an appropriate error message.

Figure 10.1 Tuition Billing Program (Screen I-O)

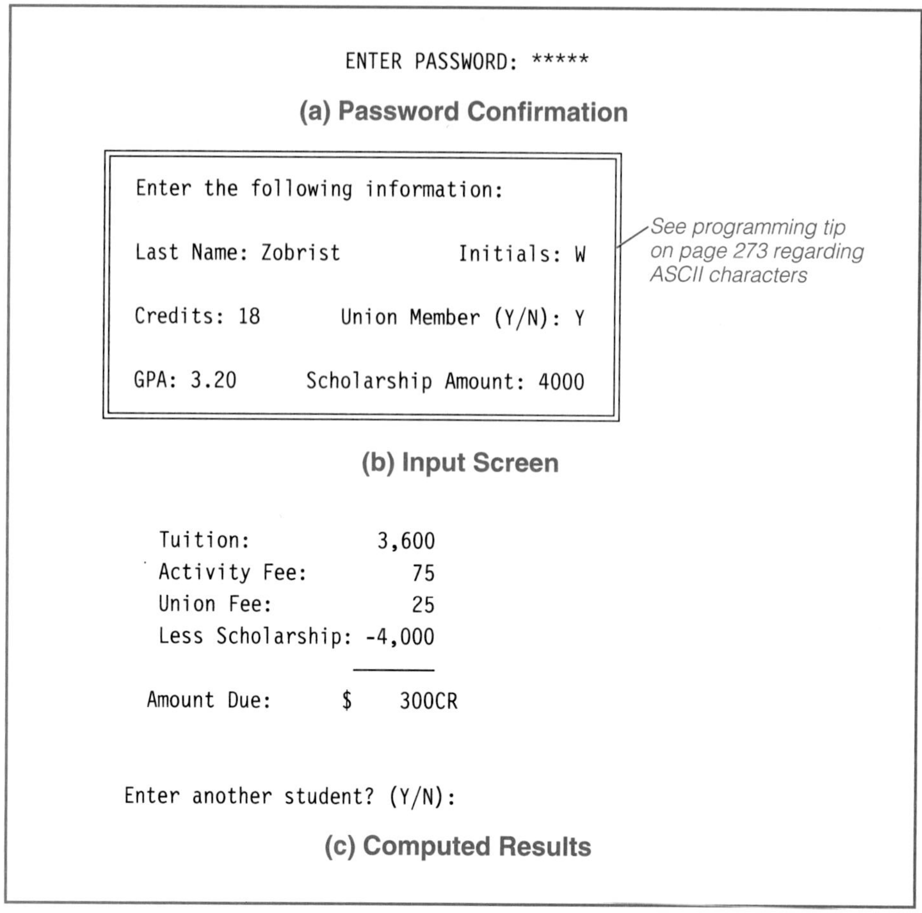

ENTER PASSWORD: *****
(a) Password Confirmation
Enter the following information:
Last Name: Zobrist
Initials: W
Credits: 18
Union Member (Y/N): Y
GPA: 3.20
Scholarship Amount: 4000
See programming tip on page 273 regarding ASCII characters
(b) Input Screen
Tuition: 3,600
Activity Fee: 75
Union Fee: 25
Less Scholarship: -4,000
Amount Due: $ 300CR
Enter another student? (Y/N):
(c) Computed Results

3. The specifications for computing an individual student's bill are the same as in the original program:
   a. Compute the individual bill as the sum of tuition, union fee, and activity fee, minus a scholarship (if any).
   b. The tuition is $200 per credit.
   c. The union fee is $25.
   d. The activity fee is based on the number of credits taken:

ACTIVITY FEE	CREDITS
$25	6 or less
$50	7–12
$75	more than 12

   e. Award a scholarship equal to the amount in the incoming record if the GPA is greater than 2.5.
4. The requirement to compute university totals has been deleted.

Hierarchy Chart

The hierarchy chart for the screen version of the tuition billing program is shown in Figure 10.2. The highest-level module, PROCESS-STUDENT-DATA, has four

Figure 10.2 Hierarchy Chart for Tuition Billing Program (Screen Version)

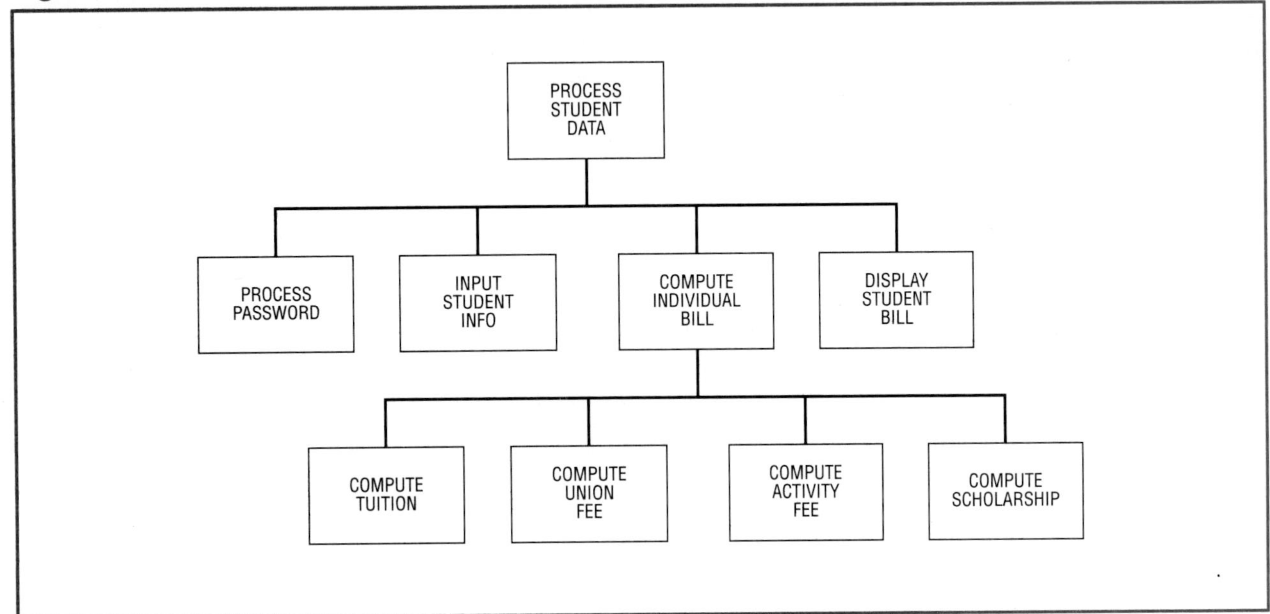

subordinates: PROCESS-PASSWORD, INPUT-STUDENT-INFO, COMPUTE-INDIVIDUAL-BILL, and DISPLAY-STUDENT-BILL. COMPUTE-STUDENT-BILL has four subordinates of its own: COMPUTE-TUITION, COMPUTE-UNION-FEE, COMPUTE-ACTIVITY-FEE, and COMPUTE-SCHOLARSHIP, all of which appeared in the original hierarchy chart.

The requirement to compute university totals has been dropped from the programming specifications, and thus the modules associated with this function that appeared in the original hierarchy chart (Figure 3.3) have been dropped from the current version.

Pseudocode

The pseudocode in Figure 10.3 contains two iterative structures, a DO UNTIL associated with obtaining the password, and a DO WHILE to process student data. The difference between the two is significant and was explained previously in Chapter 9 (see Figure 9.1). Recall, therefore, that the DO UNTIL structure tests the condition *after* executing the indicated statements and thus ensures that those statements are executed at least once. A DO WHILE, however, tests the condition *before* executing the statements, and hence the indicated statements need not be executed at all.

The user must be given *at least* one try to enter the password and hence the DO UNTIL structure is used to accept and validate (reject) the user's entry. If the user fails to enter the correct password within the allocated number of tries, the continue-processing-switch will be set to 'N', which prevents the execution of statements within the DO WHILE loop; that is, the program terminates without processing a student record.

The Completed Program

The completed program is shown in Figure 10.4 and reflects the hierarchy chart and pseudocode just discussed. It is different from all previous programs in that input is

Figure 10.3 Pseudocode for Tuition Billing Program (Screen Version)

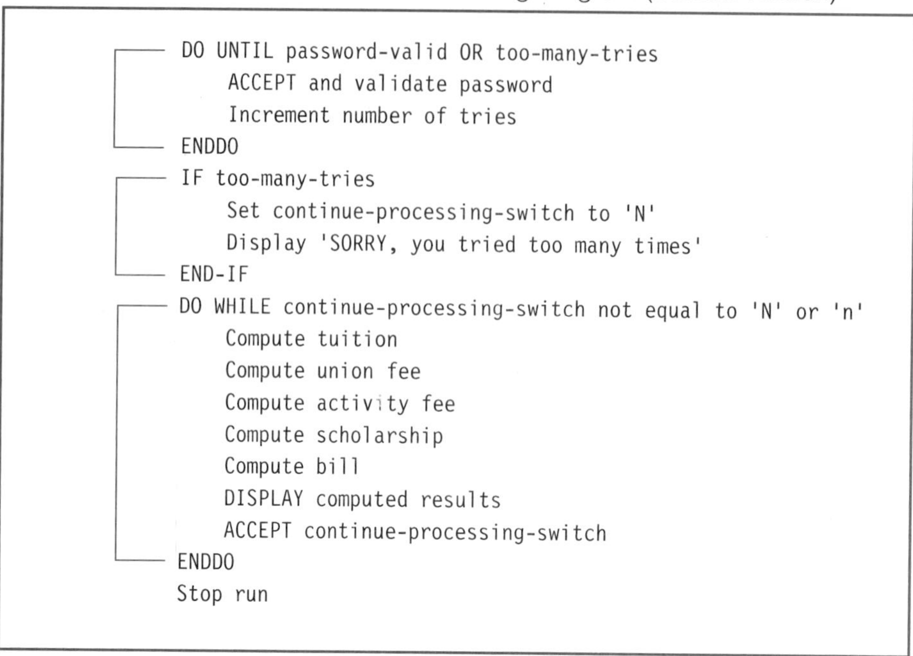

```
DO UNTIL password-valid OR too-many-tries
    ACCEPT and validate password
    Increment number of tries
ENDDO
IF too-many-tries
    Set continue-processing-switch to 'N'
    Display 'SORRY, you tried too many times'
END-IF
DO WHILE continue-processing-switch not equal to 'N' or 'n'
    Compute tuition
    Compute union fee
    Compute activity fee
    Compute scholarship
    Compute bill
    DISPLAY computed results
    ACCEPT continue-processing-switch
ENDDO
Stop run
```

received from the keyboard and output is displayed on the monitor. Thus, there are no files in this program, and hence no need for an Environment Division (and the associated SELECT statements), nor for the File Section in the Data Division. The absence of all files also means that the Procedure Division does not contain the familiar OPEN, CLOSE, READ, and WRITE statements that were present in all previous programs.

All I-O is screen based and accomplished through ACCEPT and DISPLAY statements with LINE and COLUMN clauses to control the location of the displayed fields. Different colors are used for different areas of the screen as implemented through the COLOR clauses that appear throughout the program; the available colors are defined as data names in lines 16–34, then referenced as necessary in the various ACCEPT and DISPLAY statements.

The imposition of a password is accomplished through the in-line PERFORM statement in lines 80–89, which uses the TEST AFTER clause to give the user two chances to enter the password correctly. The SECURE clause, in the ACCEPT statement of lines 87 and 88, prevents the user's response from appearing on the screen, and the AUTO clause saves the user from having to press the return key. The BLANK SCREEN clause in line 84 clears the screen before requesting the password. The program accepts either COBOL or cobol as a valid password according to the 88-level entry in line 38; it will not, however, recognize a combination of upper- and lowercase letters.

Once a valid password has been entered, the program processes students one at a time through the in-line PERFORM statement in lines 72–76, which invokes three lower-level paragraphs for each student: 200-INPUT-STUDENT-INFO, 310-COMPUTE-INDIVIDUAL-BILL, and 500-DISPLAY-STUDENT-BILL. The latter paragraph ends by obtaining the user response regarding another student (lines 189–191). Note, too, the provision for both upper- and lowercase data entry as the CONTINUE-PROCESSING-SWITCH in line 72 is compared to both 'N' and 'n'.

One last comment concerns the double line that appeared around the user's input in the screen of Figure 10.1b. This was accomplished by including the necessary ASCII (graphics) characters in the DISPLAY statements of lines 99 through 117. (See programming tip on the Alt key and numeric keypad.)

PROGRAMMING TIP

The Hidden Power of the Alt Key

Newcomers to the computer recognize the Alt key as the middle key in the Ctrl, Alt, and Del sequence to reboot the computer. It has many more uses, however, one of which is to reproduce any character within the 256 ASCII character set shown in the table below.

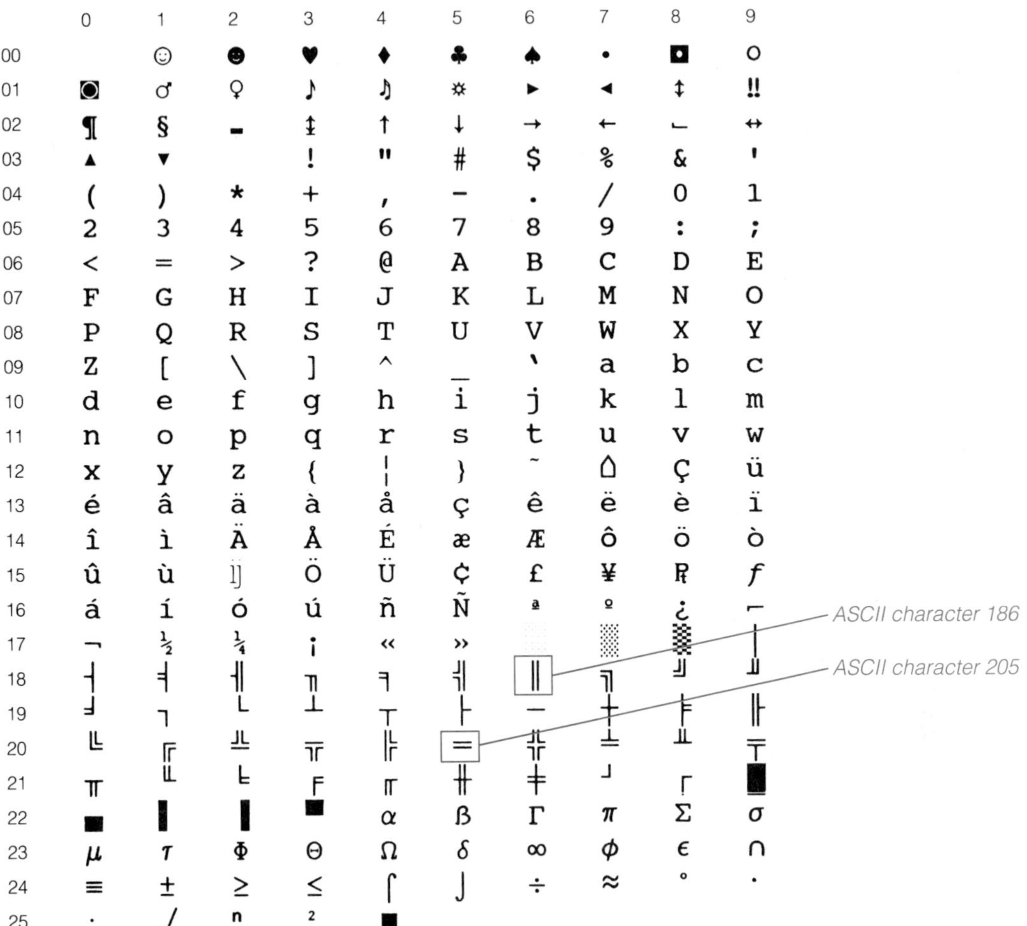

	0	1	2	3	4	5	6	7	8	9
00		☺	☻	♥	♦	♣	♠	•	◘	○
01	◙	♂	♀	♪	♫	☼	►	◄	↕	‼
02	¶	§	▬	↨	↑	↓	→	←	∟	↔
03	▲	▼		!	"	#	$	%	&	'
04	(	)	*	+	,	-	.	/	0	1
05	2	3	4	5	6	7	8	9	:	;
06	<	=	>	?	@	A	B	C	D	E
07	F	G	H	I	J	K	L	M	N	O
08	P	Q	R	S	T	U	V	W	X	Y
09	Z	[	\	]	^	_	`	a	b	c
10	d	e	f	g	h	i	j	k	l	m
11	n	o	p	q	r	s	t	u	v	w
12	x	y	z	{	¦	}	~	⌂	Ç	ü
13	é	â	ä	à	å	ç	ê	ë	è	ï
14	î	ì	Ä	Å	É	æ	Æ	ô	ö	ò
15	û	ù	ÿ	Ö	Ü	¢	£	¥	₧	ƒ
16	á	í	ó	ú	ñ	Ñ	ª	º	¿	⌐
17	¬	½	¼	¡	«	»	░	▒	▓	│
18	┤	╡	╢	╖	╕	╣	║	╗	╝	╜
19	╛	┐	└	┴	┬	├	─	┼	╞	╟
20	╚	╔	╩	╦	╠	═	╬	╧	╨	╤
21	╥	╙	╘	╒	╓	╫	╪	┘	┌	█
22	▄	▌	▐	▀	α	ß	Γ	π	Σ	σ
23	µ	τ	Φ	Θ	Ω	δ	∞	φ	ε	∩
24	≡	±	≥	≤	⌠	⌡	÷	≈	°	∙
25	·	√	^{n}	^{2}	■					

The double vertical line, for example, is found in row 18, column 6 of the table, and thus, is ASCII character 186; it is entered into a program file by *holding the Alt key down, and typing 1, 8, and 6, from the* ***numeric*** *keyboard.* In similar fashion, a double horizontal line is found in row 20, column 5, and thus is ASCII character number 205. Four other characters, corresponding to the four corners, are required to complete the box.

The printer, however, is a limiting factor, because while all of the 256 symbols will appear on an ordinary monitor, they are not necessarily supported on every printer.

Figure 10.4 Screen Version of Tuition Billing Program

```
       IDENTIFICATION DIVISION.
       PROGRAM-ID.    SCRNTUIT.
       AUTHOR.        CAROL VAZQUEZ VILLAR.

       DATA DIVISION.
       WORKING-STORAGE SECTION.
       01  STUDENT-DATA.
           05  STU-NAME.
               10  STU-LAST-NAME       PIC X(15).
               10  STU-INITIALS        PIC XX.
           05  STU-CREDITS             PIC 9(2).
           05  STU-UNION-MEMBER        PIC X.
           05  STU-SCHOLARSHIP         PIC 9(4).
           05  STU-GPA                 PIC 9V99.

       01  SCREEN-COLORS.
      * COLORS FOR FOREGROUND AND BACKGROUND
           05  BLACK                   PIC S9(4) COMP-5 VALUE 0.
           05  BLUE                    PIC S9(4) COMP-5 VALUE 1.
           05  GREEN                   PIC S9(4) COMP-5 VALUE 2.
           05  CYAN                    PIC S9(4) COMP-5 VALUE 3.
           05  RED                     PIC S9(4) COMP-5 VALUE 4.
           05  MAGENTA                 PIC S9(4) COMP-5 VALUE 5.
           05  BROWN                   PIC S9(4) COMP-5 VALUE 6.
           05  WHITE                   PIC S9(4) COMP-5 VALUE 7.
      * ADDITIONAL COLORS FOR FOREGROUND ONLY
           05  BRIGHT-BLACK            PIC S9(4) COMP-5 VALUE 8.
           05  BRIGHT-BLUE             PIC S9(4) COMP-5 VALUE 9.
           05  BRIGHT-GREEN            PIC S9(4) COMP-5 VALUE 10.
           05  BRIGHT-CYAN             PIC S9(4) COMP-5 VALUE 11.
           05  BRIGHT-RED              PIC S9(4) COMP-5 VALUE 12.
           05  BRIGHT-MAGENTA          PIC S9(4) COMP-5 VALUE 13.
           05  BRIGHT-BROWN            PIC S9(4) COMP-5 VALUE 14.
           05  BRIGHT-WHITE            PIC S9(4) COMP-5 VALUE 15.

       01  PASSWORD-VARIABLES.
           05  PASSWORD-ENTERED        PIC X(5).
               88  VALID-PASSWORD                VALUE 'COBOL' 'cobol'.
           05  TRIES-COUNTER           PIC 9.
               88  TOO-MANY-TRIES                VALUE 3.

       01  CONTINUE-PROCESSING-SWITCH  PIC X     VALUE 'Y'.

       01  INDIVIDUAL-CALCULATIONS.
           05  IND-TUITION             PIC 9(4)  VALUE ZEROS.
           05  IND-ACTIVITY-FEE        PIC 9(2)  VALUE ZEROS.
           05  IND-UNION-FEE           PIC 9(2)  VALUE ZEROS.
           05  IND-SCHOLARSHIP         PIC 9(4)  VALUE ZEROS.
           05  IND-BILL                PIC S9(6) VALUE ZEROS.

       01  DISPLAY-CALCULATIONS.
```

Colors are given mnemonic names for subsequent reference in Procedure Division

Figure 10.4 *(continued)*

```
           05  DIS-TUITION             PIC Z,ZZ9.
           05  DIS-ACTIVITY-FEE        PIC Z9.
           05  DIS-UNION-FEE           PIC Z9.
           05  DIS-SCHOLARSHIP         PIC Z,ZZ9.
           05  DIS-BILL                PIC $ZZZ,ZZ9CR.

       01  CONSTANTS-AND-RATES.
           05  PRICE-PER-CREDIT        PIC 9(3)  VALUE 200.
           05  UNION-FEE               PIC 9(2)  VALUE 25.
           05  ACTIVITY-FEES.
               10  1ST-ACTIVITY-FEE    PIC 99    VALUE 25.
               10  1ST-CREDIT-LIMIT    PIC 99    VALUE 6.
               10  2ND-ACTIVITY-FEE    PIC 99    VALUE 50.
               10  2ND-CREDIT-LIMIT    PIC 99    VALUE 12.
               10  3RD-ACTIVITY-FEE    PIC 99    VALUE 75.
           05  MINIMUM-SCHOLAR-GPA     PIC 9V9   VALUE 2.5.

       PROCEDURE DIVISION.
       000-PROCESS-STUDENT-DATA.
           PERFORM 100-PROCESS-PASSWORD.
           PERFORM UNTIL CONTINUE-PROCESSING-SWITCH = 'N' OR 'n'
               PERFORM 200-INPUT-STUDENT-INFO
               PERFORM 310-COMPUTE-INDIVIDUAL-BILL
               PERFORM 500-DISPLAY-STUDENT-BILL
           END-PERFORM.
           STOP RUN.

       100-PROCESS-PASSWORD.
           PERFORM WITH TEST AFTER
               VARYING TRIES-COUNTER FROM 1 BY 1
               UNTIL VALID-PASSWORD OR TOO-MANY-TRIES
                   DISPLAY 'ENTER PASSWORD: ' LINE 12 COLUMN 30
                       WITH BLANK SCREEN
                       FOREGROUND-COLOR BRIGHT-GREEN
                       BACKGROUND-COLOR MAGENTA
                   ACCEPT PASSWORD-ENTERED LINE 12 COLUMN 46
                       WITH REVERSE-VIDEO AUTO SECURE
           END-PERFORM.
           IF TOO-MANY-TRIES
               MOVE 'N' TO CONTINUE-PROCESSING-SWITCH
               DISPLAY 'SORRY, You tried too many times'
                  LINE 24 COLUMN 22 WITH BLINK
                     FOREGROUND-COLOR WHITE
                     BACKGROUND-COLOR RED
           END-IF.
       200-INPUT-STUDENT-INFO.
           DISPLAY ' ″″″″″″″″″″″″″″″″″″″″″″″″″″″″″″″″″″″″″″″″″″″″″»'
               AT LINE  2 COLUMN 5 WITH BLANK SCREEN
               FOREGROUND-COLOR BRIGHT-BROWN
               BACKGROUND-COLOR BLUE.
```

In-line PERFORM statement drives program

TEST AFTER clause ensures that in-line statements are executed at least once

Use of color in screen output

Figure 10.4 *(continued)*

```
           DISPLAY '″ Enter the following information:          ″'
               AT LINE  3 COLUMN 5.
           DISPLAY '″                                           ″'
               AT LINE  4 COLUMN  5.
           DISPLAY '″ Last Name:                  Initials:     ″'
               AT LINE  5 COLUMN  5.
           DISPLAY '″                                           ″'
               AT LINE  6 COLUMN  5.
           DISPLAY '″ Credits:          Union Member (Y/N):     ″'
               AT LINE  7 COLUMN  5.
           DISPLAY '″                                           ″'
               AT LINE  8 COLUMN  5.
           DISPLAY '″     GPA:          Scholarship Amount:     ″'
               AT LINE  9 COLUMN  5.
           DISPLAY '¨″″″″″″″″″″″″″″″″″″″″″″″″″″″″″″″″″″″″″″″″″″″″″…'
               AT LINE 10 COLUMN 5.
           ACCEPT STU-LAST-NAME AT LINE 5 COLUMN 18.
           ACCEPT STU-INITIALS AT LINE 5 COLUMN 45.
           ACCEPT STU-CREDITS AT LINE 7 COLUMN 16.
           ACCEPT STU-UNION-MEMBER AT LINE 7 COLUMN 45 WITH AUTO.
           ACCEPT STU-GPA AT LINE 9 COLUMN 16 WITH AUTO.
           ACCEPT STU-SCHOLARSHIP AT LINE 9 COLUMN 45.

       310-COMPUTE-INDIVIDUAL-BILL.
           PERFORM 410-COMPUTE-TUITION.
           PERFORM 430-COMPUTE-UNION-FEE.
           PERFORM 460-COMPUTE-ACTIVITY-FEE.
           PERFORM 490-COMPUTE-SCHOLARSHIP.
           COMPUTE IND-BILL = IND-TUITION + IND-UNION-FEE +
              IND-ACTIVITY-FEE - IND-SCHOLARSHIP
              SIZE ERROR DISPLAY 'SIZE ERROR FOR INDIVIDUAL BILL'
           END-COMPUTE.

       410-COMPUTE-TUITION.
           COMPUTE IND-TUITION = PRICE-PER-CREDIT * STU-CREDITS
              SIZE ERROR DISPLAY 'SIZE ERROR FOR INDIVIDUAL TUITION'
           END-COMPUTE.

       430-COMPUTE-UNION-FEE.
           IF STU-UNION-MEMBER = 'Y' or 'y'
              MOVE UNION-FEE TO IND-UNION-FEE
           ELSE
              MOVE ZERO TO IND-UNION-FEE
           END-IF.

       460-COMPUTE-ACTIVITY-FEE.
           EVALUATE TRUE
               WHEN STU-CREDITS <= 1ST-CREDIT-LIMIT
                   MOVE 1ST-ACTIVITY-FEE TO IND-ACTIVITY-FEE
               WHEN STU-CREDITS > 1ST-CREDIT-LIMIT
                   AND STU-CREDITS <= 2ND-CREDIT-LIMIT
```

IF statement checks for upper and lower case

Figure 10.4 *(continued)*

```
                    MOVE 2ND-ACTIVITY-FEE TO IND-ACTIVITY-FEE
            WHEN STU-CREDITS > 2ND-CREDIT-LIMIT
                MOVE 3RD-ACTIVITY-FEE TO IND-ACTIVITY-FEE
            WHEN OTHER
                DISPLAY 'INVALID CREDITS FOR: ' STU-NAME
        END-EVALUATE.

    490-COMPUTE-SCHOLARSHIP.
        IF STU-GPA > MINIMUM-SCHOLAR-GPA
           MOVE STU-SCHOLARSHIP TO IND-SCHOLARSHIP
        ELSE
           MOVE ZERO TO IND-SCHOLARSHIP
        END-IF.

    500-DISPLAY-STUDENT-BILL.
        MOVE IND-TUITION TO DIS-TUITION.
        DISPLAY 'Tuition:' AT LINE 12 COLUMN 10.
        DISPLAY DIS-TUITION AT LINE 12 COLUMN 29.

        MOVE IND-ACTIVITY-FEE TO DIS-ACTIVITY-FEE.
        DISPLAY 'Activity Fee:' AT LINE 13 COLUMN 10.
        DISPLAY DIS-ACTIVITY-FEE AT LINE 13 COLUMN 32.

        MOVE IND-UNION-FEE TO DIS-UNION-FEE.
        DISPLAY 'Union Fee:' AT LINE 14 COLUMN 10.
        DISPLAY DIS-UNION-FEE AT LINE 14 COLUMN 32.

        MOVE IND-SCHOLARSHIP TO DIS-SCHOLARSHIP.
        DISPLAY 'Less Scholarship: -' AT LINE 15 COLUMN 10.
        DISPLAY DIS-SCHOLARSHIP AT LINE 15 COLUMN 29.

        DISPLAY '--------' AT LINE 16 COLUMN 27.
        MOVE IND-BILL TO DIS-BILL.
        DISPLAY 'Amount Due:' AT LINE 17 COLUMN  9.
        DISPLAY DIS-BILL AT LINE 17 COLUMN 26.
        DISPLAY 'Enter another student? (Y/N):'
            AT LINE 20 COLUMN 7.
        ACCEPT CONTINUE-PROCESSING-SWITCH AT LINE 20 COLUMN 37.
```

LINE and COLUMN clause control screen output

Obtains response for next student

Car Validation and Billing Program

The concept of ***data validation*** was introduced in Chapter 8 in the form of a stand-alone edit program that processed a file of incoming transactions, rejected invalid transactions with appropriate error message(s), and wrote valid transactions to a new file; the latter was then input to a reporting program that was developed in Chapter 9. This chapter combines the data validation and reporting programs into a single program to validate data as they are entered and produce an on-screen result.

The biggest difference between this program and its predecessor(s) is that the data are validated *interactively* as they are entered, as opposed to the *batch-oriented* approach in Chapter 8. The advantage of the interactive program is that the user is given the opportunity to correct the invalid transaction at the time the error is detected, as opposed to receiving a report listing the errors. Realize, however, that interactive (screen-based) programs are restricted to low-volume applications and that their execution is far more time consuming than programs that are file-driven. Specifications follow in the usual format.

PROGRAMMING SPECIFICATIONS

Program Name: Car Validation and Billing Program (Screen Version)

Narrative: This program combines the specifications for data validation and reporting as presented earlier in Chapters 8 and 9. The fields in each incoming transaction are accepted and validated one at time, after which the bill is computed and displayed on the screen. Valid transactions are also written to an output file.

Screen Layout: See Figure 10.5 (page 280).

Processing Requirements:

1. Develop an interactive program to accept and validate car rental data, then compute and display the associated bill. The program is to execute continually until it receives a response indicating that no more records are to be processed.
2. Each incoming field is to be validated as it is entered; that is, the user cannot move to the next field until valid data have been entered in the current field. The requirements for validation were presented in Chapter 8 and are summarized below. Each transaction is to be checked for the following:
   a. A numeric contract number.
   b. The presence of both a first and last name; a middle initial is not required, but if present, the initial must be alphabetic.
   c. A valid car type where the code is one of five values; E, C, M, F, or L.
   d. A valid date in which the month is between 1 and 12, the day is consistent with the month (e.g., April 31 should be rejected), and the date is less than or equal to the system date.
   e. A valid number of days rented that is greater than zero and less than or equal to 35.
   f. Numeric values for the mileage in and out; and further, that the mileage reported when the car is turned in is greater than the mileage when the car was taken out. The number of miles driven must also pass a reasonableness test of 10 miles or more per day
   g. A numeric mileage rate less than or equal to 50 cents per day.
   h. An insurance field of either Y or N.
3. Write the validated transaction to a file as per the original program in Chapter 8.
4. Calculate the customer's bill after all fields have been validated. The amount due is a function of car type, days rented, miles driven, mileage rate, and insurance.
   a. The mileage rate is different for each customer and appears as a field in the incoming transaction; the mileage total is the mileage rate times the number of miles driven.
   b. The daily rate is a function of the type of car rented. Economy cars cost $15 a day, compact cars $20 a day, mid-size cars $24 a day, full-size cars $28 a day, and luxury cars $35 a day. The daily total is the daily rate times the number of days rented.
   c. Insurance is optional at $10.50, regardless of the type of car rented.

d. A customer's total bill consists of the mileage total, daily total, and insurance total as described in parts (a), (b), and (c).

5. Display the computed bill on the screen as per the screen layout of Figure 10.5.

6. The requirement to compute totals has been deleted.

The Screen Section

The tuition billing program illustrated the use of ACCEPT and DISPLAY statements within the Procedure Division. This approach is useful to display individual lines and/or to accept a limited number of fields as input, but awkward when you need to fill an entire screen. A second limitation of individual ACCEPT and DISPLAY statements is that they are scattered throughout the Procedure Division, making it difficult to reproduce consistent screens from program to program within a system.

The ***Screen Section*** specifies the characteristics of an entire screen in the Data Division, then accepts or displays that screen in a single statement in the Procedure Division. The Screen Section is physically the *last* section in the Data Division, and its structure is similar to that of the File and/or Working-Storage Sections. Consider:

```
level-number {screen-name} [BLANK {SCREEN}] {BELL} [BLINK]
             {FILLER     }        {LINE  }  {BEEP}

    [HIGHLIGHT] [REVERSE-VIDEO] [UNDERLINE]

    [BACKGROUND-COLOR IS data-name-1] [FOREGROUND-COLOR IS data-name-2]

    [LINE NUMBER {identifier-1}] [COLUMN NUMBER {identifier-2}]
                 {integer-1   }                 {integer-2   }

    [VALUE IS literal-1]

    {PICTURE} IS {FROM identifier-4 TO identifier-5}
    {PIC    }    {USING identifier-6              }

    [AUTO] [SECURE]
```

An appreciation for the Screen Section can best be gained by viewing sample screens and the associated COBOL entries. Consider now Figure 10.5, which displays three screens from the car validation and billing program to be developed later in the chapter. Figure 10.5a displays the opening screen, consisting entirely of prompts for the various fields. Figure 15.5b displays a completed screen for Janice Vogel with valid entries in all fields, and Figure 10.5c displays the computed results.

The screens are produced in the sequence shown; that is, the system displays the opening screen of Figure 10.5a and the user enters the fields one at a time. Each field is validated as it is entered; the user cannot move to the next field until he or she has entered a valid value for the current field. Once all fields have been entered the system computes the bill and displays the results.

An abbreviated Screen Section, extracted from the completed program at the end of the chapter, is shown in Figure 10.6. The entries in the Screen Section are similar to those in the File or Working-Storage Section; that is, they consist of group items divided into elementary items. The entry at the 01 level must specify a screen-name—for example, OPENING-SCREEN and UPDATE-SCREEN in Figure 10.6. The

Figure 10.5 Screen Layouts

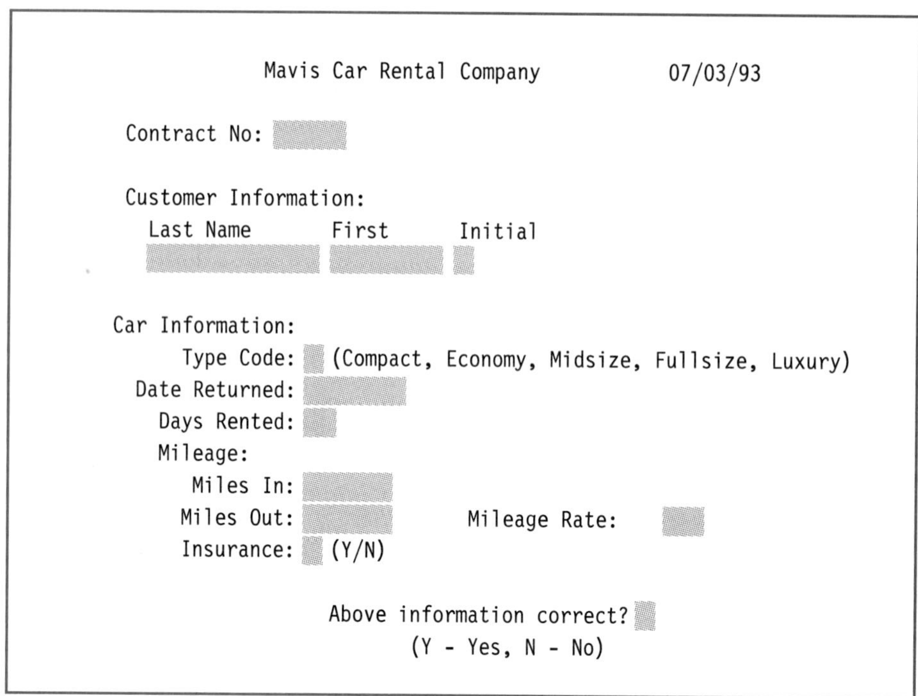

(a) Opening Screen (No Data Entered)

```
                 Mavis Car Rental Company          07/03/93

    Contract No: 886222

    Customer Information:
      Last Name        First      Initial
      VOGEL            JANICE     D

   Car Information:
         Type Code: F (Compact, Economy, Midsize, Fullsize, Luxury)
     Date Returned: 05/18/93
       Days Rented: 12
       Mileage:
          Miles In:   6,345
         Miles Out:   6,123       Mileage Rate:   .02
         Insurance: Y (Y/N)

                     Above information correct? Y
                            (Y - Yes, N - No)
```

(b) Validated Record

Figure 10.5 *(continued)*

```
                Mavis Car Rental Company           07/03/93

    Contract No: 886222

    Customer Information:
      Last Name        First      Initial
      VOGEL            JANICE     D

   Car Information:
         Type Code: F (Compact, Economy, Midsize, Fullsize, Luxury)
     Date Returned: 05/18/93                                   Totals
       Days Rented: 12            Rental Rate: $28.00         $336.00
       Mileage:
          Miles In:    6,345     Miles Driven:     222
         Miles Out:    6,123     Mileage Rate:     .02          $4.44
         Insurance: Y (Y/N)    Insurance Rate: $10.50         $126.00
                                                              ______
                                        Amount Due:           $466.44

                           Enter another record? N
                             (Y - Yes, N - No)
```

(c) Computed Bill

Figure 10.6 Abbreviated Screen Section

```
SCREEN SECTION.
01  OPENING-SCREEN.
    05  BLANK SCREEN
        BACKGROUND-COLOR BLUE  FOREGROUND-COLOR WHITE.
    05  SCREEN-PROMPTS.
    .
     .
        10  LINE  3 COLUMN  7  VALUE 'Contract No:'.
        10  LINE  5 COLUMN  7  VALUE 'Customer Information:'.
        10  LINE  6 COLUMN  9  VALUE 'Last Name'.
        10          COLUMN 25  VALUE 'First'.
        10          COLUMN 36  VALUE 'Initial'.
        10  LINE  9 COLUMN  6  VALUE 'Car Information:'.
        10  LINE 10 COLUMN 12  VALUE 'Type Code:'.
    .
     .
    05  SCREEN-INPUTS.
        10  SCR-CONTRACT-NO    PIC 9(6) USING REN-CONTRACT-NO
            LINE  3 COLUMN 20  REVERSE-VIDEO.
```

Figure 10.6 *(continued)*

```
         10  SCR-LAST-NAME       PIC X(15) USING REN-LAST-NAME
             LINE  7 COLUMN  9   REVERSE-VIDEO.
         10  SCR-FIRST-NAME      PIC X(10) USING REN-FIRST-NAME
             LINE  7 COLUMN 25   REVERSE-VIDEO.
         10  SCR-INITIAL         PIC X     USING REN-INITIAL
             LINE  7 COLUMN 36   REVERSE-VIDEO.
         10  SCR-CAR-TYPE        PIC X     USING REN-CAR-TYPE
             LINE 10 COLUMN 23   REVERSE-VIDEO AUTO.
     .
      .
 01  UPDATE-SCREEN.
     05  LINE 11 COLUMN 67       VALUE 'Totals' HIGHLIGHT.
     05  LINE 12 COLUMN 38       VALUE 'Rental Rate:' HIGHLIGHT.
     05  UPD-DAILY-RATE          PIC $$$9.99  FROM IND-DAILY-RATE
         LINE 12 COLUMN 50       HIGHLIGHT.
     05  UPD-DAILY-TOTAL         PIC $$$,$$9.99 FROM IND-DAILY-TOTAL
                 COLUMN 63       HIGHLIGHT.
     05  LINE 14 COLUMN 37       VALUE 'Miles Driven:' HIGHLIGHT.
     05  UPD-MILES-DRIVEN        PIC ZZZ,ZZ9  FROM IND-MILES-DRIVEN
                 COLUMN 50       HIGHLIGHT.
     05  UPD-MILEAGE-TOTAL       PIC $$,$$9.99
                                 FROM IND-MILEAGE-TOTAL
         LINE 15 COLUMN 64       HIGHLIGHT.
     05  LINE 16 COLUMN 35       VALUE 'Insurance Rate:' HIGHLIGHT.
     05  UPD-INSURANCE-RATE      PIC $$9.99 FROM INSURANCE-RATE
         LINE 16 COLUMN 51       HIGHLIGHT.
     05  UPD-INSURANCE-TOTAL     PIC $$,$$9.99
                                 FROM IND-INSURANCE-TOTAL
                 COLUMN 64       HIGHLIGHT.
     05  LINE 17 COLUMN 63       VALUE '----------' HIGHLIGHT.
     05  LINE 18 COLUMN 48       VALUE 'Amount Due: ' HIGHLIGHT.
     05  UPD-AMOUNT-DUE          PIC $$$$,$$9.99 FROM IND-AMOUNT-DUE
                 COLUMN 62       HIGHLIGHT.
```

screen (data) name is optional at any other level; for example, the first 05-level entry in Figure 10.6 omits the screen (data) name and specifies a blank screen with a blue background and white foreground. The next 05-level entry includes a data name, SCREEN-PROMPTS, which is divided into multiple elementary items, each of which omits the data name.

If a screen (data) name or FILLER is specified, then it must be the first word following the level name. The remaining clauses can appear in any order, but each elementary item must contain at least one of the following clauses: BELL, BLANK LINE, BLANK SCREEN, COLUMN, LINE, PICTURE, or VALUE. (The VALUE and PICTURE clauses are mutually exclusive in the Screen Section.) Any clause that appears on a group item applies to all elementary items within the group where it is allowed. If the same clause is specified at multiple levels in the hierarchy, the *lowest* level takes effect. The various optional clauses are illustrated in Figure 10.6

and function as explained previously in conjunction with the ACCEPT and DISPLAY statements.

Note, too, the correspondence between the line and column positioning within SCREEN-PROMPTS and SCREEN-INPUT; for example, a prompt for 'Contract No:' appears on line 3 and extends from column 7 to 18; the data name SCR-CONTRACT-NO is subsequently accepted in column 20 on the same line. The action of the LINE and COLUMN clauses is the same as with individual ACCEPT and DISPLAY statements: omission of the LINE clause defaults to the same line as the previously specified element. Thus the prompt for last name is displayed on line 6, column 9 followed by the prompt for first name in column 25 of the same line, followed by the initial in column 36 of the same line.

The Screen Section makes possible the definition of multiple screens within the same program as implied by the screen in Figure 10.5c, in which the computed results are displayed on the same (expanded) screen as the original inputs. Thus the Screen Section in Figure 10.6 contains a second 01 entry, UPDATE-SCREEN, with multiple entries that display both text and computed information; the latter is displayed after all data have been entered and the bill has been computed.

The **TO** clause in a screen description entry indicates an input field; the **FROM** clause indicates an output field. The **USING** clause—for example, USING REN-CONTRACT-NO—is equivalent to the combination of FROM and TO clauses each specifying the same data name. In this instance the screen input in line 3, column 20 is accepted from and/or moved to the data name SCR-CONTRACT-NO, which is defined elsewhere in the Data Division.

Hierarchy Chart

The hierarchy chart in Figure 10.7 combines the functions of the data validation and reporting programs of Chapters 8 and 9. The second-level module, PROCESS-RENTAL-RECORDS, effectively drives the program and contains subordinates to VALIDATE-RENTAL-RECORD, COMPUTE-IND-BILL, WRITE-VALID-RECORD, and INPUT-SCREEN-CONFIRM.

The validation module, VALIDATE-RENTAL-RECORD, contains a lower-level module for every validity check (identical to those in Chapter 8), each of which calls a common routine that displays the indicated error message or clears the error line. The computation module, COMPUTE-IND-BILL, has three subordinates of its own: COMPUTE-MILEAGE-TOTAL, COMPUTE-DAILY-TOTAL, and COMPUTE-INSURANCE-TOTAL. The remaining modules under PROCESS-RENTAL-RECORDS write the validated record, then determine whether another record is to be processed.

Pseudocode

The pseudocode in Figure 10.8 is driven by an overall loop to process transactions until the user elects to quit. Each new transaction begins with validation of individual fields, which continues until the user indicates that the entire screen is accurate; that is, the user is given the opportunity to change any field that has been previously validated. Within this loop, each field is validated interactively; that is, the user cannot enter the next field until the current field has been accepted as valid.

Once all fields have been entered and validated, the program moves to the computation of the bill according to the specifications presented earlier. The computed bill is displayed on the screen, the validated record is written to a valid record file, and the user is given the opportunity to process another transaction.

Figure 10.7 Hierarchy Chart

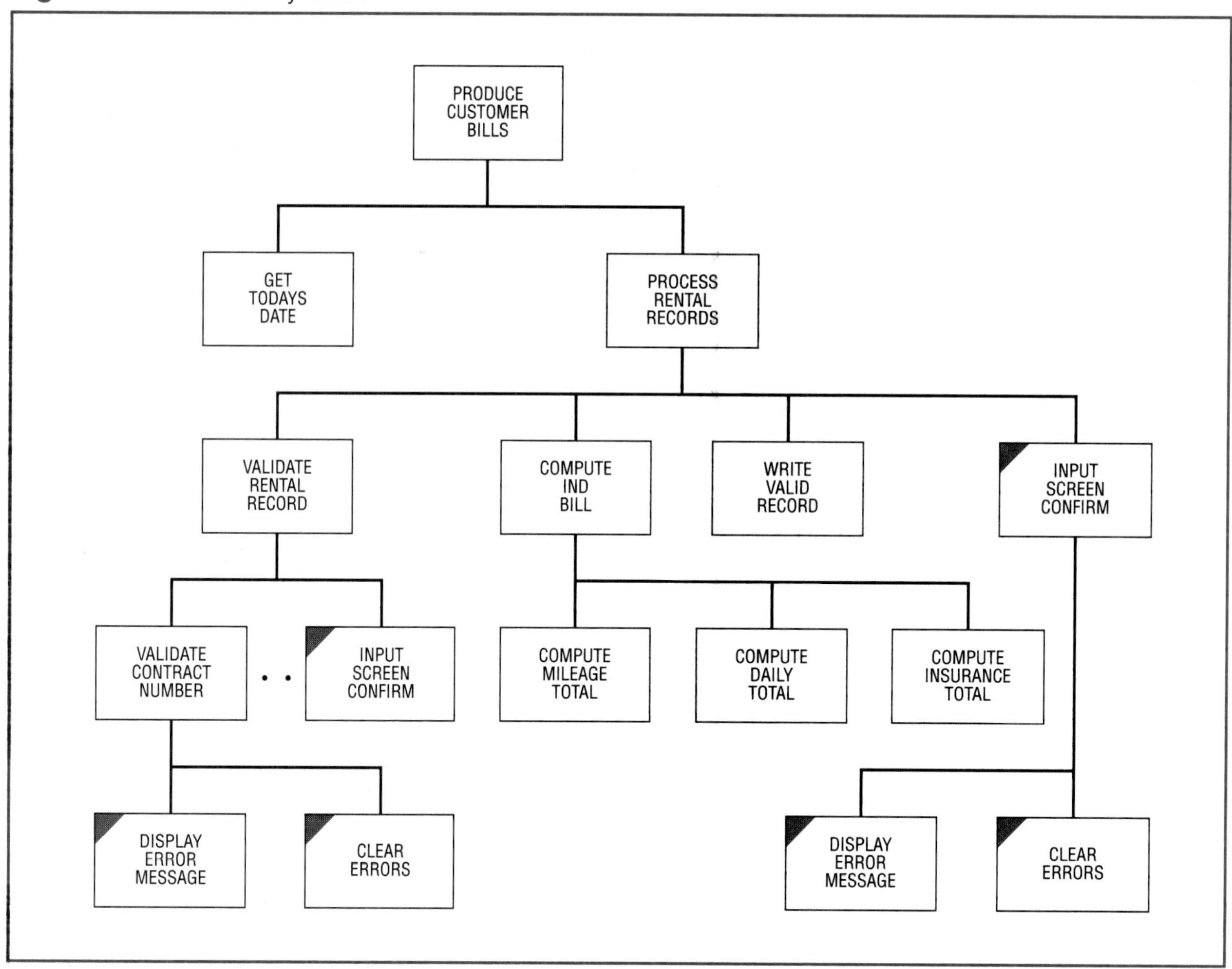

Figure 10.8 Pseudocode for Car Validation and Billing Program (Screen Version)

```
Open valid-rental-file
Get today's date
DO WHILE another record is desired
    DO UNTIL information correct
        DO UNTIL valid-field-switch = spaces
            Accept contract number
            IF contract number = zeros
                Display 'Contract number must not be zero'
                Move 'NO' to valid-field-switch
            ELSE
                Move spaces to valid-field-switch
            ENDIF
        ENDDO
```

Figure 10.8 *(continued)*

```
            DO UNTIL valid-field-switch = spaces
                Accept last-name
                IF last-name = spaces
                    Display 'Error - Missing last name'
                    Move 'NO' to valid-field-switch
                ELSE
                    Move spaces to valid-field-switch
                ENDIF
            ENDDO
            . . . Validation checks for remaining fields
            Display information correct message
            DO UNTIL valid confirmation ("Y", "y", "N", or "n")
                Accept confirm-switch
                IF valid confirmation
                    Clear previous error message
                ELSE
                    Display 'Must be "Y" or "N"'
                ENDIF
            ENDDO
        ENDDO
        Compute miles driven = miles in - miles out
        DO CASE
            Car Type E - Move economy rate to mileage rate
            Car Type C - Move compact rate to mileage rate
            Car Type M - Move midsize to mileage rate
            Car Type F - Move fullsize rate to mileage rate
            Car Type L - Move luxury rate to mileage rate
        END CASE
        Compute mileage total = miles driven * mileage rate
        Compute daily total = days rented * daily rate
        IF insurance taken
            Compute insurance = insurance rate * days rented
        END-IF
        Compute total bill = mileage amount + daily amount + insurance
        Display computed bill
        Write valid record to valid record file
        Display Another record message
        DO UNTIL valid confirmation ("Y", "y", "N", or "n")
            Accept confirm-switch
            IF valid confirmation
                Clear previous error message
            ELSE
                Display 'Must be "Y" or "N"'
            ENDIF
        ENDDO
    ENDDO
    Close valid-rental-file
    Stop run
```

The Completed Program

The completed program is shown in Figure 10.9 and includes many statements from the earlier programs in Chapters 8 and 9. The most significant difference is that I-O is screen based, with transactions entered via the keyboard and computed results displayed on the monitor, as provided through the extended Screen Section (lines 135–244). The program also creates a VALID-RENTAL-FILE as output, illustrating that the same program can contain both a File Section and a Screen Section

Figure 10.9 Car Validation and Billing Program

```
 1        IDENTIFICATION DIVISION.
 2        PROGRAM-ID.      SCRNCARS.
 3        AUTHOR.          CVV.
 4
 5        ENVIRONMENT DIVISION.
 6        INPUT-OUTPUT SECTION.
 7        FILE-CONTROL.
 8            SELECT VALID-RENTAL-FILE
 9                ASSIGN TO UT-S-SYSOUT.
10
11        DATA DIVISION.
12        FILE SECTION.
13        FD  VALID-RENTAL-FILE.
14        01  VALID-RENTAL-RECORD         PIC X(57).
15
16        WORKING-STORAGE SECTION.
17        01  RENTAL-RECORD-IN.
18            05  REN-CONTRACT-NO         PIC 9(6).
19            05  REN-NAME.
20                10  REN-LAST-NAME       PIC X(15).
21                10  REN-FIRST-NAME      PIC X(10).
22                10  REN-INITIAL         PIC X.
23            05  REN-RETURNED-DATE.
24                10  REN-RETURNED-YEAR   PIC 9(2).
25                10  REN-RETURNED-MONTH  PIC 9(2).
26                    88  VALID-MONTHS          VALUES 1 THRU 12.
27                    88  FEBRUARY              VALUE 2.
28                    88  30-DAY-MONTH          VALUES 4 6 9 11.
29                    88  31-DAY-MONTH          VALUES 1 3 5 7 8 10 12.
30                10  REN-RETURNED-DAY    PIC 9(2).
31            05  REN-CAR-TYPE            PIC X.
32                88  VALID-CAR-TYPES           VALUES 'E' 'C' 'M' 'F' 'L'.
33            05  REN-DAYS-RENTED         PIC 99.
34                88  ZERO-DAYS-RENTED          VALUE  0.
35                88  VALID-DAYS-RENTED         VALUES 1 THRU 35.
36            05  REN-MILEAGE.
37                10  REN-MILES-IN        PIC 9(6).
38                10  REN-MILES-OUT       PIC 9(6).
```

Figure 10.9 *(continued)*

```
           10  REN-MILEAGE-RATE      PIC V99.
               88  VALID-MILEAGE-RATES   VALUES 00 THRU .50.
       05  REN-INSURANCE             PIC X.
           88  VALID-INSURANCE               VALUE 'Y' 'y' 'N' 'n'.
           88  INSURANCE                     VALUE 'Y' 'y'.

   01  PROGRAM-SWITCHES-AND-CONSTANTS.
       05  MILES-PER-DAY-FACTOR      PIC 99    VALUE 10.
       05  VALID-FIELD-SWITCH        PIC XX.
           88  VALID-FIELD                   VALUE SPACES.
       05  CONFIRM-SWITCH            PIC X  VALUE SPACES.
           88  INFO-CORRECT                  VALUE 'Y' 'y'.
           88  NO-MORE-RECORDS               VALUE 'N' 'n'.
           88  VALID-CONFIRMED               VALUE 'N' 'n' 'Y' 'y'.

   01  TODAYS-DATE-INFORMATION.
       05  TODAYS-DATE.
           10  TODAYS-YEAR           PIC 99.
           10  TODAYS-MONTH          PIC 99.
           10  TODAYS-DAY            PIC 99.
       05  SCREEN-DATE               PIC X(8).

   01  CONFIRM-MESSAGES.
       05  CONFIRM-MESSAGE           PIC X(27).
       05  INFO-CORRECT-MESSAGE      PIC X(27)
             VALUE 'Above information correct? '.
       05  ANOTHER-RECORD-MESSAGE    PIC X(27)
             VALUE '     Enter Another Record? '.

   01  ERROR-MESSAGES.
       05  ERROR-MESSAGE             PIC X(40).
       05  ZERO-CONTRACT-NO-MSG      PIC X(40)
             VALUE '    CONTRACT NUMBER MUST NOT BE ZERO'.
       05  LAST-NAME-MSG             PIC X(40)
             VALUE '             MISSING LAST NAME'.
       05  FIRST-NAME-MSG            PIC X(40)
             VALUE '             MISSING FIRST NAME'.
       05  INITIAL-MSG               PIC X(40)
             VALUE '          NON ALPHABETIC INITIAL'.
       05  CAR-TYPE-MSG              PIC X(40)
             VALUE '  CAR TYPE MUST BE:  E, C, M, F, OR L'.
       05  MONTH-MSG                 PIC X(40)
             VALUE '    MONTH MUST BE BETWEEN 1 AND 12'.
       05  DAY-MSG                   PIC X(40)
             VALUE '                INVALID DAY'.
       05  FUTURE-DATE-MSG           PIC X(40)
             VALUE '      DATE HAS NOT YET OCCURRED'.
       05  NON-NUM-DAYS-RENTED-MSG PIC X(40)
             VALUE '     DAYS RENTED MUST BE NUMERIC'.
       05  ZERO-DAYS-MSG             PIC X(40)
```

User may enter upper- or lowercase response

Table of error messages established in Working-Storage

Figure 10.9 *(continued)*

```
             VALUE '      DAYS RENTED MUST BE > ZERO'.
          05  LEASING-MSG            PIC X(40)
             VALUE '      REFER TO LONG-TERM LEASING'.
          05  NON-NUM-MILES-IN-MSG   PIC X(40)
             VALUE '        NON-NUMERIC MILES IN'.
          05  NON-NUM-MILES-OUT-MSG  PIC X(40)
             VALUE '        NON-NUMERIC MILES OUT'.
          05  LESS-THAN-MILES-MSG    PIC X(40)
             VALUE '    MILEAGE IN LESS THAN MILEAGE OUT' .
          05  INVALID-MILES-MSG      PIC X(40)
             VALUE '     MILES DRIVEN UNREASONABLY LOW'.
          05  NON-NUM-RATE-MSG       PIC X(40)
             VALUE '       NON-NUMERIC MILEAGE RATE'.
          05  MILEAGE-RATE-MSG       PIC X(40)
             VALUE '       MILEAGE RATE OUT OF RANGE'.
          05  INSURANCE-MSG          PIC X(40)
             VALUE '      INSURANCE CODE MUST BE Y OR N'.
          05  YES-NO-MSG             PIC X(40)
             VALUE '           MUST BE "Y" OR "N"'.

      01  DAILY-RATES.
          05  ECONOMY-RATE             PIC 9(3)V99  VALUE 15.
          05  COMPACT-RATE             PIC 9(3)V99  VALUE 20.
          05  MID-RATE                 PIC 9(3)V99  VALUE 24.
          05  FULL-RATE                PIC 9(3)V99  VALUE 28.
          05  LUXURY-RATE              PIC 9(3)V99  VALUE 35.
          05  INSURANCE-RATE           PIC 99V99    VALUE 10.50.

      01  IND-BILL-INFORMATION.
          05  IND-MILES-DRIVEN         PIC 9(6).
          05  IND-DAILY-RATE           PIC 9(3)V99.
          05  IND-DAILY-TOTAL          PIC 9(5)V99.
          05  IND-MILEAGE-TOTAL        PIC 9(4)V99.
          05  IND-INSURANCE-TOTAL      PIC 9(4)V99.
          05  IND-AMOUNT-DUE           PIC 9(6)V99.

      01  SCREEN-COLORS.
          05  BLUE                     PIC S9(4) COMP-5 VALUE 1.
          05  CYAN                     PIC S9(4) COMP-5 VALUE 3.
          05  RED                      PIC S9(4) COMP-5 VALUE 4.
          05  MAGENTA                  PIC S9(4) COMP-5 VALUE 5.
          05  WHITE                    PIC S9(4) COMP-5 VALUE 7.
          05  BRIGHT-GREEN             PIC S9(4) COMP-5 VALUE 10.
          05  BRIGHT-MAGENTA           PIC S9(4) COMP-5 VALUE 13.
          05  BRIGHT-WHITE             PIC S9(4) COMP-5 VALUE 15.

      SCREEN SECTION.
      01  OPENING-SCREEN.
          05  BLANK SCREEN
              BACKGROUND-COLOR BLUE  FOREGROUND-COLOR WHITE.
```

Screen Section follows Working-Storage Section

Figure 10.9 *(continued)*

```
         05  SCREEN-PROMPTS.
             10  LINE  1 BLANK LINE BACKGROUND-COLOR MAGENTA.
             10          COLUMN 20  VALUE 'Mavis Car Rental Company'
                         BACKGROUND-COLOR MAGENTA
                         FOREGROUND-COLOR BRIGHT-GREEN.
             10  SCR-DATE            PIC X(8) FROM SCREEN-DATE
                         COLUMN 55 BACKGROUND-COLOR MAGENTA
                                 FOREGROUND-COLOR BRIGHT-GREEN.
             10  LINE  3 COLUMN  7  VALUE 'Contract No:'.
             10  LINE  5 COLUMN  7  VALUE 'Customer Information:'.
             10  LINE  6 COLUMN  9  VALUE 'Last Name'.
             10          COLUMN 25  VALUE 'First'.
             10          COLUMN 36  VALUE 'Initial'.
             10  LINE  9 COLUMN  6  VALUE 'Car Information:'.
             10  LINE 10 COLUMN 12  VALUE 'Type Code:'.
             10          COLUMN 25
                 VALUE '(Compact, Economy, Midsize, Fullsize, Luxury)'
                         FOREGROUND-COLOR CYAN.
             10          COLUMN 26  VALUE 'C' HIGHLIGHT.
             10          COLUMN 35  VALUE 'E' HIGHLIGHT.
             10          COLUMN 44  VALUE 'M' HIGHLIGHT.
             10          COLUMN 53  VALUE 'F' HIGHLIGHT.
             10          COLUMN 63  VALUE 'L' HIGHLIGHT.
             10  LINE 11 COLUMN  8  VALUE 'Date Returned:'.
             10          COLUMN 23  VALUE 'mm/dd/yy'
                         FOREGROUND-COLOR BRIGHT-WHITE.
             10  LINE 12 COLUMN 10  VALUE 'Days Rented:'.
             10  LINE 13 COLUMN 10  VALUE 'Mileage:'.
             10  LINE 14 COLUMN 13  VALUE 'Miles In:'.
             10  LINE 15 COLUMN 12  VALUE 'Miles Out:'.
             10          COLUMN 37  VALUE 'Mileage Rate:'.
             10  LINE 16 COLUMN 12  VALUE 'Insurance:'.
             10          COLUMN 25  VALUE '(Y/N)'
                         FOREGROUND-COLOR CYAN.

         05  SCREEN-INPUTS.
             10  SCR-CONTRACT-NO     PIC 9(6) USING REN-CONTRACT-NO
                 LINE  3 COLUMN 20   REVERSE-VIDEO.
             10  SCR-LAST-NAME       PIC X(15) USING REN-LAST-NAME
                 LINE  7 COLUMN  9   REVERSE-VIDEO.
             10  SCR-FIRST-NAME      PIC X(10) USING REN-FIRST-NAME
                 LINE  7 COLUMN 25   REVERSE-VIDEO.
             10  SCR-INITIAL         PIC X     USING REN-INITIAL
                 LINE  7 COLUMN 36   REVERSE-VIDEO.
             10  SCR-CAR-TYPE        PIC X     USING REN-CAR-TYPE
                 LINE 10 COLUMN 23   REVERSE-VIDEO AUTO.
             10  SCR-RETURNED-MONTH  PIC 99  USING REN-RETURNED-MONTH
                 LINE 11 COLUMN 23   REVERSE-VIDEO AUTO.
             10  SCR-RETURNED-DAY    PIC 99   USING REN-RETURNED-DAY
                 LINE 11 COLUMN 26   REVERSE-VIDEO AUTO.
```

Omitted LINE clause causes all three entries on line 6

Figure 10.9 *(continued)*

```
189              10  SCR-RETURNED-YEAR  PIC 99   USING REN-RETURNED-YEAR
190                  LINE 11 COLUMN 29  REVERSE-VIDEO AUTO.
191              10  SCR-DAYS-RENTED    PIC 99   USING REN-DAYS-RENTED
192                  LINE 12 COLUMN 23  REVERSE-VIDEO AUTO.
193              10  SCR-MILES-IN       PIC ZZZ,ZZ9 USING REN-MILES-IN
194                  LINE 14 COLUMN 23  REVERSE-VIDEO.
195              10  SCR-MILES-OUT      PIC ZZZ,ZZ9 USING REN-MILES-OUT
196                  LINE 15 COLUMN 23  REVERSE-VIDEO.
197              10  SCR-MILEAGE-RATE   PIC .99  USING REN-MILEAGE-RATE
198                  LINE 15 COLUMN 54  REVERSE-VIDEO.
199              10  SCR-INSURANCE      PIC X    USING REN-INSURANCE
200                  LINE 16 COLUMN 23  REVERSE-VIDEO AUTO.
201          05  LINE 24 BLANK LINE.
202          05  LINE 25 BLANK LINE.
203
204      01  UPDATE-SCREEN.
205          05  LINE 11 COLUMN 67       VALUE 'Totals' HIGHLIGHT.
206          05  LINE 12 COLUMN 38       VALUE 'Rental Rate:' HIGHLIGHT.
207          05  UPD-DAILY-RATE          PIC $$$9.99  FROM IND-DAILY-RATE
208              LINE 12 COLUMN 50       HIGHLIGHT.
209          05  UPD-DAILY-TOTAL         PIC $$$,$$9.99 FROM IND-DAILY-TOTAL
210                      COLUMN 63       HIGHLIGHT.
211          05  LINE 14 COLUMN 37       VALUE 'Miles Driven:' HIGHLIGHT.
212          05  UPD-MILES-DRIVEN        PIC ZZZ,ZZ9  FROM IND-MILES-DRIVEN
213                      COLUMN 50       HIGHLIGHT.
214          05  UPD-MILEAGE-TOTAL       PIC $$,$$9.99
215                                      FROM IND-MILEAGE-TOTAL
216              LINE 15 COLUMN 64       HIGHLIGHT.
217          05  LINE 16 COLUMN 35       VALUE 'Insurance Rate:' HIGHLIGHT.
218          05  UPD-INSURANCE-RATE      PIC $$9.99 FROM INSURANCE-RATE
219              LINE 16 COLUMN 51       HIGHLIGHT.
220          05  UPD-INSURANCE-TOTAL     PIC $$,$$9.99
221                                      FROM IND-INSURANCE-TOTAL
222                      COLUMN 64       HIGHLIGHT.
223          05  LINE 17 COLUMN 63       VALUE '----------' HIGHLIGHT.
224          05  LINE 18 COLUMN 48       VALUE 'Amount Due: ' HIGHLIGHT.
225          05  UPD-AMOUNT-DUE          PIC $$$$,$$9.99 FROM IND-AMOUNT-DUE
226                      COLUMN 62       HIGHLIGHT.
227
228      01  ERROR-LINE.
229          05  LINE 25 BLANK LINE BACKGROUND-COLOR RED.
230          05                          PIC X(40) FROM ERROR-MESSAGE
231                      COLUMN 20       HIGHLIGHT BLINK BEEP
232              FOREGROUND-COLOR BRIGHT-WHITE  BACKGROUND-COLOR RED.
233
234      01  CONFIRM-SCREEN.
235          05  LINE 24 BLANK LINE      BACKGROUND-COLOR MAGENTA.
236          05                          PIC X(27) FROM CONFIRM-MESSAGE
237              LINE 24 COLUMN 25
238              BACKGROUND-COLOR MAGENTA FOREGROUND-COLOR BRIGHT-GREEN.
```

Screen name is displayed in line 271 (callout to line 204, 01 UPDATE-SCREEN.)

Figure 10.9 *(continued)*

```
       05                         PIC X USING CONFIRM-SWITCH
           LINE 24 COLUMN 52      BLINK AUTO
           BACKGROUND-COLOR MAGENTA FOREGROUND-COLOR BRIGHT-GREEN.
       05  LINE 25 BLANK LINE BACKGROUND-COLOR MAGENTA.
       05  LINE 25 COLUMN 32      VALUE '(Y - Yes, N - No)'
           BACKGROUND-COLOR MAGENTA FOREGROUND-COLOR BRIGHT-GREEN.

   PROCEDURE DIVISION.
   000-CREATE-VALID-RENTAL-FILE.
       OPEN OUTPUT VALID-RENTAL-FILE.
       PERFORM 100-GET-TODAYS-DATE.
       PERFORM 200-INPUT-RENTAL-RECORDS
           UNTIL NO-MORE-RECORDS.
       CLOSE VALID-RENTAL-FILE.
       STOP RUN.

   100-GET-TODAYS-DATE.
       ACCEPT TODAYS-DATE FROM DATE.
       STRING TODAYS-MONTH '/' TODAYS-DAY '/' TODAYS-YEAR
           DELIMITED BY SIZE INTO SCREEN-DATE.

   200-INPUT-RENTAL-RECORDS.
       INITIALIZE RENTAL-RECORD-IN.
       PERFORM 400-VALIDATE-RENTAL-RECORD WITH TEST AFTER
           UNTIL INFO-CORRECT.
       PERFORM 500-COMPUTE-IND-BILL.
       DISPLAY UPDATE-SCREEN.
       PERFORM 600-WRITE-VALID-RECORD.
       MOVE ANOTHER-RECORD-MESSAGE TO CONFIRM-MESSAGE.
       PERFORM 700-INPUT-SCREEN-CONFIRM.

   400-VALIDATE-RENTAL-RECORD.
       DISPLAY OPENING-SCREEN.
       PERFORM 410-VALIDATE-CONTRACT-NO.
       PERFORM 420-VALIDATE-NAME.
       PERFORM 430-VALIDATE-CAR-TYPE.
       PERFORM 440-VALIDATE-DATE-RETURNED
           WITH TEST AFTER UNTIL VALID-FIELD.
       PERFORM 450-VALIDATE-DAYS-RENTED.
       PERFORM 460-VALIDATE-MILES-DRIVEN.
       PERFORM 470-VALIDATE-MILEAGE-RATE.
       PERFORM 480-VALIDATE-INSURANCE.
       MOVE INFO-CORRECT-MESSAGE TO CONFIRM-MESSAGE.
       PERFORM 700-INPUT-SCREEN-CONFIRM.

   410-VALIDATE-CONTRACT-NO.
       PERFORM WITH TEST AFTER UNTIL VALID-FIELD
           ACCEPT SCR-CONTRACT-NO
           IF REN-CONTRACT-NO = ZEROES
               MOVE ZERO-CONTRACT-NO-MSG TO ERROR-MESSAGE
```

Combination of foreground and background colors for emphasis (callout to the boxed lines `05 LINE 25 COLUMN 32 VALUE '(Y - Yes, N - No)' BACKGROUND-COLOR MAGENTA FOREGROUND-COLOR BRIGHT-GREEN.`)

DISPLAY statement references 01 entry in Screen Section (callout to `DISPLAY OPENING-SCREEN.`)

Figure 10.9 *(continued)*

```
                PERFORM 499-DISPLAY-ERROR-MESSAGE
            ELSE
                PERFORM 498-CLEAR-ERRORS
            END-IF
        END-PERFORM.

    420-VALIDATE-NAME.
        PERFORM WITH TEST AFTER UNTIL VALID-FIELD
            ACCEPT SCR-LAST-NAME
            IF REN-LAST-NAME = SPACES
                MOVE LAST-NAME-MSG TO ERROR-MESSAGE
                PERFORM 499-DISPLAY-ERROR-MESSAGE
            ELSE
                PERFORM 498-CLEAR-ERRORS
            END-IF
        END-PERFORM.
        PERFORM WITH TEST AFTER UNTIL VALID-FIELD
            ACCEPT SCR-FIRST-NAME
            IF REN-FIRST-NAME = SPACES
                MOVE FIRST-NAME-MSG TO ERROR-MESSAGE
                PERFORM 499-DISPLAY-ERROR-MESSAGE
            ELSE
                PERFORM 498-CLEAR-ERRORS
            END-IF
        END-PERFORM.
        PERFORM WITH TEST AFTER UNTIL VALID-FIELD
            ACCEPT SCR-INITIAL
            IF REN-INITIAL NOT ALPHABETIC
                MOVE INITIAL-MSG TO ERROR-MESSAGE
                PERFORM 499-DISPLAY-ERROR-MESSAGE
            ELSE
                PERFORM 498-CLEAR-ERRORS
            END-IF
        END-PERFORM.

    430-VALIDATE-CAR-TYPE.
        PERFORM WITH TEST AFTER UNTIL VALID-FIELD
            ACCEPT SCR-CAR-TYPE
            IF NOT VALID-CAR-TYPES
                MOVE CAR-TYPE-MSG TO ERROR-MESSAGE
                PERFORM 499-DISPLAY-ERROR-MESSAGE
            ELSE
                PERFORM 498-CLEAR-ERRORS
            END-IF
        END-PERFORM.

    440-VALIDATE-DATE-RETURNED.
        PERFORM WITH TEST AFTER UNTIL VALID-FIELD
            ACCEPT SCR-RETURNED-MONTH
            IF VALID-MONTHS
```

TEST AFTER clause ensures that in-line statements are executed at least once (annotation to the boxed PERFORM in 420-VALIDATE-NAME)

TEST AFTER clause ensures that in-line statements are executed at least once (annotation to the boxed PERFORM in 430-VALIDATE-CAR-TYPE)

Figure 10.9 *(continued)*

```
                  PERFORM 498-CLEAR-ERRORS
              ELSE
                  MOVE MONTH-MSG TO ERROR-MESSAGE
                  PERFORM 499-DISPLAY-ERROR-MESSAGE
              END-IF
          END-PERFORM.
          PERFORM WITH TEST AFTER UNTIL VALID-FIELD
              ACCEPT SCR-RETURNED-DAY
              IF 30-DAY-MONTH AND REN-RETURNED-DAY > 0 AND <= 30 OR
                31-DAY-MONTH AND REN-RETURNED-DAY > 0 AND <= 31 OR
                FEBRUARY AND REN-RETURNED-DAY > 0 AND <= 29
                   PERFORM 498-CLEAR-ERRORS
              ELSE
                  MOVE DAY-MSG TO ERROR-MESSAGE
                  PERFORM 499-DISPLAY-ERROR-MESSAGE
              END-IF
          END-PERFORM.
          PERFORM WITH TEST AFTER UNTIL VALID-FIELD
              ACCEPT SCR-RETURNED-YEAR
              IF REN-RETURNED-DATE > TODAYS-DATE
                  MOVE FUTURE-DATE-MSG TO ERROR-MESSAGE
                  PERFORM 499-DISPLAY-ERROR-MESSAGE
              ELSE
                  PERFORM 498-CLEAR-ERRORS
              END-IF
          END-PERFORM.

      450-VALIDATE-DAYS-RENTED.
          PERFORM WITH TEST AFTER UNTIL VALID-FIELD
              ACCEPT SCR-DAYS-RENTED
              IF ZERO-DAYS-RENTED
                  MOVE ZERO-DAYS-MSG TO ERROR-MESSAGE
                  PERFORM 499-DISPLAY-ERROR-MESSAGE
              ELSE
                  IF NOT VALID-DAYS-RENTED
                      MOVE LEASING-MSG TO ERROR-MESSAGE
                      PERFORM 499-DISPLAY-ERROR-MESSAGE
                  ELSE
                      PERFORM 498-CLEAR-ERRORS
                  END-IF
              END-IF
          END-PERFORM.

      460-VALIDATE-MILES-DRIVEN.
          PERFORM WITH TEST AFTER UNTIL VALID-FIELD
              ACCEPT SCR-MILES-IN
              ACCEPT SCR-MILES-OUT
              IF REN-MILES-IN < REN-MILES-OUT
                  MOVE LESS-THAN-MILES-MSG TO ERROR-MESSAGE
                  PERFORM 499-DISPLAY-ERROR-MESSAGE
```

TEST AFTER clause ensures that in-line statements are executed at least once

Figure 10.9 *(continued)*

```
               ELSE
                   IF REN-MILES-IN - REN-MILES-OUT <
                       MILES-PER-DAY-FACTOR * REN-DAYS-RENTED
                           MOVE INVALID-MILES-MSG TO ERROR-MESSAGE
                           PERFORM 499-DISPLAY-ERROR-MESSAGE
                   ELSE
                           PERFORM 498-CLEAR-ERRORS
                   END-IF
               END-IF
           END-PERFORM.

       470-VALIDATE-MILEAGE-RATE.
           PERFORM WITH TEST AFTER UNTIL VALID-FIELD
               ACCEPT SCR-MILEAGE-RATE
               IF NOT VALID-MILEAGE-RATES
                   MOVE MILEAGE-RATE-MSG TO ERROR-MESSAGE
                   PERFORM 499-DISPLAY-ERROR-MESSAGE
               ELSE
                   PERFORM 498-CLEAR-ERRORS
               END-IF
           END-PERFORM.

       480-VALIDATE-INSURANCE.
           PERFORM WITH TEST AFTER UNTIL VALID-FIELD
               ACCEPT SCR-INSURANCE
               IF NOT VALID-INSURANCE
                   MOVE INSURANCE-MSG TO ERROR-MESSAGE
                   PERFORM 499-DISPLAY-ERROR-MESSAGE
               ELSE
                   PERFORM 498-CLEAR-ERRORS
               END-IF
           END-PERFORM.

       498-CLEAR-ERRORS.
           INITIALIZE VALID-FIELD-SWITCH.
           DISPLAY ' ' LINE 25 WITH BLANK LINE.

       499-DISPLAY-ERROR-MESSAGE.
           MOVE 'NO' TO VALID-FIELD-SWITCH.
           DISPLAY ERROR-LINE.

       500-COMPUTE-IND-BILL.
           PERFORM 520-COMPUTE-MILEAGE-TOTAL.
           PERFORM 540-COMPUTE-DAILY-TOTAL.
           PERFORM 560-COMPUTE-INSURANCE-TOTAL.
           COMPUTE IND-AMOUNT-DUE ROUNDED
               = IND-MILEAGE-TOTAL + IND-DAILY-TOTAL
                 + IND-INSURANCE-TOTAL
               SIZE ERROR DISPLAY 'SIZE ERROR ON AMOUNT DUE FOR '
                   REN-CONTRACT-NO
           END-COMPUTE.
```

TEST AFTER clause ensures that in-line statements are executed at least once

Figure 10.9 *(continued)*

```

       520-COMPUTE-MILEAGE-TOTAL.
           COMPUTE IND-MILES-DRIVEN
               = REN-MILES-IN - REN-MILES-OUT
           END-COMPUTE.
           COMPUTE IND-MILEAGE-TOTAL ROUNDED
               = IND-MILES-DRIVEN * REN-MILEAGE-RATE
               SIZE ERROR
                 DISPLAY 'COMPUTED BILL EXCESSIVELY LARGE'
           END-COMPUTE.

       540-COMPUTE-DAILY-TOTAL.
           EVALUATE REN-CAR-TYPE
               WHEN 'E' MOVE ECONOMY-RATE TO IND-DAILY-RATE
               WHEN 'C' MOVE COMPACT-RATE TO IND-DAILY-RATE
               WHEN 'M' MOVE MID-RATE TO IND-DAILY-RATE
               WHEN 'F' MOVE FULL-RATE TO IND-DAILY-RATE
               WHEN 'L' MOVE LUXURY-RATE TO IND-DAILY-RATE
               WHEN OTHER MOVE ZEROES TO IND-DAILY-RATE
           END-EVALUATE.
           MULTIPLY IND-DAILY-RATE BY REN-DAYS-RENTED
               GIVING IND-DAILY-TOTAL
               SIZE ERROR DISPLAY 'SIZE ERROR ON RENTAL TOTAL'
           END-MULTIPLY.

       560-COMPUTE-INSURANCE-TOTAL.
           IF INSURANCE
               MULTIPLY INSURANCE-RATE BY REN-DAYS-RENTED
                   GIVING IND-INSURANCE-TOTAL
                   SIZE ERROR DISPLAY 'SIZE ERROR ON INSURANCE TOTAL'
               END-MULTIPLY
           ELSE
               MOVE ZEROES TO IND-INSURANCE-TOTAL
           END-IF.

       600-WRITE-VALID-RECORD.
           WRITE VALID-RENTAL-RECORD FROM RENTAL-RECORD-IN.

       700-INPUT-SCREEN-CONFIRM.
           DISPLAY CONFIRM-SCREEN.
           PERFORM WITH TEST AFTER UNTIL VALID-CONFIRMED
               ACCEPT CONFIRM-SCREEN
               IF VALID-CONFIRMED
                   PERFORM 498-CLEAR-ERRORS
               ELSE
                   MOVE YES-NO-MSG TO ERROR-MESSAGE
                   PERFORM 499-DISPLAY-ERROR-MESSAGE
               END-IF
           END-PERFORM.
```

EVALUATE statement determines daily rate

Indentation increases readability

The requirements for the validation of individual fields parallel those in Chapter 8, and thus the table of error messages (lines 68–107) is repeated from the validation program. The validation process is different, however, as each field is checked interactively, so that the user cannot move to the next field until a valid value has been entered for the current field.

Consider, for example, the validation of car type in lines 324–333. The TEST AFTER clause guarantees that the performed statements are executed at least once; that is, the car type is accepted into SCR-CAR-TYPE (defined in lines 183–184), then tested by the IF statement in lines 327–332. A valid car type will reset VALID-FIELD-SWITCH to 'NO', which in turn satisfies the condition in the PERFORM statement in line 325. An invalid response, however, displays the appropriate error message, then requests a new response from the user. A similar process is followed for the other fields in each transaction. An appreciation for the interactive nature of the program can best be gained by executing the program as it exists on the accompanying data disk.

The remainder of the Procedure Division is straightforward with applicable paragraphs copied from the earlier programs—for example, COMPUTE-MILEAGE-TOTAL, COMPUTE-DAILY-TOTAL, and COMPUTE-INSURANCE-TOTAL.

LIMITATIONS OF COBOL-74

The Screen Section and extended options of the ACCEPT and DISPLAY statements are *not* included in either the COBOL-74 or COBOL-85 standard, and thus there are no limitations per se in the earlier compiler. In other words, any differences that do exist are due to vendor-specific extensions, which vary significantly from compiler to compiler.

SUMMARY

Points to Remember

- The extended screen handling capabilities in the Screen Section and the ACCEPT and DISPLAY statements are not part of the COBOL-85 standard. The examples in this chapter follow the syntax of the Classroom COBOL compiler that accompanies the text, which conforms to the X-Open standard.
- The ACCEPT and DISPLAY statements display individual lines and/or accept a limited number of fields as input. Both statements contain an abundance of optional clauses, the functions of which are generally apparent from the clause itself: BLINK, BEEP, BACKGROUND-COLOR, FOREGROUND-COLOR, and so forth.
- The Screen Section facilitates the production of uniform screens within a system as an entire screen may be easily copied from one program to the next. This is in contrast to individual ACCEPT and DISPLAY statements that are scattered throughout the Procedure Division.

- The format of the Screen Section parallels that of the File and Working-Storage sections in the Data Division; that is, it consists of 01-level entries that are further divided into group and elementary items. The Screen Section must be the last section in the Data Division.
- Data validation may be implemented interactively through an in-line perform and through TEST AFTER clauses, which accept a data name, perform the indicated validation, then repeat the process until a valid field has been entered.

Key Words and Concepts

Alt key
ASCII characters
Background color
Batch-oriented program
Data validation
Foreground color
Interactive program
Password protection
Prompt
Reversed video
Screen attribute
Screen-name

COBOL Elements

ACCEPT
AUTO
BACKGROUND-COLOR
COLUMN
DISPLAY
FOREGROUND-COLOR
FROM
HIGHLIGHT
LINE
REVERSE-VIDEO
SCREEN SECTION
SECURE
TO
USING

FILL-IN

1. The Screen Section (is/is not) part of the COBOL-85 standard.
2. The typical screen displays ______________ lines of ______________ columns each.
3. The ______________ clause in the ACCEPT statement prevents the user's response from being displayed on the monitor.
4. The LINE and COLUMN clauses (are/are not) required in the ACCEPT and/or DISPLAY statements
5. The Screen Section is the (first/last) section in the Data Division.
6. The ______________ key, in conjunction with the numeric keyboard, can be used to enter any of the 256 ______________ characters into a program.
7. In general, the foreground and background colors (should/should not) be the same.
8. The (ACCEPT/DISPLAY) statement is often used in conjunction with top-down testing and/or debugging.

9. An in-line PERFORM statement, coupled with the (TEST BEFORE/TEST AFTER) clause, is used to implement interactive data validation.
10. The ______________ ______________ facilitates the production of uniform screens within a system in that its entries can be easily copied from program to program.
11. Screen I-O makes possible the implementation of (batch-oriented/interactive) programs.
12. An in-line perform, in conjunction with the TEST AFTER clause, can be used to ______________ a field as it is entered.

TRUE/FALSE

1. The same COBOL program cannot contain a Screen Section and a File Section.
2. The File Section is required in every program.
3. The LINE and/or COLUMN clauses are required in the DISPLAY statement.
4. The Screen Section is required in all programs that display output on the monitor.
5. The ACCEPT and DISPLAY statements are used for low-volume output.
6. The options and syntax for screen I-O are unlikely to change from one compiler to the next.
7. Text is typically displayed on screens in which the foreground and background colors are the same.
8. COBOL-85 makes little provision for screen I-O, and thus its implementation varies greatly from compiler to compiler.
9. The optional clauses in the ACCEPT statement can appear in any order.
10. Interactive data validation cannot be implemented in programs with extensive screen I-O.

PROBLEMS

1. Which clause is used to implement the following in an ACCEPT and/or DISPLAY statement?
   a. Invert the specified or default background and foreground colors
   b. Prevent the referenced field from being displayed on the screen
   c. Require that at least one character is entered in the referenced field
   d. Automatically position the cursor to the first character of the next field after the last character of the current field has been entered
   e. Clear the screen before accepting (displaying) a data element
   f. Emphasize the displayed field (multiple clauses are acceptable)

2. Indicate the exact effect of each of the following DISPLAY statements. Note, however, that some of the statements are invalid syntactically, in which case you should indicate the nature of the error. Other statements are valid syntactically, but most probably do not do what the programmer intended.
   a. DISPLAY
   b. DISPLAY 'COMPUTE-TUITION paragraph is entered'
   c. DISPLAY 'TUITION = IND-TUITION'
   d. DISPLAY 'TUITION = ', IND-TUITION
   e. DISPLAY 'Initials: AT LINE 5 COLUMN 5'
   f. DISPLAY 'Initials:' AT LINE 5 COLUMN 5
   g. The two statements, DISPLAY 'Less Scholarship' AT LINE 15 COLUMN 10 followed by DISPLAY 'Amount due' AT LINE 15 COLUMN 16
3. Modify the tuition billing program to accommodate the following:
   a. A new password, RTG, which should be accepted as valid in all uppercase, all lowercase, or any combination of upper- and lowercase letters.
   b. Data validation as you see fit; the program as presently written does no validation whatsoever. Suggest and implement validation checks for at least three fields.
   c. Display a total screen at the conclusion of processing that contains the number of students processed and the corresponding totals for total tuition, total activity fee, total union fee, total scholarship awarded, and the total amount due.
   d. Create a valid record file as output—that is, a file containing the valid student records that could be input into the edited version of the tuition billing program in Chapter 7.
4. Answer the following with respect to the car validation and billing program:
   a. Is the program case-sensitive; that is, is there any difference between entering an upper- or lowercase C to denote a compact car?
   b. What changes (if any) have to be made to VALUE clauses in the Data Division to make the program case-insensitive for car type?
   c. What changes (if any) have to be made in the Procedure Division to support those made in the Data Division in part (b)?
   d. What other changes (if any) are needed to make the program case-insensitive to other data names?
5. The car validation and billing program makes extensive use of the in-line PERFORM statement to validate data as it is entered.
   a. What is the minimum number of times the statements within an in-line perform (e.g., lines 305–313) will be executed?
   b. Do the PERFORM statements (e.g., lines 305–313) implement a DO WHILE or a DO UNTIL structure?
   c. What is the effect (if any) of substituting TEST BEFORE for TEST AFTER in line 305?
   d. What is the effect (if any) of removing the TEST clause in line 305?

Introduction to Tables

CHAPTER OUTLINE

OBJECTIVES

After reading this chapter you will be able to:

- Define a table and describe its use in programming.
- Use the OCCURS (at either the group or elementary level) to implement a table in COBOL.
- Use the PERFORM VARYING statement to process a table.
- Distinguish between fixed and variable length records; use the OCCURS DEPENDING ON clause to implement a variable length table.
- State the purpose of the USAGE clause.
- Differentiate between a subscript and an index.

OVERVIEW

This is the first of three chapters that deal exclusively with tables, a topic of major importance in any programming language. A table is a grouping of similar data whose values are stored in consecutive storage locations and assigned a single data name. Any reference to an individual element within a table is accomplished by a subscript or an index.

The present chapter introduces the basic statements for table processing. We begin with the OCCURS clause to define a table and show how it can be used at both the group and elementary levels. We discuss the DEPENDING ON phrase to specify a variable-length table and the concept of relative subscripting. We cover the PERFORM VARYING statement to process the elements in a table by repeatedly executing a paragraph or a series of in-line statements. We also differentiate between an index that is specified in an INDEXED BY clause and a subscript defined in Working-Storage. All of this material is summarized by the illustrative program at the end of the chapter.

Introduction to Tables

The motivation for using a table comes from examination of Figure 11.1. Let us assume that a company tabulates its sales on a monthly basis and that the sales of each month are to be referenced within a COBOL program. Without tables, as in the brute force approach of Figure 11.1a, 12 different data names are required: JAN-SALES, FEB-SALES, and so on. A table, however, enables you to define a single data name such as SALES, then subsequently refer to individual months by an appropriate subscript. SALES (2), for example, refers to the sales for the second month, February.

Figure 11.1 The Table Concept

```
01  ANNUAL-SALES-DATA.
    05  JAN-SALES           PIC 9(6).
    05  FEB-SALES           PIC 9(6).
    05  MAR-SALES           PIC 9(6).
    05  APR-SALES           PIC 9(6).
    05  MAY-SALES           PIC 9(6).
    05  JUN-SALES           PIC 9(6).
    05  JUL-SALES           PIC 9(6).
    05  AUG-SALES           PIC 9(6).
    05  SEP-SALES           PIC 9(6).
    05  OCT-SALES           PIC 9(6).
    05  NOV-SALES           PIC 9(6).
    05  DEC-SALES           PIC 9(6).
```

(a) Brute Force

```
01  ANNUAL-SALES-DATA.
    05  SALES  OCCURS  12  TIMES           PIC 9(6).
```

(b) OCCURS Clause

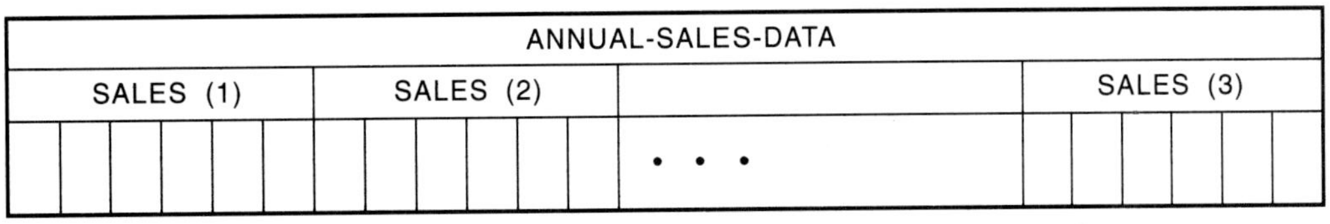

ANNUAL-SALES-DATA			
SALES (1)	SALES (2)		SALES (3)
		. . .	

(c) Storage Schematic

OCCURS Clause

The **OCCURS** clause defines the number of entries in a table and is covered in detail later in the chapter. For the time being, however, we consider only its simplest form:

```
OCCURS integer TIMES
```

The OCCURS clause is illustrated in Figure 11.1b to define a table of 12 elements, with each element in the table having the identical format; that is, each element is a six-position numeric field. The entire table takes a total of 72 positions (12 entries x 6 positions per entry), as shown in the schematic of Figure 11.1c. As indicated, individual entries in the table are referenced by the table name, SALES, and an appropriate subscript—for example, SALES (1) to refer to the first element (January sales), SALES (2) to refer to the second element (February sales), and so on.

The OCCURS clause is not permitted at the 01 level and thus the sales table was defined under the entry ANNUAL-SALES-DATA in Figure 11.1b. The 12 elements may be referenced collectively by the data name ANNUAL-SALES-DATA although such a reference is unlikely to be used.

Processing a Table

After a table has been defined, we shall want to sum the 12 monthly totals to produce an annual total. There are several approaches, the first of which is brute force:

```
COMPUTE ANNUAL-TOTAL
    = SALES (1) + SALES (2) + SALES (3)
    + SALES (4) + SALES (5) + SALES (6)
    + SALES (7) + SALES (8) + SALES (9)
    + SALES (10) + SALES (11) + SALES (12)
END-COMPUTE.
```

This technique is cumbersome to code, and defeats the purpose of defining the table in the first place, but it does explicitly illustrate the concept of table processing. Fortunately, however, there is a better way through the PERFORM VARYING statement.

PERFORM VARYING

The **PERFORM VARYING** statement causes repeated execution of a designated procedure or series of in-line statements and is the most common means of processing a table. Consider:

```
PERFORM [procedure-name-1]

    [WITH TEST {BEFORE}]
               {AFTER }

    VARYING identifier-1 FROM {literal-1   } BY {literal-2   }
                              {identifier-2}    {identifier-3}

    UNTIL condition-1

  [imperative-statement-1 END-PERFORM]
```

The TEST BEFORE/TEST AFTER clause is new to COBOL-85 and was explained in Chapter 9. The clause is optional and typically omitted; the default is TEST BEFORE and corresponds to the COBOL-74 implementation.

The PERFORM VARYING statement (with test before) *initializes* a variable, *tests a condition*, and if the condition is not satisfied, enters a loop to *execute* a procedure, *increment* a variable, and *retest* the condition (condition-1). The loop is executed repeatedly until the condition is finally satisfied, at which point the PERFORM VARYING statement ends, and control passes to the next sequential statement in the program. The sequence just described is illustrated in Figure 11.2 and is restated below:

1. Identifier-1 is initialized to the value in the **FROM** clause
2. Condition-1 is evaluated and is either true or false:
    a. If the condition is true, the PERFORM VARYING is terminated and control passes to the next sequential statement.
    b. If the condition is false, procedure-name-1 or imperative-statement-1 is executed, after which identifier-1 is incremented with the value in the **BY** clause. Condition-1 is reevaluated as either true or false with subsequent action as just described.

Figure 11.2 PERFORM VARYING (with TEST BEFORE)

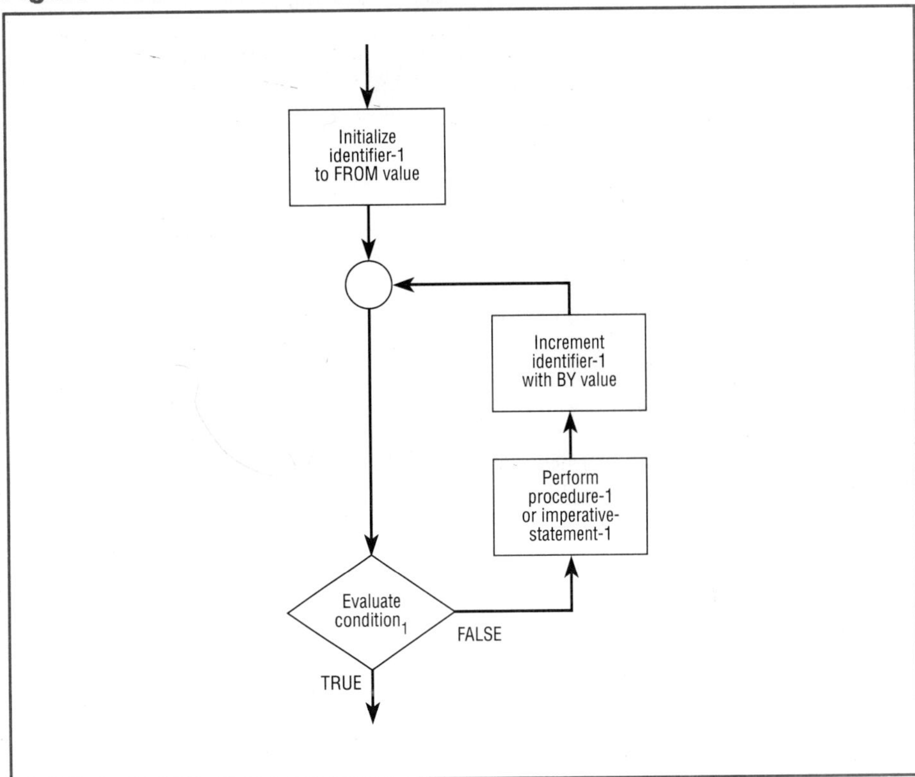

The condition in the PERFORM VARYING statement typically includes a greater than sign, rather than an equal sign, to execute the designated procedure an integer number of times; for example, the statement

```
PERFORM COMPUTE-PAYMENT
    VARYING SUBSCRIPT FROM 1 BY 1
        UNTIL SUBSCRIPT > 3
```

executes the procedure COMPUTE-PAYMENT three times. The sequence is explained as follows:

1. SUBSCRIPT is initially set to 1 and the condition SUBSCRIPT > 3 is evaluated. The condition is not true, so the designated procedure, COMPUTE-PAYMENT, is executed the first time.

2. SUBSCRIPT is incremented to 2 and the condition is retested. The condition is still not satisfied, so COMPUTE-PAYMENT is executed a second time.

3. SUBSCRIPT is incremented to 3, but the condition is still false—*3 is not greater than 3*—and hence COMPUTE-PAYMENT is executed a third (and final) time.

4. SUBSCRIPT is incremented to 4, satisfying the condition in the UNTIL clause and terminating the PERFORM statement. (Note that, had the condition been specified as SUBSCRIPT = 3, COMPUTE-PAYMENT would have been executed only twice.)

Extending this reasoning to the general case of executing a procedure N times requires a statement of the form:

```
PERFORM PARAGRAPH
    VARYING SUBSCRIPT FROM 1 BY 1
        UNTIL SUBSCRIPT > N.
```

The data name used to monitor execution—for example, SUBSCRIPT—must be explicitly defined in Working-Storage.

The PERFORM VARYING statement is illustrated a final time in Figure 11.3. The choice between performing a paragraph as in Figure 11.3a, or using an in-line perform as in Figure 11.3b, is one of personal preference. Both techniques are equally acceptable and achieve identical results.

Figure 11.3 Processing a Table

```
    MOVE ZERO TO ANNUAL-TOTAL.
    PERFORM INCREMENT-ANNUAL-TOTAL
        VARYING SALES-SUB FROM 1 BY 1
            UNTIL SALES-SUB > 12.
      .
         .
            .
INCREMENT-ANNUAL-TOTAL.
    ADD SALES (SALES-SUB) TO ANNUAL-TOTAL.
```

(a) Performing a Paragraph

```
    MOVE ZERO TO ANNUAL-TOTAL.
    PERFORM
        VARYING SALES-SUB FROM 1 BY 1
            UNTIL SALES-SUB > 12
        ADD SALES (SALES-SUB) TO ANNUAL-TOTAL
    END-PERFORM.
```

(b) In-line Perform

A Second Example

Let us consider a second example in which three sets of salary data are kept for each employee; that is, each employee record contains the employee's present salary and date on which it became effective, the previous salary and date, and the second previous salary and date. (Not all employees have all three salaries.)

It is, of course, possible to develop unique data names for each occurrence of salary information, for example,

```
05  SALARY-DATA.
    10  PRESENT-SALARY              PIC 9(6).
    10  PRESENT-SALARY-DATE         PIC 9(4).
    10  PREVIOUS-SALARY             PIC 9(6).
    10  PREVIOUS-SALARY-DATE        PIC 9(4).
    10  SECOND-PREVIOUS-SALARY      PIC 9(6).
    10  SECOND-PREVIOUS-SALARY-DATE PIC 9(4).
```

Figure 11.4 OCCURS Clause at the Group Level

```
05  SALARY-DATA OCCURS 3 TIMES.
    10  SALARY          PIC 9(6).
    10  SAL-DATE        PIC 9(4).
```

(a) COBOL Statements

SALARY-DATA(1)		SALARY-DATA(2)		SALARY-DATA(3)	
SALARY (1)	SAL-DATE(1)	SALARY (2)	SAL-DATE(2)	SALARY (3)	SAL-DATE(3)

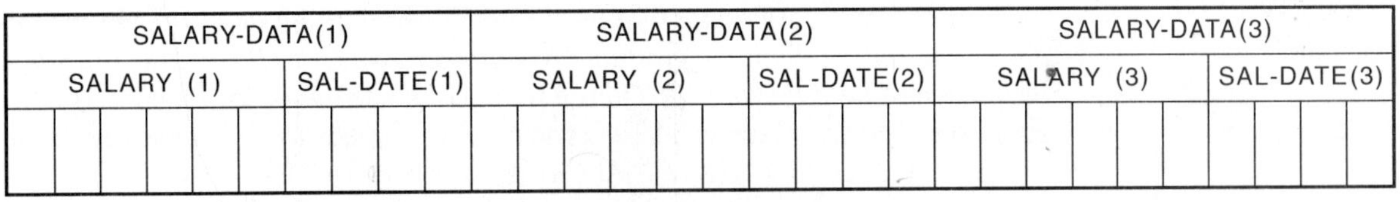

(b) Storage Schematic

Figure 11.5 OCCURS Clause at the Elementary Level

```
05  SALARY-DATA.
    10  SALARY          OCCURS  3  TIMES    PIC 9(6).
    10  SAL-DATE        OCCURS  3  TIMES    PIC 9(4).
```

(a) COBOL Statements

SALARY-DATA					
SALARY (1)	SALARY (2)	SALARY (3)	SAL-DATE(1)	SAL-DATE(2)	SAL-DATE(3)

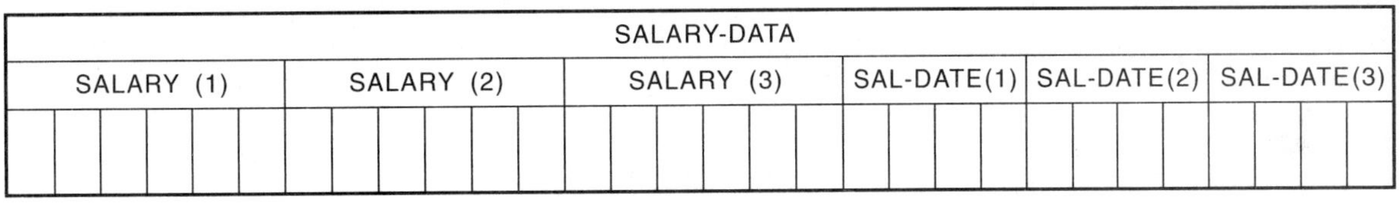

(b) Storage Schematic

What if, however, it were suddenly decided that four, five, or even ten levels of historical data were required? The situation is neatly circumvented by establishing a table that enables the programmer to define logically similar elements under a common name, and to reference the desired entry subsequently by an appropriate subscript. Hence SALARY (1) denotes the present salary, SALARY (2) the previous salary, SALARY (3) the second previous salary, and so on. Figure 11.4 shows the COBOL statements and corresponding storage allocation for such a scheme.

Figure 11.4 depicts a total of 30 storage positions for the table SALARY-DATA, with the OCCURS clause at the group level. Positions 1–6 refer to SALARY (1), positions 7–10 refer to SAL-DATE (1), and positions 1–10 collectively to SALARY-DATA (1). In similar fashion, positions 11–16 refer to SALARY (2), positions 17–20 refer to SAL-DATE (2), and positions 11–20 collectively to SALARY-DATA (2). Whenever a subscript is used, it is enclosed in parentheses.

Figure 11.5 contains an alternate implementation with two OCCURS clauses at the elementary level. A total of 30 storage positions are still assigned to the table, but the storage allocation is different; i.e., positions 1–6 contain SALARY (1), positions 7–12 contain SALARY (2), and positions 13–18 contain SALARY (3). In similar fashion, positions 19–22 correspond to SAL-DATE (1), positions 23–26 to SAL-DATE (2), and positions 27–30 to SAL-DATE (3). Either arrangement, Figure 11.4 or Figure 11.5, is appropriate; the choice is up to the programmer.

Problems with the OCCURS Clause

The most common error associated with tables is the omission of a subscript where one is required, or the inclusion of a subscript where it is not needed. The rule is very simple. *Any data name that has been defined with an OCCURS clause, or any data name subservient to a group item containing an OCCURS clause, must always be referenced with a subscript.* Failure to do so results in a compilation error. Thus all of the following are valid references with respect to the table definition of Figure 11.4: SALARY-DATA (2), SALARY (2), and SAL-DATE (2).

In the table definition of Figure 11.5, however, the OCCURS clause exists at the elementary, rather than the group, level. SALARY-DATA is referenced *without* a subscript and refers collectively to the 30 bytes in the table. SALARY and SAL-DATE are both defined with OCCURS clauses and require subscripts: SALARY (2) and SAL-DATE (2), for example.

The compiler checks only for the existence of a subscript, but not its value; for example, the entry SALARY (20) is syntactically correct in that a subscript is present, but logically incorrect as the OCCURS clause defines only three elements. The error would not be detected during compilation; it would pose a problem during execution as it references an invalid storage location with unpredictable results. Some compilers offer the option of including a ***subscript check*** whereby an error message will be produced during execution if an invalid subscript is referenced.

Rules for Subscripts

COBOL subscripts may be either variable or constant, but in either case must adhere to the following:

1. At least one space is required between the data name and the left parenthesis.

Valid:	`SALES (2)`
Invalid:	`SALES(SUB)`
Invalid:	`SALES(2)`

2. A space may not follow the left parenthesis nor precede the right parenthesis.

Valid:	`SALES (SUB)`
Valid:	`SALES (2)`
Invalid:	`SALES( 2)`
Invalid:	`SALES(2 )`

3. A subscript can be a data name or a numeric literal with an integer value. Relative subscripting—that is, a data name plus or minus an integer—is also permitted.

Valid:	`SALES (SUB + 1)`
Invalid:	`SALES (1.2)`

Relative Subscripting

Relative subscripting—that is, the ability to add or subtract an integer from a subscript—is a tremendous convenience in certain situations. The report in Figure

Figure 11.6 Relative Subscripting

CURRENT SALARY	EFFECTIVE DATE	PERCENT INCREASE
$46,000	09/93	15.0%
$40,000	09/92	11.1%
$36,000	09/91	12.5%
$32,000	09/90	

(a) Salary History

```
PERFORM VARYING SUB FROM 1 BY 1
    UNTIL SUB > 3 OR SALARY (SUB + 1) = 0
       COMPUTE PCT-SALARY-INC (SUB)
           = 100 * ((SALARY (SUB) - SALARY (SUB + 1))
           / SALARY (SUB + 1)
       END-COMPUTE
END-PERFORM.
```

(b) Computation of Percent Salary Increase

11.6a displays four levels of salary, the date on which each salary became effective, and the associated percent increase for each pair of salaries. (The percent increase is not calculated for the last salary.) Percent increase is computed according to the general formula:

$$\text{Percent Salary Increase} = \frac{\text{New Salary} - \text{Old Salary}}{\text{Old Salary}} \times 100$$

The current salary of $46,000 in Figure 11.6a reflects a 15 percent increase over the previous salary of $40,000 and was computed as follows:

$$\text{Percent Salary Increase} = \frac{46{,}000 - 40{,}000}{40{,}000} \times 100 = .15$$

The percent salary increase is a repetitive calculation that is required for each pair of salaries stored within the salary table. One (tedious) approach is to use a different formula for each pair of salaries—that is, one formula to reference SALARY (1) and SALARY (2), a second formula to reference SALARY (2) and SALARY (3), and so on. A more elegant solution is to develop a general formula that references SALARY (SUB) and SALARY (SUB + 1) as shown in Figure 11.6b.

The COMPUTE statement is executed three times if all four salaries are present. Newer employees will not have a complete salary history, however, and hence the second condition in the UNTIL clause will cease execution if an earlier salary is not present; that is, the latter condition prevents a division by zero when an earlier salary is not available.

USAGE Clause

The **USAGE** clause is intended to make a program more efficient. The clause is entirely optional as the presence (or absence) of a USAGE clause does not alter the logic of a program, but affects only the generated object code. A true understanding, therefore, requires a knowledge of assembler fundamentals which is beyond the present discussion. Suffice it to say that subscripts are best defined with a USAGE clause in one of four equivalent formats as follows:

```
05  SUBSCRIPT-1      PIC S9(4)     USAGE IS COMPUTATIONAL.
05  SUBSCRIPT-2      PIC S9(4)     COMPUTATIONAL.
05  SUBSCRIPT-3      PIC S9(4)     USAGE IS COMP.
05  SUBSCRIPT-4      PIC S9(4)     COMP.
```

OCCURS DEPENDING ON

We began the chapter with the simplest form of the OCCURS clause to define a table. The clause has several additional options, however, as shown below:

```
OCCURS {integer-1 TO integer-2 TIMES [DEPENDING ON data-name-1]}
       {integer-2 TIMES                                        }

       [{ASCENDING } KEY IS data-name-2 [data-name-3] . . .]
       [{DESCENDING}                                       ]

       [INDEXED BY index-name-1 [index-name-2] . . .]
```

The DEPENDING ON clause defines a ***variable-length table.*** This in turn produces a ***variable-length record,*** which is reflected in the RECORD CONTAINS clause of the FD as shown in Figure 11.7.

The records in STUDENT-TRANSCRIPT-FILE will vary in length from 42 to 1,131 characters, depending on the number of courses a student has completed. The minimum record length is 42 characters; 30 for name, 10 for major, and 2 for the number of courses. The records for incoming freshmen will contain the minimum 42 characters, whereas the records for upperclassmen contain an additional 11 bytes for every completed course. An arbitrary maximum of 99 courses is permitted in a record.

The advantage of ***variable-length records*** is that they allocate only as much space as necessary in the storage medium. ***Fixed-length records,*** on the other hand, assign the same (maximum) amount of disk space to every record in the file.

Figure 11.7 Variable-length Records

```
FD  STUDENT-TRANSCRIPT-FILE
    RECORD CONTAINS 42 TO 1131 CHARACTERS
    DATA RECORD IS STUDENT-RECORD.
01  STUDENT-RECORD.
    05  ST-NAME                                        PIC X(30).
    05  ST-MAJOR                                       PIC X(10).
    05  ST-COURSES-COMPLETED                           PIC 99.
    05  ST-COURSE-GRADE OCCURS 0 TO 99 TIMES
        DEPENDING ON ST-COURSES-COMPLETED.
        10  ST-COURSE-NUMBER                           PIC 9(6).
        10  ST-GRADE                                   PIC X.
        10  ST-COURSE-DATE                             PIC 9(4).
```

What, then, is the maximum number of courses? Is it five per semester, times 8 semesters, or 40 courses? What about the student who fails a course or the one with two majors, or the one who remains in the university to pursue a master's or doctoral degree? Perhaps we should allocate space for 100 courses, just to be safe. If we do, every student record will require 1,100 bytes (11 bytes per course times 100 courses). But at any given time the average student probably has completed twenty or fewer courses (that is, there are freshmen, sophomores, juniors, and seniors in the file), and hence most records would require only 220 (20 x 11) or fewer characters. In other words, approximately 900 bytes per record would be wasted in the storage medium. Multiply this by the number of students in the university, and you can quickly see the inefficiency of fixed-length records in certain applications.

Variable-length records, on the other hand, allow only as much space in each record as is actually required. Each variable-length record contains a specific field from which the length of the record can be calculated—for example, the number of completed courses, which becomes the data name specified in the OCCURS DEPENDING ON clause.

The INDEXED BY clause is covered later in this chapter (on page 321). The ASCENDING/DESCENDING KEY clause is presented in Chapter 12 in conjunction with table lookups.

The Student Transcript Program

We are ready to incorporate the basic material on table processing into an illustrative program. Specifications follow in the usual format.

PROGRAMMING SPECIFICATIONS

Program Name: Student Transcript Program

Narrative: This program processes a file of student records to produce a set of student transcripts. Each incoming record contains a variable-length table with the student's grades from the preceding semester. The program computes the grade point average for every student, prints individual transcripts for each student, and produces a table of students on the dean's list at the end of processing.

Input File(s): STUDENT-FILE

Input Record Layout:

```
01  STUDENT-RECORD.
    05  ST-NAME                                    PIC X(19).
    05  ST-NUMBER-OF-COURSES                       PIC 99.
    05  ST-COURSE-INFO OCCURS 1 TO 8 TIMES
        DEPENDING ON ST-NUMBER-OF-COURSES.
        10  ST-COURSE-NUMBER                       PIC X(3).
        10  ST-COURSE-GRADE                        PIC X.
        10  ST-COURSE-CREDITS                      PIC 9.
```

Test Data: See Figure 11.8a.

Report Layout: See Figure 11.8b and 11.8c.

Processing Requirements: 1. Read a file of student records.

Figure 11.8 Test Data and Required Output

```
BENJAMIN, L        05111A3222A2333A3444A3555B3
BORROW, J          04666B3777B3888B3999B4
MILGROM, M         06123C4456C4789C4012C4345C3678C4
```

(a) Test Data

```
NAME:BENJAMIN, L              OFFICIAL TRANSCRIPT

          COURSE # CREDITS  GRADE
             111         3     A
             222         2     A
             333         3     A
             444         3     A
             555         3     B

                AVERAGE: 3.79    *DEANS LIST*


NAME:BORROW, J                OFFICIAL TRANSCRIPT

          COURSE # CREDITS  GRADE
             666         3     B
             777         3     B
             888         3     B
             999         4     B

                AVERAGE: 3.00


NAME:MILGROM, M               OFFICIAL TRANSCRIPT

          COURSE # CREDITS  GRADE
             123         4     C
             456         4     C
             789         4     C
             012         4     C
             345         3     C
             678         4     C

                AVERAGE: 2.00
```

(b) Individual Transcripts

```
                    STUDENTS ON THE DEANS LIST

                          TOTAL    TOTAL    QUALITY
NAME                     COURSES  CREDITS    POINTS     GPA

BENJAMIN, L                 5        14        53       3.79
```

(c) The Dean's List

Figure 11.9 Calculation of Grade Point Average

COURSE	COURSE GRADE	COURSE CREDITS
Course Number 1	A	2
Course Number 2	B	4

(a) Hypothetical Grades

SUB	GRADE(SUB)	CREDITS(SUB)	MULTIPLIER	TOTAL-QUALITY-POINTS	TOTAL-CREDITS
1	A	2	4	8 (0 + 2*4)	2
2	B	4	3	20 (8 + 4*3)	6

(b) Incrementing Counters

GRADE-POINT-AVERAGE = TOTAL-QUALITY-POINTS / TOTAL-CREDITS = 20 / 6 = 3.33

(c) Calculation of Grade Point Average

2. For every record read,
   a. Calculate the grade point average (GPA) according to a four-point scale with grades of A, B, C, D, and F, worth 4, 3, 2, 1, and 0, respectively. Courses are weighted according to their credit value in computing the GPA. The number of quality points for a given course is equal to the number of credits for that course times the numeric value of that grade. The GPA is equal to the total number of quality points (for all courses) divided by the total number of credits. The computation of the GPA is further illustrated in Figure 11.9.
   b. Print the student's name, list of courses with associated grades, and computed grade point average according to the format in Figure 11.8b. Every transcript is to begin on a new page.
   c. Determine whether the student qualifies for the dean's list, which requires a GPA of 3.5 or higher; if so, print the dean's list designation on the last line of the transcript.
3. Print a list of all students on the dean's list at the end of processing as shown in Figure 11.8c.

Program Design

The development of this (or any other) program begins with a hierarchy chart that includes all necessary functions to implement the processing requirements. The output in Figure 11.8 shows individual transcripts and a composite dean's list, both of which represent major tasks to be fully expanded; thus the highest-level module in the hierarchy chart will have two subordinates, CREATE-TRANSCRIPT and WRITE-DEANS-LIST, corresponding to the major functions. Each of these is expanded further as shown in the hierarchy chart of Figure 11.10.

The CREATE-TRANSCRIPT module has four subordinates: WRITE-TRANS-HEADING, PROCESS-COURSES, WRITE-GPA, and ADD-TO-DEANS-LIST. PROCESS-COURSES, in turn, has two subordinates: INCREMENT-COUNTERS and WRITE-DETAIL-LINE. WRITE-DEANS-LIST also has two subordinates: WRITE-DEANS-LIST-HEADING and WRITE-DEANS-LIST-DETAILS. The hierarchy chart is straightforward and easy to follow with the functions of all modules readily apparent from the module names.

Figure 11.10 Hierarchy Chart for Transcript Program

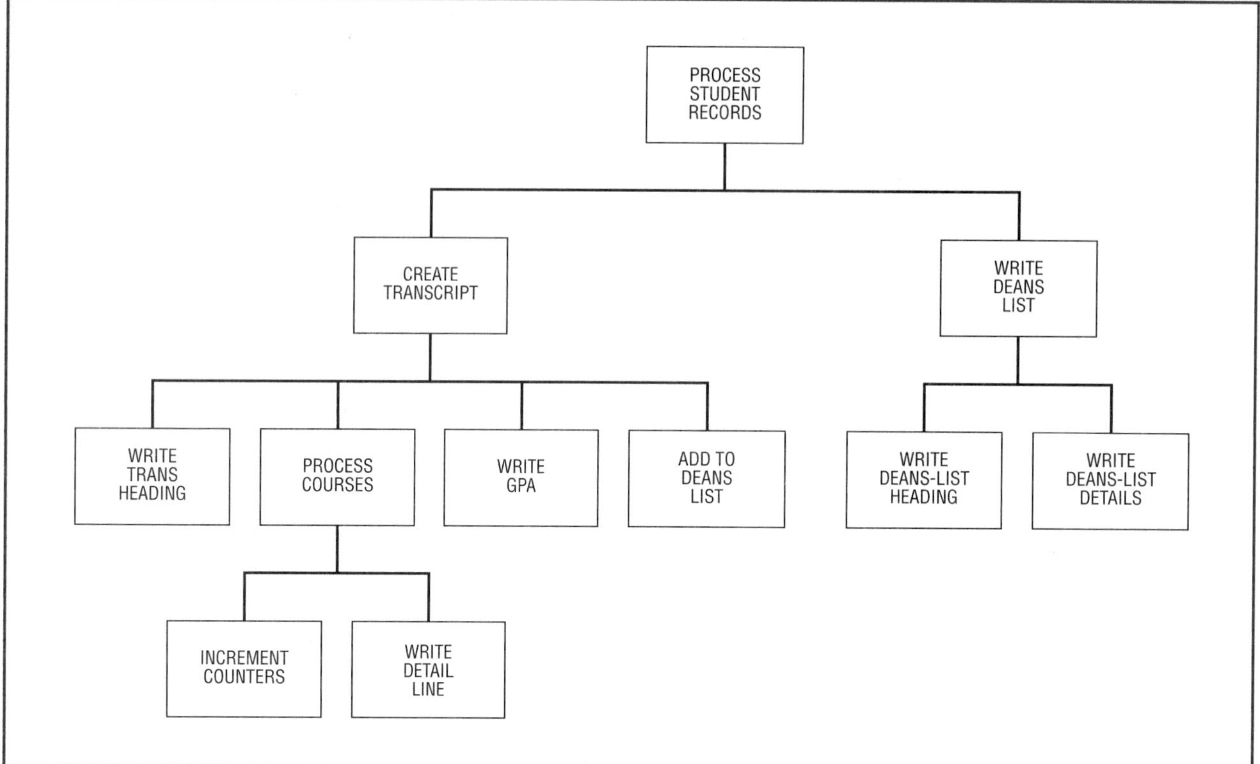

The pseudocode in Figure 11.11 uses an in-line perform to eliminate the priming read used in earlier programs. The false-condition branch in the read statement drives the program and contains the logic to compute an individual's grade point average, produce the transcript, and determine whether the individual qualifies for the dean's list.

The processing of each incoming record focuses on the production of a transcript, a process that begins with the initialization of two counters, for total quality points and total credits, respectively. Next, an inner loop is executed for every course in the current record, to determine the appropriate multiplier for the course (4 for an A, 3 for a B, and so on), to increment the counters for quality points and credits, and to write the detail line. This loop terminates after all courses (for one student) have been processed, after which the grade point average is computed by dividing the total quality points by the total number of credits.

The pseudocode next determines whether the student qualifies for the dean's list, and if so, increments the number of students on the dean's list, then moves the student's data to the appropriate place in a dean's list table. The table containing the students on the dean's list is written at the end of processing.

The Completed Program

The completed program is shown in Figure 11.12. The paragraphs in the Procedure Division correspond one to one with the modules in the hierarchy chart, and its logic in the program parallels that of the pseudocode just developed. The program complies with the processing requirements and also illustrates the various COBOL features presented earlier. Note the following:

Figure 11.11 Pseudocode for Transcript Program

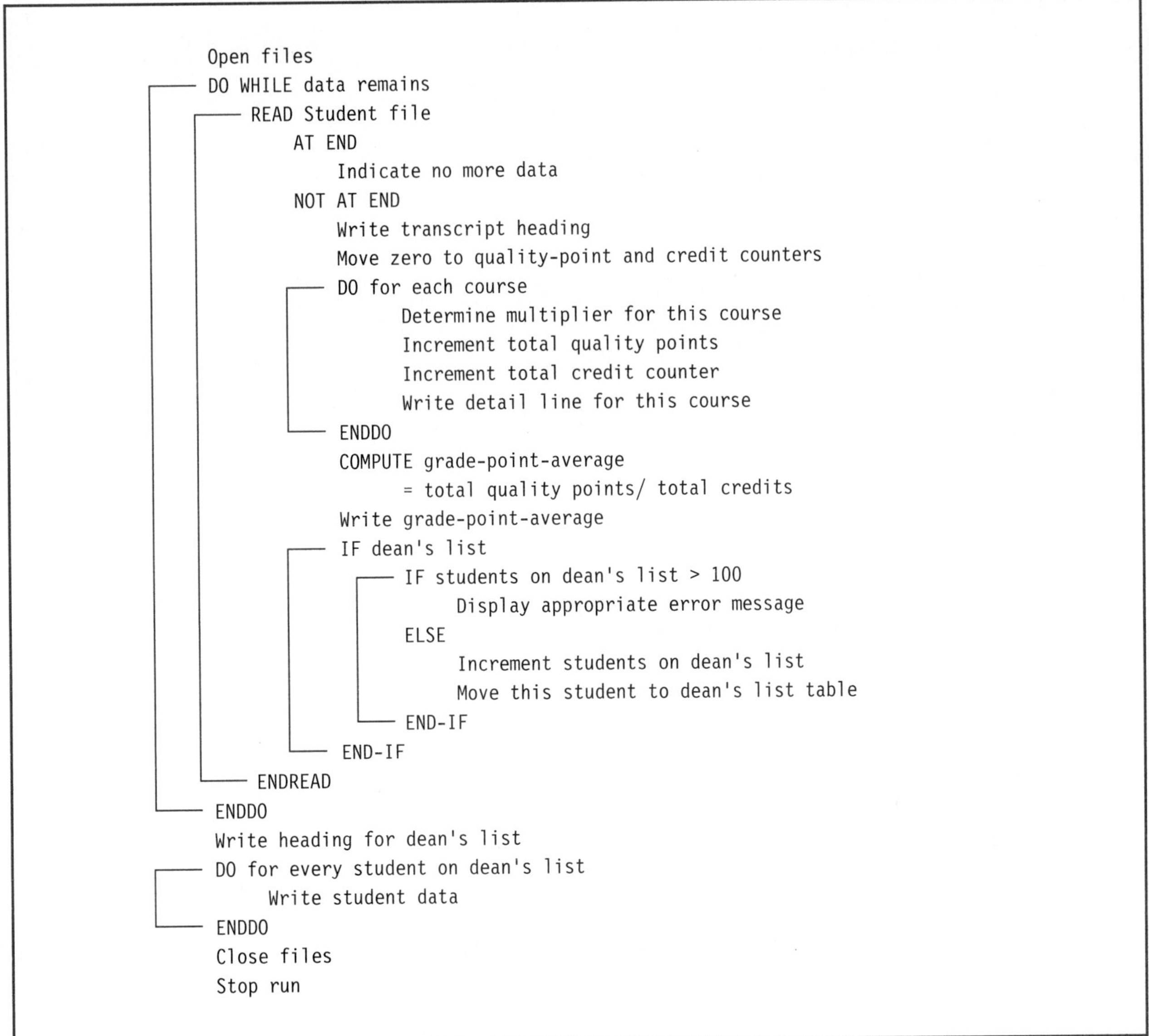

```
Open files
DO WHILE data remains
    READ Student file
        AT END
            Indicate no more data
        NOT AT END
            Write transcript heading
            Move zero to quality-point and credit counters
            DO for each course
                Determine multiplier for this course
                Increment total quality points
                Increment total credit counter
                Write detail line for this course
            ENDDO
            COMPUTE grade-point-average
                = total quality points/ total credits
            Write grade-point-average
            IF dean's list
                IF students on dean's list > 100
                    Display appropriate error message
                ELSE
                    Increment students on dean's list
                    Move this student to dean's list table
                END-IF
            END-IF
    ENDREAD
ENDDO
Write heading for dean's list
DO for every student on dean's list
    Write student data
ENDDO
Close files
Stop run
```

1. The OCCURS DEPENDING ON clause in lines 21 and 22 defines a variable-length table for the number of courses, which in turn produces a variable-length record in lines 15–17 of the FD for STUDENT-FILE.
2. The definition of two subscripts in Working-Storage—COURSE-SUB and DEAN-SUB—both of which contain the (USAGE IS) COMP clause for efficiency.
3. The in-line PERFORM statement of lines 133–140, coupled with the false-condition branch in the READ statement, drives the program by performing the paragraph 200-CREATE-TRANSCRIPT (lines 146–159) for every record in the file. This critical paragraph computes the grade point average, produces the transcript, and determines whether the student qualifies for the dean's list.

Figure 11.12 The Student Transcript Program

```
IDENTIFICATION DIVISION.
PROGRAM-ID.    TRANSCRP.
AUTHOR.        ROBERT GRAUER.

ENVIRONMENT DIVISION.
INPUT-OUTPUT SECTION.
FILE-CONTROL.
    SELECT STUDENT-FILE
        ASSIGN TO UT-S-STUDENT.
    SELECT PRINT-FILE
        ASSIGN TO UT-S-PRINT.

DATA DIVISION.
FILE SECTION.
FD  STUDENT-FILE
    RECORD CONTAINS 26 TO 61 CHARACTERS
    DATA RECORD IS STUDENT-RECORD.
01  STUDENT-RECORD.
    05  ST-NAME                 PIC X(19).
    05  ST-NUMBER-OF-COURSES    PIC 99.
    05  ST-COURSE-INFO OCCURS 1 TO 8 TIMES
        DEPENDING ON ST-NUMBER-OF-COURSES.
        10  ST-COURSE-NUMBER    PIC X(3).
        10  ST-COURSE-GRADE     PIC X.
        10  ST-COURSE-CREDITS   PIC 9.

FD  PRINT-FILE
    RECORD CONTAINS 132 CHARACTERS
    DATA RECORD IS PRINT-LINE.
01  PRINT-LINE                  PIC X(132).

WORKING-STORAGE SECTION.
01  SUBSCRIPTS.
    05  COURSE-SUB              PIC S9(4)               COMP.
    05  DEAN-SUB                PIC 9(3)    VALUE ZERO  COMP.

01  SWITCHES-AND-COUNTERS.
    05  END-OF-FILE-SWITCH      PIC X(3)    VALUE 'NO '.
    05  STUDENTS-ON-DEANS-LIST  PIC 9(3)    VALUE ZERO.

01  INDIVIDUAL-GPA-VARIABLES.
    05  IND-TOTAL-CREDITS       PIC 999.
    05  IND-TOTAL-QUAL-POINTS   PIC 999.
    05  IND-MULTIPLIER          PIC 9.
    05  IND-GRADE-POINT-AVERAGE PIC S9V99.
        88  DEANS-LIST                      VALUES 3.5 THRU 4.

01  DEANS-LIST-TABLE.
    05  DEANS-LIST-INFO OCCURS 100 TIMES.
        10  DL-NAME             PIC X(19).
```

Definition of variable-length table

COMPUTATIONAL clause increases efficiency of compiled program

Figure 11.12 *(continued)*

```
               10  DL-COURSES           PIC 99.
               10  DL-CREDITS           PIC 999.
               10  DL-QUAL-POINTS       PIC 999.
               10  DL-GPA               PIC S9V99.

       01  TRANS-HEADING-LINE-ONE.
           05  FILLER                   PIC X(6)    VALUE ' NAME:'.
           05  HDG-NAME                 PIC X(15).
           05  FILLER                   PIC X(10)   VALUE SPACES.
           05  FILLER                   PIC X(19)
                         VALUE 'OFFICIAL TRANSCRIPT'.
           05  FILLER                   PIC X(82) VALUE SPACES.

       01  TRANS-HEADING-LINE-TWO.
           05  FILLER                   PIC X(10)   VALUE SPACES.
           05  FILLER                   PIC X(9)    VALUE 'COURSE # '.
           05  FILLER                   PIC X(9)    VALUE 'CREDITS  '.
           05  FILLER                   PIC X(5)    VALUE 'GRADE'.
           05  FILLER                   PIC X(99)   VALUE SPACES.

       01  DETAIL-LINE.
           05  FILLER                   PIC X(13)   VALUE SPACES.
           05  DET-COURSE               PIC X(3).
           05  FILLER                   PIC X(9)    VALUE SPACES.
           05  DET-CREDITS              PIC 9.
           05  FILLER                   PIC X(5)    VALUE SPACES.
           05  DET-GRADE                PIC X.
           05  FILLER                   PIC X(100) VALUE SPACES.

       01  LAST-LINE.
           05  FILLER                   PIC X(16)   VALUE SPACES.
           05  FILLER                   PIC X(9)    VALUE 'AVERAGE: '.
           05  LAST-GPA                 PIC 9.99.
           05  FILLER                   PIC X(4)    VALUE SPACES.
           05  LAST-DEANS-LIST          PIC X(12)   VALUE SPACES.
           05  FILLER                   PIC X(87)   VALUE SPACES.

       01  DEANS-LIST-HEADING-LINE-ONE.
           05  FILLER                   PIC X(20)   VALUE SPACES.
           05  FILLER                   PIC X(26)
                         VALUE 'STUDENTS ON THE DEANS LIST'.
           05  FILLER                   PIC X(86)   VALUE SPACES.

       01  DEANS-LIST-HEADING-LINE-TWO.
           05  FILLER                   PIC X(25)    VALUE SPACES.
           05  FILLER                   PIC X(5)     VALUE 'TOTAL'.
           05  FILLER                   PIC X(5)     VALUE SPACES.
           05  FILLER                   PIC X(5)     VALUE 'TOTAL'.
           05  FILLER                   PIC X(4)     VALUE SPACES.
           05  FILLER                   PIC X(7)     VALUE 'QUALITY'.
```

Figure 11.12 *(continued)*

```
          05  FILLER                   PIC X(81)    VALUE SPACES.

      01  DEANS-LIST-HEADING-LINE-THREE.
          05  FILLER                   PIC X        VALUE SPACES.
          05  FILLER                   PIC X(4)     VALUE 'NAME'.
          05  FILLER                   PIC X(19)    VALUE SPACES.
          05  FILLER                   PIC X(7)     VALUE 'COURSES'.
          05  FILLER                   PIC X(3)     VALUE SPACES.
          05  FILLER                   PIC X(7)     VALUE 'CREDITS'.
          05  FILLER                   PIC X(4)     VALUE SPACES.
          05  FILLER                   PIC X(6)     VALUE 'POINTS'.
          05  FILLER                   PIC X(5)     VALUE SPACES.
          05  FILLER                   PIC X(3)     VALUE 'GPA'.
          05  FILLER                   PIC X(73)    VALUE SPACES.

      01  DEANS-LIST-DETAIL-LINE.
          05  FILLER                   PIC X        VALUE SPACES.
          05  DL-DET-NAME              PIC X(19).
          05  FILLER                   PIC X(7)     VALUE SPACES.
          05  DL-DET-TOT-COURSES       PIC Z9.
          05  FILLER                   PIC X(7)     VALUE SPACES.
          05  DL-DET-TOT-CREDITS       PIC ZZ9.
          05  FILLER                   PIC X(8)     VALUE SPACES.
          05  DL-DET-TOT-QUAL-POINTS   PIC ZZ9.
          05  FILLER                   PIC X(6)     VALUE SPACES.
          05  DL-DET-GPA               PIC 9.99.
          05  FILLER                   PIC X(72)    VALUE SPACES.

      PROCEDURE DIVISION.
      100-PROCESS-STUDENT-RECORDS.
          OPEN INPUT  STUDENT-FILE
               OUTPUT PRINT-FILE.
          PERFORM UNTIL END-OF-FILE-SWITCH = 'YES'
              READ STUDENT-FILE
                  AT END
                      MOVE 'YES' TO END-OF-FILE-SWITCH
                  NOT AT END
                      PERFORM 200-CREATE-TRANSCRIPT
              END-READ
          END-PERFORM.
          PERFORM 300-WRITE-DEANS-LIST.
          CLOSE STUDENT-FILE
                PRINT-FILE.
          STOP RUN.

      200-CREATE-TRANSCRIPT.
          PERFORM 210-WRITE-TRANS-HEADING.
          MOVE ZERO TO IND-TOTAL-QUAL-POINTS IND-TOTAL-CREDITS.
          PERFORM 220-PROCESS-COURSES
              VARYING COURSE-SUB FROM 1 BY 1
                  UNTIL COURSE-SUB > ST-NUMBER-OF-COURSES.
```

In-line PERFORM statement and false-condition branch drives the program

PERFORM VARYING statement processes all entries in course table

Figure 11.12 *(continued)*

```
    COMPUTE IND-GRADE-POINT-AVERAGE ROUNDED
        = IND-TOTAL-QUAL-POINTS / IND-TOTAL-CREDITS
        SIZE ERROR DISPLAY 'SIZE ERROR ON GPA'
    END-COMPUTE.
    PERFORM 250-WRITE-GPA.
    IF DEANS-LIST
        PERFORM 260-ADD-TO-DEANS-LIST
    END-IF.

210-WRITE-TRANS-HEADING.
    MOVE ST-NAME TO HDG-NAME.
    WRITE PRINT-LINE FROM TRANS-HEADING-LINE-ONE
        AFTER ADVANCING PAGE.
    WRITE PRINT-LINE FROM TRANS-HEADING-LINE-TWO
        AFTER ADVANCING 2 LINES.

220-PROCESS-COURSES.
    PERFORM 230-INCREMENT-COUNTERS.
    PERFORM 240-WRITE-DETAIL-LINE.

230-INCREMENT-COUNTERS.
    EVALUATE ST-COURSE-GRADE (COURSE-SUB)
       WHEN 'A'
           MOVE 4 TO IND-MULTIPLIER
       WHEN 'B'
           MOVE 3 TO IND-MULTIPLIER
       WHEN 'C'
           MOVE 2 TO IND-MULTIPLIER
       WHEN 'D'
           MOVE 1 TO IND-MULTIPLIER
       WHEN OTHER
           MOVE 0 TO IND-MULTIPLIER
           DISPLAY 'INVALID COURSE GRADE'
    END-EVALUATE.
    COMPUTE IND-TOTAL-QUAL-POINTS = IND-TOTAL-QUAL-POINTS
        + ST-COURSE-CREDITS (COURSE-SUB) * IND-MULTIPLIER
        SIZE ERROR DISPLAY 'SIZE ERROR ON TOTAL QUALITY POINTS'
    END-COMPUTE.
    ADD ST-COURSE-CREDITS (COURSE-SUB) TO IND-TOTAL-CREDITS
        SIZE ERROR DISPLAY 'SIZE ERROR ON TOTAL CREDITS'
    END-ADD.

240-WRITE-DETAIL-LINE.
    MOVE ST-COURSE-NUMBER (COURSE-SUB) TO DET-COURSE.
    MOVE ST-COURSE-CREDITS (COURSE-SUB) TO DET-CREDITS.
    MOVE ST-COURSE-GRADE (COURSE-SUB) TO DET-GRADE.
    WRITE PRINT-LINE FROM DETAIL-LINE.

250-WRITE-GPA.
    MOVE IND-GRADE-POINT-AVERAGE TO LAST-GPA.
```

COURSE-SUB varies during execution of WRITE-DETAIL-LINE

Figure 11.12 *(continued)*

```
       IF DEANS-LIST
           MOVE '*DEANS LIST*' TO LAST-DEANS-LIST
       ELSE
           MOVE SPACES TO LAST-DEANS-LIST
       END-IF.
       WRITE PRINT-LINE FROM LAST-LINE
           AFTER ADVANCING 2 LINES.

   260-ADD-TO-DEANS-LIST.
       IF STUDENTS-ON-DEANS-LIST > 100
           DISPLAY 'DEAN LIST TABLE EXCEEDED'
       ELSE
           ADD 1 TO STUDENTS-ON-DEANS-LIST
           ADD 1 TO DEAN-SUB
           MOVE ST-NAME TO DL-NAME (DEAN-SUB)
           MOVE ST-NUMBER-OF-COURSES TO DL-COURSES (DEAN-SUB)
           MOVE IND-TOTAL-CREDITS TO DL-CREDITS (DEAN-SUB)
           MOVE IND-TOTAL-QUAL-POINTS TO DL-QUAL-POINTS (DEAN-SUB)
           MOVE IND-GRADE-POINT-AVERAGE TO DL-GPA (DEAN-SUB)
       END-IF.

   300-WRITE-DEANS-LIST.
       PERFORM 310-WRITE-DEANS-LIST-HEADINGS.
       PERFORM 320-WRITE-DEANS-LIST-DETAILS
           VARYING DEAN-SUB FROM 1 BY 1
               UNTIL DEAN-SUB > STUDENTS-ON-DEANS-LIST.

   310-WRITE-DEANS-LIST-HEADINGS.
       WRITE PRINT-LINE FROM DEANS-LIST-HEADING-LINE-ONE
           AFTER ADVANCING PAGE.
       WRITE PRINT-LINE FROM DEANS-LIST-HEADING-LINE-TWO
           AFTER ADVANCING 2 LINES.
       WRITE PRINT-LINE FROM DEANS-LIST-HEADING-LINE-THREE.
       MOVE SPACES TO PRINT-LINE.
       WRITE PRINT-LINE.

   320-WRITE-DEANS-LIST-DETAILS.
       MOVE DL-NAME (DEAN-SUB) TO DL-DET-NAME.
       MOVE DL-COURSES (DEAN-SUB) TO DL-DET-TOT-COURSES.
       MOVE DL-CREDITS (DEAN-SUB) TO DL-DET-TOT-CREDITS.
       MOVE DL-QUAL-POINTS (DEAN-SUB) TO DL-DET-TOT-QUAL-POINTS.
       MOVE DL-GPA (DEAN-SUB) TO DL-DET-GPA.
       WRITE PRINT-LINE FROM DEANS-LIST-DETAIL-LINE.
```

Increments number of entries in variable-length table (ADD 1 TO STUDENTS-ON-DEANS-LIST)

Produces the dean's list (PERFORM 320-WRITE-DEANS-LIST-DETAILS … UNTIL DEAN-SUB > STUDENTS-ON-DEANS-LIST)

4. The computation of the grade point average is described as follows:
   a. The counters IND-TOTAL-QUALITY-POINTS and IND-TOTAL-CREDITS are set to zero by the MOVE ZERO statement in line 148.
   b. The PERFORM VARYING statement in lines 149–151 executes the paragraph 220-PROCESS-COURSES, which in turn performs two lower-level paragraphs for every course in the current record, one course at a time.
   c. Each time the paragraph 230-INCREMENT-COUNTERS is executed, the course multiplier is determined (4 for an A, 3 for a B, and so on), after which the cumulative values of the quality points and credits are updated.
   d. The PERFORM VARYING terminates, after which the GPA is determined in lines 152–155.
5. The definition of a counter STUDENTS-ON-DEANS-LIST (line 39) and the definition of the associated DEANS-LIST-TABLE in lines 48–54 to hold data for qualifying students. The IF statement in lines 157–159 determines whether the current student qualifies for the dean's list, then executes paragraph 260-ADD-TO-DEANS-LIST (lines 210–221) to increment the counter and move the student's values to the appropriate place in the table.
6. The PERFORM VARYING statement in lines 225–227 to produce the dean's list based on the number of students (i.e., the final value of STUDENTS-ON-DEANS-LIST) and the entries in the table.

Indexes Versus Subscripts

The transcript program just completed illustrates the basics of table processing, and as such goes a long way toward increasing your proficiency in COBOL. There is, however, a good deal more to learn about tables, and so we return to the syntax of the OCCURS clause shown earlier in the chapter.

The OCCURS clause includes an optional INDEXED BY entry to define an ***index*** for use with a particular table. An index is conceptually the same as a subscript in that both reference an entry in a table. Indexes, however, produce more efficient object code and are preferred (by some programmers) for that reason. The difference is subtle; an index represents a ***displacement*** (the number of positions into a table), whereas a subscript indicates an occurrence. Consider:

```
05  ST-COURSE-INFO OCCURS 10 TIMES
    INDEXED BY COURSE-INDEX.
    10  ST-COURSE-NUMBER           PIC X(3).
    10  ST-COURSE-GRADE            PIC X.
    10  ST-COURSE-CREDITS          PIC 99.
```

The COBOL statements establish a table with 10 entries which occupy a total of 60 positions in memory. Valid subscripts for ST-COURSE-INFO are 1, 2, 3, . . . 10, because the table entries occur 10 times. The first occurrence of ST-COURSE-INFO is at the start of the table (displacement zero), the second occurrence begins 6 bytes into the table, the third occurrence 12 bytes into the table, and so on. The value of the index is the value of the displacement, that is, the number of positions into a table to the entry in question; hence valid displacements for ST-COURSE-INFO are 0, 6, 12, . . . 54.

Fortunately, you need not be concerned with the actual value (displacement) of an index, and can regard it conceptually as a subscript. In other words, you will indicate index values of 1, 2, 3, and so on, which will be converted by the compiler to internal displacements of 0, 6, 12, and so on. Indexes can not, however, be initialized with a MOVE statement, nor can they be incremented with an ADD statement. The SET statement is used instead.

The SET Statement

The **SET** statement has two formats and is used only with indexes.

Format 1

```
SET {identifier-1 [, identifier-2] . . . }  TO {identifier-3 }
    {index-name-1 [, index-name-2] . . . }     {index-name-3 }
                                               {integer-1    }
```

Format 2

```
SET index-name-4 [, index-name-5] . . . {UP BY  } {identifier-4}
                                        {DOWN BY} {integer-2   }
```

Figures 11.13 and 11.14 compare indexes and subscripts. Figure 11.13a depicts the definition of a table without an index, which in turn requires the definition of a subscript elsewhere in the Data Division. Figure 11.13b uses a PERFORM VARYING statement to manipulate this table (in conjunction with COURSE-SUBSCRIPT), while Figure 11.13c shows the PERFORM TIMES statement to accomplish the same objective. The latter is yet another form of the PERFORM statement and performs the designated procedure (or in-line statement) the indicated number of times. It is less convenient than a comparable PERFORM VARYING statement as the programmer has to vary the subscript (index) explicitly.

Figure 11.14 contains parallel code, except that the table is defined in Figure 11.14a with an index (so there is no need to define a subscript). Figure 11.14b is virtually identical to its predecessor in that the PERFORM VARYING statement can manipulate either subscripts or indexes. Finally, Figure 11.14c shows the alternate (less desirable) way to process the table. Observe, therefore, the use of SET statements to initialize and increment the index (as opposed to the MOVE and ADD statements in Figure 11.13c.

Indexing is not required in COBOL, and thus you can choose between subscripts and indexes in any given application. Indeed, you may wonder why bother with indexes at all, if they provide the same capability as subscripts. The answer is twofold:

1. Indexes provide more efficient object code than subscripts.
2. Indexes are required for SEARCH and SEARCH ALL, two powerful statements that are presented in Chapter 12.

Differences between indexes and subscripts are summarized in Table 11.1.

Table 11.1 Indexes versus Subscripts

INDEXES	SUBSCRIPTS
Defined with a specific table; can be used only with the table with which they are defined	Defined in Working-Storage; the same subscript can be used with multiple tables although this is not recommended
Initialized and incremented via the SET statement; can also be manipulated in PERFORM statements	May not be used with SET statements (MOVE and ADD are used instead); can also be manipulated in PERFORM statements
Provide more efficient object code than subscripts	USAGE IS COMPUTATIONAL makes subscripts more efficient, although indexes are still faster

Figure 11.13 Indexes versus Subscripts (Subscripts)

```
    05  ST-NUMBER-OF-COURSES          PIC 99.
    05  ST-COURSE-INFO OCCURS 1 TO 8 TIMES
        DEPENDING ON ST-NUMBER-OF-COURSES.
        10  ST-COURSE-NUMBER          PIC X(3).
        10  ST-COURSE-GRADE           PIC X.
        10  ST-COURSE-CREDITS         PIC 99.
    .
     .
      .
    05  COURSE-SUBSCRIPT              PIC S9(4)  COMP.
```

Subscript defined separately in Working-Storage

(a) Table Definition

```
    PERFORM WRITE-COURSE-DATA
        VARYING COURSE-SUBSCRIPT FROM 1 BY 1
            UNTIL COURSE-SUBSCRIPT > ST-NUMBER-OF-COURSES.
    .
     .
      .
WRITE-COURSE-DATA.
    MOVE ST-COURSE-NUMBER (COURSE-SUBSCRIPT) TO PL-NUMBER.
    MOVE ST-COURSE-GRADE (COURSE-SUBSCRIPT) TO PL-GRADE.
    WRITE PRINT-LINE FROM PRINT-LINE-ONE
        AFTER ADVANCING 1 LINE.
```

(b) PERFORM VARYING

```
    MOVE 1 TO COURSE-SUBSCRIPT.
    PERFORM WRITE-COURSE-DATA ST-NUMBER-OF-COURSES TIMES.
    .
     .
      .
WRITE-COURSE-DATA.
    MOVE ST-COURSE-NUMBER (COURSE-SUBSCRIPT) TO PL-NUMBER.
    MOVE ST-COURSE-GRADE (COURSE-SUBSCRIPT) TO PL-GRADE.
    WRITE PRINT-LINE FROM PRINT-LINE-ONE
        AFTER ADVANCING 1 LINE.
    ADD 1 TO COURSE-SUBSCRIPT.
```

(c) PERFORM TIMES

Figure 11.14 Indexes versus Subscripts (Indexes)

```
05  ST-NUMBER-OF-COURSES            PIC 99.
05  ST-COURSE-INFO OCCURS 1 TO 8 TIMES
    DEPENDING ON ST-NUMBER-OF-COURSES
    INDEXED BY COURSE-INDEX.
    10  ST-COURSE-NUMBER            PIC X(3).
    10  ST-COURSE-GRADE             PIC X.
    10  ST-COURSE-CREDITS           PIC 99.
```

Index is defined with table

(a) Table Definition

```
PERFORM WRITE-COURSE-DATA
    VARYING COURSE-INDEX FROM 1 BY 1
        UNTIL COURSE-INDEX > ST-NUMBER-OF-COURSES.
.
  .
    .
WRITE-COURSE-DATA.
    MOVE ST-COURSE-NUMBER (COURSE-INDEX) TO PL-NUMBER.
    MOVE ST-COURSE-GRADE (COURSE-INDEX) TO PL-GRADE.
    WRITE PRINT-LINE FROM PRINT-LINE-ONE
        AFTER ADVANCING 1 LINE.
```

(b) PERFORM VARYING

```
SET COURSE-INDEX TO 1.
PERFORM WRITE-COURSE-DATA ST-NUMBER-OF-COURSES TIMES.
.
  .
    .
WRITE-COURSE-DATA.
    MOVE ST-COURSE-NUMBER (COURSE-INDEX) TO PL-NUMBER.
    MOVE ST-COURSE-GRADE (COURSE-INDEX) TO PL-GRADE.
    WRITE PRINT-LINE FROM PRINT-LINE-ONE
        AFTER ADVANCING 1 LINE.
    SET COURSE-INDEX UP BY 1.
```

Index is initialized by a SET statement

(c) PERFORM TIMES

LIMITATIONS OF COBOL-74

COBOL-85 introduced several minor changes in conjunction with table processing. The new compiler allows seven levels of subscripting as opposed to the earlier limit of three, but given that the typical programmer seldom uses three-level tables, this extension is of little practical benefit. (Multiple-level tables are covered in Chapter 13.) The OCCURS DEPENDING ON clause may specify a value of zero, whereas at least one occurrence was required in COBOL-74.

A more significant change is the introduction of relative subscripting (as explained in Figure 11.6), enabling the reference DATA-NAME (SUBSCRIPT ± integer). Relative subscripting was not permitted in COBOL-74 (although relative indexing was).

SUMMARY

Points to Remember

- A table is a grouping of similar data whose values are stored in contiguous storage locations and assigned a single name. Tables are implemented in COBOL through the OCCURS clause with subscripts or indexes used to reference individual items in a table. The OCCURS DEPENDING ON clause implements a variable-length table.
- An index is conceptually the same as a subscript but provides more efficient object code. Indexes are manipulated with the SET statement, whereas subscripts are initialized with a MOVE statement and incremented with an ADD statement.
- The PERFORM VARYING statement manipulates an index or a subscript to execute a procedure or series of in-line statements. Omission of the TEST BEFORE and TEST AFTER clauses defaults to TEST BEFORE and corresponds to the COBOL-74 implementation.
- The PERFORM TIMES statement also provides for repeated execution of a procedure or in-line statement, but requires the programmer to explicitly vary the value of the subscript or index.
- The optional USAGE IS COMPUTATIONAL clause is used to improve the efficiency of a program's generated object code, but does not affect its logic.

Key Words and Concepts

Displacement
Fixed-length record
Index
Relative indexing
Relative subscripting
Subscript
Table
Variable-length record
Variable-length table

COBOL Elements

```
BY
FROM
INDEXED BY
OCCURS
OCCURS DEPENDING ON
PERFORM TIMES
PERFORM VARYING
SET
TEST AFTER
TEST BEFORE
UNTIL
USAGE IS COMPUTATIONAL
```

FILL-IN

1. A table is defined through the ______________ clause.
2. Entries in a table may be referenced by either a ________________ or an ________________.
3. A ________________ length table is defined by the ________________ ______________ ______________ clause.
4. The USAGE clause is a (required/optional) entry for a subscript.
5. A table (must/may) be defined with an index.
6. (Subscripts/indexes) are manipulated with a SET statement.
7. Arithmetic (is/is not) permitted for subscripts and indexes.
8. ______________ levels of subscripting are permitted in COBOL-85.
9. The TEST BEFORE clause (changes/does not change) the effect of a PERFORM VARYING statement.
10. The OCCURS DEPENDING ON, ASCENDING/DESCENDING KEY, and INDEXED BY clauses are (optional/required) entries in an OCCURS clause.

TRUE/FALSE

1. Tables are established by a DIMENSION statement.
2. The same entry may not contain both an OCCURS clause and a PICTURE clause.
3. When using subscripts, a space is required between a data name and the left parenthesis.
4. The USAGE clause is required when defining a subscript in Working-Storage.
5. The entry, DATA-NAME (0) would not cause a compilation error, provided that an OCCURS clause had been used in the associated definition.

6. The same subscript can be used to reference different tables.
7. The same index can be used to reference different tables
8. A subscript may be a constant or a variable.
9. All records in the same file must be the same length.
10. The SET statement is used to manipulate subscripts or indexes.
11. An index may be modified by either an ADD or a MOVE statement.
12. The PERFORM VARYING statement may manipulate both subscripts and indexes.

PROBLEMS

1. Indicate which entries are incorrectly subscripted. Assume that SUB1 has been set to 5, and that the following entry applies:

   ```
   05 SALES-TABLE OCCURS 12 TIMES PIC 9(5).
   ```

   a. SALES-TABLE (1)
   b. SALES-TABLE (15)
   c. SALES-TABLE (0)
   d. SALES-TABLE (SUB1)
   e. SALES-TABLE(SUB1)
   f. SALES-TABLE (5)
   g. SALES-TABLE (SUB1, SUB2)
   h. SALES-TABLE (3)
   i. SALES-TABLE (3)
   j. SALES-TABLE (SUB1 + 1)

2. How many times will PARAGRAPH-A be executed by each of the following PERFORM statements?

   a.
   ```
   PERFORM PARAGRAPH-A
         VARYING SUBSCRIPT FROM 1 BY 1
             UNTIL SUBSCRIPT > 5.
   ```

   b.
   ```
   PERFORM PARAGRAPH-A
         VARYING SUBSCRIPT FROM 1 BY 1
             WITH TEST BEFORE
                 UNTIL SUBSCRIPT > 5.
   ```

   c.
   ```
   PERFORM PARAGRAPH-A
         VARYING SUBSCRIPT FROM 1 BY 1
             WITH TEST AFTER
                 UNTIL SUBSCRIPT > 5.
   ```

   d.
   ```
   PERFORM PARAGRAPH-A
         VARYING SUBSCRIPT FROM 1 BY 1
             UNTIL SUBSCRIPT = 5.
   ```

   e.
   ```
   PERFORM PARAGRAPH-A
         VARYING SUBSCRIPT FROM 1 BY 1
             WITH TEST BEFORE
                   UNTIL SUBSCRIPT = 5.
   ```

f.
```
PERFORM PARAGRAPH-A
    VARYING SUBSCRIPT FROM 1 BY 1
        WITH TEST AFTER
            UNTIL SUBSCRIPT = 5.
```

3. Given the following Working-Storage entries:

```
01  SAMPLE-TABLES.
    05  FIRST-TABLE OCCURS 10 TIMES
        INDEXED BY FIRST-INDEX.
        10  FIRST-TABLE-ENTRY        PIC X(5).
    05  SECOND-TABLE OCCURS 10 TIMES
        INDEXED BY SECOND-INDEX.
        10  SECOND-TABLE-ENTRY       PIC X(5).

01  SUBSCRIPT-ENTRIES.
    05  FIRST-SUBSCRIPT              PIC 9(4).
    05  SECOND-SUBSCRIPT             PIC 9(4).
```

Indicate whether the following table references are valid syntactically.

a. FIRST-TABLE-ENTRY (FIRST-INDEX)

b. FIRST-TABLE-ENTRY (FIRST-SUBSCRIPT)

c. SECOND-TABLE-ENTRY (FIRST-INDEX)

d. SECOND-TABLE-ENTRY (SECOND-INDEX)

e. SECOND-TABLE-ENTRY (FIRST-SUBSCRIPT)

f. SECOND-TABLE-ENTRY (SECOND-SUBSCRIPT)

g. FIRST-TABLE-ENTRY (FIRST-INDEX + 1)

h. FIRST-TABLE-ENTRY (FIRST-SUBSCRIPT + 1)

Indicate whether the following Procedure Division statements are valid.

i. MOVE 1 TO FIRST-SUBSCRIPT

j. SET FIRST-SUBSCRIPT TO 1

k. MOVE 1 TO FIRST-INDEX

l. SET FIRST-INDEX TO 1

m. SET FIRST-INDEX UP BY 1

n. ADD 1 TO FIRST-INDEX

4. Use the general format of the OCCURS clause to determine whether the following are valid entries (the level number has been omitted in each instance):

a. `TABLE-ENTRY OCCURS 4 TIMES.`

b. `TABLE-ENTRY OCCURS 4.`

c.
```
TABLE-ENTRY OCCURS 3 TO 30 TIMES
  DEPENDING ON NUMBER-OF-TRANS.
```

d.
```
TABLE-ENTRY OCCURS 5 TIMES
  INDEXED BY TABLE-INDEX.
```

e.
```
TABLE-ENTRY OCCURS 5 TIMES
  SUBSCRIPTED BY TABLE-SUBSCRIPT.
```

f.
```
TABLE-ENTRY OCCURS 5 TO 50 TIMES
    DEPENDING ON NUMBER-OF-TRANSACTIONS
    INDEXED BY TABLE-INDEX.
```

g.
```
TABLE-ENTRY OCCURS 6 TIMES
    ASCENDING KEY TABLE-CODE
    INDEXED TABLE-INDEX.
```

h.
```
TABLE-ENTRY OCCURS 6 TIMES
    ASCENDING KEY TABLE-CODE-1
    DESCENDING KEY TABLE-CODE-2 INDEXED BY TABLE-INDEX.
```

5. How many storage positions are allocated for each of the following table definitions? Show an appropriate schematic indicating storage assignment for each table.

a.
```
01  STATE-TABLE.
    05  STATE-NAME OCCURS 50 TIMES          PIC X(15).
    05  STATE-POPULATION OCCURS 50 TIMES    PIC 9(8).
```

b.
```
01  STATE-TABLE.
    05  NAME-POPULATION OCCURS 50 TIMES.
        10  STATE-NAME                      PIC X(15).
        10  STATE-POPULATION                PIC 9(8).
```

6. Show Procedure Division statements to determine the largest and smallest population in POPULATION-TABLE. (Assume the table has been initialized elsewhere.) Move these values to BIGGEST and SMALLEST, respectively. Move the state names to BIG-STATE and SMALL-STATE, respectively. POPULATION-TABLE is defined as follows:

```
01  POPULATION-TABLE.
    05  POPULATION-AND-NAME OCCURS 50 TIMES
        INDEXED BY POP-INDEX.
        10  POPULATION     PIC 9(8).
        10  STATE-NAME     PIC X(15).
```

Table Lookups

CHAPTER OUTLINE

OBJECTIVES

After reading this chapter you will be able to:

- Define a table lookup and describe why it is used.
- Distinguish between a numeric, alphabetic, and alphanumeric code; describe several attributes of a good coding system.
- Distinguish between a sequential table lookup, a binary table lookup, and direct access to table entries.
- Distinguish between a table that is hard coded versus one that is input loaded.
- State the purpose of the VALUE, OCCURS, and REDEFINES clauses as they pertain to table definition and initialization.
- Define a range-step table.
- Code SEARCH and SEARCH ALL statements to implement table lookups.

OVERVIEW

One-level tables, subscripts, and indexes were introduced in Chapter 11. This chapter extends that information to include table lookups—the conversion of incoming data from a concise, coded format to a descriptive and more meaningful result.

The System Concepts section begins with a discussion of codes, then proceeds to techniques for table organization, table initialization, and table lookups. The body of the chapter covers the COBOL implementation of the conceptual material, and includes the REDEFINES, VALUE, and OCCURS clauses, and the SEARCH and SEARCH ALL statements. All of this material is effectively summarized in a COBOL program at the end of the chapter.

System Concepts

Figure 12.1 depicts a table of student major ***codes*** and the associated descriptions. Records in the storage medium contain a two-position code, whereas printed reports display the descriptive (expanded) value. The conversion is accomplished through a ***table lookup***, with the obvious advantage that less space is required to store codes rather than descriptive values. (Consider the implications for large files with thousands, perhaps millions of records.)

A second, perhaps more important, reason for using codes is to assign records to consistent classes. It is a simple matter for a data-entry clerk to look up a *unique* code for a Computer Information Systems major (e.g., 24 in Figure 12.1), and different clerks will always obtain the same code for the same major. It is far less likely that different clerks will always use identical spellings for a given major; even the same individual is apt to use different spellings at different times, especially when one begins to abbreviate. By assigning a code, rather than a descriptive value, individuals

Figure 12.1 Table of Major Codes

02	ART HISTORY
04	BIOLOGY
19	CHEMISTRY
21	CIVIL ENGINEERING
24	COMP INF SYS
32	ECONOMICS
39	FINANCE
43	MANAGEMENT
49	MARKETING
54	STATISTICS

with the same major will have a common identifying characteristic that can be subsequently processed by a program.

Types of Codes

The codes in a table may be ***numeric***, ***alphabetic***, or ***alphanumeric***. A numeric code consists entirely of digits; for example, the zip code is a numeric code familiar to all Americans. A three-digit numeric code has 1,000 possible values (from 0 through 999). In similar fashion, four- and five-digit numeric codes have 10,000 and 100,000 values, respectively.

Alphabetic codes contain only letters—for example, state abbreviations. A two-position alphabetic code has 676 possible values. (Each character can assume one of 26 values, A through Z. Thus, a two-position alphabetic code has $26 \times 26 = 26^2 = 676$ possible values. In similar fashion, a three-position alphabetic code has $26^3 =$ 17,576 possible values.)

Alphanumeric codes contain both letters and numbers—for example, license plates. Alphanumeric codes offer the advantage of providing a greater number of combinations than either pure numeric or pure alphabetic codes. A three-digit numeric code has 1,000 (10^3) variations, a three-digit alphabetic code has 17,576 (26^3) possibilities, but a three-position alphanumeric code (in which each character can be either a letter or number) has 46,656 (36^3) choices. Table 12.1 summarizes the various types of codes.

TABLE 12.1 Types of Table Codes

	SYMBOLS	NUMBER OF POSSIBLE VALUES		
CODE TYPE	**USED**	**1 POSITION**	**2 POSITIONS**	**n POSITIONS**
Numeric	0–9	$10^1 = 10$	$10^2 = 100$	10^n
Alphabetic	A–Z	$26^1 = 26$	$26^2 = 676$	26^n
Alphanumeric	A–Z, 0–9	$36^1 = 36$	$36^2 = 1{,}296$	36^n

Characteristics of Codes

A good coding system is ***precise***, ***mnemonic***, and ***expandable***. A precise code is unique; that is, it should not be possible to select alternative choices from a table of codes for a given entry. Indeed, codes are often assigned because the original attribute is not unique. Universities, for example, assign student numbers because different students may have the same name.

Good codes are mnemonic, that is, easy to remember. State abbreviations are alphabetic rather than numeric for this reason. Thus NY and TX are inherently easier to learn as abbreviations for New York and Texas than random two-digit numbers.

A coding system should also be expandable so that future additions can be easily handled. It is poor design, for example, to allocate only two positions in a record for a numeric branch office code, if 98 unique branch offices already exist.

Sequential Table Lookup

A ***table lookup*** occurs when an incoming code is compared to entries in a table in order to convert the code to an expanded value. In a ***sequential*** table lookup the entries in the table are checked in order, as shown in Figure 12.2.

Figure 12.2 Sequential Table Lookup

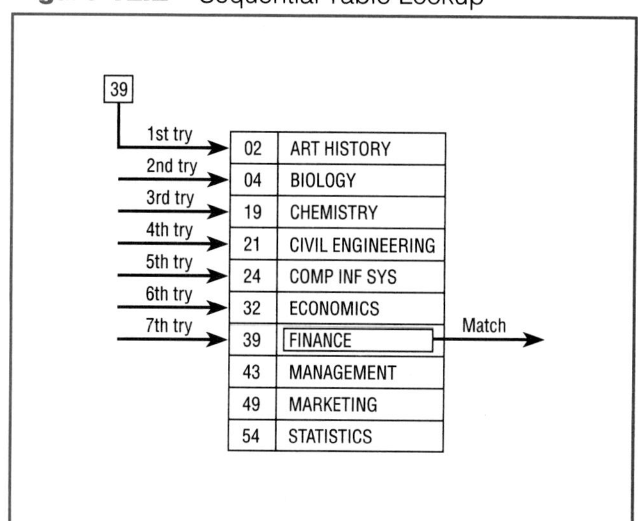

Assume, for example, an incoming code of 39. A sequential lookup begins with the first entry, then the second entry, and so on until a match is found or the table is exhausted. In this instance, 7 tries are required. On the average, a sequential table lookup requires N/2 tries (where N is the number of entries in the table) to find a match, assuming that each entry is equally likely.

The codes in Figure 12.2 were arranged sequentially. An alternative form of table organization, by ***frequency of occurrence***, is sometimes used to reduce the number of trials needed to find a match in a sequential lookup. Assume, for example, that Computer Information Systems is the most common major, followed by Management. It is reasonable, therefore, to list these majors first and second in the table. In other words, majors are listed according to the likelihood of finding a match, rather than by a strict numeric sequence. The codes in the table are still examined in order, but the table itself has been rearranged.

Many tables follow a so-called 80/20 rule; that is, 80% of the matches come from 20% of the entries. (For example, 80% of the questions raised in class may come from 20% of the students; 80% of the United States population lives in 20% of the states, and so on. The numbers 80 and 20 are approximate, but the concept is valid over a surprising number of applications.)

Organization by frequency of occurrence requires a knowledge of code probabilities that is often unavailable. Sequential organization is therefore more common.

Binary Table Lookup

A binary lookup makes the number of comparisons relatively independent of where in the table the match occurs, but requires that the entries in the table be in sequence (either ascending or descending). The action of a binary lookup is illustrated in Figure 12.3.

Figure 12.3 Binary Lookup

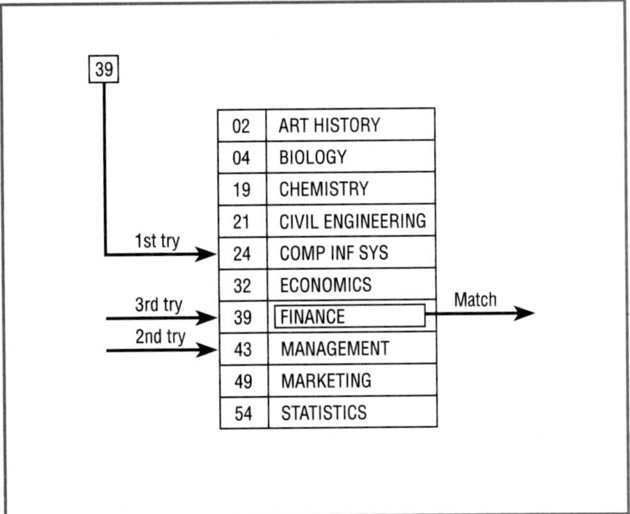

A binary search begins in the *middle* of the table, for example, at the fifth entry in Figure 12.3, and eliminates half the table with every comparison. The search then proceeds as follows:

1. Is the value of the incoming entry (the code you want to find) greater than the middle entry in the table? The answer is yes in this example in that 39 (the incoming code) is greater than 24 (the value of the middle entry). The search algorithm therefore eliminates table entries one through five.
2. There are five remaining entries (positions 6–10) that could yet contain a value equal to the incoming code. The middle (eighth) entry is selected and the comparison is made again; that is, is the value of incoming code 39 greater than the value of the eighth (middle) entry of 43? It isn't, which eliminates table entries eight through 10.
3. There are two remaining entries (positions 6–7). The middle (seventh) entry is selected, and its value of 39 matches that of the incoming code. The search is terminated.

A total of three comparisons was required to match the incoming code, 39. (If 32 had been the incoming entry, four comparisons would have been needed, but this is the *maximum* number that would ever be required for a 10-position table.) A sequential lookup, on the other hand, required seven comparisons until a match was found on 39.

If all 10 entries in a table have an equal chance of occurring, the *average* number of comparisons for a sequential search on a table of 10 entries is five. This is greater than the *maximum* number for a binary search. Indeed, as table size increases, the advantage of the binary search increases dramatically. Table 12.2 shows the maximum number of comparisons for tables with 8 to 4,095 entries.

TABLE 12.2 Required Number of Comparisons for Binary Search

NUMBER OF ELEMENTS		MAXIMUM NUMBER OF COMPARISONS
8–15	(less than 2^4)	4
16–31	(less than 2^5)	5
32–63	(less than 2^6)	6
64–127	(less than 2^7)	7
128–255	(less than 2^8)	8
256–511	(less than 2^9)	9
512–1023	(less than 2^{10})	10
1024–2047	(less than 2^{11})	11
2048–4095	(less than 2^{12})	12

Positional Organization and Direct Lookups

A ***positional table*** is a sequential table with a *consecutive* set of numeric codes. It permits immediate retrieval of a table value at the expense of unused storage space. Figure 12.4 depicts positional organization and the associated ***direct lookup***.

The table in Figure 12.4 is considerably larger than the sequential table in Figures 12.2 and 12.3. Fifty-four entries are present in Figure 12.4, as opposed to 10 in the earlier tables. Observe also that codes are not stored in a positional table; that is, the value of the associated code is the position of the descriptive value within the table. Hence, ART HISTORY is stored in the second position and has an associated code of 2; BIOLOGY is stored in the fourth position with an associated code of 4; and so forth. As can be seen, this arrangement results in considerable empty (wasted) space, as only 10 of the 54 table entries contain descriptive values.

The advantage of a positional table is that a match is found immediately; for example, to obtain the descriptive value for an incoming code of 39, you go *directly* to the 39th entry in the table. (Prudent practice dictates that the programmer ensure the incoming code is valid, that is, within the table's range, before attempting a direct lookup.)

Initializing a Table

A table is initialized in one of two ways, by hard coding it into a program, or by reading its values from a file. (A table may also be initialized through the COPY statement, which is presented in Chapter 16.) Both techniques are discussed in detail.

Hard Coding

A table may be ***hard-coded*** directly in a program as shown in Figure 12.5. This is accomplished through a combination of the VALUE, OCCURS, and REDEFINES clauses, which are explained below:

VALUE Assigns an initial value to a specified area in memory.

REDEFINES Assigns another name to previously allocated memory locations.

Figure 12.4 Positional Organization and Direct Lookup

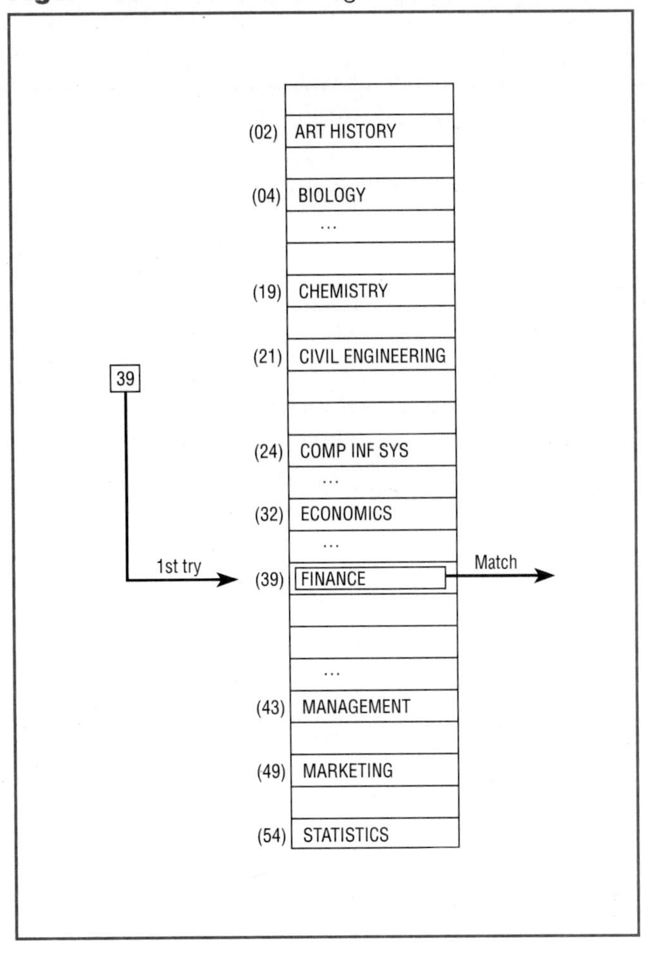

Figure 12.5 Initialization via Hard Coding

```
01  MAJOR-VALUE.
    05  FILLER            PIC X(14)    VALUE '02ART HISTORY'.
    05  FILLER            PIC X(14)    VALUE '04BIOLOGY'.
    05  FILLER            PIC X(14)    VALUE '19CHEMISTRY'.
    05  FILLER            PIC X(14)    VALUE '21CIVIL ENG'.
    05  FILLER            PIC X(14)    VALUE '24COMP INF SYS'.
    05  FILLER            PIC X(14)    VALUE '32ECONOMICS'.
    05  FILLER            PIC X(14)    VALUE '39FINANCE'.
    05  FILLER            PIC X(14)    VALUE '43MANAGEMENT'.
    05  FILLER            PIC X(14)    VALUE '49MARKETING'.
    05  FILLER            PIC X(14)    VALUE '54STATISTICS'.

01  MAJOR-TABLE REDEFINES MAJOR-VALUE.
    05  MAJORS OCCURS 10 TIMES.
        10  MAJOR-CODE    PIC 9(2).
        10  EXP-MAJOR     PIC X(12).
```

Figure 12.6 Table Initialization (Storage Schematic)

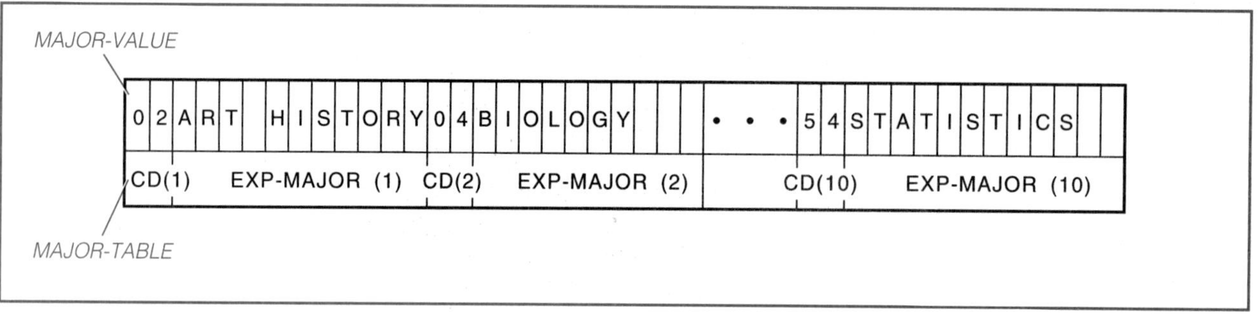

OCCURS Establishes a table, that is, permits different locations to be referenced by the same data name, but with different subscripts.

The need for the VALUE and OCCURS clauses is somewhat intuitive, whereas the REDEFINES clause is more obscure. The 01 entry MAJOR-VALUE contains 10 successive FILLER entries, each with a different VALUE clause, which collectively initialize 140 consecutive positions with the indicated values. The first two positions under MAJOR-VALUE contain 02, positions 3–14 contain ART HISTORY, positions 15 and 16 contain 04, positions 17–28 contain BIOLOGY, and so on.

The REDEFINES clause assigns a different name (MAJOR-TABLE) to these same 140 positions, and the subsequent OCCURS clause creates a table with 10 occurrences. The first two positions in the table are designated MAJOR-CODE (1) and contain 02, the first major code. Positions 3–14 are known as EXP-MAJOR (1) and contain ART HISTORY, and so on. The conceptual view of these storage locations is shown in Figure 12.6.

Input-loaded Tables

Initialization of a table through hard coding is a commonly used technique, but one that presents problems in program maintenance when the table changes. Any change to a hard-coded table requires a corresponding change in the program, which in turn requires that the program be recompiled and retested. Moreover, if the same table is used in multiple programs, then the same change has to be made in *every* program that uses the table, a time-consuming and error-prone procedure.

A better technique is to initialize the table dynamically, by reading values from a file when the program is executed. This is known as an ***input-loaded table*** and is illustrated in Figure 12.7. The Data Division entries in Figure 12.7a establish space for the variable-length major table without assigning values; the latter is accomplished at execution time by the Procedure Division entries in Figure 12.7b. (The statements in Figure 12.7b use the in-line PERFORM statement and false-condition branch of the READ statement to process a file until its records are exhausted.)

The process is further illustrated by Figure 12.8, in which records from the external file (containing the table codes and descriptive values) are read one at a time and moved to the appropriate table entries. The first record in MAJOR-CODE-FILE contains the first code and descriptive value, 02 and ART HISTORY, respectively, which are moved into MAJOR-CODE (1) and EXP-MAJOR (1). Subsequent table values are moved in similar fashion.

The advantage of an input-loaded table (over one that is hard coded) is that any change to the table is accommodated by modifying the file that contains the table values. The program (or programs) that access that table are unaffected.

Figure 12.7 Input-Loaded Table

```
FD  MAJOR-CODE-FILE
    RECORD CONTAINS 14 CHARACTERS
    DATA RECORD IS MAJOR-CODE-RECORD.
01  MAJOR-CODE-RECORD.
    05  INCOMING-FILE-CODE     PIC 9(2).
    05  INCOMING-FILE-NAME     PIC X(12).
   .
     .
       .
WORKING-STORAGE SECTION.
01  MAJOR-TABLE.
    05  MAJORS OCCURS 1 TO 10 TIMES
        DEPENDING ON NUMBER-OF-MAJORS
        INDEXED BY MAJOR-INDEX.
        10  MAJOR-CODE           PIC 9(2).
        10  EXP-MAJOR            PIC X(12).

01  NUMBER-OF-MAJORS             PIC 99     VALUE ZERO.
```

(a) Data Division Entries

```
OPEN INPUT MAJOR-CODE-FILE.
PERFORM VARYING MAJOR-INDEX FROM 1 BY 1
    UNTIL MAJOR-INDEX > 10
       OR END-OF-MAJOR-FILE = 'YES'
    READ MAJOR-CODE-FILE
       AT END
           MOVE 'YES' TO END-OF-MAJOR-FILE
       NOT AT END
           ADD 1 TO NUMBER-OF-MAJORS
           MOVE INCOMING-FILE-CODE TO MAJOR-CODE (MAJOR-INDEX)
           MOVE INCOMING-FILE-NAME TO EXP-MAJOR (MAJOR-INDEX)
    END-READ
END-PERFORM.
IF MAJOR-INDEX > 10
    DISPLAY 'MAJOR TABLE TOO SMALL'
END-IF.
CLOSE MAJOR-CODE-FILE.
```

(b) In-Line Perform

Table Lookups

Once a table has been established, the table lookup procedure is coded in the Procedure Division. We illustrate four alternative COBOL techniques: PERFORM VARYING, SEARCH, SEARCH ALL, and Direct Access to table entries.

Figure 12.8 Input-Loaded Tables

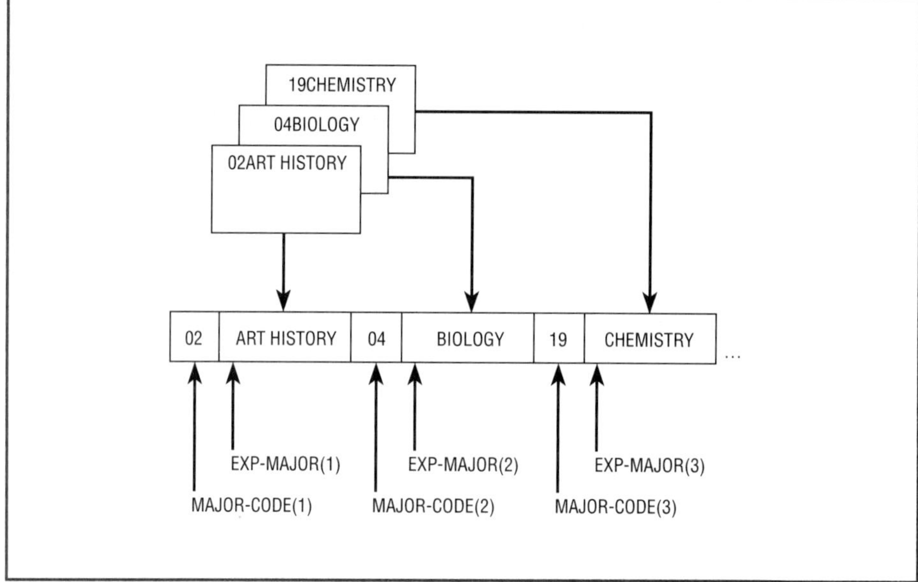

PERFORM VARYING Statement

Figure 12.9 contains the COBOL statements to implement the sequential table lookup of Figure 12.2. Entries in the table are compared sequentially to the incoming code ST-MAJOR-CODE with one of two outcomes. Either a match is found, in which case the corresponding descriptive value is moved to the output area, or the incoming code is not in the major table, which produces an appropriate error message.

The check for an invalid code is accomplished by comparing the value of the subscript WS-MAJOR-SUB, to the number of entries in the table. This type of error checking is extremely important and is one way of distinguishing between professional work and sloppy coding. (What would happen if the check were not included and an unknown code did appear?) Observe also the need to initialize both switches prior to the lookup, and how the switches are reset when the search is terminated.

SEARCH Statement

The SEARCH statement implements a sequential table lookup and is easier to use than the corresponding PERFORM VARYING statement. SEARCH has the following syntax:

```
SEARCH identifier-1 [VARYING {index-name-1}]
                             {identifier  }

     [AT END imperative-statement-1]

     WHEN condition-1 {imperative-statement-2}
                      {NEXT SENTENCE         }

    [WHEN condition-2 {imperative-statement-3}] . . .
                      {NEXT SENTENCE         }

[END-SEARCH]
```

Figure 12.9 Sequential Lookup with PERFORM VARYING

```
WORKING-STORAGE SECTION.

01  TABLE-PROCESSING-ELEMENTS.
    05  WS-MAJOR-SUB            PIC S9(4)    USAGE IS COMP.
    05  WS-FOUND-MAJOR-SWITCH   PIC X(3)     VALUE 'NO'
    05  WS-END-OF-TABLE-SWITCH  PIC X(3)     VALUE 'NO'.

01  MAJOR-VALUE.
    05  FILLER                  PIC X(14)    VALUE '02ART HISTORY'.
    05  FILLER                  PIC X(14)    VALUE '04BIOLOGY'.
    05  FILLER                  PIC X(14)    VALUE '19CHEMISTRY'.
    05  FILLER                  PIC X(14)    VALUE '21CIVIL ENG'.
    05  FILLER                  PIC X(14)    VALUE '24COMP INF SYS'.
    05  FILLER                  PIC X(14)    VALUE '32ECONOMICS'.
    05  FILLER                  PIC X(14)    VALUE '39FINANCE'.
    05  FILLER                  PIC X(14)    VALUE '43MANAGEMENT'.
    05  FILLER                  PIC X(14)    VALUE '49MARKETING'.
    05  FILLER                  PIC X(14)    VALUE '54STATISTICS'.

01  MAJOR-TABLE REDEFINES MAJOR-VALUE.
    05  MAJORS OCCURS 10 TIMES.
        10  MAJOR-CODE          PIC 9(2).
        10  EXP-MAJOR           PIC X(12).
  .
    .
      .
PROCEDURE DIVISION.
    MOVE 'NO' TO WS-FOUND-MAJOR-SWITCH  WS-END-OF-TABLE-SWITCH.
    PERFORM FIND-MAJOR
        VARYING WS-MAJOR-SUB FROM 1 BY 1
            UNTIL WS-END-OF-TABLE-SWITCH = 'YES'
               OR WS-FOUND-MAJOR-SWITCH = 'YES'.
  .
    .
      .
FIND-MAJOR.
    IF WS-MAJOR-SUB > 10
        MOVE 'YES' TO WS-END-OF-TABLE-SWITCH
        MOVE 'UNKNOWN' TO HDG-MAJOR
    ELSE
        IF ST-MAJOR-CODE = MAJOR-CODE (WS-MAJOR-SUB)
            MOVE 'YES' TO WS-FOUND-MAJOR-SWITCH
            MOVE EXP-MAJOR (WS-MAJOR-SUB) TO HDG-MAJOR
        END-IF
    END-IF.
```

PROGRAMMING TIP

Restrict Subscripts and Switches to a Single Use

Data names defined as switches and/or subscripts should be restricted to a single use. Consider:

Poor Code

```
01    SUBSCRIPT                        PIC S9(4)    COMP.
01    EOF-SWITCH                       PIC X(3)     VALUE SPACES.

      PERFORM INITIALIZE-TITLE-FILE
          UNTIL EOF-SWITCH = 'YES'.
      MOVE SPACES TO EOF-SWITCH.
      PERFORM PROCESS-EMPLOYEE-RECORDS
          UNTIL EOF-SWITCH = 'YES'.
      PERFORM COMPUTE-SALARY-HISTORY
          VARYING SUBSCRIPT FROM 1 BY 1
              UNTIL SUBSCRIPT > 3.
      PERFORM FIND-MATCH-TITLE
          VARYING SUBSCRIPT FROM 1 BY 1
              UNTIL SUBSCRIPT > 100.
```

Improved Code

```
01    PROGRAM-SUBSCRIPTS.
      05 TITLE-SUBSCRIPT               PIC S9(4)    COMP.
      05 SALARY-SUBSCRIPT              PIC S9(4)    COMP.
01    END-OF-FILE-SWITCHES.
      05 END-OF-TITLE-FILE-SWITCH      PIC X(3)     VALUE SPACES.
      05 END-OF-EMPLOYEE-FILE-SWITCH   PIC X(3)     VALUE SPACES.

      PERFORM INITIALIZE-TITLE-FILE
          UNTIL END-OF-TITLE-FILE-SWITCH = 'YES'.
      PERFORM PROCESS-EMPLOYEE-RECORDS
          UNTIL END-OF-EMPLOYEE-FILE-SWITCH = 'YES'.
      PERFORM COMPUTE-SALARY-HISTORY
          VARYING SALARY-SUBSCRIPT FROM 1 BY 1
              UNTIL SALARY-SUBSCRIPT > 3.
      PERFORM FIND-MATCHING-TITLE
          VARYING TITLE-SUBSCRIPT FROM 1 BY 1
              UNTIL TITLE-SUBSCRIPT > 100.
```

At the very least, the improved code offers superior documentation. By restricting data names to a single use, one automatically avoids such nondescript entries as EOF-SWITCH or SUBSCRIPT. Of greater impact, the improved code is more apt to be correct in that a given data name is modified or tested in fewer places within a program. Finally, if bugs do occur, the final values of the unique data names (TITLE-SUBSCRIPT and SALARY-SUBSCRIPT) will be of much greater use than the single value of SUBSCRIPT.

Identifier-1 in the SEARCH statement designates a table that contains both the OCCURS and INDEXED BY clauses. AT END is optional, but strongly recommended, to detect invalid or unknown codes. The WHEN clause specifies both a condition and an imperative sentence; the latter is executed when the condition is satisfied (that is, when a match is found.) Control passes to the statement immediately following the SEARCH statement after the WHEN condition is satisfied or the AT END clause is reached. (The VARYING option is covered in Chapter 13.)

The SEARCH statement is illustrated in Figure 12.10 (which implements the identical logic of Figure 12.9). The table definition includes the INDEXED BY clause, which is required by the SEARCH statement, and establishes values through hard coding.

The SEARCH statement compares, in sequence, entries in the MAJORS table to ST-MAJOR-CODE. If no match is found (that is, if the AT END condition is

Figure 12.10 SEARCH Statement (Sequential Lookup)

```
01  MAJOR-VALUE.
    05  FILLER             PIC X(14)    VALUE '02ART HISTORY'.
    05  FILLER             PIC X(14)    VALUE '04BIOLOGY'.
    05  FILLER             PIC X(14)    VALUE '19CHEMISTRY'.
    05  FILLER             PIC X(14)    VALUE '21CIVIL ENG'.
    05  FILLER             PIC X(14)    VALUE '24COMP INF SYS'.
    05  FILLER             PIC X(14)    VALUE '32ECONOMICS'.
    05  FILLER             PIC X(14)    VALUE '39FINANCE'.
    05  FILLER             PIC X(14)    VALUE '43MANAGEMENT'.
    05  FILLER             PIC X(14)    VALUE '49MARKETING'.
    05  FILLER             PIC X(14)    VALUE '54STATISTICS'.

01  MAJOR-TABLE REDEFINES MAJOR-VALUE.
    05  MAJORS OCCURS 10 TIMES
        INDEXED BY MAJOR-INDEX.        <-- INDEXED BY clause required
        10  MAJOR-CODE     PIC 9(2).       in table definition
        10  EXP-MAJOR      PIC X(12).
  .
    .
      .
PROCEDURE DIVISION.
  .
    .
      .
    SET MAJOR-INDEX TO 1.              <-- SET statement establishes
    SEARCH MAJORS                          starting point
        AT END
            MOVE 'UNKNOWN' TO HDG-MAJOR
        WHEN ST-MAJOR-CODE = MAJOR-CODE (MAJOR-INDEX)
            MOVE EXP-MAJOR (MAJOR-INDEX) TO HDG-MAJOR
    END-SEARCH.
```

reached), then UNKNOWN is moved to HDG-MAJOR. However, if a match does occur, [that is, if ST-MAJOR-CODE = MAJOR-CODE (MAJOR-INDEX)], the appropriate major is moved to HDG-MAJOR. The search is terminated, and control passes to the statement following the SEARCH.

The statement SET MAJOR-INDEX TO 1 is necessary to indicate the point in the table where the search is to begin, and appears before the SEARCH statement. Recall also that the SET statement must be used to modify an index; that is, it is *incorrect* to say MOVE 1 TO MAJOR-INDEX.

SEARCH ALL Statement

The SEARCH ALL statement implements a binary lookup, and is presented below:

```
SEARCH ALL identifier-1

      [AT END imperative-statement-1]

      WHEN condition-1 {imperative-statement-2}
                       {NEXT SENTENCE         }

[END SEARCH]
```

As with a sequential search statement, SEARCH ALL requires the associated table be defined with an index. In addition, *the codes in the table must be in sequence* (either ascending or descending).

The implementation of a binary search is shown in Figure 12.11, and is very similar in appearance to Figure 12.10. Observe, however, the KEY clause in the table definition to indicate the sequence in which codes appear. (In the event that codes in the table are out of sequence, COBOL will not indicate an explicit error, but the results of the search will be incorrect.) Note too that since SEARCH ALL determines its own starting position in the table, a SET statement is not used in conjunction with a binary lookup. The differences between SEARCH and SEARCH ALL are summarized in Table 12.3.

TABLE 12.3 SEARCH versus SEARCH ALL

SEARCH	SEARCH ALL
Implements a sequential lookup	Implements a binary lookup
Requires a SET statement prior to SEARCH, to establish the initial position in the table	Does not require an initial SET statement (calculates its own starting position)
Does not require codes in the table to be in any special sequence	Requires codes to be in (ascending or descending) sequence on the associated KEY clause in the table definition
Contains an optional VARYING clause (See Figure 13.18)	Does not contain a VARYING clause
May specify more than one WHEN clause	Restricted to a single WHEN clause

Direct Lookup

A positional table results in wasted space but permits a far faster table lookup in that you go *directly* to the appropriate table entry. Implementation of a direct lookup is shown in Figure 12.12.

Figure 12.11 SEARCH ALL Statement (Binary Lookup)

```
01  MAJOR-VALUE.
    05  FILLER              PIC X(14)    VALUE '02ART HISTORY'.
    05  FILLER              PIC X(14)    VALUE '04BIOLOGY'.
    05  FILLER              PIC X(14)    VALUE '19CHEMISTRY'.
    05  FILLER              PIC X(14)    VALUE '21CIVIL ENG'.
    05  FILLER              PIC X(14)    VALUE '24COMP INF SYS'.
    05  FILLER              PIC X(14)    VALUE '32ECONOMICS'.
    05  FILLER              PIC X(14)    VALUE '39FINANCE'.
    05  FILLER              PIC X(14)    VALUE '43MANAGEMENT'.
    05  FILLER              PIC X(14)    VALUE '49MARKETING'.
    05  FILLER              PIC X(14)    VALUE '54STATISTICS'.

01  MAJOR-TABLE REDEFINES MAJOR-VALUE.
    05  MAJORS OCCURS 10 TIMES
        ASCENDING KEY IS MAJOR-CODE
        INDEXED BY MAJOR-INDEX.
        10  MAJOR-CODE      PIC 9(2).
        10  EXP-MAJOR       PIC X(12).
    .
     .
      .
PROCEDURE DIVISION.
    .
     .
      .
     SEARCH ALL MAJORS
         AT END
             MOVE 'UNKNOWN' TO HDG-MAJOR
         WHEN MAJOR-CODE (MAJOR-INDEX) = ST-MAJOR-CODE
             MOVE EXP-MAJOR (MAJOR-INDEX) TO HDG-MAJOR
     END-SEARCH.
```

ASCENDING KEY required for binary search

The codes themselves are not stored in the table of descriptive values as the *position* of an entry within the table corresponds to its associated code. The direct lookup is in essence a single MOVE statement in which the descriptive value in the indicated table position is chosen. The associated IF statement ensures that the incoming code lies within the range of the table.

Range-Step Tables

A ***range-step table*** is used when the same table value is applicable to multiple search arguments—that is, when there is no longer a one-to-one correspondence between a table value and the search argument. The computation of federal income tax is a well-known example as the same tax rate is applied to an entire tax bracket; that is, there is one tax rate for all incomes less than $20,000, a different rate for incomes between $20,000 and $40,000, and so on.

The scholarship table in Figure 12.13a is another example of a range-step table in which the amount of financial aid depends on a student's grade point

Figure 12.12 Direct Access to Table Entries

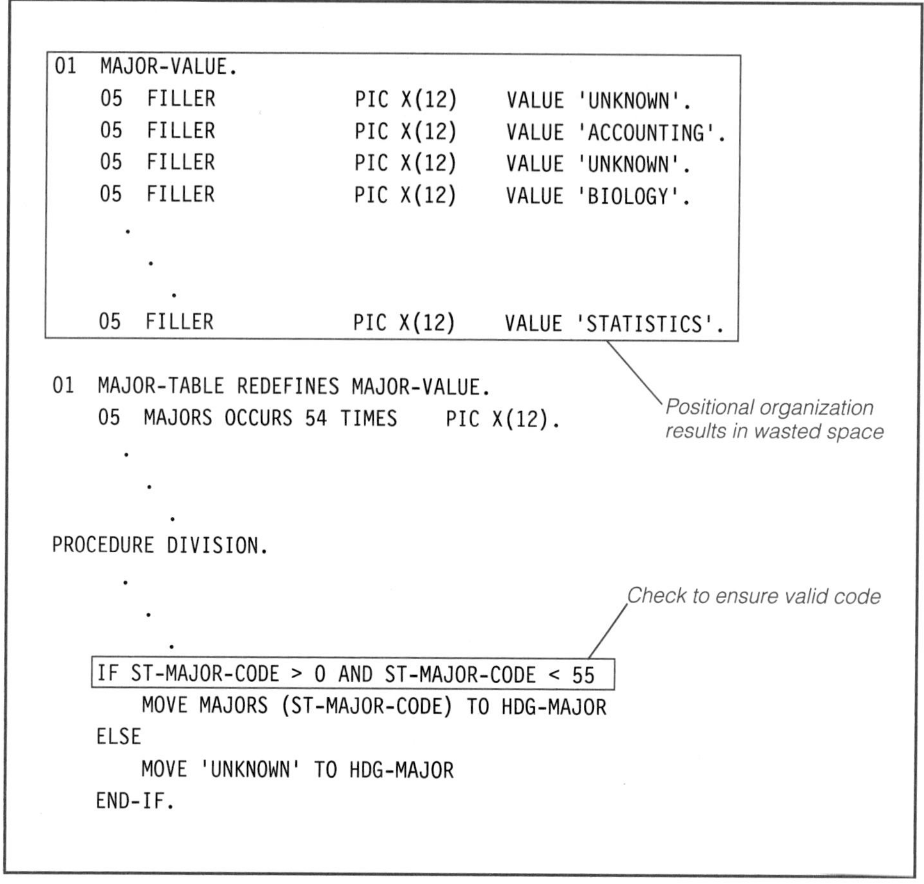

```
01  MAJOR-VALUE.
    05  FILLER              PIC X(12)    VALUE 'UNKNOWN'.
    05  FILLER              PIC X(12)    VALUE 'ACCOUNTING'.
    05  FILLER              PIC X(12)    VALUE 'UNKNOWN'.
    05  FILLER              PIC X(12)    VALUE 'BIOLOGY'.
      .
        .
          .
    05  FILLER              PIC X(12)    VALUE 'STATISTICS'.

01  MAJOR-TABLE REDEFINES MAJOR-VALUE.
    05  MAJORS OCCURS 54 TIMES    PIC X(12).
      .
        .
          .
PROCEDURE DIVISION.
      .
        .
          .
    IF ST-MAJOR-CODE > 0 AND ST-MAJOR-CODE < 55
        MOVE MAJORS (ST-MAJOR-CODE) TO HDG-MAJOR
    ELSE
        MOVE 'UNKNOWN' TO HDG-MAJOR
    END-IF.
```

Positional organization results in wasted space
Check to ensure valid code

Figure 12.13 Range-step Table

Grade Point Average	Scholarship Percentage
3.75 - 4.00	100
3.50 - 3.74	75
3.25 - 3.49	50
3.00 - 3.24	33
2.75 - 2.99	25
2.50 - 2.74	15

(a) Scholarship Table

average. Students with a GPA between 2.50 and 2.74 receive a scholarship of 15%, students with a GPA between 2.75 and 2.99 an award of 25%, and so on.

The COBOL implementation is shown in Figure 12.13b. The scholarship table is hard coded and parallels the earlier example in Figure 12.5. The GPA table includes the minimum grade point average and corresponding scholarship amount for each of the six table entries. (There is no need to include the corresponding maximum grade point average).

Figure 12.13 *(continued)*

```
 01  SCHOLARSHIP-TABLE.
     05  GPA-SCHOLARSHIP-PERCENTAGES.
         10  FILLER                PIC X(6)     VALUE '375100'.
         10  FILLER                PIC X(6)     VALUE '350075'.
         10  FILLER                PIC X(6)     VALUE '325050'.
         10  FILLER                PIC X(6)     VALUE '300033'.
         10  FILLER                PIC X(6)     VALUE '275025'.
         10  FILLER                PIC X(6)     VALUE '250015'.
     05  GPA-TABLE REDEFINES GPA-SCHOLARSHIP-PERCENTAGES
             OCCURS 6 TIMES
             INDEXED BY GPA-INDEX.
         10  GPA-MINIMUM           PIC 9V99.
         10  SCHOLARSHIP-PCT       PIC 999.
 .
   .
     .
     SET GPA-INDEX TO 1.
     SEARCH GPA-TABLE
         AT END
             MOVE ZERO TO SCHOLARSHIP-AWARD
         WHEN STUDENT-GPA >= GPA-MINIMUM (GPA-INDEX)
             MOVE SCHOLARSHIP-PCT (GPA-INDEX) TO SCHOLARSHIP-AWARD
     END-SEARCH.
```

Range-step table uses a >= condition

(b) COBOL Implementation

The SEARCH statement implements a sequential search similar to the earlier example in Figure 12.10. Note, however, that the WHEN condition uses a greater than or equal condition in accordance with the definition of the range-step table.

A Complete Example

We are ready now to incorporate the material on table lookups and initialization procedures into a complete example. Specifications are as follows:

PROGRAMMING SPECIFICATIONS

Program Name: Tables

Narrative: This program fully illustrates table processing. Two distinct means for initialization (hard coding and input loaded tables) are shown, as are three techniques for table lookups (sequential, binary, and direct access to table entries).

Input File(s): EMPLOYEE-FILE

TITLE-FILE

Employee Record:

COLUMNS	FIELD	PICTURE
1–20	Name	X(20)
21–24	Title Code	X(4)
25–27	Location Code	X(3)
28	Education Code	9
29–34	Employee Salary	9(6)

Title Record:

COLUMNS	FIELD	PICTURE
1–4	Title Code	X(4)
5–19	Descriptive Value	X(15)

Test Data: See Figure 12.14a for TITLE-FILE. See Figure 12.14b for EMPLOYEE-FILE.

Report Layout: See Figure 12.14c.

Processing Requirements:

1. Process an employee file, with each record containing the employee's salary as well as *coded* data on an employee's location, education, and title.
2. The table of location codes is to be hard-coded into the program and expanded via a sequential search. Location codes and their descriptive values are shown below:

CODE	CITY
ATL	Atlanta
BOS	Boston
CHI	Chicago
DET	Detroit
KC	Kansas City
LA	Los Angeles
MIN	Minneapolis
NY	New York
PHI	Philadelphia
SF	San Francisco

3. The education codes are to be stored in a positional table and expanded via a direct lookup. Education codes and their descriptive values are shown below:

CODE	EDUCATION
1	Some high school
2	High school diploma
3	Two-year degree
4	Four-year degree
5	Some graduate work
6	Master's degree
7	Doctorate degree
8	Other

4. The table of title codes is to be read from a file and expanded via a binary search. The title codes and their descriptive values were shown earlier in Figure 12.14a.
5. The amount of life insurance is determined by the employee's salary according to the following range-step table:

Figure 12.14 Test Data and Report

```
1000PROGRAMMER
1500DATA BASE
2000OPERATOR
2999SYSTEMS ANALYST
3499DATA DICTIONARY
```

(a) Title File

```
JACKIE CLARK        2999CHI4025000
MARGOT HUMMER       1000LA 6080000
PERCY GARCIA        2999IND3015000
CATHY BENWAY        3499ATL5110000
LOUIS NORIEGA       0100NC 9035000
JUD MCDONALD        1500ATL3065000
NELSON KERBEL       1000PHI3038000
```

(b) Employee File

EMPLOYEE	LOCATION	TITLE	EDUCATION	SALARY	LIFE INS
JACKIE CLARK	CHICAGO	SYSTEMS ANALYST	4YR DEGREE	$25,000	$80,000
MARGOT HUMMER	LOS ANGELES	PROGRAMMER	MASTERS	$80,000	$250,000
PERCY GARCIA	UNKNOWN	SYSTEMS ANALYST	2YR DEGREE	$15,000	$40,000
CATHY BENWAY	ATLANTA	DATA DICTIONARY	SOME GRAD	$110,000	$500,000
LOUIS NORIEGA	UNKNOWN	UNKNOWN	UNKNOWN	$35,000	$80,000
JUD MCDONALD	ATLANTA	DATA BASE	2YR DEGREE	$65,000	$175,000
NELSON KERBEL	PHILADELPHIA	PROGRAMMER	2YR DEGREE	$38,000	$80,000

(c) Report

SALARY RANGE	LIFE INSURANCE
<= $ 20,000	$ 40,000
$ 20,001–$ 40,000	$ 80,000
$ 40,001–$ 75,000	$ 175,000
$ 75,001–$ 100,000	$ 250,000
$ 100,001–$ 200,000	$ 500,000

6. Print a detail line for each employee with descriptive information for location, education, title, and life insurance. Single-space this report.

Program Design

The hierarchy chart for the table lookup is shown in Figure 12.15. The highest-level module, PRODUCE-EMPLOYEE-REPORT, contains three subordinates to initialize the title table (the specifications called for an input-loaded table), write a heading

Figure 12.15 Hierarchy Chart for Table-Lookup Program

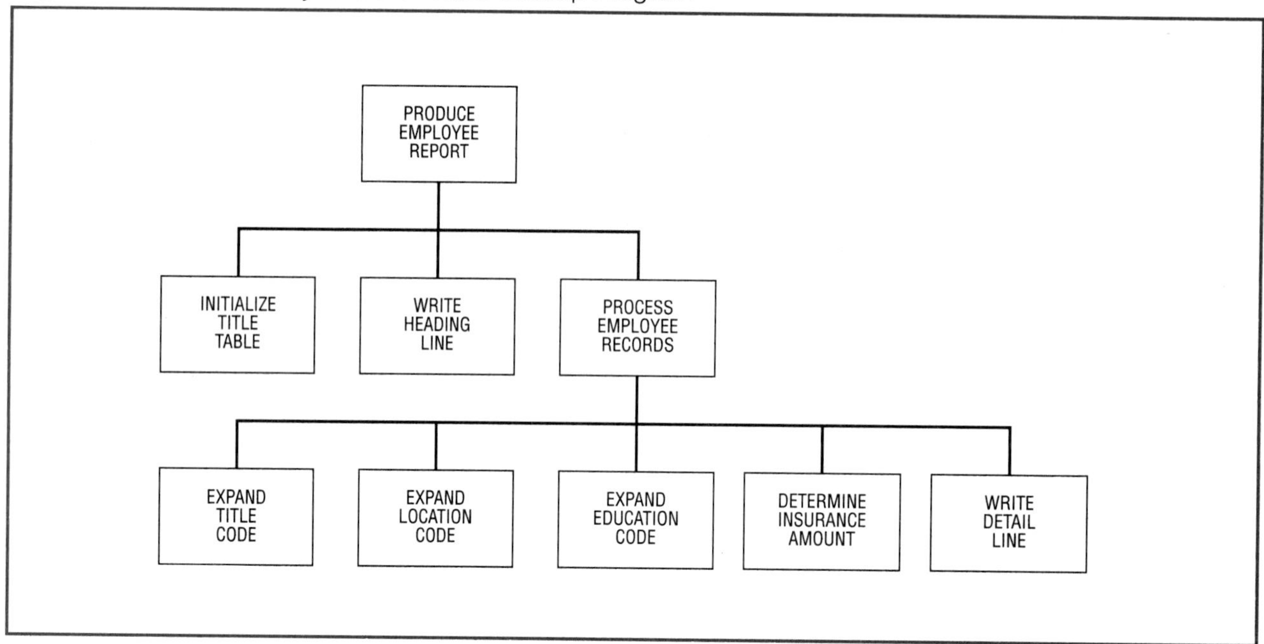

line, and process employee records; the latter includes four lower modules for the four table lookups.

The associated pseudocode is shown in Figure 12.16 and uses the in-line perform and false-condition branch first to process both the title and employee files. The title file is processed first and includes a check to ensure that the size of the title table is not exceeded. After the last record from the title file has been read, the employee file is opened and processed in its entirety. Each incoming employee record has its title, location, and education codes expanded, the amount of insurance determined, and a detail line written.

The Completed Program

The completed program is shown in Figure 12.17. The paragraphs in the Procedure Division correspond one to one with the modules in the hierarchy chart, and its logic in the program parallels that of the pseudocode just developed. The program complies with the processing requirements and also illustrates the various COBOL features presented earlier. Note the following:

1. The use of three SELECT statements for EMPLOYEE-FILE, PRINT-FILE, and TITLE-FILE; the latter is used to dynamically load the title table.

2. Omission of all optional clauses in the FD entries in the Data Division; that is, the FD contains only the file name. The optional reserved word FILLER is also omitted throughout the Data Division (see Limitations of COBOL-74 on page 357).

3. The use of READ INTO and WRITE FROM throughout the Procedure Division; this is not a requirement of table processing per se, but a coding style used throughout the text.

4. The definition of the location table in lines 43–59 through combination of the VALUES, OCCURS, and REDEFINES clauses. The location table includes the INDEXED BY clause as required by the SEARCH statement in lines 190–196.

Figure 12.16 Pseudocode for Table-Lookup Program

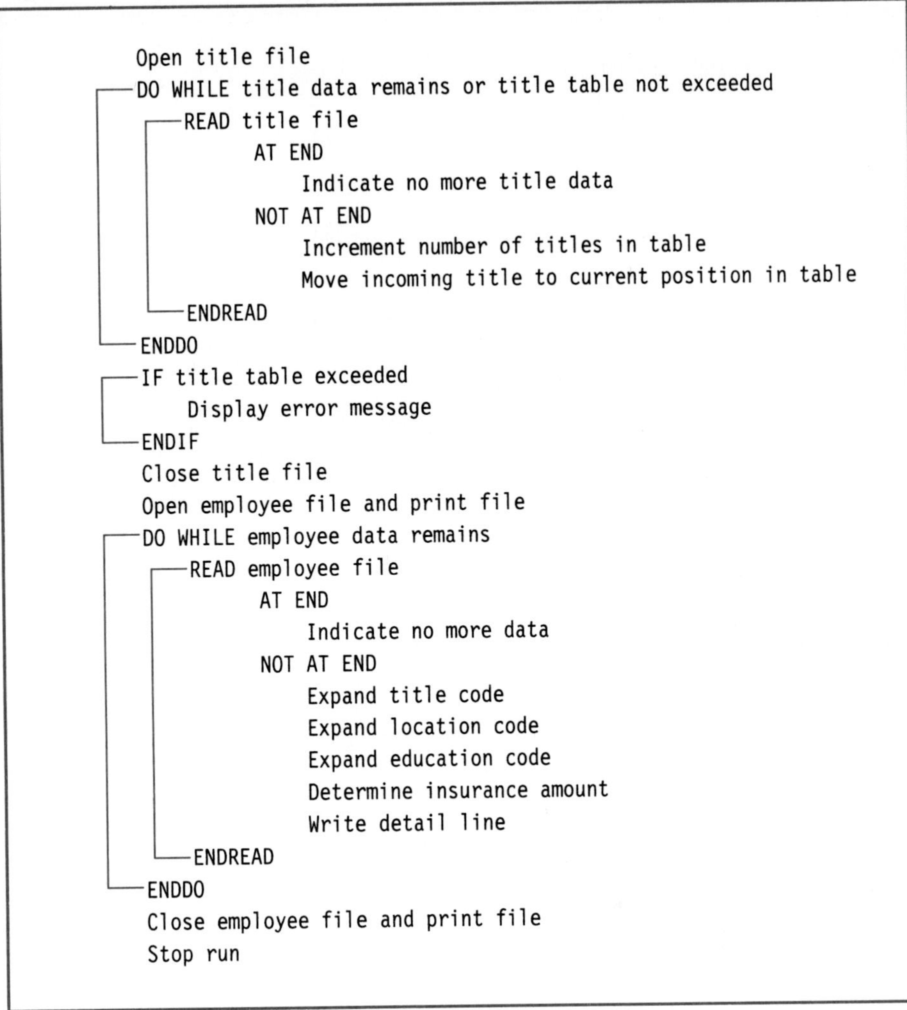

```
Open title file
DO WHILE title data remains or title table not exceeded
    READ title file
        AT END
            Indicate no more title data
        NOT AT END
            Increment number of titles in table
            Move incoming title to current position in table
    ENDREAD
ENDDO
IF title table exceeded
    Display error message
ENDIF
Close title file
Open employee file and print file
DO WHILE employee data remains
    READ employee file
        AT END
            Indicate no more data
        NOT AT END
            Expand title code
            Expand location code
            Expand education code
            Determine insurance amount
            Write detail line
    ENDREAD
ENDDO
Close employee file and print file
Stop run
```

Figure 12.17 Table-Lookup Program

```
IDENTIFICATION DIVISION.
PROGRAM-ID.    TABLES.
AUTHOR.        ROBERT GRAUER

ENVIRONMENT DIVISION.
INPUT-OUTPUT SECTION.
FILE-CONTROL.
    SELECT EMPLOYEE-FILE
        ASSIGN TO UT-S-SYSIN.
    SELECT PRINT-FILE
        ASSIGN TO UT-S-PRINT.
    SELECT TITLE-FILE
        ASSIGN TO UT-S-TITLES.

DATA DIVISION.
```

Separate file is used to initialize title table

Figure 12.17 *(continued)*

```
       FILE SECTION.
       FD  TITLE-FILE.
       01  TITLE-IN                   PIC X(19).

       FD  EMPLOYEE-FILE.
       01  EMPLOYEE-RECORD            PIC X(34).

       FD  PRINT-FILE.
       01  PRINT-LINE                 PIC X(132).

       WORKING-STORAGE SECTION.
       01                             PIC X(14)
               VALUE 'WS BEGINS HERE'.

       01  PROGRAM-SWITCHES-AND-COUNTERS.
           05  END-OF-TITLE-FILE      PIC X(3)   VALUE 'NO '.
           05  END-OF-EMP-FILE        PIC X(3)   VALUE 'NO '.
           05  NUMBER-OF-TITLES       PIC 999    VALUE ZEROS.

       01  TITLE-TABLE.
           05  TITLES OCCURS 1 TO 999 TIMES
               DEPENDING ON NUMBER-OF-TITLES
               ASCENDING KEY IS TITLE-CODE
               INDEXED BY TITLE-INDEX.
               10  TITLE-CODE         PIC X(4).
               10  TITLE-NAME         PIC X(15).

       01  LOCATION-VALUE.
           05                         PIC X(16)  VALUE 'ATLATLANTA'.
           05                         PIC X(16)  VALUE 'BOSBOSTON'.
           05                         PIC X(16)  VALUE 'CHICHICAGO'.
           05                         PIC X(16)  VALUE 'DETDETROIT'.
           05                         PIC X(16)  VALUE 'KC KANSAS CITY'.
           05                         PIC X(16)  VALUE 'LA LOS ANGELES'.
           05                         PIC X(16)  VALUE 'MINMINNEAPOLIS'.
           05                         PIC X(16)  VALUE 'NY NEW YORK'.
           05                         PIC X(16)  VALUE 'PHIPHILADELPHIA'.
           05                         PIC X(16)  VALUE 'SF SAN FRANCISCO'.

       01  LOCATION-TABLE REDEFINES LOCATION-VALUE.
           05  LOCATIONS OCCURS 10 TIMES
               INDEXED BY LOCATION-INDEX.
               10  LOCATION-CODE      PIC X(3).
               10  LOCATION-NAME      PIC X(13).

       01  EDUCATION-TABLE.
           05  EDUCATION-VALUES.
               10                     PIC X(10)     VALUE 'SOME HS'.
               10                     PIC X(10)     VALUE 'HS DIPLOMA'.
```

Different switches are defined for different files

ASCENDING KEY clause required for subsequent binary search

Location table is initialized through combination of OCCURS, VALUES, and REDEFINES clauses

Figure 12.17 *(continued)*

```
               10                 PIC X(10)     VALUE '2YR DEGREE'.
               10                 PIC X(10)     VALUE '4YR DEGREE'.
               10                 PIC X(10)     VALUE 'SOME GRAD'.
               10                 PIC X(10)     VALUE 'MASTERS'.
               10                 PIC X(10)     VALUE 'PH. D.'.
               10                 PIC X(10)     VALUE 'OTHER'.
           05  EDU-NAME REDEFINES EDUCATION-VALUES
                  OCCURS 8 TIMES    PIC X(10).

       01  SALARY-INSURANCE-TABLE.
           05  INSURANCE-VALUES.
               10                 PIC X(12)     VALUE '020000040000'.
               10                 PIC X(12)     VALUE '040000080000'.
               10                 PIC X(12)     VALUE '075000175000'.
               10                 PIC X(12)     VALUE '100000250000'.
               10                 PIC X(12)     VALUE '200000500000'.
           05  INSURANCE-TABLE REDEFINES INSURANCE-VALUES
                   OCCURS 5 TIMES
                   INDEXED BY INSURANCE-INDEX.
               10  SALARY-MAXIMUM  PIC 9(6).
               10  INSURANCE-AMOUNT PIC 9(6).

       01  HEADING-LINE.
           05                     PIC X(2)      VALUE SPACES.
           05                     PIC X(10)     VALUE 'EMPLOYEE'.
           05                     PIC X(10)     VALUE SPACES.
           05                     PIC X(8)      VALUE 'LOCATION'.
           05                     PIC X(7)      VALUE SPACES.
           05                     PIC X(5)      VALUE 'TITLE'.
           05                     PIC X(12)     VALUE SPACES.
           05                     PIC X(10)     VALUE 'EDUCATION'.
           05                     PIC X(4)      VALUE SPACES.
           05                     PIC X(6)      VALUE 'SALARY'.
           05                     PIC X(3)      VALUE SPACES.
           05                     PIC X(8)      VALUE 'LIFE INS'.
           05                     PIC X(47)     VALUE SPACES.

       01  DASHED-LINE.
           05                     PIC X(85)     VALUE ALL '-'.
           05                     PIC X(47)     VALUE SPACES.

       01  DETAIL-LINE.
           05  DET-NAME           PIC X(20).
           05                     PIC XX        VALUE SPACES.
           05  DET-LOCATION       PIC X(13).
           05                     PIC XX        VALUE SPACES.
           05  DET-TITLE          PIC X(15).
           05                     PIC XX        VALUE SPACES.
           05  DET-EDUCATION      PIC X(10).
           05                     PIC XXX       VALUE SPACES.
```

FILLER optional in COBOL-85

Figure 12.17 *(continued)*

```
        05  DET-SALARY          PIC $$$$,$$$.
        05                      PIC XX         VALUE SPACES.
        05  DET-INSURANCE       PIC $$$$,$$$.
        05                      PIC X(47)      VALUE SPACES.

    01  WS-EMPLOYEE-RECORD.
        05  EMP-NAME            PIC X(20).
        05  EMP-TITLE-CODE      PIC X(4).
        05  EMP-LOC-CODE        PIC X(3).
        05  EMP-EDUC-CODE       PIC 9.
        05  EMP-SALARY          PIC 9(6).

    01 WS-TITLE-RECORD.
        05  TITLE-IN-CODE       PIC X(4).
        05  TITLE-IN-NAME       PIC X(15).

    PROCEDURE DIVISION.
    100-PRODUCE-EMPLOYEE-REPORT.
        PERFORM 200-INITIALIZE-TITLE-TABLE.
        OPEN INPUT EMPLOYEE-FILE
             OUTPUT PRINT-FILE.
        PERFORM 300-WRITE-HEADING-LINES.
        PERFORM UNTIL END-OF-EMP-FILE = 'YES'
            READ EMPLOYEE-FILE INTO WS-EMPLOYEE-RECORD
                AT END
                    MOVE 'YES' TO END-OF-EMP-FILE
                NOT AT END
                    PERFORM 400-PROCESS-EMPLOYEE-RECORDS
            END-READ
        END-PERFORM.
        CLOSE EMPLOYEE-FILE
              PRINT-FILE.
        STOP RUN.

    200-INITIALIZE-TITLE-TABLE.
        OPEN INPUT TITLE-FILE.
        PERFORM VARYING TITLE-INDEX FROM 1 BY 1
            UNTIL END-OF-TITLE-FILE = 'YES'
                OR TITLE-INDEX > 999
            READ TITLE-FILE INTO WS-TITLE-RECORD
                AT END
                   MOVE 'YES' TO END-OF-TITLE-FILE
                NOT AT END
                   ADD 1 TO NUMBER-OF-TITLES
                   MOVE TITLE-IN-CODE TO TITLE-CODE (TITLE-INDEX)
                   MOVE TITLE-IN-NAME TO TITLE-NAME (TITLE-INDEX)
            END-READ
        END-PERFORM.
        IF TITLE-INDEX > 999
            DISPLAY 'SIZE OF TITLE TABLE IS EXCEEDED'
```

Title table is initialized dynamically (PERFORM 200-INITIALIZE-TITLE-TABLE.)

Checks that table size is not exceeded (OR TITLE-INDEX > 999)

Figure 12.17 *(continued)*

```
           END-IF.
           CLOSE TITLE-FILE.

       300-WRITE-HEADING-LINES.
           WRITE PRINT-LINE FROM HEADING-LINE
               AFTER ADVANCING PAGE.
           WRITE PRINT-LINE FROM DASHED-LINE
               AFTER ADVANCING 1 LINE.

       400-PROCESS-EMPLOYEE-RECORDS.
           PERFORM 420-EXPAND-TITLE-CODE.
           PERFORM 430-EXPAND-LOCATION-CODE.
           PERFORM 440-EXPAND-EDUCATION-CODE.
           PERFORM 450-DETERMINE-INSURANCE-AMOUNT.
           PERFORM 470-WRITE-DETAIL-LINE.

       420-EXPAND-TITLE-CODE.
           SEARCH ALL TITLES
               AT END
                   MOVE 'UNKNOWN' TO DET-TITLE
               WHEN TITLE-CODE (TITLE-INDEX) = EMP-TITLE-CODE
                   MOVE TITLE-NAME (TITLE-INDEX) TO DET-TITLE
           END-SEARCH.

       430-EXPAND-LOCATION-CODE.
           SET LOCATION-INDEX TO 1.
           SEARCH LOCATIONS
               AT END
                   MOVE 'UNKNOWN' TO DET-LOCATION
               WHEN EMP-LOC-CODE = LOCATION-CODE (LOCATION-INDEX)
                   MOVE LOCATION-NAME (LOCATION-INDEX) TO DET-LOCATION
           END-SEARCH.

       440-EXPAND-EDUCATION-CODE.
           IF EMP-EDUC-CODE < 1 OR > 8
               MOVE 'UNKNOWN' TO DET-EDUCATION
           ELSE
               MOVE EDU-NAME (EMP-EDUC-CODE) TO DET-EDUCATION
           END-IF.

       450-DETERMINE-INSURANCE-AMOUNT.
           IF EMP-SALARY IS NUMERIC
               SET INSURANCE-INDEX TO 1
               SEARCH INSURANCE-TABLE
                   AT END
                       MOVE ZERO TO DET-INSURANCE
                   WHEN EMP-SALARY <= SALARY-MAXIMUM (INSURANCE-INDEX)
                       MOVE INSURANCE-AMOUNT (INSURANCE-INDEX)
                           TO DET-INSURANCE
               END-SEARCH
```

Binary search (lines 182–187)

Sequential search (lines 190–196)

Direct access to table entries (lines 199–203)

Range-step table uses <= condition (line 211)

Figure 12.17 *(continued)*

```
215           ELSE
216               DISPLAY 'INCOMING SALARY NOT NUMERIC'
217               MOVE ZERO TO DET-INSURANCE
218           END-IF.
219
220       470-WRITE-DETAIL-LINE.
221           MOVE SPACES TO PRINT-LINE.
222           MOVE EMP-NAME TO DET-NAME.
223           MOVE EMP-SALARY TO DET-SALARY.
224           WRITE PRINT-LINE FROM DETAIL-LINE
225               AFTER ADVANCING 1 LINE.
```

5. The definition of the education table (lines 61–72) as a positional table; that is, the education codes themselves (1, 2, ... ,8) are *not* entered in the table, and the incoming employee education code is expanded via direct access to a table entry in the MOVE statement of line 202. (The IF statement in line 199 is executed prior to the MOVE to ensure a valid education code.)
6. The definition of the insurance table (lines 74–85), which includes an INDEXED BY clause as required by the subsequent SEARCH statement. Note, too, the WHEN clause in line 211 includes a less than or equal condition consistent with the implementation of a range-step table.
7. The definition of the title table as input loaded in lines 35–41; that is, the OCCURS clause merely allocates spaces for the table but does not assign values to it; the latter is done dynamically in lines 150–166 of the Procedure Division. Note, too, the inclusion of the INDEXED BY and ASCENDING KEY clauses that are required by the SEARCH ALL statement in lines 182–187.

The flow in the Procedure Division is straightforward and easy to follow. The PERFORM statement in line 133 initializes the title table, after which the employee and print files are opened and a heading line is written. The combination of the in-line perform and false-condition branch in lines 137 through 144 processes employee records until the file is exhausted.

LIMITATIONS OF COBOL-74

The optional END-SEARCH scope terminator is new to COBOL-85 and terminates the conditional portion of the SEARCH and SEARCH ALL statements.

The word FILLER is optional, making possible Data Division entries of the form:

```
01  MAJOR-VALUE.
    05                    PIC X(14)    VALUE '02ART HISTORY'.
    05                    PIC X(14)    VALUE '04BIOLOGY'.
    05                    PIC X(14)    VALUE '19CHEMISTRY'.
        .
          .
            .
```

The entries look strange initially, but make perfect sense when you realize that data names defined as FILLER are not referenced in the Procedure Division; that is, omission of the word FILLER has no effect on the remainder of a program.

SUMMARY

Points to Remember

- Codes may be alphabetic, numeric, or alphanumeric. A good coding system will be precise, mnemonic, and expandable.
- The VALUE, OCCURS, and REDEFINES clauses are used in combination to define and initialize a table within a COBOL program.
- A table lookup may be implemented sequentially, in binary fashion, or through direct access to table entries.
- A range-step table occurs when there is no one-to-one correspondence between a table value and the search argument.
- Tables may be initialized through hard coding or dynamically loaded at execution time.
- A SEARCH statement is used to implement a sequential lookup. The statement requires the INDEXED BY clause in the table definition.
- A SEARCH ALL statement is used to implement a binary lookup. The statement requires the INDEXED BY and KEY clauses in the table definition, and requires the keys in the table to be in either ascending or descending sequence.

Key Words and Concepts

Alphabetic code
Alphanumeric code
Binary table lookup
Direct access to table entries
Hard coding
Index
Input-loaded table
Mnemonic code
Numeric code
Positional organization
Precise code
Range-step table
Sequential table lookup
Subscript
Table lookup

COBOL Elements

ASCENDING KEY
AT END
DESCENDING KEY
END-SEARCH
INDEXED BY
OCCURS
PERFORM VARYING
REDEFINES
SEARCH
SEARCH ALL
SET
VALUE
WHEN

FILL-IN

1. A two-position numeric code has ______________ combinations; a two-position alphabetic code has ______________; and a two-position alphanumeric code has ______________.
2. A ______________ table lookup does not require its entries to be in any special order, whereas a binary table lookup requires that the entries be in either ______________ or ______________ sequence.
3. If a table is ______________ ______________, then the program in which it is found must be recompiled in order to change the table.
4. An ______________ ______________ table makes it possible to change entries in the table without recompiling the program.
5. Direct access to table entries is possible only if the table has ______________ organization.
6. A sequential table lookup in a table of 500 elements could require as many as ______________ tries, whereas a binary lookup for the same table would take no more than ______________ tries.
7. The ______________ clause gives another name to previously allocated space.
8. A sequential table lookup is implemented by the ______________ statement, whereas a binary lookup is implemented by ______________ ______________.
9. The ASCENDING/DESCENDING ______________ clause is required in the table definition if a binary table lookup is to be implemented.
10. The ______________ statement appears before a sequential search, but is not used prior to a binary search.
11. The ______________ clause is required in a table's definition if either a sequential or binary search is used.

12. The REDEFINES clause (must/may) be used when initializing a table.
13. If the wrong number of subscripts are used with a particular data name, a (compilation/execution) error will result.
14. A SET statement (is/is not) used before a SEARCH ALL statement, as the binary algorithm calculates its own starting position.
15. A ______________ ______________ table occurs when there is no longer a one-to-one correspondence between a table value and the search argument.

TRUE/FALSE

1. A binary search over a table of 500 elements requires 9 or fewer comparisons.
2. A sequential search over a table of 500 elements could require 500 comparisons.
3. Direct access to table entries requires no comparisons.
4. The SEARCH statement requires an index.
5. SEARCH ALL denotes a binary search.
6. There are no additional requirements of table organization in order to implement a binary rather than a sequential search.
7. An index (that is, displacement) of zero refers to the first element in a table.
8. A subscript of zero refers to the first element in a table.
9. An index cannot be manipulated by a MOVE statement.
10. PERFORM VARYING can manipulate both indexes and subscripts.
11. A SEARCH statement can contain only a single WHEN clause.
12. The ASCENDING (DESCENDING) KEY clause is required whenever the SEARCH statement is applied to a table.
13. The INDEXED BY clause is required whenever the SEARCH statement is applied to a table.
14. The same index can be applied to many tables.
15. The same subscript can be applied to many tables.
16. An index and a subscript can be applied to the same table.
17. The REDEFINES clause provides another name for previously allocated space.
18. The REDEFINES clause must be used in initializing a table.
19. A binary search could be applied to a table if its elements were arranged in descending (rather than ascending) sequence.
20. A numeric code of four digits provides a greater number of possibilities than a three-digit alphabetic code.
21. Codes are used for reasons other than to conserve space.
22. Alphabetic codes are more likely to be mnemonic than numeric codes.
23. Numeric codes, such as Social Security numbers, should not be unique to accommodate individuals with the same last name.
24. Positionally organized tables require the first code to begin at 1.

25. Positionally organized tables require numeric codes.
26. Positionally organized tables often result in large amounts of wasted space.
27. A range-step table requires a one-to-one correspondence between the table value and search argument.
28. The federal income tax table is an example of a range-step table.

PROBLEMS

1. How many unique codes can be developed from a four-position numeric code? From a four-position alphabetic code? From a four-position alphanumeric code?
2. Ask a friend to pick a number from 1 to 2,000. What is the maximum number of guesses required to find the number if
   a. a binary search is used?
   b. a sequential search is used?

   Answer parts (a) and (b), if the selected number is between 1 and 4,000.
3. What, if anything, is wrong with the following table definition?

```
01  MONTH-TABLE.
    05  MONTH OCCURS 12 TIMES           PIC X(4).
    05  MONTH-VALUES REDEFINES MONTH    PIC X(36)
        VALUE 'JANFEBMARAPRMAYJUNJULAUGSEPOCTNOVDEC'.
```

4. The DAY-OF-WEEK phrase was introduced in Chapter 9 (page 242) to obtain a one-position code corresponding to the day of the week. An alternate way of expanding the code (as opposed to the EVALUATE statement in Chapter 9) is to use a positional table and direct lookup.
   a. Use the data names in Figure 12.18 to write the appropriate ACCEPT statement.
   b. Write the necessary statements to implement a direct lookup on the table of Figure 12.18.

Figure 12.18 DAY-OF-WEEK Table

```
01  DAY-CODE-VALUE          PIC 9.

01  DAY-HEADING.
    05  FILLER              PIC X(9)     VALUE 'TODAY IS '.
    05  TODAYS-DAY          PIC X(9).

01  DAY-OF-WEEK-VALUE.
    05  FILLER              PIC X(9)     VALUE 'MONDAY'.
    05  FILLER              PIC X(9)     VALUE 'TUESDAY'.
    05  FILLER              PIC X(9)     VALUE 'WEDNESDAY'.
    05  FILLER              PIC X(9)     VALUE 'THURSDAY'.
    05  FILLER              PIC X(9)     VALUE 'FRIDAY'.
    05  FILLER              PIC X(9)     VALUE 'SATURDAY'.
    05  FILLER              PIC X(9)     VALUE 'SUNDAY'.

01  DAY-OF-WEEK-TABLE REDEFINES MAJOR-VALUE.
    05  DAY OCCURS 7 TIMES     PIC X(9).
```

5. Given the following table definition:

```
01  LOCATION-VALUE.
    05  FILLER              PIC X(16)  VALUE '010ATLANTA'.
    05  FILLER              PIC X(16)  VALUE '020BOSTON'.
    05  FILLER              PIC X(16)  VALUE '030CHICAGO'.
    05  FILLER              PIC X(16)  VALUE '040DETROIT'.
    05  FILLER              PIC X(16)  VALUE '050KANSAS CITY'.
    05  FILLER              PIC X(16)  VALUE '060LOS ANGELES'.
    05  FILLER              PIC X(16)  VALUE '070NEW YORK'.
    05  FILLER              PIC X(16)  VALUE '080PHILADELPHIA'.
    05  FILLER              PIC X(16)  VALUE '090SAN FRANCISCO'.
    05  FILLER              PIC X(16)  VALUE '045DENVER'.
01  LOCATION-TABLE REDEFINES LOCATION-VALUE.
    05  LOCATION OCCURS 10 TIMES
        ASCENDING KEY IS LOCATION-CODE
        INDEXED BY LOCATION-INDEX.
        10  LOCATION-CODE   PIC X(3).
        10  LOCATION-NAME   PIC X(13).
```

and the following Procedure Division code:

```
    SET LOCATION-INDEX TO 1.
    SEARCH LOCATION
        AT END
            DISPLAY '*ERROR IN SEQUENTIAL SEARCH FOR DENVER'
        WHEN LOCATION-CODE (LOCATION-INDEX) = '045'
            DISPLAY 'SEQUENTIAL SEARCH OK FOR DENVER'
    END-SEARCH.
    SEARCH LOCATION
        AT END
            DISPLAY '*ERROR IN SEQUENTIAL SEARCH FOR NEW YORK'
        WHEN LOCATION-CODE (LOCATION-INDEX) = '070'
            DISPLAY 'SEQUENTIAL SEARCH OK FOR NEW YORK'
    END-SEARCH.
```

a. Indicate the output that will be produced.

b. Code a binary search statement to expand code 045 for Denver. Do you expect any trouble in the execution of that statement?

Multilevel Tables

CHAPTER OUTLINE

OBJECTIVES

After reading this chapter you will be able to:

- Describe a conceptual (user's) view of one-, two-, and three-level tables; implement (that is, define and initialize) one-, two-, and three-level tables in COBOL.
- Differentiate between the VALUE, OCCURS, and REDEFINES clauses as they relate to table definition and initialization.
- Distinguish between errors in compilation versus errors in execution; give an example of each as it pertains to multilevel table processing.
- Explain the operation of a PERFORM VARYING statement; develop suitable examples to process tables in one, two, and three dimensions.
- Use the VARYING option of the SEARCH statement; nest SEARCH statements within one another for multilevel-table lookups.

OVERVIEW

COBOL-85 allows multilevel tables of up to seven dimensions as opposed to the earlier limit of three in COBOL-74. Most applications do not require anything beyond a three-level table, and thus our coverage is limited to two- and three-level tables. The underlying concepts are identical regardless of a table's complexity, and hence our approach to multilevel tables will be a simple extension of the single-level problem.

We begin with a one-level example and develop it completely. This material reviews some discussion from the previous chapter, but is included nonetheless, in order to build the parallel between one-, two-, and three-level examples. Our presentation reexamines the OCCURS, VALUE, and REDEFINES clauses in the Data Division, and the PERFORM VARYING statement in the Procedure Division. We then extend the discussion to two and three dimensions and present complete programs to illustrate all statements.

The chapter concludes with a third program to implement table lookups in a multilevel table. The example introduces the VARYING option of the SEARCH statement and also nests SEARCH statements within one another.

System Concepts

Figure 13.1a depicts the user's view of a table of starting salaries within a company. In this example, an employee starts at one of 10 salaries, depending on the responsibility level for his or her job. A junior account executive, for example, may be designated as having a responsibility level of 1, whereas a divisional manager may be assigned level 10. The 10 salaries together comprise a salary table, with individual values designated by a subscript. The starting salary at responsibility level four, for example, is $30,000.

Figure 13.1 Multilevel Tables

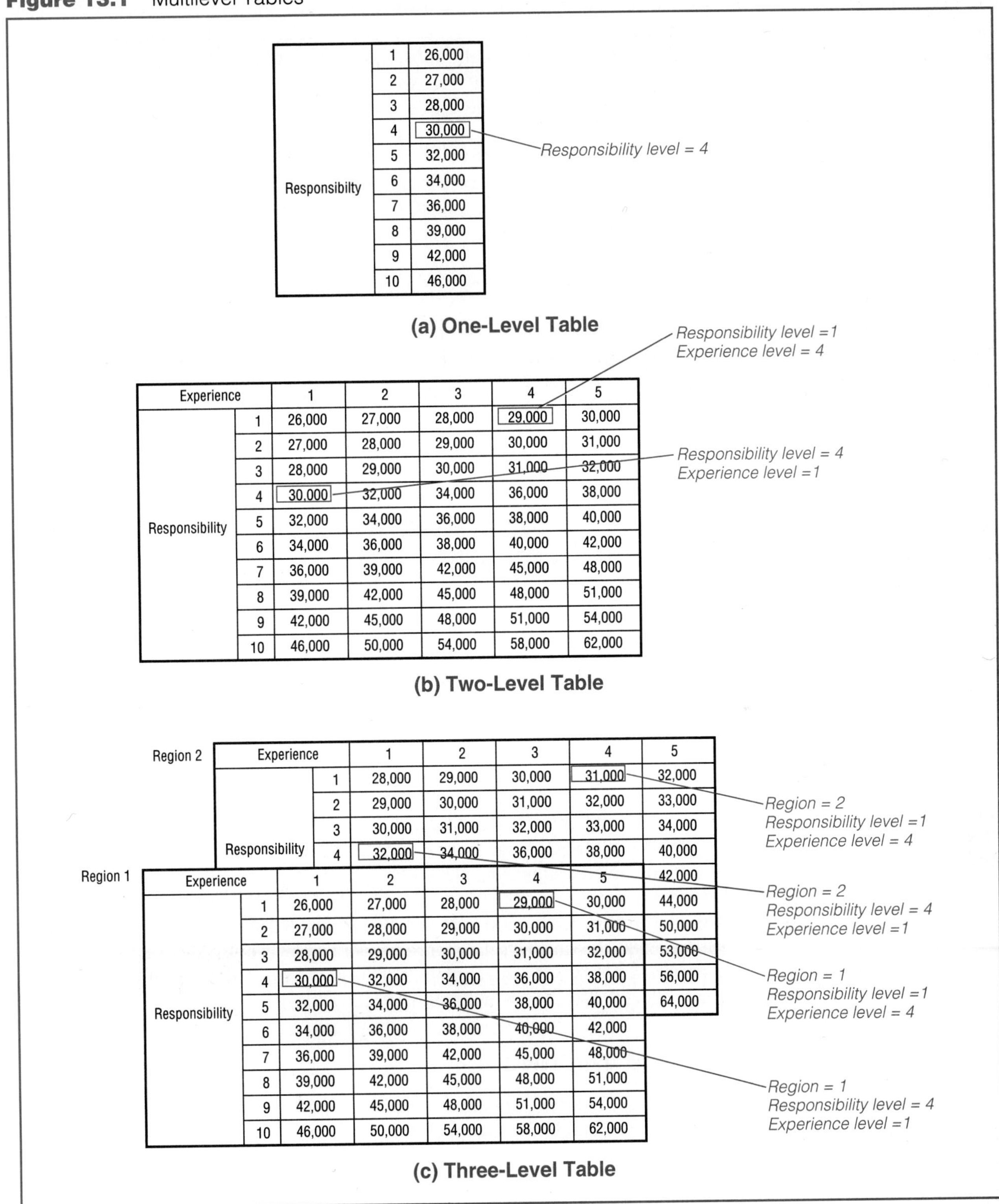

Responsibilty		
	1	26,000
	2	27,000
	3	28,000
	4	30,000
	5	32,000
	6	34,000
	7	36,000
	8	39,000
	9	42,000
	10	46,000

(a) One-Level Table

Experience		1	2	3	4	5
Responsibility	1	26,000	27,000	28,000	29,000	30,000
	2	27,000	28,000	29,000	30,000	31,000
	3	28,000	29,000	30,000	31,000	32,000
	4	30,000	32,000	34,000	36,000	38,000
	5	32,000	34,000	36,000	38,000	40,000
	6	34,000	36,000	38,000	40,000	42,000
	7	36,000	39,000	42,000	45,000	48,000
	8	39,000	42,000	45,000	48,000	51,000
	9	42,000	45,000	48,000	51,000	54,000
	10	46,000	50,000	54,000	58,000	62,000

(b) Two-Level Table

Region 2

Experience		1	2	3	4	5
Responsibility	1	28,000	29,000	30,000	31,000	32,000
	2	29,000	30,000	31,000	32,000	33,000
	3	30,000	31,000	32,000	33,000	34,000
	4	32,000	34,000	36,000	38,000	40,000
						42,000
						44,000
						50,000
						53,000
						56,000
						64,000

Region 1

Experience		1	2	3	4	5
Responsibility	1	26,000	27,000	28,000	29,000	30,000
	2	27,000	28,000	29,000	30,000	31,000
	3	28,000	29,000	30,000	31,000	32,000
	4	30,000	32,000	34,000	36,000	38,000
	5	32,000	34,000	36,000	38,000	40,000
	6	34,000	36,000	38,000	40,000	42,000
	7	36,000	39,000	42,000	45,000	48,000
	8	39,000	42,000	45,000	48,000	51,000
	9	42,000	45,000	48,000	51,000	54,000
	10	46,000	50,000	54,000	58,000	62,000

(c) Three-Level Table

Figure 13.1b extends the user's view to two dimensions, in which salary is a function of two variables, responsibility and experience. The additional variable enables individuals with the same responsibility to be assigned different salaries, depending on experience. An individual at responsibility level four, for example, earns one of five salaries ($30,000, $32,000, $34,000, $36,000, or $38,000), depending on his or her experience level (which varies from one to five, respectively.) Two subscripts are necessary to designate a specific value in a two-level table; it should be apparent that the order of the subscripts is important; that is, the entry in row 4, column 1 ($30,000) is different from the entry in row 1, column 4 ($29,000).

Figure 13.1c extends the user's view to a third dimension, region, in which salary is a function of three variables; region (based on cost of living), responsibility, and experience. Any reference to a specific entry in a three-level table requires three subscripts, and again the order is important. Look again at Figure 13.1c and verify that the salary for region 1, responsibility 4, and experience 1 is $30,000, while the entry in region 2, responsibility 4, and experience 1 is $32,000.

COBOL Implementation

A table is initialized either by hard-coding it in a program or by dynamically loading it at execution time. Once initialized, the entries in a table can be accessed through a PERFORM VARYING or SEARCH statement, and these statements are applicable to tables in one, two, or three dimensions. We have, however, for the sake of simplicity, chosen to focus on hard-coding and the PERFORM VARYING statement. As previously indicated, our approach will be to develop the material for the simplest application (one-level tables), and then extend the concepts to two and three dimensions.

One-Level Tables

Figure 13.2 depicts three different views of the one-level table shown earlier in Figure 13.1. Figure 13.2a repeats the user's view in which salary is a function of responsibility, Figure 13.2b contains the COBOL statements to define and initialize the table in COBOL, and Figure 13.2c shows the resulting storage allocation.

Figure 13.2b creates the 01 entry SALARY-VALUES with 10 successive VALUE clauses that initialize 50 consecutive locations in memory. The first five locations contain 26000, the next five contain 27000, and so on.

The REDEFINES clause assigns another name, SALARY-TABLE, to these same 50 locations, and the subsequent OCCURS clause establishes the table. (The OCCURS clause cannot appear on the 01 level and hence SALARY is defined under SALARY-TABLE.) The first five positions in SALARY-VALUES are renamed SALARY (1) and contain 26000, the starting salary for responsibility level one. The next five positions are renamed SALARY (2) and contain 27000, and so on. The conceptual view of the storage allocation is shown in Figure 13.2c.

PERFORM VARYING

The PERFORM VARYING statement (explained previously in Chapter 11) processes the elements in a table. For example, the statement

```
PERFORM WRITE-STARTING-SALARY
    VARYING RESPONSIBILITY-SUB FROM 1 BY 1
        UNTIL RESPONSIBILITY-SUB > 10
```

executes the procedure WRITE-STARTING-SALARY 10 times, changing the value of RESPONSIBILITY-SUB each time the procedure is executed. The PERFORM VARYING statement initializes (increments) a subscript (index), tests a condition, then performs the designated procedure, depending on whether the condition is true. In the example, RESPONSIBILITY-SUB is initialized to 1, and the condition

Figure 13.2 One-level Table

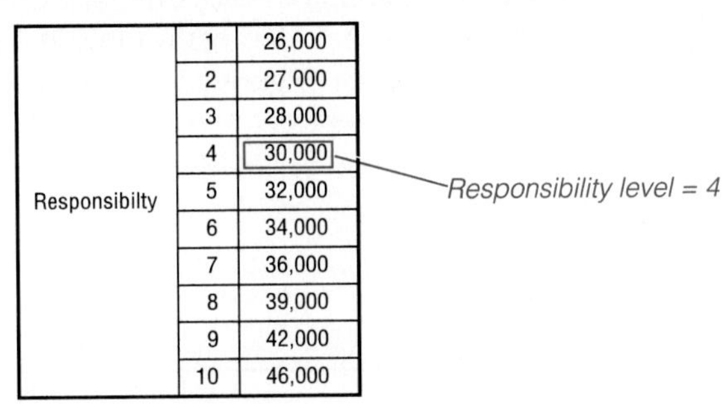

Responsibilty		
	1	26,000
	2	27,000
	3	28,000
	4	30,000
	5	32,000
	6	34,000
	7	36,000
	8	39,000
	9	42,000
	10	46,000

(a) User's View

```
01 SALARY-VALUES.
    05 FILLER     PIC X(5)     VALUE '26000'.
    05 FILLER     PIC X(5)     VALUE '27000'.
    05 FILLER     PIC X(5)     VALUE '28000'.
    05 FILLER     PIC X(5)     VALUE '30000'.
    05 FILLER     PIC X(5)     VALUE '32000'.
    05 FILLER     PIC X(5)     VALUE '34000'.
    05 FILLER     PIC X(5)     VALUE '36000'.
    05 FILLER     PIC X(5)     VALUE '39000'.
    05 FILLER     PIC X(5)     VALUE '42000'.
    05 FILLER     PIC X(5)     VALUE '46000'.

01 SALARY-TABLE REDEFINES SALARY-VALUES.
    05 SALARY OCCURS 10 TIMES        PIC 9(5).
```

(b) Initialization via the REDEFINES and VALUES Clauses

SALARY-TABLE									
SALARY (1)	SALARY (2)	SALARY (3)	SALARY (4)	SALARY (5)	SALARY (6)	SALARY (7)	SALARY (8)	SALARY (9)	SALARY (10)
2 6 0 0 0	2 7 0 0 0	2 8 0 0 0	3 0 0 0 0	3 2 0 0 0	3 4 0 0 0	3 6 0 0 0	3 9 0 0 0	4 2 0 0 0	4 6 0 0 0
SALARY-VALUES									

(c) Storage Schematic

RESPONSIBILITY-SUB > 10 is evaluated. The condition is not satisfied, so the designated procedure, WRITE-STARTING-SALARY, is executed for the first time. RESPONSIBILITY-SUB is incremented to 2, and the condition is retested. The condition is still false, so WRITE-STARTING-SALARY is executed a second time. The loop (testing, executing, and incrementing) continues for values of RESPONSIBILITY-SUB of 3, 4, 5, and so on, until RESPONSIBILITY-SUB reaches 10. Even then the condition is still not satisfied, because *10 is **not** greater than 10,* and so WRITE-STARTING-SALARY is executed a tenth (and last) time. RESPONSIBILITY-SUB is incremented to 11, the condition is finally satisfied (11 > 10), and the PERFORM VARYING is terminated.

Two-Level Tables

All of this material is easily extended to two levels as shown in Figure 13.3. Figure 13.3a repeats the user's view of the table in which salary is a function of both responsibility and experience, Figure 13.3b shows the COBOL definition and initialization, and Figure 13.3c depicts the storage allocation.

Figure 13.3 Two-level Tables

Experience		1	2	3	4	5
Responsibility	1	26,000	27,000	28,000	29,000	30,000
	2	27,000	28,000	29,000	30,000	31,000
	3	28,000	29,000	30,000	31,000	32,000
	4	30,000	32,000	34,000	36,000	38,000
	5	32,000	34,000	36,000	38,000	40,000
	6	34,000	36,000	38,000	40,000	42,000
	7	36,000	39,000	42,000	45,000	48,000
	8	39,000	42,000	45,000	48,000	51,000
	9	42,000	45,000	48,000	51,000	54,000
	10	46,000	50,000	54,000	58,000	62,000

Responsibility level = 1
Experience level = 4

Responsibility level = 4
Experience level = 1

(a) User's View

```
01 SALARY-VALUES.
   05 FILLER    PIC X(25)      VALUE '2600027000280002900030000'.
   05 FILLER    PIC X(25)      VALUE '2700028000290003000031000'.
   05 FILLER    PIC X(25)      VALUE '2800029000300003100032000'.
   05 FILLER    PIC X(25)      VALUE '3000032000340003600038000'.
   05 FILLER    PIC X(25)      VALUE '3200034000360003800040000'.
   05 FILLER    PIC X(25)      VALUE '3400036000380004000042000'.
   05 FILLER    PIC X(25)      VALUE '3600039000420004500048000'.
   05 FILLER    PIC X(25)      VALUE '3900042000450004800051000'.
   05 FILLER    PIC X(25)      VALUE '4200045000480005100054000'.
   05 FILLER    PIC X(25)      VALUE '4600050000540005800062000'.

01 SALARY-TABLE REDEFINES SALARY-VALUES.
   05 RESPONSIBILITY OCCURS 10 TIMES.
      10  EXPERIENCE OCCURS 5 TIMES.
          15  SALARY                  PIC 9(5).
```

(b) Initialization via the REDEFINES and VALUES Clauses

SALARY-TABLE										
RESPONSIBILITY (1)						RESPONSIBILITY (10)				
Exp (1)	Exp (2)	Exp (3)	Exp (4)	Exp (5)		Exp (1)	Exp (2)	Exp (3)	Exp (4)	Exp (5)
2 6 0 0 0	2 7 0 0 0	2 8 0 0 0	2 9 0 0 0	3 0 0 0 0	...	4 6 0 0 0	5 0 0 0 0	5 4 0 0 0	5 8 0 0 0	6 2 0 0 0
SALARY-VALU ES										

(c) Storage Schematic

Establishment of a two-level table requires two OCCURS clauses, each at a different level, in the table definition as shown:

```
01  SALARY-TABLE.
    05  RESPONSIBILITY  OCCURS 10 TIMES.
        10  EXPERIENCE  OCCURS  5 TIMES.
            15  SALARY                  PIC 9(5).
```

The above entries establish a 50-element table (10 rows and 5 columns) with each element assigned five memory locations (according to the PICTURE clause). There are a total of 250 memory locations (10 x 5 x 5) allocated to the table as shown in Figure 13.3c. The first 25 locations contain the salaries for the five experience levels at the first responsibility level. Locations 1–5 contain the salary at responsibility level 1, experience level 1; locations 6–10 contain the salary at responsibility level 1, experience level 2; and so on. In similar fashion, locations 26–50 refer to the salaries for the five experience levels at responsibility level 2; locations 51–75 to the salaries at the five experience levels for responsibility level 3; and so on.

As in the one-level example, the table is initialized through combination of the OCCURS, VALUE, and REDEFINES clauses. This time, however, each VALUE clause fills an entire row (consisting of five experience levels or 25 positions in all). The first VALUE clause fills the first 25 locations (corresponding to the five experience levels for responsibility one), the second VALUE clause fills locations 26–50 (the five experience levels for responsibility two), and so on. The order of the VALUE clauses is critical and coincides with Figure 13.3a. The resulting storage allocation is shown in Figure 13.3c and further clarifies the discussion.

Errors in Compilation

Newcomers to multilevel tables find it all too easy to use the wrong number of subscripts, specify subscripts in improper sequence, and/or supply an invalid subscript value (that is, a value beyond the definition in the OCCURS clause.) The rule is very simple, namely that the number of subscripts is equal to the number of OCCURS clauses used to define the entry and further, that the order of subscripts corresponds to the order of the OCCURS clauses.

Consider again the table definition in Figure 13.3b, observing that SALARY is subordinate to EXPERIENCE, that EXPERIENCE is subordinate to RESPONSIBILITY, and that both RESPONSIBILITY and EXPERIENCE were defined with an OCCURS clause. In other words an OCCURS clause appears in *both* group items prior to the definition of SALARY, and thus *two* subscripts will be required for all Procedure Division references to SALARY. Any reference to SALARY that does not include two subscripts will be flagged during compilation. SALARY (1,4) is a valid reference to indicate the element in row 1, column 4 of the two-level table; SALARY (1) is *invalid* and will be flagged accordingly.

The compiler, however, is concerned only with syntax (namely that the proper number of subscripts is supplied), and not with the values of those subscripts. In other words, a reference to SALARY (20, 20) would not produce a compilation error, because it contains two subscripts and is syntactically valid. It would, however, cause problems during execution as the subscript values are inconsistent with the table definition. (The execution results are unpredictable.)

COBOL also allows reference to data names at different ***hierarchical levels*** of a table (although such reference may not make sense logically). Thus the definition of a two-dimensional table automatically allows reference to other one-dimensional tables. Refer again to the storage schematic of Figure 13.3c and/or the examples below to clarify the issue.

SALARY (6, 5)	A valid entry in all respects, which refers to salary responsibility level 6, experience level 5. The data name SALARY must always be referenced with two subscripts.
SALARY (5, 6)	Syntactically correct in that SALARY has two subscripts. The entry will compile cleanly but will cause problems in execution because it refers to responsibility and experience levels of 5 and 6, respectively, which are inconsistent with the table definition.
SALARY-TABLE	Refers to the entire table of 50 elements (250 locations). SALARY-TABLE is referenced without any subscripts.
RESPONSIBILITY (1)	Refers collectively to the five experience levels for the first level of salary responsibility; RESPONSIBILITY is referenced with a single subscript.
EXPERIENCE (6, 5)	A valid entry equivalent to SALARY (6,5); the entries are equivalent because SALARY is the only elementary item defined under the group item EXPERIENCE.

PERFORM VARYING

The PERFORM VARYING statement was introduced in Chapter 11 in conjunction with processing a one-level table. Its syntax is easily extended to process a two-level table as shown below. Consider:

```
PERFORM [procedure-name-1] [WITH TEST {BEFORE}]
                                      {AFTER }

    VARYING {identifier-1} FROM {identifier-2} BY {literal-2   }
            {index-name-1}      {index-name-2}    {identifier-3}
                                {literal-1   }
        UNTIL condition-1

  [ AFTER {identifier-4} FROM {identifier-5} BY {identifier-6}
          {literal-3   }      {index-name-3}    {literal-5   }
                              {literal-4   }
        UNTIL condition-2                                      ] . . .

[imperative-statement-1 END PERFORM]
```

The PERFORM VARYING statement accommodates a two-level table through inclusion of the **AFTER** clause that varies two subscripts (indexes) simultaneously. As in the case of a one-level table, the TEST BEFORE/TEST AFTER clause is optional and is typically omitted; the default is TEST BEFORE and corresponds to the COBOL-74 implementation.

The PERFORM VARYING statement executes a designated procedure as in Figure 13.4a, or the statements in an in-line perform as in Figure 13.4b. Either way two subscripts are used as shown in Figure 13.4c. RESPONSIBILITY-SUB is varied from 1 to 10, in conjunction with EXPERIENCE-SUB changing from 1 to 5, so that the performed statements are executed 50 times in all.

The *bottom* subscript (EXPERIENCE-SUB in this example) is varied first. Thus RESPONSIBILITY-SUB is initially set to 1 while EXPERIENCE-SUB is varied from 1 to 5. RESPONSIBILITY-SUB is then incremented to 2, while EXPERIENCE-SUB

Figure 13.4 PERFORM VARYING with Two Subscripts

```
    PERFORM INITIALIZE-SALARIES
        VARYING RESPONSIBILITY-SUB FROM 1 BY 1
            UNTIL RESPONSIBILITY-SUB > 10
        AFTER EXPERIENCE-SUB FROM 1 BY 1
            UNTIL EXPERIENCE-SUB > 5.
    .
       .
          .
INITIALIZE-SALARIES.
    MOVE ZERO TO SALARY (RESPONSIBILITY-SUB, EXPERIENCE-SUB).
```

(a) Performing a Paragraph

```
    PERFORM
        VARYING RESPONSIBILITY-SUB FROM 1 BY 1
            UNTIL RESPONSIBILITY-SUB > 10
        AFTER EXPERIENCE-SUB FROM 1 BY 1
            UNTIL EXPERIENCE-SUB > 5
                MOVE ZERO TO SALARY (RESPONSIBILITY-SUB, EXPERIENCE-SUB)
    END-PERFORM.
```

(b) In-Line Perform

Responsibility Subscript	Experience Subscript	
1	1	RESPONSIBILITY-SUB is set to 1 while EXPERIENCE-SUB varies from 1 to 5
1	2	
1	3	
1	4	
1	5	
2	1	RESPONSIBILITY-SUB is set to 2 while EXPERIENCE-SUB varies from 1 to 5
2	2	
2	3	
2	4	
2	5	
.		
.		
.		
10	1	RESPONSIBILITY-SUB reaches 10 and EXPERIENCE-SUB varies from 1 to 5
10	2	
10	3	
10	4	
10	5	

(c) Variation of Subscripts

Figure 13.5 Varying Column and/or Row Subscripts

Question: What is the average salary for responsibility level three?
Answer: Sum the five salaries in row three of the salary table, then divide that total by five.

```
MOVE ZERO TO TOTAL-SALARY.
PERFORM
    VARYING EXPERIENCE-SUB FROM 1 BY 1
        UNTIL EXPERIENCE-SUB > 5
            ADD SALARY (3, EXPERIENCE-SUB) TO TOTAL-SALARY
END-PERFORM.
COMPUTE AVERAGE-SALARY = TOTAL-SALARY / 5.
```

(a) Varying a Column Subscript

Question: What is the average salary for experience level four?
Answer: Sum the 10 salaries in column four of the salary table, then divide that total by 10.

```
MOVE ZERO TO TOTAL-SALARY.
PERFORM
    VARYING RESPONSIBILITY-SUB FROM 1 BY 1
        UNTIL EXPERIENCE-SUB > 10
            ADD SALARY (RESPONSIBILITY-SUB, 4) TO TOTAL-SALARY
END-PERFORM.
COMPUTE AVERAGE-SALARY = TOTAL-SALARY / 10.
```

(b) Varying a Row Subscript

Question: What is the average salary over all responsibility and experience levels?
Answer: Sum all 50 salaries in the table, then divide that total by 50.

```
MOVE ZERO TO TOTAL-SALARY.
PERFORM
    VARYING RESPONSIBILITY-SUB FROM 1 BY 1
        UNTIL RESPONSIBILITY-SUB > 10
    AFTER EXPERIENCE-SUB FROM 1 BY 1
        UNTIL EXPERIENCE-SUB > 5
            ADD SALARY (RESPONSIBILITY-SUB, EXPERIENCE-SUB) TO TOTAL-SALARY
END-PERFORM.
COMPUTE AVERAGE-SALARY = TOTAL-SALARY / 50.
```

(c) Varying Both Subscripts

is again varied from 1 to 5. The process continues until all 50 combinations have been reached.

It is not necessary to always vary both subscripts in a two-level table; that is, you can hold the row constant and vary the column, or keep the column constant and vary the row. Indeed, different types of information are obtained according to the subscript that is used. Figure 13.5a, for example, varies the column subscript (EXPERIENCE-SUB) while keeping the row constant, to obtain the average starting salary at the third responsibility level. In similar fashion, Figure 13.5b varies the row subscript (RESPONSIBILITY-SUB) while keeping the column constant, to obtain the average starting salary for the fourth experience level. Figure 13.5c varies both subscripts to compute the average salary over all 50 row-column combinations.

A Sample Program

We incorporate the material on two-level tables into a COBOL program. Specifications follow in the usual format.

PROGRAMMING SPECIFICATIONS

Program Name: Two-Level Tables

Narrative: This program illustrates the definition, initialization, and processing of two-level tables, building directly on the examples just presented. The specifications call for the processing of an employee file and the printing of each individual's salary, based on his or her responsibility and experience. In addition, the number of employees in each responsibility/experience combination is to be computed.

Input File(s): EMPLOYEE-FILE

Input Record Layout:

```
01  EMPLOYEE-RECORD.
    05  EMP-NAME                            PIC X(15).
    05  EMP-SALARY-DETERMINANTS.
        10  EMP-RESP                        PIC 99.
        10  FILLER                          PIC X.
        10  EMP-EXP                         PIC 99.
        10  FILLER                          PIC X(3).
    05  FILLER                              PIC X(5).
```

Test Data:

```
ADAMS          04 01
BAKER          01 04
BROWN          08 02
CHARLES        09 02
DAVIDSON       09 04
DAVIS          10 04
EPSTEIN        04 05
FRANKEL        03 03
GOODMAN        03 03
GULFMAN        03 05
HATHAWAY       07 02
INGLES         03 01
JACKSON        06 03
JORDAN         06 03
KING           07 02
LIPMAN         07 01
LOWELL         01 04
```

Report Layout: See Figure 13.6.

Processing Requirements:

1. Read a file of employee records, and for each record:
   a. Determine the employee's starting salary as a function of responsibility and experience.
   b. Print a detail line for this employee showing his or her name and starting salary.
2. Compute the number of employees for each responsibility-experience combination. This requires creation of a 10-by-5 table to store the number of individuals in each responsibility-experience combination, and implies that as each employee record is

Figure 13.6 Output of Two-Level Program

```
STARTING SALARIES OF ALL NEW EMPLOYEES

ADAMS        $30,000
BAKER        $29,000
BROWN        $42,000
CHARLES      $45,000
DAVIDSON     $51,000
DAVIS        $58,000
EPSTEIN      $38,000
FRANKEL      $30,000
GOODMAN      $30,000
GULFMAN      $32,000
HATHAWAY     $39,000
INGLES       $28,000
JACKSON      $38,000
JORDAN       $38,000
KING         $39,000
LIPMAN       $36,000
LOWELL       $29,000
```

(a) Detail Report

```
                 STARTING SALARY SUMMARY REPORT

                                EXPERIENCE
RESPONSIBILITY      1       2       3       4       5

      1             0       0       0       2       0
      2             0       0       0       0       0
      3             1       0       2       0       1
      4             1       0       0       0       1
      5             0       0       0       0       0
      6             0       0       2       0       0
      7             1       2       0       0       0
      8             0       1       0       0       0
      9             0       1       0       1       0
     10             0       0       0       1       0
```

(b) Summary Report

read, the corresponding table entry (the particular responsibility-experience combination) has to be incremented by one.

3. When all employees have been processed, print the table containing the number of employees in each category as shown in Figure 13.6b.

Program Design

The report layout in Figure 13.6 requires both a ***detail report*** containing a line for every employee, as well as a ***summary report*** displaying the total number of employees in each of the 50 responsibility-experience combinations. The program will evaluate each incoming record to determine in which of the 50 categories the employee fits, then increment the appropriate counter. At the conclusion of processing—after all employee records have been read—the table of 50 totals will be printed as the summary report.

The functions needed in the eventual program are shown in the expanded hierarchy chart of Figure 13.7. The purpose of the individual modules should be apparent from the module name and/or the eventual COBOL program (shown later in the chapter).

The pseudocode in Figure 13.8 is succinct and is restricted to the basic building blocks of structured programming. The initial statements open the files and write an appropriate heading. The program is driven by a loop that determines the appropriate responsibility/experience combination for each employee record, writes the detail line, and increments the appropriate counter. The summary report is written after this loop has ended (when all employee records have been processed).

The Completed Program

Much of the completed program in Figure 13.9 is already familiar as it repeats the COBOL statements used in the explanation of two-level tables. The COBOL statements to define the salary table (lines 42–57), appeared earlier in Figure 13.3b and were discussed fully at that time. A second two-level table, for the number of employees in each category, is defined in lines 59–62; the definition uses the OCCURS

Figure 13.7 Hierarchy Chart for Two-Level Program

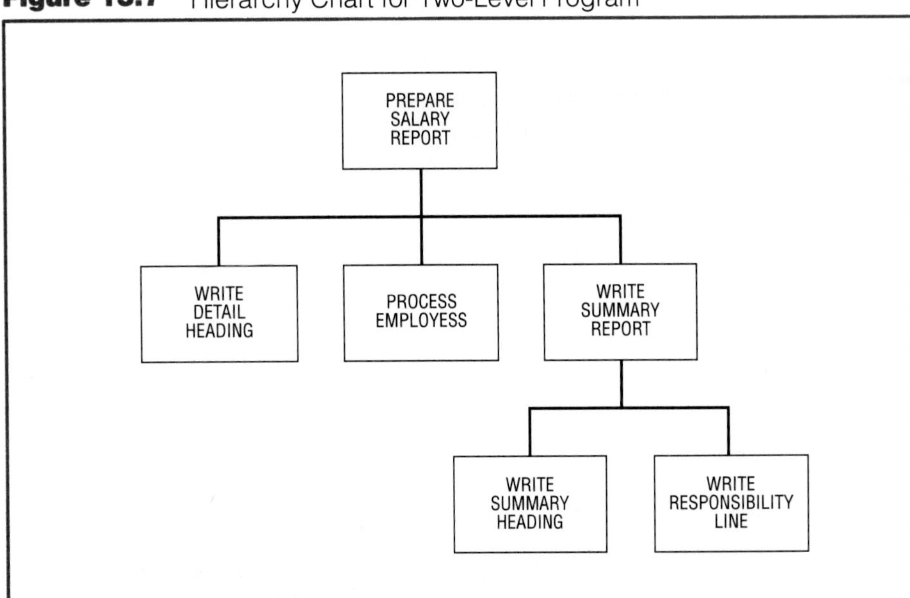

Figure 13.8 Pseudocode for Two-Level Program

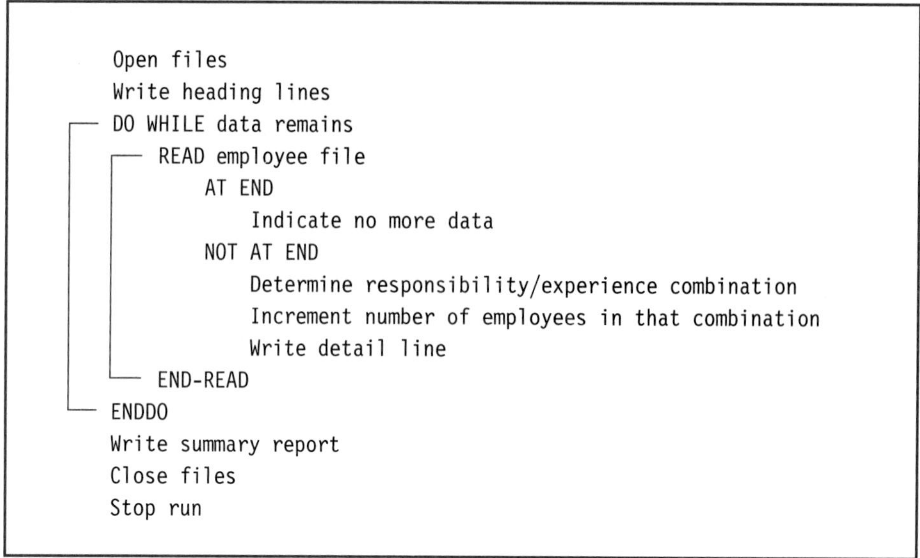

```
Open files
Write heading lines
DO WHILE data remains
    READ employee file
        AT END
            Indicate no more data
        NOT AT END
            Determine responsibility/experience combination
            Increment number of employees in that combination
            Write detail line
    END-READ
ENDDO
Write summary report
Close files
Stop run
```

Figure 13.9 Two-Level Program

```
IDENTIFICATION DIVISION.
PROGRAM-ID.    2LVTABLE.
AUTHOR.        ROBERT T. GRAUER.

ENVIRONMENT DIVISION.
INPUT-OUTPUT SECTION.
FILE-CONTROL.
    SELECT EMPLOYEE-FILE
          ASSIGN TO UT-S-SYSIN.
    SELECT PRINT-FILE
          ASSIGN TO UT-S-SYSOUT.

DATA DIVISION.
FILE SECTION.
FD  EMPLOYEE-FILE
    DATA RECORD IS EMPLOYEE-RECORD.
01  EMPLOYEE-RECORD                   PIC X(23).

FD  PRINT-FILE
    DATA RECORD IS PRINT-LINE.
01  PRINT-LINE                        PIC X(132).

WORKING-STORAGE SECTION.
01  FILLER                            PIC X(14)
        VALUE 'WS BEGINS HERE'.

01  WS-EMPLOYEE-RECORD.
    05  EMP-NAME                      PIC X(15).
```

Figure 13.9 *(continued)*

```
           05  EMP-SALARY-DETERMINANTS.
               10  EMP-RESP                        PIC 99.
               10  FILLER                          PIC X.
               10  EMP-EXP                         PIC 99.
               10  FILLER                          PIC X(3).

       01  PROGRAM-SUBSCRIPTS.
           05  RESP-SUB                            PIC S9(4) COMP.
           05  EXP-SUB                             PIC S9(4) COMP.

       01  WS-END-OF-DATA-SWITCH                   PIC X(3)   VALUE SPACES.
           88  END-OF-DATA                                    VALUE 'YES'.

       01  SALARY-VALUES.
           05  FILLER  PIC X(25)   VALUE '2600027000280002900030000'.
           05  FILLER  PIC X(25)   VALUE '2700028000290003000031000'.
           05  FILLER  PIC X(25)   VALUE '2800029000300003100032000'.
           05  FILLER  PIC X(25)   VALUE '3000032000340003600038000'.
           05  FILLER  PIC X(25)   VALUE '3200034000360003800040000'.
           05  FILLER  PIC X(25)   VALUE '3400036000380004000042000'.
           05  FILLER  PIC X(25)   VALUE '3600039000420004500048000'.
           05  FILLER  PIC X(25)   VALUE '3900042000450004800051000'.
           05  FILLER  PIC X(25)   VALUE '4200045000480005100054000'.
           05  FILLER  PIC X(25)   VALUE '4600050000540005800062000'.

       01  SALARY-TABLE REDEFINES SALARY-VALUES.
           05  RESPONSIBILITY OCCURS 10 TIMES.
               10  EXPERIENCE OCCURS 5 TIMES.
                   15  SALARY                  PIC 9(5).

       01  NUMBER-OF-EMPLOYEES-TABLE.
           05  NUMBER-RESPONSIBILITY OCCURS 10 TIMES.
               10  NUMBER-EXPERIENCE OCCURS 5 TIMES.
                   15  NUMB-EMP        PIC 99        VALUE ZERO.

       01  DETAIL-REPORT-HEADING-LINE.
           05  FILLER                      PIC X(9)    VALUE SPACES.
           05  FILLER                      PIC X(39)
                   VALUE 'STARTING SALARIES OF ALL NEW EMPLOYEES'.
           05  FILLER                      PIC X(82)   VALUE SPACES.

       01  DETAIL-LINE-1.
           05  FILLER                      PIC X(12)   VALUE SPACES.
           05  DET-EMP-NAME                PIC X(15).
           05  FILLER                      PIC X(4)    VALUE SPACES.
           05  DET-SALARY                  PIC $99,999.
           05  FILLER                      PIC X(94)   VALUE SPACES.

       01  SUMMARY-REPORT-HEADING-LINE-1.
           05  FILLER                      PIC X(24)   VALUE SPACES.
```

Used as subscripts into summary table

Two-level salary is hard coded

Two-level summary table is defined and initialized to zero

Figure 13.9 *(continued)*

```
           05  FILLER                  PIC X(39)
                   VALUE 'STARTING SALARY SUMMARY REPORT'.
           05  FILLER                  PIC X(69)  VALUE SPACES.

       01  SUMMARY-REPORT-HEADING-LINE-2.
           05  FILLER                  PIC X(36)  VALUE SPACES.
           05  FILLER                  PIC X(10)  VALUE 'EXPERIENCE'.
           05  FILLER                  PIC X(86)  VALUE SPACES.

       01  SUMMARY-REPORT-HEADING-LINE-3.
           05  FILLER                  PIC X(5)   VALUE SPACES.
           05  FILLER                  PIC X(14)  VALUE 'RESPONSIBILITY'.
           05  FILLER                  PIC X(48)
                 VALUE '      1         2         3         4         5'.
           05  FILLER                  PIC X(65)  VALUE SPACES.

       01  SUMMARY-LINE-1.
           05  FILLER                  PIC X(9).
           05  SUMMARY-RESPONSIBILITY PIC Z(4).
           05  FILLER                  PIC X(4)   VALUE SPACES.
           05  SUMMARY-TOTAL-VALUES OCCURS 5 TIMES.
               10  FILLER              PIC X(4).
               10  SUMMARY-NUMBER      PIC Z(4)9.
           05  FILLER                  PIC X(70).

       PROCEDURE DIVISION.
       100-PREPARE-SALARY-REPORT.
           OPEN INPUT EMPLOYEE-FILE
               OUTPUT PRINT-FILE.
           PERFORM 200-WRITE-DETAIL-REPORT-HDG.
           PERFORM UNTIL END-OF-DATA
               READ EMPLOYEE-FILE INTO WS-EMPLOYEE-RECORD
                   AT END
                       MOVE 'YES' TO WS-END-OF-DATA-SWITCH
                   NOT AT END
                       PERFORM 300-PROCESS-EMPLOYEES
           END-PERFORM.
           PERFORM 400-WRITE-SUMMARY-REPORT.
           CLOSE EMPLOYEE-FILE
                 PRINT-FILE.
           STOP RUN.

       200-WRITE-DETAIL-REPORT-HDG.
           WRITE PRINT-LINE FROM DETAIL-REPORT-HEADING-LINE
               AFTER ADVANCING PAGE.
           MOVE SPACES TO PRINT-LINE.
           WRITE PRINT-LINE.

       300-PROCESS-EMPLOYEES.
           ADD 1 TO NUMB-EMP (EMP-RESP, EMP-EXP).
```

Program driven by in-line perform and false-condition branch

Increments number of employees in summary table

Figure 13.9 *(continued)*

```
129          MOVE EMP-NAME TO DET-EMP-NAME.
130          MOVE SALARY (EMP-RESP, EMP-EXP) TO DET-SALARY.
131          WRITE PRINT-LINE FROM DETAIL-LINE-1.
132
133      400-WRITE-SUMMARY-REPORT.
134          PERFORM 500-WRITE-SUMMARY-HEADING.
135          PERFORM 520-WRITE-RESPONSIBILITY-LINE
136              VARYING RESP-SUB FROM 1 BY 1
137                  UNTIL RESP-SUB > 10.
138
139      500-WRITE-SUMMARY-HEADING.
140          WRITE PRINT-LINE FROM SUMMARY-REPORT-HEADING-LINE-1
141              AFTER ADVANCING PAGE.
142          WRITE PRINT-LINE FROM SUMMARY-REPORT-HEADING-LINE-2
143              AFTER ADVANCING 2 LINES.
144          WRITE PRINT-LINE FROM SUMMARY-REPORT-HEADING-LINE-3.
145          MOVE SPACES TO PRINT-LINE.
146          WRITE PRINT-LINE.
147
148      520-WRITE-RESPONSIBILITY-LINE.
149          MOVE SPACES TO SUMMARY-LINE-1.
150          PERFORM VARYING EXP-SUB FROM 1 BY 1
151             UNTIL EXP-SUB > 5
152                  MOVE NUMB-EMP (RESP-SUB, EXP-SUB)
153                      TO SUMMARY-NUMBER (EXP-SUB)
154          END-PERFORM.
155          MOVE RESP-SUB TO SUMMARY-RESPONSIBILITY.
156          WRITE PRINT-LINE FROM SUMMARY-LINE-1.
```

Prints a detail line for each employee (line 131)

Writes summary headings (lines 140–146)

In-line perform moves five experience levels to responsibility line (lines 150–154)

clauses to allocate space for the table, but omits the REDEFINES clause, because (unlike the salary table) the number of employees is computed during processing. The 50 elements in the table are initialized to zero by the VALUE ZERO clause in line 62. (See limitations of COBOL-74 at the end of the chapter.)

The Procedure Division follows both the hierarchy chart and pseudocode. The key to the program is the ADD statement in line 128, which increments the number of employees for the particular responsibility-experience combination. The subscript values in this statement are taken directly from the incoming employee record, which defines EMP-RESP and EMP-EXP in lines 30 and 32, respectively. The detail line for the individual employee is written in lines 129–131.

The summary report is produced after the end of file has been reached by the PERFORM WRITE-SUMMARY-REPORT statement of line 116. The heading lines are written in lines 140–146, after which the paragraph WRITE-RESPONSIBILITY-LINE is executed 10 times (once for each responsibility level) in lines 148–156. The latter paragraph contains its own PERFORM VARYING statement to write each of the five experience totals for each of the 10 responsibility levels.

Three-Level Tables

The material on two-level tables is easily extended to a third dimension. We continue therefore with our two-level example, in which salary is a function of responsibility and experience, but this time add a third determinant, region (due to different costs of living in different areas of the country). Figure 13.10a depicts the user's view showing salary as a function of three variables (region, responsibility, and experience), Figure 13.10b contains the COBOL definition, and Figure 13.10c shows the storage allocation.

Establishment of a three-level table requires three OCCURS clauses in the table definition:

```
01  SALARY-TABLE.
    05  REGION OCCURS 2 TIMES.
        10  RESPONSIBILITY OCCURS 10 TIMES.
            15  EXPERIENCE OCCURS  5 TIMES.
                20  SALARY                          PIC 9(5).
```

These entries establish a 100-element table (2 x 10 x 5) with each element assigned five memory locations (according to the PICTURE clause). Thus there are a total of 500 memory locations allocated to the table as indicated in Figure 13.10c. The first 25 locations refer to the five experience levels at the first responsibility level in the first region; the next 25 locations to the five experience levels at the second responsibility level in the first region, and so on.

As in the two-level example, the table is initialized through combinations of the OCCURS, VALUE, and REDEFINES clauses. Each VALUE clause fills an entire row (consisting of five experience elements or 25 positions in all), with 20 such statements needed to initialize all 500 storage locations. The first VALUE clause fills the first 25 locations (corresponding to the five experience levels for responsibility one in region one), the second VALUE clause fills locations 26–50 (the five experience levels for responsibility two in region one), and so on. The order of the VALUE clauses is critical and coincides with Figure 13.10a. The resulting storage allocation is shown in Figure 13.10c and further clarifies the discussion.

Once again you must be careful to use the correct number of subscripts, as well as specify the subscripts in the proper order. The rule is the same as for two-level tables, namely that the number of subscripts is equal to the number of OCCURS clauses used to define the entry, and further, that the order of the subscripts corresponds to the order of the OCCURS clauses.

Return to the table definition of Figure 13.10b, observing that three OCCURS clauses are associated with SALARY, and hence three subscripts are necessary; that is, SALARY is subordinate to REGION, RESPONSIBILITY, and EXPERIENCE, each of which was defined with its own OCCURS clause. Hence any Procedure Division reference to SALARY must include three subscripts—for example, SALARY (2, 4, 1) to indicate the salary for region 2, responsibility 4, and experience 1.

As is the case with one- and two-level tables, the compiler is concerned only with syntax (that the proper number of subscripts is supplied), and not with the values of those subscripts. A reference to SALARY (3, 1, 1) would not produce a compilation error because it is syntactically valid. It would, however, cause problems during execution because the subscript value for region 3 is inconsistent with the table definition. The execution results are unpredictable.

COBOL also permits reference at different hierarchical levels, so that the definition of a three-level table automatically allows reference to other one- and two-dimensional tables (although such references may not make sense logically). Refer again to the storage schematic in Figure 13.10c and/or the examples below to further clarify this discussion.

Figure 13.10 Three-level Tables

Region 2

Experience		1	2	3	4	5
Responsibility	1	28,000	29,000	30,000	31,000	32,000
	2	29,000	30,000	31,000	32,000	33,000
	3	30,000	31,000	32,000	33,000	34,000
	4	32,000	34,000	36,000	38,000	40,000
						42,000
						44,000
						50,000
						53,000
						56,000
						64,000

Region 1

Experience		1	2	3	4	5
Responsibility	1	26,000	27,000	28,000	29,000	30,000
	2	27,000	28,000	29,000	30,000	31,000
	3	28,000	29,000	30,000	31,000	32,000
	4	30,000	32,000	34,000	36,000	38,000
	5	32,000	34,000	36,000	38,000	40,000
	6	34,000	36,000	38,000	40,000	42,000
	7	36,000	39,000	42,000	45,000	48,000
	8	39,000	42,000	45,000	48,000	51,000
	9	42,000	45,000	48,000	51,000	54,000
	10	46,000	50,000	54,000	58,000	62,000

(a) User's View

```
01 SALARY-VALUES.
   05 REGION-ONE.
      10 FILLER      PIC X(25)     VALUE '2600027000280002900030000'.
      10 FILLER      PIC X(25)     VALUE '2700028000290003000031000'.
      10 FILLER      PIC X(25)     VALUE '2800029000300003100032000'.
      10 FILLER      PIC X(25)     VALUE '3000032000340003600038000'.
      10 FILLER      PIC X(25)     VALUE '3200034000360003800040000'.
      10 FILLER      PIC X(25)     VALUE '3400036000380004000042000'.
      10 FILLER      PIC X(25)     VALUE '3600039000420004500048000'.
      10 FILLER      PIC X(25)     VALUE '3900042000450004800051000'.
      10 FILLER      PIC X(25)     VALUE '4200045000480005100054000'.
      10 FILLER      PIC X(25)     VALUE '4600050000540005800062000'.
   05 REGION-TWO.
      10 FILLER      PIC X(25)     VALUE '2800029000300003100032000'.
      10 FILLER      PIC X(25)     VALUE '2900030000310003200033000'.
      10 FILLER      PIC X(25)     VALUE '3000031000320003300034000'.
      10 FILLER      PIC X(25)     VALUE '3200034000360003800040000'.
      10 FILLER      PIC X(25)     VALUE '3400036000380004000042000'.
      10 FILLER      PIC X(25)     VALUE '3600038000400004200044000'.
      10 FILLER      PIC X(25)     VALUE '3800041000440004700050000'.
      10 FILLER      PIC X(25)     VALUE '4100044000470005000053000'.
      10 FILLER      PIC X(25)     VALUE '4400047000500005300056000'.
      10 FILLER      PIC X(25)     VALUE '4800052000560006000064000'.

01 SALARY-TABLE REDEFINES SALARY-VALUES.
   05 REGION OCCURS 2 TIMES.
      10 RESPONSIBILITY OCCURS 10 TIMES.
         15 EXPERIENCE OCCURS 5 TIMES.
            20 SALARY              PIC 9(5).
```

(b) Initialization via the REDEFINES and VALUES Clauses

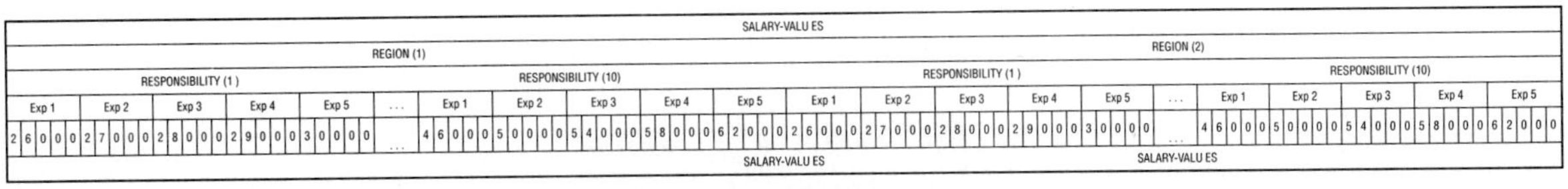

SALARY-VALU ES																						
REGION (1)											REGION (2)											
RESPONSIBILITY (1)						RESPONSIBILITY (10)					RESPONSIBILITY (1)						RESPONSIBILITY (10)					
Exp 1	Exp 2	Exp 3	Exp 4	Exp 5	...	Exp 1	Exp 2	Exp 3	Exp 4	Exp 5	Exp 1	Exp 2	Exp 3	Exp 4	Exp 5	...	Exp 1	Exp 2	Exp 3	Exp 4	Exp 5	
2 6 0 0 0	2 7 0 0 0	2 8 0 0 0	2 9 0 0 0	3 0 0 0 0	...	4 6 0 0 0	5 0 0 0 0	5 4 0 0 0	5 8 0 0 0	6 2 0 0 0	2 6 0 0 0	2 7 0 0 0	2 8 0 0 0	2 9 0 0 0	3 0 0 0 0	...	4 6 0 0 0	5 0 0 0 0	5 4 0 0 0	5 8 0 0 0	6 2 0 0 0	
SALARY-VALU ES											SALARY-VALU ES											

(c) Storage Schematic

SALARY (1, 2, 3)	A valid reference in all respects, which refers to the salary for region 1, responsibility 2, and experience 3. SALARY must always be referenced with three subscripts.
SALARY (2, 12, 7)	Syntactically correct in that SALARY has three subscripts. The entry compiles cleanly but will cause problems in execution, because it refers to responsibility and experience levels of 12 and 7, respectively, which are inconsistent with the table definition.
SALARY-TABLE	Refers to the entire table of 100 elements (500 memory locations in all). SALARY-TABLE is referenced without any subscripts.
REGION (1)	Refers collectively to the 10 responsibility levels, each containing five experience levels associated with the first region; REGION is referenced with a single subscript.
RESPONSIBILITY (1, 2)	Refers collectively to the five experience levels for responsibility level 2 for region 1; RESPONSIBILITY is referenced with two subscripts.
EXPERIENCE (1, 2, 3)	A valid entry equivalent to SALARY (1, 2, 3); the entries are equivalent because SALARY is the only elementary item defined under the group item EXPERIENCE.

PERFORM VARYING

The syntax of the PERFORM VARYING statement shows the AFTER clause enclosed in brackets and followed by three dots to indicate the clause can be repeated. Accordingly, three-level tables are processed with a PERFORM VARYING statement that includes two AFTER clauses as shown in Figure 13.11. The statement may execute either a designated procedure as in Figure 13.11a, or a series of in-line statements as in Figure 13.11b.

As in the two-level example, all possible combinations of the three subscripts are executed, causing the designated statements to be executed a total of 100

Figure 13.11 PERFORM VARYING with Three Subscripts

```
    PERFORM INITIALIZE-SALARIES
        VARYING REGION-SUB FROM 1 BY 1
            UNTIL REGION-SUB > 2
        AFTER RESPONSIBILITY-SUB FROM 1 BY 1
            UNTIL RESPONSIBILITY-SUB > 10
        AFTER EXPERIENCE-SUB FROM 1 BY 1
            UNTIL EXPERIENCE-SUB > 5.
 .
   .
     .
INITIALIZE-SALARIES.
    MOVE ZERO TO SALARY (REGION-SUB, RESPONSIBILITY-SUB, EXPERIENCE-SUB).
```

(a) Performing a Paragraph

Figure 13.11 *(continued)*

```
PERFORM
    VARYING REGION-SUB FROM 1 BY 1
        UNTIL REGION-SUB > 2
    AFTER RESPONSIBILITY-SUB FROM 1 BY 1
        UNTIL RESPONSIBILITY-SUB > 10
    AFTER EXPERIENCE-SUB FROM 1 BY 1
        UNTIL EXPERIENCE-SUB > 5
            MOVE ZERO TO SALARY (REGION-SUB, RESPONSIBILITY-SUB, EXPERIENCE-SUB)
END-PERFORM.
```

(b) In-Line Perform

Region Subscript	Responsibility Subscript	Experience Subscript	
1	1	1	REGION-SUB and RESPONSIBILITY-SUB are both set to 1 while EXPERIENCE-SUB varies from 1 to 5
1	1	2	
1	1	3	
1	1	4	
1	1	5	
1	2	1	REGION-SUB remains at 1 while RESPONSIBILITY-SUB is incremented to 2 and EXPERIENCE-SUB is again varied from 1 to 5
1	2	2	
1	2	3	
1	2	4	
1	2	5	
.	.	.	
1	10	1	At the 50th iteration, REGION-SUB is still set to 1, but RESPONSIBILITY-SUB has reached 10
1	10	2	
1	10	3	
1	10	4	
1	10	5	
2	1	1	REGION-SUB is incremented to 2, RESPONSIBILITY-SUB is reset to 1 while EXPERIENCE-SUB varies from 1 to 5
2	1	2	
2	1	3	
2	1	4	
2	1	5	
.	.	.	
2	10	1	At the 100th iteration, REGION-SUB reaches 2, RESPONSIBILITY-SUB reaches 10 and EXPERIENCE-SUB reaches 5
2	10	2	
2	10	3	
2	10	4	
2	10	5	

(c) Variation of Subscripts

(2 × 10 × 5) times. The *bottom* subscript (EXPERIENCE-SUB in the example) is varied first, then the middle subscript (RESPONSIBILITY-SUB), and finally the top subscript (REGION-SUB). The sequence in which the 100 combinations are executed is shown in Figure 13.11.

A Sample Program

We incorporate the material on three-level tables into our previous sample COBOL program on two-level tables. The specifications have been updated and are presented in their entirety.

PROGRAMMING SPECIFICATIONS

Program Name: Three-Level Tables

Narrative: This program extends the example on two-level tables to a third dimension in that salary is now a function of three variables (region, responsibility, and experience). As in the earlier program, a detail report is required showing the salary of each employee. In addition a summary report containing the number of employees in each region/responsibility/experience combination is to be produced.

Input File(s): EMPLOYEE-FILE

Input Record Layout:

```
01  EMPLOYEE-RECORD.
    05  EMP-NAME                          PIC X(15).
    05  EMP-SALARY-DETERMINANTS.
        10  EMP-RESP                      PIC 99.
        10  FILLER                        PIC X.
        10  EMP-EXP                       PIC 99.
        10  FILLER                        PIC X(3).
        10  EMP-REGION                    PIC 99.
    05  FILLER                            PIC X(5).
```

Test Data:

```
ADAMS          04 01 01
BAKER          01 04 01
BROWN          08 02 02
CHARLES        09 02 02
DAVIDSON       09 04 02
DAVIS          10 04 01
EPSTEIN        04 05 02
FRANKEL        03 03 01
GOODMAN        03 03 01
GULFMAN        03 05 01
HATHAWAY       07 02 01
INGLES         03 01 01
JACKSON        06 03 01
JORDAN         06 03 01
KING           07 02 01
LIPMAN         07 01 01
LOWELL         01 04 02
```

Report Layout: See Figure 13.12.

Figure 13.12 Output of Three-Level Program

STARTING SALARIES OF ALL NEW EMPLOYEES

ADAMS	$30,000
BAKER	$29,000
BROWN	$44,000
CHARLES	$47,000
DAVIDSON	$53,000
DAVIS	$58,000
EPSTEIN	$40,000
FRANKEL	$30,000
GOODMAN	$30,000
GULFMAN	$32,000
HATHAWAY	$39,000
INGLES	$28,000
JACKSON	$38,000
JORDAN	$38,000
KING	$39,000
LIPMAN	$36,000
LOWELL	$31,000

(a) Detail Report

STARTING SALARY SUMMARY REPORT - REGION 1

	EXPERIENCE				
RESPONSIBILITY	1	2	3	4	5
1	0	0	0	1	0
2	0	0	0	0	0
3	1	0	2	0	1
4	1	0	0	0	0
5	0	0	0	0	0
6	0	0	2	0	0
7	1	2	0	0	0
8	0	0	0	0	0
9	0	0	0	0	0
10	0	0	0	1	0

STARTING SALARY SUMMARY REPORT - REGION 2

	EXPERIENCE				
RESPONSIBILITY	1	2	3	4	5
1	0	0	0	1	0
2	0	0	0	0	0
3	0	0	0	0	0
4	0	0	0	0	1
5	0	0	0	0	0
6	0	0	0	0	0
7	0	0	0	0	0
8	0	1	0	0	0
9	0	1	0	1	0
10	0	0	0	0	0

(b) Summary Report

Processing Requirements:

1. Read a file of employee records, and for each record:
   a. Determine the employee's starting salary as a function of region, responsibility, and experience.
   b. Print a detail line for this employee showing his or her name and starting salary.
2. Compute the number of employees for each *region-responsibility-experience* combination. This requires creation of a 2 x 10 x 5 table to store the number of individuals in each region-responsibility-experience combination, and implies that as each employee record is read, the corresponding table entry is incremented by one.
3. When all employees have been processed, print the table containing the number of employees in each category as shown in Figure 13.12b.

The Completed Program

The extension of the original program from two to three dimensions is so direct that the hierarchy chart and pseudocode are virtually unchanged. The completed program is shown in Figure 13.13, and should already appear familiar, as it repeats the COBOL statements used in the explanation of three-level tables. The COBOL statements to define the salary table (lines 44–73), appeared earlier in Figure 13.10b and were discussed fully at that time. Observe also the definition of a second

Figure 13.13 Three-Level Program

```
 1        IDENTIFICATION DIVISION.
 2        PROGRAM-ID.    3LVTABLE.
 3        AUTHOR.        ROBERT T. GRAUER.
 4
 5        ENVIRONMENT DIVISION.
 6        INPUT-OUTPUT SECTION.
 7        FILE-CONTROL.
 8            SELECT EMPLOYEE-FILE
 9                ASSIGN TO UT-S-SYSIN.
10            SELECT PRINT-FILE
11                ASSIGN TO UT-S-SYSOUT.
12
13        DATA DIVISION.
14        FILE SECTION.
15        FD  EMPLOYEE-FILE
16            DATA RECORD IS EMPLOYEE-RECORD.
17        01  EMPLOYEE-RECORD                PIC X(23).
18
19        FD  PRINT-FILE
20            DATA RECORD IS PRINT-LINE.
21        01  PRINT-LINE                     PIC X(132).
22
23        WORKING-STORAGE SECTION.
24        01  FILLER                         PIC X(14)
25                VALUE 'WS BEGINS HERE'.
26
27        01  WS-EMPLOYEE-RECORD.
```

Figure 13.13 *(continued)*

```
        05  EMP-NAME                           PIC X(15).
        05  EMP-SALARY-DETERMINANTS.
            10  EMP-RESP                       PIC 99.
            10  FILLER                         PIC X.
            10  EMP-EXP                        PIC 99.
            10  FILLER                         PIC X.
            10  EMP-REG                        PIC 99.

    01  PROGRAM-SUBSCRIPTS.
        05  RESP-SUB                           PIC S9(4) COMP.
        05  EXP-SUB                            PIC S9(4) COMP.
        05  REG-SUB                            PIC S9(4) COMP.

    01  WS-END-OF-DATA-SWITCH                  PIC X(3)  VALUE SPACES.
        88  END-OF-DATA                                  VALUE 'YES'.

    01  SALARY-VALUES.
        05  REGION-ONE.
            10  FILLER  PIC X(25)  VALUE '2600027000280002900030000'.
            10  FILLER  PIC X(25)  VALUE '2700028000290003000031000'.
            10  FILLER  PIC X(25)  VALUE '2800029000300003100032000'.
            10  FILLER  PIC X(25)  VALUE '3000032000340003600038000'.
            10  FILLER  PIC X(25)  VALUE '3200034000360003800040000'.
            10  FILLER  PIC X(25)  VALUE '3400036000380004000042000'.
            10  FILLER  PIC X(25)  VALUE '3600039000420004500048000'.
            10  FILLER  PIC X(25)  VALUE '3900042000450004800051000'.
            10  FILLER  PIC X(25)  VALUE '4200045000480005100054000'.
            10  FILLER  PIC X(25)  VALUE '4600050000540005800062000'.

        05  REGION-TWO.
            10  FILLER  PIC X(25)  VALUE '2800029000300003100032000'.
            10  FILLER  PIC X(25)  VALUE '2900030000310003200033000'.
            10  FILLER  PIC X(25)  VALUE '3000031000320003300034000'.
            10  FILLER  PIC X(25)  VALUE '3200034000360003800040000'.
            10  FILLER  PIC X(25)  VALUE '3400036000380004000042000'.
            10  FILLER  PIC X(25)  VALUE '3600038000400004200044000'.
            10  FILLER  PIC X(25)  VALUE '3800041000440004700050000'.
            10  FILLER  PIC X(25)  VALUE '4100044000470005000053000'.
            10  FILLER  PIC X(25)  VALUE '4400047000500005300056000'.
            10  FILLER  PIC X(25)  VALUE '4800052000560006000064000'.

    01  SALARY-TABLE REDEFINES SALARY-VALUES.
        05  REGION OCCURS 2 TIMES.
            10  RESPONSIBILITY OCCURS 10 TIMES.
                15  EXPERIENCE OCCURS 5 TIMES.
                    20  SALARY                 PIC 9(5).

    01  NUMBER-OF-EMPLOYEES-TABLE.
        05  NUMBER-REGION OCCURS 2 TIMES.
            10  NUMBER-RESPONSIBILITY OCCURS 10 TIMES.
```

Used as subscripts into summary table

Three-level salary table

Figure 13.13 *(continued)*

```
                  15  NUMBER-EXPERIENCE OCCURS 5 TIMES.
                      20  NUMB-EMP       PIC 99      VALUE ZERO.

       01  DETAIL-REPORT-HEADING-LINE.
           05  FILLER                   PIC X(9)    VALUE SPACES.
           05  FILLER                   PIC X(39)
                   VALUE 'STARTING SALARIES OF ALL NEW EMPLOYEES'.
           05  FILLER                   PIC X(82)   VALUE SPACES.

       01  DETAIL-LINE-1.
           05  FILLER                   PIC X(12)   VALUE SPACES.
           05  DET-EMP-NAME             PIC X(15).
           05  FILLER                   PIC X(4)    VALUE SPACES.
           05  DET-SALARY               PIC $99,999.
           05  FILLER                   PIC X(94)   VALUE SPACES.

       01  SUMMARY-REPORT-HEADING-LINE-1.
           05  FILLER                   PIC X(24)   VALUE SPACES.
           05  FILLER                   PIC X(39)
                   VALUE 'STARTING SALARY SUMMARY REPORT - REGION'.
           05  SUM-REGION-NUMBER        PIC ZZZ9.
           05  FILLER                   PIC X(65)   VALUE SPACES.

       01  SUMMARY-REPORT-HEADING-LINE-2.
           05  FILLER                   PIC X(36)   VALUE SPACES.
           05  FILLER                   PIC X(10)   VALUE 'EXPERIENCE'.
           05  FILLER                   PIC X(86)   VALUE SPACES.

       01  SUMMARY-REPORT-HEADING-LINE-3.
           05  FILLER                   PIC X(5)    VALUE SPACES.
           05  FILLER                   PIC X(14)   VALUE 'RESPONSIBILITY'.
           05  FILLER                   PIC X(48)
                 VALUE '       1         2         3         4         5'.
           05  FILLER                   PIC X(65)   VALUE SPACES.

       01  SUMMARY-LINE-1.
           05  FILLER                   PIC X(9).
           05  SUMMARY-RESPONSIBILITY PIC Z(4).
           05  FILLER                   PIC X(4)    VALUE SPACES.
           05  SUMMARY-TOTAL-VALUES OCCURS 5 TIMES.
               10  FILLER               PIC X(4).
               10  SUMMARY-NUMBER       PIC Z(4)9.
           05  FILLER                   PIC X(70).

       PROCEDURE DIVISION.
       100-PREPARE-SALARY-REPORT.
           OPEN INPUT EMPLOYEE-FILE
               OUTPUT PRINT-FILE.
           PERFORM 200-WRITE-DETAIL-REPORT-HDG.
```

Figure 13.13 *(continued)*

```
        PERFORM UNTIL END-OF-DATA
            READ EMPLOYEE-FILE INTO WS-EMPLOYEE-RECORD
                AT END
                    MOVE 'YES' TO WS-END-OF-DATA-SWITCH
                NOT AT END
                    PERFORM 300-PROCESS-EMPLOYEES
        END-PERFORM.
        PERFORM 400-WRITE-SUMMARY-REPORT
            VARYING REG-SUB FROM 1 BY 1
                UNTIL REG-SUB > 2.
        CLOSE EMPLOYEE-FILE
              PRINT-FILE.
        STOP RUN.

    200-WRITE-DETAIL-REPORT-HDG.
        WRITE PRINT-LINE FROM DETAIL-REPORT-HEADING-LINE
            AFTER ADVANCING PAGE.
        MOVE SPACES TO PRINT-LINE.
        WRITE PRINT-LINE.

    300-PROCESS-EMPLOYEES.
        ADD 1 TO NUMB-EMP (EMP-REG, EMP-RESP, EMP-EXP).
        MOVE EMP-NAME TO DET-EMP-NAME.
        MOVE SALARY (EMP-REG, EMP-RESP, EMP-EXP) TO DET-SALARY.
        WRITE PRINT-LINE FROM DETAIL-LINE-1.

    400-WRITE-SUMMARY-REPORT.
        MOVE REG-SUB TO SUM-REGION-NUMBER.
        PERFORM 500-WRITE-SUMMARY-HEADING.
        PERFORM 520-WRITE-RESPONSIBILITY-LINE
            VARYING RESP-SUB FROM 1 BY 1
                UNTIL RESP-SUB > 10.

    500-WRITE-SUMMARY-HEADING.
        WRITE PRINT-LINE FROM SUMMARY-REPORT-HEADING-LINE-1
            AFTER ADVANCING PAGE.
        WRITE PRINT-LINE FROM SUMMARY-REPORT-HEADING-LINE-2
            AFTER ADVANCING 2 LINES.
        WRITE PRINT-LINE FROM SUMMARY-REPORT-HEADING-LINE-3.
        MOVE SPACES TO PRINT-LINE.
        WRITE PRINT-LINE.

    520-WRITE-RESPONSIBILITY-LINE.
        MOVE SPACES TO SUMMARY-LINE-1.
        PERFORM VARYING EXP-SUB FROM 1 BY 1
           UNTIL EXP-SUB > 5
               MOVE NUMB-EMP (REG-SUB, RESP-SUB, EXP-SUB)
                        TO SUMMARY-NUMBER (EXP-SUB)
        END-PERFORM.
        MOVE RESP-SUB TO SUMMARY-RESPONSIBILITY.
        WRITE PRINT-LINE FROM SUMMARY-LINE-1.
```

Program driven by in-line perform and false condition branch

Increments number of employees in summary table

Prints a detail line for each employee

Invoked twice—once for each region

Invoked 10 times—once for each responsibility level

In-line perform moves five experience levels to appropriate region and responsibility

three-level table, for the number of employees in each category in lines 75–79; the definition uses the OCCURS clauses to allocate space for the table, but omits the REDEFINES clause, because (unlike the salary table) the number of employees is computed during processing. The 100 elements in the table are initialized to zero by the VALUE ZERO clause in line 79. (See limitations of COBOL-74 at the end of the chapter.)

The Procedure Division of Figure 13.13 follows both the hierarchy chart and pseudocode. The key to the program is the ADD statement of line 148, which increments the number of employees for the particular region/responsibility/experience combination. The subscript values in this statement are taken directly from the incoming employee record, which define EMP-REG, EMP-RESP, and EMP-EXP. The detail line for the individual employee is created in lines 149–151.

The summary report is produced after the end of file has been reached by the PERFORM statement of lines 134–136, which executes the paragraph WRITE-SUMMARY-REPORT twice, once for each region. The heading lines are written (statements 160–167), after which the paragraph WRITE-RESPONSIBILITY-LINE is executed 10 times (once for each responsibility level) in lines 171–175. The latter paragraph contains its own PERFORM VARYING statement to write the five experience totals for each responsibility level.

Table Lookups

The examples thus far took advantage of a direct lookup in which the table elements were referenced directly by the value of the subscript; that is, the examples used numeric subscripts for responsibility and experience that corresponded directly to the row and column of the table. This is not always true as indicated by the example in Figure 13.14.

The table in Figure 13.14a depicts a user's view in which quarterly sales are recorded for every branch within the corporation. The COBOL implementation in Figure 13.14b establishes BRANCH as a one-level table with 25 rows; it also establishes QUARTERLY-SALES as a two-level table consisting of 25 rows and 4 columns. Any reference to BRANCH-NAME requires a single subscript (index)— for example, BRANCH-NAME (2) to obtain the branch-name in the second row. Any reference to QUARTERLY-SALES requires two subscripts (indexes) to indicate the branch and quarter—for example, QUARTERLY-SALES (2, 1), QUARTERLY-SALES (2, 2), QUARTERLY-SALES (2, 3), and QUARTERLY-SALES (2, 4) to reference the four sales figures for the branch in row two. Figure 13.14c shows the corresponding storage schematic.

Assume now that we want to obtain the annual sales for a specific branch, for example, Boston. An individual could tell at a glance that the data for Boston are in the second row of the table and would know automatically to sum the figures in row two to obtain the annual sales. The computer, however, has to first search the table of branch names to locate the proper row before summing the quarterly sales. The process is illustrated in Figure 13.4d, which contains the Procedure Division statements necessary to obtain the annual sales for Boston.

The SET statement is required prior to a sequential search in order to begin the search in row one of the BRANCH table. The SEARCH statement varies BRANCH-INDEX until a match is found on branch name; the WHEN clause includes a PERFORM VARYING statement that varies QUARTERLY-INDEX from one to four in the appropriate (BRANCH-INDEX) row in order to obtain the annual total. Note, too, the use of scope terminators (END-ADD, END-PERFORM, and END-SEARCH) and how the various statements are nested within one another.

Figure 13.14 Two-Level Table Lookup

Branch Name	1st Quarter	2nd Quarter	3rd Quarter	4th Quarter
Atlanta	$100,000	$200,000	$300,000	$400,000
Boston	$50,000	$150,000	$250,000	$350,000
Chicago	$150,000	$165,000	$400,000	$275,000
. . .				
San Diego	$25,000	$50,000	$75,000	$100,000

(a) User's View

```
01  SALES-TABLE REDEFINES SALES-DATA.
    05  BRANCH OCCURS 25 TIMES
        INDEXED BY BRANCH-INDEX.
        10  BRANCH-NAME                   PIC X(12).
        10  QUARTERLY-SALES     OCCURS 4 TIMES
            INDEXED BY QUARTERLY-INDEX    PIC 9(6).
```

(b) Table Definition

SALES-TABLE								
BRANCH (1)				...	BRANCH (25)			
BRANCH NAME (1)	QUARTERLY SALES (1,1)	...	QUARTERLY SALES (1,4)		BRANCH NAME (25)	QUARTERLY SALES (25,1)	...	QUARTERLY SALES (25,4)
PIC X(12)	PIC 9(6)		PIC 9(6)		PIC X(12)	PIC 9(6)		PIC 9(6)

(c) Storage Schematic

```
MOVE ZEROS TO ANNUAL-TOTAL.
SET BRANCH-INDEX TO 1.
SEARCH BRANCH
   AT END
       DISPLAY 'Boston not in table'
   WHEN BRANCH-NAME (BRANCH-INDEX) = 'Boston'
       PERFORM VARYING QUARTERLY-INDEX FROM 1 BY 1
           UNTIL QUARTERLY-INDEX > 4
               ADD QUARTERLY-SALES (BRANCH-INDEX, QUARTERLY-INDEX)
                   TO ANNUAL-TOTAL
               SIZE ERROR
                   DISPLAY 'ANNUAL TOTAL TOO LARGE'
               END-ADD
       END-PERFORM
END-SEARCH.
```

(d) SEARCH Statement

A Calorie Counter's Delight

We come now to our final example, which ties together material from several previous chapters. The specifications call for an interactive program that accepts information from the console and displays the results on the monitor. Specifications follow in the usual format.

PROGRAMMING SPECIFICATIONS

Program Name: A Calorie Counter's Delight

Narrative: Develop a program that will prompt the operator for an age and weight, then display the number of calories needed to maintain that weight. The table of daily maintenance calories is given in the second processing requirement.

Input File(s): None; input will be accepted from the console.

Report Layout: None; output will be displayed on the monitor.

Processing Requirements:

1. Prompt the user for age and weight; validate the parameters immediately as they are input and prompt the user continually until valid values are received. Age must be between 18 and 75 years, inclusive; weight between 90 and 165 pounds, inclusive.
2. Display the calories required to maintain the indicated weight according to the table below.

DAILY MAINTENANCE CALORIES TABLE

WEIGHT (POUNDS)		**AGE RANGE** (YEARS)		
FROM	**TO**	**18–35**	**36–55**	**56–75**
90	99	1,700	1,500	1,300
100	110	1,850	1,650	1,400
111	121	2,000	1,750	1,550
122	128	2,100	1,900	1,600
129	132	2,150	1,950	1,650
133	143	2,300	2,050	1,800
144	154	2,400	2,150	1,850
155	165	2,550	2,300	1,950

3. Ask the user whether s/he wishes to input another set of parameters; if yes, repeat steps one and two above; if not, terminate the program.

Range-Step Tables

The concept of a range-step table was introduced in the previous chapter and is essential to the solution of the present problem. A range-step table occurs when the same table value—for example, 1,700 calories—is applicable to many search arguments—for example, any weight between 90 and 99 pounds coupled with any age between 18 and 35. We need to recognize, therefore, that two range-step tables, for weight and age, are necessary in addition to the calorie maintenance table.

Our solution is shown in Figure 13.15. The user's view of the three tables is shown in Figure 13.15a and the COBOL implementation in Figure 13.15b. The

Figure 13.15 Range-step Tables

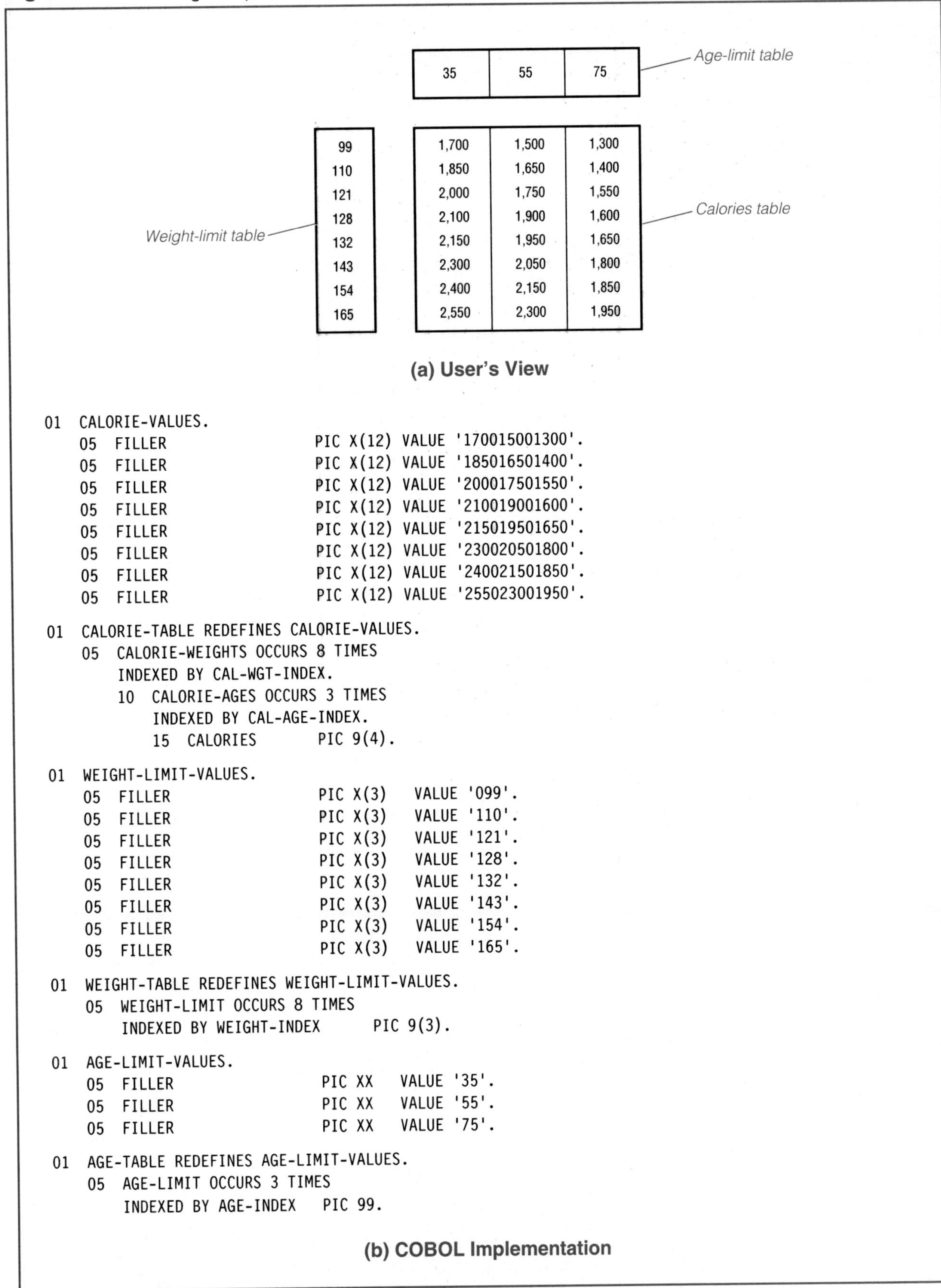

(a) User's View

```
01  CALORIE-VALUES.
    05  FILLER                  PIC X(12) VALUE '170015001300'.
    05  FILLER                  PIC X(12) VALUE '185016501400'.
    05  FILLER                  PIC X(12) VALUE '200017501550'.
    05  FILLER                  PIC X(12) VALUE '210019001600'.
    05  FILLER                  PIC X(12) VALUE '215019501650'.
    05  FILLER                  PIC X(12) VALUE '230020501800'.
    05  FILLER                  PIC X(12) VALUE '240021501850'.
    05  FILLER                  PIC X(12) VALUE '255023001950'.

01  CALORIE-TABLE REDEFINES CALORIE-VALUES.
    05  CALORIE-WEIGHTS OCCURS 8 TIMES
        INDEXED BY CAL-WGT-INDEX.
        10  CALORIE-AGES OCCURS 3 TIMES
            INDEXED BY CAL-AGE-INDEX.
            15  CALORIES        PIC 9(4).

01  WEIGHT-LIMIT-VALUES.
    05  FILLER                  PIC X(3)   VALUE '099'.
    05  FILLER                  PIC X(3)   VALUE '110'.
    05  FILLER                  PIC X(3)   VALUE '121'.
    05  FILLER                  PIC X(3)   VALUE '128'.
    05  FILLER                  PIC X(3)   VALUE '132'.
    05  FILLER                  PIC X(3)   VALUE '143'.
    05  FILLER                  PIC X(3)   VALUE '154'.
    05  FILLER                  PIC X(3)   VALUE '165'.

01  WEIGHT-TABLE REDEFINES WEIGHT-LIMIT-VALUES.
    05  WEIGHT-LIMIT OCCURS 8 TIMES
        INDEXED BY WEIGHT-INDEX      PIC 9(3).

01  AGE-LIMIT-VALUES.
    05  FILLER                  PIC XX   VALUE '35'.
    05  FILLER                  PIC XX   VALUE '55'.
    05  FILLER                  PIC XX   VALUE '75'.

01  AGE-TABLE REDEFINES AGE-LIMIT-VALUES.
    05  AGE-LIMIT OCCURS 3 TIMES
        INDEXED BY AGE-INDEX   PIC 99.
```

(b) COBOL Implementation

Figure 13.16 Hierarchy Chart

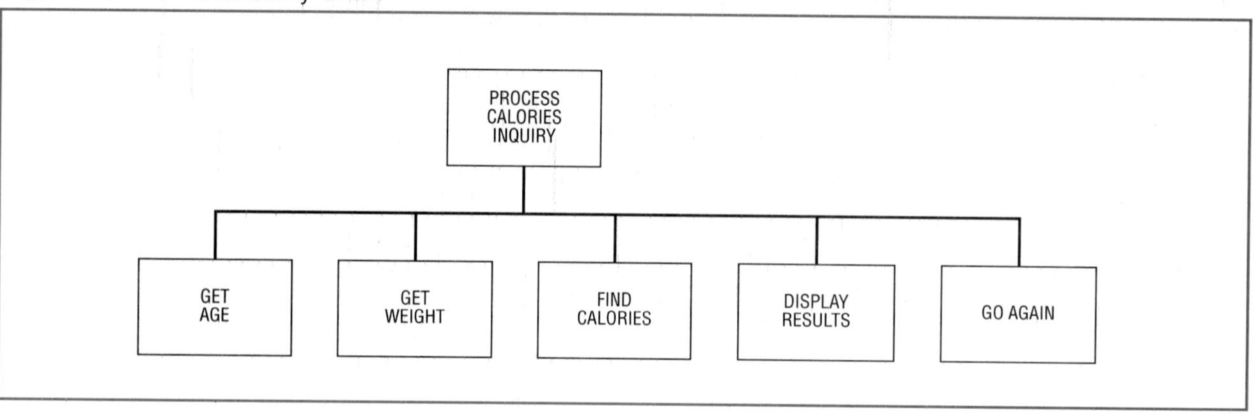

definition of the CALORIE-TABLE is straightforward and uses the OCCURS, VALUE, and REDEFINES clauses as explained earlier. The WEIGHT-LIMIT table stores only the upper limit for each weight class because the ranges overlap from one class to the next—that is, 90–99 pounds, 100–110 pounds, 111–121 pounds, and so on. In similar fashion the age-limit table stores only the upper limit for each age class.

The hierarchy chart in Figure 13.16 contains the modules to get the user's age and weight, determine the number of calories, display the results, then determine whether the entire process is to be repeated. The pseudocode in Figure 13.17 continually prompts the user until a valid age is received, then prompts the user for a valid weight. The ***nested search*** statement mimics the process a person would follow to determine the number of calories based on weight and age—that is, to search the weight limits in the various rows, then go across the appropriate row to search the age limits for that weight. Note, too, the less than or equal condition in the search argument, which checks only the upper limit in each weight (age) class.

The Completed Program

The completed program is shown in Figure 13.18 and parallels the pseudocode and hierarchy chart just discussed. Several features of the program merit attention.

1. The definition of CALORIE-TABLE in lines 17–32 as a two-level 8 x 3 table; the indexes CAL-WGT-INDEX and CAL-AGE-INDEX are defined with the table to reference the row and column, respectively.

2. The definition of two range-step tables for weight and age limits in lines 34–46 and lines 48–55, and referenced by WEIGHT-INDEX and AGE-INDEX, respectively.

3. The ***nested* SEARCH *statements*** in lines 82–94, which identify the row containing the weight limit (from the one-level weight-limit table), the column containing the age limit (from the one-level age-limit table), then reference the corresponding row and column in the calorie table to display the answer.

4. The SET statement in line 81 that initializes WEIGHT-INDEX (from the weight-limit table) *and* CAL-WGT-INDEX (from the two-level calorie table); the **SEARCH VARYING** statement in line 82 manipulates these indexes in conjunction with one another so that when the weight limit is found in the

Figure 13.17 Pseudocode

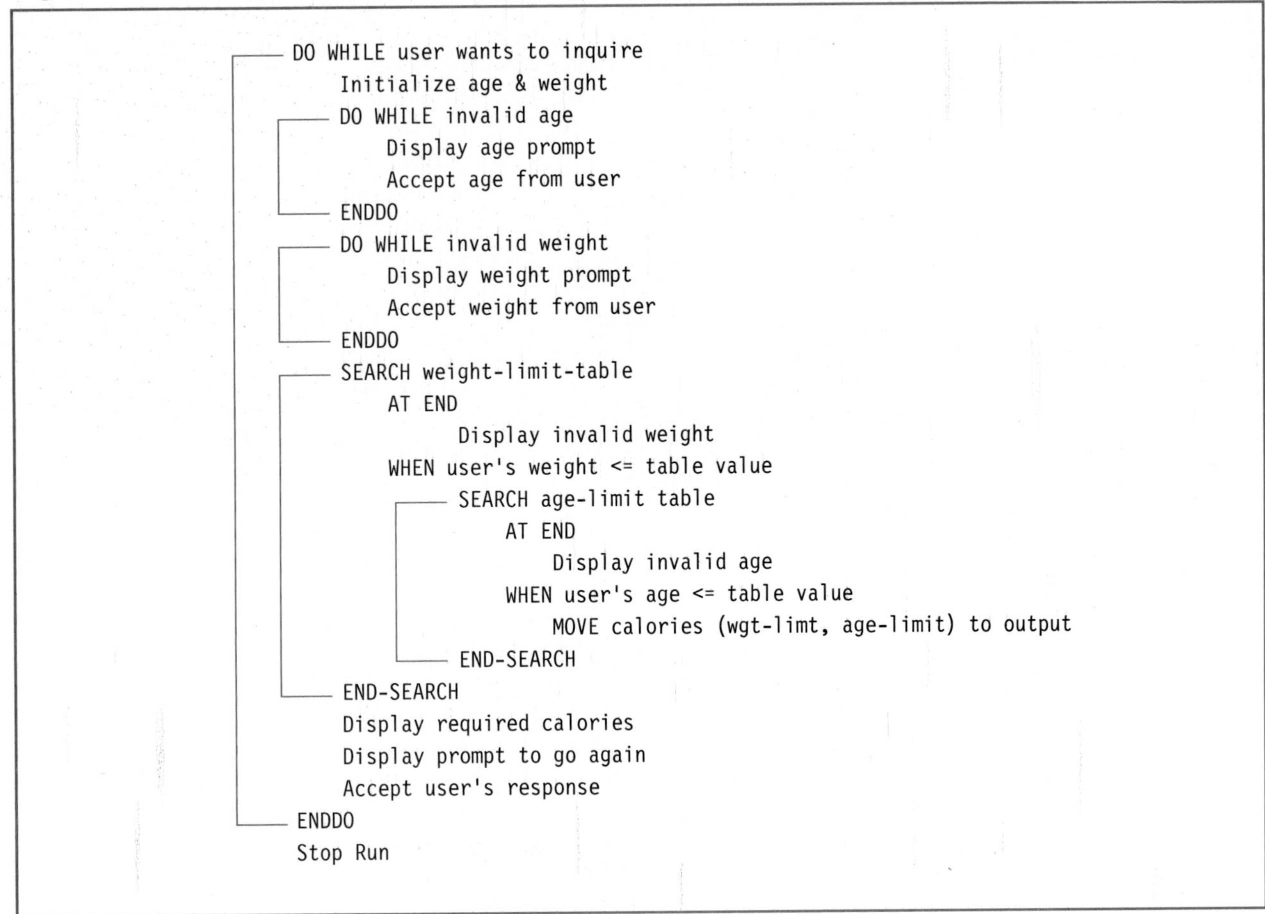

```
DO WHILE user wants to inquire
    Initialize age & weight
    DO WHILE invalid age
        Display age prompt
        Accept age from user
    ENDDO
    DO WHILE invalid weight
        Display weight prompt
        Accept weight from user
    ENDDO
    SEARCH weight-limit-table
        AT END
              Display invalid weight
        WHEN user's weight <= table value
              SEARCH age-limit table
                  AT END
                      Display invalid age
                  WHEN user's age <= table value
                      MOVE calories (wgt-limt, age-limit) to output
              END-SEARCH
    END-SEARCH
    Display required calories
    Display prompt to go again
    Accept user's response
ENDDO
Stop Run
```

Figure 13.18 Calories Program

```
IDENTIFICATION DIVISION.
PROGRAM-ID.    CALORIE.
AUTHOR.        CVV.

DATA DIVISION.
WORKING-STORAGE SECTION.
01  INDIVIDUAL-DATA.
    05  IND-AGE              PIC 99.
        88  VALID-AGE                  VALUE 18 THRU 75.
    05  IND-WEIGHT           PIC 9(3).
        88  VALID-WEIGHT               VALUE 90 THRU 165.

01  PROGRAM-VARIABLES.
    05  CALORIES-NEEDED      PIC Z,ZZ9 VALUE ZEROS.
    05  GO-AGAIN-SWITCH      PIC X.

01  CALORIE-VALUES.
    05  FILLER                PIC X(12) VALUE '170015001300'.
```

Definition of two-level table

Figure 13.18 *(continued)*

```
       05  FILLER               PIC X(12) VALUE '185016501400'.
       05  FILLER               PIC X(12) VALUE '200017501550'.
       05  FILLER               PIC X(12) VALUE '210019001600'.
       05  FILLER               PIC X(12) VALUE '215019501650'.
       05  FILLER               PIC X(12) VALUE '230020501800'.
       05  FILLER               PIC X(12) VALUE '240021501850'.
       05  FILLER               PIC X(12) VALUE '255023001950'.

   01  CALORIE-TABLE REDEFINES CALORIE-VALUES.
       05  CALORY-WEIGHTS OCCURS 8 TIMES
           INDEXED BY CAL-WGT-INDEX.
           10  CALORY-AGES OCCURS 3 TIMES
               INDEXED BY CAL-AGE-INDEX.
               15  CALORIES     PIC 9(4).

   01  WEIGHT-LIMIT-VALUES.
       05  FILLER               PIC X(3)   VALUE '099'.
       05  FILLER               PIC X(3)   VALUE '110'.
       05  FILLER               PIC X(3)   VALUE '121'.
       05  FILLER               PIC X(3)   VALUE '128'.
       05  FILLER               PIC X(3)   VALUE '132'.
       05  FILLER               PIC X(3)   VALUE '143'.
       05  FILLER               PIC X(3)   VALUE '154'.
       05  FILLER               PIC X(3)   VALUE '165'.

   01  WEIGHT-TABLE REDEFINES WEIGHT-LIMIT-VALUES.
       05  WEIGHT-LIMIT OCCURS 8 TIMES
           INDEXED BY WEIGHT-INDEX      PIC 9(3).

   01  AGE-LIMIT-VALUES.
       05  FILLER               PIC XX   VALUE '35'.
       05  FILLER               PIC XX   VALUE '55'.
       05  FILLER               PIC XX   VALUE '75'.

   01  AGE-TABLE REDEFINES AGE-LIMIT-VALUES.
       05  AGE-LIMIT OCCURS 3 TIMES
           INDEXED BY AGE-INDEX   PIC 99.

   PROCEDURE DIVISION.
   PROCESS-CALORIE-INQUIRY.
       PERFORM UNTIL GO-AGAIN-SWITCH = 'n' OR 'N'
           MOVE ZEROS TO IND-AGE IND-WEIGHT
           PERFORM GET-AGE
               UNTIL VALID-AGE
           PERFORM GET-WEIGHT
               UNTIL VALID-WEIGHT
           PERFORM FIND-CALORIES
           PERFORM DISPLAY-RESULTS
           PERFORM GO-AGAIN
       END-PERFORM.
       DISPLAY 'May all your calories be non-fat'.
```

Definition of two-level table

Prompts user continually until valid age and weight are entered

Figure 13.18 *(continued)*

```
70          STOP RUN.
71
72      GET-AGE.
73          DISPLAY 'Enter Age (18-75): ' NO ADVANCING.
74          ACCEPT IND-AGE.
75
76      GET-WEIGHT.
77          DISPLAY 'Enter Weight (90-165): ' NO ADVANCING.
78          ACCEPT IND-WEIGHT.
79
80      FIND-CALORIES.
81          SET WEIGHT-INDEX CAL-WGT-INDEX TO 1.
82          SEARCH WEIGHT-LIMIT VARYING CAL-WGT-INDEX
83             AT END
84                 DISPLAY 'Weight not found in table'
85             WHEN IND-WEIGHT <= WEIGHT-LIMIT (WEIGHT-INDEX)
86                 SET AGE-INDEX CAL-AGE-INDEX TO 1
87                 SEARCH AGE-LIMIT VARYING CAL-AGE-INDEX
88                     AT END
89                         DISPLAY 'Age not found in table'
90                     WHEN IND-AGE <= AGE-LIMIT (AGE-INDEX)
91                         MOVE CALORIES (CAL-WGT-INDEX, CAL-AGE-INDEX)
92                         TO CALORIES-NEEDED
93                 END-SEARCH
94          END-SEARCH.
95
96      DISPLAY-RESULTS.
97          DISPLAY ' '.
98          DISPLAY CALORIES-NEEDED ' calories/day will maintain '
99          'a weight of ' IND-WEIGHT ' pounds at age ' IND-AGE.
100         DISPLAY ' '.
101
102     GO-AGAIN.
103         DISPLAY 'Go again? (Y/N) ' NO ADVANCING.
104         ACCEPT GO-AGAIN-SWITCH.
```

Nested SEARCH statements use VARYING option

first table, the corresponding row is set in the second table. The SET statement in line 86 and the SEARCH VARYING statement in line 87 function in similar fashion for the age limit and corresponding column in the calorie table.

5. The MOVE statement in line 91 is a direct lookup that uses values of CAL-WGT-INDEX and CAL-AGE-INDEX established by the nested SEARCH statements.
6. The various ACCEPT and DISPLAY statements throughout the program that utilize screen I-O.

LIMITATIONS OF COBOL-74

Seven levels of subscripting are permitted in COBOL-85 as opposed to the earlier limit of three; most applications, however, do not require even three-level tables.

COBOL-85 facilitates the initialization of a table in which all elements have the same value by allowing the VALUE clause to be specified in the same entry as an OCCURS clause. (The technique was illustrated in lines 61–62 of Figure 13.9.) This was not permitted in COBOL-74, which required a PERFORM VARYING statement or REDEFINES clause to achieve the same result.

The optional END-SEARCH scope terminator is new to COBOL-85 and terminates the conditional portion of the SEARCH and SEARCH ALL statements; the scope terminator makes it possible to nest SEARCH statements.

SUMMARY

Points to Remember

- Multilevel tables of up to seven levels are possible in COBOL-85 although most applications use tables of only one, two, or three dimensions.
- The entries in multiple-level tables may be referenced in different hierarchical levels. The number of subscripts (indexes) needed is equal to the number of OCCURS clauses in the entry definition.
- Tables at any level may be initialized through a combination of the OCCURS, VALUES, and REDEFINES clauses. The OCCURS clause allocates space for the table, the VALUE clause places data in these locations, and the REDEFINES clause assigns another name to previously allocated space.
- Multilevel tables can be manipulated by using the PERFORM VARYING statement with the addition of the appropriate AFTER clause(s). The bottom subscript (index) is always manipulated first.
- The SEARCH VARYING statement manipulates the indexes in two tables in conjunction with one another; the technique is often used with range-step tables, in which the table arguments are stored in a separate table.

Key Words and Concepts

Compilation error
Detail report
Execution error
Hierarchical level
Nested search statement
Range-step table
Summary report
Three-level table
Two-level table
User view

COBOL Elements

AFTER
BY
END-SEARCH
OCCURS
PERFORM VARYING
REDEFINES
SEARCH VARYING
UNTIL
VALUE

FILL-IN

1. A two-level table requires two ______________ clauses in its definition.
2. In a PERFORM VARYING statement with two subscripts, the (bottom/top) subscript is varied first.
3. COBOL-85 permits a maximum of ______________ subscripts.
4. If a Procedure Division reference is made to FIELD-ONE (SUB1, SUB2), SUB1 refers to the ______________ level OCCURS clause, whereas SUB2 refers to the ______________ level OCCURS clause.
5. In COBOL-74 a VALUE clause (may/may not) be used in conjunction with an ______________ clause to initialize a table, and so a ______________ clause is used as well.
6. The statement:

```
PERFORM PARAGRAPH-A
    VARYING SUB1 FROM 1 BY 1 UNTIL SUB1 > 5
        AFTER SUB2 FROM 1 BY 1 UNTIL SUB2 > 6.
```

   will perform PARAGRAPH-A a total of ______________ times.
7. The PERFORM statement of question 6 begins execution by setting SUB1 to 1, and varying SUB2 from ______________ to ______________, after which SUB1 will be incremented to ______________, and SUB2 will again vary from ______________ to ______________.
8. Given the COBOL definition:

```
01  CORPORATION.
    05  REGION  OCCURS 4 TIMES.
        10  STATE  OCCURS 5 TIMES.
            15  CITY  OCCURS 6 TIMES  PIC 9(6).
```

   A total of ______________ elements are present in the table.
9. Answer with respect to the table of question 8. Any reference to REGION requires ______________ subscript(s), a reference to STATE requires ______________ subscript(s), and a reference to CITY requires ______________ subscript(s).

TRUE/FALSE

1. A maximum of seven OCCURS clauses in a given table is permitted in COBOL-85.
2. A given entry may contain both an OCCURS clause and a PICTURE clause.
3. A given entry may contain both an OCCURS clause and a VALUE clause.

4. The REDEFINES clause is required whenever a table is initialized.
5. A PERFORM VARYING statement may vary indexes as well as subscripts.
6. Referencing a data name with two subscripts, when only a single OCCURS clause appears in the table definition, produces a compilation error.
7. Referencing a data name with a subscript value of 50, when the OCCURS clause indicates only 10 entries, produces a compilation error.
8. SEARCH statements may be nested.
9. The VARYING, FROM, BY, and AFTER clauses are mandatory in a PERFORM statement.
10. A PERFORM VARYING statement will always execute the designated procedure at least once.

PROBLEMS

1. Write out the 12 pairs of values that will be assumed by SUB-1 and SUB-2 as a result of the statement:

```
PERFORM 10-PROCESS-TABLE
    VARYING SUB-1 FROM 1 BY 1
        UNTIL SUB-1 > 4
    AFTER SUB-2 FROM 1 BY 1
        UNTIL SUB-2 > 3.
```

2. Indicate the 24 sets of values that will be assumed by SUB-1, SUB-2, and SUB-3 as a result of the following statement. Remember that the bottom subscript is varied first.

```
PERFORM 10-PROCESS-TABLE
    VARYING SUB-1 FROM 1 BY 1
        UNTIL SUB-1 > 3
    AFTER SUB-2 FROM 1 BY 1
        UNTIL SUB-2 > 2
    AFTER SUB-3 FROM 1 BY 1
        UNTIL SUB-3 > 4.
```

3. Given the following table definition:

```
01  CORPORATE-DATA.
    05  COMPANY OCCURS 10 TIMES.
        10  DIVISION-NAME          PIC X(15).
        10  YEARLY-FINANCIAL-DATA OCCURS 4 TIMES.
            15  REVENUE            PIC 9(7)
            15  NET-INCOME         PIC 9(7).
```

a. Indicate an appropriate storage schematic.

b. State whether the following are valid or invalid references, and if invalid, indicate whether the problem occurs during compilation or execution:

   i. CORPORATE-DATA
   ii. COMPANY
   iii. COMPANY (8)
   iv. DIVISION-NAME (8)
   v. DIVISION-NAME (12)

vi. YEARLY-FINANCIAL-DATA (4)
vii. REVENUE (10, 4)
viii. NET-INCOME (10,4)
ix. REVENUE (4, 10)

4. A corporation monitors monthly sales for its six branch offices according to the following table definition:

```
01  CORPORATE-SALES-TABLE.
    05  BRANCH-OFFICE OCCURS 6 TIMES.
        10  BRANCH-NAME            PIC X(10).
        10  MONTHS OCCURS 12 TIMES.
            15  SALES-AMOUNT       PIC 9(6).
```

   a. Indicate the appropriate storage schematic.
   b. Write a PERFORM VARYING statement to determine the annual sales for the third branch office.
   c. Write a PERFORM VARYING statement to determine the corporate sales for May.
   d. Write a PERFORM VARYING statement to determine the corporate sales for the entire year.
   e. Develop an FD, corresponding record description, and associated Procedure Division statements, to read the data for CORPORATE-SALES-TABLE from a file of six records; that is, each incoming record has the 12 monthly sales for a particular branch office.
   f. Develop an FD, corresponding record description, and associated Procedure Division statements, to read the data for CORPORATE-SALES-TABLE from a file of 12 records; that is, each incoming record has the six branch office amounts for a particular month.

5. Your professor has two sections of COBOL. Each section has 40 students. Each student is expected to submit six projects and take three examinations. Develop a file structure suitable to all of this data in a single table.

6. The following table was suggested to tabulate enrollments for the various colleges within a university. Each college, such as the College of Engineering, has multiple majors: Mechanical Engineering, Electrical Engineering, and so on.

```
01  ENROLLMENT-DATA.
    05  COLLEGE OCCURS 3 TIMES.
        10  MAJOR OCCURS 50 TIMES.
            15  YEAR OCCURS 4 TIMES.
                20  NUMBER-OF-STUDENTS      PIC 9(4).
```

   a. Indicate an appropriate storage schematic.
   b. State whether the following are valid or invalid references, and if invalid, indicate whether the problem occurs during compilation or execution:
      i. ENROLLMENT-DATA
      ii. COLLEGE (1)
      iii. MAJOR (1)
      iv. YEAR (1)
      v. NUMBER-OF-STUDENTS (1)
      vi. NUMBER-OF-STUDENTS (1, 2, 3)
      vii. NUMBER-OF-STUDENTS (4, 5, 6)

c. Write PERFORM VARYING statements to determine:
   i. The total number of students in the university.
   ii. The total number of seniors in the first college.
   iii. The total number of students in the first major of the first college.
   iv. The total number of freshmen (year 1) in the first college.
   v. The total number of freshmen in the university.

Sorting

CHAPTER OUTLINE

OBJECTIVES

After reading this chapter you will be able to:

- Distinguish between an internal sort, a utility sort, and the COBOL SORT statement.
- Differentiate between an ascending and a descending sort; between major, intermediate, and minor keys; and between primary, secondary, and tertiary keys.
- Define collating sequence; discuss the most significant differences between EBCDIC and ASCII and how the collating sequence affects fields with an embedded sign.
- Explain the syntax of the COBOL SORT statement, and the supporting RELEASE, RETURN, and SD statements.
- Explain the use of INPUT PROCEDURE to sort on a calculated field, and/or to selectively pass records to the sort work file.
- Distinguish between a merge and a sort.

OVERVIEW

Sorting (the rearrangement of data) is one of the most frequent operations in data processing, making it possible to present data in a variety of sequences according to the analysis required. Transactions may be listed alphabetically, alphabetically by location, in ascending or descending sequence by account balance, and so on. The sorting procedure itself is accomplished in one of three ways:

1. An internal sort, in which the programmer develops his or her own logic within the application program. (This approach is typically not used by the COBOL programmer.)
2. A utility sort, in which an independent sort program is executed outside of the application program as a separate step.
3. The COBOL SORT statement, in which control is passed to the independent sort program from within the COBOL program. (Our discussion deals exclusively with this approach.)

We begin the chapter by developing the general concepts associated with sorting, then present the necessary statements to implement sorting within a COBOL program. We develop two parallel programs to illustrate variations within the SORT statement and conclude with a brief discussion of merging, which is a special case of sorting.

System Concepts

A ***sort key*** is a field within a record that determines how the file is to be arranged. Several keys may be specified in a single sort, as in the case of a departmental census in which employees are to appear alphabetically within department. In other words, the file is to be rearranged (that is, sorted) so that all employees in the same department appear together, and further, so that employees in the same department appear alphabetically. Department is a more important key than employee name; thus department is considered the ***major key*** and employee name the ***minor key***. (Other, equally correct, terminology refers to department as the ***primary key*** and name as the ***secondary key***.)

Sorting is done in one of two sequences: ***ascending*** (low to high) or ***descending*** (high to low). Listing employees in increasing order of salary is an example of an ascending sort, whereas listing them in decreasing order (that is, with the highest salary first) represents a descending sort. *Any sort on an alphabetic field, (employee name, for example) is always perceived as an ascending sort.* (An ascending sort is assumed if the sequence is not specified.)

To be absolutely sure of this terminology, consider Figure 14.1. Figure 14.1a lists unsorted data for 12 students. Figure 14.1b displays these records after they have been sorted by name only. Figure 14.1c shows a primary sort on year (descending) and a secondary sort on name. Thus, all students in year four are listed first (in alphabetical order), then all students in year three, and so on. Finally, Figure 14.1d illustrates primary, secondary, and tertiary sorts. All business majors are listed first, then all engineering majors, and finally all liberal arts majors. Within each major, students are listed by year in descending order and are also listed alphabetically within year.

Collating Sequence

The sequencing of numeric items is done strictly according to their algebraic values; for example, −10 is less than +5, which is less than +10. The length of a numeric field does not enter into the comparison; for example, a four-digit integer field equal to 0099 is less than a three-digit field equal to 100.

The sequencing of alphabetic and/or alphanumeric fields is more subtle with fields of different length—for example, GREEN and GREENFIELD. The sorting algorithm compares the two names one character at a time, from left to right and determines that the first five letters, G, R, E, E, and N, are the same in both names. The shorter field (GREEN in the example) is then extended with blanks so that comparison may continue. A blank, however, is always considered smaller than any other letter, so that GREEN will be placed ahead of GREENFIELD.

The sorting of alphanumeric fields is further complicated when the sort key contains letters and numbers. Comparison still proceeds from left to right, but which alphanumeric key should come first, 111 or AAA? Surprisingly, either answer could be correct, depending on the ***collating sequence*** in effect. Collating sequence is defined as the ordered list (from low to high) of all valid characters and is a function of manufacturer; IBM mainframes use **EBCDIC,** whereas almost every other computer, including the PC, uses **ASCII.** Both sequences are shown in Figure 14.2 for selected characters.

As can be seen from Figure 14.2, the number one 1 comes *after* the letter A in EBCDIC, but *before* the letter A in ASCII. In other words, in an alphanumeric sort a key of 111 will precede a key of AAA under the ASCII collating sequence, but follow it under EBCDIC. It is imperative, therefore, that you be aware of the collating sequence in effect when alphanumeric keys are specified. This is especially true in a

Figure 14.1 Sorting Vocabulary

Primary Key: Name (Ascending)

NAME	YEAR	MAJOR
Smith	1	Liberal arts
Jones	4	Engineering
Adams	3	Business
Howe	2	Liberal arts
Frank	1	Engineering
Epstein	2	Engineering
Zev	4	Business
Benjamin	4	Business
Grauer	3	Liberal arts
Crawford	2	Engineering
Deutsch	4	Business
Makoske	1	Business

(a) Unsorted Data

NAME	YEAR	MAJOR
Adams	3	Business
Benjamin	4	Business
Crawford	2	Engineering
Deutsch	4	Business
Epstein	2	Engineering
Frank	1	Engineering
Grauer	3	Liberal arts
Howe	2	Liberal arts
Jones	4	Engineering
Makoske	1	Business
Smith	1	Liberal arts
Zev	4	Business

(b) Sorted Data, One Key

Primary Key: Year (Descending)
Secondary Key: Name (Ascending)

NAME	YEAR	MAJOR
Benjamin	4	Business
Deutsch	4	Business
Jones	4	Engineering
Zev	4	Business
Adams	3	Business
Grauer	3	Liberal arts
Crawford	2	Engineering
Epstein	2	Engineering
Howe	2	Liberal arts
Frank	1	Engineering
Makoske	1	Business
Smith	1	Liberal arts

(c) Sorted Data, Two Keys

Primary Key: Major (Ascending)
Secondary Key: Year (Descending)
Tertiary Key: Name (Ascending)

NAME	YEAR	MAJOR
Benjamin	4	Business
Deutsch	4	Business
Zev	4	Business
Adams	3	Business
Makoske	1	Business
Jones	4	Engineering
Crawford	2	Engineering
Epstein	2	Engineering
Frank	1	Engineering
Grauer	3	Liberal arts
Howe	2	Liberal arts
Smith	1	Liberal arts

(d) Sorted Data, Three Keys

multivendor environment, as when on-site mini- or microcomputers offload to an IBM mainframe.

Embedded Sign

The collating sequence has yet an additional consequence with signed numeric fields. Arithmetic operations require positive and negative numbers, and hence, when we do arithmetic with pencil and paper, we precede the numbers with plus

Figure 14.2 EBCDIC and ASCII Collating Sequences

EBCDIC		ASCII	
	(space)		(space)
.	(period)	“	(quotation mark)
<	(less than)	$	(currency symbol)
(	(left parenthesis)	’	(apostrophe)
+	(plus symbol)	(	(left parenthesis)
$	(currency symbol)	)	(right parenthesis)
*	(asterisk)	*	(asterisk)
)	(right parenthesis)	+	(plus symbol)
;	(semicolon)	,	(comma)
–	(hyphen, minus symbol)	–	(hyphen, minus symbol)
/	(slash)	.	(period, decimal point)
,	(comma)	/	(slash)
>	(greater than)		0 through 9
’	(apostrophe)	;	(semicolon)
=	(equal sign)	<	(less than)
“	(quotation mark)	=	(equal sign)
	a through z (lower case)	>	(greater than)
	A through Z (upper case)		A through Z (upper case)
	0 through 9		a through z (lower case)

Figure 14.3 Embedded Signs (ASCII versus EBCDIC)

(a) ASCII

Digit	Character	Digit	Character
+1	1	–1	!
+2	2	–2	“
+3	3	–3	#
+4	4	–4	$
+5	5	–5	%
+6	6	–6	&
+7	7	–7	’
+8	8	–8	(
+9	9	–9	)
+0	0	–0	Space

(b) EBCDIC

Digit	Character	Digit	Character
+1	A	–1	J
+2	B	–2	K
+3	C	–3	L
+4	D	–4	M
+5	E	–5	N
+6	F	–6	O
+7	G	–7	P
+8	H	–8	Q
+9	I	–9	R
+0	{	–0	}

and minus signs. The computer, however, embeds the sign within the low-order digit of the number according to the table in Figure 14.3. The advantage of an ***embedded sign*** is that a position is saved in the storage medium; for example, only one position is needed for a single-digit numeric field versus two (one for the digit and one for the sign) if the sign were stored separately.

Figure 14.4 Embedded Signs (ASCII versus EBCDIC)/II

```
  Name         Account Balance
John Doe           $1,005
Mary Smith         $1,005CR
Frank Coulter      $2,000
Erik Parker        $2,000CR
```

(a) Report

```
John Doe           1005
Mary Smith         100%
Frank Coulter      2000
Erik Parker        200
```

Law-order character is a space

(b) Data (ASCII)

```
John Doe           100E
Mary Smith         100N
Frank Coulter      200{
Erik Parker        200}
```

(c) Data (EBCDIC)

The effect of the collating sequence is seen in Figure 14.4. Figure 14.4a contains a simple report in which John Doe and Mary Smith have positive and negative balances of $1,005. The data that produce the report are shown in Figure 14.4b for ASCII and in Figure 14.4c for EBCDIC. The record for Mary Smith contains a percent sign in the lower-order digit under ASCII according to the character for -5 in Figure 14.3a, but an upper case N under EBCDIC as indicated in Figure 14.3b.

The optional **SIGN** clause (entered after the PICTURE clause) makes it possible to embed the sign as the leading rather than the trailing character, and/or to establish a separate position for the sign. Consider:

```
[[SIGN IS] {LEADING } [SEPARATE CHARACTER]]
           {TRAILING}
```

The vast majority of applications, however, embed the sign as the trailing character (the default action taken by COBOL) as was illustrated in Figure 14.4.

COBOL Implementation

The COBOL requirements for implementing a sort center on the SORT statement. In addition, you must be familiar with an SD (sort description) and with the RELEASE and RETURN statements.

SORT Statement

The syntax for the **SORT** statement is as follows:

```
SORT file-name-1

    {ON {DESCENDING} KEY {data-name-1} . . .} . . .
        {ASCENDING }

    [WITH DUPLICATES IN ORDER]

    [COLLATING SEQUENCE IS alphabet-name]

    {INPUT PROCEDURE IS procedure-name-1 [{THRU   } procedure-name-2]}
    {USING {fine-name-2}                  [{THROUGH}                 ]}

    {OUTPUT PROCEDURE IS procedure-name-3 [{THRU   } procedure-name-4]}
    {GIVING {file-name-3}                  [{THROUGH}                 ]}
```

Multiple sort keys are listed in the order of importance, with the major (primary) key listed first. Thus, the statement:

```
SORT STUDENT-FILE
    ASCENDING KEY STUDENT-MAJOR
    DESCENDING KEY YEAR-IN-SCHOOL
    ASCENDING KEY STUDENT-NAME
```

corresponds to the order of the keys in Figure 14.1d. (STUDENT-MAJOR is the primary key, YEAR-IN-SCHOOL is the secondary key, and STUDENT-NAME is the tertiary key.) As can be seen from the general syntax, KEY is an optional reserved word, so that the preceding statement could have been written as:

```
SORT STUDENT-FILE
    ASCENDING STUDENT-MAJOR
    DESCENDING YEAR-IN-SCHOOL
    ASCENDING STUDENT-NAME
```

When consecutive keys have the same sequence (both ascending or both descending), ASCENDING (or DESCENDING) need not be repeated. Hence, if it were necessary to obtain a master list of students in ascending order by year in school, and alphabetically within year, you could code:

```
SORT STUDENT-FILE
    ASCENDING YEAR-IN-SCHOOL
              STUDENT-NAME
```

The **WITH DUPLICATES IN ORDER** phrase in the SORT statement ensures that the sequence of records with duplicate keys in the output file will be identical to the sequence of the records in the input file. The phrase is illustrated in Figure 14.9, which appears later in the chapter.

The **COLLATING SEQUENCE** clause allows you to change the collating sequence; that is, you can specify ASCII on an IBM mainframe or EBCDIC on a PC. (Implementation of an alternate collating sequence is less than straightforward, and you should consult an appropriate vendor manual if you wish to use one.)

The SORT statement requires a choice between **INPUT PROCEDURE** and **USING,** and between **OUTPUT PROCEDURE** and **GIVING,** resulting in four possible combinations: USING/GIVING, USING/OUTPUT PROCEDURE, INPUT PROCEDURE/GIVING, and INPUT PROCEDURE/OUTPUT PROCEDURE. The choice between the different options depends on the specific application. (The chapter contains two listings for USING/GIVING and INPUT PROCEDURE/OUTPUT PROCEDURE.)

The difference between USING and INPUT PROCEDURE is that INPUT PROCEDURE requires the programmer to do the I/O to and from the sort utility, whereas the USING option does the I/O automatically. INPUT PROCEDURE is thus a more general technique in that it permits sorting on a ***calculated field***, a field not contained in the input record. Assume, for example, that an employee record contains the present and previous salary, but not the percent of salary increase. The USING option can sort on either salary, but not on the salary increase because the latter is a calculated field that it is not present in the input record.

The INPUT PROCEDURE also allows you to *selectively* pass records to the sort utility, a desirable practice in instances where only some of the records in an input file are to appear in a subsequent report. Sorting is time consuming and thus, it is highly inefficient to sort an entire file only to eliminate records after sorting. It is far better to select the records prior to the sort by using the INPUT PROCEDURE.

The difference between OUTPUT PROCEDURE and GIVING is the status of the sorted file. The OUTPUT PROCEDURE uses a *temporary* work file, which disappears after the program ends so that the results of the sort are lost. The GIVING option creates a *permanent* file containing the sorted results that remains after the program has ended.

SD (Sort Description)

The first file in the SORT statement references the ***sort work file*** that was previously defined in an **SD** (Sort Description) statement in the Data Division. The SD is analogous to an FD except that it refers to a sort work file, rather than an ordinary file used for I/O. The SD has the general syntax:

```
SD file-name-1

   [RECORD CONTAINS [integer-1 TO] integer-2 CHARACTERS]

   [DATA {RECORD IS  } {data-name-1} . . .]
   [     {RECORDS ARE}                    ]
```

RELEASE and RETURN

The **RELEASE** and **RETURN** statements are required in the INPUT and OUTPUT PROCEDURE, respectively. The RELEASE statement is analogous to a WRITE statement and writes a record to the sort work file (the file defined in the SD).

```
RELEASE record-name [FROM identifier]
```

The RELEASE statement appears in the INPUT PROCEDURE. The RETURN statement, on the other hand, is analogous to a READ statement and appears in the OUTPUT PROCEDURE. It has the format:

```
RETURN file-name [INTO identifier]
    [AT END imperative-statement-1]
   [NOT AT END imperative-statement-2]
[END-RETURN]
```

The RETURN statement reads a record from the sort work file (the file defined in the SD) for subsequent processing in the program.

The SORT statement and its related statements can be integrated into any COBOL program. We proceed to develop a typical application, with specifications in the usual format. In actuality we present two separate programs, to illustrate both the INPUT PROCEDURE/OUTPUT PROCEDURE and USING/GIVING options of the SORT statement.

PROGRAMMING SPECIFICATIONS

Program Name: Sort Programs

Narrative: The specifications call for *two* programs to illustrate the USING/GIVING and INPUT PROCEDURE/OUTPUT PROCEDURE options of the SORT statement. The programs use the same data file but produce different reports.

Input File(s): SALES-FILE

Input Record Layout:

```
01  SALES-RECORD-IN.
    05  SR-ACCOUNT-NUMBER        PIC 9(6).
    05  FILLER                   PIC X.
    05  SR-NAME                  PIC X(15).
    05  SR-SALES                 PIC S9(4).
    05  FILLER                   PIC XX.
    05  SR-COMMISSION-PERCENT    PIC V99.
    05  FILLER                   PIC XX.
    05  SR-LOCATION              PIC X(15).
    05  SR-REGION                PIC X(11).
```

Test Data: See Figure 14.5.

Report Layout: See Figure 14.6a and 14.6b. The report layout—the heading, detail, and total lines—is the same for both programs, but the contents of the reports—the specific records as well as the sequence of those records—are different.

Processing Requirements:

1. Develop two parallel programs, each of which processes a file of sales records and computes the commission due for each incoming transaction. The amount of the commission is equal to the sales amount times the commission percentage.
2. The first program is to use the USING/GIVING option to produce a master list of *all* incoming records. The records are to be in sequence by region, location, and name as shown in Figure 14.6a.
3. The second program is to use the INPUT PROCEDURE/OUTPUT PROCEDURE option and list only the transactions with a commission greater than $100. The records are to appear in decreasing order of commission as shown in Figure 14.6b.

Figure 14.5 Test Data (ASCII Format)

```
000069 BENWAY     023!  10  CHICAGO         MIDWEST
000100 HUMMER     010'  05  CHICAGO         MIDWEST
000101 CLARK      1500  10  TRENTON         NORTHEAST
000104 CLARK      0500  03  TRENTON         NORTHEAST
100000 JOHNSON    030#  06  ST. PETERSBURG  SOUTHEAST
130101 CLARK      3200  20  TRENTON         NORTHEAST
203000 HAAS       8900  05  ST. LOUIS       MIDWEST
248545 JOHNSON    0345  14  ST. PETERSBURG  SOUTHEAST
277333 HAAS       009(  08  ST. LOUIS       MIDWEST
400000 JOHNSON    070)  08  ST. PETERSBURG  SOUTHEAST
444333 ADAMS      100%  01  NEW YORK        NORTHEAST
444444 FEGEN      0100  02  ST. PETERSBURG  SOUTHEAST
475365 HAAS       0333  05  ST. LOUIS       MIDWEST
476236 FEGEN      037&  03  ST. PETERSBURG  SOUTHEAST
476530 BENWAY     023%  05  CHICAGO         MIDWEST
555555 FEGEN      0304  05  ST. PETERSBURG  SOUTHEAST
555666 ADAMS      2003  20  NEW YORK        NORTHEAST
576235 CLARK      0100  03  TRENTON         NORTHEAST
583645 KARLSTROM  0145  04  BALTIMORE       NORTHEAST
649356 HUMMER     0345  05  CHICAGO         MIDWEST
694446 HUMMER     0904  10  CHICAGO         MIDWEST
700039 MARCUS     0932  10  BALTIMORE       NORTHEAST
750020 MARCUS     0305  05  BALTIMORE       NORTHEAST
800396 KARLSTROM  3030  09  BALTIMORE       NORTHEAST
878787 JOHNSON    1235  12  ST. PETERSBURG  SOUTHEAST
987654 ADAMS      2005  10  NEW YORK        NORTHEAST
988888 BENWAY     0450  01  CHICAGO         MIDWEST
999340 BENWAY     0334  30  CHICAGO         MIDWEST
```

Figure 14.6 Sorted Reports

```
                              SALES ACTIVITY REPORT        04/21/93          PAGE  1

 REGION     LOCATION          NAME          ACCOUNT #        SALES     COMMISSION
MIDWEST     CHICAGO           BENWAY          000069      $  231-       $   23-
MIDWEST     CHICAGO           BENWAY          476530      $  235-       $   12-
MIDWEST     CHICAGO           BENWAY          988888      $  450        $    5
MIDWEST     CHICAGO           BENWAY          999340      $  334        $  100
MIDWEST     CHICAGO           HUMMER          000100      $  107-       $    5-
MIDWEST     CHICAGO           HUMMER          649356      $  345        $   17
MIDWEST     CHICAGO           HUMMER          694446      $  904        $   90
MIDWEST     ST. LOUIS         HAAS            203000      $8,900        $  445
MIDWEST     ST. LOUIS         HAAS            277333      $   98-       $    8-
MIDWEST     ST. LOUIS         HAAS            475365      $  333        $   17
```

(a) By Region, Location, and Name (All Records)

Figure 14.6 *(continued)*

SALES ACTIVITY REPORT 04/21/93 PAGE 3

REGION	LOCATION	NAME	ACCOUNT #	SALES	COMMISSION
NORTHEAST	TRENTON	CLARK	576235	$ 100	$ 3
SOUTHEAST	ST. PETERSBURG	FEGEN	444444	$ 100	$ 2
SOUTHEAST	ST. PETERSBURG	FEGEN	476236	$ 376-	$ 11-
SOUTHEAST	ST. PETERSBURG	FEGEN	555555	$ 304	$ 15
SOUTHEAST	ST. PETERSBURG	JOHNSON	100000	$ 303-	$ 18-
SOUTHEAST	ST. PETERSBURG	JOHNSON	248545	$ 345	$ 48

```
57-
148
2,540
```

SALES ACTIVITY REPORT 04/21/93 PAGE 2

REGION	LOCATION	NAME	ACCOUNT #	SALES	COMMISSION
NORTHEAST	BALTIMORE	KARLSTROM	583645	$ 145	$ 6
NORTHEAST	BALTIMORE	KARLSTROM	800396	$3,030	$ 273
NORTHEAST	BALTIMORE	MARCUS	700039	$ 932	$ 93
NORTHEAST	BALTIMORE	MARCUS	750020	$ 305	$ 15
NORTHEAST	NEW YORK	ADAMS	444333	$1,005-	$ 10-
NORTHEAST	NEW YORK	ADAMS	555666	$2,003	$ 401
NORTHEAST	NEW YORK	ADAMS	987654	$2,005	$ 201
NORTHEAST	TRENTON	CLARK	000101	$1,500	$ 150
NORTHEAST	TRENTON	CLARK	000104	$ 500	$ 15
NORTHEAST	TRENTON	CLARK	130101	$3,200	$ 640

(a) By Region, Location, and Name (All Records)

SALES ACTIVITY REPORT 04/21/93 PAGE 1

REGION	LOCATION	NAME	ACCOUNT #	SALES	COMMISSION
NORTHEAST	TRENTON	CLARK	130101	$3,200	$ 640
MIDWEST	ST. LOUIS	HAAS	203000	$8,900	$ 445
NORTHEAST	NEW YORK	ADAMS	555666	$2,003	$ 401
NORTHEAST	BALTIMORE	KARLSTROM	800396	$3,030	$ 273
NORTHEAST	NEW YORK	ADAMS	987654	$2,005	$ 201
NORTHEAST	TRENTON	CLARK	000101	$1,500	$ 150
SOUTHEAST	ST. PETERSBURG	JOHNSON	878787	$1,235	$ 148
		*** COMPANY TOTAL =		$ 21,873	$ 2,258

(b) By Decreasing Commision (Commission > $100)

USING/GIVING Option

The specifications are similar to those of any other reporting program that requires a combination of heading, detail, and total lines. The hierarchy chart and pseudocode for the USING/GIVING option are shown in Figures 14.7 and 14.8, respectively. The hierarchy chart contains many of the modules found in earlier programs—for example, GET-TODAYS-DATE, WRITE-HEADING-LINES, and WRITE-DETAIL-LINE. In addition, it contains the module SORT-SALES-FILE to sequence records in the sales file.

Figure 14.7 Hierarchy Chart (USING/GIVING)

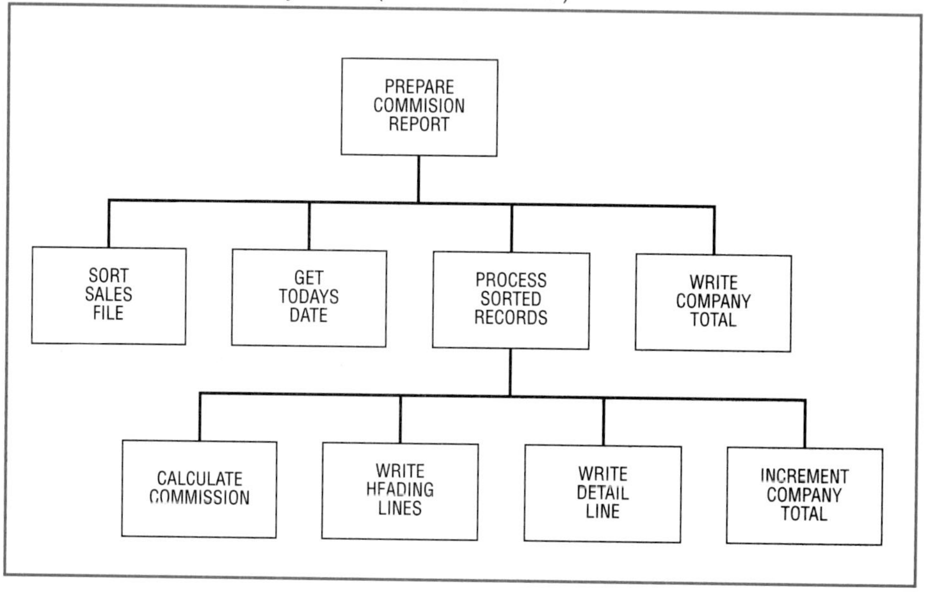

Figure 14.8 Pseudocode (USING/GIVING)

```
Sort Sales File
Open Sorted Sales File, Print File
Get today's date
DO WHILE sorted data remains
    READ Sorted Sales File
        AT END
            Indicate no more data
        NOT AT END
            Calculate commission
            IF line count greater than lines per page
                Initialize line count to 1
                Increment page count
                Write heading lines
            END-IF
            Write detail line
            Increment company total
    END READ
ENDDO
Write company total
Close files
Stop run
```

The pseudocode in Figure 14.8 contains a sort statement prior to the main loop, which contains the in-line perform and false-condition branch used in all other programs. The sales commission is calculated for each incoming record, a detail line is written, and the company total is incremented. The pseudocode also contains the logic to implement a page heading routine as explained previously in Chapter 9.

The USING/GIVING format is illustrated in Figure 14.9. The SORT statement in lines 149–155 references three files—SORT-WORK-FILE, SALES-FILE, and, SORTED-SALES-FILE—each of which has the identical record layout. The SORT statement implicitly opens SALES-FILE and reads every record in that file, releasing each record as it is read to the sort work file. It then sequences the sort work file according to designated keys and writes the newly ordered file to SORTED-SALES-FILE. The programmer does not open or close SORT-WORK-FILE or SALES-FILE as this is done by the SORT statement.

Figure 14.9 SORT Program (USING/GIVING)

```
1    IDENTIFICATION DIVISION.
2    PROGRAM-ID.    SORT1.
3    AUTHOR.        CVV.
4
5    ENVIRONMENT DIVISION.
6    INPUT-OUTPUT SECTION.
7    FILE-CONTROL.
8        SELECT SALES-FILE
9            ASSIGN TO UT-S-SYSIN.
10       SELECT PRINT-FILE
11           ASSIGN TO UT-S-SYSOUT.
12       SELECT SORT-WORK-FILE
13           ASSIGN TO UT-S-SORTWK01.
14       SELECT SORTED-SALES-FILE
15           ASSIGN TO UT-S-SORTED.
16
17   DATA DIVISION.
18   FILE SECTION.
19   FD  SALES-FILE
20       RECORD CONTAINS 58 CHARACTERS
21       DATA RECORD IS SALES-RECORD.
22   01  SALES-RECORD                  PIC X(58).
23
24   FD  PRINT-FILE
25       RECORD CONTAINS 132 CHARACTERS
26       DATA RECORD IS PRINT-LINE.
27   01  PRINT-LINE                    PIC X(132).
28
29   SD  SORT-WORK-FILE
30       RECORD CONTAINS 58 CHARACTERS
31       DATA RECORD IS SORT-RECORD.
32   01  SORT-RECORD.
33       05  SORT-ACCOUNT-NUMBER       PIC 9(6).
```

Sort work file is defined in ordinary SELECT statement

Sort work file is defined in an SD

Sort keys present in incoming record

Figure 14.9 *(continued)*

```
           05  FILLER                     PIC X.
           05  SORT-NAME                  PIC X(15).
           05  FILLER                     PIC X(10).
           05  SORT-LOCATION              PIC X(15).
           05  SORT-REGION                PIC X(11).

       FD  SORTED-SALES-FILE
           RECORD CONTAINS 58 CHARACTERS
           DATA RECORD IS SORTED-SALES-RECORD.
       01  SORTED-SALES-RECORD            PIC X(58).

       WORKING-STORAGE SECTION.
       01  FILLER                         PIC X(14)
               VALUE 'WS BEGINS HERE'.

       01  SALES-RECORD-IN.
           05  SR-ACCOUNT-NUMBER          PIC 9(6).
           05  FILLER                     PIC X.
           05  SR-NAME                    PIC X(15).
           05  SR-SALES                   PIC S9(4).
           05  FILLER                     PIC XX.
           05  SR-COMMISSION-PERCENT      PIC V99.
           05  FILLER                     PIC XX.
           05  SR-LOCATION                PIC X(15).
           05  SR-REGION                  PIC X(11).

       01  TODAYS-DATE-AREA.
           05  TODAYS-YEAR                PIC 99.
           05  TODAYS-MONTH               PIC 99.
           05  TODAYS-DAY                 PIC 99.

       01  PROGRAM-SWITCHES.
           05  DATA-REMAINS-SWITCH        PIC X(3)     VALUE 'YES'.
               88  NO-DATA-REMAINS                     VALUE 'NO'.

       01  PAGE-AND-LINE-COUNTERS.
           05  LINE-COUNT                 PIC 9(2)     VALUE 11.
           05  PAGE-COUNT                 PIC 9(2)     VALUE ZEROS.
           05  LINES-PER-PAGE             PIC 9(2)     VALUE 10.

       01  INDIVIDUAL-CALCULATIONS.
           05  IND-COMMISSION             PIC S9(4).

       01  COMPANY-TOTALS.
           05  COMPANY-SALES-TOT          PIC S9(6)    VALUE ZEROES.
           05  COMPANY-COMM-TOT           PIC S9(6)    VALUE ZEROES.

       01  HDG-LINE-ONE.
           05  FILLER                     PIC X(25)    VALUE SPACES.
           05  FILLER                     PIC X(21)
```

Sort keys present in incoming record

Figure 14.9 *(continued)*

```
             VALUE 'SALES ACTIVITY REPORT'.
        05  FILLER                      PIC X(8)    VALUE SPACES.
        05  HDG-DATE                    PIC X(8).
        05  FILLER                      PIC X(10)   VALUE SPACES.
        05  FILLER                      PIC X(5)    VALUE 'PAGE '.
        05  HDG-PAGE                    PIC Z9.
        05  FILLER                      PIC X(53)   VALUE SPACES.

    01  HDG-LINE-TWO.
        05  FILLER                      PIC X(7)    VALUE ' REGION'.
        05  FILLER                      PIC X(5)    VALUE SPACES.
        05  FILLER                      PIC X(8)    VALUE 'LOCATION'.
        05  FILLER                      PIC X(11)   VALUE SPACES.
        05  FILLER                      PIC X(4)    VALUE 'NAME'.
        05  FILLER                      PIC X(10)   VALUE SPACES.
        05  FILLER                      PIC X(11)   VALUE 'ACCOUNT # '.
        05  FILLER                      PIC X(5)    VALUE SPACES.
        05  FILLER                      PIC X(5)    VALUE 'SALES'.
        05  FILLER                      PIC X(3)    VALUE SPACES.
        05  FILLER                      PIC X(10)   VALUE 'COMMISSION'.
        05  FILLER                      PIC X(53)   VALUE SPACES.

    01  DETAIL-LINE.
        05  DET-REGION                  PIC X(11).
        05  FILLER                      PIC X       VALUE SPACES.
        05  DET-LOCATION                PIC X(15).
        05  FILLER                      PIC X(3)    VALUE SPACES.
        05  DET-NAME                    PIC X(15).
        05  FILLER                      PIC X(2)    VALUE SPACES.
        05  DET-ACCOUNT-NUMBER          PIC 9(6).
        05  FILLER                      PIC X(5)  VALUE SPACES.
        05  DET-SALES                   PIC $Z,ZZ9-.
        05  FILLER                      PIC X(7)    VALUE SPACES.
        05  DET-COMMISSION              PIC $Z,ZZ9-.
        05  FILLER                      PIC X(50)   VALUE SPACES.

    01  COMPANY-TOTAL-LINE.
        05  FILLER                      PIC X(31)   VALUE SPACES.
        05  FILLER                      PIC X(25)
              VALUE '*** COMPANY TOTAL = '.
        05  COMPANY-SALES-TOTAL         PIC $Z(3),ZZ9-.
        05  FILLER                      PIC X(5)    VALUE SPACES.
        05  COMPANY-COMM-TOTAL          PIC $Z(3),ZZ9-.
        05  FILLER                      PIC X(51)   VALUE SPACES.

    PROCEDURE DIVISION.
    100-PREPARE-COMMISSION-REPORT.
        PERFORM 210-SORT-SALES-RECORDS.
        OPEN INPUT SORTED-SALES-FILE
             OUTPUT PRINT-FILE.
```

Opens the sorted file to produce report

Figure 14.9 *(continued)*

```
    PERFORM 230-GET-TODAYS-DATE.
    PERFORM UNTIL NO-DATA-REMAINS
        READ SORTED-SALES-FILE INTO SALES-RECORD-IN
            AT END
                MOVE 'NO' TO DATA-REMAINS-SWITCH
            NOT AT END
                PERFORM 250-PROCESS-SORTED-RECORDS
        END-READ
    END-PERFORM.
    PERFORM 290-WRITE-COMPANY-TOTAL.
    CLOSE SORTED-SALES-FILE
          PRINT-FILE.
    STOP RUN.

210-SORT-SALES-RECORDS.
    SORT SORT-WORK-FILE
        ASCENDING KEY SORT-REGION
                      SORT-LOCATION
                      SORT-NAME
        WITH DUPLICATES IN ORDER
        USING SALES-FILE
        GIVING SORTED-SALES-FILE.

230-GET-TODAYS-DATE.
    ACCEPT TODAYS-DATE-AREA FROM DATE.
    STRING TODAYS-MONTH '/' TODAYS-DAY '/' TODAYS-YEAR
       DELIMITED BY SIZE INTO HDG-DATE.

250-PROCESS-SORTED-RECORDS.
    PERFORM 310-CALCULATE-COMMISSION.
    IF LINE-COUNT > LINES-PER-PAGE
        PERFORM 330-WRITE-HEADING-LINES
    END-IF.
    PERFORM 350-WRITE-DETAIL-LINE.
    PERFORM 370-INCREMENT-COMPANY-TOTAL.

290-WRITE-COMPANY-TOTAL.
    MOVE COMPANY-SALES-TOT TO COMPANY-SALES-TOTAL.
    MOVE COMPANY-COMM-TOT TO COMPANY-COMM-TOTAL.
    WRITE PRINT-LINE FROM COMPANY-TOTAL-LINE
        AFTER ADVANCING 2 LINES.

310-CALCULATE-COMMISSION.
    COMPUTE IND-COMMISSION ROUNDED =
        SR-SALES * SR-COMMISSION-PERCENT
        SIZE ERROR DISPLAY 'SIZE ERROR ON COMMISSION FOR '
            SR-NAME
    END-COMPUTE.

330-WRITE-HEADING-LINES.
```

All three files must have identical length and record layout

Figure 14.9 *(continued)*

```
184          MOVE 1 TO LINE-COUNT.
185          ADD 1 TO PAGE-COUNT.
186          MOVE PAGE-COUNT TO HDG-PAGE.
187          WRITE PRINT-LINE FROM HDG-LINE-ONE
188              AFTER ADVANCING PAGE.
189          WRITE PRINT-LINE FROM HDG-LINE-TWO
190              AFTER ADVANCING 2 LINES.
191
192      350-WRITE-DETAIL-LINE.
193          MOVE SR-REGION TO DET-REGION.
194          MOVE SR-LOCATION TO DET-LOCATION.
195          MOVE SR-NAME TO DET-NAME.
196          MOVE SR-ACCOUNT-NUMBER TO DET-ACCOUNT-NUMBER.
197          MOVE SR-SALES TO DET-SALES.
198          MOVE IND-COMMISSION TO DET-COMMISSION.
199          WRITE PRINT-LINE FROM DETAIL-LINE.
200          ADD 1 TO LINE-COUNT.
201
202      370-INCREMENT-COMPANY-TOTAL.
203          ADD SR-SALES TO COMPANY-SALES-TOT.
204          ADD IND-COMMISSION TO COMPANY-COMM-TOT.
```

Three keys—SORT-REGION, SORT-LOCATION, and SORT-NAME—are specified in lines 150–152 as the primary, secondary, and tertiary key, respectively. The WITH DUPLICATES IN ORDER phrase keeps records with duplicate keys in the same sequence as the input file. Note, therefore, that since the input file in Figure 14.5 is already in sequence by account number, records with the same region, location, and name will be in sequence by account number as well.

After the file has been sorted, control returns to the OPEN statement in line 132, which opens SORTED-SALES-FILE as input and PRINT-FILE as output. The remainder of the Procedure Division reads records from the sorted file in order to produce the report of Figure 14.6a. Its logic parallels that of any other reporting program that produces a combination of heading, detail, and total lines.

INPUT PROCEDURE/OUTPUT PROCEDURE Option

The hierarchy chart to implement the INPUT PROCEDURE/OUTPUT PROCEDURE option is shown in Figure 14.10. It contains the identical modules as its predecessor for the USING/GIVING option, but the placement of the modules (the subordinate relationships and associated span of control) is significantly different.

The most obvious change is the sort module itself, which sits atop the hierarchy chart in Figure 14.10, but which is subordinate to PREPARE-COMMISSION-REPORT in Figure 14.7. This is because the SORT statement effectively drives the INPUT PROCEDURE/OUTPUT PROCEDURE option as it calls the respective procedures. A second major change is the placement of CALCULATE-COMMISSION, which is subordinate to the sort module in Figure 14.10, because the commission is calculated

Figure 14.10 Hierarchy Chart (INPUT PROCEDURE/OUTPUT PROCEDURE)

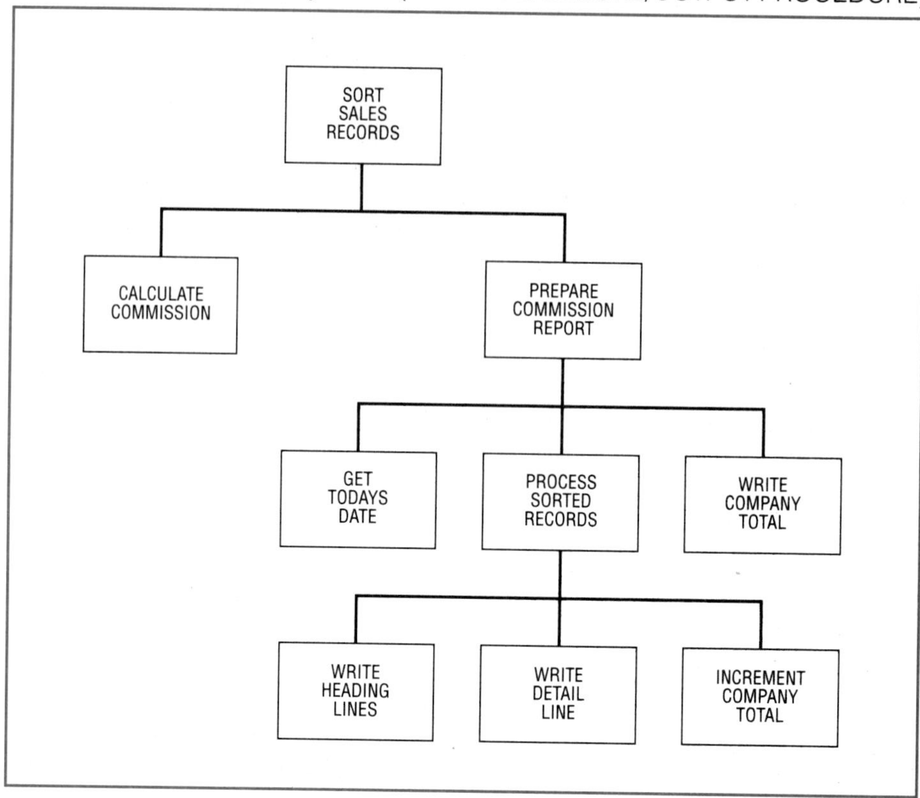

prior to sorting, and only those records with sufficient commission are written to the sort work file. In the earlier hierarchy chart, however, every record in the incoming file appears in the report; the commission is calculated after sorting so that CALCULATE-COMMISSION is subordinate to PROCESS-SORTED-RECORDS.

The pseudocode in Figure 14.11 contains two loops, whereas its predecessor in Figure 14.8 contained only one. This is because the USING/GIVING option does the I/O for the programmer and thus is transparent to the programmer. However, INPUT PROCEDURE/OUTPUT PROCEDURE requires the programmer to do the I/O and this is reflected in the pseudocode. The initial loop opens the (unsorted) sales file, calculates the commission for each incoming record, then selectively releases records to the sort work file. The second loop (which corresponds to the only loop in Figure 14.8) reads records from the sorted file and prepares the report.

The program containing the INPUT PROCEDURE/OUTPUT PROCEDURE format is illustrated in Figure 14.12. Explanation begins with the SORT statement itself, lines 125–128, which references a sort work file defined in an SD in lines 27–37 of the Data Division. SORT-WORK-FILE is to be sorted on SORT-COMMISSION, a calculated field that is not contained in the incoming sales record.

The INPUT PROCEDURE/OUTPUT PROCEDURE involves several implicit transfers of control as follows:

1. Control passes from the SORT statement to the INPUT PROCEDURE, which reads records from an input file and builds the sort work file.
2. When the INPUT PROCEDURE is finished, control passes to the sort utility, which sorts the work file created by the INPUT PROCEDURE.

Figure 14.11 Pseudocode (INPUT PROCEDURE/OUTPUT PROCEDURE)

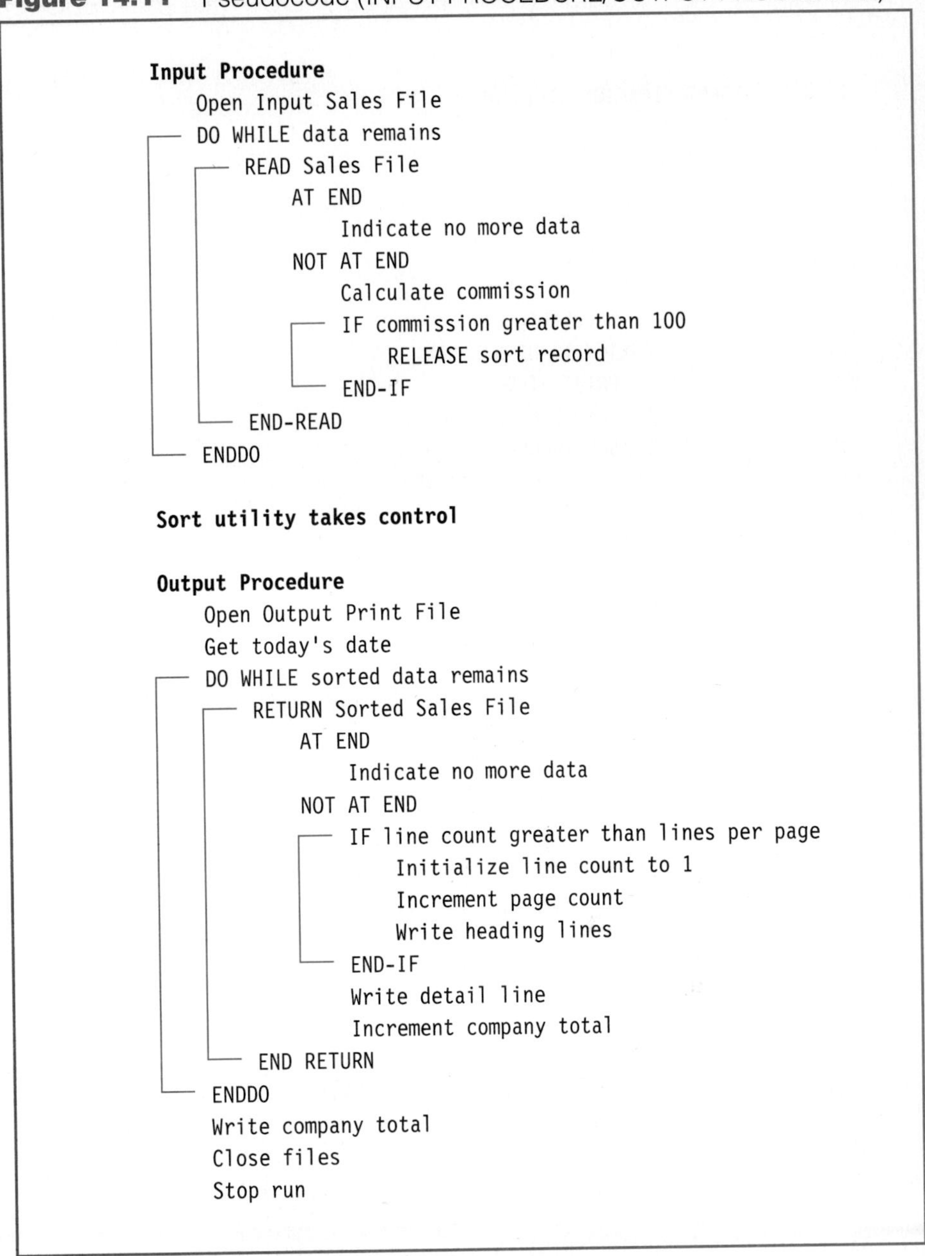

```
Input Procedure
    Open Input Sales File
    DO WHILE data remains
        READ Sales File
            AT END
                Indicate no more data
            NOT AT END
                Calculate commission
                IF commission greater than 100
                    RELEASE sort record
                END-IF
        END-READ
    ENDDO

Sort utility takes control

Output Procedure
    Open Output Print File
    Get today's date
    DO WHILE sorted data remains
        RETURN Sorted Sales File
            AT END
                Indicate no more data
            NOT AT END
                IF line count greater than lines per page
                    Initialize line count to 1
                    Increment page count
                    Write heading lines
                END-IF
                Write detail line
                Increment company total
        END RETURN
    ENDDO
    Write company total
    Close files
    Stop run
```

3. After the sort has taken place, control passes to the OUTPUT PROCEDURE, which reads records from the sorted file in order to produce the required report.
4. When the OUTPUT PROCEDURE is finished, control returns to the statement directly (physically) following the actual SORT statement.

The INPUT PROCEDURE is the paragraph 100-CALCULATE-COMMISSION and extends from lines 131 to 148. It begins by opening SALES-FILE, after which the combination of the in-line PERFORM and false condition branch processes records until the file is empty. The commission is calculated for each incoming record, and

Figure 14.12 SORT Program (INPUT PROCEDURE/OUTPUT PROCEDURE)

```
IDENTIFICATION DIVISION.
PROGRAM-ID.   SORT2.
AUTHOR.       CVV.

ENVIRONMENT DIVISION.
INPUT-OUTPUT SECTION.
FILE-CONTROL.
    SELECT SALES-FILE
        ASSIGN TO UT-S-SYSIN.
    SELECT PRINT-FILE
        ASSIGN TO UT-S-SYSOUT.
    SELECT SORT-WORK-FILE
        ASSIGN TO UT-S-SORTWK01.

DATA DIVISION.
FILE SECTION.
FD  SALES-FILE
    RECORD CONTAINS 57 CHARACTERS
    DATA RECORD IS SALES-RECORD.
01  SALES-RECORD                     PIC X(57).

FD  PRINT-FILE
    RECORD CONTAINS 132 CHARACTERS
    DATA RECORD IS PRINT-LINE.
01  PRINT-LINE                       PIC X(132).

SD  SORT-WORK-FILE
    RECORD CONTAINS 62 CHARACTERS
    DATA RECORD IS SORT-RECORD.
01  SORT-RECORD.
    05  SORT-ACCOUNT-NUMBER          PIC 9(6).
    05  FILLER                       PIC X.
    05  SORT-NAME                    PIC X(15).
    05  FILLER                       PIC X(10).
    05  SORT-LOCATION                PIC X(15).
    05  SORT-REGION                  PIC X(11).
    05  SORT-COMMISSION              PIC S9(4).

WORKING-STORAGE SECTION.
01  FILLER                           PIC X(14)
        VALUE 'WS BEGINS HERE'.

01  SALES-RECORD-IN.
    05  SR-ACCOUNT-NUMBER            PIC 9(6).
    05  FILLER                       PIC X.
    05  SR-NAME                      PIC X(15).
    05  SR-SALES                     PIC S9(4).
    05  FILLER                       PIC XX.
    05  SR-COMMISSION-PERCENT        PIC V99.
    05  FILLER                       PIC XX.
    05  SR-LOCATION                  PIC X(15).
```

SD defines sort work file

Calculated field not found in input record

Figure 14.12 *(continued)*

```
           05  SR-REGION                  PIC X(11).
           05  SR-COMMISSION              PIC S9(4).

       01  TODAYS-DATE-AREA.
           05  TODAYS-YEAR                PIC 99.
           05  TODAYS-MONTH               PIC 99.
           05  TODAYS-DAY                 PIC 99.

       01  PROGRAM-SWITCHES.
           05  DATA-REMAINS-SWITCH        PIC X(3)   VALUE 'YES'.
               88  NO-DATA-REMAINS                   VALUE 'NO'.
           05  SORTED-DATA-REMAINS-SW     PIC X(3)   VALUE 'YES'.
               88  NO-SORTED-DATA-REMAINS            VALUE 'NO'.

       01  PAGE-AND-LINE-COUNTERS.
           05  LINE-COUNT                 PIC 9(2)   VALUE 11.
           05  PAGE-COUNT                 PIC 9(2)   VALUE ZEROS.
           05  LINES-PER-PAGE             PIC 9(2)   VALUE 10.

       01  COMPANY-TOTALS.
           05  COMPANY-SALES-TOT          PIC S9(6)   VALUE ZEROES.
           05  COMPANY-COMM-TOT           PIC S9(6)   VALUE ZEROES.

       01  HDG-LINE-ONE.
           05  FILLER                     PIC X(25)  VALUE SPACES.
           05  FILLER                     PIC X(21)
                 VALUE 'SALES ACTIVITY REPORT'.
           05  FILLER                     PIC X(8)   VALUE SPACES.
           05  HDG-DATE                   PIC X(8).
           05  FILLER                     PIC X(10)  VALUE SPACES.
           05  FILLER                     PIC X(5)   VALUE 'PAGE '.
           05  HDG-PAGE                   PIC Z9.
           05  FILLER                     PIC X(53)  VALUE SPACES.

       01  HDG-LINE-TWO.
           05  FILLER                     PIC X(7)    VALUE ' REGION'.
           05  FILLER                     PIC X(5)    VALUE SPACES.
           05  FILLER                     PIC X(8)    VALUE 'LOCATION'.
           05  FILLER                     PIC X(11)   VALUE SPACES.
           05  FILLER                     PIC X(4)    VALUE 'NAME'.
           05  FILLER                     PIC X(10)   VALUE SPACES.
           05  FILLER                     PIC X(11)   VALUE 'ACCOUNT #'.
           05  FILLER                     PIC X(5)    VALUE SPACES.
           05  FILLER                     PIC X(5)    VALUE 'SALES'.
           05  FILLER                     PIC X(3)    VALUE SPACES.
           05  FILLER                     PIC X(10)   VALUE 'COMMISSION'.
           05  FILLER                     PIC X(53)   VALUE SPACES.

       01  DETAIL-LINE.
           05  DET-REGION                 PIC X(11).
           05  FILLER                     PIC X       VALUE SPACES.
```

Figure 14.12 *(continued)*

```
           05  DET-LOCATION              PIC X(15).
           05  FILLER                    PIC X(3)     VALUE SPACES.
           05  DET-NAME                  PIC X(15).
           05  FILLER                    PIC X(2)     VALUE SPACES.
           05  DET-ACCOUNT-NUMBER        PIC 9(6).
           05  FILLER                    PIC X(5)    VALUE SPACES.
           05  DET-SALES                 PIC $Z,ZZ9-.
           05  FILLER                    PIC X(7)     VALUE SPACES.
           05  DET-COMMISSION            PIC $Z,ZZ9-.
           05  FILLER                    PIC X(50)    VALUE SPACES.

       01  COMPANY-TOTAL-LINE.
           05  FILLER                    PIC X(31)    VALUE SPACES.
           05  FILLER                    PIC X(25)
                 VALUE '*** COMPANY TOTAL = '.
           05  COMPANY-SALES-TOTAL       PIC $Z(3),ZZ9-.
           05  FILLER                    PIC X(5)     VALUE SPACES.
           05  COMPANY-COMM-TOTAL        PIC $Z(3),ZZ9-.
           05  FILLER                    PIC X(51)    VALUE SPACES.

       PROCEDURE DIVISION.
       0000-SORT-SALES-RECORDS.
           SORT SORT-WORK-FILE
               DESCENDING KEY SORT-COMMISSION
               INPUT PROCEDURE 100-CALCULATE-COMMISSION
               OUTPUT PROCEDURE 200-PREPARE-COMMISSION-REPORT.
           STOP RUN.

       100-CALCULATE-COMMISSION.
           OPEN INPUT SALES-FILE.
           PERFORM UNTIL NO-DATA-REMAINS
               READ SALES-FILE INTO SALES-RECORD-IN
                   AT END
                       MOVE 'NO' TO DATA-REMAINS-SWITCH
                   NOT AT END
                       COMPUTE SR-COMMISSION ROUNDED =
                           SR-SALES * SR-COMMISSION-PERCENT
                           SIZE ERROR DISPLAY 'ERROR ON COMMISSION FOR '
                           SR-NAME
                       END-COMPUTE
                       IF SR-COMMISSION > 100
                           RELEASE SORT-RECORD FROM SALES-RECORD-IN
                       END-IF
               END-READ
           END-PERFORM.
           CLOSE SALES-FILE.

       200-PREPARE-COMMISSION-REPORT.
           OPEN OUTPUT PRINT-FILE.
           PERFORM 230-GET-TODAYS-DATE.
```

Sales are listed by calculated commission (DESCENDING KEY SORT-COMMISSION)

Control returns here after SORT statement (STOP RUN.)

INPUT PROCEDURE (100-CALCULATE-COMMISSION.)

RELEASE statement writes record to work file

Records are conditionally written to work file (IF SR-COMMISSION > 100 … END-IF)

OUTPUT PROCEDURE (200-PREPARE-COMMISSION-REPORT.)

Figure 14.12 *(continued)*

```
    PERFORM UNTIL NO-SORTED-DATA-REMAINS
        RETURN SORT-WORK-FILE INTO SALES-RECORD-IN
            AT END
                MOVE 'NO' TO SORTED-DATA-REMAINS-SW
            NOT AT END
                PERFORM 250-PROCESS-SORTED-RECORDS
        END-RETURN
    END-PERFORM.
    PERFORM 290-WRITE-COMPANY-TOTAL.
    CLOSE PRINT-FILE.

230-GET-TODAYS-DATE.
    ACCEPT TODAYS-DATE-AREA FROM DATE.
    STRING TODAYS-MONTH '/' TODAYS-DAY '/' TODAYS-YEAR
       DELIMITED BY SIZE INTO HDG-DATE.

250-PROCESS-SORTED-RECORDS.
    IF LINE-COUNT > LINES-PER-PAGE
        PERFORM 330-WRITE-HEADING-LINES
    END-IF.
    PERFORM 350-WRITE-DETAIL-LINE.
    PERFORM 370-INCREMENT-COMPANY-TOTAL.

290-WRITE-COMPANY-TOTAL.
    MOVE COMPANY-SALES-TOT TO COMPANY-SALES-TOTAL.
    MOVE COMPANY-COMM-TOT TO COMPANY-COMM-TOTAL.
    WRITE PRINT-LINE FROM COMPANY-TOTAL-LINE
        AFTER ADVANCING 2 LINES.

330-WRITE-HEADING-LINES.
    MOVE 1 TO LINE-COUNT.
    ADD 1 TO PAGE-COUNT.
    MOVE PAGE-COUNT TO HDG-PAGE.
    WRITE PRINT-LINE FROM HDG-LINE-ONE
        AFTER ADVANCING PAGE.
    WRITE PRINT-LINE FROM HDG-LINE-TWO
        AFTER ADVANCING 2 LINES.

350-WRITE-DETAIL-LINE.
    MOVE SR-REGION TO DET-REGION.
    MOVE SR-LOCATION TO DET-LOCATION.
    MOVE SR-NAME TO DET-NAME.
    MOVE SR-ACCOUNT-NUMBER TO DET-ACCOUNT-NUMBER.
    MOVE SR-SALES TO DET-SALES.
    MOVE SR-COMMISSION TO DET-COMMISSION.
    WRITE PRINT-LINE FROM DETAIL-LINE.
    ADD 1 TO LINE-COUNT.

370-INCREMENT-COMPANY-TOTAL.
    ADD SR-SALES TO COMPANY-SALES-TOT.
    ADD SR-COMMISSION TO COMPANY-COMM-TOT.
```

RETURN statement reads records from sort work file

only those records with a commission greater than $100 are written (released) to the sort work file. The INPUT PROCEDURE ends by closing SALES-FILE, after which control passes to the sort utility. The sort work file is neither opened nor closed explicitly by the programmer as that is done by the sort utility.

The OUTPUT PROCEDURE is the paragraph 200-PREPARE-COMMISSION-REPORT and extends from lines 150 to 162. It begins by opening PRINT-FILE, after which the combination of the in-line PERFORM and false-condition branch processes records until the sort work file is empty. The report is produced by using many of the identical paragraphs from the earlier program. The OUTPUT PROCEDURE ends by closing PRINT-FILE after which control passes to the STOP RUN statement in line 129 immediately under the SORT statement.

Comparing Options

The differences between the two COBOL programs is highlighted by comparing the generated reports in Figure 14.6. Figure 14.6a was produced by the USING/GIVING option and lists *all records* in sequence by region, location, and name. Figure 14.6b lists a subset of *selected records* in decreasing order of commission, a calculated field. The following are other differences between the two programs:

1. Figure 14.9 sorts on three fields, SORT-REGION, SORT-LOCATION, and SORT-NAME, each of which is contained in the incoming record. Figure 14.12 sorts on SORT-COMMISSION, a calculated field not found in the incoming record.
2. The USING option in Figure 14.9 does the I/O for the programmer; that is, it opens SALES-FILE, reads and writes every record from this file to the sort work file, then closes SALES-FILE when the sort work file has been created.
3. The INPUT PROCEDURE in Figure 14.12 requires the programmer to do the I/O; that is, the programmer has to open SALES-FILE, read records from the input file and write (release) them to the sort work file, then close the input file.
4. The GIVING option in Figure 14.9 creates a permanent file, SORTED-SALES-FILE, that contains the results of the sort; the OUTPUT PROCEDURE in Figure 14.12 creates a temporary work file that disappears when the program terminates. The GIVING option uses an extra file; that is, four files are present in Figure 14.9 versus three in Figure 14.12.
5. The OUTPUT PROCEDURE uses a RETURN statement in lines 154–159 because the sorted records are read from the sort work file. This is in contrast to the READ statement in lines 136–141 of Figure 14.9, which reads records from SORTED-SALES-FILE, an ordinary file defined in an FD.
6. The record lengths in Figure 14.9 of SORT-FILE, SALES-FILE, and SORTED-SALES-FILE, must be the same (58 characters). The record lengths of SORT-FILE and SALES-FILE in Figure 14.12 are different.

MERGE Statement

Merging files is a special case of sorting. The **MERGE** statement takes several input files, which have identical record formats and which have been sorted in the same sequence, and combines them into a single output file (device type and blocking may differ for the various files). A merge achieves the same results as sorting, but more efficiently; that is, the several input files to a merge could also be concatenated as a single input file to a sort. The advantage of the merge over a sort is in execution speed; a merge will execute faster because its logic realizes that the several input files are already in order.

The format of the MERGE statement is as follows:

```
MERGE file-name-1

     { ON {DESCENDING} KEY {data-name-1} . . . } . . .
          {ASCENDING }

     [COLLATING SEQUENCE IS alphabet-name]

      USING file-name-2 [file-name-3] . . .

     {OUTPUT PROCEDURE IS procedure-name-1 [{THRU   } procedure-name-2]}
     {                                      [{THROUGH}                 ]}
     {GIVING {file-name-4} . . .                                        }
```

File-name-1 must be specified in an SD. Rules for ASCENDING (DESCENDING) KEY, COLLATING SEQUENCE, USING/GIVING, and OUTPUT PROCEDURE are identical to those of the SORT statement.

Unlike the SORT statement, however, there is no INPUT PROCEDURE option. In other words you must specify USING, and list all files from which incoming records will be chosen. Hence every record in every file specified in USING will appear in the merged file. However, you do have a choice between GIVING and OUTPUT PROCEDURE.

None of the files specified in a MERGE statement can be open when the statement is executed, as the merge operation implicitly opens them. In similar fashion, the files will be automatically closed by the MERGE.

An example of a MERGE statement is shown below:

```
MERGE WORK-FILE
    ON ASCENDING CUSTOMER-ACCOUNT-NUMBER
        DESCENDING AMOUNT-OF-SALE
    USING
        MONDAY-SALES-FILE
        TUESDAY-SALES-FILE
        WEDNESDAY-SALES-FILE
        THURSDAY-SALES-FILE
        FRIDAY-SALES-FILE
    GIVING
        WEEKLY-SALES-FILE.
```

WORK-FILE is defined in a COBOL SD. WEEKLY-SALES-FILE, MONDAY-SALES-FILE, TUESDAY-SALES-FILE, and so on are each specified in both FD and SELECT statements. These files must be in sequence and are both opened and closed by the merge operation.

The primary key is CUSTOMER-ACCOUNT-NUMBER (ascending), and the secondary key is AMOUNT-OF-SALE (descending). All records with the same account number will be grouped together with the highest sale for each account number listed first. Records with identical keys in one or more input files will be listed in the order in which the files appear in the MERGE statement itself. Hence, in the event of a tie on both account number and amount of sale, Monday's transactions will appear before Tuesday's, and so on.

LIMITATIONS OF COBOL-74

The SORT statement in COBOL-74 is significantly more restrictive than its counterpart in COBOL-85. In particular:

1. The INPUT (OUTPUT) PROCEDURE in COBOL-74 was required to be a *section* rather than a paragraph, which necessitated that other paragraphs in the program be organized into sections as well.
2. The INPUT (OUTPUT) PROCEDURE in COBOL-74 could not transfer control to points outside the designated procedure, requiring the use of a GO TO statement within the procedure. The GO TO statement was directed to an EXIT paragraph at the end of the section.

Both of these restrictions have been removed from COBOL-85 as illustrated in the INPUT PROCEDURE/OUTPUT PROCEDURE example in Figure 14.12. An additional change in COBOL-85 is the introduction of the WITH DUPLICATES IN ORDER phrase, which was not present in the earlier compiler.

SUMMARY

Points to Remember

- Sorting is done in one of two sequences, ascending or descending. Multiple sort keys are listed in order of importance— primary, secondary, and tertiary; or major, intermediate, and minor.
- Two collating sequences are in common use, EBCDIC (on IBM mainframes) and ASCII (on the PC and other mainframes). The difference is significant when an alphanumeric key is used and/or with an embedded sign in a numeric field.
- The SORT statement has four combinations: INPUT PROCEDURE/OUTPUT PROCEDURE, USING/GIVING, USING/OUTPUT PROCEDURE, and INPUT PROCEDURE/GIVING.
- The INPUT PROCEDURE requires the programmer to do the I/O associated with the sort work file, whereas the USING option does the I/O automatically. The advantage of the INPUT PROCEDURE is the ability to sort on a calculated field and/or to selectively pass records to the sort work file.
- The INPUT PROCEDURE contains a RELEASE statement to transfer (write) records to the sort work file; the OUTPUT PROCEDURE contains a RETURN statement to read the sorted data.
- The GIVING option specifies a permanent file that remains after the program has ended and that contains the sorted results; the OUTPUT PROCEDURE uses a temporary work file, which is deleted after the program has ended.

- Regardless of which option is chosen, file-name-1 of the SORT statement must be described in an SD. Further, each key (that is, data name) appearing in the SORT statement must be described in the sort record.
- If the USING / GIVING option is used, file-name-2 and file-name-3 each require an FD. The record sizes of file names 1, 2, and 3 must all be the same.

Key Words and Concepts

ASCII
Ascending sort
Calculated field
Collating sequence
Descending sort
EBCDIC
Embedded sign
Intermediate key
Major key
Minor key
Primary key
Secondary key
Sort key
Sort work file
Temporary work file
Tertiary key
Utility sort program

COBOL Elements

ASCENDING KEY
DESCENDING KEY
DUPLICATES IN ORDER
GIVING
INPUT PROCEDURE
MERGE
OUTPUT PROCEDURE
RELEASE
RETURN
SD
SIGN IS LEADING SEPARATE CHARACTER
SIGN IS TRAILING SEPARATE CHARACTER
SORT
USING

FILL-IN

1. A sort ______________ is a field within a record that determines how the file is to be arranged.
2. The most important key is known as the ______________ or ______________ key.
3. ______________ and ______________ are widely used collating sequences.
4. If records in a file have been sorted by salary so that the employee with the highest salary appears first, the records are in ______________ sequence by salary.
5. If a file has been sorted by state, city within state, and employee within city, then state, city, and name are the ______________, ______________, and ______________ keys, respectively.
6. In a sort on an alphanumeric part number, AAA would precede 111 using the ______________ collating sequence, but follow it under ______________.
7. The USING option may be used with either ______________ or ______________ ______________.

8. The _____________ statement is analogous to WRITE and appears in the _____________ _____________.

9. A sort work file must be defined in a _____________ statement in the Environment Division and in an _____________ in the Data Division.

10. An embedded sign (requires/does not require) an extra position within a signed field.

11. The default placement of a sign is as the (leading/trailing) character in a(n) (embedded/separate) position.

12. The _____________ _____________ may be used to sort on a _____________ field, and also to _____________ pass records to the sort work file to increase efficiency.

13. The MERGE statement requires that its input files have _____________ record layouts.

14. The MERGE statement (does/does not) permit the INPUT PROCEDURE option.

TRUE/FALSE

1. The SORT statement cannot be used on a calculated field.
2. If USING is specified in the SORT statement, then GIVING must also be specified.
3. If INPUT PROCEDURE is specified in the SORT statement, then OUTPUT PROCEDURE is also required.
4. Only one ascending and one descending key are permitted in the SORT statement.
5. Major key and primary key are synonymous.
6. Minor key and secondary key are synonymous.
7. RELEASE and RETURN are associated with the USING/GIVING option.
8. RELEASE is present in the INPUT PROCEDURE.
9. RETURN is specified in the OUTPUT PROCEDURE.
10. If a record is released, it is written to the sort file.
11. If a record is returned, it is read from the sort file.
12. If USING/GIVING is used, the sorted file must contain every record in the input file.
13. If INPUT PROCEDURE/OUTPUT PROCEDURE is used, the sorted file must contain every record in the input file.
14. XYZ will always come before 123 in an alphanumeric sort.
15. ADAMS will always appear before ADAMSON, regardless of collating sequence.
16. The file specified immediately after the word MERGE must be defined in an MD rather than an SD.
17. The MERGE statement can specify INPUT PROCEDURE/OUTPUT PROCEDURE.
18. The MERGE statement can specify USING/GIVING.
19. The MERGE statement can be applied to input files with different record layouts.
20. The sort work file (the file defined in the SD) is a temporary file and does not exist after the COBOL program has finished execution.

PROBLEMS

1. Given the following data:

Name	Location	Department
Milgrom	New York	1000
Samuel	Boston	2000
Isaac	Boston	2000
Chandler	Chicago	2000
Lavor	Los Angeles	1000
Elsinor	Chicago	1000
Tater	New York	2000
Craig	New York	2000
Borow	Boston	2000
Kenneth	Boston	2000
Renaldi	Boston	1000
Gulfman	Chicago	1000

Rearrange the data according to the following sorts:

a. Major field: department (descending); minor field: name (ascending).

b. Primary field: department (ascending); secondary field: location (ascending); tertiary field: name (ascending).

2. Given the statement

```
SORT SORT-FILE
    ASCENDING KEY STUDENT-MAJOR DESCENDING YEAR-IN-SCHOOL
    ASCENDING STUDENT-NAME
USING FILE-ONE
GIVING FILE-TWO.
```

a. What is the major key?

b. What is the minor key?

c. Which file will be specified in an SD?

d. Which file will contain the sorted output?

e. Which file(s) will be specified in a SELECT?

f. Which file contains the input data?

g. Which file must contain the data names STUDENT-NAME, YEAR-IN-SCHOOL, and STUDENT-MAJOR?

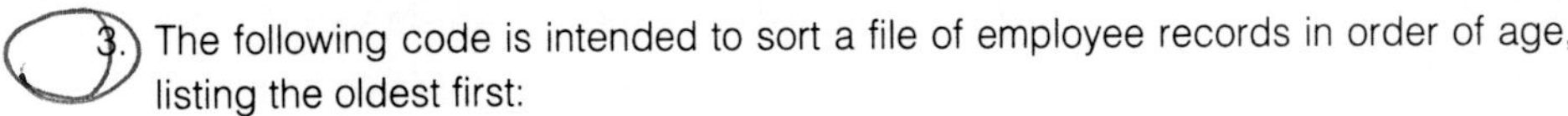

3. The following code is intended to sort a file of employee records in order of age, listing the oldest first:

```
FD  EMPLOYEE-FILE
      .
       .
01  EMPLOYEE-RECORD.
    05  EMP-NAME              PIC X(25).
    05  EMP-BIRTH-DATE.
        10  EMP-BIRTH-MONTH   PIC 99.
        10  EMP-BIRTH-YEAR    PIC 99.
    05  FILLER                PIC X(51).
```

```
SD  SORT-FILE
        .
        .
01  SORT-RECORD.
    05  FILLER              PIC X(20).
    05  SORT-BIRTH-DATE.
        10  SORT-BIRTH-MONTH  PIC 99.
        10  SORT-BIRTH-YEAR   PIC 99.
    05  FILLER              PIC X(56).

PROCEDURE DIVISION.
    SORT SORT-FILE
        DESCENDING KEY SORT-BIRTH-MONTH SORT-BIRTH-YEAR
        USING EMPLOYEE-FILE
        GIVING ORDERED-FILE.
```

There are three distinct reasons why the intended code will not work. Find and correct the errors.

4. The registrar has asked for a simple report listing students by year, and alphabetically within year. Thus all freshmen are to appear first, followed by all sophomores, juniors, seniors, and graduate students. The incoming record has the following layout:

```
01  STUDENT-RECORD.
    05  ST-NAME         PIC X(15).
    05  ST-MAJOR        PIC X(15).
    05  ST-YEAR         PIC XX.
    05  ST-CREDITS      PIC 99.
    05  ST-COLLEGE      PIC X(10).
```

The ST-YEAR field uses the codes, FR, SO, JR, SR, and GR for freshman, sophomore, junior, senior, and graduate student, respectively. Develop the Procedure Division code to accomplish the desired sort. (It is not as easy as it looks.)

5. Indicate the form of the SORT statement (USING, INPUT PROCEDURE, GIVING, OUTPUT PROCEDURE) that would most likely be used for the following applications:
   a. Conversion of an incoming inventory file that has its part numbers in ASCII sequence to a new file, having its numbers in EBCDIC sequence.
   b. Preparation of a report to select all graduating seniors (those with completed credits totaling 90 or more), listed in order of decreasing grade point average.
   c. A data-validation program that reads unedited transactions, rejects those with invalid data, and prepares a sorted transaction file containing only valid records.
   d. A program to prepare mailing labels in zip code order from a customer list.

6. Given the statement:

```
MERGE WORK-FILE
    ASCENDING ACCOUNT-NUMBER
    DESCENDING AMOUNT-OF-SALE
USING
    JANUARY-SALES
    FEBRUARY-SALES
    MARCH-SALES
GIVING
    FIRST-QUARTER-SALES.
```

a. Which file(s) are specified in an SD?

b. Which file(s) are specified in an FD?

c. Which file(s) contain the key ACCOUNT-NUMBER?

d. What is the primary key?

e. What is the secondary key?

f. If a record on the JANUARY-SALES file has the identical ACCOUNT-NUMBER as a record on the FEBRUARY-SALES file, which record would come first on the merged file?

g. If a record on the JANUARY-SALES file has the identical AMOUNT-OF-SALE as a record on the FEBRUARY-SALES file, which record would come first on the merged file?

h. If a record on the JANUARY-SALES file has the identical AMOUNT-OF-SALE and ACCOUNT-NUMBER as a record on the FEBRUARY-SALES file, which record would come first on the merged file?

7. Given the following COBOL definition:

```
05  TRANSACTION-DATE.
    10  TRANS-MONTH       PIC 99.
    10  TRANS-DAY         PIC 99.
    10  TRANS-YEAR        PIC 99.
```

Write a portion of the SORT statement necessary to put transactions in sequence, with the earliest transaction listed first. Are there any problems in your solution when the century changes? Should you be concerned about those problems now?

8. The registrar requires an alphabetical list of graduating seniors. The report will be generated from the student master file, which contains every student in the school, in social security number sequence.

Two approaches have been suggested. The first uses the USING/GIVING option to sort the file alphabetically, after which the desired records are selected for inclusion in the report. The second selects the desired records in the INPUT PROCEDURE, after which the file is sorted and the report prepared in the OUTPUT PROCEDURE.

Both approaches will produce a correct report. Is there any reason to choose one over the other?

Control Breaks

CHAPTER OUTLINE

OBJECTIVES

After reading this chapter you will be able to:

- Define control break; distinguish between a single control break and a multilevel control break.
- Explain the relationship between sorting and control breaks.
- Design a hierarchy chart and pseudocode to implement any number of control breaks; evaluate the hierarchy chart with respect to completeness, functionality, and span of control.
- Use a general purpose algorithm to write a COBOL program for any number of control breaks.
- Develop COBOL programs for one-, two-, and three-level control breaks.
- Distinguish between rolling and running totals.

OVERVIEW

This chapter does not introduce any new COBOL per se, but uses the COBOL you already know to present one of the most important applications in data processing, that of control breaks. A control break is defined as a change in a designated field, which in turn requires that the incoming file be in sequence by the designated field. There is, therefore, a close relationship between sorting and control breaks, a relationship that will be stressed throughout the chapter.

The logic associated with control breaks is more complex than many of the examples presented earlier in the text. The difficulty, if any, stems from a rush into coding a program, without giving suitable thought to its design. Accordingly, we emphasize the importance of proper design, and the use of hierarchy charts and pseudocode, to simplify the eventual coding.

Control breaks may be implemented at several levels, just as a file may be sorted on multiple keys. The system concepts section distinguishes between one-, two-, and three-level control breaks, each of which is developed in a separate program.

System Concepts

This chapter continues the example of Chapter 14, beginning with a review of the file in Figure 15.1 (shown previously as Figure 14.5). Six fields are present in every record: account number, salesperson, sales amount, commission percentage, location, and region. The sales amount contains an embedded sign to reflect negative numbers (i.e., returns rather than sales) as previously discussed. Recall, too, that the commission amount is determined by multiplying the commission percentage (contained in the record) by the sales amount.

Figure 15.1 Transaction File (The sales amount shows ASCII rather than EBCDIC characters.)

Acct Num	Salesperson	Sales Amount	Comm Pct	Location	Region
000069	BENWAY	023!	10	CHICAGO	MIDWEST
000100	HUMMER	010'	05	CHICAGO	MIDWEST
000101	CLARK	1500	10	TRENTON	NORTHEAST
000104	CLARK	0500	03	TRENTON	NORTHEAST
100000	JOHNSON	030#	06	ST. PETERSBURG	SOUTHEAST
130101	CLARK	3200	20	TRENTON	NORTHEAST
203000	HAAS	8900	05	ST. LOUIS	MIDWEST
248545	JOHNSON	0345	14	ST. PETERSBURG	SOUTHEAST
277333	HAAS	009(	08	ST. LOUIS	MIDWEST
400000	JOHNSON	070)	08	ST. PETERSBURG	SOUTHEAST
444333	ADAMS	100%	01	NEW YORK	NORTHEAST
444444	FEGEN	0100	02	ST. PETERSBURG	SOUTHEAST
475365	HAAS	0333	05	ST. LOUIS	MIDWEST
476236	FEGEN	037&	03	ST. PETERSBURG	SOUTHEAST
476530	BENWAY	023%	05	CHICAGO	MIDWEST
555555	FEGEN	0304	05	ST. PETERSBURG	SOUTHEAST
555666	ADAMS	2003	20	NEW YORK	NORTHEAST
576235	CLARK	0100	03	TRENTON	NORTHEAST
583645	KARLSTROM	0145	04	BALTIMORE	NORTHEAST
649356	HUMMER	0345	05	CHICAGO	MIDWEST
694446	HUMMER	0904	10	CHICAGO	MIDWEST
700039	MARCUS	0932	10	BALTIMORE	NORTHEAST
750020	MARCUS	0305	05	BALTIMORE	NORTHEAST
800396	KARLSTROM	3030	09	BALTIMORE	NORTHEAST
878787	JOHNSON	1235	12	ST. PETERSBURG	SOUTHEAST
987654	ADAMS	2005	10	NEW YORK	NORTHEAST
988888	BENWAY	0450	01	CHICAGO	MIDWEST
999340	BENWAY	0334	30	CHICAGO	MIDWEST

The records in Figure 15.1 are in sequence by account number, so that the transactions associated with any particular salesperson are scattered throughout the file. What if, however, we wanted to know the total sales and/or commission amount for a particular salesperson or for every salesperson? The easiest way to produce such a report would be to sort the file by salesperson so that all of the transactions for each salesperson appear together. It would then be a simple matter to look at all the transactions for Adams in order to compute his total sales and commission, then look at the transactions for Benway, then for Clark, etc. This is precisely what is meant by control break processing.

The records in Figure 15.2a have been sorted by salesperson in order to produce the report of Figure 15.2b. A ***control break***, defined as a change in a ***control field*** (salesperson in the example), occurs when the value of the control field changes from record to record—for example, when we go from the last transaction for Adams to the first transaction for Benway, and again from the last transaction for Benway to the first transaction for Clark. The detection of a control break signals the creation of one or more ***control totals,*** which in this example would be the sales and commissions for a given salesperson.

Figure 15.2 One-Level Control Break

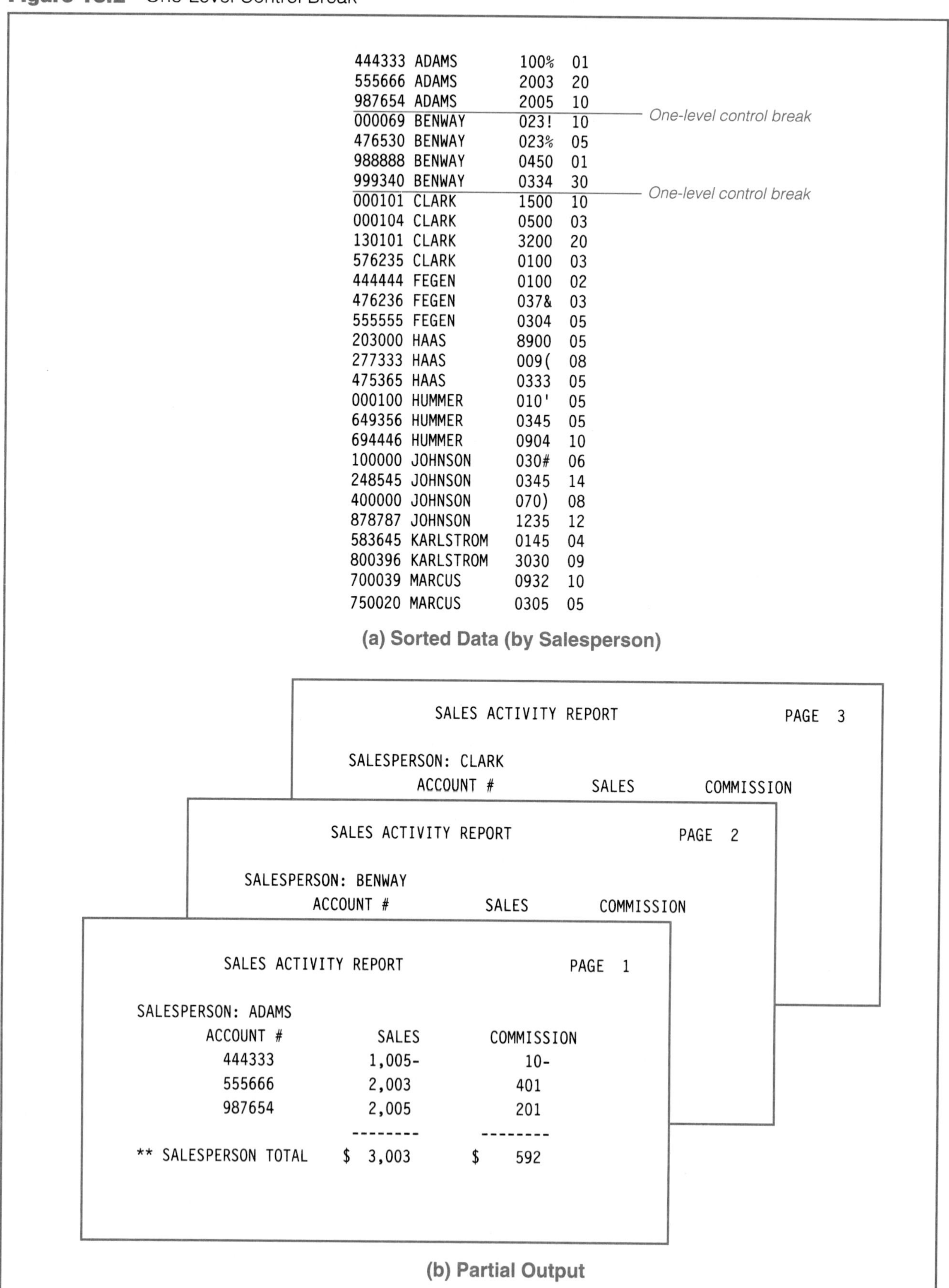

444333 ADAMS 100% 01
555666 ADAMS 2003 20
987654 ADAMS 2005 10
000069 BENWAY 023! 10
476530 BENWAY 023% 05
988888 BENWAY 0450 01
999340 BENWAY 0334 30
000101 CLARK 1500 10
000104 CLARK 0500 03
130101 CLARK 3200 20
576235 CLARK 0100 03
444444 FEGEN 0100 02
476236 FEGEN 037& 03
555555 FEGEN 0304 05
203000 HAAS 8900 05
277333 HAAS 009(08
475365 HAAS 0333 05
000100 HUMMER 010' 05
649356 HUMMER 0345 05
694446 HUMMER 0904 10
100000 JOHNSON 030# 06
248545 JOHNSON 0345 14
400000 JOHNSON 070) 08
878787 JOHNSON 1235 12
583645 KARLSTROM 0145 04
800396 KARLSTROM 3030 09
700039 MARCUS 0932 10
750020 MARCUS 0305 05
One-level control break
One-level control break
SALES ACTIVITY REPORT PAGE 3
SALESPERSON: CLARK
ACCOUNT # SALES COMMISSION
SALES ACTIVITY REPORT PAGE 2
SALESPERSON: BENWAY
ACCOUNT # SALES COMMISSION
SALES ACTIVITY REPORT PAGE 1
SALESPERSON: ADAMS
ACCOUNT # SALES COMMISSION
444333 1,005- 10-
555666 2,003 401
987654 2,005 201
-------- --------
** SALESPERSON TOTAL $ 3,003 $ 592

(a) Sorted Data (by Salesperson)

(b) Partial Output

A ***two-level control break*** is illustrated in Figure 15.3. The data in Figure 15.3a have been sorted by location, and by salesperson within location, in order to produce the report in Figure 15.3b. All salespersons in the same location appear together, as do all transactions for the same salesperson. A one-level control break occurs from Karlstrom to Marcus as salesperson changes, but location does not. A two-level control break occurs from Marcus to Benway, when the values of two control fields, salesperson and location, change simultaneously. The two-level control break produces two sets of control totals: the sales and commission totals for Marcus, as well as the sales and commission totals for all salespersons in Baltimore.

A ***three-level control break*** is shown in Figure 15.4. The data in Figure 15.4a have been sorted by region, location within region, and salesperson within location, in order to produce the report of Figure 15.4b. A one-level control break occurs from Benway to Hummer as salesperson changes, but location and region do not. A two-level control break occurs from Hummer to Haas when salesperson and location change simultaneously but regions remains constant, and a three-level control break occurs from Haas to Karlstrom as all three fields change together.

There is no theoretical limit to the number of control breaks that can be computed; there is a practical limit, however, in that most people lose track after three (or at most four) levels. Regardless of the number of control breaks in effect, the file used to create the control totals must be in sequence according to the designated control fields.

Figure 15.3 Two-Level Control Break

```
583645 KARLSTROM   0145  04  BALTIMORE
800396 KARLSTROM   3030  09  BALTIMORE
----------------------------------------- One-level control break
700039 MARCUS      0932  10  BALTIMORE
750020 MARCUS      0305  05  BALTIMORE
----------------------------------------- Two-level control break
000069 BENWAY      023!  10  CHICAGO
476530 BENWAY      023%  05  CHICAGO
988888 BENWAY      0450  01  CHICAGO
999340 BENWAY      0334  30  CHICAGO
000100 HUMMER      010'  05  CHICAGO
649356 HUMMER      0345  05  CHICAGO
694446 HUMMER      0904  10  CHICAGO
444333 ADAMS       100%  01  NEW YORK
555666 ADAMS       2003  20  NEW YORK
987654 ADAMS       2005  10  NEW YORK
203000 HAAS        8900  05  ST. LOUIS
277333 HAAS        009(  08  ST. LOUIS
475365 HAAS        0333  05  ST. LOUIS
444444 FEGEN       0100  02  ST. PETERSBURG
476236 FEGEN       037&  03  ST. PETERSBURG
555555 FEGEN       0304  05  ST. PETERSBURG
100000 JOHNSON     030#  06  ST. PETERSBURG
248545 JOHNSON     0345  14  ST. PETERSBURG
400000 JOHNSON     070)  08  ST. PETERSBURG
878787 JOHNSON     1235  12  ST. PETERSBURG
000101 CLARK       1500  10  TRENTON
000104 CLARK       0500  03  TRENTON
130101 CLARK       3200  20  TRENTON
576235 CLARK       0100  03  TRENTON
```

(a) Sorted Data (by Location and Salesperson)

Figure 15.3 *(continued)*

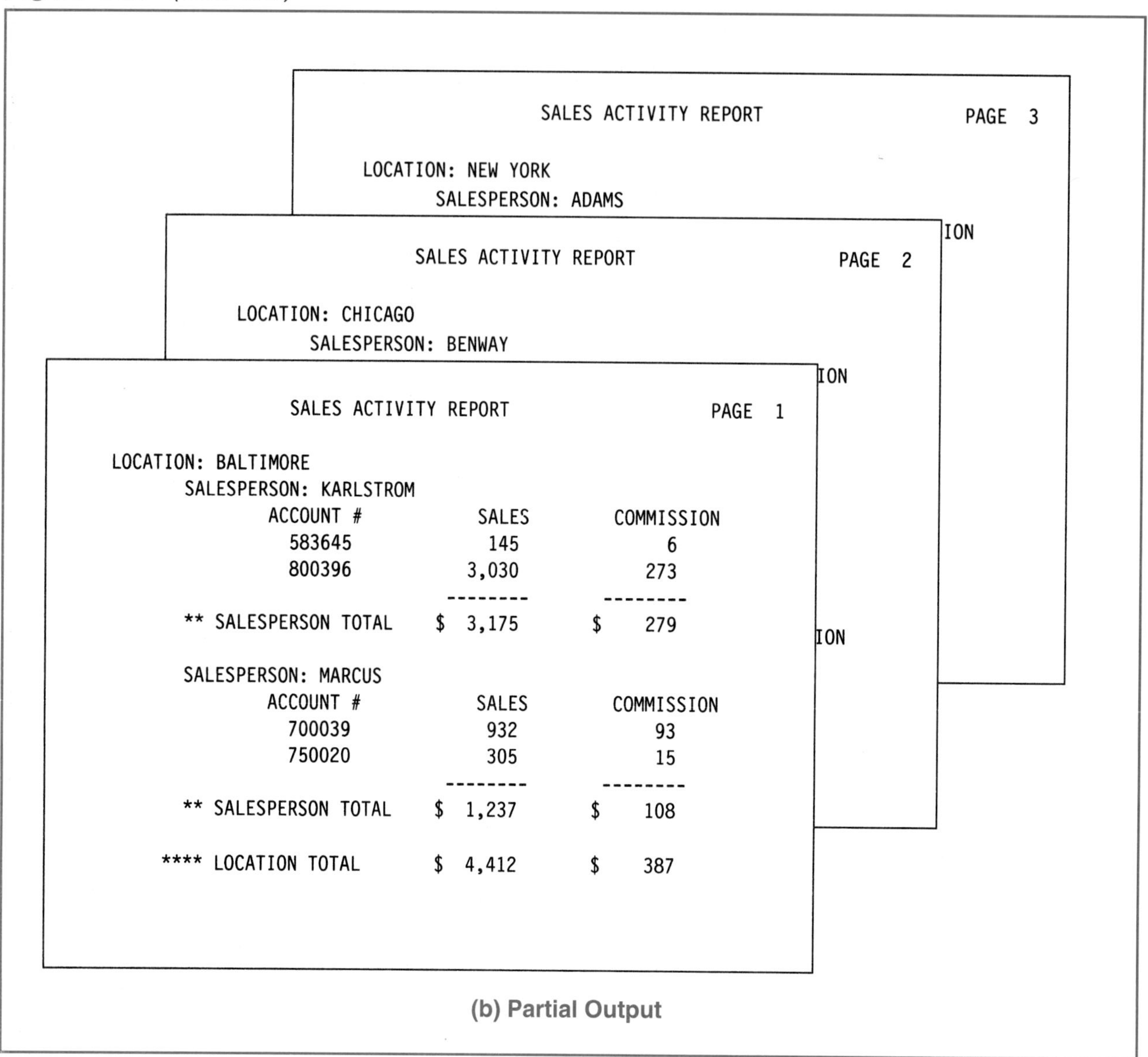

```
                SALES ACTIVITY REPORT                    PAGE  3

  LOCATION: NEW YORK
       SALESPERSON: ADAMS

                SALES ACTIVITY REPORT                    PAGE  2

  LOCATION: CHICAGO
       SALESPERSON: BENWAY

                SALES ACTIVITY REPORT                    PAGE  1

  LOCATION: BALTIMORE
       SALESPERSON: KARLSTROM
             ACCOUNT #          SALES          COMMISSION
              583645              145                   6
              800396            3,030                 273
                             --------            --------
       ** SALESPERSON TOTAL   $  3,175         $      279

       SALESPERSON: MARCUS
             ACCOUNT #          SALES          COMMISSION
              700039              932                  93
              750020              305                  15
                             --------            --------
       ** SALESPERSON TOTAL   $  1,237         $      108

     **** LOCATION TOTAL      $  4,412         $      387
```

(b) Partial Output

Running versus Rolling Totals

Each of the reports in Figures 15.2 through 15.4 computes totals at one or more levels (at salesperson, location, region, and company), according to the number of control breaks. The company totals are printed at the end of processing and appear on the last page of each report, but are not visible in the individual figures. (The total sales for the company and corresponding commission are $23,906 and $2,540, respectively.)

Consider for a moment how the computations might be accomplished in the one-level report of Figure 15.2b. There is only one way to compute the total for individual salespersons—by initializing the total for each new salesperson to zero, then adding the amount on every transaction for that salesperson to his or her total. There are, however, two ways to compute the company total—by adding the value for every transaction to a ***running company total***, or by waiting for a break on salesperson and then adding, or ***rolling,*** the salesperson total to the company total. The latter is more efficient in that fewer additions are performed.

Similar reasoning applies to the two-level report of Figure 15.3b, in which the location total can be computed two different ways—by adding the value of each incoming transaction to a running location total, or by waiting for a control break on salesperson, then rolling the salesperson total to the location total. In similar fashion, the company total may be obtained in three ways. First, by adding the value of every incoming transaction to a running company total. Second, by rolling the salesperson total into the company total after a one-level break on salesperson. Or third, by rolling the location total into the company total after a two-level break on location. The third approach is the most efficient.

You should be able to extend this logic to the three-level report of Figure 15.4b, which maintains a running total for each salesperson, then rolls the salesperson total into the location total (after a break on salesperson), rolls the location total into the region total (after a break on location), and finally rolls the region total into the company total (after a break on region).

Figure 15.4 Three-Level Control Break

```
000069 BENWAY      023!  10  CHICAGO         MIDWEST
476530 BENWAY      023%  05  CHICAGO         MIDWEST
988888 BENWAY      0450  01  CHICAGO         MIDWEST
999340 BENWAY      0334  30  CHICAGO         MIDWEST
---------------------------------------------------- One-level control break
000100 HUMMER      010'  05  CHICAGO         MIDWEST
649356 HUMMER      0345  05  CHICAGO         MIDWEST
694446 HUMMER      0904  10  CHICAGO         MIDWEST
---------------------------------------------------- Two-level control break
203000 HAAS        8900  05  ST. LOUIS       MIDWEST
277333 HAAS        009(  08  ST. LOUIS       MIDWEST
475365 HAAS        0333  05  ST. LOUIS       MIDWEST
---------------------------------------------------- Three-Level control break
583645 KARLSTROM   0145  04  BALTIMORE       NORTHEAST
800396 KARLSTROM   3030  09  BALTIMORE       NORTHEAST
700039 MARCUS      0932  10  BALTIMORE       NORTHEAST
750020 MARCUS      0305  05  BALTIMORE       NORTHEAST
444333 ADAMS       100%  01  NEW YORK        NORTHEAST
555666 ADAMS       2003  20  NEW YORK        NORTHEAST
987654 ADAMS       2005  10  NEW YORK        NORTHEAST
000101 CLARK       1500  10  TRENTON         NORTHEAST
000104 CLARK       0500  03  TRENTON         NORTHEAST
130101 CLARK       3200  20  TRENTON         NORTHEAST
576235 CLARK       0100  03  TRENTON         NORTHEAST
444444 FEGEN       0100  02  ST. PETERSBURG  SOUTHEAST
476236 FEGEN       037&  03  ST. PETERSBURG  SOUTHEAST
555555 FEGEN       0304  05  ST. PETERSBURG  SOUTHEAST
100000 JOHNSON     030#  06  ST. PETERSBURG  SOUTHEAST
248545 JOHNSON     0345  14  ST. PETERSBURG  SOUTHEAST
400000 JOHNSON     070)  08  ST. PETERSBURG  SOUTHEAST
878787 JOHNSON     1235  12  ST. PETERSBURG  SOUTHEAST
```

(a) Sorted Data (by Region, Location, and Salesperson)

Figure 15.4 *(continued)*

```
                         SALES ACTIVITY REPORT                  PAGE  3

     REGION: SOUTHEAST
             LOCATION: ST. PETERSBURG
```

```
                         SALES ACTIVITY REPORT                  PAGE  2

     REGION: NORTHEAST
             LOCATION: BALTIMORE
```

```
                         SALES ACTIVITY REPORT                  PAGE  1

     REGION: MIDWEST
             LOCATION: CHICAGO
                    SALESPERSON: BENWAY
                           ACCOUNT #          SALES         COMMISSION
                             000069            231-             23-
                             476530            235-             12-
                             988888            450               5
                             999340            334             100
                                            --------       --------
                    ** SALESPERSON TOTAL  $     318        $     70

                    SALESPERSON: HUMMER
                           ACCOUNT #          SALES         COMMISSION
                             000100            107-              5-
                             649356            345              17
                             694446            904              90
                                            --------       --------
                    ** SALESPERSON TOTAL  $   1,142        $    102

                  **** LOCATION TOTAL     $   1,460        $    172

             LOCATION: ST. LOUIS
                    SALESPERSON: HAAS
                           ACCOUNT #          SALES         COMMISSION
                             203000          8,900             445
                             277333             98-              8-
                             475365            333              17
                                            --------       --------
                    ** SALESPERSON TOTAL  $   9,135        $    454

                  **** LOCATION TOTAL     $   9,135        $    454

                ****** REGION TOTAL       $  10,595        $    626
```

(b) Partial Output

One-Level Control Breaks

The development of the one- (two- and three-) level programs is not difficult given a clear understanding of the requirements and the distinction between running and rolling totals. We begin with the specifications for the one-level program.

PROGRAMMING SPECIFICATIONS

Program Name: One-Level Control Break

Narrative: The specifications are for the one-level control break program. Changes to the specifications to accommodate two- and three-level control breaks are provided later in the chapter.

Input File(s): SALES-FILE

Input Record Layout:

```
01  SALES-RECORD-IN.
    05  SR-ACCOUNT-NUMBER          PIC 9(6).
    05  FILLER                     PIC X.
    05  SR-NAME                    PIC X(15).
    05  SR-SALES                   PIC S9(4).
    05  FILLER                     PIC XX.
    05  SR-COMMISSION-PERCENT      PIC V99.
    05  FILLER                     PIC XX.
    05  SR-LOCATION                PIC X(15).
    05  SR-REGION                  PIC X(11).
```

Test Data: See Figure 15.1.

Report Layout: See Figure 15.2b.

Processing Requirements:

1. Sort the incoming transaction file by salesperson; use the WITH DUPLICATES IN ORDER phrase of the SORT statement to keep the sorted file in sequence by transaction number within salesperson.
2. Process transactions until a control break is encountered on salesperson, then for each new salesperson:
   a. Initialize the total sales and commission for that salesperson to zero.
   b. Print a heading for this salesperson on a new page.
3. Process all transactions for each salesperson as follows:
   a. Compute the commission for each transaction by multiplying the amount of the sale by the commission percentage.
   b. Print a detail line for each transaction containing the account number, sales amount, and computed commission.
   c. Increment the total sales and commissions for that salesperson by the corresponding amounts for this transaction.
4. Print a total line for each salesperson whenever salesperson changes. Print dashes as indicated between the last detail line and the total line.
5. Increment the company totals with the salesperson's accumulated totals as salesperson changes.
6. Print the company totals after all records have been processed.

Hierarchy Chart

The report in Figure 15.2b contains a heading line prior to the first transaction for each salesperson, detail lines containing the sales and commission for the individual transactions, and a total line after all transactions for each salesperson. The company total appears at the end of the report (but is not visible in Figure 15.2b).

All of these functions are recognized in the hierarchy chart of Figure 15.5a, which was developed in stages, beginning at the top and working down to the bottom. The functions at every level in the hierarchy chart are divided into component functions that appear on the next lower-level. The lower-level functions are further subdivided into other functions on a still lower-level, until finally the lowest-level functions cannot be further subdivided.

The module at the top (or first level) of the hierarchy chart, PREPARE-SALES-REPORT, depicts the overall program function. It is divided into four subordinate functions, each of which was taken directly from the programming specifications. These modules are placed on the second level of the hierarchy chart:

1. SORT-TRANSACTION-FILE to sort the transaction file (as indicated in item 1 of the processing requirements)
2. READ-SORTED-SALES-FILE to read a record from the sorted file
3. PROCESS-ONE-SALESPERSON to process each salesperson (from items 2 through 5 of the processing requirements)
4. WRITE-COMPANY-TOTAL to write the company total (from item 6 of the processing requirements)

Each of these modules is considered for further subdivision, but only PROCESS-ONE-SALESPERSON is divided into component functions for the next level. Once again, we use the processing requirements as a guide to determine the subordinate functions for the third level:

1. INITIALIZE-SALESPERSON to initialize the sales and commission amounts for this salesperson (item 2a of the processing requirements)
2. WRITE-SALESPERSON-HEADING to write a heading for each salesperson (item 2b of the processing requirements)
3. PROCESS-ONE-TRANSACTION to process the transaction (item 3 of the processing requirements)
4. WRITE-SALESPERSON-TOTAL to print the salesperson total (item 4 of the processing requirements)
5. INCREMENT-COMPANY-TOTAL to increment the company total (item 5 of the processing requirements)

Each function is evaluated for further subdivision, but only PROCESS-ONE-TRANSACTION is developed further. Repeating the earlier procedure, and again using the processing requirements, we obtain the modules for the fourth and final level:

1. CALCULATE-COMMISSION to calculate the commission for the transaction (item 3a of the processing requirements)
2. WRITE-DETAIL-LINE to write a detail line for each transaction (item 3b of the processing requirements)
3. INCREMENT-SALESPERSON-TOTAL to increment the salesperson's total (item 3c of the processing requirements)
4. READ-SORTED-SALES-FILE to read the next record and avoid an endless loop

Figure 15.5 One-Level Algorithm

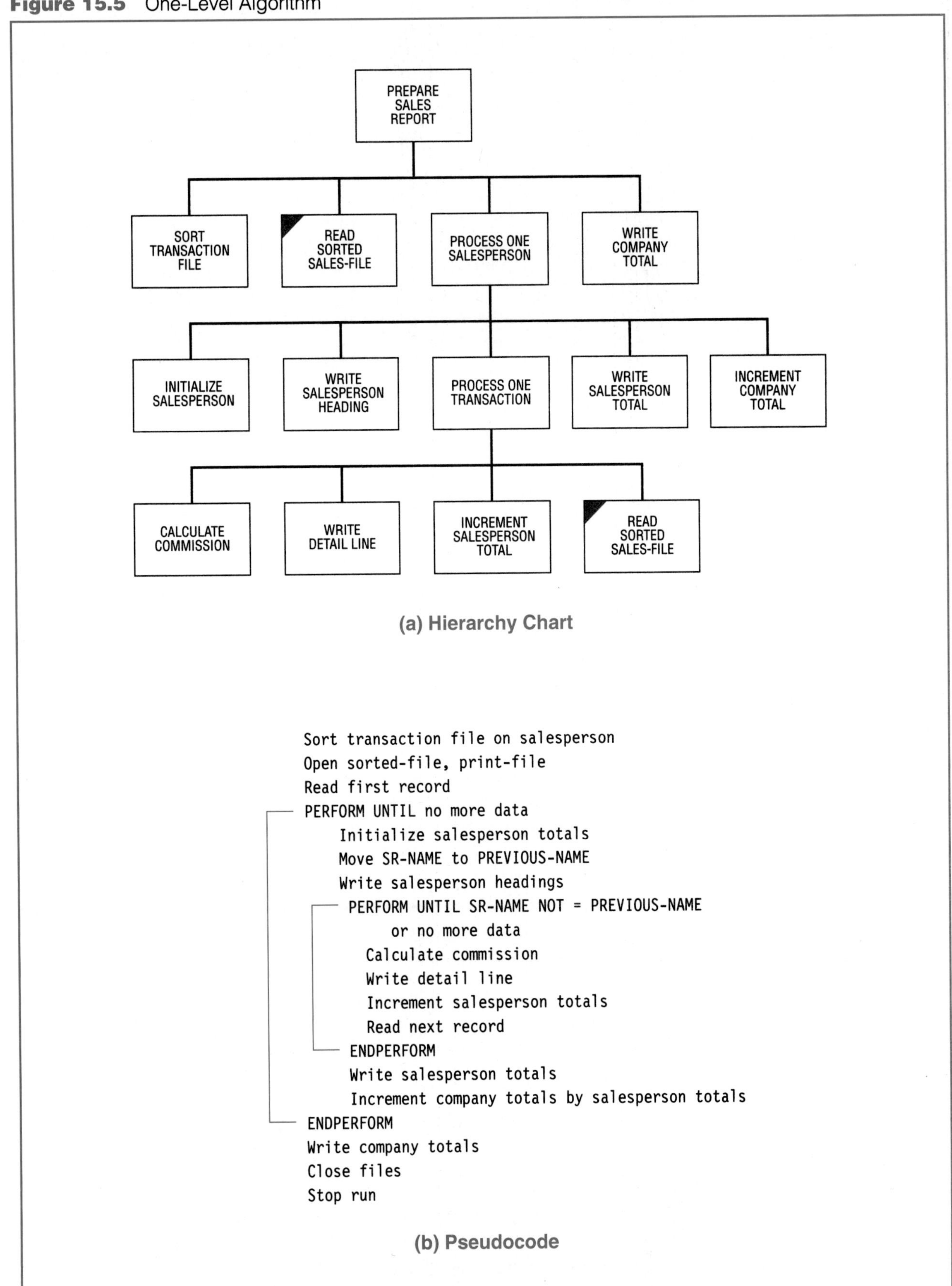
PREPARE SALES REPORT
SORT TRANSACTION FILE
READ SORTED SALES-FILE
PROCESS ONE SALESPERSON
WRITE COMPANY TOTAL
INITIALIZE SALESPERSON
WRITE SALESPERSON HEADING
PROCESS ONE TRANSACTION
WRITE SALESPERSON TOTAL
INCREMENT COMPANY TOTAL
CALCULATE COMMISSION
WRITE DETAIL LINE
INCREMENT SALESPERSON TOTAL
READ SORTED SALES-FILE
Sort transaction file on salesperson
Open sorted-file, print-file
Read first record
PERFORM UNTIL no more data
Initialize salesperson totals
Move SR-NAME to PREVIOUS-NAME
Write salesperson headings
PERFORM UNTIL SR-NAME NOT = PREVIOUS-NAME
or no more data
Calculate commission
Write detail line
Increment salesperson totals
Read next record
ENDPERFORM
Write salesperson totals
Increment company totals by salesperson totals
ENDPERFORM
Write company totals
Close files
Stop run

(a) Hierarchy Chart

(b) Pseudocode

The completed hierarchy chart is evaluated according to the criteria presented in Chapter 3—completeness, functionality, and span of control. The hierarchy chart is complete because it contains a module corresponding to every processing requirement. Its modules are functional (i.e., each module accomplishes a single task) as can be implied from the module names that consist of a verb, an adjective or two, and an object—for example, INCREMENT-SALESPERSON-TOTAL or WRITE-DETAIL-LINE.

Finally, the span of control (number of subordinate modules) is reasonably set at three or four throughout the hierarchy chart, and the relationship of the modules to one another appears to be correct. Observe, for example, that WRITE-DETAIL-LINE, INCREMENT-SALESPERSON-TOTAL, and READ-SORTED-SALES-FILE are subordinate to PROCESS-ONE-TRANSACTION, which in turn is subordinate to PROCESS-ONE-SALESPERSON, which is subordinate to PREPARE-SALES-REPORT. There is no other reasonable way to relate these functions, all of which are required to maintain completeness.

Pseudocode

The pseudocode in Figure 15.5b introduces specific COBOL data names, such as SR-NAME and PREVIOUS-NAME, that enable the program to detect a control break. In other words, a COBOL statement cannot simply process records until a control break occurs, but must specify precisely how to determine when the value of salesperson changes. Thus in order to detect a control break, the program compares the name on the record just read to the name on the previous record; that is, it compares SR-NAME to PREVIOUS-NAME, and detects a break when the values are different.

The pseudocode sorts the transaction file according to salesperson, reads the first transaction record, then executes the statements in the outer loop for every salesperson until the entire file has been processed. The (sales and commission) totals for each new salesperson are initialized, then an inner loop is executed until a control break is detected. The inner loop processes all transactions for the current salesperson by calculating the commission amount, writing a detail line, and incrementing the running salesperson totals. The inner loop is terminated by the control break—that is, when SR-NAME is not equal to PREVIOUS-NAME—after which the sales and commission totals for the salesperson are written and rolled into the corresponding company totals.

It is now a simple matter to write the required program.

The Completed Program

The completed program in Figure 15.6 is straightforward and easy to follow, especially after the preceding discussion on hierarchy charts and pseudocode. Note especially the relationship of the hierarchy chart in Figure 15.5a to the paragraphs in the Procedure Division. The modules in the hierarchy chart correspond one to one with the paragraphs in the program. Observe also that each level in the hierarchy chart corresponds to a COBOL PERFORM statement.

The Working-Storage Section contains multiple 01 entries for the various print lines required by the program. There are multiple heading lines, a detail line, and two total lines. Working-Storage also contains separate counters for the salesperson and company totals, as well as a switch, PREVIOUS-NAME, to detect the control break on salesperson.

The SORT statement (lines 151–156) specifies SORT-NAME as the primary key in accordance with the requirements of the control break on salesperson. The

WITH DUPLICATES IN ORDER phrase keeps the transactions for a given salesperson in sequence by account number because the input file (Figure 15.1) was already in sequence by this field.

Figure 15.6 One-Level Control Break Program

```
IDENTIFICATION DIVISION.
PROGRAM-ID.    ONELEVEL.
AUTHOR.        CVV.

ENVIRONMENT DIVISION.
INPUT-OUTPUT SECTION.
FILE-CONTROL.
    SELECT SALES-FILE
        ASSIGN TO UT-S-SYSIN.
    SELECT PRINT-FILE
        ASSIGN TO UT-S-SYSOUT.
    SELECT SORT-WORK-FILE
        ASSIGN TO UT-S-SORTWK01.
    SELECT SORTED-SALES-FILE
        ASSIGN TO UT-S-SORTED.

DATA DIVISION.
FILE SECTION.
FD  SALES-FILE
    RECORD CONTAINS 58 CHARACTERS
    DATA RECORD IS SALES-RECORD.
01  SALES-RECORD                    PIC X(58).

FD  PRINT-FILE
    RECORD CONTAINS 132 CHARACTERS
    DATA RECORD IS PRINT-LINE.
01  PRINT-LINE                      PIC X(132).

SD  SORT-WORK-FILE
    RECORD CONTAINS 58 CHARACTERS
    DATA RECORD IS SORT-RECORD.
01  SORT-RECORD.
    05  SORT-ACCOUNT-NUMBER         PIC 9(6).
    05  FILLER                      PIC X.
    05  SORT-NAME                   PIC X(15).
    05  FILLER                      PIC X(10).
    05  SORT-LOCATION               PIC X(15).
    05  SORT-REGION                 PIC X(11).

FD  SORTED-SALES-FILE
    RECORD CONTAINS 58 CHARACTERS
    DATA RECORD IS SORTED-SALES-RECORD.
01  SORTED-SALES-RECORD             PIC X(58).
```

Figure 15.6 *(continued)*

```
       WORKING-STORAGE SECTION.
       01  FILLER                       PIC X(14)
               VALUE 'WS BEGINS HERE'.

       01  SALES-RECORD-IN.
           05  SR-ACCOUNT-NUMBER        PIC 9(6).
           05  FILLER                   PIC X.
           05  SR-NAME                  PIC X(15).
           05  SR-SALES                 PIC S9(4).
           05  FILLER                   PIC XX.
           05  SR-COMMISSION-PERCENT    PIC V99.
           05  FILLER                   PIC XX.
           05  SR-LOCATION              PIC X(15).
           05  SR-REGION                PIC X(11).

       01  PROGRAM-SWITCHES-AND-COUNTERS.
           05  DATA-REMAINS-SW          PIC X(3)    VALUE 'YES'.
               88  NO-DATA-REMAINS                  VALUE 'NO'.
           05  PREVIOUS-NAME            PIC X(15)   VALUE SPACES.
           05  PAGE-COUNT               PIC 99      VALUE ZEROES.

       01  CONTROL-BREAK-TOTALS.
           05  INDIVIDUAL-TOTALS.
               10  IND-COMMISSION       PIC S9(4).
           05  SALESPERSON-TOTALS.
               10  SALESPERSON-SALES-TOT PIC S9(6).
               10  SALESPERSON-COMM-TOT  PIC S9(6).
           05  COMPANY-TOTALS.
               10  COMPANY-SALES-TOT    PIC S9(6)   VALUE ZEROS.
               10  COMPANY-COMM-TOT     PIC S9(6)   VALUE ZEROS.

       01  REPORT-HEADING-LINE.
           05  FILLER                   PIC X(25)   VALUE SPACES.
           05  FILLER                   PIC X(21)
                 VALUE 'SALES ACTIVITY REPORT'.
           05  FILLER                   PIC X(19)   VALUE SPACES.
           05  FILLER                   PIC X(5)    VALUE 'PAGE '.
           05  HDG-PAGE                 PIC Z9.
           05  FILLER                   PIC X(60)   VALUE SPACES.

       01  SALESPERSON-HEADING-LINE-ONE.
           05  FILLER                   PIC X(15)   VALUE SPACES.
           05  FILLER                   PIC X(13)
                 VALUE 'SALESPERSON: '.
           05  HDG-NAME                 PIC X(15).
           05  FILLER                   PIC X(89)   VALUE SPACES.

       01  SALESPERSON-HEADING-LINE-TWO.
           05  FILLER                   PIC X(23)   VALUE SPACES.
```

Signed fields are used in all computations

Figure 15.6 *(continued)*

```
           05  FILLER                   PIC X(11)    VALUE 'ACCOUNT .
           05  FILLER                   PIC X(9)     VALUE SPACES.
           05  FILLER                   PIC X(5)     VALUE 'SALES'.
           05  FILLER                   PIC X(8)     VALUE SPACES.
           05  FILLER                   PIC X(10)    VALUE 'COMMISSION'.
           05  FILLER                   PIC X(66)    VALUE SPACES.

       01  DETAIL-LINE.
           05  FILLER                   PIC X(25)    VALUE SPACES.
           05  DET-ACCOUNT-NUMBER       PIC 9(6).
           05  FILLER                   PIC X(9)     VALUE SPACES.
           05  DET-SALES                PIC Z(3),ZZ9-.
           05  FILLER                   PIC X(7)     VALUE SPACES.
           05  DET-COMMISSION           PIC Z(3),ZZ9-.
           05  FILLER                   PIC X(69)    VALUE SPACES.

       01  DASHED-LINE.
           05  FILLER                   PIC X(40)    VALUE SPACES.
           05  FILLER                   PIC X(8)     VALUE ALL '-'.
           05  FILLER                   PIC X(7)     VALUE SPACES.
           05  FILLER                   PIC X(8)     VALUE ALL '-'.
           05  FILLER                   PIC X(69)    VALUE SPACES.

       01  SALESPERSON-TOTAL-LINE.
           05  FILLER                   PIC X(15)    VALUE SPACES.
           05  FILLER                   PIC X(21)
                 VALUE '** SALESPERSON TOTAL'.
           05  FILLER                   PIC X(3)     VALUE SPACES.
           05  SALESPERSON-SALES-TOTAL  PIC $Z(3),ZZ9-.
           05  FILLER                   PIC X(6)     VALUE SPACES.
           05  SALESPERSON-COMM-TOTAL   PIC $Z(3),ZZ9-.
           05  FILLER                   PIC X(69)    VALUE SPACES.

       01  COMPANY-TOTAL-LINE.
           05  FILLER                   PIC X(9)     VALUE SPACES.
           05  FILLER                   PIC X(22)
                 VALUE '******** COMPANY TOTAL'.
           05  FILLER                   PIC X(8)     VALUE SPACES.
           05  COMPANY-SALES-TOTAL      PIC $Z(3),ZZ9-.
           05  FILLER                   PIC X(6)     VALUE SPACES.
           05  COMPANY-COMM-TOTAL       PIC $Z(3),ZZ9-.
           05  FILLER                   PIC X(69)    VALUE SPACES.

       PROCEDURE DIVISION.
       100-PREPARE-SALES-REPORT.
           PERFORM 200-SORT-TRANSACTION-FILE.
           OPEN INPUT SORTED-SALES-FILE
                OUTPUT PRINT-FILE.
           PERFORM 220-READ-SORTED-SALES-FILE.
           PERFORM 240-PROCESS-ONE-SALESPERSON
```

Editing reflects signed fields (DET-SALES, DET-COMMISSION)

Highest-level module in hierarchy chart (100-PREPARE-SALES-REPORT)

Figure 15.6 *(continued)*

```
                UNTIL NO-DATA-REMAINS.
            PERFORM 260-WRITE-COMPANY-TOTAL.
            CLOSE SORTED-SALES-FILE
                  PRINT-FILE.
            STOP RUN.

        200-SORT-TRANSACTION-FILE.
            SORT SORT-WORK-FILE
                ASCENDING KEY
                    SORT-NAME
                WITH DUPLICATES IN ORDER
                USING SALES-FILE
                GIVING SORTED-SALES-FILE.

        220-READ-SORTED-SALES-FILE.
            READ SORTED-SALES-FILE INTO SALES-RECORD-IN
                AT END MOVE 'NO' TO DATA-REMAINS-SW
            END-READ.

        240-PROCESS-ONE-SALESPERSON.
            PERFORM 300-INITIALIZE-SALESPERSON.
            PERFORM 320-WRITE-SALESPERSON-HEADING.
            PERFORM 340-PROCESS-ONE-TRANSACTION
                UNTIL SR-NAME NOT EQUAL PREVIOUS-NAME
                            OR NO-DATA-REMAINS.
            PERFORM 360-WRITE-SALESPERSON-TOTAL.
            PERFORM 380-INCREMENT-COMPANY-TOTAL.

        260-WRITE-COMPANY-TOTAL.
            MOVE COMPANY-SALES-TOT TO COMPANY-SALES-TOTAL.
            MOVE COMPANY-COMM-TOT TO COMPANY-COMM-TOTAL.
            WRITE PRINT-LINE FROM COMPANY-TOTAL-LINE
                AFTER ADVANCING 2 LINES.

        300-INITIALIZE-SALESPERSON.
            MOVE SR-NAME TO PREVIOUS-NAME.
            INITIALIZE SALESPERSON-TOTALS.

        320-WRITE-SALESPERSON-HEADING.
            ADD 1 TO PAGE-COUNT.
            MOVE PAGE-COUNT TO HDG-PAGE.
            WRITE PRINT-LINE FROM REPORT-HEADING-LINE
                AFTER ADVANCING PAGE.
            MOVE SR-NAME TO HDG-NAME.
            WRITE PRINT-LINE FROM SALESPERSON-HEADING-LINE-ONE
                AFTER ADVANCING 2 LINES.
            WRITE PRINT-LINE FROM SALESPERSON-HEADING-LINE-TWO
                AFTER ADVANCING 1 LINE.

        340-PROCESS-ONE-TRANSACTION.
            PERFORM 400-CALCULATE-COMMISSION.
```

Sort statement required to place transactions in sequence

Heading written prior to each new salesperson

Detection of control break

Total for this salesperson written after control break is detected

Figure 15.6 *(continued)*

```
          PERFORM 420-WRITE-DETAIL-LINE.
          PERFORM 440-INCRMENT-SALESPERSON-TOTAL.
          PERFORM 220-READ-SORTED-SALES-FILE.

      360-WRITE-SALESPERSON-TOTAL.
          WRITE PRINT-LINE FROM DASHED-LINE
              AFTER ADVANCING 1 LINE.
          MOVE SALESPERSON-SALES-TOT TO SALESPERSON-SALES-TOTAL.
          MOVE SALESPERSON-COMM-TOT TO SALESPERSON-COMM-TOTAL.
          WRITE PRINT-LINE FROM SALESPERSON-TOTAL-LINE
              AFTER ADVANCING 1 LINE.
          MOVE SPACES TO PRINT-LINE.
          WRITE PRINT-LINE
              AFTER ADVANCING 1 LINE.

      380-INCREMENT-COMPANY-TOTAL.
          ADD SALESPERSON-SALES-TOT TO COMPANY-SALES-TOT.
          ADD SALESPERSON-COMM-TOT TO COMPANY-COMM-TOT.

      400-CALCULATE-COMMISSION.
          COMPUTE IND-COMMISSION ROUNDED =
              SR-SALES * SR-COMMISSION-PERCENT
              SIZE ERROR DISPLAY 'SIZE ERROR ON COMMISSION FOR '
                  SR-NAME
          END-COMPUTE.

      420-WRITE-DETAIL-LINE.
          MOVE SR-ACCOUNT-NUMBER TO DET-ACCOUNT-NUMBER.
          MOVE SR-SALES TO DET-SALES.
          MOVE IND-COMMISSION TO DET-COMMISSION.
          WRITE PRINT-LINE FROM DETAIL-LINE.

      440-INCRMENT-SALESPERSON-TOTAL.
          ADD SR-SALES TO SALESPERSON-SALES-TOT.
          ADD IND-COMMISSION TO SALESPERSON-COMM-TOT.
```

Salesperson totals are rolled into company totals

Salesperson totals are accumulated through running totals

Two-Level Control Breaks

The reports in Figures 15.2, 15.3, and 15.4 presented a logical progression of one, two, and three control breaks—for salesperson; location and salesperson; and region, location, and salesperson, respectively. This section extends the hierarchy chart, pseudocode, and COBOL program for the one-level application to include a second control break.

Hierarchy Chart

The development of the two-level hierarchy chart is best accomplished as an extension of its existing one-level counterpart. One easy way to anticipate the changes is to compare the one- and two-level reports in Figures 15.2b and 15.3b, then consider the following questions with respect to the hierarchy chart of Figure 15.5a:

1. What additional (i.e., new) modules are necessary?
2. Which existing modules (if any) have to be modified?
3. Which existing modules (if any) have to be deleted?

Every module that appeared in the one-level hierarchy chart will also appear in its two-level counterpart; that is, no modules will be deleted because every function in the one-level application is also required in the two-level example. In addition, several new functions have to be added to accommodate the control break on location. These include:

1. PROCESS-ONE-LOCATION to process all salespersons in one location
2. INITIALIZE-LOCATION to initialize the sales and commission amounts for this location
3. WRITE-LOCATION-HEADING to print a location heading prior to each new location
4. INCREMENT-LOCATION-TOTAL to increment the sales and commission totals for each location
5. WRITE-LOCATION-TOTAL to print the location totals after a control break on location

Changes will also be required in the logic of some existing modules; for example, the module SORT-TRANSACTION-FILE must now reflect a sort on location and salesperson within location. A more subtle change is in WRITE-SALESPERSON-HEADING, which previously began the report for each salesperson on a new page, but which now lists all salespersons in one location on the same page.

The computation of the company total changes as well. The one-level example waited for a control break on salesperson, then rolled the salesperson total into the company total. Although the same approach could be used in the two-level example, it is more efficient to wait for a control break on location, then roll the location total into the company total.

The hierarchy chart for the two-level problem is shown in Figure 15.7a, with the additional and/or modified modules shaded for emphasis. The placement of the new modules is important, and you should notice that the module PROCESS-ONE-LOCATION appears on the second level of the hierarchy chart; this in turn forces the existing module PROCESS-ONE-SALESPERSON, and all of its subordinates, down a level.

Figure 15.7b is subject to the same design considerations as its predecessor, namely, completeness, functionality, and span of control. All design criteria appear satisfactory and the hierarchy chart is finished.

Pseudocode

The pseudocode for the one-level control example is expanded to its two-level counterpart in Figure 15.7b. New and/or modified statements are highlighted to be consistent with the associated hierarchy chart.

The sort statement includes location as an additional key as previously indicated. The major change, however, is the modification of the outer loop to include a series of repetitive statements for each new location that initialize the location totals, write the location heading, and process all salespersons in that location. The detection of a control break on location occurs when SR-LOCATION is unequal to PREVIOUS-LOCATION, and produces the location total, which is then rolled into the company total.

Figure 15.7 Two-Level Algorithm

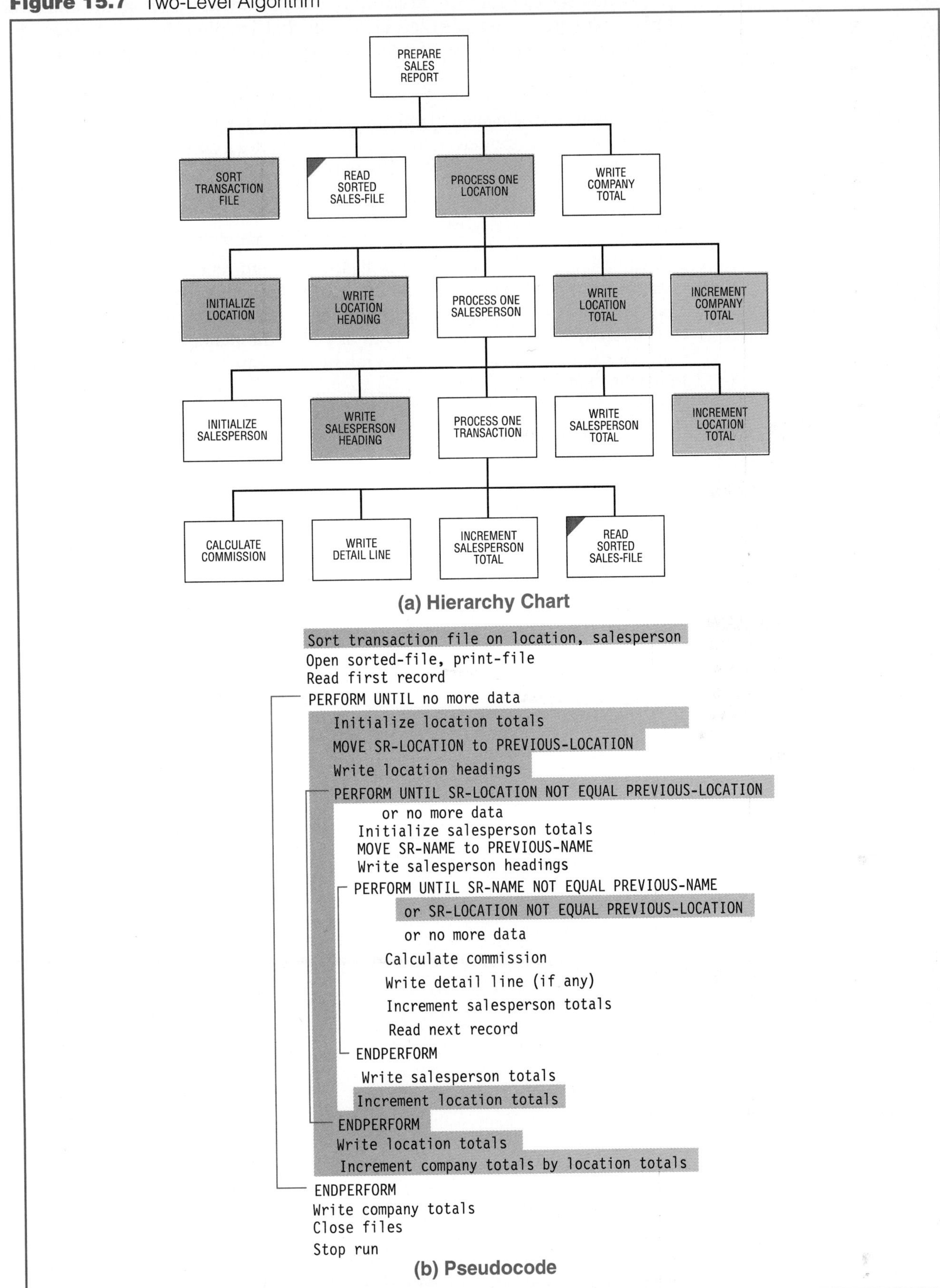
PREPARE SALES REPORT
SORT TRANSACTION FILE
READ SORTED SALES-FILE
PROCESS ONE LOCATION
WRITE COMPANY TOTAL
INITIALIZE LOCATION
WRITE LOCATION HEADING
PROCESS ONE SALESPERSON
WRITE LOCATION TOTAL
INCREMENT COMPANY TOTAL
INITIALIZE SALESPERSON
WRITE SALESPERSON HEADING
PROCESS ONE TRANSACTION
WRITE SALESPERSON TOTAL
INCREMENT LOCATION TOTAL
CALCULATE COMMISSION
WRITE DETAIL LINE
INCREMENT SALESPERSON TOTAL
READ SORTED SALES-FILE
(a) Hierarchy Chart
Sort transaction file on location, salesperson
Open sorted-file, print-file
Read first record
PERFORM UNTIL no more data
Initialize location totals
MOVE SR-LOCATION to PREVIOUS-LOCATION
Write location headings
PERFORM UNTIL SR-LOCATION NOT EQUAL PREVIOUS-LOCATION
or no more data
Initialize salesperson totals
MOVE SR-NAME to PREVIOUS-NAME
Write salesperson headings
PERFORM UNTIL SR-NAME NOT EQUAL PREVIOUS-NAME
or SR-LOCATION NOT EQUAL PREVIOUS-LOCATION
or no more data
Calculate commission
Write detail line (if any)
Increment salesperson totals
Read next record
ENDPERFORM
Write salesperson totals
Increment location totals
ENDPERFORM
Write location totals
Increment company totals by location totals
ENDPERFORM
Write company totals
Close files
Stop run
(b) Pseudocode

Within each location, there is a second loop (carried over from the one-level application) to process all salespersons in that location. Note, however, the ***compound condition*** in the test for a control break on salesperson that now includes both salesperson and location. This dual test is necessary in the unusual instance where the last salesperson in the current location and the first salesperson in the next location have the same name. (A general rule for the detection of a control break requires a compound condition, which includes a check for the level you are on, as well as any levels above the current level.)

The Completed Program

The completed program is shown in Figure 15.8 and reflects all of the indicated changes. Once again, we call your attention to the relationship between the hierarchy chart in Figure 15.7a and the paragraphs in the Procedure Division. The modules in the hierarchy chart correspond one to one with the paragraphs in the program. Observe also that each level in the hierarchy chart can be matched with a COBOL PERFORM statement.

Figure 15.8 Two-Level Control Break Program

```
IDENTIFICATION DIVISION.
PROGRAM-ID.    TWOLEVEL.
AUTHOR.        CVV.

ENVIRONMENT DIVISION.
INPUT-OUTPUT SECTION.
FILE-CONTROL.
    SELECT SALES-FILE
        ASSIGN TO UT-S-SYSIN.
    SELECT PRINT-FILE
        ASSIGN TO UT-S-SYSOUT.
    SELECT SORT-WORK-FILE
        ASSIGN TO UT-S-SORTWK01.
    SELECT SORTED-SALES-FILE
        ASSIGN TO UT-S-SORTED.

DATA DIVISION.
FILE SECTION.
FD  SALES-FILE
    RECORD CONTAINS 58 CHARACTERS
    DATA RECORD IS SALES-RECORD.
01  SALES-RECORD                    PIC X(58).

FD  PRINT-FILE
    RECORD CONTAINS 132 CHARACTERS
    DATA RECORD IS PRINT-LINE.
01  PRINT-LINE                      PIC X(132).

SD  SORT-WORK-FILE
    RECORD CONTAINS 58 CHARACTERS
    DATA RECORD IS SORT-RECORD.
```

Figure 15.8 *(continued)*

```
       01  SORT-RECORD.
           05  SORT-ACCOUNT-NUMBER       PIC 9(6).
           05  FILLER                    PIC X.
           05  SORT-NAME                 PIC X(15).
           05  FILLER                    PIC X(10).
           05  SORT-LOCATION             PIC X(15).
           05  SORT-REGION               PIC X(11).

       FD  SORTED-SALES-FILE
           RECORD CONTAINS 58 CHARACTERS
           DATA RECORD IS SORTED-SALES-RECORD.
       01  SORTED-SALES-RECORD           PIC X(58).

       WORKING-STORAGE SECTION.
       01  FILLER                        PIC X(14)
               VALUE 'WS BEGINS HERE'.

       01  SALES-RECORD-IN.
           05  SR-ACCOUNT-NUMBER         PIC 9(6).
           05  FILLER                    PIC X.
           05  SR-NAME                   PIC X(15).
           05  SR-SALES                  PIC S9(4).
           05  FILLER                    PIC XX.
           05  SR-COMMISSION-PERCENT     PIC V99.
           05  FILLER                    PIC XX.
           05  SR-LOCATION               PIC X(15).
           05  SR-REGION                 PIC X(11).

       01  PROGRAM-SWITCHES-AND-COUNTERS.
           05  DATA-REMAINS-SW           PIC X(3)     VALUE 'YES'.
               88  NO-DATA-REMAINS                    VALUE 'NO'.
           05  PREVIOUS-NAME             PIC X(15)    VALUE SPACES.
           05  PREVIOUS-LOCATION         PIC X(15)    VALUE SPACES.
           05  PAGE-COUNT                PIC 99       VALUE ZEROES.

       01  CONTROL-BREAK-TOTALS.
           05  INDIVIDUAL-TOTALS.
               10  IND-COMMISSION        PIC S9(4).
           05  SALESPERSON-TOTALS.
               10  SALESPERSON-SALES-TOT PIC S9(6).
               10  SALESPERSON-COMM-TOT  PIC S9(6).
           05  LOCATION-TOTALS.
               10  LOCATION-SALES-TOT    PIC S9(6).
               10  LOCATION-COMM-TOT     PIC S9(6).
           05  COMPANY-TOTALS.
               10  COMPANY-SALES-TOT     PIC S9(6)    VALUE ZEROS.
               10  COMPANY-COMM-TOT      PIC S9(6)    VALUE ZEROS.

       01  REPORT-HEADING-LINE.
           05  FILLER                    PIC X(25)    VALUE SPACES.
```

Used to detect control break on location (callout to PREVIOUS-LOCATION)

Location counters are added to two-level program (callout to LOCATION-TOTALS)

Figure 15.8 *(continued)*

```
    05  FILLER                      PIC X(21)
          VALUE 'SALES ACTIVITY REPORT'.
    05  FILLER                      PIC X(19)   VALUE SPACES.
    05  FILLER                      PIC X(5)    VALUE 'PAGE '.
    05  HDG-PAGE                    PIC Z9.
    05  FILLER                      PIC X(60)   VALUE SPACES.

01  LOCATION-HEADING-LINE.
    05  FILLER                      PIC X(8)    VALUE SPACES.
    05  FILLER                      PIC X(10)
          VALUE 'LOCATION: '.
    05  HDG-LOCATION                PIC X(19)   VALUE SPACES.
    05  FILLER                      PIC X(95)   VALUE SPACES.

01  SALESPERSON-HEADING-LINE-ONE.
    05  FILLER                      PIC X(15)   VALUE SPACES.
    05  FILLER                      PIC X(13)
          VALUE 'SALESPERSON: '.
    05  HDG-NAME                    PIC X(15).
    05  FILLER                      PIC X(89)   VALUE SPACES.

01  SALESPERSON-HEADING-LINE-TWO.
    05  FILLER                      PIC X(23)   VALUE SPACES.
    05  FILLER                      PIC X(11)   VALUE 'ACCOUNT # '.
    05  FILLER                      PIC X(9)    VALUE SPACES.
    05  FILLER                      PIC X(5)    VALUE 'SALES'.
    05  FILLER                      PIC X(8)    VALUE SPACES.
    05  FILLER                      PIC X(10)   VALUE 'COMMISSION'.
    05  FILLER                      PIC X(66)   VALUE SPACES.

01  DETAIL-LINE.
    05  FILLER                      PIC X(25)   VALUE SPACES.
    05  DET-ACCOUNT-NUMBER          PIC 9(6).
    05  FILLER                      PIC X(9)    VALUE SPACES.
    05  DET-SALES                   PIC Z(3),ZZ9-.
    05  FILLER                      PIC X(7)    VALUE SPACES.
    05  DET-COMMISSION              PIC Z(3),ZZ9-.
    05  FILLER                      PIC X(69)   VALUE SPACES.

01  DASHED-LINE.
    05  FILLER                      PIC X(40)   VALUE SPACES.
    05  FILLER                      PIC X(8)    VALUE ALL '-'.
    05  FILLER                      PIC X(7)    VALUE SPACES.
    05  FILLER                      PIC X(8)    VALUE ALL '-'.
    05  FILLER                      PIC X(69)   VALUE SPACES.

01  SALESPERSON-TOTAL-LINE.
    05  FILLER                      PIC X(15)   VALUE SPACES.
    05  FILLER                      PIC X(21)
          VALUE '** SALESPERSON TOTAL'.
```

Location heading is added to two-level program

Figure 15.8 *(continued)*

```
          05  FILLER                   PIC X(3)     VALUE SPACES.
          05  SALESPERSON-SALES-TOTAL  PIC $Z(3),ZZ9-.
          05  FILLER                   PIC X(6)     VALUE SPACES.
          05  SALESPERSON-COMM-TOTAL   PIC $Z(3),ZZ9-.
          05  FILLER                   PIC X(69)    VALUE SPACES.

      01  LOCATION-TOTAL-LINE.
          05  FILLER                   PIC X(13)    VALUE SPACES.
          05  FILLER                   PIC X(19)
                VALUE '**** LOCATION TOTAL'.
          05  FILLER                   PIC X(7)     VALUE SPACES.
          05  LOCATION-SALES-TOTAL     PIC $Z(3),ZZ9-.
          05  FILLER                   PIC X(6)     VALUE SPACES.
          05  LOCATION-COMM-TOTAL      PIC $Z(3),ZZ9-.
          05  FILLER                   PIC X(69)    VALUE SPACES.

      01  COMPANY-TOTAL-LINE.
          05  FILLER                   PIC X(9)     VALUE SPACES.
          05  FILLER                   PIC X(22)
                VALUE '******** COMPANY TOTAL'.
          05  FILLER                   PIC X(8)     VALUE SPACES.
          05  COMPANY-SALES-TOTAL      PIC $Z(3),ZZ9-.
          05  FILLER                   PIC X(6)     VALUE SPACES.
          05  COMPANY-COMM-TOTAL       PIC $Z(3),ZZ9-.
          05  FILLER                   PIC X(69)    VALUE SPACES.

      PROCEDURE DIVISION.
      100-PREPARE-SALES-REPORT.
          PERFORM 200-SORT-TRANSACTION-FILE.
          OPEN INPUT SORTED-SALES-FILE
              OUTPUT PRINT-FILE.
          PERFORM 220-READ-SORTED-SALES-FILE.
          PERFORM 240-PROCESS-ONE-LOCATION
              UNTIL NO-DATA-REMAINS.
          PERFORM 260-WRITE-COMPANY-TOTAL.
          CLOSE SORTED-SALES-FILE
                PRINT-FILE.
          STOP RUN.

      200-SORT-TRANSACTION-FILE.
          SORT SORT-WORK-FILE
              ASCENDING KEY
                  SORT-LOCATION
                  SORT-NAME
              WITH DUPLICATES IN ORDER
              USING SALES-FILE
              GIVING SORTED-SALES-FILE.

      220-READ-SORTED-SALES-FILE.
          READ SORTED-SALES-FILE INTO SALES-RECORD-IN
```

Location total line is added to two-level program

Keys in SORT statement match control breaks

Figure 15.8 *(continued)*

```
                AT END MOVE 'NO' TO DATA-REMAINS-SW
            END-READ.

        240-PROCESS-ONE-LOCATION.
            PERFORM 300-INITIALIZE-LOCATION.
            PERFORM 320-WRITE-LOCATION-HEADING.
            PERFORM 340-PROCESS-ONE-SALESPERSON
                UNTIL SR-LOCATION NOT EQUAL PREVIOUS-LOCATION
                        OR NO-DATA-REMAINS.
            PERFORM 360-WRITE-LOCATION-TOTAL.
            PERFORM 380-INCREMENT-COMPANY-TOTAL.

        260-WRITE-COMPANY-TOTAL.
            MOVE COMPANY-SALES-TOT TO COMPANY-SALES-TOTAL.
            MOVE COMPANY-COMM-TOT TO COMPANY-COMM-TOTAL.
            WRITE PRINT-LINE FROM COMPANY-TOTAL-LINE
                AFTER ADVANCING 2 LINES.

        300-INITIALIZE-LOCATION.
            MOVE SR-LOCATION TO PREVIOUS-LOCATION.
            INITIALIZE LOCATION-TOTALS.

        320-WRITE-LOCATION-HEADING.
            ADD 1 TO PAGE-COUNT.
            MOVE PAGE-COUNT TO HDG-PAGE.
            WRITE PRINT-LINE FROM REPORT-HEADING-LINE
                AFTER ADVANCING PAGE.
            MOVE SR-LOCATION TO HDG-LOCATION.
            WRITE PRINT-LINE FROM LOCATION-HEADING-LINE
                AFTER ADVANCING 2 LINES.

        340-PROCESS-ONE-SALESPERSON.
            PERFORM 400-INITIALIZE-SALESPERSON.
            PERFORM 420-WRITE-SALESPERSON-HEADING.
            PERFORM 440-PROCESS-ONE-TRANSACTION
                UNTIL SR-NAME NOT EQUAL PREVIOUS-NAME
                   OR SR-LOCATION NOT EQUAL PREVIOUS-LOCATION
                        OR NO-DATA-REMAINS.
            PERFORM 460-WRITE-SALESPERSON-TOTAL.
            PERFORM 480-INCREMENT-LOCATION-TOTAL.

        360-WRITE-LOCATION-TOTAL.
            MOVE LOCATION-SALES-TOT TO LOCATION-SALES-TOTAL.
            MOVE LOCATION-COMM-TOT TO LOCATION-COMM-TOTAL.
            WRITE PRINT-LINE FROM LOCATION-TOTAL-LINE
                AFTER ADVANCING 1 LINE.
            MOVE SPACES TO PRINT-LINE.
            WRITE PRINT-LINE
                AFTER ADVANCING 1 LINE.

        380-INCREMENT-COMPANY-TOTAL.
```

Location heading written for each new location (PERFORM 320-WRITE-LOCATION-HEADING.)

Location total written after control break detected (PERFORM 360-WRITE-LOCATION-TOTAL.)

Detects control break if salespersons in two locations have the same name (OR SR-LOCATION NOT EQUAL PREVIOUS-LOCATION)

Figure 15.8 *(continued)*

```
           ADD LOCATION-SALES-TOT TO COMPANY-SALES-TOT.
           ADD LOCATION-COMM-TOT TO COMPANY-COMM-TOT.

       400-INITIALIZE-SALESPERSON.
           MOVE SR-NAME TO PREVIOUS-NAME.
           INITIALIZE SALESPERSON-TOTALS.

       420-WRITE-SALESPERSON-HEADING.
           MOVE SR-NAME TO HDG-NAME.
           WRITE PRINT-LINE FROM SALESPERSON-HEADING-LINE-ONE
               AFTER ADVANCING 1 LINE.
           WRITE PRINT-LINE FROM SALESPERSON-HEADING-LINE-TWO
               AFTER ADVANCING 1 LINE.

       440-PROCESS-ONE-TRANSACTION.
           PERFORM 500-CALCULATE-COMMISSION.
           PERFORM 520-WRITE-DETAIL-LINE.
           PERFORM 540-INCRMENT-SALESPERSON-TOTAL.
           PERFORM 220-READ-SORTED-SALES-FILE.

       460-WRITE-SALESPERSON-TOTAL.
           WRITE PRINT-LINE FROM DASHED-LINE
               AFTER ADVANCING 1 LINE.
           MOVE SALESPERSON-SALES-TOT TO SALESPERSON-SALES-TOTAL.
           MOVE SALESPERSON-COMM-TOT TO SALESPERSON-COMM-TOTAL.
           WRITE PRINT-LINE FROM SALESPERSON-TOTAL-LINE
               AFTER ADVANCING 1 LINE.
           MOVE SPACES TO PRINT-LINE.
           WRITE PRINT-LINE
               AFTER ADVANCING 1 LINE.

       480-INCREMENT-LOCATION-TOTAL.
           ADD SALESPERSON-SALES-TOT TO LOCATION-SALES-TOT.
           ADD SALESPERSON-COMM-TOT TO LOCATION-COMM-TOT.

       500-CALCULATE-COMMISSION.
           COMPUTE IND-COMMISSION ROUNDED =
               SR-SALES * SR-COMMISSION-PERCENT
               SIZE ERROR DISPLAY 'SIZE ERROR ON COMMISSION FOR '
                   SR-NAME
           END-COMPUTE.

       520-WRITE-DETAIL-LINE.
           MOVE SR-ACCOUNT-NUMBER TO DET-ACCOUNT-NUMBER.
           MOVE SR-SALES TO DET-SALES.
           MOVE IND-COMMISSION TO DET-COMMISSION.
           WRITE PRINT-LINE FROM DETAIL-LINE.

       540-INCRMENT-SALESPERSON-TOTAL.
           ADD SR-SALES TO SALESPERSON-SALES-TOT.
           ADD IND-COMMISSION TO SALESPERSON-COMM-TOT.
```

Location totals are rolled into company totals
Salesperson totals are rolled into location totals

The Working-Storage Section contains every statement from the previous program plus additional entries to accommodate the second control break. The location heading and total lines are defined in lines 89–94 and 138–146, respectively. There are new counters for the location totals, LOCATION-SALES-TOT, and LOCATION-COMM-TOT, and a new data name, PREVIOUS-LOCATION, to detect the control break on location. The new entries are shaded in the listing for emphasis.

The SORT statement (lines 172–178) specifies two keys, SORT-LOCATION and SORT-NAME, to sort the transaction file by location and salesperson within location. The WITH DUPLICATES IN ORDER phrase keeps the transactions for a given salesperson in sequence by account number since the input file (Figure 15.1) was already in sequence by account number.

The remaining statements in the Procedure Division are straightforward and easy to follow, given the earlier discussion of the hierarchy chart and associated pseudocode. Observe, for example, the paragraph to increment the company totals (lines 232–234), in which location totals are rolled into the company totals. Note, too, the compound condition in the PERFORM statement of lines 216–219 to detect a control break on salesperson.

Three-Level Control Breaks

We return to the reports of Figures 15.2, 15.3, and 15.4, which showed the progression of one-, two-, and three-level control breaks. This time, we will expand the hierarchy chart, pseudocode, and COBOL program from two to three levels.

Hierarchy Chart

The three-level hierarchy chart will be developed as an extension of the existing two-level hierarchy chart. Accordingly, we will compare the two- and three-level reports in Figures 15.3b and 15.4b, then consider the following questions with respect to the existing chart:

1. What additional (i.e., new) modules are necessary?
2. Which existing modules (if any) have to be modified?
3. Which existing modules (if any) have to be deleted?

Every module that appeared in the two-level hierarchy chart will also appear in the three-level version; no modules will be deleted because every function from the two-level example is also required in the three-level example. Several new functions are necessary to accommodate the control break on region. These include:

1. PROCESS-ONE-REGION to process all locations in one region
2. INITIALIZE-REGION to initialize the sales and commission totals for this region
3. WRITE-REGION-HEADING to print a region heading for each new region
4. INCREMENT-REGION-TOTAL to increment the sales and commission totals for each region
5. WRITE-REGION-TOTAL to print region totals after a break on region

Changes will also be required in the logic of some existing modules—for example, a change in SORT-TRANSACTION-FILE to reflect a sort on region, location within region, and salesperson within location. It will also be necessary to change WRITE-LOCATION-HEADING, which previously began the report for each location on a new page, but which now lists all locations in the same region on the same page.

The computation of the company totals also changes. The two-level example waited for a control break on location, then rolled the location total into the company total. The same approach could be used in the three-level example, but it is more efficient to wait for a control break on region, then roll the region total into the company total.

The hierarchy chart for the three-level problem is shown in Figure 15.9a, with the additional and/or modified modules shaded for emphasis. The placement of the new modules is important, and you should notice that the module PROCESS-ONE-REGION appears on the second level of the hierarchy chart, which in turn forces the existing module PROCESS-ONE-LOCATION, and all of its subordinates, down a level.

Figure 15.9b is subject to the same design considerations as its predecessor, namely, completeness, functionality, and span of control. All design criteria appear satisfactory and the hierarchy chart is finished.

Figure 15.9 Three-Level Algorithm

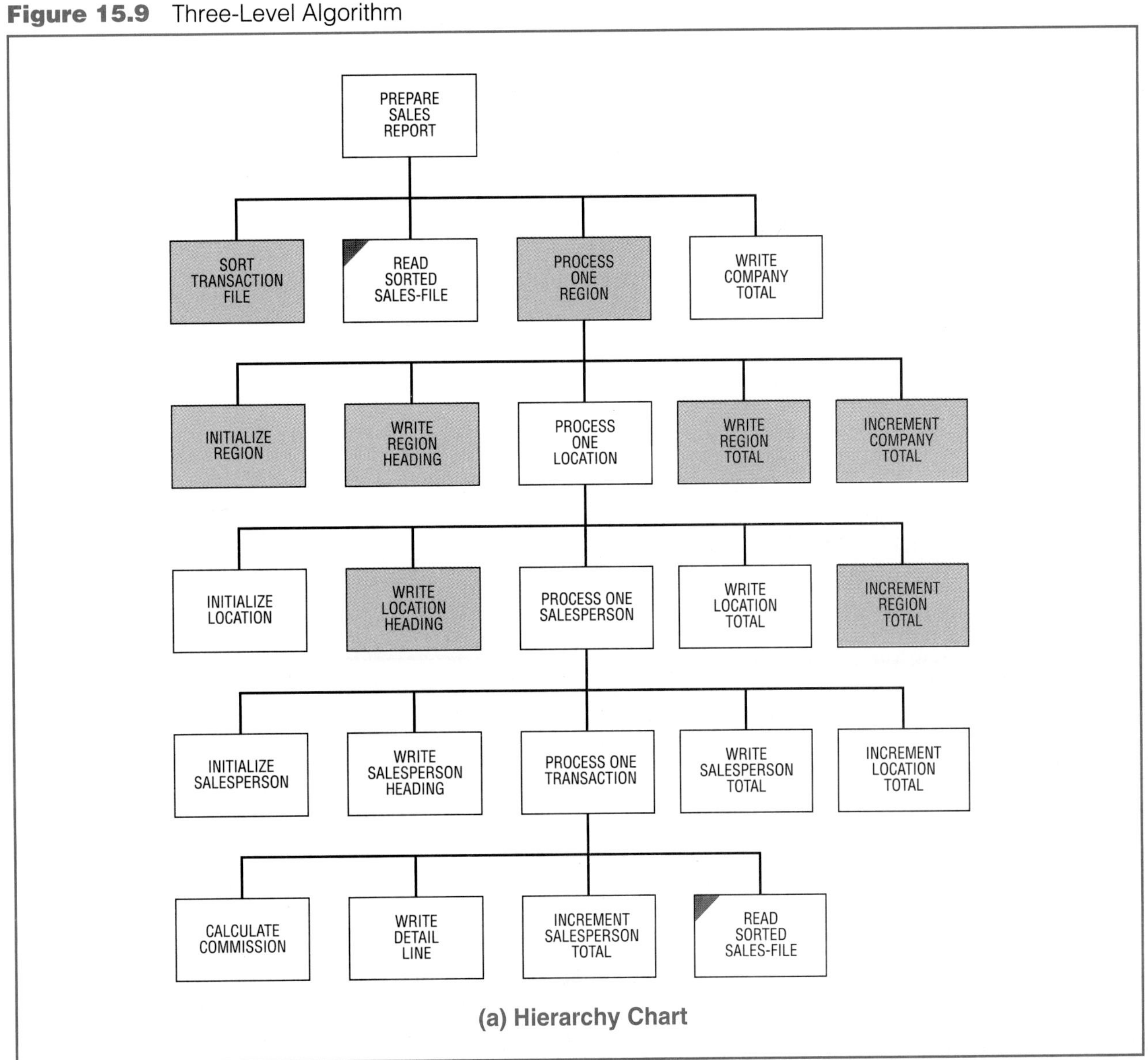

(a) Hierarchy Chart

Figure 15.9 *(continued)*

```
Sort transaction file on region, location, and salesperson
Open sorted-file, print-file
Read first record
PERFORM UNTIL no more data
    Initialize region totals
    MOVE SR-REGION to PREVIOUS-REGION
    Write region heading
    PERFORM UNTIL REGION NOT EQUAL PREVIOUS-REGION
            or no more data
        Initialize location totals
        MOVE SR-LOCATION to PREVIOUS-LOCATION
        Write location heading
        PERFORM UNTIL SR-LOCATION NOT EQUAL PREVIOUS-LOCATION
                or SR-REGION NOT EQUAL PREVIOUS-REGION
                or no more data
            Initialize salesperson totals
            MOVE SR-NAME to PREVIOUS-NAME
            Write salesperson heading
            PERFORM UNTIL SR-NAME NOT EQUAL PREVIOUS-NAME
                    or SR-LOCATION NOT EQUAL PREVIOUS-LOCATION
                    or SR-REGION NOT EQUAL PREVIOUS-REGION
                    or no more data
                Calculate commission
                Write detail line
                Increment salesperson totals
                Read next record
            ENDPERFORM
            Write salesperson totals
            Increment location totals
        ENDPERFORM
        Write location totals
        Increment region totals
    ENDPERFORM
    Write region totals
    Increment company totals by region totals
ENDPERFORM
Write company totals
Close files
Stop run
```

(b) Pseudocode

Pseudocode

The pseudocode for the two-level control break is expanded to its three-level counterpart in Figure 15.9b. New and/or modified statements are highlighted to be consistent with the associated hierarchy chart.

The sort statement includes region as an additional key as previously indicated. The major change, however, is the modification of the outer loop to include a series of repetitive statements for each new region that initialize the region totals, write the region heading, and process all locations in that region. The detection of a control break on region occurs when SR-REGION is unequal to PREVIOUS-REGION, and produces the region total, which is then rolled into the company total.

Within each region, there is a second loop (carried over from the two-level application) to process all locations in that region. A compound condition, that includes location and region, is necessary to detect a control break on location in the unusual instance where the last location in the current region and the first location in the next region have the same name. (This is in accordance with the general rule to detect a control break, which includes a compound condition that checks the level you are on, as well as any levels above the current level. Note, therefore, the compound condition associated with a control break on salesperson that includes salesperson, location, and region.)

The Completed Program

The completed program is shown in Figure 15.10 and reflects all of the indicated changes. Once again, we call your attention to the relationship between the hierarchy chart in Figure 15.9a and the paragraphs in the Procedure Division. The modules in the hierarchy chart correspond one to one with the paragraphs in the program. Observe also that each level in the hierarchy chart can be matched with a COBOL PERFORM statement.

The Working-Storage Section contains every statement from the previous program plus additional entries to accommodate the second control break. The region heading and total lines are defined in lines 93–96 and 157–165, respectively. There are new counters for the region totals, REGION-SALES-TOT, and REGION-COMM-TOT, and a new data name, PREVIOUS-REGION, to detect the control break on region. The new entries are shaded in the listing for emphasis.

The SORT statement (lines 191–198) specifies three keys—SORT-REGION, SORT-LOCATION, and SORT-NAME—to sort the transaction file by region, location within region, and salesperson within location. The WITH DUPLICATES IN ORDER phrase keeps the transactions for a given salesperson in sequence by account number since the input file (Figure 15.1) was already in sequence by account number.

The remaining statements in the Procedure Division are straightforward and easy to follow given the earlier discussion of the hierarchy chart and associated pseudocode. Observe, for example, the paragraph to increment the company totals (lines 249–251), in which region totals are rolled into the company totals. Note, too, the compound condition in the PERFORM statement of lines 236–239 to detect a control break on salesperson.

Figure 15.10 Three-Level Control Break Program

```
1        IDENTIFICATION DIVISION.
2        PROGRAM-ID.    THRLEVEL.
3        AUTHOR.        CVV.
4
5        ENVIRONMENT DIVISION.
```

Figure 15.10 *(continued)*

```
       INPUT-OUTPUT SECTION.
       FILE-CONTROL.
           SELECT SALES-FILE
               ASSIGN TO UT-S-SYSIN.
           SELECT PRINT-FILE
               ASSIGN TO UT-S-SYSOUT.
           SELECT SORT-WORK-FILE
               ASSIGN TO UT-S-SORTWK01.
           SELECT SORTED-SALES-FILE
               ASSIGN TO UT-S-SORTED.

       DATA DIVISION.
       FILE SECTION.
       FD  SALES-FILE
           RECORD CONTAINS 58 CHARACTERS
           DATA RECORD IS SALES-RECORD.
       01  SALES-RECORD                     PIC X(58).

       FD  PRINT-FILE
           RECORD CONTAINS 132 CHARACTERS
           DATA RECORD IS PRINT-LINE.
       01  PRINT-LINE                       PIC X(132).

       SD  SORT-WORK-FILE
           RECORD CONTAINS 58 CHARACTERS
           DATA RECORD IS SORT-RECORD.
       01  SORT-RECORD.
           05  SORT-ACCOUNT-NUMBER          PIC 9(6).
           05  FILLER                       PIC X.
           05  SORT-NAME                    PIC X(15).
           05  FILLER                       PIC X(10).
           05  SORT-LOCATION                PIC X(15).
           05  SORT-REGION                  PIC X(11).

       FD  SORTED-SALES-FILE
           RECORD CONTAINS 58 CHARACTERS
           DATA RECORD IS SORTED-SALES-RECORD.
       01  SORTED-SALES-RECORD              PIC X(58).

       WORKING-STORAGE SECTION.
       01  FILLER                           PIC X(14)
               VALUE 'WS BEGINS HERE'.

       01  SALES-RECORD-IN.
           05  SR-ACCOUNT-NUMBER            PIC 9(6).
           05  FILLER                       PIC X.
           05  SR-NAME                      PIC X(15).
```

Figure 15.10 *(continued)*

```
          05  SR-SALES                 PIC S9(4).
          05  FILLER                   PIC XX.
          05  SR-COMMISSION-PERCENT    PIC V99.
          05  FILLER                   PIC XX.
          05  SR-LOCATION              PIC X(15).
          05  SR-REGION                PIC X(11).

      01  PROGRAM-SWITCHES-AND-COUNTERS.
          05  DATA-REMAINS-SW          PIC X(3)    VALUE 'YES'.
              88  NO-DATA-REMAINS                  VALUE 'NO'.
          05  PREVIOUS-NAME            PIC X(15)   VALUE SPACES.
          05  PREVIOUS-LOCATION        PIC X(15)   VALUE SPACES.
          05  PREVIOUS-REGION          PIC X(11)   VALUE SPACES.
          05  PAGE-COUNT               PIC 99      VALUE ZEROES.

      01  CONTROL-BREAK-TOTALS.
          05  INDIVIDUAL-TOTALS.
              10  IND-COMMISSION       PIC S9(4).
          05  SALESPERSON-TOTALS.
              10  SALESPERSON-SALES-TOT PIC S9(6).
              10  SALESPERSON-COMM-TOT PIC S9(6).
          05  LOCATION-TOTALS.
              10  LOCATION-SALES-TOT   PIC S9(6).
              10  LOCATION-COMM-TOT    PIC S9(6).
          05  REGION-TOTALS.
              10  REGION-SALES-TOT     PIC S9(6).
              10  REGION-COMM-TOT      PIC S9(6).
          05  COMPANY-TOTALS.
              10  COMPANY-SALES-TOT    PIC S9(6)   VALUE ZEROS.
              10  COMPANY-COMM-TOT     PIC S9(6)   VALUE ZEROS.

      01  REPORT-HEADING-LINE.
          05  FILLER                   PIC X(25)   VALUE SPACES.
          05  FILLER                   PIC X(21)
                  VALUE 'SALES ACTIVITY REPORT'.
          05  FILLER                   PIC X(19)   VALUE SPACES.
          05  FILLER                   PIC X(5)    VALUE 'PAGE '.
          05  HDG-PAGE                 PIC Z9.
          05  FILLER                   PIC X(60)   VALUE SPACES.

      01  REGION-HEADING-LINE.
          05  FILLER                   PIC X(8)    VALUE 'REGION: '.
          05  HDG-REGION               PIC X(11)   VALUE SPACES.
          05  FILLER                   PIC X(113)  VALUE SPACES.

      01  LOCATION-HEADING-LINE.
          05  FILLER                   PIC X(8)    VALUE SPACES.
```

Region is an additional control field

Used to detect control break on region

Region totals are added to three-level program

Region heading is added to three-level program

Figure 15.10 *(continued)*

```
           05  FILLER                     PIC X(10)
                  VALUE 'LOCATION: '.
           05  HDG-LOCATION               PIC X(19)    VALUE SPACES.
           05  FILLER                     PIC X(95)    VALUE SPACES.

       01  SALESPERSON-HEADING-LINE-ONE.
           05  FILLER                     PIC X(15)    VALUE SPACES.
           05  FILLER                     PIC X(13)
                  VALUE 'SALESPERSON: '.
           05  HDG-NAME                   PIC X(15).
           05  FILLER                     PIC X(89)    VALUE SPACES.

       01  SALESPERSON-HEADING-LINE-TWO.
           05  FILLER                     PIC X(23)    VALUE SPACES.
           05  FILLER                     PIC X(11)    VALUE 'ACCOUNT .
           05  FILLER                     PIC X(9)     VALUE SPACES.
           05  FILLER                     PIC X(5)     VALUE 'SALES'.
           05  FILLER                     PIC X(8)     VALUE SPACES.
           05  FILLER                     PIC X(10)    VALUE MMISSION'.
           05  FILLER                     PIC X(66)    VALUE SPACES.

       01  DETAIL-LINE.
           05  FILLER                     PIC X(25)    VALUE SPACES.
           05  DET-ACCOUNT-NUMBER         PIC 9(6).
           05  FILLER                     PIC X(9)     VALUE SPACES.
           05  DET-SALES                  PIC Z(3),ZZ9-.
           05  FILLER                     PIC X(7)     VALUE SPACES.
           05  DET-COMMISSION             PIC Z(3),ZZ9-.
           05  FILLER                     PIC X(69)    VALUE SPACES.

       01  DASHED-LINE.
           05  FILLER                     PIC X(40)    VALUE SPACES.
           05  FILLER                     PIC X(8)     VALUE ALL '-'.
           05  FILLER                     PIC X(7)     VALUE SPACES.
           05  FILLER                     PIC X(8)     VALUE ALL '-'.
           05  FILLER                     PIC X(69)    VALUE SPACES.

       01  SALESPERSON-TOTAL-LINE.
           05  FILLER                     PIC X(15)    VALUE SPACES.
           05  FILLER                     PIC X(21)
                  VALUE '** SALESPERSON TOTAL'.
           05  FILLER                     PIC X(3)     VALUE SPACES.
           05  SALESPERSON-SALES-TOTAL    PIC $Z(3),ZZ9-.
           05  FILLER                     PIC X(6)     VALUE SPACES.
           05  SALESPERSON-COMM-TOTAL     PIC $Z(3),ZZ9-.
           05  FILLER                     PIC X(69)    VALUE SPACES.

```

Figure 15.10 *(continued)*

```
       01  LOCATION-TOTAL-LINE.
           05  FILLER                     PIC X(13)    VALUE SPACES.
           05  FILLER                     PIC X(19)
                  VALUE '**** LOCATION TOTAL'.
           05  FILLER                     PIC X(7)     VALUE SPACES.
           05  LOCATION-SALES-TOTAL       PIC $Z(3),ZZ9-.
           05  FILLER                     PIC X(6)     VALUE SPACES.
           05  LOCATION-COMM-TOTAL        PIC $Z(3),ZZ9-.
           05  FILLER                     PIC X(69)    VALUE SPACES.

       01  REGION-TOTAL-LINE.
           05  FILLER                     PIC X(11)    VALUE SPACES.
           05  FILLER                     PIC X(19)
                  VALUE '****** REGION TOTAL'.
           05  FILLER                     PIC X(9)    VALUE SPACES.
           05  REGION-SALES-TOTAL         PIC $Z(3),ZZ9-.
           05  FILLER                     PIC X(6)     VALUE SPACES.
           05  REGION-COMM-TOTAL          PIC $Z(3),ZZ9-.
           05  FILLER                     PIC X(69)    VALUE SPACES.

       01  COMPANY-TOTAL-LINE.
           05  FILLER                     PIC X(9)     VALUE SPACES.
           05  FILLER                     PIC X(22)
                  VALUE '******** COMPANY TOTAL'.
           05  FILLER                     PIC X(8)     VALUE SPACES.
           05  COMPANY-SALES-TOTAL        PIC $Z(3),ZZ9-.
           05  FILLER                     PIC X(6)     VALUE SPACES.
           05  COMPANY-COMM-TOTAL         PIC $Z(3),ZZ9-.
           05  FILLER                     PIC X(69)    VALUE SPACES.

       PROCEDURE DIVISION.
       100-PREPARE-SALES-REPORT.
           PERFORM 200-SORT-TRANSACTION-FILE.
           OPEN INPUT SORTED-SALES-FILE
               OUTPUT PRINT-FILE.
           PERFORM 220-READ-SORTED-SALES-FILE.
           PERFORM 240-PROCESS-ONE-REGION
               UNTIL NO-DATA-REMAINS.
           PERFORM 260-WRITE-COMPANY-TOTAL.
           CLOSE SORTED-SALES-FILE
                 PRINT-FILE.
           STOP RUN.

       200-SORT-TRANSACTION-FILE.
           SORT SORT-WORK-FILE
               ASCENDING KEY
                   SORT-REGION
```

Region total line is added to three-level program

Keys in SORT statement match control breaks

Figure 15.10 *(continued)*

```
               SORT-LOCATION
               SORT-NAME
           WITH DUPLICATES IN ORDER
           USING SALES-FILE
           GIVING SORTED-SALES-FILE.

       220-READ-SORTED-SALES-FILE.
           READ SORTED-SALES-FILE INTO SALES-RECORD-IN
               AT END MOVE 'NO' TO DATA-REMAINS-SW
           END-READ.

       240-PROCESS-ONE-REGION.
           PERFORM 300-INITIALIZE-REGION.
           PERFORM 320-WRITE-REGION-HEADING.
           PERFORM 340-PROCESS-ONE-LOCATION
               UNTIL SR-REGION NOT EQUAL PREVIOUS-REGION
                   OR NO-DATA-REMAINS.
           PERFORM 360-WRITE-REGION-TOTAL.
           PERFORM 380-INCREMENT-COMPANY-TOTAL.

       260-WRITE-COMPANY-TOTAL.
           MOVE COMPANY-SALES-TOT TO COMPANY-SALES-TOTAL.
           MOVE COMPANY-COMM-TOT TO COMPANY-COMM-TOTAL.
           WRITE PRINT-LINE FROM COMPANY-TOTAL-LINE
               AFTER ADVANCING 2 LINES.

       300-INITIALIZE-REGION.
           MOVE SR-REGION TO PREVIOUS-REGION.
           INITIALIZE REGION-TOTALS.

       320-WRITE-REGION-HEADING.
           ADD 1 TO PAGE-COUNT.
           MOVE PAGE-COUNT TO HDG-PAGE.
           WRITE PRINT-LINE FROM REPORT-HEADING-LINE
               AFTER ADVANCING PAGE.
           MOVE SR-REGION TO HDG-REGION.
           WRITE PRINT-LINE FROM REGION-HEADING-LINE
               AFTER ADVANCING 2 LINES.

       340-PROCESS-ONE-LOCATION.
           PERFORM 400-INITIALIZE-LOCATION.
           PERFORM 420-WRITE-LOCATION-HEADING.
           PERFORM 440-PROCESS-ONE-SALESPERSON
               UNTIL SR-LOCATION NOT EQUAL PREVIOUS-LOCATION
                   OR SR-REGION NOT EQUAL PREVIOUS-REGION
                       OR NO-DATA-REMAINS.
           PERFORM 460-WRITE-LOCATION-TOTAL.
```

Keys in SORT statement match control breaks

Region heading written for each new region

Region total written after control break detected

Figure 15.10 *(continued)*

```
        PERFORM 480-INCREMENT-REGION-TOTAL.

    360-WRITE-REGION-TOTAL.
        MOVE REGION-SALES-TOT TO REGION-SALES-TOTAL.
        MOVE REGION-COMM-TOT TO REGION-COMM-TOTAL.
        WRITE PRINT-LINE FROM REGION-TOTAL-LINE
            AFTER ADVANCING 1 LINE.

    380-INCREMENT-COMPANY-TOTAL.
        ADD REGION-SALES-TOT TO COMPANY-SALES-TOT.
        ADD REGION-COMM-TOT TO COMPANY-COMM-TOT.

    400-INITIALIZE-LOCATION.
        MOVE SR-LOCATION TO PREVIOUS-LOCATION.
        INITIALIZE LOCATION-TOTALS.

    420-WRITE-LOCATION-HEADING.
        MOVE SR-LOCATION TO HDG-LOCATION.
        WRITE PRINT-LINE FROM LOCATION-HEADING-LINE
            AFTER ADVANCING 1 LINE.

    440-PROCESS-ONE-SALESPERSON.
        PERFORM 500-INITIALIZE-SALESPERSON.
        PERFORM 520-WRITE-SALESPERSON-HEADING.
        PERFORM 540-PROCESS-ONE-TRANSACTION
            UNTIL SR-NAME NOT EQUAL PREVIOUS-NAME
                OR SR-LOCATION NOT EQUAL PREVIOUS-LOCATION
                    OR SR-REGION NOT EQUAL PREVIOUS-REGION
                        OR NO-DATA-REMAINS.
        PERFORM 560-WRITE-SALESPERSON-TOTAL.
        PERFORM 580-INCREMENT-LOCATION-TOTAL.

    460-WRITE-LOCATION-TOTAL.
        MOVE LOCATION-SALES-TOT TO LOCATION-SALES-TOTAL.
        MOVE LOCATION-COMM-TOT TO LOCATION-COMM-TOTAL.
        WRITE PRINT-LINE FROM LOCATION-TOTAL-LINE
            AFTER ADVANCING 1 LINE.
        MOVE SPACES TO PRINT-LINE.
        WRITE PRINT-LINE
            AFTER ADVANCING 1 LINE.

    480-INCREMENT-REGION-TOTAL.
        ADD LOCATION-SALES-TOT TO REGION-SALES-TOT.
        ADD LOCATION-COMM-TOT TO REGION-COMM-TOT.

    500-INITIALIZE-SALESPERSON.
        MOVE SR-NAME TO PREVIOUS-NAME.
```

Region totals are rolled into company totals (annotating the two ADD statements in 380-INCREMENT-COMPANY-TOTAL)

Location totals are rolled into region totals (annotating the two ADD statements in 480-INCREMENT-REGION-TOTAL)

Figure 15.10 *(continued)*

```
           INITIALIZE SALESPERSON-TOTALS.

       520-WRITE-SALESPERSON-HEADING.
           MOVE SR-NAME TO HDG-NAME.
           WRITE PRINT-LINE FROM SALESPERSON-HEADING-LINE-ONE
               AFTER ADVANCING 1 LINE.
           WRITE PRINT-LINE FROM SALESPERSON-HEADING-LINE-TWO
               AFTER ADVANCING 1 LINE.

       540-PROCESS-ONE-TRANSACTION.
           PERFORM 600-CALCULATE-COMMISSION.
           PERFORM 620-WRITE-DETAIL-LINE.
           PERFORM 640-INCREMENT-SALESPERSON-TOTAL.
           PERFORM 220-READ-SORTED-SALES-FILE.

       560-WRITE-SALESPERSON-TOTAL.
           WRITE PRINT-LINE FROM DASHED-LINE
               AFTER ADVANCING 1 LINE.
           MOVE SALESPERSON-SALES-TOT TO SALESPERSON-SALES-TOTAL.
           MOVE SALESPERSON-COMM-TOT TO SALESPERSON-COMM-TOTAL.
           WRITE PRINT-LINE FROM SALESPERSON-TOTAL-LINE
               AFTER ADVANCING 1 LINE.
           MOVE SPACES TO PRINT-LINE.
           WRITE PRINT-LINE
               AFTER ADVANCING 1 LINE.

       580-INCREMENT-LOCATION-TOTAL.
           ADD SALESPERSON-SALES-TOT TO LOCATION-SALES-TOT.
           ADD SALESPERSON-COMM-TOT TO LOCATION-COMM-TOT.

       600-CALCULATE-COMMISSION.
           COMPUTE IND-COMMISSION ROUNDED =
               SR-SALES * SR-COMMISSION-PERCENT
               SIZE ERROR DISPLAY 'SIZE ERROR ON COMMISSION FOR '
                   SR-NAME
           END-COMPUTE.

       620-WRITE-DETAIL-LINE.
           MOVE SR-ACCOUNT-NUMBER TO DET-ACCOUNT-NUMBER.
           MOVE SR-SALES TO DET-SALES.
           MOVE IND-COMMISSION TO DET-COMMISSION.
           WRITE PRINT-LINE FROM DETAIL-LINE.

       640-INCRMENT-SALESPERSON-TOTAL.
           ADD SR-SALES TO SALESPERSON-SALES-TOT.
           ADD IND-COMMISSION TO SALESPERSON-COMM-TOT.
```

Salesperson totals are rolled into location totals

PROGRAMMING TIP

How to Write a Control Break Program

The algorithm for one-, two-, and three-level control breaks follows a general pattern that can be adopted for any control break application and/or any number of levels. We suggest, therefore, that you review the hierarchy chart, pseudocode, and/or COBOL programs that were developed in this chapter and see how those examples fit a general pattern.

Start by determining the number of levels in the application, their relative importance (sort order), and corresponding field names. Identify the field names that will be used to detect a control break at each level—for example, **SR-REGION, SR-LOCATION**, and **SR-NAME** in the three-level example used in the text.

Modify the hierarchy chart, pseudocode, and COBOL listings from the chapter to accommodate your specific application. Begin with the highest (most important) level and do the following for every level:

1. Initialize the control totals for this level
2. Initialize the field name to detect a control break at this level with the previous value
3. Write the heading for this level (if any)
4. Process this level until the field name at this level is not equal to the previous value

   OR the field name at a higher level is not equal to the previous value

   OR no data remains
5. Write this level's total (if required)
6. Increment the next higher level's total (rolling total)

At the lowest (transaction) level:

1. Perform the necessary calculations (if any)
2. Write a detail line (if any)
3. Increment the lowest level's total (running total)
4. Read the next record

LIMITATIONS OF COBOL-74

There are no specific enhancements in COBOL-85 intended to facilitate the processing of control breaks. Accordingly, all of the listings in this chapter could be made to run under COBOL-74 with only minor modification, such as the removal of the END-READ scope terminator, and the WITH DUPLICATES clause in the sort statement; the latter would require an additional sort key on account number.

SUMMARY

Points to Remember

- A control break is a change in a designated (control) field; any file used to process control breaks must be in sequence according to the control field.
- Control breaks may occur at multiple levels; for example, a two-level control break occurs when two control fields change simultaneously; in similar fashion a three-level control break occurs when three control fields change simultaneously.
- There is no theoretical limit to the number of control breaks; there is a practical limit, however, in that most people lose track after three (or at most four) levels.
- Programs for one-, two-, and three-level control breaks are developed according to a general algorithm; the importance of a hierarchy chart and pseudocode in the design process cannot be over-emphasized.
- A running total is incremented by the value of the corresponding field in every transaction; a rolling total is incremented by a lower-level-control total only after a control break has occurred; rolling totals are more efficient than running totals.

Key Words and Concepts

Compound condition
Control field
Control total
Control break
Hierarchy chart
One-level control break
Pseudocode
Rolling total
Running total
Three-level control break
Two-level control break

FILL-IN

1. A ______________ in a designated field is known as a ______________ ______________.
2. Any file used to process control breaks must be in ______________ according to the control fields.
3. It (is/is not) possible for data in a given record to produce a control break on more than one field.
4. Control break processing (is/is not) limited to one level.
5. A program's hierarchy chart is best developed (before/after) the program is written.
6. The more significant field in a two-level control break application is known as the ______________ field, whereas the less significant field is the ______________ field.

7. (Pseudocode/hierarchy charts) depict a program's logic and decision-making sequence.
8. A COBOL program to process control breaks (requires/does not require) the file to be in sequence.
9. Running totals are (more/less) efficient than rolling totals.
10. A ______________ total increments the value of a counter after every record.
11. A ______________ total increments the value of a counter after a control break.

TRUE/FALSE

1. Control break processing is restricted to a single level.
2. Input to a control break program need not be in any special order.
3. Modules in a hierarchy chart and paragraphs in a COBOL program correspond one to one.
4. A hierarchy chart depicts decision-making logic.
5. Each level in a hierarchy chart corresponds to a COBOL PERFORM statement.
6. A two-level control break occurs when two control fields change simultaneously.
7. A three-level control break implies the occurrence of one- and two-level control breaks as well.
8. A three-level control breaks requires that three control totals be computed at each level.
9. Rolling totals is a more efficient means of computation than running totals
10. A rolling total increments a counter for every transaction.

PROBLEMS

1. Return once more to the two-level program in Figure 15.8 and note that the PERFORM statement to detect a break in salesperson (lines 188–190) includes the clause SR-LOCATION NOT EQUAL PREVIOUS-LOCATION. Why? (What would happen if this clause were not present and the last salesperson in one location had the same name as the first salesperson in the next location?) State a generalized rule for the compound condition in PERFORM statements that is needed to detect control breaks.
2. What would be the consequences of omitting the SORT statement in the one-level control break program of Figure 15.6; that is, describe the appearance of the resulting report if the unsorted transaction file of Figure 15.1 were used in lieu of the sorted file in Figure 15.2a. Explain in general terms the consequences of omitting the SORT statement in any of the programs contained in the chapter.
3. The one-level program of Figure 15.6 uses the data names SALESPERSON-SALES-TOT and COMPANY-SALES-TOT to accumulate totals.
   a. Which data name(s) are computed as a *running* total? When, and by what amount, is the total incremented?
   b. Which data name(s) are computed as a *rolling* total? When, and by what amount, is the total incremented?

c. Repeat parts (a) and (b) for the two-level program of Figure 15.8. Answer for the data names SALESPERSON-SALES-TOT, LOCATION-SALES-TOT, and COMPANY-SALES-TOT.

d. Repeat parts (a) and (b) for the three-level program of Figure 15.10. Answer for the data names SALESPERSON-SALES-TOT, LOCATION-SALES-TOT, REGION-SALES-TOT, and COMPANY-SALES-TOT.

4. The hypothetical Continental University is composed of multiple colleges, with each college divided into multiple departments. The central administration wants to know the total number of students in a variety of categories and uses a university-wide ENROLLMENT-FILE to compute the desired totals. The following fields are present in each enrollment record: COLLEGE, DEPARTMENT, YEAR, NUMBER-OF-STUDENTS. Identify the control fields and sorting sequence to produce each of the following reports. (Each report is to be treated independently.)

   a. The number of students in each year
   b. The number of students in each department
   c. The number of students in each college
   d. The number of students in each college and within college, the number of students in each department
   e. The number of students in each college and within college, the number of students in each year

Subprograms

CHAPTER OUTLINE

OBJECTIVES

After reading this chapter you will be able to:

- Define a subprogram and describe its implementation in COBOL.
- Distinguish between a called and calling program; describe the use of a hierarchy chart to show the relationship of programs within a system.
- State the purpose of the COPY statement; indicate where it may be used within a program and how it can be used to pass a parameter list.
- Distinguish between the BY CONTENT and BY REFERENCE clauses as they relate to subprograms.
- Explain the function of the INITIAL phrase in the PROGRAM-ID paragraph.
- Describe the purpose of the linkage-editor; explain the meaning of an unresolved external reference.

OVERVIEW

This chapter introduces the concept of subprograms in order to develop a system of programs associated with physical fitness. Each program is compiled as a separate entity, after which the individual object programs are linked together to produce a single load module. The chapter includes material on all necessary COBOL elements as well as a conceptual discussion on the role of the link program (linkage-editor).

The COBOL presentation begins with the CALL statement and associated parameter list in the calling program, then presents the relationship with data names defined in the LINKAGE SECTION of the called program. It describes the different ways of passing parameters, either BY REFERENCE or BY CONTENT, and introduces the COPY statement as a means of simplifying program development.

The chapter also serves as an effective review of earlier material in that the various subprograms utilize many features from previous chapters. Thus, we once again emphasize the importance of data validation from Chapter 8, illustrate advanced statements from the Procedure Division as covered in Chapter 9, review the screen I/O capabilities presented in Chapter 10, and incorporate material on both one- and two-level tables from Chapters 11 through 13.

Subprograms

The PERFORM statement has been used throughout the text to divide a program into functional paragraphs, each of which is executed as necessary from elsewhere within the program. The individual paragraphs are developed in stages and implemented in hierarchical fashion through top-down testing. The individual paragraphs are, in effect, subroutines that are written, compiled, and executed within the main program.

Alternatively, the performed routines may be developed as independent entities, known as ***subprograms,*** that are written and compiled separately from the ***main (calling) program.*** The subprograms within the same system may even be written by different programmers, but they are always executed under control of the main program. Subprograms bring to a system all the advantages of modularity that functional paragraphs bring to a program; for example, a change in one subprogram should not affect the internal workings of another subprogram nor the overall flow of the system. And, like the paragraphs in a program, the subprograms in a system may be developed and tested in top-down fashion.

A subprogram contains the four divisions of a regular program, and in addition, a LINKAGE SECTION in its Data Division to hold the data passed to and from the calling program. Figure 16.1 contains statements extracted from the listings at the end of the chapter to illustrate the use of subprograms. In this example, the calling program contains the logic to accept personal data from a user regarding the individual's height, age, and sex. It passes control to the sub (called) program WGTSUB, which determines the ideal range for the person's weight based on the data received. The CALL statement in the calling program matches the entry in the PROGRAM-ID paragraph of the called program (WGTSUB).

The CALL statement transfers control to the first executable statement in the called program. The CALL statement contains a USING clause, which specifies the data on which the called program is to operate. The called program in turn contains a USING clause in its Procedure Division header, indicating which data it is to receive from the calling program. The data names in either USING clause are known collectively as the ***parameter*** or ***argument list.***

The data names in the two parameter lists can (but need not) be the same, but the order and structure of data names within the list is critical. The first item in the parameter list of the calling program is FITNESS-RECORD, and corresponds to the first item in the parameter list of the called program, which is also called FITNESS-RECORD. In similar fashion, the second and third items in the calling program (WEIGHT-FROM and WEIGHT-TO) correspond to the second and third items in the subroutine (LS-WEIGHT-FROM and LS-WEIGHT-TO). The picture clauses of the individual parameters (arguments) are the same, but the data names are different.

The arguments in the calling program are defined either in the File Section or in Working-Storage, whereas the arguments in the called program must be defined in the ***Linkage Section.*** The parameters in either program must be defined as 01 or elementary items; that is, group items (other than 01 entries) cannot be passed to a subprogram.

Execution of the CALL statement in the main program transfers control to the first executable statement of the subprogram, which executes exactly as a regular COBOL program; the latter is terminated by an EXIT PROGRAM statement that returns control to the calling program at the statement immediately after the CALL.

Called and Calling Programs

The example in Figure 16.1 included only two programs, one calling program and one called program. More complex arrangements are also possible, for example:

Figure 16.1 COBOL Statements for a Subprogram

```
IDENTIFICATION DIVISION.
PROGRAM-ID.    FITNESS.
    .
    .
DATA DIVISION.
FILE SECTION.
FD  FITNESS-FILE
    DATA RECORD IS FITNESS-RECORD.
01  FITNESS-RECORD.
    05  FULL-NAME               PIC X(19).
    05  HEIGHT                  PIC 99.
    05  SEX                     PIC X.
    05  AGE                     PIC 99.
    .
    .
WORKING-STORAGE SECTION.
    .
    .
    05  WEIGHT-FROM             PIC 9(3).
    05  WEIGHT-TO               PIC 9(3).
    .
    .
PROCEDURE DIVISION.
    .
    .
    CALL WGTSUB
        USING FITNESS-RECORD, WEIGHT-FROM, WEIGHT-TO
    END-CALL.
    .
    .
```

Transfers control to first executable statement in called program

(a) Main Program

```
IDENTIFICATION DIVISION.
PROGRAM-ID.    WGTSUB.
    .
    .
LINKAGE SECTION.
01  LS-WEIGHT-FROM              PIC 9(3).
01  LS-WEIGHT-TO                PIC 9(3).
01  FITNESS-RECORD.
    05  FULL-NAME               PIC X(19).
    05  HEIGHT                  PIC 99.
    05  SEX                     PIC X.
    05  AGE                     PIC 99.
    .
    .
PROCEDURE DIVISION
    USING FITNESS-RECORD, LS-WEIGHT-FROM, LS-WEIGHT-TO.
    .
    .
    EXIT PROGRAM.
```

Contains the arguments for the subprogram

Returns control to calling program

(b) Subprogram

1. One program can call multiple subprograms; for example, program A can call programs B, C, D, and E.
2. One program can be called from different programs; for example, program F can be called from programs B and C.

3. The same program can be both a called and calling program; for example, program A calls program B, which in turn calls program F. (Program B is both a called and calling program.)

A hierarchy chart depicts the relationship of various programs to one another within a system, just as it shows the relationship of paragraphs within a program. The hierarchy chart in Figure 16.2, for example, illustrates the relationships just expressed. Thus, program A sits at the top of the hierarchy chart and calls programs B, C, D, and E. Program F is shown twice in the hierarchy chart, indicating that it (program F) is called from programs B and C. Programs B and C function as both called and calling programs; they are called from program A and in turn call program F.

Figure 16.2 Called and Calling Programs

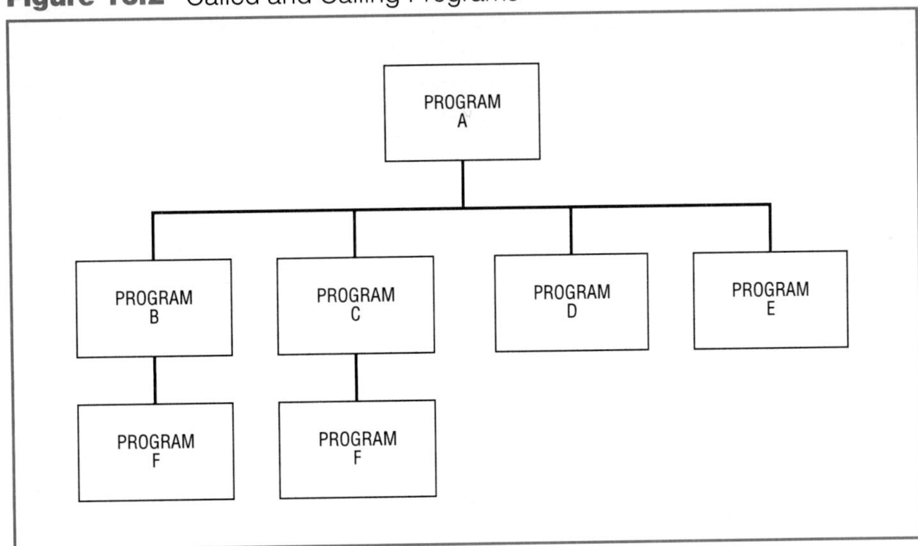

The COPY Statement

The data names used within different programs of the same system are often interrelated because the same file is apt to be referenced by several programs. The **COPY** statement facilitates the development of such programs by allowing the programmer to code a one-line COPY statement, which brings the associated entries into the COBOL program.

Figure 16.3 contains a COPY statement in which the programmer coded the line COPY TRAINCPY in line 27. The COBOL compiler locates the file TRAINCPY, and brings in lines 28–34 as though the programmer had coded them explicitly. The compiler inserts a C after the statement number in the source listing to indicate a copied statement.

A COPY statement may be used anywhere within a COBOL program, *except that the text being copied cannot contain another COPY.* The syntax of the COPY statement is simply:

```
COPY text-name
```

Figure 16.3 The COPY Statement

```
          COPY TRAINCPY.
       01 TRAINING-ARGUMENTS.
          05 TRAINING-INPUTS.
             10 TRAIN-AGE                PIC 99.
             10 TRAIN-FITNESS-LEVEL      PIC X.
          05 TRAINING-RANGES.
             10 TRAIN-OVERALL-RANGE      PIC X(5).
             10 TRAIN-FITNESS-RANGE      PIC X(5).
```

where text-name is the name of a file (member, or element) that exists independently of the COBOL program. A COPY statement is not restricted to subprograms; it can be used with any COBOL program. COPY statements offer the following advantages:

1. Individual programmers need not code the extensive Data Division entries that can make COBOL so tedious; a programmer can code a one-line COPY statement, and the compiler will bring the proper entries into the program.
2. Any change that affects multiple programs is made only once, in the library version of the COPY element. Subsequent compilations of all programs containing a COPY statement for that element will automatically bring in the updated version.
3. Programming errors are reduced through standardization and common definition of data elements. All fields within a record description (or other copied element) in one program will always be correct and consistent with the definition in other programs using the same copied element.

Calling BY CONTENT and BY REFERENCE

One of the most important principles of structured design is program independence, which minimizes (eliminates) the effect one program has on another. The optional **USING BY CONTENT** phrase prevents the values of parameters created in the calling program from being changed by the called program. Consider:

```
CALL program [USING {[BY REFERENCE] identifier-2 . . .} . . .]
                    { BY CONTENT    identifier-3 . . .}

[END-CALL]
```

and an example:

```
CALL 'SUBRIN'  USING FIELD-A
   BY CONTENT FIELD-B FIELD-C
   BY REFERENCE FIELD-D.
```

The CALL statement passes four arguments, FIELD-A, FIELD-B, FIELD-C, and FIELD-D, to a subprogram that manipulates any or all of these parameters (referring to them by its own data names as defined in its LINKAGE SECTION). However, the USING BY CONTENT phrase will restore the values of FIELD-B and FIELD-C to their initial values when control is returned to the calling program, despite any changes made to the corresponding parameters by the called program.

PROGRAMMING TIP

Use COPY To Pass Parameters

The order of arguments in the **CALL USING** and **PROCEDURE DIVISION USING** clauses of the calling and called programs is critical. You can reduce the chance for error by using a **COPY** clause to pass parameters as shown. Consider:

Poor Code:

```
CALL 'WGTSUB'
   USING HEIGHT, SEX, AGE, WEIGHT-FROM, WEIGHT-TO
END-CALL.

PROCEDURE DIVISION
   USING LS-HEIGHT, LS-SEX, LS-AGE, LS-WGT-FROM, LS-WGT-TO.
```

Improved Code:

```
     COPY WGTLST.
C 01 WEIGHT-TABLE-ARGUMENTS.
C        05  WT-HEIGHT         PIC 99.
C        05  WT-SEX            PIC X.
C        05  WT-AGE            PIC 99.
C        05  WT-FROM           PIC 9(3).
C        05  WT-TO             PIC 9(3)

     CALL 'WGTSUB'
        USING WEIGHT-TABLE-ARGUMENTS
     END-CALL.

  LINKAGE SECTION.
     COPY WGTLST.
C 01 WEIGHT-TABLE-ARGUMENTS.
C        05  WT-HEIGHT         PIC 99.
C        05  WT-SEX            PIC X.
C        05  WT-AGE            PIC 99.
C        05  WT-FROM           PIC 9(3).
C        05  WT-TO             PIC 9(3).

     PROCEDURE DIVISION
        USING WEIGHT-TABLE-ARGUMENTS.
```

Use of the single **01** parameter facilitates coding in the **USING** clauses and also makes them immune to change. Use of the same **COPY** member in both programs eliminates any problem with listing arguments in the wrong order or inconsistent definition through different pictures.

No such restriction is placed on the value of FIELD-A, which will retain any value computed in the called program. The value of FIELD-D will also reflect changes made by the called program, as it (FIELD-D) was specified in a **USING BY REFERENCE** phrase; that is, USING BY REFERENCE is equivalent to a CALL statement with neither phrase.

INITIAL Clause

The **INITIAL** clause in the PROGRAM-ID paragraph restores a program to its initial state each time it is called; that is, all data names in Working-Storage are reset to their original values via any VALUE clauses that are present. Consider:

```
PROGRAM-ID. program-name [IS INITIAL PROGRAM].
```

The INITIAL clause makes it possible to start with an original (unmodified) copy of a called program every time it is executed. Alternatively, omission of the phrase causes every execution of a called program to begin with the values established in the latest (previous) execution. (The INITIAL clause is not supported by the Link program supplied with CA-Realia Classroom COBOL.)

A System for Physical Fitness

The material on subprograms will be incorporated into a system for physical fitness that obtains input from a user, determines various aspects of the individual's fitness, then displays the results at the end of processing. The individual programs illustrate the transfer of control and passing of parameters between a called and calling program, and also review COBOL material from earlier chapters as described in the chapter overview.

PROGRAMMING SPECIFICATIONS

Program Name: Physical Fitness System

Narrative: The specifications call for a series of programs that constitute a system for physical fitness. A screen I/O program will accept and verify various inputs from a user, such as age, sex, and height, then pass control to a series of subprograms to compute the desired weight and target heart range at different levels of fitness.

Input Files: There are no input or output files as all data are entered and displayed interactively via screen I/O. Figure 16.4 contains a sample screen for a hypothetical individual named Mr. Fit. The inputs provided by Mr. Fit are highlighted in the top half of the screen. The diagnostic messages produced by the system show Mr. Fit's weight of 185 to be within the desired range for his age, sex, and height. The system also suggests a target (10-second) heart rate (after exercise) between 27 and 30 in accordance with his advanced fitness level.

Processing Requirements:

1. Develop a series of programs that constitute a system for physical fitness as described below:
   a. A main program to govern the overall system and pass control to various subprograms as appropriate
   b. A subprogram to accept and validate an individual's personal data
   c. A subprogram to compute a goal weight based on an individual's sex, height, and age.
   d. A subprogram to compute a target heart rate (after sustained cardiovascular exercise) based on age and fitness level
   e. A subprogram to display the computed results for weight and target heart rate
2. The main program is to control the overall system by passing (receiving) control from the various subprograms. The system is to execute continually—that is, for multiple individuals—until it receives a response that no one else wishes to use the system.

3. The input program is to accept the following fields as indicated in Figure 16.4: Name, Age, Sex, Weight, Height, and Fitness level. Validation checks are required as follows:
   a. A name must be entered
   b. Age must be 18 or higher
   c. Sex must be male or female; the system should accept both upper- and lowercase letters as valid characters.
   d. Height is to be entered in inches and must be consistent with the tables available to the system; valid male heights are between 60 and 76 inches; valid female heights must be between 54 and 74 inches.
   e. The fitness level should be entered as a single letter, B, I, or A, corresponding to Beginner, Intermediate, or Advanced. The system should accept both upper- and lowercase letters as valid characters.

   The input program is to display appropriate prompts and error messages for each of these fields. In addition, it should also display the current time as shown in the upper right portion of Figure 16.4.
4. The goal weight is determined from a person's sex, height, and age as shown in the tables of Figure 16.5.
5. The minimum and maximum target (training) heart ranges, expressed for a 10-second period after exercise, are determined from an individual's age according to the formulas:

   ```
   Minimum target (10 seconds) = .60 * (220 – AGE) / 6
   Maximum target (10 seconds) = .90 * (220 – AGE) / 6
   ```

   The target range can also be adjusted according to the individual's fitness level and the range between the maximum and minimum values; that is, those at a beginner's level of fitness should aim for a target heart range in the lower third of the interval, those with intermediate fitness in the middle third, and those at an advanced level in the upper third.

Figure 16.4 Fitness Screen

```
      Personal Fitness Evaluation                         11:53:10

  Full Name: Mr. Fit

  Age: 22            Weight: 185          Fitness Level: A
  Sex (M/F): M       Height: 74            B - Beginner
                                           I - Intermediate
                                           A - Advanced

  Your Goal Weight Range: 163-196
    CONGRATULATIONS! You are within the range

  Training Heart Rate Range Information (10 Second)
    Overall Heart Rate Range: 20-30
    Adjusted for Fitness Level: 27-30


        Another Person (Y/N):
```

Figure 16.5 Table of Goal Weights

Height (in inches)	Age (in years)				
	18	19-20	21-22	23-24	25 & Over
54	83-99	84-101	85-103	86-104	88-106
55	84-100	85-102	86-104	88-105	90-107
56	86-101	87-103	88-105	90-106	92-108
57	89-102	90-104	91-106	92-108	94-110
58	91-105	92-106	93-109	94-111	96-113
59	93-109	94-111	95-113	96-114	99-116
60	96-112	97-113	98-115	100-117	102-119
61	100-116	101-117	102-119	103-121	105-122
62	104-119	105-121	106-123	107-125	108-126
63	106-125	107-126	108-127	109-129	111-130
64	109-130	110-131	111-132	112-134	114-135
65	112-133	113-134	114-136	116-138	118-139
66	116-137	117-138	118-140	120-142	122-143
67	121-140	122-142	123-144	124-146	126-147
68	123-144	124-146	126-148	128-150	130-150
69	130-148	131-150	132-152	133-154	134-155
70	134-151	135-154	136-156	137-158	138-159
71	138-155	139-158	140-160	141-162	142-163
72	142-160	143-162	144-164	145-166	146-167
73	146-164	147-166	148-168	149-170	150-171
74	150-168	151-170	152-172	153-174	154-175

(a) Goal Weights for Women

Height (in inches)	Age (in years)				
	18	19-20	21-22	23-24	25 & Over
60	109-122	110-133	112-135	114-137	115-138
61	112-126	113-136	115-138	117-140	118-141
62	115-130	116-139	118-140	120-142	121-144
63	118-135	119-143	121-145	123-147	124-148
64	120-145	122-147	124-149	126-151	127-152
65	124-149	125-151	127-153	129-155	130-156
66	128-154	129-156	131-158	133-160	134-161
67	132-159	133-161	134-158	136-165	138-166
68	135-163	136-165	138-167	140-169	142-170
69	140-163	141-169	142-171	144-173	146-174
70	143-170	144-173	146-175	148-178	150-179
71	147-177	148-179	150-181	152-183	154-184
72	151-180	152-184	154-186	156-188	158-189
73	155-187	156-189	158-190	160-193	162-194
74	160-192	161-194	163-196	165-198	167-199
75	165-198	166-199	168-201	170-203	172-204
76	170-202	171-204	173-206	175-208	177-209

(b) Goal Weights for Men

Hierarchy Chart

The hierarchy chart has been used throughout the text to indicate the required functions within a COBOL program. It can also be used to indicate the relationship of programs within a system as shown in Figure 16.6.

Figure 16.6 Hierarchy Chart of the Overall System

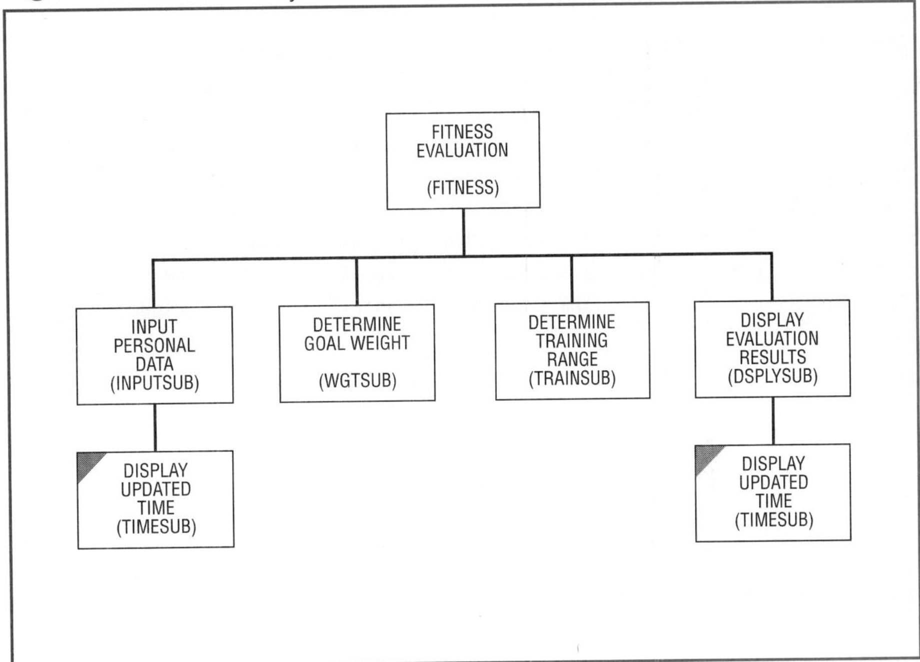

The module at the top of the hierarchy chart, FITNESS-EVALUATION, is the main program for the overall system; it has four subordinates (subprograms) in accordance with the processing specifications: INPUT-PERSONAL-DATA, DETERMINE-GOAL-WEIGHT, DETERMINE-TRAINING-RANGE, and DISPLAY-EVALUATION-RESULTS. (The entries in parentheses correspond to the name of the program as it appears in the PROGRAM-ID paragraph.) A sixth program, DISPLAY-UPDATED-TIME, is subordinate to the programs to accept and display the data.

Pseudocode

The logic for the overall system (main program) is contained in the pseudocode of Figure 16.7. The main program is driven by a single loop to process multiple individuals (as per the second processing specification) until a negative response is received regarding continuation. This is consistent with the corresponding prompt at the bottom of Figure 16.4, which asks whether there is another user.

The logic within the loop is straightforward and passes control from one subprogram to the next in sequential fashion. Note, however, the requirement to establish a parameter list prior to calling each subprogram, and further, how the parameter lists for the different subprograms contain different variables. Observe also that the parameter list for the last program references *another-person-switch,* which determines whether execution is to continue.

Figure 16.7 Pseudocode

```
DO WHILE user wants to continue

    CALL INPUTSUB subprogram to get personal information

    Establish parameter list (height, age, sex, weight-from, weight-to)
        for WGTSUB program
    Call WGTSUB program to determine weight goals

    Establish parameter list (age, fitness-level, overall-range,
        fitness-range) for TRAINSUB program
    Call TRAINSUB program to determine training ranges

    Establish parameter list (training ranges, weight-goals,
        another-person-switch) for DSPLYSUB program
    Call DSPLYSUB program to display results and request continuation

ENDDO
Stop run
```

The Completed Programs

The next several pages contain listings for the completed programs according to the description in Table 16.1. We have, however, in the interest of space, omitted the pseudocode and hierarchy chart for the individual programs.

Main Program (FITNESS)

The main program in Figure 16.8 contains neither an Environment Division nor a File Section as all input/output operations are accomplished via the screen. The Working-Storage Section consists largely of four COPY statements corresponding to the parameter lists for each of the four called programs. The programmer codes a single statement, such as COPY INPUTREC in line 10. The compiler locates the file INPUTREC and brings in lines 11 through 26 as though the programmer had coded them explicitly.

The mainline paragraph in lines 69–76 corresponds exactly to the pseudocode in Figure 16.7. The INITIALIZE statement in line 79 clears the parameters passed to the input program and is necessary so that the input values from one user are not carried over to the next user. The CALL statement in lines 80–82 transfers control to the input subprogram, using a single parameter, INPUT-INFORMATION, which is copied into both programs.

A different parameter list is created immediately prior to calling each of the remaining subprograms; for example, lines 85–87 move the data names for age, height, and sex—obtained from the input subprogram—to the corresponding data names in the parameter list for the weight program. Observe also how the CALL statement uses a single 01 entry, WEIGHT-ARGUMENTS, as the parameter list and further, how the entry is copied into the program (line 40). The same technique is used prior to the CALL statement for the training program in lines 95–97, and prior to the CALL statement for the final display program in lines 105–107.

Table 16.1 Physical Fitness System

PROGRAM-ID	CALLED/CALLING PROGRAMS	FIGURE #	DESCRIPTION
FITNESS	Calls INPUTSUB, WGTSUB, TRAINSUB, and DSPLYSUB	Figure 16.8	The main program governs the overall system; it passes control to the input subprogram, which accepts input from the user, passes control to the weight and training programs, then passes control to the display subprogram that displays the calculated results. The main program executes continually until the user elects to exit.
INPUTSUB	Called from FITNESS; calls TIMESUB	Figure 16.9	The input subprogram obtains all required inputs from the user (name, age, sex, height, and fitness level), validating each field as it is entered. The program reviews the screen section that was first presented in Chapter 10.
WGTSUB	Called from FITNESS	Figure 16.10	The weight subprogram accepts an individual's sex, height, and age, then determines a range for the person's desired weight. The program reviews two-level tables as presented in Chapter 12.
TRAINSUB	Called from FITNESS	Figure 16.11	The training subprogram determines an individual's target heart rate according to age and fitness level. The program reviews various Procedure Division statements and scope terminators from earlier chapters.
DSPLYSUB	Called from FITNESS; calls TIMESUB	Figure 16.12	The display subprogram updates the original screen created by the input program, using various options for the ACCEPT and DISPLAY statements, thus reviewing additional material from Chapter 10.
TIMESUB	Called from INPUTSUB and DSPLYSUB	Figure 16.13	The time subprogram is included to show that a subprogram need not contain a Linkage Section, and further that it can be called from multiple calling programs. It also illustrates the means of obtaining the current time from the system and reference modification.

Figure 16.8 Fitness Program

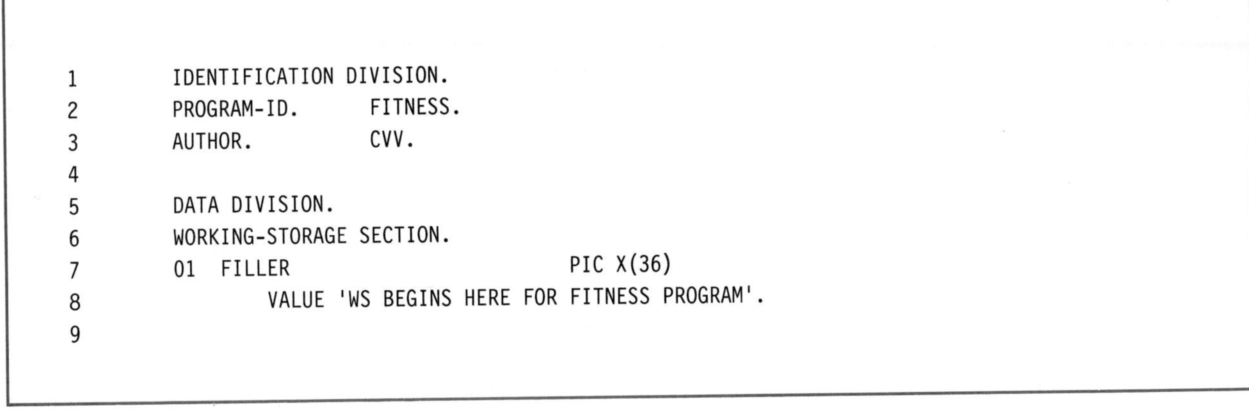

```
IDENTIFICATION DIVISION.
PROGRAM-ID.      FITNESS.
AUTHOR.          CVV.

DATA DIVISION.
WORKING-STORAGE SECTION.
01  FILLER                      PIC X(36)
        VALUE 'WS BEGINS HERE FOR FITNESS PROGRAM'.

```

Figure 16.8 *(continued)*

```
          COPY INPUTREC.
      01  INPUT-INFORMATION.
          05  INP-FULL-NAME             PIC X(30).
              88  MISSING-NAME              VALUE SPACES.
          05  INP-AGE                   PIC 99.
              88  INVALID-AGES              VALUES 0 THRU 17.
          05  INP-SEX                   PIC X.
              88  VALID-SEX                  VALUES 'M' 'm' 'F' 'f'.
              88  MALE                       VALUES 'M' 'm'.
              88  FEMALE                     VALUES 'F' 'f'.
          05  INP-HEIGHT                PIC 99.
          05  INP-WEIGHT                PIC 9(3).
              88  INVALID-WEIGHTS
                    VALUES 0 THRU 70 500 THRU 999.
          05  INP-FITNESS-LEVEL         PIC X.
              88  VALID-FITNESS-LEVELS
                    VALUES 'B' 'I' 'A' 'b' 'i' 'a'.

          COPY TRAINCPY.
      01  TRAINING-ARGUMENTS.
          05  TRAINING-INPUTS.
              10  TRAIN-AGE                 PIC 99.
              10  TRAIN-FITNESS-LEVEL       PIC X.
                  88  BEGINNER                  VALUE 'B' 'b'.
                  88  INTERMEDIATE              VALUE 'I' 'i'.
                  88  ADVANCED                  VALUE 'A' 'a'.
          05  TRAINING-RANGES.
              10  TRAIN-OVERALL-RANGE       PIC X(5).
              10  TRAIN-FITNESS-RANGE       PIC X(5).

          COPY WGTCOPY.
      01  WEIGHT-ARGUMENTS.
          05  WEIGHT-TABLE-INPUTS.
              10  WGT-HEIGHT                PIC 99.
              10  WGT-AGE                   PIC 99.
              10  WGT-SEX                   PIC X.
                  88  MALE                      VALUE 'M' 'm'.
                  88  FEMALE                    VALUE 'F' 'f'.
          05  WEIGHT-GOALS.
              10  GOAL-WGT-FROM             PIC 999.
              10  GOAL-WGT-TO               PIC 999.

          COPY DISPCPY.
      01  DISPLAY-ARGUMENTS.
          05  DISP-TRAINING-RANGES.
              10  DISP-TRAIN-OVERALL-RANGE  PIC X(5).
              10  DISP-TRAIN-FITNESS-RANGE  PIC X(5).
          05  DISP-WEIGHT-GOALS.
              10  DISP-GOAL-WGT-FROM        PIC ZZ9.
              10  DISP-GOAL-WGT-TO          PIC ZZ9.
```

Record description is copied into program

Lowercase responses are accepted

Figure 16.8 *(continued)*

```
           05  DISP-INPUT-WEIGHT              PIC 9(3).
           05  ANOTHER-PERSON-SWITCH          PIC X  VALUE SPACES.
               88  NO-MORE-PERSONS                VALUE 'N' 'n'.
               88  VALID-ANOTHER                  VALUE 'N' 'n' 'Y' 'y'.

       01  FILLER                         PIC X(32)
               VALUE 'WS ENDS HERE FOR FITNESS PROGRAM'.

       PROCEDURE DIVISION.
       000-FITNESS-EVALUATION.
           PERFORM UNTIL NO-MORE-PERSONS
               PERFORM 100-INPUT-PERSONAL-DATA
               PERFORM 200-GOAL-WEIGHT-RANGE
               PERFORM 300-TRAIN-RATE-RANGE
               PERFORM 400-DISPLAY-RESULTS
           END-PERFORM.
           STOP RUN.

       100-INPUT-PERSONAL-DATA.
           INITIALIZE INPUT-INFORMATION.
           CALL 'INPUTSUB'
               USING INPUT-INFORMATION
           END-CALL.

       200-GOAL-WEIGHT-RANGE.
           MOVE INP-AGE TO WGT-AGE.
           MOVE INP-HEIGHT TO WGT-HEIGHT.
           MOVE INP-SEX TO WGT-SEX.
           CALL 'WGTSUB'
               USING WEIGHT-ARGUMENTS
           END-CALL.

       300-TRAIN-RATE-RANGE.
           MOVE INP-AGE TO TRAIN-AGE.
           MOVE INP-FITNESS-LEVEL TO TRAIN-FITNESS-LEVEL.
           CALL 'TRAINSUB'
               USING TRAINING-ARGUMENTS
           END-CALL.

       400-DISPLAY-RESULTS.
           MOVE TRAIN-OVERALL-RANGE TO DISP-TRAIN-OVERALL-RANGE.
           MOVE TRAIN-FITNESS-RANGE TO DISP-TRAIN-FITNESS-RANGE.
           MOVE GOAL-WGT-FROM TO DISP-GOAL-WGT-FROM.
           MOVE GOAL-WGT-TO TO DISP-GOAL-WGT-TO.
           MOVE INP-WEIGHT TO DISP-INPUT-WEIGHT.
           CALL 'DSPLYSUB'
               USING DISPLAY-ARGUMENTS
           END-CALL.
```

CALL statement transfers control to called (sub)program

CALL statement transfers control to called (sub)program

Input Program (INPUTSUB)

The input program in Figure 16.9 reviews data validation and screen I/O as presented in Chapter 10. It also functions as a subprogram, and hence the Linkage Section in lines 53–70 which defines the data names passed from the calling (fitness) program. Note the relationship between the CALL statement in the calling program (lines 80–82 in Figure 16.8) and the Procedure Division header in line 120 of this program, both of which contain the 01 entry, INPUT-INFORMATION. The latter is copied into both programs in accordance with the programming tip on page 481.

The input program also contains a second COPY statement, COPY COLORCPY, to define the various colors available with screen I/O. The Screen Section defines an input screen consistent with the display shown earlier in Figure 16.4; it also utilizes various features of screen I/O (line and column positioning, reverse video, and underlining) as presented in Chapter 10.

The Procedure Division accepts and validates the input parameters, one at a time, in accordance with the table of error messages defined in lines 37–48. Each parameter is processed in a separate paragraph, which utilizes the DO UNTIL (TEST AFTER) construct described earlier in Chapters 9 and 10.

Figure 16.9 Input Subprogram

```
1         IDENTIFICATION DIVISION.
2         PROGRAM-ID.        INPUTSUB.
3         AUTHOR.            CVV.
4
5         DATA DIVISION.
6         WORKING-STORAGE SECTION.
7         01   FILLER                      PIC X(38)
8                   VALUE 'WS BEGINS HERE FOR SUBPROGRAM INPUTSUB'.
9
10        01  PROGRAM-SWITCHES.
11            05  VALID-FIELD-SWITCH       PIC XX.
12                88  VALID-FIELD                VALUE SPACES.
13            05  CONFIRM-SWITCH           PIC X.
14                88  ALL-DATA-VALID             VALUE 'Y' 'y'.
15
16            COPY COLORCPY.
17C       01  SCREEN-COLORS.
18C      * COLORS FOR FOREGROUND AND BACKGROUND
19C           05  BLACK                    PIC S9(4) COMP-5 VALUE 0.
20C           05  BLUE                     PIC S9(4) COMP-5 VALUE 1.
21C           05  GREEN                    PIC S9(4) COMP-5 VALUE 2.
22C           05  CYAN                     PIC S9(4) COMP-5 VALUE 3.
23C           05  RED                      PIC S9(4) COMP-5 VALUE 4.
24C           05  MAGENTA                  PIC S9(4) COMP-5 VALUE 5.
25C           05  BROWN                    PIC S9(4) COMP-5 VALUE 6.
26C           05  WHITE                    PIC S9(4) COMP-5 VALUE 7.
27C      * ADDITIONAL COLORS FOR FOREGROUND ONLY
28C           05  BRIGHT-BLACK             PIC S9(4) COMP-5 VALUE 8.
29C           05  BRIGHT-BLUE              PIC S9(4) COMP-5 VALUE 9.
30C           05  BRIGHT-GREEN             PIC S9(4) COMP-5 VALUE 10.
31C           05  BRIGHT-CYAN              PIC S9(4) COMP-5 VALUE 11.
```

Entry in PROGRAM-ID paragraph matches CALL statement in calling (FITNESS) program

Figure 16.9 *(continued)*

```
           05  BRIGHT-RED                  PIC S9(4) COMP-5 VALUE 12.
           05  BRIGHT-MAGENTA              PIC S9(4) COMP-5 VALUE 13.
           05  BRIGHT-BROWN                PIC S9(4) COMP-5 VALUE 14.
           05  BRIGHT-WHITE                PIC S9(4) COMP-5 VALUE 15.

       01  ERROR-VALUES-TABLE.
           05  ERROR-MESSAGE-VALUES.
               10  PIC X(30) VALUE '      Name must be Entered'.
               10  PIC X(30) VALUE '       Age must be over 17'.
               10  PIC X(30) VALUE '       Sex must be M or F'.
               10  PIC X(30) VALUE '  Weight must be > 70 & < 500'.
               10  PIC X(30) VALUE '  Male Height must be 60"-76"'.
               10  PIC X(30) VALUE ' Female Height must be 54"-74"'.
               10  PIC X(30) VALUE 'Fitness Level must be B I or A'.
           05  ERROR-MESSAGE-TABLE REDEFINES ERROR-MESSAGE-VALUES.
               10  ERROR-MESSAGE OCCURS 7 TIMES
                   INDEXED BY ERROR-INDEX PIC X(30).

       01  FILLER                          PIC X(36)
               VALUE 'WS ENDS HERE FOR SUBPROGRAM INPUTSUB'.

       LINKAGE SECTION.
           COPY INPUTREC.
       01  INPUT-INFORMATION.
           05  INP-FULL-NAME               PIC X(30).
               88  MISSING-NAME                  VALUE SPACES.
           05  INP-AGE                     PIC 99.
               88  INVALID-AGES                  VALUES 0 THRU 17.
           05  INP-SEX                     PIC X.
               88  VALID-SEX                      VALUES 'M' 'm' 'F' 'f'.
               88  MALE                           VALUES 'M' 'm'.
               88  FEMALE                         VALUES 'F' 'f'.
           05  INP-HEIGHT                  PIC 99.
           05  INP-WEIGHT                  PIC 9(3).
               88  INVALID-WEIGHTS
                       VALUES 0 THRU 70 500 THRU 999.
           05  INP-FITNESS-LEVEL           PIC X.
               88  VALID-FITNESS-LEVELS
                       VALUES 'B' 'I' 'A' 'b' 'i' 'a'.

       SCREEN SECTION.
       01  INPUT-SCREEN.
           05  BLANK SCREEN FOREGROUND-COLOR WHITE
                            BACKGROUND-COLOR BLUE.
           05  SCREEN-PROMPTS.
               10  LINE  1 COLUMN 9
                   VALUE 'Personal Fitness Evaluation'.
               10  LINE  3 COLUMN  4  VALUE 'Full Name:'.
               10  LINE  5 COLUMN  4  VALUE 'Age:'.
               10  LINE  5 COLUMN 22  VALUE 'Weight:'.
```

Linkage Section contains arguments of called program

Must be the last section in the Data Division

Figure 16.9 *(continued)*

```
            10  LINE  5 COLUMN 44  VALUE 'Fitness Level:'.
            10  LINE  6 COLUMN  4  VALUE 'Sex (M/F):'.
            10  LINE  6 COLUMN 22  VALUE 'Height:'.
            10  LINE  6 COLUMN 45  VALUE 'B - Beginner    '
                FOREGROUND-COLOR BLACK BACKGROUND-COLOR CYAN.
            10  LINE  7 COLUMN 45  VALUE 'I - Intermediate'
                FOREGROUND-COLOR BLACK BACKGROUND-COLOR CYAN.
            10  LINE  8 COLUMN 45  VALUE 'A - Advanced    '
                FOREGROUND-COLOR BLACK BACKGROUND-COLOR CYAN.

        05  SCREEN-INPUTS.
            10  SCR-FULL-NAME     LINE  3 COLUMN 15  PIC X(30)
                USING INP-FULL-NAME REVERSE-VIDEO.
            10  SCR-AGE           LINE  5 COLUMN  9  PIC 99
                USING INP-AGE REVERSE-VIDEO REQUIRED AUTO.
            10  SCR-WEIGHT        LINE  5 COLUMN 30  PIC 999
                USING INP-WEIGHT REVERSE-VIDEO REQUIRED AUTO.
            10  SCR-FITNESS-LEVEL LINE  5 COLUMN 59  PIC X
                USING INP-FITNESS-LEVEL REVERSE-VIDEO AUTO.
            10  SCR-SEX           LINE  6 COLUMN 15  PIC X
                USING INP-SEX    REVERSE-VIDEO AUTO.
            10  SCR-HEIGHT        LINE  6 COLUMN 30  PIC 99
                USING INP-HEIGHT REVERSE-VIDEO REQUIRED AUTO.

    01  CONFIRM-SCREEN.
        05  LINE 23 COLUMN  13 UNDERLINE
            FOREGROUND-COLOR BRIGHT-GREEN
            BACKGROUND-COLOR MAGENTA
            VALUE 'Is the above information correct? '.
        05  LINE 24 COLUMN 21
            FOREGROUND-COLOR GREEN
            BACKGROUND-COLOR MAGENTA
            VALUE '   (Y - Yes, N - No)   '.
        05  SCR-CONFIRM       LINE 23 COLUMN 49  PIC X
            FOREGROUND-COLOR BRIGHT-MAGENTA
            BACKGROUND-COLOR GREEN
            USING CONFIRM-SWITCH.

    PROCEDURE DIVISION USING INPUT-INFORMATION.
    000-INPUT-PERSONAL-DATA.
        INITIALIZE PROGRAM-SWITCHES.
        PERFORM UNTIL ALL-DATA-VALID
            DISPLAY INPUT-SCREEN
            CALL 'TIMESUB'
            PERFORM 200-VALIDATE-DATA
            PERFORM 300-CONFIRM-INPUT-SCREEN
        END-PERFORM.
        EXIT PROGRAM.

    200-VALIDATE-DATA.
```

INITIALIZE statement resets all program switches

EXIT PROGRAM returns control to calling program

Figure 16.9 *(continued)*

```
           PERFORM 210-VALIDATE-NAME.
           PERFORM 220-VALIDATE-AGE.
           PERFORM 230-VALIDATE-SEX.
           PERFORM 240-VALIDATE-WEIGHT.
           PERFORM 250-VALIDATE-HEIGHT.
           PERFORM 260-VALIDATE-FITNESS-LEVEL.

       210-VALIDATE-NAME.
           PERFORM WITH TEST AFTER UNTIL VALID-FIELD
               ACCEPT SCR-FULL-NAME
               IF MISSING-NAME
                   SET ERROR-INDEX TO 1
                   PERFORM 299-DISPLAY-ERROR-MESSAGE
               ELSE
                   PERFORM 288-CLEAR-ERRORS
               END-IF
           END-PERFORM.

       220-VALIDATE-AGE.
           PERFORM WITH TEST AFTER UNTIL VALID-FIELD
               ACCEPT SCR-AGE
               IF INVALID-AGES
                   SET ERROR-INDEX TO 2
                   PERFORM 299-DISPLAY-ERROR-MESSAGE
               ELSE
                   PERFORM 288-CLEAR-ERRORS
               END-IF
           END-PERFORM.

       230-VALIDATE-SEX.
           PERFORM WITH TEST AFTER UNTIL VALID-FIELD
               ACCEPT SCR-SEX
               IF VALID-SEX
                   PERFORM 288-CLEAR-ERRORS
               ELSE
                   SET ERROR-INDEX TO 3
                   PERFORM 299-DISPLAY-ERROR-MESSAGE
               END-IF
           END-PERFORM.

       240-VALIDATE-WEIGHT.
           PERFORM WITH TEST AFTER UNTIL VALID-FIELD
               ACCEPT SCR-WEIGHT
               IF INVALID-WEIGHTS
                   SET ERROR-INDEX TO 4
                   PERFORM 299-DISPLAY-ERROR-MESSAGE
               ELSE
                   PERFORM 288-CLEAR-ERRORS
               END-IF
           END-PERFORM.
```

In-line perform with TEST AFTER clause validates data as they are entered

Figure 16.9 *(continued)*

```

 250-VALIDATE-HEIGHT.
     PERFORM WITH TEST AFTER UNTIL VALID-FIELD
         ACCEPT SCR-HEIGHT
         EVALUATE TRUE ALSO INP-HEIGHT
             WHEN MALE ALSO NOT 60 THRU 76
                 SET ERROR-INDEX TO 5
                 PERFORM 299-DISPLAY-ERROR-MESSAGE
             WHEN FEMALE ALSO NOT 54 THRU 74
                 SET ERROR-INDEX TO 6
                 PERFORM 299-DISPLAY-ERROR-MESSAGE
             WHEN OTHER
                 PERFORM 288-CLEAR-ERRORS
         END-EVALUATE
     END-PERFORM.

 260-VALIDATE-FITNESS-LEVEL.
     PERFORM WITH TEST AFTER UNTIL VALID-FIELD
         ACCEPT SCR-FITNESS-LEVEL
         IF VALID-FITNESS-LEVELS
             PERFORM 288-CLEAR-ERRORS
         ELSE
             SET ERROR-INDEX TO 7
             PERFORM 299-DISPLAY-ERROR-MESSAGE
         END-IF
     END-PERFORM.

 288-CLEAR-ERRORS.
     INITIALIZE VALID-FIELD-SWITCH.
     DISPLAY ' ' LINE 24 WITH BLANK LINE.

 299-DISPLAY-ERROR-MESSAGE.
     CALL 'TIMESUB'.
     MOVE 'NO' TO VALID-FIELD-SWITCH.
     DISPLAY ERROR-MESSAGE (ERROR-INDEX)
        LINE 24 COLUMN 25 WITH HIGHLIGHT BLINK BEEP
        FOREGROUND-COLOR BRIGHT-WHITE
        BACKGROUND-COLOR RED.

 300-CONFIRM-INPUT-SCREEN.
     DISPLAY CONFIRM-SCREEN.
     ACCEPT SCR-CONFIRM.
```

Weight-range Program (WGTSUB)

The weight-range program in Figure 16.10 reviews material on multilevel programs as presented in Chapter 13. The Working-Storage Section defines two tables, for men and women's weights, in accordance with the user's view as presented in Figure 16.5. Subsequent statements in the Procedure Division determine the suggested range for an individual's weight, based on sex, height, and age.

The sex, height, and age are contained within the 01 entry WEIGHT-ARGUMENTS that is passed as an argument to the subprogram by the CALL statement in lines 88–90 of the fitness (main) program in Figure 16.8, and which coincides with the Procedure Division header in line 101 of this program. The parameter list consists of a single 01 entry, which is copied into both the calling and called program. Note the COPY statement in the Linkage Section of this program (lines 89–99,) and the corresponding COPY statement in the fitness program (lines 40–50 in Figure 16.8). Note, too, the use of COPY statements to initialize and define the tables for male and female weights, in lines 10 and 38, respectively.

Figure 16.10 Weight Subprogram

```
1     IDENTIFICATION DIVISION.
2     PROGRAM-ID.       WGTSUB.
3     AUTHOR.           CVV.
4
5     DATA DIVISION.
6     WORKING-STORAGE SECTION.
7     01   FILLER                         PIC X(36)
8              VALUE 'WS BEGINS HERE FOR SUBPROGRAM WGTSUB'.
9
10        COPY MALEWGT.
11C   01  MALE-WEIGHT-VALUES.
12C       05     PIC X(30)  VALUE  '109122110133112135114137115138'.
13C       05     PIC X(30)  VALUE  '112126113136115138117140118141'.
14C       05     PIC X(30)  VALUE  '115130116139118140120142121144'.
15C       05     PIC X(30)  VALUE  '118135119143121145123147124148'.
16C       05     PIC X(30)  VALUE  '120145122147124149126151127152'.
17C       05     PIC X(30)  VALUE  '124149125151127153129155130156'.
18C       05     PIC X(30)  VALUE  '128154129156131158133160134161'.
19C       05     PIC X(30)  VALUE  '132159133161134158136165138166'.
20C       05     PIC X(30)  VALUE  '135163136165138167140169142170'.
21C       05     PIC X(30)  VALUE  '140163141169142171144173146174'.
22C       05     PIC X(30)  VALUE  '143170144173146175148178150179'.
23C       05     PIC X(30)  VALUE  '147177148179150181152183154184'.
24C       05     PIC X(30)  VALUE  '151180152184154186156188158189'.
25C       05     PIC X(30)  VALUE  '155187156189158190160193162194'.
26C       05     PIC X(30)  VALUE  '160192161194163196165198167199'.
27C       05     PIC X(30)  VALUE  '165198166199168201170203172204'.
28C       05     PIC X(30)  VALUE  '170202171204173206175208177209'.
29C
30C   01  MALE-WEIGHT-TABLE REDEFINES MALE-WEIGHT-VALUES.
31C       05  MALE-HEIGHTS OCCURS 17 TIMES
32C           INDEXED BY MALE-HGT-INDEX.
33C           10  MALE-AGES OCCURS 5 TIMES
34C               INDEXED BY MALE-AGE-INDEX.
35C               15  MALE-WGT-FROM     PIC 9(3).
36C               15  MALE-WGT-TO       PIC 9(3).
```

Entry in PROGRAM-ID paragraph matches CALL statement in calling program

Weight tables are copied into program

Figure 16.10 *(continued)*

```
           COPY FEMWGT.
       01  FEMALE-WEIGHT-VALUES.
           05      PIC X(30)  VALUE  '083099084101085103086104088106'.
           05      PIC X(30)  VALUE  '084100085102086104088105090107'.
           05      PIC X(30)  VALUE  '086101087103088105090106092108'.
           05      PIC X(30)  VALUE  '089102090104091106092108094110'.
           05      PIC X(30)  VALUE  '091105092106093109094111096113'.
           05      PIC X(30)  VALUE  '093109094111095113096114099116'.
           05      PIC X(30)  VALUE  '096112097113098115100117102119'.
           05      PIC X(30)  VALUE  '100116101117102119103121105122'.
           05      PIC X(30)  VALUE  '104119105121106123107125108126'.
           05      PIC X(30)  VALUE  '106125107126108127109129111130'.
           05      PIC X(30)  VALUE  '109130110131111132112134114135'.
           05      PIC X(30)  VALUE  '112133113134114136116138118139'.
           05      PIC X(30)  VALUE  '116137117138118140120142122143'.
           05      PIC X(30)  VALUE  '121140122142123144124146126147'.
           05      PIC X(30)  VALUE  '123144124146126148128150130150'.
           05      PIC X(30)  VALUE  '130148131150132152133154134155'.
           05      PIC X(30)  VALUE  '134151135154136156137158138159'.
           05      PIC X(30)  VALUE  '138155139158140160141162142163'.
           05      PIC X(30)  VALUE  '142160143162144164145166146167'.
           05      PIC X(30)  VALUE  '146164147166148168149170150171'.
           05      PIC X(30)  VALUE  '150168151170152172153174154175'.

       01  FEMALE-WEIGHT-TABLE REDEFINES FEMALE-WEIGHT-VALUES.
           05  FEMALE-HEIGHTS OCCURS 21 TIMES
               INDEXED BY FEMALE-HGT-INDEX.
               10  FEMALE-AGES OCCURS 5 TIMES
                   INDEXED BY FEMALE-AGE-INDEX.
                   15  FEMALE-WGT-FROM  PIC 9(3).
                   15  FEMALE-WGT-TO    PIC 9(3).

       01  AGE-LIMIT-VALUES.
           05                          PIC 99    VALUE 18.
           05                          PIC 99    VALUE 20.
           05                          PIC 99    VALUE 22.
           05                          PIC 99    VALUE 24.
           05                          PIC 99    VALUE 99.
       01  AGE-TABLE REDEFINES AGE-LIMIT-VALUES.
           05  AGE-LIMIT OCCURS 5 TIMES
               INDEXED BY AGE-INDEX    PIC 99.

       01  CONSTANTS-AND-VARIABLES.
           05  MALE-HGT-ADJUST-CONSTANT    PIC 99    VALUE 59.
           05  FEMALE-HGT-ADJUST-CONSTANT  PIC 99    VALUE 53.
           05  ADJUSTED-HEIGHT             PIC 99.

       01  FILLER                         PIC X(34)
                VALUE 'WS ENDS HERE FOR SUBPROGRAM WGTSUB'.
```

Weight tables are copied into program

Figure 16.10 *(continued)*

```
       LINKAGE SECTION.
           COPY WGTCOPY.
       01  WEIGHT-ARGUMENTS.
           05  WEIGHT-TABLE-INPUTS.
               10  WGT-HEIGHT               PIC 99.
               10  WGT-AGE                  PIC 99.
               10  WGT-SEX                  PIC X.
                   88  MALE                         VALUE 'M' 'm'.
                   88  FEMALE                       VALUE 'F' 'f'.
           05  WEIGHT-GOALS.
               10  GOAL-WGT-FROM            PIC 999.
               10  GOAL-WGT-TO              PIC 999.

       PROCEDURE DIVISION USING WEIGHT-ARGUMENTS.
       FIND-GOAL-WEIGHT.
           EVALUATE TRUE
               WHEN MALE
                   PERFORM FIND-MALE-WEIGHT-RANGE
               WHEN FEMALE
                   PERFORM FIND-FEMALE-WEIGHT-RANGE
               WHEN OTHER
                   DISPLAY 'INVALID SEX ENTERED'
                   INITIALIZE WEIGHT-GOALS
           END-EVALUATE.
           EXIT PROGRAM.

       FIND-MALE-WEIGHT-RANGE.
           COMPUTE ADJUSTED-HEIGHT =
               WGT-HEIGHT - MALE-HGT-ADJUST-CONSTANT
               SIZE ERROR DISPLAY 'SIZE ERROR ADJUSTED HEIGHT'
           END-COMPUTE.
           SET MALE-AGE-INDEX AGE-INDEX TO 1.
           SET MALE-HGT-INDEX TO ADJUSTED-HEIGHT.
           SEARCH AGE-LIMIT VARYING MALE-AGE-INDEX
               AT END DISPLAY 'MALE AGE NOT FOUND'
                   INITIALIZE WEIGHT-GOALS
               WHEN
                   WGT-AGE <= AGE-LIMIT (AGE-INDEX)
                   SET MALE-AGE-INDEX TO AGE-INDEX
                   MOVE MALE-WGT-FROM (MALE-HGT-INDEX, MALE-AGE-INDEX)
                       TO GOAL-WGT-FROM
                   MOVE MALE-WGT-TO (MALE-HGT-INDEX, MALE-AGE-INDEX)
                       TO GOAL-WGT-TO
           END-SEARCH.

       FIND-FEMALE-WEIGHT-RANGE.
           COMPUTE ADJUSTED-HEIGHT =
               WGT-HEIGHT - FEMALE-HGT-ADJUST-CONSTANT
               SIZE ERROR DISPLAY 'SIZE ERROR ADJUSTED HEIGHT'
```

Linkage Section contains arguments of called program (annotation to LINKAGE SECTION.)

EXIT PROGRAM returns control to calling program (annotation to EXIT PROGRAM.)

Figure 16.10 *(continued)*

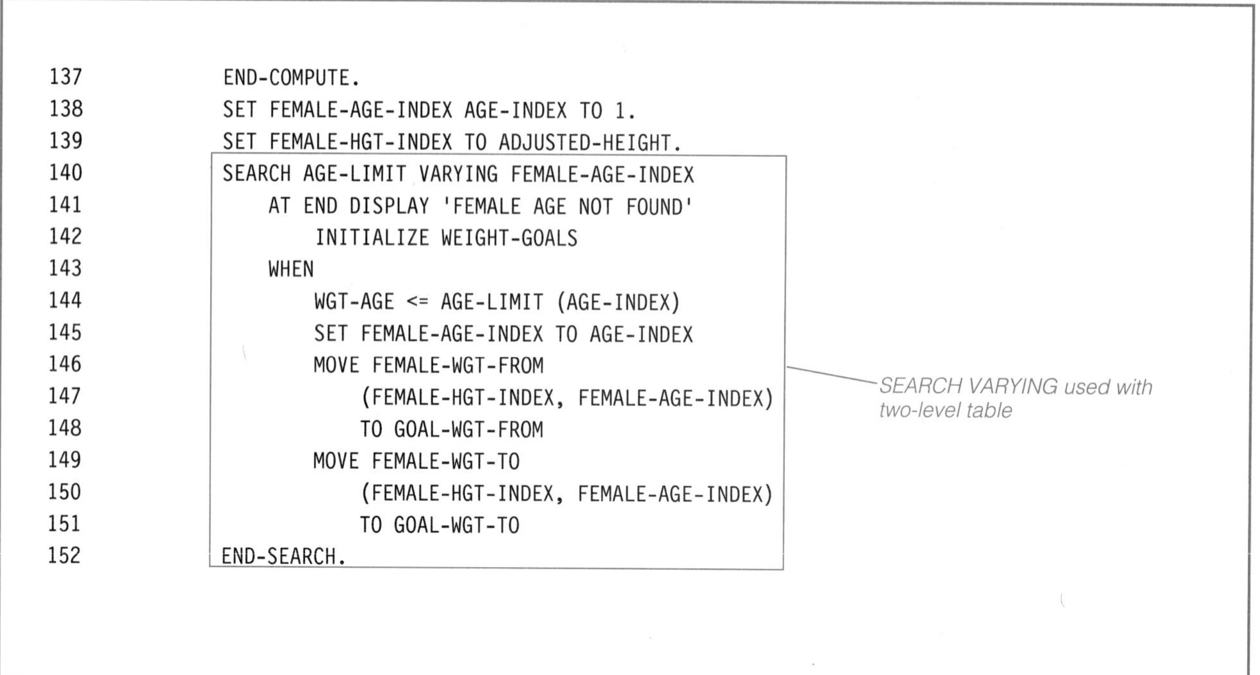

```
        END-COMPUTE.
        SET FEMALE-AGE-INDEX AGE-INDEX TO 1.
        SET FEMALE-HGT-INDEX TO ADJUSTED-HEIGHT.
        SEARCH AGE-LIMIT VARYING FEMALE-AGE-INDEX
            AT END DISPLAY 'FEMALE AGE NOT FOUND'
                INITIALIZE WEIGHT-GOALS
            WHEN
                WGT-AGE <= AGE-LIMIT (AGE-INDEX)
                SET FEMALE-AGE-INDEX TO AGE-INDEX
                MOVE FEMALE-WGT-FROM
                    (FEMALE-HGT-INDEX, FEMALE-AGE-INDEX)
                    TO GOAL-WGT-FROM
                MOVE FEMALE-WGT-TO
                    (FEMALE-HGT-INDEX, FEMALE-AGE-INDEX)
                    TO GOAL-WGT-TO
        END-SEARCH.
```

SEARCH VARYING used with two-level table

Training Program (TRAINSUB)

The training program in Figure 16.11 calculates an individual's target heart rate (after exercise) according to the formulas given in the programming specifications. The program uses the SIZE ERROR phrase and associated END-COMPUTE scope terminator in several places in the Procedure Division. It also uses the EVALUATE statement to determine the specific training range according to the user's fitness level.

The means for passing parameters between this program and the fitness program, which calls it, parallels the procedure for the other subprograms. Thus, the Linkage Section contains a COPY statement (line 29) to define the 01 parameters that constitute the parameter list; note, too, the correspondence between the Procedure Division header in this program and the CALL statement in the fitness program.

Display Program (DSPLYSUB)

The display program in Figure 16.12 uses DISPLAY statements rather than a Screen Section to control the displayed output in accordance with earlier material from Chapter 10. The means for passing parameters between this program and the fitness program parallel the procedure for the other subprograms. The Linkage Section contains a COPY statement (line 52) to define the single 01 parameter, which constitutes the parameter list in the Procedure Division header of lines 65–66.

Observe also the presence of the identical COPY statement found in the input program (line 21) to obtain the definition of foreground and background colors.

Figure 16.11 Training Subprogram

```
IDENTIFICATION DIVISION.
PROGRAM-ID.      TRAINSUB.
AUTHOR.          CVV.

DATA DIVISION.
WORKING-STORAGE SECTION.

01  FILLER                          PIC X(38)
        VALUE 'WS BEGINS HERE FOR SUBPROGRAM TRAINSUB'.

01  RATES-AND-CONSTANTS.
    05  TRAIN-CONSTANT              PIC 999  VALUE 220.
    05  LOW-RATE                    PIC V9   VALUE .6.
    05  HIGH-RATE                   PIC V9   VALUE .9.

01  RANGE-CALCULATIONS.
    05  OVERALL-RANGES.
        10  OVERALL-HIGH            PIC 99.
        10  OVERALL-LOW             PIC 99.
    05  FITNESS-RANGES.
        10  FITNESS-HIGH            PIC 99.
        10  FITNESS-LOW             PIC 99.
    05  RANGE-INTERVAL              PIC 9.

01  FILLER                          PIC X(36)
        VALUE 'WS ENDS HERE FOR SUBPROGRAM TRAINSUB'.

LINKAGE SECTION.
    COPY TRAINCPY.
01  TRAINING-ARGUMENTS.
    05  TRAINING-INPUTS.
        10  TRAIN-AGE                   PIC 99.
        10  TRAIN-FITNESS-LEVEL         PIC X.
            88  BEGINNER                       VALUE 'B' 'b'.
            88  INTERMEDIATE                   VALUE 'I' 'i'.
            88  ADVANCED                       VALUE 'A' 'a'.
    05  TRAINING-RANGES.
        10  TRAIN-OVERALL-RANGE         PIC X(5).
        10  TRAIN-FITNESS-RANGE         PIC X(5).

PROCEDURE DIVISION
    USING TRAINING-ARGUMENTS.
FIND-TRAIN-RANGE.
    PERFORM COMPUTE-OVERALL-RANGES.
    PERFORM COMPUTE-FITNESS-RANGES.
    EXIT PROGRAM.
```

Literals used for debugging

Program parameters are copied into Linkage section

EXIT PROGRAM returns control to calling program

Figure 16.11 *(continued)*

```

COMPUTE-OVERALL-RANGES.
    COMPUTE OVERALL-LOW ROUNDED =
        (TRAIN-CONSTANT - TRAIN-AGE) * LOW-RATE / 6
        SIZE ERROR DISPLAY 'SIZE ERROR ON LOW RANGE'
    END-COMPUTE.
    COMPUTE OVERALL-HIGH ROUNDED =
        (TRAIN-CONSTANT - TRAIN-AGE) * HIGH-RATE / 6
        SIZE ERROR DISPLAY 'SIZE ERROR ON HIGH RANGE'
    END-COMPUTE.
    STRING OVERALL-LOW '-' OVERALL-HIGH DELIMITED BY SIZE
        INTO TRAIN-OVERALL-RANGE
    END-STRING.

COMPUTE-FITNESS-RANGES.
    COMPUTE RANGE-INTERVAL =
        (OVERALL-HIGH - OVERALL-LOW) / 3
        SIZE ERROR DISPLAY 'SIZE ERROR ON RANGE INTERVAL'
    END-COMPUTE.
    EVALUATE TRUE
        WHEN BEGINNER
            MOVE OVERALL-LOW TO FITNESS-LOW
            COMPUTE FITNESS-HIGH ROUNDED =
                OVERALL-LOW + RANGE-INTERVAL
                SIZE ERROR DISPLAY 'SIZE ERROR HIGH FITNESS'
            END-COMPUTE
        WHEN INTERMEDIATE
            COMPUTE FITNESS-LOW ROUNDED =
                OVERALL-LOW + RANGE-INTERVAL
                SIZE ERROR DISPLAY 'SIZE ERROR LOW FITNESS'
            END-COMPUTE
            COMPUTE FITNESS-HIGH ROUNDED =
                OVERALL-HIGH - RANGE-INTERVAL
                SIZE ERROR
                    DISPLAY 'SIZE ERROR HIGH FITNESS'
            END-COMPUTE
        WHEN ADVANCED
            COMPUTE FITNESS-LOW ROUNDED =
                OVERALL-HIGH - RANGE-INTERVAL
                SIZE ERROR DISPLAY 'SIZE ERROR LOW FITNESS'
            END-COMPUTE
            MOVE OVERALL-HIGH TO FITNESS-HIGH
        WHEN OTHER
            DISPLAY 'INVALID FITNESS LEVEL SEE VALIDATION'
    END-EVALUATE.
    STRING FITNESS-LOW '-' FITNESS-HIGH DELIMITED BY SIZE
        INTO TRAIN-FITNESS-RANGE
    END-STRING.
```

Figure 16.12 Display Subprogram

```
IDENTIFICATION DIVISION.
PROGRAM-ID.      DSPLYSUB.
AUTHOR.          CVV.

DATA DIVISION.
WORKING-STORAGE SECTION.
01   FILLER                       PIC X(38)
         VALUE 'WS BEGINS HERE FOR SUBPROGRAM UPDTESUB'.

01  DISPLAY-MESSAGES.
    05  OVER-WEIGHT-COMMENT       PIC X(41)
        VALUE '  OH! NO! Your weight exceeds the range'.
    05  UNDER-WEIGHT-COMMENT      PIC X(41)
        VALUE ' EAT UP! Your weight is below the range'.
    05  IN-WEIGHT-COMMENT         PIC X(41)
        VALUE 'CONGRATULATIONS! You are within the range'.
    05  WEIGHT-COMMENT            PIC X(41).
    05  ANOTHER-MESSAGE           PIC X(14)
          VALUE 'Must be Y or N'.

    COPY COLORCPY.
 01  SCREEN-COLORS.
* COLORS FOR FOREGROUND AND BACKGROUND
     05  BLACK                    PIC S9(4) COMP-5 VALUE 0.
     05  BLUE                     PIC S9(4) COMP-5 VALUE 1.
     05  GREEN                    PIC S9(4) COMP-5 VALUE 2.
     05  CYAN                     PIC S9(4) COMP-5 VALUE 3.
     05  RED                      PIC S9(4) COMP-5 VALUE 4.
     05  MAGENTA                  PIC S9(4) COMP-5 VALUE 5.
     05  BROWN                    PIC S9(4) COMP-5 VALUE 6.
     05  WHITE                    PIC S9(4) COMP-5 VALUE 7.
* ADDITIONAL COLORS FOR FOREGROUND ONLY
     05  BRIGHT-BLACK             PIC S9(4) COMP-5 VALUE 8.
     05  BRIGHT-BLUE              PIC S9(4) COMP-5 VALUE 9.
     05  BRIGHT-GREEN             PIC S9(4) COMP-5 VALUE 10.
     05  BRIGHT-CYAN              PIC S9(4) COMP-5 VALUE 11.
     05  BRIGHT-RED               PIC S9(4) COMP-5 VALUE 12.
     05  BRIGHT-MAGENTA           PIC S9(4) COMP-5 VALUE 13.
     05  BRIGHT-BROWN             PIC S9(4) COMP-5 VALUE 14.
     05  BRIGHT-WHITE             PIC S9(4) COMP-5 VALUE 15.

 01  MESSAGE-COLORS.
     05  FORE-COLOR               PIC S9(4) COMP-5.
     05  BACK-COLOR               PIC S9(4) COMP-5.

 01  GOAL-WEIGHT-RANGE            PIC X(7).

 01  FILLER                       PIC X(36)
```

Screen colors are copied into program

Figure 16.12 *(continued)*

```
           VALUE 'WS ENDS HERE FOR SUBPROGRAM UPDTESUB'.

 LINKAGE SECTION.
     COPY DISPCPY.
 01  DISPLAY-ARGUMENTS.
     05  DISP-TRAINING-RANGES.
         10  DISP-TRAIN-OVERALL-RANGE   PIC X(5).
         10  DISP-TRAIN-FITNESS-RANGE   PIC X(5).
     05  DISP-WEIGHT-GOALS.
         10  DISP-GOAL-WGT-FROM         PIC ZZ9.
         10  DISP-GOAL-WGT-TO           PIC ZZ9.
     05  DISP-INPUT-WEIGHT              PIC 9(3).
     05  ANOTHER-PERSON-SWITCH          PIC X  VALUE SPACES.
         88  NO-MORE-PERSONS                VALUE 'N' 'n'.
         88  VALID-ANOTHER                  VALUE 'N' 'n' 'Y' 'y'.

 PROCEDURE DIVISION
     USING DISPLAY-ARGUMENTS.
 000-UPDATE-PERSONAL-DATA.
     PERFORM 100-DETERMINE-WEIGHT-COMMENT.
     PERFORM 200-UPDATE-SCREEN.
     CALL 'TIMESUB'.
     PERFORM 300-INPUT-ANOTHER-PERSON.
     EXIT PROGRAM.

 100-DETERMINE-WEIGHT-COMMENT.
     EVALUATE TRUE
         WHEN DISP-INPUT-WEIGHT < DISP-GOAL-WGT-FROM
             MOVE UNDER-WEIGHT-COMMENT TO WEIGHT-COMMENT
             MOVE MAGENTA TO BACK-COLOR
             MOVE BLACK TO FORE-COLOR
         WHEN DISP-INPUT-WEIGHT > DISP-GOAL-WGT-TO
             MOVE OVER-WEIGHT-COMMENT TO WEIGHT-COMMENT
             MOVE RED TO BACK-COLOR
             MOVE BLACK TO FORE-COLOR
         WHEN OTHER
             MOVE IN-WEIGHT-COMMENT TO WEIGHT-COMMENT
             MOVE GREEN TO BACK-COLOR
             MOVE BLACK TO FORE-COLOR
     END-EVALUATE.

 200-UPDATE-SCREEN.
     STRING DISP-GOAL-WGT-FROM '-' DISP-GOAL-WGT-TO
         DELIMITED BY SIZE
         INTO GOAL-WEIGHT-RANGE
     END-STRING.
     DISPLAY
         'Your Goal Weight Range: ' LINE 11 COLUMN 4
         GOAL-WEIGHT-RANGE LINE 11 COLUMN 28 WITH HIGHLIGHT.
     DISPLAY
```

Call to another subprogram (annotation pointing to `CALL 'TIMESUB'.`)

Figure 16.12 Display Subprogram

```
         WEIGHT-COMMENT LINE 12 COLUMN 6 WITH BLINK
             FOREGROUND-COLOR FORE-COLOR
             BACKGROUND-COLOR BACK-COLOR.
     DISPLAY
        'Training Heart Rate Range Information (10 Second)'
             LINE 14 COLUMN 4.
     DISPLAY
        'Overall Heart Rate Range: '
             LINE 15 COLUMN  6
         DISP-TRAIN-OVERALL-RANGE COLUMN 32 WITH HIGHLIGHT
         'Adjusted for Fitness Level: ' LINE 16 COLUMN 6
         DISP-TRAIN-FITNESS-RANGE COLUMN 34 WITH HIGHLIGHT.
     DISPLAY ' '  LINE 23 COLUMN 1 WITH BLANK LINE.
     DISPLAY ' '  LINE 24 COLUMN 1 WITH BLANK LINE.

 300-INPUT-ANOTHER-PERSON.
     DISPLAY 'Another Person? (Y/N): ' LINE 24 COLUMN 10
         WITH FOREGROUND-COLOR BRIGHT-GREEN
              BACKGROUND-COLOR MAGENTA.
     PERFORM WITH TEST AFTER UNTIL VALID-ANOTHER
         ACCEPT ANOTHER-PERSON-SWITCH LINE 24 COLUMN 33
             WITH FOREGROUND-COLOR BRIGHT-GREEN
                  BACKGROUND-COLOR MAGENTA
         IF VALID-ANOTHER
             DISPLAY ' '  LINE 24 WITH BLANK LINE
         ELSE
             DISPLAY ANOTHER-MESSAGE
                 LINE 24 COLUMN 38 WITH HIGHLIGHT BLINK
                 FOREGROUND-COLOR BRIGHT-WHITE
                 BACKGROUND-COLOR RED
         END-IF
     END-PERFORM.
```

In-line perform accepts and validates response regarding additional processing

Time Program (TIMESUB)

The program to update the displayed time (Figure 16.13) uses the ACCEPT statement to obtain the current time containing hours, minutes, seconds, and hundredths of a second as per the discussion in Chapter 8. Reference modification is used in conjunction with an INSPECT statement to truncate hundredths of a second in the displayed time.

The program is called from two other programs as per the system hierarchy chart in Figure 16.6. This program is different from the other subprograms in that it does not contain any parameters; the program is completely self-contained as it obtains the current time from the system, and then displays the results directly on the monitor.

Figure 16.13 Time Subprogram

```
IDENTIFICATION DIVISION.
PROGRAM-ID.     TIMESUB.
AUTHOR.         CVV.

DATA DIVISION.
WORKING-STORAGE SECTION.
01   FILLER                        PIC X(37)
         VALUE 'WS BEGINS HERE FOR SUBPROGRAM TIMESUB'.

01  TIME-VARIABLES.
    05  THE-TIME                   PIC 9(8).
    05  HH-MM-SS                   PIC 99B99B99.

01  FILLER                         PIC X(35)
         VALUE 'WS ENDS HERE FOR SUBPROGRAM TIMESUB'.

PROCEDURE DIVISION.
000-UPDATE-TIME.
    ACCEPT THE-TIME FROM TIME.
    MOVE THE-TIME (1:6) TO HH-MM-SS.
    INSPECT HH-MM-SS REPLACING ALL ' ' BY ':'.
    DISPLAY HH-MM-SS LINE 1 COLUMN 60.
    EXIT PROGRAM.
```

Preference modification truncates time

The Linkage Editor

Beginning COBOL programmers often take the ***link program*** (or ***linkage editor*** as it is called on IBM mainframes) for granted, because it functions transparently as the middle step in the compile, link, and execute sequence. Knowledge of the link program assumes greater importance, however, in systems of multiple programs as in the fitness example just presented. Accordingly, we review the compile, link, and execute sequence that was first presented in Chapter 2.

Three distinct programs are associated with the execution of a single COBOL program, a relationship that was shown earlier in Figure 2.3. The COBOL compiler translates a source program into an object (machine language) program; the link program combines the object program with object modules from other COBOL programs and/or vendor-supplied I/O routines to create an executable load module; and finally, the load module accepts the input data and produces the desired results.

Consider now a slightly different scenario in which a system of three COBOL programs (a main program and two subprograms) is to be developed. This time, a total of five steps is required in order to execute the main program:

1. Compile the main program
2. Compile the first subprogram
3. Compile the second subprogram
4. Link the three object programs to produce a load module
5. Execute the load module

It is not necessary, however, to repeat the entire five-step sequence every time the system undergoes additional testing. What if, for example, the subprograms have been successfully debugged, and only the main program is being changed? Can you see that it is inherently wasteful to continually recompile the subprograms if they remain the same? In other words, if only the main program changes, couldn't we just compile the main program (step 1), then link the object program to the existing object programs for the subprograms (step 4), and then execute the resulting load module (step 5)?

Other variations are also possible; for example, if the first subprogram changes but the other two remain the same, the run stream would consist of steps two, four, and five as only the first subprogram would have to be recompiled. Another variation would consist solely of step five, to execute the load module (without recompilation or linking) when all testing has been completed.

Figure 16.14 illustrates the compile, link, and execute sequence for the fitness system developed earlier in the chapter. Figure 16.14a displays the file names of the six programs in the system (as they might appear on a PC); the COB extension indicates a COBOL source program.

Figure 16.14b depicts a conceptual view of the associated run stream. Each of the six programs is compiled separately in steps 1 through 6, the individual object modules are linked together in step 7, and the resulting load module is executed in step 8. Figure 16.14c indicates the presence of the six object modules (extension OBJ) that are produced as a result of the individual compilations.

Figure 16.14d shows the two additional files produced by the link program. FITNESS.MAP contains the descriptive information produced by the link program and is analogous to a COBOL listing produced by the compiler. FITNESS.EXE is the resulting load module that is eventually executed.

Problems with the Linkage Editor

Students are often frustrated in their attempt to produce a load module with multiple subprograms. Consider, for example, Figure 16.15, which contains—in outline form—a COBOL main (calling) program and two sub (called) programs. Observe, however, that there is an *inconsistency* between the CALL statement of the main program and the PROGRAM-ID paragraph of the first subprogram; that is, the main program is calling **SUB1,** whereas the PROGRAM-ID paragraph refers to **SUBRTN1.** This in turn produces the error message in Figure 16.15d.

The exact wording of the error message will vary from system to system; for example, the linkage editor on an IBM mainframe will cite an ***unresolved external reference,*** whereas the link program on a PC may reference an ***undefined symbol.*** Regardless of the system, however, the link program will not execute cleanly, despite the fact that all three programs compiled without error.

The reason for the problem becomes apparent when we again consider the functions of the COBOL compiler and the link program. The compiler translates COBOL source statements to machine language, and thus, must accept statements that call other (external) programs—for example, CALL SUB1. The compiler cannot access SUB1 directly, and trusts in the link program to locate the appropriate object module and produce an executable load module. The unresolved external reference detected by the link program means there was a call for a program named SUB1, but that the object module for SUB1 could not be found.

Return to the original COBOL listing of Figure 16.15a and observe once again the inconsistency between the CALL statement in the main program (CALL SUB1) and the PROGRAM-ID paragraph in the subprogram (SUBRTN1). Make the entries consistent (i.e., change SUB1 to SUBRTN1) and the problem is solved.

Figure 16.14 The Compile, Link, and Execute Sequence

```
DSPLYSUB COB
FITNESS  COB
INPUTSUB COB
TIMESUB  COB
WGTCOPY  COB
WGTSUB   COB
```

(a) Directory before Compilation

```
Step 1: Compile fitness program (FITNESS.COB)
Step 2: Compile input program (INPUTSUB.COB)
Step 3: Compile weight goals program (WGTSUB.COB)
Step 4: Compile training program (TRAINSUB.COB)
Step 5: Compile format time program (TIMESUB.COB)
Step 6: Compile final display program (DSPLYSUB.COB)

Step 7: Link the object programs

Step 8: Execute the load module
```

(b) The Run Stream (Conceptual View)

```
DSPLYSUB COB     DSPLYSUB OBJ
FITNESS  COB     FITNESS  OBJ
INPUTSUB COB     INPUTSUB OBJ
TIMESUB  COB     TIMESUB  OBJ
WGTCOPY  COB     TRAINSUB OBJ
WGTSUB   COB     WGTSUB   OBJ
```

(c) Directory after Compilation

```
FITNESS  MAP
FITNESS  EXE
```

(d) Directory after Linking (Additional Files Only)

LIMITATIONS OF COBOL-74

The optional BY REFERENCE and BY CONTENT phrases were not present in COBOL-74. The omission of both phrases defaults to CALLING BY REFERENCE and is the equivalent of the CALL statement in COBOL-74. The INITIAL phrase in the PROGRAM-ID paragraph is also new to COBOL-85. The optional scope terminator, END-CALL, is also new.

Two other minor changes do not add any additional capability per se, but simplify the use of subprograms. These are:

1. EXIT PROGRAM (to return control to the calling program) need not be the only statement in a paragraph, as was required in COBOL-74.
2. An elementary item may appear in the parameter list as opposed to the COBOL-74 restriction to 01- or 77-level entries.

Figure 16.15 Problems with the Linkage Editor

```
IDENTIFICATION DIVISION.
PROGRAM-ID.    MAINPROG.
    .
      .
PROCEDURE DIVISION.
    .
      .
        .
    CALL 'SUB1' USING PARAMETER-1.
    CALL 'SUBRTN2' USING PARAMETER-2.
```

CALL statement inconsistent with PROGRAM-ID paragraph of first subroutine

(a) Main Program

```
IDENTIFICATION DIVISION.
PROGRAM-ID.    SUBRTN1.
    .
      .
PROCEDURE DIVISION
    USING PARAMETER-1.
    .
      .
    EXIT PROGRAM.
```

(b) First Subroutine

```
IDENTIFICATION DIVISION.
PROGRAM-ID.    SUBRTN2.
    .
      .
PROCEDURE DIVISION
    USING PARAMETER-2.
    .
      .
    EXIT PROGRAM.
```

(c) Second Subroutine

```
ERROR - SUB1 IS AN UNRESOLVED EXTERNAL REFERENCE
```

(d) Error Message

SUMMARY

Points to Remember

- A sub (called) program is a program that is written and compiled independently of other programs but which is executed under the control of a main (calling) program.
- A hierarchy chart shows the relationship of paragraphs within a COBOL program or programs within a system. The subprograms that comprise a system are developed in stages and tested in top-down fashion just as the paragraphs within a program.
- The CALL statement in a calling program transfers control to the first executable statement in the called program. The EXIT PROGRAM statement returns control from the called program to the calling program.
- The argument list is specified in the CALL USING statement of the calling program and in the Procedure Division header of the called program. The data names in the parameter lists can be, but do not have to be, the same.
- The COPY statement inserts statements into a COBOL program (from a copy library) during compilation, as though the statements had been coded directly in the program itself. A COPY statement may appear anywhere within a program except within another COPY statement.
- CALLING BY CONTENT prevents the value of a passed parameter modified in the calling program from being changed in the called program; CALLING BY REFERENCE, however, will change the variable in the calling program.
- The INITIAL phrase in the PROGRAM-ID paragraph restores a program to its initial state each time it is called; that is, all data names are reset to their original values via any VALUE clauses that are present.
- The linkage editor (link program) combines the object modules produced by compilation of one or more programs with vendor-supplied I/O routines to produce a load module.

Key Words and Concepts

Argument list
Called program
Calling program
Linkage editor (link program)
Load module
Main program
Parameter list
Subprogram
Undefined symbol
Unresolved external reference

COBOL Elements

```
BY CONTENT
BY REFERENCE
CALL USING
COPY
END-CALL
EXIT PROGRAM
INITIAL
LINKAGE SECTION
PROCEDURE DIVISION USING
```

FILL-IN

1. A called program returns control to its calling program via an ______________ ______________ statement.
2. The LINKAGE SECTION appears in the (calling/called) program, and indicates that space for these data names has already been allocated in the (calling/called) program.
3. The order of arguments in the USING clauses of the called and calling programs (is/is not) important.
4. If program A calls program B, then program A is the main or ______________ program and program B is the sub or ______________ program.
5. If program A calls program B and program B calls program C, then program B is (both/neither) a called and a calling program.
6. A COBOL program (may/may not) call multiple subprograms.
7. A ______________ statement is used to bring in text from a file on disk into a COBOL program.
8. Specification of the (BY CONTENT/BY REFERENCE) phrase ensures that the original values will be restored when control is returned to the calling program.
9. Specification of the (BY CONTENT/BY REFERENCE) phrase does not restore the values and thus functions identically to the COBOL-74 implementation.
10. The ______________ phrase in the PROGRAM-ID paragraph restores the data names in a called program to their initial values.
11. The PERFORM statement is to a paragraph as the ______________ statement is to a subprogram.

TRUE/FALSE

1. The COPY clause is permitted only in the Data Division.
2. The Linkage Section appears in the calling program.
3. Data names in CALL . . . USING and PROCEDURE DIVISION USING . . . must be the same.
4. A called program contains only the Data and Procedure Divisions.
5. The COPY statement can be used on an FD only.
6. A COPY statement takes effect during the linking phase of the compile, link, and execution sequence.
7. A program can contain only one CALL statement.
8. The same program can function as both a called and a calling program.
9. The parameter list may contain group items at other than a 01 level.
10. A hierarchy chart can be used to show the relationship of paragraphs in a program or programs in a system.
11. A CALL statement must include either the BY REFERENCE or BY CONTENT phrase.
12. A CALL statement must contain at least one parameter.

PROBLEMS

1. Answer the following questions with respect to the hierarchy chart in Figure 16.16:
   a. Which programs are calling programs?
   b. Which programs are called programs?
   c. Which programs are both called and calling programs?
   d. Which programs contain a CALL statement?
   e. Which programs contain a Linkage Section?
   f. Which programs might contain a COPY statement?
   g. Which programs might contain an INITIAL clause?

Figure 16.16 Hierarchy Chart for Problem 1

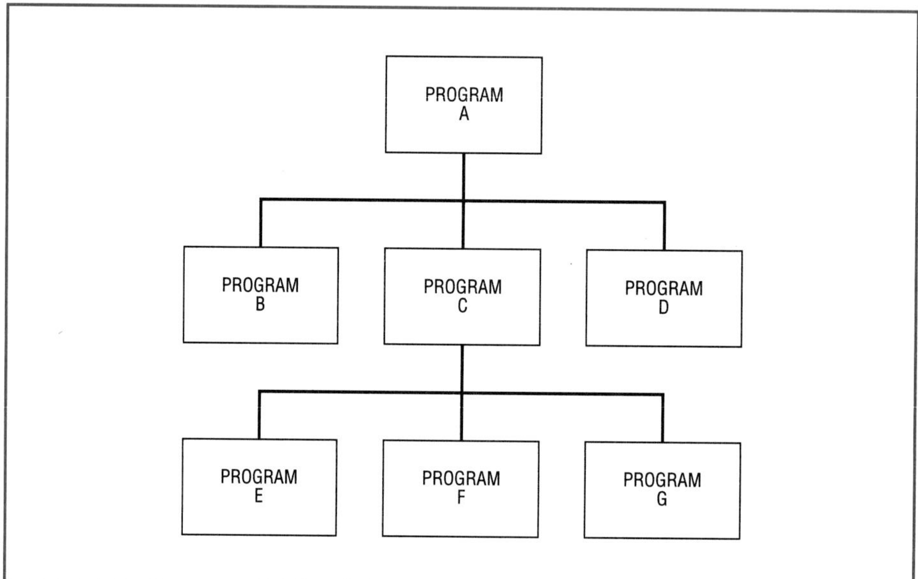

2. Figure 16.17 shows a partial listing of a called and calling program in which the first three Procedure Division statements of the subprogram initialize various counters and switches.
   a. Are these statements redundant with the existing VALUE clauses; that is, what would be the effect (if any) of removing the MOVE statements from the subprogram?
   b. What would be the effect (if any) of removing the MOVE ZERO statements, replacing them with VALUE ZERO clauses in the Data Division, and including the INITIAL phrase in the PROGRAM-ID header of the called program?
   c. Which Procedure Division statement could be substituted for the MOVE ZERO statements with no other changes to the program?

Figure 16.17 Skeleton Programs for Problem 2

```
IDENTIFICATION DIVISION.
PROGRAM-ID.    MAINPROG.
   .
    .
PROCEDURE DIVISION.
   .
    .
    CALL 'SUB1' USING PARAMETER-LIST.
```

(a) Main Program

```
IDENTIFICATION DIVISION.
PROGRAM-ID.    SUB1.
   .
    .
WORKING-STORAGE SECTION.
01  SUB-COUNTERS-AND-SWITCHES.
    05  FIRST-COUNTER          PIC 9(3)    VALUE ZERO.
    05  SECOND-COUNTER         PIC 9(3)    VALUE ZERO.
    05  TABLE-LOOKUP-SWITCH    PIC X(3)    VALUE SPACES.

PROCEDURE DIVISION
    USING PARAMTER-LIST.
   .
    .
RESET-DATA-ITEMS.
    MOVE ZEROS TO FIRST-COUNTER.
    MOVE ZEROS TO SECOND-COUNTER.
    MOVE SPACES TO TABLE-LOOKUP-SWITCH.
   .
    .
```

(b) Subprogram

3. Answer the following with respect to the COBOL fragment of Figure 16.18.
   a. What are the ending values for each of the six data names (that is, for A, B, C, D, E, and F)?
   b. What is the effect, if any, of removing the BY CONTENT phrase in the CALL statement?
   c. What is the effect, if any, of removing the BY REFERENCE phrase in the CALL statement?

Figure 16.18 COBOL Skeleton for Problem 3

```
    MOVE ZEROS TO A, B, C.
    CALL SUBRTN
        USING A
            BY CONTENT B
            BY REFERENCE C
    END-CALL.
```

(a) Calling Program

```
PROGRAM-ID.    SUBRTN.

PROCEDURE DIVISION
    USING D, E, F.
        .
            .
    MOVE 10 TO D, E, F
    EXIT PROGRAM.
```

(b) Called Program

4. Answer the following with respect to the COBOL skeleton in Figure 16.19.
   a. Indicate the necessary steps in a conceptual run stream to compile, link, and execute all three programs.
   b. Which steps would have to be repeated in the run stream of part (a), given that the subprograms were working perfectly, but that the main program needs modification?
   c. Which steps would have to be repeated in the run stream of part (a), given that the only change was in the copy member INPUTREC?
   d. What problems, if any, would arise in connection with the CALL statement for PROGA? In which step (compilation, linking, or execution) would the problem arise (be detected)?
   e. What problems, if any, would arise in connection with the CALL statement for PROGB? In which step (compilation, linking, or execution) would the problem arise (be detected)?
5. Explain how the concept of top-down testing can be applied to the fitness system as depicted by the hierarchy chart of Figure 16.6.

Figure 16.19 COBOL Programs for Problem 4

```
        IDENTIFICATION DIVISION.
        PROGRAM-ID.    MAINPROG.

        WORKING-STORAGE SECTION.
            COPY INPUTREC
C       01  INPUT-DATA.
C           05  INPUT-NAME        PIC X(15).
          .
            .
        01  PASSED-PARAMETERS.
            05  PARM-A            PIC 9(4).
            05  PARM-B            PIC XX.

        PROCEDURE DIVISION.

            CALL 'PROGA' USING PARM-A, PARM-B, INPUT-DATA.
            CALL 'PROGB' USING PARM-A.
```

(a) Main Program

```
        IDENTIFICATION DIVISION.
        PROGRAM-ID.    PROGA.

        LINKAGE SECTION.
            COPY INPUTREC
C       01  INPUT-DATA.
C           05  INPUT-NAME        PIC X(15).
          .
            .
        01  NEW-DATA-NAMES.
            05  NEW-NAME-A       PIC XX.
            05  NEW-NAME-B       PIC 9(4).

        PROCEDURE DIVISION
            USING NEW-NAME-A, NEW-NAME-B, INPUT-DATA.
```

(b) First Subroutine

```
        IDENTIFICATION DIVISION.
        PROGRAM-ID.    PROG-B.

        LINKAGE SECTION.
        01 PASSED-PARAMETERS.
           05  PARM-A             PIC 9(4).

        PROCEDURE DIVISION
            USING PARM-A.
```

(b) Second Subroutine

Sequential File Maintenance

CHAPTER OUTLINE

OBJECTIVES

After reading this chapter you will be able to:

- Describe the file maintenance operation; distinguish between the old master, transaction, and new master files.
- Describe the three transaction types associated with file maintenance.
- Differentiate between sequential and nonsequential file maintenance.
- Describe at least three types of errors that can be detected in a stand-alone edit program; list two errors that cannot be detected in such a program.
- Discuss the balance line algorithm.
- Define top-down testing; explain how a program may be tested before it is completely coded.

OVERVIEW

A large proportion of data-processing activity is devoted to file maintenance. Although printed reports are the more visible result of data processing, all files must be maintained to reflect the changing nature of the physical environment. In every system new records can be added, while existing records can be changed or deleted.

The chapter begins with a discussion of system concepts, emphasizing the importance of data validation in the maintenance process. It continues with coverage of the balance line algorithm, a completely general procedure for sequential file maintenance. The resulting program is implemented in stages through top-down testing. The initial version of the program contains several program stubs and validates the interaction among the higher-level paragraphs in the hierarchy chart. The second, and completed, version fulfills the requirements of the case study.

System Concepts

In its simplest form, file maintenance implies the existence of three files, an ***old master file***, a ***transaction file***, and a ***new master file***, which is produced as a consequence of processing the first two files with one another. The situation is depicted in Figure 17.1, which contains a system flowchart for the traditional ***sequential update***.

Figure 17.2 is an expanded version of Figure 17.1 with hypothetical data included. The old master and transaction files are both in sequence according to the same field (key), in this example, by social security number. The transaction file contains information on how the old master file is to be changed—that is, whether new records are to be ***added***, or existing records ***changed*** or ***deleted***. During the update process, every record in the old master file will be copied intact to the new master file, unless the update program detects a transaction for that record. The output produced by the program consists of the new master file and various error messages if problems are encountered.

Figure 17.1 Sequential Update

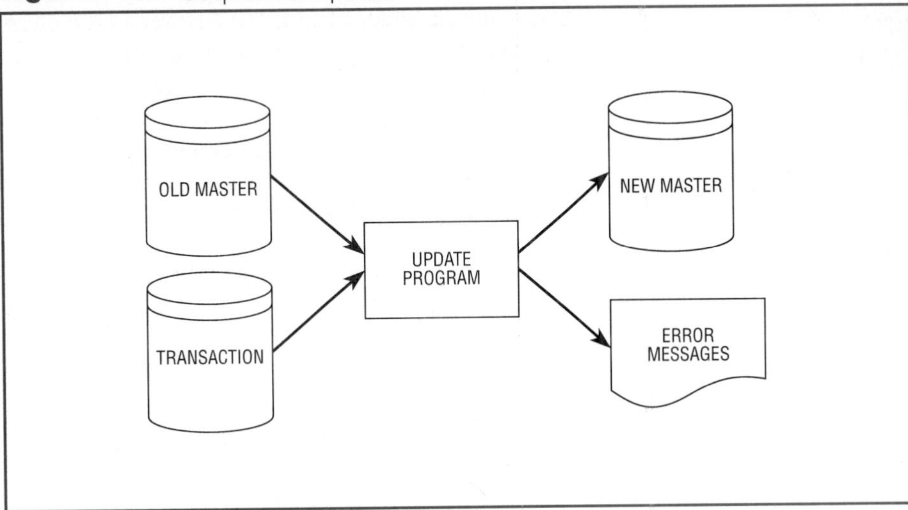

Figure 17.2 Sequential Update with Data Files

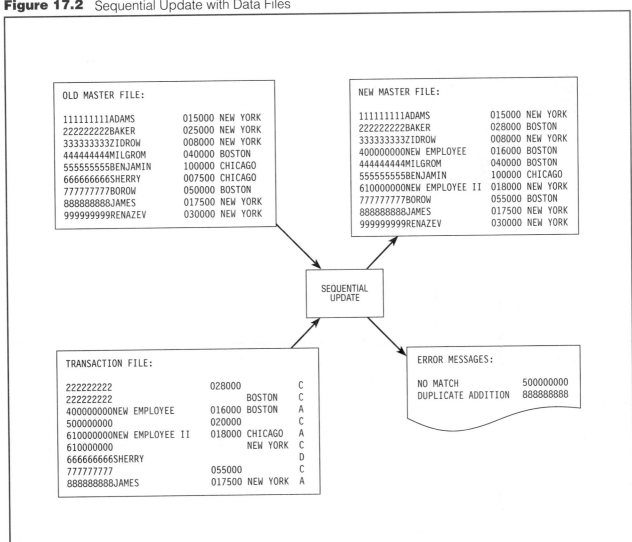

```
OLD MASTER FILE:

111111111ADAMS          015000 NEW YORK
222222222BAKER          025000 NEW YORK
333333333ZIDROW         008000 NEW YORK
444444444MILGROM        040000 BOSTON
555555555BENJAMIN       100000 CHICAGO
666666666SHERRY         007500 CHICAGO
777777777BOROW          050000 BOSTON
888888888JAMES          017500 NEW YORK
999999999RENAZEV        030000 NEW YORK
```

```
NEW MASTER FILE:

111111111ADAMS                015000 NEW YORK
222222222BAKER                028000 BOSTON
333333333ZIDROW               008000 NEW YORK
400000000NEW EMPLOYEE         016000 BOSTON
444444444MILGROM              040000 BOSTON
555555555BENJAMIN             100000 CHICAGO
610000000NEW EMPLOYEE II      018000 NEW YORK
777777777BOROW                055000 BOSTON
888888888JAMES                017500 NEW YORK
999999999RENAZEV              030000 NEW YORK
```

SEQUENTIAL UPDATE

```
TRANSACTION FILE:

222222222                     028000          C
222222222                            BOSTON   C
400000000NEW EMPLOYEE         016000 BOSTON   A
500000000                     020000          C
610000000NEW EMPLOYEE II      018000 CHICAGO  A
610000000                            NEW YORK C
666666666SHERRY                               D
777777777                     055000          C
888888888JAMES                017500 NEW YORK A
```

```
ERROR MESSAGES:

NO MATCH             500000000
DUPLICATE ADDITION   888888888
```

Every record in the old master file contains four fields: social security number, name, salary, and location. The records in the old master are in sequence by social security number, the value of which must be *unique* for every record in the file. Records in the transaction file are also in sequence by social security number, and three types of transactions (additions, changes, and deletions) are present. The update procedure must be general enough to accommodate multiple transactions for the same record; for example, employee 222222222 has two records in the transaction file, both of which are corrections.

Records with a transaction type of **A** are to be added to the new master file in their entirety. (Thus, New Employee, with social security number 400000000, does not appear on the old master but has been added to the new master.) Records with a transaction type of **D** are to be deleted. (Hence, Sherry, with social security number 666666666, appears in the old master but not the new master.) Records with a transaction code of **C** indicate a change in the value of a specific field(s) and contain only the social security number and field(s) to be changed. (Accordingly, Baker, with social security number 222222222, has had his salary and location changed to $28,000 and Boston, respectively.)

Note, too, that in addition to the records for which there is activity, the old master contains several records for which there is no corresponding transaction; for example, there are no transactions for records with social security numbers of 333333333 and 999999999. Such records are simply copied intact to the new master.

All of these illustrations assume that the transaction file is valid in and of itself by virtue of a previously executed ***stand-alone edit*** program. In other words, the validation of the incoming transaction file has already been accomplished in an earlier program. This enables simplified logic in the maintenance program, as it can assume that all transactions contain a valid code (A, C, or D), that the transactions are in sequence by social security number, that additions contain all necessary fields, and so on. (Data validation was first introduced in Chapter 8.)

There are, however, two types of errors that cannot be detected in the stand-alone edit, and which must be checked in the update program itself. These are the attempted correction or deletion of a nonexistent old master record (a ***no match***), and the addition of a new record that is already in the old master file (a ***duplicate addition***). The transaction file in Figure 17.2 illustrates both errors (with transactions 500000000 and 888888888, respectively).

Sequential versus Nonsequential Processing

This chapter is concerned entirely with a ***sequential update*** whereby every record in the old master is copied to the new master regardless of whether or not it changes. This technique is perfectly adequate when there is substantial activity in the old master file (that is, when many records change), but inefficient if only a few changes are made to the existing master file.

By contrast, a ***nonsequential update*** uses a single master file, which functions as both the old and new master. The records in the transaction file are processed one at a time, in no particular sequence, and matched against the existing master file. Nonsequential processing works best with low-activity files because unchanged records are left alone; that is, only those master records with a matching transaction record are written (rewritten) in the master file. Nonsequential processing is discussed in Chapter 18.

Periodic Maintenance

All file maintenance is done *periodically*, with the frequency depending on the application. A file of student transcripts is updated only a few times a year; a bank's checking transactions are updated daily, with other types of systems being updated

Figure 17.3 Two-period Sequential Update

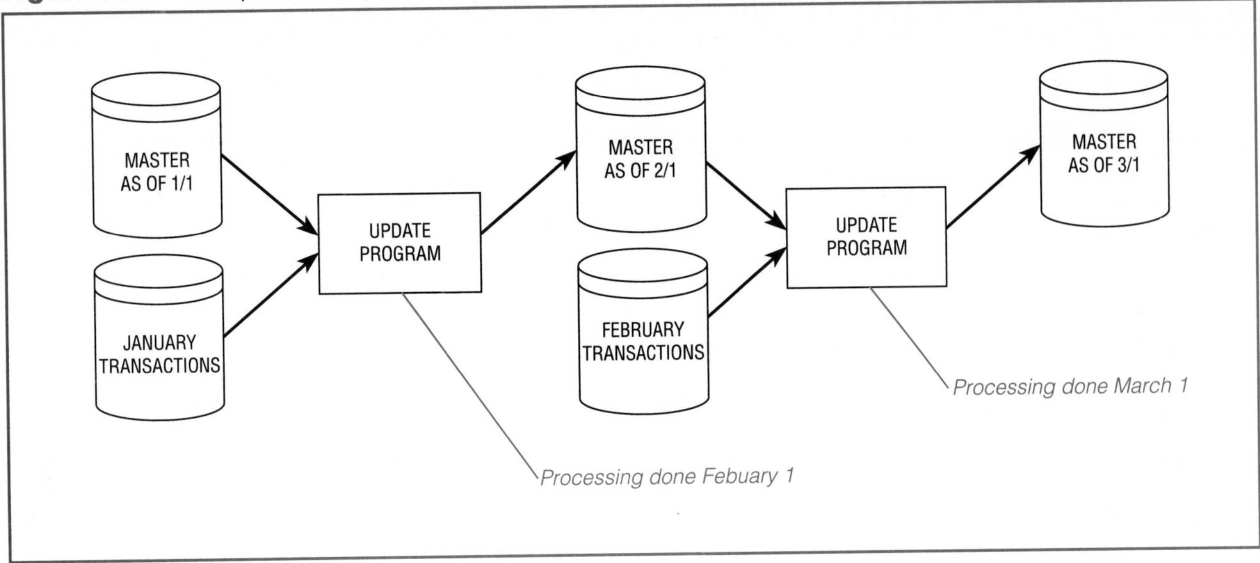

weekly or monthly. (Real-time applications, which process transactions as they occur, are covered in conjunction with nonsequential processing in the next chapter.)

A monthly cycle is depicted in Figure 17.3, beginning with a master file on January 1. Transactions are collected (batched) during the month of January. Then, on February 1, the master file of January 1 (now the old master) is processed with the transactions accrued during January, to produce a new master as of February 1. The process continues from month to month. Transactions are collected during February. On March 1, we use the file created February 1 as the old master, run it against the February transactions, and produce a new master as of March 1. The process continues indefinitely.

Figure 17.3 also serves as a basis for discussion of how ***backup procedures*** are implemented. Consider, for example, the situation on March 1 after the update has been run. The installation now has three ***generations*** of the master file; the file just produced (current master), the file produced on February 1st (previous master), and the original master file of January 1st (second previous master).

The availability of previous generations of the master file enables re-creation of the update process, should the need arise. Thus, an installation could rerun the update of March 1st, provided it retained the February master and associated transaction file. It could also go back a generation and recreate the February master, given that it retained the original January master and its associated transaction file. The number of generations that are retained depends on the individual installation, but will seldom be fewer than three. This type of backup is referred to as a ***grandfather-father-son*** strategy (with apologies to women).

Data Validation

The need for ***data validation*** is paramount, regardless of whether processing is done sequentially or nonsequentially, or how many generations of backup are retained. The example in Figure 17.2 simply assumed a valid transaction file, an assumption that is far too unrealistic in practice. Accordingly we introduce concepts of data validation within the basis of a COBOL case study.

Figure 17.4 expands the sequential update of Figure 17.1 to include a separate step for data validation, in which the transaction file is first input to a stand-alone

Figure 17.4 Sequential Update with Data Validation

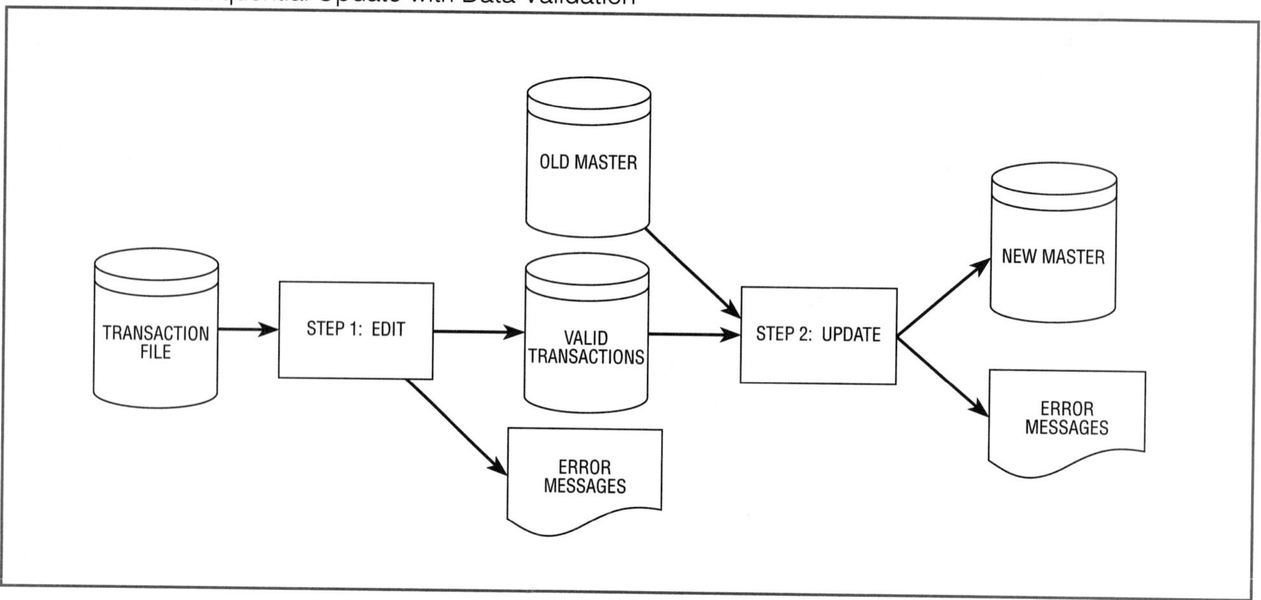

edit program. This program checks transactions for several errors (invalid transaction codes, incomplete additions, and so on), and only those transactions that pass all validity checks will be written to the output (valid) transaction file. The latter is then input to the sequential update.

In effect, Figure 17.4 is a blueprint for the remainder of the chapter. We begin with specifications for the edit program, develop the program completely, present a second set of specifications for the file maintenance (update) program, and develop that program in the second half of the chapter.

PROGRAMMING SPECIFICATIONS

Program Name: Data Validation

Narrative: This program illustrates typical types of data validation, which are implemented in a stand-alone edit program.

Input File(s): TRANSACTION-FILE

Input Record Layout:

```
01 TRANSACTION-RECORD.
   05  TR-SOC-SEC-NUMBER                  PIC X(9).
   05  TR-NAME.
       10  TR-LAST-NAME                   PIC X(15).
       10  TR-INITIALS                    PIC XX.
   05  TR-LOCATION-CODE                   PIC X(3).
   05  TR-COMMISSION-RATE                 PIC 99.
   05  TR-SALES-AMOUNT                    PIC 9(5).
   05  TR-TRANSACTION-CODE                PIC X.
       88  ADDITION        VALUE 'A'.
       88  CORRECTION      VALUE 'C'.
       88  DELETION        VALUE 'D'.
```

Test Data: See Figure 17.5a.

Output Files: VALID-TRANSACTION-FILE

ERROR-FILE

Output Record Layout: Identical to the input record layout.

Processing Requirements:

1. Process a file of incoming transactions, rejecting any (and all) invalid transactions with an appropriate error message. Each transaction is to be checked for the following:
   a. Sequence—The transactions are supposed to be in ascending sequence according to social security number by virtue of a previous program. (Multiple transactions with the same social security number are allowed). Accordingly, this program is not to sort the transaction file but to implement logic to ensure that the transactions are in fact in order. (Sorting is time consuming and should not be repeated if the transactions are already in order.)
   b. Valid transaction code—Only three types of transaction codes are permitted: A, C, or D, denoting additions, corrections, and deletions, respectively. Any other transaction code (including a blank) is to be rejected.
   c. Completeness—Additions are to contain the employee's name and initials, location, and commission rate. All fields are to be checked with individual messages written for any missing field(s). Corrections must contain a value for the sales amount.
   d. Data types—TR-COMMISSION-RATE (required for an addition) and TR-SALES-AMOUNT (required for a correction) must be numeric fields. A violation of either condition requires a specific error message.
   e. Valid location code—Additions are to contain a valid location code—that is, a location code of ATL, BOS, NYC, PHI, or SF (corresponding to the entries in a location codes table to be embedded within the program).
2. All valid transactions are to be written to a VALID-TRANSACTION-FILE, which will be created as an output file by the program. Invalid transactions may be discarded after the appropriate error message has been printed.

The function of the edit program is best understood by examining Figure 17.5, which contains the input transaction file, associated error messages, and the output (valid) transaction file. Fourteen transactions were input to the edit program (Figure 17.5a), but only eight of these passed all validity checks and thus made it to the output file (Figure 17.5c). You may find it useful to review each of the rejected transactions in conjunction with the associated error message in Figure 17.5b.

Figure 17.5 Valid Transaction File

```
000000000BOROW          JSATL07      A
000000000BOROW          JS      10000C
000000000BOROW          JS      20000C
100000000GRABER         P       30000
222222222NEW GUY        RT           A
333333333ESMAN          TNNY 09      A
400000000MOLDOF         BLATL15      A
444444444RICHARDS       IM      05000C
555555555JORDAN           BOS07      A
700000000MILGROM        A            D
666666666JOHNSON        M NYC12      A
800000000VAZQUEZ        C       55000C
```

Figure 17.5 *(continued)*

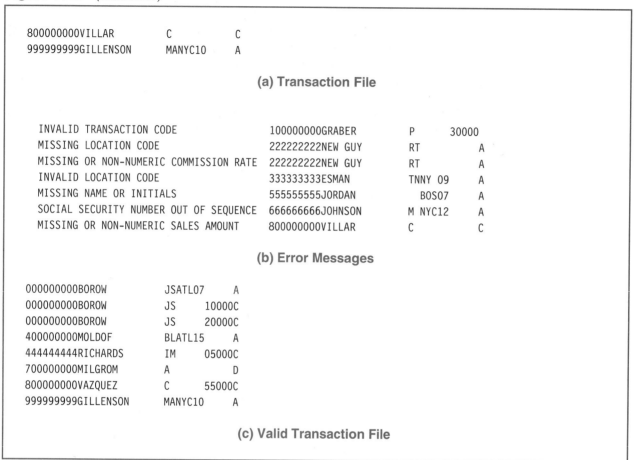

```
800000000VILLAR        C         C
999999999GILLENSON     MANYC10   A
```

(a) Transaction File

```
INVALID TRANSACTION CODE                  100000000GRABER      P      30000
MISSING LOCATION CODE                     222222222NEW GUY     RT          A
MISSING OR NON-NUMERIC COMMISSION RATE    222222222NEW GUY     RT          A
INVALID LOCATION CODE                     333333333ESMAN       TNNY 09     A
MISSING NAME OR INITIALS                  555555555JORDAN        BOS07     A
SOCIAL SECURITY NUMBER OUT OF SEQUENCE    666666666JOHNSON     M NYC12     A
MISSING OR NON-NUMERIC SALES AMOUNT       800000000VILLAR      C           C
```

(b) Error Messages

```
000000000BOROW         JSATL07      A
000000000BOROW         JS      10000C
000000000BOROW         JS      20000C
400000000MOLDOF        BLATL15      A
444444444RICHARDS      IM      05000C
700000000MILGROM       A            D
800000000VAZQUEZ       C       55000C
999999999GILLENSON     MANYC10      A
```

(c) Valid Transaction File

Figure 17.6 Hierarchy Chart for Data Validation Program

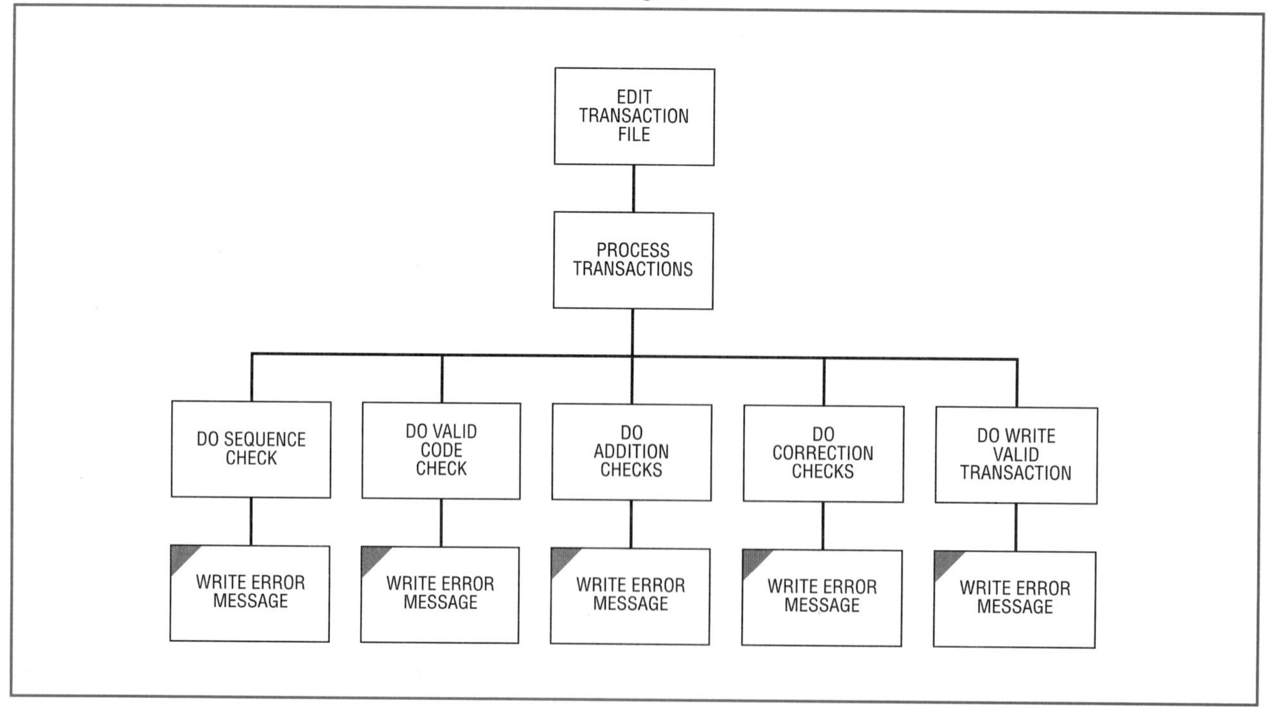

Designing the Program

The edit program is developed along the same lines as any other program, first by designing a hierarchy chart to include the functions required by the program, and then by developing pseudocode to embrace sequence and decision-making logic.

The hierarchy chart in Figure 17.6 is straightforward and should not present any difficulty. Note, however, that the module WRITE-ERROR-MESSAGE is called from several places in the program because the function is subservient to each of the error-checking modules. We have decided, therefore, to place these statements in a separate routine, rather than repeat the identical code in multiple places throughout the program.

The pseudocode for the data validation program is shown in Figure 17.7. Each incoming transaction is assumed to be valid initially, so that 'YES' is moved to

Figure 17.7 Pseudocode for Data Validation Program

```
Open files
DO while data remains
    READ transaction file
        AT END
            Indicate no more data
        NOT AT END
            Move 'YES' to valid-record-switch
            IF trans-social-security < previous-social-security
                Move 'NO' to valid-record-switch
                Write error message
            ENDIF
            Move trans-social-security to previous-social-security
            IF transaction-code is not valid
                Move 'NO' to valid-record-switch
                Write error message
            ENDIF
            IF addition
                IF transaction fails addition-check(s)
                    Move 'NO' to valid-record-switch
                    Write error message(s)
                ENDIF
            ELSE
                IF correction
                    IF sales-amount not numeric
                        Move 'NO' to valid-record-switch
                        Write error message
                    ENDIF
                ENDIF
            ENDIF
            IF valid-record-switch = 'YES'
                Write valid-transaction-record
            ENDIF
    ENDREAD
ENDDO
Close files
Stop run
```

VALID-RECORD-SWITCH. The transaction is then subjected to the various editing requirements, any one of which could cause VALID-RECORD-SWITCH to be set to 'NO'. Only if the transaction passes all of the individual checks (that is, if VALID-RECORD-SWITCH is still set to 'YES') is it written to the valid record file at the end of the loop.

The Completed Program

The completed program is shown in Figure 17.8. One technique worthy of special mention is the establishment of a table for the error messages (lines 47 through 64) and the subsequent printing of an error message in the paragraph 400-WRITE-ERROR-MESSAGE (lines 167–172).

Figure 17.8 The Edit Program

```
1    IDENTIFICATION DIVISION.
2    PROGRAM-ID.   EDIT.
3    AUTHOR.       ROBERT GRAUER.
4
5    ENVIRONMENT DIVISION.
6    INPUT-OUTPUT SECTION.
7    FILE-CONTROL.
8        SELECT TRANSACTION-FILE
9            ASSIGN TO UT-S-TRANS.
10       SELECT VALID-TRANSACTION-FILE
11           ASSIGN TO UT-S-VALTRANS.
12       SELECT ERROR-FILE
13           ASSIGN TO UT-S-ERRORS.
14
15   DATA DIVISION.
16   FILE SECTION.
17   FD  TRANSACTION-FILE
18       DATA RECORD IS TRANSACTION-RECORD.
19   01  TRANSACTION-RECORD                   PIC X(37).
20
21   FD  VALID-TRANSACTION-FILE
22       DATA RECORD IS VALID-TRANSACTION-RECORD.
23   01  VALID-TRANSACTION-RECORD             PIC X(37).
24
25   FD  ERROR-FILE
26       DATA RECORD IS ERROR-RECORD.
27   01  ERROR-RECORD                         PIC X(132).
28
29   WORKING-STORAGE SECTION.
30   01  FILLER                               PIC X(14)
31           VALUE 'WS BEGINS HERE'.
32
33   01  WS-TRANSACTION-RECORD.
34       05  TR-SOC-SEC-NUMBER                PIC X(9).
35       05  TR-NAME.
```

Valid transactions are written to separate file

Figure 17.8 *(continued)*

```
            10  TR-LAST-NAME                PIC X(15).
            10  TR-INITIALS                 PIC XX.
        05  TR-LOCATION-CODE                PIC X(3).
        05  TR-COMMISSION-RATE              PIC 99.
        05  TR-SALES-AMOUNT                 PIC 9(5).
        05  TR-TRANSACTION-CODE             PIC X.
            88  ADDITION       VALUE 'A'.
            88  CORRECTION     VALUE 'C'.
            88  DELETION       VALUE 'D'.
            88  VALID-CODES    VALUES 'A', 'C', 'D'.

    01  ERROR-VALUES-TABLE.
        05  ERROR-VALUES.
            10  FILLER                      PIC X(40)
                VALUE 'SOCIAL SECURITY NUMBER OUT OF SEQUENCE'.
            10  FILLER                      PIC X(40)
                VALUE 'INVALID TRANSACTION CODE'.
            10  FILLER                      PIC X(40)
                VALUE 'MISSING NAME OR INITIALS'.
            10  FILLER                      PIC X(40)
                VALUE 'MISSING LOCATION CODE'.
            10  FILLER                      PIC X(40)
                VALUE 'INVALID LOCATION CODE'.
            10  FILLER                      PIC X(40)
                VALUE 'MISSING OR NON-NUMERIC COMMISSION RATE'.
            10  FILLER                      PIC X(40)
                VALUE 'MISSING OR NON-NUMERIC SALES AMOUNT'.
        05  ERROR-TABLE REDEFINES ERROR-VALUES.
            10  ERROR-MESSAGE OCCURS 7 TIMES PIC X(40).

    01  LOCATION-VALUES-TABLE.
        05  LOCATION-VALUES.
            10  FILLER                      PIC X(3)  VALUE 'ATL'.
            10  FILLER                      PIC X(3)  VALUE 'BOS'.
            10  FILLER                      PIC X(3)  VALUE 'NYC'.
            10  FILLER                      PIC X(3)  VALUE 'PHI'.
            10  FILLER                      PIC X(3)  VALUE 'SF '.
        05  LOCATION-TABLE REDEFINES LOCATION-VALUES.
            10  LOCATION OCCURS 5 TIMES
                INDEXED BY LOCATION-INDEX   PIC X(3).

    01  WS-ERROR-LINE.
        05  FILLER                          PIC X(2).
        05  EL-REASON                       PIC X(40).
        05  EL-TRANSACTION                  PIC X(37).
        05  FILLER                          PIC X(54).

    01  WS-SWITCHES-AND-DATANAMES.
        05  WS-EOF-SWITCH                   PIC X(3)  VALUE 'NO '.
        05  WS-VALID-RECORD-SWITCH          PIC X(3)  VALUE SPACES.
```

Error messages are grouped in a common table

Figure 17.8 *(continued)*

```
           05  WS-PREVIOUS-SOC-SEC-NUMBER        PIC X(9)  VALUE SPACES.
           05  WS-ERROR-CODE                     PIC 99.

       PROCEDURE DIVISION.
       100-EDIT-TRANSACTION-FILE.
           OPEN INPUT TRANSACTION-FILE
               OUTPUT VALID-TRANSACTION-FILE
                      ERROR-FILE.
           PERFORM UNTIL WS-EOF-SWITCH = 'YES'
               READ TRANSACTION-FILE INTO WS-TRANSACTION-RECORD
                   AT END
                       MOVE 'YES' TO WS-EOF-SWITCH
                   NOT AT END
                       PERFORM 210-PROCESS-TRANSACTIONS
               END-READ
           END-PERFORM.
           CLOSE TRANSACTION-FILE
                 VALID-TRANSACTION-FILE
                 ERROR-FILE.
           STOP RUN.

       210-PROCESS-TRANSACTIONS.
           MOVE 'YES' TO WS-VALID-RECORD-SWITCH.
           PERFORM 300-DO-SEQUENCE-CHECK.
           PERFORM 310-DO-VALID-CODE-CHECK.
           IF ADDITION
               PERFORM 320-DO-ADDITION-CHECKS
           ELSE
               IF CORRECTION
                   PERFORM 330-DO-CORRECTION-CHECKS
               END-IF
           END-IF.
           IF WS-VALID-RECORD-SWITCH = 'YES'
               PERFORM 340-WRITE-VALID-TRANSACTION
           END-IF.

       300-DO-SEQUENCE-CHECK.
           IF TR-SOC-SEC-NUMBER < WS-PREVIOUS-SOC-SEC-NUMBER
               MOVE 1 TO WS-ERROR-CODE
               PERFORM 400-WRITE-ERROR-MESSAGE
           END-IF.
           MOVE TR-SOC-SEC-NUMBER TO WS-PREVIOUS-SOC-SEC-NUMBER.

       310-DO-VALID-CODE-CHECK.
           IF NOT VALID-CODES
               MOVE 2 TO WS-ERROR-CODE
               PERFORM 400-WRITE-ERROR-MESSAGE
           END-IF.

       320-DO-ADDITION-CHECKS.
```

In-line perform and false-condition branch drives the program

Transaction is assumed valid initially

Only valid transactions are written to output file

Appropriate subscript is moved to WS-ERROR-CODE

Figure 17.8 *(continued)*

```
        IF TR-LAST-NAME = SPACES OR TR-INITIALS = SPACES
            MOVE 3 TO WS-ERROR-CODE
            PERFORM 400-WRITE-ERROR-MESSAGE
        END-IF.
        IF TR-LOCATION-CODE = SPACES
            MOVE 4 TO WS-ERROR-CODE
            PERFORM 400-WRITE-ERROR-MESSAGE
        ELSE
            SET LOCATION-INDEX TO 1
            SEARCH LOCATION
                AT END
                    MOVE 5 TO WS-ERROR-CODE
                    PERFORM 400-WRITE-ERROR-MESSAGE
                WHEN TR-LOCATION-CODE = LOCATION (LOCATION-INDEX)
                    NEXT SENTENCE
            END-SEARCH
        END-IF.
        IF TR-COMMISSION-RATE NOT NUMERIC
            MOVE 6 TO WS-ERROR-CODE
            PERFORM 400-WRITE-ERROR-MESSAGE
        END-IF.

    330-DO-CORRECTION-CHECKS.
        IF TR-SALES-AMOUNT NOT NUMERIC
            MOVE 7 TO WS-ERROR-CODE
            PERFORM 400-WRITE-ERROR-MESSAGE
        END-IF.

    340-WRITE-VALID-TRANSACTION.
        WRITE VALID-TRANSACTION-RECORD FROM WS-TRANSACTION-RECORD.

    400-WRITE-ERROR-MESSAGE.
        MOVE 'NO ' TO WS-VALID-RECORD-SWITCH.
        MOVE SPACES TO WS-ERROR-LINE.
        MOVE ERROR-MESSAGE (WS-ERROR-CODE) TO EL-REASON.
        MOVE WS-TRANSACTION-RECORD TO EL-TRANSACTION.
        WRITE ERROR-RECORD FROM WS-ERROR-LINE.
```

SEARCH statement nested in IF statement

All error messages are produced by a common routine

The use of an ***error message table*** enables the programmer to see at a glance all of the errors checked by the program, and further to format those messages in identical fashion. It also facilitates the use of a common routine to display the individual messages, rather than having to duplicate code throughout the program. Observe, therefore, that each error routine moves an appropriate subscript value to WS-ERROR-CODE upon detection of an error, which is then used by 400-WRITE-ERROR-MESSAGE to display the appropriate error.

Is data validation worth the extra time and trouble? Any programmer who has ever been called at two in the morning will answer strongly in the affirmative. Put another way, diligent application of data validation (sometimes known as ***defensive programming***) minimizes the need for subsequent debugging. All debugging techniques, no matter how sophisticated, suffer from the fact that they are applied *after* a problem has occurred. The inclusion of data validation within a system attempts to detect the (inevitable) errors that will occur *before* they produce a problem.

Sequential File Maintenance

We are now ready to proceed with the main objective of the chapter, the development of a program for sequential file maintenance. Specifications follow in the usual format.

PROGRAMMING SPECIFICATIONS

Program Name: Sequential Update

Narrative: This program implements the traditional sequential update via the balance line algorithm.

Input Files: TRANSACTION-FILE

OLD-MASTER-FILE

Input Record Layout:

```
01  TRANSACTION-RECORD.
    05  TR-SOC-SEC-NUMBER                 PIC X(9).
    05  TR-NAME.
        10  TR-LAST-NAME                  PIC X(15).
        10  TR-INITIALS                   PIC XX.
    05  TR-LOCATION-CODE                  PIC X(3).
    05  TR-COMMISSION-RATE                PIC 99.
    05  TR-SALES-AMOUNT                   PIC 9(5).
    05  TR-TRANSACTION-CODE               PIC X.
        88  ADDITION        VALUE 'A'.
        88  CORRECTION      VALUE 'C'.
        88  DELETION        VALUE 'D'.

01  OLD-MASTER-RECORD.
    05  OM-SOC-SEC-NUMBER                 PIC X(9).
    05  OM-NAME.
        10  OM-LAST-NAME                  PIC X(15).
        10  OM-INITIALS                   PIC XX.
    05  OM-LOCATION-CODE                  PIC X(3).
    05  OM-COMMISSION-RATE                PIC 99.
    05  OM-YEAR-TO-DATE-SALES             PIC 9(8).
```

Output File: NEW-MASTER-FILE

Output Record Layout: Identical to old master record.

Test Data: See Figure 17.9a (Old Master File) and Figure 17.9b (Valid Transaction File).

Processing Requirements:

1. Develop a sequential update program to process an incoming transaction file and the associated old master file to produce a new master file.
2. The transaction file is assumed to be valid in and of itself by virtue of a stand-alone edit program. Hence, each transaction has a valid transaction code (A, C, or D), numeric

Figure 17.9 Test Data

```
100000000GRABER         P ATL1500000000
200000000RUBIN          MABOS0800020000
300000000ANDERSON       IRBOS1000113000
400000000MOLDOF         BLATL1500000000
500000000GLASSMAN       JSNYC1000045000
600000000GRAUER         RTNYC0800087500
700000000MILGROM        A SF 0900120000
800000000VAZQUEZ        C ATL1200060000
900000000CLARK          E NYC0700002500
```

(a) Old Master

```
000000000BOROW          JSATL07      A
000000000BOROW          JS      10000C
000000000BOROW          JS      20000C
400000000MOLDOF         BLATL15      A
444444444RICHARDS       IM      05000C
700000000MILGROM        A            D
800000000VAZQUEZ        C       55000C
999999999GILLENSON      MANYC10      A
```

(b) Valid Transaction File (Output of Edit Program)

fields are numeric, and so on. Nevertheless, the update program must check (and flag) two kinds of errors that could not be detected in the stand-alone edit, as they require interaction with the old master file. These are:

a. Duplicate additions, in which the social security number of a transaction coded as an addition already exists in the old master,

b. No matches, in which the social security number of a transaction coded as either a deletion or a correction, does not exist in the old master.

3. Transactions coded as additions are to be added to the new master file in their entirety, and will contain a value for every field in the transaction record (except for TR-SALES-AMOUNT). The value of YEAR-TO-DATE-SALES in the new master record is to be initialized to zero.

4. Transactions coded as deletions are to be removed from the master file. These transactions contain only the social security number and transaction code.

5. Transactions coded as corrections contain only the social security number, name, and the transaction sales amount (TR-SALES-AMOUNT). The value of TR-SALES-AMOUNT on the incoming transaction is to be *added* to the value in the YEAR-TO-DATE-SALES field in the master record.

6. Any old master record for which there is no corresponding transaction is to be copied intact to the new master.

The Balance Line Algorithm

Every COBOL book has confronted the problem of a sequential update. Barry Dwyer[1] details a general and elegant solution to the problem known as the ***balance line***

1. B. Dwyer, "One More Time—How to Update a Master File," **Communications of the ACM,** vol. 24, no.1 (January 1981).

algorithm. To understand this solution, realize that the logic in a sequential update is more difficult than what has been encountered in previous chapters because there are multiple input files. The essence of the problem, then, is to determine whether to read from the old master file, the transaction file, or both. The solution is handled neatly in the balance line algorithm by the concept of an active key.

The ***active key*** is the smaller of the old master key and transaction key currently being processed. Thus, if the transaction key is less than the old master key, the active key is equal to the transaction key; if the transaction and old master keys are equal, the active key is equal to either; finally, if the old master key is less than the transaction key, the active key is the old master. (Note how easily the technique can be extended to multiple transaction files; the active key is always defined as the smallest value of all keys currently processed.)

The active key determines which records are admitted to the update process, and is illustrated with respect to the data in Figure 17.9. At the start of execution, the initial social security numbers for the old master and transaction records are 100000000 and 000000000, respectively, yielding an active key of 000000000. Thus, only the transaction record is considered for processing, while the old master record is held in abeyance. The algorithm processes this transaction, then reads another record from the transaction file, again with social security number 000000000. The keys are compared and again the transaction key is less than the master key, leaving the active key unchanged. After this transaction is processed, a third transaction is read, also with social security number 000000000, with the same results.

The fourth transaction with social security number 400000000 is read and produces a new active key of 100000000, which is the lesser of the old master (100000000) and transaction (400000000) social security numbers. The old master record is admitted to the update process, while the transaction record is held. The process continues in this fashion until eventually both files are out of data.

The balance line algorithm is expressed in pseudocode in Figure 17.10. The initial records are read from each file, and the first active key is determined. Next the major loop is executed until both the old master and transaction files are out of data. (**HIGH-VALUES** is a COBOL figurative literal and denotes the largest possible value. It is a convenient way of forcing ***end-of-file*** conditions, as will be seen when test data are examined later in the chapter.)

Within the outer loop, the key of the old master record is compared to the active key. If these values are equal, the old master record is moved (but **not** written) to the new master file, and another record is read from the old master file. We are not, however, finished with the original master record as it must be determined if any transactions exist for that record. Accordingly an inner loop is executed, which processes all transactions whose key is equal to the active key. (The transaction file is read repeatedly in the inner loop after each transaction is processed.) When the transaction key no longer equals the active key, a check is made to see if a deletion was processed, and if not, the new master record is written. The next active key is chosen, and the outer loop continues.

Figure 17.10 does not include the logic to accommodate error processing; that is, although the transaction file is assumed to be valid in and of itself, there are additional errors that come to light only in the actual updating process. Specifically, the update program must reject transactions that attempt to add records that already exist in the old master (duplicate additions), and must also reject transactions that attempt to change or delete records that do not exist (a no match).

The easiest way to accomplish this error processing is through the assignment of an ***allocation status*** to every value of the active key; that is, the value of the key is either allocated or it is not. If the allocation status is on, the record belongs in the file; if the allocation status is off, the record does not belong. Deletion of an existing record changes the status from on to off, whereas addition of a new record alters the

Figure 17.10 Balance Line Algorithm

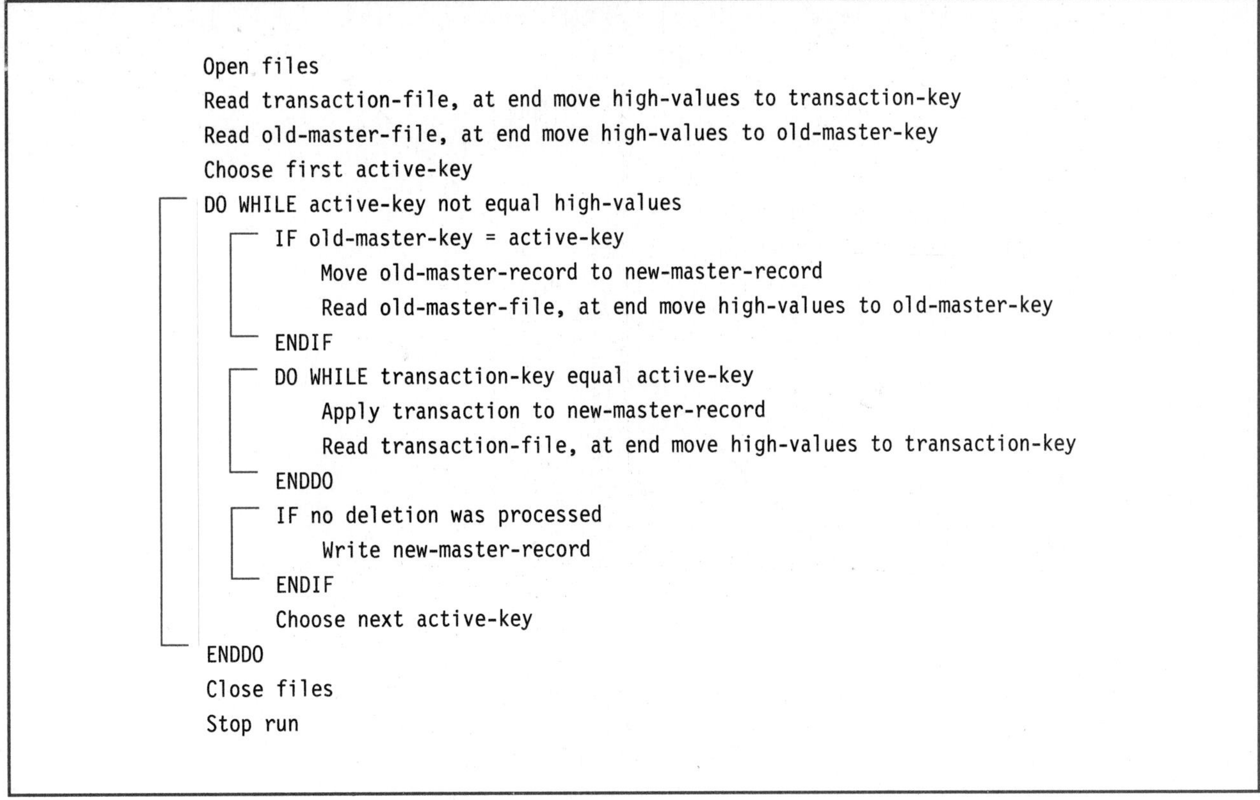

```
Open files
Read transaction-file, at end move high-values to transaction-key
Read old-master-file, at end move high-values to old-master-key
Choose first active-key
DO WHILE active-key not equal high-values
    IF old-master-key = active-key
        Move old-master-record to new-master-record
        Read old-master-file, at end move high-values to old-master-key
    ENDIF
    DO WHILE transaction-key equal active-key
        Apply transaction to new-master-record
        Read transaction-file, at end move high-values to transaction-key
    ENDDO
    IF no deletion was processed
        Write new-master-record
    ENDIF
    Choose next active-key
ENDDO
Close files
Stop run
```

status from off to on. Any attempt to add a record whose status is already on signifies a duplicate addition. In similar fashion, attempting to change or delete a record whose allocation status is off also signifies an error, as the transaction key is not present in the old master.

Figure 17.11 expands the pseudocode of Figure 17.10 to include RECORD-KEY-ALLOCATED-SWITCH to accommodate this discussion. A record is written to the new master file only when RECORD-KEY-ALLOCATED-SWITCH is set to YES. In other words, deletions are accomplished simply by setting the switch to NO and not writing the record.

You should be convinced of the total generality of Figure 17.11 and, further, that multiple transactions for the same key may be presented in any order. For example, if an addition and correction are input in that order, the record will be added and corrected in the same run. However, if the correction precedes the addition, then the correction will be flagged as a no match, and only the addition will take effect. Two additions for the same key will result in adding the first and flagging the second as a duplicate add. An addition, correction, and deletion may be processed in that order for the same transaction. A deletion followed by an addition may also be processed but will produce an error message, indicating an attempt to delete a record that is not in the old master.

Designing the Hierarchy Chart

Recall that pseudocode and a hierarchy chart depict different things. Pseudocode indicates sequence and decision-making logic, whereas a hierarchy chart depicts function, indicating what has to be done, but not necessarily when. Accordingly, we

Figure 17.11 Expanded Balance Line Algorithm

```
Open files
Read transaction-file, at end move high-values to transaction-key
Read old-master-file, at end move high-values to old-master-key
Choose first active-key
DO WHILE active-key not equal high-values
    IF old-master-key = active-key
        Move 'yes' to record-key-allocated-switch
        Move old-master-record to new-master-record
        Read old-master-file, at end move high-values to old-master-key
    ELSE (active-key is not in old-master-file)
        Move 'no' to record-key-allocated switch
    ENDIF
    DO WHILE transaction-key equal active-key
        DO CASE transaction-code
            CASE addition
                IF record-key-allocated-switch = 'yes'
                    Write 'error - duplicate addition'
                ELSE (active-key is not in old-master-file)
                    Move transaction-record to new-master-record
                    Move 'yes' to record-key-allocated-switch
                ENDIF
            CASE correction
                IF record-key-allocated-switch = 'yes'
                    Process correction
                ELSE (active-key is not in old-master-file)
                    Write 'error - no matching record'
                ENDIF
            CASE deletion
                IF record-key-allocated-switch = 'yes'
                    Move 'no' to record-key-allocated-switch
                ELSE (active-key is not in old-master-file)
                    Write 'error - no matching record'
                ENDIF
        END CASE
        Read transaction-file, at end move high-values to transaction-key
    END DO
    IF record-key-allocated-switch = 'yes'
        write new-master-record
    ENDIF
    Choose next active-key
END DO
Close files
Stop run
```

begin by listing the functional modules necessary to accomplish a sequential update using the balance line algorithm:

Overall Program Function	UPDATE-MASTER-FILE
Functional Modules	READ-TRANSACTION-FILE READ-OLD-MASTER-FILE CHOOSE-ACTIVE-KEY PROCESS-ACTIVE-KEY BUILD-NEW-MASTER WRITE-NEW-MASTER APPLY-TRANSACTIONS-TO-MASTER ADD-NEW-RECORD CORRECT-OLD-RECORD DELETE-OLD-RECORD

The hierarchy chart in Figure 17.12 is developed in top-down fashion, beginning with the overall program function, UPDATE-MASTER-FILE. Development of a hierarchy chart requires explicit specification of the function of each module, which should be apparent from the module name, consisting of a verb, one or two adjectives, and an object. Nevertheless, the module functions are described in depth:

UPDATE-MASTER-FILE — The mainline routine that drives the entire program. It opens the program files, invokes

Figure 17.12 Hierarchy Chart for Sequential Update

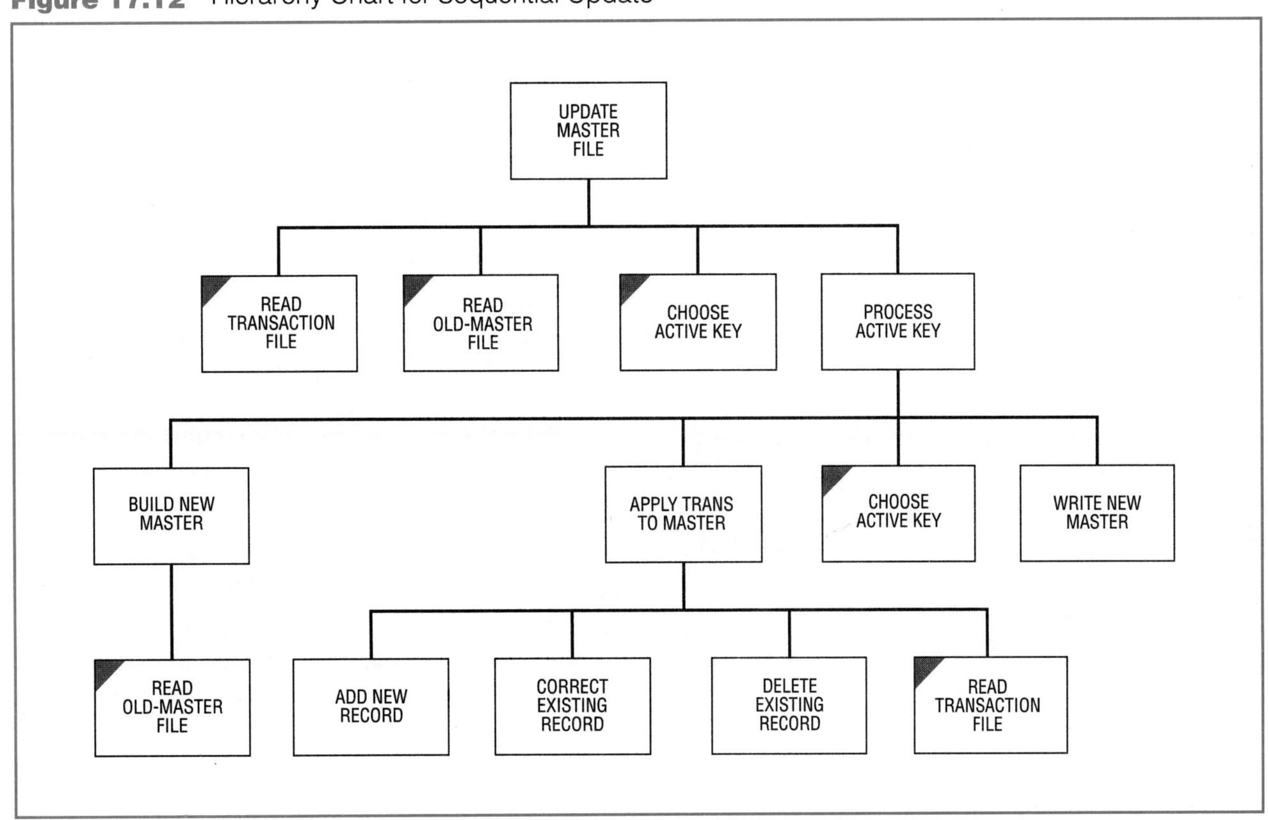

subordinate routines to do an initial read from each input file, and determines the first active key. It invokes PROCESS-ACTIVE-KEY until all files are out of data, closes the files, and terminates the run.

READ-TRANSACTION-FILE	Reads a record from the transaction file and moves HIGH-VALUES to the transaction key when the file is empty. This module is performed from more than one place in the program as indicated by the shading in the upper left-hand corner.
READ-OLD-MASTER-FILE	Reads a record from the old master file and moves HIGH-VALUES to the old master key when the file is empty. This module is performed from more than one place in the program as indicated by the shading in the upper left-hand corner.
CHOOSE-ACTIVE-KEY	Determines the active key for the balance line algorithm from the current values of the old master and transaction records. This module is also performed from more than one place.
PROCESS-ACTIVE-KEY	Performs up to four subordinates according to the value of active key. All four subordinates are invoked when the keys on the old master and transaction files equal the active key, and no deletions were processed.
BUILD-NEW-MASTER	Moves the current old master record to a corresponding new master record. This module is mandated by the nature of a sequential update, which requires that every record in the old master file be copied to the new master file, regardless of whether the record changes.
WRITE-NEW-MASTER	Writes a new master record, and is performed only after all transactions for that record have been processed.
APPLY-TRANS-TO-MASTER	Performs one of three subordinates to add, correct, or delete a record according to the current transaction code. Regardless of the transaction type, the module invokes READ-TRANSACTION-FILE to obtain the next transaction and executes repeatedly as long as the transaction key equals the active key.
ADD-NEW-RECORD	Lowest-level module to add a new record, which will set RECORD-KEY-ALLOCATED-SWITCH to YES.
CORRECT-OLD-RECORD	Lowest-level module to update (correct) the year-to-date sales total in an existing master record.
DELETE-OLD-RECORD	Lowest-level module to delete a record, which will set RECORD-KEY-ALLOCATED-SWITCH to NO.

Top-Down Testing

Top-down testing implies that the highest (most difficult) modules in a hierarchy chart be tested earlier, and more often, than the lower-level (and often trivial) routines. It requires that testing begin as soon as possible, and well before the program is finished. Testing a program before it is completed is accomplished by coding lower-level modules as program stubs, that is, abbreviated versions of completed modules.

The major advantage in this approach is that testing begins sooner in the development cycle. Errors that do exist are found earlier and consequently are easier to correct. Later versions can still contain bugs, but the more difficult problems will already have been resolved in the initial tests.

Figure 17.9 (shown previously) contains sufficient data to adequately test the update program. All transaction types are present with multiple transactions present for the same transaction record (000000000). There is a duplicate addition (400000000) that should be flagged as an error, as well as an attempted correction on a nonexisting social security number (444444444).

It is highly desirable that a person other than the programmer, preferably the user, supply the test data. The latter individual does not know how the program actually works, and thus is in a better position to make up objective data. In addition, the user knows the original specification and is not subject to distortions from the analysis phase. The programmer, on the other hand, is biased, either consciously or subconsciously, and will generate data to accommodate his or her program or interpretation of the specifications. We should also mention that anticipated results are best computed *before* testing begins. Otherwise, it is too easy to assume the program works, because the output "looks right." Indeed, trainees are often so overjoyed merely to get output that they conclude the testing phase upon receiving their first printout.

The Stubs Program

Figure 17.13 contains the stubs program for a sequential update implemented according to the balance line algorithm. It is *complete* in that it contains a paragraph for every module in the hierarchy chart of Figure 17.12, yet *incomplete* because several of the lower-level modules exist only as ***program stubs***, that is, abbreviated paragraphs.

Figure 17.13 uses only two files, the old master and transaction, with record descriptions corresponding to the programming specifications. The new master file is not referenced explicitly in the program; instead, the paragraphs 0060-BUILD-NEW-MASTER and 0080-WRITE-NEW-MASTER contain DISPLAY statements to indicate that they have been executed. Indeed, the program contains many such DISPLAY statements to facilitate testing by indicating program flow.

Consider the test data in Figure 17.9, in conjunction with the program in Figure 17.13 and its associated output (Figure 17.14). The program begins by reading the first record from each file, social security numbers 000000000 and 100000000 for the transaction and old master, respectively. The active key is the smaller of the two, social security number 000000000, and corresponds to the transaction value. The paragraph 0070-APPLY-TRANS-TO-MASTER is entered for the first transaction, after which the lower-level paragraph 0090-ADD-NEW-RECORD is invoked. The second and third transactions also have a social security number of 000000000, so that 0070-APPLY-TRANS-TO-MASTER is executed twice more, each time followed by 0100-CORRECT-EXISTING-RECORD. Finally, when the transaction key no longer

Figure 17.13 Stubs Program

```
IDENTIFICATION DIVISION.
PROGRAM-ID.   SEQSTUB.
AUTHOR.       ROBERT GRAUER.

ENVIRONMENT DIVISION.
INPUT-OUTPUT SECTION.
FILE-CONTROL.
    SELECT TRANSACTION-FILE
        ASSIGN TO UT-S-VALTRANS.
    SELECT OLD-MASTER-FILE
        ASSIGN TO UT-S-OLDMAST.

DATA DIVISION.
FILE SECTION.
FD  TRANSACTION-FILE
    DATA RECORD IS TRANSACTION-RECORD.
01  TRANSACTION-RECORD                       PIC X(37).

FD  OLD-MASTER-FILE
    DATA RECORD IS OLD-MAST-RECORD.
01  OLD-MAST-RECORD                          PIC X(39).

WORKING-STORAGE SECTION.
01  FILLER                                   PIC X(14)
        VALUE 'WS BEGINS HERE'.

01  WS-TRANS-RECORD.
    05  TR-SOC-SEC-NUMBER                    PIC X(9).
    05  TR-NAME.
        10  TR-LAST-NAME                     PIC X(15).
        10  TR-INITIALS                      PIC XX.
    05  TR-LOCATION-CODE                     PIC X(3).
    05  TR-COMMISSION-RATE                   PIC 99.
    05  TR-SALES-AMOUNT                      PIC 9(5).
    05  TR-TRANSACTION-CODE                  PIC X.
        88  ADDITION         VALUE 'A'.
        88  CORRECTION       VALUE 'C'.
        88  DELETION         VALUE 'D'.

01  WS-OLD-MAST-RECORD.
    05  OM-SOC-SEC-NUMBER                    PIC X(9).
    05  OM-NAME.
        10  OM-LAST-NAME                     PIC X(15).
        10  OM-INITIALS                      PIC XX.
    05  OM-LOCATION-CODE                     PIC X(3).
    05  OM-COMMISSION-RATE                   PIC 99.
    05  OM-YEAR-TO-DATE-SALES                PIC 9(8).

01  WS-BALANCE-LINE-SWITCHES.
    05  WS-ACTIVE-KEY                        PIC X(9).
    05  WS-RECORD-KEY-ALLOCATED-SWITCH       PIC X(3).
```

Two input files are required

Three transaction types are permitted

Figure 17.13 *(continued)*

```

PROCEDURE DIVISION.
0010-UPDATE-MASTER-FILE.
    OPEN INPUT TRANSACTION-FILE
               OLD-MASTER-FILE.
    PERFORM 0020-READ-TRANSACTION-FILE.
    PERFORM 0030-READ-OLD-MASTER-FILE.
    PERFORM 0040-CHOOSE-ACTIVE-KEY.
    PERFORM 0050-PROCESS-ACTIVE-KEY
        UNTIL WS-ACTIVE-KEY = HIGH-VALUES.
    CLOSE TRANSACTION-FILE
          OLD-MASTER-FILE.
    STOP RUN.

0020-READ-TRANSACTION-FILE.
    READ TRANSACTION-FILE INTO WS-TRANS-RECORD
        AT END MOVE HIGH-VALUES TO TR-SOC-SEC-NUMBER
    END-READ.

0030-READ-OLD-MASTER-FILE.
    READ OLD-MASTER-FILE INTO WS-OLD-MAST-RECORD
        AT END MOVE HIGH-VALUE TO OM-SOC-SEC-NUMBER
    END-READ.

0040-CHOOSE-ACTIVE-KEY.
    IF TR-SOC-SEC-NUMBER LESS THAN OM-SOC-SEC-NUMBER
        MOVE TR-SOC-SEC-NUMBER TO WS-ACTIVE-KEY
    ELSE
        MOVE OM-SOC-SEC-NUMBER TO WS-ACTIVE-KEY
    END-IF.

0050-PROCESS-ACTIVE-KEY.
    DISPLAY '    '.
    DISPLAY '    '.
    DISPLAY 'RECORDS BEING PROCESSED'.
    DISPLAY '  TRANSACTION SOC SEC #: ' TR-SOC-SEC-NUMBER.
    DISPLAY '  OLD MASTER SOC SEC #:  ' OM-SOC-SEC-NUMBER.
    DISPLAY '  ACTIVE KEY:            ' WS-ACTIVE-KEY.
    DISPLAY '    '.

    IF OM-SOC-SEC-NUMBER = WS-ACTIVE-KEY
        MOVE 'YES' TO WS-RECORD-KEY-ALLOCATED-SWITCH
        PERFORM 0060-BUILD-NEW-MASTER
    ELSE
        MOVE 'NO' TO WS-RECORD-KEY-ALLOCATED-SWITCH
    END-IF.

    PERFORM 0070-APPLY-TRANS-TO-MASTER
        UNTIL WS-ACTIVE-KEY NOT EQUAL TR-SOC-SEC-NUMBER.

    IF WS-RECORD-KEY-ALLOCATED-SWITCH = 'YES'
```

Initial reads

Determines active key

DISPLAY statements facilitate testing

Figure 17.13 *(continued)*

```
            PERFORM 0080-WRITE-NEW-MASTER
        END-IF.

        PERFORM 0040-CHOOSE-ACTIVE-KEY.

    0060-BUILD-NEW-MASTER.
        DISPLAY '0060-BUILD-NEW-MASTER ENTERED'.
        PERFORM 0030-READ-OLD-MASTER-FILE.

    0070-APPLY-TRANS-TO-MASTER.
        DISPLAY '0070-APPLY-TRANS-TO-MASTER ENTERED'
                '    TRANSACTION CODE: '  TR-TRANSACTION-CODE.

        EVALUATE TRUE
            WHEN ADDITION
                PERFORM 0090-ADD-NEW-RECORD
            WHEN CORRECTION
                PERFORM 0100-CORRECT-EXISTING-RECORD
            WHEN DELETION
                PERFORM 0110-DELETE-EXISTING-RECORD
            WHEN OTHER
                DISPLAY 'INVALID TRANSACTION CODE'
        END-EVALUATE.

        PERFORM 0020-READ-TRANSACTION-FILE.

    0080-WRITE-NEW-MASTER.
        DISPLAY '0080-WRITE-NEW-MASTER ENTERED'.

    0090-ADD-NEW-RECORD.
        DISPLAY '0090-ADD-NEW-RECORD ENTERED'.
        IF WS-RECORD-KEY-ALLOCATED-SWITCH = 'YES'
            DISPLAY '  ERROR-DUPLICATE ADDITION: ' TR-SOC-SEC-NUMBER
        ELSE
            MOVE 'YES' TO WS-RECORD-KEY-ALLOCATED-SWITCH
        END-IF.

    0100-CORRECT-EXISTING-RECORD.
        DISPLAY '0100-CORRECT-EXISTING-RECORD ENTERED.'
        IF WS-RECORD-KEY-ALLOCATED-SWITCH = 'YES'
            NEXT SENTENCE
        ELSE
            DISPLAY '  ERROR-NO MATCHING RECORD: ' TR-SOC-SEC-NUMBER
        END-IF.

    0110-DELETE-EXISTING-RECORD.
        DISPLAY '0110-DELETE-EXISTING-RECORD ENTERED'.
        IF WS-RECORD-KEY-ALLOCATED-SWITCH = 'YES'
            MOVE 'NO' TO WS-RECORD-KEY-ALLOCATED-SWITCH
        ELSE
            DISPLAY '  ERROR-NO MATCHING RECORD: ' TR-SOC-SEC-NUMBER
        END-IF.
```

DISPLAY statement indicates paragraph has been called

Determines which lower-level module to execute

Partially coded paragraphs

RECORD-KEY-ALLOCATED-SWITCH controls deletion

Figure 17.14 Truncated Output of Stubs Program

```
RECORDS BEING PROCESSED
  TRANSACTION SOC SEC #: 000000000
  OLD MASTER SOC SEC #:  100000000
  ACTIVE KEY:            000000000

0070-APPLY-TRANS-TO-MASTER ENTERED    TRANSACTION CODE: A
0090-ADD-NEW-RECORD ENTERED
0070-APPLY-TRANS-TO-MASTER ENTERED    TRANSACTION CODE: C
0100-CORRECT-EXISTING-RECORD ENTERED.
0070-APPLY-TRANS-TO-MASTER ENTERED    TRANSACTION CODE: C
0100-CORRECT-EXISTING-RECORD ENTERED.
0080-WRITE-NEW-MASTER ENTERED

RECORDS BEING PROCESSED
  TRANSACTION SOC SEC #: 400000000
  OLD MASTER SOC SEC #:  100000000
  ACTIVE KEY:            100000000

0060-BUILD-NEW-MASTER ENTERED
0080-WRITE-NEW-MASTER ENTERED

RECORDS BEING PROCESSED
  TRANSACTION SOC SEC #: 400000000
  OLD MASTER SOC SEC #:  200000000
  ACTIVE KEY:            200000000

0060-BUILD-NEW-MASTER ENTERED
0080-WRITE-NEW-MASTER ENTERED

RECORDS BEING PROCESSED
  TRANSACTION SOC SEC #: 400000000
  OLD MASTER SOC SEC #:  300000000
  ACTIVE KEY:            300000000

0060-BUILD-NEW-MASTER ENTERED
0080-WRITE-NEW-MASTER ENTERED

RECORDS BEING PROCESSED
  TRANSACTION SOC SEC #: 400000000
  OLD MASTER SOC SEC #:  400000000
  ACTIVE KEY:            400000000

0060-BUILD-NEW-MASTER ENTERED
0070-APPLY-TRANS-TO-MASTER ENTERED    TRANSACTION CODE: A
0090-ADD-NEW-RECORD ENTERED
  ERROR-DUPLICATE ADDITION: 400000000
0080-WRITE-NEW-MASTER ENTERED
    .
        .
            .
RECORDS BEING PROCESSED
  TRANSACTION SOC SEC #: 999999999
  OLD MASTER SOC SEC #:
  ACTIVE KEY:            999999999

0070-APPLY-TRANS-TO-MASTER ENTERED    TRANSACTION CODE: A
0090-ADD-NEW-RECORD ENTERED
0080-WRITE-NEW-MASTER ENTERED
```

equals the active key, that is, when the fourth transaction (Moldof, with social security number 400000000) is read, the paragraph 0080-WRITE-NEW-MASTER is executed to write the new (and corrected) record to the new master file.

The next determination of the active key compares the transaction just read (social security number 400000000) to the current old master social record (social security number 100000000), producing an active key of 100000000. The program decides there are no transactions for this old master record and copies it immediately to the new master file, as implied by the paragraphs 0060-BUILD-NEW-MASTER and 0080-WRITE-NEW-MASTER. The next two determinations of the active key (for old master records 200000000 and 300000000) produce a similar result. The fifth determination of the active key finds the same social security number in both files in conjunction with an attempted addition in the transaction file, producing an error message for a duplicate addition.

By now you should be gaining confidence that the program is working correctly, because the paragraphs are executing in proper sequence for the test data. We can say therefore that the initial testing has concluded successfully and move on to developing the completed program.

The Completed Program

Once the stubs program has been tested and debugged, it is relatively easy to complete the program because the most difficult portion has already been written. We know that the interaction between modules works correctly; that the program will correctly read from the old master, transaction file, or both; that it will apply multiple transactions to the same master record; and that it will properly perform the appropriate lower-level module to add, correct, or delete a record.

Figure 17.15 contains the expanded update program, which defines an additional FD for the NEW-MASTER-FILE as well as completed paragraphs for the addition and correction routines. The DISPLAY statements associated with the testing procedure have also been deleted.

The files associated with the completed program are shown in Figure 17.16. Figures 17.16a and 17.16b repeat the original test data (for convenience), whereas Figures 17.16c and 17.16d contain the actual output. You should take a moment to verify the results to satisfy yourself that the program is working correctly. Observe in particular how multiple transactions were applied to a single old record (Borow), how Borow and Gillenson were successfully added to the new master, and how Milgrom was deleted. The two error messages correctly reflect both errors, an attempted duplicate addition and a nonmatching social security number.

Figure 17.15 Completed Sequential Update

```
IDENTIFICATION DIVISION.
PROGRAM-ID.   SEQUPDT.
AUTHOR.       ROBERT GRAUER.

ENVIRONMENT DIVISION.
INPUT-OUTPUT SECTION.
FILE-CONTROL.
    SELECT TRANSACTION-FILE
        ASSIGN TO UT-S-VALTRANS.
    SELECT OLD-MASTER-FILE
        ASSIGN TO UT-S-OLDMAST.
```

Figure 17.15 *(continued)*

```
         SELECT NEW-MASTER-FILE
             ASSIGN TO UT-S-NEWMAST.

     DATA DIVISION.
     FILE SECTION.
     FD  TRANSACTION-FILE
         DATA RECORD IS TRANSACTION-RECORD.
     01  TRANSACTION-RECORD                     PIC X(37).

     FD  OLD-MASTER-FILE
         DATA RECORD IS OLD-MAST-RECORD.
     01  OLD-MAST-RECORD                        PIC X(39).

     FD  NEW-MASTER-FILE
         DATA RECORD IS NEW-MAST-RECORD.
     01  NEW-MAST-RECORD                        PIC X(39).

     WORKING-STORAGE SECTION.
     01  FILLER                                 PIC X(14)
             VALUE 'WS BEGINS HERE'.

     01  WS-TRANS-RECORD.
         05  TR-SOC-SEC-NUMBER                  PIC X(9).
         05  TR-NAME.
             10  TR-LAST-NAME                   PIC X(15).
             10  TR-INITIALS                    PIC XX.
         05  TR-LOCATION-CODE                   PIC X(3).
         05  TR-COMMISSION-RATE                 PIC 99.
         05  TR-SALES-AMOUNT                    PIC 9(5).
         05  TR-TRANSACTION-CODE                PIC X.
             88  ADDITION        VALUE 'A'.
             88  CORRECTION      VALUE 'C'.
             88  DELETION        VALUE 'D'.

     01  WS-OLD-MAST-RECORD.
         05  OM-SOC-SEC-NUMBER                  PIC X(9).
         05  OM-NAME.
             10  OM-LAST-NAME                   PIC X(15).
             10  OM-INITIALS                    PIC XX.
         05  OM-LOCATION-CODE                   PIC X(3).
         05  OM-COMMISSION-RATE                 PIC 99.
         05  OM-YEAR-TO-DATE-SALES              PIC 9(8).

     01  WS-NEW-MAST-RECORD.
         05  NM-SOC-SEC-NUMBER                  PIC X(9).
         05  NM-NAME.
             10  NM-LAST-NAME                   PIC X(15).
             10  NM-INITIALS                    PIC XX.
         05  NM-LOCATION-CODE                   PIC X(3).
         05  NM-COMMISSION-RATE                 PIC 99.
```

Output file has been added (SELECT NEW-MASTER-FILE ASSIGN TO UT-S-NEWMAST)

Three transaction types (88 ADDITION, CORRECTION, DELETION)

Record layouts are identical (WS-OLD-MAST-RECORD and WS-NEW-MAST-RECORD)

Figure 17.15 *(continued)*

```
           05  NM-YEAR-TO-DATE-SALES             PIC 9(8).

       01  WS-BALANCE-LINE-SWITCHES.
           05  WS-ACTIVE-KEY                     PIC X(9).
           05  WS-RECORD-KEY-ALLOCATED-SWITCH    PIC X(3).

       PROCEDURE DIVISION.
       0010-UPDATE-MASTER-FILE.
           OPEN INPUT TRANSACTION-FILE
                      OLD-MASTER-FILE
               OUTPUT NEW-MASTER-FILE.
           PERFORM 0020-READ-TRANSACTION-FILE.
           PERFORM 0030-READ-OLD-MASTER-FILE.
           PERFORM 0040-CHOOSE-ACTIVE-KEY.
           PERFORM 0050-PROCESS-ACTIVE-KEY
               UNTIL WS-ACTIVE-KEY = HIGH-VALUES.
           CLOSE TRANSACTION-FILE
                 OLD-MASTER-FILE
                 NEW-MASTER-FILE.
           STOP RUN.

       0020-READ-TRANSACTION-FILE.
           READ TRANSACTION-FILE INTO WS-TRANS-RECORD
               AT END MOVE HIGH-VALUES TO TR-SOC-SEC-NUMBER
           END-READ.

       0030-READ-OLD-MASTER-FILE.
           READ OLD-MASTER-FILE INTO WS-OLD-MAST-RECORD
               AT END MOVE HIGH-VALUE TO OM-SOC-SEC-NUMBER
           END-READ.

       0040-CHOOSE-ACTIVE-KEY.
           IF TR-SOC-SEC-NUMBER LESS THAN OM-SOC-SEC-NUMBER
               MOVE TR-SOC-SEC-NUMBER TO WS-ACTIVE-KEY
           ELSE
               MOVE OM-SOC-SEC-NUMBER TO WS-ACTIVE-KEY
           END-IF.

       0050-PROCESS-ACTIVE-KEY.
           IF OM-SOC-SEC-NUMBER = WS-ACTIVE-KEY
               MOVE 'YES' TO WS-RECORD-KEY-ALLOCATED-SWITCH
               PERFORM 0060-BUILD-NEW-MASTER
           ELSE
               MOVE 'NO' TO WS-RECORD-KEY-ALLOCATED-SWITCH
           END-IF.

           PERFORM 0070-APPLY-TRANS-TO-MASTER
               UNTIL WS-ACTIVE-KEY NOT EQUAL TR-SOC-SEC-NUMBER.

           IF WS-RECORD-KEY-ALLOCATED-SWITCH = 'YES'
               PERFORM 0080-WRITE-NEW-MASTER
```

Processing terminates when the active key is HIGH-VALUES: i.e., when both files are empty (annotation to lines 76–77)

Applies multiple transactions to a single master record (annotation to lines 108–109)

Figure 17.15 *(continued)*

```
    END-IF.

    PERFORM 0040-CHOOSE-ACTIVE-KEY.

0060-BUILD-NEW-MASTER.
    MOVE WS-OLD-MAST-RECORD TO WS-NEW-MAST-RECORD.
    PERFORM 0030-READ-OLD-MASTER-FILE.

0070-APPLY-TRANS-TO-MASTER.
    EVALUATE TRUE
        WHEN ADDITION
            PERFORM 0090-ADD-NEW-RECORD
        WHEN CORRECTION
            PERFORM 0100-CORRECT-EXISTING-RECORD
        WHEN DELETION
            PERFORM 0110-DELETE-EXISTING-RECORD
        WHEN OTHER
            DISPLAY 'INVALID TRANSACTION CODE'
    END-EVALUATE.

    PERFORM 0020-READ-TRANSACTION-FILE.

0080-WRITE-NEW-MASTER.
    WRITE NEW-MAST-RECORD FROM WS-NEW-MAST-RECORD.

0090-ADD-NEW-RECORD.
    IF WS-RECORD-KEY-ALLOCATED-SWITCH = 'YES'
        DISPLAY '  ERROR-DUPLICATE ADDITION: ' TR-SOC-SEC-NUMBER
    ELSE
        MOVE 'YES' TO WS-RECORD-KEY-ALLOCATED-SWITCH
        MOVE SPACES TO WS-NEW-MAST-RECORD
        MOVE TR-SOC-SEC-NUMBER TO NM-SOC-SEC-NUMBER
        MOVE TR-NAME TO NM-NAME
        MOVE TR-LOCATION-CODE TO NM-LOCATION-CODE
        MOVE TR-COMMISSION-RATE TO NM-COMMISSION-RATE
        MOVE ZEROS TO NM-YEAR-TO-DATE-SALES
    END-IF.

0100-CORRECT-EXISTING-RECORD.
    IF WS-RECORD-KEY-ALLOCATED-SWITCH = 'YES'
        ADD TR-SALES-AMOUNT TO NM-YEAR-TO-DATE-SALES
    ELSE
        DISPLAY '  ERROR-NO MATCHING RECORD: ' TR-SOC-SEC-NUMBER
    END-IF.

0110-DELETE-EXISTING-RECORD.
    IF WS-RECORD-KEY-ALLOCATED-SWITCH = 'YES'
        MOVE 'NO' TO WS-RECORD-KEY-ALLOCATED-SWITCH
    ELSE
        DISPLAY '  ERROR-NO MATCHING RECORD: ' TR-SOC-SEC-NUMBER
    END-IF.
```

Expanded from program stub (annotation to 0090-ADD-NEW-RECORD)

Precludes writing a new master record (annotation to lines IF WS-RECORD-KEY-ALLOCATED-SWITCH = 'YES' / MOVE 'NO' TO WS-RECORD-KEY-ALLOCATED-SWITCH)

Figure 17.16 Output of the Sequential Update

```
100000000GRABER        P ATL1500000000
200000000RUBIN         MABOS0800020000
300000000ANDERSON      IRBOS1000113000
400000000MOLDOF        BLATL1500000000
500000000GLASSMAN      JSNYC1000045000
600000000GRAUER        RTNYC0800087500
700000000MILGROM       A SF 0900120000
800000000VAZQUEZ       C ATL1200060000
900000000CLARK         E NYC0700002500
```

(a) Old Master

```
000000000BOROW         JSATL07      A
000000000BOROW         JS      10000C
000000000BOROW         JS      20000C
400000000MOLDOF        BLATL15      A
444444444RICHARDS      IM      05000C
700000000MILGROM       A            D
800000000VAZQUEZ       C       55000C
999999999GILLENSON     MANYC10      A
```

(b) Valid Transaction File

```
000000000BOROW         JSATL0700030000
100000000GRABER        P ATL1500000000
200000000RUBIN         MABOS0800020000
300000000ANDERSON      IRBOS1000113000
400000000MOLDOF        BLATL1500000000
500000000GLASSMAN      JSNYC1000045000
600000000GRAUER        RTNYC0800087500
800000000VAZQUEZ       C ATL1200115000
900000000CLARK         E NYC0700002500
999999999GILLENSON     MANYC1000000000
```

(c) New Master File

```
ERROR-DUPLICATE ADDITION: 400000000
ERROR-NO MATCHING RECORD: 444444444
```

(d) Error Messages

SUMMARY

Points to Remember

- File maintenance is a necessity of every system and enables three types of transactions. New records may be added, while existing records may be changed or deleted.
- A sequential update copies every record from the old master file to the new master, regardless of whether it changes. By contrast, a nonsequential update uses a single file as both the old and new master. Sequential processing is best when the master file is active and has substantial activity; nonsequential processing is more efficient for inactive files with less activity.
- Data validation is an essential component of file maintenance. The transaction file is typically run through a stand-alone edit prior to the maintenance program to check for valid codes, complete records, and so on. The update program must still check for duplicate additions and/or no matches (that is, transactions entered as corrections or deletions for records that are not present in the master file).
- The balance line algorithm is a general approach to sequential file maintenance. The algorithm allows multiple transactions from one or more transaction files, to reference a single master record.
- Top-down testing was demonstrated through use of a stub program. Early testing ensures that modules are performed in proper sequence and facilitates the correction of any errors detected.

Key Words and Concepts

Active key
Addition
Allocation status
Backup
Balance line algorithm
Correction
Data validation
Defensive programming
Deletion
Duplicate addition
End-of-file condition
Error message table
Grandfather-father-son
Hierarchy chart
New master file
No match
Nonsequential update
Old master file
Periodic file maintenance
Program stub
Record-key allocated switch
Sequential update
Stand-alone edit program
Stub program
Test data
Top-down testing and implementation
Transaction file

COBOL Element

HIGH-VALUES

FILL-IN

1. In a sequential update, ______________ record in the old master (except those slated for deletion) is copied (rewritten) to the new master, regardless of whether it changes.
2. Incoming transactions to a sequential update have generally been validated in a ______________ ______________ program.
3. The balance line algorithm (does/does not) require every record in the old master file to have a unique key.
4. The balance line algorithm (does/does not) require every record in the transaction file to have a unique key.
5. In general, the three transaction types that are input to a sequential update are ______________, ______________ and ______________.
6. The RECORD-KEY-ALLOCATED-SWITCH is used in checking for two types of errors: ______________ additions, and/or ______________.
7. An incomplete addition (can/can not) be detected in a stand-alone edit program.
8. An invalid transaction code (can/can not) be detected in a stand-alone edit program.
9. An incorrectly entered social security number on an otherwise valid transaction (can/can not) be detected in a stand-alone edit program.
10. Top-down testing requires that the ______________ levels in a hierarchy chart be tested ______________ and more often than the lower-level routines.
11. In order to implement top-down testing, a ______________ program is developed, which contains several one-line paragraphs consisting of ______________ statements.
12. The grandfather-father-son backup scheme implies that at least ______________ generations of files are kept.
13. ______________ ______________ is a figurative literal used to force the end-of-file condition.

TRUE/FALSE

1. The balance line algorithm requires a unique key for every record in the old master file.
2. Transactions to the balance line algorithm must be presented in the following order: additions, changes, deletions.
3. The balance line algorithm permits multiple transactions for the same master record and can be generalized to any number of transaction files.
4. A program must be completely coded before any testing can begin.
5. The high-level modules in a hierarchy chart should be tested first.
6. One can logically assume that input to a maintenance program will be valid.

7. One need not check for duplicate additions if the transaction file has been run through a stand-alone edit program.
8. A module in a hierarchy chart can be performed from more than one place.
9. Pseudocode and hierarchy charts depict the same thing.
10. A program stub may consist of a one-line DISPLAY paragraph.
11. Test data are best designed by the programmer writing the program.
12. Top-down testing can begin before a program is completely finished.
13. The balance line algorithm is restricted to a single transaction file.
14. A hierarchy chart contains decision-making logic.

PROBLEMS

1. The transaction file in Figure 17.9b has both name and initials entered on correction transactions in addition to the social security number. Is this necessary according to the specifications and subsequent COBOL implementation (Figure 17.15)? Describe both an advantage and a disadvantage of entering the name and initials.
2. The specifications of the update program do not discuss how to change (i.e., correct) the social security number of an existing record. With respect to Figure 17.9a, for example, how could the social security number of Sugrue, who already exists in the old master file, be changed to 100000001? Discuss two different approaches, with an advantage and a disadvantage for each.
3. What problems, if any, do you see with each of the following? (Assume no data validation has been done.)

   a.
   ```
   IF SEX = 'M'
       ADD 1 TO NUMBER-OF-MEN
   ELSE
       ADD 1 TO NUMBER-OF-WOMEN
   END-IF.
   ```

   b.
   ```
   SEARCH LOCATION-TABLE
       WHEN INCOMING-LOCATION-CODE = LOCATION (LOC-INDEX)
           MOVE EXPANDED-LOCATION (LOC-INDEX) TO PRINT-LOCATION
   END-SEARCH.
   ```

Indexed Files

CHAPTER OUTLINE

OBJECTIVES

After reading this chapter you will be able to:

- Describe how an index file enables both sequential and/or nonsequential retrieval of individual records.
- Define the specific terms associated with IBM's VSAM implementation of indexed files.
- Discuss the clauses in the SELECT statement for an indexed file; indicate which clauses are optional and which are required.
- Define file status bytes; state how they may be used to verify the success of an I/O operation.
- Differentiate between the READ statements for sequential and nonsequential access of an indexed file.
- Differentiate between the WRITE, REWRITE, and DELETE statements as they apply to file maintenance of an indexed file.
- Describe the syntax of the START statement and give a reason for its use.
- Distinguish between the primary and alternate keys of an indexed file, and the requirements for each.

OVERVIEW

This chapter covers all major aspects of indexed files, a type of file organization that permits both sequential and nonsequential access to individual records. It begins with a general discussion of how indexed files work, with particular reference to IBM's VSAM implementation. Different vendors use different terminology, but the underlying concepts are the same, namely, a series of indexes that access individual records on a sequential or random basis. More importantly, the COBOL syntax is identical for all vendors who adhere to the ANS 85 standard.

The chapter includes three programs that illustrate all of the COBOL elements associated with this type of file organization. The first shows how to create an indexed file, the second continues with the file maintenance example of the previous chapter, and the last illustrates how individual records may be accessed by multiple keys—for example, name and social security number.

System Concepts

Although different vendors have different physical implementations of indexed files, and consequently different terminology, the principles are the same; namely, a series of ***indexes*** that allow individual records to be accessed either sequentially or nonsequentially. This section provides an intuitive discussion of how an indexed file actually works.

In reality, the physical implementation of an indexed file is of little or no concern to the programmer. The operating system establishes and maintains the indexes, and the programmer is concerned primarily with accessing the file through the appropriate COBOL elements. Nevertheless, a conceptual understanding is of benefit in developing a more competent and better-rounded individual. Accordingly, we consider IBM's VSAM implementation.

A VSAM file or data set is divided into ***control areas*** and ***control intervals.*** A control interval is a continuous area of auxiliary storage. A control area contains one or more control intervals. A control interval is independent of the physical device on which it resides; that is, a control interval that takes exactly one track of a given direct access device might require more or less than one track if the file were moved to another type of device).

A VSAM file is defined with an index so that individual records may be located on a random basis, with entries in the index known as index records. The lowest-level index is called the ***sequence set.*** Records in all higher levels are collectively called the ***index set***.

An entry in a sequence set contains the highest key in a control interval and a vertical pointer to that interval. An entry in an index set contains the highest key in the index record at the next lower level and a vertical pointer to the sequence set. These concepts are made clearer by examination of Figure 18.1.

Figure 18.1 shows 28 records hypothetically distributed in a VSAM data set. The entire file consists of three control areas; each area in turn contains three control intervals. The shaded areas shown at the end of each control interval contain information required by VSAM. The index set has only one level of indexing. There are three entries in the index set, one for each control area. Each entry in the index

Figure 18.1 Initial VSAM Data Set

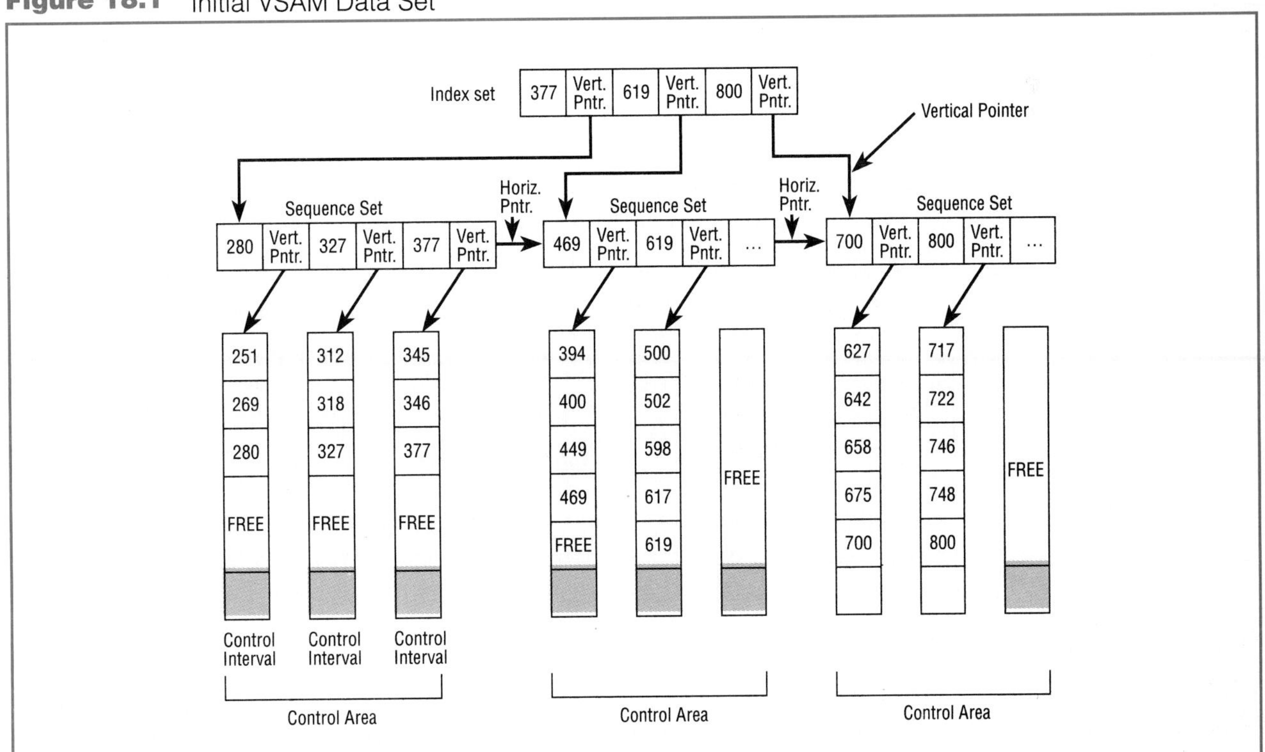

set contains the highest key in the corresponding control area; thus 377, 619, and 800 are the highest keys in the first, second, and third control areas, respectively. Each control area has its own sequence set. The entries in the first sequence set show the highest keys of the control intervals in the first control area to be 280, 327, and 377, respectively. Note that the highest entry in the third control interval, 377, corresponds to the highest entry in the first control area of the index set.

Figure 18.1 illustrates two kinds of pointers, vertical and horizontal. Vertical pointers are used for direct access to an individual record. For example, assume that the record with a key of 449 is to be retrieved. VSAM begins at the highest level of index (that is, at the index set). It concludes that record key 449, *if* it is present, is in the second control area (377 is the highest key in the first area, whereas 619 is the highest key in the second control area). VSAM follows the vertical pointer to the sequence set for the second control area and draws its final conclusion: record key 449, *if* it exists, will be in the first control interval of the second control area.

Horizontal pointers are used for sequential access only. In this instance, VSAM begins at the first sequence set and uses the horizontal pointer to get from that sequence set record to the one containing the next highest key. Put another way, the vertical pointer in a sequence set points to data; the horizontal pointer indicates the sequence set containing the next highest record.

Figure 18.1 contains several allocations of ***free space***, which are distributed in one of two ways: as free space within a control interval or as a free control interval within a control area. In other words, as VSAM loads a file, empty space is deliberately left throughout the file. This is done to facilitate subsequent insertion of new records.

Figure 18.2 shows the changes brought about by the addition of two new records, with keys of 410 and 730, to the file of Figure 18.1. Addition of the first record, key 410, poses no problem, as free space is available in the control interval

Figure 18.2 Control Interval Split

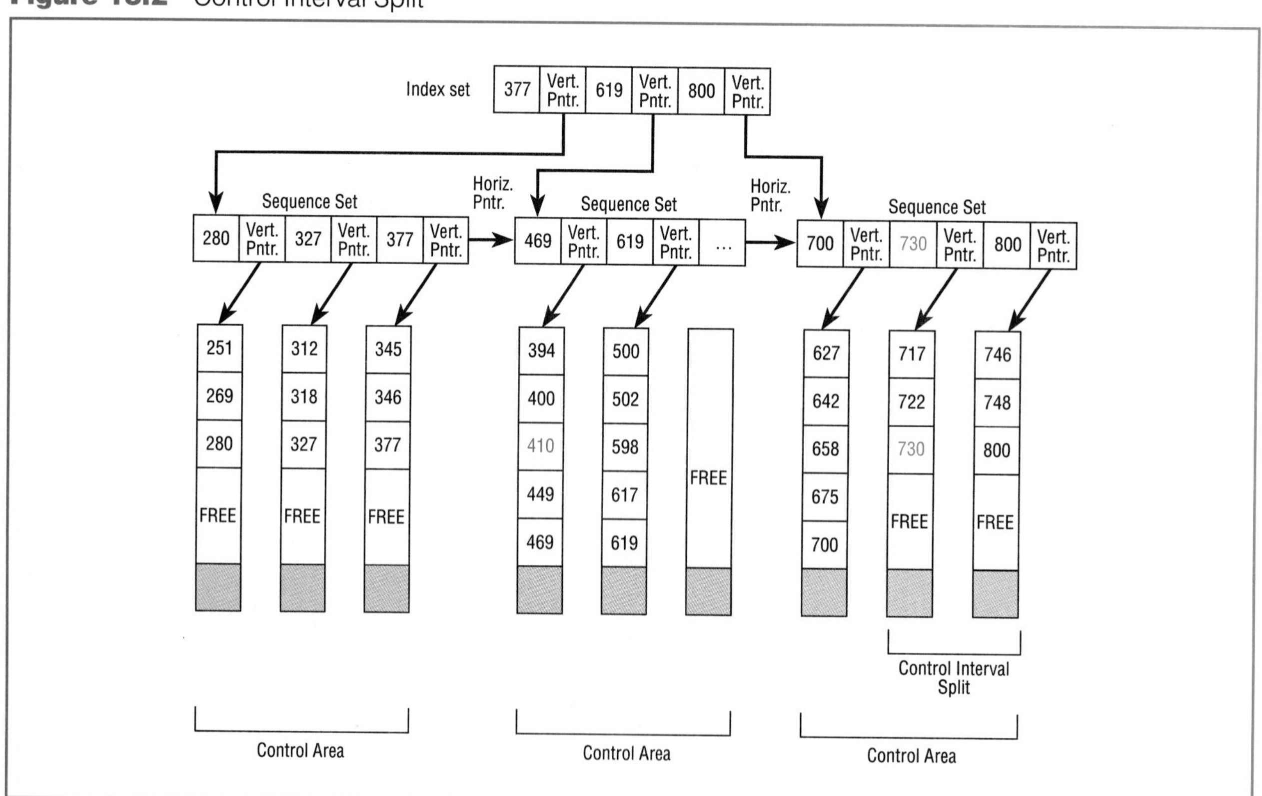

where the record belongs. Record 410 is inserted into its proper place and the other records in that control interval are moved down.

The addition of record key 730 requires different action. The control interval that should contain this record is full in Figure 18.1. Consequently VSAM causes a ***control interval split***, in which some of the records in the previously filled control interval are moved to an empty control interval in the same control area. Entries in the sequence set for the third control area will change, as shown in Figure 18.2. This makes considerable sense when we realize that each record in a sequence set contains the key of the highest record in the corresponding control interval. Thus the records in the sequence set must reflect the control interval split. Note that after a control interval split, subsequent additions are facilitated, as free space is again readily available.

Figure 18.3 shows the results of including three additional records, with keys of 316, 618, and 680. Record 316 is inserted into free space in the second control interval of the first control area, with the other records initially in this interval shifted down. Record 618 causes a control interval split in the second control area.

Record 680 also requires a control interval split except that there are no longer any free control intervals in the third control area. Accordingly, a ***control area split*** is initiated, in which some of the records in the old control area are moved into a new control area at the end of the data set. Both the old and the new control areas will have free control intervals as a result of the split. In addition, the index set has a fourth entry, indicating the presence of a new control area. The sequence set is also expanded to accommodate the fourth control area.

Figure 18.3 Control Area Split

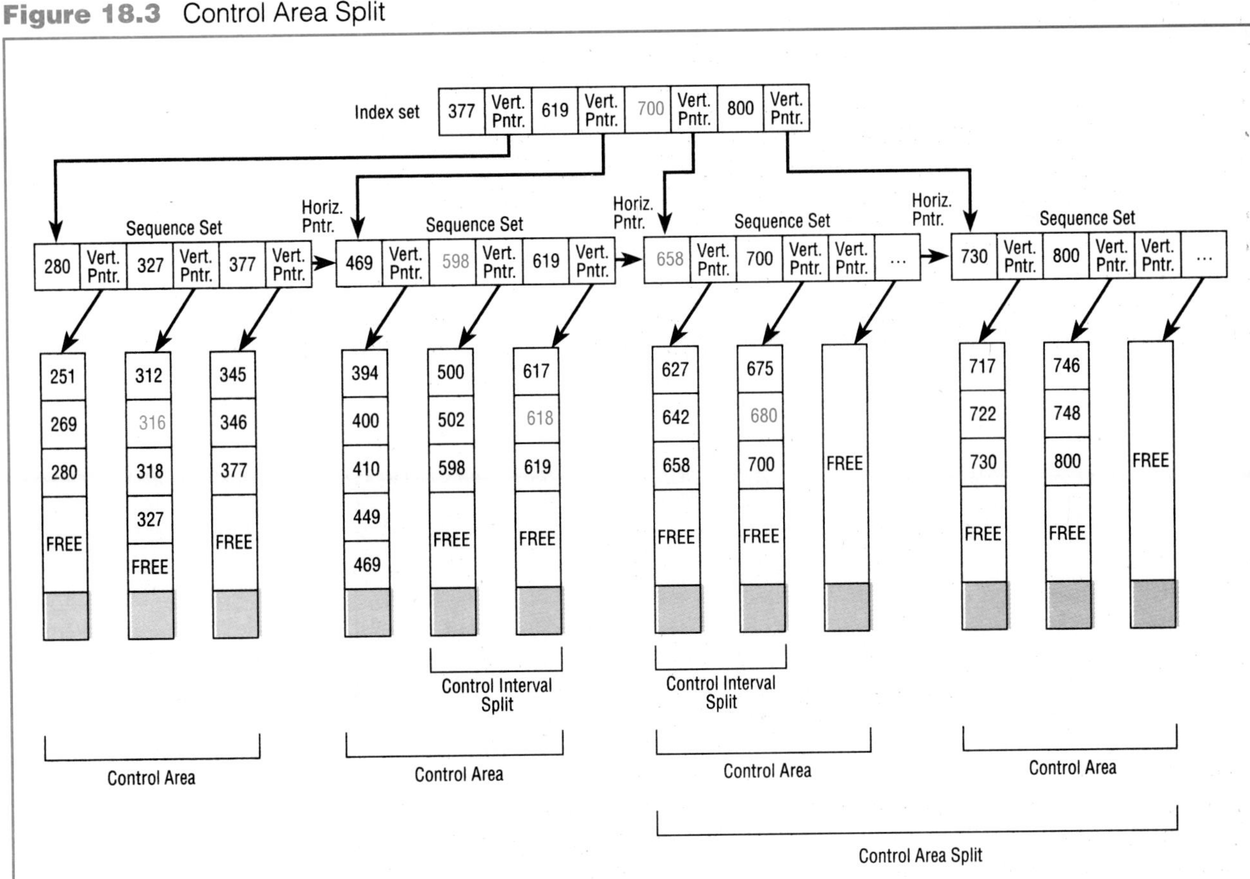

COBOL Implementation

The COBOL implementation of an indexed file centers on the SELECT statement in the Environment Division. Consider:

```
SELECT file-name

    ASSIGN TO {implementor-name-1}
              {literal-1         } . . .

    [RESERVE integer-1 [AREA ]]
                       [AREAS]

    [ORGANIZATION IS] INDEXED

    [                 {SEQUENTIAL}]
    [ACCESS MODE IS   {RANDOM    }]
    [                 {DYNAMIC   }]

    RECORD KEY IS data-name-1

    [ALTERNATE RECORD KEY IS data-name-2 [WITH DUPLICATES]] . . .

    [FILE STATUS IS data-name-3]
```

Three clauses are required: ASSIGN, ORGANIZATION IS INDEXED, and RECORD KEY. The function of the **ASSIGN** clause is the same as with a sequential file—to tie a programmer-chosen file name to a system name. The **ORGANIZATION IS INDEXED** clause indicates an indexed file and needs no further explanation.

The **RECORD KEY** clause references a field defined in the FD for the indexed record whose value must be unique for each record in the file. The value of the record key is used by the operating system to establish the necessary indexes for the file, which in turn enables the random retrieval of individual records.

The remaining entries—RESERVE integer AREAS, ACCESS MODE, ALTERNATE RECORD KEY, and FILE STATUS—are optional. The **RESERVE integer AREAS** clause functions identically as with a sequential file, to increase processing efficiency by allocating alternate I/O areas (or buffers) for the file. If the clause is omitted, the number of alternate areas defaults to the vendor's implementation, which is adequate in most instances. Specification of RESERVE ZERO AREAS will slow processing but will save an amount of storage equal to the buffer size. This is generally done only on smaller systems when the amount of main memory is limited.

The meaning of **ACCESS MODE** is apparent when either sequential or random (nonsequential) access is specified. ACCESS IS DYNAMIC allows a file to be read both sequentially and nonsequentially in the same program and is illustrated in Figure 18.12 later in the chapter.

ALTERNATE RECORD KEY provides a second path for random access. Unlike the record key, which must be unique for every record, the alternate key may contain duplicate values. This capability is extremely powerful and gives COBOL some limited facility for data base management. You could, for example, specify an account number as the record key and a person's name as the alternate key. Realize, however, that while the alternate key is powerful, it is expensive in terms of overhead, in that a second set of indexes must be maintained by the operating system and thus, the feature should not be used indiscriminately. The ALTERNATE RECORD KEY clause is illustrated in Figure 18.12 at the end of the chapter.

The **FILE STATUS** clause is available for any type of file organization and allows the programmer to distinguish between the many different types of I/O error conditions. The concept was first introduced in Chapter 6 in connection with debugging (see page 158). The operating system automatically returns a two-position field known as the ***I/O status*** (or file status bytes) to the data name designated in the FILE STATUS clause. The value of the file status bytes may be interrogated by the programmer, who is thus able to more closely monitor the results of any I/O operation.

Table 18.1 lists the various file status codes and their meaning. The use of file status codes is illustrated in the ensuing program to create an indexed file.

Table 18.1 File Status Codes

Code	Meaning
00	A successful input/output operation is performed with no further information available.
04	A READ is successful, but the length of the record being processed does not conform to the fixed file attributes for that file.
05	An OPEN is successful, but the referenced optional file is not present at open time.
07	An input/output statement is successful; however, for a CLOSE with NO REWIND, REEL/UNIT, or FOR REMOVAL or for an OPEN with NO REWIND the referenced file is on a nonreel/unit medium.
10	A sequential READ is attempted and no next logical record exists because (1) the end of file has been reached; or (2) an optional input file is not present.
14	A sequential READ is attempted and the number of significant digits in the record number is larger than the size of the key data item described for the file.
15	A sequential READ statement is attempted for the first time on an optional file that is not present.
21	A sequence error exists for a sequentially accessed indexed file.
22	An attempt is made to write or rewrite a record that would create a duplicate prime record key or duplicate alternate record key without the DUPLICATES phrase.
23	An attempt is made to randomly access a record that does not exist in the file, or a START or random READ is attempted on an optional input file that is not present.
24	An attempt is made to write beyond the externally defined boundaries.
25	A START statement or a random READ statement has been attempted on an optional file that is not present.
30	A permanent error exists and no further information is available concerning the input/output operation.
34	A permanent error exists because of a boundary violation; an attempt is made to write beyond the externally defined boundaries.
35	A permanent error exists because an OPEN with the INPUT, I/O, or EXTEND phrase is attempted on a nonoptional file that is not present.
37	A permanent error exists because an OPEN is attempted on a file and that file will not support the open mode specified: (1) EXTEND or OUTPUT phrase specified but not supported by the file; (2) I/O phrase is specified, but input and output operations are not supported by the file; or (3) INPUT phrase is specified, but the file will not support READ operations.
38	A permanent error exists because an OPEN is attempted on a file previously closed with a lock.
39	The OPEN is unsuccessful because a conflict has been detected between the fixed file attributes and the ones specified for that file in the program.
41	An OPEN statement is attempted for a file in the open mode.
42	A CLOSE statement is attempted for a file not in the open mode.
43	In the sequential access mode, the last input/output statement executed for the file prior to the execution of a DELETE or REWRITE statement was not a successfully executed READ statement.
44	A boundary violation exists because of an attempt to: (1) write or rewrite a record that is larger than the largest or smaller than the smallest record allowed by the RECORD IS VARYING clause of the associated file-name, or (2) rewrite a record and the record is not the same size as the record being replaced.
46	A sequential READ is attempted on a file open in the input or I/O mode and no valid next record has been established because the preceding: (1) START was unsuccessful, (2) READ was unsuccessful but did not cause an at-end condition, or (3) READ caused an at-end condition.
47	The execution of a READ or START is attempted on a file not open in the input or I/O mode.
48	The execution of a WRITE is attempted on a file not open in the I/O, output, or extend mode.
49	The execution of a DELETE or REWRITE statement is attempted on a file not open in the I/O mode.

Creating an Indexed File

Our first program creates an indexed file from sequential data, and in so doing, illustrates both the SELECT statement in the Environment Division and the use of the FILE STATUS bytes in the Procedure Division. It is important to realize that unlike sequential files, which can be created (or displayed) with an ordinary text editor or word processor, indexed files require a special procedure to create the associated indexes, and hence the need for this program. The COBOL program is not difficult and serves as a good introduction to indexed files. Specifications follow in the usual format.

PROGRAMMING SPECIFICATIONS

Program Name: Creating an Indexed File

Narrative: This program copies the data from an incoming sequential file to an output indexed file. The logic is trivial in nature as the program is intended primarily to illustrate the SELECT statement for indexed files and the use of FILE STATUS bytes.

Input File(s): SEQUENTIAL-FILE

Input Record Layout:

```
01  SEQUENTIAL-RECORD.
    05  SEQ-SOC-SEC-NUMBER                  PIC X(9).
    05  SEQ-REST-OF-RECORD                  PIC X(30).
```

Output File: INDEXED-FILE

Output Record Layout:

```
01  INDEXED-RECORD.
    05  IND-SOC-SEC-NUMBER                  PIC X(9).
    05  IND-REST-OF-RECORD                  PIC X(30).
```

Test Data:

```
100000000GRABER          P ATL1500000000
200000000RUBIN           MABOS0800020000
300000000ANDERSON        IRBOS1000113000
222222222PANZER          S NYC0600000000
400000000MOLDOF          BLATL1500000000
500000000GLASSMAN        JSNYC1000045000
600000000GRAUER          RTNYC0800087500
700000000MILGROM         A SF 0900120000
800000000VAZQUEZ         C ATL1200060000
900000000CLARK           E NYC0700002500
```

Processing Requirements:

1. Copy the records in an incoming sequential file to an equivalent indexed file. The record layouts in both files are the same, with the first nine positions serving as the record key.
2. Display the FILE STATUS bytes after every I/O operation associated with the indexed file (OPEN, CLOSE, and WRITE).
3. Verify that the newly created indexed file has its records in sequence, and further, that every record contains a unique value for the record key. Note, for example, that the record for Panzer in the test data is out of sequence and should be flagged accordingly.

Pseudocode

The logic for this program is simple indeed as indicated in the programming specifications. In essence all we do is read a record from the sequential file, write it to the indexed file, and repeat the loop until the sequential file is out of data. We do not have to concern ourselves with building the indexes per se, as this is done automatically through the appropriate COBOL statements. The logic for the program is depicted in the pseudocode of Figure 18.4.

Figure 18.4 Pseudocode for Creating Indexed File

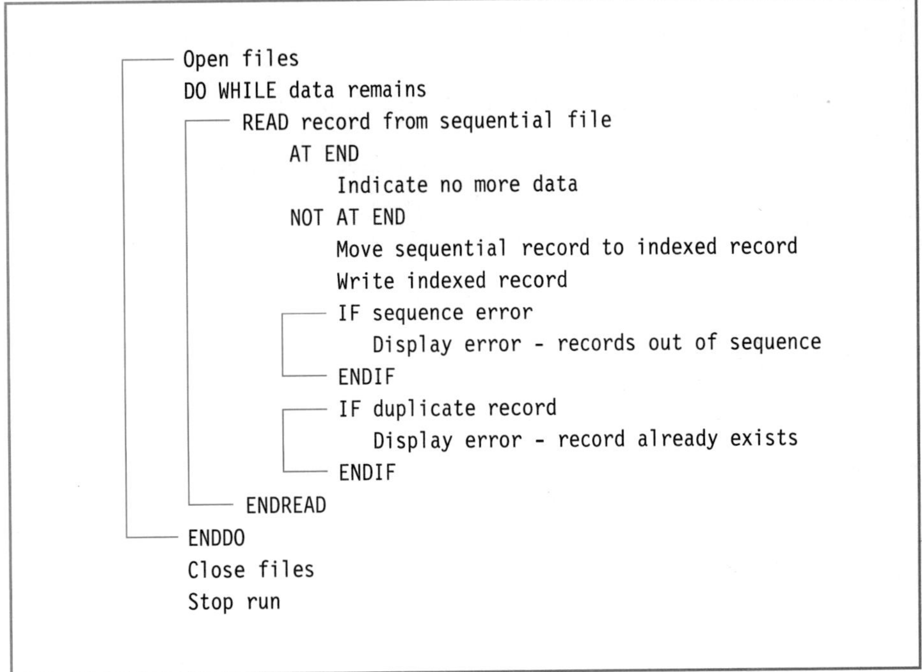

```
Open files
DO WHILE data remains
    READ record from sequential file
        AT END
            Indicate no more data
        NOT AT END
            Move sequential record to indexed record
            Write indexed record
            IF sequence error
                Display error - records out of sequence
            ENDIF
            IF duplicate record
                Display error - record already exists
            ENDIF
    ENDREAD
ENDDO
Close files
Stop run
```

The Completed Program

Figure 18.5 displays the completed program and contains little that is new in the way of COBOL other than the SELECT statement of lines 10 through 15. As indicated in the previous discussion, the ASSIGN, ORGANIZATION IS INDEXED, and RECORD KEY clauses are required, while the ACCESS IS SEQUENTIAL and FILE STATUS clauses are optional (and included here for purposes of illustration).

The RECORD KEY clause designates a field within the indexed record (IND-SOC-SEC-NUM) that will be used by the operating system to build the necessary indexes. Observe, therefore, that IND-SOC-SEC-NUM is referenced in two places, in the RECORD KEY clause of line 14 and in the FD for the indexed file in line 30.

The optional FILE STATUS clause of line 15 designates a two-position data name, INDEXED-STATUS-BYTES, which in turn is defined in Working-Storage (line 35). The operating system automatically updates the file status bytes after every I/O operation, making the result available to the program via the data name INDEXED-STATUS-BYTES. This, in turn, makes it possible to closely monitor the success (or failure) of various statements within the program.

To illustrate the utility of the file status bytes, return to the test data in the programming specifications, *noting that the record for Panzer is out of sequence.* The logic in the Procedure Division reads a record from the sequential file and

Figure 18.5 Program to Create an Indexed File

```
IDENTIFICATION DIVISION.
PROGRAM-ID.    CREATE.
AUTHOR.        ROBERT GRAUER.

ENVIRONMENT DIVISION.
INPUT-OUTPUT SECTION.
FILE-CONTROL.
    SELECT SEQUENTIAL-FILE
        ASSIGN TO UT-S-SEQUENCE.
    SELECT INDEXED-FILE
        ASSIGN TO DA-INDMAST
        ORGANIZATION IS INDEXED
        ACCESS IS SEQUENTIAL
        RECORD KEY IS IND-SOC-SEC-NUM
        FILE STATUS IS INDEXED-STATUS-BYTES.

DATA DIVISION.
FILE SECTION.
FD  SEQUENTIAL-FILE
    RECORD CONTAINS 39 CHARACTERS
    DATA RECORD IS SEQUENTIAL-RECORD.
01  SEQUENTIAL-RECORD.
    05  SEQ-SOC-SEC-NUM            PIC X(9).
    05  SEQ-REST-OF-RECORD         PIC X(30).

FD  INDEXED-FILE
    RECORD CONTAINS 39 CHARACTERS
    DATA RECORD IS INDEXED-RECORD.
01  INDEXED-RECORD.
    05  IND-SOC-SEC-NUM            PIC X(9).
    05  IND-REST-OF-RECORD         PIC X(30).

WORKING-STORAGE SECTION.
01  END-OF-FILE-SWITCH             PIC X(3)      VALUE 'NO'.
01  INDEXED-STATUS-BYTES           PIC XX.

PROCEDURE DIVISION.
0010-UPDATE-MASTER-FILE.
    OPEN INPUT SEQUENTIAL-FILE
        OUTPUT INDEXED-FILE.
    DISPLAY 'OPEN STATEMENT EXECUTED'.
    DISPLAY '    FILE STATUS BYTES = ', INDEXED-STATUS-BYTES.
    DISPLAY ' '.
    PERFORM UNTIL END-OF-FILE-SWITCH = 'YES'
        READ SEQUENTIAL-FILE
            AT END
                MOVE 'YES' TO END-OF-FILE-SWITCH
            NOT AT END
                MOVE SEQ-SOC-SEC-NUM TO IND-SOC-SEC-NUM
                MOVE SEQ-REST-OF-RECORD TO IND-REST-OF-RECORD
                WRITE INDEXED-RECORD
                    INVALID KEY PERFORM 0020-EXPLAIN-WRITE-ERROR
                END-WRITE
                DISPLAY 'WRITE STATEMENT EXECUTED FOR  '
                    SEQUENTIAL-RECORD
```

SELECT statement includes ORGANIZATION, ACCESS, RECORD KEY and FILE STATUS clauses
RECORD KEY is defined within INDEXED-RECORD
File status bytes defined in Working-Storage
In-line perform and false-condition branch drive program

Figure 18.5 Program to Create an Indexed File

```
56                    DISPLAY '    FILE STATUS BYTES = '
57                        INDEXED-STATUS-BYTES
58                    DISPLAY ' '
59            END-READ
60        END-PERFORM.
61        CLOSE SEQUENTIAL-FILE
62              INDEXED-FILE.
63        DISPLAY 'CLOSE STATEMENT EXECUTED'.
64        DISPLAY '    FILE STATUS BYTES = ', INDEXED-STATUS-BYTES.
65        DISPLAY ' '.
66        STOP RUN.
67
68    0020-EXPLAIN-WRITE-ERROR.
69        IF INDEXED-STATUS-BYTES = '21'
70            DISPLAY 'ERROR (SEQUENCE) FOR      ' SEQUENTIAL-RECORD
71        END-IF.
72        IF INDEXED-STATUS-BYTES = '22'
73            DISPLAY 'ERROR (DUPLICATE KEY) FOR ' SEQUENTIAL-RECORD
74        END-IF.
```

File status bytes may be interrogated and displayed

copies it to the indexed file, repeating the loop until the sequential file is empty. A problem will result, however, because the indexed file requires its records to be in sequence, which is not true in this example. Accordingly it is good technique to include an **INVALID KEY** clause in the WRITE statement of lines 51 through 53, which is executed if, and only if, an error is detected. The paragraph performed as a consequence of the error, 0020-EXPLAIN-WRITE-ERROR (lines 68–74), interrogates the file status bytes to reveal the exact cause of the problem.

Output of the program is shown in Figure 18.6 and consists entirely of display output produced at various points in the program. The first and last lines show the results of the OPEN and CLOSE statements, respectively; both operations executed successfully as evidenced by file status bytes of 00. Note, too, how file status bytes of 00 are displayed for every *successful* write operation, but that a value of 21, corresponding to an out-of-sequence record, is displayed for Panzer.

Additional COBOL Elements

Several statements in the Procedure Division are uniquely associated with indexed files or have extended formats for indexed files. These include OPEN, READ, WRITE, REWRITE, and DELETE. We will discuss each of these statements in isolation, then include them in the illustrative programs that follow.

OPEN

The **I-O** clause of the OPEN statement, OPEN I-O, is required when updating indexed files. Consider:

```
       { INPUT }
OPEN   { OUPUT }  file-name
       { I-O   }
```

Figure 18.6 Display Output of Create Program

```
OPEN STATEMENT EXECUTED                          OPEN statement executed without error
    FILE STATUS BYTES = 00

WRITE STATEMENT EXECUTED FOR  100000000GRABER          P ATL1500000000
    FILE STATUS BYTES = 00

WRITE STATEMENT EXECUTED FOR  200000000RUBIN           MABOS0800020000
    FILE STATUS BYTES = 00

WRITE STATEMENT EXECUTED FOR  300000000ANDERSON        IRBOS1000113000
    FILE STATUS BYTES = 00

ERROR (SEQUENCE) FOR       222222222PANZER         S NYC0600000000
WRITE STATEMENT EXECUTED FOR  222222222PANZER          S NYC0600000000   Sequence error for Panzer
    FILE STATUS BYTES = 21

WRITE STATEMENT EXECUTED FOR  400000000MOLDOF          BLATL1500000000
    FILE STATUS BYTES = 00

WRITE STATEMENT EXECUTED FOR  500000000GLASSMAN        JSNYC1000045000
    FILE STATUS BYTES = 00

WRITE STATEMENT EXECUTED FOR  600000000GRAUER          RTNYC0800087500
    FILE STATUS BYTES = 00

WRITE STATEMENT EXECUTED FOR  700000000MILGROM         A SF 0900120000
    FILE STATUS BYTES = 00

WRITE STATEMENT EXECUTED FOR  800000000VAZQUEZ         C ATL1200060000
    FILE STATUS BYTES = 00

WRITE STATEMENT EXECUTED FOR  900000000CLARK           E NYC0700002500
    FILE STATUS BYTES = 00

CLOSE STATEMENT EXECUTED                         CLOSE statement executed without error
    FILE STATUS BYTES = 00
```

INPUT and OUTPUT are used when an indexed file is accessed or created. In nonsequential maintenance, however, the *same* indexed file functions as both the old and new master files, and hence is both an input and an output file. The file is opened as an I-O file—for example, OPEN I-O INDEXED-FILE—to enable it to serve both functions in the same program; that is, you may read records from the file (input), as well as write records to the file (output).

READ

The **READ** statement has two distinct formats, for sequential and nonsequential access, respectively. These are:

Format 1 (Sequential Access)

```
READ file-name [NEXT] RECORD [INTO identifier-1]
    [AT END imperative-statement-1]
    [NOT AT END imperative-statement-2]
[END-READ]
```

Format 2 (Nonsequential Access)

```
READ file-name RECORD [INTO identifier-1]
    [KEY IS data-name-1]
    [INVALID KEY imperative-statement-1]
    [NOT INVALID KEY imperative-statement-2]
[END-READ]
```

The first format, for sequential access, has been used throughout the text and should present no difficulty. (The NEXT phrase is discussed in conjunction with the ACCESS IS DYNAMIC clause of the SELECT statement, and is illustrated in Figure 18.12 toward the end of the chapter.)

The second format, for nonsequential access, *must be preceded by a MOVE statement, in which the key of the desired record is moved to the data name designated as the RECORD KEY in the SELECT statement.* Consider:

```
SELECT INDEXED-FILE
    ASSIGN TO DA-INDEXED
    ORGANIZATION IS INDEXED
    ACCESS IS RANDOM
    RECORD KEY IS IND-SOC-SEC-NUM.
  .
    .
    MOVE 888888888 TO IND-SOC-SEC-NUM.
    READ INDEXED-FILE INTO WS-INPUT-AREA
        INVALID KEY
            DISPLAY 'Record 888888888 is not in the indexed file'
        NOT INVALID KEY
      .
        .
    END-READ.
```

The value of the desired record is moved to the data name designated as the record key

statements to process record 888888888

The READ statement accesses the indexed file nonsequentially in an attempt to retrieve the record whose key is 888888888. If the record is in the file, it will be read and made available in WS-INPUT-AREA (as well as in the record area within the FD for INDEXED-FILE). If, however, the record does not exist, the INVALID KEY condition is raised and the indicated error message is displayed.

The **KEY IS** clause is necessary if multiple keys are specified in the SELECT statement (that is, if ALTERNATE RECORD KEY is included). Consider:

```
SELECT INDEXED-FILE
    ASSIGN TO DA-INDEXED
    ORGANIZATION IS INDEXED
    RECORD KEY IS IND-SOC-SEC-NUM
    ACCESS IS RANDOM
    ALTERNATE RECORD KEY IS IND-NAME WITH DUPLICATES.
.
  .
MOVE 'Smith' TO IND-NAME.
READ INDEXED-FILE INTO WS-WORK-AREA
    KEY IS IND-NAME
```

The value of the desired record is moved to the specified key

```
        INVALID KEY
            DISPLAY 'Smith is not in the file'
        NOT INVALID KEY
            .
              .
                .
    END-READ.
```

As in the case of a single key, the READ statement is preceded by a MOVE statement in which the desired value is moved to the appropriate key field. The file is then searched nonsequentially for the value specified (Smith in the example). The INVALID KEY condition is activated if the record cannot be found.

WRITE

The **WRITE** statement also has an optional INVALID KEY clause, as you already know from the COBOL program to create an indexed file (Figure 18.5). Consider:

```
WRITE record-name [FROM identifier-1]
    [INVALID KEY imperative statement-1]
    [NOT INVALID KEY imperative-statement-2]
[END-WRITE]
```

Specification of ACCESS IS SEQUENTIAL (in the SELECT statement) to create the indexed file requires that incoming records be in sequential order, and further, each record is required to have a unique key. The INVALID KEY condition is raised if either of these requirements is violated.

REWRITE

The **REWRITE** statement replaces existing records when a file has been opened as an I/O file, as in the case of nonsequential maintenance. Its syntax is similar to that of the WRITE statement:

```
REWRITE record-name [FROM identifier-1]
    [INVALID KEY imperative statement-1]
    [NOT INVALID KEY imperative-statement-2]
[END-REWRITE]
```

The INVALID KEY condition is raised if the record key of the last record read does not match the key of the record to be replaced.

DELETE

The DELETE statement removes a record from an indexed file. Consider:

```
DELETE file-name RECORD
    [INVALID KEY imperative statement-1]
    [NOT INVALID KEY imperative-statement-2]
[END-DELETE]
```

The DELETE statement is appropriate only for files opened in the I/O mode.

Maintaining an Indexed File

The distinction between ***sequential*** and ***nonsequential*** file maintenance was presented in the previous chapter, but is repeated here for emphasis. A sequential update uses two distinct master files, an old and a new master, with every record in the old master rewritten to the new master regardless of whether it changes. A nonsequential update uses a single master file that functions as both the old and new master, and only the records that change are rewritten. A sequential update is driven by the relationship between the old master and transaction files, whereas a nonsequential update is driven solely by the transaction file; that is, transactions are processed until the transaction file is empty. Finally, a sequential update requires the transaction file to be in sequence, whereas the transactions for a nonsequential update can be in any order.

The sequential update was developed in Chapter 17 through implementation of the balance line algorithm. We continue now with a parallel problem for nonsequential processing.

PROGRAMMING SPECIFICATIONS

Program Name: Nonsequential Update

Narrative: This program parallels the update program of Chapter 17 except that the master file is accessed nonsequentially, and thus the transaction file need not be in sequence. In addition, the balance line algorithm does not apply.

Input File: TRANSACTION-FILE

Input Record Layout:

```
01 TRANSACTION-RECORD.
    05  TR-SOC-SEC-NUMBER                  PIC X(9).
    05  TR-NAME.
        10  TR-LAST-NAME                   PIC X(15).
        10  TR-INITIALS                    PIC XX.
    05  TR-LOCATION-CODE                   PIC X(3).
    05  TR-COMMISSION-RATE                 PIC 99.
    05  TR-SALES-AMOUNT                    PIC 9(5).
    05  TR-TRANSACTION-CODE                PIC X.
        88  ADDITION         VALUE 'A'.
        88  CORRECTION       VALUE 'C'.
        88  DELETION         VALUE 'D'.
```

Input/Output File: INDEXED-FILE

Input Record Layout:

```
01  IND-MASTER-RECORD.
    05  IND-SOC-SEC-NUMBER                 PIC X(9).
    05  IND-NAME.
        10  IND-LAST-NAME                  PIC X(15).
        10  IND-INITIALS                   PIC XX.
    05  IND-LOCATION-CODE                  PIC X(3).
    05  IND-COMMISSION-RATE                PIC 99.
    05  IND-YEAR-TO-DATE-SALES             PIC 9(8).
```

Test Data: See Figure 18.7a and 18.7b.

Figure 18.7 Test Data for Nonsequential Update

```
100000000GRABER        P ATL1500000000
200000000RUBIN         MABOS0800020000
300000000ANDERSON      IRBOS1000113000
400000000MOLDOF        BLATL1500000000
500000000GLASSMAN      JSNYC1000045000
600000000GRAUER        RTNYC0800087500
700000000MILGROM       A SF 0900120000
800000000VAZQUEZ       C ATL1200060000
900000000CLARK         E NYC0700002500
```

(a) Indexed File (before Update)

```
444444444RICHARDS      IM      05000C
700000000MILGROM       A            D
000000000BOROW         JSATL07      A
000000000BOROW         JS      10000C
000000000BOROW         JS      20000C
400000000MOLDOF        BLATL15      A
800000000VAZQUEZ       C       55000C
999999999GILLENSON     MANYC10      A
```

Transactions are not in sequential order (boxed: 700000000MILGROM and 000000000BOROW records)

(b) Transaction File

```
000000000BOROW         JSATL0700030000
100000000GRABER        P ATL1500000000
200000000RUBIN         MABOS0800020000
300000000ANDERSON      IRBOS1000113000
400000000MOLDOF        BLATL1500000000
500000000GLASSMAN      JSNYC1000045000
600000000GRAUER        RTNYC0800087500
800000000VAZQUEZ       C ATL1200115000
900000000CLARK         E NYC0700002500
999999999GILLENSON     MANYC1000000000
```

(c) Indexed File (after Update)

```
ERROR-NO MATCHING RECORD: 444444444
ERROR-DUPLICATE ADDITION: 400000000
```

(d) Error Messages

Processing Requirements:

1. Develop a nonsequential update program to process an incoming transaction file and update the associated indexed file. The processing requirements parallel those of the sequential update program of Chapter 17 with the following changes:
   a. There is only a single master file (the indexed file), which functions as both the old and new master files.
   b. The transaction file need not be in sequential order.
   c. The balance line algorithm does not apply.
2. The transaction file is assumed to be valid in and of itself by virtue of a stand-alone edit program. Hence, each transaction has a valid transaction code (A, C, or D), numeric fields are numeric, and so on. Nevertheless, the update program must check (and flag) two kinds of errors that could not be detected in the stand-alone edit, as they require interaction with the old master file. These are:
   a. Duplicate additions, in which the social security number of a transaction coded as an addition already exists in the old master,
   b. No matches, in which the social security number of a transaction coded as either a deletion or a correction does not exist in the old master.
3. Transactions coded as additions are to be added to the new master file in their entirety, and will contain a value for every field in the transaction record (except for TR-SALES-AMOUNT). The value of IND-YEAR-TO-DATE-SALES in the new master record is to be initialized to zero.
4. Transactions coded as deletions are to be removed from the master file. These transactions contain only the social security number and transaction code.
5. Transactions coded as corrections contain only the social security number,name, and the transaction sales amount (TR-SALES-AMOUNT). The value of TR-SALES-AMOUNT on the incoming transaction is to be *added* to the value in the IND-YEAR-TO-DATE-SALES field in the master record.

Figure 18.7 contains the indexed and transaction files before the update, the indexed file after the update has been run, and the associated error messages (for duplicate additions and no matches). The data parallel the example in Chapter 17 except that the transaction file is no longer in sequence. Nevertheless, the updated indexed file is the same in both examples; that is, Borow and Gillenson have been added, Milgrom has been deleted, and Vazquez has had her record changed. Note, however, that the error messages in Figure 18.7d are reversed (from those in Chapter 17) to match the order in which the transactions were processed.

Hierarchy Chart

The hierarchy chart of Figure 18.8 is simpler than its counterpart for sequential processing; it also contains four modules that were present in the hierarchy chart of Chapter 17. In other words, regardless of whether the master file is accessed sequentially or nonsequentially, it is still necessary to apply transactions to the master file, to add records to the indexed file, and to correct and/or delete existing records.

Conspicuous by its absence, however, is the module to CHOOSE-ACTIVE-KEY, because the nonsequential update is driven entirely by the transaction file. The program processes the transaction file until there are no more transactions; that is, there is no need for an active key to determine whether the record from the transaction file or the old master file will be admitted to the update process because the balance line algorithm does not apply. (See problem 7.)

Figure 18.8 Hierarchy Chart for Nonsequential Update Program

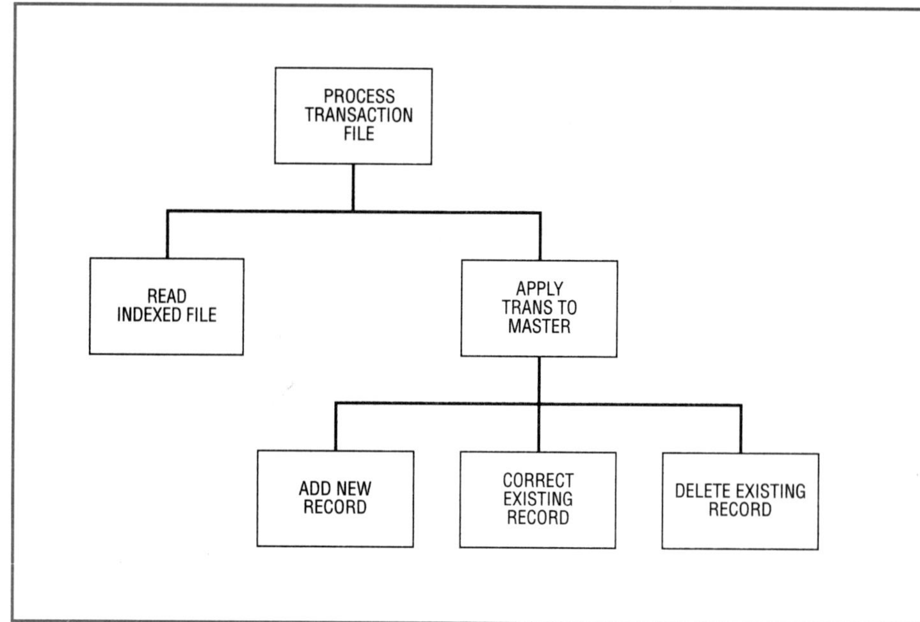

Pseudocode

The pseudocode for the nonsequential update is driven entirely by the transaction file, which reads a transaction, determines whether or not the corresponding social security number is in the indexed file, then processes the transaction as appropriate. The logic is simpler than that of the balance line algorithm, which had to determine whether the next record was to be read from the transaction file, the old master file, or both.

The pseudocode reads a record from the transaction file and immediately does a random read on the indexed file. The social security number from the transaction file is, or is not, present in the indexed file, which determines the value of the record-key-allocated-switch. The transaction is then processed according to the transaction code (addition, deletion, or correction) and the value of the record-key-allocated-switch. The process continues until the transaction file is exhausted.

The Completed Program

The completed program is shown in Figure 18.10. The SELECT statement for the INDEXED-FILE (lines 10–14) contains the required ORGANIZATION IS INDEXED and RECORD KEY clauses, and specifies ACCESS IS RANDOM. INDEXED-FILE is opened as an I/O file in line 63 because it serves as both the old and new master file; that is, it is read from and written to.

The READ statement for the indexed file (lines 79–84) is preceded by a MOVE statement, in which the key of the transaction record is moved to IND-SOC-SEC-NUM, the field defined as the RECORD KEY. The indexed file is read in an attempt to find this record, and the INVALID KEY condition is triggered if the value is not in the file.

The contents of the lowest-level modules, ADD-NEW-RECORD, CORRECT-EXISTING-RECORD and DELETE-EXISTING-RECORD, have been modified slightly (from their counterparts in the sequential update) to include the appropriate I/O statements and contain WRITE, REWRITE, and DELETE statements, respectively.

Figure 18.9 Pseudocode for Nonsequential Update Program

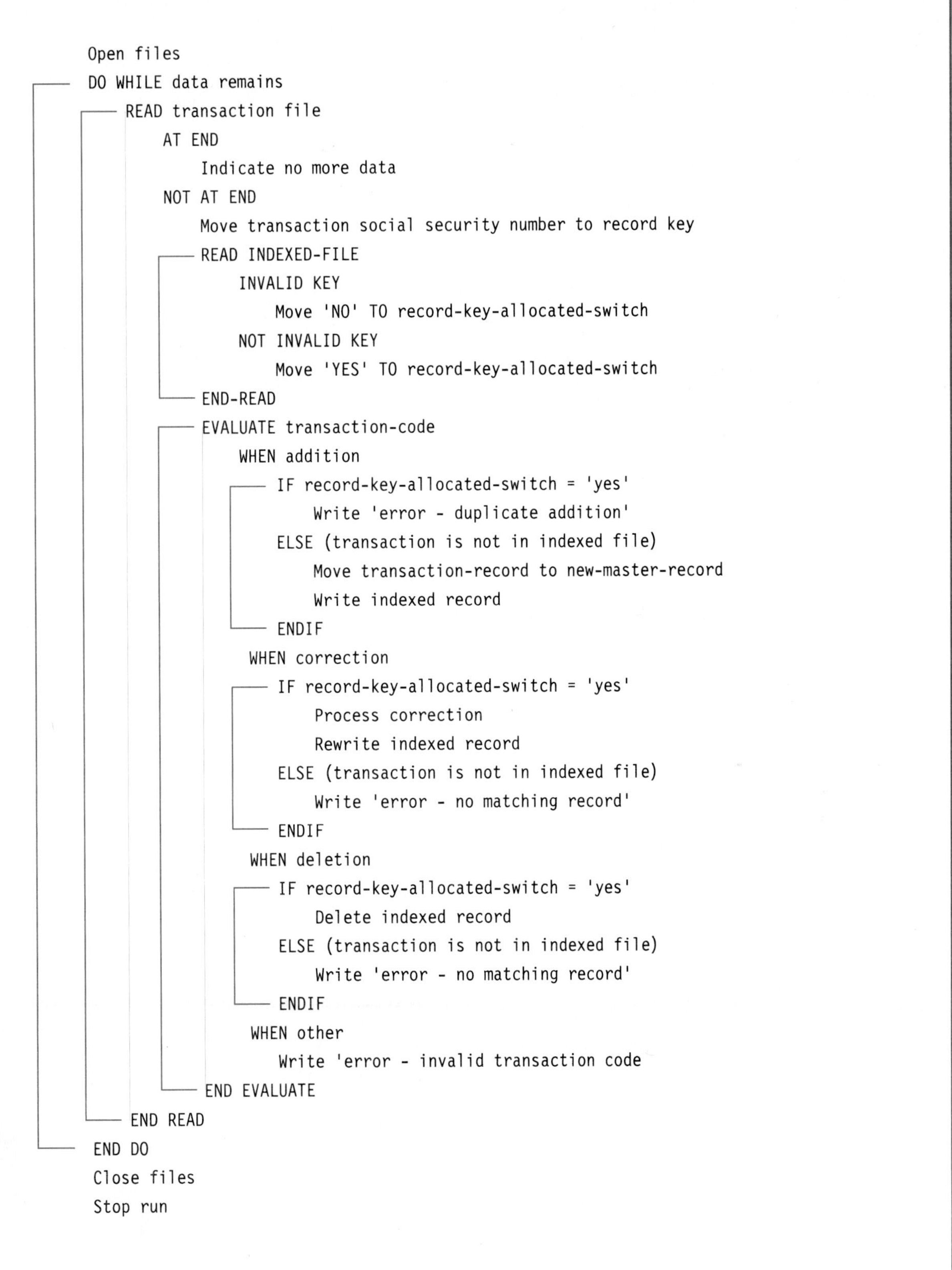

```
Open files
DO WHILE data remains
    READ transaction file
        AT END
            Indicate no more data
        NOT AT END
            Move transaction social security number to record key
            READ INDEXED-FILE
                INVALID KEY
                    Move 'NO' TO record-key-allocated-switch
                NOT INVALID KEY
                    Move 'YES' TO record-key-allocated-switch
            END-READ
            EVALUATE transaction-code
                WHEN addition
                    IF record-key-allocated-switch = 'yes'
                        Write 'error - duplicate addition'
                    ELSE (transaction is not in indexed file)
                        Move transaction-record to new-master-record
                        Write indexed record
                    ENDIF
                WHEN correction
                    IF record-key-allocated-switch = 'yes'
                        Process correction
                        Rewrite indexed record
                    ELSE (transaction is not in indexed file)
                        Write 'error - no matching record'
                    ENDIF
                WHEN deletion
                    IF record-key-allocated-switch = 'yes'
                        Delete indexed record
                    ELSE (transaction is not in indexed file)
                        Write 'error - no matching record'
                    ENDIF
                WHEN other
                    Write 'error - invalid transaction code
            END EVALUATE
    END READ
END DO
Close files
Stop run
```

Figure 18.10 Nonsequential Update Program

```
IDENTIFICATION DIVISION.
PROGRAM-ID.    NONSEQUP.
AUTHOR.        ROBERT GRAUER.

ENVIRONMENT DIVISION.
INPUT-OUTPUT SECTION.
FILE-CONTROL.
    SELECT TRANSACTION-FILE
        ASSIGN TO UT-S-VALTRANS.
    SELECT INDEXED-FILE
        ASSIGN TO DA-INDMAST
        ORGANIZATION IS INDEXED
        ACCESS IS RANDOM
        RECORD KEY IS IND-SOC-SEC-NUM.

DATA DIVISION.
FILE SECTION.
FD  TRANSACTION-FILE
    RECORD CONTAINS 37 CHARACTERS
    DATA RECORD IS TRANSACTION-RECORD.
01  TRANSACTION-RECORD               PIC X(37).

FD  INDEXED-FILE
    RECORD CONTAINS 39 CHARACTERS
    DATA RECORD IS INDEXED-RECORD.
01  INDEXED-RECORD.
    05  IND-SOC-SEC-NUM              PIC X(9).
    05  IND-REST-OF-RECORD           PIC X(30).

WORKING-STORAGE SECTION.
01  FILLER                           PIC X(14)
        VALUE 'WS BEGINS HERE'.

01  WS-TRANS-RECORD.
    05  TR-SOC-SEC-NUMBER            PIC X(9).
    05  TR-NAME.
        10  TR-LAST-NAME             PIC X(15).
        10  TR-INITIALS              PIC XX.
    05  TR-LOCATION-CODE             PIC X(3).
    05  TR-COMMISSION-RATE           PIC 99.
    05  TR-SALES-AMOUNT              PIC 9(5).
    05  TR-TRANSACTION-CODE          PIC X.
        88  ADDITION       VALUE 'A'.
        88  CORRECTION     VALUE 'C'.
        88  DELETION       VALUE 'D'.

01  WS-MASTER-RECORD.
    05  MA-SOC-SEC-NUMBER            PIC X(9).
    05  MA-NAME.
        10  MA-LAST-NAME             PIC X(15).
```

SELECT statement for INDEXED-FILE

Figure 18.10 *(continued)*

```
               10  MA-INITIALS                 PIC XX.
           05  MA-LOCATION-CODE                PIC X(3).
           05  MA-COMMISSION-RATE              PIC 99.
           05  MA-YEAR-TO-DATE-SALES           PIC 9(8).

       01  PROGRAM-SWITCHES.
           05  END-OF-FILE-SWITCH              PIC X(3)      VALUE 'NO '.
           05  RECORD-KEY-ALLOCATED-SWITCH     PIC X(3)      VALUE 'NO '.

       PROCEDURE DIVISION.
       0010-PROCESS-TRANSACTION-FILE.
           OPEN INPUT TRANSACTION-FILE
                  I-O INDEXED-FILE.
           PERFORM UNTIL END-OF-FILE-SWITCH = 'YES'
               READ TRANSACTION-FILE INTO WS-TRANS-RECORD
                   AT END
                       MOVE 'YES' TO END-OF-FILE-SWITCH
                   NOT AT END
                       PERFORM 0020-READ-INDEXED-FILE
                       PERFORM 0030-APPLY-TRANS-TO-MASTER
               END-READ
           END-PERFORM.
           CLOSE TRANSACTION-FILE
                 INDEXED-FILE.
           STOP RUN.

       0020-READ-INDEXED-FILE.
           MOVE TR-SOC-SEC-NUMBER TO IND-SOC-SEC-NUM.
           READ INDEXED-FILE INTO WS-MASTER-RECORD
               INVALID KEY
                   MOVE 'NO ' TO RECORD-KEY-ALLOCATED-SWITCH
               NOT INVALID KEY
                   MOVE 'YES' TO RECORD-KEY-ALLOCATED-SWITCH
           END-READ.

       0030-APPLY-TRANS-TO-MASTER.
           EVALUATE TRUE
               WHEN ADDITION
                   PERFORM 0090-ADD-NEW-RECORD
               WHEN CORRECTION
                   PERFORM 0100-CORRECT-EXISTING-RECORD
               WHEN DELETION
                   PERFORM 0110-DELETE-EXISTING-RECORD
               WHEN OTHER
                   DISPLAY 'INVALID TRANSACTION CODE'
           END-EVALUATE.

       0090-ADD-NEW-RECORD.
           IF RECORD-KEY-ALLOCATED-SWITCH = 'YES'
               DISPLAY '  ERROR-DUPLICATE ADDITION: ' TR-SOC-SEC-NUMBER
```

In-line perform and false-condition branch drive the program

Nonsequential READ statement

EVALUATE statement determines transaction processing

Figure 18.10 *(continued)*

```
          ELSE
              MOVE SPACES TO WS-MASTER-RECORD
              MOVE TR-SOC-SEC-NUMBER TO MA-SOC-SEC-NUMBER
              MOVE TR-NAME TO MA-NAME
              MOVE TR-LOCATION-CODE TO MA-LOCATION-CODE
              MOVE TR-COMMISSION-RATE TO MA-COMMISSION-RATE
              MOVE ZEROS TO MA-YEAR-TO-DATE-SALES
              WRITE INDEXED-RECORD FROM WS-MASTER-RECORD
          END-IF.

      0100-CORRECT-EXISTING-RECORD.
          IF RECORD-KEY-ALLOCATED-SWITCH = 'YES'
              ADD TR-SALES-AMOUNT TO MA-YEAR-TO-DATE-SALES
              REWRITE INDEXED-RECORD FROM WS-MASTER-RECORD
          ELSE
              DISPLAY '  ERROR-NO MATCHING RECORD: ' TR-SOC-SEC-NUMBER
          END-IF.

      0110-DELETE-EXISTING-RECORD.
          IF RECORD-KEY-ALLOCATED-SWITCH = 'YES'
              DELETE INDEXED-FILE
          ELSE
              DISPLAY '  ERROR-NO MATCHING RECORD: ' TR-SOC-SEC-NUMBER
          END-IF.
```

Modified to use appropriate I/O statements

Alternate Record Key

Our earlier discussion of the SELECT statement included the **ALTERNATE RECORD KEY** phrase to enable a second path for retrieving records from an indexed file. Unlike the record key, which must be unique, the alternate key may contain duplicate values. This capability is illustrated in the third and final program of the chapter, the specifications of which follow in the usual format.

PROGRAMMING SPECIFICATIONS

Program Name: Alternate Indexes

Narrative: This program illustrates primary and alternate indexes, as well as nonsequential retrieval on either type of key. It does no useful processing per se, other than to illustrate COBOL syntax

Input File: INDEXED-FILE

Input Record Layout:

```
01 INDEXED-RECORD.
   05  IND-SOC-SEC-NUMBER              PIC X(9).
   05  IND-NAME                        PIC X(15).
   05  IND-REST-OF-RECORD              PIC X(16).
```

Figure 18.11 Alternate Keys

```
100000000GRAUER
100000001GRAUER
100000002GRAUER
300000000MILGROM
300000001MILGROM
300000002MILGROM
400000000GRAUER
500000000JONES
600000000SMITH
700000000MILGROM
```

(a) The Indexed File

```
PRIMARY KEY OK - 300000001

ALTERNATE KEY - MILGROM        300000000
ALTERNATE KEY - MILGROM        300000001
ALTERNATE KEY - MILGROM        300000002
ALTERNATE KEY - MILGROM        700000000
```

(b) Displayed Output

Test Data: See Figure 18.11a.

Report Layout: There is no formal report produced by this program; instead DISPLAY statements are used to indicate the results as in Figure 18.11b.

Processing Requirements:

1. The social security and name fields are designated as the primary and secondary keys, respectively. The value of the social security number is unique, whereas the value of name is not.
2. Execute a random read for the record whose social security number is 300000001, displaying an appropriate message to indicate whether or not the record was found.
3. Execute a random read to find the first record whose name is Milgrom, then read sequentially to display all other records with this value in the secondary key.

Figure 18.12 contains the completed program corresponding to these specifications. The SELECT statement in lines 8–13 designates IND-SOC-SEC-NUM and IND-NAME as the primary (record) and alternate key, respectively. The record key is (and must always be) unique, but the alternate key need not be; hence the **WITH DUPLICATES** phrase is included in the SELECT statement. Both fields are defined within the FD for INDEXED-FILE in lines 21 and 22, respectively. The **ACCESS IS DYNAMIC** phrase (line 11) indicates both random and sequential retrieval within the same program.

Figure 18.12 Alternate Index Program

```
IDENTIFICATION DIVISION.
PROGRAM-ID.   ALTINDEX.
AUTHOR.       ROBERT GRAUER.

ENVIRONMENT DIVISION.
INPUT-OUTPUT SECTION.
FILE-CONTROL.
    SELECT INDEXED-FILE
        ASSIGN TO DA-ALTINDEX
        ORGANIZATION IS INDEXED
        ACCESS IS DYNAMIC
        RECORD KEY IS IND-SOC-SEC-NUM
        ALTERNATE RECORD KEY IS IND-NAME WITH DUPLICATES.

DATA DIVISION.
FILE SECTION.
FD  INDEXED-FILE
    RECORD CONTAINS 40 CHARACTERS
    DATA RECORD IS INDEXED-RECORD.
01  INDEXED-RECORD.
    05  IND-SOC-SEC-NUM          PIC X(9).
    05  IND-NAME                 PIC X(15).
    05  IND-REST-OF-RECORD       PIC X(16).

WORKING-STORAGE SECTION.
01  END-OF-FILE-SWITCH           PIC X(3)    VALUE SPACES.

PROCEDURE DIVISION.
0010-DISPLAY-INDEXED-RECORDS.
    OPEN INPUT INDEXED-FILE.
    PERFORM 0020-RETRIEVE-BY-PRIMARY-KEY.
    PERFORM 0030-RETRIEVE-BY-SECONDARY-KEY.
    CLOSE INDEXED-FILE.
    STOP RUN.

0020-RETRIEVE-BY-PRIMARY-KEY.
    MOVE '300000001' TO IND-SOC-SEC-NUM.
    READ INDEXED-FILE
        INVALID KEY
            DISPLAY 'RECORD NOT FOUND - 300000001'
        NOT INVALID KEY
            DISPLAY 'PRIMARY KEY OK - ', IND-SOC-SEC-NUM
    END-READ.
    DISPLAY ' '.

0030-RETRIEVE-BY-SECONDARY-KEY.
    MOVE 'MILGROM' TO IND-NAME.
    READ INDEXED-FILE KEY IS IND-NAME
        INVALID KEY
            DISPLAY 'RECORD NOT FOUND - MILGROM'
```

Indicates both random and sequential retrieval (ACCESS IS DYNAMIC)

Nonunique alternate key (ALTERNATE RECORD KEY IS IND-NAME WITH DUPLICATES.)

Keys defined within index record (IND-SOC-SEC-NUM, IND-NAME)

Primary key retrieval (0020-RETRIEVE-BY-PRIMARY-KEY)

Secondary key retrieval (READ INDEXED-FILE KEY IS IND-NAME)

Figure 18.12 *(continued)*

```
51              NOT INVALID KEY
52                  PERFORM 0040-RETRIEVE-DUPLICATES
53                      UNTIL IND-NAME NOT EQUAL 'MILGROM'
54                      OR END-OF-FILE-SWITCH = 'YES'
55          END-READ.
56
57      0040-RETRIEVE-DUPLICATES.
58          DISPLAY 'ALTERNATE KEY - ' IND-NAME, IND-SOC-SEC-NUM.
59          READ INDEXED-FILE NEXT RECORD
60              AT END
61                  MOVE 'YES' TO END-OF-FILE-SWITCH
62          END-READ.
```

Successful retrieval

The Procedure Division illustrates the retrieval of records on either field. Lines 36–44 contain the logic for the primary key and have already been covered in the program for a nonsequential update. The READ statement of lines 38–43 is preceded by a MOVE statement in which the key of the desired record (300000001 in the example) is moved to the data name designated as the RECORD KEY in the SELECT statement. If the record is in the file, it will be read into the data name INDEXED-RECORD; and the false-condition branch, NOT INVALID KEY, will indicate the primary key was found. If the record is not in the file, the INVALID KEY condition will be activated to display an appropriate error message.

Lines 46–55 contain a parallel procedure based on the alternate key, but with three important differences:

1. The key value (MILGROM) is moved to the ALTERNATE RECORD KEY (IND-NAME rather than IND-SOC-SEC-NUM).
2. The KEY IS phrase is used to indicate the retrieval is on the alternate rather than the primary key.
3. Successful retrieval causes the execution of 0040-RETRIEVE-DUPLICATES, which retrieves all records for MILGROM. The NEXT RECORD phrase (line 59) in the READ statement indicates sequential retrieval.

The DISPLAY output produced by the program is shown in Figure 18.11b. The first message indicates the successful retrieval based on the primary key (produced by the paragraph 0020-RETRIEVE-BY-PRIMARY-KEY). The second set of messages reflects all records for Milgrom.

Concatenated Key

The record key in an indexed file may be specified as a group item rather than an elementary item, producing what is known as a ***concatenated key***, that is, a key consisting of two (or more) keys strung together to form a single value. Consider, for example, a system for bank loans with a concatenated key defined as follows:

```
05  CUSTOMER-LOAN-NUMBER.
    10  CUSTOMER-NUMBER        PIC 9(6).
    10  LOAN-NUMBER            PIC 9(3).
```

In this example CUSTOMER-LOAN-NUMBER is a group item and consists of the elementary items, CUSTOMER-NUMBER and LOAN-NUMBER. Every value of the record key (CUSTOMER-LOAN-NUMBER) must be unique, but there can be several loans for the same customer, with each loan assigned a new loan number. Customer 111111, for example, may have two outstanding loans, with record keys of 111111001 and 111111004, respectively. (Loans 002 and 003 may have been previously paid off.) The problem is to retrieve all loans for a given customer, which leads to a discussion of the START statement.

The START Statement

The **START** statement moves nonsequentially (randomly) into an indexed file to the first record whose value is equal to, greater than, or not less than the value contained in the identifier. The INVALID KEY condition is raised if the file does not contain a record meeting the specified criterion. Syntactically, the START statement has the form:

```
                     ┌     ┌IS EQUAL TO                   ┐            ┐
                     │     │IS =                          │            │
                     │     │IS GREATER THAN               │            │
                     │     │IS >                          │            │
START file-name      │ KEY<│IS NOT LESS THAN              │> identifier│
                     │     │IS NOT <                      │            │
                     │     │IS GREATER THAN OR EQUAL TO   │            │
                     └     └IS >=                         ┘            ┘

     [INVALID KEY imperative-statement-1]

     [NOT INVALID KEY imperative-statement-2]

     [END-START]
```

The START statement can be used in conjunction with a concatenated key as shown in Figure 18.13. *Note, however, that START only moves to the designated record, but does **not** read the record.* In other words, a READ statement is required immediately following START. The subsequent PERFORM statement will then retrieve all loans for the customer in question.

LIMITATIONS OF COBOL-74

The READ, DELETE, WRITE, REWRITE, and START statements contain both an optional scope terminator and a false-condition branch. As indicated throughout the text, these elements are new to COBOL-85 and were not available in COBOL-74.

Sixteen I/O status codes (i.e., the majority of the entries in Table 18.1) are new to COBOL-85. The new codes (04, 05, 07, 15, 24, 25, 34, 35, 37, 38, 39, 41, 42, 43, 46, and 49) were added to eliminate the need for vendor-specific file status codes that treated the same error condition in different ways.

Figure 18.13 The START Statement

```
SELECT LOAN-FILE
    ASSIGN TO DA-LOANS
    ORGANIZATION IS INDEXED
    ACCESS MODE IS DYNAMIC
    RECORD KEY IS CUSTOMER-LOAN-NUMBER.
.
  .
    .
FD  LOAN-FILE
    RECORD CONTAINS 120 CHARACTERS
    DATA RECORD IS LOAN-RECORD.
01  LOAN-RECORD.
    05  CUSTOMER-LOAN-NUMBER.
        10  CUSTOMER-NUMBER         PIC 9(6).
        10  LOAN-NUMBER             PIC 9(3).
.
  .
    .
PROCEDURE DIVISION.
.
  .
    .
    MOVE 333333000 TO CUSTOMER-LOAN-NUMBER.
    START LOAN-FILE
        KEY IS GREATER THAN CUSTOMER-LOAN-NUMBER
        INVALID KEY DISPLAY 'CUSTOMER 333333 NOT IN FILE'
    END-START.

    READ LOAN-FILE NEXT RECORD
        AT END
            MOVE 'YES' TO END-OF-FILE-SWITCH
    END-READ.

    PERFORM UNTIL CUSTOMER-NUMBER NOT EQUAL 333333
        OR END-OF-FILE-SWITCH = 'YES'
            DISPLAY LOAN-RECORD
            READ LOAN-FILE NEXT RECORD
                AT END
                    MOVE 'YES' TO END-OF-FILE-SWITCH
            END-READ
    END-PERFORM.
```

Record key is concatenated, consisting of customer number and loan number

START statement finds the first loan for customer 333333

PERFORM statement finds all subsequent loans

SUMMARY

Points to Remember

- Indexed files permit sequential and/or nonsequential access to records within a file. Different vendors have different physical implementations, but the COBOL syntax to access an indexed file is the same for all compilers adhering to the ANS 85 standard. VSAM (Virtual Storage Access Method) is IBM's implementation for indexed files.
- The SELECT statement for an indexed file has seven clauses: three clauses (ASSIGN, ORGANIZATION IS INDEXED, and RECORD KEY) are required, and the other four (RESERVE AREAS, ACCESS MODE, ALTERNATE RECORD KEY, and FILE STATUS) are optional.
- The RECORD KEY clause in the SELECT statement specifies a field (defined within the FD of the indexed record) whose value must be unique; the value of the optional alternate record key can contain duplicate values.
- The Procedure Division has several statements uniquely associated with indexed files, and/or extends the formats of other statements to accommodate indexed files. These include OPEN I-O, READ . . . INVALID KEY, WRITE . . . INVALID KEY, and DELETE.
- The transaction file does not have to be in sequence when updating an indexed file as the latter can be accessed nonsequentially. The INVALID KEY clause will be activated if the transaction record is not found.
- The updated indexed file cannot be used as the old master to retest the update program with the same input as previously; you must retain (create) a copy of the original indexed file for repeated testing.
- A concatenated key consists of two or more fields strung together. Concatenated keys are frequently used in conjunction with the START statement, which moves nonsequentially to the first record satisfying a specified condition.

Key Words and Concepts

Concatenated key
Control area
Control area split
Control interval
Control interval split
False-condition branch
Free space
Index set
Indexed file
I/O status
Multiple keys
Nonsequential access
Scope terminator
Sequence set
Sequential access
VSAM organization

COBOL Elements

ACCESS IS DYNAMIC
ACCESS IS RANDOM
ACCESS IS SEQUENTIAL
ACCESS MODE
ALTERNATE RECORD KEY
DELETE
END-DELETE
END-READ
END-START
END-REWRITE
END-WRITE
FILE STATUS
INVALID KEY
NOT INVALID KEY
OPEN I-O
ORGANIZATION IS INDEXED
RECORD KEY
RESERVE AREAS
REWRITE
START
WITH DUPLICATES
WRITE . . . INVALID KEY

FILL-IN

1. ______________ files make it possible to retrieve records sequentially and/or nonsequentially.
2. An active file is best updated sequentially, whereas ______________ processing should be used for inactive files.
3. ______________ is the IBM specific implementation of COBOL's ______________ file organization.
4. In IBM's VSAM implementation, a ______________ ______________ contains one or more ______________ ______________.
5. In IBM's VSAM implementation, each entry in a sequence set contains the ______________ key for the associated control interval.
6. The SELECT statement for indexed files requires three clauses: ______________, ______________, and ______________.
7. An indexed file requires the primary key to be ______________, but allows ______________ values for its ______________ key.
8. Records are added to an indexed file through the ______________ statement; existing records are changed through ______________ and removed by the ______________ statement.
9. The FILE STATUS clause is (optional/required) and requires that a ______________ byte area be defined in ______________ ______________.
10. FILE STATUS bytes of ______________ indicate a successful I/O operation, whereas ______________ indicates an end-of-file condition.
11. The ______________ statement allows one to enter an indexed file randomly and read sequentially from that point on.
12. A random (nonsequential) READ statement is preceded by a MOVE statement in which the desired key is moved to the field defined as the ______________ ______________.
13. Specification of ACCESS IS ______________ permits both sequential and nonsequential access of an indexed file in the same program.
14. When a file is open in the ______________ mode, it may be read from and written to.

TRUE/FALSE

1. ALTERNATE RECORD KEY should always be specified for indexed files to allow for future expansion.
2. The FILE STATUS clause is permitted only for indexed files.
3. A READ statement must contain either the AT END or INVALID KEY clause.
4. Inclusion of the INTO clause in a READ statement is not recommended, as it requires additional storage space.
5. RESERVE 0 AREAS is recommended to speed up processing of an indexed file that is processed sequentially.
6. The value of RECORD KEY must be unique for every record in an indexed file.
7. The value of ALTERNATE RECORD KEY must be unique for every record in an indexed file.
8. The FILE STATUS clause is a mandatory entry in the SELECT statement for an indexed file.
9. An indexed file can be accessed sequentially and nonsequentially in the same program.
10. The first byte of an indexed record should contain either LOW- or HIGH-VALUES.
11. WRITE and REWRITE can be used interchangeably.
12. Records in an indexed file are deleted by moving HIGH-VALUES to the first byte.
13. The COBOL syntax for IBM VSAM files conforms to the ANS 85 standard.
14. Active files are best updated nonsequentially.

PROBLEMS

1. Describe the changes to Figure 18.3 if record keys 401, 723, 724, and 725 were added. What would happen if record keys 502 and 619 were deleted?
2. Assume that record key 289 is to be inserted in the first control area of the VSAM data set in Figure 18.3. Logically, it could be added as the last record in the first control interval or the first record in the second control interval. Is there a preference?

   In similar fashion, should record 620 be inserted as the last record in the third interval of the second area or as the first record in the first interval of the third area?

   Finally, will record 900 be inserted as the last record in the fourth control area, or will it require creation of a fifth control area? Can you describe in general terms how VSAM adds records at the end of control areas and/or control intervals?
3. Indicate whether each of the following SELECT statements is valid syntactically and logically. (Some of the statements have more than one error.)

   a.
```
SELECT INDEXED-FILE
    ASSIGN DA-INDEXED
    ORGANIZATION INDEXED
    RECORD IND-SOC-SEC-NUM.
```

b.
```
SELECT INDEXED-FILE
    ASSIGN TO DA-INDEXED
    RECORD KEY IS IND-SOC-SEC-NUM WITH NO DUPLICATES
    ALTERNATE KEY IS IND-NAME WITH DUPLICATES.
```

c.
```
SELECT INDEXED-FILE
    ASSIGN TO DA-INDEXED
    RESERVE 5 AREAS
    ORGANIZATION IS INDEXED
    ACCESS IS SEQUENTIAL
    RECORD KEY IS IND-SOC-SEC-NUM WITH DUPLICATES
    ALTERNATE RECORD KEY IS IND-NAME
    FILE STATUS IS FILE-STATUS-BYTES.
```

d.
```
SELECT INDEXED-FILE
    ASSIGN TO DA-INDEXED
    ORGANIZATION IS INDEXED
    ACCESS MODE RANDOM
    RECORD KEY IS IND-SOC-SEC-NUM, IND-NAME.
```

4. Given the COBOL definition:

```
    05  FILE-STATUS-BYTES              PIC 99.
```

What is wrong with the following entries?

a.
```
IF FILE-STATUS-BYTES EQUAL '10'
    DISPLAY 'END OF FILE HAS BEEN REACHED'
END-IF
```

b.
```
IF FILE STATUS-BYTES EQUAL 10
    DISPLAY 'ERROR - DUPLICATE KEY'
END-IF
```

c.
```
IF FILE-STATUS-BYTE EQUAL 1
    DISPLAY 'END OF FILE HAS BEEN REACHED'
END-IF
```

d.
```
IF FILE STATUS BYTES EQUAL 10
    DISPLAY 'END OF FILE HAS BEEN REACHED'
END-IF
```

5. Indicate whether each of the following entries is valid syntactically and logically. (Assume INDEXED-FILE and INDEXED-RECORD are valid as a file name and a record name, respectively.)

a.
```
OPEN INPUT INDEXED-FILE
     OUTPUT INDEXED-FILE.
```

b.
```
READ INDEXED-FILE.
```

c.
```
READ INDEXED-FILE
    AT END MOVE 'YES' TO END-OF-FILE-SWITCH.
END-READ.
```

d.
```
READ INDEXED-FILE
    AT END
        MOVE 'YES' TO END-OF-FILE-SWITCH
    NOT AT END
        PERFORM PROCESS-RECORD
END-READ.
```

e.
```
READ INDEXED-FILE
    AT END MOVE 21 TO FILE-STATUS-BYTES.
```

f.
```
READ INDEXED-FILE
    INVALID KEY
        DISPLAY 'RECORD IS IN FILE'
    NOT INVALID KEY
        DISPLAY 'RECORD IS NOT IN FILE'
END-READ.
```

g.
```
WRITE INDEXED-RECORD.
```

h.
```
WRITE INDEXED-RECORD
    INVALID KEY
        DISPLAY 'INVALID KEY'
    NOT INVALID KEY
        PERFORM CONTINUE-PROCESSING
END-WRITE.
```

i.
```
REWRITE INDEXED-RECORD
    INVALID KEY
        DISPLAY 'INVALID KEY'
        PERFORM ERROR-PROCESSING
END-REWRITE.
```

j.
```
REWRITE INDEXED-FILE.
```

k.
```
DELETE INDEXED-RECORD.
```

l.
```
DELETE INDEXED-FILE.
```

6. Figure 18.14a contains a slightly modified paragraph from the nonsequential update program of Figure 18.10, which produces the compiler diagnostics in Figure 18.14b. Why do the errors occur?
7. The balance line algorithm was not used for the nonsequential update program (Figure 18.10) developed in the chapter. The resulting program worked correctly, but it can be made more efficient by changing its logic to include the concept of the active key.
   a. What are the advantages of including the additional logic and using the balance line algorithm?
   b. What are the disadvantages to this approach?
   c. Modify the hierarchy chart and pseudocode of Figures 18.8 and 18.9 to accommodate the algorithm.

Figure 18.14 Debugging Exercise

```
60      PROCEDURE DIVISION.
61      0010-UPDATE-MASTER-FILE.
62          OPEN INPUT TRANSACTION-FILE
63                 I-O INDEXED-FILE.
64          PERFORM UNTIL END-OF-FILE-SWITCH = 'YES'
65              READ TRANSACTION-FILE INTO WS-TRANS-RECORD
66                  AT END
67                      MOVE 'YES' TO END-OF-FILE-SWITCH
68                  NOT AT END
69                      PERFORM 0020-READ-INDEXED-FILE
70                      PERFORM 0030-APPLY-TRANS-TO-MASTER.
71              END-READ
72          END-PERFORM
```

(a) Modified Procedure Division

```
64 W Explicit scope terminator END- 'PERFORM' assumed present
71 E No corresponding active scope for 'END-READ'
72 E No corresponding active scope for 'END-PERFORM'
```

(b) Error Messages

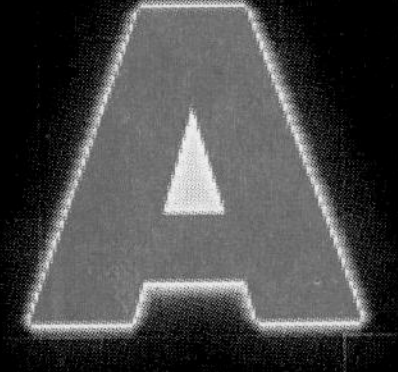

CA-Realia® Classroom COBOL and Data Disk

Overview: This appendix describes in summary form the use of CA-Realia® Classroom COBOL and the associated data disk that accompanies this text. Additional instructions are provided in the form of hands-on exercises in Appendix B and are referenced as appropriate. The CA-Realia disk contains the Classroom COBOL compiler, the batch files to compile and link a COBOL program, and the utility programs described below. The data disk contains the CA-Realia editor (RED), every COBOL program in the text, and data files for all projects in Appendix F.

Utilities: The educational versions of four utility programs are provided in conjunction with Classroom COBOL and are installed with the compiler in the REALCOB subdirectory. The utilities include a link program, editor, interactive debugger, and indexed utility to create and/or print indexed files. The link program, **LINK.EXE**, is executed as the middle step in the compile, link, and execute sequence. The editor, **RED**, is designed specifically for COBOL programs and is illustrated in exercise 3 of Appendix B. The interactive debugger, **REALDBUG**, displays program statements as they are executed and is described in exercise 4 of Appendix B. The indexed utility, **REALCOPY,** creates and/or prints indexed files and is illustrated in exercise 5 of Appendix B.

Hardware Requirements: Classroom COBOL is very powerful, yet altogether modest in its hardware requirements. It requires a minimum of 160Kb of free memory and DOS 3.2 or higher. A hard disk is not required provided you have a high-density floppy drive.

Limitations of Classroom COBOL: Classroom COBOL is fully functional and limited only by the size of the program it can accept. In particular:

1. Programs for compilation cannot be larger than 500 statements. (Comments do not count.) You can, however, *use subprograms to overcome this limitation*; that is, program A can call program B, which in turn can call program C, and so on.
2. Execution time files cannot exceed 64Kb.
3. All programs, regardless of size, must compile in the available memory.

Installation of CA-Realia Software: Insert the CA-Realia disk into drive A. Type **A:** to make drive A the default drive, then type the command **REALINST** to begin the installation procedure. Follow the instructions displayed on the monitor to complete the installation. Once the installation is complete, you should modify the PATH command in the AUTOEXEC.BAT file (on the root directory) to reflect the REALCOB subdirectory. You should also add the command SHELL=C:\COMMAND.COM/E:1200/P to the CONFIG.SYS file (also on the root directory) to increase the environment space needed to contain the SET statements issued in conjunction with COBOL programs. Finally, you need to copy the CA-Realia editor (RED) from the data disk to the REALCOB subdirectory. The installation procedure is further illustrated in exercise 1 of Appendix B.

Installation of the Data Disk: The data disk contains the CA-Realia editor (RED), every COBOL program that appears in the text, all associated data files, as well as data files for all projects in Appendix F. You will find it convenient to copy the data disk to the hard disk, provided you have your own computer and are not sharing it with other students in a laboratory situation. (You can still use the data disk even if you are sharing a computer; just place it into drive A every time you access the COBOL compiler.) To copy the files on the data disk to the hard disk, place the data disk into drive A, type **A:** to make the disk in drive A the default, then type INSTALL followed by the letter of the drive where you want the data files—for example, **INSTALL C** to install the data disk on drive C.

The CA-Realia Editor (RED): Classroom COBOL is accompanied by its own editor which is designed specifically for COBOL programs. You can, however, use any ASCII editor—for example, EDIT in DOS 5.0, or a word processor provided you save the COBOL program as an ASCII file. RED is illustrated in exercise 3 in Appendix B.

Compile, Link, and Go Sequence: The compile, link, and execute sequence is described fully in exercise 2 in Appendix B and summarized below. The exercise requires you to change to the subdirectory containing the program and associated data files. In addition, you may need to change the default drive, depending on whether or not you copied the data disk to the hard drive. Thus,

Type **C:** and press ↵ if you copied the data disk to the hard disk
or Type **A:** and press ↵ if you are using the data disk in drive A

The remaining commands are typical for any COBOL program; for example, to compile, link, and execute the program SENIOR.COB, which uses one input file and produces one report as output, and which is located in the subdirectory \DATADISK\CHAPTR02, enter the following:

`CD \DATADISK\CHAPTR02 ↵`	Changes to the subdirectory containing the COBOL program
`C SENIOR ↵`	Uses the batch file C.BAT to compile the program SENIOR.COB. (Assumes the existence of a DOS path command to the REALCOB subdirectory)
`L SENIOR ↵`	Uses the batch file L.BAT to link the object module produced by the compiler and produce an executable load module. (Assumes the existence of a DOS path command to the REALCOB subdirectory)
`SET SYSIN=SENIOR.DAT ↵`	Ties the COBOL SELECT statement to the input data file SENIOR.DAT found in the subdirectory
`SET SYSOUT=SENIOR.RPT[N] ↵`	Ties the COBOL SELECT statement to the output report produced by the program
`SENIOR ↵`	Executes the program

Batch Files: The compile, link, and execute sequence uses our batch files, C.BAT and L.BAT, to simplify the required DOS commands. You can, however, create your own batch files to simplify the execution (testing) of the same program from one session to the next, especially when multiple SET statements are required. Thus, if you were to create an additional batch file such as SAVETIME.BAT containing the necessary SET statements, all you would need to do is type the name of the batch file, SAVETIME, every time you want to execute the SET statements. (See ONE.BAT, TWO.BAT, and THREE.BAT in the CHAPTR15 subdirectory for batch files pertaining to one-, two-, and three-level control breaks, respectively.)

Windows: Classroom COBOL may be run from a DOS window within the Windows environment. Open the Main Group, double click on the MS-DOS icon to obtain the C prompt, then issue commands as described above. If you see the message *Insufficient Memory* when attempting to compile, exit Windows completely and run from DOS.

File Status Codes: File status codes are defined within the COBOL standard to indicate the nature of an execution error. One very common error is a missing and/or incorrect SET statement. Recall that the purpose of the COBOL SELECT statement is to tie a programmer-chosen file name such as STUDENT-FILE to a system name such as SYSIN, and that the DOS SET statement associates that system name with a file on disk such as SENIOR.DAT. Should you forget to include the proper SET statements and/or misspell either the system name or DOS file name, you will be confronted with an error message of the form:

```
RCL0002: File status 35 on C:SENIR.DAT
    Error detected at offset 0042 in segment 00 of program SENIOR
```

The message indicates that the program could not find the file SENIR.DAT; the problem was produced by an improper SET statement, which misspelled the name of the data file as SENIR.DAT rather than SENIOR.DAT. The complete list of file status codes is found on page 555.

Debugging: REALDBUG, the interactive debugger, is invaluable and fully illustrated in exercise 4 in Appendix B. The debugger enables you to see program statements as they are executed, display intermediate results, set break points, and so on.

Subprograms: The use of a subprogram(s) requires that the subprogram(s) be compiled as a separate entity, then linked together with the main program to form a single load module. For example, to compile, link, and execute a main program and two subprograms (all of which are assumed to be in the same directory), enter the commands below:

`C MAIN ↵`	Compiles the main program
`C SUB1 ↵`	Compiles the first subprogram
`C SUB2 ↵`	Compiles the second subprogram
`L MAIN+SUB1+SUB2 ↵`	Links the three separate object modules produced by the individual compilations into a single load module
`SET statements ↵`	One SET statement for every COBOL SELECT statement in the main and/or subprograms
`MAIN ↵`	Executes the load module

COPY Statement: The file containing the COPY member must have the extension **COB,** the same extension used for COBOL programs. There are no additional requirements provided the COPY member(s) is in the same directory as the COBOL program. Some programmers, however, prefer to place all COPY members in a single directory, such as C:\COPYLIB, so that the members can be accessed by any COBOL program. This is turn requires the specification of an additional SET statement; **SET SYSLIB=;C:\COPYLIB** *prior* to compilation. (The semicolon immediately after the equal sign indicates the compiler is to look in the current directory for the COPY member; the other directory indicates the common library for all COPY members.)

SORT Statement: There are no additional requirements in support of the COBOL SORT statement other than the SET statements for the associated files; for example, a SORT statement with USING/GIVING option requires three SET statements for the input, output, and sort-work files, respectively.

Indexed Files: Indexed files enable nonsequential access to individual records and thus cannot be created nor viewed in the normal fashion, such as with the DOS TYPE command. Accordingly, the REALCOPY utility is provided to facilitate access to indexed files and is described in exercise 5 of Appendix B.

Compiler Switches: The action of the compiler can be altered at compile time through use of switches and/or compiler directives. Compiler switches are specified by a slash after the program name; for example, C SENIOR /Q will compile the program SENIOR.COB with the Q (quotation mark) switch in effect. Consider:

- `/C` Checks subscripts; the generated code ensures that the execution time values for all subscripts and indexes are within the proper range (not less than one and not greater than the maximum occurrence number)
- `/D` Implements the equivalent of a data-exception check on IBM 370 type mainframe by checking that nonbinary operands have valid sign and decimal digit values
- `/H` Generates debugger information in the form of a symbol table produced as an additional file during compilation with extension SYM. The /H switch is included in the C.BAT file
- `/K` Prohibits lowercase letters, treating them as invalid characters as required by the COBOL-74 standard
- `/Q` Sets quote mode; specifies that nonnumeric literals are to be enclosed in quotation marks (the ANSI standard) as opposed to apostrophes
- `/R` Reduces the length of the LST file from 132 characters to 80. The /R switch is included in the C.BAT file
- `/U` Generates a cross-reference listing of unreferenced items only; can be used in conjunction with the /X switch to produce a cross reference of both referenced and unreferenced items
- `/X` Generates a cross-reference listing of referenced items; the cross-reference listing was illustrated in Figure 6.6 in Chapter 6

EBCDIC versus ASCII: Classroom COBOL will compile under the EBCDIC (rather than default ASCII) collating sequence by entering the compiler directive SET COBDIREC=EBCDIC *prior* to compilation. The difference between the two collating sequences, and their effects on sorting and signed numbers, was explained in Chapter 14.

More about the Data Disk: The data disk contains the subdirectory DATADISK, which in turn is further divided into additional subdirectories corresponding to the chapters in the book. The contents of the data disk are shown in Figure A.1.

All of the files used in conjunction with a particular chapter appear together in the corresponding subdirectory—for example, \DATADISK\CHAPTR05 for the programs in Chapter 5. The following conventions apply to the files on the data disk.

1. The extension COB signifies a COBOL program (in ASCII format) suitable for input to Classroom COBOL or for uploading on a mainframe; the file name matches the entry in the PROGRAM-ID paragraph of the program (or the referenced name in a COPY statement).

2. The extension DAT signifies a data file; file names that begin with PRJ signify the data file for the end-of-chapter project; for example, PRJ07-03.DAT contains the data for Project 3 in Chapter 7.

3. The extension BAT signifies a batch file containing all of the SET commands needed for the programs in a given directory.

```
A:\
  COPYFILE.MSG
  COPYRITE.TXT
  ERROR.MSG
  FINISHED.MSG
  INSTALL.BAT
  INVALID.MSG
  WARNMD.MSG
  RED.EXE
  CHAPTR02
    FIRSTTRY.COB
    FIRSTTRY.DAT
    SENIOR.DAT
    SENIOR74.COB
    SENIOREE.COB
    SENIORCE.COB
    PRJ02-01.DAT
    PRJ02-02.DAT
    PRJ02-03.DAT
    PRJ02-04.DAT
    PRJ02-05.DAT
    PRJ02-06.DAT
    PRJ02-07.DAT
    SENIOR.COB
  CHAPTR03
    TUITION.DAT
    TUITION3.COB
    PRJ03-01.DAT
    PRJ03-02.DAT
    PRJ03-03.DAT
    PRJ03-04.DAT
    PRJ03-05.DAT
    PRJ03-06.DAT
    PRJ03-07.DAT
    PRJ03-08.DAT
  CHAPTR05
    TUITION.DAT
    TUITION5.COB
  CHAPTR06
    TUIT6COM.COB
    TUIT6EXE.COB
    TUITION.DAT
  CHAPTR07
    TUITION7.DAT
    TUITION7.COB
    PRJ07-01.DAT
    PRJ07-02.DAT
    PRJ07-03.DAT
    PRJ07-04.DAT
    PRJ07-06.DAT
    PRJ07-07.DAT
    PRJ07-09.DAT
  CHAPTR08
    CARS.DAT
    CARSETS.BAT
    PRJ08-01.DAT
    PRJ08-02.DAT
    PRJ08-03.DAT
    PRJ08-04.DAT
    VALCARS.DAT
    PRJ08-05.DAT
    PRJ08-06.DAT
    PRJ08-07.DAT
    VALCARS.COB
    PRJ08-08.DAT
    PRJ08-09.DAT
  CHAPTR09
    VALCARS.DAT
    CARSRPT.COB
  CHAPTR10
    SCRNCARS.COB
    SCRNTUIT.COB
  CHAPTR11
    STUDENT.DAT
    TRANSCRP.COB
    PRJ11-01.DAT
    PRJ11-03.DAT
    PRJ11-04.DAT
    PRJ11-05.DAT
    PRJ11-06.DAT
  CHAPTR12
    TABLES.COB
    TABLES.DAT
    TITLES.DAT
    TABLESX.BAT
    PRJ12-02.DAT
    PRJ12-03.DAT
    PRJ12-04.DAT
    PRJ12-06.DAT
    PRJ12-08.DAT
    PRJ12-09.DAT
    PRJ12-07.DAT
  CHAPTR13
    2LVTABLE.COB
    TABLES.BAT
    TABLES.DAT
    3LVTABLE.COB
    CALORIES.COB
    PRJ13-01.DAT
    PRJ13-02.DAT
    PRJ13-03.DAT
  CHAPTR14
    SORT1.COB
    SORTIN.DAT
    XSORT1.BAT
    XSORT2.BAT
    SORT2.COB
    PRJ14-01.DAT
    PRJ14-02.DAT
    PRJ14-03.DAT
    PRJ14-04.DAT
    PRJ14-05.DAT
    PRJ14-06.DAT
    PRJ14-07.DAT
    PRJ14-08.DAT
  CHAPTR15
    ONE.BAT
    SORTED.DAT
    TWO.BAT
    SORTIN.DAT
    THREE.BAT
    THRLEVEL.COB
    TWOLEVEL.COB
    ONELEVEL.COB
  CHAPTR16
    INPUTSUB.COB
    COLORCPY.COB
    TIMESUB.COB
    TRAINSUB.COB
    MALEWGT.COB
    FEMWGT.COB
    WGTSUB.COB
    LFIT.BAT
    INPUTREC.COB
    PRJ16-01.DAT
    TRAINCPY.COB
    WGTCOPY.COB
    FITNESS.COB
    DISPCPY.COB
    DSPLYSUB.COB
    16-1STAT.DAT
  CHAPTR17
    EDIT.COB
    EDITSETS.BAT
    OLDMAST.DAT
    SEQSTUB.COB
    SEQUPDT.COB
    TRANS.DAT
    VALTRANS.DAT
    MAS17-02.DAT
    MAS17-03.DAT
    MAS17-04.DAT
    MAS17-08.DAT
    TRN17-02.DAT
    TRN17-03.DAT
    TRN17-04.DAT
    TRN17-05.DAT
    TRN17-08.DAT
    TRN17-06.DAT
    TRN17-07.DAT
  CHAPTR18
    ALTINDEX.COB
    ALTINPUT.DAT
    CREATE.COB
    NONSEQUP.COB
    NONSETS.BAT
    SEQUENCE.DAT
    VALTRANS.DAT
    INDMAST.DAT
    ALTINDEX.DAT
    MAS18-08.DAT
    TRN18-08.DAT
```

Hands-on Exercises

Overview: This appendix consists of five hands-on exercises, which provide detailed instruction on Classroom COBOL and the associated utilities. The exercises are straightforward and offer step-by-step instructions to make you proficient in the use of the CA-Realia software.

Exercise 1: Installation

Exercise 2: Compile, link, and execute a COBOL program

Exercise 3: RED—The CA-Realia® editor

Exercise 4: REALDBUG—The interactive debugger

Exercise 5: REALCOPY—Creating and printing indexed files

HANDS-ON EXERCISE 1:

Installation

Discussion: The installation procedure assumes you are familiar with the DOS concept of ***subdirectories***, which divide a disk into separate (logical) areas, much as a book is divided into chapters. Hence one portion of the disk (one subdirectory) will be established for the CA-Realia software, while other subdirectories will be created for the COBOL programs and associated data files. The installation procedure will also set a ***path*** to the newly created REALCOB subdirectory, enabling DOS to execute these programs from whichever subdirectory you happen to be in. With this in mind the installation procedure will do the following:

1. Create a subdirectory on drive C (C:\REALCOB), then copy all of the CA-Realia files from drive A into the newly created subdirectory on drive C.
2. Direct you to modify and/or create the CONFIG.SYS file on the root directory of drive C to increase the allocated space for environmental variables, that is, the SET commands required for the various files in your COBOL program.
3. Direct you to modify and/or create the AUTOEXEC.BAT file on the root directory of drive C to include a PATH command that references the subdirectory containing Classroom COBOL.

Step 1: Boot the System

Boot the system as you would for any other program and end at the DOS prompt. If you are running under Windows, open the Main Group, then double click on the MS-DOS icon to arrive at the DOS prompt.

Step 2: Install Classroom COBOL

Place the CA-Realia disk into drive A, then enter the commands:

```
A: ↵
REALINST ↵
```

The first command makes drive A the default drive. The second command executes the installation program, REALINST, which asks you where to install the CA-Realia software. Press return if you are content with the default selection, C:\REALCOB, or enter another drive and/or directory as you see fit. Follow the instructions displayed on the monitor to complete the installation.

Step 3a: Additional Installation Procedure (CONFIG.SYS)

Classroom COBOL requires the presence of a CONFIG.SYS file in the root directory on drive C. It is quite likely that this file already exists (in which case you may or may not have to add an additional command); if, however, a CONFIG.SYS file is not present, you will to have to create the file at this time. To see if the CONFIG.SYS file is present, enter the command:

```
TYPE C:\CONFIG.SYS ↵
```

whereupon the system will either display the contents of the existing CONFIG.SYS file, or respond with the message, *File not found - CONFIG.SYS.* If the file exists, check to see that it contains the FILES and SHELL commands shown below, and if not, modify the existing CONFIG.SYS file to include these commands. (Be sure to save the modified file as an ASCII file.)

If, on the other hand, your system does not contain a CONFIG.SYS file, you need to create one with the following commands:

```
CD C:\ ↵
COPY CON: CONFIG.SYS ↵
FILES=20 ↵
SHELL=C:\COMMAND.COM/E:1200/P ↵
```
Press the **F6** key followed by the enter key

Verify that you have created the CONFIG.SYS file by repeating the TYPE command you issued previously—**TYPE C:\CONFIG.SYS**—to display the CONFIG.SYS file on your monitor.

Step 3b: Additional Installation Procedure (AUTOEXEC.BAT)

The procedure to compile, link, and execute a COBOL program (described in the next exercise) requires the existence of a PATH command, which is best specified in the AUTOEXEC.BAT file on the root directory. Again, it is quite likely that your system already contains this file, which can be verified with the command:

```
TYPE C:\AUTOEXEC.BAT ↵
```

As in the previous step, the system will either display the contents of the existing AUTOEXEC.BAT file, or it will respond with the message, *File not found - AUTOEXEC.BAT.* It is more than likely that your system already has an existing

AUTOEXEC.BAT file, in which case you need to modify (add) the existing PATH command to include an additional subdirectory indicating the directory for Classroom COBOL. (The path you specify must be consistent with your choice of directory during installation—for example, C:\REALCOB if you accepted the default drive and directory in step 2.)

If, on the other hand, your system does not contain an AUTOEXEC.BAT file, you need to create one with the following commands:

```
CD C:\ ↵
COPY CON: AUTOEXEC.BAT ↵
PATH C:\REALCOB ↵
```

Press the **F6** key followed by the enter key

Verify that you have created the AUTOEXEC.BAT file by repeating the TYPE command you issued previously—**TYPE C:\AUTOEXEC.BAT**—to display the AUTOEXEC.BAT file on your monitor.

Step 3c: Additional Installation Procedure (the Data Disk)

The data disk contains the CA-Realia editor, every COBOL program that appears in the text, all associated data files, as well as data files for projects at the end of each chapter. You will find it convenient to copy the data disk to the hard disk, provided you have your own computer and are not sharing it with other students in a laboratory situation. (You can still use the data disk even if you are sharing a computer by placing it into drive A every time you access the COBOL compiler.) If you do have your own computer, however, we suggest you copy the data disk to the hard drive at this time by doing the following:

1. Place the data disk into drive A
2. Type **A:** (to change to drive A)
3. Type INSTALL followed by the drive name—for example, **INSTALL C** to install the data disk on drive C

Step 3d: Additional Installation Procedure—the CA-Realia Editor (RED)

Although you can use any ASCII editor or word processor to create and edit COBOL programs, we suggest you install the CA-Realia editor because it is specifically tailored to the needs of the COBOL programmer. Accordingly:

1. Check that the data disk is still in drive A
2. Type **C:** to change to drive C
3. Type **CD C:\REALCOB** to change to the REALCOB subdirectory
4. Type **COPY A:\RED.EXE** to copy the editor from the data disk in drive A to the REALCOB subdirectory

Step 4: Verify the Installation

Change to the root directory of drive C with the command, **CD C:** to verify that you have in fact accomplished what you set out to do by viewing the files in this directory. Enter the command **DIR/P** (the /P will cause the monitor to pause if the root directory contains more files than can be seen at one time.) The contents of the root directory will, of course, depend on your particular computer, but in any event, it should contain entries for the REALCOB and DATADISK subdirectories (if you copied the convenience disk to your hard drive), and also the CONFIG.SYS and AUTOEXEC.BAT files.

Step 5: Change to the REALCOB Subdirectory

Type **CD \REALCOB**, then type **DIR** to view the contents of this subdirectory, which should contain the files shown below:

```
Directory of C:\REALCOB
C        BAT        22 10-17-92    8:50a
CLEAN    BAT        86 01-09-93    9:32a
L        BAT        31 02-12-92   11:57a
LINK     EXE     49808 02-28-92   12:07p
REALCOB  EXE    775061 03-30-93    2:51p
REALCOPY EXE     80704 03-19-93    3:48p
REALDBUG EXE    160583 03-30-93    4:11p
REALDOS  LIB    198656 03-18-93    4:00p
RED      EXE     64079 03-18-93    4:10p
```

If you do not see the very last file, RED.EXE, return to the additional installation procedure described in step 3d. The REALCOB directory contains the program (COM) files for the compiler, editor, debugger, and link program. It also contains two batch files, C.BAT and L.BAT, to compile and link a COBOL program, and a third batch file, CLEAN.BAT, to erase excess files at the end of the exercises.

Step 6: View the Data Disk

You can also view the contents of the convenience disk, but the commands depend on whether or not you copied the convenience disk to the hard drive in step 3c. Thus, if you copied the data disk to the hard disk:

Type **CD C:\DATADISK** and press ↵
Type **DIR** and press ↵

If, however, you did not copy the data disk to the hard disk:

Place the data disk into drive A
Type **A:** and press ↵
Type **DIR** and press ↵

Either way you will see a list of subdirectories corresponding to the different chapters in the book, with each subdirectory containing the files associated with that chapter.

HANDS-ON EXERCISE 2:

Compile, Link, and Execute a COBOL Program

Discussion: This exercise takes advantage of batch files to shorten the commands needed to compile and link a COBOL program. A batch file, such as C.BAT or L.BAT, contains one or more DOS commands, which are executed collectively by entering the name of the file (C or L in the example). In other words, a batch file may be viewed as a program consisting of individual DOS commands.

The batch file C.BAT consists of the single line, REALCOB/RH %1,,[N] to invoke the compiler. (The purpose of the R and H compiler switches was explained in Appendix A; the [N] eliminates tabs from the source listing.) The key to the batch file is the %1, which indicates a DOS ***replaceable parameter*** (variable). In other words DOS will substitute whatever value you supply in conjunction with the batch command for the %1. Hence if you type the command C SENIOR, DOS replaces the %1 with SENIOR, producing the command REALCOB /RH SENIOR,,[N]. As you can see, batch files make life easier by saving time and reducing the chance for error in entering complicated commands.

Step 1: Change to the Appropriate Directory

Boot the system, ending at the DOS prompt. The selection of a default drive and directory depends on the location of the COBOL files, that is, on whether or not you copied the data disk to the hard disk in step 3c of the previous exercise. Thus, if you copied the data disk to the hard disk in step 3c of the installation:

1. Type **C:** and press ↵
2. Type CD \DATADISK\CHAPTR02 and press ↵

If, however, you did not copy the data disk to the hard disk:

1. Place the data disk into drive A
2. Type **A:** and press ↵
3. Type **CD \CHAPTR02** and press ↵

Step 2: Create the Program File

Normally you would have to create the file containing the COBOL program. We have, however, made life easier by including all of the illustrative COBOL programs and associated data files on the data disk. Type **DIR** to verify the existence of these files, which this time will display the contents of the CHAPTR02 subdirectory; two of the files, SENIOR.COB and SENIOR.DAT, will be used in this exercise.

Step 3: Create the File of Test Data

Normally, you would have to create a second file containing the test data. As we have already indicated, this has been done for you as the file SENIOR.DAT already exists on the data disk.

Step 4: Compile the Program

Type **C SENIOR** to compile the program. This simple command invokes the batch file C.BAT (containing the command that invokes Classroom COBOL) in conjunction with the COBOL program SENIOR.COB. The following messages will appear on the monitor as compilation takes place:

```
CA-Realia Classroom COBOL Version 4.200
Copyright (c) 1993 Computer Associates International, Inc..
19:17:07 Pass 1
 .
   .
19:17:08 End of compilation
```

Step 5: View the Results of Compilation

Type the command **DIR SENIOR.*** to see the various files created as a result of the compilation. You should see the original program file SENIOR.COB, as well as three additional SENIOR files with extensions OBJ, LST, and SYM. The first file,

SENIOR.OBJ, is the object (machine language) program that will be input to the link program. The second file, SENIOR.LST, contains the COBOL listing and associated compilation messages. The final file, SENIOR.SYM, contains a symbol table used by the interactive debugger (see exercise 4).

The program will compile without error because you are using our file from the data disk. Note, however, that when you enter your own program in other exercises, you are apt to make mistakes that result in one or more compilation errors. This in turn requires you to return to the editor to correct your program, after which you have to check for compilation errors, and if necessary reedit the program, recompile, and so on, until you have a clean compile.

You can obtain a hard copy of the listing with the command **TYPE SENIOR.LST>LPT1**. (The TYPE command displays the contents of the indicated file on the monitor; the greater than sign redirects the output to the printer, which produces the hard copy.)

Step 6: Link the Program

After the program has compiled cleanly (that is, there are no compilation errors), you are ready to link the object program just created to produce the executable load module. Type **L SENIOR** to invoke the L.BAT file, which in turn executes the link program. Type **DIR SENIOR.*** to view the additional files created by the linkage editor, which now include SENIOR.MAP and SENIOR.EXE; the latter is the load module that will be executed in step 8.

Step 7: Enter the Necessary SET Commands

A DOS SET command is required for every file in the COBOL program. Thus, since the engineering senior program used two files, two SET statements are required. Enter the commands *exactly* as they appear (there are no spaces on either side of the equal sign):

```
SET SYSIN=SENIOR.DAT ↵
SET SYSOUT=SENIOR.RPT[N] ↵
```

To better understand the nature of these critically important statements, consider the SELECT statements that appeared in the engineering senior program:

```
SELECT STUDENT-FILE ASSIGN TO UT-S-SYSIN.
SELECT PRINT-FILE ASSIGN TO UT-S-SYSOUT.
```

The COBOL SELECT statement ties a programmer-chosen filename such as STUDENT-FILE, to a system name such as SYSIN. The DOS SET command then ties system name, SYSIN, to the actual file (data) as it exists on disk. In other words the COBOL program is reading records from the file STUDENT-FILE, which is now associated with the data file SENIOR.DAT. In similar fashion, the program will write its report to PRINT-FILE, which will be contained in the file SENIOR.RPT. (You can also type SET, with no additional parameters, to display the DOS environmental variables and see if they are correct.)

Step 8: Execute the Program

Type **SENIOR** to execute the SENIOR.EXE load module (i.e., the COBOL program), which is to read the student records file and produce the list of engineering seniors as output. Enter the command **TYPE SENIOR.RPT** to display the report on the monitor. You should see the single heading line, followed by the name of the qualified seniors, Orville Wright and John Roebling.

You can obtain hard copy of the report by using the greater than sign to redirect output to the printer; enter the command **TYPE SENIOR.RPT>LPT1** to produce a printed copy of the report.

Step 9: Erase Unnecessary Files

The exercise began with two files, SENIOR.COB and SENIOR.DAT, containing the program and data files, respectively. It ended with an additional six files, with extensions of LST, OBJ, SYM, MAP, EXE, and RPT. We suggest you delete the latter six files to conserve space on your disk through individual ERASE (DEL) commands, or through our CLEAN.BAT utility, which has been installed in the REALCOB directory. Type **CLEAN SENIOR** at the DOS prompt to erase the files; do not delete SENIOR.COB or SENIOR.DAT, or you will be unable to recreate the exercise.

HANDS-ON EXERCISE 3:

RED—The CA-Realia® Editor

Discussion: The exercises in this appendix use the COBOL programs that exist on our data disk, but sooner or later you will have to create your own programs. You can use the DOS EDIT command (available in DOS 5.00 or higher), or any other editor with which you are familiar. You can also use a word processor (e.g., WordPerfect) provided you save the program as an ASCII (text file; e.g., Ctrl+F5 in WordPerfect). Alternatively, you can use the CA-Realia editor, RED, which is tailored to the requirements of COBOL. (The editor is contained on the data disk and was installed in step 3d in hands-on Exercise 1.)

The CA-Realia editor is extremely powerful, but there is no need to learn all of its commands. Indeed, you can probably use it immediately, with what you already know about another editor—for example, insertion and replacement. You can then use the extensive on-line help facility as necessary, to master the more sophisticated commands and gain proficiency.

The exercise that follows shows how to load the editor, how to find and correct compilation errors, how to make changes, and how to save the edited program. It also introduces the on-line help facility to explore some of the more sophisticated features that enable you to create and/or modify COBOL programs more efficiently.

Step 1: Change to the Appropriate Subdirectory

Change to the CHAPTR02 subdirectory as described in step 1 of the preceding exercise. Type **C SENIORCE** to compile the engineering senior program found in this directory, which produces the following error messages on the screen:

```
60 W Period assumed before 'IF'

63 E Undefined symbol 'WRTE'

64 E No corresponding active scope for 'END-IF'
```

Don't worry about the compilation errors because we have deliberately selected this program to illustrate one of the best features of the editor—its ability to find and correct compilation errors. The editor uses the existing LST file produced by the compilation, and which contains the list of compilation errors, to position you at the line(s) within the COBOL program where the error(s) are detected.

Step 2: Load RED

Type **RED SENIORCE.COB/N** to load the editor and produce the screen of Figure B.1a. (The /N in the command to load the editor is important as it prevents tabs from being inserted into the COBOL program, which become a problem only if you return to a different editor.) The status line at the bottom of the screen contains the program name; the vertical lines above the status line show the predetermined tab stops (discussed in step 12).

Step 3: Correct Compilation Errors

Press **Alt+E** to position the cursor at the first compilation error as shown in Figure B.1b; the IF statement is highlighted, with the associated error message, *Period assumed before IF*, shown at the bottom of the screen. Use the arrow keys to move to the paragraph header, and enter a period after the paragraph name.

Press **Alt+E** until you come to the next error and associated message, *Undefined symbol WRTE.* Insert the missing I (press the Ins key if necessary to toggle to the insert mode). Press **Alt+E** a final time to display the last error, *No corresponding active scope for END-IF.* Remove the period after WRITE PRINT-LINE to correct the error.

Step 4: Save the Corrected Program

Press **Alt+F1** to save the corrected program and return to the DOS prompt. Type **C SENIORCE** to recompile the program and verify that the compilation errors have been corrected. Type **RED SENIORCE.COB/N** to reenter the editor and continue with the exercise.

Step 5: The Delete and Undelete Commands

Move to the beginning of the program. Press **F4** to delete the first line of the program, then press **F4** twice more to delete the remainder of the Identification Division. Press **Alt+F4** to restore the last deleted line, then press **Alt+F4** as needed to restore the other lines. You have just learned two very important keys, F4 to delete a line, and Alt+F4 to undelete a line.

Step 6: On-line Help (Function Keys)

Press **Alt+W** (as indicated at the bottom of Figure B.1a) to produce the list of function keys shown in Figure B.1c. The list appears overwhelming at first, but is less intimidating when you recognize what you already know such as F4 to delete a line. Press and hold the Alt key as instructed in the lower right portion of the screen to bring up additional function key definitions—for example, Alt+F4 to undelete a line. Release the Alt key to return to the screen of Figure B.1c. Press Alt+W to toggle the display of function keys on or off as you like.

Step 7: Move and Copy Commands

You can move and/or copy one or more statements within a program through combination of the F5, F6, F7, and F8 function keys that provide the cut, copy, and paste functions common to all editors. Start with the F6 key to mark the range of statements (Alt+F6 cancels the range), then use F5 or F8 to cut or copy the block to the buffer. Move the cursor to the new position, then press F7 to paste contents of the buffer into the program. Experiment as you see fit with the move and copy command, then abandon the edit as described in the next step.

Figure B.1 The CA-Realia Editor (RED)

```
IDENTIFICATION DIVISION.
PROGRAM-ID.         SENIORCE.
AUTHOR.             ROBERT GRAUER.

ENVIRONMENT DIVISION.
INPUT-OUTPUT SECTION.
FILE-CONTROL.
    SELECT STUDENT-FILE
         ASSIGN TO UT-S-SYSIN.
    SELECT PRINT-FILE
         ASSIGN TO UT-S-SYSOUT.

DATA DIVISION.
FILE SECTION.
FD  STUDENT-FILE
    RECORD CONTAINS 43 CHARACTERS
    DATA RECORD IS STUDENT-IN.
01  STUDENT-IN.
    05  STU-NAME                 PIC X(25).
    05  STU-CREDITS              PIC 9(3).
    05  STU-MAJOR                PIC X(15).

FD  PRINT-FILE

RED Version 4.201  seniorce.cob                 Alt-W for on screen help
```

(a) Opening Screen

```
    END-READ.
    PERFORM WRITE-HEADING-LINE.
    PERFORM PROCESS-RECORDS
        UNTIL DATA-REMAINS-SWITCH = 'NO'.
    CLOSE STUDENT-FILE
          PRINT-FILE.
    STOP RUN.

WRITE-HEADING-LINE.
    MOVE HEADING-LINE TO PRINT-LINE.
    WRITE PRINT-LINE.

PROCESS-RECORDS
    IF STU-CREDITS > 110 AND STU-MAJOR = 'ENGINEERING'
        MOVE STU-NAME TO PRINT-NAME
        MOVE DETAIL-LINE TO PRINT-LINE
        WRTE PRINT-LINE.
    END-IF.
    READ STUDENT-FILE
        AT END MOVE 'NO' TO DATA-REMAINS-SWITCH
    END-READ.

0138 W Period assumed before 'IF'
```

(b) Correcting Compilation Errors

Step 8: Abandon the Edit

Any editor must provide the ability to quit without saving. Press **Alt+F2**, then answer **yes**, to abandon the edit and negate all changes. Unlike other editors, however, RED includes a recovery capability in the event of a system crash by recording your

Figure B.1 *(continued)*

```
         PROGRAM-ID.        SENIORCE.
         AUTHOR.            ROBERT GRAUER.

         ENVIRONMENT DIVISION.
         INPUT-OUTPUT SECTION.
         FILE-CONTROL.
             SELECT STUDENT-FILE
                 ASSIGN TO UT-S-SYSIN.
             SELECT PRINT-FILE
                 ASSIGN TO UT-S-SYSOUT.

         DATA DIVISION.
         FILE SECTION.
         FD  STUDENT-FILE
             RECORD CONTAINS 43 CHARACTERS
             DATA RECORD IS STUDENT-IN.
         01  STUDENT-IN.
             05  STU-NAME              PIC X(25).

RED Version 4.201  seniorce.cob      C=07   M  I=00067 O=00000 H=00048 B1=00004
F1  Scroll up          F2  Scroll down      Esc    Enter command
F3  Insert line        F4  Delete line      Alt-H  Full help information
F5  Delete to buffer   F6  Mark range       Alt-W  Help window on/off
F7  Insert buffer      F8  Copy to buffer   Alt-F1 Terminate edit
F9  Duplicate char     F10 Duplicate field  Alt key for other Alt-Fn definitions
```

(c) Help Screen (Function Keys)

changes in a special journal file that is written to the disk every 60 seconds. (See the recovery help screen for additional information.)

Step 9: A Change in Specifications

Let us assume that the requirements of the original program have been changed to print the name and major of all students with at least 110 credits. This in turn requires a change to the IF statement to alter the selection criteria and a corresponding change to the heading and detail lines within the Data Division to include the student's major. The modifications could be made by using the basics of insertion and replacement, but we will continue to explore more powerful commands within the editor.

Step 10: On-line Help (Main Menu)

Type **RED SENIORCE.COB/N** to reenter the editor, then press **Alt+H** to produce the main help menu of Figure B.1d. Type a *lowercase* **c** to produce the secondary help screen in Figure B.1e. Follow the on-screen instructions that tell you to type an *uppercase* S to produce the help screen for the Search command shown in Figure B.1f. Press a *lowercase* **x** to exit help and return to the program.

Step 11: The Search Command

Check that the cursor is at the beginning of the program. Press **Esc** to enter the command mode, then type **S IF** followed by the **enter** key, to search for the first occurrence of the character string IF, which takes you to the IF contained within

Figure B.1 *(continued)*

```
CA-Realia Source Editor Version 4.201  000000
Copyright (c) 1992 Computer Associates International, Inc.

Select help topic. During edit, Alt-H gets this help screen.
  a - Main help menu (you are looking at it)
  b - Buffer handling
  c - Command processing
  d - DOS command used to load RED and use of files
  e - Error messages
  f - Function key usage
  g - General information on the organization of RED
  h - Help information available
  i - Increased screen size option (for EGA)
  k - Keyword option (for COB/CBL files)
  l - Locating error messages (for COB/CBL files)
  m - File formats
  n - Numbering operation (for COB files)
  o - Summary of command line switch options
  p - P switch for controlling numeric pad (NumLock)
  r - Recovery facilities
  s - Special handling of comments in COB/CBL files
  t - Tab handling
  u - Usage of message line
  w - Option for controlling "snow" on screen
  x - Exit from help
```

(d) Main Help Screen

```
CA-Realia Source Editor Version 4.201  000000

COMMAND PROCESSING

RED Commands are entered by pressing the ESC key. This will blank the message
line at the bottom of the screen for entry of a command. During command entry,
the left and right cursor keys and backspace keys can be used, as well as Ins
and Del in the normal manner. In addition Home resets the cursor to the start of
the line, and Ctrl End (ERASE END LINE) is active. Entry of a command is
terminated by pressing the Enter key. Pressing the ESC key during entry of a
command causes the command to be abandoned. See also description of REPEAT
COMMAND (End key) function. Commands start with a single letter (upper or lower
case):

  B - Search backwards to key     N - Search to line number
  D - Delete lines                R - Replace string
  G - Global replace string       S - Search forwards to key
  H - Hex data entry              T - Set tabs
  M - Merge file

Press the corresponding upper case command letter for a detailed description of
the command.

Press x to exit from help, a to return to main help menu
```

(e) Secondary Help Screen (Command Processing)

IDENTIFICATION DIVISION. This is obviously not the character string we are searching for, so you need to reenter the search command—that is, press **Esc** followed by **S IF**. (Alternatively, you can enter S /IF, where the slash indicates a whole word; we learned this feature by consulting the help screen for the Search command in Figure B.1f.) Use the Del key to delete the AND clause within the IF statement.

Figure B.1 *(continued)*

```
CA-Realia Source Editor Version 4.201  000000

S COMMAND - SEARCH FORWARDS

The S command searches forward from the current position until a specified key
is located. The form of the command is:

  S key

The key is a string of characters surrounded by quotes, with any quote within
the string appearing doubled. If the key is preceded by / (slash), then the key
will only match if it is a word, i.e. if it is surrounded by blanks or special
characters. If the key is preceded by \ (reverse slash), then it will only match
at the start of the line (possibly preceded by blanks). If the key does not
start with / \ or quote, and contains no blanks, then the surrounding quotes may
optionally be omitted.

Examples:

  S '* *'         search for two asterisks separated by a blank
  S/themselves    search for word themselves
  S\xyz:          search for string xyz: at start of line
  S               null key never matches = go to end of file

Press x to exit from help, a to return to main help menu
```

(f) Help Screen (Search Command)

Step 12: Setting and Clearing Tabs

The set and clear tab commands can be used to good advantage to insert and/or modify the additional statements. Press **Esc** to enter the command mode, then type **T 8,12,16,36,50** followed by the **enter** key to set tabs in the positions corresponding to columns used in our program. (Alternatively you can move the cursor to a specific column and press Alt+T to set a single tab stop, or press Alt+C to clear a single tab if you make a mistake.)

Move the cursor to the end of the line containing the FILLER entry for 'STUDENT NAME', then press the **enter** key to insert a new line into the program. Modify the heading and detail lines within the Data Division to include the student's major as indicated below. Press the **tab** key as appropriate to move to columns 36 and 50 for the PICTURE and VALUE clauses, respectively. Note, too, you will have to insert a MOVE statement within the scope of the IF, to MOVE STU-MAJOR TO PRINT-MAJOR.

```
01 HEADING-LINE.
   05 FILLER          PIC X(10)   VALUE SPACES.
   05 FILLER          PIC X(12)   VALUE 'STUDENT NAME'.
   05 FILLER          PIC X(18)   VALUE SPACES.
   05 FILLER          PIC X(5)    VALUE 'MAJOR'.
   05 FILLER          PIC X(87)   VALUE SPACES.

01 DETAIL-LINE.
   05 FILLER          PIC X(8)    VALUE SPACES.
   05 PRINT-NAME      PIC X(25).
   05 FILLER          PIC X(4)    VALUE SPACES.
   05 PRINT-MAJOR     PIC X(15).
   05 FILLER          PIC X(80)   VALUE SPACES.
```

Additional lines

Step 13: Test the Changes

Press **Alt+F1** to save the corrected program and return to the DOS prompt. Type **C SENIORCE** to compile, then **L SENIORCE** to link the program if it compiles cleanly. Enter the statements **SET SYSIN=SENIOR.DAT** and **SET SYSOUT=SENIORCE.RPT[N]**, then type **SENIORCE** to execute the modified program. Type the command **TYPE SENIORCE.RPT** to see the report after the program executes.

Step 14: A Tip for the More Advanced Programmer

It is often useful (in debugging) to negate the effects of a statement, without deleting the statement from the program. This is accomplished by commenting out the indicated lines—that is, by placing an asterisk in column 7 to convert the indicated line to a comment. Use the **F6** key to mark the indicated range of statements, then press **Alt+I** to comment (uncomment) the highlighted range.

Step 15: On Your Own

The exercise has demonstrated the basic commands to create and/or modify a COBOL program. More importantly, perhaps, it has introduced the extensive on-line help facility, which contains all the documentation you need to master RED. As with any program, practice makes perfect.

HANDS-ON EXERCISE 4:

REALDBUG—The Interactive Debugger

Discussion: The interactive debugger monitors the execution of a COBOL program, allowing you to pause at any time to display the value of a data name or take other action. It is similar in concept to inserting DISPLAY statements at specific points within a program, except it is more flexible and easier to use. The best time to learn the debugger is when you don't have to, that is, to practice on a program that works correctly.

In essence the debugger lets you choose between executing one statement at a time, versus executing multiple statements until a range (break point) is reached. Either way, you can display the value of a data name(s), resume execution, then pause again to display the value of the (same or different) data name(s). At any given time you are either in the program window from where you issue debugging commands, or in a view (or watch) window from where you examine the value of a data name.

The debugger is extremely powerful and it will take you a while to master all of its commands. Nevertheless, you can accomplish a great deal with just two commands, Advance and View, to advance one statement at a time and view the values of the associated data names. Other commands provide additional capability as described below:

- The Look and View commands offer alternate ways to display the value of a data name within a view window. The Look command prompts you for the specific data name, whereas the View command requires you to position the cursor on the data name within the listing. You can also establish a watch window to continually display the value of any data name throughout the execution of the program.
- The Find and Where commands offer different ways to move within the program window to the line where the data (paragraph) name is defined. The

Find command (like the Look command) prompts you for the data (paragraph) name, whereas the Where command requires you to position the cursor on the data (paragraph) name within the listing.

- The Advance command executes one statement at a time versus the Trace command, which executes the entire program, highlighting each line as it is executed. The Range command establishes break points (ranges) in the program and is used in conjunction with the Go command to execute statements until a range is encountered. The Quit command exits the debugger.
- The Mode command sets the various options used in the debugger; for example, you can throttle (slow down) the execution of the Trace command, use the Autoview command to automatically display data names as statements are executed, and/or display (suppress) the hexadecimal values of the displayed data names.
- The cursor, PgDn, and PgUp keys scroll anywhere within the program window; alternatively you can type a specific line number to move the cursor to a different place in the listing. The Execute command repositions the cursor on the next statement to be executed.

One final point before we begin is that the debugger contains significantly more capability than can be demonstrated in a single exercise. Accordingly you are referred to the extensive on-line help facility for additional information. Press **Alt+F1** to get a list of high-level topics that lead to specific screens. Press **F1** at any time to obtain a list of commands that are effective from the specific window. Press the **Esc** key to exit help.

Step 1: Change to the Appropriate Directory

The selection of the default drive and directory depends on the location of the COBOL files, that is, on whether or not you copied the data disk. Thus, if you copied the data disk to the hard disk:

1. Type **C:** and press ↵
2. Type **CD \DATADISK\CHAPTR05** and press ↵

If, however, you did not copy the data disk to the hard disk

1. Place the data disk in drive A
2. Type **A:** and press ↵
3. Type **CD \CHAPTR05** and press ↵

Step 2: Compile and Link the Program

Type **C TUITION5** and **L TUITION5** to compile and link the TUITION5.COB program just as you normally would. Enter the appropriate SET commands, **SET SYSIN=TUITION.DAT** and **SET SYSOUT=TUITION.RPT[N].**

Step 3: Invoke the Debugger

To invoke the debugger on a *monochrome* monitor, enter the following command:

```
REALDBUG TUITION5 /MI
```

To invoke the debugger on a *color* monitor, enter the following command:

```
REALDBUG TUITION5
```

Figure B.2 The Interactive Debugger

```
RealDBUG 4.200|Enter next Listing command ... Press F1 for Help
                                    TUITION5
121|      05  FILLER                PIC X(49) VALUE SPACES.
122|
123| PROCEDURE DIVISION.
124| PREPARE-TUITION-REPORT.
125|     OPEN INPUT STUDENT-FILE
126|          OUTPUT PRINT-FILE.
127|     PERFORM WRITE-HEADING-LINE.
128|     PERFORM READ-STUDENT-FILE.
129|     PERFORM PROCESS-STUDENT-RECORD
130|          UNTIL DATA-REMAINS-SWITCH = 'NO'.
131|     PERFORM WRITE-UNIVERSITY-TOTALS.
132|     CLOSE STUDENT-FILE
133|           PRINT-FILE.
134|     STOP RUN.
135|
136| WRITE-HEADING-LINE.
137|     MOVE HEADING-LINE TO PRINT-LINE.
138|     WRITE PRINT-LINE
139|         AFTER ADVANCING PAGE.
140|     MOVE SPACES TO PRINT-LINE.
141|     WRITE PRINT-LINE.
141|     WRITE PRINT-LINE.
```

(a) The Opening Screen

You will see the screen in Figure B.2a with the OPEN (first executable) statement highlighted.

Step 4: The Advance Command

Type **A** (Advance) to execute the current COBOL statement, which moves the highlight to the next executable statement, the PERFORM statement on line 127. Type **A** to execute this statement, then continue to advance in the program until you come to the COMPUTE statement in line 163.

Step 5: The View and Ctrl+View Commands

Position the cursor on the data name PRICE-PER-CREDIT within the COMPUTE statement on line 163, then type **V** to view the contents of this field in a view window at the bottom of the screen. Press **Esc** (enter or space) to leave the view window and return to the program, move the cursor to STU-CREDITS, then press **V** to see the value of this data name. Press **Esc** to return to the program window, but this time press **Ctrl+V** to see the value of all three data names in the COMPUTE statement as shown in Figure B.2b.

Step 6: The Mode Command

The values of the data names are displayed in both decimal and hexadecimal; the latter is confusing and we suggest you eliminate the hexadecimal display through the mode command. Type **M** to bring up the mode window, type **X** to toggle (on or off) the hexadecimal display, then press **enter** to return to the view window. The hexadecimal values should be gone.

Figure B.2 *(continued)*

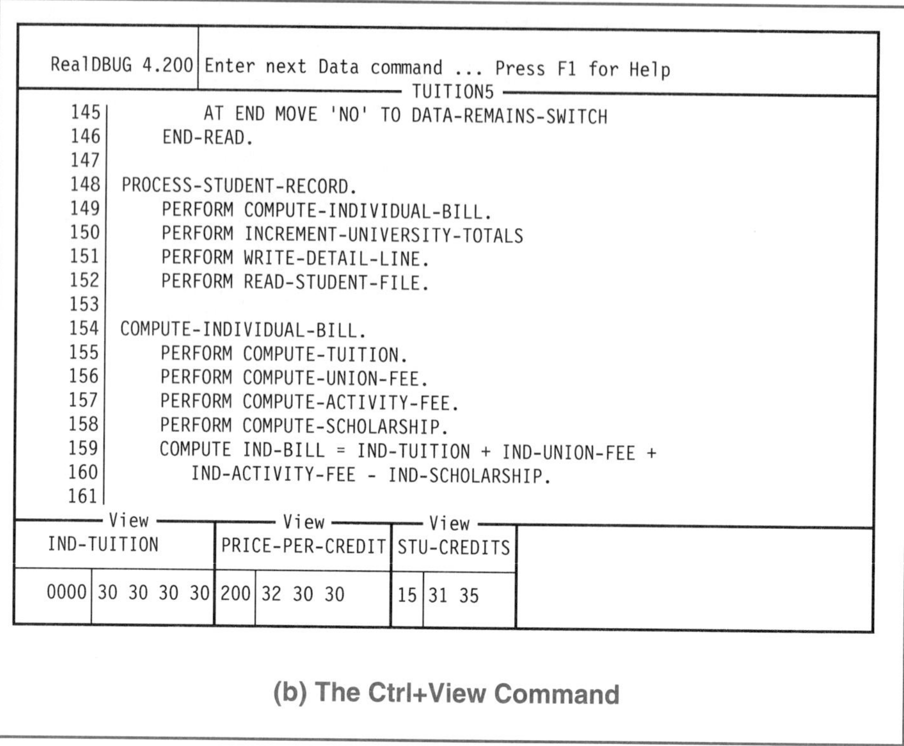

(b) The Ctrl+View Command

Step 7: The Range and Go Commands

Press **enter** to return to the program window. Check that the cursor is still on the COMPUTE statement, then type **R** *twice* to establish a one-line range (break point). Type **A** to execute the next statement in the program, then type **G** to execute the Go command, which proceeds until the first range, such as the COMPUTE statement, is reached. Execute the Advance command once again, then the Go command to appreciate the difference: Advance executes a single statement, whereas the Go command advances to the next highlighted range.

Step 8: The Find and Range Commands

Type **F** to execute the Find command and type **READ-STUDENT-FILE** when prompted for the data/procedure name. Move the cursor down one line to the READ statement, type **R** to set the beginning of the range, move the cursor to the END-READ scope terminator, and type **R** a second time to set the end of the range. There are now two ranges in the program.

Type **G** to execute the Go command, which moves from range to range within the program, and/or from statement to statement within the highlighted range. Execute the Go command three or four more times, noting that the action of the command depends on where it is executed; that is, the Go command advances to the next range only if it is executed outside a highlighted range (or on the last line of the highlighted range), but advances a single line when executed within a highlighted range.

Step 9: The Help Command

Press **F1** (at any time) to display the context-sensitive help window shown in Figure B.2c, which lists the available commands. You can obtain help on any

Figure B.2 (continued)

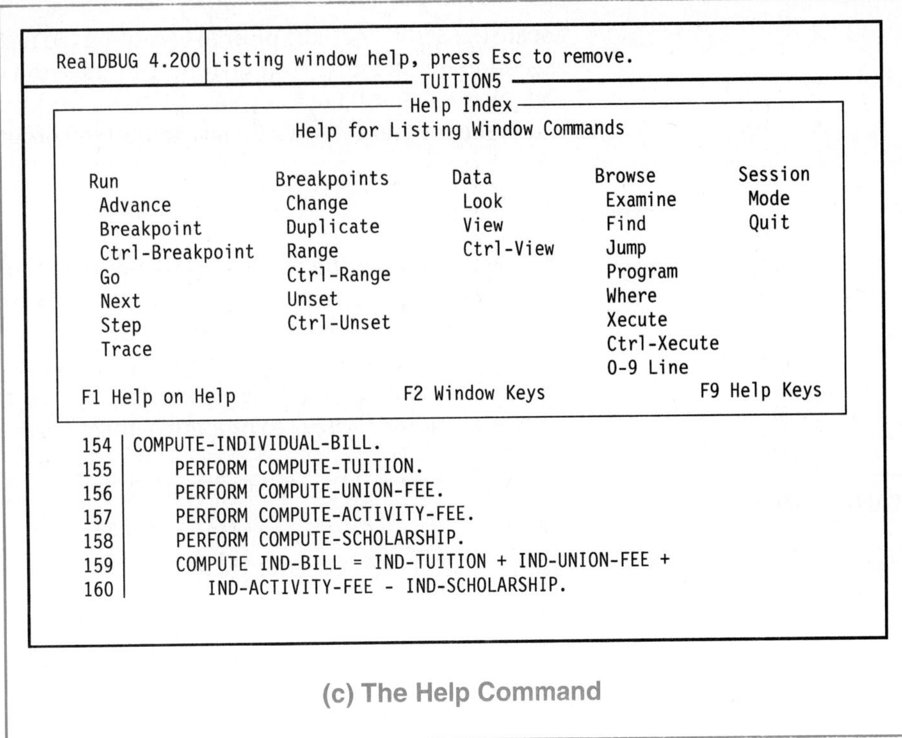

(c) The Help Command

command by typing the highlighted letter; for example, type **G** to display information about the Go command. Press **Esc** to exit help.

Step 10: Watch Windows

Type **L** to look at a particular data name, then type **STU-LAST-NAME** in response to the prompt; the last name of the current student will be displayed in the view window at the bottom of the screen. Press Esc to return to the program. Type A to advance one line in the program.

Type **L**, followed by STU-LAST-NAME as previously, but this time type **W** to create a watch window that remains permanently on the screen. Return to the program window, then create a second watch window for STU-CREDITS. (Type **L**, **STU-CREDITS**, **W** to change the view window to a watch window, then return to the program window.) Execute the Go command several times, noticing how the watch windows remain on the screen and change to reflect the current student.

Step 11: The Unset Command

Type **U** to unset both ranges. (If you are outside a range you will be prompted to unset all ranges. If you are within a range, you will unset that range only.) Type **G** a final time. This time you will be taken to the STOP RUN statement since there are no ranges set in the program. The debugger displays the message that the program has terminated and a STOP RUN was executed.

Step 12: The Quit Command

Type **Q** to quit the program, followed by **Y** to confirm. Type **REALDBUG TUITION5** (as in step 3) to reenter the debugger and continue with the exercise.

Step 13: The Trace Command

Locate the Scroll Lock key prior to executing the next command so that you can halt execution if necessary. Ready? Type **T** to trace the execution of the entire program and press the **Scroll Lock** key to stop. If you were too slow—that is, you reached the end of the program—you will have to quit the program and reenter the debugger.

Step 14: The Throttle

Press **M** to execute the mode command, type **S** to slow (throttle) the trace, then enter a value from 1 to 9; the higher the value, the slower the program; we suggest a throttle of 5 to 7. Press the **enter** key to return to your program, then type **T** to rexecute the trace command, which now proceeds at a slower speed than before. You can press Scroll Lock as before to stop the trace and return control to the program window. Type Q to quit the debugger a final time.

HANDS-ON EXERCISE 5:

REALCOPY—A Utility for Indexed Files

Discussion: Indexed files permit sequential and nonsequential access to individual records, making the structure of an indexed file more complicated than the sequential files used throughout the book. Accordingly, indexed files require special treatment as they cannot be created or viewed in the normal fashion such as with the DOS TYPE command. One solution is to write a "quick and dirty" COBOL program every time you need to create and/or print an indexed file; a more efficient approach is to use the REALCOPY utility.

The exercise implements the nonsequential update program described in Chapter 18, which requires three distinct uses of the REALCOPY utility. It is used in step 3b to create the indexed file, in step 4 to print the newly created indexed file before the update has taken place, and in step 6 to print the indexed file after the update. REALCOPY is also used in steps 7 and 8 in conjunction with the ALTERNATE RECORD key.

Step 1: Change to the Appropriate Directory

The selection of a default drive and directory depends on the location of the COBOL files, that is, on whether or not you copied the data disk to the hard disk in step 3c of the previous exercise. Thus, if you copied the data disk to the hard disk in step 3c of the installation:

1. Type **C:** and press ↵
2. Type **CD \DATADISK\CHAPTR18** and press ↵

If, however, you did not copy the data disk to the hard disk

1. Place the data disk into drive A
2. Type **A:** and press ↵
3. Type **CD \CHAPTR18** and press ↵

Step 2: Establish the Environment

Type **NONSETS** to execute the NONSETS.BAT file included in this subdirectory. The batch file contains all of the SET statements required throughout the exercise. You can verify that the environment has been properly set, by typing **SET** (with no parameters) at the DOS prompt. You will then see the entire DOS environment including the following four entries: SEQUENCE=SEQUENCE.DAT, VALTRANS=VALTRANS.DAT[N], INDMAST=INDMAST.DAT, and ALTINDEX=ALTINDEX.DAT.

Step 3a: Create the Indexed File by Using a COBOL Program

Use **C CREATE**, **L CREATE**, and **CREATE** to compile, link, and execute the program CREATE.COB from Figure 18.5 in the text. (You do not have to enter the individual SET statements because of the batch file in step 2.)

Step 3b: Create the Indexed File by Using the REALCOPY Utility Program

An indexed file is created more easily with the REALCOPY utility than with a COBOL program. Type the command, **REALCOPY SEQUENCE.DAT[U39] INDMAST.DAT[X]** to create the indexed file INDMAST.DAT from the sequential file SEQUENCE.DAT. You will be prompted for three responses:

1. Record type: Enter **F** for fixed length.
2. Primary key: Enter **0/9** for the offset and length, respectively. The *offset* is the relative position within the record where the key begins, with the first position corresponding to an offset of zero. The *length* of the key is 9 as there are 9 positions in the social security number.
3. Alternate key: Press the **return** key.

The REALCOPY program will not execute cleanly, however, because the input file (SEQUENCE.DAT) contains an out-of-sequence record (social security number, 222222222) that causes the program to terminate. Accordingly, you need to delete the erroneous record from the SEQUENCE.DAT file; realize, however, that since SEQUENCE.DAT is a sequential file, you can use any editor to accomplish the task. Delete the record, then rerun the REALCOPY utility.

Step 4: Print the Indexed File (before the Update)

The REALCOPY utility will print the contents of an indexed file regardless of how it was created. Type the command **REALCOPY INDMAST.DAT[X] CON[N]** to view the contents of the newly created indexed file on your monitor. You should see the nine records shown earlier in Figure 18.7a.

Step 5: Compile, Link, and Execute the Nonsequential Update Program

Use **C NONSEQUP**, **L NONSEQUP**, and **NONSEQUP** to compile, link, and execute the program NONSEQUP.COB from Figure 18.10 in the text. (You do not have to enter any SET commands because of the batch file in step 2.)

Step 6: Print the Indexed File (after the Update)

Enter the command **REALCOPY INDMAST.DAT[X] CON[N]** to print the contents of the indexed file after the update. (This is exactly the same command as in step 4.) This time you will see 10 records in the file, which should correspond exactly to the file shown earlier in Figure 18.7c.

Step 7: Alternate Indexes

The REALCOPY utility can also be used in conjunction with a secondary (alternate) index. Type the command **REALCOPY ALTINPUT.DAT[U40] ALTINDEX.DAT[X]** to create a second indexed file, ALTINDEX.DAT, from the sequential file ALTINPUT.DAT. You will see the identical prompts to those displayed earlier in step 3b. Thus:

1. Record type: Type **F** for a fixed-length record.
2. Primary key: Type **0/9** as the offset and length for the primary key.
3. Alternate key 01: Type **9/15/D** as the offset, length, and characteristics for the secondary key; the offset is 9, the length is 15, and duplicates are permitted.
4. Alternate key 02: Press the **return** key.

Step 8: Print the Alternate Index File

Type **REALCOPY ALTINDEX.DAT[X] CON[N]** to print the newly created indexed file, which produces the following display on your monitor:

```
RealCOPY CA-Realia File Copying Utility Educational Version 4.20
Copyright (C) Computer Associates Int'l, Inc. 1993. All rights reserved.

Input File      File type [x]     Record Length     40 fixed.
Output file     File type [n]     Record Length     40 variable.

100000000GRAUER
100000001GRAUER
100000002GRAUER
300000000MILGROM
300000001MILGROM
300000002MILGROM
400000000GRAUER
500000000JONES
600000000SMITH
700000000MILGROM
Records Copied: 10.
```

The value of the primary key (social security number) is unique, but the secondary (name) key is not; that is, there are multiple records with the same last name. Use **C ALTINDEX**, **L ALTINDEX**, and **ALTINDEX** to compile, link, and execute the program ALTINDEX.COB from Figure 18.12 in the text.

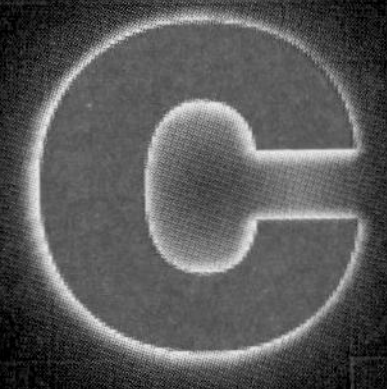

Reserved Words

ACCEPT
ACCESS
ADD
ADVANCING
AFTER
ALL
ALPHABET
ALPHABETIC
ALPHABETIC-LOWER
ALPHABETIC-UPPER
ALPHANUMERIC
ALPHANUMERIC-EDITED
ALSO
ALTER
ALTERNATE
AND
ANY
ARE
AREA
AREAS
ASCENDING
ASSIGN
AT
AUTHOR

BEFORE
BINARY
BLANK
BLOCK
BOTTOM
BY

CALL
CANCEL
CD
CF
CH
CHARACTER
CHARACTERS
CLASS
CLOCK-UNITS
CLOSE
COBOL
CODE
CODE-SET
COLLATING
COLUMN
COMMA
COMMON
COMMUNICATION
COMP
COMPUTATIONAL
COMPUTE
CONFIGURATION
CONTAINS
CONTENT
CONTINUE
CONTROL
CONTROLS
CONVERTING
COPY
CORR
CORRESPONDING
COUNT
CURRENCY

DATA
DATE
DATE-COMPILED
DATE-WRITTEN
DAY
DAY-OF-WEEK
DE
DEBUG-CONTENTS
DEBUG-ITEM
DEBUG-LINE
DEBUG-NAME
DEBUG-SUB-1
DEBUG-SUB-2
DEBUG-SUB-3
DEBUGGING
DECIMAL-POINT
DECLARATIVES
DELETE
DELIMITED
DELIMITER
DEPENDING
DESCENDING
DESTINATION
DETAIL
DISABLE
DISPLAY
DIVIDE
DIVISION
DOWN
DUPLICATES
DYNAMIC

EGI
ELSE
EMI
ENABLE
END
END-ADD
END-CALL
END-COMPUTE
END-DELETE
END-DIVIDE
END-EVALUATE
END-IF
END-MULTIPLY
END-OF-PAGE
END-PERFORM
END-READ
END-RECEIVE
END-RETURN
END-REWRITE
END-SEARCH
END-START
END-STRING
END-SUBTRACT
END-UNSTRING
END-WRITE
ENTER
ENVIRONMENT
EOP
EQUAL
ERROR
ESI
EVALUATE
EVERY
EXCEPTION
EXIT
EXTEND
EXTERNAL

FALSE
FD
FILE
FILE-CONTROL
FILLER
FINAL
FIRST
FOOTING
FOR
FROM

GENERATE
GIVING
GLOBAL
GO
GREATER
GROUP

HEADING
HIGH-VALUE
HIGH-VALUES

I-O
I-O-CONTROL
IDENTIFICATION
IF
IN
INDEX
INDEXED
INDICATE
INITIAL
INITIALIZE
INITIATE
INPUT
INPUT-OUTPUT
INSPECT
INSTALLATION
INTO
INVALID
IS

JUST
JUSTIFIED

KEY

LABEL
LAST
LEADING
LEFT
LENGTH
LESS
LIMIT
LIMITS
LINAGE
LINAGE-COUNTER
LINE
LINE-COUNTER
LINES
LINKAGE
LOCK
LOW-VALUE
LOW-VALUES

MEMORY
MERGE
MESSAGE
MODE
MODULES
MOVE
MULTIPLE
MULTIPLY

NATIVE
NEGATIVE
NEXT
NO
NOT
NUMBER
NUMERIC
NUMERIC-EDITED

OBJECT-COMPUTER
OCCURS
OF
OFF
OMITTED
ON
OPEN
OPTIONAL
OR
ORDER
ORGANIZATION
OTHER
OUTPUT
OVERFLOW

PACKED-DECIMAL
PADDING
PAGE
PAGE-COUNTER
PERFORM
PF
PH
PIC
PICTURE
PLUS
POINTER
POSITION
POSITIVE
PRINTING
PROCEDURE
PROCEDURES
PROCEED
PROGRAM
PROGRAM-ID
PURGE

QUEUE
QUOTE
QUOTES

RANDOM
RD
READ
RECEIVE
RECORD
RECORDS
REDEFINES
REEL
REFERENCE
REFERENCES
RELATIVE
RELEASE
REMAINDER
REMOVAL
RENAMES
REPLACE
REPLACING
REPORT
REPORTING
REPORTS
RERUN
RESERVE
RESET
RETURN
REVERSED
REWIND
REWRITE
RF
RH
RIGHT
ROUNDED
RUN

SAME
SD
SEARCH
SECTION
SECURITY
SEGMENT
SEGMENT-LIMIT
SELECT
SEND
SENTENCE
SEPARATE
SEQUENCE
SEQUENTIAL
SET
SIGN
SIZE
SORT
SORT-MERGE
SOURCE
SOURCE-COMPUTER
SPACE
SPACES
SPECIAL-NAMES
STANDARD
STANDARD-1
STANDARD-2
START
STATUS
STOP
STRING
SUB-QUEUE-1
SUB-QUEUE-2
SUB-QUEUE-3
SUBTRACT
SUM
SUPPRESS
SYMBOLIC
SYNC
SYNCHRONIZED

TABLE
TALLYING
TAPE
TERMINAL
TERMINATE
TEST
TEXT
THAN
THEN
THROUGH
THRU
TIME
TIMES
TO
TOP
TRAILING
TRUE
TYPE

UNIT
UNSTRING
UNTIL
UP
UPON
USAGE
USE
USING

VALUE
VALUES
VARYING

WHEN
WITH
WORDS
WORKING-STORAGE
WRITE

ZERO
ZEROES
ZEROS

+
-
*
/
**
>
<
=
>=
<=

COBOL-85 Reference Summary

This appendix contains the composite language skeleton of the revised version of the American National Standard COBOL. It is intended to display complete and syntactically correct formats.

The leftmost margin on pages 612 through 620 is equivalent to margin A in a COBOL source program. The first indentation after the leftmost margin is equivalent to margin B in a COBOL source program.

On pages 621 through 631 the leftmost margin indicates the beginning of the format for a new COBOL verb. The first indentation after the leftmost margin indicates continuation of the format of the COBOL verb. The appearance of the italic letter ***S***, ***R***, ***I***, or ***W*** to the left of the format for the verbs CLOSE, OPEN, READ, and WRITE indicates the **Sequential** I-O module, **Relative** I-O module, **Indexed** I-O module, or Report **Writer** module in which that general format is used. The following formats are presented:

Identification Division

```
IDENTIFICATION DIVISION.

PROGRAM-ID. program-name [IS {|COMMON |} PROGRAM]
                              {|INITIAL|}

[AUTHOR. [comment-entry] . . . ]

[INSTALLATION. [comment-entry] . . . ]

[DATE-WRITTEN. [comment-entry] . . . ]

[DATE-COMPILED. [comment-entry] . . . ]

[SECURITY. [comment-entry] . . . ]
```

Environment Division

```
[ENVIRONMENT DIVISION.

[CONFIGURATION SECTION.

[SOURCE-COMPUTER. [computer-name [WITH DEBUGGING MODE] . ] ]

[OBJECT-COMPUTER. [computer-name

    [PROGRAM COLLATING SEQUENCE IS alphabet-name-1]

    [SEGMENT-LIMIT IS segment-number] . ] ]

[SPECIAL-NAMES. [ [implementor-name-1

        {IS mnemonic-1 [ON STATUS IS condition-name-1 [OFF STATUS IS condition-name-2] ]}
        {IS mnemonic-name-2 [OFF STATUS IS condition-name-2 [ON STATUS IS condition-name-1] ]} ] . . .
        {[ON STATUS IS condition-name-1 [OFF STATUS IS condition-name-2] ]}
        {[OFF STATUS IS condition-name-2 [ON STATUS IS condition-name-1] ]}

    [ALPHABET alphabet-name-1 IS

        {STANDARD-1                                                      }
        {STANDARD-2                                                      }
        {NATIVE                                                          }
        {implementor-name-2                                              } ] . . .
        {{literal-1 [{THROUGH} literal-2                ]}              }
        {{           [{THRU   }                          ]} . . .        }
        {{           [{ALSO literal-3} . . .             ]}              }

[SYMBOLIC CHARACTERS {{{symbolic-character-1} . . . {IS } {integer-1} . . . } . . . [IN alphabet-name-2] }] . . .
                                                     {ARE}

[CLASS class-name IS {literal-4 [{THROUGH} literal-5]} . . . ] . . .
                                [{THRU   }          ]

[CURRENCY SIGN IS literal-6]

[DECIMAL-POINT IS COMMA]. ] ] ]

[INPUT-OUTPUT SECTION.

FILE-CONTROL.

    {file-control-entry} . . .
```

Environment Division *(continued)*

```
[I-O-CONTROL.

  [RERUN [ON {file-name-1          }] EVERY {{[END OF] {REEL} OF file-name-2}}] ...
  [          {implementor-name-1   }]       {{         {UNIT}               }}
                                            {{integer-1 RECORDS             }}
                                            {integer-2 CLOCK-UNITS           }
                                            {condition-name-1                }

  [[SAME [RECORD    ] AREA FOR file-name-1 {file-name-2} ... ] ...          ]
  [[     [SORT      ]                                        ]              ]
  [[     [SORT-MERGE]                                        ]              ] ]
  [                                                                         ]
  [[MULTIPLE FILE TAPE CONTAINS                                  ] ...     .]
  [[      {file-name-3 [POSITION IS integer-1] } ...             ]          ]
```

File Control Entry

SEQUENTIAL FILE

```
SELECT [OPTIONAL] file-name-1

    ASSIGN TO {implementor-name-1} ...
              {literal-1         }

    [RESERVE integer-1 [AREA ]]
                       [AREAS]

    [ [ORGANIZATION IS] SEQUENTIAL]

    [PADDING CHARACTER IS {data-name-1}]
                          {literal-2  }

    [RECORD DELIMITER IS {STANDARD-1        }]
                         {implementor-name-2}

    [ACCESS MODE IS SEQUENTIAL]

    [FILE STATUS IS data-name-2] .
```

RELATIVE FILE

```
SELECT [OPTIONAL] file-name-1

    ASSIGN TO {implementor-name-1} ...
              {literal-1         }

    [RESERVE integer-1 [AREA ]]
                       [AREAS]

    [ORGANIZATION IS] RELATIVE

    [ACCESS MODE IS {SEQUENTIAL [RELATIVE KEY IS data-name-1]}]
    [               {{RANDOM }                               }]
    [               {{DYNAMIC} RELATIVE KEY IS data-name-1   }]

    [FILE STATUS IS data-name-2] .
```

File Control Entry *(continued)*

INDEXED FILE

```
SELECT [OPTIONAL] file-name-1

    ASSIGN TO {implementor-name-1}
              {literal-1          } . . .

   [RESERVE integer-1 [AREA ]]
                      [AREAS]

   [ORGANIZATION IS] INDEXED

   [ACCESS MODE IS {SEQUENTIAL}]
                   {RANDOM    }
                   {DYNAMIC   }

   RECORD KEY IS data-name-1

   [ALTERNATE RECORD KEY IS data-name-2 [WITH DUPLICATES]] . . .

   [FILE STATUS IS data-name-3] .
```

SORT OR MERGE FILE

```
SELECT file-name-1 ASSIGN TO {implementor-name-1}
                             {literal-1          } . . .
```

Data Division

```
[DATA DIVISION.
[FILE SECTION.
[file-description-entry
{record-description-entry} . . . ] . . .
[sort-merge-file-description-entry
{record-description-entry} . . . ] . . .
[report-file-description-entry] . . . ]
[WORKING-STORAGE SECTION.
[77-level-description-entry]
[record-description-entry  ] . . . ]
[LINKAGE SECTION.
[77-level-description-entry]
[record-description-entry  ] . . . ]
[COMMUNICATION SECTION.
[communication-description-entry
[record-description-entry] . . . ] . . . ]
[REPORT SECTION.
[report-description-entry
{record-group-description-entry} . . . ] . . . ] ]
```

File Description Entry

SEQUENTIAL FILE

```
FD  file-name-1
    [IS EXTERNAL]
    [IS GLOBAL]
    [BLOCK CONTAINS [integer-1 TO] integer-2 {RECORDS   }]
                                             {CHARACTERS}
    [       {CONTAINS integer-3 CHARACTERS                                            }]
    [RECORD {IS VARYING IN SIZE [ [FROM integer-4] [TO integer-5] CHARACTERS]         }]
    [       {      [DEPENDING ON data-name-1]                                         }]
    [       {CONTAINS integer-6 TO integer-7 CHARACTERS                               }]
    [LABEL {RECORD IS  } {STANDARD}]
    [      {RECORDS ARE} {OMITTED }]
    [VALUE OF {implementor-name-1 IS {data-name-2}} . . . ]
    [                                {literal-1  }        ]
    [DATA {RECORD IS  } {data-name-3} . . . ]
    [     {RECORDS ARE}                     ]
    [LINAGE IS {data-name-4} LINES [WITH FOOTING AT {data-name-5}]   ]
    [          {integer-8  }                        {integer-9  }    ]
    [    [LINES AT TOP {data-name-6}] [LINES AT BOTTOM {data-name-7}]]
    [                  {integer-10 }                   {integer-11 } ]
    [CODE-SET IS alphabet-name-1] .
```

RELATIVE FILE

```
FD  file-name-1
    [IS EXTERNAL]
    [IS GLOBAL]
    [BLOCK CONTAINS [integer-1 TO] integer-2 {RECORDS   }]
                                             {CHARACTERS}
    [       {CONTAINS integer-3 CHARACTERS                                            }]
    [RECORD {IS VARYING IN SIZE [ [FROM integer-4] [TO integer-5] CHARACTERS]         }]
    [       {      [DEPENDING ON data-name-1]                                         }]
    [       {CONTAINS integer-6 TO integer-7 CHARACTERS                               }]
    [LABEL {RECORD IS  } {STANDARD}]
    [      {RECORDS ARE} {OMITTED }]
    [VALUE OF {implementor-name-1 IS {data-name-2}} . . . ]
    [                                {literal-1  }        ]
    [DATA {RECORD IS  } {data-name-3} . . . ] .
    [     {RECORDS ARE}                     ]
```

File Description Entry *(continued)*

SORT-MERGE FILE

```
SD file-name-1

  [        {CONTAINS integer-1 CHARACTERS                                         }]
  [RECORD  {IS VARYING IN SIZE [ [FROM integer-2] [TO integer-3] CHARACTERS]      }]
  [        {    [DEPENDING ON data-name-1]                                        }]
  [        {CONTAINS integer-4 TO integer-5 CHARACTERS                            }]

  [DATA {RECORD IS   } {data-name-2} . . . ]
  [     {RECORDS ARE }                     ]
```

REPORT FILE

```
FD file-name-1
  [IS EXTERNAL]
  [IS GLOBAL]

  [BLOCK CONTAINS [integer-1 TO] integer-2 {RECORDS   }]
  [                                        {CHARACTERS}]

  [        {CONTAINS integer-3 CHARACTERS                                         }]
  [RECORD  {IS VARYING IN SIZE [ [FROM integer-4] [TO integer-5] CHARACTERS]      }]
  [        {    [DEPENDING ON data-name-1]                                        }]
  [        {CONTAINS integer-6 TO integer-7 CHARACTERS                            }]

  [LABEL {RECORD IS  } {STANDARD}]
  [      {RECORDS ARE} {OMITTED }]

  [VALUE OF {implementor-name-1 IS {data-name-2}} . . . ]
  [         {                      {literal-1  }}       ]

  [CODE-SET IS alphabet-name-1]

  {REPORT IS   } {report-name-1} . . .
  {REPORTS ARE }
```

INDEXED FILE

```
FD file-name-1
  [IS EXTERNAL]
  [IS GLOBAL]

  [BLOCK CONTAINS [integer-1 TO] integer-2 {RECORDS   }]
  [                                        {CHARACTERS}]

  [        {CONTAINS integer-3 CHARACTERS                                         }]
  [RECORD  {IS VARYING IN SIZE [ [FROM integer-4] [TO integer-5] CHARACTERS]      }]
  [        {    [DEPENDING ON data-name-1]                                        }]
  [        {CONTAINS integer-6 TO integer-7 CHARACTERS                            }]

  [LABEL {RECORD IS  } {STANDARD}]
  [      {RECORDS ARE} {OMITTED }]

  [VALUE OF {implementor-name-1 IS {data-name-2}} . . . ]
  [         {                      {literal-1  }}       ]

  [DATA {RECORD IS   } {data-name-3} . . . ] .
  [     {RECORDS ARE }                     ]
```

Data Description Entry

FORMAT 1

```
level-number [data-name-1]
             [FILLER     ]

    [REDEFINES data-name-2]

    [IS EXTERNAL]

    [IS GLOBAL]

    [{PICTURE} IS character-string]
    [{PIC    }                    ]

    [           {BINARY         }]
    [           {COMPUTATIONAL  }]
    [           {COMP           }]
    [[USAGE IS] {DISPLAY        }]
    [           {INDEX          }]
    [           {PACKED-DECIMAL }]

    [[SIGN IS] {LEADING } [SEPARATE CHARACTER]]
    [          {TRAILING}                      ]

    [OCCURS integer-2 TIMES                                             ]
    [    [{ASCENDING } KEY IS {data-name-3} . . .] . . .                ]
    [    [{DESCENDING}                           ]                      ]
    [    [INDEXED BY {index-name-1} . . . ]                             ]
    [OCCURS integer-1 TO integer-2 TIMES DEPENDING ON data-name-4       ]
    [    [{ASCENDING } KEY IS {data-name-3} . . .] . . .                ]
    [    [{DESCENDING}                           ]                      ]
    [    [INDEXED BY {index-name-1} . . . ]                             ]

    [{SYNCHRONIZED} [LEFT ]]
    [{SYNC        } [RIGHT]]

    [{JUSTIFIED} RIGHT]
    [{JUST     }      ]

    [BLANK WHEN ZERO]

    [VALUE IS literal-1] .
```

FORMAT 2

```
66 data-name-1 RENAMES data-name-2 [{THROUGH} data-name-3] .
                                   [{THRU   }            ]
```

FORMAT 3

```
88 condition-name-1 {VALUE IS  } {literal-1 [{THROUGH} literal-2]} . . . .
                    {VALUES ARE} {          [{THRU   }          ]}
```

Communication Description Entry

FORMAT 1

```
CD cd-name-1

                           [ [SYMBOLIC QUEUE IS data-name-1]
                             [SYMBOLIC SUB-QUEUE-1 IS data-name-2]
                             [SYMBOLIC SUB-QUEUE-2 IS data-name-3]
                             [SYMBOLIC SUB-QUEUE-3 IS data-name-4]
                             [MESSAGE DATE IS data-name-5]
                             [MESSAGE TIME IS data-name-6]
                             [SYMBOLIC SOURCE IS data-name-7]
   FOR [INITIAL] INPUT       [TEXT LENGTH IS data-name-8]
                             [END KEY IS data-name-9]
                             [STATUS KEY IS data-name-10]
                             [MESSAGE COUNT IS data-name-11] ]
                           [data-name-1, data-name-2, data-name-3,
                             data-name-4, data-name-5, data-name-6,
                             data-name-7, data-name-8, data-name-9,
                             data-name-10, data-name-11]
```

FORMAT 2

```
CD cd-name-1 FOR OUTPUT
   [DESTINATION COUNT IS data-name-1]
   [TEXT LENGTH IS data-name-2]
   [STATUS KEY IS data-name-3]
   [DESTINATION TABLE OCCURS integer-1 TIMES
      [INDEXED BY {index-name-1} . . . ] ]
   [ERROR KEY IS data-name-4]
   [SYMBOLIC DESTINATION IS data-name-5] .
```

FORMAT 3

```
CD cd-name-1

                         [ [MESSAGE DATE IS data-name-1]
                           [MESSAGE TIME IS data-name-2]
                           [SYMBOLIC TERMINAL IS data-name-3]
   FOR [INITIAL] I-O       [TEXT LENGTH IS data-name-4]
                           [END KEY IS data-name-5]
                           [STATUS KEY IS data-name-6] ]
                         [data-name-1, data-name-2, data-name-3,
                           data-name-4, data-name-5, data-name-6]
```

Report Description Entry

```
RD  report-name-1
    [IS GLOBAL]
    [CODE literal-1]
    [ {CONTROL IS  } {{data-name-1} . . .           } ]
    [ {CONTROLS ARE} {FINAL [data-name-1] . . .     } ]
    [PAGE [LIMIT IS  ] integer-1 [LINE ] [HEADING integer-2]
          [LIMITS ARE]           [LINES]
       [FIRST DETAIL integer-3] [LAST DETAIL integer-4]
       [FOOTING integer-5] ] .
```

Report Group Description Entry

FORMAT 1

```
01  [data-name-1]
    [ LINE NUMBER IS {integer-1 [ON NEXT PAGE]} ]
    [                {PLUS integer-2          } ]
    [                {integer-3     } ]
    [ NEXT GROUP IS  {PLUS integer-4} ]
    [                {NEXT PAGE     } ]
                {REPORT HEADING}                                }
                {RH            }                                }
                {PAGE HEADING}                                  }
                {PH          }                                  }
                {CONTROL HEADING} {data-name-2}                 }
                {CH             } {FINAL      }                 }
    TYPE IS     {DETAIL}                                        }
                {DE    }                                        }
                {CONTROL FOOTING} {data-name-3}                 }
                {CF             } {FINAL      }                 }
                {PAGE FOOTING}                                  }
                {PF          }                                  }
                {REPORT FOOTING}                                }
                {RF            }                                }
    [ [USAGE IS] DISPLAY] .
```

FORMAT 2

```
level-number  [data-name-1]
    [ LINE NUMBER IS {integer-1 [ON NEXT PAGE]} ]
    [                {PLUS integer-2          } ]
    [ [USAGE IS] DISPLAY] .
```

Report Group Description Entry *(continued)*

FORMAT 3

```
level-number  [data-name-1]

    {PICTURE}
    {PIC    }  IS  character-string

    [ [USAGE  IS]  DISPLAY]

    [[SIGN  IS]  {LEADING }  SEPARATE  CHARACTER]
    [            {TRAILING}                      ]

    [{JUSTIFIED}  RIGHT]
    [{JUST     }       ]

    [BLANK  WHEN  ZERO]

    [LINE  NUMBER  IS  {integer-1  [ON  NEXT PAGE]}]
    [                  {PLUS  integer-2           }]

    [COLUMN  NUMBER  IS  integer-3]

    {SOURCE  IS  identifier-1                                              }
    {VALUE  IS  literal-1                                                  }
    {{SUM  {identifier-2} . . .  [UPON  {data-name-2} . . . ] } . . .      }
    {                                                                      }
    {    [RESET  ON  {data-name-3}]                                        }
    {    [           {FINAL      }]                                        }

    [GROUP  INDICATE] .
```

Procedure Division

FORMAT 1

```
[PROCEDURE DIVISION  [USING  {data-name-1} . . . ] .
[DECLARATIVES.
{section-name  SECTION  [segment-number] .
    USE statement.
[paragraph-name.
    [sentence] . . . ] . . . } . . .
END DECLARATIVES.]
{section-name  SECTION  [segment-number] .
[paragraph-name.
    [sentence] . . . ] . . . } . . . ]
```

FORMAT 2

```
[PROCEDURE DIVISION  [USING  {data-name-1} . . . ] .
[paragraph-name.
    [sentence] . . . } . . . ]
```

COBOL Verbs

```
ACCEPT identifier-1 [FROM mnemonic-name-1]
```

```
                               ⎧DATE       ⎫
ACCEPT identifier-2 FROM ⎨DAY        ⎬
                               ⎪DAY-OF-WEEK⎪
                               ⎩TIME       ⎭
```

```
ACCEPT cd-name-1 MESSAGE COUNT
```

```
ADD {identifier-1} . . . TO {identifier-2 [ROUNDED] } . . .
    {literal-1   }
    [ON SIZE ERROR imperative-statement-1]
    [NOT ON SIZE ERROR imperative-statement-2]
    [END-ADD]
```

```
ADD {identifier-1} . . . TO {identifier-2}
    {literal-1   }          {literal-2   }
    GIVING {identifier-3} [ROUNDED] } . . .
    [ON SIZE ERROR imperative-statement-1]
    [NOT ON SIZE ERROR imperative-statement-2]
    [END-ADD]
```

```
ADD {CORRESPONDING} identifier-1 TO identifier-2 [ROUNDED]
    {CORR         }
    [ON SIZE ERROR imperative-statement-1]
    [NOT ON SIZE ERROR imperative-statement-2]
    [END-ADD]
```

```
ALTER {procedure-name-1 TO [PROCEED TO] procedure-name-2} . . .
```

```
CALL {identifier-1} [USING {[BY REFERENCE] {identifier-2} . . .} . . . ]
     {literal-1   }        {BY CONTENT {identifier-2} . . .     }
    [ON OVERFLOW imperative-statement-1] [END-CALL]
```

```
CALL {identifier-1} [USING {[BY REFERENCE] {identifier-2} . . .} . . . ]
     {literal-1   }        {BY CONTENT {identifier-2} . . .     }
    [ON EXCEPTION imperative-statement-1]
    [NOT ON EXCEPTION imperative-statement-2]
    [END-CALL]
```

COBOL Verbs *(continued)*

```
CANCEL {identifier-1} . . .
       {literal-1   }
```

S W

```
       {                [{REEL} [FOR REMOVAL]]  }
CLOSE  { file-name-1    [{UNIT}              ]  } . . .
       {                [                    ]  }
       {                [WITH {NO REWIND}    ]  }
       {                [     {LOCK     }    ]  }
```

R I

```
CLOSE {file-name-1} [WITH LOCK] } . . .
```

```
COMPUTE {identifier-1 [ROUNDED] } . . . = arithmetic-expression-1
    [ON SIZE ERROR imperative-statement-1]
    [NOT ON SIZE ERROR imperative-statement-2]
    [END-COMPUTE]
```

```
CONTINUE
```

```
DELETE file-name-1 RECORD
    [INVALID KEY imperative-statement-1]
    [NOT INVALID KEY imperative-statement-2]
    [END-DELETE]
```

```
        {INPUT [TERMINAL]}
DISABLE {I-O TERMINAL    } cd-name-1 [WITH KEY {identifier-1}]
        {OUTPUT          }           [         {literal-1   }]
```

```
DISPLAY {identifier-1} . . . [UPON mnemonic-name-1] [WITH NO ADVANCING]
        {literal-1   }
```

```
DIVIDE {identifier-1} INTO {identifier-2 [ROUNDED] } . . .
       {literal-1   }
    [ON SIZE ERROR imperative-statement-1]
    [NOT ON SIZE ERROR imperative-statement-2]
    [END-DIVIDE]
```

```
DIVIDE {identifier-1} INTO {identifier-2}
       {literal-1   }      {literal-2   }
    GIVING {identifier-3 [ROUNDED] } . . .
    [ON SIZE ERROR imperative-statement-1]
    [NOT ON SIZE ERROR imperative-statement-2]
    [END-DIVIDE]
```

COBOL Verbs *(continued)*

```
DIVIDE {identifier-1} BY {identifier-2}
       {literal-1   }    {literal-2   }

    GIVING {identifier-3 [ROUNDED] } . . .
    [ON SIZE ERROR imperative-statement-1]
    [NOT ON SIZE ERROR imperative-statement-2]
    [END-DIVIDE]
```

```
DIVIDE {identifier-1} INTO {identifier-2} GIVING identifier-3 [ROUNDED]
       {literal-1   }      {literal-2   }

    REMAINDER identifier-4
    [ON SIZE ERROR imperative-statement-1]
    [NOT ON SIZE ERROR imperative-statement-2]
    [END-DIVIDE]
```

```
DIVIDE {identifier-1} BY {identifier-2} GIVING identifier-3 [ROUNDED]
       {literal-1   }    {literal-2   }

    REMAINDER identifier-4
    [ON SIZE ERROR imperative-statement-1]
    [NOT ON SIZE ERROR imperative-statement-2]
    [END-DIVIDE]
```

```
       {INPUT [TERMINAL]}
ENABLE {I-O TERMINAL    } cd-name-1 [WITH KEY {identifier-1}]
       {OUTPUT          }                     {literal-1   }
```

```
         {identifier-1}  [      {identifier-2}]
         {literal-1   }  [      {literal-2   }]
EVALUATE {expression-1}  [ALSO  {expression-2}] . . .
         {TRUE        }  [      {TRUE        }]
         {FALSE       }  [      {FALSE       }]

  { {WHEN
     {ANY                                                                                      }
     {condition-1                                                                              }
     {TRUE                                                                                     }
     {FALSE                                                                                    }
     {      {{identifier-3            } [{THROUGH} {identifier-4            }]]}               }
     {[NOT] {{literal-3               } [{THRU   } {literal-4               }]]}               }
     {      {{arithmetic-expression-1 } [          {arithmetic-expression-2 }]]}               }
```

COBOL Verbs *(continued)*

```
    [ALSO
        { ANY
        { condition-2
        { TRUE
        { FALSE
        { [NOT] { identifier-5                } [ { THROUGH } { identifier-6                } ] } ] . . . } . . .
        {       { literal-5                   } [ { THRU    } { literal-6                   } ] }
        {       { arithmetic-expression-3     } [             { arithmetic-expression-4     } ] }

    imperative-statement-1} . . .
  [WHEN OTHER  imperative-statement-2]
  [END-EVALUATE]
```

```
EXIT
```

```
EXIT PROGRAM
```

```
GENERATE { data-name-1   }
         { report-name-1 }
```

```
GO TO [procedure-name-1]
```

```
GO TO {procedure-name-1} . . . DEPENDING ON identifier-1
```

```
IF condition-1 THEN { {statement-1} . . . } { ELSE {statement-2} . . . [END-IF] }
                    { NEXT SENTENCE        } { ELSE NEXT SENTENCE                 }
                                             { END-IF                             }
```

```
INITIALIZE {identifer-1} . . .

   [ REPLACING { { ALPHABETIC           }                                     } . . . ]
   [           { { ALPHANUMERIC         }                                     }       ]
   [           { { NUMERIC              } DATA BY { identifier-2 }            }       ]
   [           { { ALPHANUMERIC-EDITED  }         { literal-1    }            }       ]
   [           { { NUMERIC-EDITED       }                                     }       ]
```

```
INITIATE {report-name-1} . . .
```

```
INSPECT identifier-1 TALLYING

  { identifier-2 FOR { CHARACTERS [ { BEFORE } INITIAL { identifier-4 } ] . . .                            } . . . } . . .
  {                  {            [ { AFTER  }         { literal-2    } ]                                  }       }
  {                  { { ALL     } { { identifier-3 } [ { BEFORE } INITIAL { identifier-4 } ] . . . } . . . }       }
  {                  { { LEADING } { { literal-1    } [ { AFTER  }         { literal-2    } ]       }       }       }
```

COBOL Verbs *(continued)*

```
INSPECT identifier-1 REPLACING

  { CHARACTERS BY {identifier-5} [{BEFORE} INITIAL {identifier-4}] . . .                              }
  {               {literal-3   } [{AFTER }         {literal-2   }]                                    }
  { {ALL    } { {identifier-3} BY {identifier-5} [{BEFORE} INITIAL {identifier-4}] . . . } . . .     } . . .
  { {LEADING} { {literal-1   }    {literal-3   } [{AFTER }         {literal-2   }]       }           }
  { {FIRST  }                                                                                         }


INSPECT identifier-1 TALLYING

  {                   { CHARACTERS [{BEFORE} INITIAL {identifier-4}] . . .                               } }
  { identifier-2 FOR  {            [{AFTER }         {literal-2   }]                                     } } . . . } . . .
  {                   { {ALL    } { {identifier-3} [{BEFORE} INITIAL {identifier-4}] . . . } . . .       } }
  {                   { {LEADING} { {literal-1   } [{AFTER }         {literal-2   }]       }             } }

  REPLACING

    { CHARACTERS BY {identifier-5} [{BEFORE} INITIAL {identifier-4}] . . .                              }
    {               {literal-3   } [{AFTER }         {literal-2   }]                                    }
    { {ALL    } { {identifier-3} BY {identifier-5} [{BEFORE} INITIAL {identifier-4}] . . . } . . .     } . . .
    { {LEADING} { {literal-1   }    {literal-3   } [{AFTER }         {literal-2   }]       }           }
    { {FIRST  }                                                                                         }


INSPECT identifier-1 CONVERTING {identifier-6} TO {identifier-7}
                                {literal-4   }    {literal-5   }

  [{BEFORE} INITIAL {identifier-4}] . . .
  [{AFTER }         {literal-2   }]


MERGE file-name-1 {ON {ASCENDING } KEY {data-name-1} . . . } . . .
                  {   {DESCENDING}                         }

  [COLLATING SEQUENCE IS alphabet-name-1]

  USING file-name-2 {file-name-3} . . .

  { OUTPUT PROCEDURE IS procedure-name-1 [{THROUGH} procedure-name-2] }
  {                                      [{THRU   }                 ] }
  { GIVING {file-name-4} . . .                                         }


MOVE {identifier-1} TO {identifier-2} . . .
     {literal-1   }


MOVE {CORRESPONDING} identifier-1 TO identifier-2
     {CORR         }


MULTIPLY {identifier-1} BY {identifier-2 [ROUNDED] } . . .
         {literal-1   }

  [ON SIZE ERROR imperative-statement-1]
  [NOT ON SIZE ERROR imperative-statement-2]
  [END-MULTIPLY]
```

COBOL Verbs *(continued)*

```
MULTIPLY {identifier-1} BY {identifier-2 [ROUNDED] } . . .
         {literal-1   }

    [ON SIZE ERROR imperative-statement-1]
    [NOT ON SIZE ERROR imperative-statement-2]
    [END-MULTIPLY]
```

```
MULTIPLY {identifier-1} BY {identifier-2}
         {literal-1   }    {literal-2   }

    GIVING {identifier-3 [ROUNDED] } . . .
    [ON SIZE ERROR imperative-statement-1]
    [NOT ON SIZE ERROR imperative-statement-2]
    [END-MULTIPLY]
```

```
S       OPEN {INPUT {file-name-1 [WITH NO REWIND] } . . .  } . . .
             {OUTPUT {file-name-2 [WITH NO REWIND] } . . . }
             {I-O {file-name-3} . . .                      }
             {EXTEND {file-name-4} . . .                   }
```

```
R I     OPEN {INPUT {file-name-1} . . .   } . . .
             {OUTPUT {file-name-2} . . .  }
             {I-O {file-name-3} . . .     }
             {EXTEND {file-name-4} . . .  }
```

```
W       OPEN {OUTPUT {file-name-1 [WITH NO REWIND] } . . .} . . .
             {EXTEND {file-name-2} . . .                  }
```

```
PERFORM [procedure-name-1 [{THROUGH} procedure-name-2]]
                          [{THRU   }                 ]

    [imperative-statement-1 END-PERFORM]
```

```
PERFORM [procedure-name-1 [{THROUGH} procedure-name-2]]
                          [{THRU   }                 ]

    {identifier-1} TIMES [imperative-statement-1 END-PERFORM]
    {integer-1   }
```

```
PERFORM [procedure-name-1 [{THROUGH} procedure-name-2]]
                          [{THRU   }                 ]

    [WITH TEST {BEFORE}] UNTIL condition-1
    [          {AFTER }]

    [imperative-statement-1 END-PERFORM]
```

COBOL Verbs *(continued)*

```
PERFORM [procedure-name-1 [{THROUGH | THRU} procedure-name-2]]

    [WITH TEST {BEFORE | AFTER}]

    VARYING {identifier-2 | index-name-1} FROM {identifier-3 | index-name-2 | literal-1}

        BY {identifier-4 | literal-2} UNTIL condition-1

    [AFTER {identifier-5 | literal-3} FROM {identifier-6 | index-name-4 | literal-3}

        BY {identifier-7 | literal-4} UNTIL condition-2] . . .

    [imperative-statement-1 END-PERFORM]
```

```
PURGE cd-name-1
```

S R I

```
READ file-name-1 [NEXT] RECORD [INTO identifier-1]
    [AT END imperative-statement-1]
    [NOT AT END imperative-statement-2]
    [END-READ]
```

R

```
READ file-name-1 RECORD [INTO identifier-1]
    [INVALID KEY imperative-statement-3]
    [NOT INVALID KEY imperative-statement-4]
    [END-READ]
```

I

```
READ file-name-1 RECORD [INTO identifier-1]
    [KEY IS data-name-1]
    [INVALID KEY imperative-statement-3]
    [NOT INVALID KEY imperative-statement-4]
    [END-READ]
```

```
RECEIVE cd-name-1 {MESSAGE | SEGMENT} INTO identifier-1
    [NO DATA imperative-statement-1]
    [WITH DATA imperative-statement-2]
    [END-RECEIVE]
```

```
RELEASE record-name-1 [FROM identifier-1]
```

COBOL Verbs *(continued)*

```
RETURN file-name-1 RECORD [INTO identifier-1]
    AT END imperative-statement-1
    [NOT AT END imperative-statement-2]
    [END-RETURN]
```

S

```
REWRITE record-name-1 [FROM identifier-1]
```

RI

```
REWRITE record-name-1 [FROM identifier-1]
    [INVALID KEY imperative-statement-1]
    [NOT INVALID KEY imperative-statement-2]
    [END-REWRITE]
```

```
SEARCH identifier-1 [VARYING {identifier-2 | index-name-2}]
    [AT END imperative-statement-1]
    {WHEN condition-1 {imperative-statement-2 | NEXT-SENTENCE}} . . .
    [END-SEARCH]
```

```
SEARCH ALL identifier-1 [AT END imperative-statement-1]
    WHEN {data-name-1 {IS EQUAL TO | IS =} {identifier-3 | literal-1 | arithmetic-expression-1}
          | condition-name-2}
    [AND {data-name-2 {IS EQUAL TO | IS =} {identifier-4 | literal-2 | arithmetic-expression-2}
          | condition-name-2}] . . .
    {imperative-statement-2 | NEXT SENTENCE}
    [END-SEARCH]
```

```
SEND cd-name-1 FROM identifier-1
```

```
SEND cd-name-1 [FROM identifier-1] {WITH identifier-2 | WITH ESI | WITH EMI | WITH EGI}
    [{BEFORE | AFTER} ADVANCING {{identifier-3 | integer-1} [LINE | LINES]
                                 | {mnemonic-name-1 | PAGE}}]
    [REPLACING LINE]
```

COBOL Verbs *(continued)*

```
                                       {index-name-2}
SET {index-name-1} . . .  TO           {identifier-2}
    {identifier-1}                     {integer-1   }

SET {index-name-3} . . . {UP BY  }  {identifier-3}
                         {DOWN BY}  {integer-2   }

SET {{mnemonic-name-1} . . . TO {ON }} . . .
                                {OFF}

SET {condition-name-1} . . . TO TRUE

SORT file-name-1 {ON {ASCENDING } KEY {data-name-1} . . . } . . .
                     {DESCENDING}

    [WITH DUPLICATES IN ORDER]
    [COLLATING SEQUENCE IS alphabet-name-1]

    {INPUT PROCEDURE IS procedure-name-1 [{THROUGH} procedure-name-2]}
    {                                     {THRU   }                  }
    {USING [file-name-2] . . .                                       }

    {OUTPUT PROCEDURE IS procedure-name-3 [{THROUGH} procedure-name-4]}
    {                                      {THRU   }                  }
    {GIVING [file-name-3] . . .                                       }

                        [     {IS EQUAL TO                 }             ]
                        [     {IS =                        }             ]
                        [     {IS GREATER THAN             }             ]
START file-name-1       [ KEY {IS >                        } data-name-1 ]
                        [     {IS NOT LESS THAN            }             ]
                        [     {IS NOT <                    }             ]
                        [     {IS GREATER THAN OR EQUAL TO }             ]
                        [     {IS >=                       }             ]

    [INVALID KEY imperative-statement-1]
    [NOT INVALID KEY imperative-statement-2]
    [END-START]

STOP {RUN      }
     {literal-1}
```

COBOL Verbs *(continued)*

```
STRING { {identifier-1} . . . DELIMITED BY {identifier-2} } . . .
         {literal-1   }                    {literal-2   }
                                           {SIZE        }
    INTO identifier-3
    [WITH POINTER identifier-4]
    [ON OVERFLOW imperative-statement-1]
    [NOT ON OVERFLOW imperative-statement-2]
    [END-STRING]
```

```
SUBTRACT {identifier-1} . . . FROM {identifier-3 [ROUNDED] } . . .
         {literal-1   }
    [ON SIZE ERROR imperative-statement-1]
    [NOT ON SIZE ERROR imperative-statement-2]
    [END-SUBTRACT]
```

```
SUBTRACT {identifier-1} . . . FROM {identifier-2}
         {literal-1   }            {literal-2   }
    GIVING {identifier-3} [ROUNDED] } . . .
    [ON SIZE ERROR imperative-statement-1]
    [NOT ON SIZE ERROR imperative-statement-2]
    [END-SUBTRACT]
```

```
SUBTRACT {CORRESPONDING} identifier-1 FROM identifier-2 [ROUNDED]
         {CORR         }
    [ON SIZE ERROR imperative-statement-1]
    [NOT ON SIZE ERROR imperative-statement-2]
    [END-SUBTRACT]
```

```
SUPPRESS PRINTING
```

```
TERMINATE {report-name-1} . . .
```

```
UNSTRING identifier-1
    [DELIMITED BY [ALL] {identifier-2} [OR [ALL] {identifier-3} ] . . . ]
                        {literal-1   }           {literal-2   }
    INTO {identifier-4 [DELIMITER IN identifier-5] [COUNT IN identifier-6] } . . .
    [WITH POINTER identifier-7]
    [TALLYING IN identifier-8]
    [ON OVERFLOW imperative-statement-1]
    [NOT ON OVERFLOW imperative-statement-2]
    [END-UNSTRING]
```

COBOL Verbs *(continued)*

```
                                                              {file-name-1} . . .
                                                              INPUT
USE [GLOBAL] AFTER STANDARD {EXCEPTION} PROCEDURE ON        { OUTPUT
                            {ERROR    }                       I-O
                                                              EXTEND
```

```
USE [GLOBAL] BEFORE REPORTING identifier-1
```

```
                          cd-name-1
                          [ALL REFERENCES OF] identifier-1
USE FOR DEBUGGING ON    { file-name-1                       } . . .
                          procedure-name-1
                          ALL PROCEDURES
```

S

```
WRITE record-name-1 [FROM identifier-1]

    [                      [{identifier-2} [LINE ]]]
    [{BEFORE}  ADVANCING  {[{integer-1   } [LINES]]}]
    [{AFTER }             { {mnemonic-name-1}      }]
    [                     { {PAGE           }      }]

    [AT {END-OF-PAGE} imperative-statement-1]
    [   {EOP        }                       ]

    [NOT AT {END-OF-PAGE} imperative-statement-2]
    [       {EOP        }                       ]

    [END-WRITE]
```

R I

```
WRITE record-name-1 [FROM identifier-1]
    [INVALID KEY imperative-statement-1]
    [NOT INVALID KEY imperative-statement-2]
    [END-WRITE]
```

COPY and REPLACE Statements

```
COPY text-name-1 [{OF} library-name-1]
                 [{IN}               ]

    [            {{== pseudo-text-1 ==}      {== pseudo-text-2 ==}}     ]
    [ REPLACING  {{identifier-1       }  BY  {identifier-2       }} . . .]
    [            {{literal-1          }      {literal-2          }}     ]
    [            {{word-1             }      {word-2             }}     ]
```

```
REPLACE {== pseudo-text-1 == BY == pseudo-text-2 ==} . . .
```

```
REPLACE OFF
```

Conditions

RELATION CONDITION

```
                            ⎧IS [NOT] GREATER THAN         ⎫
                            ⎪IS [NOT] >                    ⎪
                            ⎪IS [NOT] LESS THAN            ⎪
⎧identifier-1             ⎫ ⎪IS [NOT] <                    ⎪ ⎧identifier-2             ⎫
⎪literal-1                ⎪ ⎪IS [NOT] EQUAL TO             ⎪ ⎪literal-2                ⎪
⎨arithmetic-expression-1  ⎬ ⎨IS [NOT] =                    ⎬ ⎨arithmetic-expression-2  ⎬
⎩index-name-1             ⎭ ⎪IS GREATER THAN OR EQUAL TO   ⎪ ⎩index-name-2             ⎭
                            ⎪IS >=                         ⎪
                            ⎪IS LESS THAN OR EQUAL TO      ⎪
                            ⎩IS <=                         ⎭
```

CLASS CONDITION

```
                       ⎧NUMERIC         ⎫
                       ⎪ALPHABETIC      ⎪
identifier-1 IS [NOT]  ⎨ALPHABETIC-LOWER⎬
                       ⎪ALPHABETIC-UPPER⎪
                       ⎩class-name      ⎭
```

CONDITION-NAME CONDITION

```
condition-name-1
```

SWITCH-STATUS CONDITION

```
condition-name-1
```

SIGN CONDITION

```
                                     ⎧POSITIVE⎫
arithmetic-expression-1  IS  [NOT]   ⎨NEGATIVE⎬
                                     ⎩ZERO    ⎭
```

NEGATED CONDITION

```
NOT condition-1
```

COMBINED CONDITION

```
condition-1  ⎧⎧AND⎫ condition-2⎫ . . .
             ⎩⎩OR ⎭            ⎭
```

ABBREVIATED COMBINED RELATION CONDITION

```
relation-condition ⎧⎧AND⎫ [NOT] [relational-operator] object⎫ . . .
                   ⎩⎩OR ⎭                                   ⎭
```

Qualification

FORMAT 1

```
                     { { {IN} data-name-2 } ... [ {IN} {file-name} ] }
{data-name-1     }   { { {OF}             }     [ {OF} {cd-name  } ] }
{condition-name  }   { {IN} {file-name}                              }
                     { {OF} {cd-name  }                              }
```

FORMAT 2

```
paragraph-name {IN} section-name
               {OF}
```

FORMAT 3

```
text-name {IN} library-name
          {OF}
```

FORMAT 4

```
LINAGE-COUNTER {IN} report-name
               {OF}
```

FORMAT 5

```
{PAGE-COUNTER} {IN} report-name
{LINE-COUNTER} {OF}
```

FORMAT 6

```
              { {IN} data-name-4 [ {IN} report-name ] }
data-name-3   { {OF}             [ {OF}             ] }
              { {IN} report-name                      }
              { {OF}                                  }
```

Miscellaneous Formats

SUBSCRIPTING

```
{condition-name-1}  ( {integer-1                        }     )
{data-name-1     }  ( {data-name-2  [ {±} integer-2]    } . . . )
                    ( {index-name-1 [ {±} integer-3]    }     )
```

REFERENCE MODIFICATION

```
data-name-1 (leftmost-character-position: [length])
```

IDENTIFIER

```
                                            [        {cd-name    } ]
data-name-1 [ {IN} data-name-2 ] . . .      [ {IN}   {file-name  } ]
            [ {OF}             ]            [ {OF}   {report-name} ]

    [ ( {subscript} . . . ) ] [ (leftmost-character-position: [length] ) ]
```

Nested Source Programs

```
IDENTIFICATION DIVISION.
PROGRAM-ID. program-name-1 [IS INITIAL PROGRAM ] .
[ENVIRONMENT DIVISION. environment-division-content]
[DATA DIVISION. data-division-content]
[PROCEDURE DIVISION. procedure-division-content]
[ [nested-source-program] . . .
END PROGRAM program-name-1.]
```

NESTED-SOURCE-PROGRAM

```
IDENTIFICATION DIVISION.
PROGRAM-ID. program-name-2 [IS { | COMMON  | } PROGRAM ] .
                           [   { | INITIAL | }         ]
[ENVIRONMENT DIVISION. environment-division-content]
[DATA DIVISION. data-division-content]
[PROCEDURE DIVISION. procedure-division-content]
[nested-source-program] . . .
END PROGRAM program-name-2.
```

A Series of Source Programs

```
{IDENTIFICATION DIVISION.
PROGRAM-ID. program-name-3 [IS INITIAL PROGRAM ] .
[ENVIRONMENT DIVISION. environment-division-content]
[DATA DIVISION. data-division-content]
[PROCEDURE DIVISION. procedure-division-content]
[nested-source-program] . . .
END PROGRAM program-name-3.} . . .
IDENTIFICATION DIVISION.
PROGRAM-ID. program-name-4 [IS INITIAL PROGRAM ] .
[ENVIRONMENT DIVISION. environment-division-content]
[DATA DIVISION. data-division-content]
[PROCEDURE DIVISION. procedure-division-content]
[ [nested-source-program] . . .
END PROGRAM program-name-4.]
```

Answers to Odd-Numbered Exercises

Chapter 1

Fill-in

1. Input, processing, output
3. Flowchart
5. Decision
7. Programmer-supplied-name
9. Relational
11. Fields

True/False

1. False. Nonnumeric literals may contain numbers, letters, or special characters.
3. False. A dataname may contain hyphens.
5. True.
7. True.
9. False. They must appear in order: IDENTIFICATION, ENVIRONMENT, DATA, and PROCEDURE.
11. True.
13. False. They must be told exactly what to do, and the instructions take the form of a computer program.
15. False. A diamond indicates a decision; a rectangle implies straight forward processing.
17. False. Reserved words are restricted to a preassigned use.
19. False. The rules for pseudocode are at the discretion of the programmer.

Chapter 2

Fill -in

1. Compiler, source, object (machine)
3. A margin
5. 12, 72
7. Editor (word processor)
9. Debugging
11. Linker
13. Different
15. Execution

True/False

1. False. A compiler translates a problem-oriented language into a machine oriented language.
3. True.
5. True.
7. False. Division headers may begin anywhere in the A margin (columns 8 to 11), although many people begin them in column 8.
9. False. Paragraph names begin in the A margin.

11. False. A clean compile means only that the program has been translated into machine language; it says nothing about whether the logic of the program is correct.
13. True.
15. False. Each text editor has its own unique commands.
17. False. The compiler produces an object module which is input to the linker, which in turn produces the load module.

Chapter 3

Fill-in

1. Sequence, selection, and iteration
3. One, one
5. Hierarchy chart
7. Completeness, functionality, and span of control
9. Pseudocode
11. Span of control
13. Bohm, Jacopini
15. Top down

True/False

1. False. It may still contain logic errors, but presumably fewer than non-structured code.
3. False. Initialization and termination are too vague and do not follow the verb, adjective, object convention for naming paragraphs.
5. True.
7. False. It is an extension to sequence, selection, and iteration.
9. False. The rules of pseudocode are at the discretion of the programmer, although individual shops may impose standards.
11. False. Testing should begin as soon as possible with the aid of program stubs.
13. False. The name implies that the paragraph is doing three distinct things, as opposed to having a single function.
15. False. Program testing should be ongoing throughout the life of the project.
17. False. The optimal number of modules is a function of the program's design.

Chapter 4

Fill-in

1. Identification
3. Braces
5. Programmer supplied
7. SELECT
9. PICTURE
11. FILE, WORKING-STORAGE
13. may not
15. BLOCK CONTAINS, logical, physical

True/False

1. True.
3. False. Square brackets indicate the entry is optional.
5. False. Some modification, generally in the Environment Division is required.
7. False. It will have a picture clause if it is an elementary item.
9. False. A group item never has a picture clause.
11. False. The determination of whether a data item is a group or elementary item depends on the definition of subordinate data items.
13. True.
15. False. Technically, a program may be written without a File Section, although this is unusual.
17. False. It is optional as indicated by the brackets in the COBOL notation.

Chapter 5

Fill-in

1. COMPUTE
3. ROUNDED
5. Before
7. Does not
9. STOP RUN
11. N + 1
13. AFTER ADVANCING PAGE
15. One, left, right
17. Decimal alignment
19. May not
21. SIZE ERROR

True/False

1. True.
3. False. An ADD statement must contain one word or the other.
5. True.
7. False. The use of BY or INTO determines which operand is the dividend, and which one is the divisor.
9. True.
11. False. If multiplication and division are both present, the order of operations is from left to right.
13. True.
15. True.
17. False. STOP RUN is the last statement executed, but it need not be (and usually isn't) the last physical statement in the program.
19. False. The READ statement specifies a file name.
21. False. They are required whenever a file is present. (Strictly speaking, if a program did not reference any files, then the statements would not be used).
23. True.
25. False. ROUNDED is an optional clause in all the arithmetic statements.
27. False. It is an optional clause.

Chapter 6

Fill-in

1. Compilation
3. Execution
5. Compiles
7. Structured walkthrough
9. Detection, correction
11. Cross reference listing

True/False

1. False. A clean compile means only that the program has been successfully translated into machine language.
3. False. The compiler checks for syntax only and has no way of determining the validity of a program's logic.
5. True.
7. True.
9. False. Spaces are generally required after punctuation symbols, but not before.
11. False. A data name may contain hyphens, letters, or digits only.
13. False. One reads a file and writes a record.
15. False. Walkthroughs should be held for everyone.
17. False. A walkthrough should take a maximum of two hours.

Chapter 7

Fill-in

1. Coding standards
3. Floating, fixed
5. V, S
7. Verb, adjective, object
9. Indentation
11. Negative

True/False

1. False. Indentation is used to improve the readability of a program.
3. False. Coding standards are a function of the individual shop.
5. False. Data names should be meaningful to simplify program maintenance, an activity which takes far more time than initial coding and data entry.
7. False. Comments should be used with caution, and always for a specific purpose; a common fault of beginners is to over comment.
9. False. The name implies that the paragraph is performing two functions.
11. False. A VALUE clause is used only to assign an initial value; for example for heading lines in Working-Storage. (VALUE clauses are not permitted in the FILE SECTION.)
13. False. The assignment of CR and/or DB depends on the accounting system in use.
15. False. One or the other should be selected, depending on the accounting system.
17. True.
19. True.

Chapter 8

Fill-in

1. Validated (checked)
3. Numeric
5. Completeness
7. 88
9. END-IF

True/False

1. False. The output of the edit program is input to the reporting program.
3. True.
5. False. The alphabetic class test can be applied to only alphabetic or alphanumeric data.
7. True.
9. True.
11. False. DAY and DATE imply the Julian and calendar dates, respectively.

Chapter 9

Fill-in

1. Two
3. Section
5. Qualified, OF, IN
7. STRING, UNSTRING, and INSPECT
9. BEFORE, AFTER
11. In-line

True/False

1. True.
3. False. An in-line perform does not specify a procedure.
5. False. CORRESPONDING is always optional.
7. False. The CORRESPONDING option has several fine points, but level number is not one of them.
9. False. It is an optional statement which is not favored by the authors.
11. True.

Chapter 10

Fill-in

1. Is not
3. SECURE
5. Last
7. Should not
9. TEST BEFORE
11. Interactive

True/False

1. False. Both sections may appear in the same program.
3. False. The clauses are optional.
5. True.
7. False. The text would be illegible; i.e., it would blend into the background.
9. True.

Chapter 11

Fill-in

1. OCCURS
3. Variable, OCCURS DEPENDING ON
5. May
7. Is
9. Does not change

True/False

1. False. Tables are established through an OCCURS clause.
3. True.
5. True. However if a subscript does assume a zero value, it would indicate a logic error in the program.
7. False. An index can be used only with the table for which it was defined.
9. False. Variable length records means that records in a file are of different lengths.
11. False. An index is modified by a SET or PERFORM statement.

Chapter 12

Fill-in

1. 100, 676, 1296
3. Hard-coded
5. Positional
7. REDEFINES
9. KEY
11. INDEXED BY
13. Compilation
15. Range step

True/False

1. True.
3. True.
5. True.
7. True.
9. True.
11. False. Examination of the COBOL syntax shows an additional WHEN clause enclosed in brackets.
13. True.
15. True. Good practice however, dictates that a separate subscript be used for every table.

17. True.
19. True.
21. True.
23. False. All codes should be unique.
25. True.
27. False. A range step table occurs when a one-to-one correspondence no longer exists.

Chapter 13

Fill-in

1. OCCURS
3. Seven
5. May not, OCCURS, REDEFINES
7. 1, 6, 2, 1, 6
9. 1, 2, 3

True/False

1. True.
3. True in COBOL-85, but not in COBOL-74.
5. True.
7. False. The program would compile cleanly, but produce problems during execution.
9. False. The clauses are all optional

Chapter 14

Fill-in

1. Key
3. EBCDIC, ASCII
5. Primary (major), secondary (intermediate), tertiary (minor)
7. GIVING, OUTPUT PROCEDURE
9. SELECT, SD
11. Trailing, embedded
13. Identical

True/False

1. False. It can be used on a calculated field if INPUT PROCEDURE is specified.
3. False. INPUT PROCEDURE may also be specified with GIVING.
5. True.
7. False. They are associated with INPUT PROCEDURE and OUTPUT PROCEDURE, respectively.
9. True.
11. True.
13. False. The INPUT PROCEDURE is used if you want to selectively pass records to the sort work file; for example, to increase efficiency by sorting on fewer records.
15. True.
17. False. INPUT PROCEDURE is not used with the MERGE statement.
19. False. The MERGE statement requires that all input files have identical record layouts and appear in the same sequence.

Chapter 15

Fill-in

1. Change, control break
3. Is
5. Before
7. Pseudocode
9. Less
11. Rolling

True/False

1. False. Control breaks can theoretically extend to any number of levels, although they lose meaning after three or four
3. True.
5. True.
7. True.
9. True.

Chapter 16

Fill-in

1. EXIT PROGRAM
3. Is
5. Both
7. COPY
9. BY REFERENCE
11. CALL

True/False

1. False. The COPY statement is permitted anywhere except within another COPY.
3. False. They can be the same, but there is no COBOL requirement stating they must be the same.
5. False. The COPY statement is permitted anywhere except within another COPY.
7. False. A program may call several subprograms.
9. False. All parameters must be elementary items except for those passed at the 01 level.
11. False. Both are optional; omission of both phrases defaults to calling BY REFERENCE which is equivalent to a CALL statement in COBOL-74.

Chapter 17

Fill-in

1. Every
3. Does
5. Additions, changes (corrections), deletions
7. Can
9. Can not
11. Stubs, DISPLAY
13. HIGH-VALUES

True/False

1. True.
3. True.
5. True.
7. False. Duplicate additions can only be checked against the master file; i.e., during the actual update.
9. False. Pseudocode is procedural in nature and indicates sequence and decision making. Hierarchy charts are functional and indicate what has to be done, not necessarily when or if.
11. False. The programmer is biased (either consciously or unconsciously), as he or she wrote the program and knows what it does or doesn't do. Ideally test data should be designed by the user, but this is often difficult to achieve.
13. False. The balance line algorithm may be used with multiple transaction files (as was done in the chapter).

Chapter 18

Fill-in

1. Indexed
3. VSAM, indexed
5. Highest
7. Unique, duplicate, alternate (secondary)
9. Optional, two, WORKING-STORAGE
11. START
13. DYNAMIC

True/False

1. False. Specification of ALTERNATE RECORD KEY will require substantial amounts of overhead in retrieving records from an indexed file; it should not be used indiscriminately.
3. False. The COBOL notation places both clauses in brackets to indicate optional entries. Logically however one of the two conditions must pertain, and consequently either clause should be specified. (The authors find these clauses easier to follow than testing the equivalent FILE STATUS entries.)
5. False. Specification of zero alternate areas will slow processing.
7. False. The ALTERNATE RECORD KEY need not be unique, as per the WITH DUPLICATES clause.
9. True.
11. False. They have different functions; to enter a new record and to change an existing record.
13. True.

PROGRAMMING SPECIFICATIONS

Project 2-1

Program Name: Employee Selection Program

Narrative: Write a program to process a file of employee records. Print the name of every employee who earns $20,000 or more, works in New York, and is younger than 30.

Input File: EMPLOYEE-FILE

Input Record Layout:

Employee Record					
Name	Salary		Location		Age
1 … 17	18 … 23	24	25 … 36	37 38	39 40

Test Data:

```
         1         2         3         4         5         6
12345678901234567890123456789012345678901234567890123456789012345
DICK TRAUM       025000 NEW YORK      40
KEN ANDERSON     042000 NEW YORK      29
MARSHAL CRAWFORD 023000 MINNEAPOLIS   32
HARRY WICKS      019000 NEW YORK      28
DICK TRACY       034500 CHICAGO       26
FEARLESS FOSDICK 019500 NEW YORK      31
MARYANNE COULTER 022300 MIAMI         37
JOHN SMITH       025000 NEW YORK      30
PETER BROWN      022500 NEW YORK      26
ED BAKER         020000 NEW YORK      29
```

Report Layout:

```
           1         2         3         4         5         6
  12345678901234567890123456789012345678901234567890123456789012345
1
2     XXXXXXXXXXXXXXXXX 999999 99
3             |             |    |
4            name        salary age
5
```

Processing Requirements:

1. Read a file of employee records.
2. For each record read, determine whether that employee earns $20,000 or more, works in New York, and is younger than 30.
3. Print the name and associated data of every employee who meets the requirements in item 2 above. Double-space detail lines.
4. Are any problems caused by using age as an input field? Are any problems caused by spelling out "New York" in the input data, rather than using an abbreviated code?

Project 2-2

Program Name: Inter-City Piano Program

Narrative: Write a program for the Inter-City Piano Company. The program is to process a file of customer records and produce a list of people eligible for a discount in buying a piano.

Input File: CUSTOMER-LESSON-FILE

Input Record Layout:

Customer Lesson Record				
Last Name	First Name	# of Lesson		Purchase Indicator
1 ... 15	16 ... 25	26 ... 28	29	30

Test Data:

```
12345678901234567890123456789012345678901234567890123456789012345
CRAWFORD       SHERRY    011 N
KARVAZY        KAREN     017 Y
MORSE          KENNETH   014 N
PLUMETREE      MICHELE   027 N
SLY            MATTHEW   019 N
POWERS         NANCY     024 Y
BLAKELY        KRISTEN   008 Y
```

Report Layout:

```
  12345678901234567890123456789012345678901234567890123456789012345
1
2           XXXXXXXXXX XXXXXXXXXXXXXXX   999
3               |            |            |
4           first name   last name      lesson
5
```

Processing Requirements:

1. Read a file of customer records.
2. For every record read, determine whether that person is eligible for a discount to buy a piano. Individuals who have taken 15 or more lessons and have not yet purchased a piano qualify. Do not consider as eligible anyone with a "Y" in position 30 of the input record which indicates that a piano has already been purchased.
3. Print the names of all qualified individuals according to item 2 above. Single-space the output. (Do not print the names of individuals who are not eligible.)

Project 2-3

Program Name: Delinquent Accounts

Narrative: Write a program to process a corporation's account file to select a list of problem accounts. The generated list will then be brought to the attention of the comptroller.

Input File: CUSTOMER-ACCOUNT-FILE

Input Record Layout:

Customer Account Record						
Name		Account No.		Account Owed		Days Overdue
1 ... 15	16	17 ... 22	23	24 ... 28	29	30 ... 32

Test Data:

```
ACME ENTERPRISE 111111 01000 010
BAKER BROTHERS  222222 20000 030
BENJAMIN CO     333333 00500 015
FRANKEL CORP    444444 27500 045
CLARK PROGRESS  555555 32000 005
MARSHAK BOOKS   666666 03500 060
KARLSTROM INC   777777 00100 045
MILGROM THEATRE 888888 15000 014
SPRINGS WATER   999999 20000 007
```

Report Layout: Design your own report layout.

Processing Requirements:

1. Read a file of customer account records.
2. Determine if the record is a problem account. An account is considered a problem if the amount owed is over 20,000 or the account is more than 30 days overdue.
3. Print the name and associated information (account number, amount owed, and days overdue) of all problem accounts. Space this information reasonably over a print line. Double-space the report.

Project 2-4

Program Name: Shoe Inventory Program

Narrative: Write a program to process a file of shoe inventory records and produce a list of shoes that need reordering.

Input File: SHOE-INVENTORY-FILE

Input Record Layout:

Shoe Inventory Record			
Vendor Name	Style No.	Quantity on Hand	Reorder Quantity
1 … 12	13 … 18	19 … 22	23 … 26

Test Data:

```
BASS        12121204500300
BRUNO MAGLI 23232305000500
KEDS        34343407000750
JOAN & DAVID45454500500025
LA GEAR     56565605000550
FLORSHEIM   67676701000075
NIKE        78787803000200
REEBOK      89898907000800
```

Report Layout:

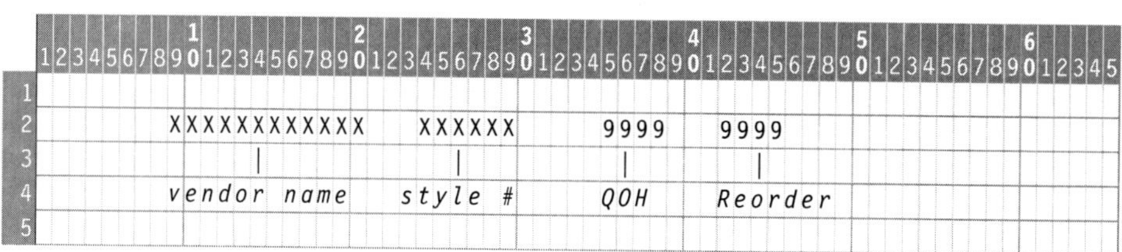

Processing Requirements:

1. Read a file of shoe inventory records.
2. For each record read, determine whether a particular shoe style should be reordered. Shoes should be reordered when the quantity on hand falls below the reorder quantity.
3. Print the vendor name, style number, quantity on hand, and reorder quantity for only the shoes that should be reordered.

Project 2-5

Program Name: Mailing List Program

Narrative: Write a program to process a file of mailing list records and produce a mailing list.

Input File: MAILING-LIST-FILE

Input Record Layout:

Mailing List Record			
Name	Street Address	City and State	Zip
1 … 20	21 … 45	46 … 63	64 … 68

Test Data:

```
         1         2         3         4         5         6
12345678901234567890123456789012345678901234567890123456789012345678
ROBERT T. GRAUER    60 PACIFIC COAST HWY     SANTA BARBARA, CA 93101
JANE DOE            123 SOUTH STREET         CHARLOTTE, NC     28203
JOHN SMITH          21 JUMP STREET           AUSTIN, TX        78701
DEBRA L. FEIT       59 BROADWAY              NEW YORK, NY      10006
MEGAN J. ALVORD     9 SOUTH SHORE DRIVE      BEVERLY HILLS, CA 90210
GEORGE BERENS       73 WEST FLAGLER          MIAMI, FL         33130
GARY FEIN           45 MAIN STREET W         CHICAGO, IL       60648
CAROL VAZQUEZ VILAR 9 ROAD TO HANA           MAUI, HI          96713
```

Report Layout:

```
          1         2         3         4         5         6
12345678901234567890123456789012345678901234567890123456789012345
1
2          XXXXXXXXXXXXXXXXXXXX - name
3          XXXXXXXXXXXXXXXXXXXXXXXXX -- street address
4          XXXXXXXXXXXXXXXXXX XXXXX
5                   |         |
6             city & state   zip
```

Processing Requirements:

1. Read a file of mailing list records.
2. For each record read, create a mailing label. Double-space between each record.

Project 2-6

Program Name: Student Admission Program

Narrative: Write a program to process a file of student records eligible for admission into college.

Input File: STUDENT-FILE

Input Record Layout:

Student Record			
Soc Sec No.	Last Name	High School GPA	SAT Score
1 ... 9	10 ... 24	25 *(2 decimals)* 27	28 ... 31

Test Data:

```
         1         2         3         4         5         6
12345678901234567890123456789012345678901234567890123456789012345
111111111DONAHUE        2550850
222222222HALL           3451000
333333333RIVERS         2000950
444444444LETTERMAN      3001100
555555555RAPHAEL        3501350
666666666LENO           3751450
777777777RIVERA         2350800
888888888WINFREY        3201300
999999999MILLER         2851000
```

Report Layout:

```
         1         2         3         4         5         6
12345678901234567890123456789012345678901234567890123456789012345
1
2     XXXXXXXXX   XXXXXXXXXXXXXXX    XXX
3             |              |          |
4           ssn          last name   YES or NO
5
```

Processing Requirements:

1. Read a file of student records.
2. For each record read:
   a. Calculate an overall index by multiplying the GPA by the GPA multiplier of 200 and then adding that amount to the SAT score.
   b. Compare the overall index to an admission criteria of 1500; if the overall index is equal to or greater than the admission criteria, the student is admitted ("YES").

3. Print the social security number, name, and either a "YES" or "NO" for all records in the file. Double-space the report.

Project 2-7

Program Name: Telephone Long Distance Carrier Program

Narrative: Write a program to process a file of telephone records to produce a report list of customers who are *not* using ET&T as a long distance carrier.

Input File: TELEPHONE-FILE

Input Record Layout:

Telephone Record			
Name	Area Code	Phone No.	Long Distance Carrier
1 … 18	19 … 21	22 … 28	29 … 35

Test Data:

```
         1         2         3         4         5         6
12345678901234567890123456789012345678901234567890123456789012345
MARYANN BARBER    3055557634AT&T
JOEL STUTZ        4076341234ET&T
ROBERT PLANT      3124374962SPRINT
GREGG ELOFSON     2032469368MCI
SARA RUSHINEK     2126662916ET&T
MARK GILLENSON    3163969476TELTEC
DAVID HERTZ       6132463618MCI
JOHN STEWART      8133246846TELTEC
```

Report Layout:

```
         1         2         3         4         5         6
12345678901234567890123456789012345678901234567890123456789012345
1
2    XXXXXXXXXXXXXXXXXX      (XXX) XXX-XXXX    XXXXXXX
3             |                |       |          |
4           name             area   phone #   long distance
5                            code              carrier
```

Processing Requirements:

1. Read a file of telephone records.
2. For each record read, determine whether the long distance carrier is ET&T or not.
3. Print the name, complete phone number, and the current long distance carrier of the records that are *not* using ET&T.

PROGRAMMING SPECIFICATIONS

Project 3-1

Program Name: Annual Compensation Report

Narrative: Develop the hierarchy chart and either flowchart, pseudocode, or Warnier-Orr diagram for a program to process a file of employee pay records, and compute and print the annual earnings of each employee. In addition, compute and print the average compensation of both monthly and hourly employees. The Identification, Environment, and Data Divisions for this project can be developed after Chapter 4. Completion of the project requires you to finish Chapter 5 in order to do the Procedure Division.

Input File: EMPLOYEE-FILE

Input Record Layout:

Employee Record			
Soc Sec No.	Name & Initials	Compensation Rate	Compensation Code
1 … 9	10 … 24	25 … 29	30

Test Data:

```
111111111GRAUER         RT01200M
222222222JONES          JJ00006H
333333333MILGROM        EA00005H
444444444RICHARDS       IM02100M
555555555JEFFRIES       JB00005H
666666666STEVEN         SS03700M
777777777BROWN          BB00008H
888888888BAKER          ED02500M
999999999SUGRUE         PK01500M
000000000VAZQUEZ        C 02350M
```

Report Layout:

```
1                                   ANNUAL COMPENSATION REPORT
2
3                     NAME               RATE      METHOD      ANNUAL AMT
4
5               XXXXXXXXXXXXXXX      99999           X            99999

         AVERAGE ANNUAL WAGE FOR HOURLY EMPLOYEES    = 99999
         AVERAGE ANNUAL WAGE FOR MONTHLY EMPLOYEES   = 99999
```

Processing Requirements:

1. Print a suitable heading line at the beginning of the report.
2. Read a file of employee pay records.
3. For every record read,
   a. Determine how the employee is paid, either hourly or monthly, according to the Compensation code of H and M, respectively. (The value in the compensation rate field is the employee's hourly or monthly compensation rate.)
   b. Calculate the employee's annual compensation. Hourly employees work 40 hours per week, 52 weeks per year. Monthly employees receive their monthly salary for 12 months.
   c. Print a detail line for each employee, showing his or her annual compensation. Single-space detail lines.
4. After all records have been read, compute the average annual compensation of all hourly employees; also compute the average of all monthly employees. Print these values at the conclusion of the report.

Project 3-2

Program Name: Shipments Report

Narrative: Develop the hierarchy chart and either flowchart, pseudocode, or Warnier-Orr diagram for a program to process a file of shipment records from three distinct warehouses; determine the anticipated revenue due each warehouse. The Identification, Environment, and Data Divisions for this project can be developed after Chapter 4. Completion of the project requires you to finish Chapter 5 in order to do the Procedure Division.

Input File: SHIPMENT-FILE

Input Record Layout:

Shipment Record					
Shipping Date			Revenue	Warehouse	Authorization
Month	Day	Year			
1 2	3 4	5 6	7 ... 13	14	15 ... 34

Test Data:

```
         1         2         3         4         5         6
12345678901234567890123456789012345678901234567890123456789012345
021293003000OCRUSS FALLOWES
021493007000OCRUSS FALLOWES
021993000250OBDALE MANDRONA
022193004400OCRAY DELODI
022893001070OAPAUL ARON
030293000020OCART COOPER
030293000460OBDALE MANDRONA
030993000480OBDALE MANDRONA
030993009200OARAY DELODI
```

Report Layout:

```
         1         2         3         4         5         6
123456789012345678901234567890123456789012345678901234567890123456
1  SHIPMENT      ANTICIPATED      WAREHOUSE       PERSON WHO
2    DATE           REVENUE                       AUTHORIZED
3 -----------------------------------------------------------------
4   99/99/99            9999999          X       XXXXXXXXXXXXXXXXXXXX
5

       TOTAL REVENUE FOR WAREHOUSE A  = 9999999
       TOTAL REVENUE FOR WAREHOUSE B  = 9999999
       TOTAL REVENUE FOR WAREHOUSE C  = 9999999
```

Processing Requirements:

1. Print a suitable heading line at the beginning of the report.
2. Read a file of shipment records.
3. For each record read,
   a. Determine which warehouse, A, B, or C, shipped the furniture and increment the appropriate warehouse total.
   b. Print a detail line for that record, containing all input fields with appropriate editing. Double-space the detail lines.
4. After all records have been read, print the total revenue for each warehouse.

Project 3-3

Program Name: Payroll Report

Narrative: Develop the hierarchy chart and either flowchart, pseudocode, or Warnier-Orr diagram to process a file of employee pay records, compute and print individual payroll calculations, and compute and print company totals. The Identification, Environment, and Data Divisions for this project can be developed after Chapter 4. Completion of the project requires you to finish Chapter 5 in order to do the Procedure Division.

Input File: EMPLOYEE-FILE

Input Record Layout:

Employee Record				
Soc Sec No.	Name		Hourly Rate	Hours Worked
	Last	Initials		
1 ... 9	10 ... 22	23 24	25 ... 27	28 29

Test Data:

```
         1         2         3         4         5         6
123456789012345678901234567890123456789012345678901234567890123456
111111111GRAUER      RT01035
222222222JONES       JJ01540
333333333MILGROM     EA00545
444444444RICHARDS    IM01150
555555555JEFFRIES    JB05530
666666666STEVENS     SS00735
777777777BROWN       BB08025
888888888BAKER       ED02530
999999999SUGRUE      PK01525
000000000VAZQUEZ     C 04050
```

Report Layout:

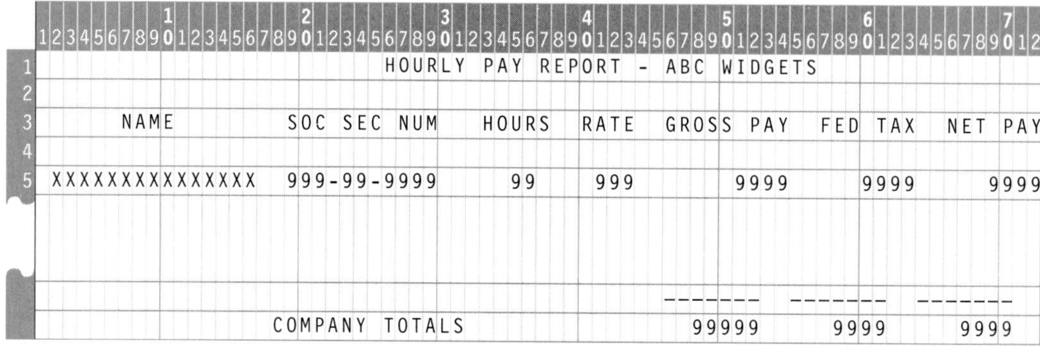

HOURLY PAY REPORT - ABC WIDGETS
NAME
SOC SEC NUM
HOURS
RATE
GROSS PAY
FED TAX
NET PAY
XXXXXXXXXXXXXXX
999-99-9999
99
999
9999
9999
9999

COMPANY TOTALS
99999
9999
9999

Processing Requirements:

1. Print a suitable heading line at the beginning of the report.
2. Read a file of employee pay records.
3. For every record read,
   a. Calculate the gross pay as follows:
      Straight time for the first 40 hours
      Time and a half for the next 8 hours (more than 40 and up to 48 hours)
      Double time for anything over 48 hours
   b. Calculate federal withholding tax as follows:
      18% on first $200 of gross
      20% on amounts between $200 and less than $240
      22% on amounts between $240 and less than $280
      24% on amounts over $280
   c. Calculate net pay as gross pay minus federal tax.
   d. Print a detail line for each employee, with suitable editing in all fields. Double-space detail lines.
   e. Increment company totals for gross pay, federal withholding, and net pay.
4. When all records have been read, print the company totals for all items in part 3e.

Project 3-4

Program Name: Savings Dividends

Narrative: Develop the hierarchy chart and either flowchart, pseudocode, or Warnier-Orr diagram for a program to process a file of savings account records and compute and print a dividend report for each account and a total. The Identification, Environment, and Data Divisions for this project can be developed after Chapter 4. Completion of the project requires you to finish Chapter 5 in order to do the Procedure Division.

Input File: SAVINGS-FILE

Input Record Layout:

Savings Record			
Account No.	Name	Amount	Term
1 ... 8	9 ... 24	25 ... 31	32 33

Test Data:

```
11000-01MILGROM         004556018
23000-05PETERS          003067016
31001-02SMITH           002589012
43045-03JONES           006988024
51005-01VILLAR          000455006
35010-02HANSEN          010936036
```

Report Layout:

```
    ACCOUNT                                SAVINGS     DIVIDEND       TOTAL
    NUMBER        NAME                      AMOUNT         PAID     SAVINGS

    XXXXXXXX      XXXXXXXXXXXXXXXX         9999999      9999999    99999999

                                         ---------    ---------   ---------
                      TOTALS              99999999     99999999   999999999
```

Processing Requirements:

1. Print a heading at the beginning of the report.
2. Read a file of savings account records.
3. Process each record read by:
   a. Determining the interest rate as follows:
      (1) 6% interest on terms of 6 months or less.
      (2) 7% interest on terms of more than 6 months but less than 12.
      (3) 8% interest on terms of more than 12 months but less than 18.

(4) 9% interest on terms of more than 18 months but less than 24.

(5) 10% interest on terms of more than 24 months but less than 30.

(6) 12% interest on terms of more than 30 months.

b. Calculating the dividend to be paid by multiplying the amount by the interest rate.

c. Calculating the total savings by adding the interest to be paid to the account amount.

d. Incrementing savings totals for savings amount, dividend paid, and total savings.

e. Printing a detail line for each record read.

4. Print a total line at the end of the report.

Project 3-5

Program Name: Grade Point Listing

Narrative: Develop the hierarchy chart and either flowchart, pseudocode, or Warnier-Orr diagram for a program to process a file of student records and produce the appropriate report. The Identification, Environment, and Data Divisions for this project can be developed after Chapter 4. Completion of the project requires you to finish Chapter 5 in order to do the Procedure Division.

Input File: STUDENT-FILE

Input Record Layout:

<table>
<tr><th colspan="5">Student Record</th></tr>
<tr><td rowspan="2">Name & Initials</td><td colspan="2">Grade Point Data</td><td colspan="2">Birth Date</td></tr>
<tr><td>Cumulative Points</td><td>Cumulative Credits</td><td>Month</td><td>Year</td></tr>
<tr><td>1 … 20</td><td>21 … 23</td><td>24 … 26</td><td>27 28</td><td>29 30</td></tr>
</table>

Test Data:

```
         1         2         3         4         5         6
12345678901234567890123456789012345678901234567890123456789012345
ADAMS, J            1500500974
MILGROM, I          2000750775
LEE, B              0000000775
GROSSMAN, M         3501100474
GROSSMAN, I         2500800376
BOROW, J            0600500772
JOHNSON, L          0250180771
FRANKEL, L          0900280366
VILLAR, M           2250550758
MARSHAK, K          1200850368
SUGRUE, P           3001151245
```

Report Layout:

```
         1         2         3         4         5         6
12345678901234567890123456789012345678901234567890123456789012345
1                  STUDENT G.P.A. REPORT
2
3    STUDENT NAME           DEAN'S LIST    PROBATION
4  XXXXXXXXXXXXXXXXXXXX        YES
5
6  XXXXXXXXXXXXXXXXXXXX                          YES

                TOTAL STUDENTS ON DEAN'S LIST =  999
                TOTAL STUDENTS ON PROBATION   =  999
```

Processing Requirements:

1. Print the indicated heading at the start of processing.
2. Read a file of student records, and for every record read:
   a. Calculate the student's grade point average. The average is computed by dividing the cumulative points field by the cumulative credits field.
   b. Determine whether the student is on the dean's list; students with a grade point average of 3.00 or higher are on the dean's list.
   c. Determine whether the student is on academic probation; students with a grade point average of less than 1.50 are on probation. Incoming freshmen, with a grade point average of 0.00, are not to be considered on probation.
   d. Print a detail line for every student containing the student's name, and whether or not the student is on the dean's list or academic probation. (Print "YES" in the appropriate column on that student's detail line.) Follow the report layout for appropriate spacing. Double-space detail lines.
3. When all records have been read, print the total number of students on the dean's list and the total number on probation. Two separate total lines are required.

Project 3-6

Program Name: Inventory Parts List

Narrative: Develop the hierarchy chart and either flowchart, pseudocode, or Warnier-Orr diagram for a program to produce an inventory report. The Identification, Environment, and Data Divisions for this project can be developed after Chapter 4. Completion of the project requires you to finish Chapter 5 in order to do the Procedure Division.

Input File: INVENTORY-FILE

Input Record Layout:

Inventory Record				
Part Name	Quantity on Hand	Amount Received	Amount Shipped	Unit Price
1 … 20	21 … 23	24 … 26	27 … 29	30 … 33

Test Data:

```
WIDGETS, SIZE S      1500500960070
WIDGETS, SIZE M      2000750760080
WIDGETS, SIZE L      0005004000090
WHOSIWHATSIS         3501100460100
GIZMOS, TYPE A       2500800360200
GIZMOS, TYPE B       0000500250300
GADGETS, SIZE S      0250180260015
GADGETS, SIZE L      0900280350025
```

Report Layout:

```
                              ***  INVENTORY REPORT  ***

                         BEGINNING   RECEIVED   SHIPPED   ENDING    UNIT     TOTAL
    PART NAME            ON HAND                          ON HAND   PRICE    VALUE

XXXXXXXXXXXXXXX            999         999        999       999      9999  9999999


                                                                          ---------
            TOTAL VALUE OF ALL INVENTORY                                   99999999
```

Processing Requirements:

1. Read a file of inventory records, and for every record read:
   a. Determine the quantity on hand at the end of the period. This is equal to the quantity on hand at the start of the period (contained in the input record), plus the amount received, minus the amount shipped.
   b. Determine the value of the inventory on hand at the end of the period. This is equal to the unit price (contained in the input record) multiplied by the quantity on hand at the end of the period [computed in part a.].
   c. Print a detail line for every part containing the part name, quantity on hand at the beginning of the period, the amount shipped, the amount received, the quantity on hand at the end of the period, the unit price, and the value of the inventory at the end of the period. Double-space detail lines.
2. When all records have been read, print the total value of all inventory on hand at the end of the period.

Project 3-7

Program Name: Money Changer

Narrative: The ACME Widget Corporation has decided to pay its employees in cash rather than by check. Develop the hierarchy chart and either flowchart, pseudocode, or Warnier-Orr diagram for a program to read a file of payroll amounts and determine the required number of bills in each denomination. The Identification, Environment, and Data Divisions for this project can be developed after Chapter 4. Completion of the project requires you to finish Chapter 5 in order to do the Procedure Division.

Input File: PAYROLL-FILE

Input Record Layout:

Payroll Record		
Employee Name	Soc Sec No.	Gross Pay
1 ... 18	19 ... 27	28 ... 30

Test Data:

```
JOHN SMITH        123456789350
JESSICA GRAUER    333444555475
CHANDLER LAVOR    987654321178
JEFFRY BOROW      777668888219
MARION MILGROM    999887777341
LYNN FRANKEL      492336789492
KARL KARLSTROM    333228888314
KATHY MARSHAK     245347878368
RHODA HAAS        111111111305
JIM FEGEN         222222222522
MARIO VILLAR      333333333378
```

Report Layout:

Line	Employee Name	Soc Sec No.	$100	$50	$20	$10	$5	$1	PAY
1	EMPLOYEE NAME		$100	$50	$20	$10	$5	$1	PAY
2									
3	XXXXXXXXXXXXXXXXXX	XXX-XX-XXXX	9	9	9	9	9	9	999
4									
5	XXXXXXXXXXXXXXXXXX	XXX-XX-XXXX	9	9	9	9	9	9	999
			---	---	---	---	---	---	---
	TOTALS		99	99	99	99	99	99	999

Processing Requirements:

1. Read a file of employee pay records.
2. For each record read:
   a. Determine the number of bills of each denomination required to pay the employee in cash, rather than by check. (Do not include cents in your computation.)
   b. Use denominations of $100, $50, $20, $10, $5, and $1. Pay employees in the highest denominations possible; e.g., an employee with a gross pay of $300 should be paid with three $100 bills rather than six $50 bills.
   c. Maintain a running total of the total payroll as well as the number of bills in each denomination for the company as a whole.
   d. Print a detail line for each employee according to the report format. Double-space detail lines.
3. When all records have been read, print a total line for the company according to specification 2c. above.

Project 3-8

Program Name: Real Estate Sales

Narrative: Develop the hierarchy chart and either flowchart, pseudocode, or Warnier-Orr diagram for a program to process a file of real estate records and produce a monthly report based on transaction types, commissions paid, and summary. The Identification, Environment, and Data Divisions for this project can be developed after Chapter 4. Completion of the project requires you to finish Chapter 5 in order to do the Procedure Division.

The sales commission on any real estate sale is 6 percent of the total sale and is divided equally between the listing and selling agencies. This produces three possible sales types, which in turn determine the commissions paid to the company and its agents.

1. *The company both sells and lists the property (CO-CO).* The agent who listed the property receives 25 percent of the total (6 percent) commission, and the remaining 75 percent of the commission is divided equally (50 percent each) between the agent who sold the property and the company.
2. *The company sells the property listed by an outside agency (CO-OUT).* The agent who sells the property listed by an outside agency receives 70 percent of the commission due to the company (the commission due to the company is 3 percent of the total sales price, or one half of the total 6 percent commission). The company retains the remaining 30 percent of the 3 percent commission to the selling agency.
3. *An outside agency sells the property that was listed by the company (OUT-CO).* The company receives 50 percent of the sales commission (3 percent of the total price), which is split equally between the company and the listing agent.

Input File: REAL-ESTATE-FILE

Input Record Layout:

Real Estate Record									
Salesperson	Date			CO-CO		CO-OUT		OUT-CO	
	Month	Day	Year	Amount	Status	Amount	Status	Amount	Status
1 ... 12	13 14	15 16	17 18	19 ... 24	25	26 ... 31	32	33 ... 38	39

Test Data:

```
ALVORD      080393138500C0000000123900K
VILLAR      080593215500C130300C234000C
VAZQUEZ     080593345500C123000C273400C
GARCIA      080893134500K145000C295600C
GRAUER      081093234000C395000C124400K
ALVORD      081293000000230000C234000K
VAZQUEZ     081593138500K234000K0000000
GARCIA      081793245000C123000C398400K
VILLAR      081894345000C0000000278400C
GRAUER      082193234500C145500K225000C
GARCIA      082293245500V178000C298600K
GRAUER      083093263500C0000000169600C
ALVORD      083193423000C130000K247000C
```

Report Layout:

```
         1         2         3         4         5         6         7
1234567890123456789012345678901234567890123456789012345678901234567890
1               LOTSA HOUSES REALTY COMPANY
2
3                       PROPERTY SOLD    PROPERTY SOLD     OUTSIDE SALE
4 DATE   SALESPERSON      CO LISTING    OUTSIDE LISTING     CO LISTING
5-------  ------------    -------------   ---------------    ------------
6 MM/DD   XXXXXXXXXXXX        999999          999999              999999

-------  ------------    -------------   ---------------    ------------
       TOTAL SALES:        9999999         9999999           9999999
       GROSS TO LOTSA:     9999999         9999999           9999999
       COMMISSIONS PAID:   9999999         9999999           9999999
       NET TO LOTSA:       9999999         9999999           9999999
       MONTHLY SUMMARY
         TOTAL SALES:      9999999
         COMMISSIONS PAID: 9999999
         NET TO LOTSA:     9999999
```

Processing Requirements:

1. Print the appropriate report headings as shown in the report layout.
2. Read a file of real estate records and process each record read by:
   a. Incrementing each of the three sales type totals with closed sales only. A closed sale is denoted by a "C" in the appropriate STATUS field.
   b. Printing a detail line of the closed sales for each sales type.
3. For all three sales types:
   a. Process the total sales by:
      (1) Printing the total sales for each of the three types of sale.
   b. Process the gross commission to the company by:
      (1) Calculating the gross commissions to the company for each of the three sales types as described in the program narrative.
      (2) Printing the calculated gross commissions for each sales type.
   c. Process the commissions paid by:
      (1) Calculating the commissions paid for each of the three sales types as described in the program narrative.
      (2) Printing the calculated commissions paid for each sales type.
   d. Process the net commissions to the company by:
      (1) Calculating the net commissions to the company for each of the three sales types as described in the program narrative.
      (2) Printing the calculated net commissions for each sales type.
4. Process the monthly summary by:
   a. Printing the total sales for the month.
   b. Printing the total commission paid for the month.
   c. Printing the total net commission to the company for the month.

PROGRAMMING SPECIFICATIONS

Projects 4-1 through 4-8

Program Name: Annual Compensation Report, Shipments Report, Payroll Report, Savings Dividends, Grade Point Listing, Inventory Parts List, Money Changer, and Real Estate Sales

Narrative: The specifications for these projects were introduced in Chapter 3, at which time you were to attempt the hierarchy charts, pseudocode, flowcharts, and/or Warnier-Orr diagrams. Now we ask you to develop the Identification, Environment, and Data Divisions, but completion of the projects requires you to finish Chapter 5 in order to do the Procedure Division.

PROGRAMMING SPECIFICATIONS

Projects 5-1 through 5-8

Program Name: Annual Compensation Report, Shipments Report, Payroll Report, Savings Dividends, Grade Point Listing, Inventory Parts List, Money Changer, and Real Estate Sales

Narrative: The specifications for these projects were introduced in Chapter 3, at which time you were to attempt the hierarchy charts, pseudocode, flowcharts, and/or Warnier-Orr diagrams. Completion of Chapter 4 enabled you to code the first three COBOL divisions. Now you are expected to develop the Procedure Division and complete the projects.

PROGRAMMING SPECIFICATIONS

Project 7-1

Program Name: Annual Compensation Report

Narrative: The specifications for this project were introduced in Chapter 3. The input record and data file have been updated to include two decimal places in the compensation rate field, which requires that the annual compensation be extended to two decimal places as well. Use COBOL's editing facility to dress up the reports produced by these changes. Redo the report layout, using any editing features you deem appropriate.

Input File: EMPLOYEE-FILE

Input Record Layout:

Employee Record			
Soc Sec No.	Name & Initial	Compensation Rate	Compensation Code
1 ... 9	10 ... 24	25 *(2 decimals)* 31	32

Test Data:

```
         1         2         3         4         5         6
12345678901234567890123456789012345678901234567890123456789012345
111111111GRAUER       RT0120025M
222222222JONES        JJ0000650H
333333333MILGROM      EA0000575H
444444444RICHARDS     IM0210000M
555555555JEFFRIES     JB0000555H
666666666STEVEN       SS0370045M
777777777BROWN        BB0000895H
888888888BAKER        ED0250010M
999999999SUGRUE       PK0150090M
000000000VAZQUEZ      C 0235033M
```

Report Layout: Use the Report Layout from Project 3-1 and modify it to look good, using the editing facility ($, commas, decimal points, etc.).

Project 7-2

Program Name: Shipments Report

Narrative: The specifications for this project were introduced in Chapter 3. The input record and data file have been updated to include two decimal places in the revenue field. Use COBOL's editing facility to dress up the reports produced by these changes. Redo the report layout, using any editing features you deem appropriate.

Input File: SHIPMENT-FILE

Input Record Layout:

Shipment Record					
Shipping Date			Revenue	Warehouse	Authorization
Month	Day	Year			
1 2	3 4	5 6	7 *(2 decimals)* 15	16	17 ... 36

Test Data:

```
         1         2         3         4         5         6
12345678901234567890123456789012345678901234567890123456789012345
021293003000050CRUSS FALLOWES
021493007000055CRUSS FALLOWES
021993000250075BDALE MANDRONA
022193004400025CRAY DELODI
022893001070038APAUL ARON
030293000020099CART COOPER
030293000460044BDALE MANDRONA
030993000480027BDALE MANDRONA
030993009200098ARAY DELODI
```

Report Layout: Use the Report Layout from Project 3-2 and modify it to look good, using the editing facility ($, commas, decimal points, etc.).

Project 7-3

Program Name: Extended Payroll Report

Narrative: The specifications for this project were introduced in Chapter 3. The input record and data file have been updated to include two decimal places in the hourly rate and hours worked fields, mandating a similar change in the gross rate, federal tax, and net pay. Use COBOL's editing facility to dress up the reports produced by these changes. Redo the report layout, using any editing features you deem appropriate.

Input File: EMPLOYEE-FILE

Input Record Layout:

Employee Record				
Soc Sec No.	Name		Hourly Rate	Hours Worked
	Last	Initials		
1 ... 9	10 ... 22	23 24	25 *(2 decimals)* 29	30 *(2 decimals)* 33

Test Data:

```
         1         2         3         4         5         6
12345678901234567890123456789012345678901234567890123456789012345
111111111GRAUER      RT0102535550
222222222JONES       JJ0150040 75
333333333MILGROM     EA0057545 50
444444444RICHARDS    IM0110050000
555S55555JEFFRIES    JB0555030 25
666666666STEVENS     SS0078035 00
777777777BROWN       BB0802525 50
888888888BAKER       ED0254530 75
999999999SUGRUE      PK0153525 00
000000000VAZQUEZ     C 0405050 25
```

Report Layout: Use the Report Layout from Project 3-3 and modify it to look good, using the editing facility ($, commas, decimal points, etc.). Don't forget to show the calculated averages from additional processing requirement #1.

Additional Requirements:

1. Add a "COMPANY AVERAGES" line at the end of the report.
2. As an aid in maintainability, define the overtime rates, overtime thresholds, tax rates, and tax thresholds as constants in Working-Storage. Use the corresponding data names in your calculations and comparisons instead of the actual values. For example:

   Change: `IF HOURS-WORKED <= 40`

   To: `IF HOURS-WORKED <= STRAIGHT-TIME`

3. Update your program and verify your results, then make the following changes. (Hint: You should need to change the values in only one place in your program.)
   a. Calculate the gross pay as follows:
      Straight time for the first 35 hours
      Time and a half for the next 7 hours (more than 35 and up to 42 hours)
      Double time for anything over 42 hours
   b. Calculate federal withholding tax as follows:
      10% on first $100 of gross

15% on amounts between $100 and less than $150

20% on amounts between $150 and less than $200

25% on amounts over $200

After the above changes are made, rerun the program to get new results and verify them with your projected answers.

4. Note that the hourly rate and hours worked have been extended to two decimal places. You should also extend all the other calculated amounts to two decimal places.

Project 7-4

Program Name: Extended Savings Dividends

Narrative: The specifications for this project were introduced in Chapter 3. The input record and data file have been updated to include two decimal places in the amount field, mandating a similar change in the fields for the dividend and total savings. Use COBOL's editing facility to appropriately dress up the reports produced by these changes. Redo the report layout, using any editing features you deem appropriate.

Input File: SAVINGS-FILE

Input Record Layout:

Savings Record			
Account No.	Name	Amount	Term
1 ... 8	9 ... 25	26 *(2 decimals)* 34	35 36

Test Data:

```
         1         2         3         4         5         6
12345678901234567890123456789012345678901234567890123456789012345

11000-01MILGROM          00450000518
23000-05PETERS           00300000016
31001-02SMITH            00258005712
43045-03JONES            00698009024
51005-01VILLAR           00045003906
35010-02HANSEN           01090002936
```

Report Layout: Use the Report Layout from Project 3-4 and modify it to look good, using the editing facility ($, commas, decimal points, etc.). Don't forget to show the calculated average from additional processing requirement two.

Additional Requirements:

1. As an aid in maintainability, define the six interest rates in Working-Storage and use these data names in your calculations instead of the raw percentage rates. For example, for a six month or less account term, change the computation

   Change: `COMPUTE IND-DIVIDEND-PAID = SAV-AMOUNT * .06`

   To: `COMPUTE IND-DIVIDEND-PAID = SAV-AMOUNT * UPTO-6MO-RATE`

   where UPTO-6MO-RATE is defined in Working-Storage with a value of .06.

2. Calculate and print the average savings amount for all savings accounts processed.
3. The savings amount has been extended to two decimal places; extend all other calculated amounts to two decimal places as well.

Update the program and verify your results, then make the following changes. (Hint: You should need to change each rate in only one place in the program.)

(1) 7% interest on 6 months or less.
(2) 8% interest on more than 6 months but up to 12.
(3) 9% interest on more than 12 months but up to 18.
(4) 10% interest on more than 18 months but up to 24.
(5) 11% interest on more than 24 months but up to 30.
(6) 14% interest on more than 30 months.

Project 7-5

Program Name: Grade Point Listing

Narrative: The specifications for this project were introduced in Chapter 3. Use COBOL's editing facility to dress up the reports produced by these changes. Redo the report layout, using any editing features you deem appropriate.

Project 7-6

Program Name: Inventory Parts List

Narrative: The specifications for this project were introduced in Chapter 3. The input record and data file have been updated to include two decimal places in the unit price field, mandating a similar extension in the total value. Use COBOL's editing facility to dress up the reports produced by these changes. Redo the report layout, using any editing features you deem appropriate.

Input File: INVENTORY-FILE

Input Record Layout:

Inventory Record				
Part Name	Quantity on Hand	Amount Received	Amount Shipped	Unit Price
1 ... 20	21 ... 23	24 ... 26	27 ... 29	30 *(2 decimals)* 35

Test Data:

```
WIDGETS, SIZE S     150050096007050
WIDGETS, SIZE M     200075076008075
WIDGETS, SIZE L     000500400009034
WHOSIWHATSIS        350110046010000
GIZMOS, TYPE A      250080036020055
GIZMOS, TYPE B      000050025030087
GADGETS, SIZE S     025018026001599
GADGETS, SIZE L     090028035002565
```

Project 7-7

Program Name: Money Changer

Narrative: The specifications for this project were introduced in Chapter 3. The input record and data file have been updated to include 2 decimal places in the gross pay field; accordingly extend the pay to 2 decimal places. Use COBOL's editing facility to appropriately dress up the reports produced by these changes. Accordingly redo the report layout, using any editing features you deem appropriate.

Input File: PAYROLL-FILE

Input Record Layout:

Payroll Record		
Employee Name	Soc Sec No.	Gross Pay
1 … 18	19 … 27	28 *(2 decimals)* 32

Test Data:

```
JOHN SMITH        12345678935050
JESSICA GRAUER    33344455547577
CHANDLER LAVOR    98765432117855
JEFFRY BOROW      77766888821983
MARION MILGROM    99988777734122
LYNN FRANKEL      49233678949237
KARL KARLSTROM    33322888831444
KATHY MARSHAK     24534787836828
RHODA HAAS        11111111130598
JIM FEGEN         22222222252244
MARIO VILLAR      33333333337869
```

Processing Requirements: Extend the calculations to determine the proper number of coins with which to pay the individual. Use quarters, dimes, nickels, and pennies in your computations.

Project 7-8

Program Name: Extended Real Estate Sales

Narrative: The specifications for this project were introduced in Chapter 3. Use COBOL's editing facility to dress up the reports produced by these changes. Redo the report layout, using any editing features you deem appropriate.

Input File: REAL-ESTATE-FILE

Input Record Layout: Same as project 3-8

Report Layout: Use the Report Layout from Project 3-8 and modify it to look good, using the editing facility ($, commas, decimal points, etc.).

Processing Requirements:

1. As an aid in maintainability, define the gross and commission rate for all three sales types in Working-Storage and use these data names in your calculations. For example, change the gross to company

   Change:
   ```
   COMPUTE TOT-GROSS-CO-CO = TOT-SALES-CO-CO * .06
   ```
   To:
   ```
   COMPUTE TOT-GROSS-CO-CO = TOT-SALES-CO-CO *
                             GROSS-CO-CO-RATE
   ```

   where GROSS-CO-CO-RATE is defined in Working-Storage with a value of .06.

2. Print the gross percent to the company for each of the three sales types as shown on the report layout.
3. Print the commission percent paid out for each of the three sales types as shown on the report layout.

Update the program and verify your results, then make the following changes. (Hint: You should need to change each rate in only one place in the program.)

The sales commission on any real estate sale is 8 percent of the total sale and is divided equally between the listing and selling agencies. This produces three possible sales types, which in return determine the commissions paid to the company and its agents.

1. *The company both sells and lists the property (CO-CO).* The agent who listed the property receives 35 percent of the total (8 percent) commission, and the remaining 65 percent of the commission is divided equally (50 percent each) between the agent who sold the property and the company.
2. *The company sells the property listed by an outside agency (CO-OUT).* The agent who sells the property listed by an outside agency receives 60 percent of the commission due to the company (the commission due to the company is 4 percent of the total sales price, or one half of the total 8 percent commission). The company retains the remaining 40 percent of the 4 percent commission to the selling agency.
3. *An outside agency sells the property that was listed by the company (OUT-CO).* The company receives 50 percent of the sales commission (4 percent of the total price), which is split equally between the company and the listing agent.

Project 7-9

Program Name: Car Sales Program

Narrative: Develop the hierarchy chart and either flowchart or pseudocode for a program to process a file of car sales records to produce a commission report.

Input File: CAR-SALES-FILE

Input Record Layout:

Car Sales Record						
Invoice No.	Type Information			Sales Information		
	Year	Make	Model	Asking Price	Sold Price	Salesperson
1 ... 5	6 7	8 ... 18	19 ... 31	32 ... 37	38 ... 43	44 ... 50

Test Data:

```
         1         2         3         4         5         6
12345678901234567890123456789012345678901234567890123456789012345

7817592NISSAN     PATHFINDER   012996011999WILLCOX
1485190ACURA      LEGEND COUPE 015990014567SCHULZ
5747693CHEVROLET  CORVETTE ZR1 044988040100MORIN
5868192BMW        535I         027990026200TORRES
8564493LOTUS      ESPRIT       073500073250WENDEL
8746588FERRARI    TESTAROSSA   105000097500FIXLER
2548991NISSAN     300ZX        009682008714JONES
2554493RANGEROVER 4 DOOR       029775027860MORIN
7246293MERCEDES   560SEC       068900066900CULVER
5684393CADILLAC   FLEETWOOD    019988018999TORRES
1574688ROLLS ROYCECORNICHE     079500070599WILLCOX
1484284FERRARI    308GTB       048500046299FIXLER
2558593JAGUAR     XJS CONV     040000035650CULVER
4791491ALFA ROMEO SPYDER       012000011298WENDEL
2853293LEXUS      LS400        038988037988SCHULZ
1654190PORSCHE    911 CABRIOLET037988035988JONES
```

Report Layout:

```
                                                  VERY VERY NICE CARS INC.
                                                     COMMISSION REPORT

                              CAR        CAR            CAR          ASKING      PRICE      % OF       COMM       NET TO
   INVOICE #   SALESPERSON   YEAR       MAKER          MODEL          PRICE       SOLD     ASKING      PAID       DEALER

     ZZZZ9      XXXXXXX       99    XXXXXXXXXXX   XXXXXXXXXXXXX    ZZZ,ZZ9     ZZZ,ZZ9      99       ZZ,ZZ9     ZZZ,ZZ9



                                                                         ----------                 ---------  ----------
                                                                         $Z,ZZZ,ZZ9                 $ZZZ,ZZ9   $Z,ZZZ,ZZ9
```

Processing Requirements:

1. Print a heading at the beginning of the report.
2. Read a file of Car Sales records.
3. For each record read:
   a. Calculate the percent of the asking price at which the car was sold. For example, a $10,000 car which sold for $9,500, sold for 95% of the asking price. Note: Allow for decimal places in your calculations, but do not print them in your report as shown in the report layout.
   b. Calculate the commission paid to the salesperson as follows:
      (1) For any car sold above 95 percent of the asking price the salesperson receives a 5% commission rate. In addition, the salesperson is paid a bonus equal to 40% of the amount in excess of 95%. For example, a $10,000 car selling at $9,800 yields a commission of $610.00 ($490.00 + $120.00).
      (2) For any car sold between 90 and 95 percent of the asking price the salesperson's 5% commission is reduced by 10% for every percentage point below 95%. For example, a $10,000 car selling at $9,400 results in 94% of the asking price and a 4.5% commission rate; therefore the commission paid is $423.00.
      (3) For any car sold below 90 percent of the asking price the amount below 90% comes straight out of the salesperson's remaining commission at the 90% level as calculated in paragraph (2)—that is, 2.5% of the asking price is all that's left to play with. For example, a $10,000 car selling at $8,900 yields a commission of only $122.50 ($222.50 - $100.00).
   c. Calculate the Net to the Dealer, assuming the dealer's markup is 25%—that is, the asking price is the dealer's cost plus 25%. For example, a $10,000 car selling at $9,400 yields a net of $977.00 since the cost to the dealer was $8000.00.
   d. Print a detail line for each record. Double-space all detail lines.
   e. Increment appropriate totals as shown on the report layout.
4. As an aid in maintainability, define the 5% commission rate, the 40% bonus rate, 95% upper level, 90% lower level, the 10% reduction per percentage point below the lower level, and the 25% markup as constants in Working-Storage. Use the corresponding data names in your calculations instead of the actual values. For example:

   To:

   ```
   COMPUTE IND-BONUS ROUNDED = BONUS-RATE * CAR-ASKING=
      PRICE * (IND-PERCENT-ASKING - UPPER-LEVEL)

   COMPUTE IND-COMM-PAID ROUNDED = CAR-PRICE-SOLD
      * COMM-RATE + IND-BONUS
   ```

5. **The Final Challenge!** Once you have verified that your program works with the original rates, determine what effect a *6%* commission rate, a *50%* bonus, a *15%* reduction for every percentage point below the upper level, and a *30%* markup would have on the net to the dealer as well as commissions paid by making the appropriate changes in Working-Storage and rerunning the program. Make sure you hand in both reports (.RPT). If this was *your* dealership, which rates would you choose?
6. Print the totals when all records have been processed.

PROGRAMMING SPECIFICATIONS

Project 8-1

Program Name: Doctor Visits Validation Program

Narrative: This program will validate a patient file and produce both an error report and a valid file.

Input File: PATIENT-FILE

Input Record Layout:

POSITIONS	FIELD	PICTURE
1-15	LAST-NAME	X(15)
16-25	FIRST-NAME	X(10)
26-50	REASON-FOR-SEEING-DOCTOR	X(25)
51-55	AMOUNT-PAID	9(3)V99

Test Data:

```
         1         2         3         4         5         6
12345678901234567890123456789012345678901234567890123456789012345
JONES          TOM                                 03600
KING           SARAH     EARACHE                   00100
WHITBECK       KENNETH   SORE SHOULDER             03600
DAY            BILL      UNEXPLAINED DIZZINESS     05000
POLLACK        MARY      HEADACHE
               LIZA      FOOT PROBLEMS             03075
SCHEUR         HELEN     PNEUMONIA REVISIT         03000
MCKEON         DICK      GENERAL PHYSICAL          1000A
GROSSMAN       IVY       BRONCHITIS                00800
STACY          MEREDITH  NOSE BLEED                02000
BASS           CAROL     NAUSEA                    03800
McGOVERN       JOHN      EYE INFECTION             01500
VAZQUEZ VILLAR CAROL     GESTATION                 00050
```

Report Layout: Design your own report layout, subject to the problem specifications.

Processing Requirements:

1. Read a file of patient records.
2. Validate each patient record for all of the following:
   a. The incoming field, AMOUNT-PAID, must be numeric. If not, display an appropriate error message that contains the entire input record.
   b. The incoming record must contain data in all fields, that is, LAST-NAME, FIRST-NAME, REASON-FOR-SEEING-DOCTOR, and AMOUNT-PAID. If any field is missing, display a single message, "INCOMING RECORD MISSING DATA," followed by the input record.
   c. Amount paid should be between $15.00 and $100.00, inclusive; if not, display an error message and the input record.
3. No further processing is required for any records that are invalid according to specifications in item 2.
4. Each valid record is to be written to a file to be used in Project 9-1.

Project 8-2

Program Name: Stock Transactions Validation Program

Narrative: This project will validate a stock transaction file and produce both a valid stock file and an error report.

Input File: STOCK-TRANSACTION-FILE

Input Record Layout:

```
01  STOCK-RECORD.
    05  ST-TRANSACTION-INFORMATION.
        10 ST-TRANSACTION-SHARES          PIC 9(3).
        10 ST-TRANSACTION-STOCK           PIC X(14).
    05  ST-PURCHASE-INFORMATION.
        10  ST-PURCHASE-PRICE             PIC 9(5)V99.
        10  ST-PURCHASE-DATE.
            15  ST-PURCHASE-YEAR          PIC 99.
            15  ST-PURCHASE-MONTH         PIC 99.
            15  ST-PURCHASE-DAY           PIC 99.
    05  ST-SALE-INFORMATION.
        10  ST-SALE-PRICE                 PIC 9(5)V99.
        10  ST-SALE-DATE.
            15  ST-SALE-YEAR              PIC 99.
            15  ST-SALE-MONTH             PIC 99.
            15  ST-SALE-DAY               PIC 99.
```

Test Data:

```
         1         2         3         4         5         6
123456789012345678901234567890123456789012345678901234567890123456

100XYZ CORP      2000000920115300000093010 3
200ABC CORP      12000009303052200000920305
100ACME WIDGETS  11500009211095000000930331
100BOROW ASSOC   005000092022900000048
300LEE ENTERPRISE45000009313229000000930422
200NATL GADGET   0100A009205151100000920631
100NATL GISMO    10000009306181200000930606
400AMER WIDGETS  09000009307070800000930906
350MILGROM POWER 10000009004052500000930431
200PARKER INC    0030000920731010000A930428
100SHELLY CO     003000090043100002 00
200STEVENS INC   20000009308312200000930922
```

Report Layout: Design your own report layout. Be sure to comply with all the processing requirements.

Processing Requirements:

1. Read a file of stock records.
2. Validate each input record for all of the following:
   a. The month, day, and year of both the purchase and sale date must be numeric.
   b. The month must be a valid value, that is, between 1 and 12, inclusive.
   c. The day cannot exceed the maximum days in the corresponding month.
   d. The date of sale cannot be earlier than the date of purchase.
   e. The dollar amount of both purchase and sale must be numeric.
3. Design an appropriate report layout. Invalid transactions are to be displayed with an appropriate error message. If a given transaction contains more than one invalid field,

multiple error messages are required. No further processing is required for invalid transactions.

4. Each valid transaction is to be written to a file to be used in Project 9-2.

Project 8-3

Program Name: Payroll Validation Program

Narrative: Develop a program to validate a payroll file and produce both a valid payroll file and an error report.

Input File: PAYROLL-FILE

Input Record Layout:

```
01  PAYROLL-RECORD.
    05  PAY-SOC-SEC-NUM              PIC 9(9).
    05  PAY-NAME.
        10  PAY-LAST                 PIC X(14).
        10  PAY-FIRST                PIC X(12).
        10  PAY-INITIAL              PIC X.
    05  PAY-INFO.
        10  PAY-HOURLY-RATE          PIC 9(3)V99.
        10  PAY-HOURS-WORKED         PIC 9(3)V99.
        10  PAY-SALARY-TYPE          PIC X.
        10  PAY-DEPENDENTS           PIC 99.
        10  PAY-TAX-STATUS           PIC 9.
        10  PAY-INSURANCE            PIC X.
    05  PAY-YTD-INFO.
        10  PAY-YTD-EARNINGS         PIC 9(6)V99.
        10  PAY-YTD-TAXES            PIC 9(5)V99.
        10  PAY-YTD-FICA             PIC 9(4)V99.
        10  PAY-YTD-INSURANCE        PIC 9(4)V99.
```

Test Data:

```
         1         2         3         4         5         6         7
123456789012345678901234567890123456789012345678901234567890123456789012345678
100000000                            01000 4000H  3D023150220114340134512050000
111111111BOYER         WARD        E0150004000S013B027000000548524202770045000
200000000MERA          SASHA       X0140004500S045B
222222222DAVERSA       NICK        A0055004000S014A009900000148500074349063000
300000000MENENDEZ      LOURDES     Y0235004000X152C045298220891300025053057500
333333333FRENCH        MICHELLE    P0650003500H082B117000002671139878670108000
400000000BARBER        MARYANN      A18000400LH06 AA85927400719262143290900000
444444444GEHLE         SHELLY      T0157504350H002Z028350000444055212909000000
500000000GRAUER        ROBERT      T1500 46000 052Z029104050513950214890000000
555555555RICO          CHERYL      S0074505200H013C013410000201150100709045000
600000000                                04000S10AB009900000137650073436060000
666666666ROWE          CANDACE     M0300004200S031A054000001232438040554090000
700000000HEMMERDE CLARKRICHARD      06500     H008Z116000002571143854320000000
777777777SHIM          ANNA        M0080004800H044C014400000229106108144090000
800000000STUTZ         JOEL         005500500H0L11 0991500       075607
888888888VASQUEZ       DONNA       A0237504000M022C042750000848813321053058500
900000000PLANT         ROBERT       0075005300S0130014410000210050100090045000
999999999VAZQUEZ VILLARCAROL        0180004000M053B032400000699724243324108000
```

Report Layout: Design your report layout based on the requirements below.

Processing Requirements:

1. Read a file of sales payroll records.
2. Validate each input record for all of the following:
   a. The incoming record must contain data for the following fields: social security number, name, hourly rate, hours worked, salary type, number of dependents, tax status, and insurance. If any field is missing, display the message "INCOMING RECORD MISSING DATA" and the input record.
   b. The incoming fields of hourly rate, hours worked, number of dependents, tax status, ytd earnings, taxes, fica, and insurance must be numeric. If not, display an appropriate error message that contains the entire input record.
   c. The salary type must be either hourly or salaried (H or S). If it is not, display an appropriate error message, such as "INVALID SALARY TYPE FOR", the social security number, name, and salary type. (Hint: Use a condition name test.)
   d. *Salaried* employees are not paid overtime; therefore hours worked for salaried employees cannot be over 40 hours. Use the message "NO OVERTIME FOR SALARIED EMPLOYEES", the social security number, name, and hours worked.
   e. The tax status must be valid (1 through 4). Use the message "INVALID TAX STATUS FOR", the social security number, name, and tax status. (Hint: Use a condition name test.)
   f. The insurance type must be valid (A, B, C, or Z). Use the message "INVALID INSURANCE FOR", the social security number, name, and insurance type. (Hint: Use a condition name test.)
   g. A reasonable number of dependents; flag any record where the number of dependents is over 10. (Hint: Use a condition name test.)
3. Any record that fails any validity test is to be rejected with no further processing, other than displaying the appropriate error message(s). It is possible that a record may contain more than one error (flag all errors). Valid records are to be written to a new file to be used in Projects 9-3 and 16-3.

Project 8-4

Program Name: Car Sales Commissions Validation Program

Narrative: This project will validate a file of car sales records and produce both a valid car file and an error report.

Input File: CAR-SALES-FILE

Input Record Layout:

FIELD NAME	POSITIONS	FIELD TYPE
Location	1 - 11	Alphanumeric
Branch	12 - 15	Numeric
Salesperson	16 - 25	Alphanumeric
Customer Name	26 - 35	Alphanumeric
Sale Date	36 - 41	Numeric
Sale Amount	42 - 47	Numeric
Commission Rate	48 - 50	Numeric
Car Model	51 - 63	Alphanumeric
Car Year	64 - 67	Numeric

Test Data:

```
         1         2         3         4         5         6
1234567890123456789012345678901234567890123456789012345678901234567

BROWARD    1234SHIM      REIMAN    131292 18725002SAAB 900     1992
MONROE     4528VASQUEZ   HAFEZ     101392 32875003JAGUAR XJS   1991
DADE       4679DAVERSA             111492030554005INFINITI Q45 1991
BROWARD    1234SHIM      PORTO     103293025575004MB 300E      1916
MONROE     4528BOYER               063393  8125004MAZDA 626    1991
BROWARD    1234GEHLE     LARSH     111293020475003PEUGOT 505GLS1991
DADE       9879FRENCH              092892022750003BMW 325iX    1991
BROWARD    1234GEHLE     HOLME      93192014700002PRELUDE SI   1992
DADE       9879FRENCH    DEGGS     013193013025004NISS MAXIMA  1992
BROWARD    1234GEHLE     MORENO    101293 17125  5TOY SUPRA    1991
DADE       0124RICO      GORMAN    103192035500184LEXUS LS400  1992
MONROE     4528VASQUEZ   HWANG     123192 25000  4LEGEND C LS  1990
BROWARD    4567ROWE      TOCKMAN   010491053150006BMW 750iL    1992
DADE       0124RICO      CHUA       81593014700004TOY CAMRY DE 1991
DADE       9879FRENCH    SPEARS    101693023975001NISSAN 300Z  1992
MONROE     4528BOYER     AUGUSMA   041093069799002MB 500 SL    1991
DADE       4679DAVERSA   RENESCA   104292004950002HYUN EXCEL G 1991
BROWARD    4567ROWE      VIERA     11 592010300002STERLG 825SL 1990
MONROE     4528BOYER     LOUIS     102992 12175104MAZ RX7 GXL  1991
BROWARD    4567ROWE      PINEDA    122493016100  3AUDI QUATTRO 1990
DADE       0124RICO      DILEGO    112693012800004MAZDA MIATA  1991
```

Report Layout: Design your own report layout, subject to the processing requirements.

Processing Requirements:

1. Read a file of car sales records.
2. Validate each input record for all of the following:
   a. The incoming record must contain data for the following fields: location, branch, salesperson, customer, sale amount, commission rate, and model year. If any field is missing, display a single message "INCOMING RECORD MISSING DATA", followed by the input record.
   b. The incoming fields of branch, sale date, sale amount, and commission rate must be numeric. If not, display an appropriate error message that contains the entire input record.
   c. Valid dates (sale date): month must be between 1 and 12, inclusive; day should be in conjunction with the month; and year must be the current year or the year before. Display a suitable message "INVALID MONTH", "INVALID DAY", and/or "INVALID YEAR", followed by the input record.
   d. A reasonable commission rate: flag any record where the rate is not between 0% and 100%. Use the message "INVALID COMMISSION RATE", followed by the input record.
   e. A reasonable car year: flag any record where the car year is not between 1930 and 1995, inclusive. Use the message "INVALID CAR YEAR", followed by the input record.
3. Any record that fails any validity test is to be rejected with no further processing, other than displaying the appropriate error message(s). It is possible that a record may contain more than one error (all errors are to be flagged).
4. Valid records are to be written to a file to be used in Project 9-4.

Project 8-5

Program Name: Invoice Validation Program

Narrative: Write a data validation program that will validate an invoice file and produce both a valid invoice file and an error report.

Input File: INVOICE-FILE

Input Record Layout:

```
01  INVOICE-RECORD-IN.
    05  INV-INVOICE-NO          PIC X(4).
    05  INV-DATE.
        10  INV-MONTH           PIC 9(2).
        10  INV-DAY             PIC 9(2).
        10  INV-YEAR            PIC 9(2).
    05  INV-CUSTOMER-INFO.
        10  INV-CUST-NAME       PIC X(10).
        10  INV-CUST-ADDRESS    PIC X(10).
        10  INV-CUST-CITY       PIC X(10).
        10  INV-CUST-STATE      PIC XX.
        10  INV-CUST-ZIP        PIC X(5).
```

Test Data:

```
         1         2         3         4         5         6
12345678901234567890123456789012345678901234567890123456789012345
2467100493Scully    20 Main StChicago   IL60666
38451312  Minnie              Disney    TZ
1578081293Schultz   45 5th St Los AngeleCA90024
3446123193Goofy     Main St   Orlando   FX39575
0342091093Culver    1 Sunny LnSeattle   WA98008
4790111293Perez     4 Long Dr New OrleanLA79345
    09  93          NoName St Somewhere   49576
6836070493Fixler    3 42nd St New York  NY10020
234G  3293Pluto     2 Dog Dr  Dogville  PR67453
4807031893Morin     9 7th Ave Newark    NJ07632
0498063093Munroe    10 Long StTulsa     OK59345
6234      Mickey    Disney St           FL33480
```

Report Layout: Develop your own report layout in compliance with the processing requirements.

Processing Requirements:

1. Read a file of invoice records.
2. Validate each input record field for all of the following:
   a. **Invoice No:**
      (1) If the invoice number is missing, print an appropriate error message:

      `Record missing data in INVOICE NO field for: Smith`

      (2) *If the invoice number is not missing*, verify that the value is numeric; if not, display an error message:

      `Nonnumeric INVOICE NO for: Smith      Invoice No: ABC4`

   b. **Date:**
      (1) If the invoice date (i.e., Month, Day, or Year) is missing, print an appropriate error message:

      `Record missing data in INVOICE DATE field for: Smith`

(2) *If the invoice date is not missing*, verify that the month is valid (i.e., 1 thru 12); error message:

```
Invalid MONTH for: Smith        Invoice No: 1234 Month: 20
```

(Hint: Use a condition name test for valid months.)

(3) Verify that the day is valid (i.e., cannot exceed the maximum days in the corresponding month); error message:

```
Invalid DAY for: Smith        Invoice No: 1234 Month: 12 Day: 35
```

(Hint: Yes, use another condition name test for valid days.)

(4) Verify that the year is valid; the year must be either the current or previous year; error message:

```
Invalid YEAR for: Smith    Invoice No: 1234  Year: 95
```

(5) If the date is valid, then verify the complete date against today's date; error message:

```
Invalid DATE for: Smith  Invoice No: 1234 Month: 12 Day: 31 Year: 95
```

c. **Name:** If the name is missing, print an appropriate error message:

```
Record missing data in NAME field for Invoice No: 1234
```

d. **Address:** If the city is missing, print an appropriate error message:

```
Record missing data in ADDRESS field for: Smith Invoice No: 1234
```

e. **City:** If the address is missing, print an appropriate error message:

```
Record missing data in CITY field for: Smith  Invoice No: 1234
```

f. **State:**

(1) If the state is missing, print an appropriate error message:

```
Record missing data in STATE field for: Smith  Invoice No: 1234
```

(2) If the state is not missing, then verify that it is a valid state. Valid States are AK, AL, AR, AZ, CA, CO, CT, DC, DE, FL, GA, HI, IA, ID, IL, IN, KS, KY, LA, MA, MD, ME, MI, MN, MO, MS, MT, NC, ND, NE, NH, NJ, NM, NV, NY, OH, OK, OR, PA, RI, SC, SD, TN, TX, UT, VA, VT, WA, WI, WV, and WY; error message:

```
Invalid STATE for: Smith    Invoice No: 1234 State: AT
```

(Hint: Another condition name test for valid states.)

g. **Zip:**

(1) If the zip is missing, print an appropriate error message:

```
Record missing data in ZIP field for: Smith      Invoice No: 1234
```

(2) *If the zip is not missing*, verify that the value is numeric; if not, display an error message:

```
Nonnumeric ZIP for: Smith       Invoice No: 1234 Zip: 08307
```

3. Any record that fails any validity test is to be rejected with no further processing, other than displaying or printing the error message(s). It is possible that a record may contain more than one error (flag all errors except where noted).
4. Valid records are to be written to a new file to be used in Project 9-5.

Project 8-6

Program Name: Student Record Validation Program

Narrative: Write a data validation program that will validate a student file and produce both a valid student file and an error report.

Input File: STUDENT-FILE

Input Record Layout:

```
01  STUDENT-RECORD.
    05  STU-ID                       PIC X(9).
    05  STU-NAME                     PIC X(16).
    05  STU-SCHOOL-INFORMATION.
        10  STU-SCHOOL-CODE          PIC X(3).
        10  STU-MAJOR-CODE           PIC X(3).
        10  STU-AID-TYPE             PIC X.
        10  STU-GPA                  PIC 9V999.
        10  STU-CREDIT-HOURS         PIC 99.
```

Test Data:

```
         1         2         3         4         5         6
12345678901234567890123456789012345678901234567890123456789012345

235980890Kostner, Kevin  BUSMKTS349908
293765635Roberts, Julia  COMMKTG365710
328576407Murphy, Eddie   COMPHYS249912
         Smith, John     MDDECOZ000003
378575600Baldwin, Alec   MUSEEGS    0G
397575906Hawn, Goldie    MEDBIOG345015
427496794Russell, Kurt   ARTCISG369018
434562734Tweety Bird     BUSFINS387103
459797G01Stallone, Sly   COMPHYL210500
470876493Gable, Clark    EMGBIOL250L
475673723Bird, Big       LAWSTAS300509
492729475Freeman, Morgan MUSCISG379012
524956063Newman, Paul    MEDSTAS332101
540394065Redford, Robert ARTACCL267510
S84784755                ENGSTTL310520
586432980Runner, Road    COMACCL250006
593639456Davis, Geena    BUSFINS299911
635968690Sarandon, Susan ENGSTAG349909
658294585Douglas, MichealBUSMKTS300004
693764956Hitchcock, Al   MISACCL355500
732947566Mouse, Mickey   MUSCISS400016
740685676Bunny, Bugs     MEDPHYS350002
753546833Duck, Donald    LAYMKTL2499
769048304Streep, Merril  ARTFINS397002
779309498Goldberg, Woopi LAWMKTG289918
794784830Grant, Cary     MESEEGL2399 G
816274855Crystal, Billy  COMBIOL300105
826495896Letterman, DavidCOMCISS300116
834858653Clark, Dick     BUSFINS379817
843020375Williams, Robin ENGENGS276910
924649576ET              EEGENGZ400112
967707888Hall, Arsenio   COMMKTG398017
```

Report Layout: Develop your own report layout in compliance with the processing requirements.

Processing Requirements:

1. Read a file of student records.
2. Validate each input record field for all of the following:
   a. **Name:** If the name is missing, print an appropriate error message:

      `Record missing data in NAME field for Student ID: 123456789`

   b. **Student ID:**

      (1) If the student ID is missing, print an appropriate error message:

      `Record missing data in STUDENT ID field for: Smith, AB`

      (2) Verify that the value is numeric; if not, display an error message:

      `Nonnumeric STUDENT ID for: Smith, AB Student ID: 123456789`

   c. **GPA:**

      (1) If the GPA is missing, print an appropriate error message:

      `Record missing data in GPA field for: Smith, AB Student ID: 123456789`

      (2) *If the GPA is not missing*, verify that the value is numeric; if not, display an error message:

      `Nonnumeric GPA for: Smith, AB Student ID: 123456789  GPA: ABCD`

      (3) *If the GPA is numeric*, then verify that the GPA is between 2.5 and 4.0, inclusively (students with a GPA below 2.5 are ineligible for any kind of aid); if not, display an error message:

      `GPA out of limits for: Smith, AB  Student ID: 123456789 GPA: 5000`

   d. **Credit Hours:**

      (1) If the credit hours are missing, print an appropriate error message:

      `Record missing data in CREDIT HOURS field for: Smith, AB Student ID: 123456789`

      (2) *If the credit hours are not missing*, verify that the value is numeric; if not, display an error message:

      `Nonnumeric CREDIT HOURS for: Smith, AB Student ID: 123456789  Credit Hours: AB`

      (3) *If the credit hours are numeric*, then verify that the hours are between 1 and 18, inclusively; if not, display an error message:

      `CREDIT HOURS out of limits for: Smith, AB  Student ID: 123456789 Credit Hours: 22`

   e. **Codes:**

      (1) Valid school codes are ART, BUS, COM, ENG, LAW, MED, and MUS; error message:

      `Invalid SCHOOL for: Smith, AB  Student ID: 123456789 Major: ABC`

      (2) Valid major codes are ACC, BIO, ECO, ENG, FIN, CIS, MKT, PHY, and STA; error message:

      `Invalid MAJOR for: Smith, AB  Student ID: 123456789 MAJOR: ABC`

      (3) Valid aid types are S, G, and L; error message:

      `Invalid AID TYPE for: Smith, AB   Student ID: 123456789 Aid Type: Z`

3. Any record that fails any validity test is to be rejected with no further processing, other than displaying or printing the appropriate error message(s). It is possible that a record may contain more than one error (all errors are to be flagged except where noted).
4. Valid records are to be written to a new file, which will be used in Projects 9-6 and 16-2.

Project 8-7

Program Name: Salary Report Validation Program

Narrative: Write a data validation program that will validate a salary file and produce a valid salary file.

Input File: SALARY-FILE

Input Record Layout:

```
01  SALARY-RECORD.
    05  SAL-SOC-SEC-NO              PIC X(9).
    05  SAL-NAME-AND-INITIALS       PIC X(15).
    05  SAL-BIRTH-DATE.
        10  SAL-BIRTH-MONTH         PIC 9(2).
        10  SAL-BIRTH-YEAR          PIC 9(2).
    05  SAL-LOCATION-CODE           PIC X(3).
    05  SAL-EDUCATION-CODE          PIC 9.
    05  SAL-TITLE-DATA.
        10  SAL-TITLE-CODE          PIC 9(3).
        10  SAL-TITLE-DATE.
            15  SAL-TITLE-MONTH     PIC 9(2).
            15  SAL-TITLE-YEAR      PIC 9(2).
    05  SAL-RATING                  PIC 9.
    05  SAL-SALARY                  PIC 9(6).
```

Test Data:

```
         1         2         3         4         5         6
12345678901234567890123456789012345678901234567890123456789012345

125896790Beckeles, GG   0357MIA404003902054000
235980890Bennett, JA    1667LA 406003444046700
293765635Blaney, WC     0467CHI504004885078027
312458697Chatani, DH    0654NY 605006904123000
328576407Chen, EI       0959MIA204002911045999
         Crumity, TR    1663AT 407106915083078
378575600Dailey, TP     0566ATL508007842067200
397575906Feuer, D       0571CHI309006844090680
427496794Garcia, A      0668LA 607002872018050
459797808Gonzalez, L    0274NY 309008855030480
470876493Gutierrez, CM  0367ATL210001904027090
492729475Jackson, NL    0466MIA304003904140980
524956063Largesse, CL   0259CHI405011873030856
540394065Levy, MS       0560LA 203012891037452
S84784755               0265ATL015014923350001
593639456Moscatelli, EJ 0367ATL207012855050120
635968690Murata, Y      0670MIA502002894038546
658294585Nilsson, P     0175CHI206003915036456
693764956Pauncefort, C  0571LA 507002742063740
732947566Raffle, AG     0668LA 205007795046589
740685G7GRobinson, PJ   1277NYC507007950
769048304Rodriguez, AM  1167MIA503003791028345
779309498Sanchez, MC    0759NY 208007904047242
794784830Schand, MI     0472LAX709006917 06490
816274855Shinawatra, R  0356CHI410007893036478
826495896Tozzi, GA      0351ATL408007825192375
834858653Villar, CV     0838MIA501002555350000
843020375Wilcoxon, B    0457ATL507004874047566
924649576Yadav, S       0461MIA209012901037856
967707888Yau, SC        0367CHI310003892238745
```

Report Layout: Develop your own report layout in compliance with the processing requirements.

Processing Requirements:

1. Read a file of salary records.
2. Validate each input record field for all of the following:
   a. **Name:** If the name is missing, print an appropriate error message:
      `Record missing data in NAME field for Soc Sec No: 123456789`

   b. **Soc Sec No:**
      (1) If the social security number is missing, print an appropriate error message:
      `Record missing data in SOC SEC NO field for: Smith, AB`

      (2) *If the social security number is not missing*, verify that the value is numeric; if not, display an error message:
      `Nonnumeric SOC SEC NO for: Smith, AB     Soc Sec No: ABCD6789`

   c. **Salary:**
      (1) If the salary is missing, print an appropriate error message:
      `Record missing data in SALARY field for: Smith, AB     Soc Sec No: 123456789`

      (2) *If the salary is not missing*, verify that the value is numeric; if not, display an error message:
      `Nonnumeric SALARY for: Smith, AB      Soc Sec No: 123456789 Salary: 083078`

      (3) If the salary is numeric, then verify that salary is over $10,000 and under $350,000; if not, display an error message:
      `SALARY out of limits (under $010000 or over $350000) for: Smith, AB`
      `Soc Sec No: 123456789 Salary: 350001`

   d. **Codes:**
      (1) Valid location codes are MIA, CHI, LA, NY, and ATL; error message:
      `Invalid LOCATION for: Smith, AB     Soc Sec No: 123456789 Location: AT`

      (2) Valid education codes are 1 through 6; error message:
      `Invalid EDUCATION for: Smith, AB      Soc Sec No: 123456789 Education: 0`

      (3) Valid title codes are 010, 020, 030, 040, 050, 060, 070, 080, 090, and 100; error message:
      `Invalid TITLE for: Smith, AB        Soc Sec No: 123456789 Title: 150`

      (4) Valid ratings are 1 through 5; error message:
      `Invalid RATING for: Smith, AB        Soc Sec No: 123456789 Rating: 0`

   e. **Birth Date and Age:**
      (1) Verify that the values in the birth date are valid; error message:
      `Invalid BIRTH MONTH for: Smith, AB      Soc Sec No: 123456789 Birth Month: 16`

      (2) Verify the employee is not under 16 years of age; error message:
      `AGE under 16 for: Smith, AB        Soc Sec No: 123456789 Age: 13`

   f. **Title Date:**
      (1) Verify that the title month is valid; error message:
      `Invalid TITLE MONTH for: Smith, AB       Soc Sec No: 123456789 Title Month: 20`

      (2) Verify that the title year is valid; the company was established in 1955; therefore no employee should have had a title before that year; error message:
      `TITLE YEAR before 1955 for: Smith, AB   Soc Sec No: 123456789 Title Year: 44`

(3) Verify that the title year is valid; therefore no employee should have had a title year beyond the current year; error message:

```
TITLE YEAR beyond 1993 for: Smith, AB   Soc Sec No: 123456789 Title Year: 95
```

(4) If the title year is valid, then verify the complete title date against today's date; error message:

```
Invalid TITLE DATE for: Smith, AB  Soc Sec No: 123456789 Month: 06 Year: 91
```

3. Any record that fails any validity test is to be rejected with no further processing, other than displaying or printing the appropriate error message(s). It is possible that a record may contain more than one error (all errors are to be flagged except where noted).

4. Valid records are to be written to a new file to be used in Projects 9-7 and 16-3.

Project 8-8

Program Name: Stock Validation Program

Narrative: Write a data validation program that will validate a stock file and produce both a valid stock file and an error report.

Input File: STOCK-FILE

Input Record Layout:

```
01  STOCK-RECORD-IN.
    05  STOCK-INFO.
        10  STOCK-NAME                PIC X(8).
        10  STOCK-EXCHANGE-CODE       PIC 9.
        10  STOCK-INDUSTRY-CODE       PIC X(3).
    05  STOCK-CURRENT-INFO.
        10  STOCK-PRICE               PIC 9(3)V9(3).
        10  STOCK-PE                  PIC 9(3).
        10  STOCK-DIVIDEND            PIC 9V99.
    05  STOCK-PROJECTION-INFO.
        10  STOCK-RISK-CODE           PIC 9.
        10  STOCK-GROWTH-RATE         PIC 9V9(4).
        10  STOCK-SHARES-TO-BUY       PIC 9(4).
```

Test Data:

```
         1         2         3         4         5         6
12345678901234567890123456789012345678901234567890123456789012345

Hhhhhhh 0BEE001000999555600100
Aaaaaaa 1BAN0123400122220054320000
Anheus  1BEE 527500161123005000015
AT&T    1TEL0421250881324025500100
BellSo  1TEL0477500152764029750065
Chevron 1OIL0727500243304009500050
Chryslr 1AUT0200000150602003000025
Compq   1CMP0287500382303015500025
Eeeeeee 1ELL1500000118900000000168
Exxon   1OIL0627500142883007000035
Fffffff 1F&L      0102500100010000
Kellogg 1FOO0583750221123024550010
Kmart   1RET0460000111763005000005
GenEl   1ELE0775000152203009500050
```

```
GnMotr  1AUT0441250153312006750010
IBM     1CMP0903750134843011000050
Marriot 1F&L0180000230283005000020
McDonld 1F&L0465000190404013500010
Norwst  1AIR0377500121002004500015
Reebok  1RET0235000090302007750075
Sears   1RET0425000152003011500050
SwBell  1TEL0603750122923007000030
Upjohn  1DRU0326250111364008000025
USWst   1AIR0356250122121004500025
Wendys  1F&L0120000220244029500050
Bankrs  2BAN0022750080581003200030
Iomega  2ELE0065000090503006750040
Maxwel  2F000130000130404007000010
Oracle  2CMP0155000552253012000010
PolkAu  2ELE0062500350752005500025
Seagate 2ELE0171253431303008900045
        3TEL1250000345500045450200
Ccccccc 3BEN0125500120153012340250
CmceBk  3BAN0155000050152004000019
LdmkB   3BAN0000630070101003250500
Ddddddd 4dru0000000204551023000750
Excel   4CMP0117500280244035000075
Ggggggg 4air0100000227500000250100
LilVern 4RET0140000140052006500050
Luria   4RET0071250290952007500025
Metrbk  4BAN0112500090603004000050
Skywst  4AIR0077500200053005000035
Sonesta 4F&L0055000021003008900050
Trustco 4BAN0270000120602004000010
Tyson   4F000186250170043005500025
Bbbbbbb 5SD 0013450120751125001500
```

Report Layout: Develop your own report layout in compliance with the processing requirements.

Processing Requirements:

1. Read a file of stock records.
2. Validate each input record field for all of the following:
   a. **Stock Name:** If the name is missing, print an appropriate error message:

      `Record missing data in NAME field Industry Code: XXX`

   b. **Exchange Code:**

      (1) Verify that the value is numeric; if not, display an error message:

      `Nonnumeric EXCHANGE CODE for Stock: XXXXXXXX`

      (2) *If the **exchange code** is numeric*, verify that the code is valid. Valid exchanges are 1 through 4.

      Error message: `Invalid EXCHANGE for Stock: XXXXXXXX  Exchange: X`

      (Hint: Use condition name test for valid exchanges.)

   c. **Industry Code:** Verify that the industry code is valid. Valid industry codes are: AIR, AUT, BAN, BEE, CMP, DRU, ELE, F&L, FOO, OIL, RET, S&L, and TEL.

      Error message: `Invalid INDUSTRY CODE for Stock: XXXXXXXX Industry: XXX`

      (Hint: Use condition name test for valid types.)

d. **PE and Dividend:** Verify that these values are numeric; if not, display the appropriate error message:

```
Nonnumeric PE for Stock: XXXXXXXX  PE: 999

Nonnumeric DIVIDEND for Stock: XXXXXXXX  Dividend: 9.99
```

e. **Price and Shares to Buy**

(1) Verify that these values are numeric; if not, display the appropriate error message:

```
Nonnumeric PRICE for Stock: XXXXXXXX  Price: 999.999

Nonnumeric SHARES TO BUY for Stock: XXXXXXXX  Shares to Buy: 9999
```

(2) Verify that both are not zero; if either is zero, display an error message:

Zero Price and/or Shares to Buy for Stock: XXXXXXXX Price: 999.999 Shares: 9999

(3) *Finally, when both the* ***price*** *and* ***shares to buy*** *are numeric and not zero,* verify that the potential stock purchase is not over the limit of $25,000. That is, if the product of the stock price and the shares to buy exceeds $25,000, the record should be rejected. Display the following error message:

```
Total Purchase exceeds limit for Stock: XXXXXXXX Limit: 9999999
```

f. **Risk Code and Growth Rate:**

(1) Verify that the value is numeric; if not, display the appropriate error message:

```
Nonnumeric RISK CODE for Stock: XXXXXXXX  Risk Code: X

Nonnumeric GROWTH RATE for Stock: XXXXXXXX  Growth Rate: XXXXX
```

(2) *If the* ***risk code*** *or* ***growth rate*** *is numeric,* verify that the codes are valid. Valid risk codes are 1 through 5. Valid growth rates are .01% through 100%. Appropriate error messages are:

```
Invalid RISK CODE for Stock: XXXXXXXX  Risk Code: X

Invalid GROWTH RATE for Stock: XXXXXXXX  Growth Rate: 9.9999
```

(Hint: Use a condition name test for valid risks and growth rates.)

3. Any record that fails any validity test is to be rejected with no further processing, other than displaying or printing the appropriate error message(s). It is possible that a record may contain more than one error (all errors are to be flagged except where noted).

4. Valid records are to be written to a file to be used in Projects 9-8, 16-4, and 17-6.

Project 8-9

Program Name: Electricity Bill Validation Program

Narrative: Write a data validation program that will validate an electric file and produce a valid electric file.

Input File: ELECTRIC-FILE

Input Record Layout:

```
01  ELECTRIC-RECORD-IN.
    05  EL-ACCOUNT-NO                  PIC X(6).
    05  EL-ACCOUNT-TYPE.
        10  EL-TYPE-CODE               PIC X.
        10  EL-CATEGORY-CODE           PIC XX.
        10  EL-DEMAND-CODE             PIC X.
        10  EL-TIME-OF-USE-CODE        PIC X.
    05  EL-METER-INFO.
        10  EL-KW-DEMAND-LEVEL         PIC 9(4).
        10  EL-SERVICE-USED-FROM-DATE.
            15  EL-FROM-YEAR           PIC 99.
            15  EL-FROM-MONTH          PIC 99.
            15  EL-FROM-DAY            PIC 99.
        10  EL-SERVICE-USED-TO-DATE.
            15  EL-TO-YEAR             PIC 99.
            15  EL-TO-MONTH            PIC 99.
            15  EL-TO-DAY              PIC 99.
        10  EL-METER-READ-INFO.
            15  EL-CURRENT-READING     PIC 9(5).
            15  EL-PREVIOUS-READING    PIC 9(5).
```

Test Data:

```
         1         2         3         4         5         6
123456789012345678901234567890123456789012345678901234567890123456

342545RRSN10000920123920222357483 4953
```

```
342545RRSN1000092012392022235748349 53
```

```
342545RRSN100009201239202223574834953
238945CCSX134679202219203223908134576
689353RRSN200009201279202290023401002
466567CGSS100459202259203264024232934
000000CCSL121999203159201100235703465
465758CCSL234569111319112140045602345
763645CGSN100009201249202158349372452
11111lRRSN101239202279202260667805678
457686CGSM105129202019203033613335688
487653CGSN200009202239203280038737846
222222CCSM221959614339205305675402466
333333CGSS105509106299111l12344457575
349766CGSS204999201229202160034662745
456977CGSL255539203079203150064303245
444444CCSS200259201189214123774275638
945766CCSL121459202219203225545544544
457897CGSM209379202259203220042502145
555555CCSX115909108329206151242547426
460674CGSM107509201209202193423421212
906654RRSN200009201159202140033500856
548645CCSL221009203099203290036404742
666666CGSS100009205309106321242424244
486467RRSN100009112319201314586723745
859734CGSM205009202189203200136409736
146557CGSL123459201189202229721995984
387643CCSM119999201179202106453342345
777777XXXX123459213289412120532506643
984545CGSN1     91090391100490302897 34
895098CGSL120009201169202199427483423
567455CGSX142439201069202084932845834
387464CCSM105009202029203035845333845
345456CGSS100309112089201087348773464
```

```
463454CGSL22382920301920327093471O374
888888CCSM20311910935920811086463643l
436355CCSM218219201149203010863818346
234557RRSN100009202279203251727417234
      CGSL256789205309205291234202345
489753CGSX120009201139202105394739843
487635CCSL120019111129201119475384653
784567CGSX256899103149203310238409549
845543CGSN200009202139203250089503453
387454CCSL220039201179202150189310763
999999CGSS111309202139112313521535218
223456CCSM114569202239203237844673523
348756CCSX121509111119112117864265987
345464RRSN200009201309203220045804975
646757CCSM212349203019203270003002985
758346CGSX221239202029203151038400384
457466CCSX231239112129201230278818236
ZZZZZZCGSN200009602159602163642686637
545465CGSS200509105199106200002300384
346768CCSL143569202179203174598545643
859567CCSX255749107209108200453400454
```

Report Layout: Develop your own report layout in compliance with the processing requirements.

Processing Requirements:

1. Read a file of electric records.
2. Validate each input record field for all of the following:
   a. **Account No:**
      (1) If the account number is missing, print an appropriate error message:
      `Record missing data in ACCOUNT NO field Account Type: RRSN1`
      (2) *If the* ***account number*** *is not missing*, then verify that the value is numeric; if not, display an error message:
      `Nonnumeric ACCOUNT NO for Account No: 123456`
   b. **Account Type:** Verify that the account type is a valid account type. Valid account types are RRSN1, RRSN2, CGSN1, CGSN2, CGSS1, CGSS2, CGSM1, CGSM2, CGSL1, CGSL2, CGSX1, CGSX2, CCSM1, CCSM2, CCSL1, CGCL2, CGCX1, CCSX2;
      Error message: `Invalid ACCOUNT TYPE for Account: 123456 Type: XXXXX`
      (Hint: Use a condition name test for valid types.)
   c. **KW Demand Level:**
      (1) Verify that the value is numeric; if not, display an error message:
      `Nonnumeric KW DEMAND LEVEL for Account No: 123456`
      (2) *If the* ***kw demand level*** *is numeric*, then verify that the value is consistent with the demand code in the account type as shown below:

Demand Code	KW Demand Level Range
N	n/a (0)
S	21-499
M	500-1999
L	2000-9999
X	2000-9999

Error Message:

```
Inconsistent DEMAND CODE & DEMAND LEVEL for Account No: 123456
Demand Code: S  Demand Level: 545
```

d. **Service Used From and To Dates:**

(1) Verify that the from or to month is valid (i.e., 1 thru 12); error message:

```
   Invalid FROM MONTH for Account No: 123456 Month: 20
or Invalid TO MONTH for Account No: 123456 Month: 20
```

(2) Verify that the from or to day is valid (i.e., cannot exceed the maximum days in the corresponding month); error message:

```
   Invalid FROM DAY for Account No: 123456 Month: 12 Day: 35
or Invalid TO DAY for Account No: 123456 Month: 12 Day: 35
```

(Hint: Use a condition name test for valid months and days.)

(3) Verify that the from or to year is valid; the year must be either the current or previous year; error message:

```
   Invalid FROM YEAR for Account No: 123456  Year: 95
or Invalid TO YEAR for Account No: 123456  Year: 95
```

(4) If the from or to date is valid, then verify the complete date (year, month, and day) against today's date; error message:

```
   Invalid FROM DATE for Account No: 123456 Mon: 05 Day: 31 Yr: 95
or Invalid TO DATE for Account No: 123456 Mon: 05 Day: 31 Yr: 95
```

(5) Verify that the from date is prior to the to date; error message:

```
FROM DATE is not prior to TO DATE for Account No: 123456
Current Date: 920325 Previous Date: 920220
```

e. **Current and Previous Readings:** Verify that the value is numeric; if not, display an error message:

```
   Nonnumeric CURRENT READING for Account No: 123456 Current Reading: 346C4
or Nonnumeric PREVIOUS READING for Account No: 123456 Previous Reading: 346C4
```

3. Any record that fails any validity test is to be rejected with no further processing, other than displaying or printing the appropriate error message(s). It is possible that a record may contain more than one error (all errors are to be flagged except where noted).

4. Valid records are to be written to a file to be used in Projects 9-9, 16-5, and 17-7.

PROGRAMMING SPECIFICATIONS

Project 9-1

Program Name: Doctor Visits Report Program

Narrative: This program accepts the valid output file produced by Project 8-1 as input and produces a report as output.

Input File: PATIENT-FILE

Input Record Layout: Identical to the output record of Project 8-1.

Test Data: Use the output file of valid records created in Project 8-1 as input.

Report Layout: Design your own report layout, subject to the processing requirements.

Processing Requirements:

1. Read a file of valid patient records.
2. Write an appropriate heading at the top of each page showing the date the report was run and page number.
3. Write a detail line for each patient showing all of the information in the input record. Print 5 patients per page.
4. Write a total line for the amount paid when all patients have been processed.

Project 9-2

Program Name: Stock Transactions Report Program

Narrative: This program accepts the valid output file produced by Project 8-2 as input and produces a report as output.

Input File: STOCK-TRANSACTION-FILE

Input Record Layout: Identical to the output record of Project 8-2.

Test Data: Use the output file of valid records created in Project 8-2 as input.

Report Layout:

```
                                        We Make U Money, Inc.                                  Page Z9
                                  Stock Activity Report as of MM/DD/YY

                                Purchase Info                           Sell Info                 Profit
                      --------------------------------     -----------------------------        / Loss
Stock          Shares   Date    Price/Share      Total     Date    Price/Share      Total

XXXXXXXXXXXXXX   ZZ9  MM/DD/YY  ZZ,ZZ9.99    ZZZ,ZZ9.99  MM/DD/YY  ZZ,ZZ9.99 ZZZ,ZZZ9.99     ---,--9.99
      .           .      .          .             .          .         .          .               .
      .           .      .          .             .          .         .          .               .
      .           .      .          .             .          .         .          .               .
                -----                      ------------                       ------------ ------------
 Totals         Z,ZZ9                      Z,ZZZ,ZZ9.99                       Z,ZZZ,ZZ9.99 -,---,--9.99
```

Processing Requirements:

1. Read a file of valid stock records.
2. Write the appropriate headings showing the date and page number.
3. For each record read:
   a. Calculate the
      (1) total purchase by multiplying the number of shares by the purchase price per share.
      (2) total sale by multiplying the shares by the selling price per share.
      (3) profit/loss by subtracting the total purchase from the total sale.

b. String the record's purchase and sale date into a month, day, and year format.
c. Write a detail line for every transaction; print 4 transactions per page.

4. Write totals as shown in the report layout after all records are processed.

Project 9-3

Program Name: Payroll Report Program

Narrative: This program accepts the valid output file produced by Project 8-3 as input and produces a report as output.

Input File: PAYROLL-FILE

Input Record Layout: Identical to the output record of Project 8-3.

Test Data: Use the output file of valid records created in Project 8-3 as input.

Report Layout:

```
                     HardWorkers of America as of mm/dd/yy            Page Z9

Name                                Gross Pay      Taxes  Insurance     Net Pay

last name, first name             $$$,$$9.99    $$$9.99    $$$9.99  $$$,$$9.99
         .                                 .          .          .           .
         .                                 .          .          .           .
         .                                 .          .          .           .
                                 $$$$,$$9.99 $$,$$9.99  $$,$$9.99 $$$$,$$9.99
```

Processing Requirements:

1. Read a file of valid payroll records.
2. Write the appropriate headings showing the date and page number.
3. For each input record read:
   a. Calculate the gross pay as:
      (1) Straight time for the first 40 hours worked
      (2) Time and a half for hours worked over 40

      Note: Salaried workers DO NOT get overtime.
   b. Calculate the deductions:
      (1) Federal withholding tax is based on the gross pay.
         (a) 18% on the first $400
         (b) 23% on amounts over $400 and up to $600, inclusive
         (c) 25% on amounts over $600
      (2) FICA is 6.2% of the gross pay.

(3) Insurance as indicated below depending on the Plan Type.

Plan	Amount Deducted
A	$5
B	$8
C	$10
Z	$0 (no insurance)

c. Calculate net pay by subtracting all of the deductions (tax, FICA, and insurance) from the gross pay.

d. Write a detail line for each employee. String the name as shown in the report layout. Print only 5 employees per page.

4. Write totals as shown on the report layout after ten records have been processed.

Project 9-4

Program Name: Car Sales Commissions Report Program

Narrative: This program accepts the valid output file produced by Project 8-4 as input and produces a report as output.

Input File: CAR-SALES-FILE

Input Record Layout: Identical to the output record of Project 8-4.

Test Data: Use the output file of valid records created in Project 8-4 as input.

Report Layout:

```
                        Very Very Nice Cars, Inc.                   Page Z9
                       Commission Report MM/DD/YY

Salesperson     Date          Car               Sale    Commission     Net

XXXXXXXXXX   MM/DD/YY  'YY XXXXXXXXXXXX    ZZZ,ZZ9     ZZZ,ZZ9     ZZZ,ZZ9
     .           .       .      .             .           .           .
     .           .       .      .             .           .           .
     .           .       .      .             .           .           .
                                        ---------- ---------- ----------
                                         Z,ZZZ,ZZ9  Z,ZZZ,ZZ9  Z,ZZZ,ZZ9
```

Processing Requirements:

1. Read a file of valid car sales records.
2. Write the appropriate headings showing the current date and page.
3. For each record read:

   a. Calculate the commission paid to the salesperson by multiplying the commission rate by the sale amount.

   b. Calculate the net to the company by subtracting the commission paid from the sale amount.
   c. Write a detail line, printing 8 sales per page. Use reference modification to show only the last two digits in the car year on the report line.
4. Write totals as shown on the report layout after all the records have been processed.

Project 9-5

Program Name: Invoice Mailing Labels Program

Narrative: This program accepts the valid output file produced by Project 8-5 as input and produces a mailing label as output.

Input File: INVOICE-FILE

Input Record Layout: Identical to the output record of Project 8-5.

Test Data: Use the output file of valid records created in Project 8-5 as input.

Report Layout:

```
Scully                          Schultz
20 Main St                      45 5th St
Chicago, IL 60666               Los Angeles, CA 90024
```

Processing Requirements:

1. Read a file of valid invoice records.
2. For each input record read create a mailing label.
   a. String the city, state, and zip as shown in the report layout.
   b. Print the labels in two columns as shown in the report layout.

Project 9-6

Program Name: Student Record Report Program

Narrative: This program accepts the valid output file produced by Project 8-6 as input and produces a report as output.

Input File: STUDENT-FILE

Input Record Layout: Identical to the output record of Project 8-6.

Test Data: Use the output file of valid records created in Project 8-6 as input.

Report Layout:

```
                              Smart U                              Page Z9
                      Student Aid Report 99/99/99

                                                Credit   Total     Total    Tuition
StudentID  Name                 School   Aid    Hours   Tuition      Aid        Due

999999999  XXXXXXXXXXXXXXX       XXX      X      Z9    ZZZ,ZZ9   ZZZ,ZZ9    ZZZ,ZZ9
    .           .                 .       .      .        .         .          .
    .           .                 .       .      .        .         .          .
    .           .                 .       .      .        .         .          .
                                                ---   ---------  ---------  ---------
                                                ZZ9   Z,ZZZ,ZZ9  Z,ZZZ,ZZ9  Z,ZZZ,ZZ9
```

Processing Requirements:

1. Read a file of valid student records.
2. Write appropriate headings showing the current date and page number.
3. For each input record read:
   a. Calculate total tuition based on $300 per credit.
   b. Calculate total aid based on the GPA as follows:

GPA	% Aid
2.5 to 3.0	60%
3.1 to 3.5	70%
3.6 to 4.0	80%

   c. Calculate the tuition due by subtracting the total aid from the total tuition.
   d. Write a detail line with the information shown on the report layout, printing 10 students per page.
4. Write the totals shown on the report layout after all the records have been processed.

Project 9-7

Program Name: Salary Report Program

Narrative: This program accepts the valid output file produced by Project 8-7 as input and produces a report as output.

Input File: SALARY-FILE

Input Record Layout: Identical to the output record of Project 8-7.

Test Data: Use the output file of valid records created in Project 8-7 as input.

Report Layout: Develop your own report layout in compliance with the processing requirements.

Processing Requirements:

1. Read a file of valid salary records.
2. Write an appropriate heading showing the current date and page number.
3. For each input record read write a detail line showing all of the information in the record. Print 10 employees per page.
4. Write a total for the salary amounts after all records have been processed.

Project 9-8

Program Name: Stock Purchases Report Program

Narrative: This program accepts the valid output file produced by Project 8-8 as input and produces a report as output.

Input File: STOCK-FILE

Input Record Layout: Identical to the output record of Project 8-8.

Test Data: Use the output file of valid records created in Project 8-8 as input.

Report Layout:

```
                  Stock Purchases               Page Z9
                day of Week MM/DD/YY

Name      Exchange   Shares     Price        Total
XXXXXXXX   XXX        Z,ZZ9   $ZZ9.999   $ZZ,ZZ9.99
   .        .           .        .             .
   .        .           .        .             .
   .        .           .        .             .
                     ------              -----------
                     ZZ,ZZ9              $ZZZ,ZZ9.99
```

Processing Requirements:

1. Read a file of valid stock records.
2. Write an appropriate heading, showing the page, day of week, and current date.
3. For each input record read:
   a. Calculate the total by multiplying the shares to buy by the stock price.
   b. Write a detail line showing all of the information on the report layout, printing 10 stocks per page.
4. When all the records are processed, print totals as shown on the report layout.

Project 9-9

Program Name: Electricity Bill Report Program

Narrative: This program accepts the valid output file produced by Project 8-9 as input and produces a report as output.

Input File: ELECTRIC-FILE

Input Record Layout: Identical to the output record of Project 8-9.

Test Data: Use the output file of valid records created in Project 8-9 as input.

Report Layout:

```
                       Bright Power & Light                        Page Z9
                      Residential Kilowatt Usage

  Account Info     Service Used   Meter Readings       Total   Estimated
---------------    ------------   -----------------  Kilowatt     Bill
Number     Type    From   To      Previous  Current  Hrs Used
999999     XXXXX   MM/DD MM/DD     ZZ,ZZ9    ZZ,ZZ9    ZZ,ZZ9   Z,ZZ9.99
   .         .       .     .         .         .         .          .
   .         .       .     .         .         .         .          .
   .         .       .     .         .         .         .          .
                                                     -------   --------
                                                     ZZZ,ZZ9  ZZ,ZZ9.99
```

Processing Requirements:

1. Read a file of valid electric records.
2. Write an appropriate heading showing the page number.
3. For each input record read:
   a. If the account category is residential:
      (1) Calculate the total kilowatt hours used by subtracting the previous reading from the current reading.
      (2) Calculate an estimated bill:

      The first 750 kw hours used will be charged at 3.922¢ per kw hour.

      Additional kw hours used will be charged at 4.922¢.

   b. Print a detail line showing the information in the report layout.
4. Write the totals shown on the report layout after all records have been processed.

PROGRAMMING SPECIFICATIONS

Projects 10-1 through 10-9

Program Name: Doctor Visits, Stock Transactions, Payroll, Car Sales Commissions, Invoice Mailing Labels, Student Record, Salary, Stock Purchases, and Electricity Bill

Narrative: These projects combine the requirements of projects 8-1 through 8-9 and 9-1 through 9-9 as presented earlier in Chapters 8 and 9. The fields in each incoming record transaction are accepted and validated one at a time, after which the necessary computations are done and the report is displayed on the screen.

Test Data: Use one or more records from the original data in Chapter 8.

Screen Layout: Design your own input and output screen layout (based on the record layout in projects 8-1 through 8-9 and report layout in projects 9-1 through 9-9).

Processing Requirements:

1. Display a screen to input and validate a record, repeating the appropriate validations in the corresponding projects in Chapter 8.
2. Display the calculated information from the corresponding projects in Chapter 9 on the screen.
3. Optional: write the validated input records to a file after displaying it on the screen.

PROGRAMMING SPECIFICATIONS

Project 11-1

Program Name: Employee Profiles

Narrative: The requirements of this project are typical of compensation reports done in large organizations, which compare individuals with similar skills to one another. (The project is expanded to include material on table lookups in Project 12-1 at the end of the next chapter.)

Input File: EMPLOYEE-FILE

Input Record Layout:

```
01  EMPLOYEE-RECORD.
    05  EMP-SOC-SEC-NUMBER                PIC X(9).
    05  EMP-NAME-AND-INITIALS             PIC X(16).
    05  EMP-DATE-OF-BIRTH.
        10  EMP-BIRTH-MONTH               PIC 99.
        10  EMP-BIRTH-YEAR                PIC 99.
    05  EMP-DATE-OF-HIRE.
        10  EMP-HIRE-MONTH                PIC 99.
        10  EMP-HIRE-YEAR                 PIC 99.
    05  EMP-SEX                           PIC X.
    05  EMP-SALARY-DATA OCCURS 3 TIMES.
        10  EMP-SALARY                    PIC 9(5).
        10  EMP-SALARY-TYPE               PIC X.
        10  EMP-SALARY-DATE.
            15  EMP-SALARY-MONTH          PIC 99.
            15  EMP-SALARY-YEAR           PIC 99.
        10  EMP-SALARY-GRADE              PIC 9.
    05  EMP-TITLE-DATA.
        10  EMP-TITLE-CODE                PIC XX.
        10  EMP-TITLE-DATE.
            15  EMP-TITLE-MONTH           PIC 99.
            15  EMP-TITLE-YEAR            PIC 99.
    05  EMP-LOCATION-CODE                 PIC 99.
    05  EMP-EDUCATION-CODE                PIC 9.
```

Test Data:

```
         1         2         3         4         5         6         7
1234567890123456789012345678901234567890123456789012345678901234567890123456
100000000DOE           J 12440991M33000M0992331500H09913           350991104
200000000WILCOX        PA10581191M29000M1192227500H11912           351191104
400000000LEVINE        S 01500890F31000M0892229000M0891228000M02912320890104
500000000SMITHERS      M 03500172M48000M0892745500M0891740000M08894280588204
600000000SUPERPROG     S 04571091F59000H10916                      501091106
700000000LEE           B 10530277F40000P0592837500M0291835000M02907400589405
800000000PERSNICKETY   P 08550392M25600H03923                      500392306
900000000MILGROM       MB11550989F32000M1192329000M0591227500M05891321189103
```

Report Layout: The report below shows required information and illustrative calculations for A. B. Jones. Print your report according to these general specifications, but do not be concerned about exact line and column positions on a page. (See item 2b in the processing requirements for additional guidelines.)

```
                         PERSONNEL PROFILE
              NAME:  JONES A.B.       SOC-SEC-NO.:  123-45-6789
              AGE:   21.4 YEARS       HIRE DATE:     1/91
--------------------------------------------------------------------------
SALARY   DATE  TYPE  % INC.   MBI    RSI     GRADE   MIDPOINT  % MIDPOINT
$24,200  7/94   P     10.0      6    20.0%     4     $28,000       86.4
$22,000  1/94   M     10.0     12    10.0%     3     $21,000      104.7
$20,000  1/93   H                              3     $21,000       95.2
```

Processing Requirements:

1. Read a file of employee records.
2. For every record read:
   a. Compute and print the employee's age, using the date of birth and date of execution. (The age calculation will be approximate, as the input birth date contains only the month and year.)
   b. Print all indicated fields with appropriate editing. Print three employees per page; leave six blank lines between employees.
   c. Print all associated salary information as described in items 3–6.
3. Each employee has a salary history with 1, 2, or 3 levels of salary data, denoting present, previous, and second previous salary, respectively. Not every employee will have all three salaries indicated, but every employee must have a present salary.
4. Associated with every salary is a salary grade, indicative of the level of responsibility in the company (for example, the janitor and president might have grade levels of 1 and 9, respectively). Each grade has an associated average salary, or midpoint. The salary midpoint is computed by multiplying the grade by $7,000. The percent of grade midpoint is found by dividing the salary by the grade midpoint and multiplying by 100.
5. Associated with every pair of salaries are three fields: percent salary increase, months between increase (MBI), and annual rate of salary increase (RSI).

a. Percent salary increase is found by subtracting the old salary from the new salary, dividing by the old salary, and multiplying by 100. For example, new and old salaries of $22,000 and $20,000 yield a percent increase of 10%.
b. Months between increase (MBI) is simply the number of months between the two salary dates.
c. Annual rate of salary increase (RSI) is computed by converting the percent salary increase to a 12-month basis; for example, 10% after 6 months is equivalent to an annual rate of 20%; 10% after 2 years is an annual rate of 5%.

6. Calculate percent salary increase, MBI, and RSI for each pair of salaries as appropriate. Realize, however, that not every employee will have all three salary levels, and hence the calculations cannot be made in every instance. Use an OCCURS clause, subscripts, and a PERFORM VARYING statement to do the calculations. Be sure to include a suitable test to avoid the computation if historical data are not present.

Project 11-2

Program Name: Benefit Statement

Narrative: Most employees do not realize the value of their fringe benefits, which often run to 30% of their annual salaries. Accordingly, benefit statements are often prepared to remind employees how well (their employer thinks) they are being treated. Develop a program to read a file of confidential employee data and to compute and print the fringe benefits for each employee.

Input File: EMPLOYEE-FILE

Input Record Layout: Use the same record layout as for Project 11-1.

Test Data: Use the same test data as for Project 11-1.

Report Layout:

```
                    Employee Benefit Statement
NAME: XXXXXXXXXXXXXXX                              BIRTH DATE: 99/99
 ANNUAL SALARY: $$$,$$9                             HIRE DATE: 99/99
------------------------- Sick Pay Benefit ------------------------------
WEEKS AT FULL PAY: Z9       WEEKS AT HALF PAY: Z9
------------------------- Retirement Benefit ----------------------------
COMPANY CONTRIBUTES: $$$,$$9  INTEREST RATE: .99  AMT AT AGE 65: $$,$$$,$$9
------------------------ Life Insurance = $$$$,$$9 -----------------------
```

Processing Requirements:

1. Read a file of employee records, preparing an individual benefit statement for every record. Each individual statement is to appear on a separate page.

2. For every record read:
   a. Calculate the retirement benefit based on an annual company contribution for each employee. The contribution is equal to 5% of the first $15,000 of salary plus 3% on any salary in excess of $15,000. Hence the company would contribute $840 annually for an employee earning $18,000 (5% of 15,000 = 750, plus 3% of 3,000 = 90). The money is invested for the employees and assumed to earn 8% annually. Use the following formula:

$$\text{Amount at age 65} = \frac{\left((1+i)^n - 1\right)}{i}$$

   where i = interest rate (for example, .08) and n = years until age 65 (specify the ROUNDED option of any arithmetic statement used in computing n).
   b. Calculate the life insurance benefit as twice an employee's annual salary if the employee earns $23,000 or less; it is three times the annual salary for those earning more than $23,000.
   c. Calculate the amount of sick pay, which is dependent on the individual's length of service. An employee is entitled to one week of full pay and an additional two weeks of half pay, for every year (or fraction thereof) of employment. The maximum benefit, however, is 10 weeks of full salary and 20 of half salary, which is reached after 10 years. (An employee with two years' service, for example, is entitled to two weeks full pay and an additional four weeks of half pay.)
   d. Use the individual's present salary, EMP-SALARY (1), in all benefit calculations.

Project 11-3

Program Name: Furniture Shipments

Narrative: This program will create an invoice for each furniture record, displaying customer information and the individual items ordered. When all the records are processed, print a summary report showing totals for each warehouse. (The project is expanded to include material on table lookups in Project 12-3 in the next chapter.)

Input File: FURNITURE-FILE

Input Record Layout:

```
01 FURNITURE-RECORD.
    05  FURN-INVOICE-NO                     PIC 9(5).
    05  FURN-CUSTOMER-NAME-N-INITIALS       PIC X(18).
    05  FURN-DELIVERY-INFO.
        10  FURN-DELIVERY-WAREHOUSE         PIC X.
        10  FURN-DELIVERY-DATE              PIC 9(6).
    05  FURN-ORDER-INFO.
        10  FURN-DEPOSIT-PERCENT            PIC 9V99.
        10  FURN-NO-ITEMS-ORDERED           PIC 9.
        10  FURN-ITEMS-ORDERED  OCCURS 1 TO 3 TIMES
                DEPENDING ON FURN-NO-ITEMS-ORDERED.
            15  FURN-ITEM                   PIC X(10).
            15  FURN-COST                   PIC 9(4)V99.
            15  FURN-WEIGHT                 PIC 9(3).
```

Test Data:

```
         1         2         3         4         5         6         7         8         9
1234567890123456789012345678901234567890123456789012345678901234567890123456789012345678901

23485EDELSTEIN, M      A061092005272" SOFA  230000100LOVESEAT  130000080
12834ALIAS, Y          B07249200042SOFA TABLE060000050END TABLE 054550035
79845RAHIM, S          A09279200073DRESSER   430000095ARMOIRE   550000100NIGHTSTAND030000045
59789KELLY, C          B08249200032DESK      059590075DESK CHAIR039550045
85778WILSON, D         C07129200123DINING TBL3575501356 CHAIRS  127800200CONSOLE   222550115
47597GUDAT, G          A062892008272" SOFA  2300000100CHAIR     054500050
58684HYMOWITZ, A       C10289200091ARMOIRE   5500000100
48577BOOZ, B           C12129200283CREDENZA  1235000125DESK      045000098DESK CHAIR054500050
56749HENNESSY, L       A09099200041POOL TABLE2300000250
95877MOHD-RAZALLI      B011293078172" SOFA  1395590075
38476THOMPSON, J       A09239200091CHAIR     05450000050TTOMAN  035000040
48565JACOMINO, R       A09239200102CHAIR     054500005072" SOFA 230000100
67566DESCHPELLES, M    B07049200092SOFA TABLE0600000130END TABLE054550035
09777SANCHEZ-CARRION, VC08129200022ARMOIRE   5500000100CREDENZA 123500250
48576WENNEMAN, M       B08169200041DRESSER   4300000095
45337AL-DAKHIL, A      A07229200051POOL TABLE2300002500
47567HARDING, J        C082292002272" SOFA  2300001200CHAIR     054500050
```

Report Layout:

```
              MANSIONS FURNITURE, INC.
                  CUSTOMER INVOICE

INVOICE #:  XXXXX                    WAREHOUSE: X
CUSTOMER NAME: XXXXXXXXXXXX, X.      SHIP DATE: MM/DD/YY

   ITEM          WEIGHT        COST
   XXXXXXXXXX       ZZ9   $$,$$9.99
    .
      .
        .
                 ------  ----------
  SUBTOTAL        Z,ZZ9  $$$,$$9.99
  SHIPPING CHARGES          $$$9.99
  TOTAL                  $$$,$$9.99
  LESS DEPOSIT           $$$,$$9.99
  BALANCE DUE            $$$,$$9.99
```

```
              MANSIONS FURNITURE, INC.
                 WAREHOUSE SUMMARY

   WAREHOUSE       WEIGHT          COST
       A              ZZ9     $$,$$9.99
       B              ZZ9     $$,$$9.99
       C              ZZ9     $$,$$9.99
                   ------    ----------
   TOTAL            Z,ZZ9    $$$,$$9.99
```

Processing Requirements:

1. Read a file of furniture shipment records.
2. For each record read:
   a. Print headings as shown on the report layout. Use the STRING statement to add a period after the first name initial in the name.
   b. Process each item ordered by
      (1) Printing a detail line as shown on the report layout.
      (2) Incrementing the weight and cost totals for the customer.
   c. When the items for one customer have been processed:
      (1) Calculate the shipping charges as follows: the first 500 pounds are charged at $2.00 per pound; additional pounds over 500 are charged at $1.75 per pound.
      (2) Calculate an intermediate total by adding the shipping charges to the cost totals.
      (3) Calculate the deposit by multiplying the total [calculated in (2) above] by the deposit percent.
      (4) Calculate the balance due by subtracting the deposit from the total.
      (5) Print the balance due as shown in the report layout.
   d. Increment the totals for the appropriate warehouse in the summary table with the above information.
3. After all records have been read, print the summary table showing totals for each warehouse (as shown on the report layout).

Project 11-4

Program Name: Computer Status Report

Narrative: This program will create an individual status report for each record in the file. When all the records have been processed, print a summary report showing totals for each status. (The project is expanded to include material on table lookups in Project 12-4 in the next chapter.)

Input File: COMPUTER-FILE

Input Record Layout:

```
01  COMPUTER-RECORD.
    05  COM-INVOICE-NO                PIC 9(5).
    05  COM-CUSTOMER-NAME             PIC X(18).
    05  COM-PAYMENT-METHOD            PIC XX.
    05  COM-SHIP-INFO.
        10  COM-SHIP-STATUS           PIC X.
        10  COM-SHIP-CHARGE           PIC 99V99.
    05  COM-COMPONENT-INFO.
        10  COM-NO-COMPONENTS         PIC 9.
        10  COM-COMPONENTS  OCCURS 1 TO 4 TIMES
               DEPENDING ON COM-NO-COMPONENTS.
            15  COM-COMPONENT         PIC X(12).
            15  COM-COST              PIC 9(4).
```

Test Data:

```
         1         2         3         4         5         6         7         8         9
12345678901234567890123456789012345678901234567890123456789012345678901234567890123456789012345

12834Blanco, Erick     AM145502486 33MHz   19952400 Modem  0099
79845Casali, Joseph    AM375002386 33MHz   1595Laser Printr1399Tape BU 120 0189
59789Davis, Kevin      VI165502486 33MHz   2095Laser Pritnr1399
85778Demler, Linda     CO380254386 33MHz   2049Dot Matrix  0169Coprocessor 0099Modem/FAX   0119
47597EChavarria, FelipeCK265002486 33MHz   2379Tape BU 250 0250
58684Flemming, Sharon  MC145002425 Notebook2395Dot Matrix  0169
48577Gonzalez, Maria   VI135003486DX2 50MHz2295Modem/FAX   0119Sound Blstr 0139
56749Katan, Maharan    CK245001325 Notebook1895
95877Parmenter, Donita CO335002486 25MHz   1995CD/ROM      0345
38476Pinkwasser, Randi VI389004486DX2 66MHz29959600 Modem  0299Dot Matrix  0169Sound Blstr 0139
37586Stewart, Roberto  CK250002386 25MHz   1295FAX         1279
```

Report Layout:

```
                    FLY BY NITE COMPUTERS, INC.
                           STATUS REPORT

INVOICE #:  XXXXX                       STATUS: X
CUSTOMER NAME: XXXXXXXXXXXXXXXX         PAYMENT METHOD: XX

       COMPONENT                         COST
       XXXXXXXXXXXX                  $$,$$9.99
         .
            .
               .
                                    ----------
      SUBTOTAL                      $$$,$$9.99
      SHIPPING CHARGES                  $$$9.99
      TOTAL                         $$$,$$9.99
```

```
                    FLY BY NITE COMPUTERS, INC.
                        SUMMARY BY STATUS

     STATUS     ITEMS     SHIP CHARGES         COST
       1          Z9       $$,$$9.99        $$,$$9.99
       2          Z9       $$,$$9.99        $$,$$9.99
       3          Z9       $$,$$9.99        $$,$$9.99
                 ----     ----------       ----------
     TOTAL       ZZ9       $$,$$9.99       $$$,$$9.99
```

Processing Requirements:

1. Read a file of customer records.
2. For each record read:
   a. Print the report for each customer on a separate page; print headings as shown on the report layout.
   b. Process each component ordered by
      (1) Printing a detail line as shown on the report layout.
      (2) Incrementing the cost totals for that customer.

c. When all items for one customer have been processed:
   (1) Calculate the customer total by adding the shipping charges to the cost totals.
   (2) Print the customer total lines as shown in the report layout.

d. Increment the appropriate status in the summary table with the above information.

3. After all records have been read, print the a summary table showing totals for each status (as shown on the report layout).

Project 11-5

Program Name: Credit Report

Narrative: This program produces a credit report for store accounts. The store offers three types of accounts: 20, 40, or 60; a customer may have one of each. The report will show detail lines for each type of account for each customer. The last page is a summary of payments, purchases, interest charged, and current balance by account type.

Input File: CREDIT-FILE

Input Record Layout:

```
01  CREDIT-RECORD.
    05  CR-ACCOUNT-NO                  PIC 9(7).
    05  CR-NAME-AND-INITIALS           PIC X(18).
    05  CR-NO-OF-ACCOUNTS              PIC 9.
    05  CR-TRANSACTIONS OCCURS 1 TO 3 TIMES
            DEPENDING ON CR-NO-OF-ACCOUNTS.
        10  CR-TYPE                    PIC 99.
        10  CR-BALANCE                 PIC 9(4)V99.
        10  CR-PAYMENT                 PIC 9(4)V99.
        10  CR-PURCHASES               PIC 9(4)V99.
```

Test Data:

```
         1         2         3         4         5         6         7         8
12345678901234567890123456789012345678901234567890123456789012345678901234567890123456

1234520STUTZ, JD           12005860003430004544 4
1957620FROST, RD           14004534505000000505 5
2947660BARBER, MM          3200233900100000095454004753403150003421260233412233412043332
3856740GOLDSMITH, KN       240023434012334034323603423303623300 05443
4209540GRAUER, RG          3200342220234221853444006344403000003433260556412034212064523
4908560PLANT, RK           2200343000343000223236004340005000000000 0
5748920ELOFSON, GS         240086400056400034223606754003754000045334
6847660STEWART, JB         16005560000560016454 3
7457620GILLENSON, ML       14006551300551303543 4
8466740RUSHINEK, SF        220045334005000123434600745540845540453 34
9436560VAZQUEZ VILLAR, C 3200453450500000034454006566606500000455060054656044656043534
```

Report Layout:

```
                NEEDLESS MARKUP STORES ACCOUNT CREDIT REPORT                  PAGE Z9

 ACCOUNT # 9999999    NAME: XXXXXXXXXXXXXXXXXX

   TYPE    PREVIOUS                        INTEREST    CURRENT       CREDIT  AVAILABLE
            BALANCE   PAYMENT PURCHASES     CHARGE    BALANCE        LIMIT     CREDIT

    99     Z,ZZ9.99  Z,ZZ9.99  Z,ZZ9.99     ZZ9.99   Z,ZZ9.99CR  Z,ZZ9.99   Z,ZZ9.99
    99     Z,ZZ9.99  Z,ZZ9.99  Z,ZZ9.99     ZZ9.99   Z,ZZ9.99CR  Z,ZZ9.99   Z,ZZ9.99
    99     Z,ZZ9.99  Z,ZZ9.99  Z,ZZ9.99     ZZ9.99   Z,ZZ9.99CR  Z,ZZ9.99   Z,ZZ9.99
                     --------- ---------- --------  ----------
   TOTALS           ZZ,ZZ9.99 ZZ,ZZ9.99  Z,ZZ9.99  ZZ,ZZ9.99CR
    .
      .
        .
```

```
              NEEDLESS MARKUP STORES ACCOUNT TYPE SUMMARY

     TYPE                                   INTEREST       CURRENT
                  PAYMENT     PURCHASES      CHARGE        BALANCE

      20         Z,ZZ9.99     Z,ZZ9.99       ZZ9.99       Z,ZZ9.99CR
      40         Z,ZZ9.99     Z,ZZ9.99       ZZ9.99       Z,ZZ9.99CR
      60         Z,ZZ9.99     Z,ZZ9.99       ZZ9.99       Z,ZZ9.99CR
                ---------    ---------     --------      ---------
    TOTALS      ZZ,ZZ9.99    ZZ,ZZ9.99     Z,ZZ9.99     ZZ,ZZ9.99CR
```

Processing Requirements:

1. Read a file of credit records.
2. Develop a page heading routine which prints 5 accounts on every page.
3. For each record read:
   a. Print the appropriate account headings.
   b. Process each account type by
      (1) Calculating the monthly interest charge on the account based on the account balance after the payment has been applied. (To make life a lot easier, use simple interest and a rate of 18.5%.)
      (2) Calculating the current balance by adding the interest charge and purchases and subtracting the payment. (Note: a customer could overpay the account, therefore you should remember to make the field signed and display it as such on the report as shown in the report layout or as desired.)
      (3) Determining the credit limit for each account as follows:

Type	Credit Limit
20	$1,500
40	$3,500
60	$5,000

(4) Calculating the available credit on the account by subtracting the current balance from the credit limit determined in (3).

(5) Printing a detail line as shown on the report layout.

(6) Incrementing the appropriate totals.

c. When all accounts for one customer have been processed, print the total lines as shown in the report layout.

d. Increment the appropriate account type in the summary table with the above information.

4. After all records have been read, print a summary table showing totals for each account type (as shown on the report layout).

Project 11-6

Program Name: Software Cost Analysis

Narrative: The program will determine the following:

1. The break-even units and revenue for each software product.
2. The break-even units and revenue for each software product if a $50,000 profit is desired.
3. The break-even units and revenue for each software product if the selling price is reduced by 25%.

Input File: SOFTWARE-FILE

Input Record Layout:

```
01  SOFTWARE-RECORD.
    05  SOFT-PROGRAM-INFO.
        10  SOFT-PRODUCT-LINE               PIC X.
        10  SOFT-PRODUCT-NO                 PIC 9(4).
        10  SOFT-PROGRAM-NAME               PIC X(18).
    05  SOFT-VARIABLE-COSTS.
        10  SOFT-PREP-COSTS.
            15  SOFT-LOADING-PER-DISK       PIC 9V99.
            15  SOFT-NO-DISKS-USED          PIC 99.
        10  SOFT-MANUAL-PRINTING            PIC 99V99.
        10  SOFT-SHIPPING-N-HANDLING        PIC 99V99.
    05  SOFT-SELL-PRICE                     PIC 999V99.
    05  SOFT-FIXED-COST                     PIC 9(5).
```

Test Data:

```
         1         2         3         4         5         6
12345678901234567890123456789012345678901234567890123456789012345

G4695Flight Simulator    150011000032503950250000
B3764WordPerfect 5.1     225113550102526900230000
G1634Leisure Suit Larry100021085020003995200000
U3476Fastback Plus       175011500035011950210000
G6424ChessMaster         050010750055003500180000
B4676Word 2.0            250085550085029975300000
M9775Automap 2.0         075010825025004900180000
G2555Police Quest        075020455044504555050000
D4954PowerPoint 2.0      225103500095029900080000
U7558PROCOMM Plus 2.01   075011050052506900075000
B2154Excel 4.0           265072575102529975287500
E5775Mickeys ABCs        080010350022502900030000
B75841-2-3 3.1 Plus      245084550055539900358000
D2585Harvard Graphics    215052525072539995345000
E6555KidPix              025010540025003500036500
B4954Quattro Pro 4.0     195064500125031950359500
U7588The Norton Desktop100021850075011500270000
```

Report Layout:

```
                         Nexus Software Inc.
                  Product Cost Analysis as of 99/99/99
                  based on Total Fixed Costs:  $ZZ,ZZ9

     Product Line: X
     Product Name: XXXXXXXXXXXXXXXXXX
     Sell Price: ZZ9.99    Total Variable Cost: ZZ9.99
                                Units     Revenue
         Breakeven              Z,ZZ9  ZZZ,ZZ9.99
         Profit: $$$,$$9.99     Z,ZZ9  ZZZ,ZZ9.99
         Price Decline: Z9%     Z,ZZ9  ZZZ,ZZ9.99
           .
             .
               .
```

```
                    Nexus Software Inc.
                   Product Cost Analysis
          Summary Report by Product Line as of 99/99/99

     Product   Breakeven      Profit:       Price
      Line                    $ZZ,ZZ9     Decline: Z9%

       X       $$$$,$$9      $$$$,$$9      $$$$,$$9
       .           .             .             .
       .           .             .             .
       .           .             .             .
     Totals $$,$$$,$$9    $$,$$$,$$9    $$,$$$,$$9
```

Processing Requirements:

1. Read a file of software records.
2. For each record read:
   a. Calculate the total variable costs for each product using the data in each record; include an additional cost of $1.00 for the disk itself. The software preparation costs will be the loading cost per disk multiplied by the number of disks used; don't forget to add the cost of the blank disk(s) by multiplying the cost of a blank disk by the number of disks used.
   b. Create a three-item table containing units and revenues. This table should hold break-even units and revenue calculated as described below:
      (1) Calculate the break-even point and revenue for each product.
      (2) Calculate the required number of units and associated revenue to yield a $50,000 profit for each product.
      (3) Calculate the price decline break-even units and revenue if the selling price is reduced by 25%.
   c. Print a detail line for each record as shown on the report layout. Design your detail line with a table that mimics the information calculated in item b. above.
   d. Increment the appropriate revenue totals in your summary table.
3. After all records have been read, print the summary report and totals on a separate page as shown on the report layout. This will require you to create a table to hold all the product lines and revenue information.

PROGRAMMING SPECIFICATIONS

Project 12-1

Program Name: Employee Profiles

Narrative: This project continues the employee profile program of Project 11-1 by introducing additional material on table lookups.

Input File: EMPLOYEE-FILE and TITLE-FILE (see processing requirement 3)

Input Record Layout: Use the same record layout as Project 11-1.

Test Data: Use the same test data as Project 11-1.

Report Layout: Expand the report layout of the earlier project to include space for the various table lookups. You may display the information anywhere you deem appropriate.

Processing Requirements:

1. The education table is to be initialized through hard-coding and expanded through a direct lookup according to the following table:

Code	Description	Code	Description
1	Some High School	5	Some Grad School
2	High School Diploma	6	Master's Degree
3	Two Year Degree	7	Ph. D.
4	Four Year Degree	8	Other Graduate Degree

2. The location table is to be initialized through hard-coding and expanded with a sequential search according to the following table:

Code	Description	Code	Description
05	Atlanta	30	Los Angeles
10	Boston	35	Minneapolis
15	Chicago	40	New York
20	Detroit	45	Philadelphia
25	Kansas City		

3. The title table is to be input loaded and expanded with a binary search according to the following table:

Code	Title
15	Accountant
18	Senior Accountant
30	Jr. Programmer
32	Senior Programmer
40	Analyst
45	Senior Analyst
50	Programming Manager

Project 12-2

Program Name: Student Profile Program

Narrative: Develop a program to print a set of student profiles, showing detailed information on each student. Among other functions, the program is to convert an incoming set of codes for each student to an expanded, and more readable, format.

Input File: STUDENT-FILE and COURSE-FILE (see processing requirement 12)

Input Record Layout:

```
01  STUDENT-RECORD-IN.
    05  STU-SOC-SEC-NUMBER                          PIC 9(9).
    05  STU-NAME-AND-INITIALS.
        10  STU-LAST-NAME                           PIC X(18).
        10  STU-INITIALS                            PIC XX.
    05  STU-DATE-OF-BIRTH.
        10  STU-BIRTH-MONTH                         PIC 99.
        10  STU-BIRTH-YEAR                          PIC 99.
    05  STU-SEX                                     PIC X.
    05  STU-MAJOR-CODE                              PIC X(3).
    05  STU-SCHOOL-CODE                             PIC 9.
    05  STU-CUMULATIVE-CREDITS                      PIC 999.
```

```
05  STU-CUMULATIVE-POINTS                    PIC 999.
05  STU-UNION-MEMBER-CODE                    PIC X.
05  STU-SCHOLARSHIP                          PIC 999.
05  STU-DATE-OF-ENROLLMENT                   PIC 9(4).
05  STU-COURSES-THIS-SEMESTER OCCURS 7 TIMES.
    10  STU-COURSE-NUMBER       PIC XXX.
    10  STU-COURSE-CREDITS      PIC 9.
```

Test Data:

```
         1         2         3         4         5         6         7         8
12345678901234567890123456789012345678901234567890123456789012345678901234567890
100000000ALBERT            A 01740MSTA1059118Y01509921002200330044004501360026011
200000000BROWN             B 0275FSTA1089275N025099210022003300044004
300000000CHARLES           GG0675MHIS2109286Y100099350135033504350535063
400000000SMITH             D 0776FXXX2090269N010099210022003300044194
500000000BAKER             EF1074MGEN3032049Y0000994222333334443
600000000GULFMAN           SF1173FELE4029059N000099320033333444355536663675270001
700000000BOROW             JS1275MIEN3030090Y00009922223
800000000MILGROM           MB0376F   5015045Y000099311131383150316003
900000000MILLER            K 0174MFRL2015054Y0000993111314031503
999919999WAYNE             N 0473FHIS2090270Y0000994501350335043505 3
```

Report Layout:

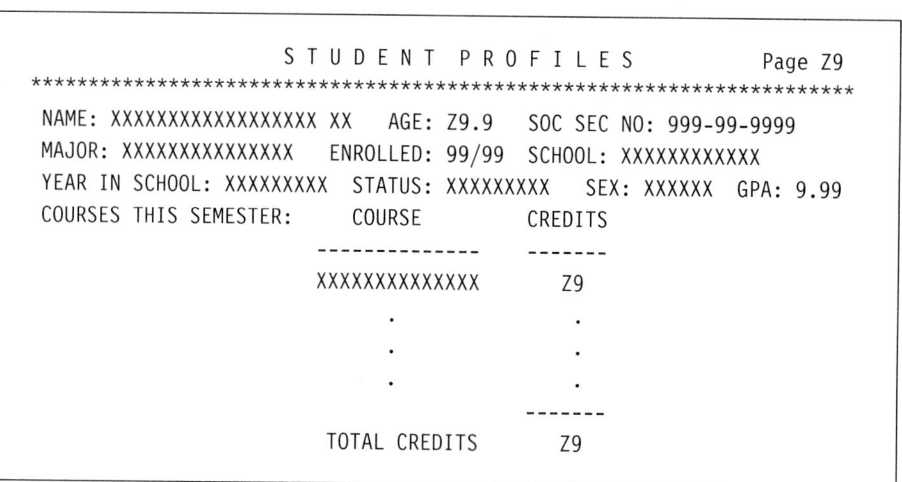

```
                    S T U D E N T   P R O F I L E S          Page Z9
***********************************************************************
NAME: XXXXXXXXXXXXXXXXXX XX   AGE: Z9.9   SOC SEC NO: 999-99-9999
MAJOR: XXXXXXXXXXXXXXX   ENROLLED: 99/99  SCHOOL: XXXXXXXXXXXX
YEAR IN SCHOOL: XXXXXXXXX  STATUS: XXXXXXXXX   SEX: XXXXXX  GPA: 9.99
COURSES THIS SEMESTER:      COURSE              CREDITS
                         --------------         -------
                         XXXXXXXXXXXXXX            Z9
                               .                    .
                               .                    .
                               .                    .
                                                -------
                          TOTAL CREDITS            Z9
```

Processing Requirements:

1. Process a file of student records, printing a complete student profile for each record.
2. Two students are to appear on each page, with eight blank lines after the last line of the first profile on each page. The page number and literal heading S T U D E N T P R O F I L E S are to appear only before the first profile on each page.
3. The detailed layout for each profile can be seen from the report layout. Additional specifications are given in items 4–11.
4. Student age is to be calculated from date of birth and date of program execution.

5. The social security number requires the insertion of hyphens; accomplish this by defining an output picture containing blanks in appropriate positions and then replace the blanks through the INSPECT verb.

6. The status of the student is either part-time or full-time. Part-time students take fewer than 12 credits per semester.

7. GPA is defined as the cumulative points divided by the cumulative credits and does not include credits taken this semester. Calculate this field to two decimal places.

8. Year in school is a function of cumulative credits and again does not include credits taken this semester. Freshmen have completed fewer than 30; sophomores between 30 and 59, inclusive; juniors between 60 and 89, inclusive; and seniors 90 or more.

9. The incoming STU-SCHOOL-CODE is to be expanded via a direct lookup. Hard-code the following table in your program:

CODE	SCHOOL	CODE	SCHOOL
1	BUSINESS	3	ENGINEERING
2	LIBERAL ARTS	4	EDUCATION

10. The incoming STU-MAJOR-CODE is to be expanded via a sequential search. Hard-code the following major table:

CODE	MAJOR	CODE	MAJOR
STA	STATISTICS	ECO	ECONOMICS
FIN	FINANCE	FRL	FOREIGN LANG
MKT	MARKETING	EEN	ELECTRICAL ENG
MAN	MANAGEMENT	MEN	MECHANICAL ENG
EDP	DATA PROCESSING	CEN	CHEMICAL ENG
PHY	PHYSICS	IEN	INDUSTRIAL ENG
ENG	ENGLISH	ELE	ELEMENTARY EDUC
BIO	BIOLOGY	SEE	SECONDARY EDUC
HIS	HISTORY	SPE	SECONDARY EDUC

11. Expand each value of STU-COURSE-NUMBER to an expanded course name using a binary search. An incoming record contains up to seven courses; blanks (that is, spaces) appear in an incoming record with fewer than seven courses.

12. The table of course codes is to be established by reading values from a separate COURSE-FILE, with the following format: course code in positions 1–3 and course

name in positions 4–18. The maximum table length is 100 courses, and the table of course codes appears below:

CODE	COURSE	CODE	COURSE
100	ENGLISH I	503	EUR HISTORY
111	COMPUTER SCI	504	ECONOMICS
140	SPANISH I	505	POL SCIENCE
150	MUSIC	506	CREATIVE WRIT
160	ART APPREC	555	EDUC THEORY
200	BIOLOGY	601	COBOL
222	CHEMISTRY	666	PSYCHOLOGY
300	CALCULUS	675	SPECIAL EDUC
333	ELECT ENG 1	700	THESIS
501	AM HISTORY		

Project 12-3

Program Name: Furniture Shipments

Narrative: This program takes Project 11-3 and adds table lookups for warehouse and item information.

Input File: FURNITURE-FILE and ITEM-FILE (see processing requirement 1a)

Input Record Layout:

```
01  FURNITURE-RECORD.
    05  FURN-INVOICE-NO                    PIC 9(5).
    05  FURN-CUSTOMER-NAME-N-INITIALS      PIC X(18).
    05  FURN-DELIVERY-INFO.
        10  FURN-DELIVERY-WAREHOUSE        PIC X.
        10  FURN-DELIVERY-DATE             PIC 9(6).
    05  FURN-ORDER-INFO.
        10  FURN-DEPOSIT-PERCENT           PIC 9V99.
        10  FURN-NO-ITEMS-ORDERED          PIC 9.
        10  FURN-ITEMS-ORDERED  OCCURS 1 TO 3 TIMES
                DEPENDING ON FURN-NO-ITEMS-ORDERED.
            15  FURN-ITEM-NO               PIC 9(4).
```

Test Data:

```
                  1         2         3         4         5         6
         1234567890123456789012345678901234567890123456789012345678901234 5
23485EDELSTEIN, M      A06109200521345138 6
12834ALIAS, Y          B07249200421787179 8
79845RAHIM, S          A0927920073230023502375
59789KELLY, C          B08249200323609365 0
85778WILSON, D         C0712920123457545904598
47597GUDAT, G          A06289200821345139 7
58684HYMOWITZ, A       C102892009123 50
48577BOOZ, B           C1212920283459936093650
56749HENNESSY, L       A090992004155 00
95877MOHD-RAZALLI      B011293078113 45
38476THOMPSON, J       A09239200911397139 9
48565JACOMINO, R       A09239201021397134 5
67566DESCHPELLES, M    B07049200921787179 8
09777SANCHEZ-CARRION, VC08129200222350459 9
48576WENNEMAN, M       B081692004123 00
45337AL-DAKHIL, A      A072292005155 00
47567HARDING, J        C08229200221345139 7
```

Report Layout: Use the same report layout as Project 11-3, but expand the warehouse from the table lookups in both the detail and summary reports. Include the item number in the detail report.

Processing Requirements:

1. Follow the same processing requirements as Project 11-3 with the following changes.
   a. Note that the item description, item cost, and item weight have been replaced in the input record layout by a single item number. Determine the description, cost, and weight via a binary lookup. Initialize the following table by reading values from a separate ITEM-FILE and input-load it:

Item #	Description	Cost	Weight	Item #	Description	Cost	Weight
1345	72" Sofa	$2,300.00	100	2375	Nightstand	$300.00	45
1386	Love Seat	$1,300.00	80	3609	Desk	$450.00	98
1397	Chair	$545.00	50	3650	Desk Chair	$395.50	45
1399	Ottoman	$350.00	40	4575	Dining Table	$3,575.50	135
1787	Sofa Table	$600.00	50	4590	6 Dining Chairs	$1,278.00	200
1798	End Table	$545.50	35	4598	Console	$2,225.50	115
2300	Dresser	$4,300.00	95	4599	Credenza	$1,235.00	250
2350	Armoire	$5,500.00	100	5500	Pool Table	$2,300.00	250

   b. The warehouse code is to be expanded via a sequential lookup. Hard-code the following table in your program:

Warehouse Code	Description
A	Miami
B	N. Carolina
C	New York

Project 12-4

Program Name: Computer Status Report

Narrative: This program takes Project 11-4 and adds table lookups for payment method, status, and component information.

Input File: COMPUTER-FILE and COMPONENT-FILE (see processing requirement 1a)

Input Record Layout:

```
01  COMPUTER-RECORD.
    05  COM-INVOICE-NO              PIC 9(5).
    05  COM-CUSTOMER-NAME           PIC X(18).
    05  COM-PAYMENT-METHOD          PIC XX.
    05  COM-SHIP-INFO.
        10  COM-SHIP-STATUS         PIC X.
        10  COM-SHIP-CHARGE         PIC 99V99.
    05  COM-COMPONENT-INFO.
        10  COM-NO-COMPONENTS       PIC 9.
        10  COM-COMPONENTS  OCCURS 1 TO 4 TIMES
                DEPENDING ON COM-NO-COMPONENTS.
            15  COM-COMPONENT-NO    PIC 9(4).
```

Test Data:

```
         1         2         3         4         5         6
12345678901234567890123456789012345678901234567890123456789012345
12834Blanco, Erick     AM14550243306250
79845Casali, Joseph    AM37500233050008120
59789Davis, Kevin      VI16550243305000
85778Demler, Linda     CO380254330055009201675O
47597Echavarria, FelipeCK26500243308250
58684Flemming, Sharon  MC14500245005500
48577Gonzalez, Maria   VI13500345006750930O
56749Katan, Maharan    CK2450013250
95877Parmenter, Donita CO33500242509001
38476Pinkwasser, Randi VI3890044660650055009300
37586Stewart, Roberto  CK25000232507000
```

Report Layout: Use the same report layout as Project 11-4, but expand the status and payment method from the table lookups in both the detail and summary reports. Include the component number in the detail line.

Processing Requirements:

1. Follow the same processing requirements as Project 11-4 with the following changes.
   a. Note that the component description and cost have been replaced in the input record layout by a single component number. Determine the description and cost via a binary lookup for the detail report. Initialize the following table by reading values from a separate COMPONENT-FILE and input-load it:

Component	Description	Cost	Component	Description	Cost
3250	386 25MHz	$1,295.00	6250	2400 BAUD Modem	$99.00
3330	386 33MHz	$1,595.00	6500	9600 BAUD Modem	$299.00
3400	386 DX40	$2,049.00	6750	Modem/FAX Card	$119.00
4250	425 Notebook	$1,995.00	7000	FAX	$1,279.00
4330	486 33MHz	$1,995.00	8120	Tape Backup Unit 120	$189.00
4500	486 DX2 50MHz	$2,295.00	8250	Tape Backup Unit 250	$250.00
4660	486 DX2 66MHz	$1,895.00	9001	CD/ROM	$345.00
5000	Laser Printer	$1,399.00	9201	Coprocessor	$99.00
5500	Dot Matrix Printer	$169.00	9300	Sound Blaster	$139.00

b. The status code (printed in both the detail and summary reports) is to be expanded via a binary lookup. Hard-code the following table in your program:

Status	Description
1	Assembly
2	Packing
3	Testing

c. The payment method code is to be expanded via a sequential lookup. Hard-code the following table in your program:

Payment Code	Method of Payment
AM	American Express
MC	MasterCard
VI	Visa
CO	COD
CK	Check

Project 12-5

Program Name: Credit Report

Narrative: This program takes Project 11-5 and adds table lookups for the interest rate, credit limit, and account type.

Input File: CREDIT-FILE

Input Record Layout: Use the same record layout as Project 11-5.

Test Data: Use the same test data as Project 11-5.

Report Layout: Use the same report layout as Project 11-5, but expand the account type with the appropriate description.

Processing Requirements: 1. Follow the same processing requirement as Project 11-5 with the following changes.

a. Determine the description, credit limit, and interest rate via a sequential lookup. Hard-code the following table:

Type	Description	Credit Limit	Interest Rate
20	Regular	$1,500	18.5%
40	3Pay	$3,500	0%
60	Household	$5,500	17.5%

Project 12-6

Program Name: Software Cost Analysis

Narrative: This program takes Project 11-6 and adds table lookups for product line description.

Input File: SOFTWARE-FILE

Input Record Layout: Use the same record layout as Project 11-6.

Test Data: Use the same test data as Project 11-6.

Report Layout: Use the same report layout as Project 11-6, but expand the product line with the appropriate description.

Processing Requirements: 1. Use the processing requirements from Project 11-6 and add the following:

a. The product line code should be expanded in the summary report using the following code definitions:

Code	Product Line	Code	Product Line
G	Games	D	Drawing/Graphics
B	Business Applications	E	Educational
U	Utility Applications	M	Miscellaneous

b. Today's date is to be printed as shown on the report layout. The current month is to be expanded via a direct lookup. Hard-code the following table in your program:

Month	Expanded Month	Month	Expanded Month
1	January	7	July
2	February	8	August
3	March	9	September
4	April	10	October
5	May	11	November
6	June	12	December

Project 12-7

Program Name: Catalog Orders Program

Narrative: Develop a program to calculate the total orders and the total handling charges for the Regal Catalog Company's monthly orders. The order file has been sorted by date.

Input File: CATALOG-ORDER-FILE and HANDLING-CLASS-FILE (see processing requirement 7)

Input Record Layout:

```
01  CATALOG-ORDER-RECORD.
    05  CAT-ITEM-NO                        PIC 9(4).
    05  CAT-DATE.
        10  CAT-MONTH                      PIC 99.
        10  CAT-DAY                        PIC 99.
        10  CAT-YEAR                       PIC 99.
    05  CAT-QUANTITY                       PIC 9(3).
    05  CAT-PRICE                          PIC 9(3)99.
    05  CAT-HANDLING-CLASS                 PIC X.
```

Test Data:

```
         1         2         3         4         5         6
123456789012345678901234567890123456789012345678901234567890123456789012345
441401048901011545A
177801208901047995G
313101298904004995E
118301318901008995D
476502058902008925F
599202148901007945C
518602188901043500F
347502228902008995E
834402288901005495B
```

Report Layout: Design your own report layout in accordance with the processing specifications.

Processing Requirements:

1. Process a file of catalog orders to determine the monthly total for orders and handling charges.
2. Print the month's orders with five blank lines between each month. Print an appropriate heading at the beginning of each new month.
3. The detailed layout can be determined from the report layout. Additional specifications are given in items 4–7.
4. The incoming CAT-MONTH is to be expanded via a direct lookup. Hard-code the following table in your program:

Month	Expanded Month	Month	Expanded Month
1	January	7	July
2	February	8	August
3	March	9	September
4	April	10	October
5	May	11	November
6	June	12	December

5. The incoming CAT-ITEM-NO is to be expanded via a binary search. Input-load the following item table:

Item No.	Item Description	Item No.	Item Description
1183	Portable Phone	4414	Chess Set
1778	20" Television	4765	Table Lamp
2686	Coffee Maker	5186	35mm Camera
3131	Ceiling Fan	5992	Tennis Racquet
3475	Bedspread	8344	Vase

6. Total price is calculated by multiplying the quantity by the price per item.
7. The incoming CAT-HANDLING-CLASS is to be expanded via a sequential search. The table for handling classes is to be established by reading values from a separate HANDLING-CLASS-FILE, with the following format: handling class code in position 1 and handling charges in positions 2–5. The maximum table length is 26. The table of class codes is shown:

Code	Handling Charges
A	6.25
B	12.00
C	14.25
D	16.50
E	18.50
F	21.25
G	25.50

Project 12-8

Program Name: Check Register

Narrative: The dollar amount of any check is written out in words, in addition to appearing as a number. This project is intended to accomplish that conversion.

Input File: CHECKING-ACCOUNT-FILE

Input Record Layout:

```
01  CHECKING-RECORD.
    05  CHECK-NUMBER               PIC 9(4).
    05  CHECK-AMOUNT               PIC 9(5).
```

Test Data:

```
111101234
222245000
333345200
444445986
666645906
777700689
888800089
999900008
100001000
200000100
300023000
```

Report Layout: The resulting report need not be elaborate. All that is required is a single detail line for each input record, containing the dollar amount and associated conversion.

Processing Requirements:

1. Read a file of checking account records.
2. For each record read:
   a. Convert the dollar amount to a written amount, with the word "dollars" appended at the end; for example, 234 should be converted to TWO HUNDRED THIRTY-FOUR DOLLARS.
   b. Cents are not included; that is, all incoming amounts are integer amounts. The maximum dollar amount to be converted is 99,999.
   c. The report is to contain one line for each record, with the amount expressed in both numbers and words.

PROGRAMMING SPECIFICATIONS

Project 13-1

Program Name: Grade Distributions

Narrative: The registrar's office is trying to determine whether a student's GPA (grade point average) improves with age and/or year in school. Accordingly, develop a program to process a set of student records, and print the necessary information in tabular form.

Input File: STUDENT-FILE

Input Record Layout:

```
01  STUDENT-RECORD-IN.
    05  STU-PERSONAL-INFO.
        10  STU-SOC-SEC-NUMBER          PIC 9(9).
        10  STU-NAME-AND-INITIALS.
            15  STU-LAST-NAME           PIC X(18).
            15  STU-INITIALS            PIC XX.
        10  STU-DATE-OF-BIRTH.
            15  STU-BIRTH-MONTH         PIC 99.
            15  STU-BIRTH-YEAR          PIC 99.
        10  STU-SEX                     PIC X.
    05  STU-SCHOOL-INFO.
```

```
          10  STU-MAJOR-CODE               PIC X(3).
          10  STU-SCHOOL-CODE              PIC 9.
          10  STU-CUMULATIVE-CREDITS       PIC 999.
          10  STU-CUMULATIVE-POINTS        PIC 999.
          10  STU-UNION-MEMBER-CODE        PIC X.
          10  STU-SCHOLARSHIP              PIC 999.
          10  STU-DATE-OF-ENROLLMENT       PIC 9(4).
      05  STU-COURSE-INFO.
          10  STU-COURSES-THIS-SEMESTER OCCURS 7 TIMES.
              15  STU-COURSE-NUMBER        PIC XXX.
              15  STU-COURSE-CREDITS       PIC 9.
```

Test Data:

```
         1         2         3         4         5         6         7         8
12345678901234567890123456789012345678901234567890123456789012345678901234567890

100000000ALBERT            A 0171MSTA1059118Y01509921002200330044004501360026011
200000000BROWN             B 0270FSTA1089275N025099210022003300440004
300000000CHARLES           GG0672MHIS2109286Y100099350135033504350535063
400000000SMITH             D 0770FXXX2090269N010099210022003300441194
500000000BAKER             EF1072MGEN3032049Y00009942223333334443
600000000GULFMAN           SF1173FELE4029059N00009932003333344435553666367527001
700000000BOROW             JS1275MIEN3030090Y0000992222 3
800000000MILGROM           MB0376F    5015045Y00009931113138315031603
900000000MILLER            K 0174MFRL2015054Y00009931113140 31503
999919999WAYNE             N 0472FHIS2090270Y0000994501350335043505 3
```

Report Layout:

```
               GRADE DISTRIBUTIONS BY AGE AND YEAR

                          AVERAGE GPA

                  UNDER 21          21 AND OVER

     FRESHMAN       9.99               9.99
     SOPHOMORE      9.99               9.99
     JUNIOR         9.99               9.99
     SENIOR         9.99               9.99
```

Processing Requirements:

1. Process a file of student records, and for each record read:
   a. Calculate the student's age from the date of execution and the student's birth date.
   b. Year in school is a function of cumulative credits and does not include the credits taken this semester. Freshmen have completed fewer than 30 credits; sophomores between 30 and 59, inclusive; juniors between 60 and 89, inclusive; and seniors 90 or more.
   c. The GPA is defined as the cumulative points divided by the cumulative credits and does not include credits taken this semester. Calculate this field to two decimal places.
   d. Determine the age and year classification as implied by the 4 x 2 table in the report layout; that is, determine in which of the eight age-year combinations the record belongs, and increment an appropriate counter.

2. When all records have been read, print the required table. In order to compute the necessary statistics, you will have to maintain two 4 x 2 tables. The entries in one table will be a cumulative total of the GPA for each age-year combination. The entries in the second table will be number of students in the age-year combination. At the conclusion of processing, divide the eight entries in the first table by their corresponding entries in the second table.

Project 13-2

Program Name: Movies

Narrative: Develop a program to compute the amount due the hundreds of movie extras who participated in the latest Hollywood extravaganza.

Input File: MOVIE-EXTRA-FILE

Input Record Layout:

POSITIONS	FIELD	PICTURE
1–9	SOC-SEC-NUMBER	9(9)
10–27	NAME	X(18)
28–29	MOVIE-EXPERIENCE	99
30	TYPE-ROLE	X
31–34	HOURS-WORKED	999V9
35–36	EXPANDED-ROLE	XX

Test Data:

```
         1         2         3         4         5         6
12345678901234567890123456789012345678901234567890123456789012345

000000001JONES, J.         00G0800GN
000000002JONES, ROY        02F0450FA
000000003WILLIAMS, JOHN    01E0450EA
000000004FOSTER, RAYMOND   11B0425BN
000000005HIGH, LUCY        08A0450AR
000000006HARDING, HOWARD   04A0450AV
000000007ZHE, KEVIN        05D0450DN
000000008JENNINGS, VIVIAN  D0200DA
000000009ROOSEVELT, TIMOTHY07E0230XX
000000010TRUELOVE, BILL    09G0450EN
```

Report Layout:

```
                        HOLLYWOOD EXTRAVAGANZA, INC.                              PAGE Z9

SOC SEC NO   MOVIE EXTRA            EXP   ROLE   HOURLY-RATE  REG-HOURS  EXTRA-HOURS    PAY
999-99-9999  XXXXXXXXXXXXXXXXXXXX   99     X       $Z9.99       ZZ9.9        Z9      $$,$$9.99
    .             .                  .     .         .            .          .           .
    .             .                  .     .         .            .          .           .
    .             .                  .     .         .            .          .           .
```

Processing Requirements:

1. Process a file of pay records for movie extras, to determine the pay owed to each individual.

2. An hourly pay scale is used, with the individual's hourly rate a function of the type of role and his or her experience in previous movies. The following table contains the pay scale and is to be hard-coded in your program:

Type of Role	Previous experience (number of movies)						
	0	1	2	3	4	5-7	8 and Up
A	20.00	25.00	30.00	32.00	34.00	38.00	40.00
B	14.00	17.00	18.00	19.00	21.00	23.00	24.00
C	7.00	7.00	7.50	8.00	8.50	8.50	9.00
D	4.00	4.00	5.00	5.50	5.50	6.00	6.00
E	3.75	4.50	5.00	5.25	5.25	5.50	5.50
F	3.50	3.50	3.50	3.75	3.75	3.75	4.00

The number of previous movies for an individual must be converted into a number from 1 to 7, so that it can be used as a subscript for access into the table.

3. Incoming pay records are to be checked for valid data; specifically:
   a. Verify that the value in MOVIE-EXPERIENCE is numeric; if not, display an error message and do no further processing for that record.
   b. Verify that the value in TYPE-ROLE is valid (i.e., A, B, C, D, E, or F); if not, display an error message and do no further processing for that record.

4. Each employee is to receive, as a bonus, a number of extra hours (not appearing on the employee's pay record), for which the employee will be paid at his or her regular hourly rate. The number of extra hours is a function of the EXPANDED-ROLE field in the incoming record as shown in the following table:

Expanded Role	Extra Hours	Expanded Role	Extra Hours
AA	01	DN	08
AV	01	DR	09
BA	03	EA	14
BN	05	EN	03
CA	05	ER	03
CN	04	FA	01
DA	08	FN	06

5. The bonus table for extra hours is in ascending sequence by the expanded role field. Use a binary search to determine the number of extra hours an individual will receive; that is, if a match is found, take the hours shown in the table and add it to the hours in the incoming record to determine pay. If no match is found, do not add any extra hours. An individual with no extra hours will be paid just for the number of hours on his or her incoming record.

6. The printed report should print no more than four valid records per page. (The employees with invalid data should be displayed in a separate error report.) Double-space between detail lines.

Project 13-3

Program Name: Two-level Tables

Narrative: This program illustrates two-level tables and PERFORM VARYING in two dimensions. Incoming employee records are checked for one of three locations and one of two performance levels, producing six location-performance combinations. The average salary for each of these six combinations is computed.

Input File: EMPLOYEE-FILE

Input Record Layout:

```
01  EMPLOYEE-RECORD-IN.
    05  EMP-PERSONAL-INFO.
        10  EMP-SOC-SEC-NUM         PIC X(9).
        10  EMP-NAME-AND-INITIALS   PIC X(16).
        10  EMP-DATE-OF-BIRTH.
            15  EMP-BIRTH-MONTH     PIC 9(2).
            15  EMP-BIRTH-YEAR      PIC 9(2).
    05  EMP-COMPANY-INFO.
        10  EMP-DATE-OF-HIRE.
            15  EMP-HIRE-MONTH      PIC 9(2).
            15  EMP-HIRE-YEAR       PIC 9(2).
        10  EMP-LOCATION-CODE       PIC 9(2).
        10  EMP-EDUCATION-CODE      PIC 9.
        10  EMP-TITLE-DATA.
            15  EMP-TITLE-CODE      PIC 9(3).
            15  EMP-TITLE-DATE      PIC 9(4).
        10  EMP-PERFORMANCE         PIC 9.
        10  EMP-SALARY              PIC 9(5).
```

Test Data:

```
         1         2         3         4         5         6
12345678901234567890123456789012345678901234567890123456789012345

354679876KERBEL, NX      07590190802564068311 5500
264480529CLARK, JS       11600791303999018412 5300
223340090HUMMER, MR      07520292806734068314 3980
556667856BENWAY, CX      09591192605999018413 2554
667893343FITZPATRICK, DT 04570693803878018422 1550
433556767NORIEGA, LA     11600491602453068321 8500
455399829VOGEL, VD       03600693803233068312 4825
688773423BEINHORN, CB    09800892304455068312 9850
100334234GARCIA, PJ      07590190602564068321 2000
899843328TOWER, DR       05600790303999018411 9000
776338380MCDONALD, J     07531190806734068315 4380
```

Report Layout:

```
                LOCATION/PERFORMANCE AVERAGE SALARY REPORT

LOCATION          HIGH PERFORMANCE          LOW PERFORMANCE
MIAMI                 ZZ,ZZ9.99               ZZ,ZZ9.99
LOS ANGELES           ZZ,ZZ9.99               ZZ,ZZ9.99
NEW YORK              ZZ,ZZ9.99               ZZ,ZZ9.99
```

Processing Requirements:

1. Read a file of employee records.
2. For each record read, determine if the employee is in Miami (code 30), Los Angeles (code 60), or New York (code 80) and has a performance rating of 1 (high performance) or 2 (low performance). Any employee meeting both requirements—that is, an employee with a valid location and performance rating—is a qualified employee. No further processing is necessary for nonqualified employees.
3. Establish a 3-by-2 table to compute salary statistics for the 6 location-performance combinations. Rows 1, 2, and 3 are for Miami, Los Angeles, and New York. Columns 1 and 2 designate high and low performance, respectively.
4. For each qualified employee:
   a. Determine the appropriate row-column (i.e., location-performance) combination.
   b. Increment the total of all employee salaries for that row-column combination by this employee's salary.
   c. Increment the number of employees in that row-column combination by 1.
5. When all employees have been processed, divide the total salaries for each combination by the number of employees in that combination, producing the average salary for that combination. Produce the required report shown in the report layout, showing the six values of average salary.

Project 13-4

Program Name: Three-level Tables

Narrative: This program extends the previous project to illustrate three-level tables and PERFORM VARYING in three dimensions. Incoming employee records are checked for one of three locations, one of six education codes, and one of two performance levels, producing 36 location-education-performance combinations. The average salary for each of these 36 combinations is computed.

Input File: EMPLOYEE-FILE

Input Record Layout: Same as Project 13-3.

Test Data: Same as Project 13-3.

Report Layout:

```
              AVERAGE SALARY REPORT FOR LOCATION: MIAMI

EDUCATION LEVEL   HIGH PERFORMANCE            LOW PERFORMANCE
  GRADE SCHOOL         ZZ,ZZ9.99                  ZZ,ZZ9.99
  HIGH SCHOOL          ZZ,ZZ9.99                  ZZ,ZZ9.99
  ASSOCIATE            ZZ,ZZ9.99                  ZZ,ZZ9.99
  BACHELOR             ZZ,ZZ9.99                  ZZ,ZZ9.99
  MASTER               ZZ,ZZ9.99                  ZZ,ZZ9.99
  DOCTORATE            ZZ,ZZ9.99                  ZZ,ZZ9.99
```

```
              AVERAGE SALARY REPORT FOR LOCATION: LOS ANGELES

EDUCATION LEVEL   HIGH PERFORMANCE            LOW PERFORMANCE
  GRADE SCHOOL         ZZ,ZZ9.99                  ZZ,ZZ9.99
  HIGH SCHOOL          ZZ,ZZ9.99                  ZZ,ZZ9.99
  ASSOCIATE            ZZ,ZZ9.99                  ZZ,ZZ9.99
  BACHELOR             ZZ,ZZ9.99                  ZZ,ZZ9.99
  MASTER               ZZ,ZZ9.99                  ZZ,ZZ9.99
  DOCTORATE            ZZ,ZZ9.99                  ZZ,ZZ9.99
```

```
              AVERAGE SALARY REPORT FOR LOCATION: NEW YORK

EDUCATION LEVEL   HIGH PERFORMANCE            LOW PERFORMANCE
  GRADE SCHOOL         ZZ,ZZ9.99                  ZZ,ZZ9.99
  HIGH SCHOOL          ZZ,ZZ9.99                  ZZ,ZZ9.99
  ASSOCIATE            ZZ,ZZ9.99                  ZZ,ZZ9.99
  BACHELOR             ZZ,ZZ9.99                  ZZ,ZZ9.99
  MASTER               ZZ,ZZ9.99                  ZZ,ZZ9.99
  DOCTORATE            ZZ,ZZ9.99                  ZZ,ZZ9.99
```

Processing Requirements:

1. Read a file of employee records.
2. For each record read, determine if the employee is in Miami, Los Angeles, or New York; has an education code of 1 through 6 for Grade School, High School, Associate, Bachelor, Master, and Doctorate; and has a performance rating of 1 (high performance) or 2 (low performance). Any employee meeting all three requirements—that is, an employee with a valid location, education, and performance rating—is a qualified employee. No further processing is necessary for nonqualified employees.
3. Establish a 3-by-6-by-2 table to compute salary statistics for the 36 location-education-performance combinations. Each location contains rows 1 through 6 for Grade School, High School, Associate, Bachelor, Master, and Doctorate; and columns 1 and 2 designate high and low performance, respectively.
4. For each qualified employee:
   a. Determine the appropriate row-column (i.e., education-performance) combination for each location.
   b. Increment the total of all employee salaries for that row-column combination for each location by this employee's salary.

c. Increment the number of employees in that row-column combination for that location by 1.

5. When all employees have been processed, divide the total salaries for each combination by the number of employees in that combination, producing the average salary for that combination. Produce the required report shown in the report layout, showing the 36 values of average salary, printing every location on a separate page.

Project 13-5

Program Name: Payroll Program

Narrative: Develop a program to print complete paycheck (including a check stub) and a payroll journal reflecting all checks printed.

Input File: PAYROLL-FILE

Input Record Layout:

```
01  PAYROLL-RECORD-IN.
    05  PAY-SOC-SEC-NUM          PIC 9(9).
    05  PAY-NAME.
        10  PAY-LAST             PIC X(14).
        10  PAY-FIRST            PIC X(12).
        10  PAY-INITIAL          PIC X.
    05  PAY-INFO.
        10  PAY-HOURLY-RATE      PIC 9(3)V99.
        10  PAY-HOURS-WORKED     PIC 9(3)V99.
        10  PAY-SALARY-TYPE      PIC X.
        10  PAY-DEPENDENTS       PIC 99.
        10  PAY-TAX-STATUS       PIC 9.
        10  PAY-INSURANCE        PIC X.
    05  PAY-YTD-INFO.
        10  PAY-YTD-EARNINGS     PIC 9(6)V99.
        10  PAY-YTD-TAXES        PIC 9(5)V99.
        10  PAY-YTD-FICA         PIC 9(4)V99.
        10  PAY-YTD-INSURANCE    PIC 9(3)V99.
```

Test Data: Use the validated payroll file from Project 8-3.

Report Layout:

```
                                ANDREW INC.                                              PAGE Z9
                       PAYROLL JOURNAL AS OF 99/99/99
                                                                 DEDUCTIONS
                                                  GROSS    ------------------------------
SOC SEC NO    NAME                              EARNINGS     TAXES      FICA   INSURANCE    NET PAY
999-99-9999   XXXXXXXXXXXXXX, XXXXXXXXXXXX X.  ZZ,ZZ9.99  Z,ZZ9.99  Z,ZZ9.99    Z9.99    ZZ,ZZ9.99
     .                     .                        .          .         .         .            .
     .                     .                        .          .         .         .            .
     .                     .                        .          .         .         .            .
                                               ---------- --------- ---------  -------   ----------
                                               ZZZ,ZZ9.99 ZZ,ZZ9.99 ZZ,ZZ9.99   ZZ9.99   ZZZ,ZZ9.99
```

Processing Requirements:

1. Read a file of payroll records.
2. For each record read calculate:
   a. Gross earnings, which is dependent on salary type (salaried or hourly) and can be calculated in one of two ways:
      (1) Salaried employees are not paid overtime. Gross pay for salaried employees is rate of pay multiplied by the standard 40 hours. If hours exceed 40, place an asterisk (*) next to the hours worked in the detail line of the payroll journal and calculate the gross earnings using 40 hours.
      (2) Hourly employees are paid overtime at a rate of time and a half for hours beyond 40 through 48 and double time for hours beyond 48.
   b. The yearly taxes, which are dependent on two factors: tax status and yearly salary. This amount is divided by 52 to obtain the weekly tax deduction.
      (1) The tax status is used to determine the proper tax table. Establish a two-level table with the following information to determine the taxes deducted (you may pick the type of initialization and lookup technique):

Head of Household				
Yearly salary over -	but not over	The tax is:		of the amount over -
0	24,850	$0	+ 15%	$0
24,850	64,200	$3,727.50	+ 28%	24,850
64,200	128,810	14,745.50	+ 33%	64,200

Married Filing Jointly				
Yearly salary over -	but not over	The tax is:		of the amount over -
0	30,950	$0	+ 15%	$0
30,950	74,800	$4,642.50	+ 28%	30,950
74,800	128,810	16,934.50	+ 33%	74,800

Single				
Yearly salary over -	but not over	The tax is:		of the amount over -
0	18,500	$0	+ 15%	$0
18,500	44,900	$2,782.50	+ 28%	18,500
44,900	93,130	10,160.50	+ 33%	44,900

Married Filing Separately				
Yearly salary over -	but not over	The tax is:		of the amount over -
0	15,475	$0	+ 15%	$0
15,475	37,425	$2,321.50	+ 28%	15,475
37,425	117,895	8,467.50	+ 33%	37,425

(2) Yearly salary for both salaried and hourly employees is estimated based on a 40-hour week and a 52-week year.

c. FICA deduction, which is calculated as 7.51% of gross pay for the first $56,000. After year-to-date earnings reach $56,000, no FICA will be deducted.

d. Insurance deducted, which is also determined by the type of insurance plan and number of dependents. Determine the insurance deducted via a table lookup in the following two-level table:

Number of Dependents	Health Plan		
	Blue Cross	**AvMed**	**Humana**
1	14.00	10.00	10.00
2	15.00	12.00	12.00
3	20.00	15.00	15.00
4	23.00	18.00	18.00
5	25.00	24.00	24.00

Note: Beyond 5 dependents the cost of the plan remains the same. Therefore, an employee with 8 dependents pays the 5-dependent rate. No insurance is deducted for those with a Z (NO-INSURANCE).

e. Net earnings, which is calculated as gross earnings minus deductions (taxes, FICA [if any], and insurance [if any]).

3. Print a payroll journal detail line as shown in the report layout. Use the STRING statement to print the employee name in the following format:

   lastname, firstname initial

4. Print a heading on top of each new page. Each page is to contain 10 employees. The date of execution should appear on the heading as indicated.

5. When all records have been read, print totals for hours worked, gross pay, all deductions (taxes deducted, FICA deducted, insurance deducted), and net pay.

Project 13-6

Program Name: Extended Student Profile Program

Narrative: This program continues the student profile program of Project 12-2 by adding a summary report. The summary report will utilize a three-dimensional table to accumulate totals for each school, major within school, and year in school within major.

Input File: STUDENT-FILE and COURSE-FILE from Project 12-2

Input Record Layout: Use the same record layout as Project 12-2.

Test Data: Use the same test data as Project 12-2.

Report Layout:

```
                      S T U D E N T   P R O F I L E S          Page Z9
                   Summary Report for School of XXXXXXXXXX as of 99/99/99
***********************************************************************
                         Major: XXXXXXXXXXXXXXX
                            Number of       Total      Average
   Year in School           Students       Credits     Credits
     Freshman                  ZZ9          ZZ,ZZ9      Z,ZZ9
     Sophomore                  .             .           .
     Junior                     .             .           .
     Senior                     .             .           .
                            ---------    ----------   --------
   Totals                     Z,ZZ9         ZZZ,ZZ9     ZZ,ZZ9

***********************************************************************
                         Major: XXXXXXXXXXXXXXX
                            Number of       Total      Average
   Year in School           Students       Credits     Credits
       .                        .             .           .

  School of XXXXXXXXXX        ZZ,ZZ9     Z,ZZZ,ZZ9     ZZZ,ZZ9
```

Processing Requirements:

1. The following are additional processing requirements to Project 12-2 for the summary report:
   a. Create a 4 x 18 x 4 (3-dimensional) table to accumulate number of students and total credits for the appropriate school-major-year (in school) combination.
   b. When all records have been processed, print the summary as shown in the report layout. Each school should begin on a new page.

PROGRAMMING SPECIFICATIONS

Project 14-1

Program Name: Sorted Mucho Bucks Salary Report

Narrative: Develop a program to process pay records for the Mucho Bucks Company to produce salary totals. This large corporation has offices in several cities. Its personnel are also grouped into functional departments, and a given department can appear in more than one city and/or have multiple managers.

Input File: EMPLOYEE-FILE

Input Record Layout:

```
01  EMPLOYEE-RECORD-IN.
    05  EMP-NAME                        PIC X(10).
    05  EMP-SALARY                      PIC 9(5).
    05  EMP-DEDUCTION-PERCENTAGE        PIC 9V9(4).
    05  EMP-DEPARTMENT                  PIC 9(3).
    05  EMP-LOCATION                    PIC 9.
    05  EMP-MANAGER                     PIC X(10).
```

Test Data:

```
         1         2         3         4         5         6
123456789012345678901234567890123456789012345678901234567890123456789012345
WEBER     180000085025 02STUTZ
```

```
WEBER     18000008502502STUTZ
JACKSON   21000013003503RUSHNEK
WHEELER   24000010003002GILLENSON
BABSON    24000035002504VAZQUEZ
JONES     35000008501001VILLAR
TYLER     36000012302502STUTZ
KELLER    29000014503004ALVORD
GOODMAN   22000007753002ELOFSON
LEWIS     22000100002504VAZQUEZ
SMITH     24000005252001BARBER
HAYES     27000012502004ALVORD
DAVIS     25000012503503PLANT
ADAMS     25000004751001GRAUER
GORDON    22500085003002ELOFSON
ELSWORTH  28000012003503PLANT
CHARLES   27000006501001VILLAR
JOHNSON   28000012002004ALVORD
HAYWARD   31000025503503PLANT
ALLEN     30000018502001BARBER
BAKER     28000009751001GRAUER
```

Report Layout:

```
                      MUCHO BUCKS COMPANY                        PAGE Z9

   LOCATION  DEPARTMENT  EMPLOYEE         SALARY   DEDUCTION      NET PAY

   XXXXXXXX  XXXXXXXXXX  XXXXXXXXXX     $$$,$$9     $$$,$$9      $$$,$$9
      .          .             .            .           .            .
      .          .             .            .           .            .
      .          .             .            .           .            .
                                     ----------  ----------   ----------
     MUCHO BUCKS TOTAL               $$,$$$,$$9  $$,$$$,$$9   $$,$$$,$$9
```

Processing Requirements:

1. Sort the incoming employee file by location and within location by department.
2. Read the file of sorted employee records, and for each record read:
   a. Calculate the deduction by multiplying the salary by the deduction percentage.
   b. Expand the department number via a sequential table lookup:

DEPARTMENT #	DEPARTMENT NAME
100	Payroll
200	EDP
250	Marketing
300	Payroll
350	Sales

   c. Expand the location code via a direct lookup:

LOCATION CODE	LOCATION NAME
1	Atlanta
2	Boston
3	Chicago
4	Detroit

d. Print a detail line containing the information as shown in the report layout.

e. Increment the company totals.

3. Print the Mucho Bucks totals at the conclusion of the report.

Project 14-2

Program Name: Sorted Brokerage Report

Narrative: Write a program to process a brokerage firm's records in order to determine the commission earned for each customer.

Input File: CUSTOMER-FILE

Input Record Layout:

```
01  CUSTOMER-RECORD-IN.
    05  CUST-BROKER-NAME            PIC X(10).
    05  CUST-ACCOUNT-INFO.
        10  CUST-ACCOUNT-NO         PIC 9(4).
        10  CUST-ACCOUNT-TYPE       PIC 9.
    05  CUST-BRANCH                 PIC 99.
    05  CUST-CUSTOMER-NAME          PIC X(10).
    05  CUST-BALANCE                PIC 9(6)V99.
```

Test Data:

```
         1         2         3         4         5         6
12345678901234567890123456789012345678901234567890123456789012345
ANTONIO   3333120BARNEY    00023452
STEINMAN  8888310BARBER    00123456
MOLDOF    4444210GRAUER    01000000
ANTONIO   6666120GARCIA    00344444
MOLDOF    4444110GRAUER    00110050
STEINMAN  5555110SMITH     00112000
ANTONIO   6666220GARCIA    01066666
STEINMAN  5555210SMITH     00114321
GIBBS     1212110MASON     00356000
MOLDOF    7777110ALVORD    00232656
ANTONIO   3333220BARNEY    00123342
GIBBS     9999110GREGORY   01020000
ANTONIO   6666220JONES     00233333
GIBBS     9999210GREGORY   02340000
STEINMAN  8888210BARBER    00050000
GIBBS     1212210MASON     02135000
MOLDOF    7777210ALVORD    00025600
GIBBS     1212310MASON     00234000
STEINMAN  8888110BARBER    00678900
ANTONIO   6666320JONES     01155555
```

Report Layout:

```
                         FLY BY NITE BROKERAGE                    PAGE Z9
                          COMMISSION REPORT

 BRANCH    BROKER        ACCT TYPE         ACCT #   BALANCE     COMMISSION
XXXXXXXX XXXXXXXXXX XXXXXXXXXXXXXXXXXXX  9999  $$$$,$$9.99   $$,$$9.99
   .        .              .                .        .             .
   .        .              .                .        .             .
   .        .              .                .        .             .
                                               -------------  ----------
 FLY BY NITE TOTALS                            $$,$$$,$$9.99  $$$,$$9.99
```

Processing Requirements:

1. Sort the incoming broker file by branch, within branch by broker, and within broker by account type.
2. Read the file of sorted brokerage commission records, and for each record read:
   a. Determine the commission as follows: balances of $500 or less will be charged a minimum $20 commission fee. Balances over $500 will be charged a 4% commission fee.
   b. Print the commission information in that record on a detail line.
      (1) Expand the branch office via a sequential table lookup:

BRANCH OFFICE	BRANCH NAME
10	Chicago
20	New York

      (2) Expand the account type via a direct table lookup:

ACCOUNT TYPE	ACCOUNT TYPE NAME
1	Retirement
2	Checking Privileges
3	Stock Only

   c. Increment the appropriate totals as shown on the report layout.
3. After all records have been read, print a total line for Fly by Nite Brokerage.

Project 14-3

Program Name: Sorted Car Sales Program

Narrative: Develop a program to process a sales file in order to determine the amount earned by each salesperson.

Input File: SALES-FILE

Input Record Layout:

```
01  SALES-RECORD-IN.
    05  SA-DEALER              PIC X(8).
    05  SA-BRANCH              PIC 9(3).
    05  SA-SALESPERSON         PIC X(10).
    05  SA-SALES-INFO.
        05  SA-CUSTOMER        PIC X(10).
        05  SA-SALE-PRICE      PIC 9(6).
        05  SA-COMMISSION-RATE PIC 9V99.
    05  SA-CAR-INFO.
        10  SA-CAR-MAKE        PIC X(8).
        10  SA-CAR-MODEL       PIC X(8).
        10  SA-CAR-YEAR        PIC 9(4).
```

Test Data:

```
         1         2         3         4         5         6
12345678901234567890123456789012345678901234567890123456789012345

BROWARD 010GEHLE     MORENO    016125005TOYOTA  SUPRA   1990
DADE    110DAVERSA   RENESCA   004950002HYUNDAI EXCEL G 1990
BROWARD 020ROWE      VIERA     014300002STERLING825SL   1989
DADE    100RICO      GORMAN    038500004LEXUS   400 LS  1992
BROWARD 010SHIM      PORTO     025575004M BENZ  300E    1988
DADE    110FRENCH    DEGGS     009025004NISSAN  MAXIMA  1988
MONROE  210BOYER     PIRES     006125004MAZDA   626     1988
DADE    100RICO      CHUA      010700004TOYOTA  CAMRY DE1990
BROWARD 020ROWE      PINEDA    009200003AUDI    5000    1988
DADE    110DAVERSA   MCDONALD  040000005INFINITIQ45     1992
BROWARD 010GEHLE     LARSH     012475003PUEGOT  505GLS  1990
DADE    110FRENCH    SPEARS    010975001NISSAN  300Z    1988
BROWARD 020ROWE      TOCKMAN   027150006BMW     635 CSI 1988
MONROE  210BOYER     AUGUSMA   039799002M BENZ  560 SL  1988
BROWARD 010GEHLE     HOLME     9013700002HONDA  PRELUDE 1990
MONROE  210BOYER     LOUIS     010175004MAZDA   RX7 GXL 1990
BROWARD 010SHIM      REINMAN   009725002SAAB    900     1988
DADE    100RICO      DILEGO    015800004MAZDA   MIATA   1992
MONROE  210VASQUEZ   HAFEZ     032875003JAGUAR  XJ6     1990
DADE    110FRENCH    GRAHE     014750003BMW     325 ES  1988
MONROE  210VASQUEZ   HWANG     023000004LEGEND  COUPE LS1988
```

Report Layout:

```
                          VERY VERY NICE CARS INC.                        PAGE Z9

                        CAR INFORMATION                             COMMISSION      NET TO
DEALER   SALESPERSON  YEAR  MAKE     MODEL    CUSTOMER      PRICE      PAID         DEALER

XXXXXXXX XXXXXXXXXX   9999 XXXXXXXX XXXXXXXX XXXXXXXXXX ZZZ,ZZ9    ZZ,ZZ9.99     ZZZ,ZZ9.99
   .         .          .     .       .          .         .           .              .
   .         .          .     .       .          .         .           .              .
   .         .          .     .       .          .         .           .              .
                                                      ---------- ----------- -------------
 VERY VERY NICE CARS TOTALS                           $Z,ZZZ,ZZ9 $ZZZ,ZZ9.99 $Z,ZZZ,ZZ9.99
```

Processing Requirements:

1. Sort the incoming sales file by dealer, within dealer by salesperson, and within year by car make.
2. Read the file of sorted sales records, and for each record read:
   a. Calculate the commission paid to the salesperson by multiplying the sale amount by the commission rate.
   b. Calculate the net to the dealer by subtracting the commission from the sale amount.
   c. Print a detail line for each sale.
   d. Increment the totals as shown on the report layout.
3. After all records have been read, print Very Very Nice Cars totals. Skip three lines prior to printing the company total.

Project 14-4

Program Name: Sorted Bonus Program

Narrative: Write a program to process a bonus file to determine which employees are eligible for a bonus and the bonus amount.

Input File: BONUS-FILE

Input Record Layout:

```
01  BONUS-RECORD-IN.
    05  BO-MANU-PLANT       PIC XX.
    05  BO-DEPARTMENT       PIC X(8).
    05  BO-EMPLOYEE         PIC X(15).
    05  BO-MANAGER          PIC X(10).
    05  BO-SALARY           PIC 99999.
    05  BO-PERCENTAGE       PIC 9V99.
    05  BO-ELIGIBILTY       PIC X.
```

Test Data:

```
         1         2         3         4         5         6
123456789012345678901234567890123456789012345678901234567890123456
TNInteriorKnowles, CD    GARCIA    30100008Y
KYFenders Price, MD      VILLAR    24000000N
OHTrim    Inniss, ML     SPENCER   32000012Y
KYFenders Kanning, DS    VILLAR    28000008Y
OHPaint   Prates, LS     ALVORD    29000015Y
KYInteriorSangastiano, LAFEIN      32000011Y
TNTrim    Gibbs, GJ      JONES     26000006Y
KYFenders Barnabas, SJ   GRAUER    30000010Y
TNInteriorDavis, JL      GARCIA    31000007Y
OHPaint   Montes, J      ALVORD    27000012Y
KYFenders Lamania, NC    GRAUER    32000005Y
TNTrim    Romero, CM     WILLIAMS  32000018Y
OHPaint   Simonton, DM   ALVORD    25000000N
TNTrim    Wilson, RJ     JONES     24000000N
OHPaint   Keiler, M      SMITH     28000006Y
TNInteriorTwinn, SA      JAMES     22000004Y
OHPaint   Chua, CE       SMITH     31000007Y
KYInteriorAl-Askar, EK   BARBER    30100009Y
OHTrim    Cardone, J     FRANK     32000008Y
```

```
KYInteriorWinter, EK     FEIN       22000000N
TNTrim    Hess, AM       WILLIAMS   36000014Y
OHTrim    Boberg, DM     FRANK      36000012Y
KYInteriorBehrend, TR    BARBER     31000005Y
OHTrim    Smith, GM      FRANK      26000000N
KYFenders Giberson, CJ   GRAUER     34000015Y
TNTrim    Clasen, CC     JONES      32000010Y
OHTrim    Al-Khuwiter, A SPENCER    24000011Y
TNInteriorAlberni, WJ    JAMES      32000010Y
KYInteriorChilders, RL   BARBER     35000012Y
TNInteriorWarren, AE     JAMES      35000011Y
```

Report Layout:

```
                    FASSSTCARS MANUFACTURERS                         PAGE Z9

  PLANT  DEPT      MANAGER      SOC SEC NO    SALARY   BONUS      TOTAL
   XX   XXXXXXXX  XXXXXXXXXX   999-99-9999   ZZ,ZZ9   Z,ZZ9    ZZZ,ZZ9
   .      .           .             .           .        .          .
   .      .           .             .           .        .          .
   .      .           .             .           .        .          .
                                             --------- -------  ---------
    FASSSTCARS TOTALS                        Z,ZZZ,ZZ9  ZZ,ZZ9 Z,ZZZ,ZZ9
```

Processing Requirements:

1. Sort the incoming bonus file by plant, within plant by department, and within department by manager. Sort only the employees that are eligible for a bonus, that is, those that contain a "Y" in the eligibility field.
2. Read the file of sorted bonus records, and for each record read:
   a. Calculate the bonus amount by multiplying the salary by the bonus percentage.
   b. Calculate the total compensation by adding the salary and the bonus.
   c. Print a detail line as shown on the report layout.
   d. Increment the appropriate totals as shown on the report layout.
3. After all records have been read, print totals for Fassstcars.

Project 14-5

Program Name: Sorted Store Sales Commissions Program

Narrative: Develop a program to process sales records for the Needless Markup company. The report is to show sales, commissions paid, and net sales for each transaction.

Input File: SALES-FILE

Input Record Layout:

```
01 SALES-RECORD.
   05 SAL-PERSON-NAME          PIC X(10).
   05 SAL-DATE.
      10 SAL-MONTH             PIC 9(2).
      10 SAL-DAY               PIC 9(2).
```

```
        10  SAL-YEAR                   PIC 9(2).
    05  SAL-AMOUNT                     PIC 9(5)V99.
    05  SAL-COMMISSION-RATE            PIC V99.
    05  SAL-STORE-NUMBER               PIC 9(2).
    05  SAL-DEPARTMENT-NAME            PIC X(12).
```

Test Data:

```
ADAMS     0422900214000603DESIGNER
HILL      0431900009800501SPORTSWEAR
SMITH     0428900008000502LINGERIE
HARRISON  0423900002600504SPORTSWEAR
HILL      0409900036900401SHOES & BAGS
HARRISON  0418900012550504SPORTSWEAR
HILL      0415900026300401SHOES & BAGS
CLARK     0424900000455504LINGERIE
TURNER    0418900007500302ACCESSORIES
JONES     0425900025600501SPORTSWEAR
ADAMS     0416900839600603DESIGNER
CLARK     0415900047800504SPORTSWEAR
SMITH     0425900015500502LINGERIE
JONES     0430900015799501SPORTSWEAR
JONES     0403900023099401SHOES & BAGS
ADAMS     0408900031500503SPORTSWEAR
LUDLUM    0426900612099603DESIGNER
ADAMS     0405900083600503SPORTSWEAR
SMITH     0412900004525302ACCESSORIES
VANBERGER 0429900005500502LINGERIE
CLARK     0409900023799504SPORTSWEAR
HARRISON  0429900022500504LINGERIE
HARRISON  0430900249825604DESIGNER
```

Report Layout:

```
                    NEEDLESS MARKUP       99/99/99                        PAGE Z9

    STORE       DEPARTMENT    SALESPERSON   DATE        SALES    COMMISSION  NET SALES
XXXXXXXXXXXX  XXXXXXXXXXXX    XXXXXXXXXX  99/99/99    ZZ,ZZ9.99    Z,ZZ9.99  ZZ,ZZ9.99
     .              .              .         .            .           .          .
     .              .              .         .            .           .          .
     .              .              .         .            .           .          .
                                                     ----------   ---------  ----------
NEEDLESS MARKUP TOTALS                                ZZZ,ZZ9.99  ZZ,ZZ9.99  ZZZ,ZZ9.99
```

Processing Requirements:

1. Sort the incoming sales file by store, within store by department, and within department by salesperson.
2. Read the file of sorted sales records, and for each record read:
   a. Calculate the commission by multiplying the sales amount by the commission rate.
   b. Calculate the net sales by subtracting the commission from the sale amount.
   c. Expand the store code via a direct lookup:

LOCATION CODE	LOCATION NAME
1	Bal Harbor
2	Dadeland
3	The Galleria
4	Worth Avenue

d. Print a detail line for each record.

e. Increment the totals for sale amount, commission paid, and net sales.

3. Print the totals at the end of the report.

Project 14-6

Program Name: Sorted Zoo Program

Narrative: Write a program to process a zoo's inventory file.

Input File: ZOO-FILE

Input Record Layout:

```
01  ZOO-RECORD.
    05  ZOO-SPECIES              PIC X(8).
    05  ZOO-TYPE                 PIC X(11).
    05  ZOO-GROUP                PIC X(7).
    05  ZOO-SEX                  PIC X.
    05  ZOO-QUANTITY             PIC 99.
    05  ZOO-ACQUISITION-LEVEL    PIC 99.
    05  ZOO-SPECIE-VALUE         PIC 9(6)V99.
```

Test Data:

```
         1         2         3         4         5         6
12345678901234567890123456789012345678901234567890123456789012345

Whale   Humpback   Mammal F010012509001
Tiger   White      Mammal F050166008508
Parrot  Macaw      Bird   M050006600005
Tiger   White      Mammal M070156008505
Parrot  Macaw      Bird   F120007509915
Bear    Black Bear Mammal M000102330502
Ray     Manta      Fish   F040004004002
Whale   Killer     Mammal F020045005002
Ray     Manta      Fish   M020004500504
Whale   Killer     Mammal M010042005001
Shark   Great WhiteFish   F010120120004
Tiger   Bengal     Mammal M020040209002
Shark   Mako       Fish   F020008990002
Whale   Humpback   Mammal M000017509001
Bear    Grizzly    Mammal F030090000002
Shark   Mako       Fish   M060009500508
Bear    Black Bear Mammal F030102330503
Parrot  Cockatoo   Bird   F450003050430
Bear    Grizzly    Mammal M040091010003
Shark   Great WhiteFish   M040113000004
Tiger   Bengal     Mammal F100020508008
```

Report Layout:

```
               Wild Kingdom Zoo Inventory Report  99/99/99          Page Z9
                                                                    No. to
 Group   Species    Type      Sex    Value  Quantity      Total    Acquire
XXXXXXX XXXXXXXX  XXXXXXXXXXX  X  ZZZ,ZZ9.99   Z9      ZZZ,ZZ9.99    Z9
   .       .          .        .     .          .            .        .
   .       .          .        .     .          .            .        .
   .       .          .        .     .          .            .        .
                                               ----   ------------   ----
Total for Wild Kingdom                          ZZ9   Z,ZZZ,ZZ9.99    ZZ9
```

Processing Requirements:

1. Sort the incoming animal file by group, within group by species, and within species by type.
2. Read the file of sorted animal records, and for each record read:
   a. Calculate the value of each animal (quantity times value).
   b. Determine whether acquisition of addition animals is justified; the zoo should acquire more animals if the acquisition level is below the quantity level.
   c. Print animal information in that record and calculated values on a detail line.
   d. Accumulate the animal quantity totals, total values, and acquisition totals.
3. After all records have been read, print totals for Wild Kingdom.

Project 14-7

Program Name: Sorted PC Software Program

Narrative: Write a program to process a PC software file to determine totals for PC software totals.

Input File: PC-SOFTWARE-FILE

Input Record Layout:

```
01  PC-SOFTWARE-RECORD-IN.
    05  PC-ORDER-INFO.
        10  PC-ORDER-NO             PIC 9(5).
        10  PC-ORDER-TYPE           PIC X.
        10  PC-CUSTOMER-NAME        PIC X(16).
    05  PC-PURCHASE-INFO.
        10  PC-QUANTITY             PIC 999.
        10  PC-PRICE                PIC 9(3)V99.
        10  PC-DATE                 PIC 9(6).
    05  PC-PROGRAM-INFO.
        10  PC-PROGRAM-ID.
            15  PC-PROGRAM-NO       PIC 9(4).
            15  PC-PLATFORM-CODE    PIC X.
        10  PC-PROGRAM-NAME         PIC X(16).
        10  PC-VENDOR               PIC X(16).
```

Test Data:

```
         1         2         3         4         5         6         7
1234567890123456789012345678901234567890123456789012345678901234567890123

02634PZeuqzav-Ralliv  015028990203935514WEntertainmnt PacMicrosoft
79456PRacal Datacomm  003334950201935653D1-2-3 2.4       Lotus
74523PAmerican Express008019001222923338WMoney 2.0       Microsoft
13473PRacal Datacomm  035084950924923146DNorton Anti-ViruSymantec
34342RNeiman Marcus   025328950925928000WPersuasion 2.1  Aldus
63452PAmerican Express010099000116933424W1-2-3 Upgrade   Lotus
53623PRacal Datacomm  035249000130935799WAmiPro 3.0      Lotus
43646PNeiman Marcus   018325000103939695DBorland C++ 3.1 Borland Int'l
43623PRacal Datacomm  030099000222933424W1-2-3 Upgrade   Lotus
27345RNeiman Marcus   003139001015926223WGallery Effects Aldus
58424RAmerican Express005334950116935653D1-2-3 2.4       Lotus
64564PNeiman Marcus   015498950925921332WPagemaker 5.0   Aldus
47635PZeuqzav-Ralliv  015038950203932858DFlight SimulatorMicrosoft
46353PRacal Datacomm  075099991221922359WNorton Desktop  Symantec
63454PZeuqzav-Ralliv  015299000203932856WExcel 4.0       Microsoft
84563RRacal Datacomm  085099991221923784WNorton Backkup  Symantec
45364PZeuqzav-Ralliv  015299000203937387WPowerPoint 3.0  Microsoft
44535PRacal Datacomm  055348951223923523WFreelance 2.0   Lotus
34593PZeuqzav-Ralliv  015299000203936195WWord 2.0        Microsoft
74387PNeiman Marcus   018318501007926242DQuattro Pro 4.0 Borland Int'l
24256PRacal Datacomm  005399000201935417D1-2-3 3.1 Plus  Lotus
75357RNeiman Marcus   015529951125921514DParadox 4.0     Borland Int'l
24246RAmerican Express010399000120935417D1-2-3 3.1 Plus  Lotus
34534RRacal Datacomm  020335001014922755W1-2-3           Lotus
23333PAmerican Express050335000116932755W1-2-3           Lotus
32453PRacal Datacomm  125089000215937010WWindows 3.1     Microsoft
74387PNeiman Marcus   005199001217927540WIntelliDraw  1.0Aldus
85634RAmerican Express015348950226933523WFreelance 2.0   Lotus
43244PAmerican Express020129001120922735WWorks 2.0       Microsoft
49785PZeuqzav-Ralliv  055023000113931162DMickey&Friends  Walt Disney Comp
43352PRacal Datacomm  025445951114927388WProject 3.0     Microsoft
47633PZeuqzav-Ralliv  015029000113932629DMickey's 123's  Walt Disney Comp
56352PNeiman Marcus   025089001016921624WVisual Basic 2.0Microsoft
46523PZeuqzav-Ralliv  015032000203938731WDashboard 1.0   Hewlett-Packard
43274PRacal Datacomm  090479001214926188DFoxPro 2.0      Microsoft
26342PZeuqzav-Ralliv  015029000113932624DMickey's ABC's  Walt Disney Comp
26437PNeiman Marcus   095059001226921620DMS-DOS 6 UpgradeMicrosoft
37466PAmerican Express125059001016921620DMS-DOS 6 UpgradeMicrosoft
47324RNeiman Marcus   045095001114922904DWorks 2.0       Microsoft
26437PRacal Datacomm  045059001016921620DMS-DOS 6 UpgradeMicrosoft
24364PZeuqzav-Ralliv  015109000203938101WNewWave 4.0     Hewlett-Packard
63454PNeiman Marcus   035299000217932856WExcel 4.0       Microsoft
94534PZeuqzav-Ralliv  015034000203936649WStar Trek:ScreenBerkeley Systems
48536PNeiman Marcus   055299000217937387WPowerPoint 3.0  Microsoft
73623PRacal Datacomm  010269001222923804DWordPerfect 5.1 WordPerfect Corp
```

Report Layout:

```
                         Software R Us, Inc. 99/99/99                                  PAGE Z9

Customer         Vendor            Platform  Program           Quantity   Price     Total
XXXXXXXXXXXXXXX  XXXXXXXXXXXXXXXX  XXXXXXX   XXXXXXXXXXXXXXXX       ZZ9  ZZ9.99    ZZ9.99
     .                 .               .            .                 .      .         .
     .                 .               .            .                 .      .         .
     .                 .               .            .                 .      .         .
                                                                   -------          --------
Total for Software R Us                                              Z,ZZ9          Z,ZZ9.99
```

Processing Requirements:

1. Sort the incoming PC software file by customer, within customer by vendor, and within vendor by platform.
2. Read the file of sorted PC software records, and for each record read:
   a. Calculate the total for each program by multiplying the quantity by the price.
   b. Determine whether the order is either a purchase (P) or a return (R) by examining the order type field. If the order is a return, then the quantity and total calculated should be negated. Make sure your report will show this (use CR, DB, +, or – editing symbols).
   c. Print information in that record and total on a detail line. Expand the platform code as follows: "D" for "DOS", and "W" for "Windows". Print the platform name only for the first detail line.
   d. Accumulate totals for quantity and total.
3. After all the records have been read, print company totals for Software R Us.

Project 14-8

Program Name: Video Program

Narrative: Write a program to process a video file to determine totals for video rental and sales revenue.

Input File: VIDEO-FILE

Input Record Layout:

```
01  VIDEO-RECORD-IN.
    05  VID-TITLE-INFO.
        10  VID-TITLE           PIC X(19).
        10  VID-CATEGORY        PIC X(11).
        10  VID-RATING          PIC X(5).
    05  VID-RENTAL-INFO.
        10  VID-RENTAL-FEE      PIC 99V99.
        10  VID-RENTED          PIC 9(3).
    05  VID-SELL-INFO.
        10  VID-SELL-PRICE      PIC 9(3)V99.
        10  VID-SOLD            PIC 9(3).
        10  VID-RETURNED        PIC 9(3).
    05  VID-STORE               PIC X(10).
```

Test Data:

```
         1         2         3         4         5         6
12345678901234567890123456789012345678901234567890123456789012345

Rocky Horror        Drama       PG-13020040005995101050Coco Grove
Dirty Harry         Action      R    017501002000025002Miami
Basic Instinct      New ReleaseR    030020003995099002Hialeah
My Girl             Drama       PG   020007002000060005Miami Bch
Cutting Edge        Drama       PG-13025010002000035008Coco Grove
Lethal Weapon III   Action      R    030015002995103000Miami
Candy Man           New ReleaseR    030020005995105040Hialeah
Cape Fear           Drama       R    020008001995020002Miami Bch
Nighmare on Elm St  Horror      R    025006001995006006Ft. Laud
ET                  Childrens   G    015006001995045012Hialeah
Caddy Shack         Comedy      PG   010004501095023005Miami
Caddy Shack         Comedy      PG   010004501095023005Coco Grove
Final Analysis      Suspense    R    030012002995076003Miami Bch
Dr. Giggles         New ReleaseR    030030007795092030Hialeah
Star Wars II        Action      G    017505001995050020Miami
Wayne's World       Comedy      PG   030005001595045055Miami
Care Bears          Childrens   G    010007500995035003Hialeah
Halloween           Horror      PG-13025004001995090095Ft. Laud
Dances with Wolves  Drama       R    030010004995010000Coco Grove
The Blues Brothers  Comedy      PG   020001001095015005Coco Grove
One Flew Over...    Drama       R    017502501095009000Coco Grove
The Birds           Horror      PG-13015001001495010000Ft. Laud
The Fly             Suspense    R    020007502995065005Miami Bch
Pinnochio           Childrens   G    010003501495080003Hialeah
The Little Mermaid  Childrens   G    025020001995098003Hialeah
To Kill a Mocking..Drama       PG   010001000995002001Miami Bch
Sneakers            New ReleaseR    030040007500125000Hialeah
The Shining         Suspense    R    015001501500010004Ft. Laud
T2 - Judgement Day  New ReleaseR    030035003995135001Hialeah
Hell Raiser II      Horror      R    015007701095075080Ft. Laud
Wayne's World       Comedy      PG   030005001595045055Coco Grove
Star Wars           Action      G    017505001495030010Miami
Beauty & the Beast  Childrens   G    030020001995200000Hialeah
```

Report Layout:

```
                BlokBuzter Monthly Video Rentals & Sales 99/99/99              PAGE Z9

                                                 Rental Information          Sell Information
                                           -----------------------------  --------------------------
Category     Rating  Movie Title           Fee  # Rented      Revenue   Price    Net       Revenue
XXXXXXXXXXX  XXXXX   XXXXXXXXXXXXXXXXXXX  Z9.99      ZZ9       ZZ9.99  ZZ9.99    ZZ9        ZZ9.99
    .          .           .                .         .            .       .       .             .
    .          .           .                .         .            .       .       .             .
    .          .           .                .         .            .       .       .             .
                                                 -------  -----------          -------  -----------
Total for BlokBuzter                               Z,ZZ9    Z,ZZ9.99             Z,ZZ9     Z,ZZ9.99
```

Processing Requirements:

1. Sort the incoming video file by store, within each store by rating, and within each rating by movie title.
2. Read the file of sorted video records, and for each record read:
   a. Calculate the rental revenue by multiplying the rental fee by the number of times rented.

b. Calculate the net sales by subtracting the videos returned from the videos sold. Returns are accepted from other stores so your net could be negative! Make sure your report will show this (use CR, DB, +, or – editing symbols).

c. Calculate the sales revenue for each movie by multiplying the selling price by the net sales.

d. Print a detail line.

e. Accumulate totals as indicated on the report layout.

3. After all the records have been read, print totals for BlokBuzter.

PROGRAMMING SPECIFICATIONS

Project 15-1

Program Name: Mucho Bucks Salary Control Break (Continuation of Project 14-1)

Narrative: Write a control break program to process pay records for the Mucho Bucks Company to produce salary totals by manager, department, and location. The choice between a two- or three-level report is between you and your instructor.

Input File: EMPLOYEE-FILE

Input Record Layout: Use the same record layout as Project 14-1.

Test Data: Use the same test data as Project 14-1.

Two-level Report Layout:

```
                         MUCHO BUCKS COMPANY                 PAGE Z9
                  SALARY REPORT FOR DEPARTMENT: XXXXXXXXXX

MANAGER: XXXXXXXXXX
    EMPLOYEE                         SALARY    DEDUCTION     NET PAY
    XXXXXXXXXX                      $$$,$$9      $$$,$$9     $$$,$$9
        .                              .            .           .
        .                              .            .           .
        .                              .            .           .
                                 ----------   ----------  ----------
TOTAL FOR manager name           $$,$$$,$$9   $$,$$$,$$9  $$,$$$,$$9

TOTAL FOR department name        $$,$$$,$$9   $$,$$$,$$9  $$,$$$,$$9

TOTAL FOR MUCHO BUCKS            $$,$$$,$$9   $$,$$$,$$9  $$,$$$,$$9
```

Three-level Report Layout:

```
                    MUCHO BUCKS COMPANY                        PAGE Z9
              SALARY REPORT FOR LOCATION: XXXXXXXXXXXX

DEPARTMENT: XXXXXXXXXX
MANAGER       EMPLOYEE                  SALARY   DEDUCTION     NET PAY
XXXXXXXXXX    XXXXXXXXXX               $$$,$$9     $$$,$$9     $$$,$$9
                  .                       .           .           .
                  .                       .           .           .
                  .                       .           .           .
                                    ----------  ----------  ----------
TOTAL FOR manager name              $$,$$$,$$9  $$,$$$,$$9  $$,$$$,$$9

TOTAL FOR department name           $$,$$$,$$9  $$,$$$,$$9  $$,$$$,$$9

TOTAL FOR location name             $$,$$$,$$9  $$,$$$,$$9  $$,$$$,$$9

TOTAL FOR MUCHO BUCKS               $$,$$$,$$9  $$,$$$,$$9  $$,$$$,$$9
```

Two-level Processing Requirements:

1. Sort the incoming employee file by department, and within department by manager.
2. Read the file of sorted employee records, and for each record read:
   a. Print a detail line as shown in the report layout using the processing requirements for Project 14-1.
   b. Increment the manager, department, and company totals as appropriate.
   c. Begin every department on a new page with an appropriate heading containing the department name and page number of the report.
   d. Print manager and department headings whenever the fields change.
   e. Print manager and department totals whenever the fields change.
3. Print the Mucho Bucks total on a separate page at the conclusion of the report.

Three-level Extension: Extend the report to include a third (higher-level) control break on location as shown in the report format. Begin each location on a new page (expand the location code in the location heading) and include multiple departments in the same location on the same page. Be sure to modify the format of the heading and detail lines, to change the SORT statement to include the extra level control break, and to modify the program to increment all totals as necessary.

Project 15-2

Program Name: Brokerage Control Break (Continuation of Project 14-2)

Narrative: Write a control break program to process a brokerage firm's records to produce totals by account type, broker, and branch. The choice between a two- or three-level report is between you and your instructor.

Input File: CUSTOMER-FILE

Input Record Layout: Use the same record layout as Project 14-2.

Test Data: Use the same test data as Project 14-2.

Two-level Report Layout:

```
                    FLY BY NIGHT BROKERAGE              PAGE Z9
              COMMISSION REPORT BROKER: XXXXXXXXXX

ACCOUNT TYPE: XXXXXXXXXXXXXXXXXXX
ACCT #       CUSTOMER             BALANCE        COMMISSION
 9999       XXXXXXXXXX          $$$$,$$9.99      $$,$$9.99
  .             .                    .               .
  .             .                    .               .
  .             .                    .               .
                               -------------   ------------
 TOTAL FOR account type        $$,$$$,$$9.99     $$$,$$9.99
                               -------------   ------------
 TOTAL FOR broker name         $$,$$$,$$9.99     $$$,$$9.99
                               -------------   ------------
 TOTAL FOR FLY BY NITE         $$,$$$,$$9.99     $$$,$$9.99
```

Three-level Report Layout:

```
                          FLY BY NIGHT BROKERAGE                  PAGE Z9
                    COMMISSION REPORT BRANCH: XXXXXXXX

BROKER: XXXXXXXXXX
   ACCT TYPE          ACCT #  CUSTOMER        BALANCE       COMMISSION
XXXXXXXXXXXXXXXXXXX    9999  XXXXXXXXXX    $$$$,$$9.99       $$,$$9.99
                        .        .              .               .
                        .        .              .               .
                        .        .              .               .
                                          -------------    ------------
 TOTAL FOR account type                   $$,$$$,$$9.99      $$$,$$9.99
                                          -------------    ------------
 TOTAL FOR broker name                    $$,$$$,$$9.99      $$$,$$9.99
                                          -------------    ------------
 TOTAL FOR branch name                    $$,$$$,$$9.99      $$$,$$9.99
                                          -------------    ------------
 TOTAL FOR FLY BY NITE                    $$,$$$,$$9.99      $$$,$$9.99
```

Two-level Processing Requirements:

1. Sort the incoming customer file by broker, and within broker by account type.
2. Read the file of sorted customer records, and for each record read:
   a. Print a detail line as shown in the report layout using the processing requirements for Project 14-2.
   b. Increment the account type, broker, and company totals as appropriate.
   c. Begin every broker on a new page with an appropriate heading containing the broker name and page number of the report.

d. Print account type and broker headings whenever the fields change.

e. Print account type and broker totals whenever the fields change.

3. Print the Fly by Nite total at the conclusion of the report.

Three-level Extension: Extend the report to include a third (higher-level) control break on branch as shown in the report format. Begin each branch on a new page (expand the branch code in the branch heading) and include multiple brokers in the same branch on the same page. Be sure to modify the format of the heading and detail lines, to change the SORT statement to include the extra level control break, and to modify the program to increment all totals as necessary.

Project 15-3

Program Name: Car Sales Control Break (Continuation of Project 14-3)

Narrative: Develop a control break program to process a sales file in order to determine totals by year, salesperson, and dealer. The choice between a two- or three-level report is between you and your instructor.

Input File: SALES-FILE

Input Record Layout: Use the same record layout as Project 14-3.

Test Data: Use the same test data as Project 14-3.

Two-level Report Layout:

```
                          VERY VERY NICE CARS INC.                  PAGE Z9
          salesperson name COMMISSION REPORT AS OF 99/99/99

YEAR: 9999
  CAR INFORMATION                                    COMMISSION         NET TO
   MAKE      MODEL          CUSTOMER   PRICE           PAID             DEALER
 XXXXXXXX XXXXXXXX        XXXXXXXXXX  ZZZ,ZZ9      ZZ,ZZ9.99       ZZZ,ZZ9.99
    .         .                .          .            .                .
    .         .                .          .            .                .
    .         .                .          .            .                .
 **  TOTAL FOR year                 $Z,ZZZ,ZZ9  $ZZZ,ZZ9.99  $Z,ZZZ,ZZ9.99

 *   TOTAL FOR salesperson name     $Z,ZZZ,ZZ9  $ZZZ,ZZ9.99  $Z,ZZZ,ZZ9.99
                                    ----------  -----------  -------------
 VERY VERY NICE CARS TOTALS         $Z,ZZZ,ZZ9  $ZZZ,ZZ9.99  $Z,ZZZ,ZZ9.99
```

Three-level Report Layout:

```
                         VERY VERY NICE CARS INC.                    PAGE Z9
               dealer name COMMISSION REPORT AS OF 99/99/99

SALESPERSON: XXXXXXXXXX
  CAR INFORMATION       CUSTOMER               COMMISSION      NET TO
YEAR MAKE     MODEL                    PRICE      PAID         DEALER

9999 XXXXXXXX XXXXXXXX  XXXXXXXXXX  ZZZ,ZZ9    ZZ,ZZ9.99     ZZZ,ZZ9.99
        .        .          .          .          .              .
        .        .          .          .          .              .
        .        .          .          .          .              .
***  TOTAL FOR year              $Z,ZZZ,ZZ9  $ZZZ,ZZ9.99  $Z,ZZZ,ZZ9.99

 **  TOTAL FOR salesperson name  $Z,ZZZ,ZZ9  $ZZZ,ZZ9.99  $Z,ZZZ,ZZ9.99

 *   TOTAL FOR dealer name       $Z,ZZZ,ZZ9  $ZZZ,ZZ9.99  $Z,ZZZ,ZZ9.99
                                 ----------  -----------  -------------
 VERY VERY NICE CARS TOTALS      $Z,ZZZ,ZZ9  $ZZZ,ZZ9.99  $Z,ZZZ,ZZ9.99
```

Two-level Processing Requirements:

1. Sort the incoming sales file by salesperson, and within salesperson by year.
2. Read the file of sorted sales records and for each record read:
   a. Print a detail line as shown in the report layout using the processing requirements for Project 14-3.
   b. Increment the year, salesperson, and company totals as appropriate.
   c. Begin every salesperson on a new page with an appropriate heading containing the salesperson name, current date, and page number of the report.
   d. Print year and salesperson headings whenever the fields change.
   e. Print year and salesperson totals whenever the fields change.
3. Print the Very Very Nice Cars totals on a separate page at the conclusion of the report.

Three-level Extension: Extend the report to include a third (higher-level) control break on dealer as shown in the report format. Begin each dealer on a new page and include multiple salespersons in the same dealer on the same page. Be sure to modify the format of the heading and detail lines, to change the SORT statement to include the extra level control break, and to modify the program to increment all totals as necessary.

Project 15-4

Program Name: Bonus Control Break Program (Continuation of Project 14-4)

Narrative: Write a control break program to process a bonus file to determine bonus totals by manager, department, and plant. The choice between a two- or three-level report is between you and your instructor.

Input File: BONUS-FILE

Input Record Layout: Use the same record layout as Project 14-4.

Test Data: Use the same test data as Project 14-4.

Two-level Report Layout:

```
                 FASSSTCARS MANUFACTURERS                  PAGE Z9
            BONUS REPORT FOR DEPARTMENT: XXXXXXXX

MANAGER: XXXXXXXXXX
SOC SEC NO      EMPLOYEE                     SALARY  BONUS     TOTAL
999-99-9999    XXXXXXXXXXXXXXX               ZZ,ZZ9  Z,ZZ9   ZZZ,ZZ9
     .                 .                        .      .         .
     .                 .                        .      .         .
     .                 .                        .      .         .
                                          --------- ------- ---------
** TOTAL FOR manager name                 Z,ZZZ,ZZ9  ZZ,ZZ9 Z,ZZZ,ZZ9
                                          --------- ------- ---------
*** TOTAL FOR department name             Z,ZZZ,ZZ9  ZZ,ZZ9 Z,ZZZ,ZZ9
                                          --------- ------- ---------
TOTAL FOR FASSSTCARS                      Z,ZZZ,ZZ9  ZZ,ZZ9 Z,ZZZ,ZZ9
```

Three-level Report Layout:

```
                 FASSSTCARS MANUFACTURERS                  PAGE Z9
               BONUS REPORT FOR PLANT: XX

DEPARTMENT: XXXXXXXX
MANAGER     SOC SEC NO    EMPLOYEE          SALARY  BONUS     TOTAL
XXXXXXXXXX  999-99-9999   XXXXXXXXXXXXXXX  ZZ,ZZ9  Z,ZZ9   ZZZ,ZZ9
                 .               .             .      .         .
                 .               .             .      .         .
                 .               .             .      .         .
                                          --------- ------- ---------
* TOTAL FOR manager name                  Z,ZZZ,ZZ9  ZZ,ZZ9 Z,ZZZ,ZZ9
                                          --------- ------- ---------
** TOTAL FOR department name              Z,ZZZ,ZZ9  ZZ,ZZ9 Z,ZZZ,ZZ9
                                          --------- ------- ---------
*** TOTAL FOR plant name                  Z,ZZZ,ZZ9  ZZ,ZZ9 Z,ZZZ,ZZ9
                                          --------- ------- ---------
TOTAL FOR FASSSTCARS                      Z,ZZZ,ZZ9  ZZ,ZZ9 Z,ZZZ,ZZ9
```

Two-level Processing Requirements:

1. Sort the incoming bonus file, sorting only the employees that are eligible for a bonus (i.e., those that contain a "Y" in the eligibility field) by department, and within department by manager.
2. Read the file of sorted bonus records and for each record read:
   a. Print a detail line as shown in the report layout using the processing requirements for Project 14-4.
   b. Increment the manager, department, and company totals as appropriate.
   c. Begin every department on a new page with an appropriate heading containing the department name and page number of the report.

d. Print manager and department headings whenever the fields change.

e. Print manager and department totals whenever the fields change.

3. Print the FassstCars Manufacturers totals at the conclusion of the report.

Three-level Extension: Extend the report to include a third (higher-level) control break on plant as shown in the report format. Begin each plant on a new page and include multiple departments in the same plant on the same page. Be sure to modify the format of the heading and detail lines, to change the SORT statement to include the extra level control break, and to modify the program to increment all totals as necessary.

Project 15-5

Program Name: Store Sales Commissions Program (Continuation of Project 14-5)

Narrative: Write a control break program to process sales records for Needless Markup to produce totals by salesperson, department, and store. The choice between a two- or three-level report is between you and your instructor.

Input File: SALES-FILE

Input Record Layout: Use the same record layout as Project 14-5.

Test Data: Use the same test data as Project 14-5.

Two-level Report Layout:

```
                          NEEDLESS MARKUP INC     99/99/99        PAGE Z9
                  COMMISSION REPORT FOR DEPARTMENT: XXXXXXXXXXXX

     SALESPERSON: XXXXXXXXXX
                 DATE              SALES       COMMISSION      NET SALES
               99/99/99          ZZ,ZZ9.99       Z,ZZ9.99      ZZ,ZZ9.99
                  .                  .              .              .
                  .                  .              .              .
                  .                  .              .              .
                                ----------      ---------     ----------
   TOTAL FOR salesperson        ZZZ,ZZ9.99      ZZ,ZZ9.99     ZZZ,ZZ9.99
                                ----------      ---------     ----------
   TOTAL FOR department         ZZZ,ZZ9.99      ZZ,ZZ9.99     ZZZ,ZZ9.99
                                ----------      ---------     ----------
   TOTAL FOR NEEDLESS MARKUP    ZZZ,ZZ9.99      ZZ,ZZ9.99     ZZZ,ZZ9.99
```

Three-level Report Layout:

```
                         NEEDLESS MARKUP INC    99/99/99          PAGE Z9
                    COMMISSION REPORT FOR STORE: XXXXXXXXXXXX

    DEPARTMENT: XXXXXXXXXXXX
    SALESPERSON      DATE         SALES       COMMISSION       NET SALES
    XXXXXXXXXX     99/99/99     ZZ,ZZ9.99       Z,ZZ9.99       ZZ,ZZ9.99
                      .             .              .               .
                      .             .              .               .
                      .             .              .               .
                               ----------      ---------      ----------
   TOTAL FOR salesperson       ZZZ,ZZ9.99      ZZ,ZZ9.99      ZZZ,ZZ9.99
                               ----------      ---------      ----------
   TOTAL FOR department name   ZZZ,ZZ9.99      ZZ,ZZ9.99      ZZZ,ZZ9.99
                               ----------      ---------      ----------
   TOTAL FOR store name        ZZZ,ZZ9.99      ZZ,ZZ9.99      ZZZ,ZZ9.99
                               ----------      ---------      ----------
   TOTAL FOR NEEDLESS MARKUP   ZZZ,ZZ9.99      ZZ,ZZ9.99      ZZZ,ZZ9.99
```

Two-level Processing Requirements:

1. Sort the incoming sales file by department, and within department by salesperson.
2. Read the file of sorted bonus records, and for each record read:
   a. Print a detail line as shown in the report layout using the processing requirements for Project 14-5.
   b. Increment the salesperson, department, and company totals as appropriate.
   c. Begin every department on a new page with an appropriate heading containing the department name, current date, and page number of the report.
   d. Print salesperson and department headings whenever the fields change.
   e. Print salesperson and department totals whenever the fields change.
3. Print the Needless Markup total at the conclusion of the report.

Three-level Extension: Extend the report to include a third (higher-level) control break on store as shown in the report format. Begin each store on a new page (expand the store code in the store heading) and include multiple departments in the same store on the same page. Be sure to modify the format of the heading and detail lines, to change the SORT statement to include the extra level control break, and to modify the program to increment all totals as necessary.

Project 15-6

Program Name: Zoo Control Break Program (Continuation of Project 14-6)

Narrative: Write a control break program to process a zoo's inventory animal file to determine totals by group, species, and type of animal. The choice between a two- or three-level report is between you and your instructor.

Input File: ZOO-FILE

Input Record Layout: Use the same record layout as Project 14-6.

Test Data: Use the same test data as Project 14-6.

Two-level Report Layout:

```
                    WILD KINGDOM ZOO    99/99/99            PAGE Z9
                  INVENTORY REPORT - species name

TYPE: XXXXXXXXXXX
                                                             NO. TO
     SEX                   VALUE     QUANTITY     TOTAL      ACQUIRE
      F                 ZZZ,ZZ9.99      Z9     ZZZ,ZZ9.99      Z9
      M                 ZZZ,ZZ9.99      Z9     ZZZ,ZZ9.99      Z9
                                       ----   ------------    ----
 ** TOTAL FOR type name                ZZ9   Z,ZZZ,ZZ9.99     ZZ9
                                       ----   ------------    ----
  * TOTAL FOR species name             ZZ9   Z,ZZZ,ZZ9.99     ZZ9
                                       ----   ------------    ----
TOTAL FOR WILD KINGDOM                 ZZ9   Z,ZZZ,ZZ9.99     ZZ9
```

Three-level Report Layout:

```
                    WILD KINGDOM ZOO    99/99/99            PAGE Z9
                   INVENTORY REPORT - group name

SPECIE: XXXXXXXX
                                                             NO. TO
TYPE                SEX     VALUE     QUANTITY     TOTAL     ACQUIRE
XXXXXXXXXXXX         F   ZZZ,ZZ9.99      Z9     ZZZ,ZZ9.99     Z9
                     M   ZZZ,ZZ9.99      Z9     ZZZ,ZZ9.99     Z9
                                        ----   ------------   ----
*** TOTAL FOR type                      ZZ9   Z,ZZZ,ZZ9.99    ZZ9
                                        ----   ------------   ----
 ** TOTAL FOR species name              ZZ9   Z,ZZZ,ZZ9.99    ZZ9
                                        ----   ------------   ----
  * TOTAL FOR group name                ZZ9   Z,ZZZ,ZZ9.99    ZZ9
                                        ----   ------------   ----
TOTAL FOR WILD KINGDOM                  ZZ9   Z,ZZZ,ZZ9.99    ZZ9
```

Two-level Processing Requirements:

1. Sort the incoming zoo file by species, and within species by type.
2. Read a file of sorted zoo records and for each record read:
   a. Print a detail line as shown in the report layout using the processing requirements for Project 14-6.
   b. Increment the type, species, and Wild Kingdom totals as appropriate.
   c. Begin every species on a new page with an appropriate heading containing the species name, current date, and page number of the report.

d. Print type and species headings whenever the fields change.

e. Print type and species totals whenever the fields change.

3. Print the Wild Kingdom totals at the conclusion of the report.

Three-level Extension: Extend the report to include a third (higher-level) control break on group as shown in the report format. Begin each group on a new page and include multiple species in the same group on the same page. Be sure to modify the format of the heading and detail lines, to change the SORT statement to include the extra level control break, and to modify the program to increment all totals as necessary.

Project 15-7

Program Name: PC Software Control Break Program (Continuation of Project 14-7)

Narrative: Write a control break program to process a PC software file to determine totals by customer, vendor, and platform. The choice between a two- or three-level report is between you and your instructor.

Input File: PC-SOFTWARE-FILE

Input Record Layout: Use the same record layout as Project 14-7.

Test Data: Use the same test data as Project 14-7.

Two-level Report Layout:

```
                         SOFTWARE R US, INC      99/99/99        PAGE Z9
                       SALES REPORT FOR vendor name

PLATFORM: XXXXXXX
CUSTOMER          PROGRAM NAME        DATE    QUANTITY    PRICE       TOTAL
XXXXXXXXXXXXXXXX XXXXXXXXXXXXXXXX 99/99/99         ZZ9   ZZ9.99      ZZ9.99
         .             .              .              .      .            .
         .             .              .              .      .            .
         .             .              .              .      .            .
                                               -------           ----------
TOTAL FOR platform                               Z,ZZ9           ZZZ,ZZ9.99
                                               -------          -----------
TOTAL FOR vendor name                            Z,ZZ9           ZZZ,ZZ9.99
                                               -------          -----------
SOFTWARE R US TOTAL                              Z,ZZ9           ZZZ,ZZ9.99
```

Three-level Report Layout:

```
                    SOFTWARE R US, INC       99/99/99         PAGE Z9
               SALES REPORT FOR customer name

VENDOR: XXXXXXXXXXXXXXX
PLATFORM   PROGRAM NAME           DATE     QUANTITY    PRICE      TOTAL
XXXXXXX    XXXXXXXXXXXXXXX      99/99/99        ZZ9   ZZ9.99     ZZ9.99
   .            .                  .             .      .           .
   .            .                  .             .      .           .
   .            .                  .             .      .           .
                                            -------          ----------
TOTAL FOR platform                            Z,ZZ9          ZZZ,ZZ9.99
                                            -------         -----------
TOTAL FOR vendor name                         Z,ZZ9          ZZZ,ZZ9.99
                                            -------         -----------
TOTAL FOR customr name                        Z,ZZ9          ZZZ,ZZ9.99
                                            -------         -----------
SOFTWARE R US TOTAL                           Z,ZZ9          ZZZ,ZZ9.99
```

Two-level Processing Requirements:

1. Sort the incoming PC software file by vendor, and within vendor by platform.
2. Read the file of sorted PC software records and for each record read:
   a. Print a detail line as shown in the report layout using the processing requirements for Project 14-7.
   b. Increment the platform, vendor, and company totals as appropriate.
   c. Begin every vendor on a new page with an appropriate heading containing the vendor name, current date, and page number of the report.
   d. Print platform and vendor headings whenever the fields change.
   e. Print platform and vendor totals whenever the fields change.
3. Print the Software R Us totals at the conclusion of the report.

Three-level Extension: Extend the report to include a third (higher-level) control break on customer as shown in the report format. Begin each customer on a new page and include multiple vendors for the same customer on the same page. Be sure to modify the format of the heading and detail lines, to change the SORT statement to include the extra level control break, and to modify the program to increment all totals as necessary.

Project 15-8

Program Name: Video Control Break Program (Continuation of Project 14-8)

Narrative: Write a control break program to process a video file to determine totals by each store, category, and rating. The choice between a two- or three-level report is between you and your instructor.

Input File: VIDEO-FILE

Input Record Layout: Use the same record layout as Project 14-8.

Test Data: Use the same test data as Project 14-8.

Two-level Report Layout:

```
                              Blokbuzter Video     99/99/99          Page Z9
                    MONTHLY VIDEO RENTALS & SALES FOR category name

RATING: XXXXXXX

                              Rental Information        Sell Information
                          ---------------------- -------------------------
MOVIE TITLE                FEE  #RENTED  REVENUE   PRICE    NET       REVENUE
XXXXXXXXXXXXXXXXXXX      Z9.99      ZZ9   ZZ9.99  ZZ9.99    ZZ9        ZZ9.99
        .                  .        .        .       .       .             .
        .                  .        .        .       .       .             .
        .                  .        .        .       .       .             .
                                 ------ ---------         ------- -----------
** TOTAL FOR rating              Z,ZZ9 Z,ZZ9.99             Z,ZZ9    Z,ZZ9.99
                                 ------ ---------         ------- -----------
 * TOTAL FOR category name       Z,ZZ9 Z,ZZ9.99             Z,ZZ9    Z,ZZ9.99
                                 ------ ---------         ------- -----------
TOTAL FOR BLOKBUZTER             Z,ZZ9 Z,ZZ9.99             Z,ZZ9    Z,ZZ9.99
```

Three-level Report Layout:

```
                              Blokbuzter Video     99/99/99           PageZ9
                    MONTHLY VIDEO RENTALS & SALES FOR store name

CATEGORY: XXXXXXXXXXX

RATING: XXXXXXX              Rental Information        Sell Information
                          ---------------------- -------------------------
MOVIE TITLE                FEE  #RENTED  REVENUE   PRICE    NET       REVENUE
XXXXXXXXXXXXXXXXXXX      Z9.99      ZZ9   ZZ9.99  ZZ9.99    ZZ9        ZZ9.99
        .                  .        .        .       .       .             .
        .                  .        .        .       .       .             .
        .                  .        .        .       .       .             .
                                 ------ ---------         ------- -----------
*** TOTAL FOR rating             Z,ZZ9 Z,ZZ9.99             Z,ZZ9    Z,ZZ9.99
                                 ------ ---------         ------- -----------
** TOTAL FOR category name       Z,ZZ9 Z,ZZ9.99             Z,ZZ9    Z,ZZ9.99
                                 ------ ---------         ------- -----------
* TOTAL FOR store name           Z,ZZ9 Z,ZZ9.99             Z,ZZ9    Z,ZZ9.99
                                 ------ ---------         ------- -----------
TOTAL FOR BLOKBUZTER             Z,ZZ9 Z,ZZ9.99             Z,ZZ9    Z,ZZ9.99
```

Two-level Processing Requirements:

1. Sort the incoming video file by category, and within category by rating.
2. Read the file of sorted video records and for each record read:
   a. Print a detail line as shown in the report layout using the processing requirements for Project 14-8.
   b. Increment the rating, category, and Blokbuzter totals as appropriate.

c. Begin every category on a new page with an appropriate heading containing the category name, current date, and page number of the report.

d. Print rating and category headings whenever the fields change.

e. Print rating and category totals whenever the fields change.

3. Print the BlokBuzter totals on a separate page at the conclusion of the report.

Three-level Extension: Extend the report to include a third (higher-level) control break on store as shown in the report format. Begin each store on a new page and include multiple categories in the same store on the same page. Be sure to modify the format of the heading and detail lines, to change the SORT statement to include the extra level control break, and to modify the program to increment all totals as necessary.

PROGRAMMING SPECIFICATIONS

Project 16-1

Program Name: Invoice Program with Subprogram

Narrative: Write a program to produce an invoice for each record in a validated invoice file.

Input File: INVOICE-FILE
STATE-FILE

Input Record Layout:

```
01  INVOICE-RECORD-IN.
    05  INV-INVOICE-NO          PIC X(4).
    05  INV-DATE.
        10  INV-MONTH           PIC 9(2).
        10  INV-DAY             PIC 9(2).
        10  INV-YEAR            PIC 9(2).
    05  INV-CUSTOMER-INFO.
        10  INV-CUST-NAME       PIC X(10).
        10  INV-CUST-ADDRESS    PIC X(10).
        10  INV-CUST-CITY       PIC X(10).
        10  INV-CUST-STATE      PIC XX.
        10  INV-CUST-ZIP        PIC X(5).
    05  INV-NO-OF-ITEMS         PIC 9.
    05  INV-ITEMS-ORDERED OCCURS 1 TO 4 TIMES
            DEPENDING ON INV-NO-OF-ITEMS.
        10  INV-ITEM-NO         PIC 9(4).
        10  INV-QUANTITY        PIC 9.

01  STATE-RECORD.
    05  ST-STATE                PIC XX.
    05  ST-ZONE                 PIC 9.
```

Test Data:

```
         1         2         3         4         5         6
12345678901234567890123456789012345678901234567890123456789012345678
2467100491Scully    20 Main StChicago   IL435353125021100115501
1578081291Schultz   45 5th St Los AngeleCA56786245002320 01
0342091091Culver    1 Sunny LnSeattle   WA55986190003
4790111290Perez     4 Long Dr New OrleanLA793452680024 5001
6836070491Fixler    3 42nd St New York  NY2000121250115503
4807031891Morin     9 7th Ave Newark    NJ30697432001900031100230002
0498063091Munroe    10 Long StTulsa     OK59345190005
```

Report Layout:

```
Date 99/99/99          Dominoe Catalog Orders        Invoice Number       9999
Ship To:        Name                               Invoice Order Date 99/99/99
                XXXXXXXXXX
                Address
                XXXXXXXXXX
                City        State   Zip
                XXXXXXXXXX  XX      XXXXX

Item No.        Description      Qty    Price Each   Total Price  Tot Ship Wt
  XXXX          XXXXXXXXXXXXXXX   9      Z,ZZ9.99     ZZ,ZZ9.99       ZZ9.99
   .               .              .         .             .              .
   .               .              .         .             .              .
   .               .              .         .             .              .
  XXXX          XXXXXXXXXXXXXXX   9      Z,ZZ9.99     ZZ,ZZ9.99       ZZ9.99
                                           Totals   $ZZZ,ZZ9.99     Z,ZZ9.99
                               Total delivery charge       ZZ9.99
                                     Handling charge         1.50
                                        Total amount  $ZZZ,ZZ9.99

                  Questions? Call Toll Free 1-800-DOMINOE
```

Processing Requirements:

1. Create an invoice, one per page, for each record read.
   a. Write appropriate invoice headings.
   b. For each item ordered:
      (1) The incoming item number is to be used to find the description, price, and shipping weight via a sequential lookup. Hard-code the following table in the program:

Item Information			
Item #	**Item Description**	**Price (each)**	**Ship Wt (each)**
1100	Handwoven Rug	129.00	9.50
1550	Crystal Frame	39.40	3.00
1250	Floor Lamp	99.00	20.30
3000	Ceiling Fan	299.00	50.01
4500	Wicker Basket	25.00	2.00
6800	Wall Clock	169.00	19.30
3200	Ceramic Figure	39.90	10.00
9000	Wood Wall Shelf	14.90	1.00

      (2) Compute the total price and total shipping weight.
      (3) Write a detail line for the item.

(4) Increment appropriate invoice totals.

c. After all the items ordered in the record have been processed, calculate the total delivery charge and the total invoice amount as follows:

(1) The total delivery charge should be calculated in a subprogram. There are two steps in obtaining the total delivery charge:

(a) You must first determine the appropriate zone. The incoming state is to be used via a binary lookup to determine the appropriate zone (there are three zones in total). Input-load this state/zone table (only once per execution of the program). The state file (16-1STAT.DAT) can be found on the data disk.

(b) The total delivery charge is based on the zone and total shipping weight. Once the correct zone has been found, it is to be used in combination with the sum of the total shipping weight as follows:

Delivery Rates				
Total Ship Wgt Range (in lbs)		**Zone Number**		
From	**To (inclusive)**	**Zone 1**	**Zone 2**	**Zone 3**
0	2	$4.00	$4.25	$4.50
2	4	$5.75	$6.25	$6.75
4	9	$7.75	$8.50	$9.25
9	20	$10.75	$12.00	$14.75
20	30	$14.00	$15.50	$18.25
30	50	$18.25	$20.75	$25.25
50	70	$21.25	$25.00	$30.50
70	999	$25.50	$29.00	$35.00

Develop a two-dimensional table to hold the above information and perform a table-lookup to determine the correct charge. Establish this table via a COPY statement. Use a direct lookup for zone dimension.

(2) The final total amount is calculated by adding the total price, the total delivery charge, and the handling charge. The current handling charge is $1.50; code this in your program so in the event this charge changes, it can be easily updated.

d. Print appropriate totals (total price, total delivery charge, handling charge, and total amount) as shown on the layout.

e. Increment the totals for price, shipping weight, total delivery charge, handling charge, and amount for the Summary Report (see #3).

2. When all records have been processed, write the Summary Report, on a separate page, of all the totals accumulated in e. (Design your summary report.)

Project 16-2

Program Name: Student Aid Report Program with Subprogram

Narrative: Write the program to print a detailed student aid report for all validated students and a summary page depicting totals for each school.

Input File: STUDENT-FILE
SCHOOL-FILE (See requirement 1b.)

Input Record Layout: Use the same record layout as Project 8-6.

Test Data: Use the validated student file from Project 8-6.

Report Layout:

Detailed Student Aid Report:

```
                                              Smart U                                         Page 1
                                         Student Aid Report                                 99/99/99

                                                                  Credit     Total      Total    Tuition
Student ID      Name            School          Type of Aid       Hours     Tuition       Aid        Due

999999999   XXXXXXXXXXXXXXX   XXXXXXXXXX       XXXXXXXXXXX          99    $ZZZ,ZZ9   $ZZZ,ZZ9   $ZZZ,ZZ9
    .             .               .                 .               .        .          .          .
    .             .               .                 .               .        .          .          .
    .             .               .                 .               .        .          .          .
```

Summary Report of Total Aid per School:

```
                                              Smart U                                         Page n
                                Summary Report of Total Aid per School                      99/99/99

                                         Total                    Total                    Tuition
School                                 Tuition                      Aid                        Due

Art                                $ZZ,ZZZ,ZZ9              $ZZ,ZZZ,ZZ9                $ZZ,ZZZ,ZZ9
 .                                           .
 .                                           .
 .                                           .
                                       =======                  =======                    =======
University Totals                 $ZZZ,ZZZ,ZZ9             $ZZZ,ZZZ,ZZ9               $ZZZ,ZZZ,ZZ9
```

Processing Requirements:

1. For each valid record read:
   a. The incoming aid type is to be expanded via a sequential lookup. The table-lookup procedure should be coded in a separate subprogram. Hard-code the following table:

Aid Type & Expanded Aid Types	
Aid Type	**Expanded Aid Type**
S	Scholarship
G	Grant
L	Loan

   b. The incoming school code is to be expanded via a binary lookup. The lookup procedure should be coded in a separate subprogram. Use the following table and input-load it in the subprogram (only once per execution of the program).

School Codes & Expanded Schools			
School Code	**Expanded School**	**School Code**	**Expanded School**
ART	Arts & Sciences	LAW	Law
BUS	Business	MED	Medicine
COM	Communications	MUS	Music
ENG	Engineering		

c. Calculate total tuition based on $300 per credit hour.

d. Calculate total aid based on the percent of total tuition. This percent is determined by a combination of credit hours and GPA as follows:

Credit Hours		GPA					
from	**to**	**from 2.5**	**to 3**	**from > 3**	**to 3.5**	**from > 3.5**	**to 4.0**
1	3	30%		40%		50%	
> 3	6	44%		52%		63%	
> 6	9	53%		64%		72%	
> 9	12	62%		75%		84%	
>12	15	70%		80%		92%	
>15	18	75%		88%		100%	

Develop a two-dimensional table to hold the above information and perform a table-lookup to determine the percent to be used. Establish this table via a COPY statement.

e. Calculate tuition due by subtracting the total aid from the total tuition.

f. Write a detail line with the information shown on the Detailed Student Aid Report, printing ten students per page.

g. Increment the school's totals for total tuition, total aid, and total due. (Establish a table to compute the aid statistics for each school that will print at the conclusion of processing, remembering that the number of schools is variable.)

3. When all records have been processed, write the Summary Report of Total Aid per School from the table established in (g).

Project 16-3

Program Name: Salary Report Program

Narrative: Write a program to print a detailed salary report and average salary summary per location for all employees in a validated salary file.

Input File: SALARY-FILE
LOCATION-FILE (See requirement 2b.)

Input Record Layout: Use the same record layout as Project 8-7.

Test Data: Use the validated salary file from Project 8-7.

Report Layout:

Detailed Salary Report:

```
                              Big Bucks, Inc.                                     Page 1
                      Detailed Salary Report for 99/99/99
Soc Sec No.     Name                Title       Location        Education       Rating     Salary
XXXXXXXXX       XXXXXXXXXXXXXXX     XXXXXXXX    XXXXXXXXXXXX    XXXXXXXXXXXX         9   $ZZZ,ZZ9
    .               .                               .               .                .
    .               .                               .               .                .
    .               .                               .               .                .
```

Summary Report of Average Salaries per Location:

```
                                        Big Bucks, Inc.                                   Page n
                     Average Salary Summary - XXXXXXXXXXXX Location for 99/99/99
Education              ---------------------------------- Rating ----------------------------------
Level                   1                2                3                 4                 5

Grade School     $ZZZ,ZZZ,ZZ9     $ZZZ,ZZZ,ZZ9     $ZZZ,ZZZ,ZZ9     $ZZZ,ZZZ,ZZ9     $ZZZ,ZZZ,ZZ9
    .                      .                .                .                .                .
    .                      .                .                .                .                .
    .                      .                .                .                .                .
Doctorate        $ZZZ,ZZZ,ZZ9     $ZZZ,ZZZ,ZZ9     $ZZZ,ZZZ,ZZ9     $ZZZ,ZZZ,ZZ9     $ZZZ,ZZZ,ZZ9
```

Processing Requirements:

1. Read a file of salary records.
2. For each record read:
   a. The incoming title code is to be expanded via a sequential lookup. The table-lookup procedure should be coded in a separate subprogram. Establish the following table via the COPY statement:

Title Codes & Expanded Titles			
Title Code	**Expanded Title**	**Title Code**	**Expanded Title**
010	President	060	DP VP
020	Vice Pres	070	DP Mgr
030	Mkt VP	080	DP Prog
040	Mkt Mgr	090	Clerk
050	Mkt Rep	100	Adm Asst

   b. The incoming location code is to be expanded via a binary lookup from the following table which is to be input-loaded. Code the lookup and initialization in a subprogram (only once per execution of the program).

Location Code	Expanded Location	Location Code	Expanded Location
MIA	Miami	NY	New York
CHI	Chicago	ATL	Atlanta
LA	Los Angeles		

c. The incoming education code is to be expanded via a direct lookup from the following table, which is to be hard-coded in your program.

Education Code	Expanded Education	Education Code	Expanded Education
1	Grade School	4	Bachelors
2	High School	5	Masters
3	Associates	6	Doctorate

d. Write a detail line with the information shown on the Detailed Salary Report, printing ten employees per page.

e. Establish a three-dimensional (5 by 6 by 5) table to compute the salary statistics for the 150 location-education-rating combinations.
   (1) Determine the appropriate row-column (i.e., education-rating) combination for each location.
   (2) Increment the employee salary total for that row-column combination for each location by the employee's salary.
   (3) Increment the number of employees in that row-column combination for that location by 1.

3. When all employees have been processed, write the Summary Report of Average Salaries per Location. Obtain the average salary by dividing the salary total for each combination by the number of employees in that combination. Print all 150 values of average salaries with every location on a separate page (i.e., 30 education-rating combinations per page).

Project 16-4

Program Name: Stock Program

Narrative: Write a program to produce a stock report for each record in a validated stock file.

Input File: STOCK-FILE
INDUSTRY-FILE (See requirement 1b.)

Input Record Layout: Use the same record layout as Project 8-8.

Test Data: Use the validated stock file from Project 8-8.

Report Layout:

```
                         Stock Evaluation Report as of 99/99/99                          Page Z9

                                           Market        Dividend         Est.  Est.  Ind
Exchange  Stock     Industry                Price   EPS     Yield    PE   Growth   PE    PE  Comments

XXXXXX    XXXXXXXX  XXXXXXXXXXXXXXX ZZ9.999   Z9.9     ZZ9.99   ZZ9  ZZ9.99%  ZZ9    Z9  XXXXXXXXXXXXX
  .          .          .              .        .         .       .      .       .     .        .
  .          .          .              .        .         .       .      .       .     .        .
  .          .          .              .        .         .       .      .       .     .        .
```

```
        Summary of Stocks to Buy as of 99/99/99

                             Market     No. of
  Exchange    Stock           Price     Shares          Total

  XXXXXX      XXXXXXXX       ZZ9.99      Z,ZZ9     ZZZ,ZZ9.99
     .           .              .          .              .
     .           .              .          .              .
     .           .              .          .              .
  Total                                 ZZ,ZZ9  $Z,ZZZ,ZZ9.99
```

Processing Requirements:

1. Read a file of stock records, and for each record read:
   a. Expand the exchange code, from the incoming record, to the appropriate exchange name as shown below. To determine the exchange name, hard-code the table in your program and implement a direct (positional) table lookup.

Exchange Code	Exchange Name
1	NYSE
2	NASDAQ
3	OTC
4	AMEX

   b. Determine the industry description and industry PE. The industry code is to be used to find the description and PE via a binary lookup. Input-load this table (only once per execution of the program).

Industry Code	Industry Description	Industry PE Range
AIR	Airline	12
AUT	Automobile	7
BAN	Bank	7
BEE	Beer	9
CMP	Computers	30
DRU	Drugs	15
ELE	Electronics	25
F&L	Food & Lodging	10
FOO	Food Products	8
OIL	Oil	12
RET	Retail	9
S&L	Savings & Loan	7
TEL	Telephone	8

c. Calculate earnings per share (EPS) by dividing the PE into the stock price.

d. Calculate the dividend yield by dividing the stock price into the dividend.

e. Determine the estimated annual rate of growth in EPS (Est. Growth) over the next 3–5 years by multiplying the annual growth rate by the risk factor. To determine the risk factor, hard-code the table in your program and implement a direct (positional) table lookup.

Risk Code	Risk Factor
1	.7
2	.8
3	.95
4	1.1
5	1.3

f. Calculate the estimated price-to-earnings ratio (Est. PE) based on the estimated annual rate of growth in EPS and the current interest rate.

(1) The current interest rate should be obtained at execution. Use appropriate DISPLAY/ACCEPT statements to prompt for the interest rate and to enter it. The current interest rate limits are from .5% to 15%. (Remember data validation.)

(2) Develop a subprogram to determine the estimated PE. Create a two-dimensional table to hold the information below and perform a table lookup to determine the appropriate PE. Establish this table via a COPY statement in your subprogram.

Estimated Annual Rate of Growth in EPS		Current Interest Rate		
from	**to**	**.5% - 7.9%**	**8% - 10.9%**	**11 - 15%**
.01%	5%	18	9	6
5.01%	10%	20	15	8
10.01%	15%	25	20	11
15.01%	20%	30	21	14
20.01%	25%	40	30	18
25.01%	30%	45	35	21
30.01%	35%	50	40	24
35.01%	130%	65	55	31

g. Determine the comments by comparing the PE in the record, estimated PE, and the industry PE.
   (1) Print "BUY NOW" in the comments column when the PE is less than both the estimated PE and the industry PE.
   (2) Print "Consider" in the comments column when the PE is less than estimated PE.
   (3) Print "Potential" in the comments column when the PE is less than the industry PE.

h. Print a detail line for the record in the file, as shown on the layout. Detail lines are to be double spaced with 10 records per page. Print appropriate headings (and page numbers) on the top of every page in the report.

i. Create a summary table to hold the stocks deemed to be bought. This table should contain the exchange, stock name, market price, and shares to purchase.

2. When all records have been processed, create the Summary Report showing all the "BUY NOW" stocks and appropriate investment totals in the headings.

Project 16-5

Program Name: Electric Program

Narrative: Write a program to produce an electric report for each record in a validated electric file.

Input File: ELECTRIC-FILE
TYPE-FILE (See requirement 1a.)

Input Record Layout: Use the same record layout as Project 8-9.

Test Data: Use the validated electric file from project 8-9.

Report Layout:

```
                                        Bright Power & Light                                         Page Z9
                                   Billing Report as of  XXX Z9, 1999

                                   Service Used     Meter Readings           Kilowatt Hours
Account                            --------------  ----------------  --------------------------        Amount
Number  Rate Schedule/Class of Service  From    To     Previous  Current  On-Peak  Off-Peak    Total      Billed

999999  XXXXXXXXXXXXXXXXXXXXXXXXXXXXXX  XXX Z9  XXX Z9   ZZ,ZZ9   ZZ,ZZ9   ZZ,ZZ9    ZZ,ZZ9   ZZ,ZZ9   ZZZ,ZZ9.99
  .             .                         .      .         .        .        .         .        .          .
  .             .                         .      .         .        .        .         .        .          .
  .             .                         .      .         .        .        .         .        .          .
                                                                          -------   -------  -------  ------------
TOTALS                                                                    ZZZ,ZZ9   ZZZ,ZZ9  ZZZ,ZZ9 $Z,ZZZ,ZZ9.99
```

Processing Requirements:

1. Read a file of electric records; for each record read:
   a. In a subprogram, determine the corresponding description, customer charge, and minimum charge. The incoming account type is to be used to find the description, customer, and minimum charges via a binary lookup. Input-load this table (only once per execution of the program).

Account Type	Description Type, Category, Demand, Time of Use	Customer Charge	Minimum Charge
CCSL1	Comm, Curt Svc, 2000+	170.00	12,670.00
CCSL2	Comm, Curt Svc, 2000+, ToU	175.00	12,699.00
CCSM1	Comm, Curt Svc, 500-1999	110.00	3,235.00
CCSM2	Comm, Curt Svc, 500-1999, ToU	120.00	3,150.99
CCSX1	Comm, Curt Svc, 2000+(TV)	400.00	13,000.00
CCSX2	Comm, Curt Svc, 2000+(TV), ToU	410.00	12,900.00
CGSL1	Comm, Gen Svc, 2000+	170.00	12,670.00
CGSL2	Comm, Gen Svc, 2000+, ToU	180.00	12,550.00
CGSM1	Comm, Gen Svc, 500-1999	41.00	3,166.00
CGSM2	Comm, Gen Svc, 500-1999, ToU	55.00	3,100.00
CGSN1	Comm, Gen Svc, non-demand	9.00	9.00
CGSN2	Comm, Gen Svc, non-demand, ToU	12.30	12.30
CGSS1	Comm, Gen Svc, 21-499	35.00	166.25
CGSS2	Comm, Gen Svc, 21-499, ToU	41.50	1,365.00
CGSX1	Comm, Gen Svc, 2000+(TV)	400.00	12,500.00
CGSX2	Comm, Gen Svc, 2000+(TV), ToU	425.00	12,900.00
RRSN1	Res, Residential Svc	5.65	5.65
RRSN2	Res, Residential Svc, ToU	8.95	8.95

b. The energy charge is determined differently for residential and commercial accounts and whether the account is or is not Time of Use:

(1) Residential Accounts

Non Time of Use

The first 750 kw hours used will be charged at 3.922¢ per kw hour.

Additional kw hours used will be charged at 4.922¢ per kw hour.

(Remember total kw hours used is the current reading minus the previous reading.)

Time of Use

The On-Peak kw hours used will be charged at 7.962¢ per kw hour.

The Off-Peak kw hours used will be charged at 2.729¢ per kw hour.

(Remember total kw hours used is the on-peak kw hours plus the off-peak kw hours.)

(2) Commercial Accounts

Non Time of Use

Develop a subprogram to determine the appropriate energy charge. Create a two-dimensional table to hold the information below and perform a table-lookup to determine the appropriate energy rates. Establish this table via a COPY statement in your subprogram. The energy charge is energy rate multiplied by the kw hours used. (Remember the kw hours used is the current reading minus the previous reading.)

Demand Type	Commercial Account Category	
	General Service (GS)	Curtailable Services (CS)
	Energy Rate	Energy Rate
N	4.564¢	
S	1.884¢	
M	1.576¢	1.473¢
L	1.573¢	1.373¢
X	1.014¢	0.945¢

Time of Use

Develop another subprogram to determine the appropriate energy and fuel rates. Create a two-dimensional table to hold the information below and perform a table-lookup to determine the appropriate energy and fuel rates. Establish this table via a COPY statement in your subprogram. The energy charge is the on-peak rate multiplied by the on-peak kw hours used plus the off-peak rate multiplied by the off-peak kw hours used. (Remember total kw hours used is the on-peak kw hours plus the off-peak kw hours.) This subprogram is almost identical to the other; debug the first before going on to this one.

Demand Type	Commercial Account Category			
	General Service (GS)		Curtailable Services (CS)	
	On-Peak	Off-Peak	On-Peak	Off-Peak
N	8.525¢	2.752¢		
S	3.846¢	1.355¢		
M	2.715¢	1.111¢	2.615¢	1.102¢
L	1.573¢.	1.066¢	2.733¢	1.046¢
X	1.082¢	0.949¢	1.062¢	0.939¢

c. The fuel charge is based on the demand code in the following table. Hard-code this table into the program and reference it via a sequential lookup.

Demand Code	Fuel Rate
N	1.824¢
S	1.824¢
M	1.823¢
L	1.816¢
X	1.769¢

d. The demand charge is calculated by multiplying the kw demand level by the demand charge. The current demand charge is $6.25. Note: Residential accounts do not have a demand charge.

e. Calculate the amount billed, which is the customer charge plus the energy charge plus the fuel charge plus the demand charge (if any). Verify the amount against the minimum charge; if amount calculated is less than the minimum charge, then use the minimum charge as the amount billed.

f. Use a hard-coded table and a direct lookup to translate the numerical From- and To- month in the record to a 3-character abbreviation (using the first 3 letters of the month) to be printed on the detail line.

g. Print a detail line for the record in the file, as shown on the layout. Detail lines are to be double spaced with 10 records per page. Print appropriate headings (and page numbers) on the top of every page in the report. Use the table in 1f. to create the format of the date as shown on the layout.

h. Increment all totals shown in the report layout.

2. When all records have been processed, write the totals accumulated in 1h.

Basic Definitions for Account Codes and Types:

Type Code: C for Commercial Accounts
R for Residential Accounts

Category Code: RS for Residential Service
GS for General Service (Commercial)
CS for Curtailable Service (Commercial)

Demand Code: Demand is the kw to the nearest whole kw, as determined from the metering equipment for the 30-minute period of the customer's greatest use.

N for non demand

S for 21–499 kw demand

M for 500–1999 kw demand

L for 2000+ kw demand

X for 2000+ Transmission Voltage kw demand

Time of Use: The energy rate is determined by the time in which the electricity is used, either On-Peak or Off-Peak. Usually the Off-Peak rate is less than the On-Peak rate.

On-Peak Hours are:

from Nov 1–Mar 31, Monday–Friday, 6am–10am & 6pm–10pm
excluding Thanksgiving, Christmas, and New Year Days
from Apr 1–Oct 31, Monday–Friday, 12noon–9pm
excluding Memorial, Independence, and Labor Days

1 for non Time of Use

2 for Time of Use

(EL-CURRENT-READING contains On-Peak kw hours used and EL-PREVIOUS-READING contains Off-Peak kw hours used.)

Project 16-6

Program Name: Extended Movies Program with Subprograms

Narrative: This program extends Project 13-2 to contain two subprograms.

Input File: MOVIE-EXTRA-FILE

Input Record Layout: Use the same record layout as Project 13-2.

Test Data: Use the same test data as Project 13-2.

Report Layout: Use the same report layout as Project 13-2.

Processing Requirements: Make the following changes to Project 13-2: the table-lookups for pay scale (processing requirement #2) and bonus (processing requirement #4) are to be implemented in a subprogram.

Project 16-7

Program Name: Extended Payroll Program with Subprogram

Narrative: This program extends Project 13-5 to contain subprograms.

Input File: PAYROLL-FILE

Input Record Layout: Use the same record layout as Project 13-5.

Test Data: Use the same test data as Project 13-5.

Report Layout: Use the same report layout as Project 13-5.

Processing Requirements: Make the following changes to Project 13-5: the table-lookups for taxes (processing requirement #2b) and insurance deduction (processing requirement #2d) are to be implemented in a subprogram.

PROGRAMMING SPECIFICATIONS

Project 17-1

Program Name: Extended Program Maintenance

Narrative: This project deals with program maintenance, in that some of the specifications for the data validation and sequential update programs presented in the chapter, have been changed as indicated below. Implement the changes in whatever program you deem appropriate.

Input File: As indicated in the chapter.

Input Record Layout: As indicated in the chapter.

Output File: NEW-MASTER-FILE

Output Record Layout: As indicated in the chapter.

Test Data: Use the existing files of Figure 17.5a and 17.9a for the unedited transaction and old master files, respectively.

Report Layout: There is no new report other than the indicated error messages.

Processing Requirements:

1. Change the stand-alone edit and/or sequential update program (as you deem appropriate) to implement all of the following:
   a. SORT the valid transaction file (at the end of the edit program or the beginning of the update program). This change also implies that out-of-sequence transactions (which are input to the edit program) are no longer invalid (assuming that is the only error).
   b. Replace lines 33–45 in the edit program, which describe the transaction file, with a COPY statement; use the same COPY statement in the sequential update program.

c. Deleted records are to be written to a new file, DELETED-RECORD-FILE, for possible recall at a future date.

d. Enable the OM-LASTNAME, OM-INITIALS, OM-LOCATION-CODE, and/or OM-COMMISSION-RATE fields in the old master to be changed if necessary. The change is accomplished by coding any (all) of these fields as a correction in the transaction file; that is, the update program is to check if a value is present in the transaction file, and if so, it will replace the value in the master file with the value in the transaction file.

e. The change involved in item d. above implies it is permissible for a correction not to contain a value in the TR-SALES-AMOUNT field. For example, the transaction,

```
800000000VILLAR          C          C
```

is now valid and implies a name change for the record in question. (The transaction was previously rejected for not containing a sales amount.)

f. The value in the commission field (on both additions and corrections) is to be between 5 and 10 inclusive; any other value is to be rejected with an appropriate error message.

2. Create additional test data (if necessary) so that all of the program modifications can be tested. Rerun both programs with the modified test data.

Project 17-2

Program Name: Student Grades Sequential File Maintenance

Narrative: Update a student master file to include information on last semester's grades.

Input File: STUDENT-MASTER-FILE
COURSE-FILE

Input Record Layout:

```
01  STUDENT-MASTER-RECORD.
    05  SM-SOC-SEC-NUMBER                PIC 9(9).
    05  SM-NAME-AND-INITIALS.
        10  SM-LAST-NAME                 PIC X(19).
        10  SM-INITIALS                  PIC XX.
    05  SM-CUMULATIVE-CREDITS            PIC 999.
    05  SM-CUMULATIVE-POINTS             PIC 999.
    05  SM-COURSES-THIS-SEMESTER OCCURS 7 TIMES.
        10  SM-COURSE-NUMBER             PIC XXX.
        10  SM-COURSE-CREDITS            PIC 9.

01  COURSE-RECORD.
    05  COURSE-SOC-SEC-NUMBER            PIC 9(9).
    05  COURSE-NUMBER                    PIC X(3).
    05  COURSE-GRADE                     PIC X.
```

Output File: NEW-STUDENT-MASTER-FILE

Output Record Layout: Same as student master record.

Test Data: **Student Master File**

```
         1         2         3         4         5         6
1234567890123456789012345678901234567890123456789012345678901234

100000000ALBERT             A 0591181002200330044004501360026011
200000000BROWN              B 0892751002200330044004
300000000CHARLES            CC10928650135033504350535063
400000000SMITH              D 0902691002200330044194
500000000BAKER              EF032049222333334443
600000000GULFMAN            SF0290592003333344435553666367527001
700000000BOROW              JB0300902223
800000000MILGROM            MB0150451113138315036013
900000000MILLER             K 015054111314031503
999999999WAYNE              N 0902705013503350435053
```

Course File:

```
         1                   1                   1
1234567890123456789  1234567890123456789  1234567890123456789

100000000100A        300000000503B        600000000444B
100000000200A        300000000504B        600000000555A
100000000300B        300000000505B        600000000666A
100000000400X        300000000507C        600000000675B
100000000501A        400000000100A        600000000700A
100000000600B        400000000200D        700000000222A
100000000601B        400000000300C        800000000111C
200000000100C        400000000400B        800000000138C
200000000200C        555555555100A        800000000150C
200000000300I        555555555200A        800000000160D
200000000400C        555555555300A        900000000111X
200000000444C        600000000200B        900000000140A
300000000501B        600000000333C        900000000150B
```

Report Layout: There is no output report other than the error messages; use whatever form you deem appropriate.

Processing Requirements:

1. Update the SM-CUMULATIVE-POINTS and SM-CUMULATIVE-CREDITS fields in the master file. Allow 4, 3, 2, 1, and 0 points for an A, B, C, D, or E, respectively. An A in a three-credit course adds 12 points and 3 credits to SM-CUMULATIVE-POINTS and SM-CUMULATIVE-CREDITS, respectively. Do not increment either field if the grade is other than A, B, C, D, or E. Display the error message, 'INVALID GRADE FOR COURSE NO XXX' with the student's name and social security number.
2. Delete students reaching 120 or more cumulative credits (graduating seniors) from the new master file. Display their names together with their grade point average in a separate report.
3. Check to ensure that every course appearing in a student's master record (in the table SM-COURSES-THIS-SEMESTER) appears in the corresponding transaction record. If a course is missing from the course (transaction) file, display the error message, 'NO GRADE FOR COURSE NO XXX' with the student's name and social security number.
4. Check that every course appearing in a transaction record appears in the student's master record. If a course is missing from the master record, display the message

'GRADE RECEIVED FOR NON-REGISTERED COURSE' with the student's name and social security number. Do not update the SM-CUMULATIVE-POINTS and SM-CUMULATIVE-CREDITS fields in the master record for this course.

5. Initialize any entry in the table SM-COURSES-THIS-SEMESTER of the master record if the course was present in a matching transaction record, and if the course had a valid grade: A, B, C, D, or E. If either of these conditions is not met, retain the course(s) with invalid data.
6. Display the transaction social security number and error message 'NO CORRESPONDING MASTER RECORD' if a social security number in the course (transaction) file does not match an existing master record.
7. Display the master social security number and the error message 'NO GRADES FOR LAST SEMESTER' if a social security number in the master does not have a matching record in the course (transaction) file.

Project 17-3

Program Name: Loan Update and Information Program

Narrative: Write a program to maintain and/or view a file of bank loans. The record key is MAST-LOAN-NUMBER, consisting of a unique six-digit customer number and a three-digit sequence number. Each loan a customer receives is assigned a new sequence number. Customer 111111, for example, may have two outstanding loans, with keys of 111111001 and 111111004. (Loans 002 and 003 may have been previously paid off.)

Input File: MASTER-LOAN-FILE
TRANSACTION-LOAN-FILE

Input Record Layout:

```
01  MASTER-LOAN-RECORD.
    05  MAST-LOAN-NUMBER.
        10  MAST-NUMBER            PIC 9(6).
        10  MAST-LOAN-SEQUENCE     PIC 9(3).
    05  MAST-LOAN-DATA.
        10  MAST-LOAN-AMOUNT       PIC 9(6).
        10  MAST-LOAN-BALANCE      PIC 9(6).
        10  MAST-LOAN-DATE         PIC 9(6).
        10  MAST-LOAN-RATE         PIC 99V99.
        10  MAST-LOAN-DUE-DATE     PIC 9(6).

01  TRANSACTION-LOAN-RECORD.
    05  TRANS-LOAN-NUMBER.
        10  TRANS-NUMBER           PIC 9(6).
        10  TRANS-LOAN-SEQUENCE    PIC 9(3).
    05  TRANS-LOAN-DATA.
        10  TRANS-LOAN-AMOUNT      PIC 9(6).
        10  TRANS-LOAN-BALANCE     PIC 9(6).
        10  TRANS-LOAN-DATE        PIC 9(6).
        10  TRANS-LOAN-RATE        PIC 99V99.
        10  TRANS-LOAN-DUE-DATE    PIC 9(6).
```

```
05  TRANS-CODE                PIC X.
    88  ADDITION                        VALUE 'A'.
    88  CORRECTION                      VALUE 'C'.
    88  DELETION                        VALUE 'D'.
    88  LOAN-DISPLAY                    VALUE 'L'.
```

Output File: NEW-MASTER-LOAN-FILE

Output Record Layout: Same as master loan record.

Test Data: **Master File:**

```
         1         2         3         4         5         6
12345678901234567890123456789012345678901234567890123456789012345

11111100101000000080000316921250031695
11111100300500000050001031911050103196
22222200101000000080000316921250031698
22222200300500000050001031921050103194
22222200401500000080001124911250112494
44444400110000010000007319110500073195
55555500101000000080000316911250031696
55555500205000000450000316921050031693
66666600101000000080000316911250031696
66666600200500000050001031911050103195
66666600401000000080000416921350041694
77777700400500000050001031911050103195
```

Transaction File:

```
         1         2         3         4         5         6
12345678901234567890123456789012345678901234567890123456789012345

888888001010000000800008019210000080191A
222222001        006000               C
222222005        007000               C
111111001010000000800003169112500316997A
111111004005000000500010319110501031996A
555555001                   10500031698C
555555002                             D
888888001015000015000                 C
666666003                             D
666666002        004500               C
222222003                       081595C
777777004                             L
777777001                             L
777777004015000                       C
```

Report Layout: Design any report you deem appropriate in conjunction with the processing specifications. (Simple DISPLAY statements will suffice for the error messages.)

Processing Requirements:

1. Sort the transaction file by loan number.
2. Process a file of sorted transactions to accomplish all of the following:
   a. Add a new loan (transaction code A)—enter all information from the transaction record to the new master record; be sure to reject duplicate additions.
   b. Delete an existing loan (transaction code D)—delete existing loan records; be sure to reject "no matches".

c. Change (correct) information on an outstanding loan (transaction code C)—transactions to correct information will contain only the loan number and the new information in specified columns. Information in the master file that does not change will not appear in the transaction record.

d. Display all information for a particular loan (transaction code L)—print a detail line in a loan report; incoming record contains only the loan number; be sure to check for "no matches".

3. All error messages ("no matches" from parts (a–d) and/or duplicate additions) are to appear in one report; information from part d. is to each appear in a separate report.

4. The FD's and record descriptions for both the master and transaction files are to be copied into the program. This requires that you establish the necessary COPY members as separate files, and bring them in at compile time.

Project 17-4

Program Name: Employee Sequential File Update

Narrative: This project and the next are more complex applications of the balance line algorithm.

Input Files: OLD-MASTER-FILE
TRANSACTION-FILE

Input Record Layouts:

```
01  OLD-MASTER-RECORD.
    05  OLD-SOC-SEC-NUMBER          PIC X(9).
    05  OLD-NAME.
        10  OLD-LAST-NAME           PIC X(12).
        10  OLD-INITIALS            PIC XX.
    05  OLD-DATE-OF-BIRTH.
        10  OLD-BIRTH-MONTH         PIC 99.
        10  OLD-BIRTH-YEAR          PIC 99.
    05  OLD-DATE-OF-HIRE.
        10  OLD-HIRE-MONTH          PIC 99.
        10  OLD-HIRE-YEAR           PIC 99.
    05  OLD-LOCATION-CODE           PIC X(3).
    05  OLD-PERFORMANCE-CODE        PIC X.
    05  OLD-EDUCATION-CODE          PIC X.
    05  OLD-TITLE-DATA OCCURS 2 TIMES.
        10  OLD-TITLE-CODE          PIC 9(3).
        10  OLD-TITLE-DATE          PIC 9(4).
    05  OLD-SALARY-DATA OCCURS 3 TIMES.
        10  OLD-SALARY              PIC 9(6).
        10  OLD-SALARY-DATE         PIC 9(4).

01  TRANSACTION-RECORD.
    05  TR-SOC-SEC-NUMBER           PIC X(9).
    05  TR-NAME.
        10  TR-LAST-NAME            PIC X(12).
        10  TR-INITIALS             PIC XX.
    05  TR-DATE-OF-BIRTH.
```

```
            10  TR-BIRTH-MONTH        PIC 99.
            10  TR-BIRTH-YEAR         PIC 99.
        05  TR-DATE-OF-HIRE.
            10  TR-HIRE-MONTH         PIC 99.
            10  TR-HIRE-YEAR          PIC 99.
        05  TR-LOCATION-CODE          PIC X(3).
        05  TR-PERFORMANCE-CODE       PIC X.
        05  TR-EDUCATION-CODE         PIC X.
        05  TR-TITLE-DATA.
            10  TR-TITLE-CODE         PIC 9(3).
            10  TR-TITLE-DATE         PIC 9(4).
        05  TR-SALARY-DATA.
            10  TR-SALARY             PIC 9(6).
            10  TR-SALARY-DATE        PIC 9(4).
        05  TR-TRANSACTION-CODE       PIC X.
            88  ADDITION                        VALUE     'A'.
            88  CORRECTION                      VALUE     'C'.
            88  DELETION                        VALUE     'D'.
```

Output File: NEW-MASTER-FILE

Output Record Layout: Identical to the old master record.

Test Data: **Old Master File:**

```
         1         2         3         4         5         6         7         8
12345678901234567890123456789012345678901234567890123456789012345678901234567890
100000000SUGRUE      PK12450888BOSE81000888        800000992 700000891
200000000CRAWFORD    MA08430973WASE220005891500585 750001092 700001091 650001090
300000000MILGROM     MB
400000000LEE           10741189NYCG4441193         340001192
500000000TATER       CR12820550CHIP33311872221185  290001092 280001091 270001090
600000000GRAUER      JE11880368WASG3331193         690001191
700000000JONES       JJ11860669BOSG89211878911186  320001091 300001090 280001089
800000000SMITH         11860448WASG33311874441186  290001091 260001090 240001089
900000000BAKER       ED11780652MIAG32111871231186  680001091 640001090 600001089
```

Transaction File:

```
         1         2         3         4         5         6
12345678901234567890123456789012345678901234567890123456789012345
100000000RUBIN       J 10701289MIA 50101292 250001292A
000000000RUBIN       J            X            7774  C
200000000CRAWFORD    MA08430973WASE22000592 750001092A
400000000LEE         BL                              C
400000000LEE           1073                          C
400000000LEE               1289                      C
400000001LEE                   MIA                   C
50000000TATER        CR                              D
55555555NEW EMPLOYEE XX                              C
55555555NEW EMPLOYEE NE09541289WASE22001292 750001292A
55555555NEW EMPLOYEE NE        NYC                   C
70000000JONES        A                      340001292C
80000000SMITH        SS             300              C
```

Report Layout: There is no report produced by this program, other than the error messages indicated in the processing requirements. The latter may be produced using DISPLAY statements with programmer discretion as to the precise layout.

Processing Requirements:

1. Develop a sequential update program to process an incoming transaction file and the associated old master file to produce a new master file.
2. Three transaction codes are permitted: A, C, and D, denoting additions, corrections, and deletions, respectively.
3. The transaction file is assumed to be valid in itself because it has been processed by a stand-alone edit program. Hence each transaction has a valid transaction code (A, C, or D), numeric fields are numeric, and so on. Nevertheless, the update program must check (and flag) two kinds of errors that could not be detected in the stand-alone edit, as they require interaction with the old master file. These are:
   a. Duplicate additions, in which the social security number of a transaction coded as an addition already exists in the old master.
   b. No matches, in which the social security number of a transaction coded as either a deletion or a correction, does not exist in the old master.
4. Transactions coded as additions are added to the new master file in their entirety. These transactions require all fields in the transaction record to be present.
5. Transactions coded as deletions are removed from the master file. These transactions need contain only the social security number and transaction code.
6. Transactions coded as corrections contain only the social security number and the corrected value of any field(s) to be changed and are handled on a parameter-by-parameter basis. For example, if birth date and location are to be corrected, the incoming transaction will contain only the social security number and corrected values of birth date and location code in the designated positions on the transaction record.
7. Any old master record for which there is no corresponding transaction is to be copied intact to the new master.

Project 17-5

Program Name: Extended Employee Sequential File Update

Narrative: This program shows the generality of the balance line algorithm by expanding the specifications in the previous project to include a second transaction file. You will find that even though a new input file has been added, there are no additional modules required for the algorithm per se. It will, however, be necessary to change the logic of CHOOSE-ACTIVE-KEY in that the active key is now the smallest of three values.

Input File: PROMOTION-FILE

Input Record Layout:

```
01  PROMOTION-RECORD.
    05  PR-SOC-SEC-NUMBER          PIC X(9).
    05  PR-NAME.
        10  PR-LAST-NAME           PIC X(12).
        10  PR-INITIALS            PIC XX.
    05  PR-SALARY-DATA.
        10  PR-SALARY              PIC 9(6).
```

```
        10  PR-SALARY-DATE         PIC 9(4).
    05  PR-TITLE-DATA.
        10  PR-TITLE-CODE          PIC 9(3).
        10  PR-TITLE-DATE          PIC 9(4).
    05  PR-PROMOTION-CODE          PIC X.
        88  SALARY-RAISE                       VALUE 'R'
        88  PROMOTION                          VALUE 'P'.
```

Test Data:

```
         1         2         3         4         5         6
12345678901234567890123456789012345678901234567890123456789012345
100000000SUGRUE      PK 900000993       R
100000000SUGRUE      PK          9990993P
400000000LEE         BL 500001193       R
666666666GLASSMAN    C  450001093       R
800000000SMITH       SS 750001093       R
```

Report Layout: Identical to the previous project.

Processing Requirements: Modify the specifications of Project 17-4 to accommodate all of the following:

1. Inclusion of a second transaction (i.e., a promotion) file to accommodate promotions and/or salary increases.
2. Salary increases are to be handled in the following manner: the transaction salary becomes the present salary in the new master, causing the present salary in the old master to become the previous salary in the new master. In similar fashion, the previous salary in the old master becomes the second previous salary in the new master. (The record layout of the master file in the programming specifications allowed three salary levels.)

   Each occurrence of salary is accompanied by a salary date in both the old master and promotion record layouts. Accordingly, the salary dates and the salaries are to be adjusted simultaneously.
3. Promotions (i.e., title changes in the new file) are to be handled in a manner analogous to salary increases. Hence the transaction title, PR-TITLE-CODE, becomes the present title in the new master, causing the present title in the old master to become the previous title in the new master. The associated dates are to be adjusted simultaneously.
4. Deletions (in the original transaction file) are to be written in their entirety to a new file, DELETED-RECORD-FILE, for possible recall at a future date.
5. All error messages are to be expanded to print the entire transaction that is in error.

Project 17-6

Program Name: Stock Sequential File Update

Narrative: Develop a sequential update program to process an incoming transaction file and the associated master stock file to produce a new master stock file.

Input File: MASTER-STOCK-FILE

TRANSACTION-FILE

Input Record Layout: Use the record layout in Project 8-8 for the MASTER-STOCK-FILE.

```
01  TRANSACTION-FILE.
    05  TR-INFO.
        10  TR-NAME             PIC X(8).
        10  TR-EXCHANGE-CODE    PIC 9.
        10  TR-INDUSTRY-CODE    PIC X(3).
    05  TR-CURRENT-INFO.
        10  TR-PRICE            PIC 9(3)V9(3).
        10  TR-PE               PIC 9(3).
        10  TR-DIVIDEND         PIC 9V99.
    05  TR-PROJECTION-INFO.
        10  TR-RISK-CODE        PIC 9.
        10  TR-GROWTH-RATE      PIC 9V9(4).
        10  TR-SHARES-TO-BUY    PIC 9(4).
    05  TRANS-CODE              PIC X.
        88  ADDITION                        VALUE 'A'.
        88  CORRECTION                      VALUE 'C'.
        88  DELETION                        VALUE 'D'.
```

Output File: NEW-MASTER-STOCK-FILE

Output Record Layout: Same as master stock file.

Test Data: Use the validated stock file from Project 8-8 as the MASTER-STOCK-FILE.

Transaction File:

```
         1         2         3         4         5         6
12345678901234567890123456789012345678901234567890123456789012345

Anheus                  200550    C
Citicorp1BAN0262500190002025500123A
Chevron 1OIL0727500243304009500050A
Compq       030550032285          C
GenEl                         0100C
GnMotr                            D
HBO     2RET0230000290302065000075A
Hilton  1F&L0497750221223055000025A
IBM                  383 01000    C
Kmart                             D
Marrion     0155000130143         C
PolkAu      005250020   4         C
Reebok            007   3     0055C
OBrien  4RET0048750150000402300110A
Seagate 2ELE0171253431303008900045A
Skywst                            D
Trustco              0653         C
Wendys  1F&L0120000220244029500050A
```

Report Layout: There is no output report other than the error messages; use whatever form you deem appropriate.

Processing Requirements:

1. Sort the master file by stock name.
2. Three transaction codes are permitted: A, C, and D, denoting additions, corrections, and deletions, respectively:

3. The transaction file is assumed to be valid in itself because it has been processed by a stand-alone edit program. Hence each transaction has a valid transaction code (A, C, or D), numeric fields are numeric, and so on. Nevertheless, the update program must check (and flag) two kinds of errors that could not be detected in the stand-alone edit, as they require interaction with the master file. These are:
   a. Duplicate additions, in which the stock name of a transaction coded as an addition already exists in the master.
   b. No matches, in which the stock name of a transaction coded as either a deletion or a correction, does not exist in the master.
4. Transactions coded as additions are added to the new master file in their entirety. These transactions require all fields in the transaction record to be present.
5. Transactions coded as deletions are removed from the master file. These transactions need contain only the stock name and transaction code.
6. Transactions coded as corrections contain only the stock name and the corrected value of any field(s) to be changed and are handled on a parameter-by-parameter basis. For example, if price and PE are to be corrected, the incoming transaction will contain only the stock name and corrected values of price and PE in the designated positions on the transaction record.
7. Any master stock record for which there is no corresponding transaction is to be copied intact to the new master.

Project 17-7

Program Name: Electric Sequential File Update

Narrative: Develop a sequential update program to process an incoming meter reading file and the associated master file to produce a new master file with updated meter readings.

Input File: MASTER-ELECTRIC-FILE
METER-READING-FILE

Input Record Layout: Use the record layout in Project 8-9 for the MASTER-ELECTRIC-FILE.

```
01  METER-READING-FILE.
    05  MET-ACCOUNT-NO                PIC X(6).
    05  MET-READ-INFO.
        10  MET-CURRENT-READING       PIC 9(5).
        10  MET-PREVIOUS-READING      PIC 9(5).
```

Output File: NEW-MASTER-ELECTRIC-FILE

Output Record Layout: Same as master electric record.

Test Data: Use the validated electric file from Project 8-9 as the MASTER-ELECTRIC-FILE.

Meter Read File:

```
         1
12345678901234567

1465579965197219
2234568545678446
2345572045617274
2389455482439081
3425453685435748
3454567598573487
3454640015000458
3467684625845985
3487567958578642
3874540085401893
3874645985458453
3875436584564533
```

```
         1
12345678901234567

4574660158902788
4576862815236133
4606743845134234
4634540844509347
4657580025600456
4864675578545867
4876359658494753
4876530015800387
4897535515853947
5474650005200023
5486450048800364
5674555189549328
```

```
         1
12345678901234567

6467570000470030
6893530014700234
7583460024810384
7636458895483493
7845670014802384
8555430048800895
8597340048801364
8950989658194274
9066540057400335
9457665712555455
9845459845490302
```

Report Layout: There is no output report other than the error messages; use whatever form you deem appropriate.

Processing Requirements:

1. Sort the master electric file by account number.
2. Apply the meter reading file to the master electric file as follows:
   a. Validate the meter reading record by checking that the current and previous reading fields are numeric; if not, display an appropriate error message.
   b. Valid meter reading records are to be applied to the master electric file as follows:
      (1) The service-used-from field in the new master becomes the service-used-to from the old master.
      (2) The service-used-to field is updated with the current date.
      (3) The previous meter reading field in the new master becomes the current meter reading of the old master.
      (4) The current meter reading information is taken from the meter reading record.
3. Display the meter reading account number and an appropriate error message if the account number does not match an existing master record.
4. Display the master account number and an appropriate error message if the account number in the master does not have a matching meter reading record.

Project 17-8

Program Name: Two-file Merge

Narrative: This project merges two sequential files to produce a third file; all three files have different record layouts.

Input Files: EMPLOYEE-MASTER-FILE
SALARY-FILE

Input Record Layout:

```
01  EMPLOYEE-MASTER-RECORD.
    05  EMP-SOC-SEC-NUMBER          PIC X(9).
    05  EMP-NAME.
        10  EMP-LAST-NAME           PIC X(15).
        10  EMP-INITIALS            PIC XX.
    05  EMP-BIRTH-DATE              PIC 9(4).
    05  EMP-HIRE-DATE               PIC 9(4).
    05  EMP-LOC-CODE                PIC X(3).
    05  EMP-TITLE-CODE              PIC 9(3).

01  SALARY-RECORD.
    05  SAL-SOC-SEC-NUMBER          PIC X(9).
    05  SAL-ANNUAL-SALARY           PIC 9(6).
```

Test Data: **Employee Master File:**

```
         1         2         3         4         5         6
12345678901234567890123456789012345678901234567890123456789012345

111111111ADAMS          JO10521082ATL111
222222222MOLDOF         ML10590484FLA222
333333333FRANKEL        LY06560589NJ 111
555555555BOROW          JE01430680NY 222
666666666MILGROM        IR03480187NY 222
888888888JONES          JJ09600684NY 222
```

Salary File:

```
         1         2         3         4         5         6
12345678901234567890123456789012345678901234567890123456789012345

111111111050000
222222222100000
444444444075000
555555555040000
777777777043500
888888888035000
999999999042000
```

Input Files: MERGED-FILE

Output Record Layout:

```
01  MERGED-DATA-RECORD.
    05  MGD-SOC-SEC-NUMBER          PIC X(9).
    05  MGD-NAME.
        10  MGD-LAST-NAME           PIC X(15).
        10  MGD-INITIALS            PIC XX.
    05  MGD-BIRTH-DATE              PIC 9(4).
    05  MGD-HIRE-DATE               PIC 9(4).
    05  MGD-LOC-CODE                PIC X(3).
    05  MGD-TITLE-CODE              PIC 9(3).
    05  MGD-ANNUAL-SALARY           PIC 9(6).
```

Report Layout: There is no report produced by this program, other than the error messages indicated in the processing requirements. The latter may be produced using DISPLAY statements with programmer discretion as to the precise layout.

Processing Requirements:

1. Write a program to merge two input files, each in sequence by social security number, to produce a third file as output.

2. In order to produce an output record with a given key, that key must be present on both input files. With respect to the test data, for example, records 111111111 and 222222222 should both appear on the merged file. A record is written to the MERGED-FILE by combining fields on the two input records as per the record layouts.

3. If a key appears on only one input file, that record key is not to appear in the MERGED-FILE. With respect to the test data, for example, record 333333333 should not appear in the MERGED-FILE, as it is not present in the SALARY-FILE. Nor should record key 444444444, as it is not present in the EMPLOYEE-MASTER-FILE.

4. Any key appearing in only one file should be flagged with an appropriate error message, for example:

```
ERROR - RECORD 333333333 NOT IN SALARY-FILE

ERROR - RECORD 444444444 NOT IN EMPLOYEE-MASTER-FILE
```

PROGRAMMING SPECIFICATIONS

Project 18-1

Program Name: Extended Program Maintenance

Narrative: Change the nonsequential update program of Figure 18.10 to accommodate the various changes in specifications listed below.

Input File: As indicated in the chapter.

Input Record Layout: As indicated in the chapter.

Test Data: Use the existing files of Figure 18.7a and 18.7b for the transaction and indexed files, respectively.

Report Layout: There is no new report other than the indicated error messages.

Processing Requirements:

1. Change the existing program to accommodate all of the following:
   a. Replace the record descriptions in Working-Storage, (lines 34–45 and 47–54 for the transaction and master files, respectively) with a COPY statement. This in turn requires you to create the necessary copy members.
   b. Deleted records are to be written to a new file, DELETED-RECORD-FILE, for possible recall at a future date.
   c. Enable the MA-LAST-NAME, MA-INITIALS, MA-LOCATION-CODE, and/or MA-COMMISSION-RATE fields in the indexed file to be changed if necessary. The change is accomplished by coding any (all) of these fields as a correction in the transaction file; that is, the update program is to check if a value is present in the transaction file, and if so, it will replace the value in the master file with the value in the transaction file.
   d. The change involved in item c. above implies it is permissible for a correction not to contain a value in the TR-SALES-AMOUNT field. For example, the transaction,

      ```
      800000000VILLAR          C          C
      ```

      is now valid and implies a name change for the record in question. (The transaction was previously rejected for not containing a sales amount.)
2. Create additional test data so that all of the program modifications can be tested. Rerun the program with the modified test data.

Projects 18-2 through 18-7

Program Name: Nonsequential File Update

Narrative: Implement the programming specifications for Projects 17-2 through 17-7 as a nonsequential (rather than a sequential) update. The file descriptions, test data, and programming specifications given with the sequential program apply here as well, except that the indexed file in this example functions as both the old and new master files in the sequential version.

Project 18-8

Program Name: Catalog Orders

Narrative: Develop an interactive program that will process additions, changes, deletions, and inquiries to an indexed file of catalog orders.

Input File: ORDER-FILE

Input Record Layout:

```
01  ORDER-RECORD-IN.
    05  ORD-NUMBER                PIC 9(6).
    05  ORD-INFO.
        10  ORD-NAME              PIC X(10).
        10  ORD-TELEPHONE         PIC 9(10).
    05  ORD-ITEMS-ORDERED  OCCURS 3 TIMES.
        10  ORD-ITEM-NUMBER       PIC 9(4).
        10  ORD-QUANTITY-ORDERED PIC 9.
```

Test Data:

```
         1         2         3         4         5         6
12345678901234567890123456789012345678901234567890123456789012345

212467Scully    3052331234125021100115501
561578Schultz   20134715354500232001
036442Culver    401345234790003
479350Perez     30597674566800245001
683736Fixler    20136218231250115503
488907Morin     4137435343320019000311002
043498Munroe    305331485490005
```

Screen Layouts: **Screen A**

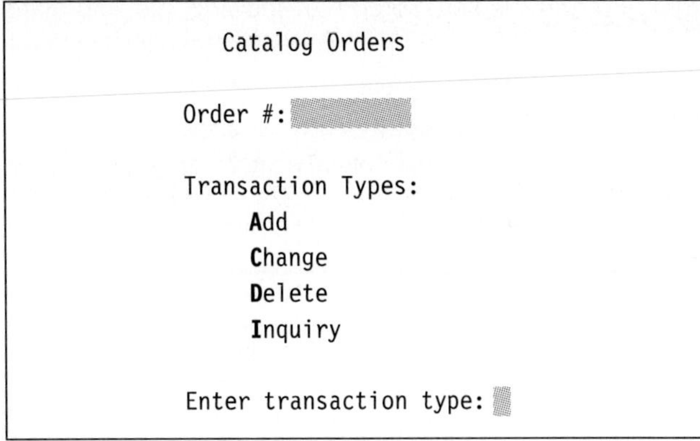

Catalog Orders
Order #:
Transaction Types:
Add
Change
Delete
Inquiry
Enter transaction type:

Screen B

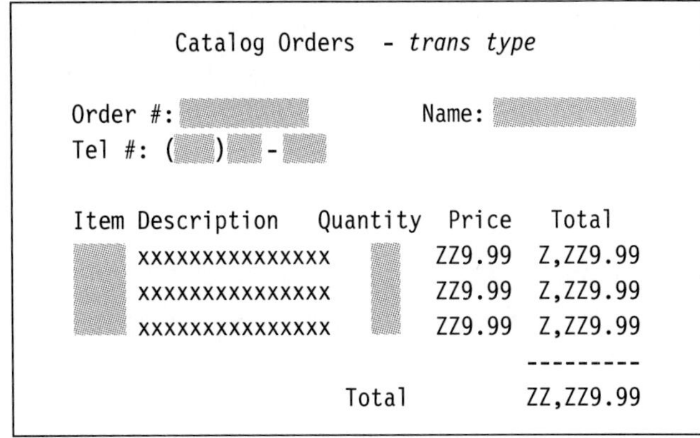

Catalog Orders - trans type
Order #:
Name:
Tel #: ( ) -
Item Description Quantity Price Total
XXXXXXXXXXXXXXX ZZ9.99 Z,ZZ9.99
XXXXXXXXXXXXXXX ZZ9.99 Z,ZZ9.99
XXXXXXXXXXXXXXX ZZ9.99 Z,ZZ9.99

Total ZZ,ZZ9.99

Processing Requirements:

1. Display Screen A to accept an order # and transaction type (valid transaction types are A, C, D, or I).
2. Depending on the transaction type, display an appropriate screen using Screen B as a model, and processing the transaction as follows:
   a. Additions:
      (1) Accept and validate the order # (don't forget to check for duplicate additions), name, telephone number (numeric), item number (valid item numbers are found in the item table, see requirement #3), and quantity (numeric).
      (2) For each valid item, look up the price and description from the item table, calculate the total (quantity multiplied by price), and display the item detail line.
      (3) When all items are entered, display a total for all ordered items.
      (4) Prompt the user for confirmation and write the record to the indexed file.
   b. Changes:
      (1) Display Screen B showing the information found in the order file.
      (2) For each item, look up and display the price and description from the item table along with the calculated total.
      (3) Allow modification to the name, telephone, item number, and quantity fields.
      (4) Validate each item changed against the item table, and for each valid item display the description and price and calculate the total.
      (5) Prompt the user for confirmation and replace the modified record in the indexed file.

c. Deletions:

(1) Display Screen B showing the information found in the order file, the corresponding information from the item table for each item, and all totals.

(2) Prompt the user for confirmation to delete, and delete the record.

d. Inquiries: Display Screen B showing the information found in the order file, the corresponding information from the item table for each item, and all totals.

3. Hard-code the following item table in the program and use a sequential lookup:

Item Information		
Item #	**Item Description**	**Price (each)**
1100	Handwoven Rug	129.00
1550	Crystal Frame	39.40
1250	Floor Lamp	99.00
3000	Ceiling Fan	299.00
4500	Wicker Basket	25.00
6800	Wall Clock	169.00
3200	Ceramic Figure	39.90
9000	Wood Wall Shelf	14.90

4. All error messages are to be displayed on the bottom of the screen and will allow the user to reenter the desired information.

Index

PLACE
STAMP
HERE

COMPUTER ASSOCIATES INTERNATIONAL, INC.
2 Executive Drive
Fort Lee, N.J. 07024

PROFESSIONAL PROGRAMMING WITH CA-Realia COBOL